Oxford University Press Digital Course Materials for

Logic

FIFTH EDITION

Stan Baronett

Carefully scratch off the silver coating to see your personal redemption code.

This code can be redeemed only once.

Once the code has been revealed, this access card cannot be returned to the publisher.

Access can also be purchased online during the registration process.

The code on this card is valid for two years from the date of first purchase. Complete terms and conditions are available at learninglink.oup.com

Access Length: 6 months from redemption of the code.

Your OUP digital course materials can be delivered several different ways, depending on how your instructor has elected to incorporate them into his or her course.

BEFORE REGISTERING FOR ACCESS, be sure to check with your instructor to ensure that you register using the proper method.

VIA YOUR SCHOOL'S LEARNING MANAGEMENT SYSTEM

Use this method if your instructor has integrated these resources into your school's Learning Management System (LMS)—Blackboard, Canvas, Brightspace, Moodle, or other.

> Log in to your instructor's course within your school's LMS.

> When you click a link to a resource that is access-protected, you will be prompted to register for access.

> Follow the on-screen instructions.

> Enter your personal redemption code (or purchase access) when prompted.

VIA OXFORD learning cloud

Use this method only if your instructor has specifically instructed you to enroll in an Oxford Learning Cloud course. **NOTE:** *If your instructor is using these resources within your school's LMS, use the Learning Management System instructions.*

> Visit the course invitation URL provided by your instructor.

> If you already have an oup.instructure.com account you will be added to the course automatically; if not, create an account by providing your name and email.

> When you click a link to a resource in the course that is access-protected, you will be prompted to register.

> Follow the on-screen instructions, entering your personal redemption code where prompted.

For assistance with code redemption, Oxford Learning Cloud registration, or if you redeemed your code using the wrong method for your course, please contact our customer support team at **learninglinkdirect.support@oup.com** or 855-281-8749.

OXFORD
UNIVERSITY PRESS

Logic

Logic

Fifth Edition

Stan Baronett

New York   Oxford
Oxford University Press

Oxford University Press is a department of the University of Oxford.
It furthers the University's objective of excellence in research, scholarship,
and education by publishing worldwide. Oxford is a registered trade mark of
Oxford University Press in the UK and certain other countries.

Published in the United States of America by Oxford University Press
198 Madison Avenue, New York, NY 10016, United States of America.

© 2022, 2019, 2016, 2013 by Oxford University Press

Cataloging-in-Publication data is on file at the Library of Congress.
ISBN: 978-0-19-760236-2

9 8 7 6 5 4 3 2 1
Printed by LSC Communications, Inc., United States of America

Brief Contents

Contents

Part IV Inductive Logic 533

Instructors interested in providing students with an opportunity for further analysis can refer them to Online Chapter 15, available at www.oup.com/he/baronett5e.

Preface

Although higher education faces many new challenges, one thing remains constant: Today's logic students want to see the relevance of logic to their lives. They need motivation to read either a print or electronic version of a textbook, and to do the exercises. Instructors of logic and critical thinking courses want their students to read the textbook and to practice the skills being taught. They want their students to come away with the ability to recognize and evaluate arguments, an understanding of formal and informal logic, and a lasting sense of why they matter. These concerns meet head-on in the classroom. This textbook is designed to help alleviate these concerns.

THE CONTINUING STORY

The focus of the fifth edition has been on continuing to fine-tune an already student-friendly and comprehensive introduction to logic book. Several passages have been reworked with an eye toward more clarity and precision. The goal, as with previous editions, has been to define, explain, and illustrate key logical concepts to provide necessary in-depth understanding for applying those concepts, so students are well equipped to tackle the exercise sets.

The driving force behind writing the fifth edition has been the continuing effort to make logic **relevant, interesting, and accessible to today's students**, without sacrificing the coverage that instructors demand and expect. An introduction to logic is often a student's only exposure to rigorous thinking and symbolism. It should prepare them for reasoning in their lives and careers. It must balance careful coverage of abstract reasoning with **clear, accessible explanations and vivid everyday examples.**

This book was written to meet all those challenges. **Relevant examples provide a bridge between formal reasoning and practical applications of logic, thereby connecting logic to student lives and future careers.** Each chapter opens with a discussion of an everyday example, often taken directly from contemporary events, to pose the problem and set the narrative tone. This provides an immediate connection between logic and real-world issues, motivating the need for logic as a tool to help with the deluge of information available today.

The challenge of any introduction to logic textbook is to connect logic to students' lives. Yet existing texts can and should do more to reinforce and improve the basic skills of reasoning we all rely on in daily life. Relevant, real-life examples are essential to making logic accessible to students, especially when they mesh seamlessly with the technical material. To accomplish this, quotes and passages from modern and classic sources illustrate the relevance of logic through some of the perennial problems that impact everyone's lives. Examples concerning the workplace, careers, sports, politics, movies, music, TV, novels, new inventions, gadgets, cell phones, transportation, newspapers, magazines, computers, speeches, science, religion, superstition, gambling, drugs, war, abortion, euthanasia, capital punishment, the role of government, taxes, military spending, and unemployment are used **to show how arguments, and thus the role of logic, can be found in nearly every aspect of life**. The examples were chosen to be interesting, thought-provoking, and relevant to students, and the writing style was crafted to engage students by connecting logic to their lives.

AN INCLUSIVE TEXT

The fourteen main chapters are designed to provide a comprehensive logic textbook, but also one that can be tailored to individual courses and their needs. The result is a full five chapters on deductive logic, but also a uniquely applied five-chapter part on inductive logic. Here separate chapters on analogical arguments, legal arguments, moral arguments, statistical arguments, and scientific arguments allow students to apply the logical skills learned in the earlier parts of the book. As with previous editions, explanations and examples have been created to facilitate student comprehension, and to show students that the logical skills they are learning do in fact have practical, real-world application. The material also provides more resources to help students when they do the exercise sets.

Since each chapter has been developed to provide maximum flexibility to instructors, some sections can be skipped without loss of continuity. In addition, those wishing for a briefer text can choose a text tailored to their course. They may choose to emphasize or omit certain chapters on formal logic or critical reasoning, and they may choose a selection of the five applied chapters to reflect their and their students' interest.

NEW TO THE FIFTH EDITION

Since student response to previous editions has been very positive, careful attention has been given to retain the style of presentation and the voice of the previous editions. Every change is designed to preserve the delicate balance of rigor with the text's overriding goal of relevance, accessibility, and student interest.

As with previous editions, the exercises are crafted to reflect the skills that are presented in each section, but also to be interesting and relevant to people's lives. There are more than 3000 exercises, many of which contain multiple parts in order for students to appreciate the importance of in-depth analysis. Some exercises were rewritten to offer more clarity, while others were replaced with completely new material. In each case, the changes reflect careful consideration of the need to provide exercises that accurately reflect the skills that students learn in each section of the book.

Part III Formal Logic   191

New: **Appendix A: Cognitive Bias** has been created to provide coverage of a topic that many instructors have requested. The decision to place this material in an appendix stemmed from the various needs of instructors. For example, some instructors want to introduce this topic early in the course, so they suggested it go in Chapter 1; others thought that it would fit nicely into Chapter 4, "Informal Fallacies"; still others want to use the material on cognitive bias, but since they don't use Chapter 4 in their custom book, they would rather have it as a separate chapter. Taking all this into consideration, we determined that the best course of action is to have the material in a separate appendix, so instructors can decide where it fits best into their course. We have also created a set of exercises for this new appendix. The exercises can be found with the book's student resources, which can be loaded into an instructor's learning management system (via **Oxford Learning Link Direct**, see p. xxi) or hosted on OUP's platform (via **Oxford Learning Cloud**, see p. xxi); they are auto-graded, with the results recorded in the instructor's gradebook.

New: **A unique set of LSAT-type exercises has been created for Appendix B: The LSAT and Logical Reasoning.** These special exercises provide an opportunity for students to directly test the skills presented in this appendix. The exercises can be found with the book's student resources, which can be loaded into an instructor's institution's learning management system (via **Oxford Learning Link Direct**, see p. xxi) or hosted on OUP's platform (via **Oxford Learning Cloud**, see p. xxi); they are auto-graded, with the results recorded in the instructor's gradebook.

New Long Proofs: Since many instructors have requested additional long proof exercises in Chapters 8 and 9, *we have added twenty-four new long proof exercises* (many requiring thirty to fifty lines). These exercises can be used to further challenge students' mastery of the rules, tactics, and strategies involved in natural deduction and predicate logic proofs. The specific exercise sets where these new long proof exercises occur are as follows: Chapter 8, Exercises 8F.IV, 8G.I, 8H.I, and 8I; Chapter 9, Exercises 9C.II, 9D.I, and 9G.2.

Chapter 1: New extended discussion and example and to illustrate different ways to create *counterexamples* to arguments (section 1F).

Chapter 4: We clarified the discussion of *false cause fallacies* to help distinguish specific types of fallacies that fall under that heading.

Chapter 5: Additional information is offered to specify how members of the subject class for **I**-propositions and **O**-propositions are to be understood regarding class inclusion or exclusion (section 5B). The discussion of *exceptive propositions* has been expanded in "Propositions Requiring Two Translations" (section 5H), to help students understand when to translate an exclusive proposition containing "only" as a compound statement. This new material helps illustrate the idea that whenever we talk or write, it is possible that part of our audience may lack some of the general knowledge regarding a factual issue that we take for granted. Thus, when a statement refers to an *individual*, sometimes it is best to spell out in detail a fact that may not be universally known to all.

Chapter 13: In 13A, the details regarding statistical arguments have been expanded. The new discussion explains how asking a few simple questions can facilitate the extraction of specific information about the *sample, population,* and *conclusion* of a statistical argument. The answers to these questions provides students with more precise analysis techniques that they can apply to the exercise sets.

Chapter 14: A new subsection in 14H, "Putting It All Together," offers a comprehensive illustration of how the three requirements for a fair test of a hypothesis can be applied to our understanding of a historical scientific case study. Mendel's research and theory offer a clear example of how a *prediction* needs to be *verifiable, nontrivial,* and *logically connected to a hypothesis* in order to provide evidence that either confirms or refutes a hypothesis.

Exercise set 14H has ten new case studies for analysis. They provide additional in-depth analysis of the important ideas, such as picking out the hypothesis, experiment, and prediction; determining whether the evidence confirms or disconfirms the hypothesis; and determining the strength of the argument by checking for any reasonable alternative explanations or other possible facts which, if uncovered, would weaken the causal claim.

SPECIAL FEATURES

The features that instructors found most useful in the fourth edition have been retained:

- Each chapter opens with a *preview*, beginning with real-life examples and outlining the questions to be addressed. It thus serves both as motivation and overview, and wherever possible it explicitly bridges both formal and informal logic to real life. For example, Chapter 1 starts with the deluge of information facing students today, to show the very need for a course in logic or critical thinking.
- Marginal definitions of key terms are provided for quick reference. Key terms appear in boldface when they are first introduced.
- The use of reference boxes has been expanded, since they have proven useful to both students and instructors. They capture material that is spread out over a number of pages in one place for easy reference.
- *Profiles in Logic* are short sketches of logicians, philosophers, mathematicians, and others associated with logic. The men and women in these sketches range in time from Aristotle and the Stoics to Christine Ladd-Franklin, the early ENIAC programmers, and others in the past century.
- Bulleted summaries are provided at the end of each chapter, as well as a list of key terms.
- The *Exercises* include a solution to the first problem in each set. Explanations are also provided where additional clarity is needed. This provides a model for students to follow, so they can see what is expected of their answers. In addition, approximately 25% of the exercises have answers provided at the back of the book.

- End-of-chapter *Logic Challenge* problems are included for each chapter. These are the kind of puzzles—like the problem of the hats, the truth teller and the liar, and the scale and the coins—that have long kept people thinking. They end chapters on a fun note, not to mention with a reminder that the challenges of logic are always lurking in plain English.
- A full glossary and index are located at the end of the book.

STUDENT AND INSTRUCTOR RESOURCES

Digital Learning Tools to Enrich and Enhance Your Course

Every new print and digital copy of *Logic*, Fifth Edition, comes with a wealth of digital teaching and learning tools to ensure your students' success in the course. These resources can be delivered directly into your learning management system (via **Oxford Learning Link Direct**) or in OUP's simple, intuitive, mobile-friendly learning platform (**Oxford Learning Cloud**). For more information on the digital learning tools in *Logic*, Fifth Edition, and how to integrate them into your course, contact your Oxford University Press representative or visit www.oup.com/he/baronett5e.

Instructor Planning and Assessment Tools

- An assignable **Proof-Checking Module** for solving symbolic proofs that allows students to enter proof solutions, check their validity, and receive feedback, both for individual lines of the proof and for a completed proof, as well as **Venn Diagram** and **Truth Table Creation Modules** that feed automatically into a gradebook that offers instructors the chance to view students' individual attempts.
- **Multiple Sets of assignable Exercises per topic and book section** with a total of around 3200 questions that feed automatically into a gradebook and offer instructors the chance to view students' individual attempts.
- A 1500 question **Test Bank**, available either as a **Test Bank course package** for use in building high-stakes assessment in your learning management system, or **in MS Word format**, for use in hard-copy exams and homework assignments, including some open-ended questions that allow students to develop extended analysis, such as drawing Venn diagrams, completing truth tables, and doing proofs.
- **PowerPoint-based Lecture Outlines for each chapter, to assist the instructor in leading classroom discussion.**

- An **Instructor's Manual**, which includes:
  - Complete answers to every set of exercises in the book—around 3000 exercises in total—including extended explanations for many of the questions that often require additional discussion and clarification.
  - Complete answers and extended explanations for every end-of-chapter "Logic Challenge."
  - A traditional "Pencil-and-Paper" version of the **Test Bank**, containing the same 1500 questions as the **Computerized Test Bank**, but converted for use in hard-copy exams and homework assignments, including some open-ended questions that allow students to develop extended analysis, such as drawing Venn diagrams, completing truth tables, and doing proofs.

Student Self-Practice Resources

- **Practice Exercises** containing roughly 1500 multiple-choice and true/false questions, which give students a chance to review what they encountered in each chapter. Each question set is preceded by a short recap of the material pertaining to the questions.
- **Interactive Flashcards** of **Key Terms** and their definitions from the book.
- **Video Tutorials** and **Light Board** Videos that work through specific example questions, bringing key concepts to life and guiding students on how to approach various problem types.
- **Chapter Guides** for reading that help students to think broadly and comparatively about the new ideas they encounter.
- **Tip Sheets** that help students to understand particularly complicated ideas presented in each chapter.
- **Bonus Chapter 15**, "Analyzing a Long Essay."

Enhanced eBook

Oxford's enhanced eBooks combine high-quality text with a rich assortment of integrated multimedia and self-practice activities to deliver a more engaging and interactive learning experience. The enhanced eBook version of *Logic*, Fifth Edition, is included within Oxford Learning Link Direct and Oxford Learning Cloud. It is also available from leading higher education eBook vendors and through Inclusive Access programs via RedShelf and VitalSource. Marginal icons in the print text indicate the presence of related self-practice questions, video tutorials, and other study resources within the enhanced eBook.

Self-Practice
Questions

Video Tutorial

Study Materials

Flexible Delivery Options

For self-study, students can access the digital materials in the **enhanced eBook** and at www.oup.com/he/baronett5e.

To reiterate, all of the digital learning tools in *Logic*, Fifth Edition can be delivered directly into your learning management system (via **Oxford Learning Link Direct**) or in OUP's simple, intuitive, mobile-friendly learning platform (**Oxford Learning Cloud**).

Oxford Learning Link Direct

Bring the digital teaching and learning tools for *Logic*, Fifth Edition, right to your institution's learning management system. Instructors and their LMS administrators simply download the Oxford Learning Link Direct Cartridge from Oxford Learning Link, and with the turn of a digital key, incorporate the digital learning tools of *Logic*, Fifth Edition directly into their LMS for assigning and grading.

Oxford Learning Cloud

Developed for instructors who do not use a learning management system or prefer an easy-to-use alternative to their school's designated LMS, Oxford Learning Cloud delivers the digital learning tools of *Logic*, Fifth Edition within a simple, intuitive, mobile-friendly, cloud-based learning platform. Learning Cloud offers pre-built courses that instructors can use "off the shelf" or customize to fit their needs. A built-in gradebook provides instructors with a convenient way to monitor student performance.

For more information on the digital teaching and learning tools in *Logic,* Fifth Edition and how to integrate them into your course, contact your Oxford University Press representative or visit www.oup.com/he/baronett5e.

ALTERNATE FORMATS AND CUSTOM EDITIONS

Because every course and professor is unique, *Logic*, Fifth Edition, is available in a variety of formats to fit any course structure or student budget.

The full text can be purchased in numerous formats:

- Print, ISBN: 9780197602362
- eBook, ISBN: 9780197602393
- Loose leaf, ISBN: 9780197602379

Additionally, access to the book's assignable student resources, which can be loaded into an instructor's institution's learning management system (via **Oxford Learning Link Direct**) or hosted on OUP's platform (via **Oxford Learning Cloud**), including a full interactive version of the text, is included with each new copy of the book in any format, and can also be purchased directly by students without the need for a print text. Please see the Instructor and Student Resources section of the preface for more information on **Oxford Learning Link Direct** and **Oxford Learning Cloud**.

For those who do not wish to assign the complete text, Alternate and Custom Editions are available in both print and digital format. Each Alternate Edition comes with answers to problems, a full glossary, and an index, as well as access to the book's assignable student resources. Please see the following ISBN information:

Logic: Concise Edition
>Chapters 1, 3, 4, 5, 6, 7, 8
>Order the print version using ISBN: 9780197602713.
>The eBook version is available from numerous eBook vendors. Look for eBook
>>ISBN: 9780197602447.

Logic: An Emphasis on Critical Thinking and Informal Logic
>Chapters 1, 2, 3, 4, 10, 11, 12, 13, 14
>The eBook version is available from numerous eBook vendors. Look for eBook
>>ISBN: 9780197602454.

Logic: An Emphasis on Formal Logic
>Chapters 1, 4, 5, 6, 7, 8, 9
>Order the print version using ISBN: 9780197602409.
>The eBook version is available from numerous eBook vendors. Look for eBook
>>ISBN: 9780197602423.

It is also possible to create a customized textbook by choosing the specific chapters necessary for a course. For more information on Alternate and Custom Editions, please contact your Oxford University Press sales representative, or call 1-800-280-0280 for details.

ACKNOWLEDGMENTS

For their very helpful suggestions throughout the writing process, I would like to thank the following reviewers:

>Mohamad Al-Hakim, Florida Gulf Coast University
>Guy Axtell, Radford University
>Ida Baltikauskas, Century College
>Joshua Beattie, California State University–East Bay
>Luisa Benton, Richland College
>Michael Boring, Estrella Mountain Community College
>Daniel Brunson, Morgan State University
>Julia R. Bursten, University of Kentucky

Jonathan Buttaci, The Catholic University of America
Jeremy Byrd, Tarrant County College
Bernardo Cantens, Moravian College
John Casey, Northeastern Illinois University
Darron Chapman, University of Louisville
Eric Chelstrom, Minnesota State University, Moorhead
Lynnette Chen, Humboldt State University
Kevin DeLapp, Converse College
Tobyn DeMarco, Bergen Community College
William Devlin, Bridgewater State University
Kristin Doneed, Anoka Ramsey Community College
Justin Donhauser, Bowling Green State University
Ian Duckles, Mesa College
David Lyle Dyas, Los Angeles Mission College
David Elliot, University of Regina
Thompson M. Faller, University of Portland
Anthony Ferrucci, Green River College
Craig Fox, California State University, Pennsylvania
Matthew Frise, Baylor University
Dimitria Electra Gatzia, University of Akron
Geoff B. Georgi, West Virginia University
David Gilboa, University of Wisconsin, Oshkosh
Cara Gillis, Pierce College
Nathaniel Goldberg, Washington and Lee University
Michael Goodman, Humboldt State University
Justin Grace, Tarrant County College Southeast Campus
John Grey, Michigan State University
Mary Gwin, San Diego Mesa College
Alicia Hall, Mississippi State University
Matthew Hallgarth, Tarleton State University
Anthony Hanson, De AnzaCollege
Merle Harton, Jr., Everglades University
John Helsel, University of Colorado,Boulder
Will Heusser, Cypress College
Ryan Hickerson, Western Oregon University
Charles Hogg, Grand Valley State University
Jeremy D. Hovda, Katholieke Universiteit Leuven
Debby D. Hutchins, Gonzaga University
Brian Huth, Kent State University
Daniel Jacobson, University of Michigan– Ann Arbor
William S. Jamison, University of Alaska Anchorage
Benjamin C. Jantzen, Virginia Polytechnic Institute & State University
Gary James Jason, California State University, Fullerton

William M. Kallfelz, Mississippi State University
Robert Larmer, University of New Brunswick
Lory Lemke, University of Minnesota–Morris
Court Lewis, Owensboro Community and Technical College
David Liebesman, Boston University
Brandon C. Look, University of Kentucky
Ian D. MacKinnon, University of Akron
Justin McBrayer, Fort Lewis College
Erik Meade, Southern Illinois University Edwardsville
Alexander Miller, Piedmont Technical College
Jonathan S. Miller, Pasadena City College
James Moore, Georgia Perimeter College
Margaret Moore, University of Tennessee
Allyson Mount, Keene State College
Nathaniel Nicol, Washington State University
Hyungrae Noh, The University of Iowa
Rosibel O'Brien-Cruz, Harold Washington College
Len Olsen, Florida Southwestern State College
Joseph B. Onyango Okello, Asbury Theological Seminary
Stephen Russell Orr, Solano Community College
Lawrence Pasternack, Oklahoma State University
James Pearson, Bridgewater State University
Christian Perring, Dowling College
Adam C. Podlaskowski, Fairmont State University
Michael Potts, Methodist University
Mark Reed, Tarrant County College
Greg Rich, Fayetteville State University
Miles Rind, Boston College
Linda Rollin, Colorado State University
Marcus Rossberg, University of Connecticut
Frank X. Ryan, Kent State University
Eric Saidel, George Washington University
Kelly Salsbery, Stephen F. Austin State University
David Sanson, Illinois State University
Stephanie Semler, Virginia Polytechnic Institute & State University
Robert Shanab, University of Nevada–Las Vegas
David Shier, Washington State University
Aeon J. Skoble, Bridgewater State University
Nancy Slonneger- Hancock, Northern Kentucky University
Basil Smith, Saddleback College
Joshua Smith, Central Michigan University
Paula Smithka, University of Southern Mississippi
Deborah Hansen Soles, Wichita State University

Charles Stein, St. Mary's College of Maryland
David Stern, University of Iowa
Tim Sundell, University of Kentucky
Eric Swanson, University of Michigan, Ann Arbor
Matthew Talbert, West Virginia University
Erin Tarver, Emory University
James Taylor, College of New Jersey
Ramon Tello, Shasta College
Joia Lewis Turner, St. Paul College
Patricia Turrisi, University of North Carolina–Wilmington
Michael Ventimiglia, Sacred Heart University
Mark C. Vopat, Youngstown State University
Reginald Williams, Bakersfield College
Mia Wood, Pierce College
Kiriake Xerohemona, Florida International University
Jeffrey Zents, South Texas College

Many thanks also to the staff at Oxford University Press:
    Andy Blitzer: Acquisitions Editor
    Rachel Boland: Assistant Editor
    Lacey Harvey: Assistant Editor
    Melissa Yanuzzi: Senior Production Editor, Print
    Michael Quilligan: Senior Media Editor
    Peter Lacey: Digital Resource Development Editor
    Molly Crowell: Digital Resource Development Assistant
    Michele Laseau: Art Director
    Sheryl Adams: Marketing Manager
    Jenobia Ser: Marketing Assistant

I also wish to thank Mary Anne Shahidi, who copyedited the manuscript, and Katie Klasmeier, who created the *Profiles in Logic* portraits.

PART I

SETTING THE STAGE

Chapter 1

What Logic Studies

Digital homework exercises for this chapter are available in your instructor's online course. For information on how to access these resources, please visit **www.oup.com/he/baronett5e**.

We live in the Information Age. The Internet provides access to millions of books and articles from around the world. Websites, blogs, and online forums contain instant commentary about events, and cell phones allow mobile access to breaking stories and worldwide communication. Cable television provides local and world news 24 hours a day. Some of the information is simply entertaining. However, we also find stories that are important to our lives. In fact, they may do more than just supply facts. They may make us want to nod in agreement or express disbelief. For example, suppose you read the following:

> The Senate recently held hearings on for-profit colleges, investigating charges that the schools rake in federal loan money, while failing to adequately educate students. Critics point to deceptive sales tactics, fraudulent loan applications, high drop-out rates, and even higher tuitions. In response, the Department of Education has proposed a "gainful employment" rule, which would cut financing to for-profit colleges that graduate (or fail) students with thousands of dollars of debt and no prospect of salaries high enough to pay them off.
>
> Jeremy Dehn, "Degrees of Debt"

If the information in this passage is accurate, then government decisions might affect thousands of people. On reading this, you would probably search for related material, to determine whether the information is correct. However, you would be concerned for more than just accuracy. You would also be asking what it means for you. Are the critics correct? Are the new rules justified, and do they address the criticism? Further research on the topic might help answer your questions.

Other types of information contain different claims. For example, in 2005, California passed a law prohibiting the sale of violent video games to minors. The law applied to games (a) in which the range of options available to a player includes killing, maiming, dismembering, or sexually assaulting an image of a human being, (b) that are offensive to prevailing standards in the community, and (c) that lack serious literary, artistic, political, or scientific value for minors. Representatives for the video game industry argued that the law was unconstitutional. The case went to the Supreme Court, where the decision was 7–2 in favor of overturning the law. Here is an excerpt of the Court's decision:

> Like protected books, plays, and movies, video games communicate ideas through familiar literary devices and features distinctive to the medium. And the basic principles of freedom of speech do not vary with a new and different communication medium. The most basic principle—that government lacks the power to restrict expression because of its message, ideas, subject matter, or content—is subject to a few limited exceptions for historically unprotected speech, such as obscenity, incitement, and fighting words. But a legislature cannot create new categories of unprotected speech simply by weighing the value of a particular category against its social costs and then punishing it if it fails the test. Therefore, video games qualify for First Amendment protection.

Adapted from *California v. Entertainment Merchants Association*

The information in this passage contains an argument. An **argument** is a group of **statements** (sentences that are either true or false) in which the conclusion is claimed to follow from the premise(s). A **premise** is the information intended to provide support for the **conclusion** (the main point of an argument). An argument can have one or more premises, but only one conclusion. In the foregoing example, the conclusion is "video games qualify for First Amendment protection." The premises are the first four sentences of the passage.

It is quite common for people to concentrate on the individual statements in an argument and investigate whether they are true or false. Since people want to know things, the actual truth or falsity of statements is important; but it is not the only important question. Equally important is the question "Assuming the premises are true, do they support the conclusion?" This question offers a glimpse of the role of logic. **Logic** is the systematic use of methods and principles to analyze, evaluate, and construct arguments.

Arguments can be simple, but they can also be quite complex. In the argument regarding video games and the First Amendment, the premises and conclusion are not difficult to recognize. However, this is not always the case. Here is an example of a complex piece of reasoning taken from the novel *Catch-22*, by Joseph Heller:

> There was only one catch and that was Catch-22, which specified that a concern for one's own safety in the face of dangers that were real and immediate was the process of a rational mind. Orr was crazy and could be grounded. All he had to do

Argument A group of statements in which the conclusion is claimed to follow from the premise(s).

Statement A sentence that is either true or false.

Premise The information intended to provide support for a conclusion.

Conclusion The statement that is claimed to follow from the premises of an argument; the main point of an argument.

Logic The systematic use of methods and principles to analyze, evaluate and construct arguments.

was ask; and as soon as he did, he would no longer be crazy and would have to fly more missions. Orr would be crazy to fly more missions and sane if he didn't, but if he was sane he had to fly them. If he flew them he was crazy and didn't have to; but if he didn't want to he was sane and had to. Yossarian was moved very deeply by the absolute simplicity of this clause of Catch-22 and let out a respectful whistle.

This passage cleverly illustrates complex reasoning. Once you know how to tease apart its premises and conclusions, you may find yourself as impressed as Yossarian.

Logic investigates the level of correctness of the reasoning found in arguments. There are many times when we need to evaluate information. Although everyone reasons, few stop to think about reasoning. Logic provides the skills needed to identify other people's arguments, putting you in a position to offer coherent and precise analysis of those arguments. Learning logical skills enables you to subject your own arguments to that same analysis, thereby anticipating challenges and criticism. Logic can help, and this book will show you how. It introduces the tools of logical analysis and presents practical applications of logic.

A. STATEMENTS AND ARGUMENTS

The terms "sentence," "statement," and "proposition" are related, but distinct. Logicians use the term "statement" to refer to a specific kind of sentence in a particular language—a *declarative sentence*. As the name indicates, we declare, assert, claim, or affirm that something is the case. In this sense every statement is either true or false, and these two possibilities are called **truth values**. For example, the statement "Water freezes at 32° F" is in English, and it is true. Translated into other languages we get the following statements:

Truth value Every statement is either true or false; these two possibilities are called *truth values.*

El agua se congela a 32° F. (Spanish)

Wasser gefriert bei 32° F. (German)

Pānī 32 digrī ēpha mēṁfreezes. (Hindi)

L'eau gèle à 32° F. (French)

Nu'ó'c đóng băng ó' 32° F. (Vietnamese)

Tubig freezes sa 32° F. (Filipino)

Air membeku pada 32° F. (Malay)

Maji hunganda yapitapo nyuzi joto 32° F. (Swahili)

The foregoing list contains eight *sentences* in eight different languages that certainly look different and, if spoken, definitely sound different. Since the eight sentences are all declarative sentences, they are all *statements*. However, the eight statements all *make the same claim*, and it is in that sense that logicians use the term "proposition." In other words, a **proposition** is the information content imparted by a statement, or, simply put, its meaning. Since each of the eight statements makes the same claim, they all have the same truth value.

Proposition The information content imparted by a statement, or, simply put, its meaning.

Although we are able to connect basic logic to ordinary language, we will not always be able to capture all the various conversational contexts, intricacies, and nuances of ordinary language. Since some statements in everyday conversation can communicate more than their informational contents, there can be a difference between what is *stated* and what is *implied*. For example, suppose you ask a stranger on the street, "Where can I get something to eat?" The stranger might reply, "There is a restaurant around the corner." The speaker *implies* that you can get something to eat at the restaurant, but the stranger did not explicitly say that. However, this does not affect the truth value of the stranger's statement: If there is a restaurant around the corner, then the statement is true; if there is not a restaurant around the corner, then the statement is false.

It is not necessary for us to know the truth value of a proposition to recognize that it must be either true or false. For example, the statement "There is a diamond ring buried fifty feet under my house" is either true or false regardless of whether or not anyone ever looks there. The same holds for the statement "Abraham Lincoln sneezed four times on his 21st birthday." We can accept that this statement must be true or false, although it is unlikely that we will ever know its truth value.

Many sentences do not have truth values. Here are some examples:

What time is it? (Question)
Clean your room now. (Command)
Please clean your room. (Request)
Let's do lunch tomorrow. (Proposal)

None of these sentences make an assertion or claim, so they are neither true nor false. Quite often we must rely on context to decide whether a sentence is being used as a statement. For example, in the song "Visions of Johanna," Bob Dylan wrote: "The ghost of 'lectricity howls in the bones of her face." Given its use of imagery, we probably should not interpret Dylan as making a claim that is either true or false. The term **inference** is used by logicians to refer to the *reasoning process* that is expressed by an argument. The act or process of reasoning from premises to a conclusion is sometimes referred to as *drawing an inference*. Arguments are created in order to establish support for a claim, and the premises are supposed to provide good reasons for accepting the conclusion.

Inference A term used by logicians to refer to the reasoning process that is expressed by an argument.

Arguments can be found in almost every part of human activity. Of course, when we use the term in a logical setting, we do not mean the kinds of verbal disputes that can get highly emotional and even violent. Logical analysis of arguments relies on rational use of language and reasoning skills. It is organized, is well thought out, and appeals to relevant reasons and justification.

Arguments arise when we expect people to know what they are talking about. Car mechanics, plumbers, carpenters, electricians, engineers, computer programmers, accountants, nurses, office workers, and managers all use arguments regularly. Arguments are used to convince others to buy, repair, or upgrade a product. Arguments can be found in political debates, and in ethical and moral disputes. Although it is common to witness the emotional type of arguments when fans discuss sports, for example, nevertheless there can be logical arguments even in that setting. For example, if fans use statistics and historical data to support their position, they can create rational and logical arguments.

B. RECOGNIZING ARGUMENTS

Studying logic enables us to master many important skills. It helps us to recognize and identify arguments correctly, in either written or oral form. In real life, arguments are rarely found in nice neat packages. We often have to dig them out, like prospectors searching for gold. We might find the premises and conclusions occurring in any order in an argument. In addition, we often encounter incomplete arguments, so we must be able to recognize arguments even if they are not completely spelled out.

An argument offers reasons in support of a conclusion. However, not all groups of sentences are arguments. A series of sentences that express *beliefs* or *opinions*, by themselves, do not constitute an argument. For example, suppose someone says the following:

> I wish the government would do something about the unemployment situation. It makes me angry to see some CEOs of large corporations getting huge bonuses while at the same time the corporation is laying off workers.

The sentences certainly let us know how the person feels. However, none of the sentences seem to offer any support for a conclusion. In addition, none of the sentences seem to be a conclusion. Of course it sometimes happens that opinions are meant to act as premises of an argument. For example, suppose someone says the following:

> I don't like movies that rely on computer-generated graphics to take the place of intelligent dialogue, interesting characters, and an intricate plot. After watching the ads on TV, I have the feeling that the new movie *Bad Blood and Good Vibes* is not very good. Therefore, I predict that it will not win any Academy Awards.

Although the first two sentences express opinions and feelings, they are offered as reasons in support of the last sentence, which is the conclusion.

Many newspaper articles are good sources of information. They are often written specifically to answer the five key points of reporting: *who, what, where, when,* and *why.* A well-written article can provide details and key points, but it need not conclude anything. Reporters sometimes simply provide information, with no intention of giving reasons in support of a conclusion. On the other hand, the editorial page of newspapers can be a good source of arguments. Editorials generally provide extensive information as *premises,* meant to support a position strongly held by the editor. The editorial page usually contains letters to the editor. Although these pieces are often highly emotional responses to social problems, some of them do contain arguments.

When people write or speak, it is not always clear that they are trying to conclude something. Written material can be quite difficult to analyze because we are generally not in a position to question the author for clarification. We cannot always be certain that what we think are the conclusion and premises are, in fact, what the author had intended. Yet we can, and should, attempt to provide justification for our interpretation. If we are speaking with someone, at least we can stop the conversation and seek clarification. When we share a common language and have similar sets of background knowledge and experiences, then we can recognize arguments when they occur by calling on those shared properties.

Since every argument must have a conclusion, it sometimes helps if we try to identify that first. Our shared language provides **conclusion indicators**—useful words that nearly all of us call on when we wish to conclude something. For example, we often use the word "therefore" to indicate our main point. Here are other words or phrases to help recognize a conclusion:

CONCLUSION INDICATORS

Therefore	Consequently	It proves that
Thus	In conclusion	It suggests that
So	It follows that	It implies that
Hence	We can infer that	We can conclude that

We can see them at work in the following examples:

1. Salaries are up. Unemployment is down. People are happy. *Therefore*, reelect me.
2. Salaries are down. Unemployment is up. People are not happy. *Consequently*, we should throw the governor out of office.
3. The book was boring. The movie based on the book was boring. The author of both the book and the screenplay is Horst Patoot. *It follows that* he is a lousy writer.

Although conclusion indicators can help us to identify arguments, they are not always available to us, as in this example:

> We should boycott that company. They have been found guilty of producing widgets that they knew were faulty, and that caused numerous injuries.

If you are not sure which sentence is the conclusion, you can simply place the word "therefore" in front of each of them to see which works best. In this case, the first sentence seems to be the point of the argument, and the second sentence seems to offer reasons in support of the conclusion. In other words, *because* the company has been found guilty of producing widgets that they knew were faulty, and that caused numerous injuries, *therefore* we should boycott the company.

In addition to identifying the conclusion, our analysis also helped reveal the premise. As with "because" in this example, a **premise indicator** distinguishes the premise from the conclusion. Here are other words or phrases that can help in recognizing an argument:

PREMISE INDICATORS

Because	Assuming that	As indicated by
Since	As shown by	Seeing that
Given that	For the reason(s) that	It follows from

When premise and conclusion indicators are not present, you can still apply some simple strategies to identify the parts of an argument. First, to help locate the conclusion, try placing the word "therefore" in front of the statements. Second, to help locate the premise or premises, try placing the word "because" in front of the statements.

In some cases you will have to read a passage a few times in order to determine whether an argument is presented. You should keep a few basic ideas in mind as you read. For one thing, at least one of the statements in the passage has to provide a reason or evidence for some other statement; in other words, it must be a premise. Second, there must be a claim that the premise supports or implies a conclusion. If a passage *expresses a reasoning process*—that the conclusion follows from the premises—then we say that it makes an **inferential claim**. The inferential claim is an objective feature of an argument, and it can be *explicit* or *implicit*. Explicit inferential claims can often be identified by the premise and conclusion indicator words and phrases discussed earlier (e.g., "because" and "therefore"). On the other hand, while implicit inferential claims do not have explicit indicator words, they still contain an inferential relationship between the premises and the conclusion. In these cases we follow the advice given earlier by supplying the words "therefore" or "because" to the statements in the passage in order to help reveal the inferential claim that is implicit.

Inferential claim If a passage expresses a reasoning process—that the conclusion follows from the premises—then we say that it makes an inferential claim.

Of course, determining whether a given passage in ordinary language contains an argument takes practice. Even the presence of an indicator word may not by itself mean that the passage contains an argument:

> He climbed the fence, threaded his stealthy way through the plants, till he stood under that window; he looked up at it long, and with emotion; then he laid him down on the ground under it, disposing himself upon his back, with his hands clasped upon his breast and holding his poor wilted flower. And *thus* he would die—out in the cold world, with no shelter over his homeless head, no friendly hand to wipe the death-damps from his brow, no loving face to bend pityingly over him when the great agony came.   Mark Twain, *Tom Sawyer*

In this passage the word "thus" (my italics) is not being used as a conclusion indicator. It simply indicates the manner in which the character would die. Here is another example:

> The modern cell phone was invented during the 1970s by an engineer working for the Motorola Corporation. However, the communications technologies that made cell phones possible had been under development *since* the late 1940s. Eventually, the ability to make and receive calls with a mobile telephone handset revolutionized the world of personal communications, with the technology still evolving in the early 21st century.   Tom Streissguth, "How Were Cell Phones Invented?"

Although the passage contains the word "since" (my italics), it is not being used as a premise indicator. Instead, it is used to indicate the period during which communications technology was developing.

We pointed out that *beliefs* or *opinions* by themselves do not constitute an argument. For example, the following passage simply *reports* information, without expressing a reasoning process:

> Approximately 2,000 red-winged blackbirds fell dead from the sky in a central Arkansas town. The birds had fallen over a 1-mile area, and an aerial survey indicated that no other dead birds were found outside of that area. Wildlife officials will examine the birds to try to figure out what caused the mysterious event.
> "Why Did 2,000 Dead Birds Fall From Sky?" Associated Press

The statements in the passage provide information about an ongoing situation, but no conclusion is put forward, and none of the statements are offered as premises.

A noninferential passage can occur when someone provides *advice* or words of wisdom. Someone may recommend that you act in a certain way, or someone may give you advice to help you make a decision. Yet if no evidence is presented to support the advice, then no inferential claim is made. Here are a few simple examples:

> In three words I can sum up everything I've learned about life: it goes on.
> > Robert Frost, as quoted in *The Harper Book of Quotations* by Robert I. Fitzhenry

> People spend a lifetime searching for happiness; looking for peace. They chase idle dreams, addictions, religions, even other people, hoping to fill the emptiness that plagues them. The irony is the only place they ever needed to search was within.
> > Ramona L. Anderson, as quoted in *Wisdom for the Soul* by Larry Chang

The passages may influence our thinking or get us to reevaluate our beliefs, but they are noninferential. The same applies to *warnings*, a special kind of advice that cautions us to avoid certain situations:

- Dangerous currents. No lifeguard on duty.
- All items left unattended will be removed.
- Unauthorized cars will be towed at owner's expense.

The truth value of these statements can be open to investigation, but there is no argument. No evidence is provided to support the statements, so the warnings, however important they may be, are not inferential.

Sometimes a passage contains *unsupported* or *loosely associated statements* that elaborate on a topic but do not make an inferential claim:

> Coaching takes time, it takes involvement, it takes understanding and patience.
> > Byron and Catherine Pulsifer, "Challenges in Adopting a Coaching Style"

> Our ability to respect others is the true mark of our humanity. Respect for other people is the essence of human rights.   Daisaku Ikeda, "Words of Wisdom"

The passages lack an inferential claim. The statements in the passages may elaborate a point, but they do not support a conclusion.

Some passages contain information that illustrates how something is done, or what something means, or even how to do a calculation. An *illustration* may be informative without making an inferential claim:

> To lose one pound of fat, you must burn approximately 3500 calories over and above what you already burn doing daily activities. That sounds like a lot of calories and you certainly wouldn't want to try to burn 3500 calories in one day. However, by taking it step-by-step, you can determine just what you need to do each day to burn or cut out those extra calories.
> > Paige Waehner, "How to Lose Weight: The Basics of Weight Loss"

The passage provides information about calories, fat, and weight loss. It illustrates what is required in order to lose one pound of fat, but it does not make an inferential claim. For another example, a passage may define a technical term:

> In order to measure the performance of one investment relative to another you can calculate the "Return on Investment (ROI)." Quite simply, *ROI* is based on returns over a certain time period (e.g., one year) and it is expressed as a percentage. Here's an example that illustrates how to perform the calculation: A 25% annual ROI would mean that a $100 investment returns $25 in one year. Thus, in one year the total investment becomes $125.
>
> "How to Calculate a Return on an Investment," eHow, Inc.

The passage defines "Return on Investment" and illustrates how to do a simple calculation. However, even though the word "thus" occurs at the beginning of the last statement, it is not a conclusion indicator in this context.

A passage might combine several of the things we have been describing—a report, an illustration, and an example—which makes it more challenging to decide whether it's an argument. Let's examine the following passage:

> Last year, more people died from selfies than shark attacks. And many more have been injured by taking their own picture. We're obsessed with proving that we *had* experiences, rather than appreciating them as they occur. We cannot admire a breathtaking mountain without inserting ourselves into the scenery. We're not living in the moment; we're making sure we can demonstrate we *had* the moment to everyone we know (and don't know). Selfies are killing our experiences.
>
> Adapted from Faith Salie, "Death by Selfie," CBS Interactive Inc.

The passage provides information about the dangers posed from taking selfies. It also describes how the proliferation of selfies has changed the way we experience life. Although the passage does not contain a conclusion indicator word or phrase, the sentence "Selfies are killing our experiences" can be used as the basis for interpreting the passage as expressing an implicit inferential claim.

There is one more topic regarding noninferential passages that needs to be explored—the role of *explanations*. That discussion will be presented in the next section.

EXERCISES 1B

Self-Practice
Questions

I. **Pick out the premises and conclusions in the following arguments. (A complete answer to the first problem in each exercise section is given as a model for you to follow. The problems marked with a star are answered in the back of the book.)**

1. Exercise helps strengthen your cardiovascular system. It also lowers your cholesterol, increases the blood flow to the brain, and enables you to think longer. Thus, there is no reason for you not to start exercising regularly.

Answer:
Premises:

    (a) Exercise helps strengthen your cardiovascular system.
    (b) It (exercise) also lowers your cholesterol.
    (c) (Exercise) increases the blood flow to the brain.
    (d) (Exercise) enables you to think longer.

Conclusion: There is no reason for you not to start exercising regularly. The indicator word "Thus" helps identify the conclusion. The other statements are offered in support of this claim.

2. If you start a strenuous exercise regimen before you know if your body is ready, you can cause serious damage. Therefore, you should always have a physical checkup before you start a rigid exercise program.

3. Since television commercials help pay the cost of programming, and because I can always turn off the sound of the commercials, go to the bathroom, or get something to eat or drink, it follows that commercials are not such a bad thing.

4. Since television commercials disrupt the flow of programs, and given that any disruption impedes the continuity of a show, consequently we can safely say that commercials are a bad thing.

⭐ 5. We should never take our friends for granted. True friends are there when we need them. They suffer with us when we fail, and they are happy when we succeed.

6. They say that "absence makes the heart grow fonder," so my teachers should really love me, since I have been absent for the last 2 weeks.

7. I think, therefore I am.
                                                 René Descartes

8. I believe that humans will evolve into androids, because we will eventually be able to replace all organic body parts with artificial parts. In addition, we will be able to live virtually forever by simply replacing the parts when they wear out or become defective.

⭐ 9. At one time Gary Kasparov had the highest ranking of any chess grand master in history. However, he was beaten in a chess tournament by a computer program called Deep Blue, so the computer program should be given a ranking higher than Kasparov.

10. It is true that $1 + 4 = 5$, and it is also true that $2 + 3 = 5$. Thus, we can conclude with certainty that $(1 + 4) = (2 + 3)$.

11. We are experiencing a loss of privacy through CCTV cameras tracking our every move. "Smart" homes and appliances can get us to change our behavior. Our children are manipulated by their toys and gadgets. Thus, humans will soon be stripped of their autonomy.

12. You should buy the digital camera at Cameras Galore. After all, you did say that you wanted the most megapixels you can get for up to $600. The digital

Video Tutorial: 1BI
Exercise #4

camera on sale today at Cameras Galore has 25 megapixels and costs $600. But the digital camera on sale at Camera Warehouse has only 18 megapixels and it costs $450.

★13. The world will end on August 6, 2045. I know this because my guru said it would, and so far everything she predicted has happened exactly as she said it would.

14. You ought to start reading more books. Reading helps you to see other points of view. Reading improves critical thinking skills. Moreover, reading makes you a more interesting person.

15. You should eat more vegetables. They contain low levels of cholesterol. They also contain low levels of sodium, fat, and trans fatty acids. High levels of those things are bad for your health.

II. Determine whether the following passages contain arguments. Explain your answers.

1. Our company has paid the highest dividends of any Fortune 500 company for the last 5 consecutive years. In addition, we have not had one labor dispute. Our stock is up 25% in the last quarter.

Answer: Not an argument. The three propositions can be used to support some other claim, but together they simply form a set of propositions with no obvious premise or conclusion.

2. Our cars have the highest resale value on the market. Customer loyalty is at an all-time high. I can give you a good deal on a new car today. You should really buy one of our cars.

3. I hate the new music played today. You can't even find a station on either AM or FM that plays decent music anymore. The movies are no better. They are just high-priced commercials for ridiculous products, designed to dupe unsuspecting, unintelligent, unthinking, unenlightened consumers.

4. We are going to have a recession. For 100 years, anytime the stock market has lost at least 20% of its value from its highest point in any fiscal year, there has been a recession. The current stock market has lost 22% of its value during the last fiscal year.

★ 5. Clare doesn't eat pork, chicken, beef, mutton, veal, venison, turkey, or fish. It follows that she must be a vegetarian.

6. Income tax revenues help pay for many important social programs, and without that money some programs would have to be eliminated. If this happens, many adults and children will suffer needlessly. That is why everyone, individuals and corporations, should not cheat on their income taxes.

7. The cost of electronic items, such as televisions, computers, and cell phones, goes down every year. In addition, the quality of the electronic products goes up every year. More and more people throughout the world will soon be able to afford at least one of those items.

Video Tutorial: 1BII
Exercise #4

8. There is biological evidence that the genetic characteristics for nonviolence have been selected over time by the species, and the height and weight of humans have increased over the centuries.

⭐ 9. He didn't create this situation of fear; he merely exploited it—and rather successfully.

Edward R. Murrow, "See It Now," CBS, March 9, 1954

10. In Italy, for thirty years under the Borgias, they had warfare, terror, murder and bloodshed, but they produced Michelangelo, Leonardo da Vinci and the Renaissance. In Switzerland, they had brotherly love, they had five hundred years of democracy and peace—and what did that produce? The cuckoo clock.

Orson Welles as Harry Lime in *The Third Man*

11. All living things (plants, animals, humans) have the ability to absorb nourishment, to grow, and to propagate. All "living creatures" (animals and humans) have in addition the ability to perceive the world around them and to move about. Moreover, all humans have the ability to think, or otherwise to order their perceptions into various categories and classes. So there are in reality no sharp boundaries in the natural world.

Jostein Gaarder, *Sophie's World*

12. *Veidt:* Will you expose me, undoing the peace millions died for? Kill me, risking subsequent investigation? Morally you're in checkmate.
Jon: Logically, I'm afraid he's right. Exposing this plot, we destroy any chance of peace, dooming Earth to worse destruction. On Mars, you demonstrated life's value. If we would preserve life here, we must remain silent.

Alan Moore and Dave Gibbons, *Watchmen*

⭐ 13. The officer shook his head, perplexed. The handprint on the wall had not been made by the librarian himself; there hadn't been blood on his hands. Besides, the print did not match his, and it was a strange print, the whorls of the fingers unusually worn. It would have been easy to match, except that they'd never recorded one like it.

Elizabeth Kostrova, *The Historian*

14. Johnny wondered if the weather would affect his plans. He worried that all the little fuses and wires he had prepared might have become damp during the night. Who could have thought of rain at this time of year? He felt a sudden shiver of doubt. It was too late now. All was set in motion. If he was to become the most famous man in the valley he had to carry on regardless. He would not fail.

Tash Aw, *The Harmony Silk Factory*

15. It may be no accident that sexual life forms dominate our planet. True, bacteria account for the largest number of individuals, and the greatest biomass. But by any reasonable measures of species diversity, or individual complexity, size, or intelligence, sexual species are paramount. And of the life forms that reproduce sexually, the ones whose reproduction is mediated by mate choice show the greatest biodiversity and the greatest complexity. Without sexual selection, evolution seems limited to the very small, the transient, the parasitic, the bacterial, and the brainless. For this reason, I think that sexual selection may be evolution's most creative force.

Geoffrey Miller, *The Mating Mind*

16. Sue hesitated; and then impulsively told the woman that her husband and herself had been unhappy in their first marriages, after which, terrified at the thought of a second irrevocable union, and lest the conditions of the contract should kill their love, yet wishing to be together, they had literally not found the courage to repeat it, though they had attempted it two or three times. Therefore, though in her own sense of the words she was a married woman, in the landlady's sense she was not.

Thomas Hardy, *Jude the Obscure*

⭐ 17. [A] distinction should be made between whether human life has a purpose and whether one's individual life is purposeful. Human life could have been created for a purpose, yet an individual's life could be devoid of purposes or meaning. Conversely, human life could have been unintended, yet an individual's life could be purposeful.

Brooke Alan Trisel, "Intended and Unintended Life"

18. In 1995, a program called Chinook won a man vs. machine world checkers championship. In 1997, Garry Kasparov, probably the best (human) chess player of all time, lost a match to an IBM computer called Deep Blue. In 2007, checkers was "solved," mathematically ensuring that no human would ever again beat the best machine. In 2011, Ken Jennings and Brad Rutter were routed on "Jeopardy!" by another IBM creation, Watson. And last March, a human champion of Go, Lee Sedol, fell to a Google program in devastating and bewildering fashion.

Oliver Roeder, "The Machines Are Coming for Poker," *FiveThirtyEight*

19. I don't know when children stop dreaming. But I do know when hope starts leaking away, because I've seen it happen. Over the years, I have spent a lot of time talking with school children of all ages. And I have seen the cloud of resignation move across their eyes as they travel through school without making any real progress. They know they are slipping through the net into the huge underclass that our society seems willing to tolerate. We must educate our children. And if we do, I believe that will be enough.

Alan Page, Minnesota Supreme Court Justice, NFL Hall of Fame Induction Speech

20. To me the similarities between the *Titanic* and *Challenger* tragedies are uncanny. Both disasters could have been prevented if those in charge had heeded the warnings of those who knew. In both cases, materials failed due to thermal effects. For the *Titanic*, the steel of her hull was below its ductile-to-brittle transition temperature; and for the *Challenger*, the rubber of the O-rings lost pliability in sub-freezing temperatures. And both tragedies provoked a worldwide discussion about the appropriate role for technology.

Mark E. Eberhart, *Why Things Break*

⭐ 21. Project Gutenberg eBooks are often created from several printed editions, all of which are confirmed as Public Domain in the U.S. unless a copyright notice is included. Thus, we do not necessarily keep eBooks in compliance with any particular paper edition.

Project Gutenberg website

22. Lab tests conducted by a team of Korean researchers revealed that when bacteria are exposed to the standard over-the-counter antibacterial ingredient known as triclosan for hours at a time, the antiseptic formulation is a more potent killer than plain soap. The problem: People wash their hands for a matter of seconds, not hours. And in real-world tests, the research team found no evidence to suggest that normal hand-washing with antibacterial soap does any more to clean the hands than plain soap.

Alan Mozes, "Which Works Better, Plain Soap or Antibacterial?" *HealthDay*

23. We are intelligent beings: intelligent beings cannot have been formed by a crude, blind, insensible being: there is certainly some difference between the ideas of Newton and the dung of a mule. Newton's intelligence, therefore, came from another intelligence.

Voltaire, *Philosophical Dictionary*

24. Churches are block-booking seats for *March of the Penguins*, which is apparently a "condemnation of gay marriage" and puts forward the case for "intelligent design," i.e., Creationism. To be honest, this is good news. If American Christians want to go public on the fact that they're now morally guided by penguins, at least we know where we all stand.   Caitlin Moran, "Penguins Lead Way"

⭐25. Authoritarian governments are identified by ready government access to information about the activities of citizens and by extensive limitations on the ability of citizens to obtain information about the government. In contrast, democratic governments are marked by significant restrictions on the ability of government to acquire information about its citizens and by ready access by citizens to information about the activities of government.

Robert G. Vaughn, "Transparency—The Mechanisms"

26. *Charlie Brown*: Why would they ban Miss Sweetstory's book?
    Linus: I can't believe it. I just can't believe it!
    Charlie Brown: Maybe there are some things in her book that we don't understand.
    Sally: In that case, they should also ban my Math book!

Charles M. Schulz, *Peanuts*

27. According to the American Academy of Arts and Sciences' recently completed Lincoln Project report, between 2008 and 2013, states reduced financial support to top public research universities by close to 30 percent. Many state legislators seem to be ignoring public opinion as they essentially starve some of the best universities—those that educate about two-thirds of American college students. [This amounts] to a pillaging of the country's greatest state universities. And that pillaging is not a matter of necessity, as many elected officials would insist—it's a matter of choice. The consequence of such policy choices is that tuition will go up and access for kids from poorer families will go down.

Adapted from Jonathan R. Cole, "The Pillaging of America's State Universities," *The Atlantic*

28. The '80s debaters tended to forget that the teaching of vernacular literature is quite a recent development in the long history of the university. (The same could be said about the relatively recent invention of art history or music as an academic research discipline.) So it is not surprising that, in such a short time, we have not yet settled on the right or commonly agreed upon way to go about it.   Robert Pippin, "In Defense of Naïve Reading"

⭐ 29. The greatest tragedy in mankind's entire history may be the hijacking of morality by religion.   Arthur C. Clarke, *Collected Essays*

30. Jokes of the proper kind, properly told, can do more to enlighten questions of politics, philosophy, and literature than any number of dull arguments.

Isaac Asimov, *Treasury of Humor*

31. The aim of argument, or of discussion, should not be victory, but progress.

Joseph Joubert, *Pensées*

32. Whenever I hear anyone arguing for slavery, I feel a strong impulse to see it tried on him personally.   Abraham Lincoln, Speech to 14th Indiana regiment, March 17, 1865

⭐ 33. The most important thing in an argument, next to being right, is to leave an escape hatch for your opponent, so that he can gracefully swing over to your side without too much apparent loss of face.   Sydney J. Harris, as quoted in *Journeys 7*

34. The logic of the world is prior to all truth and falsehood.

Ludwig Wittgenstein, *Notebooks 1914–1916*

35. I am aware that the assumed instinctive belief in God has been used by many persons as an argument for His existence. But this is a rash argument, as we should thus be compelled to believe in the existence of many cruel and malignant spirits, only a little more powerful than man; for the belief in them is far more general than in a beneficent Deity.   Charles Darwin, *The Descent of Man*

36. [T]he essential act of the Party is to use conscious deception while retaining the firmness of purpose that goes with complete honesty. To tell deliberate lies while genuinely believing in them, to forget any fact that has become inconvenient, and then, when it becomes necessary again, to draw it back from oblivion for just so long as it is needed, to deny the existence of objective reality and all the while to take account of the reality which one denies—all this is indispensably necessary.   George Orwell, *1984*

⭐ 37. For nothing requires a greater effort of thought than arguments to justify the rule of nonthought. I experienced it with my own eyes and ears after the war, when intellectuals and artists rushed like a herd of cattle into the Communist Party, which soon proceeded to liquidate them systematically and with great pleasure. You are doing the same. You are the brilliant ally of your own gravediggers.   Milan Kundera, *Immortality*

38. When you plant lettuce, if it does not grow well, you don't blame the lettuce. You look for reasons it is not doing well. It may need fertilizer, or more water, or less sun. You never blame the lettuce. Yet if we have problems with our friends or our family, we blame the other person. But if we know how to take care of them, they will grow well, like the lettuce. Blaming has no positive effect at all, nor does trying to persuade using reason and argument. That is my experience. If you understand, and you show that you understand, you can love, and the situation will change.   Thich Nhât Hanh, *Peace Is Every Step*

39. Your friends praise your abilities to the skies, submit to you in argument, and seem to have the greatest deference for you; but, though they may ask it, you never find them following your advice upon their own affairs; nor allowing you to manage your own, without thinking that you should follow theirs. Thus, in fact, they all think themselves wiser than you, whatever they may say.
                                              Viscount William Lamb Melbourne, *Lord Melbourne's Papers*

40. Violence and lawlessness spread across London . . . property and vehicles have been set on fire in several areas, some burning out of control. One reporter pointed out that in Clapham where the shopping area had been picked clean, the only shop left unlooted and untouched was the book shop.
                                              Martin Fletcher, "Riots Reveal London's Two Disparate Worlds," *NBC News*

⭐ 41. The most perfidious way of harming a cause consists of defending it deliberately with faulty arguments.   Friedrich Nietzsche, *The Gay Science*

42. I've put in so many enigmas and puzzles that it will keep the professors busy for centuries arguing over what I meant, and that's the only way of insuring one's immortality.   James Joyce, as quoted in *James Joyce* by Richard Ellmann

43. The Keynesian argument that if the private sector lacks confidence to spend, the government should spend is not wrong. But Keynes did not spell out where the government should spend. Nor did he envisage that lobbyists can influence government spending to be wasteful. Hence, every prophet can be used by his or her successors to prove their own points of view. This is religion, not science.   Andrew Sheng, "Economics Is a Religion, Not a Science"

44. All true wisdom is found on T-shirts. I wear T-shirts, so I must be wise.

⭐ 45. The National Biosafety Board has approved the release of genetically modified mosquitoes for field testing. This particular type of mosquito can spread the dengue fever and yellow fever viruses. Clinical trial at the laboratory level was successful and the biosafety committee has approved it for testing in a controlled environment. The males would be genetically modified and when mated with female mosquitoes in the environment, it is hoped the killer genes would cause the larvae to die. The regional director cautioned that care be taken in introducing a new species to the environment.
                                              Newspaper article, "Field Testing Approved for Genetically Modified Mosquitoes"

46. It may not always be immediately apparent to frustrated investors—they wish management would be more frugal and focus more on the stock price—but there's usually some calculated logic underlying Google's unconventional strategy. Google's brain trust—founders Larry Page and Sergey Brin, along with CEO Eric Schmidt—clearly think differently than most corporate leaders, and may eventually encourage more companies to take risks that might not pay off for years, if ever. Page and Brin warned potential investors when they laid out their iconoclastic approach to business before Google sold its stock in an initial public offering. "Our long-term focus may simply be the wrong business strategy," they warned. "Competitors may be rewarded for short-term tactics and grow stronger as a result. As potential investors, you should consider the risks around our long-term focus."

    Michael Liedtke, "Calculated Risks? Making Sense of Google's Seemingly Kooky Concepts"

47. Tribalism is about familiarity within the known entity. It's not about hatred of others, it's about comfort within your own, with a natural reluctance to expend the energy and time to break across the barriers and understand another group. Most of what we're quick to label racism isn't really racism. Racism is premeditated, an organized class distinction based on believed superiority and inferiority of different races. That "ism" suffix makes racism a system, just like capitalism or socialism. Racism is used to justify exclusion and persecution based on skin color, things that rarely come into play in today's NBA.

    J. A. Adande, "LeBron James, Race and the NBA"

48. Kedah Health Department employees who smoke will not be eligible for the annual excellence performance awards even if they do well in their work. The Director said, "Thirty percent or 3,900 of our 13,000 department personnel are smokers. As staff representing a health department, they should act as role models. Thus, I hope that they will quit smoking."

    Embun Majid, "Health Department Snuffs Out Excellence Awards for Smokers"

⭐ 49. Even though testing in horse racing is far superior in many respects to testing in human athletics, the concern remains among horse racing fans and industry participants that medication is being used illegally.

    Dr. Scott Palmer, "Working in the Light of Day"

50. A really educated democracy, distrustful of emotional phraseology and all the rest of the stock in trade of the exploiters of crooked thinking, devoid of reverence for ancient institutions and ancient ways of thinking, could take conscious control of our social development and could destroy these plagues of our civilizations—war, poverty, and crime—if it were determined that nothing should stand in the way of their removal [and] if we are willing to trust our own intelligences sufficiently boldly and if we want it badly enough. But the revolution must start in our own minds.

    Adapted from Robert H. Thouless, *How to Think Straight*

C. ARGUMENTS AND EXPLANATIONS

We saw that in some contexts, words such as "since" or "thus" are not used as premise or conclusion indicators. In much the same way, the word "because" is often placed in front of an **explanation**, which provides reasons for why or how an event occurred. To see the difference between an *argument* and an *explanation*, imagine that a student's cell phone starts ringing and disturbs everyone's concentration during an exam. After class, one of the students might complain:

> *Because* you failed to turn off your cell phone before entering the classroom, I think it is safe to say that your behavior shows that you are self-centered, inconsiderate, and rude.

The speaker concludes that the cell phone owner's lack of consideration reveals character flaws—"self-centered, inconsiderate, and rude." In this setting, the word "because" is used to indicate that evidence is being offered in support of a conclusion; so we have an argument.

Now, as it happens, the student whose cell phone started ringing responds using the word "because" too:

> I forgot to turn off my cell phone *because* I was almost in a car accident on my way to take the exam this morning, and I was completely distracted thinking about what happened.

In this setting, however, the word "because" is used to indicate an *explanation*. This speaker does not dispute the fact that her cell phone went off during the exam; rather, she is attempting to explain *why* it happened.

Here are two more examples to consider:

> **A.** Because you started lifting weights without first getting a physical checkup, you will probably injure your back.
> **B.** Your back injury occurred because you lifted weights without first getting a physical checkup.

The first passage contains an inferential claim. In this context the word "because" indicates that a statement is used as support for the conclusion "you will probably injure your back." The premise uses the accepted fact that the person has started lifting weights, so the premise is not in dispute. Since the person has not yet injured his or her back (and might not in the future), the conclusion can turn out to be either true or false.

However, in the second passage the word "because" is not used to indicate support for a conclusion. From the context it appears that the back injury is not in dispute, so what the passage contains is an explanation for the back injury. The explanation may be correct, or it might be incorrect, but in either case there is no argument in the second passage.

Let's work through another example. Suppose your car does not start. A friend might say, "Your car doesn't start *because* you have a dead battery." If you thought that the word "because" is acting as a premise indicator ("you have a dead battery"), then the conclusion would be, "Your car doesn't start." The problem with treating this

Explanation An explanation provides reasons for why or how an event occurred. By themselves, explanations are not arguments; however, they can form part of an argument.

example as an argument is that the alleged conclusion is not in doubt; it has already been established as true. We generally construct arguments in order to provide good reasons (premises) to support a proposition (the conclusion) *whose truth is in question.* But in this example you do not need any reasons to believe that your car doesn't start: You already know that. In general, explanations do not function directly as premises in an argument if they explain an already accepted fact.

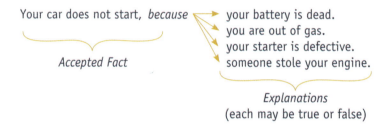

Your car does not start, *because* → your battery is dead.
　　　　　　　　　　　　　　　　　　　 you are out of gas.
　　　　　　　　　　　　　　　　　　　 your starter is defective.
　　　　　　　　　　　　　　　　　　　 someone stole your engine.

Accepted Fact

Explanations
(each may be true or false)

However, explanations can also be used to construct arguments—the goal being to *test* the explanation, to see if it is correct. Chapter 14 further develops the relationships between explanations, experiments, and predictions.

EXERCISES 1C

Self-Practice
Questions

Determine whether each of the following passages contains an *argument* or an *explanation*. Explain your answer.

　1. Bridget must have found a better job; that's why she didn't come to work today. **Answer:** Explanation. It is a fact that she did not come to work today; so an explanation is being offered.

　2. In platonic love there can be no tragedy, because in that love all is clear and pure.
　　　　　　　　　　　　　　　　　　　　　　　　　　　Leo Tolstoy, *Anna Karenina*

　3. In the nation's public policy, we too often allow ideology and political maneuvering to render facts moot, especially when those facts support inconvenient truths such as global climate change.... From public education to health care, we focus more on the politics of changing public policy than the efficacy and morality of making the changes. Consequently, our nation, a house divided, struggles to stand.
　　　Jeff Rivers, "From Sports to Politics to Life, We Must Face Our Truths, Problems and All," *The Undefeated*

　4. The job of arguing with the umpire belongs to the manager, because it won't hurt the team if he gets thrown out of the game.
　　　　　　　　　　　　　　　　　Earl Weaver, as quoted in *Home Plate* by Brenda Berstler

★ 5. Computers now write some 1 billion business press releases every year. Everything from tax returns to legal forms can be completed by machines. Clearly, artificial intelligence and robotics will eliminate many semi-skilled professions.
　　　　　　　　　　John Wasik, "How College Students Can Make Better Career Choices," *Moneywatch*

6. People generally quarrel because they cannot argue.

   Gilbert K. Chesterton, *The Collected Works of G. K. Chesterton*

7. An independent candidate will never win the presidency of the United States. This is because the two-party system of Democrats and Republicans is too powerful to let a third party get any wide base of support among the American voting public.

8. That God cannot lie is no advantage to your argument, because it is no proof that priests cannot, or that the Bible does not.

   Thomas Paine, *The Life and Works of Thomas Paine*

⭐ 9. Because it is limited in characters, texting discourages thoughtful discussion or any level of detail.

   Adapted from Daniel J Levitin, "Why the Modern World Is Bad for Your Brain," *The Guardian*

10. There has been an overall decrease in violence among humans worldwide throughout recorded history. Some biologists claim that this is because the genetic characteristics for nonviolence have been selected over time by the species.

11. Project Gutenberg is synonymous with the free distribution of electronic works in formats readable by the widest variety of computers including obsolete, old, middle-aged and new computers. It exists because of the efforts of hundreds of volunteers and donations from people in all walks of life.

   From Project Gutenberg website

12. Since there is biological evidence that the genetic characteristics for non-violence have been selected over time by the species, we should see an overall decrease in violence among humans worldwide in the coming centuries.

⭐ 13. To make Windows Phone 7 a success, Microsoft has to win over not just phone manufacturers and phone companies, but software developers. The iPhone and Android are popular in part because of the tens of thousands of tiny applications, or "apps," made by outside software developers.

   Newspaper article, "Microsoft Bets Big on New Phone Software"

14. Presently I began to detect a most evil and searching odor stealing about on the frozen air. This depressed my spirits still more, because of course I attributed it to my poor departed friend.

   Mark Twain, *How to Tell a Story, and Other Essays*

15. While it is true that science cannot decide questions of value, that is because they cannot be intellectually decided at all, and lie outside the realm of truth and falsehood. Whatever knowledge is attainable, must be attained by scientific methods; and what science cannot discover, mankind cannot know.

   Bertrand Russell, *Religion and Science*

16. "You must understand," said he, "it's not love. I've been in love, but it's not that. It's not my feeling, but a sort of force outside me has taken possession of me. I went away, you see, because I made up my mind that it could never be, you understand, as a happiness that does not come on earth; but I've struggled with myself, I see there's no living without it. And it must be settled."

Leo Tolstoy, Anna Karenina

⭐ 17. Years ago I used to think sometimes of making a lecturing trip through the antipodes and the borders of the Orient, but always gave up the idea, partly because of the great length of the journey and partly because my wife could not well manage to go with me. Mark Twain, How to Tell a Story, and Other Essays

18. Briefly, Cosmic Consciousness, according to Bucke, is a higher form of consciousness that is slowly but surely coming to the entire human race through the process of evolution. The mystics and religious leaders of the past were simply ahead of their time. Bucke believes that Cosmic Consciousness is the real source of all the world's religions. He did not believe that the cosmic state is necessarily infallible. Like the development of any faculty, it takes a long time to become perfected. And so, just because Cosmic Consciousness is the root of religious beliefs, it doesn't follow that the beliefs are necessarily correct.

Raymond Smullyan, Some Interesting Memories: A Paradoxical Life

19. It's nothing or everything, Culum. If you're prepared to be second-best, go topside now. What I'm trying to make you understand is that to be the Tai-Pan of The Noble House you have to be prepared to exist alone, to be hated, to have some aim of immortal value, and to be ready to sacrifice anyone you're not sure of. Because you're my son I'm offering you today, untried, a chance at supreme power in Asia. Thus a power to do almost anything on earth.

James Clavell, Tai-Pan

20. All the big corporations depreciate their possessions, and you can, too, provided you use them for business purposes. For example, if you subscribe to the Wall Street Journal, a business-related newspaper, you can deduct the cost of your house, because, in the words of U.S. Supreme Court Chief Justice Warren Burger in a landmark 1979 tax decision: "Where else are you going to read the paper? Outside? What if it rains?" Dave Barry, "Sweating Out Taxes"

Truth value analysis
Determines if the information in the premises is accurate, correct, or true.

Logical analysis
Determines the strength with which the premises support the conclusion.

D. TRUTH AND LOGIC

Determination of the truth value of a statement is distinct from analysis of the logic of an argument. **Truth value analysis** determines whether the information in the premises is accurate, correct, or true. **Logical analysis** determines the strength with which the premises support the conclusion. If you are not aware of the difference between the truth value of statements and the logic of an argument, then confusion can arise. Suppose you hear that the book you are now reading weighs 2000 pounds.

If you are like most people, you immediately know the statement to be false. Your decision happens so fast you could not stop it if you tried. This shows that one part of our mind is constantly analyzing information for truth value. We must recognize that our minds are constantly working on two different levels, and we must learn to keep those levels separate. In order to evaluate the logic of an argument, we must often temporarily ignore the truth values—not because they are unimportant, but simply because an analysis of the logic requires us to focus on an entirely different question. We must learn to not be distracted by trying to determine the truth value of the statements—just as when we close our eyes to concentrate on hearing something.

Of course it is important that our statements be true. However, a thorough analysis of arguments requires an active separation of the truth value from the logic. Think of what happens when children begin learning addition. For example, an elementary school teacher gave two cookies to each student at the beginning of the class. "Okay Sam," she said, "you have two cookies, and Sophie has two cookies. How many cookies do you have together?" At that point Sam started to cry. The teacher thought that Sam was embarrassed because he didn't know the answer. In fact, Sam had already eaten his two cookies. His reaction was based on knowing that the teacher's statement that he had two cookies was false, so perhaps he thought he would be in trouble for having eaten the cookies. It is easy to forget that it often takes time to learn to think abstractly.

E. DEDUCTIVE AND INDUCTIVE ARGUMENTS

Logical analysis of an argument is concerned with determining the *strength of the inferential claim*—the claim that the conclusion follows from the premises. We start with a working definition of two main classes of arguments: deductive and inductive.

> A **deductive argument** is one in which the inferential claim is that the conclusion *follows necessarily* from the premises. In other words, under the *assumption* that the premises are true it is *impossible* for the conclusion to be false.

> An **inductive argument** is one in which the inferential claim is that the conclusion is *probably true* if the premises are true. In other words, under the *assumption* that the premises are true it is *improbable* for the conclusion to be false.

To help identify arguments as either deductive or inductive, one thing we can do is look for key words or phrases. For example, the words "necessarily," "certainty," "definitely," and "absolutely" suggest a deductive argument:

> **A.** Jupiter is a planet in our solar system. Every planet in our solar system is smaller than the Sun. Therefore, it follows necessarily that Jupiter is smaller than the Sun.

The indicator word "necessarily" suggests that the argument can be classified as deductive.

On the other hand, the words "probably," "likely," "unlikely," "improbable," "plausible," and "implausible" suggest inductive arguments:

> **B.** Some parts of the United States have had severe winters for the last 10 years. The *Farmer's Almanac* predicts another cold winter next year. Therefore, probably some parts of the United States will have a severe winter next year.

Deductive argument
An argument in which the inferential claim is that the conclusion follows *necessarily* from the premises. In other words, under the *assumption* that the premises are true it is *impossible* for the conclusion to be false.

Inductive argument
An argument in which the inferential claim is that the conclusion is *probably true* if the premises are true. In other words, under the *assumption* that the premises are true it is *improbable* for the conclusion to be false.

The indicator word "probably" suggests that the argument can be classified as inductive. Of course we have to remember that specific indicator words or phrases may not always occur in ordinary language. In addition, although a passage may contain an indicator word or phrase, the person using the phrase may be misusing the term. In some instances people overstate their case, while in other instances they may not be aware of the distinction between deductive arguments and inductive arguments, so they might use terms indiscriminately. However, looking for indicator words can help in understanding an argument by letting you see how the information is arranged.

Another factor to consider when determining whether an argument is deductive or inductive is the strength of the inferential connection between the premises and the conclusion. In other words, if the conclusion does follow *necessarily* from premises that are assumed to be true, then the argument is clearly deductive. Here is an example:

> **C.** All vegetables contain vitamin C. Spinach is a vegetable. Therefore, spinach contains vitamin C.

The conclusion follows necessarily under the assumption that the premises are true. In other words, if we assume that it is true that all vegetables contain vitamin C, and if we also assume that it is true that spinach is a vegetable, then it is impossible for spinach not to contain vitamin C. Therefore, this argument can be classified as deductive. Notice once again the importance of disregarding the truth value of the premises at this point in our analysis. We are *not* claiming that the premises are in fact true. Instead, we are claiming that *under the assumption that the premises are true* it is impossible for the conclusion to be false.

There is another result of examining the actual strength of the inferential connection between the premises and the conclusion. If we determine that the conclusion of an argument follows probably from premises that are assumed to be true, then it is often best to consider the argument as inductive. Here is an example:

> **D.** The majority of plasma TVs last for 5 years. Chris just bought a new plasma TV. Therefore, Chris's new plasma TV will last 5 years.

Let's examine argument D. Under the assumption that the premises are true, the conclusion is highly likely to be true; however, it is possible that it is false. In other words, if we assume that it is true that the majority of plasma TVs last for 5 years, and if we also assume that it is true that Chris just bought a new plasma TV, then it is probable that Chris's new plasma TV will last 5 years. Therefore, this argument can be classified as inductive. Again, we are disregarding the truth value of the premises. We are not claiming that the premises are in fact true. Instead, we are claiming that *under the assumption that the premises are true*, it is probable that the conclusion is true. Therefore, argument D can be classified as inductive.

Inductive arguments amplify the scope of the information in the premises. For example, the first premise in example D provides information about plasma TVs, but it does not make a claim about every plasma TV. Nor does it make a claim about any specific TV (including Chris's TV); instead, it only states something about the majority of plasma TVs. It is in this sense that we say that the conclusion regarding Chris's TV goes beyond the information in the premises; hence it is possible that the conclusion is false even under the assumption that the premises are true.

However, this does not take away from the value of strong inductive arguments. In fact, we rely on them nearly every day. For most practical purposes, we do not have sufficient knowledge of the world to make the conclusions of our arguments follow necessarily from true premises, so we rely on evidence and experience to make many decisions. That's why knowing the likelihood of something happening can assist our rational decision making. Inductive arguments play a crucial role in our lives.

There are many kinds of inductive arguments, such as *analogical arguments, statistical arguments, causal arguments, legal arguments, moral arguments*, and *scientific arguments*. (More on these kinds of inductive arguments can be found in Part IV of this book.) Analogical arguments are based on the idea that when two things share some relevant characteristics, they probably share other characteristics as well. Here is an example:

> I previously owned two Ford station wagons. They both got good gas mileage, both needed few repairs, and both had a high resale value. I just bought a new Ford station wagon, so it will get good gas mileage, need few repairs, and have a high resale value.

Statistical arguments are based on our ability to generalize. When we observe a pattern, we often create an argument that uses a statistical regularity:

> In a survey of 1000 university students in the United States, 80% said that they expect to make more money in their lives than their parents. Therefore, the vast majority of all university students expect to make more money in their lives than their parents.

Causal arguments are arguments based on knowledge of either causes or effects. For example, a team of medical scientists may conduct experiments to determine if a new drug (the potential cause) will have a desired effect on a particular disease. In a different setting, a forensic expert might do a series of tests to determine the cause of a person's death. Causal arguments can even be found in everyday occurrences. For example, someone might say the following:

> The lamp in my room does not work. I changed the light bulb, but it still did not work. I moved the lamp to another room just in case the wall outlet was defective, but the lamp still did not work. So, it must be the wiring in the lamp that is defective.

We defined a deductive argument as one in which it is claimed that the conclusion follows necessarily from the premises. If we look once again at example C, then we can see that the conclusion does not amplify or expand the scope of the information in the premises. The first premise provides information about *every* vegetable, and the second premise states that spinach is a vegetable. Therefore, under the assumption that the premises are true, the conclusion does not go beyond what is already contained in the premises.

It should not be surprising that deductive arguments can be found in mathematics and geometry. Even simple arithmetical calculations are deductive. For example, if you assume that you can save $50 a week, then you can conclude that after 1 year (52 weeks) you will have saved $2600. When we encounter an argument that is based on mathematics, we can consider it to be deductive.

Earlier we said that many statistical arguments can be classified as inductive. Of course, there are statistical calculations that are purely mathematical in nature; in those cases, the calculations are deductive. However, when the conclusion goes beyond what is provided by the premises, the statistical argument is inductive, like our survey of 1000 university students. Since the conclusion stated something about all university students, it went beyond the scope of the premises.

Classifying arguments into different types will allow you to apply the specific evaluation techniques that will be introduced in this book. Your ability to classify an argument as deductive or inductive will continue to grow as you have the opportunity to analyze many different arguments.

EXERCISES 1E

Self-Practice
Questions

The following exercises are intended to apply your understanding of the difference between deductive and inductive arguments. Determine whether the following arguments are best classified as being deductive or inductive. Explain your answers.

1. Every insect has six legs. What's crawling on me is an insect. So what's crawling on me has six legs.

Answer: Deductive. The first premise says something definite about every insect. The second premise says that an insect is crawling on me. The conclusion follows necessarily under the assumption that both premises are true.

2. Most insects have six legs. What's crawling on me is an insect. Therefore, what's crawling on me probably has six legs.

3. The exam's range of A scores is 90–100. I got a 98 on the exam. It follows necessarily that I got an A on the exam.

4. The exam's range of A scores is 90–100. I got an A on the exam, thus I got a 98 on the exam.

⭐ 5. All fires need oxygen. There is no oxygen in that room. So there is no fire in that room.

6. Most cars are not hybrids. My instructor owns a car. It follows that my instructor's car is probably not a hybrid.

7. Carly tossed a coin ten times, and in each case it came up heads. I have a feeling that it is a trick coin. I predict the next toss will be heads.

8. Many wars were caused by a combination of strident nationalism, economic inequality, and fear of immigration. All three things are occurring today in our society. We can infer that our country will soon be involved in a war.

⭐ 9. All elements with atomic weights greater than 64 are metals. Z is an element with an atomic weight of 79. Therefore, Z is a metal.

10. It is estimated that pollution and climate change is causing approximately 1% of Earth's species to become extinct each year. Scientists have identified around two million different species. We can conclude that approximately 20,000 different species will become extinct this year.

11. Antibiotics have no effect on viruses. You have a disease that is caused by a virus. You are taking the antibiotic Q. Thus the antibiotic you are taking will have no effect on your disease.

Video Tutorial: 1EI
Exercise #11 & #12

12. Some antibiotics are effective for treating certain bacterial infections. You have a bacterial infection. You are taking the antibiotic Q. Thus the antibiotic you are taking will be effective in treating your bacterial infection.

⭐ 13. Anyone over 21 years of age can legally play the slot machines in Las Vegas. Sam is 33 years old. Sam can legally play the slot machines in Las Vegas.

14. The average temperature in July in Las Vegas is 107 degrees. I'm going to drive through Las Vegas on July 14, so I predict it will be 107 degrees that day.

15. I am a vertebrate animal because every mammal is a vertebrate animal, and I am a mammal.

16. Most fruit have seeds. I am eating an orange. All oranges are fruit, so I am eating something with seeds.

⭐ 17. Most Doberman dogs bark a lot. My cousin just got a Doberman dog. Therefore, my cousin's Doberman dog will probably bark a lot.

18. The vast majority of a survey of 600 people who identified themselves as being very religious reported that they were against capital punishment. It is safe to say that the vast majority of all Americans think the same way.

19. I started taking daily vitamins, calcium, and fish oil. I read that these supplements are correlated with longevity. Given this, I expect to live at least one hundred more years.

20. No car battery that has at least one defective cell can be repaired. Your car battery has at least one defective cell, so it cannot be repaired.

⭐ 21. It's our job to make college basketball players realize that getting an education is something that's important, because life after basketball is a real long time.
Larry Brown, Southern Methodist University basketball coach

22. Many women who used to be full-time mothers are discovering that outside work gives them friends, challenges, variety, money, independence; it makes them feel better about themselves, and therefore lets them be better parents.
Wendy Coppedge Sanford, *Ourselves and Our Children*

23. If the NBA Finals rock, then the NBA thrives. If the NBA Finals are filled with stars, then the NBA Finals rock. If the Heat make the NBA Finals, then the NBA Finals will be filled with stars. Therefore, if the Heat make the NBA Finals, then the NBA thrives.

    Dan Wheeler, adapted from "Rick Reilly's Mailbag," ESPN.com

24. Even when people think they're multitasking, what they are really doing is switching between tasks, not doing them simultaneously. And constant exposure to multiple devices at the same time isn't making people any better at it. "The more stuff you have, the less you are able to focus on individual things. There is very limited bandwidth for conscious thought," said Earl Miller, professor of neuroscience at MIT.

    Keith Wagstaff, "The 'Smart Life': How Connected Cars, Clothes and Homes Could Fry Your Brain," NBC News

★ 25. Studies indicate that when you have been forced to wait at the end of the line throughout your childhood, you tend to jump at the opportunity to be first when you grow up. So, if your last name begins with a letter near the end of the alphabet you're more likely to have a twitchy finger anxious to hit the buy button, whether for clothes or concert tickets.

    "How Your Last Name Affects Shopping Decisions," Today.com

26. What has happened in our society is we don't exist separate from our devices anymore because we've learned to do so many things dependently on our devices. One of the things that's happening with technology, which is very unfortunate, is people responding with brevity as opposed to really talking something through.   Dr. Nancy Mramor, quoted in "Texting Instead of Yelling?" USA Today

27. "The policies the United States has had for the last 41 years have become irrelevant," said Morris Panner, a former counternarcotics prosecutor in New York and at the American Embassy in Colombia, who is now an adviser at Harvard's Kennedy School of Government. "The United States was worried about shipments of cocaine and heroin for years, but whether those policies worked or not doesn't matter because they are now worried about Americans using prescription drugs."

    Damien Cave and Michael S. Schmidt, "Rise in Pill Abuse Forces New Look at U.S. Drug Fight," The New York Times

28. Civilizations rise, but there's an environmental filter that causes them to die off again and disappear fairly quickly. If you look at planet Earth, the filtering we've had in the past has been in these mass extinctions. The mass extinction we are now living through has only just begun; so much more dying is coming.

    Adapted from David Wallace-Wells, "The Uninhabitable Earth," New York Magazine

★ 29. The Supreme Court sided with the video game industry today, declaring a victor in the six-year legal match between the industry and the California lawmakers who wanted to make it a crime for anyone in the state to sell extremely violent games to kids. . . . Writing for a plurality of justices, Justice Scalia said

California's arguments "would fare better if there were a longstanding tradition in this country of specially restricting children's access to depictions of violence, but there is none." He cited numerous examples of violence in literature. "Reading Dante is unquestionably more cultured and intellectually edifying than playing 'Mortal Kombat.' But these cultural and intellectual differences are not constitutional." "[Therefore, t]he basic principles of freedom of speech . . . do not vary with a new and different communication medium," Scalia wrote in the Court's opinion, citing an earlier speech case.

Stephen Totilo, "1st Amendment Beats Ban in Video Game Battle," MSNBC.MSN.com

30. The belief in God has often been advanced as not only the greatest, but the most complete of all the distinctions between man and the lower animals. It is however impossible, as we have seen, to maintain that this belief is innate or instinctive in man. On the other hand a belief in all-pervading spiritual agencies seems to be universal; and apparently follows from a considerable advance in man's reason, and from a still greater advance in his faculties of imagination, curiosity and wonder. I am aware that the assumed instinctive belief in God has been used by many persons as an argument for His existence. But this is a rash argument, as we should thus be compelled to believe in the existence of many cruel and malignant spirits, only a little more powerful than man; for the belief in them is far more general than in a beneficent Deity. The idea of a universal and beneficent Creator does not seem to arise in the mind of man, until he has been elevated by long-continued culture.

Charles Darwin, The Descent of Man

F. DEDUCTIVE ARGUMENTS: VALIDITY AND SOUNDNESS

Logical analysis of a deductive argument is concerned with determining whether the conclusion follows necessarily from the premises. Placed in the form of a question, logical analysis of a deductive argument asks the following: "Assuming the premises are true, is it possible for the conclusion to be false?" Answering this question will provide us with some key terms with which we can dig deeper into deductive arguments.

A **valid deductive argument** is one in which, *assuming* the premises are true, it is *impossible* for the conclusion to be false. In other words, the conclusion *follows necessarily* from the premises. On the other hand, an **invalid deductive argument** is one in which, *assuming* the premises are true, it is *possible* for the conclusion to be false. In other words, the conclusion *does not follow necessarily* from the premises.

Determining the validity or the invalidity of an argument rests on logical analysis. We rely on the assumption that the premises are true in order to determine whether the conclusion necessarily follows. However, truth value does have a role in the overall analysis of deductive arguments. The determination that a deductive argument is

Valid deductive argument An argument in which, *assuming* the premises are true, it is *impossible* for the conclusion to be false. In other words, the conclusion *follows necessarily* from the premises.

Invalid deductive argument An argument in which, *assuming* the premises are true, it is *possible* for the conclusion to be false. In other words, the conclusion *does not follow necessarily* from the premises.

Sound argument A deductive argument is sound when the argument is valid, and the premises are true.

Unsound argument A deductive argument is unsound when the argument is invalid, or when at least one of the premises is false.

valid rests on the *assumption* that the premises are true. A valid deductive argument can have premises or a conclusion whose actual truth value is false. Combining logical analysis with truth value analysis provides us with two more definitions. First, when logical analysis shows that a deductive argument is valid, and when truth value analysis of the premises shows that they are all true, then the argument is **sound**. However, if the deductive argument is invalid, or if at least one of the premises is false, then the argument is **unsound**.

To determine whether a deductive argument is valid or invalid, we apply logical analysis by assuming the premises are true. If logical analysis determines that the argument is valid, then we apply truth value analysis in order to determine whether the argument is sound or unsound. The following flow chart illustrates the process:

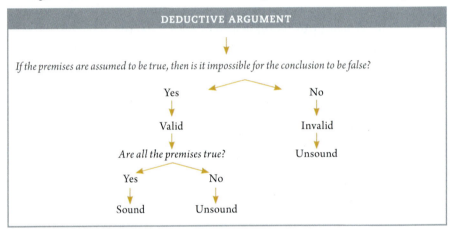

The flow chart illustrates an important point: A *valid* argument is one where it is impossible for the conclusion to be false, *assuming* the premises are true. And since a *sound* argument is one where the premises *are true*, we know that every sound argument's conclusion is true.

Argument Form

It is easy to confuse the question of the truth value of statements with the logical question of what follows from the statements. To keep the two questions clear and distinct when you analyze arguments, it can help to think about logical possibilities. To illustrate this idea, we start with a brief table listing the logical possibilities available in deductive arguments:

DEDUCTIVE ARGUMENTS			
Premises	Conclusion	Validity	Soundness
1. True	True	Valid or invalid	Sound or unsound
2. True	False	Invalid	Unsound
3. At least one is false	True	Valid or invalid	Unsound
4. At least one is false	False	Valid or invalid	Unsound

Line 2 states that a deductive argument with true premises and a false conclusion is invalid and unsound. This is a straightforward result of the previous section's discussion, so it should be easy to understand. However, lines 1, 3, and 4 can cause some confusion, so we will work slowly through them.

First, notice that under the column "Validity," deductive arguments that have the characteristics listed in lines 1, 3, and 4 are said to be *either* valid or invalid. Second, under the column "Soundness," deductive arguments that have the characteristics listed in both lines 3 and 4 are said to be unsound, but those in line 1 can be *either* sound or unsound.

Let's look at lines 3 and 4. Since both lines refer to deductive arguments that have "at least one false premise," the arguments are automatically unsound. In contrast, the deductive arguments referred to in line 1 have true premises, and since they can be *either* valid or invalid, they can be *either* sound or unsound. At this point, we are simply listing the logical possibilities. We now need to flesh out those possibilities to see how we can make the final determinations. For that we need to further explore the *logical analysis* and *truth value analysis* of some arguments.

Let's begin by looking at two arguments:

A. All dogs are cats. All cats are snakes. Therefore, all dogs are snakes.
B. No mammals are beagles. No mammals are dogs. Therefore, no beagles are dogs.

Each premise and conclusion in examples A and B relates two *classes* of objects (also called *groups* or *categories*). For example, the first premise of argument A refers to the *class of dogs* and the *class of cats*. The first premise of argument B refers to the *class of mammals* and the *class of beagles*. (Statements and arguments that use class terms are the subject of *categorical logic*, which is explored in Chapters 5 and 6.)

It should be easy to determine that all the premises and the conclusions in both A and B are false. However, since we want to focus on the *logical question of validity*, we do not want to get bogged down in truth value analysis. We need to reveal the *argument form*, which is the structure of the argument, not its content. In categorical logic, an **argument form** is an arrangement of logical vocabulary and letters that stand for class terms such that a uniform substitution of class terms for the letters results in an argument. In other words, an argument is valid or invalid based on its logical form, not on its subject matter.

To get started, we need to separate the *logical vocabulary* from the *nonlogical vocabulary* in the individual statements. For example, the first premise of argument A contains the logical vocabulary words "all" and "are," while the nonlogical vocabulary consists of the class terms "dogs" and "cats." In contrast, the first premise of argument B contains the logical vocabulary words "no" and "are," while the nonlogical vocabulary consists of the class terms "mammals" and "beagles."

Argument form In categorical logic, an argument form is an arrangement of logical vocabulary and letters that stand for class terms such that a uniform substitution of class terms for the letters results in an argument.

We can use letters to stand for the nonlogical terms "dogs" and "cats" while keeping the logical vocabulary ("all" and "are") intact to reveal the statement form of the first premise. In categorical logic, a **statement form** is an arrangement of logical vocabulary and letters that stand for class terms such that a uniform substitution of class terms for the letters results in a statement. For example, if we let D = *dogs*, and C = *cats*, then the statement form is the following: "All D are C." We can extend the technique to reveal the *argument forms* of A and B, which we will then label FA and FB. Here are the letters we will use: Let D = *dogs*, C = *cats*, S = *snakes*, M = *mammals*, and B = *beagles*.

Statement form In categorical logic, a statement form is an arrangement of logical vocabulary and letters that stand for class terms such that a uniform substitution of class terms for the letters results in a statement.

FA. All D are C.
All C are S.
All D are S.

FB. No M are B.
No M are D.
No B are D.

Notice that we introduced a horizontal line to separate the premises from the conclusion. This technique allows us to eliminate the word "Therefore." We know that an argument is constructed entirely of statements, and we know that each of the premises and the conclusion have two possible truth values (true or false). Recall that a valid argument is a deductive argument in which, assuming the premises are true, it is *impossible* for the conclusion to be false. An invalid argument is a deductive argument in which, assuming the premises are true, it is *possible* for the conclusion to be false.

We used the letters D, C, S, M, and B to stand for *dogs, cats, snakes, mammals,* and *beagles*. However, we can substitute *any* class or group term we wish for those letters, *as long as we keep the argument form intact.* A **substitution instance** of a *statement* occurs when a uniform substitution of class terms for the letters results in a statement. A substitution instance of an *argument* occurs when a uniform substitution of class terms for the letters results in an argument. For example, if we now let D = *Android phones*, C = *popular products*, and S = *inexpensive items*, we get the following substitution instance for argument form FA:

Substitution instance In categorical logic, a substitution instance of a *statement* occurs when a uniform substitution of class terms for the letters results in a statement. A *substitution instance* of an *argument* occurs when a uniform substitution of class terms for the letters results in an argument.

All Android phones are popular products.
All popular products are inexpensive items.
All Android phones are inexpensive items.

What we want to do is determine whether it is *possible* that either argument form FA or argument form FB, or both, can have true premises and a false conclusion. In order to make our task as easy as possible, we will use examples in which the truth value of the premises and conclusions are obvious to nearly everyone. For example, most people find it easier to determine the truth value of the statement "All beagles are dogs," than it is for the statement "All bivalves are mollusks." The following table supplies substitution instances for both FA and FB:

Argument Form FA—VALID		Argument Form FB—INVALID	
1. *True*	All beagles are dogs.	1. *True*	No dogs are snakes.
True	<u>All dogs are mammals.</u>	*True*	<u>No dogs are cats.</u>
True	All beagles are mammals.	*True*	No snakes are cats.
	SOUND		**UNSOUND**
2. *True*		2. *True*	No cats are beagles.
True	None exist	*True*	<u>No cats are dogs.</u>
False		*False*	No beagles are dogs.
			UNSOUND
3. *True*	All beagles are mammals.	3. *True*	No beagles are cats.
False	<u>All mammals are dogs.</u>	*False*	<u>No beagles are dogs.</u>
True	All beagles are dogs.	*True*	No cats are dogs.
	UNSOUND		**UNSOUND**
4. *True*	All dogs are mammals.	4. *True*	No cats are dogs.
False	<u>All mammals are snakes.</u>	*False*	<u>No cats are mammals.</u>
False	All dogs are snakes.	*False*	No dogs are mammals.
	UNSOUND		**UNSOUND**
5. *False*	All dogs are cats.	5. *False*	No beagles are dogs.
True	<u>All cats are mammals.</u>	*True*	<u>No beagles are cats.</u>
True	All dogs are mammals.	*True*	No dogs are cats.
	UNSOUND		**UNSOUND**
6. *False*	All cats are beagles.	6. *False*	No cats are mammals.
True	<u>All beagles are dogs.</u>	*True*	<u>No cats are dogs.</u>
False	All cats are dogs.	*False*	No mammals are dogs.
	UNSOUND		**UNSOUND**
7. *False*	All beagles are cats.	7. *False*	No mammals are cats.
False	<u>All cats are dogs.</u>	*False*	<u>No mammals are dogs.</u>
True	All beagles are dogs.	*True*	No cats are dogs.
	UNSOUND		**UNSOUND**
8. *False*	All dogs are cats.	8. *False*	No mammals are beagles.
False	<u>All cats are snakes.</u>	*False*	<u>No mammals are dogs.</u>
False	All dogs are snakes.	*False*	No beagles are dogs.
	UNSOUND		**UNSOUND**

No matter what we substitute into the form FA it is logically impossible for a false conclusion to follow from true premises. In other words, form FA can result in arguments that correspond to every combination of truth values in the table, *except number 2.* On the other hand, it is logically possible to substitute into form FB and get a false conclusion following from true premises. Form FB can result in arguments that correspond to every combination in the table, *including number 2.*

Even though the actual truth value of the original statements in both argument A and argument B were the same (false premises and a false conclusion), argument A is valid, but argument B is invalid. It is important to remember that when we evaluate arguments, we must always distinguish truth value analysis from the logical analysis.

Counterexamples

The overall analysis of a deductive argument requires two things: logical analysis and truth value analysis. Based on logical analysis deductive arguments are either valid or invalid. When we add the results of truth value analysis, deductive arguments are either sound or unsound. Most people have more experience in evaluating the truth value than the logic of an argument, simply because our formal education is heavily devoted to what is known to be true. A large part of education is the teaching of facts.

The difference between logical analysis and truth value analysis can be illustrated by the role of **counterexamples**. A counterexample to a *statement* is evidence that shows the statement is false, and it concerns truth value analysis. Suppose someone says, "No human is taller than eight feet." If we are able to find a human who is taller than eight feet, then we have evidence that the statement is false. The evidence can be considered to be a counterexample to the statement "No human is taller than eight feet."

Statements that use the words "never," "always," or the phrase "every time" are often subject to simple counterexamples. Here are some examples of statements and counterexamples:

> *Statement:* "I never get to stay home from school."
> *Counterexample:* "You stay home from school when you are sick and when we go on vacation."
> *Statement:* "He always gets to go first."
> *Counterexample:* "You went first when we rode on the roller coaster at the park last week."
> *Statement:* "The phone rings every time I'm taking a shower."
> *Counterexample:* "But you took a shower last night and the phone didn't ring."

A counterexample to an *argument* plays a different role. It shows that the conclusion does *not* follow necessarily from premises assumed to be true. A single counterexample to a deductive argument is enough to show that the argument is invalid. This should not be surprising. If you recall, every deductive argument is either valid or invalid. Therefore, it is not necessary to find more than one counterexample to a deductive argument because there are no degrees of invalidity. In other words, deductive arguments cannot be classified as *partially valid* or *semi-valid*.

Let's consider the following deductive argument:

C.   All bomohs are scam artists.
<u>All grifters are scam artists.</u>
All bomohs are grifters.

You do not need to know what either a bomoh or a grifter or a scam artist is in order to determine if the argument is valid or invalid. Whatever those things are we can begin by thinking about the argument in a logical way. The argument relates two things (bomohs and grifters) to a third thing (scam artists). Now even if we assume that every bomoh and every grifter is a scam artist, then does the conclusion follow necessarily? In other words, does it follow necessarily that every bomoh is a grifter? The first step of the analysis is to reveal the argument form. Let's substitute letters for the terms in order to reveal the form: B = *bomohs*, S = *scam artists*, and G = *grifters*.

Counterexample A counterexample to a statement is evidence that shows the statement is false. A counterexample to an argument shows that the conclusion does not follow necessarily from the premises. A single counterexample to a deductive argument is enough to show that the argument is invalid.

FC.   All B are S.
          All G are S.
          All B are G.

The second step is to substitute three terms for the letters, such that the substitution instance will be a counterexample. Let's try the following: B = *beagles*, S = *mammals*, and G = *dogs*.

D.   All beagles are mammals.
          All dogs are mammals.
          All beagles are dogs.

Truth value analysis shows that the premises and the conclusion are true, so this substitution instance is not a counterexample. At this point it can help to change our strategy, so that our thinking does not get stuck in a loop. Repeating the same approach to a problem may cause us to miss other possibilities. We might fail to see alternative paths because our minds are locked into one way of analysis. Sometimes, however, the light bulb goes on, and we instantly see the answer (the *Aha!* experience). A puzzle illustrates how this can happen.

Imagine that you are given a knife and are told to cut a cake (with no icing) into two equal pieces with one slice. You must always cut the cake in straight lines; you cannot stop a cut halfway through the cake and resume it at another place; and you cannot touch the cake in any other way. This is easily accomplished as follows:

Once you have successfully cut the cake into two equal pieces, you are then asked to cut the cake into four equal pieces with one more slice. You should be able to do this quite easily:

At this point, you are now asked to cut the cake into eight equal parts with just one more slice. Remember the rules: You must cut the cake in straight lines; you cannot start a cut in one place and resume it somewhere else; and you cannot touch the cake in any other way. Can you do it? Do you think it is impossible?

Before reading further, you should have struggled with the problem for a while in order to experience fully the possibility of attacking the problem in only one way. The puzzle, as stated, has set your mind thinking in one direction by imagining the cake as a two-dimensional object. But the cake is a three-dimensional object. It can be cut in half through its middle, leaving four pieces on top and four on the bottom, all equal to each other.

If our search for a counterexample starts with the premises, then we start by making the premises true and then seeing if the conclusion turned out to be false. Although it is generally easier to think of things that would make the premises true, we could get stuck in a loop.

However, there is a way to shorten the amount of time needed to find a counterexample, and that is to analyze an argument from the bottom up. This technique temporarily ignores the premises and instead concentrates on the conclusion. For our current example, the conclusion is "All B are G." Since we are searching for a counterexample, we must substitute terms that make the conclusion false. It helps to choose simple terms that will make the conclusion obviously false. For example, let's try the following substitutions: B = *dogs*, G = *cats*.

> All dogs are S.
> All cats are S.
> All dogs are cats.

The conclusion is clearly false. Now if we can substitute a term for the "S" in the premises, and have the premises be true, then this will produce a counterexample. But before we simply start randomly trying different terms, we should think of what we are trying to accomplish. We need to substitute something for the "S" such that both premises are true. That means that we have to think of something that both dogs and cats have in common. Well, since every dog and every cat is a mammal, we can try that and see what happens.

> **E.**   All dogs are mammals.
> All cats are mammals.
> All dogs are cats.

The premises of this argument are true and the conclusion is false, so we have created a counterexample. The counterexample shows that the argument is invalid.

Let's look at another example:

> **G.**   All bomohs are scam artists.
> All scam artists are grifters.
> All bomohs are grifters.

Here we have switched the order of the terms in the second premise. Once again, the first step is to reveal the argument form. Let's substitute the same letters we used earlier for the terms in order to reveal the form: B = *bomohs*, S = *scam artists*, and G = *grifters*.

> **FG.**   All B are S.
> All S are G.
> All B are G.

This has the same general argument form that we encountered in example FA:

> **FA.**   All D are C.
> All C are S.
> All D are S.

Since we already said that FA is a valid form, FG is valid as well. However, let's work through the argument using the bottom-up technique for additional practice. We can use the same substitutions as before: B = *dogs*, S = *mammals*, and G = *cats*.

> All dogs are mammals.
> <u>All mammals are cats.</u>
> All dogs are cats.

The conclusion is false and the first premise is true. However, the second premise is false. Therefore, this particular substitution instance is not a counterexample. At this point we can take another look at the form of argument FG. If we assume that every B is an S (premise 1), and every S is a G (premise 2), then it follows that every B must be a G. However, we might want to try another substitution instance. Let's use these: B = *human beings*, S = *mammals*, and G = *animals*.

> All human beings are mammals.
> <u>All mammals are animals.</u>
> All human beings are animals.

The premises are true, but so is the conclusion. This particular substitution instance is also not a counterexample. This brings up an interesting point. The counterexample method can be effectively used to show that an argument is invalid, but it cannot show that an argument is valid. If you think about this, it begins to make sense. Invalid arguments have counterexamples, but valid arguments do not.

In order to create a counterexample it helps to use simple terms with which you are familiar. This helps ensure that the truth value of the statements you create are generally well known to everyone. If you noticed, we used terms such as *beagles*, *mammals*, *cats*, and *dogs*. Although counterexamples are a good way to identify invalid arguments, they are sometimes difficult to create. If we are unable to create a counterexample, then this by itself does not show that the argument is valid; instead it might be that we just failed to find a counterexample. (Part III introduces additional techniques of logical analysis that are capable of showing validity.)

So far, we have been using letters to represent class terms (for example, we let D = *dogs*). We can now expand this technique to different types of statements. Let's compare the following two examples:

H. All *pizza toppings* are *delicious morsels*.
I. If *Sherry lives in Los Angeles*, then *Sherry lives in California*.

In example H, the two italicized words are *class terms*, which *by themselves* are neither true nor false. However, the two italicized parts of example I are *statements* that are either true or false (we can call them *simple statements*). In addition, example I contains the logical vocabulary words "if" and "then." Example I is a good illustration of how a *sentence* in English can contain *multiple simple statements*. Taken as a whole, example I is a *compound statement* and it, too, is either true or false.

We can use letters to represent the simple statements in example I while we keep the logical vocabulary in place. For example, if we let *L* = *Sherry lives in Los Angeles*, and *C* = *Sherry lives in California*, then we get the following for example I: If *L*, then *C*.

This technique can be applied to certain kinds of arguments. For example:

Argument J:	**Argument Form:**
If Sherry lives in Los Angeles, then Sherry lives in California.	**If *L*, then *C*.**
Sherry lives in California.	*C.*
Sherry lives in Los Angeles.	*L.*

The first premise, "If Sherry lives in Los Angeles, then Sherry lives in California," is an example of a *conditional statement*. The simple statement that follows the word "if" is referred to as the *antecedent*. The other simple statement, which follows the word "then," is referred to as the *consequent*. At this stage, the most important thing to recognize is that a conditional statement *does not assert* that either the antecedent or the consequent is true. What is asserted is that *if* the antecedent is true, *then* the consequent is true.

Given this understanding of a conditional statement, let's analyze argument J. We can start by assuming that the first premise is true. Why? Because it *does not assert* that Sherry actually lives in Los Angeles, it just asserts that *if* she lives in Los Angeles, then she lives in California. Next, let's assume that the second premise is also true, that Sherry lives in California. We can now ask: Does the conclusion follow necessarily from the two premises? No, because it is *possible* that Sherry lives in San Francisco. Thus, argument J is invalid.

The *argument form* for argument J is referred to as the *fallacy of affirming the consequent*. It is a *formal fallacy*, a logical error that occurs in the form of an argument. Formal fallacies are restricted to *deductive* arguments. (Formal fallacies are also discussed in Chapters 6–8.) In contrast to this, *informal fallacies* are mistakes in reasoning that occur in ordinary language. (Informal fallacies are discussed in Chapter 4.)

Let's look at another argument:

Argument K:	**Argument Form:**
If Sherry lives in Los Angeles, then Sherry lives in California.	**If *L*, then *C*.**
Sherry lives in Los Angeles.	*L.*
Sherry lives in California.	*C.*

Relying on our understanding of a conditional statement, we can analyze argument K. As we saw with argument J, we can start by assuming that the first premise is true. Now, *if* the second premise is also assumed to be true, then the conclusion follows necessarily. Thus, argument K is valid. The *argument form* for argument K is referred to as *modus ponens*. In order to fully appreciate this result, we need to understand that since argument K is valid, no counterexample exists. This is an important claim, and we will try to explain it with the apparatus we currently have.

Recall that we were able to create a counterexample to argument J by recognizing that even if both premises were true, it is possible that the conclusion is false (that Sherry lives in San Francisco). Let's try that with argument K. As before, we can assume that the first premise is true. Now if we assume that the second premise is true, then the conclusion follows necessarily. (You can learn about different methods for demonstrating validity, as well as other methods for showing invalidity, in Part III, "Formal Logic.")

Let's look at a few more examples:

Argument M:	**Argument Form:**
If Sherry lives in Los Angeles, then Sherry lives in California.	If *L*, then *C*.
Sherry does not live in Los Angeles.	It is not the case that *L*.
Sherry does not live in California.	It is not the case that *C*.

We have been using the letter "*L*" to represent the simple statement "Sherry lives in Los Angeles." In order to represent the statement "Sherry does *not* live in Los Angeles," we place the phrase "It is not the case that" in front of the letter "*L*." Similarly, we have been using the letter "*C*" to represent the simple statement "Sherry lives in California." In order to represent the statement "Sherry does *not* live in California," we place the phrase "It is not the case that" in front of the letter "*C*."

Let's analyze argument M. We can start by assuming that the two premises are true. Does the conclusion follow necessarily? No, because it is possible that Sherry lives in San Francisco. Thus, argument M is invalid. The *argument form* for argument M is referred to as the *fallacy of denying the antecedent*, and it is a *formal fallacy*.

Here is another example:

Argument N:	**Argument Form:**
If Sherry lives in Los Angeles, then Sherry lives in California.	If *L*, then *C*.
Sherry does not live in California.	It is not the case that *C*.
Sherry does not live in Los Angeles.	It is not the case that *L*.

Let's analyze argument N. We can start by assuming that the premises are true. Given this, the conclusion follows necessarily. Thus, argument N is valid. The *argument form* for argument N is referred to as *modus tollens*. Since argument N is valid, no counterexample exists.

We will look at two more examples.

Argument P:	**Argument Form:**
If Sherry lives in Los Angeles, then Sherry lives in California.	If *L*, then *C*.
If Sherry lives in California, then Sherry lives in the United States.	If *C*, then *U*.
If Sherry lives in Los Angeles, then Sherry lives in the United States.	If *L*, then *U*.

Let's analyze argument P. We start by assuming that the premises are true. Given this, the conclusion follows necessarily. Thus, argument P is valid. The *argument form* for argument P is referred to as *hypothetical syllogism*. Since argument P is valid, no counterexample exists.

Our last example is the following:

Argument Q:	**Argument Form:**
Sherry lives in Los Angeles or Sherry lives in San Francisco.	*L* or *S*.
Sherry does not live in Los Angeles.	It is not the case that *L*.
Sherry lives in San Francisco.	*S*.

Let's analyze argument Q. The first premise is a compound statement that contains two simple statements ("Sherry lives in Los Angeles" and "Sherry lives in San Francisco"). It also contains the logical vocabulary word "or." This kind of compound statement is called a *disjunction*, and the two nonlogical parts are called *disjuncts*. When we assert a disjunction, we claim that at least one of the two disjuncts is true. In other words, the only way a disjunction is false is if both disjuncts are false.

We can start our analysis by assuming that the first premise is true. Given this assumption, one of the disjuncts must be true. Now, *if* the second premise is true, then it eliminates the first disjunct in the first premise. Therefore, the conclusion follows necessarily. Thus, argument Q is valid. The *argument form* for argument Q is referred to as *disjunctive syllogism*. Since argument Q is valid, no counterexample exists.

Since many real-life arguments do not fall easily into a form like the examples we have been examining, we sometimes have to be creative in finding a counterexample. For example, consider this argument:

> Every student in my daughter's psychology class has at least a 3.0 average. But all the students in her calculus class have at least a 2.0 average. So it has to be that every single student in my daughter's psychology class has a higher average than every single student in my daughter's calculus class.

The first two statements are premises, and the third statement is the conclusion. Another way to create a counterexample to an argument is to construct a *model* that shows the possibility of true premises and a false conclusion. Suppose that a particular student from the psychology class has a 3.2 average. This possibility would make the first premise true. Now suppose that a particular student from the calculus class has a 3.6 average. This is possible because the claim in the second premise is that the students have *at least* a 2.0 average. In this case, the second premise is true, too, but the conclusion is false. We have created a counterexample that shows the argument is invalid.

Let's look at another example.

> Andy's puppy weighs more than Patrick's cat. This follows from the fact that Andy's puppy weighs more than ten pounds, and Patrick's cat weighs more than seven pounds.

The conclusion is the first statement. We create a counterexample to the argument by showing the possibility of true premises and a false conclusion. Suppose that Andy's puppy weighs eleven pounds. This possibility makes the premise about Andy's puppy true. Let's also suppose that Patrick's cat weighs twelve pounds. This is possible because the premise about Patrick's cat states that it weighs more than seven pounds. Given this possibility, the second premise is true. However, the conclusion is false. We have once again created a counterexample that shows the argument is invalid.

The exercises that follow will allow you to apply what you have learned about counterexamples to help analyze arguments.

Summary of Deductive Arguments

Valid argument: A deductive argument in which, *assuming* the premises are true, it is *impossible* for the conclusion to be false.

Invalid argument: A deductive argument in which, *assuming* the premises are true, it is *possible* for the conclusion to be false.

Sound argument: A deductive argument is sound when both of the following requirements are met:
1. The argument is valid (logical analysis).
2. All the premises are true (truth value analysis).

Unsound argument: A deductive argument is unsound if either or both of the following conditions hold:
1. The argument is invalid (logical analysis).
2. The argument has at least one false premise (truth value analysis).

EXERCISES 1F

I. Create a counterexample or model to show that the following deductive arguments are invalid.

Self-Practice
Questions

1. All towers less than 200 years old are skyscrapers. All buildings made of steel are skyscrapers. Therefore, all buildings made of steel are towers less than 200 years old.

Answer: If we let T = *towers less than 200 years old*, S = *skyscrapers*, and B = *buildings made of steel*, then the argument form is the following:

All T are S.
All B are S.
All B are T.

The following substitutions create a counterexample: Let T = *cats*, S = *mammals*, and B = *dogs*.

All cats are mammals.
All dogs are mammals.
All dogs are cats.

Both premises are true, and the conclusion is false. Therefore, the counterexample shows that the argument is invalid.

2. No espresso drinks are wholesome foods. No espresso drinks are caffeine-free beverages. Therefore, no wholesome foods are caffeine-free beverages.

3. All Phi Beta Kappa members are seniors in college. All Phi Beta Kappa members are liberal arts majors. Therefore, all liberal arts majors are seniors in college.

4. No student unions are places that are open 24/7. No student unions are movie theaters. Therefore, no movie theaters are places that are open 24/7.

Video Tutorial:
1FI Exercise #5

⭐ 5. All computers are electronic devices. All things that require an AC adapter are electronic devices. Therefore, all computers are things that require an AC adapter.

6. No driving vacation trips are relaxing excursions. No relaxing excursions are cheap outings. Therefore, no driving vacation trips are cheap outings.

7. All recalled products are dangerous items. All dangerous items are defective objects. Therefore, all defective objects are recalled products.

8. No skateboards are items made of wood. No items made of wood are flammable objects. Therefore, no flammable objects are skateboards.

⭐ 9. No unicorns are immortal creatures. No centaurs are immortal creatures. It follows that no unicorns are centaurs.

10. Book A has more than 200 pages. Book B has more than 500 pages. Therefore, book B has more pages than book A.

11. Movie X is longer than three hours. Movie Y is longer than two hours. Therefore, Movie X is longer than Movie Y.

12. Barney was born before 1989. Hazel was born before 1959. Thus, Hazel was born before Barney.

⭐ 13. Fidelix was born before 1990. Gil was born before 1991. Thus, Fidelix was born before Gil.

14. Maegan spent 1/3 of her yearly income on her car. Alyssa spent 1/2 of her yearly income on her car. Therefore, Alyssa spent more money on her car than Maegan.

15. Anna spent 1/2 of her yearly income on her car. Molly spent 1/3 of her yearly income on her car. Therefore, Molly spent more money on her car than Anna.

16. All psychiatrists are people with medical degrees. All people who can prescribe drugs are people with medical degrees. Therefore, all psychiatrists are people who can prescribe drugs.

⭐ 17. All strawberries are fruit. All strawberries are plants. It follows that all fruit are plants.

18. All members of the U.S. Congress are citizens of the United States. All people under 21 years of age are citizens of the United States. Therefore, no people under 21 years of age are members of the U.S. Congress.

19. All humans are things that contain carbon. All inanimate objects are things that contain carbon. Therefore, all humans are inanimate objects.

20. No coal mines are dangerous areas to work. All dangerous areas to work are places inspected by federal agencies. Therefore, no coal mines are places inspected by federal agencies.

II. First, reveal the argument form of the following deductive arguments. Second, label it as either the *fallacy of affirming the consequent, modus ponens, the fallacy of denying the antecedent, modus tollens, hypothetical syllogism, or disjunctive syllogism*. Third, create a counterexample for each of the invalid argument forms.

1. If Sam goes to the meeting, then Joe will stay home. Sam is not going to the meeting. Therefore, Joe will not stay home.

Answer: If we let *S = Sam goes to the meeting*, and *J = Joe will stay home*, then the argument form is the following:

> If *S*, then *J*.
> It is not the case that *S*.
> It is not the case that *J*.

Fallacy of denying the antecedent. The argument is invalid.

Since this is an invalid argument form, we can try to create a counterexample. We can make the letters "*S*" and "*J*" stand for *any statements that we wish*. All we need to do is create a scenario where both premises are true and the conclusion is false. Suppose that we make *S = my mom ate an apple*, and *J = my mom ate a fruit*. In addition, suppose that my mom actually ate an orange instead of an apple. Under these assumptions, the first premise would still be true (recall that the conditional statement *does not assert* that she ate an apple; it asserts only that *if* she ate an apple, then she ate a fruit). Since we assumed that she ate an orange, the second premise is also true. However, the conclusion is false because she did eat a fruit.

2. Either you take a cut in pay or we will lay you off. You did not take a cut in pay. Thus, we will lay you off.

3. If today is Adrian's birthday, then he received presents. Adrian received presents. So, today is Adrian's birthday.

4. If animals have rights, then animals can vote. Animals have rights. Therefore, animals can vote.

⭐ 5. If birds can swim, then birds are aquatic animals. Birds are not aquatic animals. Thus, birds cannot swim.

6. If bananas are fruit, then bananas are plants. If bananas are plants, then bananas use photosynthesis. So, if bananas are fruit, then bananas use photosynthesis.

7. If Mary stayed home from work, then her car is in the garage. Mary's car is in the garage. Therefore, Mary stayed home from work.

8. If it rained last night, then the street is wet. It did not rain last night. Thus, the street is not wet.

⭐ 9. Either you are lost or you are confused. You are not lost. Therefore, you are confused.

10. If Petra went swimming, then she is at the lake. Petra is not at the lake. Thus, Petra did not go swimming.

11. If your motorcycle is burning oil, then it is wasting energy. If your motorcycle is wasting energy, then it is polluting the air. So, if your motorcycle is burning oil, then it is polluting the air.

12. If Jane Blythe is a secret agent, then she is licensed to carry a gun. Jane Blythe is not a secret agent, so she is not licensed to carry a gun.

⭐ 13. If I can save $1000, then I can buy a car. I can save $1000. Thus, I can buy a car.

14. If Tommy knows several computer programming languages, then he is a computer linguist. Tommy is a computer linguist, so he knows several computer programming languages.

15. Either you completed the coursework or you failed the course. You did not complete your coursework. Therefore, you failed the course.

G. INDUCTIVE ARGUMENTS: STRENGTH AND COGENCY

Often our arguments are not expected to achieve validity. As we shall see, the results of analysis of inductive arguments are not all-or-nothing. If you recall, deductive arguments can be valid, invalid, sound, or unsound. In addition, one deductive argument cannot be more valid (or invalid) than another deductive argument. In contrast to this, one inductive argument can be classified as *stronger* or *weaker* than another inductive argument. We can compare them by how likely their respective conclusions are true, under the assumption that the premises are true. Recall that an inductive argument is one in which the inferential claim is that the conclusion is *probably true* if the premises are true. In other words, under the *assumption* that the premises are true it is *improbable* for the conclusion to be false.

Strong inductive argument An argument such that if the premises are *assumed* to be true, then the conclusion is *probably* true. In other words, the probable truth of the conclusion *follows from* the truth of the premises.

A **strong inductive argument** is such that if the premises are *assumed* to be true, then the conclusion is *probably true*. Let's look at a simple example:

> Most cars in the United States use gasoline. Therefore, my aunt's new car probably uses gasoline.

If we *assume* that the premise is true, then the conclusion is *probably* true. The important thing to consider is that the premise offers direct and relevant support, so we can say that the *probable truth* of the conclusion *follows from* the truth of the premise.

Weak inductive argument An argument such that either (a) if the premises are *assumed* to be true, then the conclusion is *probably not true*, or (b) a probably true conclusion *does not follow from the premises.*

In contrast, a **weak inductive argument** is an argument such that either (a) if the premises are *assumed* to be true, then the conclusion is *probably not true*, or (b) a probably true conclusion *does not follow from the premises.*

Let's look at a simple example of (a):

> Most cars in the United States use gasoline. Therefore, my aunt's new car probably is electric.

If we *assume* that the premise is true, then the conclusion is probably not true. Thus, the argument is weak. Notice that we are *not* claiming that the conclusion is false; we are claiming only that is *unlikely to be true*, assuming the premise is true.

The other way an inductive argument can be weak is (b) a probably true conclusion *does not follow from the premises*. This typically occurs when premises that are *irrelevant* to the conclusion do not provide any probabilistic support for the conclusion. In these cases, *even though the conclusion is probably true*, the argument is weak. Here is a simple example:

> You need a valid driver's license to legally drive an automobile. Therefore, for the near future most new automobiles will use gasoline.

There is no direct, relevant connection between the premise and the conclusion. Although the conclusion is probably true, that probability is *not* based on the assumption that the premise is true. Since the conclusion is probably true *independently of the premise*, the argument is weak. The important consideration in evaluating the strength or weakness of an inductive argument is the probabilistic support the premises give to the conclusion.

When we add truth value analysis to the results of the logical analysis, we get two additional classifications. An inductive argument is **cogent** when the argument is strong and the premises are true. On the other hand, an inductive argument is **uncogent** if either or both of the following conditions hold: The argument is weak, or the argument has at least one false premise. The following flow chart illustrates the process:

Cogent argument An inductive argument is cogent when the argument is strong and the premises are true.

Uncogent argument An inductive argument is uncogent if either or both of the following conditions hold: The argument is weak, or the argument has at least one false premise.

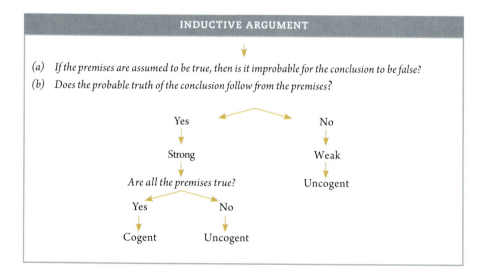

Since it is easy to confuse the question of the truth value of statements with the logical question of what follows from those statements, it is important to keep the two questions separate when you analyze arguments. To help, we start with a brief table listing the logical possibilities available in inductive arguments:

	INDUCTIVE ARGUMENTS		
Premises	Conclusion	Strength	Cogency
1. True	Probably true	Strong or weak	Cogent or uncogent
2. True	Probably false	Weak	Uncogent
3. At least one false	Probably true	Strong or weak	Uncogent
4. At least one false	Probably false	Strong or weak	Uncogent

Line 2 states that an inductive argument with true premises and a false conclusion is weak and uncogent. This is a straightforward result of the previous discussion. On the other hand, lines 1, 3, and 4 may need additional explanation.

Notice that under the column "Strength," inductive arguments that have the characteristics listed in lines 1, 3, and 4 are said to be either strong or weak. Under the column "Cogency," inductive arguments that have the characteristics listed in both lines 3 and 4 are said to be uncogent, but those in line 1 can be either cogent or uncogent.

Let's look at lines 3 and 4. Since both lines refer to inductive arguments that have at least one false premise, the arguments are automatically uncogent. In contrast, the inductive arguments referred to in line 1 have true premises, and since they can be either strong or weak, they can be either cogent or uncogent. At this point, we are simply listing the logical possibilities. We now need to flesh out those possibilities to see how we can make the final determinations. Here are some examples:

Premise/Conclusion	Strong	Weak
True premise *Probably true conclusion*	Most cars use gasoline. Therefore, probably my cousin's car uses gasoline. **COGENT**	A few cars are antiques. Therefore, probably my cousin's car uses gasoline. **UNCOGENT**
True premise *Probably false conclusion*	None exist	A few cars are antiques. Therefore, probably my cousin's car is an antique. **UNCOGENT**
False premise *Probably true conclusion*	Most new cars cost over $100,000. Therefore, probably your new Ferrari costs over $100,000. **UNCOGENT**	Most cars are antiques. Therefore, probably your car uses gasoline. **UNCOGENT**
False premise *Probably false conclusion*	Most cars are antiques. Therefore, probably your car is an antique. **UNCOGENT**	Most cars are hybrids. Therefore, probably your car is a Ferrari. **UNCOGENT**

Techniques of Analysis

Let's start with an analysis of an inductive argument:

> Most National Basketball Association most valuable players (MVPs) are at
>   least six feet tall.
> The next National Basketball Association MVP will be at least six feet tall.

The logical analysis begins by assuming that the premise is true. The key for applying the logical analysis in this example is the term "most." Under the assumption that the premise is true, the conclusion is probably true; therefore, the argument is strong. Turning now to the truth value analysis, research shows that the premise is true. Therefore, the argument is both strong and cogent.

Let's now analyze a pair of inductive arguments at the same time. Imagine that you have the following information: An opaque jar contains exactly 100 marbles. There are 99 blue marbles and 1 red marble in the jar. Next, you are told that someone has reached into the jar and picked 1 marble, and you and a friend guess what color it is. You choose blue and your friend chooses red. We can use this case to create two inductive arguments:

A.   An opaque jar contains exactly 100 marbles.
         There are 99 blue marbles in the jar.
         There is 1 red marble in the jar.
         The marble picked is blue.

B.   An opaque jar contains exactly 100 marbles.
         There are 99 blue marbles in the jar.
         There is 1 red marble in the jar.
         The marble picked is red.

Using the definitions for inductive arguments, a logical analysis shows that argument A is strong and argument B is weak. Based on the assumption that the premises are true we can calculate that the conclusion of argument A has a 99/100 chance of being true, while the conclusion of argument B has only a 1/100 chance of being true. Given this, we can say that argument A is much stronger than argument B.

Now suppose we are shown the actual marble that was picked and it is red. Is this a counterexample to argument A that would make argument A weak? And would this result suddenly render argument B strong? The answer to both questions is *No*. We determined that the premises, *if they are assumed to be true*, make the conclusion of argument A *probably true*. On the other hand, the premises, *if they are assumed to be true*, make the conclusion of argument B *not probably true*. Therefore, the single result of a red marble does not change our mind.

However, at some point new evidence can become a factor in our overall assessment. We turn now to that discussion.

The Role of New Information

In order to advance the discussion, we will continue our analysis of arguments A and B from the end of the previous section. Suppose that the red marble is returned to the jar, the jar is shaken, and a *second* pick yields a red marble again. Since we are assuming that there is only 1 red marble in the jar, the probability of this happening is $1/100 \times 1/100 = 1/10,000$—which is very small, *but not impossible*. In fact, in a very long series of picks, we would eventually expect this to happen. But now suppose that the *next five picks* all result in a red marble, and each time the red marble is returned and the jar shaken. The probability is now 1/100 multiplied by itself seven times (that is, the original two picks plus five more). Faced with the new evidence, we may need to explain why we are getting these unexpected results.

We still assume that the premises are true; this is how we are coming up with the probabilities. But at some point the actual results may cause us to *question the truth of the original premises*. Although we were told that the jar contained 99 blue marbles and 1 red marble, we might start doubting this. In fact, we might even doubt that there are any blue ones at all, or if there are 100 marbles. It could even be that this is a scam; the person picking the marble palms a red one and never really puts it back. In other words, we might start doubting the truth of any or all of the premises.

As this example shows, determining whether an inductive argument is strong or weak is not an all-or-nothing thing. Also, a single counterexample does not have the same effect on an inductive argument that it has on a deductive argument. The goals of inductive and deductive arguments are simply different.

Another interesting point to consider regarding inductive arguments is that by adding an additional premise or premises to a weak inductive argument, we can often create a new argument that is strong. For example, consider the following argument:

> There are green and black socks in the box. Thus, a sock picked at random will probably be green.

Since we do not know how many socks of each color are in the box, the premise *does not* make the conclusion highly likely to be true; thus it is a weak argument. However, suppose we are given some new information:

> There are green and black socks in the box. *Eight of the socks are green and two are black.* Thus, a sock picked at random will probably be green.

Based on the new information, there is an 8/10 chance of picking a green sock. Since the conclusion is now highly likely to be true, the addition makes this a strong argument.

On the other hand, it is also possible that new information will affect a strong inductive argument such that the added premises create a new, weak argument. For example, consider the following argument:

> I just drank a bottle of Sunrise Spring Mineral Water. Since it has been shown that most bottled water is safe, I can conclude, with some confidence, that the water was safe.

Assuming the premises are true, this is a strong argument. However, suppose we pick up the newspaper and read an article reporting the following:

> Happy Sunshine Manufacturing Corporation has announced that it is recalling all of its Sunrise Spring Mineral Water due to a suspected contamination at one of its bottling facilities. Anyone having purchased this product is advised to return it to the store of purchase for a full refund.

When added as additional premises, this new information makes the original conclusion unlikely to be true; thus its addition creates a weak argument.

Of course, not all additional information will affect an inductive argument. For example, if new information is added as a premise, *but it is irrelevant to the conclusion*, then it has no effect on the strength of the argument.

As we saw earlier, there are many types of inductive arguments. In Part IV ("Inductive Logic") we introduce techniques of analysis for several types of inductive arguments.

Summary of Inductive Arguments

Strong inductive argument: An argument such that if the premises are *assumed* to be true, then the conclusion is *probably* true. In other words, the probable truth of the conclusion *follows from* the truth of the premises.

Weak inductive argument: An argument such that either (a) if the premises are *assumed* to be true, then the conclusion is *probably not true,* or (b) a probably true conclusion *does not follow from the premises.*

Cogent argument: An inductive argument is cogent when both of the following requirements are met:
  1. The argument is strong (logical analysis).
  2. All the premises are true (truth value analysis).

Uncogent argument: An inductive argument is uncogent if either or both of the following conditions hold:
  1. The argument is weak (logical analysis).
  2. The argument has at least one false premise (truth value analysis).

EXERCISES 1G

I. Determine whether the following inductive arguments are *strong* or *weak*.

Self-Practice Questions

1. Most insects have six legs. What's crawling on me is an insect. So what's crawling on me has six legs.

Answer: Strong. If we assume the premises are true, then the conclusion is probably true.

2. The exam's range of A scores is 90–100. I got an A on the exam, thus I got a 98 on the exam.

Video Tutorial: 1GI
Exercise #5

3. There are nine red marbles and one blue marble in that jar. I randomly picked a marble from that jar. Therefore, I probably did not pick the blue marble.

4. Because most beaches are places where it is safe to swim, it is, therefore, safe for us to swim at this beach.

⭐ 5. Shane tossed a coin ten times, and in each case it came up heads. Therefore, the next toss will be heads.

6. Most elements with atomic weights greater than 64 are metals. Z is an element with an atomic weight of 79. Therefore, Z is a metal.

7. A few arthropods are venomous. I was just bitten by an arthropod. So, its bite was probably venomous.

8. Most antibiotics are effective for treating bacterial infections. You have a bacterial infection. You are taking the antibiotic Q. Thus, the antibiotic you are taking will be effective in treating your bacterial infection.

⭐ 9. Most fruit have seeds. I am eating an orange, so I am eating something with seeds.

10. Most Doberman dogs bark a lot. My cousin just got a Doberman dog. Therefore, my cousin's Doberman dog will probably bark a lot.

II. The following exercises are designed to get you to evaluate the strength of inductive arguments as the result of adding new information. You will be given an inductive argument; then additional information will be provided. Determine whether the new information *strengthens* or *weakens* the original argument. Evaluate each piece of new information independently of the others. Here is the argument:

> <u>**The lamp in your room does not work.**</u>
> **The light bulb is defective.**

1. The ceiling light works.

Answer: Strengthens the argument. If the ceiling light works, then there is electricity available in the room.

2. The lamp is plugged into the wall socket correctly.

3. Your radio is working, and it is connected to the same outlet as the lamp.

4. The ceiling light does not work.

⭐ 5. The lamp is not plugged into the wall socket correctly.

6. Your radio is not working, and it is connected to the same outlet as the lamp.

7. You replace the light bulb, and the lamp now works.

8. You replace the light bulb, and the lamp does not work.

⭐ 9. Every other electrical fixture in the room works.

10. No electrical fixture in the room works.

Apply the same kind of analysis to the next inductive argument. Evaluate the new information to decide if that particular piece of information *strengthens* or *weakens* the argument. Treat each new piece of information independently of the others.

> <u>Your car won't start.</u>
> **Your battery is dead.**

11. The headlights don't work.

Answer: Strengthens the argument. Headlights draw their power from the battery; therefore, this new evidence strengthens the argument.

12. The headlights do work.

⭐ 13. The battery is 5 years old.

14. The battery is 3 months old.

15. The horn works.

16. The horn does not work.

⭐ 17. The battery terminal clamps are loose.

18. The battery terminal clamps are tight.

19. When you jump-start the car, it starts.

20. When you jump-start the car, it does not start.

H. RECONSTRUCTING ARGUMENTS

People often take shortcuts when creating arguments. Someone might intentionally leave out important information because he or she thinks that the missing information is already understood. In such instances, we need to reconstruct the argument by filling in the missing information. For example, someone might say the following:

> The novel I just bought is by Judy Prince, so I'm sure I'm going to like it.

Even if the speaker is not someone you know well, you can probably supply the missing premise:

> The novel I just bought is by Judy Prince [and I liked every novel of hers that I have read so far], so I'm sure I'm going to like it.

Notice that we placed brackets around the missing premise in order to indicate that the additional statement was not part of the original argument. Arguments with missing premises, missing conclusions, or both are called **enthymemes**. (The term derives from two roots: "en," meaning *in*, and "thymos," which refers to the mind, literally meaning, *to keep in the mind*.) The missing information is therefore *implied*. Enthymemes are context-driven. Our recognition and subsequent reconstruction of the argument depends on the setting in which the information appears.

Enthymemes
Arguments with missing premises, missing conclusions, or both.

However, sometimes we are expected to supply missing information with which we are not necessarily familiar. For example, suppose someone says this:

> I have a Cadillac; therefore, I don't have to spend much on maintenance.

The assumption is that we will supply something like the following:

> I have a Cadillac [and Cadillacs require very little maintenance]; therefore, I don't have to spend much on maintenance.

Advertisements can be effective when they have missing conclusions. A billboard once displayed the following message:

> Banks lend money. We're a bank.

The advertisers were clever enough to know that most people would easily fill in the conclusion: "We lend money." Some clever ads say very little but imply a lot. The visual is created in order for you to mindlessly fill in the missing conclusion: "If I buy this product, then I will experience what is being depicted." (Of course, nobody falls for this.)

What we choose to supply as a missing premise or conclusion can affect the subsequent evaluation of the argument. For example, suppose someone says the following:

> Bill Gateway is rich; it follows that he cheats on his taxes.

We can fill in the missing premise in these two ways:

> (1) Bill Gateway is rich; [and since all rich people cheat on their taxes] it follows that he cheats on his taxes.
> (2) Bill Gateway is rich; [and since most rich people cheat on their taxes] it follows that he cheats on his taxes.

Because the term "rich" is vague, we need to define it for purposes of analysis. We can arbitrarily stipulate that "rich" means any individual whose income exceeds $250,000 a year. In addition, we can stipulate that "most" means at least 70%.

Let's apply logical analysis first. Reconstruction (1) makes the argument deductive, and assuming the premises are true, it is valid. Reconstruction (2) makes the argument inductive, and assuming the premises are true, it is a strong argument. Now let's apply truth value analysis. In reconstruction (1), the added premise, "all rich people cheat on their taxes," is false if even one rich person does not cheat on his or her taxes. It seems likely that at least one rich person has not cheated. Thus, the argument is valid, but probably unsound.

For reconstruction (2), the truth value of the added premise, "most rich people cheat on their taxes," is not so obvious. While many people probably have strong feelings regarding the truth or falsity of this added premise, objective evidence is necessary to decide the issue. For example, if the Internal Revenue Service (IRS) published a report stating that approximately 70% of all "rich" people (using our stipulated definition of the term) who have been audited have been found to cheat on their taxes, then this could be used as objective evidence to show the premise is true. If so, the argument is cogent. However, if the IRS published a report stating that only around 15% of all "rich" people who have been audited have been found to cheat on their taxes, then this could be used as objective evidence to show the premise is false. If so, we would classify the argument as uncogent, because at least one premise is false.

Given both analyses, we should choose the reconstructed argument that *gives the benefit of the doubt to* the person presenting the argument. In this case, reconstructing the argument as inductive is the better choice. This process is referred to as the **principle of charity**. The principle is based on a sense of fairness and an open mind. Since we expect other people to interpret and analyze our arguments in the most reasonable way, we should do the same. This principle also stresses the *concern for truth*. Reconstructing a reasonable argument *raises* the possibility that we will arrive at the truth and learn something. Reconstructing an illogical argument *reduces* the possibility that we will arrive at the truth and learn something.

Suppose someone says the following:

> Expanding educational opportunities for all Americans will require our elected representatives to allocate more tax money for education than is currently available. Without this additional funding we will not be able to compete in a fast-changing world, and our economy and standard of living will suffer. No one wants that to happen.

Based on the information given, the speaker probably wants us to conclude something like the following:

> We should allocate more tax money for education than is currently available.

If we accept the premises as *true*, then this is a strong argument. However, we can question the accuracy of the premises. For example, we can ask whether there are other ways to expand educational opportunities without raising taxes. We can also ask whether our economy and standard of living will suffer, as stated in the argument. Answering these questions will serve to help us learn something about the important issues raised by the argument.

In contrast, someone who fails to apply the principle of charity might conclude the following:

> We have to cut military spending.

This results in a weak argument since nothing in the premises directly supports the cutting of military spending. However, this reconstruction avoids the possibility of a reasonable argument that deserves serious evaluation.

There is another important aspect to deductive arguments that we should investigate. It is often quite easy to add a premise to an invalid argument, thereby creating a new valid argument. For example, consider the following:

> Frank committed a murder. Therefore, Frank committed a felony.

The argument is invalid. It requires an added premise to make it valid, as the following reconstruction shows:

> Frank committed a murder. [Every murder is a felony.] Therefore, Frank committed a felony.

Principle of charity
We should choose the reconstructed argument that gives the benefit of the doubt to the person presenting the argument.

If we add a premise to make an argument valid, then we must make sure that the new premise does not create an unsound argument. For example:

> Frank committed a felony. Therefore, Frank committed a murder.

This is an invalid argument. It can be made valid by adding a new premise:

> Frank committed a felony. [Every felony is a murder.] Therefore, Frank committed a murder.

This is a valid argument. However, not every felony is a murder (selling illegal drugs is a felony). Thus, the new premise is false, and the argument is unsound. Therefore we must be careful to add premises that not only logically support the conclusion, but that are also true.

Additional premises can affect a deductive argument, but only in one way. As we saw, it is possible to add premises to an invalid argument and create a new valid argument. However, the opposite result cannot happen. Since the original premises of a valid argument provide the necessary support to ensure that the argument is valid, no additional premise(s) can affect that outcome.

As we saw with enthymemes, context can influence our recognition and reconstruction of arguments, which is why interpretations of statements and arguments must be justified. Since it is easy to take a statement out of context and give it any interpretation we please, we often need the original context to help us settle disagreements. The more we know about the setting in which the statements and arguments were made, the people involved, and the issues at hand, the more accurate our interpretations, analyses, and evaluations will be.

Of course, not all uses of language are transparent. For instance, people often speak *rhetorically*; that is, the language they employ may be implying things that are not explicitly said. We must be careful when we interpret this kind of language, and we need to justify our reconstructions of arguments.

Although arguments are constructed out of statements, sometimes a premise or conclusion is disguised as a question. A *rhetorical question* guides and persuades the reader or the listener. Here is an example:

> Using rhetorical questions in speeches is a great way to keep the audience involved. Don't you think those kinds of questions would keep your attention?
>
> Bo Scott Bennett, *Year to Success*

The passage engages us in a dialogue, but the writer is clever enough to persuade us to accept his intended answer. Suppose someone says the following:

> You have not saved any money, you have only a part-time job, and at your age car insurance will cost you at least $2000 a year. Do you really think you can afford a car?

Although the last sentence poses a question, it should be clear from the context that the speaker's intention is to assert a conclusion: "You can't afford a car." So the rhetorical question is really a statement disguised in the form of a question. We can reconstruct the argument as follows:

> You have not saved any money. You have only a part-time job. At your age car insurance will cost you at least $2000 a year. [Therefore, you can't afford a car.]

Since we changed the rhetorical question into a statement, we placed it in brackets. In some arguments, both a premise and a conclusion appear as rhetorical questions. For example, suppose a disgruntled teenager says the following:

> I do my share of work around this house. Don't I deserve to get something in return? Why shouldn't I be allowed to go to the Weaknotes concert today?

The speaker is using two rhetorical questions for dramatic effect. Our reconstruction should reveal the assertions implied by the speaker, as follows:

> I do my share of work around this house. [I deserve to get something in return.] [Thus, I should be allowed to go to the Weaknotes concert today.]

The reconstruction gives us a clearer understanding of the argument. Here is another example of a rhetorical question appearing as part of an argument:

> Why do you waste your time worrying about your death? It won't happen during your lifetime.

Here is the reconstructed argument:

> [Your death won't happen during your lifetime. So, stop wasting your time worrying about it.]

There are other aspects of rhetorical language. For instance, suppose you tell a friend that you are trying to lose twenty-five pounds. Your friend might say the following:

> If you were really serious about losing weight, then you would not be eating that large pepperoni pizza all by yourself.

From the context, it should be clear that the speaker is observing you eating a pizza, so that fact is not in dispute. The observation is then used as the basis to imply a conclusion. In this example, the consequent of the conditional statement contains the intended premise, while the antecedent contains the intended conclusion. Here is the reconstructed argument:

> [You are eating that large pepperoni pizza all by yourself. Therefore, you are not really serious about losing weight.]

A conditional statement that is used to imply an argument is called a *rhetorical conditional*. We must take care to reconstruct a conditional statement as an argument only when we are reasonably sure that the conditional is being used rhetorically. A correct reconstruction of a conditional statement as an argument requires an understanding of the context in which the conditional appears.

A rhetorical conditional can even occur in the form of a question. Depending on the context, a rhetorical conditional can be reconstructed in different ways. For example, suppose we encounter this statement:

If you truly care about your children, then why are you neglecting them?

If the speaker happens to be a close friend or relative whose intent is to change someone's behavior, the argument might be reconstructed as follows:

[I know you care about your children. So, you have to stop neglecting them.]

On the other hand, if the speaker is a social worker who has observed repeated instances of child neglect, the argument might be reconstructed differently:

[You repeatedly neglect your children. Therefore, you do not truly care for them.]

In this case, the social worker may be using the rhetorical conditional as part of a more extended justification for removing the children from a negligent parent.

The next example adds a new dimension to our discussion of rhetorical conditionals. Suppose a parent says this to a child:

If you are smart, and I know you are, then you will do the right thing.

It is possible to reconstruct the argument and yet retain a conditional as a premise. We might want to allow the phrase "I know you are" to play a key role in our reconstruction. If so, the argument can be displayed as follows:

[If you are smart, then you will do the right thing. I know that you are smart. Thus, you will do the right thing.]

Alternatively, we might reconstruct the argument by eliminating the conditional aspect. If we interpret the phrase "I know you are" as directly asserting the antecedent, then we can place emphasis on the purely rhetorical nature of the conditional. The new reconstruction might look like this:

[You are smart; therefore, you will do the right thing.]

Whichever way we decide to reconstruct an argument, we should be prepared to justify our reconstruction by reference to the context in which it originally occurred.

Finally, it is important to remember that (1) *arguments are neither true nor false*, and (2) *statements are neither valid nor invalid nor strong nor weak*. The following chart illustrates these two points.

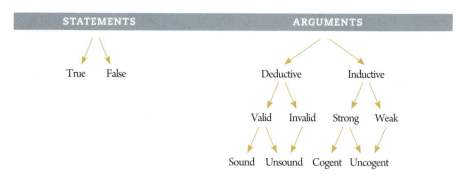

EXERCISES 1H

I. For each of the following enthymemes, supply either the missing premise(s) or the missing conclusion. Apply the *principle of charity* **to your reconstructions. Evaluate the resulting arguments, and explain your answers.**

Self-Practice
Questions

1. I am talking to a human; therefore, I am talking to a mammal.

Answer:

Reconstruction 1: Missing premise: *All humans are mammals.*

This makes the argument deductively valid. Since the added premise is true, if the first premise is true, then it is a sound argument.

Reconstruction 2: Missing premise: *The vast majority of humans are mammals.*

This makes the argument inductively strong. But since we know that all humans are mammals, this reconstruction would not be the best choice.

2. I am talking to a mammal; therefore, I am talking to a human.

3. Shane owns a Honda, so it must be a motorcycle.

4. Shane owns a motorcycle, so it must be a Honda.

⭐ 5. I have a headache. I just took two aspirins. Aspirins relieve headaches.

6. The office laser printer can print twenty pages a minute in black and white or ten pages a minute in color. It took 1 minute to print John's ten-page report on the office laser printer.

7. Viola just had a big lasagna dinner, so I know she is very happy now.

8. Since Viola just had a big lasagna dinner, it follows that she will soon be looking for the antacid tablets.

⭐ 9. Jill has a viral infection. She decided to take some penicillin. But she doesn't realize that penicillin has no effect on viruses.

10. Jill has a bacterial infection. She decided to take some penicillin. Penicillin can be effective when treating bacteria.

11. Frances must be an honest person, because she is an educated person.

12. There are ten marbles in the jar; nine red and one blue. I picked, at random, one of the marbles from the jar.

⭐ 13. Jamillah is a safe driver, so her insurance rates are low.

14. Wilma has an expensive camera, therefore she takes perfect pictures.

15. Shane is a well-prepared and diligent student. Teachers respect students who are well prepared and diligent.

16. Perform at your best when your best is required. Your best is required every day.

Video Tutorial: 1H
Exercise #11

Adapted from John Wooden's *Pyramid of Success*

⭐17. Most of us today live in cities and spend far less time outside in green, natural spaces than people did several generations ago. Various studies have found that urban dwellers with little access to green spaces have a higher incidence of psychological problems than people living near parks. But city dwellers who visit natural environments have lower levels of stress hormones immediately afterward than people who have not recently been outside.

Gretchen Reynolds, "How Walking in Nature Changes the Brain," *The New York Times*

18. When drunk in excess, alcohol damages nearly all organ systems. It is also connected to higher death rates and is involved in a greater percentage of crime than most other drugs, including heroin. But the problem is that "alcohol is too embedded in our culture and it won't go away," said Leslie King, an adviser to the European Monitoring Centre for Drugs.

Adapted from "Alcohol More Lethal than Heroin, Cocaine," Associated Press

19. Some 80,000 Western-trained Chinese scientists have returned to work in the pharmaceutical and health-care industries in China since the mid-1980s. In addition to the accelerated return of Chinese scientists, the Chinese government and private industry have instituted a surge in investment in research and development in the above mentioned fields.

Adapted from the article "China as Innovator," *Straits Times*

20. There are some things in our society and some things in our world of which I'm proud to be maladjusted, and I call upon all men of goodwill to be maladjusted to these things until the good society is realized. I must honestly say to you that I never intend to adjust myself to racial segregation and discrimination. I never intend to adjust myself to religious bigotry. I never intend to adjust myself to economic conditions that will take necessities from the many to give luxuries to the few, and leave millions of God's children smothering in an airtight cage of poverty in the midst of an affluent society.

Martin Luther King, Jr., 1963 speech

II. Reconstruct arguments based on your understanding and interpretation of the *rhetorical* aspect of the passages that follow. In each case be prepared to offer justification for your reconstruction and interpretation.

1. You already ate more than your fair share of our limited food supply; do you really want more?

Answer:

<u>You already ate more than your fair share of our limited food supply.</u>
[You do not really want more.]

The rhetorical force behind the assertion "You already ate *more* than your *fair share* of our *limited* food supply" (added emphasis) seems to be indicating that the conclusion should be negative in tone.

2. Capital punishment sometimes leads to the execution of innocent humans. As a society we cannot continue to perform such brutal acts of inhumanity. Isn't it time to change the existing laws?

3. You are not happy at your job, so why not quit?

4. If he is being accused of taking steroids now, then why has he hit approximately the same number of home runs each year since he first started playing professional baseball?

⭐ 5. If you are correct that he has not taken steroids, then how can you explain his suddenly gaining forty pounds of muscle and doubling his average home run total?

6. If the United States cannot find the number one terrorist on the list, then it cannot ever hope to eliminate the large number of cells of anonymous terrorists.

7. If you want to get in shape, then why do you sit around the house all day doing nothing?

8. If the Catholic Church really believes in the equality of women, then why aren't there any women priests?

⭐ 9. If she committed suicide by shooting herself, then why is there no trace of gunpowder on her hands?

10. If U.S. international policy is not to be a nation builder, then we wouldn't keep overthrowing governments we don't like and installing puppet leaders.

11. If you want to be financially secure in your retirement years, then why don't you have a retirement counselor?

12. You hate getting prank phone calls, so why don't you get an unlisted phone number?

⭐ 13. If you want to get rich quick, then why don't you buy more lottery tickets?

14. Does any wrong-headed decision suddenly become right when defended with religious conviction? In this age, don't we know better? If my God told me to poke the elderly with sharp sticks, would that make it morally acceptable to others?   Rick Reilly, "Wrestling with Conviction"

15. Now I know I'm fighting an uphill battle in some sense. If someone willingly chooses to be illogical, how to do you argue with them? Through logic? Clearly you cannot, because they don't subscribe to this. If someone maintains that the world is 6,000 years old and that any evidence otherwise is just a trick by God to make us think the world is older, how do I argue against this?   Tony Piro, interview at "This Week in Webcomics"

Summary

Study Materials

- Argument: A group of statements of which one (the conclusion) is claimed to follow from the others (the premises).
- Statement: A sentence that is either true or false.
- Premise(s): The information intended to provide support for a conclusion.
- Logic is the systematic use of methods and principles to analyze, evaluate, and construct arguments.
- Every statement is either true or false; these two possibilities are called "truth values."
- Proposition: The information content imparted by a statement, or, simply put, its meaning.
- Inference: The term used by logicians to refer to the reasoning process that is expressed by an argument.
- In order to help recognize arguments, we rely on premise indicator words and phrases, and conclusion indicator words and phrases.
- If a passage expresses a reasoning process—that the conclusion follows from the premises—then we say that it makes an inferential claim.
- If a passage does not express a reasoning process (explicit or implicit), then it does not make an inferential claim (it is a noninferential passage).
- Explanation: Provides reasons for why or how an event occurred. By themselves, explanations are not arguments; however, they can form part of an argument.
- Truth value analysis determines if the information in the premises is accurate, correct, or true.
- Logical analysis determines the strength with which the premises support the conclusion.
- Deductive argument: An argument in which the inferential claim is that the conclusion follows *necessarily* from the premises. In other words, under the *assumption* that the premises are true it is *impossible* for the conclusion to be false.
- Inductive argument: An argument in which the inferential claim is that the conclusion is *probably true* if the premises are true. In other words, under the *assumption* that the premises are true it is *improbable* for the conclusion to be false. In other words, the *probable truth* of the conclusion *follows from* the premises.
- Valid deductive argument: An argument in which, *assuming* the premises are true, it is *impossible* for the conclusion to be false. In other words, the conclusion *follows necessarily* from the premises.
- Invalid deductive argument: An argument in which, *assuming* the premises are true, it is *possible* for the conclusion to be false. In other words, the conclusion *does not follow necessarily* from the premises.
- When logical analysis shows that a deductive argument is valid, and when truth value analysis of the premises shows that they are all true, then the argument is sound.

- If a deductive argument is invalid, or if at least one of the premises is false (truth value analysis), then the argument is unsound.
- In categorical logic, an argument form is an arrangement of logical vocabulary and letters that stand for class terms such that a uniform substitution of class terms for the letters results in an argument.
- In categorical logic, a statement form is an arrangement of logical vocabulary and letters that stand for class terms such that a uniform substitution of class terms for the letters results in a statement.
- A substitution instance of a *statement* occurs when a uniform substitution of class terms for the letters results in a statement. A substitution instance of an *argument* occurs when a uniform substitution of class terms for the letters results in an argument.
- A counterexample to a statement is evidence that shows the statement is false, and it concerns truth value analysis. A counterexample to an argument shows that the conclusion does not follow necessarily from the premises. A single counterexample to a deductive argument is enough to show that an argument is invalid.
- Conditional statement: In English, the word "if" typically precedes the antecedent of a conditional statement, and the word "then" typically precedes the consequent.
- Fallacy of affirming the consequent: An invalid argument form; it is a formal fallacy.
- *Modus ponens*: A valid argument form.
- Fallacy of denying the antecedent: An invalid argument form; it is a formal fallacy.
- *Modus tollens*: A valid argument form.
- Hypothetical syllogism: A valid argument form.
- Disjunction: A compound statement that has two distinct statements, called disjuncts, connected by the word "or."
- Disjunctive syllogism: A valid argument form.
- Strong inductive argument: An argument such that if the premises are *assumed* to be true, then the conclusion is *probably true*. In other words, the probable truth of the conclusion *follows from* the truth of the premises.
- Weak inductive argument: An argument such that either (a) if the premises are *assumed* to be true, then the conclusion is *probably not true,* or (b) a probably true conclusion *does not follow from the premises.*
- An inductive argument is cogent when the argument is strong and the premises are true. An inductive argument is uncogent when either or both of the following conditions hold: the argument is weak, or the argument has at least one false premise.
- Enthymemes: Arguments with missing premises, missing conclusions, or both.
- Principle of charity: We should choose the reconstructed argument that gives the benefit of the doubt to the person presenting the argument.

- Rhetorical language: When we speak or write for dramatic or exaggerated effect. When the language we employ may be implying things that are not explicitly said.
- Rhetorical question: Occurs when a statement is disguised in the form of a question.
- Rhetorical conditional: A conditional statement that is used to imply an argument.

KEY TERMS

argument 3	inferential claim 8	strong inductive
argument form 31	invalid deductive	argument 44
cogent argument 45	argument 29	substitution instance 32
conclusion 3	logic 3	truth value 4
conclusion	logical analysis 22	truth value analysis 22
indicators 7	premise 3	uncogent argument 45
counterexample 34	premise indicators 7	unsound argument 30
deductive argument 23	principle of charity 53	valid deductive
enthymemes 51	proposition 4	argument 29
explanation 19	sound argument 30	weak inductive
inductive argument 23	statement 3	argument 44
inference 5	statement form 32	

LOGIC CHALLENGE: THE PROBLEM OF THE HATS

Scientists, philosophers, mathematicians, detectives, logicians, and physicians all face logical problems. How do they go about solving them? For insights, try your own hand at a challenge, the *problem of the hats*. Once you are given the facts of the case, be aware of how you attack the problem, how you take it apart, what you place emphasis on, your avenues of pursuit, and plausible conjectures. The answer requires "seeing" a key move.

Here is the challenge: A teacher comes to class with a box and shows the contents of the box to the students. It contains three white hats, two red hats, and nothing else. There happen to be only three students in this class, and the teacher tells them that he is going to blindfold each one and then place one of the five hats on each of their heads. The remaining two hats will then be placed back in the box, so no one can see them once the blindfolds are removed. If anyone can tell what color hat they have on their heads, then the teacher will give that student an A. But the students are not allowed to guess: They must be able to *prove* they have that color hat.

The teacher removes the blindfold from the first student, who is now able to see the color of the hats on the other two students—but not his own. The first student looks carefully at the other two hats, thinks silently for a while, and says he does not know the color of his hat. The teacher then removes the blindfold from the second student. He, too, looks at the hats on the other two students, thinks for a while, and says he does not know the color of his hat. (As before, this student does *not* say aloud the color of the hats he sees on the other two students' heads.) Now, just as the teacher is about to remove the blindfold from the third student, she says that she knows exactly the color of the hat on her head. In fact, she doesn't even need to see the hats of the other two students to know this.

Can you see how she did it? No information is being held back, no tricks are being played, and no word games are used. All the information necessary to solve the problem is contained in its description. There are three possibilities for you to consider. Which is correct?

1. She cannot possibly know what color hat she has on her head.
2. She has a red hat and can prove it.
3. She has a white hat and can prove it.

PART II

INFORMAL LOGIC

Chapter 2

Language Matters

Digital homework exercises for this chapter are available in your instructor's online course. For information on how to access these resources, please visit **www.oup.com/ he/baronett5e**.

Words are powerful. They can incite riots and move people to revolt, or they can create calm and soothe those in pain. They take on the aura of "magic words," like secret spells, or they can harm others by their very meaning, such as racial or religious slurs. Words can also fail us. Visiting someone in a hospital or attending a funeral is uncomfortable if we don't know what to say. Even asking for a date can be a frightening experience. We imagine that there are perfect sentences, and if we were lucky enough to utter them, then the person of our dreams would fall in love.

Skill and practice are essential in order to use language effectively—and so are clear, unambiguous, and precise definitions. Most words have multiple meanings, which helps explain why communication can misfire. Hearing or reading something in context can help, and in conversation we can often ask for clarification. But misunderstandings can have serious consequences, and a choice between two meanings of a single word can affect the course of history.

A Japanese word, *mokusatsu*, may have changed all our lives. It has two meanings: (1) to ignore, (2) to refrain from comment. The release of a press statement using the second meaning in July 1945 might have ended the war then. The Emperor was ready to end it, and had the power to do so. The cabinet was preparing to accede to the Potsdam ultimatum of the Allies—surrender or be crushed— but wanted a little more time to discuss the terms. A press release was prepared announcing a policy of *mokusatsu*, with the *no comment* implication. But it got on the foreign wires with the *ignore* implication through a mix-up in translation: "The cabinet *ignores* the demand to surrender." To recall the release would have entailed an unthinkable loss of face. Had the intended meaning been publicized, the cabinet might have backed up the Emperor's decision to surrender. In which event, there might have been no atomic bombs over Hiroshima and Nagasaki, no Russian armies in Manchuria, no Korean war to follow. The lives of tens of thousands of Japanese and American boys might have been saved. One word, misinterpreted.   Stuart Chase, *Power of Words*

Definitions play an important part in analyzing statements and arguments because terms often have numerous meanings. They do, in fact, in the title of this chapter. In "Language Matters," the word "matters" has two legitimate interpretations. It can refer to the subject of the chapter—*the use of language*—or it can refer to the significance of that subject. As we'll see, language is an important topic for the study of logic.

Ambiguity can serve a purpose, just as in the chapter title, and it can also be a great source for jokes. A *double entendre* can be funny when we recognize that a key word has both a common meaning and a risqué or suggestive one. However, when it comes to arguments, *vague, ambiguous,* or *imprecise* terms can reduce the clarity of statements and get in the way of our understanding of an argument.

A term is *vague* whenever there is no clear or distinct meaning that is attached to it. For example, the phrases "a rich person," "a fair price," and "natural preservatives" remain vague until we are given precise information regarding their intended meaning. In some cases, vagueness occurs because a term is relative to a given situation. For example, you might be considered rich in one country, but not in another. Here is another statement that uses a vague term: "The amount of nuclear waste material in the United States is quite small." What counts as "quite small"? Would the nuclear waste material fit in a tractor trailer, or would it fill up a football stadium? Descriptions like these can clarify a term's meaning.

A term is *ambiguous* if it has several meanings (each of which can be clear and distinct). For example, in the statement "He just bought a light suit," the term "light" might mean either the color of the suit or the weight of the material. We normally rely on context to alert us to which meaning is intended. For example, the terms "left" and "right" are ambiguous unless we are told which direction we are facing. In the following three examples, the term "premises" has multiple distinct meanings, but each is used in a way that eliminates ambiguity:

A. "Premises" means statements that are offered in support of a conclusion.
B. "These premises are off-limits" means that only police authorities are permitted to enter.
C. In a bill of equity case, "premises" means the preliminary or explanatory statements or facts of a document, as in a deed.

In each instance, the term "premises" was defined in a way that eliminates ambiguity, vagueness, and imprecision. Throughout this chapter, we will illustrate how language is used, along with methods that are available to clarify the words in statements and arguments. We hope you gain an appreciation of the relationship between language and logic.

A. INTENSION AND EXTENSION

Clarifying the meaning of statements requires a close look at the meaning of the terms. A **term** is either a single word or a group of words that can be the subject of a statement. A term can be a common name, a proper name, or even a descriptive phrase:

Term A single word or a group of words that can be the subject of a statement; it can be a common name, a proper name, or even a descriptive phrase.

Common Names	Proper Names	Descriptive Phrases
plant	Cleopatra	registered voters
building	Los Angeles	purple flowers
car	Mars	the director of *Inception*
mammal	Moby Dick	military personnel
money	Michael Jordan	Nobel Prize winners

In this section, we look closely at two kinds of meaning: *intension* and *extension*. First, however, we need to be sure we know what we mean by using a term.

Terms, Use, and Mention

Not all words are terms. Generally speaking, prepositions, adverbs, some adjectives, conjunctions, and ungrammatical phrases are not considered to be terms, because they are not the subject of a statement. Here are some examples:

Prepositions	**Adverbs**	**Conjunctions**
in, on, by, since	*quickly, very happily, easily*	*and, but, because, however*

Certain Adjectives
good, wise, another, rotten

Ungrammatical Phrase
a heavily into pothole thus

We can also distinguish the *use* of a word from the *mention* of a word. This distinction is helpful because it introduces a method that helps clarify some written language. Three sentences can help illustrate the difference:

- John is my brother.
- "John" is a four-letter word.
- "John" means a toilet or bathroom.

The first statement *uses* the word "John" as the subject. (Notice that the term does not appear in quotes in that statement.) Thus we say that the first statement *uses* the word "John" (without quotes) to refer to a person. However, in the second example it is not the term itself that is the subject. Instead, it is the term that appears within quotation marks that is the subject. We say that it is being *mentioned*. In other words, the subject of the first statement is a *person*, while the subject of the second statement is the *word* that appears within quotation marks. The subject of the third sentence is also the word appearing within quotation marks.

Earlier we described conjunctions, such as the word "because," as not being terms. However, "because" can still be the subject of a statement when it is enclosed in quotes and is being mentioned. Consider the following two examples:

A. The word "because" is a good premise indicator.
B. I will vote for her because she has outlined a clear strategy for economic recovery.

In the first example the word "because" (appearing in quotes) is being *mentioned*; the quoted word is the subject of the statement. However, in the second example the word "because" (appearing without quotes) is being *used*; it is not a subject.

Two Kinds of Meaning

Two kinds of meaning are associated with terms. The first is the **intension** of a term, which is specified by listing the properties or attributes that the term connotes—in other words, its *sense*. For example, to specify the intensional meaning of the term "automobile," you might provide a partial list of properties: passenger vehicle; powered by an engine; used for traveling on roads and highways. (Do not confuse the term "intension" with "intention." *Intension* is the connotation (sense) of a term, whereas *intention* is a mental determination, the intent or purpose of an action.)

The second kind of meaning associated with a term is the **extension**—the **class** or collection of objects to which the term applies. In other words, what the term denotes (its *reference*).

The term "automobile" and its meanings

Intension *(connotation):*
The properties:
passenger vehicle; powered by an engine; used for traveling on roads and highways.

Extension *(denotation):*
The class members:
all the cars in the world.

Some terms have intension but no extension. For example, the term "centaur" connotes the following properties: a creature that has a man's head, torso, and arms, but the body and legs of a horse. However, the term "centaur" has no extension; it denotes an **empty class**, or one that has zero members. We get the same result for all fictional terms. This illustrates an important general rule: *Extension is determined by intension.* To see what effect intension has on extension, take a simple example:

water; ocean; Pacific Ocean

This sequence of terms has **increasing intension**, meaning that each term after the first connotes more attributes than the previous term. Simply put, the series of terms displays an increase in specific attributes. On the other hand, the sequence of terms has **decreasing extension**, meaning that each term after the first denotes a set of objects with fewer members than the previous term. The extension of the term "water" is all the water in the world; the extension of the term "ocean" is the five recognized

---

Intension The intension of a term is specified by listing the properties or attributes that the term connotes—in other words, its sense.

Extension The class or collection of objects to which the term applies. In other words, what the term denotes (its reference).

Class A group of objects.

Empty class A class that has zero members.

Increasing intension A sequence of terms in which each term after the first connotes more attributes than the previous term.

Decreasing extension A sequence of terms in which each term after the first denotes a set of objects with fewer members than the previous term.

oceans (Arctic, Atlantic, Indian, Pacific, and the Southern or Antarctic Ocean); the extension of the term "Pacific Ocean" is one specific ocean.

Let's look at another example:

banana; fruit; food; commodity

Decreasing intension
A sequence of terms in which each term after the first connotes fewer attributes than the previous term.

Increasing extension
A sequence of terms in which each term after the first denotes a set of objects with more members than the previous term.

This sequence of terms has **decreasing intension**, meaning that each term after the first connotes fewer attributes than the previous term. In other words, the series of terms displays a decrease in specific attributes. However, the sequence of terms has **increasing extension**; each term after the first denotes a set of objects with more members than the previous term. The extension of the term "banana" is all the bananas in the world; the extension of the term "fruit" includes all types of fruit (including bananas); the extension of the term "food" is all kinds of food (including fruit); and finally, the extension of the term "commodity" is any kind of product or article of trade or commerce (including food).

Generally speaking, we will find the following to be the case:

- A series of terms that has *increasing intension* has *decreasing extension*.
- A series of terms that has *decreasing intension* has *increasing extension*.

Of course, these general rules have some exceptions. If a term denotes an empty class, then a series of terms with increasing (or decreasing) intension will not affect the extension (it will remain empty). Here is an example:

leprechaun; leprechaun with red hair; leprechaun with red hair and a green hat

The series of terms regarding leprechauns displays increasing intension, but each term in the sequence denotes an empty class. Another exception to the general rule is when the series of terms has increasing intension but the extension, while not empty, nevertheless remains the same throughout the series. Here is an example:

living horse; living horse with DNA; living horse with DNA and a central nervous system

The series of terms displays increasing intension, but all the terms in the series have the same (non-empty) extension.

Proper Names

One further point needs to be clarified. Since proper names, such as "Cleopatra," can refer to different people, they require a slightly different type of analysis. One way to think about a proper name is that it is simply a shorthand way of describing a person. The descriptions we attach to proper names are, therefore, a special kind of intension, and again will determine the extension of the term. Here is an example:

After Julius Caesar's assassination, Cleopatra, the Queen of Egypt who died in 30 BCE, aligned with Mark Antony instead of Caesar's son Augustus.

Since there are typically many different descriptions that can be used to identify the denotation of a proper name, context and a familiarity with their descriptions can help clear up any confusion. Here is another example that uses the term "Cleopatra":

> Cleopatra, the Los Angeles-based record company, recently announced that it signed Huw Lloyd-Langton to a long-term record deal.

Once again, the description attached to the proper name is used to clarify the intended denotation. Whereas the proper name "Cleopatra" denotes a person in the first example, it denotes a record company in the second example. These examples illustrate how relevant descriptions can be used to help determine the extension of a proper name.

The next two sections will explore some specific techniques used to produce definitions. We will begin by describing four intensional definition techniques—*synonymous definitions*, *word origin definitions*, *operational definitions*, and *definition by genus and difference*. This will be followed by an examination of three extensional definition techniques—*ostensive definitions*, *enumerative definitions*, and *definition by subclass*.

EXERCISES 2A

I. List some of the properties connoted by the following terms.

1. athlete

Answer: strong, fast, agile, stamina, skilled, competitor

Self-Practice Questions

2. country

3. animal

4. game

⭐ 5. president

6. mammal

7. book

8. planet

⭐ 9. plant

10. teacher

11. computer

12. city

II. Name three things denoted by the following terms.

1. athlete

Answer: Tiger Woods, Shaquille O'Neal, Tom Brady

2. magazine

3. movie

4. U.S. senator

⭐ 5. philosopher

6. novelist

7. Nobel Prize winner

8. jazz musician

⭐ 9. lake

10. extinct animal

III. Name all the things denoted by the following terms.

1. capital city of California

Answer: Sacramento

2. Nobel Prize winner in two different science fields

3. Earth continent

4. first person to step on the Moon

⭐ 5. Seven Wonders of the Ancient World

6. person who won the most Best Actress Academy Awards

7. tallest mountain on Earth

8. planet in our solar system

⭐ 9. month with 31 days

10. first person to fly solo across the Atlantic Ocean

IV. The following will require you to apply your knowledge of intension and extension to a sequence of terms.

Put the following series of terms in the order of *increasing intension*.

1. mammal, animal, pediatrician, physician, human

Answer: animal, mammal, human, physician, pediatrician

2. American sports car, Corvette, car, sports car, vehicle

3. shrub, Portland rose, plant, perennial, rose

Put the following series of terms in the order of *increasing extension*.

4. polygon, equilateral triangle, isosceles triangle, convex polygon, triangle

⭐ 5. robin, animal, thrush, flying animal, bird

6. skyscraper, office building, building, New York City skyscraper, Empire State Building

Video Tutorial: 2AIV
Exercise #6

Put the following series of terms in the order of *decreasing intension*.

7. Usain Bolt, human, track and field athlete, athlete, Olympic Gold Medal winner

8. printing, book, 20th-century fictional book, *The Grapes of Wrath*, fictional book

⭐ 9. chilled dessert, dessert, Jell-O, food, Cherry Jell-O

Put the following series of terms in the order of *decreasing extension*.

10. *In the Heat of the Night*, dramas, entertainment, Sidney Poitier movies, movies

11. painting, Vincent van Gogh's *Still Life with Flowers*, still life, art, 19th-century still life

12. human, *Apollo 11* crew member, pilot, Neil Armstrong, astronaut

B. USING INTENSIONAL DEFINITIONS

Part of the analysis of statements and arguments is evaluating the clarity of the terms involved. We saw earlier that the term "matters" can convey two meanings, as in the chapter title. In that setting the ambiguity is not out of place. However, when it comes to arguments, ambiguity should be eliminated. Much of ordinary language contains ambiguous or imprecise political terms, such as "liberal" and "conservative." Typically, statements containing these political labels suffer from being unclear. Consider the following argument:

> My opponent for governor is a liberal, so you should vote against her.

Since we have no idea what the speaker means by the term "liberal," our understanding of the argument is hindered—precisely because of the lack of clarity. An important requirement for a good argument, then, is that all the terms have an acceptable, clear, and unambiguous meaning. This is also a simple but crucial requirement for all communication; its strict adherence would eliminate many confusions and controversies. Problems related to unclear terms can lead to difficulty in determining the truth content of individual statements. In turn, these individual statement problems sometimes lead to *informal fallacies* (the subject of Chapter 4).

A **definition** assigns a meaning to a word, phrase, or symbol. Logicians use the term **definiendum** to refer to that which is being defined, and the term **definiens** to refer to that which does the defining. For example, if you look in a dictionary for the definition of the term "book" (the definiendum), you might find the following partial entry: "a printed work of fiction or nonfiction" (the definiens). In one sense then, what the definiens does is provide an alternative symbolism that has the same meaning as the definiendum. It is in this manner that we say that the definition has assigned a meaning to the definiendum. Here are some examples:

Definition A definition assigns a meaning to a word, phrase, or symbol.

Definiendum Refers to that which is being defined.

Definiens Refers to that which does the defining.

DEFINITIONS

Definiendum	Definiens
e-book	short for "electronic book"; any book published in digital form
dog-eat-dog world	ruthless competition; looking out for your own self-interest
shaman	a person claiming to use magic to cure diseases or predict the future

An **intensional** (connotative) **definition** assigns a meaning to a term by listing the properties or attributes shared by all the objects that are denoted by the term. We will examine some of the different techniques that are used for intensional definitions.

Intensional definition Assigns a meaning to a term by listing the properties or attributes shared by all the objects that are denoted by the term.

Synonymous Definitions

As the name indicates, a **synonymous definition** assigns a meaning to a term by providing another term with the same meaning; in other words, by providing a synonym. This can be a very simple and effective technique to convey the meaning of

Synonymous definition Assigns a meaning to a term by providing another term with the same meaning; in other words, by providing a synonym.

a term, as long as the synonym is readily understood. Here are a few examples of synonymous definitions:

- "Honest" means trustworthy.
- "Attorney" means lawyer.
- "Feckless" means irresponsible.
- "Adversity" means misfortune.

Since many words cannot be defined accurately by a synonym, this technique has its limitations. For example, someone might try defining "obscene" as "indecent," "offensive," or "depraved." But this word cannot be easily captured by a mere synonym, partly because of the moral and legal issues connected with its use. The Supreme Court has wrestled with trying to define the term "obscene" for legal purposes. In the case of *Miller v. California* (1973), a decision to adopt a definition had five justices in agreement. The majority opinion stated that there were three basic guidelines: "(a) whether 'the average person, applying contemporary community standards' would find that the work, taken as a whole, appeals to the prurient interest; (b) whether the work depicts or describes, in a patently offensive way, sexual conduct specifically defined by the applicable state law; and (c) whether the work, taken as a whole, lacks serious literary, artistic, political, or scientific value." Four justices dissented.

As you can see, these "guidelines" are filled with terms that need to be defined. "Average person," "contemporary community standards," "prurient interest," "sexual conduct," and "serious literary, artistic, political, or scientific value" all need to be clarified.

Word Origin Definitions

Word origin definition
Assigns a meaning to a term by investigating its origin. The study of the history, development, and sources of words is called *etymology*.

A **word origin definition** assigns a meaning to a term by investigating its origin. Since most ordinary English words originated in older languages, such as Latin, Greek, and Arabic, we can often trace the current meaning back to its original sources to see how it has changed through time. The study of the history, development, and sources of words is called *etymology*. For example, the word "etymology" itself comes from the Greek word "etymologia," which combines two root words—"etymo," meaning *true sense*, and "logos," meaning *word*. The suffix "-logy" has another common meaning—*the study of.* Although the term "etymology" originally meant *the true sense of a word*, it now means *the study of the origin of words.* The importance of investigating the origin of words is expressed by the following quote:

> The older a word, the deeper it reaches.   Ludwig Wittgenstein, *Notebooks*

Knowing the origin of a word can sometimes illustrate why the term was chosen. Here is one example:

"Malaria" means an infectious disease characterized by recurring attacks of chills and fever. The term derives from the Italian "mala," meaning bad, and "aria," meaning air. The term was used because of the mistaken belief that the disease was caused by the bad air in swampy districts. It was only during the 1890s that experiments revealed that the disease was caused by mosquitoes.

Many familiar terms use the common suffix "-logy." For example, "psychology" is now defined as the science or study of human and animal behavior. The term is derived from two Greek words: "psyche," meaning *soul*, and "logia," meaning *the study of*. The term "biology" is now defined as the science or study of living organisms. The term is derived from two Greek words: "bios," meaning *life*, and "logia," meaning *the study of*. Here is one more example of a word origin definition:

> "Philosophy" means love of wisdom. It derives from the Greek word "philosophia," which is a combination of the two root words "philo," meaning *loving*, and "sophia," meaning *wisdom or knowledge*.

Word origin definitions have a practical value as well. Anyone who has watched the National Spelling Bee will recognize the common strategy of not only asking for the definition of a word, but also asking for the language of origin of a word. Contestants who have studied the root words of a given language can use that knowledge to break down a complex word into its component parts. This can help them decide which prefix or suffix to try when piecing together the spelling of a word.

Operational Definitions

An **operational definition** defines a term by specifying a measurement procedure. For example, academic achievement is very important for many people in the field of education, including teachers, administrators, test developers, and students. An operational definition of "academic achievement" might use grade point average (GPA) as a measuring procedure. This measuring device is *quantitative* because it provides us with a range of numerical values. In most colleges, the range is from 4.0 to 0.0, with the highest (4.0) for all A's, to the lowest (0.0) for all F's.

Operational definition Defines a term by specifying a measurement procedure.

An alternative operational definition for "academic achievement" might use letters of recommendation written by teachers. This measuring device is quite different from a GPA; it is *qualitative* because its range of values is open-ended. Letters of recommendation may state the grades you received, as well as an assessment of your position relative to other students (for example, the top 10% of the class). It might also mention other important factors, such as your ability to write original essays, self-discipline, willingness to help other students, the ability to ask relevant questions and grasp abstract material, and the prospects for graduate work, to name a few.

We could rank each student in order, from those with the strongest letters of recommendation to those with the weakest. This would not be easy because we are not dealing with a straightforward quantitative method. For example, the terms "strongest" and "weakest" need to be defined. For the same reason, if we then compare two sets of student rankings for the same student body, we might be surprised to see a large variation. The two lists might not match up very well at all. Therefore, the kind of operational definition we give to a term may affect the strength of the argument in which it plays a part.

Here are a few more examples:

- "Aggression" means the number of behaviors that result in verbal threats or physical harm.
- Isaac Newton's definition of "force" is mass times acceleration.
- For some economists, "recession" means two consecutive quarters of falling GDP (gross domestic product).

Many terms denote phenomena that can be observed only indirectly, such as radioactivity. We cannot see radioactivity. We do, however, have powerful ways of measuring it, as with a Geiger counter, an instrument designed to detect radioactive particles. As in this example, we need some empirical means of measuring or performing experiments on many phenomena in order to obtain objective evidence about them. Scientists can study electrons and other subatomic particles only indirectly, in a device called a "cloud chamber," which is a sealed container containing alcohol vapor. The electrons traveling through the chamber condense the vapor, much like the vapor trails you see in the sky behind a jet airplane. In each of these examples, we

PROFILES IN LOGIC
Rudolf Carnap

Rudolf Carnap (1891–1970) was born in Germany but later became a U.S. citizen. At university, Carnap studied both physics and philosophy, which he applied to his research and allowed him to make important contributions to several areas of philosophy, including the philosophy of language. Carnap argued that because much of ordinary language is ambiguous, many philosophical problems can be resolved by a logical analysis of language, which, for Carnap, meant *formal* languages that incorporate the rules of logic and mathematics. Since formal languages offer precise meanings to statements, ambiguity is eliminated.

To help in this analysis, Carnap developed a *verifiability principle*, according to which a *statement* is meaningful only if it is verifiable; in other words, all terms must be reducible by means of definitions to observational language. A *term* is meaningful

relative to a specific theory given in a specific language. Although Carnap admitted that some theoretical terms are not reducible to observational terms, their meaning is acquired by direct connection to other terms that are observational terms. Furthermore, *observational terms* get their meaning by *operational definitions*, which are governed by how scientists actually apply them. Over time, Carnap's position was criticized by other philosophers who showed problems with Carnap's attempt to connect theoretical terms with direct empirical observations. Carnap modified his position and held that there is an *indirect connection* to observations.

A driving force guiding Carnap's work is captured in this statement: "The function of logical analysis is to analyze all knowledge, all assertions of science and of everyday life, in order to make clear the sense of each such assertion and the connections between them."

are offered strong evidence that these terms denote something that can be physically observed, albeit indirectly.

Since many terms require extraordinary evidence to convince us that they denote actual existing objects, researchers must develop strong methods of gathering indirect evidence. To help us determine if a term truly refers to objects that we can observe only indirectly, we rely on measurement, prediction, and explanation.

First, if a claim uses a term to denote a part of the physical world (however invisible it might be to our five senses), the person asserting the claim must be able to provide strong, credible evidence to back it up. This has been accomplished by devices that can detect and measure what we cannot directly observe. For example, scientists have developed barometers, thermometers, Geiger counters, cloud chambers, and cyclotrons, to name just a few inventions, in order to gather evidence. Second, these measuring devices must allow the accurate prediction of future experimental results. Finally, we must be able to explain how and why the events occur as they do. In other words, the explanations require a theoretical framework or model, as we explore in detail in Chapter 14.

Definition by Genus and Difference

We saw that an intensional definition specifies the attributes that a term connotes, and in this way it determines the class denoted by the term. Any class that has members can be divided into smaller classes called *subclasses*. For example, the class of fruit has many subclasses, such as cherries, strawberries, and apples. And each of those subclasses can be further divided. For example, the subclass of apples has several subclasses of its own, such as McIntosh, Rome, and Granny Smith. We refer to any class of objects that is being divided as the *genus* and the subclasses as *species*. (You can think of the "genus" as *general*, and the "species" as *specific*.)

The terms "genus" and "species" have a slightly different meaning in logic than they do in biology. Biological classifications are ways to relate all life in a hierarchy, sometimes referred to as the *tree of life*. For example, humans, whales, dolphins, wolves, and dogs are all members of the class *mammals*. However, humans belong to the order (subclass) *primates*; whales and dolphins belong to the order *cetacea*; wolves and dogs both belong to the order *canidae*.

Logic uses the terms "genus" and "species" in a more flexible way, so classes and subclasses do not need to remain in a rigid hierarchy. A person can be placed in many different classes and subclasses, which do not need to have a sense of higher or lower. It is possible for a person to be a mother, daughter, sister, cousin, aunt, professor, scientist, Pulitzer Prize winner, and skier. In fact, it is possible for a class to be a genus relative to one species, and yet that same class can be a species relative to a different genus. For example, the class of siblings is a genus in relation to the species *sister*. But the class of siblings happens to be a species in relation to the genus *offspring*. For our purposes, a *genus* is simply any class that is larger than any of its subclasses (*species*).

We can distinguish the different species (subclasses) of a genus by listing the attribute(s) that indicates the *difference* (or specific difference) between each species. For example, consider the genus *offspring* and two species, *son* and *daughter*. When we qualify the genus offspring by adding the term "male" we supply the difference. The combination of a term denoting the genus (in this example "offspring") with a term that connotes a specific difference (in this example "male") creates the meaning of the term that denotes the species. Here are five examples that illustrate the complete process:

DEFINIENDUM		DEFINIENS	
Species		**Difference + Genus**	
"Mother"	means	female	parent
"Bachelor"	means	unmarried	adult male
"Igloo"	means	snow	house
"Triangle"	means	three-sided	polygon
"Gelding"	means	castrated	male horse

PROFILES IN LOGIC
Ludwig Wittgenstein

What would you do if you wrote a book in which you thought you had answered all philosophical questions? Give away the substantial fortune that you inherited? Go teach primary school in a small village? That's exactly what Ludwig Wittgenstein did.

Ludwig Wittgenstein (1889–1951) came from one of the wealthiest families in Vienna. He served in the Austrian army during World War I, and during his time as a prisoner of war he began writing what came to be known as *Tractatus Logico-Philosophicus*, one of the most influential books of the last century. In it, Wittgenstein applied recent advances in logic to traditional philosophical questions—and declared them over and done. As he wrote in the preface, "I am, therefore, of the opinion that the problems have in essentials been finally solved."

The *Tractatus* is a difficult book, subject to many interpretations. Wittgenstein himself said, "I should not like my writing to spare other people the trouble of thinking." For him, the limits of thought are established by clarifying the limits of language: "What we cannot speak about we must pass over in silence."

But Wittgenstein did return to philosophy. He gave lectures to small groups of students, many of whom went on to become influential philosophers themselves. He also wrote a substantial amount of his thoughts in a series of notebooks. Although he withheld publishing anything else during his lifetime, his *Philosophical Investigations* became enormously influential. Despite Wittgenstein's best efforts, philosophical questions are still being asked.

As the examples illustrate, a **definition by genus and difference** assigns a meaning to a term (the *species*) by establishing a *genus* and combining it with the attribute (the specific *difference*) that distinguishes the members of that species.

C. USING EXTENSIONAL DEFINITIONS

We will now examine some of the different techniques that are used for extensional definitions. An **extensional** (denotative) **definition** assigns meaning to a term by indicating the class members denoted by the term. We will describe three ways of assigning meaning by extensional definitions—*ostensive definitions, enumerative definitions*, and *definitions by subclass*.

Ostensive Definitions

An **ostensive definition** involves demonstrating the term—for example, by pointing to a member of the class that the term denotes. (The word "ostensive" comes from the Latin word "ostendere," which means *to show*.) Suppose a car mechanic tells you that you need a new alternator, but you have never seen one. The mechanic could provide an ostensive definition by either pointing to the alternator (if it is still attached to the engine) or letting you see the alternator (if it has been detached from the engine). The act of showing someone an object is the basis for most ostensive definitions in everyday life.

Ostensive definitions are used to introduce children to many terms by showing some examples of what the term denotes. Children are often introduced to words by repeatedly connecting a word to pictures of the objects denoted by the term. Ostensive definitions are also used to teach a foreign language by pointing to an object and repeating a word. An ostensive definition is called for whenever you hold an object or point to it and ask, "What is this called?" The answer to the question will be a term associated with that class of objects.

Ostensive definitions require nonverbal behavior—pointing, gesturing, drawing a picture, or showing a photograph. Ostensive definitions show what an object looks like, but they do not provide synonyms or redefine the term by giving alternate meanings. Ostensive definitions are used typically when only a small number of the members of a class are available; this sets limitations on their effectiveness. For example, it is possible that a child who has learned the term "deer" through an ostensive definition will then point to a moose and say "deer." Similarly, when we point to an object, it is not always apparent what we are emphasizing. Is it the shape of the object, its color, or the material out of which it is made? Although ostensive definitions provide some information regarding the extension of a term, they do not provide information regarding the intension of a term.

Definition by genus and difference
Assigns a meaning to a term (the species) by establishing a genus and combining it with the attribute that distinguishes the members of that species.

Extensional definition
Assigns meaning to a term by indicating the class members denoted by the term.

Ostensive definition
Involves demonstrating the term—for example, by pointing to a member of the class that the term denotes.

Enumerative Definitions

Enumerative definition Assigns a meaning to a term by naming the individual members of the class denoted by the term.

An **enumerative definition** assigns a meaning to a term by naming the individual members of the class denoted by the term. Here are a few examples:

- "New England" means Connecticut, Maine, Massachusetts, New Hampshire, Rhode Island, and Vermont.
- "The Knights of the Round Table" means the group that includes Sir Galahad, Sir Lancelot, and Sir Gawain, among others.

The first example illustrates a complete enumeration of the members of the class that the term "New England" denotes because every member of the class is included in the definition. The second example, however, provides only a partial enumeration of the members of the class denoted (many members of the class are left out of the definition).

Both partial and complete enumerations can be useful; the context in which the definition occurs provides direction as to which type is appropriate. For example, a complete enumeration of all the members of the class of stars is impractical since there are hundreds of billions of stars in our galaxy alone. However, a complete enumeration of the members of the class of U.S. senators who voted for (or against) a particular bill is something that would be easy to compile and may be important for deciding future elections.

Definition by Subclass

Definition by subclass Assigns a meaning to a term by naming subclasses (species) of the class denoted by the term.

A **definition by subclass** assigns a meaning to a term by naming subclasses (*species*) of the class denoted by the term. (This differs from an enumerative definition where individual members were named.) A definition by subclass can be partial or complete (it is complete only when the subclasses named include the entire extension). Here are a few examples:

- "Music" means rock, blues, jazz, hip-hop, country, classical, and so forth.
- "Movie genre" means comedy, action, drama, film noir, romance, horror, along with others.
- "Coal" means lignite, subbituminous, bituminous, and anthracite.

The subclasses named in the first definition, when taken together, do not include all the members of the class, so it is a partial definition. The same is true of the second definition. However, the subclasses named in the third definition, when taken together, do include all the members of the class, and therefore is a complete definition.

As we saw with enumerative definitions, both partial and complete definitions by subclass can be useful. Once again, the context in which the definition occurs can provide a direction as to which type is appropriate. For example, a complete definition by subclass of all the species of insects is impractical. After all, there are more than a million species, with probably a lot more yet to be discovered. However, a complete definition by subclass of the members of the class of coal might be useful in determining how much of each type exists and its potential as future sources of energy.

DEFINITIONAL TECHNIQUES

Synonymous definition Assigns a meaning to a term by providing another term with the same meaning; in other words, by providing a synonym.

Word origin definition Assigns a meaning to a term by investigating its origin. The study of the history, development, and sources of words is called *etymology*.

Operational definition Defines a term by specifying a measurement procedure.

Definition by genus and difference Assigns a meaning to a term (the species) by establishing a genus and combining it with the attribute that distinguishes the members of that species.

Ostensive definition Involves demonstrating the term—for example, by pointing to a member of the class that the term denotes.

Enumerative definition Assigns a meaning to a term by naming the individual members of the class denoted by the term.

Definition by subclass Assigns a meaning to a term by naming subclasses (species) of the class denoted by the term.

EXERCISES 2C

Determine whether the following are synonymous definitions, word origin (etymological) definitions, operational definitions, definitions by genus and difference, ostensive (demonstrative) definitions, enumerative definitions, or definitions by subclass.

Self-Practice Questions

1. "Felony" means murder, rape, and arson, among other things.
Answer: Subclass

2. "Dentist" is a term derived from the Latin word "dens," meaning *tooth*.

3. "Typhoon" means a tropical hurricane that occurs in Asia and the Pacific Ocean.

4. See that big green thing in front of you? That's an oak tree.

⭐ 5. "Hat" means headgear.

6. "Intelligence" means the score a person receives on the Stanford-Binet I.Q. Test.

7. "Country" means something such as the United States, Mexico, Italy, Indonesia, or Japan.

8. "Epistemology" is a term derived from the Greek word "episteme," meaning *knowledge*, and the suffix "-ology," meaning *the study of*.

⭐ 9. "Natural language" means something such as English, Spanish, French, Chinese, or Hindi.

10. Look where I'm pointing; that's your car's alternator.

11. "Novice" means beginner.

Video Tutorial: 2C
Exercise #9

12. "Piano" means a musical stringed instrument set in a vertical or horizontal frame, played by depressing keys that cause hammers to strike the strings and produce audible vibrations.

⭐13. "Virus" means chicken pox, smallpox, measles, polio, and the like.

14. "Atmospheric pressure" means the reading found on a barometer.

15. The plant next to the shed is a bougainvillea.

16. "Abode" means residence.

⭐17. "Construction equipment" means bulldozer, crane, pile driver, dredger, grader, and the like.

18. "Metaphysics" comes from the Greek words "meta," meaning *after*, and "physika," meaning *natural things*. The name was used by Andronicus of Rhodes in 70 BCE simply as a reference to the books written by Aristotle that happened to be placed in order after his works on physics. It has since come to mean the study of first principles and is even used by some to refer to any investigation that is outside the physical realm.

19. "Biomass" means organic materials used as renewable energy sources, such as wood, crops, and waste.
Clean-energy-ideas.com

20. "Element" means something such as hydrogen, helium, carbon, or oxygen.

⭐21. There is a question that some people use to summarize the concerns of medieval scholars: "How many angels can dance on the head of a pin?" Wendell Johnson is credited with offering this answer: "Bring me a pin, and some angels, and we'll soon find out."

22. "Goods and services" means (in the area of trademarks) chemicals, machinery, hand tools, advertising, transportation, storage, to name only a few.
Adapted from About.com

23. "Laborer" means worker.

24. If I know that someone means to explain a color-word to me, then "That is called 'sepia'" will help me to understand the word.
Ludwig Wittgenstein, *Philosophical Investigations*

⭐25. "Rock opera" means something such as *Quadrophenia*, *The Wall*, *The Rise and Fall of Ziggy Stardust and the Spiders from Mars*, or *Operation: Mindcrime*.

26. The popular definition of tragedy is heavy drama in which everyone is killed in the last act; comedy being light drama in which everyone is married in the last act.
George Bernard Shaw, "Tolstoy: Tragedian or Comedian?"

27. "Logic" can be defined as the study of the methods of reasoning and the evaluation of arguments. The term is derived from the Greek word "logikos," which means *pertaining to speaking or reasoning*. In turn, the word "logikos" was derived from the word "logos," which means *word*, *idea*, or *reason*.

28. To find the length of an object, we have to perform certain physical operations. The concept of length is therefore fixed when the operations by which length is measured are fixed: that is, the concept of length involves as much as and nothing more than the set of operations by which length is determined.

    Percy W. Bridgman, *The Logic of Modern Physics*

⭐29. She showed me what the word "pungent" meant by holding a durian under my nose and letting me smell it.

30. "Patent classification system" means Class 2 Apparel; Class 7 Compound tools; Class 14 Bridges, and many others.   Adapted from the U.S. Patent Office

31. The most common way to find out whether you're overweight or obese is to figure out your body mass index (BMI). BMI is an estimate of body fat, and it's a good gauge of your risk for diseases that occur with more body fat. The overweight group is anyone with a BMI over 25.

    U.S. Department of Health and Human Services

32. "President of the United States" means someone such as George Washington, Abraham Lincoln, Franklin D. Roosevelt, or John F. Kennedy.

⭐33. "Salary" means wages.

34. "O.K." means acceptable or agreeable (also spelled *okay*). It is a facetious phonetic spelling of *oll korrect* which was meant to represent *all correct*. It was first used in Boston in 1839, then used in 1840 by Democrat partisans of Martin Van Buren during his election, who allegedly named their organization the *O.K. Club* in allusion to the initials of "Old Kinderhook," Van Buren's nickname, derived from his birthplace Kinderhook, New York.

    Adapted from *The Random House Dictionary*

35. White lies are at the other end of the spectrum of deception from lies in a serious crisis. They are the most common and the most trivial forms that duplicity can take. The fact that they are so common provides their protective coloring. And their very triviality, when compared to more threatening lies, makes it seem unnecessary or even absurd to condemn them. Some consider all well-intentioned lies, however momentous, to be white; I shall adhere to the narrower usage: a white lie, in this sense, is a falsehood not meant to injure anyone, and of little moral import.   Sissela Bok, *Lying: Moral Choice in Public and Private Life*

D. APPLYING DEFINITIONS

The techniques used so far also apply to how definitions can be used in ordinary language. However, many examples found in newspapers, magazines, novels, and other sources do not typically follow the format used in this chapter. In fact, they often make a point of the ambiguity that our techniques so far are designed to avoid.

Generally speaking, many everyday sources do not use quotation marks to indicate that a term is being defined. In addition, by convention some writers use quotation marks differently from how they were introduced in this chapter. For example, an author might use quotation marks to emphasize that a word is being used sarcastically:

That was certainly a "beautiful" dress she had on tonight.

Or a writer might use scare quotes around a phrase to indicate irony. In spoken language, we may even use our hands to mimic the appearance of written scare quotes—the gesture referred to as "air quotes."

Later in this chapter, we introduce techniques that can help clarify statements and arguments in ordinary language. These techniques, such as paraphrasing, will incorporate ideas that you have learned thus far, such as intension, extension, and definitions. For now, though, we need to look more closely at definitions from sources as they typically appear.

Stipulative Definitions

Stipulative definition
Introduces a new meaning to a term or symbol.

Stipulations help avoid mistakes in interpretation by specifying precise points of reference or measuring devices. A **stipulative definition** does more: It introduces an entirely new meaning. When the new meaning applies to a familiar term or symbol, confusion can easily occur. For example, if a child says, "These pants are tight!" his or her parent might naturally think the following: "I will take them back and get you a larger size." From the child's perspective, the parent is woefully out of touch. The child then enlightens the parent by exclaiming, "You don't get it. *Tight* means *cool!*"

People using a new term for the first time establish the meaning. Yet the term and its meanings can still be modified by others for their own purposes. For example, when Apple introduced the iPod, it coined a new word and at the same time provided a stipulative definition: a portable digital audio player with the capacity to store thousands of audio files. Since that time, Apple has introduced even more new words with stipulative definitions. For example, you can now get many different types of iPhones: iPhone 6s, iPhone 7, iPhone 8, and iPhone 12. Whenever scientists discover new things about the world, they may create new terms or symbols, along with new definitions, or they may use old terms but provide new stipulative definitions. For example, Nobel Prize laureate Murray Gell-Mann coined the term "quark" to refer to the elementary particles that combine to make up protons, neutrons, and other subatomic particles. The six kinds of quarks make a great illustration of the arbitrary nature of stipulative definitions. Physicists refer to them as having six "flavors": *up, down, charm, strange, top,* and *bottom.* Of course, the playful nature of these names also shows the importance of having easy-to-remember terms if we are to communicate at all.

In addition to intensional definition techniques, stipulative definitions can also use all three types of extensional definitions of a term. For example, a speaker can assign the new meaning of a term by pointing to an object denoted by the term (an ostensive definition). On the other hand, an enumerative definition may be offered, identifying individual members either partially or completely. Finally, a definition by subclass may be given (again, either partial or complete).

Stipulative definitions are proposals to create a new term or to use an old term in a new way. The proposals can be accepted, rejected, modified, or even ignored. However, there are some drawbacks to excessive stipulations of a term. If the meaning of a term is stretched so that it denotes nearly anything, then the term loses its informative value. For example, if everything is "tall," then the term provides no information. Another example, "awesome," means something that inspires a sense of wonder or reverence. But this colloquial meaning can easily mean anything that is great or excellent. In an interview (adapted slightly here), a U.S. Olympic Gold Medal winner managed to apply it to everything from a *game* and his *teammates* to *feelings*, a *crowd*, *opponents*, and an *experience*:

> The game was awesome.   My teammates were awesome.
> It felt awesome.   The crowd was awesome.
> The other team was awesome.   The whole experience was awesome.

At some point the term "awesome" loses its informative power, and it winds up having no more meaning than "Wow!"

Since stipulative definitions are specific but arbitrary, care must be taken when introducing them in an argument. The possibility of confusion can compound mistakes in interpretation, analysis, understanding, and the evaluation of an argument containing stipulated terms. That is why all terms in a good argument are clearly understood or expressly defined, given the context in which the argument occurs. For example, the most modern meaning of the word "mouse" began as a stipulative definition among computer users. Given the widespread acceptance of the new meaning and the reference of the term, and the hundreds of millions of computer users around the world, the directive "Move the mouse to position the cursor at the beginning of the word you want to delete" would rarely be understood as telling you to manipulate a small rodent.

Lexical Definitions

Like the definition of a mouse as a device to position the cursor, over time a stipulative definition can go from use by a small group of people to widespread acceptance. At this point the term is included among *lexical definitions*.

A **lexical definition** is a definition based on the common use of a word, term, or symbol. The definitions found in dictionaries provide the common meanings of terms and are examples of lexical definitions. "Lexical" means the common vocabulary of a given language as determined by the actual use in a community of

Lexical definition A definition based on the common use of a word, term, or symbol.

speakers and writers. Unlike stipulative definitions, a lexical definition is useful if it accurately reports the way a term is commonly used; otherwise it is not very useful.

Since most terms have multiple meanings, we often rely on lexical definitions to clear up any ambiguity that can lead to a misunderstanding. For example, a lexical definition of "career" might include "a way of making a living" or "a paid occupation"; but it can also mean the general progress of a part of life, such as "my career as a student." A lexical definition of "ornament" might be "a decorative object." However, the term "ornament" can be used to indicate an inanimate object (such as a piece of jewelry), or it can be used to indicate an attractive person who accompanies someone to a function.

The lexical definitions found in many dictionaries often use all four types of intensional definitions. First, a lexical definition might provide information regarding the intension of a term by genus and difference. For example, a dictionary might provide the following information for the term "puppy": *genus*—dog; *difference*—very young. Second, since lexical definitions sometimes offer synonyms as part of the definition, they facilitate the creation of new sentences using alternative words for the term being defined. Third, lexical definitions found in dictionaries typically supply the etymology of a term. And finally, a lexical definition might provide an operational definition.

In addition to intensional definitions, many dictionaries often use all three types of extensional definition techniques. First, they might provide an ostensive definition by an illustration or a picture of the objects denoted by the term. Second, an enumerative definition may identify the individual members (again, either partial or complete). Third, a dictionary may supply a definition by subclass.

When we consult a lexical definition, we have the opportunity to clear up any ambiguity—and we should, whenever we encounter ambiguity in statements and arguments. We rely on lexical definitions to provide accurate guidelines to correct and incorrect usage as determined by a community using a common language.

Functional Definitions

Functional definition
Specifies the purpose or use of the objects denoted by the term.

A **functional definition** specifies the *purpose* or *use* of the objects denoted by the term. For example, a functional definition of the term "cup" can be "a small open container used to hold liquid or solids." Although cups are used mostly for liquids (e.g., coffee, tea, juice, or water), they are also used in cooking (e.g., a cup of sugar or flour). Since a functional definition concentrates on specifying how something is used, it often omits any mention of the material out of which the object is composed. For example, a cup can be made of glass, plastic, cardboard, wood, and many other materials, as long as it performs its function correctly. In fact, you can always *cup your hands* temporarily to hold water.

We use functional definitions to define the normal use of objects that have been created or designed for specific purposes. For example, if you have your car inspected, you might be told that you need a new alternator. If you have no idea what an alternator does, you can ask the mechanic. She probably will tell you that the alternator supplies electrical power throughout the car. Also, the alternator is necessary to recharge the battery after you start the car, since power is temporarily taken from the battery. This intensional definition does not tell you what an alternator looks like. Still, it provides an adequate description of the function of an alternator. Of course, if you ask to see an alternator, the mechanic can point to it in the engine compartment or show you one that is not already connected to an engine. In fact, a functional definition of many simple objects, unlike an alternator, can be given by extension. For example, the best way to illustrate the function of a saw, a hammer, or a doorstopper is to see the tool in action.

Precising Definitions

A **precising definition** reduces the vagueness and ambiguity of a term by providing a sharp focus, often a technical meaning, for a term. Precising definitions can be found in settings that require very distinct and specific meanings of terms, such as law, science, medicine, or manufacturing.

Precising definition
Reduces the vagueness and ambiguity of a term by providing a sharp focus, often a technical meaning, for a term.

A legal setting might rely on a precise definition of what constitutes a "dangerous weapon" or "illegal drug." A different legal situation might rely on a precising definition of "burglary": *the breaking and unwarranted entry into the dwelling place of another person with the intention of committing a felony.* Law enforcement officers can use this definition in meeting the requirements for arresting a suspect. At a trial, debate over technical matters internal to the definition may continue as well. For example, the word "breaking" seems to imply the use of force. Nevertheless, some states have interpreted it loosely to include any fraudulent entry—for example, telling the person at the door that you are from the gas company and are there to check for leaks. (Notice the similarity of the words "intension" and "intention." As we saw, "intension" refers to the meaning of a term, while "intention," in a legal setting, means what a person has set his or her mind to doing.)

In science, terms such as "energy," "momentum," and "mass" must have precise definitions. A scientific definition of "energy" includes some discussion of how "*matter can do work by its mass, electric charge,* or *motion.*" The italicized terms would themselves need precising definitions to convey a complete understanding.

Medical settings also rely on precise definitions. Doctors must often make ethical decisions regarding the status of a critically ill patient. And that can require a precise determination of when a human being is dead. Although this is a highly controversial topic, nevertheless there have been attempts to offer precise definitions of the term "dead" as it pertains to humans. (You can imagine a similar debate over the definition of when human life begins.) Here is one example:

The National Conference of Commissioners on Uniform State Laws in 1980 formulated the Uniform Determination of Death Act. It states that: "An individual who has sustained either (1) irreversible cessation of circulatory and

> respiratory functions, or (2) irreversible cessation of all functions of the entire brain, including the brain stem, is dead. A determination of death must be made in accordance with accepted medical standards." This definition was approved by the American Medical Association in 1980 and by the American Bar Association in 1981.
>
> MedicineNet, Inc.

This precising definition is an operational definition. It specifies medical procedures that are to be used to determine if the term "dead" applies. Precising definitions are used in many other areas as well. For example, the U.S. Census Bureau has crafted a precising definition of "poverty" based on family income. The definition was used in 2010 to determine the poverty rate in the United States.

> Size of family unit: 1 person—$11,136; 2 people—$14,220; 3 people—$17,378 (the list continues at roughly $3000–$4000 increments per added person).

The Census Bureau also provides the method that they used to calculate the different thresholds:

> The preliminary estimates of the weighted average poverty thresholds for 2010 are calculated by multiplying the 2009 weighted average thresholds by a factor of 1.016403, the ratio of the average annual Consumer Price Index for All Consumers (CPI-U) for 2010 to the average annual CPI-U for 2009.

Once again, we can see that this kind of precising definition is an operational definition. It establishes the meaning of the term "poverty" by specifying monetary thresholds that will be used to determine the number of households in each category, and thus the overall poverty rate in the United States in the year 2010.

As the examples illustrate, precising definitions clarify meaning by eliminating vagueness and ambiguity. Extensional definitions are not useful as precising definitions, because they do not eliminate the potential for vagueness. That is because intension determines extension—and not the other way around.

Since precising definitions are not simply arbitrary assignments of meanings, they differ from stipulative definitions. A stipulative definition can be a way of hiding your intended meaning from those not in your small group. When used this way, a stipulative definition is meant to exclude others from understanding what you mean. In contrast, a precising definition is meant to include as many people as possible by focusing on legitimate, useful, accurate, clear, and direct meaning.

Theoretical Definitions

Theoretical definition
Assigns a meaning to a term by providing an understanding of how the term fits into a general theory.

A **theoretical definition** assigns a meaning by providing an understanding of how the term fits into a general theory. Take some illustrations from science. For example, the term "inheritance" can mean *the estate that passes to an heir*, or it can mean *the characteristics transmitted from parents to their offspring*. The second meaning concerns biology and has been the subject of both theoretical and experimental research for centuries. One of the first modern biological theories of inheritance was formulated by Gregor Mendel in the 19th century. It illustrates the role of theoretical definitions:

- "Factor" means the hereditary unit in which a characteristic (trait) is transmitted from one generation to the next.
- "The first principle of inheritance" means that each individual inherits two factors, one from each parent.
- "The second principle of inheritance" means that the factors are inherited randomly from each parent.
- "The third principle of inheritance" means that if two traits are inherited that cannot both be displayed, then the trait that is displayed is called "dominant" and the other is called "recessive."

Mendel's theoretical definitions clearly provide intensional meanings for terms. But the terms could just as well have denoted classes with zero extension. Mendel himself could not know for sure until he began his experiments. In fact, we now use the term "allele" in place of Mendel's term "factor," and the resulting pair of alleles (one from each parent) is now called a "gene." This illustrates an important connection between theoretical definitions and precising definitions. If a theory is successful, then scientists can develop precise definitions for many of the concepts suggested by the theory (e.g., the modern precising definitions of "gene"). The resulting precising definitions (using operational techniques) then pave the way for additional specific ways to measure the objects, which in turn open up new avenues for testing.

Not all theoretical definitions stand the test of time. For example, the term "phlogiston" was originally defined as "the element or particles that exist in a physical body and which are released during combustion." Part of the reasoning behind theorizing that such an element existed was that most material gives off heat and smoke during combustion, so something has to be released into the atmosphere. Also, it was known that if you place a candle in an enclosed space, then the candle soon stops burning. The phlogiston theory explained this by claiming that phlogiston saturates the enclosed space until no more room is available for the release of new particles. This sounds entirely plausible. However, you probably have never heard of phlogiston because we now know that the term denotes an empty class; there is no phlogiston. The discovery of oxygen signaled the end of the phlogiston theory. The candle goes out in an enclosed space not because phlogiston fills the space, but rather because fires need oxygen and all the available oxygen has been used up.

Scientific theories can be understood as sets of *abstract theoretical definitions*. For example, Isaac Newton's definition of the term "gravity" is "an attractive force between bodies that have mass." One of the component terms in this definition is "force," which itself needs defining. Newton's definition of "force" is contained in his three laws of motion. (The first law is "Every object in a state of uniform motion tends to remain in that state of motion unless an external force is applied to it.") Newton's theory is, therefore, the complete set of related theoretical definitions.

A close look at theoretical definitions reveals their main purpose—to provide a way of imagining consequences that can be experimentally tested. It is in this capacity that theoretical definitions can be fruitful. In other words, a theoretical definition can only plant a seed in our imagination. But a precising definition is created in order to be directly applied. Precising definitions offer direct procedures and criteria for determining whether something falls under a certain category. (Who, for example, meets the criteria that define "poverty"?) Theoretical definitions do not function that way. They do not provide a means of direct application. In fact, some highly abstract theories cannot be tested because the technical apparatus has not yet been invented. It took many decades to invent the necessary machinery required to test much of quantum theory. More recently, some physicists, including Stephen Hawking, believe that M-theory will be the final "theory of everything." As of now, however, M-theory remains purely theoretical.

If a theoretical definition is fruitful, then scientists can gain knowledge of how a particular part of the world works. They can attain varying degrees of usefulness or they can be completely useless, as many theories have proven to be. Therefore, we can speak of a theoretical definition as being like an abstract tool. And just as many tools turned out to have no significant utility and were soon discarded, the same fate has befallen many theories. This is why experimentation is so important in helping us learn about the world. What experiments and testing do is to provide the means of determining the success, failure, or limitations of a theory. We can learn from success, but also from failure. (Chapter 14 returns to how theories are tested.)

Persuasive Definitions

Persuasive definition
Assigns a meaning to a term with the direct purpose of influencing attitudes or opinions.

A **persuasive definition** assigns a meaning to a term with the direct purpose of influencing attitudes or opinions. The goal is to persuade the listener or reader to adopt either a favorable or unfavorable response toward whatever is denoted by the term. We will discuss two types of persuasive definitions, those that use *emotional language*, and those that use *figurative language*.

Let's start with a few examples that illustrate opposite sides of a contentious issue:

- "National health care" means that the government decides whether you live or die.
- "National health care" means that we get the same medical care that greedy politicians get.

Both definitions fail to offer specific information about the actual policies behind the health-care program. Instead, each definition is crafted to influence a specific attitude and arouse a particular emotional response toward the issue.

Let's look at another example.

> Life seems to be an experience in ascending and descending. You think you're beginning to live for a single aim—for self-development, or the discovery of cosmic truths—when all you're really doing is to move from place to place as if devoted primarily to real estate.   Margaret Anderson, *The Fiery Fountains*

The writer is presenting a persuasive definition. It is meant to get us to see that our so-called progress through life may not be as wonderful as it might appear. It offers an alternative vision of life that might cause us to rethink our attitude toward our goals and dreams.

We might come across a persuasive definition that is very subtle, especially if the writer is very gifted and creative. Although the definition might be hidden inside the passage, it can be quite powerful. Here is an example:

> I thought if war did not include killing, I'd like to see one every year.
>
> Maya Angelou, *Gather Together in My Name*

The author presents an interesting way of defining the term "war." Angelou's way of presenting the issue is meant to get us to realize that, among other things, wars cause death; and she believes that should be enough to persuade us to abandon the practice.

A persuasive definition might be offered as a way to *reinforce* or *change* an opinion. Political speeches are often laced with persuasive definitions that are meant either to create a positive attitude toward a position (or group) or else to disparage the opposing position (or group). However, some debates concern the definition of "politics" itself:

> Politics is the art of the possible.　　　Otto Von Bismarck, *Complete Works*, vol. 7
> Politics is not the art of the possible. It consists in choosing between the disastrous and the unpalatable.　　　John Kenneth Galbraith, *Letter to President Kennedy*

Von Bismarck's definition is meant to place the practice of politics in a positive light. The word "art" suggests that politics is something that skilled artisans can perfect in order to create beneficial results through negotiation. In contrast, Galbraith's definition casts politics in a negative light by contradicting Von Bismarck's claim and elaborates directly on the shortcomings of politics.

The overall goal of a persuasive definition is not to provide direct or accurate information regarding the intension or extension of a term, but instead to influence our thinking about an issue. This is why persuasive definitions are used extensively in politics. Given this, it is not surprising to find that people who rely on a persuasive definition are rarely interested in whether the definition is accurate; they are concerned simply with the definition's effectiveness as persuasion.

Figurative definitions offer metaphors in place of the attributes normally given through an intensional meaning. They function differently than an informative definition, which provides accurate information regarding how a term is normally used. Consider this definition of "accordion":

> Accordion: An instrument in harmony with the sentiments of an assassin.
>
> Ambrose Bierce, *The Devil's Dictionary*

Bierce's definition relies on your being familiar with the way an accordion looks and sounds. It is humorous only if you already understand the lexical definition:

> "Accordion" means a portable wind instrument having a large bellows for forcing air through small metal reeds, a keyboard for the right hand, and buttons for sounding single bass notes or chords for the left hand.
>
> *The Random House Dictionary*

Here is another definition that uses both figurative and emotional language.

> Religion is the sigh of the oppressed creature, the heart of a heartless world, and the soul of soulless conditions. It is the opium of the people.
>
> Karl Marx, *A Contribution to the Critique of Hegel's Philosophy of Right*

The terms "sigh," "oppressed," "heartless," and "soulless" are emotionally charged. And the term "opium" is used figuratively; it is meant to evoke a hopeless addiction to the "drug" of religion.

Persuasive definitions are often used in arguments. However, a persuasive definition that relies solely on an emotional response, or uses figurative language, does not offer a good, objective reason as support for a conclusion. (This is discussed further in Chapter 4, "Informal Fallacies.")

TYPES OF DEFINITIONS

Stipulative definition Introduces a new meaning to a term or symbol.

Lexical definition A definition based on the common use of a word, term, or symbol.

Functional definition Specifies the purpose or use of the objects denoted by the term.

Precising definition Reduces the vagueness and ambiguity of a term by providing a sharp focus, often a technical meaning, for a term.

Theoretical definition Assigns a meaning to a term by providing an understanding of how the term fits into a general theory.

Persuasive definition Assigns a meaning to a term with the direct purpose of influencing attitudes or opinions.

EXERCISES 2D

Self-Practice
Questions

Determine whether the following definitions are stipulative, lexical, precising, theoretical, functional, or persuasive.

1. "Mouse" means a small rodent, or a device for moving the cursor across a computer monitor.

Answer: Lexical

2. Properly speaking, history is nothing but the crimes and misfortunes of the human race.   Pierre Bayle, "Manicheans"

3. "Horn" means a device on a moving vehicle used to get the attention of people and animals.

4. "n00b" means a novice gamer or a newcomer to video games.

⭐ 5. "Momentum" means the impetus of an object in motion.

6. But if you want to be free, you've got to be a prisoner. It's the condition of freedom—true freedom.   Aldous Huxley, *Eyeless in Gaza*

7. "Water molecule" means two atoms of hydrogen and one atom of oxygen.

8. "Scissors" means a device used to cut material or paper.

⭐ 9. "Love" means a strong attraction, devotion, or attachment to a person.

10. "Area of a triangle" means 1/2 base × height.

11. From now on, "late" means anytime after 10:30 PM.

12. "Freedom" is just another word for nothing left to lose.

From the song "Me and Bobby McGee"

⭐13. "Right to privacy" means the control of access to undocumented personal information.

14. "Barometer" means an instrument that measures atmospheric pressure.

15. "Purr" means a low, murmuring sound expressive of satisfaction.

16. "E-cigarettes" means plastic and metal devices that heat a liquid nicotine solution in a disposable cartridge.   Adapted from the Associated Press

⭐17. "No" means no.

18. No one is more dangerous than he who imagines himself pure in heart: for his purity, by definition, is unassailable.   James Baldwin, *Nobody Knows My Name*

19. "Substance" means the fundamental constituent of existence.

20. "Science" means the systematic knowledge gained through observation and experiment.

⭐21. A "derivative" is the rate of change of a function at a specific value of x.

Lawrence Spector, "The Math Page"

22. Definition of a classic: a book everyone is assumed to have read and often thinks they have.   Alan Bennett, *Independent*

23. "Semantics" means the study of the meaning or the interpretation of words and sentences in a language.

24. The difference between gratitude and attribution is not negligible; one displays humility, the other hubris. It seems like a basic tenet of Christianity to give glory to God, quite another to pronounce that God was giving glory to *you*.

Tim Keown, ESPN

⭐25. "Fraud" is the intentional use of deceit, a trick or some dishonest means to deprive another of his/her/its money, property or a legal right.   Law.com

26. "Grue" is the property of an object that makes it appear green if observed before some future time t, and blue if observed afterward.

Nelson Goodman, *The New Riddle of Induction*

27. Freedom is nothing else but a chance to be better.

Albert Camus, *Resistance, Rebellion, and Death*

▷

Video Tutorial: 2D
Exercise #13

28. "Biofuel" means fuel produced from renewable biomass material, commonly used as an alternative, cleaner fuel source.   Clean-energy-ideas.com

⭐29. [I]f you want a stronger version of "good," what sense is there in having a whole string of vague useless words like "excellent" and "splendid" and all the rest of them? "Plusgood" covers the meaning, or "doubleplusgood" if you want something stronger still. Of course we use those forms already, but in the final version of Newspeak there'll be nothing else.   George Orwell, *1984*

30. A colorimeter is a machine that measures the way an object either reflects or transmits light across the visible spectrum, and records the values which correlate with the way the human eye sees color.
                    Technical Definition, Sample 1, quoted at www.engl.nie.edu

31. A Coffee Dialogue:
    Customer: I'll have a small coffee.
    Salesperson: I'm sorry; we only have *Tall, Grande, Venti,* or our newest size, *Trenta.*
    Customer: What's the smallest?
    Salesperson: That would be *Tall.*
    Customer: So "Tall" means small?
    Salesperson: In a manner of speaking.

32. "Alternator" means a device used for producing electrical current.

⭐33. "Microscope" means an instrument invented to magnify objects too small to be seen under normal conditions.

34. It's a rare parent who can see his or her child clearly and objectively. At a school board meeting I attended … the only definition of a gifted child on which everyone in the audience could agree was "mine."
                    Jane Adams, *I'm Still Your Mother*

35. "Malaria" means the disease caused by the bite of an anopheles mosquito infected with any of four protozoans of the genus *Plasmodium.*
                    Collins Dictionary

36. Psycho-analysis pretends to investigate the Unconscious. The Unconscious by definition is what you are not conscious of. But the Analysts already know what's in it—they should, because they put it all in beforehand.
                    Saul Bellow, *The Dean's December*

⭐37. "Syntax" means the study of the grammatical rules of a language.

38. There are two words in the English language that the sports world just can't seem to get right. The first is "ironic," which often gets confused with "coincidental." The second is "redemption," which often gets confused with "The guy who got in trouble in the offseason is playing really well now."
                    LZ Granderson, "Ben Roethlisberger's Redemption"

39. Absolute, True, and Mathematical Time, of itself, and from its own nature flows equably without regard to anything external, and by another name is called Duration.

   Isaac Newton, Principia

40. History for multiculturalists is not a succession of dissolving texts, but a tense tangle of past actions that have reshaped the landscape, distributed the nation's wealth, established boundaries, engendered prejudices, and unleashed energies.

   Joyce Appleby, "Recovering America's Historic Diversity"

⭐41. Virus and spyware definitions are files that Security Essentials uses to identify malicious or potentially unwanted software on your computer.

   Microsoft Security Essentials

42. A jerk, then, is a man (or woman) who is utterly unable to see himself as he appears to others. He has no grace, he is tactless without meaning to be, he is a bore even to his best friends, he is an egotist without charm. All of us are egotists to some extent, but most of us—unlike the jerk—are perfectly and horribly aware of it when we make asses of ourselves. The jerk never knows.

   Sydney J. Harris, "A Definition of a Jerk"

43. "Life" means the property or quality that distinguishes living organisms from dead organisms and inanimate matter, manifested in functions such as metabolism, growth, reproduction, and response to stimuli or adaptation to the environment originating from within the organism.

   The American Heritage Dictionary of the English Language

44. An electronic message is "spam" if (A) the recipient's personal identity and context are irrelevant because the message is equally applicable to many other potential recipients; and (B) the recipient has not verifiably granted deliberate, explicit, and still-revocable permission for it to be sent.

   The Spamhaus Project Ltd.

⭐45. Religion can be defined as a system of beliefs and practices by means of which a group of people struggles with the ultimate problems of human life. It expresses their refusal to capitulate to death, to give up in the face of frustration, to allow hostility to tear apart their human aspirations.

   J. Milton Yinger, The Scientific Study of Religion

46. "Dementia" is the significant loss of intellectual abilities such as memory capacity, severe enough to interfere with social or occupational functioning. The criteria for diagnosis of dementia include impairment of attention, orientation, memory, judgment, language, motor and spatial skills, and function.

   Adapted from Medterms.com

47. The effect is further enhanced because human lips are "everted," meaning that they purse outward. This trait sets us apart from other members of the animal kingdom. Unlike other primates, the soft, fleshy surface of our lips remains exposed, making their shape and composition intensely alluring.

   Sheril Kirshenbaum, The Science of Kissing

48. Challenged with a 100 million euro ($133 million) deficit, one western German city has introduced a day tax on prostitutes to help whittle down its budget gap. The new "pleasure tax" requires prostitutes in Dortmund to purchase a 6 euro "day ticket" for each day they work, or face a potential fine. Such taxes are not unusual in Germany where prostitution is legal and sex workers must pay tax on their income. Cologne introduced a 150 euro "pleasure tax" on sex workers in 2004 and later added a 6 euro day tax option for part-time prostitutes.

Reuters

★49. There was a time when "universe" meant "all there is." Everything. The whole shebang. The notion of more than one universe, more than one everything, would seemingly be a contradiction in terms. Yet a range of theoretical developments has gradually qualified the interpretation of "universe." To a physicist, the word's meaning now largely depends on context. Sometimes "universe" still connotes absolutely everything.   Brian Greene, *The Hidden Reality*

50. Civil disobedience is a moral weapon in the fight for justice. But how can disobedience ever be moral? Well I guess that depends on one's definition of the words. In 1919, in India, ten thousand people gathered in Amritsar to protest the tyranny of British rule. General Reginald Dyer trapped them in a courtyard and ordered his troops to fire into the crowd for ten minutes. Three hundred seventy-nine died—men, women, children, shot down in cold blood. Dyer said he had taught them "a moral lesson." Gandhi and his followers responded not with violence, but with an organized campaign of noncooperation. Government buildings were occupied. Streets were blocked with people who refused to rise, even when beaten by police. Gandhi was arrested. But the British were soon forced to release him. He called it a "moral victory." The definition of moral: Dyer's "lesson" or Gandhi's victory. You choose.

James Farmer, Jr., "Resolved: Civil Disobedience Is a Moral Weapon in the Fight for Justice"

E. GUIDELINES FOR INFORMATIVE DEFINITIONS

Ordinary language relies heavily on lexical definitions. Conversations between friends and relatives assume, for the most part, a common agreement on the everyday meaning of words. If a misunderstanding occurs because a term is ambiguous or vague, then the people involved can often clarify the intended meaning. A conversation among coworkers can be informal, regarding non-work-related topics, or it can include technical terms that rely on precise definitions (e.g., a medical procedure to be performed).

Since definitions are used in a variety of settings and for many different purposes, there is no single rule to which every definition must conform. For example, definitions used in poetry, novels, music, or jokes often use metaphors. They do not have to be truthful, informative, or even accurate in order to be effective. However, if our goal is to impart correct and accurate information, then our definitions should follow definite guidelines. Also, if definitions are to play a role in arguments, then ambiguity, vagueness, and any other source of imprecision need to be eliminated. Fortunately, eight guidelines can make the construction of informative definitions easier.

1. An informative definition should use quotation marks appropriately.

We have already offered a few examples from written sources that did not use quotation marks around a term being defined. However, definitions that are meant to be informative should follow the pattern used in this chapter. Here is an example:

> Life is the sum of the forces that resist death.   Gustav Eckstein, *The Body Has a Head*

This can be easily changed to match the format we have used:

> "Life" means the sum of the forces that resist death.

Here are a few more examples:

- A Sicilian pizza is made with a thick crust.
- "Sicilian pizza" means a pizza made with a thick crust.
- A dune buggy is a small open vehicle with low-pressure tires for riding on sandy beaches.
- "Dune buggy" means a small open vehicle with low-pressure tires for riding on sandy beaches.

In each instance, the ordinary language sentence was rewritten in order to place the definiendum within quotation marks. This lets the reader know that the term is being mentioned (the quoted term is the subject).

2. An informative definition should include the essential meaning of a term.

If a definition is to impart information, then it should include the fundamental attributes associated with the objects denoted by the term. The essential properties are what distinguish the objects being referred to from other things. Consider the following example.

> "Television" means plasma, LCD, or LED.

Although the definition does provide extensional meaning through subclasses, it does not give any information about the essential properties of a television (intensional meaning). The next example provides an intensional meaning of the term.

> "Television" means a device for receiving electrical signals and converting them into moving images and sound.

There are many other objects that require a functional definition to provide the essential meaning (e.g., pneumatic jackhammer, computer, and cyclotron). However, an essential definition of "child" would not include a functional definition because we do not define humans by specifying that they serve any distinct purpose.

3. An informative definition should not be too broad or too narrow.

Definitions that are too broad will allow things to be included that should be excluded. For example:

> "Horse" means a large animal that humans often ride.

The definition is too broad. It allows camels and elephants to be included, since they both fit the definition provided. Here is another example of the same term:

> "Horse" means a stallion.

This definition is too narrow. It eliminates females and the young of both sexes. Once again, if a definition is to provide accurate information, then it needs to be such that it includes all and only those objects that are correctly associated with the term's denotation. The following example illustrates this point.

> "Horse" means a quadruped belonging to the same family as zebras and donkeys; individuals typically have a long mane along the back of the neck; a few of the many breeds are appaloosa, mustang, and thoroughbred.

4. An informative definition should not be circular.

In order for a definition to be informative, it must provide substantial material that enlarges our understanding of a term. Some ordinary language definitions fail because they define a term by using the term itself.

> "Addict" means someone who is addicted to a drug.

The definition is circular because it uses the term "addict" as part of the definition. If you do not know already what the term "addict" means, then the proposed definition is not informative. Here are a few more examples:

- "Chemist" means someone who studies chemistry.
- "Length" means how long something is.

Both of these definitions are circular because they assume as part of the definition the very thing they are meant to define. The following are examples of how the three examples can be rewritten to eliminate circularity:

- "Addict" means someone who is physiologically or psychologically dependent on a substance or activity; some examples of addiction are drug, alcohol, and gambling.
- "Chemist" means someone who studies the properties, composition, reactions, and transformations of elementary substances; inorganic chemistry studies all compounds except those containing carbon; organic chemistry is the study of substances found in living organisms.
- "Length" means the extent of something when measured from end to end (also called "linear," meaning *represented by a line*); some common measuring devices for length are centimeters, inches, feet, yards, and meters.

Since the definition of "length" included measuring devices, it illustrates how an operational definition can help clarify the meaning of certain terms.

5. An informative definition should be affirmative and not negative.

We can convey some meaning by contrasting the objects denoted by a term with other objects. For example:

> "Honest" means someone who is not a cheat.

Yet such a definition fails to provide intensional meaning. A definition should make sure to include relevant properties normally associated with the objects it denotes, like this:

> "Honest" means someone who is trustworthy and reliable in their intentions and actions.

Let's look at another negative definition.

> "Normal" means someone who is not insane.

It can be rewritten as follows:

> "Normal" means conforming to a certain standard or convention; in medicine, it refers to someone free from disease; in psychiatry or psychology, it refers to someone free from any mental disorders.

Of course there are exceptions to this rule; in ordinary language situations, a negative definition can be quite adequate to the task. Here are a few simple examples.

- "Dead" means no longer living.
- "Bald tire" means a tire that does not have any tread.

The context in which the definition is used should provide a guide to the appropriateness of a negative definition.

6. An informative definition should not use ambiguous or vague language.

We have seen how ambiguity and vagueness can make a definition less effective and how we can avoid those mistakes. Ambiguity arises when a definition can be reasonably interpreted in more than one way. Here is an example:

> "Fanatic" means true believer.

The term "true believer" can mean a person with deep, genuine, and sincere beliefs. However, it can also mean a person whose belief is simply true. The first interpretation emphasizes the sincerity of the belief; the second interpretation emphasizes the truth value of the belief. The definition does not provide a sufficient context to eliminate the ambiguity.

Vagueness results from a definition that fails to delineate precisely what objects are denoted by a term. For example:

> "Capitalism" means the economic system whereby individuals control the wealth.

The term "individuals" is vague in this definition. Does it refer only to individuals, or are small companies and large corporations included? Does the term "wealth" include property as well as money? What role, if any, does a government have in the economic system defined? The definition is not very informative because it leaves too many unanswered questions.

7. An informative definition should not use emotionally charged or figurative language.

Definitions that rely on emotionally charged language generally fail to provide the essential attributes that are required for intensional meaning. The next example illustrates this point:

> To establish justice in a sinful world is the whole sad duty of the political order.
>
> Reinhold Niebuhr, *On Politics*

The definition uses the words "sinful" and "sad" to establish an emotional response in the reader. The definition may be effective for its intended purpose, but it does not provide either intensional or extensional meaning for the term "political order."

Let's look at another example:

> Ask any die-hard what conservatism is; he'll tell you that it's true socialism.
>
> Aldous Huxley, *Eyeless in Gaza*

The definition contains the term "die-hard," which is usually associated with a person who holds stubbornly to a position; it is intended to elicit an emotional response. Also, the term "true" in this setting is used to assert that there is only one correct interpretation of the terms involved.

Figurative definitions offer metaphors in place of the essential attributes normally given through an intensional meaning. Consider this example:

> Art is a fruit that grows in man, like a fruit on a plant, or a child in its mother's womb.
>
> Jean Arp, "Art Is a Fruit"

The use of figurative language is intended to be evocative and poetic; it is not intended to be informative. Therefore, it functions differently from a lexical definition.

8. An informative definition should include a context whenever necessary.

Many common words have more than one meaning. In order to avoid misunderstanding, it sometimes helps to provide the context, often in parentheses:

- "Bank" means (in geography) the dry land bordering a stream or river.
- "Bank" means (in flying) an aircraft's angle of inclination during a turn.
- "Bank" means (in finance) a business involved in saving and lending people's money.
- "Bank" means (in pool or billiards) a cue shot that strikes a side or end cushion.

Once again, the setting in which the definition occurs should provide you with clues regarding whether or not you should include an explicit reference to a context.

EXERCISES 2E

Analyze the following passages using the *Guidelines for Informative Definitions.* Explain why you think that one, more than one, or none of the guidelines are applicable to each passage.

Self-Practice
Questions

1. Reality is that which, when you stop believing in it, doesn't go away.

   Philip K. Dick, *How to Build a Universe That Doesn't Fall Apart Two Days Later*

Answer: The definition uses irony to make its point, so it does not attempt to be informative by providing a lexical or precising definition. However, we can add quotation marks (using Guideline 1): "Reality" means that which, when you stop believing in it, doesn't go away.

2. One definition of man is "an intelligence served by organs."

   Ralph Waldo Emerson, "Works and Days"

3. "Politician" means an elected official who likes to spend other people's money.

4. The definition of the individual was: a multitude of one million divided by one million.

   Arthur Koestler, *Darkness at Noon*

⭐ 5. It is from the womb of art that criticism was born.

   Charles Baudelaire, "Salon of 1846"

Video Tutorial: 2E
Exercise #5

6. A philanthropist is a man whose charity increases directly as the square of the distance.

   George Eliot, *Middlemarch*

7. I guess the definition of a lunatic is a man surrounded by them.

   Ezra Pound, Quoted in *Charles Olson and Ezra Pound*

8. Retaliation is related to nature and instinct, not to law. Law, by definition, cannot obey the same rules as nature.

   Albert Camus, *Resistance, Rebellion and Death*

⭐ 9. Grade point average (GPA) means the number determined by dividing the total grade points achieved by the number of credits earned.

10. It is the greatest happiness of the greatest number that is the measure of right and wrong.

    Jeremy Bentham, *Fragment of Government*

11. Tall means anyone who can eat peanuts off my head.

12. To be "conscious" means not simply to be, but to be reported, known, to have awareness of one's being added to that being.

    William James, "How Two Minds Can Know the Same Thing"

⭐13. To say the word Romanticism is to say modern art—that is, intimacy, spirituality, color, aspiration towards the infinite, expressed by every means available to the arts.

    Charles Baudelaire, "Salon of 1846"

14. Journalists write news stories based on the material, and then provide a link to the supporting documentation to prove our stories are true.

    Charlie Savage, "U.S. Tries to Build Case for Conspiracy by WikiLeaks"

15. The human mind is so complex and things are so tangled up with each other that, to explain a blade of straw, one would have to take to pieces an entire universe. . . . A definition is a sack of flour compressed into a thimble.

Rémy De Gourmont, "Glory and the Idea of Immortality"

16. If a thousand men were not to pay their tax-bills this year, that would not be as violent and bloody measure as it would be to pay them and enable the State to commit violence and shed innocent blood. This is, in fact, the definition of a peaceable revolution, if any such is possible.

Henry David Thoreau, *On the Duty of Civil Disobedience*

⭐17. Whereas Smith noted that renegotiations or extensions of rookie contracts were "banned" until after the third year, a management official said the proposal "allows" for those renegotiations or extensions after the third year.

Chris Mortensen and Adam Schefter, "Sources: Sides Could Talk This Week"

18. By intuition is meant the kind of intellectual sympathy by which one places oneself within an object in order to coincide with what is unique in it and consequently inexpressible. Analysis, on the contrary, is the operation which reduces the object to elements already known, that is, to elements common both to it and other objects.

Henri Bergson, *An Introduction to Metaphysics*

19. The needs of a society determine its ethics, and in the Black American ghettos the hero is that man who is offered only the crumbs from his country's table but by ingenuity and courage is able to take for himself a Lucullan feast.

Maya Angelou, *I Know Why the Caged Bird Sings*

20. Physics is experience, arranged in economical order.

Ernst Mach, "The Economical Nature of Physics"

F. COGNITIVE AND EMOTIVE MEANING

We saw in Chapter 1 that sentences can be used for a variety of reasons, such as asking a question, providing information, making a request, or giving an order. Language also serves as a vehicle for expressing feelings through songs, poetry, stories, proverbs, jokes, and even lies. We will focus on two functions of language—to convey information and to express emotion.

Language that is used to convey information has **cognitive meaning**, while language that is used to express emotion or feelings has **emotive meaning**. Consider two examples:

A. It's already 7:00. He is late for the appointment.
B. It's already 7:00. He is late for the appointment. I am fed up with his nonsense; he is completely untrustworthy, self-centered, and useless.

Cognitive meaning
Language that is used to convey information has cognitive meaning.

Emotive meaning
Language that is used to express emotion or feelings has emotive meaning.

The two statements in A convey information, so they both have cognitive meaning. Although the first two statements in B convey information, the third statement is more complex. The phrase "I am fed up with his nonsense" has emotive meaning, and the terms "completely untrustworthy, self-centered, and useless" are value judgments. A **value judgment** is a claim that a particular human action or object has some degree of importance, worth, or desirability. However, the claim that the person referred to in B is "completely untrustworthy, self-centered, and useless" has terms that are vague and that need to be clearly defined. In addition, we are provided with no evidence to support the claim, other than that the person was once late for an appointment. Therefore, the value claim and the cognitive meaning are obscured by the emotive language.

Value judgment A claim that a particular human action or object has some degree of importance, worth, or desirability.

Let's look at two more examples:

> A stem cell is an unspecialized cell found in fetuses, embryos, and some adult body tissues that has the potential to develop into specialized cells or divide into other stem cells. Stem cells from fetuses or embryos can develop into any type of differentiated cells, while those found in mature tissues develop only into specific cells. Stem cells can potentially be used to replace tissue damaged or destroyed by disease or injury, but the use of embryonic stem cells for this purpose is controversial.
>
> *The American Heritage Science Dictionary*

> [This] would allow scientists to create an embryonic clone for the purposes of extracting the stem cells from that embryo, a procedure that will cause the embryo's immediate demise. The stem cells may then be used for experimental treatments on another human being with a disease. Let's see, creating a human being for the purposes of killing that person for another human being's health, sounds an awfully lot like cannibalism, only worse. ... [T]he procedure would not merely use tissue from human embryos, it would destroy them. That's like saying removing someone's heart is just using their tissue.
>
> C. Ben Mitchell, "Biotech Cannibalism"

The first passage provides a definition of the term "stem cells" (an unspecialized cell) and also provides information regarding its sources (fetuses, embryos, and some adult body tissues). There is also information regarding the potential uses of the different kinds of stem cells. The passage illustrates an extended use of cognitive meaning.

The second passage also has examples of cognitive meaning—for example, "The stem cells may then be used for experimental treatments on another human being with a disease." However, it also has examples of emotive meaning—for example, "the embryo's immediate demise," and "sounds an awfully lot like cannibalism, only worse." There is even sarcasm laced with emotion: "That's like saying removing someone's heart is just using their tissue."

These two passages again illustrate that statements can contain both cognitive and emotive meaning. Look again at "[This] would allow scientists to create an embryonic clone for the purposes of extracting the stem cells from that embryo, a procedure that will cause the embryo's immediate demise." The first part of the sentence has cognitive meaning, and the second part contains both cognitive and emotive meaning. However, the emotional force of the language can sometimes make it difficult to distinguish or extract the cognitive meaning. We can extract the cognitive meaning of the phrase "a procedure that will cause the embryo's immediate demise" by looking closely at certain key words. The term "embryo" can be defined as the stage of development (in humans) up to the second month in the womb. The term "fetus" can be defined as the stage of development (in humans) occurring after the second month in the womb. We can replace the term "demise" with the more neutral term "death." The cognitive meaning can then be distinguished by paraphrasing the original: "a procedure that causes the death of the embryo."

There is another important use of emotive language in the second passage. The author first uses the term "embryo" but then switches to the term "human": "Let's see, creating a human being for the purposes of killing that person." The author has maneuvered the reader from "the embryo's immediate demise" to "killing that person." Since it is controversial whether an embryo is a *person*, the author is unjustified in simply substituting the term "person" for "embryo." (The terms are not synonymous.)

Since we want to focus on the informational content of the statements in an argument, emotionally charged language interferes with analysis. The emotive meaning of a statement can sometimes override and obscure the cognitive meaning and any value judgments that are made. Also, a vague claim can hide behind the emotionally charged language with the result that the evidence needed to support the claim is overlooked. (Chapter 12 offers a detailed discussion of value judgments.)

EXERCISES 2F

Self-Practice
Questions

Determine whether the following passages contain phrases expressing cognitive meaning, emotive meaning, or both. Explain your answers.

1. Americans gave nearly $300 billion to charities last year, a 1% increase when adjusted for inflation.

Answer: Cognitive meaning. The passage provides information regarding the percentage of increase in charitable contributions.

2. Gambling is for suckers. As P. T. Barnum said, "There's a sucker born every minute." State lotteries bleed hard-earned money from those least able to afford it. The corrupt officials who voted to allow those obscene games should be sent to jail. I'll be happy to turn the key and lock them up.

3. The two new integrated resorts and casinos in Singapore have each generated over $100 million in profits per month since they opened. At this rate they will each be able to pay off their start-up costs in 5 years.

4. The independent assessment committee was satisfied that adequate measures were taken by the local authorities to meet all foreseeable contingencies.

⭐ 5. The Great Pyramid of Giza is the only thing that still exists among the Seven Wonders of the Ancient World.

6. The powers-that-be were ridiculously unprepared for the huge crowd last night. The resulting chaos caused immense suffering and put precious lives in extreme peril. Some heads should roll over this tragedy.

7. At some point, if you don't want to worry about teams in minor markets, don't put teams in minor markets, or don't leave teams in minor markets if they're truly minor. Socialism, communism, whatever you want to call it, is never the answer.

   Hank Steinbrenner, co-owner of the New York Yankees, quoted in the Associated Press

8. It is the business of thought to define things, to find the boundaries; thought, indeed, is a ceaseless process of definition.

   Vance Palmer, in *Intimate Portraits*, ed. H. P. Heseltine

⭐ 9. As much as we want to keep everybody, we've already made these guys very, very rich, and I don't feel we owe anybody anything monetarily. Some of these players are wealthier than their bosses.

   Hank Steinbrenner, quoted at CBSSports.com

10. It brings us one step closer to the brink of war, because I don't think the North would seek war by intention, but war by accident, something spiraling out of control has always been my fear.   Peter Beck, quoted at Guardian.co.uk

Video Tutorial: 2F
Exercise #10

11. The utopian male concept which is the premise of male pornography is this— since manhood is established and confirmed over and against the brutalized bodies of women, men need not aggress against each other; in other words, women absorb male aggression so that men are safe from it.

   Andrea Dworkin, *The Root Cause*

12. By contrast with history, evolution is an unconscious process. Another, and perhaps a better way of putting it would be to say that evolution is a natural process, history a human one. … Insofar as we treat man as a part of nature—for instance in a biological survey of evolution—we are precisely not treating him as a historical being. As a historically developing being, he is set over against nature, both as a knower and as a doer.   Owen Barfield, *History, Guilt, and Habit*

⭐13. The man who can roust the excitement and the enthusiasm of the coordination of the players is the one who will come through, the one that can bring their team to that high expectation of unity, solidarity and togetherness and performing above and beyond the call of duty, he will be the big, big winner Sunday.

   Don King, boxing promoter, quoted at ESPN.go.com

14. Ah, California, my home sweet home. Did anyone catch the California Horse Racing Board's meeting the other day, during which the commissioners were asked to choose between bald-faced corporatism and open-handed charity? Okay, maybe it wasn't as simple as that, but contrary conclusions are hard to draw.

   Jay Hovdey, *Daily Racing Form*

15. Choosing the wrong policy can have consequences. For example, when comparing breast cancer treatment coverage under three California policies, the study found that a patient would spend nearly $4,000 for a typical treatment under one policy or as much as $38,000 under another even though both policies had similar deductibles and out-of-pocket limits.

Susan Jaffe, "Speak Plain English, *Health Insurers Told,*" *Kaiser Health News*

G. FACTUAL AND VERBAL DISPUTES

Factual dispute
Occurs when people disagree on a matter that involves facts.

A **factual dispute** occurs when people disagree on a matter that involves facts. For example, one person might claim that Benjamin Franklin must have been a U.S. president because his picture is on the $100 bill, while another person claims that Franklin was not a U.S. president. This dispute can be resolved by consulting historical or biographical sources. Here is another example of a factual dispute:

- Our state legislature should pass a law authorizing capital punishment because it is an effective deterrent to violent crime.
- Our state legislature should not pass a law authorizing capital punishment because it has not been shown to be an effective deterrent to violent crime.

The dispute concerns the factual question of whether or not capital punishment is an effective deterrent to violent crime. Each side in the dispute needs to provide relevant scientific evidence in support of its position.

A factual dispute can involve emotional language. It occurs when people agree on certain facts and terms but express their feelings toward the facts in different ways. For example:

- Executing violent criminals is morally acceptable because those people are worthless and commit despicable acts against peace-loving, innocent humans.
- Executing violent criminals is morally unacceptable because even though those people are as bad as you say, we should open our hearts, and learn to love and forgive.

The disputants seem to agree on the terms "worthless," "despicable acts," and "peace-loving." However, their emotional responses to these terms differ, as do their value judgments regarding how we should act toward violent criminals.

Verbal dispute
Occurs when a vague or ambiguous term results in a linguistic misunderstanding.

A **verbal dispute** occurs when a vague or ambiguous term results in a linguistic misunderstanding. In other words, statements that are thought to be about the objects denoted by certain key terms instead involve a dispute about the terms themselves. These kinds of disputes are resolved not by investigating the facts, but by an investigation of the definitions. Suppose someone is a "small bookmaker." Is his occupation illegal? Since the term "bookmaker" can mean either "a person who makes books" or "a person who accepts illegal wagers on sporting events" (often referred to as a "bookie"), the dispute hinges on an ambiguity arising from an unclear context. Disputes of this nature are easily cleared up once the correct meaning is identified.

However, there are more complicated kinds of verbal disputes. A term might be used when there is some overall agreement on its intension, but disagreement as to its extension. For example, some disputes have involved the question of whether a certain belief system qualifies as a "religion." Legal, governmental, and moral issues are all involved. A religion that is recognized by the government has certain privileges, such as being exempt from paying taxes. The disputes can sometimes be resolved by clarifying the intension of the term (which will further determine the extension), so that the court can make a decision. However, deciding the legal question will not necessarily satisfy everyone, because religious issues often evoke emotional responses.

Sometimes the parties involved cannot agree on a definition. Although most governments condemn acts of terrorism, we often hear that "one person's terrorist is another person's freedom fighter." In more formal language, a United Nations report in 2010 stated that "some delegations pointed out the necessity to distinguish between acts of terrorism and the legitimate struggle of people in the exercise of their right to self-determination."

In a report to the United Nations General Assembly, the Secretary-General offered this definition:

> Any action constitutes terrorism if it is intended to cause death or serious bodily harm to civilians or non-combatants with the purpose of intimidating a population or compelling a Government or an international organization to do or abstain from doing any act.
>
> *In Larger Freedom: Towards Development, Security and Human Rights for All,* March 21, 2005

The United Nations has still not adopted a definition of "terrorism." The contentious issues involving the term "terrorism" are not merely verbal. However, even if a verbal agreement could be reached, the emotive meaning, political divisions, and value judgments that get attached to the term still need to be settled.

EXERCISES 2G

Determine whether the following disputes are factual, verbal, or some combination of the two. Also, point out any emotional language that might be involved.

Self-Practice
Questions

1. A: Drinking one glass of red wine a day has been linked with a lower risk of heart disease.

    B: Excessive alcohol consumption has been linked to liver disease.

Answer: Verbal dispute. Person A talks about the effects of "drinking one glass of red wine a day," while person B talks about the effects of "excessive alcohol consumption." The dispute is not about the facts related to their respective claims.

2. A: All humans are created equal.

    B: That can't be. We all have a unique DNA profile.

3. A: You were fired because of your poor work performance.
   B: I was fired because the supervisor didn't like me.

4. A: My parents are in heaven.
   B: There is no heaven.

Video Tutorial: 2G
Exercise #5

⭐ 5. A: The capital city of Korea is Seoul.
   B: You are wrong. The capital city of Korea is Pyongyang.

6. A: There is a higher incidence of child leukemia near nuclear power plants compared to the rest of the United States.
   B: Nuclear power plants provide the best opportunity to free ourselves from oil dependency.

7. A: Here, have a martini.
   B: It's not a martini because it was not made with dry vermouth.
   A: But a martini doesn't have to be made with dry vermouth.

8. A: This is my new car.
   B: That's not new. It's at least 5 years old.

⭐ 9. A: Don't ask her whether you should take the job or not—make your own decision.
   B: I am making my own decision—I have decided to ask her what I should do.

10. A: Sales will increase if we upgrade customer service because customers will feel that we care about their satisfaction.
    B: I disagree. Sales will decrease if we upgrade customer service because it will make it too easy for customers to return products after they used them for a while.

11. A: Our business is booming. Total sales are up 13% over last year.
    B: Our business is not booming. Profit is down 3% from last year.

12. A: Did you see his last movie? What an actor; he's a genius.
    B: I read somewhere that his I.Q. is only 110, so he's definitely not in the genius range.

⭐13. A: I don't think, I know.
    B: I don't think you know either.

14. A: The contract proposal offered by the company is reasonable.
    B: The contract proposal is just their way of further exploiting the working class.

15. A: No radio station east of the Mississippi can use the letter "K" as its first call letter.
    B: Oh really; then what about KDKA? It's in Pittsburgh, Pennsylvania.

16. A: The proposed tax hike is too high. The individuals who invest their hard-earned money in businesses that provide all the jobs are being robbed of that which is their sacred right to keep. The government is like a thief who steals rather than works. Taxes are immoral because they take what

rightfully belongs to someone and give it to those too lazy or not talented enough to compete. We should be able to do whatever we want with what we earn instead of being subjected to onerous taxation spiraling out of control. The government wants higher and higher taxes the way an addict tries to satisfy an insatiable desire.

B: The proposed tax hike is not too high. In fact, it is not enough. The rich people in this country are getting away with murder when it comes to paying their fair share. Big corporations need to fleece the public to ensure obscene profits for their shareholders, who then turn around and purchase luxury items that flaunt their wealth with lifestyles that rival the most decadent periods in human history.

⭐17. Some years ago, being with a camping party in the mountains, I returned from a solitary ramble to find every one engaged in a ferocious metaphysical dispute. The corpus of the dispute was a squirrel—a live squirrel supposed to be clinging to one side of a tree-trunk; while over against the tree's opposite side a human being was imagined to stand. This human witness tries to get sight of the squirrel by moving rapidly round the tree, but no matter how fast he goes, the squirrel moves as fast in the opposite direction, and always keeps the tree between himself and the man, so that never a glimpse of him is caught. The resultant metaphysical problem now is this: *Does the man go round the squirrel or not?* He goes round the tree, sure enough, and the squirrel is on the tree; but does he go round the squirrel? In the unlimited leisure of the wilderness, discussion had been worn threadbare. Every one had taken sides, and was obstinate; and the numbers on both sides were even.

William James, *What Pragmatism Means*

18. In his System of Nature, A.D. 1776, Linnaeus declares, "I hereby separate the whales from the fish." … The grounds upon which Linnaeus would fain have banished the whales from the waters, he states as follows: "On account of their warm bilocular heart, their lungs, their movable eyelids, their hollow ears." … I take the good old fashioned ground that the whale is a fish, and call upon holy Jonah to back me. This fundamental thing settled, the next point is, in what internal respect does the whale differ from other fish. Above, Linnaeus has given you those items. But in brief, they are these: lungs and warm blood; whereas, all other fish are lungless and cold blooded.   Herman Melville, *Moby Dick*

19. M: An argument isn't just contradiction.
A: It can be.
M: No it can't. An argument is a connected series of statements intended to establish a proposition.
A: No it isn't.
M: Yes it is! It's not just contradiction.
A: Look, if I argue with you, I must take up a contrary position.
M: Yes, but that's not just saying "No it isn't."
A: Yes it is!
M: No it isn't!

A: Yes it is!

M: Argument is an intellectual process. Contradiction is just the automatic gainsaying of any statement the other person makes. *(short pause)*

A: No it isn't.

M: It is.

A: Not at all.

Monty Python, "The Argument Sketch"

20. A: In 1982, 82 percent of college graduates read novels or poems for pleasure; two decades later, only 67 percent did. And more than 40 percent of Americans under 44 did not read a single book—fiction or nonfiction—over the course of a year. The proportion of 17-year-olds who read nothing (unless required to do so for school) more than doubled between 1984 and 2004. This time period, of course, encompasses the rise of personal computers, Web surfing and video games.

Susan Jacoby, "The Dumbing of America"

B: Susan Jacoby presents a compelling, though perhaps naïve and myopic, view of intellectualism and the persistence of literature in the 21st century. Like so many nervous academics of our age, Jacoby provides a view compounded by urgent pollster data, alarming statistics, and factoids heralding in the age of ignorance at the hands of the digital revolution. A concern about whether young people are wasting their minds has been intermittently fashionable throughout history. If Jacoby contends that "video" is eroding our intellect, I encourage her to immerse herself in the story of Wikipedia. This is a place where today's youth, in phenomenal numbers, are helping professors and graduate students to build a repository of living knowledge from all corners of this planet. This is not a project for the next decade or the century. It is a project for all time.

Jimmy Wales, the founder of Wikipedia, "We're Smarter than You Think"

Study Materials

Summary

- Term: A single word or a group of words that can be the subject of a statement; it can be a common name, a proper name, or even a descriptive phrase.
- Clarifying the meaning of a statement requires a close look at the meaning of the terms involved. Vague, ambiguous, or imprecise terms can reduce the clarity of individual statements and arguments.
- Intension: The intension of a term is specified by listing the properties or attributes that the term connotes—in other words, its sense.
- Class: A group of objects.
- Extension: The class or collection of objects to which the term applies. In other words, what the term denotes (its reference).
- A sequence of terms can have increasing intension, decreasing intension, increasing extension, or decreasing extension.

- Empty class: A class that has zero members.
- A definition assigns a meaning to a word, phrase, or symbol. Logicians use the term "definiendum" to refer to that which is being defined, and the term "definiens" to that which does the defining.
- Intensional definition: Assigns a meaning to a term by listing the properties or attributes shared by all the objects that are denoted by the term.
- Synonymous definition: Assigns a meaning to a term by providing another term with the same meaning; in other words, by providing a synonym.
- Word origin definition: A meaning can be assigned to a term by investigating its origin. The study of the history, development, and sources of words is called *etymology*.
- Operational definition: Defines a term by specifying a measurement procedure.
- Definition by genus and difference: Assigns a meaning to a term (the species) by establishing a genus and combining it with the attribute that distinguishes the members of that species.
- Extensional definition: Assigns meaning to a term by indicating the class members denoted by the term.
- Ostensive definition: Involves demonstrating the term—for example, by pointing to a member of the class that the term denotes.
- Enumerative definition: Assigns meaning to a term by naming the individual members of the class denoted by the term.
- Definition by subclass: Assigns meaning to a term by naming subclasses (species) of the class denoted by the term.
- Stipulative definition: Introduces a new meaning to a term or symbol.
- Lexical definition: A definition based on the common use of a word, term, or symbol.
- Functional definition: Specifies the purpose or use of the objects denoted by the term.
- Precising definition: Reduces the vagueness and ambiguity of a term by providing a sharp focus, often a technical meaning, for a term.
- Theoretical definition: Assigns a meaning to a term by providing an understanding of how the term fits into a general theory.
- Persuasive definition: Assigns a meaning to a term with the direct purpose of influencing attitudes or opinions.
- There are eight guidelines that are meant to facilitate the construction of informative definitions.
- Cognitive meaning: Language that is used to convey information.
- Emotive meaning: Language that is used to express emotion or feelings.
- Value judgment: A claim that a particular human action or object has some degree of importance, worth, or desirability.
- Factual dispute: Occurs when people disagree on a matter which involves facts.
- Verbal dispute: Occurs when a vague or ambiguous term results in a linguistic misunderstanding.

KEY TERMS

class   69
cognitive meaning   102
decreasing extension   69
decreasing intension   70
definiendum   73
definiens   73
definition   73
definition by genus and
   difference   79
definition by subclass   80
emotive meaning   102
empty class   69

enumerative
   definition   80
extension   69
extensional definition   79
factual dispute   106
functional definition   86
increasing extension   70
increasing intension   69
intension   69
intensional definition   73
lexical definition   85
operational definition   75

ostensive definition   79
persuasive definition   90
precising definition   87
stipulative definition   84
synonymous
   definition   73
term   68
theoretical definition   88
value judgment   103
verbal dispute   106
word origin
   definition   74

LOGIC CHALLENGE: THE PATH

A person walks up a mountain path in Tibet to visit a monastery in order to gain enlightenment. She starts out on her journey at 7:00 AM and arrives at the monastery 8 hours later. A monk hands her a note and tells her not to read it until she returns to the bottom of the mountain. The next morning she starts down the path at 7:00 AM. She is anxious to read the note, and since she is able to walk downhill very fast, she arrives at the bottom in 4 hours. She opens the note and reads the following:

> On your journey down the path you passed one spot at the exact same time that you passed it when you went up the path.

Is the note correct? Explain your answer.

Chapter 3

Diagramming Arguments

Digital homework exercises for this chapter are available in your instructor's online course. For information on how to access these resources, please visit **www.oup.com/he/baronett5e.**

A diagram of an argument, like a road map, is a visual tool. It offers a graphic depiction of the argument's structure, and it allows us to follow a path from point A (the premises) to point B (the conclusion). It highlights connections—the connections between the statements that make up the argument. It takes a passage and extracts all the premises, numbers them, and then connects them to the conclusion. You can consult the numbers as you make those connections in the passage yourself.

Maps are especially helpful for long trips, and diagrams are especially useful for extended arguments. If you are on a road trip, you might find that you can get to your destination by several different routes, each through a different city. Similarly, an argument might contain premises that work independently of each other in support of the conclusion. On the other hand, when tracing a route on a map, you might find there is only one way to get where you want to go, and the route takes you through several stops along the way. In the same way, you might need all the premises of an argument, because they work together to support the conclusion.

A road map might show that you cannot get to your destination—or at least not easily, because some roads are not yet completed. In the same manner, some arguments are missing a premise or a conclusion, either intentionally or unintentionally. In those cases, we need to add the missing information based on our overall understanding. If we add a missing premise, then we are building a bridge, to connect the existing premises to the conclusion. If we add a missing conclusion, then we are providing a final destination. Of course, our diagram will have to distinguish the information we are given from what we have added to complete the argument. This chapter applies diagramming to both simple and extended arguments.

A. THE BASICS OF DIAGRAMMING ARGUMENTS

Once we have located an argument, we can create a diagram—a map of the premises and conclusion. There are a few basic techniques for creating diagrams, and they can be used as building blocks for diagramming extended arguments. For example, suppose you read this simple argument: "You do not take care of your dog. Therefore, you will not be able to accept the responsibility of owning a car." The first step in creating a diagram is to number the statements as they appear (disregarding, at this point, whether they are premises or conclusions).

> [1] You do not take care of your dog. Therefore, [2] you will not be able to accept the responsibility of owning a car.

The passage contains the conclusion indicator "therefore," so we can determine that statement 2 is the conclusion. The next step is to diagram the argument by connecting the premise to the conclusion with an arrow:

1
↓
2

Simple diagram A diagram consisting of a single premise and a single conclusion.

The result is a **simple diagram** consisting of a single premise and a single conclusion. When there is more than one premise, the premises may act independently in support of the conclusion. **Independent premises** are such that the falsity of one does not nullify the support the others give to the conclusion. We can illustrate this by adding other premises to our example:

Independent premises Premises are independent when the falsity of one would not nullify any support the others would give to the conclusion.

> [1] You will not be able to accept the responsibility of owning a car because [2] you do not take care of your dog, [3] you don't clean your room, and [4] you do not handle your money responsibly.

Independent premises can be captured in a **convergent diagram**. Here is the convergent diagram for our example:

Convergent diagram A diagram that reveals the occurrence of independent premises.

2   3   4
↘ ↓ ↙
1

Each of the three premises has its own arrow, because each premise offers independent support for the conclusion. In other words, each premise, by itself, offers a reason to accept the conclusion. Even if one or two of the premises are shown to be false, at least one arrow would remain.

Dependent premises Premises are dependent when they work together to support a conclusion. In other words, the falsity of one dependent premise weakens the support that the other dependent premises give to the conclusion.

There are other ways that premises can act to support a conclusion. **Dependent premises** work together to support a conclusion. In other words, the falsity of one dependent premise weakens the support that the other dependent premises give to the conclusion. For example:

> [1] Lead was found in the paint in that apartment building. [2] Lead poisoning can occur in children who ingest small amounts of lead over a long period of time. Thus, [3] the children living in those apartments should be tested for lead poisoning.

The conclusion, "the children living in those apartments should be tested for lead poisoning," is supported by the two premises *working together*. Each premise depends on the other to offer strong support for the conclusion. Premise 1 tells us that lead was found in the paint in the building, which, *by itself*, doesn't seem to strongly support the conclusion. Similarly, although premise 2 tells us that lead poisoning can occur in children who ingest small amounts of lead over a long period of time, premise 2, *by itself*, doesn't seem to strongly support the conclusion. However, when the two premises are *linked together* their joint information combines to support the conclusion. This is illustrated by the following diagram:

The diagram links premise 1 and premise 2 to show that they work together to support the conclusion. Dependent premises create a **linked diagram**. Notice the difference between a linked diagram and a convergent diagram in which each *independent* premise has its own arrow connecting it to the conclusion.

Linked diagram A diagram that reveals the occurrence of dependent premises.

Let's look at another example:

> [1] The movie version of *The Lord of the Rings* used some of the original dialogue from the books, [2] it used the language Tolkien invented, [3] it used the characters he created, [4] it kept the overall plot, and [5] the settings were the same as in the books. Therefore, [6] the movie trilogy *The Lord of the Rings* captured most of the spirit of the original books.

Here premises 1 through 5 are linked to support the conclusion, that the movies captured most of the spirit of the original books.

It is also possible that one premise supports more than one conclusion. Consider this argument:

> [1] The new movie *Son of Avatar* will be the highest grossing movie in history. Therefore, [2] it is sure to win multiple Academy Awards, and [3] some of the actors will be among the highest paid in the industry. We can also conclude that [4] the director will get to do anything he wants in the near future.

In this passage, one premise is being used to support three separate conclusions, resulting in a **divergent diagram**:

Divergent diagram A diagram that shows a single premise supporting independent conclusions.

Finally, some passages contain a series of arguments, in which a conclusion from one argument becomes a premise in the next one. For example:

> [1] The government just cut taxes and [2] put a freeze on the minimum wage. [3] This combination is sure to create higher unemployment. Of course, [4] that will lead to a drop in gross domestic sales. [5] This will surely cause a recession.

Serial diagram A diagram that shows that a conclusion from one argument is a premise in a second argument.

This results in a **serial diagram**:

Statements 1 and 2 are linked (conjoined) to support 3, which is an intermediate conclusion. Statement 3 then is a premise for statement 4, which is another intermediate conclusion. Finally, 4 is a premise for 5, the conclusion of the argument.

B. DIAGRAMMING EXTENDED ARGUMENTS

Extended arguments can require diagrams that combine two of our diagramming techniques, as in this example:

> [1] Asbestos has been found in many of the recently built homes and apartments in this city. [2] Asbestos has been found to cause cancer in humans. Also, [3] high levels of arsenic have been found in the city's drinking water supply. [4] Arsenic has been found to cause cancer in humans. Thus, [5] we can expect to see a rise in the cancer rate in the coming years.

Statement 1 tells us that asbestos has been found in many of the recently built homes and apartments in this city, which by itself doesn't strongly support the conclusion. On the other hand, statement 2 tells us that asbestos has been found to cause cancer in humans, which again by itself doesn't strongly support the conclusion. By working together, they offer stronger support than each individually. Upon close examination, statements 3 and 4 work similarly to 1 and 2. Our diagram will reflect this analysis.

As the diagram shows, 1 and 2 work together, so they are dependent premises that form a linked diagram when connected to 5 by way of an arrow. Likewise, 3 and 4

work together, so they, too, are dependent premises that form a linked diagram when connected to 5 by way of a separate arrow. Finally, the two arrows indicate the presence of a convergent diagram.

Extended arguments often require diagrams that combine more than two of our diagramming techniques, as in this example:

> [1] My working overtime each day for the next three weeks, and [2] my coming in on weekends, [3] will guarantee that I will finish the report early. Of course, [4] it is also possible that working a normal 40-hour week will lead to the same result. Therefore, [5] finishing the report early will lead to a bigger paycheck. [6] It could also lead to a promotion.

(A) The arrow from 1 and 2 to 3 indicates the presence of a linked diagram (dependent premises).
(B) The two arrows, one from 1 and 2 to 3, and the other from 4 to 3, indicate the presence of a convergent diagram (independent premises).
(C) The two arrows, one leading from 3 to 5, and the other from 3 to 6, indicate the presence of a divergent diagram.
(D) The entire diagram reveals the presence of a serial diagram.

Finally, if we add or change material from a passage, then our diagram has to reflect that change. We place the new statement in brackets to distinguish it from the given information. Here is an example:

> [1] The idea that space and time may form a closed surface without boundary also has profound implications for the role of God in the affairs of the universe. [2] So long as the universe had a beginning, we could suppose it had a creator. But [3] if the universe is really completely self-contained, having no boundary or edge, it would have neither beginning nor end; [4] it would simply be. What place, then, for a creator?   Stephen W. Hawking, *A Brief History of Time*

The final sentence of the passage is a rhetorical question that we can rewrite as a numbered statement:

> [5] [There is no place for a creator.]

We can now diagram the argument.

2. For the last 10 years the best picture Oscar has gone to a drama. A comedy has no chance of winning the Oscar for best picture this year.

3. An independent candidate will never win the presidency of the United States. This is because the two-party system of Democrats and Republicans is too powerful to let a third party get any wide base of support among the American voting public.

4. That God cannot lie is no advantage to your argument, because it is no proof that priests can not, or that the Bible does not.

Thomas Paine

⭐ 5. Sue hesitated; and then impulsively told the woman that her husband and herself had been unhappy in their first marriages, after which, terrified at the thought of a second irrevocable union, and lest the conditions of the contract should kill their love, yet wishing to be together, they had literally not found the courage to repeat it, though they had attempted it two or three times. Therefore, though in her own sense of the words she was a married woman, in the landlady's sense she was not.

Thomas Hardy, *Jude the Obscure*

6. Since there is biological evidence that the genetic characteristics for nonviolence have been selected over time by the species, we should see an overall decrease in violence among humans worldwide in the coming centuries.

7. Project Gutenberg eBooks are often created from several printed editions, all of which are confirmed as Public Domain in the U.S. unless a copyright notice is included. Thus, we do not necessarily keep eBooks in compliance with any particular paper edition.

Project Gutenberg website

8. Stepan Arkadyevitch had learned easily at school, thanks to his excellent abilities, but he had been idle and mischievous, and therefore was one of the lowest in his class.

Leo Tolstoy, *Anna Karenina*

⭐ 9. We are intelligent beings: intelligent beings cannot have been formed by a crude, blind, insensible being: there is certainly some difference between the ideas of Newton and the dung of a mule. Newton's intelligence, therefore, came from another intelligence.

Voltaire, *Philosophical Dictionary*

10. Kedah Health Department employees who smoke will not be eligible for the annual excellence performance awards even if they do well in their work. The Director said, "Thirty percent or 3,900 of our 13,000 department personnel are smokers. As staff representing a health department, they should act as role models. Thus, I hope that they will quit smoking."

Embun Majid, "Health Department Snuffs Out Excellence Awards for Smokers"

11. The '80s debaters tended to forget that the teaching of vernacular literature is quite a recent development in the long history of the university. (The same could be said about the relatively recent invention of art history or music as an academic research discipline.) So it is not surprising that, in such a short

time, we have not yet settled on the right or commonly agreed upon way to
go about it.   Robert Pippin, "In Defense of Naïve Reading"

12. The officer shook his head, perplexed. The handprint on the wall had not been
made by the librarian himself; there hadn't been blood on his hands. Besides,
the print did not match his, and it was a strange print, the whorls of the fingers
unusually worn. It would have been easy to match, except that they'd never
recorded one like it.   Elizabeth Kostrova, *The Historian*

⭐13. After supper she got out her book and learned me about Moses and the Bulrushers, and I was in a sweat to find out all about him; but by and by she let it
out that Moses had been dead a considerable long time; so then I didn't care
no more about him, because I don't take no stock in dead people.

                                                  Mark Twain, *Huckleberry Finn*

14. To me the similarities between the *Titanic* and *Challenger* tragedies are
uncanny. Both disasters could have been prevented if those in charge had
heeded the warnings of those who knew. In both cases, materials failed due to
thermal effects. For the *Titanic*, the steel of her hull was below its ductile-to-
brittle transition temperature; and for the *Challenger*, the rubber of the O-rings
lost pliability in sub-freezing temperatures. And both tragedies provoked a
worldwide discussion about the appropriate role for technology.

                                                  Mark E. Eberhart, *Why Things Break*

15. Your friends praise your abilities to the skies, submit to you in argument, and
seem to have the greatest deference for you; but, though they may ask it, you
never find them following your advice upon their own affairs; nor allowing
you to manage your own, without thinking that you should follow theirs. Thus,
in fact, they all think themselves wiser than you, whatever they may say.

                                   Viscount William Lamb Melbourne, *Lord Melbourne's Papers*

16. I stated above that I am among those who reject the notion that a full-fledged
human soul comes into being the moment that a human sperm joins a human
ovum to form a human zygote. By contrast, I believe that a human soul—and,
by the way, it is my aim in this book to make clear what I mean by this slippery, shifting word, often rife with religious connotations, but here not having
any—comes slowly into being over the course of years of development. It may
sound crass to put it this way, but I would like to suggest, at least metaphori-
cally, a numerical scale of "degrees of souledness." We can initially imagine it
as running from 0 to 100, and the units of this scale can be called, just for the
fun of it, "hunekers." Thus you and I, dear reader, both possess 100 hunekers
of souledness, or thereabouts.   Douglas Hofstadter, *I Am a Strange Loop*

⭐17. It may be no accident that sexual life forms dominate our planet. True, bacteria account for the largest number of individuals, and the greatest biomass.
But by any reasonable measures of species diversity, or individual complexity,

Video Tutorial: 3BII
Exercise #17

size, or intelligence, sexual species are paramount. And of the life forms that reproduce sexually, the ones whose reproduction is mediated by mate choice show the greatest biodiversity and the greatest complexity. Without sexual selection, evolution seems limited to the very small, the transient, the parasitic, the bacterial, and the brainless. For this reason, I think that sexual selection may be evolution's most creative force.

Geoffrey Miller, The Mating Mind

18. I don't know when children stop dreaming. But I do know when hope starts leaking away, because I've seen it happen. Over the years, I have spent a lot of time talking with school children of all ages. And I have seen the cloud of resignation move across their eyes as they travel through school without making any real progress. They know they are slipping through the net into the huge underclass that our society seems willing to tolerate. We must educate our children. And if we do, I believe that will be enough.

Alan Page, Minnesota Supreme Court Justice, NFL Hall of Fame Induction Speech

19. The Keynesian argument that if the private sector lacks confidence to spend, the government should spend is not wrong. But Keynes did not spell out where the government should spend. Nor did he envisage that lobbyists can influence government spending to be wasteful. Hence, every prophet can be used by his or her successors to prove their own points of view. This is religion, not science.

Andrew Sheng, "Economics Is a Religion, Not a Science"

III. Identify and number the premises and conclusions in the following passages, and then diagram the argument.

1. We will soon get more oil from areas of our country that were once protected by law. However, it has been projected that the amount of oil will be too small to have any serious effect on the overall oil supply. Although coal production will be raised, the amount will not meet the increased amount of energy that will be needed. In addition, new legislation has eliminated the requirement for the automobile industry to increase gas mileage in their new cars. So, it seems that gasoline prices will not go down in the near future.

Answer: [1] We will soon get more oil from areas of our country that were once protected by law. However, [2] it has been projected that the amount of oil will be too small to have any serious effect on the overall oil supply. [3] Although coal production will be raised, [4] the amount will not meet the increased amount of energy that will be needed. In addition, [5] new legislation has eliminated the requirement for the automobile industry to increase gas mileage in their new cars. So, [6] it seems that gasoline prices will not go down in the near future.

2. Driving a car without a seatbelt is dangerous. Statistics show you are 10 times more likely to be injured in an accident if you are not wearing a seat belt. Besides, in our state you can get fined $100 if you are caught not wearing one. You ought to wear one even if you are driving a short distance.

3. Jean studied at least 10 hours for the exam, and she got an A. Bill studied at least 10 hours for the exam, and he got an A. Sue studied at least 10 hours for the exam, and she got an A. Jim studied at least 10 hours for the exam. Jim probably got an A on the exam.

4. Fathers and mothers have lost the idea that the highest aspiration they might have for their children is for them to be wise—as priests, prophets or philosophers are wise. Specialized competence and success are all that they can imagine.

    Allan Bloom, *The Closing of the American Mind*

⭐ 5. Death is not an event in life: we do not live to experience death. If we take eternity to mean not infinite temporal duration but timelessness, then eternal life belongs to those who live in the present. Our life has no end in just the way in which our visual field has no limits.

    Ludwig Wittgenstein, *Tractatus Logico-Philosophicus*

Video Tutorial: 3BIII
Exercise #5

6. But while college debt has proven a financial chokehold for some people, a four-year degree is still great insurance, especially in a tough job market: The unemployment rate for people with a bachelor's degree or higher was 4.5 percent in July, compared to 10.1 percent for those with only a high school diploma.

    Allison Linn, "Is It Worth It to Go to College?"

7. We measure the success of schools not by the kinds of human beings they promote, but by whatever increases in reading scores they chalk up. We have allowed quantitative standards, so central to the adult economic system, to become the principal yardstick for our definition of our children's worth.

    Kenneth Keniston, "The 11-Year-Olds of Today Are the Computer Terminals of Tomorrow"

8. We have discovered dozens and dozens of artfully disguised items that have posed a risk. The threats are real, the stakes are high, and we must prevail. When it comes to the Transportation Security Administration (TSA), we are the last line of defense. Therefore, full-body scanners and enhanced pat-downs are necessary to catch nonmetallic security threats.

    John Pistole, Head of the TSA, quoted at Washingtonpost.com

⭐ 9. Because there is a law such as gravity, the universe can and will create itself from nothing. Spontaneous creation is the reason there is something rather than nothing, why the universe exists, why we exist. It is not necessary to invoke God to light the blue touch paper and set the universe going.

    Stephen Hawking and Leonard Mlodinow, *The Grand Design*

Video Tutorial: 3BIII
Exercise #9

10. Because robots can stage attacks with little immediate risk to the people who operate them, opponents say that robot warriors lower the barriers to warfare, potentially making nations more trigger-happy and leading to a new technological arms race. "Wars will be started very easily and with minimal costs" as automation increases, predicted Wendell Wallach, a scholar at the Yale Interdisciplinary Center for Bioethics and chairman of its technology and ethics study group.   John Markoff, "U.S. Military Recruits Robots for Combat"

11. Although we like to think of young children's lives as free of troubles, they are in fact filled with disappointment and frustration. Children wish for so much, but can arrange so little of their own lives, which are so often dominated by adults without sympathy for the children's priorities. That is why children have a much greater need for daydreams than adults do. And because their lives have been relatively limited they have a greater need for material from which to form daydreams.   Bruno Bettelheim, "Children and Television"

12. I know that this world exists. That I am placed in it like my eye in its visual field. That something about it is problematic, which we call its meaning. This meaning does not lie in it but outside of it. That life is the world. That my will penetrates the world. That my will is good or evil. Therefore that good and evil are somehow connected with the meaning of the world.

    Ludwig Wittgenstein, *Journal*

⭐ 13. The line that I am urging as today's conventional wisdom is not a denial of consciousness. It is often called, with more reason, a repudiation of mind. It is indeed a repudiation of mind as a second substance, over and above body. It can be described less harshly as an identification of mind with some of the faculties, states, and activities of the body. Mental states and events are a special subclass of the states and events of the human or animal body.

    Willard Van Orman Quine, *Quiddities*

14. During the next few decades, many Haitian species of plants and animals will become extinct because the forests where they live, which originally covered the entire country, are nearly gone. The decline of frogs in particular, because they are especially vulnerable, is a biological early-warning signal of a dangerously deteriorating environment. When frogs start disappearing, other species will follow and the Haitian people will suffer, as well, from this environmental catastrophe.   "Scientists: Haiti's Wildlife Faces Mass Extinction," *Our Amazing Planet*

15. In fact, in a backward way, Vick has been the best thing to happen to pit bulls. "It's very true," says John Goodwin of the Humane Society of the United States. "For the big picture, Michael has been a tipping point. Since his case, there have been 30 new laws enacted all over the country toughening dog fighting penalties. Raids [on dog fighting rings] were up twice as much in 2008—after Vick—as they were in 2006, before him. There's much more awareness. People see it now and call it in."   Rick Reilly, "Time to Forgive Vick Is Here"

16. Institutionalized rejection of difference is an absolute necessity in a profit economy which needs outsiders as surplus people. As members of such an economy, we have all been programmed to respond to the human differences between us with fear and loathing and to handle that difference in one of three ways: ignore it, and if that is not possible, copy it if we think it is dominant, or destroy it if we think it is subordinate. But we have no patterns for relating across our human differences as equals. As a result, those differences have been misnamed and misused in the service of separation and confusion.

Audre Lorde, "Age, Race, Class, and Sex: Women Redefining Difference"

⭐ 17. It has only just begun to dawn on us that in our own language alone, not to speak of its many companions, the past history of humanity is spread out in an imperishable map, just as the history of the mineral earth lies embedded in the layers of its outer crust. But there is this difference between the record of the rocks and the secrets which are hidden in language: whereas the former can only give us knowledge of outward dead things—such as forgotten seas and the bodily shapes of prehistoric animals—language has preserved for us the inner living history of man's soul. It reveals the evolution of consciousness.

Owen Barfield, *History in English Words*

18. Logic is not concerned with human behavior in the same sense that physiology, psychology, and social sciences are concerned with it. These sciences formulate laws or universal statements which have as their subject matter human activities as processes in time. Logic, on the contrary, is concerned with relations between factual sentences (or thoughts). If logic ever discusses the truth of factual sentences it does so only conditionally, somewhat as follows: if such-and-such a sentence is true, then such-and-such another sentence is true. Logic itself does not decide whether the first sentence is true, but surrenders that question to one or the other of the empirical sciences.

Rudolf Carnap, "Logic"

19. We learned that in addition to the noxious chemicals in our pricey blowouts, there were sketchy ingredients in just about everything we used—from our daily shampooing to our biweekly manicures. We also learned that only 11 percent of the 10,500 ingredients determined by the Food and Drug Administration (FDA) to be in use by the cosmetics industry have been tested for safety by a publicly accountable agency. Of the ones we do know about, some are flat-out dangerous to our health, others are questionable at best, and most are doing almost nothing to improve the quality, feel, and health of our skin and hair. So not only are these products wreaking some unspeakable havoc on our bodies, they're also making us look worse.

Siobhan O'Connor and Alexandra Spunt, *No More Dirty Looks*

20. All logical truth and all truths that logic can warrant must turn upon meaning in the sense of intension. Because logic and the logically certifiable comprise only such facts as are independent of all particular experience and are capable

of being known with certainty merely through clear and cogent thinking. The same must hold of any analytic truth: if it is capable of being known by taking thought about it, then it must be independent of meaning in the sense of extension and turn upon meanings only in the sense of intension.

Clarence Lewis, "The Modes of Meaning"

⭐ 21. It is a commonplace that all religion expresses itself in mythological or metaphorical terms; it says one thing and means another; it uses imagery to convey truth. But the crucial fact about religion is not that it is metaphor, but that it is unconscious metaphor. No one can express any thought without using metaphors, but this does not reduce all philosophy and science to religion, because the scientist knows that his metaphors are merely metaphors and that the truth is something other than the imagery by which it is expressed, whereas in religion the truth and the imagery are identified. To repeat the Creed as a religious act it is necessary not to add "All this I believe in a symbolical or figurative sense": to make that addition is to convert religion into philosophy.

R. G. Collingwood, "Outlines of a Philosophy of Art"

22. Leprosy is a disease caused by the bacteria *mycobacterium leprae*, which causes damage to the skin and the peripheral nervous system. Unfortunately, the history of leprosy and its interaction with man is one of suffering and misunderstanding. The newest research suggests that at least as early as 4000 B.C. individuals had been infected with the bacteria, while the first known written reference to the disease was found on Egyptian papyrus in about 1550 B.C. The disease was well recognized in ancient China, Egypt, and India, and there are several references to the disease in the Bible. Because the disease was poorly understood, very disfiguring, slow to show symptoms, and had no known treatment, many cultures thought the disease was a curse or punishment from the gods. Consequently, leprosy was left to be "treated" by priests or holy men, not physicians.

Adapted from "Leprosy (Hansen's Disease)," MedicineNet, Inc.

23. The biggest misconception when discussing Los Angeles' attractiveness as a market is thinking every NFL owner would salivate at the prospect of having a team in the second biggest media market in the country and the entertainment capital of the world. That is simply not the case in the NFL's egalitarian model, in which all national revenues are equally divided among the 32 teams. In the NFL, the amount of money a team can generate from its stadium with as little risk as possible is what NFL owners are after. So if they can get their state, city, or county to completely subsidize the stadium while giving 100 percent of the revenue to the owner, as is the case in many NFL cities, that's the best possible deal. That would never happen in Los Angeles, and therefore moving an NFL team to L.A. has never made financial sense for an owner with a better deal in a smaller market. Arash Markazi, "A 16-Year Rocky Relationship"

Summary

Study Materials

- Diagramming premises and conclusions displays the relationships between all the parts of an argument.
- The first step in diagramming an argument is to number the statements as they appear in the argument. The next step is to diagram the relationships by connecting the premises to the conclusion with an arrow.
- Simple diagram: A diagram consisting of a single premise and a single conclusion.
- Premises are independent when the falsity of any one would not nullify the support the others give to the conclusion.
- Convergent diagram: Reveals the occurrence of independent premises.
- Dependent premises work together to support a conclusion. In other words, the falsity of one dependent premise weakens the support that the other dependent premises give to the conclusion.
- Linked diagram: Reveals the occurrence of dependent premises.
- Divergent diagram: Shows a single premise used to support independent conclusions.
- Serial diagram: Shows a conclusion from one argument that becomes a premise in a second argument.

KEY TERMS

LOGIC CHALLENGE: THE TRAIN TO VEGAS

You live in Los Angeles and decide to spend New Year's Eve in Las Vegas. You board the nonstop express train and consult the timetable for departures and arrivals. You read that it takes exactly 5 hours to get from Los Angeles to Las Vegas and the same length of time for the return trip. You also read that a train leaves each of the two cities every hour on the hour, and a train arrives in each of the two cities every hour on the hour. Now suppose for the sake of accuracy and precision of reasoning that every train runs perfectly on time. (Yes, this is a fantasy.)

The express trains have their own private set of tracks, so you will only pass those express trains that left Las Vegas. You decide to count the number of trains that you will pass on the trip. Your train leaves at 3:00 PM, and just as you are departing, sure enough a train from Las Vegas arrives. You begin counting with the train that just arrived, so it is train number 1.

How many express trains will you see by the end of your trip?

Chapter 4

Informal Fallacies

Digital homework exercises for this chapter are available in your instructor's online course. For information on how to access these resources, please visit **www.oup.com/he/baronett5e**.

We run into arguments everywhere—even when we are not looking for them. For example, you might be watching television, listening to the news, or watching a sporting event when you hear the following:

> For a number of years, seven-time Tour de France bicycle champion Lance Armstrong has been accused of using performance-enhancing drugs. An article in the French newspaper *L'Equipe* alleged that six of Armstrong's urine samples from the 1999 race were retested and found to contain the drug erythropoietin (EPO). If EPO is injected it can give an athlete a tremendous performance boost; however, it had already been banned by the Tour de France in 1999.
>
> Both the newspaper that published the report and the Tour de France race are owned by Amaury Sport Organization (ASO). In his response to the accusation by the newspaper, Armstrong said, "My question is how ASO can own the paper and the race."
>
> Adapted from Philip Hersh, "Armstrong, Defenders Not Forthright," *Chicago Tribune*

Armstrong's response avoided the question of his possible use of the drug, and shifted any potential wrongdoing to ASO. He deflected our attention away by implying that since the newspaper and the race have the same owner, they have formed a conspiracy against him. We now know that Armstrong finally admitted to using illegal doping techniques, and he has been stripped of all his Tour de France titles. Nevertheless, when asked how he felt about winning the races illegally, Armstrong said, "I feel that I won the races. . . . I know that is not a popular answer, but the reality is that . . . it was just a messy time," referring to widespread doping in cycling. "It was basically an arms race, and we all played ball that way." Armstrong tried to justify his behavior by saying that *because everyone did it*, he still considers himself the winner of the races.

We often encounter arguments that appear to be correct, but on close inspection they lack real merit. Trying to pin down why can be a challenge—or part of the game. Here is an example from a popular television show:

> *Homer:* Not a bear in sight. The Bear Patrol must be working like a charm!
> *Lisa:* That's specious reasoning, Dad.
> *Homer:* Thank you, dear.
> *Lisa:* By your logic I could claim that this rock keeps tigers away.
> *Homer:* Oh, how does it work?
> *Lisa:* It doesn't work.
> *Homer:* Uh-huh.
> *Lisa:* It's just a stupid rock.
> *Homer:* Uh-huh.
> *Lisa:* But I don't see any tigers around, do you?
> *Homer:* Lisa, I want to buy your rock.
>
> From "Much Apu About Nothing," *The Simpsons*

Homer has committed a fallacy, and he is not going to give it up without a fight.

The term "fallacy" derives from a Latin word meaning *to deceive*. (Another label for fallacies is revealing—"*non sequitur*," which literally means *it does not follow*.) Fallacious arguments are often misleading or deceptive, but they can also be unintentional. They can also be intentionally comic, like in *The Simpsons*. Clearly fallacious reasoning is often used in literature, movies, and jokes to point out the irrelevancy or absurdity of a statement or an argument.

Arguments purport to offer evidence for a conclusion, but they can fail, and some special cases of failure are classified as fallacies. A **formal fallacy** is a logical error that occurs in the form or structure of an argument. Formal fallacies are restricted to deductive arguments, and an understanding of deductive analysis and logical form makes it possible to recognize and understand them. (Formal fallacies were introduced in Chapter 1. They are developed in detail in Chapters 6, 7, and 8.) An **informal fallacy** is a mistake in reasoning that occurs in ordinary language and concerns the content of the argument rather than its form. Informal fallacies include mistakes of relevance, assumption, ambiguity, and diversion. In addition, some informal fallacies are persuasive because they involve fear, anger, pity, or even admiration. If we adopt fallacious reasoning, then we reduce our ability to reason properly, and if we accept other people's fallacious reasoning, then we erode our ability to critically assess arguments.

Good arguments have premises that are relevant and establish logical, reasonable ties to the conclusion. However, some informal fallacies use irrelevant premises. Although these fallacies have reasoning flaws, they can be psychologically persuasive. Other kinds of fallacies rely on assumptions that have not been justified. These fallacies assume the truth of a claim that has not been supported. When we uncover the unwarranted assumption, then we show the fallacious nature of the argument. Some fallacies misuse generalizations. The mistakes include making a generalization

Formal fallacy A logical error that occurs in the form or structure of an argument; it is restricted to deductive arguments.

Informal fallacy A mistake in reasoning that occurs in ordinary language and concerns the content of the argument rather than its form.

on the basis of insufficient or biased evidence. Other fallacies misapply the methods of science to make unsubstantiated cause-effect claims. We shall meet them all in this chapter.

The classification of fallacies into small groups is meant to help you recognize similarities among certain fallacies. These groups rely on the concept of "family resemblance," where the members of a group share some common characteristic. However, since this is *not* meant to be a rigid method of categorization, you can expect to see some general concepts, such as relevance, appear in more than one group. For example, we talked earlier about good arguments having *relevant* premises. But fallacies can suffer from an "irrelevancy" in many different ways. Therefore, the use of small groups is meant to help you to recognize a characteristic common to all members of a group, and to distinguish the specific characteristics of each group member.

A. WHY STUDY FALLACIES?

If you are aware of the existence of fallacies, and understand the specific nature of fallacious reasoning, then you can recognize examples in everyday life. Recognition, and the ability to expose the reasoning flaws in fallacies, arms you against the psychological power of persuasion that often accompanies fallacious reasoning.

Fallacies are instances of flawed reasoning whose premises do not offer good grounds for believing the conclusion. Although none of us wants to believe what is false, we are all, on occasion, subject to the powers of persuasion. We must guard against such things as deception, the prejudice of stereotypes, and the acceptance of ungrounded beliefs. Unfortunately, it is often relatively easy and common to accept poor reasoning for a strongly held belief. But it is not enough to have strong beliefs; we must also have strong reasons and strong arguments to support our beliefs. By studying fallacies you will be less likely to make these mistakes. Since we are all inundated with information on a daily basis, we need to have critical thinking skills that we can apply naturally and consistently, whether in the area of politics, advertisements, work, school, or even personal relationships.

Each type of fallacy has a specific flaw, yet there are some general aspects that allow us to group related fallacies together. Knowing how to recognize and analyze instances of fallacies protects us from their illogical lure and gives us a better understanding and appreciation of instances of good reasoning.

B. FALLACIES BASED ON PERSONAL ATTACKS OR EMOTIONAL APPEALS

Both the *truth of a statement* and the *strength of an argument* should be judged on objective grounds. We can reject a *statement* if we have credible, objective evidence that contradicts the claim. However, we should *not* reject a statement merely because we have a strong opinion against it. We need to back up our rejection with factual evidence. We can reject an *argument* if we base our criticism on logical analysis and truth value analysis. For example, the argument might be *invalid* (deductive) or *weak* (inductive). On the other hand, the argument might be valid but *unsound*, or else it might be strong but *uncogent*. However, when an argument is rejected based solely on an *attack against the person* making the argument, not on the merits of the argument itself, then a fallacy occurs. We will explore four types of fallacies based on personal attacks and then look at three types of fallacious appeals to emotion that attempt to get us to accept a conclusion. These kinds of arguments employ psychological tactics that draw on group solidarity, or the desire to belong to a group.

Fallacies Based on Personal Attacks

1. AD HOMINEM ABUSIVE

The **ad hominem abusive** fallacy is distinguished by an attack on alleged character flaws of a person instead of the person's argument. ("*Ad hominem*" means *against the person*.) Generally speaking, a person's character is irrelevant to the determination of the truth or falsity of her claims, or the strength of her argument. Clear cases of *ad hominem* abusive are not difficult to recognize. The personal attacks use either spoken or written derogatory and abusive terms such as *arrogant, overrated, stupid, liar, lazy, radical*, and *loser*. The verbal or written insults rely on disrespectful language or scornful abuse whose intent is to harm a person's credibility or reputation. These character assassinations divert attention away from the logical determination of the strength of an argument, and instead denigrate the character of the person making the argument. Here are some examples:

> **Ad hominem abusive**
> The fallacy is distinguished by an attack on alleged character flaws of a person instead of the person's argument.

- You should not believe what he says about our economy because he is a left-leaning, card-carrying radical.
- She is old, out of touch with reality, and belongs in a loony bin. So, you cannot accept her advice on marriage.
- Don't listen to his criticism of our senator. After all, he is too young and probably experimented with illegal drugs when he was in college.

In all these cases, the reason to reject someone's statement or position is based on irrelevant information. In the first example, an economic argument should be judged on the merits of the advice and strength of the argument presented, not by vague labels denigrating a person's character. In the second example, the age of the person offering advice has no bearing on the strength or weakness of her argument. Furthermore, no evidence is given to show that the person has any mental impairment that might affect her reasoning. Finally, in the third example, the criticism of the senator should be judged on the logical strength of the arguments and the factual nature of the claims. The person's age or alleged college experiences are irrelevant to the merits of his argument. In addition, these kinds of personal attacks typically contain no supporting evidence. All of the fallacies fail because they avoid a logical analysis of whether the opponent's arguments are valid or invalid (deductive), strong or weak (inductive). The fallacies also avoid a truth value analysis of whether the opponent's premises are true or false, and whether the arguments are sound or unsound, cogent or uncogent.

2. AD HOMINEM CIRCUMSTANTIAL

Ad hominem circumstantial When someone's argument is rejected based on the circumstances of the person's life.

The ***ad hominem* circumstantial** fallacy occurs when someone's argument is rejected based on the circumstances of a person's life. Circumstances are different from character. For example, political affiliation, educational institution, place of birth, religious affiliation, and income are circumstances connected to people's lives. When we insinuate that someone's circumstances dictate the truth or falsity of their claims or the strength of their arguments, then we are once again attacking the person rather than the claim. These kinds of attacks also include the use of negative stereotypes, such as racial, sexual, or religious stereotypes, and can be subtle or overtly dismissive. However, they do not advance anyone's cause. A reference to any kind of stereotype is irrelevant to the determination of the strength of an argument. Here is an example:

> Of course Senator Hilltop argues that my administration's tax proposals are bad for the country. But since her party lost the last election, her opinions have no credibility.

The passage clearly shows that Senator Hilltop's reasons for why she is against the tax proposals, whether good or not, are not even being considered. This is an obvious instance of *ad hominem* circumstantial; it attacks the senator's party affiliation instead of her argument.

The following two arguments illustrate the same point:

- You told us why you are against raising taxes. But we know the real reason is that you are a billionaire, and you want to hold on to as much of your money as you can.
- I heard your argument why you are against euthanasia. But you failed to point out the real reason: You are a physician, so you make money only if terminally ill people are kept alive as long as possible.

In the first example, no details of the argument against raising taxes are addressed. Instead, the rejection of the argument rests entirely on the person's wealth. In the second example, the physician's argument is rejected, not by any logical analysis or counterexample, but simply by the circumstances of the person being a physician.

3. POISONING THE WELL

Poisoning the well The fallacy occurs when a person is attacked *before* she has a chance to present her case.

A third version of *ad hominem* argument, called **poisoning the well**, occurs when a person is attacked *before* she has a chance to present her case. The attacker mentions something about the opponent's character or life and uses that information to warn the audience not to believe anything they hear or read. For example:

> Before you read her article "Stop All Wars," you should know that she was arrested six times for protesting in front of the Pentagon and White House. She also has been investigated by the FBI for possible ties to peace movements in other countries, some of which resulted in violence. It is crystal clear that these kinds of people are dangerous and want to destroy our Constitution and take away our basic freedoms. We must not let them.

As illustrated by the passage, the fallacy uses abusive or circumstantial evidence to paint a negative opinion of someone before that person has a chance to make her case. This can be an effective way to influence an audience, but it has no logical credibility.

4. TU QUOQUE

The fourth type of *ad hominem* fallacy is known as **tu quoque** (meaning *you too* or *look who's talking*). It is distinguished by the specific attempt of one person to avoid the issue at hand by claiming the other person is a hypocrite. In other words, the fallacy occurs when someone points to the discrepancy between another person's *claim* and *actions* as a basis for discrediting the other person's *claim*. For example:

> You have been lecturing me about not joining a gang. But Dad, you were a gang member, and you never went to jail. So, I'll make my own decision about joining a gang.

The premises are used to imply the following: *Dad, you are a hypocrite.* This result is then used to reject the dad's arguments: *Because you are a hypocrite, I can disregard your lectures.* As we can see from the reconstructed argument, the conclusion is the result of a *tu quoque* fallacy. The fallacy occurs because the argument attacks the dad, not the dad's arguments.

Another example comes from the political world. If a U.S. senator criticizes the human rights failings of China by offering a detailed description of recorded UN inquiries, a Chinese representative might say the following:

> The senator should look in his own backyard. What about the complete disregard of the universal rights of people who the U.S. government incarcerates without any recourse to courts or a lawyer? What about the U.S. policy of spying on its own citizens without a court order? The senator should not throw stones when he lives in a glass house. Let me remind him that "whoever is without sin let him cast the first stone."

Other than stringing together a number of clichés, this response offers no rational rebuttal of the assertions of human rights violations.

Instances of *tu quoque* fallacies occur quite often in personal arguments. For example, a child might say the following:

> Mom, I don't know why you keep pressuring me to give up smoking. You keep showing me statistics proving that smoking is bad for my health, that it will shorten my life, that it costs too much money. But you started smoking at my age and only recently quit. How can you honestly tell me to stop?

Since there are many good reasons to support the conclusion that someone should stop smoking, these reasons must be rationally argued against. To attack the person making the argument rather than the argument is to commit the fallacy.

Ad hominem fallacies follow a similar pattern:

a. Person X presents an argument.
b. Person Y attacks the character or circumstances of person X.
c. Based solely on the attack against person X, person Y rejects person X's argument.

Tu quoque The fallacy is distinguished by the specific attempt of one person to avoid the issue at hand by claiming the other person is a hypocrite.

The general pattern illustrates the importance of recognizing that any criticism of a person's argument should be restricted to their argument and should not be based on *ad hominem* attacks. (The pattern is slightly different for *poisoning the well* fallacies, where the person under attack has yet to make her argument.) All *ad hominem* fallacies rest on the same kind of reasoning errors—the rejection of an opponent's argument by criticizing a person's character or circumstances, and the absence of any logical or factual analysis of the opponent's argument.

When the fallacy does not occur: There are some instances where an argument might appear to commit an *ad hominem* fallacy but it does not. For example, if someone has previously been exposed as a liar based on contradictions in statements given under oath, then there are objective grounds for suspicion about any current or future *statements*. Likewise, if the person presents an argument, we might have reason to question the accuracy of some of his premises. In that case, pointing out specific instances of an untrustworthy character would not be fallacious since there are objective grounds for doubting the person's claims. It is important to acknowledge that by rejecting a known liar's claim we are *not* saying that his claims are in fact false; we are simply saying that we have a good reason not to believe him.

Another exception is when someone's argument is *not* under consideration, but his or her character is being described. For example:

> Bernard Madoff was guilty of one of the most infamous financial frauds in history. The evidence against him was so strong that he pled guilty to eleven felonies, including money laundering, perjury, and wire fraud. The perjury charge means that he is a liar. He is also a cheat and a person without conscience, with no sympathy for his victims. By any moral sense, Madoff is a most despicable character.

Although the passage does conclude something about Madoff's character, it *does not* reject any of Madoff's arguments. Thus, it is not an instance of an *ad hominem* argument.

Fallacies Based on Emotional Appeals

Some arguments rely solely on the arousal of a strong emotional state or psychological reaction to get us to accept a conclusion. This fallacious tactic has been used by tyrants and bigots throughout history, with devastating social effects. It often appeals to a mob mentality, an "us against them" attitude, with a fixation on fear or hate. Exposing the fallacy can sometimes be the first step in defeating this potentially harmful social ill.

The first type of appeal to emotion that we will cover relies on the desire to belong to a group that is admired, or appeal to the people. This tactic is used effectively by many advertisements. The next kind of appeal to emotion covered relies exclusively on our sense of pity and mercy. Finally, we will address an appeal to emotion that relies on fear or the heavy hand of force to sway people to agree to a conclusion they might not otherwise accept.

5. APPEAL TO THE PEOPLE

The fallacy of **appeal to the people** occurs when an argument manipulates a psychological need or desire, such as the desire to belong to a popular group, or the need for group solidarity, so that the reader or listener will accept the conclusion. However, the avoidance of objective evidence in favor of an emotional response defeats the goal of a rational investigation of truth. We will look at three forms of the fallacy.

The first form makes an emotional appeal based on the psychological force of *group solidarity*. An arguer who uses an emotional response based on the power of one's connection to a group is also known to be "rallying the troops." Appeals to the people are usually laced with emotionally charged words that arouse strong feelings for or against some deep-seated belief. For example:

> We must not let our country be taken over by illegal aliens. After all, they knowingly and brazenly broke the law by entering illegally, so they are nothing but criminals. They will continue to flout our laws, steal our jobs, and threaten our very way of life.

The passage has a series of emotionally charged phrases: "brazenly broke the law," "nothing but criminals," "flout our laws," and "threaten our very way of life." This kind of emotional appeal can be dangerous because mob psychology is often violent. In groups, people will often do things they would not do alone. The group offers a psychological protective shield that insulates individual members from having to think for themselves. The phrase "to run amok" captures the irrational aspect of mob mentality.

Political pollsters also use the appeal to the people tactic. They can manipulate poll questions so that the appeal to an emotional response overrides the rational grounds for a person's belief. Here is an example of a rhetorical, or loaded, question:

> Public schoolteachers are demanding a pay raise and threaten to strike if they don't get it. A prolonged strike will jeopardize our children's future. In addition, some economists predict that any substantial pay raise will result in an unbalanced budget, which in turn will lead to an increase in taxes. Although the school year lasts only 180 days, the teachers get paid 12 months a year, whether or not school is in session. So are you for or against a pay raise for public school teachers?

Although the final sentence is a rhetorical question, it is obvious that it is disguised as a statement: *You should be against a pay raise for public schoolteachers.* The language employed is meant to appeal to the emotions of taxpayers and voters. The terms "demanding," "threaten," "prolonged strike," and "jeopardize" are used to evoke a sense of dire consequences and to provoke anger. The argument offers negative consequences of a teachers' pay raise, but only as possibilities, not as facts. Also, the mention of higher taxes serves to fuel the emotions of voters.

A second form of appeal to the people draws on an individual's desire to belong to a popular group. This form of the fallacy is called the *bandwagon effect*. The fallacy derives its name from the emotions involved in joining a movement merely because it is popular (to "jump on the bandwagon"). Advertisements often prey on the appeal

Appeal to the people
The fallacy occurs when an argument manipulates a psychological need or desire, such as the desire to belong to a popular group, or the need for group solidarity, so that the reader or listener will accept the conclusion.

of being included in a popular fad and the pressure of being left out. Here are some examples of the bandwagon effect fallacy:

- More than 80% of families have given up their old landline phones and switched to cell phones. Don't be the last to make the change. Hurry and get yours now and feel the excitement of calling from anywhere.
- The PlayBox 6 is the number one game console in America. Your friends probably own them. Why wait to use theirs? Ask your parents to get you one today.
- Hard Pink Lemonade has captured the taste of adults. Sales have tripled in the last 6 months. But don't take our word for it. Ask your friends. Better yet, get some and be the life of the next party.

Fallacious bandwagon arguments conclude that you should do something simply because "everyone else is doing it."

The third form of the appeal to the people fallacy occurs as a common thread that runs through some advertising campaigns. The idea rests on the desire of some people to belong to an *exclusive* or *elite group*. For example, many people wish to be rich or famous. This is different from the bandwagon effect, in that the desire is *not* to follow the lead of a large group but a small elite group instead. The fallacy occurs when the argument avoids objective evidence in favor of a direct emotional appeal that activates the desire.

Slick ads are created in order to arouse a desire to attain the product. Such products are often displayed being used by an exclusive group: the rich, the beautiful, the successful—in other words, the lucky few. The obvious implication is that if you use this product, you will be transformed into one of the lucky ones. Such ads push psychological buttons: the need to belong to a group, the desire to be respected, the desire to be successful, and so on. Playing upon emotions is a powerful tool that is understood and effectively used by corporations to sell their products. For example:

> You work hard. You deserve more from life. Don't get stuck in a boring routine. Driving the new turbo-charged Zephyer will have everyone looking at you. Get one and turn heads.

The desire to stand out is also powerful motivation, and it is a desire on which many advertisers design their campaigns. Here is another example:

> Why just watch sports? Why not become the athlete you know you are. HardArmour T-shirts. For the athlete deep inside you waiting to get out.

Although the tactics used in appeals to the people can often influence people's behavior, they have no logical credibility.

6. APPEAL TO PITY

Appeal to pity The fallacy results from an exclusive reliance on a sense of pity or mercy for support of a conclusion.

A second type of the fallacious appeal to emotion is the **appeal to pity**, which exclusively relies on a sense of pity or mercy for support of a conclusion. For example, a defense attorney may attempt to get the jury to sympathize with the defendant prior to deliberation. If the defendant is found guilty, then the appeal may be addressed to the judge, asking for a light sentence based on the effects that a harsh sentence would have on the defendant's family. On the other side, the prosecution may appeal to the jury to sympathize with the victim. The prosecutor may also appeal to the judge to consider the emotional devastation inflicted on the victim's family. In this way, she may persuade the judge to sentence the defendant to the maximum penalty allowed by law. However, trials are, ideally, rational decision-making processes whose goals are to weigh evidence objectively. If pity is substituted for evidence and the rule of law, then the judgment is fallacious.

Here is an example:

> Your honor, before you sentence my client for the murder of his parents, I ask you to consider his situation. He is an orphan. Perhaps you can give him the lightest punishment possible.

The premises provide no objective evidence for a light punishment. The argument is ironic since the premises ask the judge to pity the defendant because he is a self-caused orphan.

Many charities arouse a sense of pity, and perhaps even guilt, when they solicit pledges of support. These charities know that people do not always act rationally and in their own best interests. Nevertheless, any cause worthy of support should have rational, legitimate reasons, which, when understood, should be sufficient to get people to give. In addition to evoking our human sense of compassion for those who are suffering, a *legitimate* argument will not have to rely solely on pity to support its conclusion.

7. APPEAL TO FEAR OR FORCE

A third type of the fallacious appeal to emotion relies on fear or the threat of harmful consequences (physical or otherwise) and is called the **appeal to fear or force**. The perceived threat places pressure on a person or group that, when effective, causes the person or group to reluctantly accept a course of action that otherwise would be unacceptable. For example, there are recorded instances where witnesses and jurors have been threatened with physical harm to themselves or to their families if they go against a defendant. In a different setting, it has been revealed that some voters have been pressured into changing their vote by the threat of violence. However, the threat need not be so overt and directly physical. For example, a company may send out the following memo to its employees:

Appeal to fear or force
A threat of harmful consequences (physical or otherwise) used to force acceptance of a course of action that would otherwise be unacceptable.

> If the workers of this company do not agree to a 25% cut in salary, then the company may have to shut its doors. Therefore, the workers of this company must agree to a 25% cut in salary.

The premise is an obvious threat. It does not, by itself, provide objective evidence for the conclusion. If the company is in bad financial shape, then there should be objective evidence to present to the workers that shows that without the pay cut the company would be forced to close. Without this evidence, the threat by the company to close its doors unless its employees take a pay cut results in an instance of the fallacy of appeal to fear or force.

The following example illustrates the same point. A parent may threaten a child with loss of privileges or being grounded in order to achieve desired results:

> You had better get straight A's on your next report card. If you don't, then we will have to punish you. You will not be allowed to go out with your friends for a month.

It is not difficult to imagine perfectly legitimate reasons why students should get good grades. Rational, objective evidence can be used as support for why students should do well in school. However, anytime an overt or implied threat is used to convince someone to make a decision, in the absence of supporting evidence for the conclusion, the rational decision-making process is subverted.

Fallacious appeals to emotion follow a similar pattern:

a. Person A uses psychological methods known to arouse strong emotions: appeals to group solidarity; jumping on the bandwagon; the desire to belong to an admired group; a sense of pity; and fear or the threat of force.
b. Person B is expected to accept the conclusion based solely on the emotional appeal.

The general pattern illustrates the importance of recognizing that when premises are irrelevant they fail to support the conclusion.

Summary of Fallacies Based on Personal Attacks

Fallacies based on personal attacks occur when someone's argument is rejected based solely on an *attack against the person* making the argument, not on the merits of the argument itself.

1. *Ad hominem* **abusive:** The fallacy is distinguished by an attack on alleged character flaws of a person instead of the person's argument.
2. *Ad hominem* **circumstantial:** The fallacy occurs when someone's argument is rejected based on the circumstances of the person's life.
3. **Poisoning the well:** The fallacy occurs when a person is attacked *before* she has a chance to present her case.
4. *Tu quoque:* The fallacy is distinguished by the specific attempt of one person to avoid the issue at hand by claiming the other person is a hypocrite.

Summary of Fallacies Based on Emotional Appeals

Fallacies based on emotional appeals occur when an argument relies solely on the arousal of a strong emotional state or psychological reaction to get a person to accept the conclusion.

5. **Appeal to the people:** The fallacy occurs when an argument manipulates a psychological need or desire, such as the desire to belong to a popular group, or the need for group solidarity, so that the reader or listener will accept the conclusion.

6. **Appeal to pity:** The fallacy results from an exclusive reliance on a sense of pity or mercy for support of a conclusion.

7. **Appeal to fear or force:** The fallacy occurs when a threat of harmful consequences (physical or otherwise) is used to force acceptance of a course of action that would otherwise be unacceptable.

EXERCISES 4B

I. Determine whether each statement is true or false.

Self-Practice
Questions

1. *Tu quoque* is distinguished by the specific attempt of one person to avoid the issue at hand by claiming the other person is a hypocrite.

Answer: True

2. The bandwagon effect occurs when an argument uses character flaws or circumstances of people's lives to reject their claims.

3. The appeal to pity uses rational reasons in support of a controversial position.

4. A threat of harmful consequences (physical or otherwise) used to force acceptance of a course of action that would otherwise be unacceptable is a fallacy of appeal to fear or force.

⭐ 5. An example of the bandwagon effect is when an appeal is made to increase the group solidarity of an elite group.

6. An appeal to pity fallacy results from an exclusive reliance on a sense of pity or mercy for support of a conclusion.

7. An appeal to join an exclusive group is a *tu quoque* fallacy.

8. An *ad hominem* circumstantial fallacy occurs when someone's argument is rejected based on the circumstances of the person's life.

⭐ 9. A poisoning the well fallacy occurs when a person is attacked *before* she has a chance to present her case.

10. A fallacious appeal to emotion occurs when an argument relies solely on the arousal of a strong emotional state or psychological reaction to get a person to accept the conclusion.

II. Read the following passages. If an argument commits a fallacy of a personal attack or an emotional appeal, then identify the specific fallacy. If a passage does not contain a fallacy, then answer "No fallacy." Explain your answers.

1. You just bought that book, but I recommend that you don't read it. Everything he writes is false. All he does is spend time promoting his book on TV, radio talk shows, and in magazines trying to get people interested so it will become a best seller.

Answer: Poisoning the well. The fallacy occurs when a person is attacked *before* he has a chance to present his case.

2. She did not vote in the last election. In fact, she is not even registered to vote. It follows that anything she suggests about how our country should be run cannot possibly be of any concern to us.

3. You spend most of your time in your room reading books. When I was your age, I played all types of sports. So, if you don't start joining some teams, then I won't give you any more money to buy books, and I'll tear up your library card.

Video Tutorial: 4BII
Exercise #4

4. My uncle drinks a six-pack of beer a day, so I couldn't believe it when he lectured me on the dangers of alcohol. He's one to talk! Nothing he says about drinking can be true because he cannot stop drinking himself.

★ 5. My opponent says that he is well qualified for city council. But he failed to tell you that he was arrested twice. Once for protesting the war in Iraq, and once during the Occupy Wall Street demonstrations. It is obvious that he hates our country and is a liar. I urge you, therefore, to reject his candidacy.

6. OLED TVs have set the new standard in television viewing. All we ask is that you go into any of our stores and look at one yourself. We bet that you will join the millions of others who have switched.

7. Maybe you didn't know that she is an orphan. Her outrageous behavior should be excused because of her background.

8. In the past 3 months, you missed work without calling in five times, and each time you couldn't produce a doctor's note. On two occasions in 1 week, you left work early without notifying your supervisor. You fell asleep at your desk and missed two important calls from clients. Given this poor record, we have decided to let you go.

Video Tutorial: 4BII
Exercise #9

★ 9. In that newspaper article, she argued that the works of Charles Darwin caused the world's major religions to reconcile their basic beliefs with the results of science. Of course she would say that. After all, she teaches biology, so she must be an atheist.

10. Our school's football team didn't win any games last year, so if they don't win at least half the games this year we will stop participating in our district's high intermural football program.

11. My aunt just stopped eating meat, and now she is lecturing everyone to give it up. She cites all this stuff from medical journals and other scientific research showing the harmful long-term effects of eating red meat. But she ate red meat most of her life, so why should I listen to her?

12. Mr. Jenkins has submitted a detailed proposal for our city's revitalization project. I happen to know Mr. Jenkins. In my honest opinion, he is argumentative,

inflexible, and highly opinionated. Given these insurmountable obstacles, I must conclude that we should reject his proposal.

⭐ 13. This administration is proposing lots of dangerous ideas. For example, it wants to raise taxes on the wealthy; it wants to expand Medicare and Medicaid coverage to the poor; it wants to cut military spending; it wants to eliminate many capital gains deductions; and it wants to spend more money on government projects. But all their fancy speech and slick arguments are just a smokescreen to hide their true communist intentions. If we don't vote them out of office we will be slaves to their dictatorial regime.

14. You should forget that she spent both of your savings on losing lottery tickets. After all, she is penniless and unemployed.

15. Macrobiotic diets and gluten-free foods are the hottest trends among today's health-conscious and savvy people. Therefore, you should join the smart set.

16. Tomorrow night you will hear the president's budget proposal. It will be the same old, tired economic arguments as the last 4 years. The president has fooled the public for too long with false promises and unrealistic goals. Therefore, if you listen to her carefully, you will see that I am right.

⭐ 17. That physician is a male, so he couldn't possibly know anything about female health problems.

18. Your daughter was caught breaking into the school's computer lab. She said that she wanted to copy some expensive software programs to sell to her friends so she could make some money. We have no choice but to suspend her from school, pending a police investigation.

19. I know you don't want to visit your grandparents, but if you don't go, then you can't go to the concert next month. In fact, you won't be able to see your friends, except in school, for the rest of the semester.

20. She did not do well on the exams; nevertheless, you should give her an A for the course. After all, she is taking 18 credits and is holding down a full-time job.

⭐ 21. Our biology teacher tried to convince us that "creation science" is not an acceptable part of science because it doesn't fit the methods and standards of acceptable science. He is a liar and a bully who likes to see students fail. He tries to intimidate students, so there's no reason to accept his arguments.

22. I know your cousin recommends taking vitamins every day. After all, she's a pharmacist; what do you expect her to tell you?

23. The Snake Charmers have sold out every concert on their latest world tour, and their new single, "Python Mounties," reached No. 1 in the first week of its release. People everywhere are clamoring to get tickets to the upcoming concert. Don't get shut out. Hurry and get yours before your friends beat you to it.

24. You have successfully completed both the written exam and the motor vehicle operation parts as required by the state. Thus, you are eligible to get your driver's license.

⭐ 25. You are about to hear a proposal to clean up the pollution in our local river. The speaker will make some wild claims about health effects, but her evidence is suspect. Of course, she will swear that she is telling you the truth, but don't fall for her stories. It's very important that you reject her proposals.

26. If you don't break off your relationship with him, your mother and I will disinherit you. So, you'd better end the relationship now.

27. You tell me to wear a seat belt when I drive because it will protect me in case I get in an accident. I never see you wear one when you drive, so why should I wear one?

28. Our political party lost the last election, not because of our platform, but because we allowed the opposition to dictate the debate. Now is not the time to be on the defensive. We must not apologize for our beliefs, which, as you will all agree, are based on the core principles of the Founding Fathers, who fought for what they believed was right for the country. Let's not sit back and see liberty destroyed. I expect everyone to take the fight to our opponents.

⭐ 29. Fighting pollution is something everyone can do. All it takes is a few minutes of your time. For example, turn off lights that are not being used and use recycle bins. Try not to waste water. None of these simple guidelines require much time or effort.

30. His reasons for believing that humans do not need a religious basis for morality should be rejected. After all, he is an atheist, so he cannot possibly have anything relevant to say on ethical issues.

31. You need to stop wearing those clothes. Just look at some teen magazines and check out the latest fashions at the mall. No one cool wears that style anymore.

32. Of course you should pay us for protection. Here's why. If you don't, we will have to break your arms, wreck your business, and harass your customers.

⭐ 33. I'm running for school president. A lot of you know me, but perhaps you don't know my opponent. Soon she will tell you why she deserves your vote. But I want to warn you that she is very argumentative, sharply critical, and finds fault with everyone. In fact, I'll bet you that she objects to everything I say. So, stay on guard and don't fall for her negative remarks.

34. You have received this letter because someone loves you. This chain letter has been around the world fifty times. I urge you to send a copy to five close friends. Some people who have broken the chain suffered tragic consequences. So, if you don't want to suffer unnecessarily, you must not break the chain.

35. The committee to reelect Senator Hatfield is meeting this Wednesday. We will also be taking applications for volunteer projects. Therefore, if you have any fresh ideas that you would like the committee to consider, bring them to the meeting.

36. We need City Hall to fix our neighborhood. Are we just going to sit back and be ignored? Are we nobodies that the power elite can ignore? We all know the answer, so I urge you to sign the petition.

⭐ 37. Jimmy sent us an e-mail laying out the details for starting a club. But Jimmy has been known to cheat on his income tax returns. Given that, how good could his ideas be?

38. I know that Senator Wickhaven has been found guilty of harassment, but did you know that he was twice wounded in the Korean War? Since he has suffered so much for our country, he should not be punished for this crime.

39. Our cars are not for everyone. In order to fully appreciate them, you must enjoy being pampered by the finest custom-made seats, state-of-the-art sound system, and personalized temperature controls. Don't settle for the ordinary.

40. The main character in that movie was vain, superficial, self-centered, and arrogant. So, it's not surprising that his partner left him.

⭐ 41. He is not a psychiatrist, so his arguments and explanations for why some people are addicted to gambling cannot be correct.

42. After lunch today, my assistant football coach gave me some advice. He saw me drinking soda, eating a candy bar, and smoking a cigarette. He said that if I wanted to maximize my potential as an athlete, I need to give up stuff that is bad for my health. Have you ever seen that guy? He is really overweight and smokes cigars. It's obvious that he has nothing to offer to make me a top athlete.

43. Our golf establishment admits only a few new members every year. Our standards are high, but why settle for something that anyone can have? See if you have what it takes to be among a special group.

44. He failed his final exam, so don't blame him for destroying his dorm room.

⭐ 45. Since that sports reporter is a female, her analysis of what caused our team to lose the game is irrelevant.

46. My supervisor said that I should try not to miss any work days during my first 6-month evaluation period. She also said that it would help me stand out to the upper management if I volunteer to work overtime. I've been working for only 1 month, but in that time she has taken three sick days, and she never works overtime. Given her bad example, I'm not going to listen to her career advice.

47. You can't give me an F on the exam. If you do, my mother and father will be so upset they will have to be hospitalized.

48. That newspaper reporter exposed corruption in the mayor's administration. In fact, the evidence she was able to uncover led to the conviction of seven people.

She deserved the Pulitzer Prize for investigative reporting that she won this year.

★ 49. The witness has been twice convicted of perjury. Given this evidence, we should doubt the truth of his testimony.

50. Our competitors have accused us of manipulating market prices. But let me remind you that 10 years ago those very same competitors were fined $2 million for price manipulation. So, why should anyone believe their charges against us?

C. WEAK INDUCTIVE ARGUMENT FALLACIES
Generalization Fallacies

A generalization fallacy occurs when an argument relies on a mistaken use of the principles behind making a generalization. For example, it is not unusual for someone to have a negative experience with members of a group and then quickly stereotype the other members by assigning derogatory characteristics to all or most of the group. On the other hand, a generalization may be mistakenly applied to a case that is an exception to the rule. We will explore several types of generalization fallacies, but first we need to define a few terms to help our analysis.

A *sample* is part of a population. A *population* is any group of objects, not just human groups. A *representative sample* occurs when the characteristics of a sample are correctly identified and matched to the population under investigation. If the premises of an argument rely on an unrepresentative sample, intentionally or unintentionally, then they fail to provide relevant objective evidence for the conclusion. The result is a weak generalization.

8. RIGID APPLICATION OF A GENERALIZATION

Rigid application of a generalization When a generalization or rule is inappropriately applied to the case at hand. The fallacy results from the belief that the generalization or rule is universal (meaning it has no exceptions).

The fallacy of a **rigid application of a generalization** arises when a generalization is inappropriately applied to the case at hand. The fallacy results from the belief that the generalization or rule is universal (meaning it has no exceptions). In fact, many generalizations and rules have exceptions—a special case that does not fall under the general rule. We often make allowances for circumstances that permit breaking a rule. (In fact, *exceptions to the rule* are sometimes called "accidental circumstances," so the fallacy is also called the *fallacy of accident*.) Therefore, to rigidly apply an otherwise acceptable generalization, even in the face of known exceptions, is to commit the fallacy of rigid application of a rule. For example, suppose someone says the following:

> I can't believe the police didn't give the driver of that ambulance any citations. He was speeding, he went through a red light, and the ambulance swerved from lane to lane without using any turn signals.

It is true that under nonemergency circumstances the driver's behavior would be subject to penalties. However, exceptions apply to ambulance drivers, firefighters, and police when they are responding to emergencies. Therefore, the speaker in the foregoing example has rigidly applied an otherwise acceptable generalization in the face of known exceptions. The mistake in this case is the belief that there are no exceptions to the rule.

Here is another example:

> My cousin's illegal drug supply was stolen last week. Luckily, the thief was caught. Therefore, the police have to return my cousin's stolen drug supply to him.

Normally, stolen property is returned to the original owner (usually after it has been presented as evidence in the event of a trial). However, if the stolen property is illegal drugs or counterfeit money, then the property will not be returned. Therefore, the speaker in the foregoing example has rigidly applied an otherwise acceptable generalization in the face of known exceptions. Once again, the mistake is believing that there are no exceptions to the rule.

9. HASTY GENERALIZATION

In order to explore the next type of generalization fallacy, we return to an earlier example. It is common for someone to notice a few negative characteristics of the members of a particular group and, on that basis alone, conclude that the majority of the group has the same negative characteristic. However, it is improbable that such a small sample is representative of the entire group. An argument that relies on a small sample that is unlikely to represent the population commits the fallacy of **hasty generalization**. This fallacy proceeds in the opposite direction from the rigid application of a generalization. Whereas a rigid application of a generalization argues *from the general to the specific*, a hasty generalization argues *from the specific to the general*. (We saw earlier that a rigid application of a generalization is also referred to as "accident." In this regard, a hasty generalization is also referred to as "reverse or converse accident.")

Hasty generalization
An argument that relies on a small sample that is unlikely to represent the population.

Let's analyze the following argument:

> I saw a fraternity guy act rudely to a fast-food employee in the food court. Probably most fraternity and sorority members are rude and arrogant.

The premise reports the observation of a single instance, but the conclusion generalizes the observed behavior to most fraternity *and* sorority members, even though no sorority members were observed. Thus, the conclusion was based on the mistaken belief that a single observation is representative of the entire group. The evidence in this case is not adequate to make such a generalization, so the premise cannot provide a good reason to support the conclusion.

Here is another example:

> The first two students whose exams I graded each got an A. Thus, I expect all fifty students in the class to get A's on the exam.

The teacher is probably being overly optimistic. Although it is possible that all fifty students will get an A on the exam, the fallacy of hasty generalization is apparent in this case. The conclusion was based on the mistaken belief that the grades of two students are a representative sample and can therefore be generalized to all fifty students in the class.

When the fallacy does not occur: Groups of objects, such as human groups, are often quite diverse, so a small sample is unlikely to accurately represent the group. However, some groups of objects include members that are extremely similar to one another, such as certain manufactured products. For example, a flaw in the ignition switch design of certain models of General Motors (GM) cars led to the cars' shutting down all power, thus causing the deaths of at least thirteen people. Based on a small sample of reported defects, GM recalled millions of cars. Since all the ignition switches have the same design and are manufactured using the same process, the switches are all nearly identical. Therefore, this is *not* an instance of a hasty generalization.

This same reasoning process is behind the strategy of relying on quality control experts in most large manufacturing sectors. For example, a company may manufacture hundreds of thousands of a certain item in a week. If a small sample of identically made products is judged to be flawed, it is reasonable to expect that all (or most of) the members of the group are flawed. On the other hand, if a small sample of the items is judged to meet acceptable standards, then the company expects the remaining items to meet the acceptable standards. However, since these are inductive arguments, the conclusions might turn out to be false.

10. COMPOSITION

Composition There are two forms of the fallacy: (1) the mistaken transfer of an attribute of the individual *parts of an object* to the *object as a whole* and (2) the mistaken transfer of an attribute of the individual *members of a class* to the *class itself.*

Let's turn to another type of generalization fallacy. There are two forms of the fallacy of **composition**: (1) the mistaken transfer of an attribute of the individual *parts of an object* to the *object as a whole* and (2) the mistaken transfer of an attribute of the individual *members of a class* to the *class itself.* Let's look at an example of the first form. Suppose someone said the following of a seven-foot-tall basketball player:

All the cells in his body are tiny. Thus, he is tiny.

The mistake is taking an attribute that is true of the cells of the person and erroneously applying it to the whole person. The fallacy can also occur when the conclusion is not necessarily untrue, but merely in doubt:

The bricks in this building are sturdy, so the building must be sturdy.

Even if the individual bricks are sturdy (the premise), the building may not be sturdy (the conclusion). Here are three other examples:

- The thread you are using is easily torn, so the garment you are making will be easily torn.
- Each ingredient you are using tastes delicious. Therefore, the cake has to taste delicious.
- I understand every word in the poem, so I must understand what the poem is about.

All of the examples of the composition fallacy so far have concerned a possible mistaken identity—of parts of an object with the whole object (a body, a building, a garment, a cake, and a poem). However, another form of composition fallacy occurs when the attributes of individual *members of a class* are mistakenly applied to the class itself. This mistake occurs when we confuse the *distributive* and *collective* use of terms. "Distributive" means that an attribute or characteristic is claimed to be true of all or most of the *individual members* of a class of objects. In other words, the attribute is *distributed* to the *members* of the class. For example, in the statement "Motorcycles are noisy," the term "noisy" is being used distributively to refer to individual motorcycles. In contrast to this, "collective" means that an attribute or characteristic of *the individual members* of a class is claimed to be true of the *class itself*. For example, in the statement "Motorcycles make up only 5% of all vehicles on U.S. roadways," the phrase "make up only 5% of all vehicles on U.S. roadways" is being used collectively to refer to the class of motorcycles, not to the individual motorcycles. Given this information, we can now examine the second form of composition fallacy. Consider the following argument:

> More noise is produced by a motorcycle than by a car. Therefore, more noise is produced on U.S. roadways by motorcycles than by cars.

The fallacy results from the mistaken transfer of an attribute of individual motorcycles and cars to their respective classes. It may be true that an individual motorcycle makes more noise than an individual car, but since there are many times more cars than motorcycles, the conclusion does not follow.

Here is an example that clearly illustrates how the fallacy occurs:

> All the *members of my club* are high school seniors. Therefore, *my club* is a high school senior.

Although no one would make this mistake, the point is to expose how the fallacy occurs. The obvious error of applying the attribute "high school senior" to a club illustrates the difference between *distributing* the attribute to the members of the club and applying that attribute *collectively* to the club itself.

Here is one more example:

> A bus uses more gasoline than a car. Therefore, buses use more gasoline in a year than cars.

In the premise, the attribute "uses more gasoline" is claimed to hold for each *member* of the class of buses (the attribute is *distributed* throughout the individual members). However, the conclusion makes a claim about the *class itself* (the attribute is claimed to hold *collectively*).

At this point, it may seem that some composition fallacies resemble hasty generalizations. Let's look closely at the difference by comparing a hasty generalization to a fallacy of composition.

> *Hasty generalization*: Those three buses get fewer than five miles to a gallon of gasoline. Therefore, most buses probably get fewer than five miles to a gallon.

In the premise, the attribute "gets fewer than five miles to a gallon of gasoline" is claimed to hold for the three observed buses. The conclusion then *distributes* the attribute to the remaining *members* of the class, *not* to the *class itself* (collectively). So, this is an instance of hasty generalization, not a fallacy of composition.

Now compare that result with the following:

> *Composition fallacy*: All the parts of that television set are inexpensive, so that television set is inexpensive.

In the premise, the attribute "inexpensive" is claimed to hold for each *part* of the television set. However, the conclusion makes a claim about the television set *as a whole* (the attribute is claimed to hold *collectively*).

When the fallacy does not occur: We must be careful not to misapply the fallacy of composition. Not every argument that reasons from parts to a whole is fallacious. For example:

> Every thread of material of which this shirt is composed is red, so the shirt is red.

This argument does not commit the fallacy of composition; in fact, it is a strong argument.

Here is another example of an argument that does not commit the fallacy of composition:

> Since every piece of my sewing machine is made from steel, it follows that my sewing machine is steel.

Compare the earlier fallacious examples with the two exceptions. The composition fallacies are not mistakes in the structure of the argument. Rather, the context of the argument, together with our knowledge of the world, is usually needed to distinguish fallacious from nonfallacious informal arguments.

11. DIVISION

Division There are two forms of the fallacy: (1) the mistaken transfer of an attribute of an *object as a whole* to the individual *parts of the object* and (2) the mistaken transfer of an attribute of a *class* to the individual *members of the class.*

The next type of generalization fallacy is the reverse of the fallacy of composition. There are two forms of the fallacy of **division**: (1) the mistaken transfer of an attribute of an *object as a whole* to the individual *parts of the object* and (2) the mistaken transfer of an attribute of a *class* to the individual *members of the class.*

For example, suppose someone said the following of a seven-foot-tall basketball player:

> He is huge, so he must have huge cells.

The mistake is taking an attribute that is true of the whole object and erroneously applying it to the parts that make up the object. Here are three other examples of the fallacy:

- She is intelligent, so she must have smart brain cells.
- The garment is strong, so the individual threads must be strong.
- The cake tastes burnt, so you must have used burnt ingredients.

All the examples of the fallacy so far have concerned a possible mistaken identity of an object (a body, a person's intelligence, a garment, and a cake) with its parts. However, a second form of division fallacy is similar to the second form of composition fallacy. This occurs when an attribute of a class is mistakenly applied to the individual members of that class. As before, the mistake occurs when the distributive and collective uses of terms are confused. For example, in the statement "Bald eagles are disappearing," the term "disappearing" is being used collectively to refer to the class of bald eagles; individual members may still live full lives. This is illustrated by the following argument:

> My teacher said that bald eagles are disappearing. I remember seeing a bald eagle at the zoo. Therefore, we better hurry to see it before it disappears.

When the fallacy does not occur: As with the fallacy of composition, we must be careful not to misapply the fallacy of division. Not every argument that reasons from the whole object to its parts is fallacious. For example:

> That is a wooden chair, so the legs are made of wood.

This argument does not commit the fallacy of division; in fact, it is a strong argument. Here is another example:

> The book she is reading is made of paper. Therefore, the pages of the book are made of paper.

Compare the earlier fallacious examples with the two exceptions. As with composition fallacies, division fallacies are *not* mistakes in the structure of the argument. Once again, the context of the argument coupled with our general knowledge helps to distinguish fallacious from nonfallacious arguments.

12. BIASED SAMPLE

Let's turn to another type of generalization fallacy. In the fallacy of **biased sample**, an argument uses a nonrepresentative sample as support for a statistical claim about an entire population. A representative sample occurs when the characteristics of a sample are correctly identified and matched to the population under investigation. For example, consider this argument:

> Recently, a sample of 1000 Catholics in the United States revealed that 85% believe that abortion is morally wrong. Therefore, evidence shows that approximately 85% of all Americans believe that abortion is morally wrong.

Biased sample An argument that uses a nonrepresentative sample as support for a statistical claim about an entire population.

The sample is fairly large, so it is not a hasty generalization. However, the sample surveyed only Catholics in the United States, but the conclusion generalizes to *all* Americans. This illustrates how even a large sample may intentionally or unintentionally exclude segments of the entire population. This results in a nonrepresentative sample, and the argument commits the fallacy of biased sample.

Here is another example:

> A survey of 100 seniors at our university showed that 90% do not oppose a parking fee increase that will go into effect next year. Therefore, we can report that almost all students do not oppose a parking fee increase.

The sample surveyed only seniors at the university, but the conclusion generalizes to *all* students. Since seniors are unlikely to be affected by an increase in parking fees next year, the sample intentionally or unintentionally excluded segments of the entire population. The resulting biased sample does not provide good evidence for the conclusion. (Chapter 13 offers more information on statistical arguments.)

False Cause Fallacies

Scientific advances owe much to experiments that verify cause-effect relationships. Science also has methods that confirm the existence of patterns that help us to understand the world and to predict future events. False cause fallacies occur when a causal connection is assumed to exist between two events when none actually exists, or when the assumed causal connection is unlikely to exist. Since causal claims require strong evidence, a cause-effect claim based on insufficient evidence is fallacious. We will look at two types of false cause fallacies.

13. POST HOC

It is normal and helpful for us to look for connections between events; that's how we learn about the world. Scientific results are achieved by correctly identifying cause-effect connections. This is how we are able to discover the cause of diseases, how and why things deteriorate over time, how to develop helpful drugs, how certain genes are connected to risk factors, and many other types of knowledge. However, not every connection that we happen to notice reveals a true cause-effect relationship. When unwanted things happen to us, it is reasonable to seek out the cause, but we must recognize that many things we connect in our day-to-day life are just coincidences.

Superstitions develop over time when instances of individual coincidences get passed from one person to another. After a few instances are noticed, it often becomes accepted that a cause-effect relationship exists. However, this is a self-sustaining result: Only positive connections are recognized; negative instances are overlooked. A scientific approach would record the number of positive and negative instances to see if there is truly a causal connection. Instead of this, anecdotal evidence that recognizes only positive instances gets passed on, thus reinforcing the superstition. The type of fallacious reasoning that develops over time from a few coincidences is related to the *post hoc* fallacy, our next topic.

Post hoc The fallacy occurs from the mistaken assumption that just because one event occurred before another event, the first event *must have caused* the second event.

The **post hoc** fallacy occurs from the mistaken assumption that just because one event occurred after another event, the first event *must have caused* the second event. ("*Post hoc*" means *after the fact*. The fallacy is also known as "*post hoc, ergo propter hoc,*" which means *after the fact, therefore because of the fact*.) The fallacious reasoning follows this simple pattern:

> X occurred before Y, therefore X caused Y.

The simplest form of the *post hoc* fallacy is a *coincidence* that results from the accidental or chance connection between two events. For example, suppose someone says the following:

> Last week I bought a new car, and today I found out that I am being laid off at work. I shouldn't have bought that car; it brought me bad luck.

The speaker incorrectly infers that buying the new car *caused* him to be laid off. The fallacious reasoning relies on the assumption that because X occurred before Y, therefore X caused Y. However, there is no credible evidence of a cause-effect relationship between buying the new car and getting laid off.

There are more complex forms of the *post hoc* fallacy. For example, it is not unusual for someone to find either a short- or long-term pattern and to make a causal connection between two things. The fallacy lies in mistaking a statistical pattern, or *correlation*, for cause and effect. For example, you might read the following:

> Researchers have discovered that, for over 30 years, there has been a definite pattern connecting the party affiliation of the U.S. president and specific soft

drink sales. During the years when a Democrat was president, Morphiacola topped all soft drink sales. When a Republican was president, Opiacola was number one in sales. If you are an investor, we advise you to put your money on the soft drink company based on who is in the White House.

The premises fail to provide the necessary support for a true causal claim. Arguments that use *post hoc* reasoning fall prey to the mistake of confusing a *correlation* with a *cause*. Fallacies of this type can be persuasive, because unlike a mere coincidence, a regular pattern seems to have emerged. Although every cause-effect relationship reveals a strong correlation, not all strong correlations reveal cause-effect relationships. For example, there is a strong correlation between wearing bathing suits and getting wet, but wearing a bathing suit does not cause us to get wet. (For more details on the difference between a *correlation* and a *cause*, see Chapter 14.)

The pattern in the cola argument was between the party in the White House and the type of cola having the most sales. Patterns like these are also referred to as *trends* and are often the basis for gambling purposes. For example, in baseball, the National League may win four straight All-Star games. In football, the American Conference might win three consecutive Super Bowls. In roulette, a red number may come up six times in a row. However, trends are temporary, and unless some definite cause-effect relationship is independently discovered that would *explain* the trend, we should not expect the trend to continue indefinitely.

Another special form of the *post hoc* fallacy is the *common cause* fallacy, which occurs when one event is believed to cause a second event, when in fact both events are the result of a common cause. For example, someone might claim that the falling barometer is the cause of a storm, when in fact both events are caused by a change in atmospheric pressure. The following illustration reveals the common cause fallacy:

The two downward arrows indicate that the atmospheric pressure is the common cause of both the falling barometer and the storm. The arrow with the X through it shows the fallacious cause-effect claim.

Another example of the fallacy occurs when someone mistakenly thinks that a rash is causing a fever. It is quite possible that both the rash and the fever have a common cause: a virus.

There is another important point about cause-effect relationships that we need to consider. In many real-life settings, events occur because of a complex network of causal factors. Demonstrating that a true causal relationship exists requires being able to *isolate one factor* as the cause and *eliminating all other possible explanations* for the effect. This is what a good scientific experiment is able to do. Unfortunately, most people are not in a position to conduct a good experiment, so they fall prey to a mistake in believing that a complex event has a single cause, when, in fact, there might be no good evidence to support that belief.

Here is an example:

> The United States is the most successful country in history. That's why people in most Middle East countries hate us.

The argument assumes that a single factor is the cause of animosity toward the United States. The argument overlooks a complex network of factors: Social, economic, military, governmental, religious, and cultural factors probably have contributed in some degree to the current state of relations. The fallacy results from the mistaken belief that there is a single cause for the phenomenon.

Consider the following argument:

> I told you not to trust her. After all, she was born under the sign of Aquarius in the year of the Rabbit. She can't help herself; the stars dictate her behavior.

Astrology places human behavior under the influence of the planets and stars. It claims that we are causally connected to astral influences that occurred at the time of our birth and continue throughout our lives. These causal claims do not have any credible scientific evidence in their support; they are based mostly on anecdotal evidence. In addition, the general personality traits associated with astrology can be applied to anyone. The argument overlooks the role of genetics; environment; socioeconomic status; child-rearing practices; and cultural, religious, and ethical influences, all of which probably contribute to our behavior.

Here is one final example:

> Public education has been declining in the United States for the last 50 years. Students today do not know as much as their parents. The decline is caused by the steady erosion of classroom discipline ever since teachers were forbidden to punish their students.

The argument assumes that a single factor is the cause of the decline of public education in the United States. Once again, we can see that the argument overlooks a complex network of factors: Social, economic, cultural, and technological issues, as well as class size and testing standards, are only some of the factors that probably have contributed to the current state of education. The argument is another example of the mistaken belief in a single cause for a complex phenomenon.

When the fallacy does not occur: Of course, there are instances in real life where we can in fact make a good determination that a single factor was the cause of an event. For example, if you throw a rock against someone's window and the window breaks, then, for the purposes of assigning blame, the cause of the broken window is quite apparent.

In a different setting, a medical examiner can sometimes pinpoint a single cause of death, but not always. Similarly, a physician can sometimes isolate a single cause of pain, or determine that a patient is suffering from a specific disease. But this is not always the case. A set of symptoms may be connected to several different diseases, thus making it difficult for physicians to make a definite diagnosis. This is why numerous tests are conducted. The additional tests can help to eliminate some diseases; the goal being to isolate one cause.

14. SLIPPERY SLOPE

Some complex arguments attempt to link events in such a way as to create an alleged, but unsupported, chain reaction. An argument that attempts to connect a series of occurrences such that the first link leads directly to a second link, and so on, until a final unwanted situation is said to be the inevitable result is called a **slippery slope** fallacy. The arguer urges us to stop the chain reaction before it has a chance to begin, by preventing the first act from ever happening. For example, consider the following argument:

> If you start smoking marijuana for pleasure, then you will need more and more to achieve the expected high. You will begin to rely on it whenever you feel depressed. Eventually you will experiment with more powerful drugs that act faster and last longer. Of course, the amount of drug intake will have to increase to achieve the desired results. The addiction will take hold and will lead to a loss of ambition, a loss of self-esteem, the destruction of your health, and the dissolution of all social ties. Therefore, you should not start smoking marijuana.

Slippery slope An argument that attempts to connect a series of occurrences such that the first link in a chain leads directly to a second link, and so on, until a final unwanted situation is said to be the inevitable result.

The argument paints a tragic picture where smoking marijuana for pleasure starts the slide down a slippery slope leading eventually to the dissolution of all social ties. However, the alleged inevitability of the final effect needs to be supported by specific objective evidence for *each step* in the alleged causal network. Each link in the chain requires scientifically accepted evidence of a verified causal connection to the next link in the chain. Until this is established, the argument need not be accepted.

Here is another example:

> If we stop water-boarding enemy combatants, then we will lose the ability to extract important information about terrorists and their future activities. The loss of information will lead to the terrorists plotting attacks with impunity. Since we will not be able to stop or disrupt their planning, we will suffer another tragic attack on United States soil.

The argument constructs a causal chain where the elimination of water-boarding leads to another tragic attack on United States soil. Once again, the alleged inevitability of the final effect has not been supported by any evidence. Each link is asserted to be a cause of the next link in the chain, but no reasons are given to back the assertions. Therefore, without support, each causal claim is unwarranted.

When the fallacy does not occur: Real cases of chain reactions are not hard to find. For example, scientists have discovered how to create nuclear reactions by setting up a series of steps where the result is known to follow. Similarly, causal links can sometimes be found in medicine, where an initial health issue can cause a series of steps leading to the death of a patient. However, each of these kinds of cases has been meticulously researched and is backed by reliable evidence.

Summary of Weak Inductive Argument Fallacies

Generalization fallacies occur when an argument relies on a mistaken use of the principles behind making a generalization. There are five individual fallacies in this group.

8. **Rigid application of a generalization:** When a generalization or rule is inappropriately applied to the case at hand. The fallacy results from the mistaken belief that the generalization or rule is universal (meaning it has no exceptions).

9. **Hasty generalization:** An argument that relies on a small sample that is unlikely to represent the population.

10. **Composition:** There are two forms of the fallacy: (1) the mistaken transfer of an attribute of the individual *parts of an object* to the *object as a whole* and (2) the mistaken transfer of an attribute of the individual *members of a class* to the *class itself.*

11. **Division:** There are two forms of the fallacy: (1) the mistaken transfer of an attribute of an *object as a whole* to the individual *parts of the object*; and (2) the mistaken transfer of an attribute of a *class* to the individual *members of the class.*

12. **Biased sample:** An argument that uses a nonrepresentative sample as support for a statistical claim about an entire population.

False cause fallacies occur when a causal connection is assumed to exist between two events when none actually exists, or when the assumed causal connection is unlikely to exist. There are two individual fallacies in this group.

13. ***Post hoc:*** The fallacy occurs from the mistaken assumption that just because one event occurred before another event, the first event *must have caused* the second event.

14. **Slippery slope:** An argument that attempts to connect a series of occurrences such that the first link in a chain leads directly to a second link, and so on, until a final unwanted situation is said to be the inevitable result.

EXERCISES 4C

Self-Practice
Questions

I. Determine whether each statement is true or false.

1. In the fallacy of biased sample, an argument uses a nonrepresentative sample as support for a statistical claim about an entire population.

Answer: True

2. An argument that relies on a small sample that is unlikely to represent the population commits the fallacy of composition.

3. To rigidly apply an otherwise acceptable generalization, even in the face of known and understood exceptions, is to commit the fallacy of division.

4. A slippery slope fallacy is an argument that attempts to make a final event the inevitable outcome of an initial act.

⭐ 5. One way the fallacy of division can occur is by the mistaken transfer of an attribute of an *object as a whole* to the individual *parts of the object.*

6. A common cause fallacy occurs when a generalization or rule is inappropriately applied to the case at hand.

7. A coincidence results from the accidental or chance connection between two events.

8. An argument that attempts to make a final event the inevitable outcome of an initial act is called *post hoc*.

⭐ 9. A special form of the *post hoc* fallacy is the *common cause* fallacy, which occurs when one event is believed to cause a second event, when in fact both events are the result of a coincidence.

10. Demonstrating that a true causal relationship exists requires generalizing from a nonrepresentative sample to an entire population.

II. Read the following passages. If an argument commits a weak inductive argument fallacy, then identify the specific fallacy. If a passage does not contain a fallacy, then answer "No fallacy." Explain your answers.

1. Ninety-five percent of a sample of registered Republicans in one state district said that they will vote for the Republican nominee for Congress from their district. So, we can expect that all the Republican nominees in the state will get around 95% of the total votes this fall.

Answer: Biased sample. An argument that uses a nonrepresentative sample as support for a statistical claim about an entire population.

2. That ambulance didn't even stop for the red light. It went zooming right through! And the police didn't even give the driver a citation. If I did that, I would get a citation. Life just isn't fair.

3. My horoscope said I would meet someone new. Today my company hired a really good-looking salesperson and we will be working closely together. Now do you see why I read my horoscope every day?

4. For the last 50 years, whenever the American League won the World Series, there was a recession that year, but when the National League won, stock prices went up. There must be some unknown economic force at work that we don't understand.

⭐ 5. There were six cases of food poisoning from undercooked burgers at that chain of fast-food restaurants. This caused the company to change its method of cooking burgers.

6. Each grain of sand is hard, so your sand castle will be hard.

7. Our experiment tested the effect of multivitamins on the common cold. We studied 1000 people who began to experience the onset of typical cold symptoms. Daily multivitamins were given to 500 randomly selected patients in the group, while the other 500 were told not to take any multivitamins. The results show that there was no statistically significant difference between the two groups in either the severity of the cold symptoms or the length of time for the symptoms to subside. We conclude that multivitamins have no noticeable effect on the common cold.

Video Tutorial: 4CII
Exercise #7

8. I met two people from that state, and they were both rude. There must be something in the drinking water of that state that makes all the people from there so rude.

⭐ 9. If you don't clean your room, then the dirt and dust will build up. Before you know it, bacteria will grow. Whatever you touch in your room will then spread bacteria, which will contaminate the entire house. We will all wind up in the hospital, terminally ill.

10. On seven different occasions it rained the day after I washed my car. I washed my car today, so take your umbrella with you tomorrow.

11. When I need to travel to another city I have to buy my own airplane ticket. The president of the United States has Air Force One to take him wherever he wants to go, and he doesn't have to pay a penny. Therefore, I should be afforded the same opportunity.

12. She is very beautiful, so she must have a lovely appendix.

⭐ 13. All the people in my fraternity think that hazing is not a problem. So, I'm sure that the entire student population agrees with us on this issue.

14. Whenever I step in the shower, either my phone rings or someone knocks on the door. I'll have to change my bathing habits, I suppose.

15. Humans need fresh fruit and raw vegetables in order to get their daily supply of vitamins. So, you should start feeding your newborn baby some fresh fruit and raw vegetables every day.

16. If you drop out of one course this semester, you will have less than a full-time load. It will take you longer to graduate. It will delay your getting a job for another year, meaning that you won't get promoted as fast as others who graduated on time. So, you can expect to lose approximately $100,000 during your lifetime.

⭐ 17. The coroner determined that the cause of death was an overdose of toxic drugs. No evidence of foul play was found. In addition, there was no suicide note. We conclude that the death was an accident.

18. My bill at the restaurant was $4.29. I played the number 429 on the lottery today, and it came up. Therefore, it was my destiny to play that number today and win.

19. I don't recommend that you eat at that restaurant. I did not like the breakfast I had there last week. I'm sure that all of their meals are of poor quality.

20. I know for a fact that the acrylic paints that Vincent van Gogh used to create this portrait were very inexpensive. So even though his painting is hanging in a museum, it can't be very expensive.

⭐ 21. Every football player at Crestfallen High School can run two miles in under 15 minutes, so all the students at that school must be in great physical condition.

22. I had two station wagons, and they were both lemons. Thus, I'm sure that there is something in the design of station wagons that makes them all terrible vehicles.

23. I read that cars in the United States consume more gasoline each year than trucks. I guess that means that my car uses more gasoline each year than that tractor trailer over there.

24. Chicken eggs do not weigh very much. So if I eat an omelet made from fifty eggs, it will not weigh very much.

⭐ 25. A random and representative sample of registered voters shows that 70% are opposed to Proposition 13 that will be on the upcoming ballot. Given this, we project that the proposition will fail to get enough votes to pass.

26. I read that the city's closed circuit video surveillance cameras that are positioned to watch for traffic violations are being stolen. Apparently, the thieves can sell the electronic equipment to unscrupulous companies. The city then had the bright idea to install a second set of cameras to watch the ones observing the traffic. This led to the thieves stealing the second set of cameras so they wouldn't be seen stealing the traffic ones. It's obvious where this is going. Pretty soon the city will have to install a third set, and then a fourth set, and then have someone stationed 24 hours a day watching each camera. In the end, this will bankrupt the city.

27. In one of my dreams last week, I saw a car wreck, but I was not in the car. I just heard that my aunt had a fender-bender in the mall's parking lot. This shows that dreams are videos sent from the future to warn us of dangers in the present.

28. Every time I bet on our team, they lose. And every time I don't bet, they win. It follows that my betting on them causes them to lose.

⭐ 29. A large survey of SUV owners revealed that 80% believe that global warming is a hoax intended to get them to give up their vehicles. This shows that the vast majority of Americans don't believe that global warming is real.

30. When I get on a bus, it's usually first come, first served. In other words, if a seat is available, you take it. But they have a sign on the bus that asks people to give up their seats for older people, people with infirmities, or someone who is pregnant. I think it should be the same for everyone. If I'm lucky enough to get a seat, why should I have to give it up?

31. Since the 1950s, our society has become increasingly more violent. It is obvious what has caused this to happen. Check the facts. As the number of television sets bought by consumers rose every year, so did crime.

32. You forgot to water your plants for 3 weeks and now they are dead. Clearly, the lack of water caused their untimely demise.

⭐ 33. My car goes from zero to sixty miles an hour in under 5 seconds, so the windshield wipers must be able to clean the front window in under 5 seconds, too.

34. In physics class we learned that elementary particles have little or no mass. My $150 physics textbook is made up of elementary particles, thus it has little or no mass.

35. I waited 30 minutes for a bus to work, and because of that I was late. The bus system in this city is completely unreliable.

36. Sending arms to Middle East militants trying to overthrow their governments is a crazy idea. Those militants will most likely force the collapse of the current regime and then take over power. But the militants are not capable of running a complex society. This will lead to instability in the region, and then a clash of cultures. Soon we will be forced to send in troops. Russia, China, and India will get involved. This will lead to World War III.

★ 37. She began making $100,000 the year after she graduated from college, and when she took an IQ test, she scored 20 points higher than when she was in high school. See, I told you: Money makes people smarter.

Video Tutorial: 4CII
Exercise #37

38. Four of us ate at that restaurant last night. Three of us had lasagna, and one had a salad. The three who had lasagna all got severe stomach aches, but not the one who had salad. We all had the same kind of appetizers and dessert. It follows that the lasagna probably caused the stomach aches.

39. Each page of the encyclopedia weighs practically nothing, so the encyclopedia weighs practically nothing.

40. The other day my sister helped an old lady cross the street, and today she won $100 on the lottery. See, I told you that doing good deeds brings you luck.

★ 41. According to the census data, the population of that city is 10% atheists. My Uncle Sam lives there, so he must be 10% atheist.

42. My daughter was listening to some music on her headphones, and I asked her to play it for me. She said it was called "EDM," which means electronic dance music. I heard one song and asked her to stop it because it was repetitive and monotonous. I imagine all EDM sounds the same.

43. If you major in humanities, then you will stop taking math and science courses. By the time you graduate you will be locked out of all the high-paying jobs. You will have to take jobs that you could have gotten with a high-school diploma. You won't be able to contribute to an IRA, and when you finally retire, your Social Security checks will not be enough to survive.

44. Every time the barometer drops below 30, it rains. It has some mysterious power over the weather, I guess.

★ 45. You have chosen great paint colors; therefore, your house will look great.

46. On two different occasions when I missed a class the instructor gave a surprise quiz. That proves the instructor gave the quiz just because he saw that I was absent.

47. All it takes is one. If you throw your empty can on the sidewalk, then someone else will either see you do it or else think it is okay. Especially kids. Pretty soon people will throw glass and plastic bottles. Then there will be all kinds of trash. The sanitation department will not be able to keep up with the level of garbage in the streets. The rat population will grow, and when that happens, bubonic plague will not be far behind.

48. A veterinarian found that 70% of the German shepherd dogs she examined had a hip displacement before they reached 10 years of age. Given this, probably 70% of all dogs will have a hip displacement before they reach 10 years of age.

⭐ 49. The house is poorly constructed, so the material it is made of must be poorly constructed as well.

50. I tried using an electric razor for a week but it irritated my skin. Good thing I bought the cheapest one possible. This shows that all electric razors are no good.

D. FALLACIES OF UNWARRANTED ASSUMPTION OR DIVERSION

Unwarranted Assumption

Fallacies of unwarranted assumption exhibit a special kind of reasoning error: They assume the truth of some unproved or questionable claim. The fallacies become apparent when the assumptions and lack of support are exposed, thus revealing the weak points of the argument.

15. BEGGING THE QUESTION

There are several types of the fallacy of **begging the question** (*"petitio principii,"* meaning *assume at the beginning*). In one type, the fallacy occurs when a premise is simply reworded in the conclusion. In a second type, called *circular reasoning*, a set of statements seem to support each other with no clear beginning or end point. In a third type, the argument assumes certain key information that may be controversial or is not supported by facts. Cases of begging the question can go unnoticed because they often sound convincing. This should not be surprising; in some cases, the conclusion is already assumed in the premises, so on the surface it might appear to be a strong argument.

Let's look at an example:

> The Beatles are the greatest band of all time. So it is safe to say that no band has ever been better than the Beatles.

The conclusion is already assumed in the premise; it is merely worded differently. Since both the premise and the conclusion assert the same thing, no new evidence is offered to support the conclusion. Obviously, *if* the claim is true in the premise, it will be true in the conclusion, so it is valid. However, the argument begs the question

Begging the question
In one type, the fallacy occurs when a premise is simply reworded in the conclusion. In a second type, called *circular reasoning*, a set of statements seem to support each other with no clear beginning or end point. In a third type, the argument assumes certain key information that may be controversial or is not supported by facts.

because it assumes what it intends to prove. We need additional information to answer the question "What evidence is there that the Beatles are the greatest band of all time?"

Here is an example of circular reasoning:

> You can believe her because she never lies. Furthermore, since she always tells the truth, she is someone that you can believe.

Paraphrasing the argument reveals the problem:

> You can believe her. She never lies. She always tells the truth. She is someone that you can believe.

If you look closely, you can see that the second and third statements say the same thing: Saying that someone never lies is the same thing as saying that she always tells the truth. Also, the first and fourth statements say the same thing; they both say that you can believe her. Ultimately, the first statement is used to support the second statement, which in turn, is then used to support the first statement. The argument goes in a circle. But the argument begs the question "What additional evidence is there that she never lies?"

The third type of the fallacy occurs when an argument fails to supply a premise that is needed to support the conclusion. For example, if your argument relies on a controversial or unsubstantiated premise that you leave out, then you are assuming information that could be unacceptable to those you are trying to convince. Consider this argument:

> The murder of a human being is always wrong. Therefore, capital punishment is always wrong.

Most people would probably accept the premise. If clarity is needed, we could offer a definition of "murder" as "the unjustified taking of the life of a human being." Our discussion might exempt cases of self-defense, legitimate police activity while protecting the citizenry, and certain military engagements. However, the conclusion *assumes* that capital punishment is a form of murder. This assumption is often the central point on which opposing positions regarding capital punishment rest. Therefore, someone who disagrees with the conclusion can point out that the assumed premise "begs the question," in that it assumes as a good reason what is in fact an unwarranted assumption: that capital punishment is a form of murder.

As it stands, the original argument (with the single premise) is invalid. However, the reconstructed argument is valid. The fallacious nature of the argument is *not* based on the underlying logic, because *if* both premises are true, then the argument is valid. In other words, if it is true that "the murder of a human being is always wrong," and if it is also true that "capital punishment is a form of murder," then the conclusion follows necessarily. The reconstructed argument may be valid, but its soundness is in question. The fallacy occurs because the truth of the added controversial premise has been assumed. The argument lacks sufficient additional, independent reasons or facts to support the assumed premise. We need additional information to answer the question "What evidence is there that capital punishment is a form of murder?"

Here is another example:

> We are justified in going to war to defend our country from foreign aggression.
> It follows that we should go to war with Syria.

The premise is probably acceptable to most people. However, the conclusion *assumes* that Syria is actively engaged in aggression toward our country. Thus, someone who disagrees with the conclusion can point out that the assumed premise "begs the question," in that it assumes as a good reason what is in fact an unwarranted assumption: that Syria is actively engaged in aggression toward our country. We need additional information to answer the question "What evidence is there that Syria is actively engaged in aggression toward our country?" The original argument (with the single premise) is invalid, but the reconstructed argument is valid. This illustrates once again that the fallacious nature of the argument is *not* based on the underlying logic, because *if* both premises are true, then the argument is valid. The fallacy occurs because the truth of the added controversial premise has been assumed. The argument lacks sufficient additional, independent reasons or facts to support the assumed premise.

When the fallacy does not occur: The examples of arguments that beg the question contained information that needed additional support. Assumptions were made that were not backed up by additional evidence. Although the fully fleshed out arguments may be valid, they are either clearly unsound or else their soundness is under question. However, there are arguments that might appear to be instances of begging the question, but they are not. Here is an example:

> Albany is the capital of New York or Sacramento is the capital of California. It
> follows that Sacramento is the capital of California or Albany is the capital of
> New York.

The argument may be trivial but it is sound (it is valid and the premise is true). It is not an instance of begging the question because it has not assumed something that needs additional support. Here is another example:

> Buffalo is the capital of New York or San Diego is the capital of California. It
> follows that San Diego is the capital of California or Buffalo is the capital of
> New York.

Once again, the argument may be trivial but in this case it is unsound (it is valid but the premise is false). Yet again, it is not an instance of begging the question because it has not assumed something that needs additional support.

16. COMPLEX QUESTION

The fallacy of **complex question** occurs when a single question actually contains multiple parts and an unestablished hidden assumption. The questioner tries to force a single answer that, in turn, is then used against the respondent. As such, the question itself is not a fallacy, but either a "yes" or "no" answer allows the questioner to create an argument that establishes the truth of the hidden assumption. For example, suppose you are asked the following question:

> Do you still cheat on your taxes?

Complex question The fallacy occurs when a single question actually contains multiple parts and an unestablished hidden assumption.

Answering either "yes" or "no" is an admission that you did, in fact, cheat on your taxes. The key words that create the complex question are "still cheat." The unestablished hidden assumption is that you have cheated. If you answer "yes," then you establish the truth of the hidden assumption, and the questioner can then conclude that you currently cheat on your taxes and you have done so in the past. On the other hand, even if you never cheated on your taxes, answering "no" once again establishes the truth of the hidden assumption. In other words, it is an admission that you did cheat on your taxes, but you no longer do. Therefore, the questioner can use this as evidence to support the conclusion that you cheated on your taxes. Here is how the questioner's argument would look:

> I asked you if you still cheat on your taxes. You said "no." Therefore, by your own admission, you did cheat on your taxes.

The premises rely on the fact that the complex question contained two distinct questions and an unestablished hidden assumption. We can eliminate the hidden assumption by separating the two questions:

> **A.** Did you ever cheat on your taxes?
> **B.** If so, are you still cheating on your taxes?

The ability to recognize that there are actually two questions at work here allows us to avoid the trap of the complex question. Once the questions are separated, a person who never cheated on her taxes can answer "no" to question A and, by so doing, eliminate the need to answer question B. This prevents the questioner from drawing an unjustified conclusion.

Complex questions can be used to trap us in many kinds of unacceptable situations. For example, suppose someone asks:

> Aren't you going to do something about your child's terrible behavior?

The complex question hides two unestablished assumptions: (1) You agree that your child's behavior needs correcting, and (2) you are going to correct it. Therefore, if you answer "yes" to the complex question, you have admitted the child's behavior needs correcting. However, even if you answer "no" to the complex question, then you have, once again, established the truth of the hidden assumption. In other words, you are admitting that the child's behavior needs correcting. You simply are not going to do anything about it.

When the fallacy does not occur: A question that does *not* try to trap the respondent into establishing the truth of a hidden assumption is not a fallacy of complex question. For example, if you ask your roommate, "Did you see the final episode of *How I Met Your Mother*?" then your question is not hiding any assumptions. In that case, answering "yes" or "no" is a satisfactory answer.

In a legal setting, a lawyer asks many kinds of questions. If she asks a complex question, then the opposing lawyer has a chance to object. If the objection is upheld, the judge might ask that the question be rephrased. On the other hand, a lawyer might ask a witness a *leading question* such as, "Did you see anyone enter the building after the defendant left?" This kind of question is meant to set the groundwork for potential follow-up questions. So, if the witness responds "yes" to the leading question, then the lawyer can ask other questions designed to elaborate on what the witness knows. However, if the witness answers "no," then the lawyer can go on to other topics. Once again, we must pay close attention to the context at hand to determine if the complex question fallacy has occurred.

17. APPEAL TO IGNORANCE

An **appeal to ignorance** (lack of knowledge) argument makes one of two possible mistakes: (1) A claim is made that a statement *must be true* because it has not been proven to be false, or (2) a claim is made that a statement *must be false* because it has not been proven to be true. Both claims are unjustified.

An example of the first kind of mistake is this:

> UFOs must exist because no one has proven that they don't exist.

Here is an example of the second kind of mistake:

> There is definitely no life anywhere else in the universe. This follows from the fact that we have never received signals from any part of space.

The conclusion in the second example is based on a single factor—the lack of signals from outer space. But our failure to have detected any signals may simply signify our lack of sophisticated methods of detection. Also, the ability to send signals is not a necessary requirement for life to exist. Both examples illustrate that fallacies of ignorance result from a general misunderstanding of science and the role of inductive arguments. For example, for a long time it was believed that an invisible substance called "phlogiston" existed in all objects that burned. When a flame

Appeal to ignorance
An argument built on a position of ignorance claims either that (1) a statement must be true because it has not been proven to be false or (2) a statement must be false because it has not been proven to be true.

PROFILES IN LOGIC
Arthur Schopenhauer

Arthur Schopenhauer (1788–1860) is not generally regarded as a logician or a mathematician, but rather as a philosopher who devoted his life to, as he tells us, "debunking charlatans, windbags, and claptrap." Schopenhauer firmly believed that fallacies should be exposed whenever they appear. In *The Art of Controversy*, he remarks that "it would be a very good thing if every trick could receive some short and obviously appropriate name, so that when a man used this or that particular trick, he could be at once reproached for it." Indeed, hundreds of fallacies have been recognized, described, and named.

Schopenhauer is often called the philosopher of pessimism because he thought that human experience is filled with all manner of brutality, pain, and suffering. Humans are compelled to hate, love, and desire, with only temporary escapes—philosophic contemplation, art (especially music), and sympathy for the plight of others.

In addition, Schopenhauer was one of the first Western philosophers to recognize and incorporate ideas from Eastern religions, such as Buddhism. In his system of thought, we are asked to "see ourselves in all existence."

burned, the phlogiston was released until no more existed in the burning object. It was thought that if you placed a candle in a glass container, the candle will eventually go out because the phlogiston was trapped in the confined space, so no more could be released. However, decisive experiments by a scientist named Lavoisier led not only to the demise of the theory of phlogiston, but also to the discovery of oxygen.

Scientists can often make *strong arguments* that something exists or does not exist. Scientists generally use inductive reasoning to shape their arguments, so they are *not* proving the certainty of their conclusions in the sense of a valid deductive argument. Instead, scientists rely on the accumulated evidence of scientific research to make their arguments. Much of science is considered "tentative," because the arguments are not meant to be deductively valid. However, a good scientific argument is inductively strong.

If substantial evidence is available to decide an issue, then the fallacy of ignorance does not arise. For example, if a police investigation results in no credible evidence

PROFILES IN LOGIC
Francis Bacon

Francis Bacon (1561–1626) held that certain fundamental fallacies prevent us from achieving a correct understanding of nature. Bacon referred to these fallacies as "idols," by which he meant sources of misunderstanding that undermine human knowledge. However, he argued that we can learn to recognize and avoid these idols.

Bacon discussed four types of idols: (1) *Idols of the Tribe.* These are part of basic human nature, so they affect everyone. For example, our sense perceptions are easily tricked, so we need to invent precise and accurate mechanical instruments to help us understand nature. Bacon tells us that "human understanding is like a false mirror, which, receiving rays irregularly, distorts and discolors the nature of things by mingling its own nature with it." We also have the tendency to believe what we *want* to be true, rather than what *is* objectively true. (2) *Idols of the Cave.* These are specific to each individual. In a sense, each one of us is housed in the cave of our mind, where our thoughts are subject to the accidental nature of our personal experience. Over time, each of us evolves a particular view of the world, by which we judge all things. (3) *Idols of the Marketplace.* These are mistakes based on an uncritical use of language. Although we need to communicate our ideas and beliefs to others, words can be vague or ambiguous, so we must be careful. Inattention to the correct meaning of words leads to fallacious reasoning. (4) *Idols of the Theater.* These are systems of belief that have solidified over time but which rest on a false foundation. They exist in belief systems that have over time insulated themselves from objective scrutiny. They are ruled by elite groups whose authority is unquestioned by masses of followers.

In order to overcome the four idols, knowledge must be based on observation and experimentation. Bacon developed a system of thought based on an objective study of facts of nature by which we can slowly build general theories.

found linking a suspect to a crime, then no matter how strongly the police might feel about the suspect, the suspect will most likely be released. But this does not mean that we can conclude with certainty that the person is innocent; it just means that the person is *probably* not guilty of the crime. Similarly, if the verdict of a jury is that the defendant is "not guilty," then the jury is saying that the evidence presented by the prosecution was not sufficient to determine guilt *beyond a reasonable doubt*. (It is important to recognize that the legal phrase "not guilty" is not synonymous with "innocent.")

Let's return to the first example: "UFOs must exist because no one has proven that they don't exist." The person making this argument is probably using the phrase "no one has proven" to mean a deductively valid argument. Given this, the person's conclusion, "UFOs must exist," relies on a mistaken interpretation of science and, in that sense, the premise is irrelevant to the conclusion.

18. APPEAL TO AN UNQUALIFIED AUTHORITY

Arguments often rely on the opinions of experts, specialists whose education, experience, and knowledge provide relevant support for a claim. When an argument uses expert testimony that is backed by strong evidence with no hint of impropriety, then the argument is most likely strong (as long as the testimony falls within the realm of the expert's field). On the other hand, arguments that rely on the opinions of people who either have *no* expertise, training, or knowledge relevant to the issue at hand, or whose testimony is not trustworthy, are arguments that **appeal to an unqualified authority**.

A person may have the credentials of an expert, but he may be *biased* toward a certain result. For example, some physicians who worked for insurance companies have testified under oath at congressional hearings that they knowingly denied payment for many patients' treatment even though they knew that they should approve it. The physicians admitted to receiving enormous yearly commissions depending on how much money they saved the insurance company. The reason that they revealed the truth was that they could not live with the consequences of their actions: the fact that their decisions led directly to some people's death. Therefore, when those physicians used their power to deny treatment to otherwise qualified patients, they were biased in their decision making.

One of the most prevalent fallacious uses of inappropriate authority is in advertisements. Athletes, celebrities, and former politicians often endorse products to boost sales. The consumer is expected to respect the famous personalities and trust their opinion. Here is an example:

> I'm Nick Panning, quarterback of the Los Angeles Seals. I've been eating *Oaties* for breakfast since I was a kid. *Oaties* taste great, and they have all the nutrition kids need. You should get some for your kids today.

Merely being famous does not qualify someone to pronounce the merits of a product. An athlete generally has no expertise in the nutritional value of a breakfast cereal. On the other hand, a person with a Ph.D. in nutrition would presumably be in a good position to offer a fair assessment of the breakfast cereal (provided the opinion is not based on monetary compensation).

Appeal to an unqualified authority An argument that relies on the opinions of people who either have *no* expertise, training, or knowledge relevant to the issue at hand, or whose testimony is not trustworthy.

Turning once again to science, no scientist would conclude that a statement is true merely because Albert Einstein said so. Every scientific statement has to be backed up by objective evidence, and replicable results. Albert Einstein, the famous *physicist*, was asked to be the first *president* of Israel. He humbly declined, stating that he had no idea how to run a country. Such modesty is rare.

19. FALSE DICHOTOMY

False dichotomy A fallacy that occurs when it is assumed that only two choices are possible, when in fact others exist.

The fallacy of **false dichotomy** ("dichotomy" means *to cut in two parts*) occurs when it is assumed that only two choices are possible, when in fact others exist. The argument contains a premise that presents an "either . . . or . . ." choice with the assumption that no other choices are available. For example, suppose that a person defending the Patriot Act and its potential infringement on certain basic freedoms says the following:

Either we give up some traditional basic freedoms or we lose the war on terror.

The argument is missing a premise and a conclusion. Since the person is defending the Patriot Act, the missing premise might be "No one wants to lose the war on terror," and the missing conclusion is most likely "We must give up some traditional basic freedoms."

Let's reveal the argument form. If we let G = *we give up some traditional basic freedoms*, and L = *we lose the war on terror*, then we get this result:

G or L.
Not L.
G.

The argument is *valid*: *If* the premises are assumed to be true, then the conclusion follows necessarily. However, the argument is *unsound*. The fallacy occurs because the first premise is false. Since the first premise fails to acknowledge that other possibilities exist, it sets up a false dichotomy. If we are captured by the passionate nature of the assertion and its implications, then we seem to be facing a difficult choice. According to the assertion, there are only two choices. If we don't want to lose the war on terror, then we must conclude that we are willing to give up some traditional basic freedoms. On the other hand, if we are not willing to give up some traditional basic freedoms, then we must conclude that we will lose the war on terror. However, once we see that this is really an instance of the fallacy of false dichotomy, then we can reject the entire notion of having only two choices in the matter. We can argue that it is possible to win the war on terror without giving up traditional basic freedoms.

Here is another example:

He was born on a Monday or a Thursday. He was not born on a Thursday, so he was born on a Monday.

Although the argument is valid, we can question its soundness. The first premise assumes that there are only two choices, but we are not given any evidence to support that assumption. Since there are five other days of the week on which the person in question might have been born, this is an instance of a false dichotomy.

When the fallacy does not occur: Not all arguments that present two choices in one of the premises are fallacies of false dichotomy. The key determination is whether the dichotomy assumes the two choices that are offered exhaust all the possibilities available. Here is an example:

> Teddy Roosevelt was the twentieth U.S. president, or Fairbanks is the capital of Alaska. Teddy Roosevelt was not the twentieth U.S. president, so Fairbanks is the capital of Alaska.

This is a valid argument: *If* the premises are assumed to be true, then the conclusion is true. However, truth value analysis shows that the first premise and the conclusion are both false (the second premise is true), thus the argument is unsound. But since the first premise does not offer a false dichotomy, this argument, although unsound, is not fallacious.

In order to illustrate a false dichotomy, let's look at a modified example from the philosopher Arthur Schopenhauer:

> Either you agree with our country's policies or you should go live in another country. You don't agree with our country's policies. Therefore, you should go live in another country.

The argument assumes that only two possibilities exist when in fact more than two exist. In the foregoing example, only two choices are given:

(1) You agree with our country's policies.
(2) You should go live in another country.

Surely these are not the only two possibilities. A concerned citizen has the right and obligation to try to change a country's policies if they are illegal, immoral, or at least not in the best interests of the country. Certainly not every political decision will turn out to be the best for a particular country. Hence, a third possibility can be added to the example:

(3) You disagree with the country's policies, and you want to change them peacefully and legally.

Exception: Not all arguments that offer two choices are fallacious. If the two choices are in fact the only two options, then the fallacy does not occur. For example, suppose that you need to make an appointment to see a doctor and she has only 2 days available this week. We might see something like the following:

> The doctor can see you either on Tuesday or Friday. You said that Tuesday will not work for you, so I'll schedule you for Friday.

Since the two choices are in fact your only options, the argument is not an instance of false dichotomy.

Fallacies of Diversion

A fallacy of diversion occurs when the meanings of terms or phrases are changed (intentionally or unintentionally) within the argument, or when our attention is purposely (or accidentally) diverted from the issue at hand. Also known as fallacies of ambiguity, these types of fallacies depend on the fact that words or phrases can have many different meanings, and context is crucial. Ambiguity, vagueness, or any unclear use of a term can seriously affect the understanding, analysis, and evaluation of an argument. On the other hand, an arguer may divert our attention by *changing the subject*, thereby setting up an argument that avoids the actual discussion.

20. EQUIVOCATION

Equivocation The fallacy occurs when the conclusion of an argument relies on an intentional or unintentional shift in the meaning of a term or phrase in the premises.

The first fallacy of diversion we will look at, **equivocation**, occurs when the conclusion of an argument relies on an intentional or unintentional shift in the meaning of a term or phrase that was used in the premises. ("Equivocation" means to use different senses of a term or phrase.) For example, someone might say the following:

> My older brother tries hard to be cool. I told him he has the personality of a cucumber. Since a refrigerator is a good place to keep things cool, he should spend some time in there.

The term "cool" has several meanings that tend to sort themselves out in the context of particular sentences. The equivocation in this example is easy to spot, but it does show clearly how the fallacy works. Equivocation can also occur when *relative terms* such as "big" and "small" are misused. Here is another example:

> I was told that he is a big man on campus (BMOC). But big men are at least 6'4" tall. He is no more than 5'7" tall, so he can't be a BMOC.

The equivocation occurs when the relative term "big" is used in two different senses. Here are two other examples of the fallacy:

- Judy said she had a hot date last night. Her apartment can get hot unless she uses the air conditioner. Therefore, the air conditioner in her apartment must not have been working.
- That looks like a hard outfit to get into. The factory that made it must have used really hard material. So, perhaps you should wash the outfit in some fabric softener.

The first example equivocates on the term "hot," while the second example uses two different senses of the term "hard." When an argument is an equivocation fallacy, it is most likely invalid, and thus unsound. This stems from the fact that the two different meanings of a key term will not be sufficient, by themselves, to support the conclusion.

Let's look at some examples where the equivocation is not so obvious. The world of politics offers numerous examples, one of which is the issue of employment. A recent presidential administration had to respond to a huge loss of manufacturing jobs during its time in office. To counteract the statistics showing a loss of jobs, the administration proposed that some fast-food workers should be reclassified from service workers to manufacturing workers. Under the new definition, anyone who cooked a burger, placed it on a bun, added condiments, and put it in a wrapper was engaged in manufacturing a product. There would thus have been a gain in manufacturing jobs during the course of the administration's time in office. Of course, once the opposing political party found out about the idea, it was quickly dropped. The administration's argument that it had cut unemployment rested on a shift in the meaning of the term "manufacturing worker," and thus was an instance of a fallacy of equivocation.

An earlier administration hatched a similar idea. The federal government normally defines the "unemployed" as only those people who are actively collecting government unemployment checks. Under this definition, people who have either exhausted their checks or are on welfare are not considered unemployed. The unemployment rate is then calculated by finding the number of unemployed and comparing this with the total number of those employed. In addition, the entire military was not used to calculate the unemployment rate; military personnel were considered neither employed nor unemployed. However, just before a presidential election, a scheme was considered that proposed that all active military personnel should be considered employed. This would have seriously reduced the unemployment rate, favoring the incumbent administration. Once again, the idea was exposed and abandoned. The administration intentionally used two different meanings of the term "employed" designed to make it appear that their economic policies were working. The argument they tried to present was an instance of the fallacy of equivocation.

21. STRAW MAN

A fallacy can occur when attention is purposely (or accidentally) diverted from the issue at hand. In other words, statements or arguments intending one thing are subtly distorted in order to divert the emphasis to a different issue. A **straw man** fallacy occurs when an argument is misrepresented in order to create a new argument that can be easily refuted. The new argument is so weak that it is "made of straw." The arguer then falsely claims that his opponent's real argument has been defeated. The straw man fallacy relies on an act of diversion, a tactic that is common in the political arena. Candidates often attempt to distort the views of their opponents by clipping a small piece out of a speech or interview and using it out of context, creating an impression directly opposite from that of the original argument. For example, a person running for public office might say the following:

> I oppose the law that requires teaching intelligent design as an alternative to evolutionary theory in public school biology classes. Evolution is an established scientific theory and deserves to be taught in science classes. Intelligent design is not a scientific theory, and it should not be taught in science classes.

An opponent of this candidate might criticize her position this way:

> She is against the new law that mandates teaching intelligent design alongside the theory of evolution. It should be obvious to anyone that she really wants to eliminate religious beliefs. She wants to destroy one of the basic principles of the Constitution of the United States.

The opponent has created a straw man argument by taking the original statement and adding an unjustified premise, "It should be obvious to anyone that she really wants to eliminate religious beliefs." The fallacious argument concludes, "She wants to destroy one of the basic principles of the Constitution of the United States."

Straw man The fallacy occurs when someone's argument is misrepresented in order to create a new argument that can be easily refuted. The new argument is so weak that it is "made of straw." The arguer then falsely claims that his opponent's real argument has been defeated.

The straw man fallacy is often used to create a false impression that a certain group holds an unacceptable position. The argument usually refers to a vague group who supposedly holds an extreme position. Here is an example:

> The Democrats promise that a government health care system will reduce the cost of health care, but as the economist Thomas Sowell has pointed out, government health care will not reduce the cost; it will simply refuse to pay the cost. And who will suffer the most when they ration care? The sick, the elderly, and the disabled, of course. The America I know and love is not one in which my parents or my baby with Down Syndrome will have to stand in front of Obama's "death panel" so his bureaucrats can decide, based on a subjective judgment of their "level of productivity in society," whether they are worthy of health care. Such a system is downright evil.
>
> Sarah Palin, "Statement on the Current Health Care Debate"

Palin has created a straw man argument about "death panels." In so doing, she takes the hollow defeat of straw man to support her claim that the proposed government health-care plan "is downright evil." Straw man arguments like this are used by most political parties, and are a staple of television programs featuring political pundits (critics or commentators) who argue about domestic and world affairs.

22. RED HERRING

Red herring A fallacy that occurs when someone completely ignores an opponent's position and changes the subject, diverting the discussion in a new direction.

Another fallacy of diversion, the **red herring** fallacy, occurs when someone completely ignores an opponent's position. By changing the subject, the red herring "throws one off the scent," diverting the discussion in a new direction. This type of fallacy differs from the straw man fallacy in that a straw man argument is purposely created to be weak, whereas a red herring argument may in fact be strong. But because a strong red herring argument diverts our attention from the real argument, it has no bearing on an opponent's argument. Here is an example:

> Many people criticize TV as turning America into an illiterate society. How can we criticize the very medium that is the envy of countries all over the world? The entertainment quality and variety of TV programs today are greater than ever before, not to mention the enormous number of cable options available to members of the viewing audience. Thus, the critics are wrong.

Rather than presenting evidence that contradicts the claim that TV is turning America into an illiterate society, the argument diverts our attention to the entertainment value of TV. Although the evidence that is presented may be true, it fails in this case to support the conclusion.

Let's look at another example. A lot of accusations were made that Barack Obama was not born in the United States. If the accusations were true, then perhaps he is not a U.S. citizen. In that case, according to the U.S. Constitution, he is not legally allowed to be president. Critics demanded that he prove his citizenship. Obama eventually produced his birth certificate that showed he was born in Honolulu, Hawaii, and thus was indeed a U.S. citizen.

However, some critics were not satisfied. They argued that this proved nothing because the document listed Obama's father's race as *African*. In other words, if Barack Obama had dual citizenship at birth, then perhaps he does not meet the Constitution's definition of a "natural-born" citizen. The critics claimed that this possibility required a reinterpretation of the intentions of the original framers of the Constitution. The critics shifted the argument from whether Obama could offer evidence that he was a citizen by diverting the debate to an examination of the intentions of the Founding Fathers.

In this next example we will first look at an argument supporting the claim that nuclear power plants are dangerous. Next, we will see how a red herring argument is created to try to defeat the first argument.

> Nuclear power plants are dangerous. We are all aware of the recent problems with the Fukushima reactor in Japan and the extent of damage and radiation leaks. Also, the 1986 disaster in Chernobyl caused many deaths and thousands of cancer cases. There is also credible evidence linking several nuclear power plants in the United States to unusual rises in leukemia, as well as dramatic increases in birth defects to children born near the facilities.

An opponent of the argument might create a red herring argument that diverts our attention from the main issue regarding the dangers that nuclear power plants pose, and shift the argument to another issue by using words or phrases designed to "push our emotional buttons."

> The dangers of nuclear power plants have been overstated. Don't forget that we are caught in an international economic war over oil controlled by Middle Eastern dictatorial regimes that brutally punish any dissent and refuse to acknowledge democratic principles. Also, because shadowy international oil cartels manipulate oil prices, our economy and our individual rights are violated. If we want to take charge of our lives, we must build more nuclear power plants.

The argument does *not* address the dangers of nuclear power plants. It diverts our attention by talking about "Middle Eastern dictatorial regimes," and how they treat their citizens, as well as "shadowy international oil cartels" that violate individual rights. Perhaps there are strong arguments that show how the United States has access to more state-of-the-art technologies that can reduce the likelihood of future disasters and protect people from harmful radiation; however, the foregoing red herring argument does none of these things.

23. MISLEADING PRECISION

A fallacy of **misleading precision** occurs when a claim appears to be statistically significant but is not. Statistics are often used misleadingly. The following is an example that we might find in an advertisement:

> Our cookies contain 30% less fat, so you should start eating them if you want to lose weight.

Our attention is captured by the seemingly impressive statistic. The idea is to dazzle us with the precise percentage in order to divert our attention from assessing its relevance to the conclusion. However, the argument does not stand up to scrutiny. It is fair to ask, "30% less fat than what?" The asserted percentage is relative to some

Misleading precision
A claim that appears to be statistically significant but is not.

other item, and we need to know what that is in order to know if this product is really significantly lower in fat than competing products. It might be the case that the cookies have 30% less fat than they did before, but they still might contain more fat than is ideal for someone trying to lose weight.

Here is another example of the kind of claim we might find in an advertisement:

> In order to clear out inventory, we have reduced our used car prices by 20%. These prices won't last forever, so you'd better hurry in and buy one of these cars before the sale ends.

In this example we need to ask, "Reduced by 20% from what?" The car dealership might have used an outdated markup price no longer in effect in order to get an artificial reduction. Another possibility is that the dealer might have recently tried raising the cost of used cars and, if sales were slow, simply returned the prices to their previous level.

The fallacy of misleading precision can even occur in a seemingly straightforward scientific claim. Consider the following:

> The full moon affects people in strange ways. We have found that you have a 100% greater chance of being physically assaulted during a full moon than at any other time of the month.

In order to evaluate the argument, we need to know the average rate of physical assault over an extended period of time. Suppose we find that the average physical assault rate per month is 1 out of every 10,000 persons. According to the argument, the full moon rate would then be 2 out of every 10,000 persons. Although the statistics show that you have a 100% greater chance of being physically assaulted during a full moon, nevertheless the greater chance is not significant. Whenever statistics are used without a reference or comparison group, you should try to determine if this is an instance of misleading precision.

24. MISSING THE POINT

Missing the point
When premises that seem to lead logically to one conclusion are used instead to support an unexpected conclusion.

The fallacy of **missing the point** occurs when premises that seem to lead logically to one conclusion are used instead to support an unexpected conclusion. A conclusion "misses the point" when the premises do not adequately prepare us for it. For example:

> I read that it can take years to find the "black boxes" that contain crucial flight information regarding an airplane crash, and sometimes they are never found. Given this, all air travel should be suspended.

The conclusion diverts us from the direction of the premises. In fact, the evidence in the premises regarding the sometimes difficult task of locating the black boxes might be relevant to the following conclusions:

- The airline industry should adopt the latest technology whereby the black boxes can either float in water or have the capacity to send out beacon signals for more than 1 month.
- Airlines need to upgrade their airplanes with the latest GPS devices.
- The search-and-rescue teams that look for missing commercial airplanes should have the same equipment that is available to the military.

However, since the gap between the premises and conclusion that "all air travel should be suspended" is so great, we say that the argument misses the point.

Here is another example:

> The Affordable Care Act has been difficult to implement. There were system failures in which people could not log on to the government website, and even cases of people's private information being compromised. Therefore, we should never let the government try to solve social problems.

The premises provide evidence regarding the difficulty of putting the law into effect. Given this, we might expect to read conclusions like the following:

- The government should have waited until the systems were thoroughly tested.
- The government should have contracted with major computing companies to ensure that the systems were state of the art.

However, since the gap between the premises and conclusion that "we should never let the government try to solve social problems" is so great, we can say that the argument misses the point and has an irrelevant conclusion.

Summary of Fallacies of Unwarranted Assumption and Diversion

Fallacies of unwarranted assumption are arguments that assume the truth of some unproved or questionable claim.

15. **Begging the question:** In one type, the fallacy occurs when a premise is simply reworded in the conclusion. In a second type, called *circular reasoning*, a set of statements seem to support each other with no clear beginning or end point. In a third type, the argument assumes certain key information that may be controversial or is not supported by facts.

16. **Complex question:** The fallacy occurs when a single question actually contains multiple parts and an unestablished hidden assumption.

17. **Appeal to ignorance:** An argument built on a position of ignorance claims either that (1) a statement must be true because it has not been proven to be false or (2) a statement must be false because it has not been proven to be true.

18. **Appeal to an unqualified authority:** An argument that relies on the opinions of people who either have *no* expertise, training, or knowledge relevant to the issue at hand, or whose testimony is not trustworthy.

19. **False dichotomy:** The fallacy occurs when it is assumed that only two choices are possible, when in fact others exist.

A fallacy of diversion occurs when the meanings of terms or phrases are changed (intentionally or unintentionally) within the argument, or when our attention is purposely (or accidentally) diverted from the issue at hand.

20. **Equivocation:** The fallacy occurs when the conclusion of an argument relies on an intentional or unintentional shift in the meaning of a term or phrase in the premises.

21. **Straw man:** The fallacy occurs when an argument is misrepresented in order to create a new argument that can be easily refuted. The new argument is so weak that it is "made of straw." The arguer then falsely claims that his opponent's real argument has been defeated.

22. **Red herring:** The fallacy occurs when someone completely ignores an opponent's position and changes the subject, diverting the discussion in a new direction.

23. **Misleading precision:** A claim that appears to be statistically significant but is not.

24. **Missing the point:** When premises that seem to lead logically to one conclusion are used instead to support an unexpected conclusion.

EXERCISES 4D

Self-Practice
Questions

I. Determine whether each statement is true or false.

1. The appeal to an unqualified authority occurs when an argument relies on the experience, training, or knowledge of people who are experts relevant to the issue at hand.

Answer: False

2. An appeal to ignorance occurs when a claim is made that either (1) a statement must be true because it has not been proven to be false or (2) a statement must be false because it has not been proven to be true.

3. A claim that appears to be statistically significant but is not is an equivocation.

4. A complex question occurs when someone ignores an opponent's position.

⭐ 5. An argument that offers only two alternatives when in fact more exist is an example of a biased sample.

6. An argument that assumes as evidence the very thing that it attempts to prove in the conclusion begs the question.

7. A false dichotomy fallacy occurs when it is assumed that only two choices are possible, when in fact others exist.

8. The fallacy of missing the point occurs in an argument where premises that seem to lead logically to one conclusion are used instead to support an unexpected conclusion.

⭐ 9. A fallacy of equivocation mistakenly transfers an attribute of the individual parts of an object to the entire object.

10. When a claim is made that appears to be statistically significant but which, upon analysis, is not, is an example of the fallacy of red herring.

11. The red herring fallacy occurs when someone's words are taken out of context to create an argument that distorts the person's position.

12. A fallacy of equivocation can happen only if the argument intentionally uses different meanings of words or phrases.

⭐ 13. A straw man fallacy is a misapplication of statistics.

14. A claim that appears to be statistically significant, but which upon analysis is not, is the fallacy of accident.

15. A fallacy of equivocation occurs when a term has a different meaning in the premises than it has in the conclusion.

II. Read the following passages. If an argument commits a fallacy of unwarranted assumption or diversion, then identify the specific fallacy. If a passage does not contain a fallacy, then answer "No fallacy." Explain your answers.

1. She argued that we should raise taxes on people who make more than $250,000 a year. But she failed to mention that the government has a duty to protect all of its citizens, especially when we are constantly under threat of terrorists who want to see us destroyed. We can't let our guard down for a minute, so there is no reason to seriously consider her position at this time.

Answer: Straw man. The fallacy occurs when an argument is misrepresented in order to create a new argument that can be easily refuted. The new argument is so weak that it is "made of straw." The arguer then falsely claims that his opponent's real argument has been defeated.

2. Either you love your country or you are a traitor. I'm sure you are not a traitor. Therefore, you must love your country.

3. George Soros is famous because he broke the Bank of England. It follows that the Bank of England must have spent a lot of money on construction costs to fix all the broken parts of the bank.

4. Biology 1 was easy for me. Physics 1 was no problem. I think I'm going to change my major to social work.

⭐ 5. This car combines top engineering with classic styling. You can't buy a better engineered or classically styled car at any cost.

6. I believe that we are reincarnated. No one has ever been able to prove that after death our spirits don't move on to another baby.

7. The producer presented his budget for the movie. However, a lot of newspapers are going bankrupt, and so are many magazines. The cost of printing presses, newsprint, and ink is rising. Thus, we should reject his budget proposal.

8. Last week's poll showed the incumbent senator lost 10% in his overall approval rating. So, we can safely say that the incumbent senator has the lowest approval rating of any senator from this state in the last 50 years.

⭐ 9. We verified your employment history and did a credit check. I assume that you have read our repayment terms, since you signed the loan agreement form. Therefore, I am going to approve your application for a loan.

Video Tutorial: 4DII
Exercise #5

the evening hour is extended to 9 p.m. (time is based on local standards; i.e., whether the locality has adopted daylight savings time)." I think the law is clear, so you can't expect me to comply with your demands.

⭐ 41. She is a chess grand master, so when she says that Russia is manipulating the internal affairs of countries that were once part of the old Soviet Union, you should believe her.

42. I hear that Walter is handling some hot stocks right now. The new asbestos gloves I bought protect your hands from hot objects. Maybe I should give them to Walter for protection.

43. If you buy two lottery tickets, then you double your chances of hitting the jackpot. Knowing that, why would you buy just one?

44. When high school students graduate, they have a choice to make: They can either go to college or become bums. My niece decided not to go to college, so, mark my words, she will certainly become a bum.

⭐ 45. You want a raise because you have been here 2 years, your evaluations have been consistently high, you rarely miss work, and the company has experienced its highest stock dividends in the last 10 years. All of that is true, but have you forgotten that there are hundreds of thousands of people who are unemployed in this country? Any of them would be thrilled to have your job. In fact, most of them would even take less than you are making now. Given these facts, we can't justify giving you a raise.

46. Look, the picture of the Olympic basketball team is on this cereal. That proves it must be good for athletes.

47. The government's spending of our income tax money on public education without asking our permission is wrong; therefore, the government's actions are a violation of our human rights. Furthermore, since the government's actions are a violation of our human rights, it follows that the government's spending of our income tax money on public education without asking our permission is wrong.

48. The flight attendant said that the only two choices for the main entrée are chicken or fish. I don't like fish, so I'm getting the chicken.

⭐ 49. Evolution is a biological law of nature. All civilized people should obey the law. Therefore, all civilized people should obey the law of evolution.

50. You said that you don't believe in God. But here's something you overlooked. It is estimated that from 1975 to 1979, the Khmer Rouge, under the leadership of Pol Pot, killed roughly 25% of the population of Cambodia. The figure is believed to be between one and three million people out of a population of eight million. The Khmer Rouge were godless people, so ending their reign of terror was a good thing.

E. RECOGNIZING FALLACIES IN ORDINARY LANGUAGE

The examples of informal fallacies analyzed so far have been constructed to clearly reveal the mistake in reasoning. They were meant to be fairly easy to recognize—once you understand the underlying techniques. However, when you read something or hear someone talk, detecting informal fallacies may be a bit more challenging. A writer who has a fluid prose style can sometimes produce a persuasive passage merely by dazzling you with her brilliant writing. A great speaker can mesmerize his audience with the mere sound of his voice, so much so that we overlook the substance of what is being said.

For example, the great actor Laurence Olivier once gave an emotional acceptance speech at the Academy Awards:

> Mr. President and Governors of the Academy, Committee Members, fellows, my very noble and approved good masters, my colleagues, my friends, my fellow-students. In the great wealth, the great firmament of your nation's generosity, this particular choice may perhaps be found by future generations as a trifle eccentric, but the mere fact of it—the prodigal, pure, human kindness of it—must be seen as a beautiful star in that firmament which shines upon me at this moment, dazzling me a little, but filling me with warmth and the extraordinary elation, the euphoria that happens to so many of us at the first breath of the majestic glow of a new tomorrow. From the top of this moment, in the solace, in the kindly emotion that is charging my soul and my heart at this moment, I thank you for this great gift which lends me such a very splendid part in this, your glorious occasion.

This short speech left most of the audience in awe, in part because Olivier was considered perhaps the greatest Shakespearian actor and in part because of his dramatic delivery. Few people went back to read the words, which, although poetic and emotional, do not contain much of substance. The moral of the story is that we have to be careful when we encounter either impressive-sounding speech or beautifully crafted written material. This is especially true if the passages contain arguments.

Some fallacies occur because the emotional attachment to a belief overrides the demands of a clear, rational, well-supported argument. Here is one example:

> Our acceptance of abortion does not end with the killing of unborn human life; it continues on to affect our attitude toward all aspects of human life. This is most obvious in how quickly, once we accept abortion, then comes the acceptance of infanticide, the killing of babies who after birth do not come up to someone's standard of life worthy to be lived, and then on to euthanasia of the aged. If human life can be taken before birth, there is no logical reason why human life cannot be taken after birth.   Francis Schaeffer, *Who Is for Life?*

The author's position about abortion is clear. However, the attempt to discredit any acceptance of abortion leads the author to commit the slippery slope fallacy. No evidence is offered in the passage to support the (assumed) link in the chain of reasoning that "once we accept abortion, then comes the acceptance of infanticide." Similarly, the author provides no support for the next (assumed) link in the chain, namely the claim that "and then on to euthanasia of the aged." This example points out the importance of separating a belief from the possible reasons in support of a belief. It also illustrates the need to guard against the quick acceptance (or rejection) of a position based solely on our emotional attachment to a position.

The next passage contains another example of a slippery slope argument.

> Health care providers, researchers, and advocates around the country were alarmed to learn that POPLINE (POPulation information onLINE) had rendered the search term "abortion" a stopword—which directs the database to ignore the term when used in a search . . . self-censorship of a specific term like "abortion" in a scientific setting sets a dangerous precedent. . . . It's scary enough to consider the possibility that ideological searches are being performed by anonymous government employees who troll our scientific databases for the word "abortion." [The terms] "contraception," "sexuality," and "reproductive health" are the next stopwords, unless we remain vigilant and protest loudly.
>
> Pablo Rodriguez, M.D., Jennifer Aulwes, and Wayne C. Shields,
> "Abortion and the Slippery Slope," Scienceprogress.org

The authors argue that the website was directed to ignore the stopword "abortion" so the database would ignore it as a search term. The authors conclude that this form of censorship will lead to other terms being designated as stopwords. However, no evidence is offered to support their dire predictions. The argument fails to support the (assumed) links in the chain of reasoning that the terms "'contraception,' 'sexuality,' and 'reproductive health' are the next stopwords." Therefore, the argument commits the slippery slope fallacy.

Fallacies are not just the result of an emotional attachment to a moral question or to a controversial political viewpoint. In fact, they can occur in a scientific study:

> Winning the Nobel Prize adds nearly two years to your lifespan, and it's not because of the cash that goes with it. The status alone conferred on a scientist by the world's most famous prize is enough to prolong his life; in fact, the status seems to work a *health-giving magic*. The study compared Nobel Prize winners with scientists who were nominated, but did not win. The average lifespan for the winners was just over 76 years, while those who had merely been nominated lived on average for 75.8 years. The researchers found that since the amount of actual prize money won had no effect on longevity, therefore the sheer status of the award is the important factor in extending lifespan.
>
> Donald MacLeod, "Nobel Prize Winners Live Longer," *Education Guardian*

Quite often, a single piece of research gets widespread coverage because it seems to indicate some new and exciting discovery. However, advances in science occur through repeated and exhaustive trials in which many groups of researchers try to eliminate every possible explanation for an effect, leaving only one answer. Therefore, preliminary results, or studies with limited data, need to be carefully weighed. In this example, a correlation has been found, but the difference in longevity between the two groups is small. The argument to support the claim that "status causes the Nobel Prize winners to live longer" could be an instance of the *post hoc* fallacy—or simple coincidence.

Although emotional appeals are a powerful way to sway public opinion, unfortunately some of those appeals are fallacious. Most of us try to balance our feelings with reason, but it is not always easy. Strong emotions can sometimes override rational thinking and lead to disastrous results. This can be seen in the increase in political anger in the United States and the way it is broadcast over the airwaves. Incivility is on view almost daily, and rudeness, discourteous behavior, and disrespect can escalate into violence.

Many people have begun pleading for a less heated and less passionate climate in the public arena. The call is for a reduction in unhelpful rhetoric—in thinly veiled acts of retaliation, in blatant threats, in the exaggeration of apocalyptic social and political consequences, in direct insults, in misinformation and outright lies, and in an unhealthy disregard of intellectual thought and the role of reason. We can replace the negative and destructive tone with constructive and reasonable debate. Issues can be discussed based on facts and the merits of the arguments, without resorting to emotionally charged language that does nothing to advance the correctness of a position.

The call for a reduction in highly charged political discourse reached a high point following the shooting of a member of Congress in 2011. However, another member of Congress objected:

> We can't use this as a moment to try to stifle one side or the other. We can't use this as a moment to say, one side doesn't have a right to talk about the issues they are passionate about.

The response sets up a *straw man* argument by claiming that the advocates for a reduction in emotional rhetoric are saying that "one side doesn't have a right to talk about the issues they are passionate about." The speaker is arguing against a position that no one holds.

The principles of reason, intellectual honesty, and analysis that we applied to short examples can be adapted to longer passages as well. In fact, the next set of exercises allows you to apply those principles to recent events and to historically important cases, many of which are examples of extended arguments.

EXERCISES 4E

The following passages were taken from various sources. Use your understanding of all the fallacies that were presented in this chapter to determine which fallacy best fits the passage. In some cases a passage may contain more than one fallacy. If a passage does not contain a fallacy, then answer "No fallacy." Explain your answers.

Self-Practice
Questions

1. You can't speak French. Petey Bellows can't speak French. I must therefore conclude that nobody at the University of Minnesota can speak French.

Max Shulman, "Love Is a Fallacy"

Answer: Hasty generalization. The conclusion about the entire university is based on two instances.

2. It's a mistake because it is in error.

William Safire, "On Language: Take My Question Please!"

3. Over and over, they're saying something like this: "We don't know what the noise in the old house was, or the white shape in the photo. So it must be a ghost."

Alan Boyle, "Sleuth Finds the Truth in Ghost Stories," Cosmiclog.nbcnews.com

4. Either man was created just as the Bible tells us, or man evolved from inanimate chemicals and random chance.

Skeptic.org

★ 5. People for the Ethical Treatment of Animals has filed multiple complaints—including alleged animal abuse, the misuse of drugs on horses, and fraud—against trainer Steve Asmussen and his top assistant, Scott Blasi. . . . Clark Brewster, the attorney representing Asmussen and Blasi, said that he had not seen any of the complaints. . . . "Until I see the materials, it's hard to comment. It's obviously a piece completely out of context slanted for the purposes of the organization that caused somebody to deceptively be hired by the Asmussen stable."

David Grening, "PETA Accuses Asmussen Stable of Mistreating Its Horses," *Daily Racing Form*

6. "The fact that we received so much feedback to the Wolfe-Simon paper suggests to us that science is proceeding as it should," the editors said in a statement. "The study involved multiple techniques and lines of evidence, and the authors felt their conclusion was the most plausible explanation for these results when considered as a whole. We hope that the study and the subsequent exchange being published today will stimulate further experiments—whether they support or overturn this conclusion."

Alan Boyle, "Arsenic-Life Debate Hits a New Level," NBC News

7. It is the case that either the nobility of this country appear to be wealthy, in which case they can be taxed, or else they appear to be poor, in which case they are living frugally and must have immense savings, which can be taxed.

"Morton's Fork," *Encyclopedia Britannica*

8. I don't like spinach, and I'm glad I don't, because if I liked it I'd eat it, and I just hate it.

Clarence Darrow, in *Clarence Darrow: A One-Man Play*

Video Tutorial: 4E
Exercise #9

★ 9. I often read the Mexico enablers justify the 800,000 Mexicans illegally crossing the U.S. border each year, rationalizing this with a statement such as, "well it is either they stay in Mexico and starve, or risk their lives crossing the border."

"The Fulano Files," at Fulanofiles.blogspot.com

10. To be an atheist, you have to believe with absolute certainty that there is no God. In order to convince yourself with absolute certainty, you must examine all the Universe and all the places where God could possibly be. Since you obviously haven't, your position is indefensible.

Infidels.org

11. Near-perfect correlations exist between the death rate in Hyderabad, India, from 1911 to 1919, and variations in the membership of the International Association of Machinists during the same period.

David Hackett Fischer, Historians' Fallacies

12. I hardly think that 58 is the right age at which to talk about a retirement home unless there are some serious health concerns. My 85-year-old mother power-walks two miles each day, drives her car safely, climbs stairs, does crosswords, and reads the daily paper.   Letter to the editor, Time

⭐ 13. For the natives, they are near all dead of the smallpox, so as the Lord hath cleared our title to what we possess.

John Winthrop, governor, Massachusetts Colony, 1634

14. Information is what you need to make money short term. Knowledge is the deeper understanding of how things work. It's obtained only by long and inefficient study. It's gained by those who set aside the profit motive and instead possess an intrinsic desire just to know.

David Brooks, "The Moral Power of Curiosity," The New York Times

15. He's not a moron at all, he's a friend. My personal relations with the president are extremely good.   Canadian prime minister Jean Chrétien, quoted in the Canadian Press

16. Why opium produces sleep: Because there is in it a dormitive power.

Molière, The Imaginary Invalid

⭐ 17. My opponent wants to sever the Danish church from the state for his own personal sake. His motion is an attempt to take over the church and further his ecumenical theology by his usual mafia methods.

Charlotte Jorgensen, "Hostility in Public Debate"

18. I do not have much information on this case except the general statement of the agency that there is nothing in the files to disprove his Communist connections.   Richard H. Rovere, Senator Joe McCarthy

19. We took the Bible and prayer out of public schools, and now we're having weekly shootings practically. We had the '60s sexual revolution, and now people are dying of AIDS.   Christine O'Donnell, quoted in the New Statesman

20. In many ways, the process reflects the history of the Capitol and the nation, said Mr. Ritchie, the historian. "The Capitol building is an interesting conglomeration," he said. "It is a whole series of buildings put together at different times, and in that way it is a nice reflection of American democracy, which was put together piecemeal from a lot of different materials. It reflects one motto of our nation, 'E pluribus unum,' Latin for 'Out of many, one.'"

Jennifer Steinhauer, "Leaky Capitol Dome Imperiled by 1,300 Cracks, Partisan Rift," The New York Times

⭐ 21. How is education supposed to make me feel smarter? Besides, every time I learn something new, it pushes some old stuff out of my brain. Remember when I took that home winemaking course, and I forgot how to drive?

Homer Simpson, "Secrets of a Successful Marriage," The Simpsons

22. The community of Pacific Palisades is extremely wealthy. Therefore, every person living there is extremely wealthy.   Peter A. Angeles, *Dictionary of Philosophy*

23. Dear Friend, a man who has studied law to its highest degree is a brilliant lawyer, for a brilliant lawyer has studied law to its highest degree.

Oscar Wilde, *De Profundis*

24. The most stringent protection of free speech would not protect a man in falsely shouting fire in a theater and causing a panic.

Oliver Wendell Homes, Supreme Court Opinion, *Schenk v. United States*

⭐ 25. Musical chills are known as aesthetic chills, thrills, shivers, and involve a seconds-long feeling of goose bumps and tingling . . . the emotions evoked by beautiful music stimulate the hypothalamus, which controls primal drives such as hunger, sex and rage and also involuntary responses like blushing and goosebumps.

Brian Alexander, "*Messiah* Give You Chills? That's a Clue to Your Personality," MSNBC.com

26. Twenty-seven years ago, Luis Alvarez first proposed that the Cretaceous–Tertiary extinction event was caused by an asteroid that struck the earth 65.5 million years earlier. This means the dinosaurs died out 65,500,027 years ago.

Worldlingo.com

27. Should we not assume that just as the eye, hand, the foot, and in general each part of the body clearly has its own proper function, so man too has some function over and above the function of his parts?   Aristotle, *Nicomachean Ethics*

28. We will starve terrorists of funding, turn them one against another, drive them from place to place, until there is no refuge or rest. And we will pursue nations that provide aid or safe haven to terrorism. Every nation, in every region, now has a decision to make. Either you are with us, or you are with the terrorists.

George W. Bush, Sept. 20, 2001, in an address to Congress

⭐ 29. You may be interested to know that global warming, earthquakes, hurricanes, and other natural disasters are a direct effect of the shrinking numbers of Pirates since the 1800s. For your interest, I have included a graph of the approximate number of pirates versus the average global temperature over the last 200 years. As you can see, there is a statistically significant inverse relationship between pirates and global temperature.

Bobby Henderson, "Open Letter to Kansas School Board"

30. Why should farmers and plant owners expect people to take a back-breaking seasonal job with low pay and no benefits just because they happen to be offering it? If no one wants an available job—especially in extreme times—maybe the fault doesn't rest entirely with the people turning it down. Maybe the market is inefficient.

Elizabeth Dwoskin, "Why Americans Won't Do Dirty Jobs," *Bloomberg Businessweek*

31. Gerda Reith is convinced that superstition can be a positive force. "It gives you a sense of control by making you think you can work out what's going to

happen next," she says. "And it also makes you feel lucky. And to take a risk or to enter into a chancy situation, you really have to believe in your own luck. In that sense, it's a very useful way of thinking, because the alternative is fatalism, which is to say, 'Oh, there's nothing I can do.' At least superstition makes people do things."

David Newnham, "Hostages to Fortune"

32. We can't change the present or the future. . . . We can only change the past, and we do it all the time. Interview with Bob Dylan in *Rolling Stone*

⭐ 33. Morality in this nation has worsened at the same time that adherence to traditional Christian beliefs has declined. Obviously, the latter has caused the former, so encouraging Christianity will ensure a return to traditional moral standards.

About.com

34. Whether deconstruction is an art or a science, a malady or a Catch-22, it would seem to belong at honours level in university degrees. School is for basics and knowledge, certainly accompanied by critical thinking, but not in a milieu where all is relative and there are no absolutes for young people who do not have the intellectual maturity to cope with the somewhat morbid rigour of constant criticism and questioning of motives. If you go on deconstructing for long enough you will become a marshmallow or a jelly.

Kenneth Wiltshire, "In Defense of the True Values of Learning"

35. It's our job to make college basketball players realize that getting an education is something that's important, because life after basketball is a real long time. Larry Brown, Southern Methodist University basketball coach

36. *Dan Quayle:* I have far more experience than many others that sought the office of vice president of this country. I have as much experience in Congress as Jack Kennedy did when he sought the presidency. I will be prepared to deal with the people in the Bush administration, if that unfortunate event would ever occur.
Lloyd Bentsen: I served with Jack Kennedy; I knew Jack Kennedy; Jack Kennedy was a friend of mine. Senator, you're no Jack Kennedy.

The 1988 U.S. vice presidential debates

⭐ 37. I call this the "Advertiser's Fallacy" because it's so prevalent in commercials, such as the one where a famous baseball slugger gives medical advice on erectile dysfunction (that should pick up the hit count!). No. See a properly qualified doctor for ED, see Rafael Palmiero only if you want to improve your baseball swing. Joe McFaul, "Law, Evolution, Science, and Junk Science"

38. Recently, we highlighted a British journalist's story about the underside of Dubai's startling ascent. Some in Dubai called foul, including one writer who wants to remind Britons that their own country has a dark side. After all, what to think of a country in which one fifth of the population lives in poverty?

Freakonomics.com, "Dubai's Rebuttal"

39. The anti-stem-cell argument goes like this: If you permit scientists to destroy human embryos for the purpose of research, [then it goes] from there to killing human fetuses in order to harvest tissue, and from there to euthanizing disabled or terminally ill people to harvest their organs, and from there to human cloning and human-animal hybrids, and if making chimeras is okay, well then Dr. Frankenstein must also be okay, and Dr. Mengele, too, and before you know it, it's one long hapless inevitable slide from high-minded medicine to the Nazis.

Marty Kaplan, in an article at Huffingtonpost.com

40. In Aesop's fable, "the crow and the pitcher," a thirsty crow dropped stones in a pitcher to raise the water level and quench its thirst. Past experiments have shown that crows and their relatives—altogether known as corvids—are indeed "remarkably intelligent, and in many ways rival the great apes in their physical intelligence and ability to solve problems," said researcher Christopher Bird at the University of Cambridge in England.

Charles Q. Choi, "Bird's Tool Use Called 'Amazing,'" Livescience.com

⭐ 41. These are the times that try men's souls. The summer soldier and the sunshine patriot will in this crisis shrink from the service of his country; but he that stands it now deserves the love and thanks for man and woman. Tyranny, like hell, is not easily conquered; yet we have this consolation with us, that the harder the conflict, the more glorious the triumph. What we obtain too cheap, we esteem too lightly; 'tis dearness only that gives everything its value. Heaven knows how to put a proper price upon its goods; and it would be strange indeed, if so celestial an article as freedom should not be highly rated. Britain, with an army to enforce her tyranny, has declared that she has a right (not only to tax) but "to bind us in all cases whatsoever," and if being bound in that manner is not slavery, then there is no such thing as slavery upon earth.

Thomas Paine, *The Crisis*

42. Once one is caught up into the material world not one person in ten thousand finds the time to form literary taste, to examine the validity of philosophic concepts for himself, or to form what, for lack of a better phrase, I might call the wise and tragic sense of life.

F. Scott Fitzgerald

43. If the Iraqi regime is able to produce, buy, or steal an amount of highly-enriched uranium a little larger than a single softball, it could have a nuclear weapon in less than a year. And if we allow that to happen, a terrible line would be crossed. Saddam Hussein would be in a position to blackmail anyone who opposes his aggression. He would be in a position to dominate the Middle East. He would be in a position to threaten America. And Saddam Hussein would be in a position to pass nuclear technology to terrorists. Knowing these realities, America must not ignore the threat gathering against us. Facing clear evidence of peril, we cannot wait for the final proof—the smoking gun—that could come in the form of a mushroom cloud.

President George W. Bush, October 8, 2002

44. A person apparently hopelessly ill may be allowed to take his own life. Then he may be permitted to deputize others to do it for him should he no longer be able to act. The judgment of others then becomes the ruling factor. Already at this point euthanasia is not personal and voluntary, for others are acting on behalf of the patient as they see fit. This may well incline them to act on behalf of other patients who have not authorized them to exercise their judgment. It is only a short step, then, from voluntary euthanasia (self-inflicted or authorized), to directed euthanasia administered to a patient who has given no authorization, to involuntary euthanasia conducted as a part of a social policy.

J. Gay Williams, "The Wrongfulness of Euthanasia"

⭐ 45. The Supreme Court sided with the video game industry today, declaring a victor in the six-year legal match between the industry and the California lawmakers who wanted to make it a crime for anyone in the state to sell extremely violent games to kids. . . . "The basic principles of freedom of speech . . . do not vary with a new and different communication medium," [Justice] Scalia wrote in the Court's opinion.

Stephen Totilo, "1st Amendment Beats Ban in Video Game Battle," MSNBC.MSN.com

46. Once, many National Football League (NFL) teams played on Thanksgiving; to this day, high school teams play championship or rivalry games on Thanksgiving. In the 1950s, the old NFL began a tradition of having only one game on turkey day, always at Detroit. In the 1960s, a Cowboys' home date was added on Thanksgiving, to help the Dallas expansion franchise become established. Detroit and Dallas have been the traditional hosts since.

Gregg Easterbrook, ESPN.com's Page 2

47. If I were to suggest that between the Earth and Mars there is a china teapot revolving about the sun in an elliptical orbit, nobody would be able to disprove my assertion provided I were careful to add that the teapot is too small to be revealed even by our most powerful telescopes. But if I were to go on to say that, since my assertion cannot be disproved, it is an intolerable presumption on the part of human reason to doubt it, I should rightly be thought to be talking nonsense. If, however, the existence of such a teapot were affirmed in ancient books, taught as the sacred truth every Sunday, and instilled into the minds of children at school, hesitation to believe in its existence would become a mark of eccentricity and entitle the doubter to the attentions of the psychiatrist in an enlightened age or of the Inquisitor in an earlier time.

Bertrand Russell, "Is There a God?"

48. *Dorothy:* Are you doing that on purpose, or can't you make up your mind?
Scarecrow: That's the trouble. I can't make up my mind. I haven't got a brain—just straw.
Dorothy: How can you talk if you haven't got a brain?
Scarecrow: I don't know. But some people without brains do an awful lot of talking, don't they?
Dorothy: I guess you're right.

From the movie *The Wizard of Oz*

★ 49. Great college football rivalries engage the healthy, activate the disturbed, fascinate the thoughtful, amaze the detached, mystify the rational, horrify the scholarly, encourage the immature, enrich the greedy, and terrify the faint of heart.   Bill Curry, "Stoops, Brown Legacies Entangled in Red River Rivalry," ESPN.com

50. A rabid debate about security and privacy has begun. As the Edward Snowden affair enters its second month, Americans don't seem to have much appetite for the subtlety of such a debate. The Prism leak discussion has been framed repeatedly as a zero-sum game, pitting privacy on one side and security on the other. "You can't have 100 percent security and also have 100 percent privacy," President Obama said on June 7, in his principal public statement in the issue, suggesting there is some dial which forces government officials to pick one over the other.

   Bob Sullivan, "Privacy vs. Security: 'False Choice' Poisons Debate on NSA Leaks," NBC News

Study Materials

Summary

- Formal fallacy: A logical error that occurs in the form or structure of an argument and is restricted to deductive arguments.
- Informal fallacy: A mistake in reasoning that occurs in ordinary language and concerns the content of the argument rather than its form.
- *Ad hominem* abusive: The fallacy is distinguished by an attack on alleged character flaws of a person instead of the person's argument.
- *Ad hominem* circumstantial: When someone's argument is rejected based on the circumstances of the person's life.
- Poisoning the well: The fallacy occurs when a person is attacked *before* she has a chance to present her case.
- *Tu quoque*: The fallacy is distinguished by the specific attempt of one person to avoid the issue at hand by claiming the other person is a hypocrite.
- Fallacious appeal to emotion: When an argument relies solely on the arousal of a strong emotional state or psychological reaction to get us to accept the conclusion.
- Appeal to the people: The fallacy occurs when an argument manipulates a psychological need or desire, such as the desire to belong to a popular group, or the need for group solidarity, so that the reader or listener will accept the conclusion.
- Appeal to pity: The fallacy results from an exclusive reliance on a sense of pity or mercy for support of a conclusion.
- Appeal to fear or force: A threat of harmful consequences (physical or otherwise) used to force acceptance of a course of action that would otherwise be unacceptable.
- Generalization fallacy: A fallacy that occurs when an argument relies on a mistaken use of the principles behind making a generalization.

- Rigid application of a generalization: When a generalization or rule is inappropriately applied to the case at hand. The fallacy results from the belief that the generalization or rule is universal (meaning it has no exceptions).
- Hasty generalization: An argument that relies on a small sample that is unlikely to represent the population.
- Composition: There are two forms of the fallacy: (1) the mistaken transfer of an attribute of the individual *parts of an object* to the *object as a whole* and (2) the mistaken transfer of an attribute of the individual *members of a class* to the *class itself*.
- Division: There are two forms of the fallacy: (1) the mistaken transfer of an attribute of an *object as a whole* to the individual *parts of the object* and (2) the mistaken transfer of an attribute of a *class* to the individual *members of the class*.
- Biased sample: An argument that uses a nonrepresentative sample as support for a statistical claim about an entire population.
- *Post hoc*: The fallacy occurs from the mistaken assumption that just because one event occurred before another event, the first event *must have caused* the second event.
- Slippery slope: An argument that attempts to connect a series of occurrences such that the first link in a chain leads directly to a second link, and so on, until a final unwanted situation is said to be the inevitable result.
- Fallacies of unwarranted assumption: Arguments that assume the truth of some unproved or questionable claim.
- Begging the question: In one type, the fallacy occurs when a premise is simply reworded in the conclusion. In a second type, called *circular reasoning*, a set of statements seem to support each other with no clear beginning or end point. In a third type, the argument assumes certain key information that may be controversial or is not supported by facts.
- Complex question: The fallacy occurs when a single question actually contains multiple parts and an unestablished hidden assumption.
- Appeal to ignorance: An argument built on a position of ignorance claims either that (1) a statement must be true because it has not been proven to be false or (2) a statement must be false because it has not been proven to be true.
- Appeal to an unqualified authority: An argument that relies on the opinions of people who either have *no* expertise, training, or knowledge relevant to the issue at hand, or whose testimony is not trustworthy.
- False dichotomy: A fallacy that occurs when it is assumed that only two choices are possible, when in fact others exist.
- Fallacy of diversion: A fallacy that occurs when the meanings of terms or phrases are changed (intentionally or unintentionally) within the argument, or when our attention is purposely (or accidentally) diverted from the issue at hand.

- Equivocation: The fallacy occurs when the conclusion of an argument relies on an intentional or unintentional shift in the meaning of a term or phrase in the premises.
- Straw man: The fallacy occurs when someone's argument is misrepresented in order to create a new argument that can be easily refuted. The new argument is so weak that it is "made of straw." The arguer then falsely claims that his opponent's real argument has been defeated.
- Red herring: A fallacy that occurs when someone completely ignores an opponent's position and changes the subject, diverting the discussion in a new direction.
- Misleading precision: A claim that appears to be statistically significant but is not.
- Missing the point: When premises that seem to lead logically to one conclusion are used instead to support an unexpected conclusion.

KEY TERMS

LOGIC CHALLENGE: A CLEVER PROBLEM

In a certain faraway country (long, long, ago), prisoners to be executed were either shot or hanged. Prisoners were allowed to make one statement. If their statement turned out to be true, then they were hanged. If their statement turned out to be false, then they were shot. That is, until one clever prisoner put an end to the practice of execution. The prisoner made her one statement, upon which the judge was forced to set her free. What statement did she make?

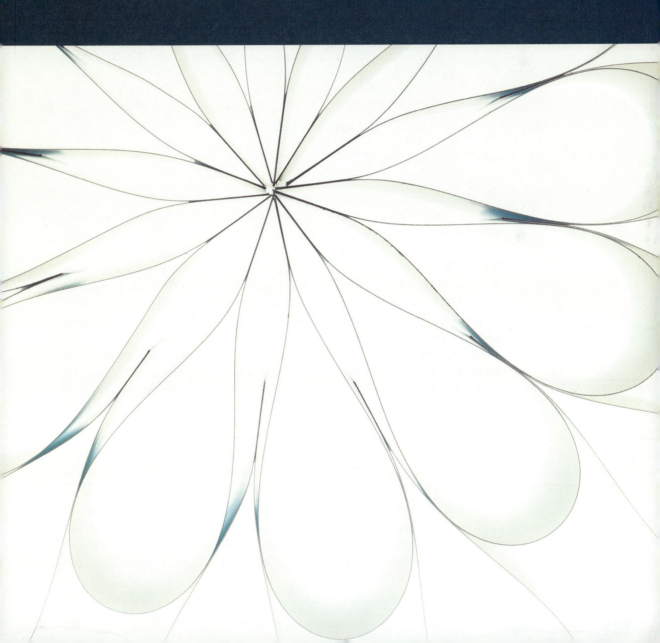

PART III

FORMAL LOGIC

Chapter 5

Categorical Propositions

Digital homework exercises for this chapter are available in your instructor's online course. For information on how to access these resources, please visit **www.oup.com/he/baronett5e.**

What if you saw a sign in a store: "No discounted items are returnable." You have just bought those new running shoes you needed—and paid full price. Are they returnable? Based on this single sign, can you conclude that *all* (or at least *some*) nondiscounted items are returnable? Is it possible that *none* of the items in the store are returnable?

Now you get an e-mail: "All graduating seniors are expected to pay their outstanding debts in full." Can you conclude that, if you are a sophomore, then you are *not* expected to pay your outstanding debts in full? Are graduating seniors the only students expected to pay their debts?

On another occasion, you happen to overhear someone talking about a restaurant: "Some of the food they serve is absolutely horrible." Can you conclude that, according to the speaker, some of the food the restaurant serves is *not* absolutely horrible?

These examples all refer to groups of objects: "discounted items," "graduating seniors," and "food the restaurant serves." Statements about groups like these are the subject of *categorical logic*. They are part of the generalizations we make every day about our experiences, about other people, and about ourselves. In fact, when it comes to politics or our futures, it is hard to resist making generalizations—but how valid are they, and what can we safely conclude when it comes to particulars? This chapter explores the foundations of categorical logic, which go back to Aristotle's fundamental work in the 4th century BCE. A thorough exploration will take us to two modern thinkers, George Boole and John Venn, whose work led to an alternative system to Aristotle's interpretations. Diagrams can guide us through arguments, and Venn showed how to picture categorical logic.

A. CATEGORICAL PROPOSITIONS

We begin with a discussion of classes, or *categories*. A **class** is a group of objects, and a *categorical proposition* relates two classes of objects. More specifically, a **categorical proposition** either affirms or denies total class inclusion, or else it affirms or denies partial class inclusion. For example:

> All stand-up comedians are witty persons.

This categorical proposition refers to two classes of objects—*stand-up comedians* and *witty persons*. In this proposition, "stand-up comedians" is the **subject term**, and "witty persons" is the **predicate term**. In addition to claiming that *all* stand-up comedians are witty persons we might instead say that *some* of them are:

> Some stand-up comedians are witty persons.

In contrast, we might say that *none* of them are:

> No stand-up comedians are witty persons.

Finally, we might say that *some* of them *are not*:

> Some stand-up comedians are not witty persons.

If we let S stand for the subject term and P stand for the predicate term in a categorical proposition, then we can say any of the following regarding S and P:

All S are P.   **Some S are P.**   **No S are P.**   **Some S are not P.**

As these examples illustrate, categorical propositions are about *class inclusion* (what objects belong to a class), as well as *class exclusion*. Centuries ago, logicians took the vowels from the Latin words "*affirmo*" (meaning *I affirm*) and "*nego*" (meaning *I deny*) and used them to designate the four types of categorical propositions:

- **A-propositions** assert that the entire subject class is included in the predicate class:
  A: All S are P.
- **I-propositions** assert that part of the subject class is included in the predicate class:
  I: Some S are P.
- **E-propositions** assert that the entire subject class is excluded from the predicate class:
  E: No S are P.
- **O-propositions** assert that part of the subject class is excluded from the predicate class:
  O: Some S are not P.

Class A group of objects.

Categorical proposition A proposition that relates two classes of objects. It either affirms or denies total class inclusion, or else it affirms or denies partial class inclusion.

Subject term The term that comes first in a standard-form categorical proposition.

Predicate term The term that comes second in a standard-form categorical proposition.

A-proposition A categorical proposition having the form "All S are P."

I-proposition A categorical proposition having the form "Some S are P."

E-proposition A categorical proposition having the form "No S are P."

O-proposition A categorical proposition having the form "Some S are not P."

Standard-form categorical proposition
A proposition that has one of the following forms: "All S are P," "Some S are P," "No S are P," "Some S are not P."

Universal affirmative
An A-proposition. It affirms that every member of the subject class is a member of the predicate class.

Universal negative
An E-proposition. It asserts that no members of the subject class are members of the predicate class.

The letters **A**, **E**, **I**, and **O** designate the four *standard forms* of categorical propositions. Since these are forms of propositions rather than actual propositions, they are neither true nor false. Replacing the S and P in a standard form with terms denoting classes of objects—the subject and predicate terms—results in a **standard-form categorical proposition** that is either true or false. For example, "All cell phones are expensive toys" is an **A**-proposition; the class terms "cell phones" and "expensive toys" replace the S and P in the standard form "All S are P." If you were to utter this proposition, then you would be claiming that *every* member of the subject class (cell phones) is a member of the predicate class (expensive toys). Since **A**-propositions affirm that every member of the subject class is a member of the predicate class, they are also called **universal affirmative** propositions.

We can substitute the terms "cell phones" and "expensive toys" for the subject and predicate of the three remaining standard forms as well. The first, "No cell phones are expensive toys" is an **E**-proposition. If you make this claim, then you are asserting that *no* members of the subject class are members of the predicate class. Since **E**-propositions assert that no members of the subject class are members of the predicate class, they are called **universal negative** propositions.

The next example, "Some cell phones are expensive toys," is an **I**-proposition. If you make this claim, then you are asserting that *at least one* member of the subject class is a member of the predicate class. Since **I**-propositions assert that *at least one* member

PROFILES IN LOGIC
Aristotle

Aristotle (384–322 BCE) is often said to have originated the study of logic, and his ideas dominated Western thought for 2000 years. His writings influenced every aspect of European culture—from politics and art to ethics and philosophy.

Aristotle wanted logic and science to complement each other, and he developed his logic, in no small part, to make scientific reasoning more solid. Aristotle's science relied on the idea of classification: To understand the things around us, we look at what they share and we rely on what we know. We therefore group them together, as a subclass of a class that is already well understood. In much the same way, Aristotle's system of logic is based on relationships

between classes. For example, the statement "All humans are mortal beings" contains a subject term ("humans") and a predicate term ("mortal beings"). It asserts that the class of humans is included in the class of mortal beings.

"All humans are mortal beings" is a *universal statement*—it applies to every one of us. But Aristotle went a step further. Because it applies to all of us, he reasoned, it is a statement about the world: The class of humans has members that actually exist. When we analyze an argument, he assumed, we are also investigating whether the statements are true. In contrast, modern logic separates the *truth of statements* from the *validity of arguments*.

of the subject class is a member of the predicate class, they are called **particular affirmative** propositions.

The final example, "Some cell phones are not expensive toys," is an **O**-proposition. If you make this claim, then you are asserting that *at least one* member of the subject class is *not* a member of the predicate class. Since **O**-propositions assert that *at least one* member of the subject class is not a member of the predicate class, they are called **particular negative** propositions.

Since Aristotle is credited with doing substantial work on the subject of categorical logic, it seems appropriate to use his name as a tool for remembering the different designations. The four vowels in "Aristotle" match the ones used in our discussion.

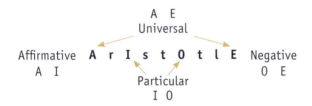

When people speak or write in ordinary language, they might not use standard-form categorical propositions. Later in this chapter you will see how ordinary language statements can be translated into standard-form categorical propositions. Since some ordinary language statements are ambiguous, translations (where appropriate) into standard-form categorical propositions can reduce the ambiguity. For now, though, we will continue exploring standard-form categorical propositions.

Particular affirmative
An I-proposition. It asserts that at least one member of the subject class is a member of the predicate class.

Particular negative
An O-proposition. It asserts that at least one member of the subject class is not a member of the predicate class.

EXERCISES 5A

Analyze each categorical proposition by doing the following: (1) Identify the subject term and predicate term of each proposition; (2) identify the categorical proposition as either A (All S are P), E (No S are P), I (Some S are P), or O (Some S are not P).

Self-Practice Questions

1. All senior citizens are people eligible for subsidized drug prescriptions.
Answer: Subject: *senior citizens*. Predicate: *people eligible for subsidized drug prescriptions*.
This is an example of an **A**-proposition.

2. Some public schools are not schools meeting national standards for excellence.

3. Some family incomes are incomes below the poverty line.

4. No private healthcare plans are easy to understand policies.

⭐ 5. All malicious murderers are evil people.

6. All public astrophysics lectures are intellectually stimulating events.

7. Some video games are not violent activities.

8. Some petty bureaucrats are tyrannical people.

⭐ 9. No lottery winners are lucky people.

10. Some diet fads are not healthy lifestyles.

11. All presidential election years are important historical times.

12. Some philosophy books are important contributions to literature.

⭐13. No amendments to the U.S. Constitution are unconstitutional acts.

14. All gamblers are superstitious people.

15. Some psychics are frauds.

B. QUANTITY, QUALITY, AND DISTRIBUTION

Quantity When we classify a categorical proposition as either universal or particular we are referring to its quantity.

Quality When we classify a categorical proposition as either affirmative or negative we are referring to its quality.

When we classify a categorical proposition as either *universal* or *particular*, we are referring to its **quantity**. Universal categorical propositions (**A** or **E**) refer to *every* member of the subject class, while particular categorical propositions (**I** or **O**) refer to *at least one* member of the subject class. When we classify a categorical proposition as either *affirmative* or *negative*, we are referring to its **quality**, which deals with class inclusion or exclusion. The affirmative categorical propositions are **A** and **I**. In **A**-propositions, *every* member of the subject class is a member of the predicate class; in **I**-propositions, *at least one* member of the subject class is a member of the predicate class. The negative categorical propositions are **E** and **O**. In **E**-propositions, *no* members of the subject class are members of the predicate class; in **O**-propositions, *at least one* member of the subject class is *not* a member of the predicate class. Once again, it is important to separate these logical issues from any determination of the actual truth value of a categorical proposition.

		Subject		Predicate	Quantity	Quality
		↓		↓	↓	↓
A:	All	S	are	P.	*universal*	*affirmative*
E:	No	S	are	P.	*universal*	*negative*
I:	Some	S	are	P.	*particular*	*affirmative*
O:	Some	S	are not	P.	*particular*	*negative*

Quantifier The words "all," "no," and "some" are quantifiers. They tell us the extent of the class inclusion or exclusion.

Copula The words "are" and "are not" are referred to as copula; they are simply forms of "to be" and serve to link (to "couple") the subject class with the predicate class.

In categorical propositions, the words "all," "no," and "some" are called **quantifiers** because they tell us the extent of the class inclusion or exclusion. The words "are" and "are not" are referred to as **copula**. They are simply forms of "to be" and serve to link (to *couple*) the subject class with the predicate class.

Quantifier   Subject   Copula   Predicate
↓   ↓   ↓   ↓
All potatoes are vegetables.

It is important to recognize that quantifiers refer to the subject class and not to the predicate class. For example, if I say "All romantic movies are good places to go on a first date," then I am asserting something about the subject class (romantic movies)—namely, that it is completely included in the predicate class (good places to go on a first date). But my assertion leaves open the extent of the predicate class.

If a categorical proposition asserts something about every member of a class, then the term designating that class is said to be **distributed**. For example, anyone uttering the proposition "All cats are mammals" makes an assertion about every member of the class of cats. Since the assertion is that *every cat* is a mammal, the subject term is distributed. On the other hand, if the proposition does not assert something about every member of a class, then the term designating that class is said to be **undistributed**. In "All cats are mammals," the predicate term is not distributed, since the word "all" does not extend its reference to mammals. In the same way, in the categorical proposition "All cats are diplomats," the subject term is distributed and the predicate term is undistributed. (Remember that this is a logical discussion. It does not address the question of truth value.)

The distinction between distributed and undistributed terms does not just apply to **A**-propositions. Let's examine the proposition "No public universities are adequately funded institutions." Since this is an **E**-proposition, the quantifier makes an assertion regarding every member of the subject class: It claims that *not even one* is a member of the predicate class. Thus, the subject term is distributed. However, unlike the results for **A**-propositions, **E**-propositions result in the predicate term being distributed. This follows because if no member of the subject class is a member of the predicate class, then the reverse must be true too. Therefore, in **E**-propositions both the subject term and predicate term are distributed.

The next example concerns **I**-propositions. If you say "Some students in this class are sophomores," then we know that the quantifier "some" refers to the subject class. Since your assertion is only that *at least one* of the students in this class is a sophomore, the subject term is not distributed. In addition, the predicate term is not distributed. Bear in mind that it is easy to misinterpret **I**-propositions. In the categorical proposition "Some students in this class are sophomores," it is *possible* for every member of the subject class to be included in the predicate class. In other words, it is possible that every student in this class is a sophomore. Recognizing this possibility eliminates a potential misunderstanding. It is incorrect to conclude "Some students in this class are *not* sophomores."

The proposition "Some cars are not fuel-efficient vehicles" is an **O**-proposition. Here again, the quantifier word "some" refers only to the subject class. If you utter this proposition, then you are asserting that *at least one* car is not a fuel-efficient vehicle. Since nothing is asserted about every member of the subject class, the subject term is not distributed. But in an interesting twist, something about the predicate class is revealed. Whenever a categorical proposition says something about *every member* of a class, then the term designating that class is distributed. In our example, since *at least one* member of the subject class is excluded from *every* member of the predicate class, then the predicate term is distributed.

Distributed If a categorical proposition asserts something about every member of a class, then the term designating that class is said to be distributed.

Undistributed If a proposition does not assert something about every member of a class, then the term designating that class is said to be undistributed.

Once again, we must be careful not to misinterpret these results. The quantifier "some" in the **O**-proposition allows the *possibility* that every member of the subject class is excluded from the predicate class. It is, therefore, incorrect to think that the proposition "Some cars are not fuel-efficient vehicles" allows you to logically conclude that "Some cars are fuel-efficient vehicles." In other words, the proposition does not rule out the possibility that every member of the subject class is excluded from the predicate class.

QUANTITY, QUALITY, AND DISTRIBUTION APPLIED TO A, E, I, AND O			
Proposition	Quantity	Quality	Term Distributed
A: All S are P.	*universal*	*affirmative*	subject
E: No S are P.	*universal*	*negative*	subject and predicate
I: Some S are P.	*particular*	*affirmative*	no distribution
O: Some S are not P.	*particular*	*negative*	predicate

A *mnemonic* is something that can be used to assist the memory. (The movie *Johnny Mnemonic* was about a person who had a cybernetic brain implant to store information.) For example, if you have studied a musical instrument you probably used the phrase "Every Good Boy Deserves Favor" to remember the notes on the treble clef—EGBDF. If it helps, you can use the following mnemonic device to remember that *subjects get distributed by universals, and predicates get distributed by negatives.*

SUPN	Subjects—Universals	Predicates—Negatives

The following illustration displays the information in this section:

QUANTITY, QUALITY, AND DISTRIBUTION	
All S are P. Universal Affirmative Subject term distributed Predicate term undistributed	**No S are P.** Universal Negative Subject term distributed Predicate term distributed
Some S are P. Particular Affirmative Subject term undistributed Predicate term undistributed	**Some S are not P.** Particular Negative Subject term undistributed Predicate term distributed

The figure uses a square to arrange the four categorical propositions. On top are the two universal propositions (**A** and **E**), and on the bottom are the two particular propositions (**I** and **O**). The left side of the square has the two affirmative propositions (**A** and **I**), and the right side has the two negative propositions (**E** and **O**). The square arranges the propositions such that the mnemonic device **SUPN** can be applied.

The first part, **SU** (subjects get distributed by universals), is illustrated by the top of the square (**A**- and **E**-propositions), and the second part, **PN** (predicates get distributed by negatives), is illustrated by the right side of the square (**E**- and **O**-propositions). That leaves the lower left side of the square (**I**-propositions) as the only categorical proposition that does not distribute at least one term. This simple square will serve as the foundation for the discussions in the remainder of the chapter.

EXERCISES 5B

I. **The following categorical propositions below are to be analyzed in three ways: (1) the correct *quantity* (*universal* or *particular*); (2) the correct *quality* (*affirmative* or *negative*); (3) the correct *distribution* (subject term distributed; predicate term distributed; both terms distributed; or neither term distributed).**

Self-Practice
Questions

1. All ice-cold soft drinks are thirst-quenching beverages.
Answer: Universal affirmative; subject term distributed; predicate term undistributed.

2. Some alternative smoking devices are not safe products.

3. No computer software programs are easily installed items.

4. Some off-road vehicles are machines that damage the environment.

⭐ 5. No tigers are vegetarians.

6. No fast-food franchises are benevolent employers.

7. Some universities are intellectual gardens.

8. Some tattoos are not acceptable fashions for parents.

⭐ 9. All body-piercing rituals are beliefs based on ancient religions.

10. No winning gamblers are probability deficient people.

11. All sugar-free pastries are foods pleasing to the palate.

12. Some gymnasium locker rooms are not aromatically pleasant places.

⭐ 13. No reality television shows are scripted programs.

14. Some tropical islands are wonderful vacation getaways.

15. No green vegetables are vitamin-deficient foods.

Video Tutorial: 5BI
Exercise #13

II. **Change the *quality* but not the *quantity* of the following categorical propositions.**

1. All board games are colorful diversions.

2. Some detectives are logical thinkers.

3. No shopping malls are convenience stores.

   4. Some swimming pools are not adequately chlorinated places.

⭐ 5. No high-definition TV shows are shows for children.

   6. All secured websites are areas protected by firewalls.

   7. Some houseplants are illegal substances.

   8. Some singers are not highly trained professionals.

⭐ 9. All karaoke bars are noisy rooms.

   10. Some race car drivers are ambidextrous people.

III. **Change the *quantity* but not the *quality* of the following categorical propositions.**

   1. Some firecrackers are not safe products.

   2. No scuba divers are claustrophobic people.

   3. All hamsters are cuddly animals.

   4. Some protein bars are quick energy snacks.

⭐ 5. All wood-burning stoves are warmth givers.

   6. Some toothpastes are fluoride dental products.

   7. No tsunamis are surfing paradises.

   8. Some fantasy magazines are not carefully written material.

⭐ 9. All tuna fish sandwiches are high-protein meals.

   10. No pickup trucks are electric vehicles.

IV. **Change both the *quality* and the *quantity* of the following categorical propositions.**

   1. All caregivers are altruistic people.

   2. Some airplane seats are uncomfortable spaces.

   3. No skydivers are people afraid of heights.

   4. Some European castles are not heated domiciles.

⭐ 5. All dancers are physically gifted athletes.

   6. No refrigerators are self-cleaning machines.

   7. Some drive-in theaters are places going out of business.

   8. Some fruit trees are not plants capable of surviving a frost.

⭐ 9. All movie special effects are scenes generated by a computer.

   10. No painful experiences are things soon forgotten.

C. EXISTENTIAL IMPORT

When a categorical proposition refers to objects that actually exist, it seems only natural to look at its truth value. For example, when we see the universal proposition "All horses are mammals," we automatically accept that horses exist, so the truth value depends on whether or not they are mammals. But consider this universal proposition: "All unicorns are mammals." We might be tempted to say the proposition is false because no unicorns exist. A proposition is said to have **existential import** if it presupposes the existence of certain kinds of objects; therefore, its truth value depends on whether the class is empty (it has no members). We know that **A**-propositions assert that the entire subject class is included in the predicate class, and **E**-propositions assert that the entire subject class is excluded from the predicate class. However, do they also assert that the subject class denotes something that actually exists? In other words, should it be assumed that *every* universal proposition has existential import?

> **Existential import**
> A proposition has existential import if it presupposes the existence of certain kinds of objects.

Logicians have dealt with this question by devising two *interpretations* of universal propositions: the *modern* and the *traditional*. The modern interpretation sets aside questions concerning the existence of the objects referred to by universal propositions. Therefore, no decision has to be made concerning the existence of members of a class (whether or not the class is empty). Given this, the **A**-proposition "All scientists are people trained in mathematics" is translated as "*If* a person is a scientist, *then* that person is trained in mathematics." The proposition "All unicorns are mammals" is translated as "*If* something is a unicorn, *then* that thing is a mammal." Under the modern interpretation, the universal **E**-proposition "No slackers are reliable workers" is translated as "*If* a person is a slacker, *then* that person is not a reliable worker." In each case, the conditional statement makes no assertion concerning the existence of members of a class.

In contrast, the traditional interpretation holds that it is *sometimes* useful to determine whether a given universal proposition has existential import. As we shall see, *if* a universal proposition does have existential import, then this leads to additional relationships between the four categorical propositions, and different methods for determining the validity or invalidity of certain categorical arguments.

Unlike universal propositions, particular categorical propositions (**I** and **O**) are always understood as having existential import under both the modern and traditional interpretations. Therefore, the question of existential import affects *only* universal propositions.

D. THE MODERN SQUARE OF OPPOSITION AND VENN DIAGRAMS

We have seen that the four types of categorical proposition forms differ in quality, quantity, or both. **Opposition** occurs whenever two categorical proposition forms have the same subject and predicate classes but differ in quality, quantity, or both.

> **Opposition** When two standard-form categorical propositions refer to the same subject and predicate classes, but differ in quality, quantity, or both.

Contradictories In categorical logic, pairs of propositions in which one is the negation of the other.

And so far, we have been concerned only with understanding the structure of these propositions. We have not considered their logical consequences. If they are taken as true or false, what can we conclude?

The first relationship we will look at is called **contradictories**, which is a pair of propositions in which one is the negation of the other (they have opposite truth values). This occurs when we recognize that it is impossible for both propositions to be true or both to be false at the same time. Contradictory categorical statements differ from each other in both quantity and quality. For example:

(1) All interstate highways are projects built with taxpayers' money. (**A**-proposition)
(2) Some interstate highways are not projects built with taxpayers' money. (**O**-proposition)

Can both of these propositions be true (or false) at the same time? The answer is "no." If the first proposition is true, then the second is false. If all interstate highways are projects built with taxpayers' money, then there cannot be even one that is *not* built with taxpayers' money. Likewise, if the second proposition is true, then the first is false. If there is at least one interstate highway that is *not* built with taxpayers' money, then it cannot be true that all of them are built with taxpayers' money.

What happens if the first proposition is false? The second proposition is true. If not every interstate highway is built with taxpayers' money, then there is at least one that is *not* built with taxpayers' money. Likewise, if the second proposition is false, then the first is true. If there is not even one interstate highway that is *not* built with taxpayers' money, then it is true that all of them are built with taxpayers' money.

For any two propositions to be truly contradictories, one of them has to be true and the other has to be false. As we saw for propositions (1) and (2), **A**- and **O**-propositions are contradictories.

E- and **I**-propositions are contradictories, too:

(3) No interstate highways are projects built with taxpayers' money. (**E**-proposition)
(4) Some interstate highways are projects built with taxpayers' money. (**I**-proposition)

If the first proposition is true then the second is false, and vice versa.

These results are illustrated in the following figure:

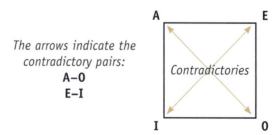

The arrows indicate the contradictory pairs:
A–O
E–I

The modern square of opposition spells out what this means. Since **A-** and **O**-propositions are contradictory, they should have opposite values for quantity, quality, and distribution. So should the contradictory propositions **E** and **I**.

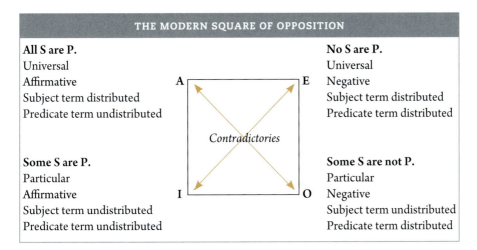

THE MODERN SQUARE OF OPPOSITION	
All S are P.	**No S are P.**
Universal	Universal
Affirmative **A**	**E** Negative
Subject term distributed	Subject term distributed
Predicate term undistributed	Predicate term distributed
Contradictories	
Some S are P.	**Some S are not P.**
Particular	Particular
Affirmative **I**	**O** Negative
Subject term undistributed	Subject term undistributed
Predicate term undistributed	Predicate term distributed

Let's see if you have grasped the idea of contradictories. Are the following two propositions contradictories?

   (5) All zoos are places where animals are treated humanely. (**A**-proposition)
   (6) No zoos are places where animals are treated humanely. (**E**-proposition)

If the first proposition is true, then the second is false. Likewise, if the second is true, then the first is false. However, if you guessed that they are contradictories, you would be wrong. To see this, consider what would happen if the first proposition were false. In that case, must the second proposition be true? If it is false that "All zoos are places where animals are treated humanely," must it be true that "No zoos are places where animals are treated humanely"? The answer is "no" because there might be *one or more* zoos where animals are treated humanely. Since this is possible, it would make the second proposition false too. Since contradictory propositions cannot both be false at the same time, we have shown that propositions (5) and (6) are not contradictories. Therefore, **A-** and **E**-propositions are not contradictories.

The modern square is now complete, but we still need to learn how to diagram our results.

Venn Diagrams

We start by relying on some ideas of the English logicians George Boole and John Venn to expand the discussion of the modern square of opposition. First, we stipulate that both **I**-propositions and **O**-propositions have existential import, because both assert the existence of at least one entity. On the other hand, both **A**-propositions and **E**-propositions *do not* have existential import.

Venn diagram A diagram that uses circles to represent categorical proposition forms.

Representations of categorical proposition forms are called **Venn diagrams**. To begin, we will use a circle to represent a class:

The area inside the circle contains every possible member of a class of objects, such as the class of video games. Continuing with this example, the area outside the circle would contain everything that is not a video game. To show that a class is empty we shade the circle completely, which indicates that it has no members:

In order to show that a class has at least one member, we can place an X anywhere inside the circle:

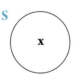

PROFILES IN LOGIC
George Boole

George Boole (1815–64) advanced the connection of logic to algebra so significantly that the subject is often called *Boolean algebra*. Boole recognized that algebraic symbols, the tools for working with numbers, could function as logical notation as well. His system applied to both categorical statements (what he called "logic of terms") and truth-functional statements as well. Boole's ideas were later developed by John Venn and were incorporated into Venn diagrams.

Boole ushered in the age of *formalism*—the idea that validity should not depend on

how we interpret the symbols in a proof, but only on the logic at work. In other words, the actual truth value of the premises and conclusion should have no bearing on validity. The rules of logic, once understood, are the only guide we need to analyze arguments. As Boole put it in the title of one of his books, he saw logic as *An Investigation of the Laws of Thought*. These ideas were the ancestors of today's computer circuitry. It is not a far step from Boolean algebra, which emphasizes the use of 0 and 1, to on-off switches.

We are now ready to complete the diagrams for our four categorical propositions. Since categorical propositions refer to the relationship between two classes, we will start by drawing two intersecting circles. With two overlapping circles, S and P, there is more to annotate. We will number each area in order to make our references clear.

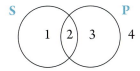

Let's see how this works for a specific case. As discussed earlier, under the modern interpretation, an **A**-proposition is to be understood as asserting "*If* something is an S, then it is also a P." Since **A**-propositions assert that every member of S is a member of P, we need to shade the area of S that is *outside* of P to indicate that it has no members. In other words, we need to shade in Area 1.

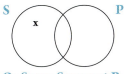

A: All S are P.

At this point, we must be careful not to misinterpret the diagram. Although the area where S and P overlap is not shaded, this does not allow us to assert that the area has members. If you may recall, under the modern interpretation, universal categorical propositions do not have existential import, so we must remain neutral about whether there are individuals in unshaded areas. Therefore, the diagram correctly represents the proposition "All S are P" (*If* something is an S, then it is also a P).

Since **A**-propositions and **O**-propositions are contradictories, **O**-propositions assert that there is at least one member of S outside the class of P. We diagram this by placing an X in the area of S that is outside P to indicate that it has at least one member. In other words, we need to place an X in Area 1.

O: Some S are not P.

If we do a side-by-side comparison of the diagrams for **A**- and **O**-propositions, we can see why they are contradictories. In the **A**-proposition diagram there are no members in Area 1, but in the **O**-proposition diagram there is at least one member in Area 1.

 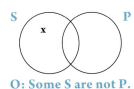

A: All S are P.   O: Some S are not P.

Let's turn to the other set of contradictories. As discussed earlier, under the modern interpretation, an **E**-proposition is to be understood as asserting "*If* something is an S, then it is *not* a P." Since **E**-propositions assert that *no* member of S is a member of P, we need to shade the area of S that overlaps with P to indicate that it has no members. In other words, we need to shade in Area 2.

E: No S are P.

Since **E**-propositions and **I**-propositions are contradictories, **I**-propositions assert that there is at least one member of S that is a member of P. We diagram this by placing an X in the area where S and P overlap. In other words, we need to place an X in Area 2.

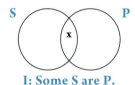

I: Some S are P.

If we do a side-by-side comparison of the diagrams for **E**- and **I**-propositions, we can see why they are contradictories. In the **E**-proposition diagram there are no members in Area 2, but in the **I**-proposition diagram there is at least one member in Area 2.

PROFILES IN LOGIC
John Venn

Although many people applied the ideas of Boolean algebra, perhaps the person with the most useful contribution was John Venn (1834–1923), who created what we now call *Venn diagrams.* If we want to analyze categorical statements and arguments, we start by simply drawing circles. Venn's system uses overlapping circles of identical size. Each circle represents one of the terms in a statement: the subject term or the predicate term. The distinct areas of the overlapping circles can then display the claims of the categorical statements. For example, shading an area indicates an empty class and is used for universal categorical statements. The letter X indicates that a class is not empty; it is used for particular categorical statements.

Venn diagrams have the advantage of uniformity: They offer a mechanical method for determining the validity (or invalidity) of categorical arguments. Venn diagrams are also used in the branch of mathematics called *set theory.* Just as two circles may overlap only a bit, two sets may have just some members in common, called their intersection. Together, the areas of both circles represent the union of sets, or all their members taken together.

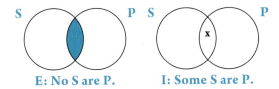

E: No S are P.   I: Some S are P.

The Venn diagrams illustrate how universal and particular categorical propositions differ when it comes to existential import. Since under the modern interpretation universal propositions do not have existential import, we must remain neutral about whether there are individuals in the unshaded areas. On the other hand, since particular categorical propositions have existential import, an X indicates that at least one individual is in that area.

Here are the Venn diagrams of the four standard-form categorical propositions:

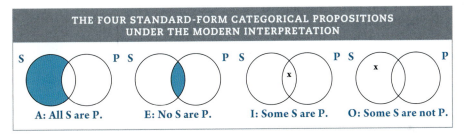

THE FOUR STANDARD-FORM CATEGORICAL PROPOSITIONS
UNDER THE MODERN INTERPRETATION

A: All S are P.   E: No S are P.   I: Some S are P.   O: Some S are not P.

EXERCISES 5D

Reveal the form of the following categorical propositions, and draw Venn diagrams to represent the relationship.

1. Some snowmen are permanent lawn fixtures.

Answer: Let S = *snowmen*, and P = *permanent lawn fixtures*. Some S are P.

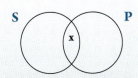

2. No airports are underground places of entertainment.

3. Some television newscasters are good actors.

4. All donuts are fat-free snacks.

⭐ 5. All psychics are frauds.

6. Some children are not offspring following in their parents' footsteps.

7. No volcanoes are currently active geologic structures.

8. Some wrestling shows are scripted events.

Lightboard Video

Self-Practice Questions

Video Tutorial: 5D Exercise #5

⭐ 9. All teachers are miserable wretches.

10. Some poems are beautifully written works of literature.

11. Some viruses are not lethal organisms.

12. No Nobel laureates are Olympic champions.

⭐ 13. All sea creatures are bivalves.

14. Some rock stars are good parents.

15. All elevators are public areas.

16. Some exotic vegetables are not edible products.

⭐ 17. Some scientific researchers are people with impeccable credentials.

18. No television commercials are events worthy of our attention.

19. All finely tuned instruments are noise emitters.

20. Some kids' toys are defective products.

⭐ 21. All French pastries are baked items.

22. Some cows are not flatulent animals.

23. No Nobel Prize winners are illiterate people.

24. Some swimmers are healthy athletes.

⭐ 25. All dogs are faithful pets.

26. No spiders are nocturnal creatures.

27. Some race car drivers are fearless competitors.

28. Some college textbooks are works of art.

⭐ 29. All teachers are inspired orators.

30. Some games of chance are sucker bets.

31. Some sandwiches are meatless foods.

32. No supercomputers are cheap electronic machines.

⭐ 33. All designer jeans are genetically engineered objects.

34. No greedy politicians are people likely to go to prison.

35. Some movie theater popcorn machines are not microwave ovens.

36. All embezzlers are social deviants.

⭐ 37. Some traffic accidents are speeding incidents.

38. All public holidays are days when banks close.

39. Some music videos are not tragedies.

40. Some fajitas are mouth-watering morsels.

⭐ 41.   No ice cream toppings are diet-friendly products.

42.   All yogurt products are healthy foods.

43.   No vegetables are vitamin-deficient produce.

44.   Some barbecue wings are undercooked meat.

⭐ 45.   All French fries are grease-laden spuds.

E. CONVERSION, OBVERSION, AND CONTRAPOSITION IN THE MODERN SQUARE

The creation and analysis of **immediate arguments** (arguments that contain only one premise), can help build a solid understanding of categorical logic. (Arguments that have more than one premise are called **mediate arguments**.) In this section, we will consider three special types of immediate argument.

Conversion

An immediate argument can be created by switching the subject and predicate terms of a given categorical proposition, a process called **conversion**. The proposition we start with is called the *convertend*, and it becomes the premise of the argument. The proposition we end up with after applying the process of conversion is called the *converse*, and it becomes the conclusion of the argument. Here is an example:

Convertend: **E**-proposition: No beer commercials are subtle advertisements.
Converse: **E**-proposition: No subtle advertisements are beer commercials.

THE METHOD OF CONVERSION
Switch the subject and predicate.
Subject ◄────────► *Predicate*

Obversion

A second type of immediate argument, called **obversion**, is formed by (1) changing the quality of the given proposition, and (2) by replacing the predicate term with its class **complement**, which is the set of objects that do not belong to a given class. For obversion, the complement is formed by attaching the prefix *non-* to the predicate term. For example, the class of milkshakes has as its complement class everything that is *not* a milkshake, the class of all non-milkshakes. The *obvertend* is the proposition we start with, so it becomes the premise of an immediate argument. The *obverse* is the proposition we wind up with, so it becomes the conclusion. Here is an example:

Obvertend: **A**-proposition: All jackhammers are weapons.
Obverse: **E**-proposition: No jackhammers are non-weapons.

Immediate argument An argument that has only one premise.

Mediate argument An argument that has more than one premise.

Conversion An immediate argument formed by interchanging the subject and predicate terms of a given categorical proposition.

Obversion An immediate argument formed by changing the quality of the given proposition, and then replacing the predicate term with its complement.

Complement The set of objects that do not belong to a given class.

The Method of Obversion

STEP 1: Change the *quality* of the given proposition.
STEP 2: Replace the *predicate term* with its *complement.*

Contraposition

Contraposition An immediate argument formed by replacing the subject term of a given proposition with the complement of its predicate term, and then replacing the predicate term of the given proposition with the complement of its subject term.

The final type of immediate argument to consider, **contraposition**, is formed by applying two steps: (1) Switch the subject and predicate terms, and (2) replace both the subject and predicate terms with their term complements. Here is an example:

| Given proposition: | **A**-proposition: | All pencils are ink-free writing tools. |
| Contrapositive: | **A**-proposition: | All non-ink-free writing tools are non-pencils. |

The Method of Contraposition

STEP 1: Switch the subject and predicate terms.
STEP 2: Replace both the subject and predicate terms with their term complements.

Diagrams

The modern square of opposition makes understanding conversion, obversion, and contraposition quite straightforward, thanks to the Venn diagrams for the four standard-form categorical propositions. Let's start with the immediate arguments for conversion:

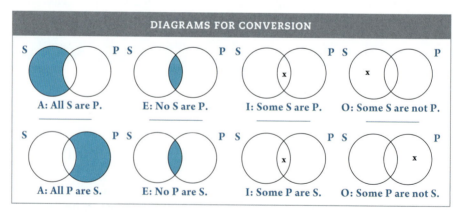

DIAGRAMS FOR CONVERSION

A: All S are P.   E: No S are P.   I: Some S are P.   O: Some S are not P.

A: All P are S.   E: No P are S.   I: Some P are S.   O: Some P are not S.

The lines separating the top and bottom diagrams can be understood as dividing the premise (above) from the conclusion (below) for the four immediate arguments. A visual inspection of the diagrams for **E** and **I** verify that these two are valid arguments. Their validity rests on the equivalence of the two diagrams (the premise and conclusion of the **E** and **I** conversions). Since we can see that the premise and conclusion of both **E** and **I** conversions are logically equivalent propositions, it is easy to understand why these are valid arguments. After all, if the premise is true, the conclusion is true too.

However, the conversion for **A**-propositions does not work. The fact that the Venn diagrams are not identical makes this easy to see. Therefore, if the premise is true, the conclusion might be false. This also helps us to understand why conversion for **O**-propositions does not work.

We have one last major hurdle to overcome for our understanding of obversion and contraposition—the prefix *non-*. Let's learn how to diagram the logic behind this prefix. Since we diagram the class designated by S as a circle, we can stipulate that everything outside that circle is non-S.

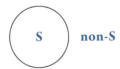

As we learned earlier, with two overlapping circles, S and P, we get four areas.

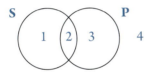

We can modify our earlier discussion by adding the prefix "non-" in the appropriate places:

- If something is in Area 1, then it is an S and a non-P.
- If something is in Area 2, then it is both an S and a P.
- If something is in Area 3, then it is a P and a non-S.
- If something is in Area 4, then it is both a non-S and a non-P.

The diagrams associated with obversion should now be easier to interpret:

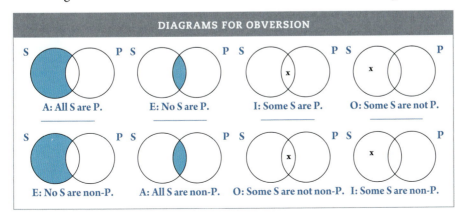

DIAGRAMS FOR OBVERSION			
A: All S are P.	E: No S are P.	I: Some S are P.	O: Some S are not P.
E: No S are non-P.	A: All S are non-P.	O: Some S are not non-P.	I: Some S are non-P.

Visual inspection verifies that the premise and conclusion of each of the four immedi-ate arguments are logically equivalent. Thus, obversion is valid for all four standard-form categorical propositions.

Let's look at the diagrams for contraposition:

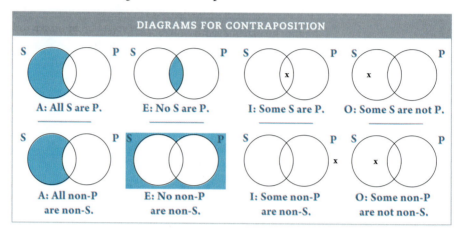

DIAGRAMS FOR CONTRAPOSITION

A: All S are P.   E: No S are P.   I: Some S are P.   O: Some S are not P.

A: All non-P are non-S.   E: No non-P are non-S.   I: Some non-P are non-S.   O: Some non-P are not non-S.

The diagrams illustrate why contraposition for **A**- and **O**-propositions produces valid immediate arguments. We can see right away the logical equivalence. We also see that contraposition produces invalid immediate arguments for both **E**- and **I**-propositions. The two diagrams for both **E**-propositions and **I**-propositions are not equivalent.

The modern square of opposition and Venn diagrams address the issues regarding existential import. This provides a method of analysis for categorical propositions and categorical arguments.

Summary of Conversion, Obversion, and Contraposition

The Method of Conversion
Switch the subject and predicate.

Subject ⟷ Predicate

The Method of Obversion

STEP 1: Change the *quality* of the given proposition.
STEP 2: Replace the *predicate term* with its *complement.*

The Method of Contraposition

STEP 1: Switch the subject and predicate terms.
STEP 2: Replace both the subject and predicate terms with their term complements.

LOGICALLY EQUIVALENT FORMS	
Conversion	
E: No S are P.	E: No P are S.
I: Some S are P.	I: Some P are S.
Obversion	
A: All S are P.	E: No S are non-P.
E: No S are P.	A: All S are non-P.
I: Some S are P.	O: Some S are not non-P.
O: Some S are not P.	I: Some S are non-P.
Contraposition	
A: All S are P.	A: All non-P are non-S.
O: Some S are not P.	O: Some non-P are not non-S.

EXERCISES 5E

I. For each of the following, provide the converse, obverse, and contrapositive of the given proposition. Also determine whether the subsequent immediate arguments are valid or invalid.

Self-Practice
Questions

1. Some games of chance are sucker bets.

Answers:

    A. *Converse*: Some sucker bets are games of chance. *Valid*

    B. *Obverse*: Some games of chance are not non-sucker bets. *Valid*

    C. *Contrapositive*: Some non-sucker bets are non-games of chance. *Invalid*

2. Some sandwiches are not meaty things.

3. No supercomputers are cheap electronic machines.

4. All designer jeans are genetically engineered objects.

⭐ 5. No greedy politicians are people likely to go to prison.

6. Some movie theater popcorn machines are not microwave ovens.

7. All embezzlers are social deviants.

8. Some traffic accidents are speeding incidents.

Video Tutorial: 5EI
Exercise #7

⭐ 9. All public holidays are days when banks close.

10. Some music videos are not tragedies.

11. Some T-bone steaks are juicy items.

12. Some fajitas are mouth-watering morsels.

⭐ 13. No ice cream toppings are diet-busters.

14. All yogurt products are healthy foods.

15. No vegetables are vitamin-deficient foods.

16. Some barbecue wings are spicy meals.

⭐ 17. All French fries are grease-laden products.

18. Some cheesecakes are sugar-free products.

19. All bananas are foods best eaten when ripe.

20. Some tofu products are delicious snacks.

⭐ 21. Some tattoos are great works of art.

22. Some sandals are not waterproof footwear.

23. No swimming pools are easy-to-clean objects.

24. All movie theater drinks are artificially sweetened products.

⭐ 25. No good deeds are acts left unrewarded.

II. **For more practice analyzing different kinds of immediate inferences, determine whether the following inferences are valid or invalid.**

1. <u>All S are P.</u>
    Some S are P.

Answer: Here is the diagram of the premise, an **A**-proposition:

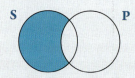

In order for the conclusion, an **I**-proposition, to be true, there would have to be an X in the area where S and P overlap. Since there is none, the immediate inference is invalid.

2. <u>All S are P.</u>
    No S are P.

3. <u>All S are P.</u>
    Some S are not P.

4. <u>No S are P.</u>
    All S are P.

⭐ 5. <u>No S are P.</u>
    Some S are P.

6. <u>No S are P.</u>
    Some S are not P.

7. <u>Some S are P.</u>
    All S are P.

8. <u>Some S are P.</u>
    No S are P.

⭐ 9. <u>Some S are P.</u>
    Some S are not P.

10. <u>Some S are not P.</u>
    All S are P.

11. <u>Some S are not P.</u>
    Some S are P.

12. <u>Some S are not P.</u>
    No S are P.

F. THE TRADITIONAL SQUARE OF OPPOSITION AND VENN DIAGRAMS

The traditional square of opposition starts out the same as the modern square of opposition when it comes to *contradictories*:

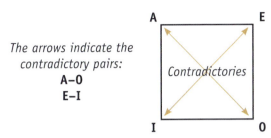

The arrows indicate the contradictory pairs:
A–O
E–I

Now consider these two propositions:

(1) All zoos are places where animals are treated humanely. (**A**-proposition)
(2) No zoos are places where animals are treated humanely. (**E**-proposition)

These two propositions are not contradictories because they both could be false at the same time. For example, if *some zoos are* places where animals are treated humanely and *some* zoos *are not* places where animals are treated humanely, then both (1) and (2) are false. Under the traditional interpretation's assumption of existence, pairs of propositions that cannot both be true at the same time, but can both be false at the same time are called **contraries**. This analysis reveals that **A**- and **E**-propositions are contraries. We can add this information to the square of opposition:

Contraries Pairs of propositions that cannot both be true at the same time, but can both be false at the same time.

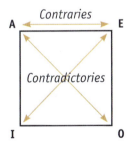

The flip side of contraries are **subcontraries**, which, under the traditional interpretation's assumption of existence cannot both be false at the same time, but can both be true at the same time. Also, if one is false, then the other must be true. The following two propositions are subcontraries:

Subcontraries Pairs of propositions that cannot both be false at the same time, but can both be true; also, if one is false, then the other must be true.

(3) Some hurricanes are storms formed in the Atlantic Ocean. (**I**-proposition)
(4) Some hurricanes are not storms formed in the Atlantic Ocean. (**O**-proposition)

It is possible for both of these propositions to be true at the same time. All that would be needed would be to find one hurricane that formed in the Atlantic Ocean and one that was not formed in the Atlantic Ocean. However, both propositions cannot be false at the same time. Why not? If proposition (3) is false, then not even one hurricane was formed in the Atlantic Ocean. If that is so, then proposition (4) must be true, because it asserts that at least one hurricane is not formed in the Atlantic Ocean. The same result is attained if we start by making proposition (4) false. Doing this would logically make proposition (3) true. We have shown that **I**- and **O**-propositions are subcontraries, and we can now add these results to the square of opposition:

One final relationship under the assumption of existence completes the traditional square of opposition. **Subalternation** is the relationship between a universal proposition (referred to as the *superaltern*) and its *corresponding* particular proposition (referred to as the *subaltern*). There are two kinds of corresponding propositions:

Subalternation
The relationship between a universal proposition (referred to as the *superaltern*) and its corresponding particular proposition (referred to as the *subaltern*).

A: All S are P	*corresponds to*	**I:** Some S are P.
E: No S are P	*corresponds to*	**O:** Some S are not P.

Under the traditional interpretation, if the universal proposition of a pair is true, then its corresponding particular will also be true. For example, if it is true that "All modern holidays are greeting-card company creations," then it is also true that "Some modern holidays are greeting-card company creations." Likewise, if it is true that "No modern holidays are greeting-card company creations," then it is also true that "Some modern holidays are not greeting-card company creations." However, the reverse does not hold. That is, if the particular proposition of a pair is true, then its corresponding universal might be true or it might be false.

Here is an example of subalternation:

(5) All musical instruments are difficult things to master. (**A**-proposition)
(6) Some musical instruments are difficult things to master. (**I**-proposition)

If the universal affirmative categorical proposition (**A**) is true, then its corresponding particular (**I**) is true, too. However, we can see that even if proposition (6), the particular affirmative (**I**) is true, then its corresponding universal (**A**) might be true or false. These same results hold for the categorical propositions **E** and **O**. For example:

(7) No musical instruments are difficult things to master. (**E**-proposition)
(8) Some musical instruments are not difficult things to master. (**O**-proposition)

As before, if proposition (7), a universal negative (**E**), is true, then its corresponding particular (**O**) is true, too. However, we can see that even if proposition (8), the particular negative (**O**), is true, then its corresponding universal (**E**) might be true or false.

Subalternation gets more interesting if we ask what happens when one member of a corresponding pair is false. On the one hand, if the universal proposition of a pair is false, then its corresponding particular partner could be true or false. For example, if it is false that "All honor students are hard workers" (**A**), then the proposition "Some honor students are hard workers" (**I**) could be either true or false. Similarly, if it is false that "No honor students are hard workers" (**E**), then the proposition "Some honor students are not hard workers" (**O**) could be either true or false. However, the reverse does not hold. That is, if the particular proposition of a pair of corresponding propositions is false, then its corresponding universal is false as well. Here is an example:

(9) All musical instruments are difficult things to master. (**A**-proposition)
(10) Some musical instruments are difficult things to master. (**I**-proposition)

If proposition (9), a universal affirmative (**A**), is false, then its corresponding particular (**I**) could be either true or false. However, we can see that if proposition (10), the particular affirmative (**I**), is false, then its corresponding universal (**A**) is false, too. These same results hold for **E**- and **O**-propositions. Here is an example:

(11) No musical instruments are difficult things to master. (**E**-proposition)
(12) Some musical instruments are not difficult things to master. (**O**-proposition)

As before, if proposition (11), a universal negative (**E**), is false, then its corresponding particular (**O**) could be either true or false. But, once again, we can see that if proposition (12), the particular negative (**O**), is false, then its corresponding universal (**E**) is false, too.

We can now complete the traditional square of opposition:

THE TRADITIONAL SQUARE OF OPPOSITION

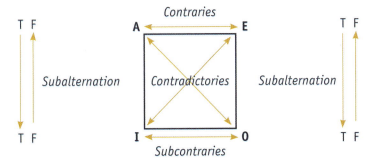

Let's try it out and see where it takes us. Suppose the following proposition is true: "All clowns are scary people" (**A**). If so, we can go around the traditional square of opposition and say something about each of the remaining three categorical proposition forms. The proposition, "No clowns are scary people" (**E**), is the contrary of the original proposition (**A**). Since contraries cannot both be true at the same time, the proposition "No clowns are scary people" (**E**) is false. Also, since the proposition "Some clowns are not scary people" (**O**) is the contradictory of the original proposition (**A**), it, too, is false. The remaining proposition, "Some clowns are scary people" (**I**), is the subaltern of the original proposition (**A**), and so it is true.

Now let's try the opposite truth value. What if the proposition "All clowns are scary people" (**A**) is false? The contrary of this proposition is "No clowns are scary people" (**E**). And going around the square, we determine that it could be true or false, so its truth value is *undetermined*. However, the proposition "Some clowns are not scary people" (**O**), the contradictory of the original proposition (**A**), must then be true. The remaining proposition, "Some clowns are scary people" (**I**), the subaltern of the original proposition (**A**), might be true or false, so its truth value is therefore *undetermined*.

EXERCISES 5F.1

Self-Practice
Questions

I. Use your understanding of the traditional square of opposition to determine the correct answer.

1. The *contradictory* of "No football players are opera singers" is:
   (a) All football players are opera singers.
   (b) Some football players are opera singers.
   (c) Some football players are not opera singers.

Answer: (b) is correct. Since "No football players are opera singers" is an **E**-proposition, its contradictory must be an **I**-proposition, which is answer (b). The correct answer cannot be (a) because it is an **A**-proposition, which is the *contrary* of an **E**-proposition. Also, (c) is not correct because it is an **O**-proposition, which is the subaltern of an **E**-proposition.

2. Are the following two propositions *contraries*?
   All yo-yos are toys better left untouched.
   No yo-yos are toys better left untouched.

3. Are the following two propositions *subcontraries*?
   Some contact lenses are gas-permeable objects.
   Some contact lenses are not gas-permeable objects.

4. True or False: In the traditional square of opposition, two contradictory categorical propositions can both be false at the same time.

⭐ 5. True or False: In the traditional square of opposition, two contrary categorical propositions can both be false at the same time.

II. Use your understanding of the traditional square to determine the correct answer: a. True, b. False, or c. Undetermined.

1. If it is false that "Some implants are easily detectable objects," then the proposition "No implants are easily detectable objects" is:

Answer: a. True. The first is an **I**-proposition, and if it is false, its contradictory **E**-proposition is true.

2. If it is false that "Some implants are easily detectable objects," then the proposition "No implants are easily detectable objects" is:

3. If it is false that "Some games are crazy inventions," then the proposition "All games are crazy inventions" is:

4. If it is true that "Some games are crazy inventions," then the proposition "All games are crazy inventions" is:

⭐ 5. If it is true that "No games are crazy inventions," then the proposition "Some games are not crazy inventions" is:

6. If it is false that "No games are crazy inventions," then the proposition "Some games are not crazy inventions" is:

III. Use your understanding of the traditional square to determine the correct answer.

1. Write the contradictory of "All sports cars are gas-guzzling machines."
Answer: Some sports cars are not gas-guzzling machines. Since the first sentence is an **A**-proposition, its contradictory is an **O**-proposition.

2. Write the contrary of "All diamond rings are expensive items."

3. What is the relationship of opposition, if any, between these two propositions?
    (a) Some foreign movies are dramas.
    (b) Some foreign movies are comedies.

4. If it is true that "Some theoretical scientists are humanists," then what can be said about the proposition "No theoretical scientists are humanists"?

⭐ 5. If it is false that "All theoretical scientists are humanists," then what can be said about the proposition "Some theoretical scientists are humanists"?

IV. For each of the following questions, you will be told the truth value of one of the four types of categorical propositions. From this information you are to determine the truth values of the other three types of categorical propositions as you go around the traditional square. Choose the correct answer: a. True, b. False, or c. Undetermined.

1. If an **A**-proposition is *true*, then you can conclude that the **E**-proposition is:
Answer: b. False. Since they are *contraries*, they cannot both be true at the same time.

2. If an **A**-proposition is *true*, then you can conclude that the **I**-proposition is:

3. If an **A**-proposition is *true*, then you can conclude that the **O**-proposition is:

4. If an **A**-proposition is *false*, then you can conclude that the **E**-proposition is:

⭐ 5. If an **A**-proposition is *false*, then you can conclude that the **I**-proposition is:

6. If an **A**-proposition is *false*, then you can conclude that the **O**-proposition is:

7. If an **E**-proposition is *true*, then you can conclude that the **A**-proposition is:

8. If an **E**-proposition is *true*, then you can conclude that the **I**-proposition is:

⭐ 9. If an **E**-proposition is *true*, then you can conclude that the **O**-proposition is:

Video Tutorial: 5FI.IV
Exercises #3 & #10

10. If an **E**-proposition is *false*, then you can conclude that the **A**-proposition is:

11. If an **E**-proposition is *false*, then you can conclude that the **I**-proposition is:

12. If an **E**-proposition is *false*, then you can conclude that the **O**-proposition is:

⭐ 13. If an **I**-proposition is *true*, then you can conclude that the **A**-proposition is:

14. If an **I**-proposition is *true*, then you can conclude that the **E**-proposition is:

15. If an **I**-proposition is *true*, then you can conclude that the **O**-proposition is:

16. If an **I**-proposition is *false*, then you can conclude that the **A**-proposition is:

⭐ 17. If an **I**-proposition is *false*, then you can conclude that the **E**-proposition is:

18. If an **I**-proposition is *false*, then you can conclude that the **O**-proposition is:

19. If an **O**-proposition is *true*, then you can conclude that the **A**-proposition is:

20. If an **O**-proposition is *true*, then you can conclude that the **E**-proposition is:

⭐ 21. If an **O**-proposition is *true*, then you can conclude that the **I**-proposition is:

22. If an **O**-proposition is *false*, then you can conclude that the **A**-proposition is:

23. If an **O**-proposition is *false*, then you can conclude that the **E**-proposition is:

24. If an **O**-proposition is *false*, then you can conclude that the **I**-proposition is:

Venn Diagrams and the Traditional Square

We can modify the way we have been drawing Venn diagrams to accommodate the traditional interpretation of universal categorical propositions. Under the traditional interpretation, an analysis of *some* categorical arguments requires determining whether a class denotes actually existing objects. Therefore, we need to introduce a new symbol to represent what we will call the "Assumption of Existence." This term is appropriate because the new symbol will be used *only* for diagramming **A**- and **E**-propositions. The symbol will be an X surrounded by a circle. Since the new symbol is used to indicate the assumption of existence only for universal propositions, it functions differently from the X in particular **I**- and **O**-propositions. We can interpret the **A**-proposition "All S are P" as follows: *If there are any members of S, they will be in the area where S and P overlap.* Under the modern interpretation, no X appears in the unshaded overlap area. However, under the traditional interpretation, we place the assumption of existence symbol in that area. In other words, the italicized clause alerts us to the *provisional* use of the circled X. Given this provisional use, we need to determine whether the circled X refers to any actually existing objects in order to determine the validity or invalidity of an argument with a universal premise.

For an **E**-proposition, since "No S are P" is logically equivalent to "No P are S," they must have identical diagrams. To ensure this, in the traditional interpretation we start by assuming that both the subject term and the predicate term have existential import. Thus, for **E**-propositions, we use two assumption of existence symbols. Here are the two new diagrams:

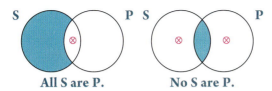

All S are P.   No S are P.

The diagrams for the particular categorical propositions (**I** and **O**) are the same as they were for the modern interpretation:

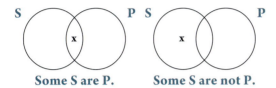

Some S are P.   Some S are not P.

Now let's look at an immediate argument and see how the two interpretations proceed.

> All improvised explosive devices are unconventional military weapons. Therefore, some improvised explosive devices are unconventional military weapons.

Using the *modern* interpretation, we start by drawing a Venn diagram of the premise:

All S are P.

Notice that no circled X appears in this diagram. Next, we check to see if the conclusion follows necessarily. Since the conclusion is an **I**-proposition, in order for it to be true there would have to be an X in the area where S and P overlap. But as we can see, there is none. Since the truth of the premise does not guarantee the truth of the conclusion, this is an invalid argument under the *modern* interpretation.

Now we will use the *traditional* interpretation. We once again start by drawing a Venn diagram of the premise:

All S are P.

Next, we check to see if the conclusion follows necessarily. Since the conclusion is an **I**-proposition, in order for it to be true there would have to be an X in the area where S and P overlap. As we can see, the circled X is in the area. At this point, the argument is *provisionally valid*, because there is one more step to complete. We need to see if the symbol represents something that actually exists. The "S" stands for *improvised explosive devices*, which are a large part of modern warfare. Therefore, in this instance, the assumption of existence symbol *does* represent something that actually exists, so the argument is *valid* under the *traditional* interpretation.

Let's examine another argument:

All perpetual motion machines are patented inventions. Therefore, some perpetual motion machines are patented inventions.

Using the *modern* interpretation, we start by drawing a Venn diagram of the premise.

All S are P.

Next, we check to see if the conclusion follows necessarily. Since the conclusion is an **I**-proposition, in order for it to be true there would have to be an X in the area where S and P overlap. But as we can see, there is none. Since the truth of the premise does not guarantee the truth of the conclusion, this is an invalid argument under the *modern* interpretation.

Now we will use the *traditional* interpretation. We start by drawing a Venn diagram of the premise.

All S are P.

Next, we check to see if the conclusion follows necessarily. Since the conclusion is an **I**-proposition, in order for it to be true there would have to be an X in the area where S and P overlap. As we can see, the assumption of existence symbol (the circled X) is in the area. At this point, the argument is only *provisionally valid*, because there is one more step to complete. We must investigate whether the circled X refers to something that actually exists. In our example, "S" stands for *perpetual motion machines*, which are purely hypothetical. An actual perpetual motion machine would have to produce more work or energy than it consumes, and this violates the laws of physics. Therefore, in this instance, the assumption of existence symbol does not represent anything that actually exists, so the argument is invalid under the *traditional* interpretation. In this case, the traditional interpretation and the modern interpretation give the same results.

As the preceding two examples illustrate, the complete traditional square of opposition holds *only under the assumption of existence*, meaning that not only does the relationship of contradictories hold, but so do contraries, subcontraries, and subalternation. However, if we determine that a universal proposition does *not* have existential import, then the relationships of contraries, subcontraries, and subalternation no longer hold. In those cases, the only relationship that still holds is contradictories.

As we can see, the major difference between the traditional and modern interpretations of universal categorical propositions is in the area of existential import. Under the traditional interpretation, determining whether or not a universal proposition refers to objects that actually exist allows some useful arguments to be valid that would otherwise be invalid under the modern interpretation. (The foregoing argument regarding improvised explosive devices is just one example.) Under the modern interpretation, validity is a purely *formal* question. To this way of thinking, the need to determine whether members of a class of objects exist adds another layer of analysis to an argument. This topic will come up again in the next chapter, when we explore categorical syllogisms, and we will have more opportunity to see how the two interpretations differ.

EXERCISES 5F.2

I. **Draw Venn diagrams for the following immediate arguments. Determine whether the arguments are valid or invalid using the traditional interpretation.**

Lightboard Video

1. No fashion models are camera-shy people. Therefore, some fashion models are not camera-shy people.

Answer: The premise is an **E**-proposition. We start by drawing a Venn diagram of the premise:

No S are P.

Next, we check to see if the conclusion follows necessarily. Since the conclusion is an **O**-proposition, in order for it to be true there has to be an X in the unshaded area of S. As we can see, the assumption of existence symbol (the circled X) is in the area. Therefore, the argument is *provisionally valid*. Now we need to see if the circled X represents something that actually exists. Since the "S" stands for *fashion models*, and they surely exist, the assumption of existence symbol does represent something that actually exists. Therefore, the argument is valid.

2. All cruise ships are romantic locations. Therefore, some cruise ships are romantic locations.

3. No centaurs are gentle creatures. Therefore, all centaurs are gentle creatures.

4. Some leprechauns are mischievous people. Therefore, no leprechauns are mischievous people.

★ 5. No former presidents of the United States are great-grandfathers. Therefore, some former presidents of the United States are great-grandfathers.

6. All former Soviet premiers are members of the KGB. Therefore, some former Soviet premiers are not members of the KGB.

7. Some used-car salespersons are honest people. Therefore, all used-car salespersons are honest people.

8. Some bank loans are low-interest loans. Therefore, some bank loans are not low-interest loans.

★ 9. Some used books are not high-priced items. Therefore, some used books are high-priced items.

10. All credit card billing statements are complex items. Therefore, some credit card billing statements are complex items.

11. Some text messages are not interesting pieces of writing. Therefore, some text messages are interesting pieces of writing.

12. All dogs are social animals. Therefore, some dogs are social animals.

★ 13. All soft drinks are acid-based beverages. Therefore, no soft drinks are acid-based beverages.

14. No batteries are perfectly efficient devices. Therefore, some batteries are perfectly efficient devices.

15. All patented inventions are physical machines. Therefore, some patented inventions are not physical machines.

16. Some sales items are defective products. Therefore, all sales items are defective products.

★ 17. All abominable snowmen are vegetarians. Therefore, some abominable snowmen are vegetarians.

18. Some canaries are not yellow birds. Therefore, all canaries are yellow birds.

19. All bathing suits are lightweight clothes. Therefore, some bathing suits are lightweight clothes.

20. Some phone apps are not secure software programs. Therefore, some phone apps are secure software programs.

II. For more practice, draw Venn diagrams for the following immediate arguments, and determine whether the inferences are *valid, provisionally valid,* or *invalid* using the *traditional interpretation.*

1. All S are P.
   Some S are P.

Answer: Here is the diagram of the premise, an **A**-proposition:

All S are P.

In order for the conclusion, an **I**-proposition, to be true, there would have to be an X in the area where S and P overlap. Since a circled X is in that area, the argument is *provisionally valid.*

2. All S are P.
   No S are P.

3. All S are P.
   Some S are not P.

4. No S are P.
   All S are P.

⭐5. No S are P.
   Some S are P.

6. No S are P.
   Some S are not P.

7. Some S are P.
   All S are P.

8. Some S are P.
   No S are P.

⭐9. Some S are P.
   Some S are not P.

10. Some S are not P.
   All S are P.

11. Some S are not P.
   Some S are P.

12. Some S are not P.
   No S are P.

G. CONVERSION, OBVERSION, AND CONTRAPOSITION IN THE TRADITIONAL SQUARE

The traditional square of opposition can also be used to analyze immediate arguments that are created by conversion, obversion, and contraposition. This will result in only two differences between the traditional and the modern square, one for conversion and one for contraposition.

Summary of Conversion, Obversion, and Contraposition

The Method of Conversion
Switch the subject and predicate.

Subject ⟵⟶ *Predicate*

The Method of Obversion

STEP 1: Change the *quality* of the given proposition.
STEP 2: Replace the *predicate term* with its *complement*.

The Method of Contraposition

STEP 1: Switch the subject and predicate terms.
STEP 2: Replace both the subject and predicate terms with their term complements.

Conversion

The traditional interpretation agrees with the modern interpretation that conversion leads to valid immediate arguments for both **E**- and **I**-propositions. The two interpretations also agree that conversion leads to invalid immediate arguments for **O**-propositions. However, they disagree when it comes to conversion for **A**-propositions. The modern interpretation holds that conversion leads to invalid immediate arguments for **A**-propositions. In contrast, the traditional interpretation uses subalternation to make conversion work *in a limited way* for **A**-propositions. Subalternation tells us that if an **A**-proposition is true, then its corresponding particular **I**-proposition is true, too. And since we already know that conversion works for **I**-propositions, we can do something called **conversion by limitation**. Here we first change a universal **A**-proposition into its corresponding particular **I**-proposition, and then we use the process of conversion on the **I**-proposition. The process looks like this:

Conversion by limitation We first change a universal A-proposition into its corresponding particular I-proposition, and then we use the process of conversion on the I-proposition.

Convertend	**A**-proposition: All spam e-mailings are invasions of your home.
Corresponding particular	**I**-proposition: Some spam e-mailings are invasions of your home.
Converse	**I**-proposition: Some invasions of your home are spam e-mailings.

Under the *traditional* interpretation, we used conversion by limitation to create a valid immediate argument. Given this, we can say that the immediate argument is *valid by limitation*.

Obversion

The traditional interpretation agrees with the modern interpretation that obversion leads to valid immediate arguments for all four standard-form categorical propositions.

Contraposition

The traditional interpretation agrees with the modern interpretation that contraposition leads to valid immediate arguments for both **A**- and **O**-propositions. The two interpretations also agree that contraposition leads to invalid immediate arguments for **I**-propositions. However, they disagree when it comes to contraposition for

E-propositions. The modern interpretation holds that contraposition leads to invalid immediate arguments for E-propositions. In contrast, the traditional interpretation uses subalternation to make contraposition work *in a limited way* for E-propositions. Subalternation tells us that if an E-proposition is true, then its corresponding particular O-proposition is true, too. And since we know that contraposition works for O-propositions, we can use **contraposition by limitation**. We first change the universal E-proposition into its corresponding particular O-proposition, and then we use the process of contraposition on the O-proposition. The process looks like this:

Given proposition:	E-proposition: No gorillas are lions.
Corresponding particular:	O-proposition: Some gorillas are not lions.
Contrapositive:	O-proposition: Some non-lions are not non-gorillas.

Under the traditional interpretation, we used contraposition by limitation to create a valid immediate argument. Given this, we can say that the immediate argument is *valid by limitation*.

Contraposition by limitation
Subalternation is used to change a universal E-proposition into its corresponding particular O-proposition. We then apply the regular process of forming a contrapositive to this O-proposition.

EXERCISES 5G

Refer back to Exercises 5E I and apply the *traditional interpretation* for conversion, obversion, and contraposition for each of the given propositions. Determine whether the subsequent immediate arguments are valid or invalid. When necessary, apply your understanding of the relevant *corresponding particular* to a given proposition to determine whether the subsequent immediate inference from that corresponding particular proposition is valid, invalid, or valid by limitation under the traditional interpretation.

Self-Practice
Questions

H. TRANSLATING ORDINARY LANGUAGE INTO CATEGORICAL PROPOSITIONS

Categorical propositions can be found in everyday life. Here is one example:

> Some football coaches are persons of character who always put their players' health first.　　Gregg Easterbrook, "Concussion Hazards Must Be Addressed"

We have already seen how logic can help us make sense of the claims all around us—but first we need to be able to paraphrase statements in ordinary language. As we are all aware, ordinary language statements can be subject to differing interpretations. Sometimes missing information requires us to reconstruct arguments based on our understanding of the context. If we can translate an ordinary language statement into a standard-form categorical proposition, then we can reduce the possibility of ambiguity. A correct translation does this by clearly formulating the subject and predicate terms, the quantity (universal or particular), and the quality (affirmative or negative).

Any translation starts with an analysis of the meaning of the ordinary language. Once we are satisfied that we understand the statement, we then construct the appropriate categorical proposition. This requires deciding on the correct quantifier (*all, no, some*), the subject term, the copula (*are, are not*), and the predicate term. Since ordinary language contains an unlimited number of possible statements, we will concentrate on a few of the types that you are most likely to encounter.

Missing Plural Nouns

Consider the following statement:

Some alcoholics are convicts.

This is a standard-form categorical proposition and contains the terms "alcoholics" and "convicts." Each of these terms is a plural noun, and each denotes a class of objects. (A *noun* is a word or group of words that refers to a person, place, or thing.) If we switch the position of the two terms, the result is again a perfectly acceptable standard-form categorical proposition:

Some convicts are alcoholics.

Now consider a second statement:

Some political parties are disorganized.

Most people would have little difficulty understanding this example. On the surface, it appears to be a standard-form categorical proposition. But this is deceiving. Let's see what happens if we switch the position of the two terms:

Some disorganized are political parties.

We no longer have an acceptable statement. The problem is that the word "disorganized" is an *adjective*, not a noun. Adjectives are used to modify nouns, and they cannot normally stand alone. Although the original statement is acceptable as far as ordinary language is concerned, in order to translate it into a standard-form categorical proposition, we have to add a plural noun, so that the resulting term will denote a class. For example:

Some political parties are disorganized groups.

The term "disorganized groups" denotes a class of objects. If we now switch the terms, we get this result:

Some disorganized groups are political parties.

When you translate ordinary language statements into standard-form categorical propositions, always make sure that the subject and predicate terms contain plural nouns.

Nonstandard Verbs

As we have seen in this chapter, standard-form categorical propositions use two forms of the verb "to be": "are" and "are not." The copula is needed to connect the subject and predicate terms; it is a linking verb. However, many ordinary language statements use other forms of the verb "to be." For a regular verb, the past tense is typically formed by adding an "-ed" ending (e.g., "talk," "talked"). But the verb "to be" is an irregular verb, which means that different tenses do not follow general rules. In fact, "to be" is considered by many language experts to be the most irregular verb in the English language. Here are a few of the forms that it takes: *is, are, was, being, been, be, will (be), would (be),* and *were.* This means that many everyday examples of ordinary language statements contain verbs that must be translated into either "are" or "are not."

Here are some examples:

Ordinary Language Statement:
All the protesters at the convention were arrested.

Standard-Form Translation:
All the protesters at the convention are people who were arrested.

Ordinary Language Statement:
Some students would prefer to cheat rather than learn the material.

Standard-Form Translation:
Some students are people who would prefer to cheat rather than learn the material.

Ordinary Language Statement:
Trespassers will be prosecuted.

Standard-Form Translation:
All trespassers are people who will be prosecuted.

As these examples illustrate, you must be careful to translate the verb into either "are" or "are not," and you must make sure that translation contains terms that denote classes.

Many ordinary language statements do not use any form of the verb "to be." In these cases you have to look closely to grasp the meaning of the statement. Here are some examples:

Ordinary Language Statement:
Some assembly required.

Standard-Form Translation:
Some parts of this item are parts that need assembling.

Ordinary Language Statement:
No pain, no gain.

Standard-Form Translation:
No exercise routines without physical pain are exercise routines offering physical gain.

Even short sentences in ordinary language can be misunderstood. The trade-off of creating translations that are lengthy and repetitive is that they offer clarity, as we shall see again in the next chapter.

Singular Propositions

Singular proposition
A proposition that asserts something about a specific person, place, or thing.

The examples so far have contained plural nouns denoting classes, but it is possible that a class has only one object. These cases occur in ordinary language in a **singular proposition**; that is, something is asserted about a specific person, place, or thing. A singular proposition can normally be translated into a universal proposition. Here is one example:

Ordinary Language Statement:
Al Gore is a Nobel Prize winner.

Standard-Form Translation:
All persons identical to Al Gore are persons who have won a Nobel Prize.

The phrase "persons identical to Al Gore" may seem odd, but there is a reason for it. Since the subject is a single individual (Al Gore), the subject term of the translation must designate a class of objects that happens to have exactly one member. There is only one person identical to Al Gore, and that is Al Gore himself. So, the phrase "persons identical to Al Gore" refers to a class of objects that has exactly one member.

The phrase "persons identical to" is called a *parameter*. A parameter must accurately represent the intended meaning of an ordinary language statement, while at the same time transforming it into a standard-form categorical proposition. Here are some parameters that you can use to translate singular propositions:

persons identical to   places identical to
things identical to   events identical to
times identical to   cases identical to

Always remember that a singular proposition refers to a *specific* person (place, thing, etc.). Given this, the phrase "identical to" is to be taken literally. There is only one Eiffel Tower, and it is in Paris. If you go to Las Vegas, you will see a structure that looks *very much like* the Eiffel Tower (at one-third the size), but there is only one tower *identical* to the Eiffel Tower.

Here are some more singular propositions in ordinary language and their translations:

Ordinary Language Statement:
Shane is good at DDR (*DanceDanceRevolution*).

Standard-Form Translation:
All persons identical to Shane are persons good at DDR (*DanceDanceRevolution*).

Ordinary Language Statement:
Hugo did not go to Hawaii last spring break.

Standard-Form Translation:
No persons identical to Hugo are persons who went to Hawaii last spring break.

Ordinary Language Statement:
My car is in Joe's garage for repairs.

Standard-Form Translation:
All things identical to my car are things in Joe's garage for repairs.

Ordinary Language Statement:
Leo was ill last night.

Standard-Form Translation:
All persons identical to Leo are persons who were ill last night.

Parameters are used when translating singular propositions. They are not needed when the ordinary language statement has plural nouns.

Adverbs and Pronouns

Some ordinary language statements contain adverbs that describe places or times. For example, in the statement "Wherever there is smoke there is fire," the word "wherever" is a *spatial* adverb. Spatial adverbs describe where something happens. Here are some spatial adverbs: *wherever, everywhere, anywhere, somewhere, nowhere, upstairs,* and *underground.*

In the statement "Whenever you are audited by the IRS, you had better get legal help," the word "whenever" is a *temporal* adverb. Temporal adverbs describe when something happens. Here are some temporal adverbs: *whenever, never, always, anytime, yesterday,* and *tomorrow.*

Translating ordinary language statements into standard-form categorical propositions using these kinds of adverbs is relatively straightforward:

Ordinary Language Statement:
Wherever there is smoke, there is fire.

Standard-Form Translation:
All places that have smoke are places that have fire.

Ordinary Language Statement:
Whenever you are audited by the IRS, you should get legal help.

Standard-Form Translation:
All times you are audited by the IRS are times that you should get legal help.

Pronouns are often used to replace nouns that are unspecified. Some ordinary language statements contain pronouns that describe unspecified persons. For example, in the statement "Whoever took my laptop is in big trouble," the pronoun "whoever" refers to an unspecified person (or persons). Here are some pronouns referring to persons: *whoever, anyone, anybody, everyone, no one,* and *someone.* In the statement "What goes around comes around," the pronoun "what" refers to an unspecified thing (or things). Here are some pronouns referring to things: *what, whatever, anything, something,* and *everything.*

Here are translations of the last two examples:

Ordinary Language Statement:
Whoever took my laptop is in big trouble.

Standard-Form Translation:
All persons who took my laptop are persons in big trouble.

Ordinary Language Statement:
What goes around comes around.

Standard-Form Translation:
All things that go around are things that come around.

"It Is False That ..."

Suppose you hear the following statement: "Every professional athlete uses steroids." This can be translated as the **A**-proposition "All professional athletes are people who use steroids." Now if you happen to believe that the proposition is false, you can say, "It is false that every professional athlete uses steroids." What your statement does is to *negate* (or deny) the original statement. Since your statement is the contradictory of an **A**-proposition, it gets translated as an **O**-proposition: "Some professional athletes are not people who use steroids."

Since **E**- and **I**-propositions are contradictory, creating a negation works much the same way. For example, the statement "It is not the case that some rings are costly jewelry" gets translated as an **E**-proposition: "No rings are costly jewelry." The phrase "It is not the case" negates the translated **I**-proposition "Some rings are costly jewelry."

Here are some useful negation phrases:

> *It is false that ...*
> *It is not the case that ...*
> *It is not true that ...*

Remember that all three of these phrases negate the statement following it. If what follows the negation phrase is an **A**-proposition, then the translation results in an **O**-proposition, and vice versa. On the other hand, if what follows the negation phrase is an **E**-proposition, then the translation results in an **I**-proposition, and vice versa.

Implied Quantifiers

Some statements in ordinary language imply something without actually saying it. Important terms are either left out on purpose or simply overlooked. In these cases we have to supply the missing terms. If the missing term is a quantifier word (*all, no, some*), then our translation into a standard-form categorical proposition must rely on a close reading of the intended meaning. Here is one example:

Sharks are predators.

The statement connects a species of animals (*sharks*) with a specific characteristic (*being a predator*). As such, it refers to the entire subject class and can be translated as follows:

All sharks are predators.

Now let's look at another example that uses the same subject (sharks):

There are sharks in the local aquarium.

It is unlikely that the person making the assertion is claiming that the entire class of sharks is in the local aquarium. Therefore, our translation will have to use the quantifier "some":

Some sharks are animals in the local aquarium.

We had to add the word "animals" because the phrase "in the local aquarium" would not by itself designate a class of objects.

How would you translate the next statement?

A professor is a human being.

Although the statement contains the phrase "a professor," it appears likely that the assertion is about every professor. It can therefore be translated as follows:

All professors are human beings.

What about this example?

A professor is not a machine.

This statement also refers to every professor, but it contains the word "not." It is tempting to translate the statement as follows:

All professors are not machines.   ***Incorrect***

The correct form of a universal affirmative categorical proposition is *All S are P*, so we cannot add the word "not" using this form. The universal negative form solves our problem:

No professors are machines.   ***Correct***

Here is one more example to consider:

A professor won the Nobel Prize.

This statement also contains the phrase "a professor" but it is unlikely that it is meant to refer to every professor. It can be translated as follows:

Some professors are winners of the Nobel Prize.

Earlier we had to make the subject term a plural noun in order for it to designate a class. Of course, if a specific professor had been named (e.g., Professor Blake), then we would have used the information regarding singular propositions to get the correct translation.

Now try a more complex example:

We will not be able to finish all the costumes by 5:00.

A quick reading might suggest that the quantifier word "all" means that this should be translated as a universal affirmative proposition. However, the word "not" indicates negation. Combining these two words gives us the phrase "not all." It is unlikely that the speaker is claiming that no costumes will be finished by 5:00. (If this had been intended, then we would expect the statement to be "We will not be able to finish *any* costume by 5:00.") Therefore, the correct quantifier is "some," and the translated statement must include the word "not":

> Some costumes are not costumes that will be finished by 5:00.

This example illustrates why ordinary language statements often require a careful reading in order to understand the meaning and to arrive at a correct translation.

Nonstandard Quantifiers

Ordinary language statements might contain quantifiers that are nonstandard, because they are not one of the following: *all, no,* or *some.* Here is an example:

> Not every investment banker is a crook.

In this statement the nonstandard quantifier "not every" probably means at least one investment banker is not a crook. Given this interpretation, the translation would be the following:

> Some investment bankers are not crooks.

Notice that we once again had to change the subject and predicate terms into plural nouns.

Here are some nonstandard quantifiers: *any, many, most, a few, one, several,* and *not every.* Let's take one from the list and look at another example:

> Not every novel about romance is interesting.

In this statement the nonstandard quantifier "not every" means that there are some novels about romance that are not interesting. Given this interpretation, the translation would be the following:

> Some novels about romance are not interesting novels.

Here is another statement in ordinary language that uses a nonstandard quantifier:

> A few movies at the mall are worth watching.

Here the quantifier "a few" is likely to mean that at least one movie at the mall is worth watching. The translation would be the following:

> Some movies at the mall are movies worth watching.

Since the phrase "worth watching" does not by itself designate a class, we had to add the term "movies" to it.

Conditional Statements

We have already encountered conditional statements when we looked at existential import. The **A**-proposition "All scientists are people trained in mathematics" can be translated as "*If* a person is a scientist, *then* that person is trained in mathematics." The **E**-proposition "No slackers are reliable workers" can be translated as "*If* a person is a slacker, *then* that person is not a reliable worker." These translations are a result of the modern interpretation of universal categorical propositions.

As you might recall from Chapter 1, the part of the conditional statement that follows the word "if" is called the *antecedent*, and the part that follows the word "then" is called the *consequent*. Here are some simple examples:

Ordinary Language Statement:
If a person has $10 in her checking account, then she is not rich.

Standard-Form Translation:
No persons having $10 in their checking account are rich persons.

Ordinary Language Statement:
If a salesperson calls on the phone, then I just hang up.

Standard-Form Translation:
All calls from salespersons are calls where I hang up.

Sometimes ordinary language statements do not have the word "if" at the beginning. When this occurs, we simply reposition the appropriate part so the antecedent comes first:

Ordinary Language Statement:
Pizza is a healthy meal if it has vegetable toppings.

Standard-Form Translation:
All pizzas with vegetable toppings are healthy meals.

Ordinary Language Statement:
A dog is not dangerous if it has been well trained.

Standard-Form Translation:
No well-trained dogs are dangerous animals.

The conditional statement "If your cup of coffee is not perfect, then you are not drinking a cup of Bigbucks coffee" poses a new kind of problem for translation. To assist us, we need to introduce *transposition*. This rule is a two-step procedure. First, we switch the positions of the antecedent and the consequent, and second, we negate both of them. Let's work through it step by step and make any additional changes in wording as we go to capture the meaning of the statement:

First Step:
If you are not drinking a cup of Bigbucks coffee, then your cup of coffee is not perfect.

Second Step:
If you are drinking a cup of Bigbucks coffee, then your cup of coffee is perfect.

Final Translation:
All cups of Bigbucks coffee are perfect cups of coffee.

Now let's look at an example that is a little more challenging. The conditional statement "If murderers do not get punished, then they do not stop their behavior" requires a bit of rewriting to capture the meaning in standard-form categorical proposition. As before, we will take it step by step and apply the rule of transposition:

First Step:
If murderers do not stop their behavior, then murderers do not get punished.

Second Step:
If murderers stop their behavior, then murderers get punished.

Final Translation:
All murderers who have stopped their behavior are murderers who have been
  punished.

In order to translate the statement "A citizen cannot be president unless the citizen is at least 35 years old," we need to understand how the word "unless" gets translated. In most statements, the word "unless" means *if not*. Substituting this into the original statement gives us this result: "A citizen cannot be president if the citizen is not at least 35 years old." Next, we can place the antecedent at the beginning of the statement: "If the citizen is not at least 35 years old, then a citizen cannot be president." We are now in a position to apply the two-step rule of transposition:

If a citizen can be president, then the citizen is at least 35 years old.

The last step completes the translation into a standard-form categorical proposition:

All citizens that can be president are citizens at least 35 years old.

Exclusive Propositions

Suppose you hear this announcement over a loudspeaker:

Only persons with tickets can enter the arena.

The announcement means that admission into the arena is limited to those holding tickets. Therefore, anyone who does not have a ticket is *excluded* from entering the arena, and we call this an *exclusive proposition*. Another way of saying this is "If a person does not have a ticket, then that person cannot enter the arena." Applying transposition to this statement, we get:

If a person can enter the arena, then that person has a ticket.

This statement can now be translated into a standard-form categorical proposition:

All persons who can enter the arena are persons that have tickets.

Here are some other words that indicate an exclusive proposition: *none but, solely, alone,* and *none except.* Let's take the first one from the list and analyze a statement that contains the words "none but":

None but students can see the movie for free.

According to the statement, anyone who is not a student is excluded from seeing the movie for free. This can be rewritten as "If a person is not a student, then that person cannot see the movie for free." Applying transposition to this statement we get:

If a person can see the movie for free, then that person is a student.

This statement can now be translated into a standard-form categorical proposition:

All persons who can see the movie for free are students.

Some ordinary language statements do not have the exclusive term at the beginning. For example, "Lottery winners get lucky only once in their lives." In these cases, we have to rewrite the terms in order to designate the correct classes:

All lottery winners are persons who get lucky once in their lives.

"The Only"

Although the words "only" and "the only" seem very much alike, they sometimes require different kinds of translations. For example, the statement "The only true friends are people who want nothing from you" can be directly translated as "All true friends are people who want nothing from you." However, if the words "the only" occurs in a different part of a statement, then you rewrite the statement by placing it and the phrase following it at the beginning. Here is an example:

Android phones are the only phones imported by her company.

The first step is to put "the only" phrase at the beginning: "The only phones imported by her company are Android phones." The final step is the translation into a standard-form categorical proposition:

All phones imported by her company are Android phones.

Propositions Requiring Two Translations

The examples so far could be translated as single statements. However, some statements need to be translated into *compound* statements, containing the word "and." For example, propositions that take the form "All except S are P" and "All but S are P" are called **exceptive propositions**. Here is one exceptive proposition: "All except those under 21 are allowed to gamble in Las Vegas." The meaning of the statement is quite clear: If you are under 21 you cannot gamble, and if you are 21 or older you can. In other words, the statement relates the predicate to both the class designated by subject term *and* to its complement. Hence the complete translation will result in a compound statement:

No under-21 persons are persons allowed to gamble in Las Vegas, and all non-under-21 persons are persons allowed to gamble in Las Vegas.

Exceptive propositions Statements that need to be translated into compound statements containing the word "and" (for example, propositions that take the form "All except S are P" and "All but S are P").

Here is another example:

Everyone but gamblers sleeps well at night.

Translation:
No gamblers are people who sleep well at night, and all non-gamblers are people who sleep well at night.

Knowing the context in which ordinary language statements occur can help in making correct translations. When we have a conversation, we can ask questions to clear up any ambiguity. This option is obviously not available when we are reading something and the author is not present. When in doubt, it is better to do more than less. In other words, if there are two reasonable interpretations of the meaning of a statement, then you had best work out the details of both. For example, suppose you read the following: "The heavy snowfall affected the turnout. Few registered voters went to the polls today." Clearly, some registered voters went to the polls and some didn't. This can be translated as a compound statement:

Some registered voters are persons who went to the polls today, and some registered voters are not persons who went to the polls today.

Earlier, the nonstandard quantifier "a few" was translated as a single **I**-proposition. ("A few movies at the mall are worth watching" was translated as "Some movies at the mall are movies worth watching.") However, sometimes "a few" should be translated as a compound statement. Again, the context is your best guide to which translation is appropriate.

Sometimes we should translate an exclusive proposition containing "only" as a compound statement. Whenever we talk or write, it is possible that part of our audience may lack some of the general knowledge regarding a factual issue that we take for granted. Thus, when a statement refers to an *individual*, sometimes it is best to spell out in detail a fact that may not be universally known to all. For example, the statement "Only Carly designed the wedding gown" makes two assertions. First, *Carly designed the wedding gown*, and second, *no one else did*. Also, since the statement asserts something about a specific person (an *individual*), our translation has to take that into account:

All persons identical to Carly are persons who designed the wedding gown, and all persons who designed the wedding gown are persons identical to Carly.

We get the same results for the statement "The only person who designed the wedding gown is Carly." In this case, the statement is equivalent to "Only Carly designed the wedding gown," and therefore it gets the same compound translation.

Here is one more example:

Barack Obama alone is the forty-fourth president of the United States.

This example contains two references. The first is to an *individual* (Barack Obama), and the second is to *an elected office*. We can translate the statement as follows:

All persons identical to Barack Obama are persons identical to the forty-fourth president of the United States, and all persons identical to the forty-fourth president of the United States are persons identical to Barack Obama.

Translations into standard-form categorical propositions often require close and careful reading, but the effort pays off by *reducing the chance of misunderstanding*. It makes us aware of the many possible ambiguities in ordinary language, and it makes our spoken and written communication more precise.

EXERCISES 5H

Translate the following ordinary language statements into standard-form categorical propositions.

Self-Practice
Questions

1. An apple is in the refrigerator.

Answer: Some apples are items in the refrigerator.

Although the statement is referring to a particular apple, the use of "some" is appropriate in this translation because it has been stipulated that it means *at least one*.

2. Any medical doctor is well educated.

3. No insects sing.

4. A flower is a plant.

⭐ 5. All happy people dance.

6. Some bears hibernate.

7. Some cars don't pollute.

8. A mango is not a vegetable.

⭐ 9. It is not the case that every novel is a satire.

10. Every office worker is under pressure to perform.

11. A tsunami is dangerous.

12. Some people don't jaywalk.

⭐ 13. Not every final exam in calculus is a challenging test.

14. Every opera is easy to understand.

15. Not every dog is friendly.

16. Any company that introduces green technology will succeed.

⭐ 17. Young children are not protected from the dangers of war.

18. Ocean levels rise whenever glaciers melt.

19. Styrofoam is 98% air.

20. Not all accidents are preventable.

⭐ 21. Every video game company hires game-testers.

Video Tutorial: 5H
Exercise #13

22. If it's all right with you, then it's all right with me.

23. A movie that depicts courage will inspire courage.

24. No good deed goes unpunished.

⭐ 25. Those who laugh last, laugh best.

26. Underpaid workers do not expect promotions.

27. None but novelists are wordsmiths.

28. A full house always beats a flush.

⭐ 29. Marie Curie is the only person to win Nobel Prizes in two different sciences.

30. A few spices are imported.

31. The people on the FBI's ten most wanted list are dangerous criminals.

32. Asteroids are the only threats to our existence on Earth.

⭐ 33. There is a diamond mine in California.

34. If you get at least eight hours of sleep, you will perform well on exams.

35. It is not true that all aerobic exercises are strenuous activities.

36. Barometers are devices for measuring atmospheric pressure.

⭐ 37. The best intentions are not defeated.

38. The Super Bowl is always the highest rated sporting event.

39. You cannot master a skill unless you practice for 10,000 hours.

40. People get depressed whenever tragedy strikes.

⭐ 41. If a religion isn't certified by the government, then it isn't legitimate.

42. All but the most loyal left the stadium.

43. A speeding violation is serious if the fine is more than $100.

44. Katharine Hepburn alone has four Academy Award best actress wins.

⭐ 45. Unless you pay your electric bill, you cannot get electricity in your apartment.

46. Whoever leaves a child in a car unattended will be arrested.

47. All vegetables except onions taste sweet.

48. Few cast members showed up for rehearsal today.

⭐ 49. Orangutans are native to Borneo.

50. If you are a credit card holder, then you are subjected to hidden charges.

51. Not all soap operas are boring.

52. Magicians are the only people capable of keeping a secret.

⭐ 53. Whatever improvement is made to the gas engine decreases our need for oil.

54. Beauty is not skin deep.

55. A practical joke is not funny if it harms someone.

56. All sharks hunt.

⭐ 57. Some people don't bowl.

58. Not every computer is expensive.

59. Most smokers wish they could quit.

60. All good things must come to an end.

⭐ 61. Beliefs worth having must withstand doubt.

62. If something is worth having, then it's worth struggling for.

63. Fair-weather friends are not trustworthy.

64. Not all that glitters is gold.

⭐ 65. Every ending is a new beginning.

66. Whoever saves even one life saves the entire world.

67. The enemy of my enemy is my friend.

68. Everything old is new again.

⭐ 69. It is false that some people over 30 years of age are not to be trusted.

70. Two snowflakes are never the same.

71. Whoever controls the media, controls the mind.
Jim Morrison, quoted in Telling It Like It Is by Paul Bowden

72. Every unhappy family is unhappy in its own way.   Leo Tolstoy, *Anna Karenina*

⭐ 73. Whoever is winning at the moment will always seem to be invincible.
George Orwell, The Orwell Reader

74. If you tell the truth, you don't have to remember anything.
Mark Twain, Notebook

75. Whoever undertakes to set himself up as a judge in Truth and Knowledge is shipwrecked by the laughter of the gods.
Albert Einstein, quoted in The Princeton Companion to Mathematics

Study Materials

Summary

- Class: A group of objects.
- Categorical proposition: Relates two classes of objects.
- Subject term: The term that comes first in a standard-form categorical proposition.
- Predicate term: The term that comes second in a standard-form categorical proposition.
- **A**-proposition: Asserts that the entire subject class is included in the predicate class ("All S are P").
- **I**-proposition: Asserts that part of the subject class is included in the predicate class ("Some S are P").
- **E**-proposition: Asserts that the entire subject class is excluded from the predicate class ("No S are P").
- **O**-proposition: Asserts that part of the subject class is excluded from the predicate class ("Some S are not P").
- "Universal" and "particular" refer to the quantity of a categorical proposition.
- "Affirmative" and "negative" refer to the quality of a categorical proposition.
- The words "all," "no," and "some" are called "quantifiers." They tell us the extent of the class inclusion or exclusion.
- The words "are" and "are not" are referred to as "copula." They are simply forms of "to be" and serve to link (to "couple") the subject class with the predicate class.
- If a categorical proposition asserts something about every member of a class, then the term designating that class is said to be *distributed*. On the other hand, if the proposition does not assert something about every member of a class, then the term designating that class is said to be *undistributed*.
- Existential import: When a proposition presupposes the existence of certain kinds of objects.
- Opposition: Occurs when two standard-form categorical propositions refer to the same subject and predicate classes but differ in quality, quantity, or both.
- Contradictories: Pairs of propositions in which one is the negation of the other. **A**- and **O**-propositions are contradictories, as are **E**- and **I**-propositions.
- Venn diagrams use circles to represent categorical proposition forms.
- Immediate argument: An argument that has only one premise.
- Mediate argument: An argument that has more than one premise.
- Conversion: An immediate argument created by interchanging the subject and predicate terms of a given categorical proposition.
- Complement: The set of objects that do not belong to a given class.

- Obversion: An immediate argument formed by changing the quality of the given proposition, and then replacing the predicate term with its complement.
- Contraposition: Formed by replacing the subject term of a given proposition with the complement of its predicate term and then replacing the predicate term of the given proposition with the complement of its subject term.
- Contraries: Pairs of propositions that cannot both be true at the same time, but can both be false at the same time. **A-** and **E**-propositions are contraries.
- Subcontraries: Pairs of propositions that cannot both be false at the same time, but can both be true; also, if one is false then the other must be true. **I-** and **O**-propositions are subcontraries.
- Subalternation: The relationship between a universal proposition (the *superaltern*) and its corresponding particular proposition (the *subaltern*).
- Conversion by limitation: When we first change a universal **A**-proposition into its corresponding particular **I**-proposition, and then we use the process of conversion on the **I**-proposition.
- Contraposition by limitation: When subalternation is used to change the universal **E**-proposition into its corresponding particular **O**-proposition. We then apply the regular process of forming a contrapositive to this **O**-proposition.
- Singular proposition: Asserts something about a specific person, place, or thing.
- Exceptive propositions: Statements that need to be translated into compound statements containing the word "and" (for example, propositions that take the form "All except S are P" and "All but S are P").

KEY TERMS

LOGIC CHALLENGE: GROUP RELATIONSHIP

The Masons are a somewhat secretive group. Based on the following information, draw a diagram using four interlocking ellipses that correctly captures the relationship between Masons and three other groups:

1. Every member of the *Scottish Rite* must be a *Mason*.
2. Every member of the *York Rite* must be a *Mason*.
3. It is possible to be a member of both the *Scottish Rite* and the *York Rite*.
4. Every *Shriner* must be a member of the *Scottish Rite*, the *York Rite*, or both.
5. *Masons* do not have to be members of the *Shriners*, or the *Scottish Rite*, or the *York Rite*.

Chapter 6

Categorical Syllogisms

Digital homework exercises for this chapter are available in your instructor's online course. For information on how to access these resources, please visit **www.oup.com/ he/baronett5e**.

Our effort to understand the logic of categorical statements gave us the ability to clarify ordinary language so that we could investigate some immediate inferences for validity. We can build on this foundation to explore complex arguments that are constructed from categorical statements. Take this, for example:

> All comedians are shy people.
> <u>Some comedians are good actors.</u>
> Some good actors are shy people.

We already saw one valuable tool, Venn diagrams, for making sense of generalizations like these—outrageous or not. But can we logically connect them? Can we make our way from the premises to the conclusion?

In addition to advancing the use of Venn diagrams, we will expand the discussion of existential import and how it affects the analysis of some arguments. We will also introduce a new set of rules that complements the use of Venn diagrams for determining validity. Finally, translating ordinary language arguments will round out the discussion of categorical logic.

A. STANDARD-FORM CATEGORICAL SYLLOGISMS

A **syllogism** is a deductive argument that has exactly two premises and a conclusion. A **categorical syllogism** is a syllogism constructed entirely of categorical propositions.

Syllogism A deductive argument that has exactly two premises and a conclusion.

Categorical syllogism A syllogism constructed entirely of categorical propositions.

It contains three different terms, each of which is used two times. Consider the same example:

All comedians are shy people.
<u>Some comedians are good actors.</u>
Some good actors are shy people.

Each of the three terms—*comedians*, *shy people*, and *good actors*—occurs twice in the categorical syllogism. By definition, the **minor term** is the subject of the conclusion (*good actors*), and the **major term** is the predicate of the conclusion (*shy people*). The term that occurs only in the premises (*comedians*) is called the **middle term**. Also, the first premise of a categorical syllogism contains the major term and it is called the **major premise**. The second premise contains the minor term, and it is called the **minor premise**.

In order to be a **standard-form categorical syllogism**, a syllogism must meet three requirements:

1. All three statements (the two premises and the conclusion) must be standard-form categorical propositions. (Any statement that is not in standard form has to be rewritten, as illustrated in Chapter 5.)
2. The two occurrences of each term must be identical and have the same sense. (This requirement eliminates instances of equivocation.)
3. The major premise must occur first, the minor premise second, and the conclusion last.

Since the syllogism at the beginning of this section meets all three requirements, it is a standard-form categorical syllogism. However, the next example fails to meet each of the three requirements.

All superstitions are religious beliefs.
<u>Some false beliefs are old superstitions.</u>
Many religious beliefs are false beliefs.

The first requirement is not met because the conclusion begins with the word "Many" (it would have to be rewritten as a standard-form proposition). The second requirement is not met because the terms "superstitions" and "old superstitions" are not identical. Finally, the third requirement is not met because the major premise occurs second, so the order of the two premises has to be switched.

THE STRUCTURE OF STANDARD-FORM CATEGORICAL SYLLOGISMS
First premise: The *major premise*.   Second premise: The *minor premise*.   Conclusion: The *minor term* is the subject, and the *major term* is the predicate.

We will examine mood and figure, and then we will look at two methods of determining whether a standard-form categorical syllogism is valid or invalid. The first method relies on the basic ideas of Venn diagrams introduced in Chapter 5. The second method uses a set of rules to determine whether a standard-form categorical syllogism is valid or invalid.

Minor term The subject of the conclusion of a categorical syllogism.

Major term The predicate of the conclusion of a categorical syllogism.

Middle term The term that occurs only in the premises of a categorical syllogism.

Major premise The first premise of a categorical syllogism (it contains the major term).

Minor premise The second premise of a categorical syllogism (it contains the minor term).

Standard-form categorical syllogism A categorical syllogism that meets three requirements: (1) All three statements must be standard-form categorical propositions. (2) The two occurrences of each term must be identical and have the same sense. (3) The major premise must occur first, the minor premise second, and the conclusion last.

B. MOOD AND FIGURE

The **mood** of a categorical syllogism consists of the type of categorical propositions involved (**A**, **E**, **I**, or **O**) and the order in which they occur. Here are some examples:

Mood The mood of a categorical syllogism consists of the type of categorical propositions involved (A, E, I, or O) and the order in which they occur.

All P are M.	All P are M.	Some P are not M.	No P are M.
All S are M.	Some S are M.	No S are M.	No S are M.
All S are P.	Some S are P.	Some S are not P.	Some S are not P.
Mood: AAA	**Mood: AII**	**Mood: OEO**	**Mood: EEO**

The middle term in the two premises can be arranged in any one of four different ways, called the **figure** of the categorical syllogism:

Figure The middle term can be arranged in the two premises in four different ways. These placements determine the figure of the categorical syllogism.

THE FOUR FIGURES OF CATEGORICAL SYLLOGISMS			
M — P S — M S — P	P M S M S P	M P M S S P	P — M M — S S P
Figure 1	**Figure 2**	**Figure 3**	**Figure 4**

Here are some examples:

All P are M.	All M are P.	Some P are not M.	No M are P.
All S are M.	Some S are M.	No M are S.	No M are S.
All S are P.	Some S are P.	Some S are not P.	Some S are not P.
AAA-2	**AII-1**	**OEO-4**	**EEO-3**

PROFILES IN LOGIC
Christine Ladd-Franklin

Christine Ladd-Franklin (1847–1930) did substantial work in symbolic logic, mathematics, physiological optics, and the theory of color vision. While at Johns Hopkins she attended the lectures of Charles S. Peirce, whose ideas on symbolic logic helped Ladd-Franklin develop her ideas. In fact, Peirce thought so much of her dissertation that he had it published in *Studies in Logic by Members of the Johns Hopkins University*. In this work, Ladd-Franklin tried to solve a problem that began with Aristotle, to find a single test that would capture all valid syllogisms. The solution requires that they all share something in common—and some general test would reveal just what. Ladd-Franklin proposed that the premises of any valid syllogism will be inconsistent with the *negation* of the conclusion. As Josiah Royce of Harvard University said of Ladd-Franklin's test, "There is no reason why this should not be accepted as the definite solution to the problem of the reduction of syllogisms."

Although her dissertation "The Algebra of Logic" was published in 1883, she was not able to receive a Ph.D. because technically she was not even enrolled at Johns Hopkins University, which at the time was all male. Only after a lifetime of important work was she finally awarded a doctorate degree in 1926.

Since there are four categorical propositions (**A**, **E**, **I**, and **O**), and since each standard-form categorical syllogism contains exactly three propositions (two premises and a conclusion), we get 4 × 4 × 4 = 64 combinations for the mood. But we also know that there are four figures to consider. Therefore, we get 64 × 4 = 256 possible standard-form categorical syllogisms.

Once we learn to apply the Venn diagram method to each of the 256 possible standard-form categorical syllogisms, we will find that fifteen are valid in both the modern and the traditional interpretation:

CATEGORICAL SYLLOGISMS VALID UNDER BOTH INTERPRETATIONS			
AAA-1	AEE-2	AII-3	AEE-4
AII-1	AOO-2	EIO-3	EIO-4
EAE-1	EAE-2	IAI-3	IAI-4
EIO-1	EIO-2	OAO-3	

However, under the traditional interpretation, which assumes existential import for universal propositions, an additional nine categorical syllogisms are *provisionally valid*:

CATEGORICAL SYLLOGISMS PROVISIONALLY VALID UNDER THE TRADITIONAL INTERPRETATION			
AAI-1	AEO-2	AAI-3	AAI-4
EAO-1	EAO-2	EAO-3	AEO-4
			EAO-4

These nine syllogisms are called "provisionally valid" because, under the *traditional* interpretation, we need to determine whether or not the term needed to make the conclusion true denotes actually existing objects. If it does, then the syllogism is valid; otherwise it is invalid.

Under the *modern* interpretation, these additional nine syllogisms are all *invalid*. You can recognize this immediately if you notice that in each case a particular conclusion follows from two universal premises. Under the modern interpretation, it would be logically impossible to get an X anywhere in the Venn diagram.

EXERCISES 6B

Self-Practice
Questions

I. Identify the major, minor, and middle terms, and the mood and figure of the following categorical syllogisms:

1. No animals are vegetarians.
   <u>All bears are animals.</u>
   No bears are vegetarians.

Answers:

1. *major term*: vegetarians; *minor term*: bears; *middle term*: animals; *mood*: **EAE**; *figure*: **1**

2. Some parents are college students.
   <u>Some politicians are not college students.</u>
   Some politicians are not parents.

3. No jet airplanes are quiet vehicles.
   <u>All jet airplanes are fast machines.</u>
   No fast machines are quiet vehicles.

4. No hot dogs are cholesterol-free foods.
   <u>Some beef products are hot dogs.</u>
   Some beef products are not cholesterol-free foods.

⭐ 5. Some cats are not independent creatures.
   <u>Some cats are not lovable pets.</u>
   Some lovable pets are not independent creatures.

6. All pastries are sweet treats.
   <u>No sweet treats are nutritious products.</u>
   No nutritious products are pastries.

7. Some comic books are not novels.
   <u>Some comic books are not fantasies.</u>
   Some fantasies are not novels.

8. All luxury resorts are secluded areas.
   <u>All five-star hotels are secluded areas.</u>
   All five-star hotels are luxury resorts.

⭐ 9. No hammers are surgical tools.
   <u>Some blunt instruments are hammers.</u>
   Some blunt instruments are not surgical tools.

Video Tutorial: 6BI
Exercise #9

10. No surfboards are paper products.
    <u>No tires are paper products.</u>
    No tires are surfboards.

11. Some games are challenging diversions.
    <u>All crossword puzzles are challenging diversions.</u>
    Some crossword puzzles are games.

12. Some colleges are commuter schools.
    <u>Some colleges are not urban schools.</u>
    Some urban schools are not commuter schools.

⭐13. All math problems are brain food.
    <u>No sporting events are math problems.</u>
    No sporting events are brain food.

14. Some paintings are abstract works of art.
    <u>Some paintings are valuable objects.</u>
    Some valuable objects are abstract works of art.

15. Some creatures are space aliens.
<u>All creatures are living organisms.</u>
Some living organisms are space aliens.

II. Determine the mood and figure of each of the following:

1. All M are P.
<u>Some M are S.</u>
Some S are P.

Answer: **AII-3**

2. No M are P.
<u>Some S are not M.</u>
Some S are not P.

3. All P are M.
<u>All S are M.</u>
All S are P.

4. Some P are M.
<u>Some S are M.</u>
Some S are P.

⭐ 5. Some M are not P.
<u>Some M are not S.</u>
Some S are not P.

6. No P are M.
<u>No M are S.</u>
No S are P.

7. All P are M.
<u>Some S are M.</u>
All S are P.

8. Some P are M.
<u>Some M are not S.</u>
Some S are not P.

⭐ 9. All M are P.
<u>No S are M.</u>
Some S are not P.

10. No M are P.
<u>Some S are M.</u>
Some S are P.

C. DIAGRAMMING IN THE MODERN INTERPRETATION

The diagrams in this part will rely on the techniques introduced in Chapter 5. If you recall, categorical propositions contain two terms and are diagrammed using a pair of overlapping circles:

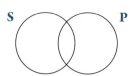

Universal propositions refer to class inclusion or exclusion. If one class is entirely included in another class (**A**-proposition) or entirely excluded from another class (**E**-proposition), then our diagrams must shade out the appropriate areas.

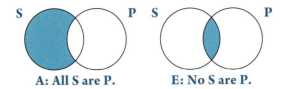

A: All S are P.   E: No S are P.

We also learned how to diagram the particular propositions **I** and **O**. Unlike universal propositions, particular propositions refer to individual members of a class. The diagrams for **I** and **O** propositions use an X to denote a specific member of a class.

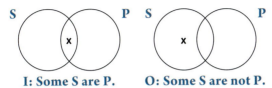

I: Some S are P.   O: Some S are not P.

When we have a single categorical proposition, we have only the relationship between two terms to consider:

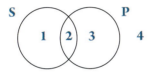

However, since standard-form categorical syllogisms have three terms (major, minor, and middle), we have to add a circle to our diagram. The added circle will create an additional four areas, which we will number accordingly:

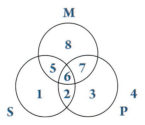

Here "**S**" stands for the class referred to by the minor term, "**P**" for the class referred to by the major term, and "**M**" for the class referred to by the middle term. We can now refer to the different areas in the diagram as follows:

- If something is in Area 1, then it is an S, a non-P, and a non-M.
- If something is in Area 2, then it is an S, a P, and a non-M.
- If something is in Area 3, then it is a P, a non-S, and a non-M.
- If something is in Area 4, then it is a non-S, a non-P, and a non-M.
- If something is in Area 5, then it is an S, an M, and a non-P.
- If something is in Area 6, then it is an S, a P, and an M.
- If something is in Area 7, then it is a P, an M, and a non-S.
- If something is in Area 8, then it is an M, a non-S, and a non-P.

The three interlocking circles might look complicated, but just a few simple tools are needed to complete the Venn diagrams. As we will soon learn, the results will allow us to determine whether a standard-form categorical syllogism is valid or invalid. And that means we can answer a crucial question: Does the conclusion follow necessarily from the premises?

To answer this question, all we need to do is diagram the two premises (major and minor); we do not need to diagram the conclusion. The reason is this: A valid syllogism's conclusion is automatically diagrammed once all the premises are diagrammed. In other words, in a valid syllogism, true premises guarantee a true conclusion. In contrast, the conclusion of an invalid syllogism does not necessarily follow from the premises. As we shall see, a correctly drawn Venn diagram will reveal just that.

Diagramming A-Propositions

We can start by diagramming **A**-propositions. Suppose the major premise is "All P are M." In that case, we need to shade the areas of P that are outside of M:

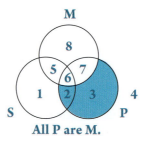

All P are M.

The S circle makes things look more complicated, but it does not change the basic principle. Since *all* the areas of P outside M must be shaded, we need to shade Areas 2 and 3.

Since the major premise contains the major term and the middle term, the only other possible **A**-proposition for it is "All M are P." To diagram this, we need to shade all the areas of M that are outside of P, Areas 5 and 8:

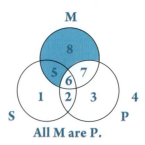

All M are P.

The same principle applies to the minor premise. In fact, there are only two more possible diagrams to consider for **A**-propositions. The minor premise can be either "All S are M" or "All M are S."

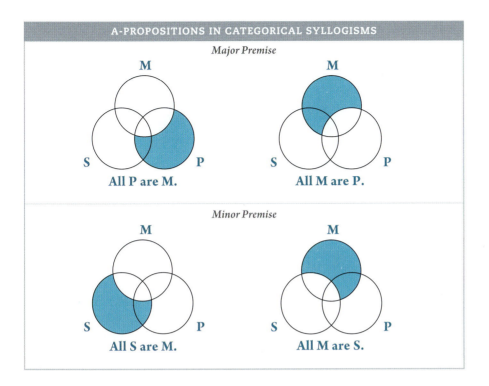

Diagramming E-Propositions

The next step is to learn how to diagram **E**-propositions. This time we will do a diagram for a possible minor premise. For example, suppose the minor premise is "No S are M." Following our basic method, we need to shade the areas of S that overlap with M, Areas 5 and 6:

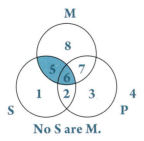

We know that the minor premise contains the minor term and the middle term, so the only other possible **E**-proposition for the minor premise is "No M are S." If you recall the basic principle from Chapter 5 regarding **E**-propositions, we can state that the diagram for "No M are S" is identical to the diagram for "No S are M." Given this, we need to consider only two possible diagrams.

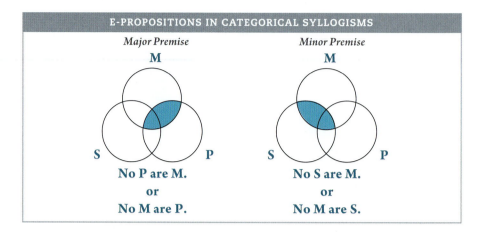

Diagramming I-Propositions

We now turn to **I**-propositions. This time, we will do a diagram for a possible major premise. For example, suppose the major premise is "Some P are M." Following our basic method, we need to place an X in the area where P and M overlap. The fact that we have three interlocking circles now complicates the process a bit, but it is easily overcome. Let's consider three possible locations:

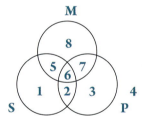

We know that the X is located somewhere in Area 6 or Area 7 (where P and M overlap). But the objects in these two areas are not the same. For example, an object in Area 6 is a P, and it is an M, and an S. However, an object in Area 7 is a P and an M, but it is *not* an S. Our problem is that the single premise "Some P are M" does not provide, by itself, enough information to place the X directly in either of those two areas. Also, we cannot place an X in both areas, because we can use only one X for each particular statement in our diagram. We solve this problem by placing the X on the line separating the two areas where the object might exist:

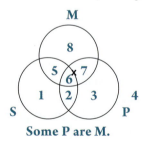

Some P are M.

The placement of X tells us that P is either in Area 6 or Area 7. What additional information would we need in order to place the X directly in Area 6 or Area 7—and not on the line separating the two? Since we are examining the possible major premise "Some P are M," the minor premise would have to be a universal proposition. There are only four possibilities to consider: "All S are M," "All M are S," "No S are M," and "No M are S." And since we know that the diagrams for the two **E**-propositions are identical, we need to draw only three diagrams.

Figure 1

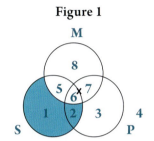

Major Premise: Some P are M.
Minor Premise: All S are M.

Figure 2

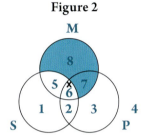

Major Premise: Some P are M.
Minor Premise: All M are S.

Figure 3

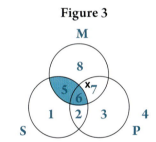

Major Premise: Some P are M.
Minor Premise: No S are M.

In Figure 1 the diagram for the minor premise "All S are M" did not shade either Area 6 or Area 7, and therefore the X remains on the line. However, in Figure 2 the diagram for the minor premise "All M are S" did shade Area 7. Since the shading indicates that Area 7 is empty (it has no members), we can now position the X in Area 6. Figure 3 reveals a third possibility. Here the diagram for the minor premise "No S are M" did shade Area 6. And since the shading indicates that Area 6 is empty (it has no members), we can position the X directly in Area 7.

We can already see a strategy emerging. If one of the premises of a categorical syllogism is a particular proposition (**I** or **O**) and one is a universal proposition (**A** or **E**), then diagram the universal one first. Although, as we saw in Figure 1, you cannot always position the X directly in an area, the strategy will help in many cases.

If you recall the basic principle from Chapter 5 regarding **I**-propositions, we can state that the diagram for "Some P are M" is identical to the diagram for "Some M are P." Given this, we need to consider only two possible diagrams.

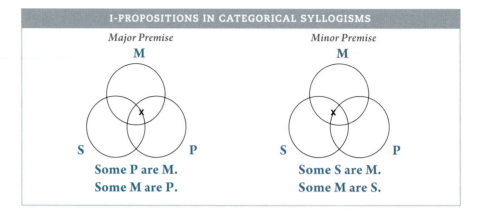

Diagramming O-Propositions

We now turn to **O**-propositions. This time we will do a diagram for a possible minor premise. For example, suppose the minor premise is "Some S are not M." Following our basic method we need to place an X in the area of S that is outside of M. Once again, we need to deal with the three interlocking circles. Let's consider three possible locations.

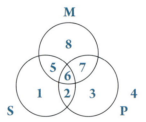

We know that the X is located somewhere in Area 1 or Area 2 (where S is outside M). But the objects in these two areas are not the same. For example, an object in Area 1 is an S, but it is not a P, and it is not an M. However, an object in Area 2 is an S, and it is a P, but it is not an M. The single premise "Some S are not M," by itself, does not provide enough information to allow us to place the X directly in either of those two areas. Also, we cannot place an X in both areas. We solve this problem by placing the X on the line separating the two possible areas where the object might exist:

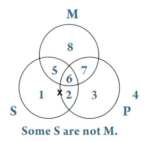

Some S are not M.

This placement of X informs us that the S is either in Area 1 or in Area 2. However, without further information we cannot yet place it in either one.

We know that the minor premise contains the minor term and the middle term, so the only other possible **O**-proposition for the minor premise is "Some M are not S." We need to draw a new diagram, applying what we have learned so far:

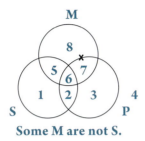

Some M are not S.

This placement of X informs us that the M referred to is either in Area 7 or in Area 8. However, without further information we cannot yet place it directly in either one.

The same principle applies to the major premise for **O**-propositions. In fact, there are only two more possible diagrams to consider. The major premise can be either "Some P are not M" or "Some M are not P":

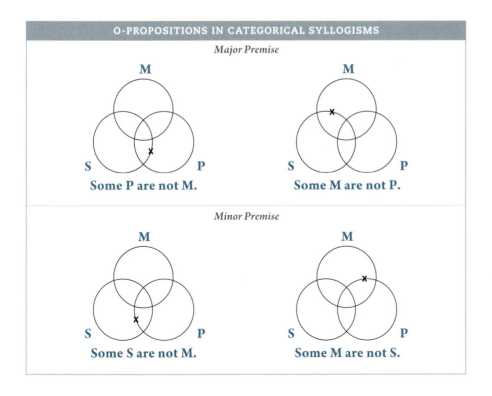

Wrapping Up the X

There is one more item to clarify. The placement of the X in a Venn diagram is restricted to certain locations. Since a particular categorical proposition refers to two classes, we must make sure the position of the X retains the reference. Let's examine a correct and incorrect Venn diagram of an **O**-proposition, "Some S are not M."

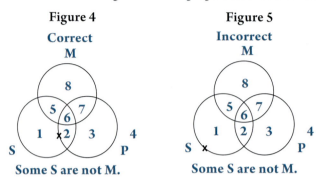

In Figure 4 the X is correctly placed on the line separating Area 1 and Area 2. This position of the X indicates that an object exists in at least one of those two areas. The important thing for us is that both Area 1 and Area 2 are outside the M circle, but they are within the S circle. However, this is not the case in Figure 5. The X is incorrectly placed on the line separating Area 1 and Area 4. This position of the X in Figure 5 indicates that an object exists in at least one of those two areas. But since the X has to be located within the S circle, this position of the X violates our requirement.

Let's examine a correct and an incorrect Venn diagram of an **I**-proposition: "Some M are P."

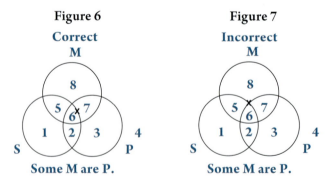

In Figure 6 the X is correctly placed on the line separating Area 6 and Area 7. This position of the X indicates that an object exists in at least one of those two areas. The important thing for us is that Area 6 and Area 7 are both within the M circle and the P circle. However, this is not the case in Figure 7. The X is incorrectly placed at the intersection of two lines. This position would mean that the X could be in any of four areas—Area 5, Area 6, Area 7, or Area 8. However, Area 5 and Area 8 are both outside the P circle. Since the X has to be located within the P circle, this position of the X violates our requirement.

We can now summarize the results:

1. The position of the X cannot be on an outside line of a circle.
2. The position of the X cannot be at the intersection of two lines.

Lightboard Video

Is the Syllogism Valid?

We are now in position to determine if a standard-form categorical syllogism is valid or invalid. Let's analyze this example:

All censored news reports are biased pieces of information.
All network news shows are censored news reports.
All network news shows are biased pieces of information.

The first step is to replace the three terms with single letters. For example, we can let C = *censored news reports* (the middle term), B = *biased pieces of information* (the major term), and N = *network news shows* (the minor term):

All C are B.
All N are C.
All N are B.

We diagram the premises by assuming they are true. (Remember: We are not yet concerned with truth values, only for a valid deduction.) Since both premises are universal propositions, we can diagram either one first. (If one of the premises were a particular proposition, then we would diagram it after the universal one.) Let's diagram the first premise (All C are B):

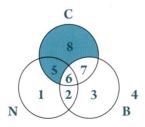

Based on the assumption of the truth of the major premise, Area 5 and Area 8 were both shaded (any area of C outside B is empty). What our diagram illustrates so far is that if anything is a C it is a member of B (Areas 6 and 7).

The next step is to diagram the information in the second premise (All N are C).

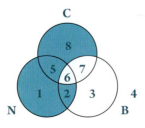

Based on the assumption of the truth of the minor premise, Area 1 and Area 2 were both shaded (any area of N outside C is empty).

The diagram is finished. In order to determine whether the syllogism is valid or invalid, ask yourself whether the diagram of the premises includes the information contained in the conclusion. In our example, the conclusion is "All N are B." The only part of the N circle left unshaded is Area 6, and it is located within the B circle. We interpret the universal proposition "All N are B" as meaning that *if* something is an N, then it is a B. The Venn diagram shows that if the premises are true, then the conclusion follows necessarily; therefore, the form of the syllogism is valid. The original categorical syllogism regarding "censored new reports" is valid as well.

Let's diagram another example to see how to determine that a standard-form categorical syllogism is invalid. Consider this argument:

> No members of the U.S. Congress are unemployed workers.
> All unemployed workers are people searching for jobs.
> No people searching for jobs are members of the U.S. Congress.

The first step is to replace the three terms with single letters. We can let C = *members of the U.S. Congress* (the major term), U = *unemployed workers* (the middle term), and J = *people searching for jobs* (the minor term):

> No C are U.
> All U are J.
> No J are C.

Since the syllogism has two universal premises, we can start with either one. Let's diagram the major premise (No C are U):

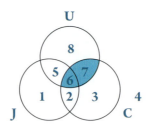

Based on the assumption of the truth of the major premise, Area 6 and Area 7 were both shaded (and both areas are empty). Now we can diagram the minor premise (All U are J):

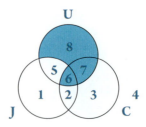

Based on the assumption of the truth of the minor premise, Area 7 and Area 8 need to be shaded. But since Area 7 was already shaded, we had only to shade Area 8.

The diagram is complete. Once again, to determine whether the syllogism is valid or invalid, we check to see if diagramming the premises created a diagram of the conclusion. In this example, the conclusion is "No J are C." In order for the conclusion to follow necessarily from the premises, *both* Area 2 and Area 6 have to be shaded (they need to be empty.) Although Area 6 is indeed shaded, Area 2 is not. Therefore, the premises have not ruled out the possibility that Area 2 has members. Since the Venn diagram has shown that it is possible for the premises to be true and the conclusion false, the syllogism form is invalid. Given this, the original categorical syllogism regarding "members of the U.S. Congress" is invalid as well.

Now let's analyze a standard-form categorical syllogism that has one universal and one particular proposition as premises.

> Some birthday gifts are expensive presents.
> All expensive presents are luxury items.
> Some luxury items are birthday gifts.

The first step is to replace the three terms with single letters. We can let B = *birthday gifts* (the major term), E = *expensive presents* (the middle term), and L = *luxury items* (the minor term):

> Some B are E.
> All E are L.
> Some L are B.

Recall that our strategy is to diagram the universal (minor) premise first (All E are L):

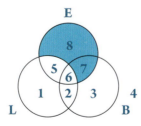

Based on the assumption of the truth of the minor premise, Area 7 and Area 8 were both shaded (both areas are empty). Now we can diagram the particular (major) premise (Some B are E):

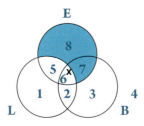

If Area 7 were not shaded, then we would have to place the X on the line separating Area 6 and Area 7. But since we applied the strategy of diagramming the universal premise first, Area 7 is already shaded. Therefore, we place the X directly into Area 6.

The diagram is finished, so we can now check for validity. In this example, the conclusion "Some L are B" is true if an X is in either Area 2 or Area 6. Since an X is located in Area 6, the Venn diagram shows that if the premises are true, then the conclusion follows necessarily. Therefore the form of the syllogism is valid. The original categorical syllogism regarding "birthday gifts" is valid as well.

Let's diagram one last case. We can now analyze a standard-form categorical syllogism in which both premises are particular propositions:

> Some designer drugs are addictive chemical substances.
> Some illegal drugs are not designer drugs.
> Some illegal drugs are not addictive chemical substances.

The first step is to replace the three terms with single letters. We can let D = *designer drugs* (the middle term), A = *addictive chemical substances* (the major term), and I = *illegal drugs* (the minor term):

> Some D are A.
> Some I are not D.
> Some I are not A.

Since both premises are particular propositions, we can diagram either one first. Let's do the major premise (Some D are A):

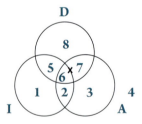

Based on the assumption of the truth of the major premise, we place an X on the line separating Area 6 and Area 7. Now we can diagram the minor premise (Some I are not D):

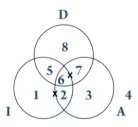

Based on the assumption of the truth of the minor premise, we place an X on the line separating Area 1 and Area 2.

The diagram is complete. In order to determine whether the syllogism is valid or invalid, we check to see if diagramming the premises created a diagram of the conclusion. In this example, the conclusion is "Some I are not A." In order for the conclusion to follow necessarily from the premises, an X would have to be directly in either Area 1 or Area 5. However, the premises have not ruled out the possibility that no X exists in either Area 1 or Area 5. Since the Venn diagram has shown that it is possible for the premises to be true and the conclusion false, the syllogism is invalid. The original categorical syllogism regarding "designer drugs" is invalid as well.

Lightboard Video

EXERCISES 6C

I. Use Venn diagrams to determine whether the following categorical syllogism forms are valid or invalid under the modern interpretation.

Self-Practice
Questions

1. All M are P.
   Some M are S.
   Some S are P.
Answer: Valid

2. No M are P.
   Some S are not M.
   Some S are not P.

3. All P are M.
   All S are M.
   All S are P.

4. Some P are M.
   Some S are M.
   Some S are P.

⭐ 5. Some M are not P.
   Some M are not S.
   Some S are not P.

6. No P are M.
   No M are S.
   No S are P.

7. All P are M.
   Some S are M.
   All S are P.

8. Some P are M.
   Some M are not S.
   Some S are not P.

⭐ 9. All M are P.
   No S are M.
   Some S are not P.

10. No M are P.
   Some S are M.
   Some S are P.

11. All M are P.
   No S are M.
   No S are P.

12. No P are M.
Some S are M.
Some S are not P.

★13. All M are P.
All S are M.
All S are P.

14. All M are P.
Some S are not M.
Some S are not P.

15. Some M are P.
All M are S.
Some S are P.

16. Some M are not P.
No S are M.
Some S are not P.

★17. All P are M.
No S are M.
All S are P.

18. Some P are M.
Some S are not M.
Some S are P.

19. Some M are not P.
All M are S.
Some S are not P.

20. No P are M.
Some M are S.
No S are P.

★21. All P are M.
Some S are not M.
No S are P.

22. Some P are M.
Some M are S.
Some S are P.

23. No M are P.
No S are M.
Some S are not P.

24. All M are P.
Some S are M.
Some S are P.

★25. All M are P.
No S are M.
Some S are P.

26. All P are M.
Some S are M.
Some S are not P.

27. All M are P.
Some S are not M.
No S are P.

28. Some M are P.
Some S are not M.
Some S are not P.

★29. No M are P.
All S are M.
All S are P.

30. Some M are P.
Some S are not M.
Some S are P.

II. Translate the following arguments into standard-form categorical syllogism forms. Then use Venn diagrams to determine whether they are valid or invalid under the modern interpretation.

1. All fast-food items are overpriced objects. No overpriced objects are nutritious products. Therefore, no nutritious products are fast-food items.

Answer: Valid. Let F = *fast-food items*, O = *overpriced objects*, and N = *nutritious products.*

All F are O.
No O are N.
No N are F.

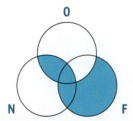

2. Some vegetables are not tasty foods. Therefore some tasty foods are not green foods, because some vegetables are not green foods.

3. All mechanical objects are noisy objects. All airplanes are noisy objects. Thus, all airplanes are mechanical objects.

4. Some pens are not useful tools. This is because some pens are leaky writing implements, and no leaky writing implements are useful tools.

⭐ 5. No septic tanks are swimming pools. No sewers are swimming pools. Therefore, no septic tanks are sewers.

6. All voice messages are distracting pieces of information. Some games people play are distracting pieces of information. So some voice messages are games people play.

7. Some universities are not expensive places to attend. Some universities are conveniently located complexes. Thus, some expensive places to attend are not conveniently located complexes.

8. No subways are reliable means of transportation. Therefore, no subways are beneficial transportation, since all reliable means of transportation are beneficial transportation.

⭐ 9. Some buildings are poorly constructed domiciles. Some buildings are architectural nightmares. So some architectural nightmares are poorly constructed domiciles.

10. All sea creatures are intelligent animals. Some sea creatures are predators. So, some intelligent animals are predators.

Video Tutorial: 6CII
Exercise #10

III. Use Venn diagrams to verify that the fifteen standard-form categorical syllogisms are valid under the modern interpretation.

1. **AAA-1**

Answer: Valid

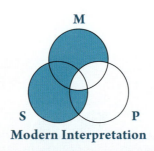

Modern Interpretation

2. **AII-1**	⭐ 9. **AII-3**
3. **EAE-1**	10. **EIO-3**
4. **EIO-1**	11. **IAI-3**
⭐ 5. **AEE-2**	12. **OAO-3**
6. **AOO-2**	⭐13. **AEE-4**
7. **EAE-2**	14. **EIO-4**
8. **EIO-2**	15. **IAI-4**

IV. Use Venn diagrams to verify that the nine additional standard-form categorical syllogisms are invalid under the modern interpretation.

1. **AAI-1**

Answer: Invalid under the modern interpretation.

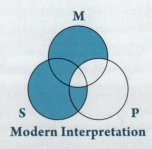

Modern Interpretation

2. **EAO-1**	6. **EAO-3**
3. **AEO-2**	7. **AAI-4**
4. **EAO-2**	8. **AEO-4**
⭐ 5. **AAI-3**	⭐ 9. **EAO-4**

D. RULES AND FALLACIES UNDER THE MODERN INTERPRETATION

While we could use Venn diagrams to test the validity of all 256 categorical syllogisms and apply them to each example, fortunately, six rules form a handy checklist to test for validity. If the syllogism does not violate any rule, then it is valid; but if it violates any of the six rules, then it is invalid. As we shall see, every violation of a rule is associated with a fallacy—a mistake in reasoning.

Rule 1: The middle term must be distributed in at least one premise.

ASSOCIATED FALLACY: UNDISTRIBUTED MIDDLE

The conclusion of a categorical syllogism asserts a relationship between the classes designated by the minor and major terms. And the premises must lay the foundation for that relationship. This can be achieved only if the premises distribute the class designated by the middle term *at least once*. Either the subject or predicate of the conclusion, or both, must be related to the entire class designated by the middle term. Otherwise the fallacy of the **undistributed middle** occurs. For example:

> All poets are creative people.
> <u>All engineers are creative people.</u>
> All engineers are poets.

Undistributed middle
A formal fallacy that occurs when the middle term in a categorical syllogism is undistributed in both premises of a categorical syllogism.

The major and minor premises are both **A**-propositions. Since the middle term "creative people" occurs as the predicate in each premise, it is undistributed in the syllogism. (Recall that **A**-propositions distribute only the subject term.) This means that the major and minor terms (which are distributed in the premises) may be related to different parts of M and not to each other. This possibility renders the syllogism invalid.

We can use a Venn diagram to verify Rule 1, letting P = *poets*, C = *creative people*, and E = *engineers*.

> All P are C.
> <u>All E are C.</u>
> All E are P.

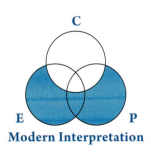

Modern Interpretation

The syllogism is invalid. For the conclusion ("All E are P") to be true, the unshaded area of E outside P has to be shaded (empty). As it stands, the diagram shows this area could have members. We can see why the middle term must be distributed in at least one premise.

Rule 2: If a term is distributed in the conclusion, then it must be distributed in a premise.

ASSOCIATED FALLACIES: ILLICIT MAJOR/ILLICIT MINOR

If a categorical proposition says something definite about every member of the class designated by a term, then the term is said to be distributed. In contrast, if the proposition does not say something definite about every member of the class designated by a term, then the term is undistributed. If neither the major term nor the minor term in the conclusion is distributed, then Rule 2 does not come into play. However, if the major term is distributed in the conclusion but not in the major premise, then the conclusion goes beyond what was asserted in the premise. This is the fallacy of an **illicit major**.

The reasoning behind the rule is clear. If the major term is distributed in the conclusion, then the conclusion makes an assertion regarding *every* member of the class designated by the major term. Hence, if the major term is not distributed in the major premise, then the premise makes an assertion regarding only *some* members of the class designated by the major term. Therefore, the conclusion goes beyond the information provided in the premises.

Let's look at an example.

> All bananas are fruit.
> <u>No strawberries are bananas.</u>
> No strawberries are fruit.

Once again, a Venn diagram can help verify the rule, letting B = *bananas*, F = *fruit*, and S = *strawberries*:

> All B are F.
> <u>No S are B.</u>
> No S are F.

Illicit major A formal fallacy that occurs when the major term in a categorical syllogism is distributed in the conclusion but not in the major premise.

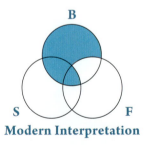

Modern Interpretation

The syllogism is invalid. For the conclusion ("No S are F") to be true, the area of S that overlaps with F would have to be shaded. As it stands, the diagram shows that this area may have members. Hence, if the major term is distributed in the conclusion, then it must be distributed in the premises.

If the minor term is distributed in the conclusion but not in the minor premise, then the conclusion goes beyond what was asserted in the premises. This is the fallacy of **illicit minor**. For example:

> All bananas are fruits.
> <u>All bananas are yellow things.</u>
> All yellow things are fruits.

The fallacy of illicit minor occurs for the same reason as the fallacy of illicit major. Both fallacies fail to observe the rule that any term that is distributed in the conclusion must be distributed in the premises.

We can diagram the syllogism by letting B = *bananas*, F = *fruits*, and Y = *yellow things*.

> All B are F.
> <u>All B are Y.</u>
> All Y are F.

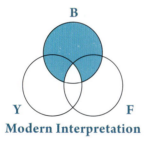

Modern Interpretation

The syllogism is invalid. For the conclusion ("All Y are F") to be true, the area of Y outside F has to be shaded. As it stands, the diagram shows that this area may have members. Hence, if the minor term is distributed in the conclusion, then it must be distributed in the premises.

Rule 3: A categorical syllogism cannot have two negative premises.

ASSOCIATED FALLACY: EXCLUSIVE PREMISES

The fallacy of **exclusive premises** rests on the principle that two negative premises will always result in an invalid syllogism. The major (negative) premise will exclude part or all of the class designated by the major term from the class designated by the middle term. The minor (negative) premise will exclude part or all of the class designated by the minor term from the class designated by the middle term. It is then

Illicit minor A formal fallacy that occurs when the minor term in a categorical syllogism is distributed in the conclusion but not in the minor premise.

Exclusive premises A formal fallacy that occurs when both premises in a categorical syllogism are negative.

impossible to deduce any kind of relationship between the classes designated by the major and minor terms, whether positive or negative. For example:

> No Facebook entries are interesting topics.
> Some blogs are not Facebook entries.
> Some blogs are not interesting topics.

A Venn diagram can help verify Rule 3, where we let F = *Facebook entries*, I = *interesting topics*, and B = *blogs*:

> No F are I.
> Some B are not F.
> Some B are not I.

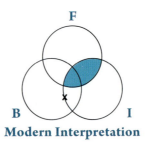

F

B   **I**

Modern Interpretation

The syllogism is invalid. For the conclusion ("Some B are not I") to be true, there has to be an X in one of the two unshaded areas of B that are outside I. As it stands, the diagram shows that it is possible that these areas have no members. Hence, a syllogism cannot have two negative premises.

Rule 4: A negative premise must have a negative conclusion.

ASSOCIATED FALLACY: AFFIRMATIVE CONCLUSION/NEGATIVE PREMISE

Since class inclusion requires an affirmative proposition, a categorical syllogism with an affirmative conclusion can validly follow only from two affirmative premises. In other words, an affirmative conclusion asserts that S is either completely or partially included in P. If one of the premises is negative, then either S or P will be excluded from the class designated by the middle term M. Since the middle term cannot connect the S and P, an affirmative conclusion cannot follow by necessity. A negative premise thus results in the fallacy of **affirmative conclusion/negative premise**.

Affirmative conclusion/negative premise A formal fallacy that occurs when a categorical syllogism has a negative premise and an affirmative conclusion.

Let's look at an example:

> No happy people are underpaid employees.
> All teachers are happy people.
> All teachers are underpaid employees.

The conclusion is a universal affirmative proposition, but one of the premises is negative. We can diagram the syllogism by letting H = *happy people*, U = *underpaid employees*, and T = *teachers*:

> No H are U.
> All T are H.
> All T are U.

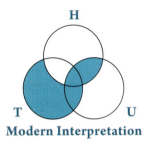

Modern Interpretation

The syllogism is invalid. For the conclusion ("All T are U") to be true, there has to be at least one area where T and U overlap that is unshaded. But as we can see, the two areas where T and U overlap are both shaded. Hence, an affirmative conclusion cannot have a negative premise.

Rule 5: A negative conclusion must have a negative premise.

ASSOCIATED FALLACY: NEGATIVE CONCLUSION/AFFIRMATIVE PREMISES

Since class exclusion requires a negative proposition, a categorical syllogism with a negative conclusion cannot validly follow from two affirmative premises that assert class inclusion. A syllogism that violates this rule commits the fallacy of **negative conclusion/affirmative premises**. In other words, a negative conclusion asserts that S is either completely or partially excluded from P. However, if both premises are affirmative, then they both assert class inclusion instead of exclusion. Therefore, the information in the premises will not be adequate for the conclusion to follow by necessity.

Negative conclusion/ affirmative premises
A formal fallacy that occurs when a categorical syllogism has a negative conclusion and two affirmative premises.

Let's look at an example:

> All carbonated drinks are bubbly beverages.
> All soft drinks are carbonated drinks.
> No soft drinks are bubbly beverages.

We can diagram the syllogism by letting C = *carbonated drinks*, B = *bubbly beverages*, and S = *soft drinks*:

> All C are B.
> All S are C.
> No S are B.

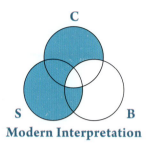

Modern Interpretation

The syllogism is invalid. For the conclusion ("No S are B") to be true, both areas where S and B overlap have to be shaded. But as we can see, one of the areas is *unshaded*. As it stands, the diagram shows that the unshaded area may have members. Hence, a negative conclusion cannot have all affirmative premises.

Rule 6: Two universal premises cannot have a particular conclusion.

ASSOCIATED FALLACY: EXISTENTIAL FALLACY

As we already know, under the modern interpretation, universal propositions do not have existential import, but particular propositions do. Therefore, under the modern interpretation, any categorical syllogism that has two universal premises and a particular conclusion will be invalid. It is logically impossible to get an X anywhere in a Venn diagram if both premises are universal propositions. But since neither premise makes an existential assertion, but the particular conclusion does, an **existential fallacy** is committed.

Existential fallacy
A formal fallacy that occurs when a categorical syllogism has a particular conclusion and two universal premises.

Let's look at an example:

All angry creatures are nihilists.
All rabid dogs are angry creatures.
Some rabid dogs are nihilists.

We can diagram the syllogism by letting A = *angry creatures*, N = *nihilists*, and D = *rabid dogs*:

All A are N.
All D are A.
Some D are N.

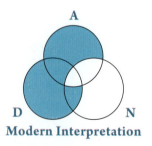

Modern Interpretation

Under the modern interpretation, the syllogism is invalid and it commits the existential fallacy. For the conclusion ("Some D are N") to be true, the unshaded area of D has to contain an X. But, as we can see in the diagram, no X appears in that area.

SUMMARY OF RULES
Rule 1: The middle term must be distributed in at least one premise.
Rule 2: If a term is distributed in the conclusion, then it must be distributed in a premise.
Rule 3: A categorical syllogism cannot have two negative premises.
Rule 4: A negative premise must have a negative conclusion.
Rule 5: A negative conclusion must have a negative premise.
Rule 6: Two universal premises cannot have a particular conclusion.

EXERCISES 6D

I. Use the six rules to discuss why the fifteen standard-form categorical syllogisms are valid under the modern interpretation.

Self-Practice
Questions

1. **AAA-1**

Answer: All six rules are met.

> Rule 1: The middle term is distributed in the first premise.
> Rule 2: The major term is not distributed in the conclusion.
> Rule 3: **AAA-1** does not have two negative premises.
> Rule 4: **AAA-1** does not have a negative premise.
> Rule 5: **AAA-1** does not have a negative conclusion.
> Rule 6: **AAA-1** does not have universal premises and a particular conclusion.

2. **AII-1**
3. **EAE-1**
4. **EIO-1**
5. **AEE-2**
6. **AOO-2**
7. **EAE-2**
8. **EIO-2**

9. **AII-3**
10. **EIO-3**
11. **IAI-3**
12. **OAO-3**
13. **AEE-4**
14. **EIO-4**
15. **IAI-4**

II. First, translate the following arguments into standard-form categorical syllogisms. Second, name the mood and figure of each. Third, use Venn diagrams and the six rules to determine whether the arguments are valid or invalid under the modern interpretation.

1. All cultures that venerate senior citizens are systems built on a strong tradition of philosophical inquiry. Some recently developed cultures are not systems

built on a strong tradition of philosophical inquiry. Therefore, some recently developed cultures are not cultures that venerate senior citizens.

Answer: Let C = *cultures that venerate senior citizens*, S = *systems built on a strong tradition of philosophical inquiry*, and R = *recently developed cultures*.

All C are S.
Some R are not S.
Some R are not C.

AOO-2. Valid under the modern interpretation. No rules are broken.

2. Some planets with oxygen are planets capable of sustaining life. Some planets outside our solar system are planets with oxygen. So, some planets outside our solar system are planets capable of sustaining life.

3. All great works of literature are creative illuminations of the human predicament. Thus, no pulp fiction novels are great works of literature, because no pulp fiction novels are creative illuminations of the human predicament.

4. All natural disasters are scientifically explainable phenomena. Some human maladies are scientifically explainable phenomena. Thus, some human maladies are natural disasters.

5. Some furry creatures are lovable pets. Some eccentric people are lovable pets. So, some eccentric people are furry creatures.

Video Tutorial: 6DII
Exercise #5

E. DIAGRAMMING IN THE TRADITIONAL INTERPRETATION

We can modify the way we have been drawing Venn diagrams to accommodate the traditional interpretation of universal categorical propositions. The major difference is that we must take into account existential import. Determining whether a class has actually existing members allows some syllogisms to be valid under the traditional interpretation that are invalid under the modern interpretation. However, we will need to investigate the assumption of existence *only* when a syllogism has a particular proposition (either **I** or **O**) as the conclusion *and* two universal premises.

A-Propositions

In Chapter 5 the circled X was introduced to represent the "**A**ssumption of **E**xistence," as illustrated in the next two diagrams:

All S are P.

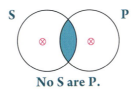

No S are P.

We start by learning how to diagram **A**-propositions in categorical syllogisms under the traditional interpretation. For example, suppose the major premise is "All P are M." Adapting our method of shading to the introduction of the assumption of existence, we get the following diagram:

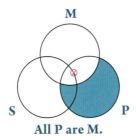

All P are M.

The areas of P outside M are shaded, and we had to place the circled X in the appropriate location. Here we need to draw on some additional information from Chapter 5. If you recall, when a categorical proposition asserts something definite about every member of a class, then the term designating that class is said to be *distributed*. For **A**-propositions, the subject term is distributed, but the predicate term is undistributed. In this case, the assumption of existence concerns the class of objects referred to by P. Therefore, we place the circled X on the line that separates the two areas where P and M overlap. The assumption of existence regarding the proposition "All P are M" refers to these two areas.

Since the major premise must contain the major term and the middle term, the only other possible **A**-proposition for the major premise is "All M are P":

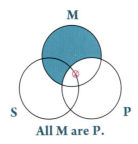

All M are P.

Once again, for **A**-propositions, the subject term is distributed, but the predicate term is undistributed. Therefore, we place the circled X on the line that separates the two areas where M and P overlap. The assumption of existence regarding the proposition, "All M are P," refers to these two areas.

The same principles apply to the minor premise, but there are only two more possible diagrams to consider. The minor premise can be either "All S are M" or "All M are S":

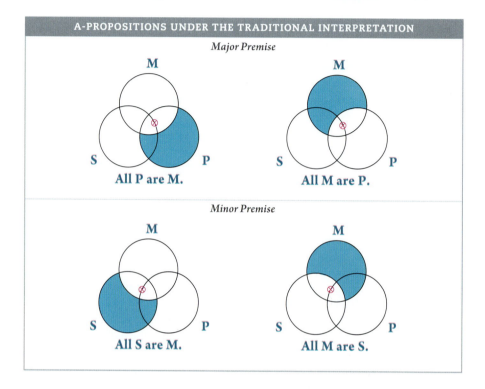

A-PROPOSITIONS UNDER THE TRADITIONAL INTERPRETATION

Major Premise

All P are M.   All M are P.

Minor Premise

All S are M.   All M are S.

E-Propositions

The next step is to learn how to diagram **E**-propositions. This time we will do a diagram for a possible minor premise. For example, suppose the minor premise is "No S are M." Following our basic method, we know that we need to shade the areas of S that overlap M. But we also need to add the symbols for the assumption of existence. We need to put one circled X in the unshaded area of S, and one circled X in the unshaded area of M:

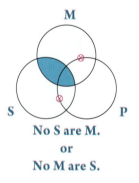

No S are M.
or
No M are S.

For the subject, S, we place a circled X on the line that separates the two areas belonging to S that are outside M. For the predicate, M, we place another circled X on the line that separates the two areas belonging to M that are outside S. Since the diagram for "No M are S" is identical to the diagram for "No S are M," the two possibilities are listed together.

These same principles apply to the major premise, so there are only two possible diagrams to consider:

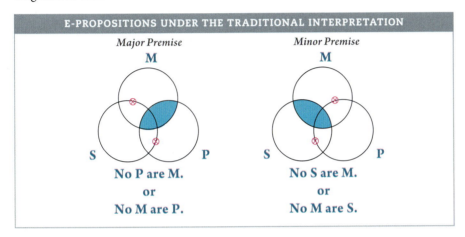

E-PROPOSITIONS UNDER THE TRADITIONAL INTERPRETATION

Major Premise

No P are M.
or
No M are P.

Minor Premise

No S are M.
or
No M are S.

We can take what we have learned and apply it to a standard-form categorical syllogism. Let's examine the following argument:

All college fraternities are environmentally conscious groups.
All environmentally conscious groups are tax-exempt organizations.
Some tax-exempt organizations are college fraternities.

If we let C = *college fraternities*, E = *environmentally conscious groups*, and T = *tax-exempt organizations*, we can reveal the argument form:

All C are E.
All E are T.
Some T are C.

We already know how to diagram this using the modern interpretation, so we can do that first (Figure 1):

Figure 1

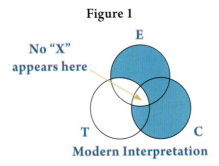

No "X"
appears here

Modern Interpretation

Under the modern interpretation, the syllogism is invalid. This should not be surprising. Under the modern interpretation, universal propositions do not assume existential import. Since both premises of the syllogism are universal propositions, diagramming them will produce only shading; therefore, no X will appear. However, the conclusion is an **I**-proposition, and for it to be true an X would have to appear in the area indicated by the arrow. Since no X appears in this area, the syllogism is invalid.

Now we will draw a Venn diagram using the traditional interpretation. This time we will diagram one premise at a time in order to get familiar with the procedure. Let's start by diagramming the major premise "All C are E":

Figure 2

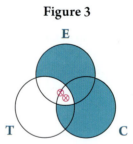

We place the circled X much as we did for **A**-propositions under the traditional interpretation. In this case, the assumption of existence concerns the class of objects referred to by C. Therefore, we place the circled X on the line that separates the two areas where C and E overlap.

The next step is to add the diagram for the minor premise "All E are T":

Figure 3

We placed a circled X on the line that separates the two areas where E and T overlap. However, because one of the areas where the original circled X might have gone has now been shaded, we are justified in moving it into the only remaining area. Since a circled X appears in the nonempty area where T and C overlap, the syllogism is at this point only "provisionally valid," because there is one more step to complete. Under the traditional interpretation, we now have to consider the assumption of existence. We must therefore investigate whether the circled X refers to something that actually exists.

In our example, the assumption of existence concerns the class of objects referred to by C (which is why we placed the circled X on the line that separated the two areas where C and E overlap). Since "C" stands for *college fraternities*, which exist, the circled X represents an actually existing object. Therefore, under the traditional interpretation the syllogism is valid.

To further illustrate the idea behind provisionally valid syllogisms under the traditional interpretation, we can examine the following argument:

> All centaurs are egoists.
> <u>All egoists are talented people.</u>
> Some talented people are centaurs.

If we let C = *centaurs*, E = *egoists*, and T = *talented people*, we can reveal the argument form:

> All C are E.
> <u>All E are T.</u>
> Some T are C.

This form is identical to the one we previously examined. Under the *modern* interpretation, we already know that it is invalid. However, under the *traditional* interpretation it is provisionally valid. Therefore, we now have to consider the assumption of existence. In this new example, "C" stands for centaurs, which do not exist. Since "C" refers to something that does not exist, the circled X does not represent an actually existing object. Therefore, under the traditional interpretation the syllogism is invalid.

In sum, the provisionally valid nature of some syllogisms under the traditional interpretation means that some argument forms can have both valid and invalid instances. Final determination then rests on the assumption of existence. The modern interpretation does not require this additional investigation.

Lightboard Video

EXERCISES 6E

I. Use Venn diagrams to determine whether the following categorical syllogism forms are valid, provisionally valid, or invalid under the traditional interpretation.

Self-Practice Questions

1. No M are P.
   <u>Some S are not M.</u>
   Some S are not P.

Answer: Invalid

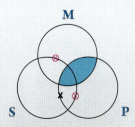

When we diagram the major (universal) premise, we shade the areas where M and P overlap, and we place one circled X on the line in the M circle and one circled X on the line in the P circle. When we diagram the minor (particular) premise, we place an X on the line in the S circle. In order for the conclusion to be true, either the X or the circled X that is on the line separating S and M would have to be directly in one of the areas of S that is outside P. However, it is possible that the X is in the area of S that is also P. It is also possible that the circled X is in the area of M that is outside S. Since this means that it is possible for the conclusion to be false while the premises are true, the syllogism is invalid. And since it is invalid, we do not need to investigate the assumption of existence.

2. All M are P.
   Some M are S.
   Some S are P.

3. All P are M.
   All S are M.
   Some S are P.

4. Some P are M.
   All S are M.
   Some S are P.

★ 5. Some M are not P.
   No M are S.
   Some S are not P.

6. No P are M.
   No M are S.
   Some S are not P.

7. All P are M.
   Some S are M.
   Some S are P.

8. All P are M.
   Some M are not S.
   Some S are not P.

★ 9. All M are P.
   No S are M.
   Some S are not P.

10. No M are P.
   Some S are M.
   Some S are P.

11. All M are P.
   No S are M.
   Some S are not P.

12. No P are M.
   Some S are M.
   Some S are not P.

★13. All M are P.
   All S are M.
   Some S are not P.

14. All M are P.
   Some S are not M.
   Some S are not P.

II. Translate the following arguments into standard-form categorical syllogism forms. Then use Venn diagrams to determine whether they are valid, provisionally valid, or invalid under the traditional interpretation.

1. All fast-food items are overpriced objects. No overpriced objects are nutritious products. Therefore, some nutritious products are not fast-food items.

Answer: Let F = *fast-food items*, O = *overpriced objects*, and N = *nutritious products*.

All F are O.
No O are N.
Some N are not F.

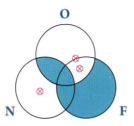

When we diagram the major premise, we shade the areas of F outside O, and place a circled X on the line in the area where F and O overlap. However, when we diagram the minor premise, we shade the areas where N and O overlap. This requires moving the first circled X from the line where F and O overlap to the unshaded area where F and O overlap. The next step is to complete the diagram for the minor premise. We place one circled X on the line where F and O overlap, and another circled X in the unshaded area of N. In order for the conclusion to be true, either an X or a circled X would have to be directly in one of the areas of N that is outside F. Since there is a circled X in this area, the argument is *provisionally valid*.

The final step of the analysis is the investigation of the assumption of existence. Since "N" stands for *nutritious products*, which exist, the circled X represents an actually existing object. Therefore, under the traditional interpretation the syllogism is valid.

2. Some vegetables are not tasty foods. So some tasty foods are not green foods, because no vegetables are green foods.

3. All mechanical objects are noisy objects. All airplanes are noisy objects. Thus, some airplanes are mechanical objects.

4. Some pens are not useful tools. This is because some pens are leaky writing implements, and no leaky writing implements are useful tools.

★ 5. No septic tanks are swimming pools. No sewers are swimming pools. Therefore, some septic tanks are not sewers.

6. All voice messages are distracting pieces of information. Some games people play are distracting pieces of information. So, some voice messages are games people play.

7. Some universities are not expensive places to attend. No universities are conveniently located complexes. Thus, some expensive places to attend are not conveniently located complexes.

8. Some squirrels are rational creatures. Therefore, some squirrels are benevolent creatures, since all rational creatures are benevolent creatures.

★ 9. Some buildings are poorly constructed domiciles. No buildings are architectural nightmares. So, some architectural nightmares are poorly constructed domiciles.

10. All sea creatures are intelligent animals. Some sea creatures are predators. So, some intelligent animals are predators.

III. Use Venn diagrams to verify that the following fifteen standard-form categorical syllogisms are valid under the traditional interpretation.

1. **AAA-1**

Answer: Valid

Traditional Interpretation

2. **AII-1**	⭐ 9. **AII-3**
3. **EAE-1**	10. **EIO-3**
4. **EIO-1**	11. **IAI-3**
⭐ 5. **AEE-2**	12. **OAO-3**
6. **AOO-2**	⭐13. **AEE-4**
7. **EAE-2**	14. **EIO-4**
8. **EIO-2**	15. **IAI-4**

IV. Use Venn diagrams to verify that the nine additional standard-form categorical syllogisms listed are *provisionally valid* under the traditional interpretation.

1. **AAI-1**

Answer: Provisionally valid under the traditional interpretation.

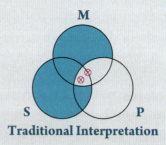

Traditional Interpretation

2. **EAO-1**	6. **EAO-3**
3. **AEO-2**	7. **AAI-4**
4. **EAO-2**	8. **AEO-4**
⭐ 5. **AAI-3**	⭐ 9. **EAO-4**

Video Tutorial: 6EIV
Exercise #7

F. RULES AND FALLACIES UNDER THE TRADITIONAL INTERPRETATION

We know that the traditional interpretation assumes that universal propositions assert existential import. Given this, it is not surprising that Rule 6 (two universal premises cannot have a particular conclusion) is applied differently under the traditional interpretation. Under the traditional interpretation, a syllogism can be provisionally valid. As long as the term needed to make the conclusion true denotes actually existing objects, then the syllogism is valid.

Let's look at an example:

> All angry creatures are nihilists.
> <u>All currently alive dodo birds are angry creatures.</u>
> Some currently alive dodo birds are nihilists.

We can diagram the syllogism by letting A = *angry creatures*, N = *nihilists*, and D = *dodo birds*:

> All A are N.
> <u>All D are A.</u>
> Some D are N.

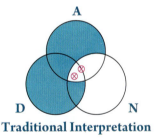

Traditional Interpretation

Under the traditional interpretation, the syllogism is provisionally valid. As the diagram shows, a circled X appears directly in the unshaded area of D that is required to make the conclusion ("Some D are N") true. Therefore, the next step is to see if the assumption of existence requirement is met. Since the subject term of the conclusion ("currently alive dodo birds") does not denote actually existing objects, the syllogism is invalid under the traditional interpretation, and it commits the existential fallacy.

EXERCISES 6F

First, translate the following arguments into standard-form categorical syllogisms. Second, name the mood and figure of each. Third, use Venn diagrams and the six rules to determine whether the arguments are valid, provisionally valid, or invalid under the traditional interpretation.

1. All cultures that venerate senior citizens are systems built on a strong tradition of philosophical inquiry. Some recently developed cultures are not systems

built on a strong tradition of philosophical inquiry. Therefore, some recently developed cultures are not cultures that venerate senior citizens.

Answer: Let C = *cultures that venerate senior citizens,* **S** = *systems built on a strong tradition of philosophical inquiry,* **and R** = *recently developed cultures.*

All C are S.
<u>Some R are not S.</u>
Some R are not C.

AOO-2. Valid. No rules are broken.

Traditional Interpretation

2. Some planets with oxygen are planets capable of sustaining life. Some planets outside our solar system are planets with oxygen. So, some planets outside our solar system are planets capable of sustaining life.

3. All great works of literature are creative illuminations of the human predicament. Thus, no pulp fiction novels are great works of literature, because no pulp fiction novels are creative illuminations of the human predicament.

4. All natural disasters are scientifically explainable phenomena. Some human maladies are scientifically explainable phenomena. Thus, some human maladies are natural disasters.

⭐ 5. Some furry creatures are lovable pets. Some eccentric people are lovable pets. So, some eccentric people are furry creatures.

G. ORDINARY LANGUAGE ARGUMENTS

As we saw in Chapter 5, ordinary language often contains statements that need to be translated into standard-form categorical propositions. They can then be analyzed using either Venn diagrams or the six rules.

Reducing the Number of Terms in an Argument

A standard-form categorical syllogism must contain exactly three different terms, and each term must occur twice in the syllogism. If an ordinary language argument contains more than three different terms, it can often be translated into a standard-form categorical syllogism. We will explore five ways to reduce the number of terms: (1) eliminating superfluous words; (2) using synonyms; (3) using class

complements; (4) using conversion, obversion, and contraposition; and (5) eliminating certain prefixes.

Sometimes all that is needed is to eliminate needless words. Suppose you encounter
the following:

> All managers are college graduates.
> <u>Some of the managers are workaholics.</u>
> Some workaholics are college graduates.

We can usually translate "of the managers" as simply "managers" to get "Some managers are workaholics." This ensures that the syllogism has exactly three different terms,
and each term is used twice.

Once the translation is complete, you can check for validity using a Venn diagram:

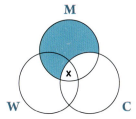

Since the syllogism does not violate any of the six rules, we have additional confirmation that it is valid.

If two of the terms in a syllogism are synonyms, then we can choose one and substitute it for the other term. For example:

> All rich people are materialistic individuals.
> <u>No materialistic individuals are altruists.</u>
> No altruists are wealthy people.

The syllogism has four terms: "rich people," "materialistic individuals," "altruists," and
"wealthy people." Since the terms "rich people" and "wealthy people" are synonyms,
you can choose either "rich people" or "wealthy people" and substitute it for the other:

> All rich people are materialistic individuals.
> <u>No materialistic individuals are altruists.</u>
> No altruists are rich people.

A Venn diagram shows the syllogism to be valid:

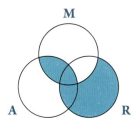

Since the syllogism does not violate any of the six rules, we have additional confirmation that it is valid.

Next, we can substitute complements for terms. As we saw in Chapter 5, the complement is the set of objects that do not belong to a given class. For example, the complements of the terms "sharp objects" and "dull objects" are "non-sharp objects" and "non-dull objects." Here is an example:

> All knives are sharp objects.
> Some knives are illegal items.
> Some legal items are dull objects.

There are five terms in the argument: "knives," "sharp objects," "illegal items," "legal items," and "dull objects." The pair of terms "sharp objects" and "dull objects" are complements, as is the pair "illegal items" and "legal items." The first step is to translate the term "dull objects" into "non-sharp objects" and the term "illegal items" into "non-legal items":

> All knives are sharp objects.
> Some knives are non-legal items.
> Some legal items are non-sharp objects.

There are still too many terms, so we have to use other methods to reduce the number to three. The major premise seems to be in order, so let's eliminate the two instances of "non-" in the minor premise and the conclusion. Since the minor premise is an **I**-proposition, we can use either conversion or obversion. Here is a summary of the methods from Chapter 5:

The Method of Conversion	The Method of Obversion	The Method of Contraposition
Switch the subject and predicate.	Step 1: Change the *quality* of the given proposition. Step 2: Replace the *predicate term* with its *complement*.	Step 1: Switch the subject and predicate terms. Step 2: Replace both the subject and predicate terms with their term complements.

If you recall, conversion is allowed on only **E**- and **I**-propositions, obversion is allowed on all four categorical propositions, and contraposition is allowed on only **A**- and **O**-propositions.

Applying obversion results in "Some weapons are not non-non-legal items," which can be reduced to "Some weapons are not legal items." The translated term ("legal items") is now identical to the minor term in the conclusion.

The conclusion is also an **I**-proposition; therefore we can apply obversion to it. The result is "Some legal items are not non-non-sharp objects," which can be reduced to "Some legal items are not sharp objects." The translated term ("sharp objects") is now identical to the major term in the premise. The final translation looks like this:

> All knives are sharp objects.
> Some knives are not legal items.
> Some legal items are not sharp objects.

We can let K = *knives*, S = *sharp objects*, and L = *legal items*:

All K are S.
Some K are not L.
Some L are not S.

A Venn diagram then shows the syllogism to be invalid:

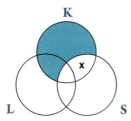

We can also see that the syllogism violates Rule 2: If a term is distributed in the conclusion, then it must be distributed in a premise. Since the major term is distributed
in the conclusion but not in the major premise, this is an instance of the fallacy of
illicit major.

If an ordinary language argument contains the prefixes "in-," "un-," or "dis-," they
can often be eliminated by substituting "non-" for each prefix. Here is an example:

All inconsiderate people are dishonorable people.
Some interesting people are considerate people.
No uninteresting people are honorable people.

The first step is to translate the prefixes using "non-":

All non-considerate people are non-honorable people.
Some interesting people are considerate people.
No non-interesting people are honorable people.

The next steps rely on our understanding of conversion, obversion, and contraposition.
Since the major premise is an **A**-proposition, we can use either obversion or contraposition. If we apply contraposition, the result is "All non-non-honorable people
are non-non-considerate people." This can be reduced to "All honorable people are
considerate people."

The minor premise seems fine as it stands, so we can move on to the conclusion.
Since the conclusion is an **E**-proposition, we can use either conversion or obversion.
If we apply obversion, the result is "All non-interesting people are non-honorable
people." We now have an **A**-proposition, so we can use contraposition. The result is
"All honorable people are interesting people."

Let's reconstruct the argument based on these results:

All honorable people are considerate people.
Some interesting people are considerate people.
All honorable people are interesting people.

We have successfully reduced the terms down to three, and they each occur twice.
However, the application of obversion and contraposition to the conclusion now has

the major premise second and the minor premise first. We need to change the order of the premises to make it a standard-form categorical syllogism. This does not affect its validity or invalidity (which is why we can diagram either the major or the minor premise first). Here is the final result:

Some interesting people are considerate people.
All honorable people are considerate people.
All honorable people are interesting people.

We can let I = *interesting people*, C = *considerate people*, and H = *honorable people*:

Some I are C.
All H are C.
All H are I.

A Venn diagram then reveals that the syllogism is invalid:

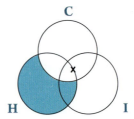

We can also see that the syllogism violates Rule 1: The middle term must be distributed in at least one premise. Since the middle term is not distributed in either premise, this is an instance of the fallacy of undistributed middle.

Let's consider another argument:

Some non-citizens pay taxes.
All taxpayers can collect Social Security.
Some non-citizens can collect Social Security.

So far, the phrases "pay taxes" and "collect Social Security" are not class terms. However, first, we can translate "pay taxes" into "taxpayers" so it matches the term in the minor premise. And second, we can translate "collect Social Security" into "people who collect Social Security" in both the minor premise and the conclusion.

The copula is missing in each statement as well, so we need to add them:

Some non-citizens are taxpayers.
All taxpayers are people who can collect Social Security.
Some non-citizens are people who can collect Social Security.

Since there are three different terms and each occurs twice, it is not necessary to eliminate the two instances of "non-." We can let non-C = *non-citizens*, T = *taxpayers*, and P = *people who can collect Social Security*:

Some non-C are T.
All T are P.
Some non-C are P.

A Venn diagram then shows the syllogism to be valid:

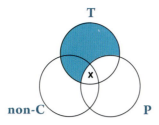

Since the syllogism does not violate any of the six rules, we have additional confirmation that it is valid.

EXERCISES 6G.1

I. The following syllogisms need to be rewritten into standard form. Use the tools discussed in this section to reduce the number of terms. Then use Venn diagrams and the six rules to determine whether the syllogisms are valid or invalid under the *modern interpretation*.

Self-Practice Questions

1. Some C are not B.
   Some non-A are B.
   Some non-C are not A.

Answer: First, use contraposition on the conclusion to obtain the following: *Some non-A are not non-non-C.* Next, rewrite to eliminate the "non-non": *Some non-A are not C.* Finally, reconstruct the syllogism:

   Some C are not B.
   Some non-A are B.
   Some non-A are not C.

The following Venn diagram shows that the syllogism is invalid.

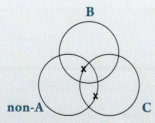

The syllogism violates Rule 2: The major term is distributed in the conclusion but not in the first premise.

2. No A are B.
   All non-A are C.
   Some non-C are not B.

3. No non-A are B.
   Some non-B are not non-C.
   Some C are not A.

4. No A are B.
    Some non-C are A.
    Some B are not C.

★ 5. Some A are non-B.
    All C are non-B.
    Some C are not A.

6. All A are B.
    Some B are not C.
    Some C are not non-A.

7. Some non-A are non-C.
    All A are B.
    Some C are non-B.

8. All non-C are B.
    No A are B.
    All C are A.

★ 9. No A are B.
    All C are A.
    All C are B.

10. No B are non-C.
    Some A are non-B.
    Some C are A.

11. All A are non-B.
    Some C are not B.
    Some non-C are A.

12. All A are B.
    Some non-B are C.
    Some C are not non-A.

★13. All C are A.
    All A are B.
    All B are C.

14. All non-A are non-C.
    No non-A are non-B.
    All C are non-B.

15. Some A are non-B.
    No C are non-A.
    Some C are not B.

II. The following arguments need to be translated and rewritten into standard form. Use the tools discussed in this section to reduce the number of terms. Then use Venn diagrams and the six rules to determine whether the syllogisms are valid or invalid under the *modern interpretation*.

1. Some TV ads are things meant to make us laugh. Therefore, some things meant to make us laugh are silly forms of entertainment, because all television ads are foolish forms of entertainment.

Answer: There are four terms: "TV ads," "things meant to make us laugh," "silly forms of entertainment," and "foolish forms of entertainment." Since "silly" and "foolish" are synonyms, we can replace one with the other. Let T = *TV ads*, L = *things meant to make us laugh*, and F = *foolish forms of entertainment*. Here is the rewritten syllogism:

All T are F.
Some T are L.
Some L are F.

The following Venn diagram shows that the syllogism is valid.

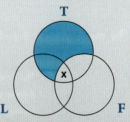

The syllogism does not violate any of the six rules.

2. All colleges without philosophy courses are institutions lacking in liberal arts programs. Every institution lacking a liberal arts program is an institution graduating students who miss out on the best ideas ever written. Thus, some colleges with philosophy courses are not institutions graduating students who miss out on the best ideas ever written.

Video Tutorial: 6GI.II
Exercise #2

3. Some over-the-counter drugs are unsafe for children. It follows that no non-prescription drugs are safe for children, because all over-the-counter drugs are not prescription drugs.

4. Some gangs are dangerous groups. That's because all gangs are mindless mobs, and some safe groups are not mindless mobs.

★ 5. All self-motivated students are using their intellectual capabilities. But no disinterested students are using their intellectual capabilities. Therefore, all self-motivated students are interested students.

6. No poorly paying jobs are sufficient to sustain a family's needs. Some well-paying jobs are not mindless careers. Thus, no jobs sufficient to sustain a family's needs are mindless careers.

7. Some managers are irresponsible employees. So, all non-managers are burdened with too much work, because all people burdened with too much work are responsible employees.

8. Some politicians are public representatives without ethical values. No public representatives with ethical values are corrupt. Therefore, some incorrupt people are politicians.

★ 9. Some preschool children are severely overweight. Some obese students are susceptible to diabetes. Therefore, some preschool children are not susceptible to diabetes.

10. Every pork-belly legislation is a waste of taxpayers' money. No reasonable law is a waste of taxpayers' money. So, no pork-belly legislation is a reasonable law.

Paraphrasing Ordinary Language Arguments

Sometimes we need to paraphrase an ordinary language argument in order to produce a standard-form categorical syllogism. Consider this argument:

> Drug tests shouldn't be used. Of course, if something is reliable, then it should be used. But unfortunately, drug tests aren't reliable.

The conclusion is "Drug tests shouldn't be used," and the other two statements are the premises. We could simply start translating any statement we wish, but it is better to have a strategy. Our aim is to translate statements so the terms match those in the other statements, if possible. Given this goal, a translation of the statement "If something is reliable, then it should be used" seems fairly straightforward. The translation is "All reliable things are things that should be used." The translation incorporated two key moves. First, since the word "reliable" does not designate a class, it was translated as "reliable things." Second, although the phrase "Of course" is often a premise indicator, it is superfluous in this context, so we eliminated it from the translation.

Now we can try to translate the other two statements to match the two available terms, "reliable things" and "things that should be used." The conclusion seems to be making a blanket statement about drug testing, so we can translate it as a universal proposition. If we try an **A**-proposition, we get "All drug tests are things that should not be used." The problem with this translation is that "things that should not be used" does not match the term "things that should be used," so we should look for an alternative. If we translate the conclusion as an **E**-proposition, the result is "No drug tests are things that should be used." Just what we want.

The remaining statement to translate is "Drug tests aren't reliable." Although the word "but" is often a premise indicator, the phrase "But unfortunately" is superfluous in this context, so we can eliminate it. Once again, we translate the statement as a universal proposition. If we translate the statement as an **E**-proposition, we get "No drug tests are reliable things." This translation results in terms that match already existing ones:

All reliable things are things that should be used.
No drug tests are reliable things.
No drug tests are things that should be used.

We can let R = *reliable things*, T = *things that should be used*, and D = *drug tests*:

All R are T.
No D are R.
No D are T.

A Venn diagram then shows that the syllogism is invalid:

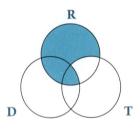

As confirmation, the syllogism violates Rule 2: If a term is distributed in the conclusion, then it must be distributed in a premise. Since the major term is distributed in the conclusion but not in the major premise, the syllogism commits the fallacy of illicit major.

Categorical Propositions and Multiple Arguments

In Chapter 5 we saw that propositions that take the form "All *except* S are P" and "All *but* S are P" are *exceptive* propositions. These propositions relate the predicate to both the class designated by the subject term and its complement. Hence, a translation results in a compound statement, containing the word "and." When an exceptive proposition occurs as a premise in a categorical syllogism, then we need to create two translations and two syllogisms. Let's look at the following argument:

> Everyone except those under 18 years of age is eligible to vote. My brother John is older than 18, so he can vote.

The conclusion of the argument is "he can vote." Based on the information in the passage, this can be translated as "All persons identical to my brother John are persons eligible to vote." The next step is to translate the exceptive proposition "Everyone except those under 18 years of age is eligible to vote." The word "Everyone" indicates that both translations will have to be universal statements. Paraphrasing the original statement gives us: "No under-18 years of age persons are persons eligible to vote" and "All non-under-18 years of age persons are persons eligible to vote." There is one more statement to translate. However, we should keep in mind that, if possible, the translation will match terms already used. Hence, the statement "My brother John is older than 18" can be translated as "No persons identical to my brother John are under-18 years of age persons." We can now put the pieces together to form two syllogisms.

A. No under-18 years of age persons are persons eligible to vote.
    No persons identical to my brother John are under-18 years of age persons.
    All persons identical to my brother John are persons eligible to vote.

This syllogism has exactly three different terms and each term is used twice. Also, the major and minor premises are in the correct location, so we do not need to change anything. We can let U = *under-18 years of age persons*, E = *persons eligible to vote*, and J = *persons identical to my brother John*:

No U are E.
No J are U.
All J are E.

A Venn diagram shows that the syllogism is invalid:

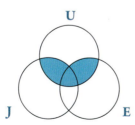

As confirmation, the syllogism violates Rule 3: A categorical syllogism cannot have two negative premises. Since this syllogism has two negative premises, it commits the fallacy of exclusive premises.

However, our analysis is not finished. Since we are dealing with an exceptive proposition, we have one more syllogism to analyze. The basic rule is that if *either* of the two syllogisms formed by translating an exceptive proposition is valid, then the original argument is valid. Here is the second syllogism:

B. All non-under-18 years of age persons are persons eligible to vote.
    No persons identical to my brother John are under-18 years of age persons.
    All persons identical to my brother John are persons eligible to vote.

Although the major and minor premises are in the correct location, there is a problem. This syllogism has four different terms, since "non-under-18 years of age persons" and "under-18 years of age persons" are not the same. We can, however, use obversion on the minor premise. The result is "All persons identical to my brother John are non-under-18 years of age persons." Now the syllogism has exactly three different terms, and each term is used twice:

All non-under-18 years of age persons are persons eligible to vote.
All persons identical to my brother John are non-under-18 years of age persons.
All persons identical to my brother John are persons eligible to vote.

We can let non-U = *non-under-18 years of age persons*, E = *persons eligible to vote*, and J = *persons identical to my brother John*:

All non-U are E.
All J are non-U.
All J are E.

The Venn diagram shows that the syllogism is valid:

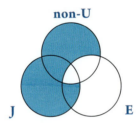

non-U

J   E

As confirmation, the syllogism does not violate any of the six rules.

EXERCISES 6G.2

The following arguments need to be translated into standard form. Use all the tools and techniques discussed so far, including reducing the number of terms and paraphrasing. Then use Venn diagrams and the six rules to determine whether the syllogisms are valid or invalid under the *modern interpretation*.

1. Not all nuclear power plants are dangerous to humans. Haskerville NP is a nuclear power plant, so it is not dangerous.

Answer: Rewrite the syllogism. Let N = *nuclear power plants*, D = *places dangerous to humans*, and H = *places identical to Haskerville NP*.

Some N are not D.
<u>All H are N.</u>
No H are D.

The following Venn diagram shows that the syllogism is invalid:

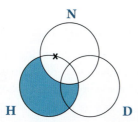

The syllogism violates Rule 1: The middle term is not distributed in at least one premise.

2. No religion can be taught in public schools. Since creationism is a religion, it cannot be taught in public schools.

3. Whenever comets appear in the sky, the stock market falls. Today, there are no comets appearing in the sky; so today the stock market will rise.

4. Shane's vehicle is not a Hummer; therefore, it gets good gas mileage, because all vehicles except Hummers get good gas mileage.

⭐ 5. Refurbished computers are not expensive, because every computer my uncle buys is refurbished, and every computer he buys is inexpensive.

6. I am not a genius, because my I.Q. is 115, and anyone who has an I.Q. over 140 is a genius.

7. Chimpanzees are conscious. That's because chimpanzees make tools, and any animal that makes tools is conscious.

8. Whoever killed Mr. Boddy had a dagger. Col. Mustard has a dagger, so he killed Mr. Boddy.

⭐ 9. Some starvation diets are effective ways to lose weight. However, starving yourself is bad for your heart. Thus, some effective ways to lose weight are bad for your heart.

10. If you have a credit card, you can buy a new television. If you can buy a new television, you can watch mind-numbing TV programs. It follows that if you have a credit card, you can watch mind-numbing TV programs.

11. Whenever the underdog wins the Super Bowl, beer sales rise. The underdog lost the Super Bowl this year, so this year beer sales will fall.

12. Most philosophy majors score high on the LSAT. Therefore, most get into the law school of their choice, because many people who score high on the LSAT get into the law school of their choice.

★13. Traditional Western philosophy is a series of footnotes to Plato. However, since Asian philosophy is not part of traditional Western philosophy, we can conclude that Asian philosophy is not a series of footnotes to Plato.

14. Only those who have the numbers 4, 10, 14, 24, 27, and 36 have won this week's lottery. I do not have those numbers, so I did not win the lottery.

15. Every college student is interested in finding their place in life. Every college student is anxious to impress their parents. So everyone interested in finding their place in life is anxious to impress their parents.

H. ENTHYMEMES

Enthymemes
Arguments with missing premises, missing conclusions, or both.

Some ordinary language arguments leave out important information. Arguments with missing premises, missing conclusions, or both are called **enthymemes**. The missing information is usually implied, so the arguments are typically best reconstructed based on knowledge of the context in which they appear. However, sometimes we do not have access to the context, so we should reconstruct the argument in order to give the benefit of the doubt to the person presenting the argument (the principle of charity). For example, suppose someone says:

> There is no good scientific evidence to support a belief in ghosts; so anyone who believes in ghosts is superstitious.

Since the word "so" is a good conclusion indicator, the missing information is a second premise. We add the missing premise (along with paraphrasing the existing information):

> Whenever there is no good scientific evidence for something, then it is a superstitious belief. There is no good scientific evidence to support anyone's belief in ghosts. So everyone's belief in ghosts is superstitious.

It is not difficult to translate the argument into a standard-form categorical syllogism:

> All beliefs that lack good scientific evidence are superstitious beliefs.
> All people's beliefs about ghosts are beliefs that lack good scientific evidence.
> All people's beliefs about ghosts are superstitious beliefs.

We can let B = *beliefs that lack good scientific evidence*, S = *superstitious beliefs*, and G = *people's beliefs about ghosts*:

> All B are S.
> All G are B.
> All G are S.

A Venn diagram shows that the syllogism is valid:

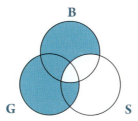

As confirmation, the syllogism does not violate any of the six rules.

An ordinary language argument might be missing both a premise and a conclusion. For example, in his inaugural address of 1933 during the Great Depression, President Franklin D. Roosevelt wanted to relieve people's worries about the ongoing economic crisis. He told the American public:

> The only thing we have to fear is fear itself.

We can fill in the missing information in the following manner:

> The only thing we have to fear is fear itself.
> <u>The economic crisis is not fear itself.</u> (*Missing premise*)
> The economic crisis is not something to be feared. (*Missing conclusion*)

As we saw in Chapter 5, "the only" can be translated as a universal affirmative proposition. Therefore, we can paraphrase the major premise, "The only thing we have to fear is fear itself," as "All things that we have to fear are things identical to fear itself." The minor premise and the conclusion should be paraphrased using the terms "things that we have to fear" and "things identical to fear itself." Hence, the minor premise can be translated as "No things identical to the economic crisis are things identical to fear itself." The conclusion can be translated as "No things identical to the economic crisis are things that we have to fear." Putting the pieces together produces the following syllogism:

> All things that we have to fear are things identical to fear itself.
> <u>No things identical to the economic crisis are things identical to fear itself.</u>
> No things identical to the economic crisis are things that we have to fear.

We can let H = *things that we have to fear*, F = *things identical to fear itself*, and E = *things identical to the economic crisis*:

> All H are F.
> <u>No E are F.</u>
> No E are H.

A Venn diagram shows that the syllogism is valid:

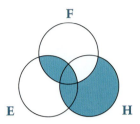

As confirmation, the syllogism does not violate any of the six rules.

We need to be careful in supplying a missing premise or conclusion, because our decisions can affect our evaluation of the argument. The next example illustrates why:

> You won't be able to finish the assigned material by tomorrow morning; therefore, you will fail the exam.

The word "therefore" is a good conclusion indicator, so the statement "You will fail the exam" can be translated as "All persons identical to you are persons who will fail the exam." Both the existing premise and the missing premise should be written, if possible, to include the terms "persons identical to you" and "persons who will fail the exam." The statement "You won't be able to finish the assigned material by tomorrow morning" can be paraphrased as "All persons identical to you are persons unable to finish the assigned material by tomorrow morning." This premise contains the minor term, "persons identical to you," so it becomes the minor premise.

The missing major premise needs to tie the information together. However, at this point we have to consider a few different possibilities. The speaker might be implying that "All persons unable to finish the assigned material by tomorrow morning are persons who will fail the exam." Another possibility is that the speaker might be implying that "Most persons unable to finish the assigned material by tomorrow morning are persons who will fail the exam." Let's examine both possibilities. The first option results in the following syllogism:

> All persons unable to finish the assigned material by tomorrow morning are persons who will fail the exam.
> All persons identical to you are persons unable to finish the assigned material by tomorrow morning.
> _____
> All persons identical to you are persons who will fail the exam.

We let A = *persons unable to finish the assigned material by tomorrow morning*, F = *persons who will fail the exam*, and Y = *persons identical to you*:

> All A are F.
> All Y are A.
> _____
> All Y are F.

A Venn diagram shows that the syllogism is valid:

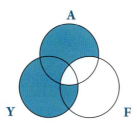

As confirmation, the syllogism does not violate any of the six rules.

Although the syllogism is valid, it may be unsound—because the major premise is likely to be false. It is possible that someone who does not finish the assigned material can still pass the exam.

Let's now try the second alternative. We will have to translate the statement "Most persons unable to finish the assigned material by tomorrow morning are persons who will fail the exam." Using the tools in Chapter 5, we can translate "most" to "some." This second option results in the following syllogism:

> Some persons unable to finish the assigned material by tomorrow morning are persons who will fail the exam.
> All persons identical to you are persons unable to finish the assigned material by tomorrow morning.
> _____
> All persons identical to you are persons who will fail the exam.

We let A = *persons unable to finish the assigned material by tomorrow morning*, F = *persons who will fail the exam*, and Y = *persons identical to you*:

> Some A are F.
> All Y are A.
> All Y are F.

A Venn diagram shows that the syllogism is invalid:

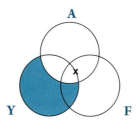

As confirmation, the syllogism violates Rule 1: The middle term must be distributed in at least one premise. Since the middle term is not distributed, the syllogism commits the fallacy of undistributed middle. The syllogism cannot be sound, even though the major premise is probably true. All that would be needed is for one person who did not finish the assigned material to fail the exam. Let's bring together the results of the two options:

1. The first syllogism is valid, but probably not sound, because the major premise is likely to be false.
2. The second syllogism is invalid and unsound, but the major premise is likely to be true.

Not all uses of language are transparent. Sometimes language is used *rhetorically*— to imply things that are not explicitly said. A premise or conclusion can be disguised as a question. For example, someone might say, "Do you think I'm that stupid?" Although the sentence poses a question, it should be clear that the speaker's intention is to make an assertion: "I'm not stupid."

A rhetorical question can be used effectively in an enthymeme because it forces the audience to supply an obvious answer. For example, you might hear the following:

We shouldn't cut taxes for the big corporations. Do you really think they care about sharing their wealth with the rest of us?

The conclusion is the first sentence, and it can be translated into a categorical proposition: "No big corporations are organizations for which we should cut taxes." The term "big corporations" will have to occur in the minor premise, and the term "organizations for which we should cut taxes" will occur in the major premise. The rhetorical question gets rewritten as "No big corporations are groups interested in sharing their

PROFILES IN LOGIC
Leonhard Euler

Leonhard Euler (1707–83), who wrote over 800 mathematical treatises, is the most prolific mathematician in history. His abilities and memory were so remarkable that he was still able to offer original contributions to nearly every area of mathematics even after he went blind.

Euler applied special diagrams, today called *Euler diagrams*, to represent logical relations. Aristotelian syllogisms deal with classes by asking what each class includes and excludes—two ideas that can be captured visually. By providing the first steps toward a rigorous proof, Euler diagrams offer an alternative to Venn diagrams and can be used as a foundation for logical analysis. Although Euler's system is perfectly suited to mathematical and logical reasoning, its flexibility allows for many other applications as well.

Euler also studied matrices—numbers or symbols arranged in rows and columns. In what he called *Latin squares*, symbols never appear twice in the same row or column. A special version of those squares is a popular pastime today. It is called Sudoku.

wealth." This is the minor premise, and the term "organizations interested in sharing their wealth" is the middle term. The major (missing) premise can be written as "All organizations for which we should cut taxes are groups interested in sharing their wealth." We can now reconstruct the argument.

> All organizations for which we should cut taxes are groups interested in sharing their wealth.
> No big corporations are groups interested in sharing their wealth.
> No big corporations are organizations for which we should cut taxes.

We let O = *organizations for which we should cut taxes*, G = *groups interested in sharing their wealth*, and B = *big corporations*:

> All O are G.
> No B are G.
> No B are O.

A Venn diagram shows that the syllogism is valid:

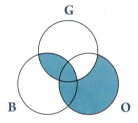

As confirmation, the syllogism does not violate any of the six rules. We leave it to you to decide on the truth value of the premises.

EXERCISES 6H

I. First, supply the missing premise or conclusion for the following enthymemes such that each one results in a valid argument. Second, translate the results into standard-form categorical syllogisms. Third, test your answers by using Venn diagrams and the six rules under the *modern interpretation.*

Self-Practice Questions

1. Anything that lacks credible evidence does not exist. Therefore, UFOs do not exist.

Answer: Rewrite the syllogism. Let L = *things that lack credible evidence*, E = *things that exist*, and U = *UFOs.*

> No L are E.
> All U are L. *Missing premise:* All UFOs are things that lack credible evidence.
> No U are E.

The following Venn diagram shows that the syllogism is valid:

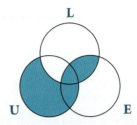

Applying the six rules verifies that the syllogism is valid:

Rule 1: The middle term is distributed in the first premise.
Rule 2: The subject term is distributed in the conclusion and in the second premise; the predicate term is distributed in the conclusion and in the first premise.
Rule 3: The syllogism does not have two negative premises.
Rule 4: The syllogism has a negative premise and a negative conclusion.
Rule 5: The syllogism has a negative conclusion and a negative premise.
Rule 6: The syllogism does not have two universal premises and a particular conclusion.

2. Religious fanatics do not believe in freedom of thought, because they think that their belief is absolutely correct.

3. The people in Congress do not deserve a raise. Don't they get enough money now?

4. Talkative students disrupt a class, so these people are unfair to the other students.

★ 5. A broken cell phone will be replaced only if it is accompanied by a sales slip. I do not have the sales slip for my broken cell phone.

6. All of the games in my room are missing pieces. Monopoly is not missing any pieces.

7. My child has experienced a substantial change in body temperature. Any substantial change in body temperature is an indication of illness.

8. Only bacterial infections are effectively treated with antibiotics, so my infection will not be effectively treated with antibiotics.

★ 9. Anyone who can successfully find their way home can learn logic. All the students in this class can successfully find their way home.

10. Capital punishment should be abolished. Why do something that fails to reduce crime?

11. Coal furnaces should be phased out, because they are a major source of air pollution.

12. The only animal with a brain the same size as humans is the dolphin. Dolphins are not fish.

★13. A few state laws are unconstitutional. They will be overturned by the Supreme Court.

14. Not all cultured pearls are expensive, but they all are beautiful.

15. Whenever the economy goes into recession people will blame the non-citizens, and the economy is going into recession this year.

16. A conscious person has certain rights, so it follows that any living person has certain rights.

★17. Some airline companies take their customers for granted, because any company that refuses to give a refund on a purchase takes their customers for granted.

18. Shouldn't all citizens fulfill mandatory duties? Then all citizens should fulfill public service.

19. I didn't ask to be born. Therefore, I don't owe anything to anyone.

20. Dancing is exercise. Therefore, dancing is good for your health.

II. The following enthymemes were adapted from newspapers, websites, and other sources. First, supply the missing premise or conclusion for the following enthymemes. Second, translate the results into standard-form categorical syllogisms. Third, test your answers by using Venn diagrams and the six rules under the *modern interpretation*. Fourth, try to make the syllogism valid. If it cannot be made valid, then explain why.

1. It is almost impossible to stop the spread of these cases (cholera), because it is so contagious.   Patrick Worsnip, "Haiti Cholera Spreading Faster Than Predicted," Reuters

Answer: Missing premise: All contagious diseases are diseases in which the spread is almost impossible to stop.

Rewritten syllogism: All contagious diseases are diseases in which the spread is almost impossible to stop. All cholera cases are contagious diseases. Therefore, all cholera cases are diseases in which the spread is almost impossible to stop.

Let T = *contagious diseases*, I = *diseases in which the spread is almost impossible to stop*, and C = *cholera cases.*

All T are I.
All C are T.
All C are I.

The following Venn diagram shows that the syllogism is valid:

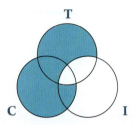

Applying the six rules verifies that the syllogism is valid:

Rule 1: The middle term is distributed in the first premise.
Rule 2: The subject term is distributed in the conclusion and in the second premise.
Rule 3: The syllogism does not have two negative premises.
Rule 4: The syllogism does not have a negative premise.
Rule 5: The syllogism does not have a negative conclusion.
Rule 6: The syllogism does not have two universal premises and a particular conclusion.

2. Henry David Thoreau said, "What is once well done is done forever." To which someone once added, "Nothing done forever is done easily."

3. Most Americans who cast their ballot in the recent midterm elections are preoccupied with the United States' economic problems. Also, most voters concerned with the country's economic problems are not people who voted on the basis of foreign policy.

Richard N. Haass, "American Foreign Policy After the Mid-Term Elections," Project-Syndicate.org

4. Keir Dillon, professional snowboarder, said, "I respect that everyone should wear a helmet. But I don't think it should be mandated."

Matt Higgins, "Head Games," ESPN.com

5. The two Koreas are still technically at war—the Korean War ended only with a truce.

Peter Beck, "Obama and South Korea Leader Agree to Hold Joint Military Exercise," MSNBC.com

6. Of the 43 horses that started in synthetic track races at Santa Anita off of prep races on dirt, not one of them won, and not every one of them was hopelessly overmatched.   Mike Watchmaker, "Beware of Breeders' Cup Generalizations," Drf.com

7. Perfection is achieved, not when there is nothing more to add, but when there is nothing left to take away.   Antoine de Saint Exupery, *Wind, Sand, and Stars*

8. An immigrant who uses a false Social Security number to get a job doesn't intend to harm anyone. It makes no sense to spend our tax dollars to imprison them for two years.   Chuck Roth, in a statement to the *New York Times*

⭐ 9. All of us failed to match our dreams of perfection. So I rate us on the basis of our splendid failure to do the impossible.

William Faulkner, *Writers at Work, First Series*, ed. Malcolm Cowley

10. If you don't dream, you're living in a memory. Who wants to live in a memory?

Chris Del Conte, quoted at Sports.espn.go.com

I. SORITES

A special type of enthymeme is a chain of arguments called a **sorites** (pronounced *soh-rhy'-teez*; from the Greek word "*sōrós*," meaning *a heap or a pile*). These arguments typically have many premises. The missing parts are intermediate conclusions each of which, in turn, becomes a premise in the next link in the chain. And if one of the links fails, so does the chain: If any syllogism in the chain is invalid, then the sorites is invalid. Let's look at an example:

> All drunk drivers are criminals.
> All drivers with blood alcohol concentration above 0.08% are drunk drivers.
> All drivers who have had the equivalent of six 12-oz. beers are drivers with blood alcohol concentrations above 0.08%.
> _____
> All drivers who have the equivalent of six 12-oz. beers are criminals.

Sorites A special type of enthymeme that is a chain of arguments. The missing parts are intermediate conclusions, each of which, in turn, becomes a premise in the next link in the chain.

We can let D = *drunk drivers*, C = *criminals*, A = *drivers with blood alcohol concentration above 0.08%*, and S = *drivers who have the equivalent of six 12-oz. beers*:

> All D are C.
> All A are D.
> All S are A.
> _____
> All S are C.

If the first two premises, "All D are C" and "All A are D," are used as the major and minor premises of a categorical syllogism, then we can supply the intermediate conclusion: "All A are C" (for "All drivers with blood alcohol concentration above 0.08% are criminals"):

> All D are C.
> All A are D.
> _____
> All A are C. (*Intermediate conclusion*)

A Venn diagram shows that the syllogism is valid:

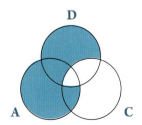

Since the syllogism does not violate any of the six rules, we have additional confirmation that it is valid.

The intermediate conclusion, "All A are C," now becomes the major premise of the next syllogism. The remaining premise of the original argument, "All S are A," becomes the minor premise, and the final conclusion is "All S are C" (which stands for "All drivers who have the equivalent of six 12-oz. beers are criminals"):

> All A are C.
> All S are A.
> All S are C.

A Venn diagram shows that the syllogism is valid:

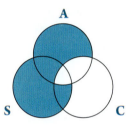

Since the syllogism does not violate any of the six rules, we have additional confirmation that it is valid.

As we already know, ordinary language arguments often require paraphrasing and reordering. Here is an example of a sorites:

> Every agreement to lift embargoes is a program designed to reduce a country's international debt. It is obvious that no weapons of mass destruction are humanitarian assistance programs. It is just as clear that some chemical weapons are not agreements to lift embargoes. Also, every program designed to reduce a country's international debt is a humanitarian assistance program. Thus, some chemical weapons are not weapons of mass destruction.

The first step is to translate the statements into standard-form categorical propositions (using paraphrasing when appropriate):

> All agreements to lift embargoes are programs designed to reduce a country's international debt.
> No weapons of mass destruction are humanitarian assistance programs.
> Some chemical weapons are not agreements to lift embargoes.
> All programs designed to reduce a country's international debt are humanitarian assistance programs.
> Some chemical weapons are not weapons of mass destruction.

The next step is to reveal the form of the argument. We let A = *agreements to lift embargoes*, P = *programs designed to reduce a country's international debt*, W = *weapons of mass destruction*, H = *humanitarian assistance programs*, and C = *chemical weapons*:

All A are P.
No W are H.
Some C are not A.
All P are H.
Some C are not W.

The next step is very important: We have to arrange the premises in the correct order. A simple method will ensure the correct outcome. First, locate the predicate in the conclusion (W); second, find the premise that contains the same letter (i.e., "No W are H"); and third, make that the first premise. The other term in this premise then becomes the next term, and its matching pair ("All P are H") becomes the next premise. We simply repeat the process until all premises are accounted for:

No W are H.
All P are H.
All A are P.
Some C are not A.
Some C are not W.

If the first two premises ("No W are H" and "All P are H") are used as the major and minor premises of a categorical syllogism, then we can supply the missing intermediate conclusion ("No P are W"):

No W are H.
All P are H.
No P are W. (*Intermediate conclusion*)

A Venn diagram shows that the syllogism is valid:

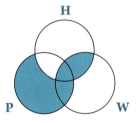

Since the syllogism does not violate any of the six rules, we have additional confirmation that it is valid. The intermediate conclusion ("No P are W") now becomes the major premise of the next syllogism. The next premise of the argument ("All A are P") becomes the minor premise, and the next intermediate conclusion is "No A are W":

No P are W.
All A are P.
No A are W. (*Intermediate conclusion*)

A Venn diagram shows that the syllogism is valid:

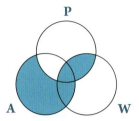

Since the syllogism does not violate any of the six rules, we have additional confirmation. The intermediate conclusion ("No A are W") now becomes the major premise of the final syllogism. The last premise of the argument ("Some C are not A") becomes the minor premise, and the final conclusion is "Some C are not W":

> No A are W.
> Some C are not A.
> Some C are not W.

Here a Venn diagram shows that the syllogism is invalid:

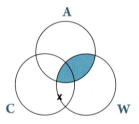

As confirmation, the syllogism violates Rule 3: A categorical syllogism cannot have two negative premises. Since the syllogism has two negative premises, it commits the fallacy of exclusive premises.

EXERCISES 6I

I. **First, put the following sorites into standard form and reduce the number of terms whenever necessary. Second, determine the intermediate conclusions. Third, use Venn diagrams and the six rules to determine whether the syllogisms are valid or invalid under the *modern interpretation*.**

1. No A are C.
   All non-D are non-B.
   No D are non-C.
   No B are A.

Answer: Rewrite the syllogism. First, apply contraposition to "All non-D are non-B" to obtain "All B are D." Second, apply obversion to "No D are non-C" to obtain "All D are C."

No A are C.
All B are D.
All D are C.
No B are A.

Next, locate the predicate in the conclusion; the premise that contains the same letter is the first premise of our constructed syllogism. The other term in this premise then becomes the next term, and its matching pair becomes the next premise.

No A are C.
All D are C.
No D are A. (*Intermediate conclusion*)

The syllogism does not violate any of the six rules.
    The following Venn diagram shows that the syllogism is valid:

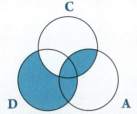

The intermediate conclusion now becomes the major premise of the final syllogism, and the remaining premise becomes the minor premise:

No D are A.
All B are D.
No B are A.

The syllogism does not violate any of the six rules.
    The following Venn diagram shows that the syllogism is valid:

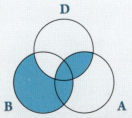

2. Some A are not C.
    No A are B.
    All D are C.
    Some B are not D.

3. Some A are C.
    All A are non-B.
    All D are B.
    Some non-D are not non-C.

4. No C are A.
    All D are C.
    Some B are A.
    Some B are not D.

★ 5. All B are D.
    No E are C.
    No A are non-C.
    All non-A are non-B.
    All D are non-E.

6. No B are C.
All A are D.
Some A are B.
Some D are E.
Some E are not C.

7. All non-C are non-E.
All B are C.
All A are non-B.
Some D are A.
Some non-E are not non-D.

8. No E are non-A.
All D are non-B.
All A are B.
No E are F.
No non-C are D.
All C are non-F.

⭐ 9. Some B are E.
All C are A.
All D are C.
No A are B.
Some E are not D.

10. No non-F are C.
All non-A are non-B.
All E are non-D.
Some B are C.
All D are non-A.
Some F are not E.

II. Rewrite each of the following sorites in standard form and reduce the number of terms whenever necessary. Second, determine the intermediate conclusions. Third, use Venn diagrams and the six rules under the *modern interpretation* to determine whether the syllogisms are valid or invalid.

1. All the clothes in my closet are old.
No popular clothes are old.
All expensive clothes are popular.
Not a single item of clothing in my closet is expensive.

Answer: Rewrite the conclusion as follows: "No clothes in my closet are expensive."
Let C = *clothes in my closet*, O = *old things*, P = *popular clothes*, and E = *expensive clothes*.

All C are O.
No P are O.
All E are P.
No C are E.

Next, we locate the predicate in the conclusion and construct a syllogism:

All E are P.
No P are O.
No O are E. (*Intermediate conclusion*)

The syllogism does not violate any of the six rules.

The following Venn diagram shows that the syllogism is valid:

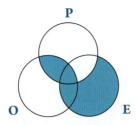

The intermediate conclusion now becomes the major premise of the final syllogism, and the remaining premise becomes the minor premise:

No O are E.
All C are O.
No C are E.

The syllogism does not violate any of the six rules.
The following Venn diagram shows that the syllogism is valid:

2. No one but an artist has an adoring public.
   No artists wonder whether they will be famous.
   No one who wonders whether he will be famous is a logic instructor.
   No logic instructor has an adoring public.

3. Fake diamonds turn dull over time.
   No polished jewelry turns dull over time.
   No expensive jewelry is unpolished jewelry.
   Fake diamonds are inexpensive jewelry.

4. All my mom's books are classics.
   No classic books have a copyright.
   All popular books are copyrighted.
   None of my mom's books are popular.

5. No famous sitcoms are controversial shows.
   All famous sitcoms are written for mass audiences.
   All X-rated movies are written for small audiences.
   All X-rated movies are controversial programs.

6. None of my dogs are overweight.
   All of my cats sleep 18 hours a day.
   All of my pets who chase other animals are cats.
   <u>None of my pets who chase other animals are overweight.</u>
   None of my dogs sleep 18 hours a day.

7. All reasoning that uses the principles of logic are well-grounded ideas.
   Irrational thinking does not use the principles of logic.
   Rational thinking is more likely to achieve correct decisions.
   <u>All decisions based on probabilities are more likely to achieve correct decisions.</u>
   All decisions based on probabilities are well-grounded ideas.

8. All satisfied restaurant customers will recommend the food to their friends.
   All dirty restaurants are health hazards.
   All satisfied restaurant customers are people who ate well-cooked food.
   No people who ate well-cooked food are health hazards.
   <u>All people who will recommend the food to their friends are repeat customers.</u>
   No dirty restaurants have repeat customers.

⭐ 9. My neighbor plays loud music.
   Drum sounds are the heart of song.
   My neighbor plays music that has a melody.
   The music that you can hear is from people who play loud music.
   <u>Music that has a melody uses drum sounds.</u>
   The only music that you can hear is the heart of song.

10. All industrial strength cleaners are toxic.
    All products that can be sold in grocery stores are tested in a public consumer's laboratory.
    Crudex is a salad dressing.
    Some industrial strength cleaners are tested in a public consumer's laboratory.
    <u>Only products that can be sold in grocery stores are salad dressings.</u>
    Crudex is not toxic.

Summary

- Syllogism: A deductive argument that has exactly two premises and a conclusion.
- Categorical syllogism: A syllogism constructed entirely of categorical propositions. It contains three different terms, each of which is used two times.
- Minor term: The subject of the conclusion of a categorical syllogism.
- Major term: The predicate of the conclusion of a categorical syllogism.

- Middle term: The term that occurs only in the premises of a categorical syllogism.
- Major premise: The first premise of a categorical syllogism contains the major term.
- Minor premise: The second premise of a categorical syllogism contains the minor term.
- In order to be a standard-form categorical syllogism, three requirements must be met: (1) All three statements must be standard-form categorical propositions. (2) The two occurrences of each term must be identical and have the same sense. (3) The major premise must occur first, the minor premise second, and the conclusion last.
- The mood of a categorical syllogism consists of the type of categorical propositions involved (A, E, I, or O) and the order in which they occur.
- The middle term can be arranged in the two premises in four different ways. These placements determine the figure of the categorical syllogism.
- There are six rules for standard-form categorical syllogisms: (1) The middle term must be distributed in at least one premise. (2) If a term is distributed in the conclusion, then it must be distributed in a premise. (3) A categorical syllogism cannot have two negative premises. (4) A negative premise must have a negative conclusion. (5) A negative conclusion must have a negative premise. (6) Two universal premises cannot have a particular conclusion.
- Undistributed middle: A formal fallacy that occurs when the middle term in a categorical syllogism is undistributed in both premises of a categorical syllogism.
- Illicit major: A formal fallacy that occurs when the major term in a categorical syllogism is distributed in the conclusion but not in the major premise.
- Illicit minor: A formal fallacy that occurs when the minor term in a categorical syllogism is distributed in the conclusion but not in the minor premise.
- Exclusive premises: A formal fallacy that occurs when both premises in a categorical syllogism are negative.
- Affirmative conclusion/negative premise: A formal fallacy that occurs when a categorical syllogism has a negative premise and an affirmative conclusion.
- Negative conclusion/affirmative premises: A formal fallacy that occurs when a categorical syllogism has a negative conclusion and two affirmative premises.
- Existential fallacy: A formal fallacy that occurs when a categorical syllogism has a particular conclusion and two universal premises.
- Enthymemes: Arguments with missing premises, missing conclusions, or both.
- Sorites: A special type of enthymeme in which the missing parts are intermediate conclusions each of which, in turn becomes a premise in the next link in the chain.

KEY TERMS

affirmative conclusion/
   negative premise   270
categorical syllogism   245
enthymemes   296
exclusive premises   269
existential fallacy   272
figure   247
illicit major   268
illicit minor   269

major premise   246
major term   246
middle term   246
minor premise   246
minor term   246
mood   247
negative conclusion/
   affirmative
   premises   271

sorites   305
standard-form categorical
   syllogism   246
syllogism   245
undistributed
   middle   267

LOGIC CHALLENGE: RELATIONSHIPS REVISITED

Suppose you are told that there are three interesting relationships among four distinct groups of objects (which we will refer to as A, B, C, and D). Here are the relationships:

- All A are B.
- All C are D.
- Some B are C.

If all three relationships are true, then which one of the five following relationships would also be true?

1. All C are B.
2. All D are A.
3. Some C are A.
4. Some D are B.
5. Some A are D.

Note: Since there are four distinct groups (referred to as A, B, C, and D), you can construct a diagram that has four interlocking ellipses. That's a big part of the challenge.

Chapter 7

Propositional Logic

Digital homework exercises for this chapter are available in your instructor's online course. For information on how to access these resources, please visit **www.oup.com/ he/baronett5e**.

Sports championships offer a chance for a city to celebrate, but they can also result in violence, looting, and even death. News coverage often shows burning cars, smashed store windows, and struggles between police and rioters. Here is one recent account:

> Fans wandered amid the chaos, some with bandanas or T-shirts pulled over their faces—either to hide their faces from police and TV cameras or to guard against the smoke, or both.
>
> "Rioters Run Wild in Vancouver After Cup Loss," Associated Press

This brief description is actually quite complex. Several simple statements are connected by a few key words. The reporter makes all of the following claims: Some fans hid their faces with bandanas *or* T-shirts pulled over their faces in order to hide from police *and* TV cameras *or* guard against smoke, *or* both. The italicized words indicate the presence of multiple statements at work. When we read the passage, we barely notice the simple words "and" and "or," and yet their role in helping us understand the reporter's claims are crucial. In fact, the words express a logical function that guides us in understanding the connection between the several claims.

Complex statements that contain words like "and" and "or" are common in ordinary language and are used in almost every form of communication—in business, in law, in politics, in academics, and in everyday conversations.

Here is another example:

> But fundamentally an organism has conscious mental states if and only if there is something that it is like to *be* that organism—something it is like *for* the organism.
>
> Thomas Nagel, "What Is It Like to Be a Bat?" *The Philosophical Review*, Vol. 83, No. 4, 1974

The passage contains another complex statement. The key logical part is the phrase "if, and only if," which indicates that multiple claims are being made. To fully understand Nagel's claims, and to offer an analysis of them, requires knowing that the word "if" has a different logical function than "only if."

Words such as "and," "or," "if," and "only if" are sometimes used imprecisely or ambiguously in ordinary language. However, propositional logic provides precise definitions. The clarity and precision of the basic language of propositional logic guides us through the analysis of many kinds of deductive arguments. This chapter explores the foundations of propositional logic and explains how it captures much of what is expressed in ordinary language. It also provides the foundation for the next two chapters.

A. LOGICAL OPERATORS AND TRANSLATIONS

In this chapter, we will learn to translate ordinary language statements using special symbols called **logical operators**, or *connectives*. The symbolic translations that we will create capture an important part of ordinary language. We will use precise guidelines for uniform translations to help reduce some of the vagueness and obscurity of everyday language. In **propositional logic** the basic elements are statements. The translations will use letters to represent statements. (If you have already worked through Chapters 5 and 6, you know that some ordinary language statements can be translated by using letters to represent class terms. In categorical logic, the basic elements are class terms which, by themselves, are neither true nor false.)

Simple and Compound Statements

In order to see how complex statements are formed, we must first distinguish between simple and compound statements. A **simple statement** is one that does not have any other statement or logical operator as a component. Here are some examples:

- Harrisburg is the capital of Pennsylvania.
- Wednesday is hump day.
- Grilled hamburgers taste delicious.
- Detective novels make great movies.

Simple statements are translated by using any uppercase letter. For example, the letter "*H*" can be used to represent the statement "Harrisburg is the capital of Pennsylvania." Although we typically pick a letter that easily identifies the statement (in this case "*H*"), any other letter would be fine. The remaining simple statements can be translated similarly. For example, the letter "*W*" can be used to represent the statement "Wednesday is hump day"; the letter "*G*" can be used to represent the

---

Logical operators
Special symbols that can be used as part of ordinary language statement translations.

Propositional logic
The basic components in propositional logic are statements.

Simple statement
One that does not have any other statement or logical operator as a component.

statement "Grilled hamburgers taste delicious"; and finally, the letter "D" can be used to represent the statement "Detective novels make great movies."

A **compound statement** is a statement that has at least one simple statement and at least one logical operator as components. Here are some examples:

1. It is not the case that drinking hot coffee reduces sweating.
2. *Hamlet* is a tragedy and *Kung Fu Panda* is a comedy.
3. Either we reduce carbon emissions or global warming will get worse.
4. If the IRS processed my return, then I should get my refund this week.
5. You will graduate if and only if you meet all university requirements.

Compound statement
A statement that has at least one simple statement and at least one logical operator as components.

These compound statements can be represented by using uppercase letters to stand for the simple statements:

1. It is not the case that D.
2. H and K.
3. Either C or G.
4. If I, then R.
5. G if and only if U.

The translation of example 4 illustrates an important point. Notice that we did the following: We let I = *the IRS processed my return*, and R = *I should get my refund this week*. Once we designate the meaning of the letter "I" in a compound statement, we cannot use that letter again. In other words, we can use the letter "I" for either "the IRS processed my return" or "I should get my refund this week," but not both. This restriction holds for arguments as well—a particular letter can stand for at most one statement.

Now it may seem odd that the translation of example 1 is considered compound. After all, it has only the single simple statement D, whereas the other four statements each have two simple statements. It consists of an affirmative statement ("drinking hot coffee reduces sweating") and the phrase "it is not the case that," which is translated by a logical operator. In fact, the expressions "and," "or," "if ... then," "only if," and "if and only if" are all translated by logical operators. Here are the translations:

Operator	Name	Compound Type	Used to Translate
~	Tilde	Negation	*not; it is not the case that*
·	Dot	Conjunction	*and; also; moreover*
∨	Wedge	Disjunction	*or; unless*
⊃	Horseshoe	Conditional	*if ... then ... ; only if*
≡	Triple bar	Biconditional	*if and only if*

We can now use the operators to translate our five examples of compound statements:

1. $\sim D$
2. $H \cdot K$
3. $C \vee G$
4. $I \supset R$
5. $G \equiv U$

A word of caution: Although the logical operators are used to translate the statements, the symbolic translations are not synonymous with the original English expressions. For example, in ordinary language the expressions "and," "or," and "if" are often vague or ambiguous. However, as we shall see, the meaning of the logical operators is precise and unambiguous. For now, we will concentrate on learning how to translate English statements using the logical operators.

Negation

The tilde symbol (~) is used to translate any ordinary language negated proposition. Some of the words and phrases that you might find in ordinary language statements are "not," "it is not the case that," "it is false that," and "it is not true that." For example, the statement "Today is not Monday" is the negation of the simple statement "Today is Monday." The word "not" and the phrase "it is not the case that" are used to deny the statement that follows them, and we refer to their use as **negation**.

> **Negation** The word "not" and the phrase "it is not the case that" are used to deny the statement that follows them, and we refer to their use as negation.

Here are some examples of English statements and their translations:

- The Eiffel Tower is not in London. ~ E
- It is false that gold is currently selling at $1000 an ounce. ~ G
- It is not the case that home foreclosures have peaked. ~ H

As the examples illustrate, the tilde is positioned directly in front of the proposition that it negates.

Conjunction

The dot symbol (·) is used to translate propositions in ordinary language that use any of the following words: "and," "both . . . and . . . ," "but," "still," "moreover," "while," "however," "also," "although," "yet," "nevertheless," and "whereas." A **conjunction** is a compound statement that has two distinct statements (called *conjuncts*) connected by the dot symbol. Here are some examples of English statements and their translations:

> **Conjunction** A compound statement that has two distinct statements (called *conjuncts*) connected by the dot symbol.

- Facebook is selling stock, and Twitter is a global phenomenon. F · T
- Music videos are dying out, and cloud computing is growing. M · C
- Honesty is the best policy, and lying is for scoundrels. H · L

Now consider this statement:

Frank and Ernest teach music.

The statement is a shorthand way of writing "Frank teaches music, and Ernest teaches music." Therefore, it can be easily translated as "F · E."

Disjunction

The wedge symbol (∨) is used to translate ordinary language statements containing the words "or," "otherwise," and the phrase "either . . . or." In addition, the word "unless" sometimes functions like the word "or." For example, the statement "You can't go to the party unless you clean your room," can be rewritten as "Either you clean your room or you can't go to the party."

A **disjunction** is a compound statement that has two distinct statements (called *disjuncts*) connected by the wedge symbol. Here are some examples of English statements and their translations:

1. You can have steak or chicken. *S* v *C*
2. She is either a Pisces or a lawyer. *P* v *L*
3. Paris is the city of lights, or Big Ben is in London. *P* v *B*
4. Unless it rains today, we will go swimming. *R* v *S*

Let's look at the first example. The ordinary language statement "You can have steak or chicken" uses a shortcut, but there are actually two distinct simple statements at work: (A) "You can have steak," and (B) "You can have chicken." Our translation, *S* v *C*, captures the compound nature of the ordinary language statement by using the wedge to form a disjunction.

Similarly, in the second example, the ordinary language statement "She is either a Pisces or a lawyer" uses a shortcut. The two distinct simple statements are: (A) "She is a Pisces," and (B) "She is a lawyer." Our translation captures the compound nature of the ordinary language statement.

In ordinary language, the word "or" has two distinct meanings. Consider these examples:

5. Either July or August has 31 days.
6. Today is Monday or today is Wednesday.

In example 5, it is possible that both July and August have 31 days. This use of "or" has an *inclusive sense* in which *both* disjuncts can be true at the same time. When we use **inclusive disjunction** we assert that *at least one* disjunct is true, and *possibly both* disjuncts are true. Given this, an inclusive disjunction is false when both disjuncts are false, otherwise it is true.

In contrast, in example 6 it is *not* possible that today can be both Monday and Wednesday. When we use **exclusive disjunction** we assert that *at least one* disjunct is true, but *not* both. In other words, we assert that the truth of one *excludes* the truth of the other. Given this, an exclusive disjunction is true when only one of the disjuncts is true; otherwise it is false. This use of "or" has an *exclusive sense* in which *both* disjuncts *cannot* be true at the same time. Here are some more examples to consider:

7. You can have either soup or salad with your meal.
8. You can have either water or soda.

There is a bit of ambiguity in both 7 and 8. However, most people will probably interpret the statements in the exclusive sense of disjunction, meaning you can have one or the other, but not both. Of course, in a real-life situation, you can always ask if you can have both soup and salad or both water and soda. If the answer is "yes," then this is a case of inclusive disjunction. However, if the answer is "no," then this is a case of exclusive disjunction.

In most real-life circumstances, the context reveals which kind of disjunction we are dealing with, if it is not obvious from the statement alone. If there is a possibility of misunderstanding through ambiguity, then it is better to spell out

Disjunction A compound statement that has two distinct statements (called *disjuncts*) connected by the wedge symbol.

Inclusive disjunction When we assert that *at least one* disjunct is true, and *possibly both* disjuncts are true. Given this, an inclusive disjunction is false when both disjuncts are false, otherwise it is true.

Exclusive disjunction When we assert that *at least one* disjunct is true, but *not* both. In other words, we assert that the truth of one *excludes* the truth of the other. Given this, an exclusive disjunction is true when only one of the disjuncts is true, otherwise it is false.

an exclusive disjunction. For example, the statement "You can have spaghetti or fish for dinner, *but not both*" identifies it as an exclusive disjunction. If we let *S* = *You can have spaghetti for dinner*, and *F* = *You can have fish for dinner*, then it can be translated as follows: $(S \lor F) \cdot \sim (S \cdot F)$.

    For the purposes of maintaining uniform translations from English, and throughout the discussion of propositional logic, the use of the wedge will assume the inclusive disjunction sense of "or."

Conditional

Conditional statement
In ordinary language, the word "if" typically precedes the *antecedent* of a conditional, and the statement that follows the word "then," is referred to as the *consequent*.

The horseshoe symbol ($\supset$) is used to translate a **conditional statement**. For example, the ordinary language statement "If you smoke two packs of cigarettes a day, then you have a high risk of getting lung cancer" can be translated as "$S \supset L$." The statement that follows the "if" is the *antecedent*, and the statement that follows the "then" is the *consequent*. Therefore, whatever phrase follows "if" must be placed first in the translation. Here are two examples to illustrate this point:

- If you wash the car, then you can go to the movies. $W \supset M$
- You can go to the movies, if you wash the car. $W \supset M$

The word "if" is a clear indicator word, one that immediately reveals the existence of a conditional statement. There are additional English words and phrases that can indicate a conditional statement. For example, consider this statement: "Whenever it snows, my water pipes freeze." This statement can be translated as "$S \supset F$." Here are more words and phrases that indicate conditionals:

Every time *P*, then *Q*.   Given that *P*, then *Q*.
Each time *P*, then *Q*.   Provided that *P*, then *Q*.
All cases where *P*, then *Q*.   In any case where *P*, then *Q*.
Anytime *P*, then *Q*.   *P* implies *Q*.
In the event of *P*, then *Q*.   On any occurrence of *P*, then *Q*.
On condition that *P*, then *Q*.   For every instance of *P*, then *Q*.

Each of these can be translated as "$P \supset Q$." Learning to recognize conditional statements makes the task of translation easier.

Distinguishing "If" from "Only If"

We already stipulated that "if" precedes the antecedent of a conditional. We can now stipulate that "only if" precedes the consequent of a conditional. Here are some examples:

- You will get the bonus only if you finish by noon. $B \supset F$
  (*B* = *You will get the bonus*, and *F* = *you finish by noon*.)
- Only if she has a 10% down payment will she get a mortgage. $M \supset P$
  (*M* = *she will get a mortgage*, and *P* = *she has a 10% down payment*.)

Here are some more examples to illustrate the many different uses of "if" and "only if":

1. *If* you win the lottery, then you will be contacted by relatives you never knew existed. $L \supset C$
   (*L = you win the lottery*, and *C = you will be contacted by relatives you never knew existed*.)
2. *Only if* you win the lottery, you will be contacted by relatives you never knew existed. $C \supset L$
3. You will be contacted by relatives you never knew existed, *if* you win the lottery. $L \supset C$
4. You will be contacted by relatives you never knew existed, *only if* you win the lottery. $C \supset L$

Sufficient and Necessary Conditions

We can use our understanding of conditional statements to explore two important concepts: *sufficient and necessary conditions*. To begin our discussion, consider this statement:

1: If you live in New Jersey, then you live in the United States. $N \supset U$

Let's look at the relationship between the antecedent and the consequent in the foregoing statement. If it is true that you live in New Jersey, then it is true that you live in the United States. In other words, living in New Jersey is *sufficient* for living in the United States. Of course, if you live in any of the other forty-nine states, then you also live in the United States. A **sufficient condition** occurs whenever one event ensures that another event is realized. In other words, the truth of the antecedent guarantees the truth of the consequent. The principle behind a sufficient condition can be captured by the phrases "is enough for" or "guarantees." Here is another example of a sufficient condition:

2: If my car engine starts, then I have gasoline. $S \supset G$

Of course, we must stipulate that it is a gasoline-powered car. Given this stipulation, if the antecedent is true, then the consequent is true.

Consider the next example:

3: If my dog is a poodle, then today is Monday. $P \supset M$

If the antecedent is true, it would *not* guarantee that the consequent is true. Therefore, this is not an example of a sufficient condition.

In contrast, a **necessary condition** means that one thing is essential, mandatory, or required in order for another thing to be realized. Consider again the statement:

4: If you live in New Jersey, then you live in the United States. $N \supset U$

Sufficient condition
Whenever one event ensures that another event is realized. In other words, the truth of the antecedent guarantees the truth of the consequent.

Necessary condition
Whenever one thing is *essential, mandatory,* or *required* in order for another thing to be realized. In other words, the falsity of the consequent ensures the falsity of the antecedent.

You cannot live in New Jersey unless you live in the United States. Given this, we can say that living in the United States is a *necessary condition* for living in New Jersey. If you *do not* live in the United States, then you *do not* live in New Jersey. This can also be written using the phrase "only if":

> 5: You live in New Jersey *only if* you live in the United States. $N \supset U$

It is important to remember that a necessary condition exists when the falsity of the consequent ensures the falsity of the antecedent.

Here is another example of a necessary condition:

> 6: My car engine starts only if I have gasoline. $S \supset G$

Once again, we stipulate that my car needs gasoline to start and run. Given this, we can see that having gasoline is a necessary condition for my car engine to start. Of course, there are many other things that are necessary for my car engine to start such as a battery, spark plugs, and ignition wires, to name only a few. So, although gasoline is not the only necessary condition for my car engine to start, it is definitely required. This example also illustrates the fact that in many real-life circumstances multiple necessary conditions are required to bring something about. The principle behind a necessary condition can be captured by the words "mandatory," "essential," and the phrase "is required for."

Let's look at one more example:

> 7: If my dog is a poodle, then today is Monday. $P \supset M$

If the consequent is false, then the antecedent might be true or false. Therefore, this is *not* an example of a necessary condition.

Biconditional

Biconditional A compound statement consisting of two conditionals—one indicated by the word "if" and the other indicated by the phrase "only if." The triple bar symbol is used to translate a biconditional statement.

The triple bar symbol (≡) is used to translate a **biconditional** statement. For example, the ordinary language statement "You will get ice cream if and only if you eat your spinach" can be translated as "$S \equiv I$." This compound statement is made up of two conditionals: One is indicated by the word "if" and the other by the phrase "only if." We can reveal the two conditionals as follows:

> If you eat your spinach, then you get ice cream, and you get ice cream only if you eat your spinach.

Notice that this compound statement is a conjunction. However, both components of the conjunction are conditionals. The first component can be translated as "$S \supset I$"; the second component can be translated as "$I \supset S$." The complete translation of this compound statement can now be given:

$$(S \supset I) \cdot (I \supset S)$$

The triple bar reduces the complexity: "$S \equiv I$."

SUMMARY OF OPERATORS AND ORDINARY LANGUAGE	
Operator	**Words and Phrases in Ordinary Language**
~	*not; it is not the case that; it is false that; it is not true that*
·	*and; both . . . and . . . ; but; still; moreover; while; however; also; moreover; although; yet; nevertheless; whereas*
v	*or; unless; otherwise; either . . . or*
⊃	*if; only if; every time; given that; each time; provided that; all cases where; in any case where; any time; supposing that; in the event of; on any occurrence of; on condition that; for every instance of*
≡	*if and only if*

EXERCISES 7A

I. Translate the following statements into symbolic form by using logical operators and uppercase letters to represent the English statements. Specify the meaning of the letters you choose in the symbolizations.

Self-Practice
Questions

1. Either it will rain tomorrow or it will be sunny.

Answer: *R* v *S.* Let *R* = *it will rain tomorrow,* and *S* = *it will be sunny.*

2. The food in that restaurant stinks, and the portions are too small.

3. Your ice is not cold.

4. If my stock portfolio is weak, then I am losing money.

⭐ 5. My car does not look great, but it gets great gas mileage.

6. If you feel great, then you look great.

7. My test score was high or I am mistaken.

8. You passed the exam only if you got at least a C.

⭐ 9. Either candy or tobacco is bad for your teeth.

10. High-paying jobs are rare, and money is scarce.

11. Today is Monday or today is Tuesday.

12. He is not a Fortune 500 CEO.

⭐ 13. Toothpaste is good for your teeth, but tobacco is not.

14. Driving too fast is hazardous to your health; and so is driving without buckling up.

15. Pizza contains all the basic food groups if, and only if, you get it with anchovies.

16. Motorcycle noise is distracting, while music in the background is soothing.

⭐ 17. My room could use a good cleaning, but I am too lazy to do anything about it.

18. You must get a passing grade on the next exam; otherwise you will fail.

19. If Carly agrees to do a job, then she will make sure it is done right.

20. Coral reefs are dying at an alarming rate around the world.

⭐ 21. I will leave a big tip only if the dinner is excellent.

22. Your paper was turned in late; however, I am willing to grant you an extension.

23. Unless you stop eating too much pepperoni, you will develop a stomach ulcer.

24. We will be protected only if we have catastrophic health insurance.

⭐ 25. It is false that Grover Cleveland was the greatest U.S. president.

26. She is happy with her box of candy; however, she would have preferred a new car.

27. Only if my apartment is well insulated is it comfortable in the winter.

28. *Citizen Kane* did not win the Academy Award for Best Picture, but it is still the greatest movie ever made.

⭐ 29. Barbara is going to lose her football bet and Johnny will get a night at the ballet.

30. My father is wise only if he is honest.

31. Either we stand in line for six hours or we go to the movie next week.

32. If I am lazy, then my room is not clean.

⭐ 33. If driving too fast is hazardous to your health, then so is driving without buckling up.

34. My father is wise and he is honest.

35. My stock portfolio is weak only if I am losing money.

36. There are not too many circus acts in Las Vegas.

⭐ 37. Only if my room could use a good cleaning, I am too lazy to do anything about it.

38. Watching paint dry is boring and so is streaming the same movie three times in a row.

39. If my father is wise, then he is honest.

40. My car is fast, if it has a turbocharger.

⭐ 41. If it rains tomorrow, then I will not have to water my plants.

42. Reading is relaxing and thinking is productive.

43. Cats and dogs make great pets.

44. The decathlon is a difficult Olympic event.

⭐ 45. My car is old, but it is still reliable.

46. Only if you are registered can you vote.

47. Either coffee or tea contains caffeine.

48. Today is Monday unless today is Tuesday. M ⌐ T deductive

II. Determine whether a *sufficient condition* exists in the following statements.

1. If Ed is a bachelor, then Ed is an adult male.

Answer: Sufficient condition. A bachelor is defined as being an unmarried adult male. Given this, if the antecedent is true (if Ed is a bachelor), then the consequent will be true as well (Ed is an adult male).

2. If Ed is an adult male, then Ed is a bachelor.

3. If there is oxygen in the room, then there is a fire in the room.

4. If there is a fire in the room, then there is oxygen in the room.

⭐ 5. If this is the month of June, then this month has exactly 30 days.

6. If this month has exactly 30 days, then this is the month of June.

7. If I live in the White House, then I am the president of the United States.

8. If I am the president of the United States, then I live in the White House.

⭐ 9. If I have exactly 100 pennies, then I have at least the equivalent of $1.

10. If I have at least the equivalent of $1, then I have exactly 100 pennies.

11. If I am over 21 years of age, then I am over 10 years of age.

12. If I am over 10 years of age, then I am over 21 years of age.

⭐ 13. If I am eating a banana, then I am eating a fruit.

14. If I am eating a fruit, then I am eating a banana.

15. If I hurt a human, then I hurt a mammal.

16. If I hurt a mammal, then I hurt a human.

III. Determine whether a *necessary condition* exists in the following statements.

1. If Ed is not an adult male, then Ed is not a bachelor.

Answer: Necessary condition. A bachelor is defined as being an unmarried adult male. Given this, if Ed is *not* an adult male, then Ed is *not* a bachelor.

2. If Ed is a not a bachelor, then Ed is not an adult male.

3. If there is not a fire in the room, then there is not oxygen in the room.

4. If there is not oxygen in the room, then there is not a fire in the room.

⭐ 5. If this month does not have exactly 30 days, then this is not the month of June.

6. If this is not the month of June, then this month does not have exactly 30 days.

7. If I am not the president of the United States, then I do not live in the White House.

8. If I do not live in the White House, then I am not the president of the United States.

⭐ 9. If I do not have at least the equivalent of $1, then I do not have exactly 100 pennies.

10. If I do not have exactly 100 pennies, then I do not have at least the equivalent of $1.

11. If I am not over 10 years of age, then I am not over 21 years of age.

12. If I am not over 21 years of age, then I am not over 10 years of age.

⭐ 13. If I am not eating a fruit, then I am not eating a banana.

14. If I am not eating a banana, then I am not eating a fruit.

15. If I do not hurt a mammal, then I do not hurt a human.

16. If I do not hurt a human, then I do not hurt a mammal.

PROFILES IN LOGIC
The Stoics

Stoic thought actually has two founders, Zeno of Citium (340–265 BCE) and Chrysippus of Soli (280–209 BCE), and no matter how you look at it, their influence has outlived them. Most of the writings of the Stoics have not survived. We know of their ideas through fragments that others have pieced together. We know about Chrysippus mostly through his great reputation as a logician. It hardly helps that, at least initially, Stoic logic was not as influential as Aristotle's system.

Unfortunately, that gives us only an incomplete picture, but it is essential to our understanding of the role of logic all the same. The Stoics did the first substantial work on what today is called *propositional logic*. The Stoics made a crucial assertion: Every statement is either true or false. Although they did not create truth tables, they did define conjunction, disjunction, negation, and conditional statements by using the two truth values—true and false. Truth-functional ideas are still essential to our understanding of logic.

The Stoics emphasized the importance of basic principles. They sought general rules that could be applied to specific kinds of arguments. For example, one of their ideas was that we can understand validity through the use of a conditional statement. This idea means that the conjunction of the premises becomes the antecedent, and the conclusion becomes the consequent. If the conditional statement is true, then the argument is valid.

B. COMPOUND STATEMENTS

In the translation of any compound statement, we must make sure to use the logical operator symbols correctly. Just as there are rules of grammar in English, there are grammatical (syntactical) rules for using symbols as well. For example, we immediately recognize that the English sentence "Carly is an excellent costume designer and a gifted pattern-maker" is grammatically correct. We also know that a different arrangement of the same words may violate rules of grammar. For example, "And excellent costume designer is an Carly gifted pattern-maker a."

Well-Formed Formulas

A few simple rules for using operator symbols ensure that the symbolic expressions that we create are grammatically correct. Such symbolic expressions are also called well-formed formulas, or *WFFs*. We define a **well-formed formula** as any grammatically correct symbolic expression. These formulas rely on the notion of **scope**, which is defined as the statement or statements that a logical operator governs.

Rule 1:

The *dot, wedge, horseshoe*, and *triple bar* symbols must go between two statements (either simple or compound).

Applying the rule ensures that "$P \cdot Q$," "$P \vee Q$," "$P \supset Q$," and "$P \equiv Q$" are all *WFFs*, where the four operators go between simple statements. Here are some examples of *WFFs* where the operators go between compound statements:

$$(P \vee Q) \supset \sim R \qquad (S \cdot P) \vee (Q \cdot S)$$

However, "$\cdot P$," "$P \cdot$," "$P Q \vee$," "$\supset P$," and "$P Q \equiv$" are not *WFFs* because in each case one of the four operators listed in the rule is not between two statements. You can use these examples as guides when you encounter other statements.

Rule 2:

The tilde ($\sim$) goes in front of the statement it is meant to negate.

Applying the rule ensures that "$\sim P$" is a *WFF*. Here are some more examples of *WFFs* using the tilde:

$$\sim (P \vee Q) \supset \sim R \qquad (S \cdot P) \vee \sim (\sim Q \cdot S)$$

However, "$P \sim$," "$(P \vee Q) \sim$," and "$\sim (S \cdot P) \sim$" are not *WFFs*.

Rule 3:

The tilde ($\sim$) cannot, *by itself*, go between two statements.

For example, "$P \sim Q$" is not a *WFF*. However, "$P \vee \sim Q$" is a *WFF*.

Rule 4:

Parentheses, brackets, and braces can be used to eliminate ambiguity in a compound statement.

Well-formed formula Any statement letter standing alone, or a compound statement such that an arrangement of operator symbols and statement letters results in a grammatically correct symbolic expression.

Scope The statement or statements that a logical operator governs.

The following three examples show how parentheses, brackets, and braces can be used:

1. Both "$P \vee (Q \cdot R)$" and "$(P \vee Q) \cdot R$" are *WFFs*. However, "$P \vee Q (\cdot R)$" is not a *WFF* because the dot does not have either a simple or compound statement directly to its left. Since the *dot* is not between two statements, Rule 1 is broken.
2. "$[(P \vee Q) \cdot (\sim R \supset S)] \vee Q$" uses both parentheses and brackets. Since no rules are broken, it is a *WFF*.
3. "$\{ [(P \vee \sim Q) \cdot (R \supset S)] \vee \sim P \} \supset \sim (R \cdot M)$" uses parentheses, brackets, and braces. Since no rules are broken, it is a *WFF*.

Alternatively, you can use just parentheses to form WFFs. Let's apply this to examples 2 and 3 above:

2a. "$((P \vee Q) \cdot (\sim R \supset S)) \vee Q$" uses just parentheses. Since no rules are broken, it is a *WFF*.
3a. "$(((P \vee \sim Q) \cdot (R \supset S)) \vee \sim P) \supset \sim (R \cdot M)$" uses just parentheses. Since no rules are broken, it is a *WFF*.

If you use just parentheses, make sure that you have an equal number of "right" and "left" ones.

The rules for *WFFs* can be summarized as follows:

A. Any statement letter standing alone is a *WFF*. (For example, "S" is a *WFF*.)
B. If "S" is a *WFF*, then "$\sim S$" is a *WFF*.
C. If "S" and "P" are *WFFs*, then "$P \cdot S$," "$P \vee S$," "$P \supset S$," and "$P \equiv S$" are all *WFFs*.
D. Nothing else is a *WFF*.
E. Parentheses, brackets, and braces can be used to eliminate ambiguity in a compound statement.

EXERCISES 7B.1

Determine whether the following arrangements of operator symbols and letters are *WFFs*. If any are not *WFFs*, point out the mistake and the rule that is violated. (Some examples may contain more than one mistake.)

1. $P \vee \sim Q$

Answer: This is a *WFF*.

2. $R \sim \vee T$

3. K

4. $K \cdot (P \sim Q)$

⭐ 5. $L \supset \sim P$

6. $L \supset \sim (P \vee \supset Q)$

7. $M (\supset P \supset Q)$

8. $(P \vee Q \supset R)$

⭐ 9. $[(P Q] \vee \sim R$

10. $\sim P (v \sim R) \cdot \sim S$

11. $P \cdot \vee Q$

12. $R \vee T \sim$

⭐ 13. $P Q$

14. $K \cdot (P \vee \sim Q)$

15. $L \sim P$

Main Operator

In order to fine-tune your knowledge of the rules for *WFFs* and to understand how to translate complex statements, we need to discuss the *main operator*. This discussion will also add to your understanding of the necessity of using parentheses, brackets, and braces to eliminate ambiguity. There are three important factors concerning the main operator:

A. The **main operator** is the operator that has the *entire* well-formed formula in its scope.

B. The main operator is either one of the four operators that go between statements or else it is the negation operator.

C. There can be only one main operator in a compound statement.

> **Main operator** The operator that has the *entire* well-formed formula in its scope.

Let's put these stipulations to work by looking at examples of compound statements:

1. $\sim R$
2. $\sim (P \vee Q)$
3. $\sim [(P \vee Q) \cdot (R \cdot S)]$

The main operator for all three examples is the tilde. The only component in example 1 is the simple statement R, and it is in the scope of the tilde. In example 2, the compound statement contained within the parentheses is in the scope of the tilde. In example 3, the compound statement contained within the brackets is in the scope of the tilde.

4. $\sim R \cdot S$
5. $(P \vee Q) \cdot R$
6. $[(P \vee \sim Q) \cdot (R \cdot S)] \cdot \sim (M \supset N)$

The main operator for examples 4–6 is the dot. In example 4, the component $\sim R$ and the component S are both in the scope of the dot. In example 5, the component to the left of the dot and the simple statement to its right are both in the scope of the dot. In example 6, the third dot from the left is the main operator; thus both the component within brackets and the component $\sim (M \supset N)$ are in the scope of the main operator.

7. $R \vee S$
8. $(P \vee Q) \supset \sim R$
9. $\{[(\sim P \vee Q) \cdot (R \cdot S)] \cdot (M \supset N)\} \equiv \sim (P \vee M)$

The main operator for example 7 is the wedge; the two simple statements, R and S are both within its scope. In example 8, the component in parentheses and the component $\sim R$ are both in the scope of the horseshoe; therefore, it is the main operator. In example 9, the component within braces to the left of the triple bar and the component to its right are both within the scope of the triple bar, which is the main operator.

There is one further point to illustrate. As mentioned earlier, there can be only one main operator in a compound statement. To see why this is necessary, consider this example:

$$P \vee Q \cdot R$$

As it stands, the compound statement is ambiguous. This is where Rule 4 comes in handy. To fully understand this, let's suppose that we are discussing the possibility that three people—Paul, Quincy, and Rita—are going to a party. Let *P = Paul will go to the party*, *Q = Quincy will go to the party*, and *R = Rita will go to the party*. If we follow Rule 1, the operators "v" and "·" in "*P* v *Q* · *R*" are *each* supposed to connect two statements (simple or compound). However, without parentheses, the *Q* gets dragged in two directions at once. Therefore, we do not know whether to connect the *Q* to the *P* or to the *R*.

There are two choices we can make: either "*P* v (*Q* · *R*)" or "(*P* v *Q*) · *R*." In either case, the ambiguity has been eliminated by the proper use of parentheses. But which is meant? The parentheses can help to explain why these are *not* identical statements. In the first choice, "*P* v (*Q* · *R*)," the wedge is the main operator. If we replace the letters with the corresponding English statements, we get this:

A. *Either* Paul will go to the party, *or both* Quincy *and* Rita will go to the party.

On the other hand, in the second choice, "(*P* v *Q*) · *R*" the dot is the main operator. If we replace the letters with the corresponding English statements we get this:

B. *Either* Paul *or* Quincy will go to the party, *and* Rita will go to the party.

A comparison of A and B shows that they are not identical statements; they do not express the same proposition.

We will add one more example. When negation is the main operator, the tilde completely governs the compound statement. For example, "~ *K*," "~ (*P* v *Q*)," and "~ [(*K* · ~*L*) ⊃ (~ *P* v *Q*)]," all have the *leftmost* negation symbol as the main operator. Now let's compare the statement "~ (*P* v *Q*)" with the statement "~ *P* v *Q*." We can use the same English substitutions for the letters that we used earlier: Let *P = Paul will go to the party*, and *Q = Quincy will go to the party*. In the first choice, the tilde is the main operator. Since the negation governs everything inside the parentheses, the statement becomes this:

C. *Neither* Paul *nor* Quincy will go to the party.

However, in the second statement the wedge is the main operator. In this case, the tilde negates only the simple statement *P*. The result is the following:

D. *Either* Paul will *not* go to the party, *or* Quincy will go to the party.

Once again we can see how the main operator ranges over the entire compound statement. These examples illustrate why there can be only one main operator in a compound statement. This also shows why we need to reduce the ambiguity in complex statements—and why the rules for *WFFs* can help.

EXERCISES 7B.2

Identify and draw a circle around the main operator in each of the following WFFs.

1. $\sim Q \vee P$

Answer: The wedge is the main operator. $\sim Q \textcircled{\vee} P$

2. $R \cdot (\sim T \vee K)$

3. $\sim K$

4. $(P \cdot \sim Q) \vee K$

⭐ 5. $L \supset \sim P$

6. $(L \supset \sim P) \supset Q$

7. $(M \vee P) \supset (Q \vee R)$

8. $[P \vee (Q \supset R)] \cdot (\sim R \vee S)$

⭐ 9. $(P \cdot Q) \vee \sim R$

10. $\sim [(P \vee \sim R) \cdot \sim S]$

11. $(\sim Q \vee P) \supset R$

12. $[R \cdot (\sim T \vee K)] \vee S$

⭐ 13. $\sim K \supset \sim P$

14. $(P \cdot \sim Q) \vee (K \supset R)$

15. $(L \supset \sim P) \cdot \sim R$

16. $[(L \supset \sim P) \supset Q] \supset \sim S$

⭐ 17. $[(M \vee P) \supset (Q \vee R)] \vee (S \cdot \sim P)$

18. $[P \vee (Q \supset R)] \supset \sim (\sim R \vee S)$

19. $(P \cdot Q) \vee (\sim R \vee S)$

20. $\sim [(P \supset \sim R) \supset (\sim S \vee Q)]$

⭐ 21. $\sim Q \cdot P$

22. $(R \cdot Q) \vee (\sim T \vee K)$

23. P

24. $(P \cdot \sim Q) \cdot K$

⭐ 25. $L \supset (\sim P \supset Q)$

Video Tutorial: 7BII
Exercise #17

Translations and the Main Operator

Whenever we translate sentences from ordinary language we must try our best to use logical operators to reduce or eliminate ambiguity. Translating complex statements from English often requires the correct placement of parentheses. One strategy to apply is to look for the main operator. Once you locate the main operator, then you can apply parentheses as needed to ensure that the components in the statement are within the scope of the main operator. Here is an example:

Either Tracy or Becky owns a DVD player, but Sophie owns one for sure.

In this example the comma helps us to locate the main operator. The word "but" indicates that the main operator is a conjunction. To the left of the comma, the statement "Either Tracy or Becky owns a DVD player" is a disjunction. To the right of the comma is the simple statement "Sophie owns one (DVD player) for sure."

We are now in position to translate the complex statement. If we let *T = Tracy owns a DVD player*, *B = Becky owns a DVD player*, and *S = Sophie owns one (DVD player) for sure*, then we can translate the statement as follows:

$$(T \vee B) \cdot S$$

The parentheses clearly separate the compound statement about Tracy and Becky from the simple statement about Sophie. Once we saw that the main operator was a *conjunction*, we then needed to place the disjunction about Tracy and Becky in parentheses. This ensured that the main operator would be the dot, and it eliminated any potential ambiguity.

The statement "Both Suzuki and Honda are Japanese-owned companies" can be translated without using parentheses, as "$S \cdot H$." Now let's compare this to a slightly different statement:

> Not both Suzuki and Honda are Japanese-owned companies.

This is a more complex statement, and it will require the use of parentheses to translate it accurately. The two statements about Suzuki and Honda are clearly joined by the conjunction word "and." However, notice that the placement of the word "not" is intended to *deny the conjunction*. In other words, since the negation is the main operator in this sentence, we must place parentheses around the conjunction. This results in the following translation:

$$\sim (S \cdot H)$$

If this seems confusing, then consider another similar example. Suppose my neighbor claims that both my cat and my dog have fleas. This can be translated as the conjunction of two simple statements: "$C \cdot D$."

Now I can *negate* my neighbor's claim by saying, "It is not the case that both my cat and my dog have fleas." Here, I am merely claiming that *at least one* of the simple statements is false. When I negate the conjunction, I am *not* necessarily saying that both the simple statements are false. Therefore, my statement gets translated by making sure the negation is the main operator: "$\sim (C \cdot D)$."

Here is another example of a complex ordinary language statement: "Neither Ford nor Chevrolet is a Japanese-owned company." Translating this statement also requires the careful placement of parentheses. One strategy to get started is to recognize that if we eliminate the letter "n" from "*neither . . . nor*" we get "*either . . . or.*" The *n*'s act as a negation device in this sentence. In other words, the statement can be rewritten as follows:

> *It is not the case* that either Ford or Chevrolet is a Japanese-owned company.

The main operator is the negation; therefore we must place parentheses around the disjunction. The translation is this: "$\sim (F \vee C)$."

EXERCISES 7B.3

Self-Practice
Questions

I. Translate the following statements into symbolic form by using logical operators and uppercase letters to represent the English statements.

1. It is not the case that Shane and Carly are hungry.
Answer: $\sim (S \cdot C)$. Let S = *Shane is hungry*, and C = *Carly is hungry*.

The conjunction "Shane and Carly are hungry" contains two simple statements: "Shane is hungry," and "Carly is hungry." However, the main operator is a negation ("It is not the case that"); therefore the tilde must be placed outside the parentheses that contain the conjunction.

2. I am not mistaken and my test score was high, and I am happy about the result.

3. He neither attended a remedial driver's education course nor did he lose his license.

4. Not both Mike and Jane wear braces on their teeth.

⭐ 5. If you can save $100 a month, then if you can afford the insurance, then you can buy a motorcycle.

6. If you exercise for 20 minutes a day and you cut out 1000 calories a day, then you will be in top physical condition in 6 months.

7. It is not the case that if you stop studying, then you will both pass the course and keep your scholarship.

8. We will reinstitute a military draft, only if either we are attacked on our soil or too few people sign up voluntarily.

⭐ 9. If neither Walter nor Sandy can drive to Pittsburgh next weekend, then Jessica will not come home, unless Jennifer is able to arrive on time.

10. It is not the case that smartphones are long-lasting or reliable.

11. If we are not careful and we don't change the oil often enough, then the engine will be ruined.

12. Either he is not allowed to go to the concert or if he finishes work on time, then he can meet us at the coffee shop.

⭐ 13. If your disc player breaks, then I will get you a new one for your birthday, or you can see about getting it fixed.

14. He did not admit to taking the camera, but if he is lying, then either he pawned it for the money or he has it in his apartment.

15. Her painting is valuable, and either she can keep it or sell it for a lot of money.

16. If soccer is the world's most popular sport, then if it catches on in the United States, then football and basketball will lose fans.

⭐ 17. It is not the case that if you will eat a lot of salads, then you will absorb a lot of vitamins, and it is not the case that if you will absorb a lot of vitamins, then you will eat a lot of salads.

18. She is athletic and creative, unless I am mistaken.

19. Johnny and Barbara will visit Las Vegas, only if Mary Lynn and Lee Ann can get a seat on the same flight.

20. Joyce has visited Hawaii, but neither Judy nor Eddie has been there.

⭐ 21. Sally got a promotion, and either Louis asks for a raise or he looks for another job.

22. Either Tommy does not have a snowmobile, or if he has skis, then he has ice skates.

23. Both slot machines and table gaming do not take credit cards.

24. Either the United States or France has a large military presence in Europe given that both Russia and Switzerland are not part of the NATO alliance.

⭐ 25. Mary does not own a motorcycle; however, if she passes the motorcycle driver's test, then either she will buy her own motorcycle or she will use Tom's.

26. If stock prices fall this year, then if unemployment rises this year, then the housing market and manufacturing jobs will suffer dire consequences.

27. It is not the case that both organic whole grain breads and organic vegetables are inexpensive, but both can be used to promote a healthy diet.

28. If the human population rises past eight billion, then our species will require more food, and if other animal species become extinct, then natural resources may become depleted. Moreover, survival may become more difficult and competition for scarce resources may become more violent.

⭐ 29. Prison populations will continue to grow and longer prison sentences will be imposed only if new laws are created and profiling is not stopped; but if punishment is seen as retribution, then punishment cannot work as a deterrence.

30. If cars and factories continue to pollute the air, then either the oceans will rise or climate change will put some life forms in jeopardy; nevertheless, we can protect future generations if, and only if, we implement sound scientific advice and curb global conspicuous consumption.

31. My university has many good instructors and resources, but if I don't take advantage of all the university has to offer, then I will have wasted both my time and my parents' money.

32. If I get a degree and find a good job, then I can save for my retirement if, and only if, the world economy does not have a meltdown and natural disasters do not wreck our infrastructure.

II. Translate the following quotes into symbolic form.

1. If you wish to make an apple pie truly from scratch, you must first invent the universe.

Carl Sagan, quoted in *Seven Wonders of the Universe That You Probably Took for Granted* by C. Renée James and Lee Jamison

Answer: Let *A = you wish to make an apple pie truly from scratch*, and *U = you must first invent the universe*: *A ⊃ U*

2. A house is not a home unless it contains food and fire for the mind as well as the body. *Margaret Fuller, quoted in Roots of Wisdom by Helen Buss Mitchell*

3. Until this moment, Senator, I think I never really gauged your cruelty or your recklessness.
Joseph Welch responding to Sen. Joseph McCarthy during the 1954 Army-McCarthy Hearings.

4. I disapprove of what you say, but I will defend to the death your right to say it.
Voltaire, quoted in The Second Sin by Thomas Stephen Szasz

⭐ 5. But a spirit of harmony will survive in America only if each of us remembers that we share a common destiny.
Barbara Jordan, quoted in Encyclopedia of Women and American Politics by Lynne E. Ford

6. Life shrinks or expands in proportion to one's courage.
Anaïs Nin, quoted in A Divine Ecology by Ian Mills

7. I hear and I forget. I see and I remember. I do and I understand.
Chinese proverb; often attributed to Confucius

8. If one man offers you democracy and another offers you a bag of grain, at what stage of starvation will you prefer the grain to the vote?
Bertrand Russell, The Basic Writings of Bertrand Russell

⭐ 9. I have not failed. I've just found 10,000 ways that won't work.
Thomas A. Edison, quoted in Dictionary of Proverbs by Grenville Kleiser

10. America is not anything if it consists of each of us. It is something only if it consists of all of us. *Woodrow Wilson, in a January 29, 1916, speech*

11. Either he's dead or my watch has stopped.
Groucho Marx, in the movie A Day at the Races

12. It is not from the benevolence of the butcher, the brewer, or the baker that we expect our dinner, but from their regard to their own interest.
Adam Smith, The Wealth of Nations

⭐ 13. If the only tool you have is a hammer, you tend to see every problem as a nail.
Abraham Maslow, quoted at Abraham-maslow.com

14. An insincere and evil friend is more to be feared than a wild beast; a wild beast may wound your body, but an evil friend will wound your mind.
Buddha, quoted in Buddha, Truth and Brotherhood by Dwight Goddard

15. The average man will bristle if you say his father was dishonest, but he will brag a little if he discovers that his great-grandfather was a pirate.
Emil Ahangarzadeh, The Secret at Mahone Bay

16. Knowledge is a great and very useful quality. *Michel de Montaigne, The Essays*

⭐ 17. The bankrupt New York City Off-Track Betting Corporation will close all of its branches in the city's five boroughs and shutter its account-wagering operation at the close of business on Friday unless the company gets some relief.
Matt Hegarty, "New York OTB Faces Friday Closing," Daily Racing Form

18. A bill of rights is what the people are entitled to against every government on earth, general or particular, and what no just government should refuse, or rest on inference.
   Thomas Jefferson, *The Papers of Thomas Jefferson*

19. Fundamentally an organism has conscious mental states if and only if there is something that it is like to *be* that organism—something it is like *for* the organism.
   Thomas Nagel, "What Is It Like to Be a Bat?"

20. Education is not the filling of a pail, but the lighting of a fire.
   William Butler Yeats, quoted in *Handbook of Reflection and Reflective Inquiry* by Nona Lyons

C. TRUTH FUNCTIONS

We know that both simple and compound propositions have truth values. The five logical operators we have introduced are "truth-functional." The truth value of any compound proposition using one or more of the five operators is a function of (that is, uniquely determined by) the truth values of its component propositions. Any such proposition is called a **truth-functional proposition**, or a truth function.

> **Truth-functional proposition** The truth value of any compound proposition using one or more of the five operators is a function of (that is, uniquely determined by) the truth values of its component propositions.

Not all ordinary language compound propositions are truth-functional. For example, the statement "Paul believes that Rhonda loves Richard" is *not* determined by the truth value of its components. The simple component statement "Rhonda loves Richard" could be true or false. But neither of the two possible truth values determines the truth value of the compound statement "Paul believes that Rhonda loves Richard." This follows because Paul might *believe* that Rhonda loves Richard whether or not Rhonda actually loves Richard. Therefore, the truth value of the simple component "Rhonda loves Richard" is not a truth-functional component of the compound statement, and the compound statement "Paul believes that Rhonda loves Richard" is not truth-functional. However, our focus is on truth-functional propositions.

We begin by defining the five logical operators that we met earlier in this chapter. Along the way we will investigate how closely the symbolic expressions that use the five operators match the meaning of ordinary language expressions.

Defining the Five Logical Operators

In the first part of the chapter, we used uppercase letters to stand for simple statements. We were then able to create compound statements by using the five operators. In order to define the logical operators, however, we need to know how to apply them to any statement—and how they determine the statement's truth value. A **statement variable** can stand for any statement, simple or compound. We use lowercase letters such as p, q, r, and s. For example, the statement variable r can stand for any of the following:

> **Statement variable** A statement variable can stand for any statement, simple or compound.

$$S$$
$$\sim P \lor Q$$
$$(R \supset P) \cdot S$$

In propositional logic, a **statement form** is an arrangement of logical operators and statement variables such that a uniform substitution of statements for the variables results in a statement. An **argument form** is an arrangement of logical operators and statement variables such that a uniform substitution of statements for the variables results in an argument. A **substitution instance** of a *statement* occurs when a uniform substitution of statements for the variables results in a statement. A substitution instance of an *argument* occurs when a uniform substitution of statements for the variables results in an argument. For example, we know from earlier that we can substitute the simple statement *S* for the statement variable *r*. We can also substitute the compound statement $(R \vee P) \cdot S$ for the statement variable *r*. In other words, any substitution of statements for statement variables can result in a statement, as long as the substitution is uniform and it is a *WFF*.

The same principle holds for statement forms that have logical operators. For example, the statement form $\sim p$ can have any of the following substitutions:

$$\sim P$$
$$\sim (M \vee N)$$
$$\sim [(R \equiv S) \cdot (P \vee Q)]$$

Each example substitutes a statement, either simple or compound, for the statement variable *p*. Also, each substitution results in a negation because the logical form that we start with, $\sim p$, is a negation.

We can now start defining the five logical operators. Each definition is given by a *truth table*. A **truth table** is an arrangement of truth values for a truth-functional compound proposition. It shows for every possible case how the truth value of the proposition is determined by the truth values of its simple components.

Negation

Negating a statement produces another statement whose truth value is the opposite of that of the first statement. Given this, the truth table definition is easy to construct:

NEGATION

p	$\sim p$
T	F
F	T

The leftmost *p* is the guide for the truth table. It lists the truth values for a statement variable. In this example, *p* stands for any statement that can be either true or false. Therefore, if *p* is true, then its negation, $\sim p$, is false, and if *p* is false, then its negation, $\sim p$, is true.

Here are two examples from ordinary language:

- Kentucky is not called the *Sunshine State*. $\sim K$
- It is not the case that Albany is the capital of New York. $\sim A$

Statement form In propositional logic, an arrangement of logical operators and statement variables such that a uniform substitution of statements for the variables results in a statement.

Argument form Refers to the structure of an argument, not to its content. In propositional logic, an argument form is an arrangement of logical operators and statement variables.

Substitution instance A substitution instance of a *statement* occurs when a uniform substitution of statements for the variables results in a statement. A substitution instance of an *argument* occurs when a uniform substitution of statements for the variables results in an argument.

Truth table An arrangement of truth values for a truth-functional compound proposition that displays for every possible case how the truth value of the proposition is determined by the truth values of its simple components.

The first compound statement is true because the simple statement K (Kentucky is called the *Sunshine State*) is false. Therefore, the negation of K is true. The second compound statement is false because the simple statement A (Albany is the capital of New York) is true. Therefore, the negation of A is false.

Conjunction

The construction of truth tables for the four remaining logical operators will be a little different than for negation, because each of them has two components. For example, the logical form for conjunction, $p \cdot q$, has two statement variables (p and q), each of which can be either true or false (two truth values). This means that the truth table will have to display four lines ($2 \times 2 = 4$):

CONJUNCTION

p	q	$p \cdot q$
T	T	T
T	F	F
F	T	F
F	F	F

An easy way to ensure that you have all the correct arrangements of truth values is to begin with the leftmost guide column (in this case, p) and divide the number of lines in half. Since we calculated that the truth table will have four lines, the first two lines under the p will have T and the last two lines F. For the next column in the guide, q, we alternate one T and one F.

A general rule to follow is this: The leftmost column has the first half of the lines as T and the second half as F. The next column to the right then cuts this in half, again alternating T and F. This continues until the final column to the left of the vertical line has one T and one F alternating with each other. This procedure will be followed when we get to more complex truth tables.

The truth table definition for conjunction (the dot) shows that a conjunction is true when both conjuncts are true; otherwise it is false. Therefore, if either one or both conjuncts are false, then the conjunction is false. A simple rule for conjunction holds for all cases: *For any compound statement containing the dot as the main logical operator to be true, both conjuncts must be true.*

Let's apply this to a simple example using ordinary language:

Today is Monday and it is raining outside.

If we let p = *today is Monday*, and q = *it is raining outside*, then the logical form of the statement is $p \cdot q$. Now, suppose that it is true that today is Monday, and it is also true that it is raining outside. Clearly, the compound statement is true. On the other hand, suppose that it is raining but today is not Monday. In that case, the *compound statement* is false even though one of its components is true. Of course, if both components are false, then the conjunction is false.

Disjunction

The truth table definition for disjunction also has four lines:

DISJUNCTION

p	q	p ∨ q
T	T	T
T	F	T
F	T	T
F	F	F

The truth table definition for disjunction (the wedge) shows that a disjunction is false when both disjuncts are false; otherwise it is true. Therefore, a disjunction is true when one disjunct is true or when both are true. As mentioned earlier in the chapter, this interpretation of the word "or" and the definition of the logical operator uses *inclusive disjunction*. Here are a few examples:

1. Memorial Day is the last Monday of May or Mount Rushmore is in South Dakota.
2. Either June or August has 31 days.
3. Either triangles have four sides or squares have three sides.

In example 1, the compound statement is true because both disjuncts are true. In example 2, the first disjunct is false, but the compound statement is true because the second disjunct is true. In example 3, since both disjuncts are false the compound statement is false.

Conditional

The truth table definition for the conditional also has four lines:

CONDITIONAL

p	q	p ⊃ q
T	T	T
T	F	F
F	T	T
F	F	T

The truth table definition for the conditional (the horseshoe) shows that a conditional is false when the antecedent is true and the consequent is false; otherwise it is true. The first two lines of the truth table seem to fit our normal expectations. For example, suppose a friend is giving you directions to Los Angeles. She tells you the following:

If you drive south on I-15, then you will get to Los Angeles.

Now suppose you drive south on I-15 and you do get to Los Angeles. In this case, since both the antecedent and consequent are true you would say that your friend's statement was true. This corresponds to the first line of the truth table. However, suppose you drive south on I-15 and you do *not* get to Los Angeles. In this case, since the antecedent is true and the consequent is false, you would say that your friend's statement was false. This corresponds to the second line of the truth table. So far the truth table matches our expectations.

Now suppose that you decide not to drive south on I-15. Perhaps you want to avoid highway driving or you just want to use back roads to see more of the countryside. Two outcomes are possible: Either you get to Los Angeles or you don't. The first of these corresponds to the third line of the truth table: false antecedent, true consequent. The second corresponds to the fourth line of the truth table: false antecedent, false consequent. According to the truth table, in both of these cases the conditional statement is true. For many people, this result is not intuitive. Let's try to clear things up.

We can start by reexamining your friend's conditional statement. For convenience, let D = *you drive south on I-15*, and L = *you will get to Los Angeles*. Your friend claims that whenever D is true, L will be true. However, it would be incorrect to assume that her statement makes the additional claim that whenever L is true, then D is true. In other words, your friend did *not* say that the *only way* to get to Los Angeles is to drive south on I-15. Therefore, if you do not drive south on I-15 (the antecedent is false), then in neither case does that make your friend's statement false. And this is just what the truth table shows.

Biconditional

The truth table definition for the biconditional also has four lines:

BICONDITIONAL

p	q	$p \equiv q$
T	T	T
T	F	F
F	T	F
F	F	T

According to the truth table, a biconditional as the main operator is true when both components have the same truth value (either both true or both false); otherwise it is false. This result can be understood if we recall that the triple bar symbol for the biconditional is a shorthand way of writing the conjunction of two conditionals:

$$(p \supset q) \cdot (q \supset p)$$

Let's see what would happen if both p and q are true. First, we need to rely on our knowledge of the truth table for conditionals, and then we need to refer to the truth table for a conjunction. The truth table for conditionals reveals that, in this instance, both conjuncts are true, and therefore the conjunction is true. This result corresponds to the first line of the biconditional truth table.

Next, let's see what would happen if both p and q are false. The truth table for conditionals reveals that in this instance both conjuncts are true, and therefore the conjunction is true. This result corresponds to the fourth line of the biconditional truth table.

What happens when p is true and q is false? The truth table for conditionals reveals that in that case the first conjunct "$p \supset q$" is false. This result, by itself, is sufficient to make the conjunction false. This result corresponds to the second line of the biconditional truth table.

Finally, what happens when p is false and q is true? The truth table for conditionals reveals that the first conjunct "$p \supset q$" is true, but the second conjunct "$q \supset p$" is false. Therefore, the conjunction is false. This result corresponds to the third line of the biconditional truth table.

Our analysis of a biconditional as the conjunction of two conditionals has provided another way to understand the truth table results. It also offered the opportunity to use the truth tables for several logical operators.

EXERCISES 7C.1

Choose the correct answer.

Self-Practice
Questions

1. If "$R \cdot S$" is true, then which of the following is correct?
   (a) R is true.
   (b) R is false.
   (c) R could be true or false.

Answer: (a) R is true. The only way for a conjunction to be true is if both conjuncts are true.

2. If "$R \cdot S$" is false, then which of the following is correct?
   (a) R is true.
   (b) R is false.
   (c) R could be true or false.

3. If "$R \lor S$" is true, then which of the following is correct?
   (a) R is true.
   (b) R is false.
   (c) R could be true or false.

4. If "$R \lor S$" is false, then which of the following is correct?
   (a) R is true.
   (b) R is false.
   (c) R could be true or false.

⭐ 5. If "$\sim R$" is false, then what is R?
   (a) R is true.
   (b) R is false.
   (c) R could be true or false.

6. If "$\sim R$" is true, then what is R?
   (a) R is true.
   (b) R is false.
   (c) R could be true or false.

7. If "$R \vee S$" is true, but R is false, then what is S?
   (a) S is true.
   (b) S is false.
   (c) S could be true or false.

8. If "$R \vee S$" is false, then can one of the disjuncts be true?
   (a) Yes
   (b) No

★ 9. If "$R \vee S$" is true, then can one of the disjuncts be false?
   (a) Yes
   (b) No

10. If "$R \cdot S$" is false, then can both conjuncts be false?
   (a) Yes
   (b) No

11. If "$R \supset S$" is true, then which of the following is correct?
   (a) R is true.
   (b) R is false.
   (c) R could be true or false.

12. If "$R \supset S$" is false, then which of the following is correct?
   (a) R is true.
   (b) R is false.
   (c) R could be true or false.

★ 13. If "$R \supset S$" is true, then which of the following is correct?
   (a) S is true.
   (b) S is false.
   (c) S could be true or false.

14. If "$R \supset S$" is false, then which of the following is correct?
   (a) S is true.
   (b) S is false.
   (c) S could be true or false.

15. If "$R \supset S$" is false, then can R be false?
   (a) Yes
   (b) No

16. If "$R \supset S$" is true, then can S be false?
   (a) Yes
   (b) No

★ 17. If "$R \equiv S$" is true, then which of the following is correct?
   (a) S is true.
   (b) S is false.
   (c) S could be true or false.

18. If "$R \equiv S$" is true, then which of the following is correct?
    (a) R is true.
    (b) R is false.
    (c) R could be true or false.

19. If "$R \equiv S$" is false, then must R be false?
    (a) Yes
    (b) No

20. If "$R \equiv S$" is false, then must S be false?
    (a) Yes
    (b) No

Operator Truth Tables and Ordinary Language

We mentioned that the truth table for the wedge establishes an *inclusive disjunction* interpretation of "or." We also pointed out that instances of *exclusive disjunction* in ordinary language can be accommodated by spelling them out more fully. Also, the conditional truth table has some less intuitive aspects that we worked through. Throughout the book, we have been balancing the practical needs of logic with its purely abstract nature.

In this sense, logic is similar to mathematics. For example, arithmetic has great practical application—everything from simple counting to balancing a checkbook. But we are all aware of the abstract nature of many branches of mathematics. Over time, mathematicians developed highly sophisticated areas of math, many of which took decades to find a useful application. In fact, some still have no practical application. However, mathematical excursions into new realms can be stimulating, just like a visit to a new country.

An introduction to logic touches on basic ideas, much like the principles of arithmetic. This is why we are often able to connect logic to ordinary language. Basic logic cannot capture *all* the nuances of ordinary language. But we would not be able to calculate the subtle changes in velocity of a moving object knowing just basic arithmetic. To do that, we would need some calculus. In the same way, while the truth tables for the five logical operators do capture much of ordinary language, we can expect some exceptions.

Start with conjunction. In many cases, the order of the conjuncts is irrelevant to its meaning. Here are two examples:

Steve is an accountant and he lives in Omaha. $A \cdot O$
Steve lives in Omaha and he is an accountant. $O \cdot A$

Constructing truth tables for these two statements will reveal an important point:

A	O	A · O
T	T	T
T	F	F
F	T	F
F	F	F

O	A	O · A
T	T	T
T	F	F
F	T	F
F	F	F

The column of truth values under the dot for "$A \cdot O$" is identical to the column of truth values for "$O \cdot A$." This means that the two statements are *logically equivalent*. (We will have more to say about *logical equivalence* later in this chapter.) Therefore, we can use either of the conjunctions to capture the meaning of both the ordinary language statements.

Now look at two more examples:

Shirley got her IRS refund this week and bought a new TV. $I \cdot T$
Shirley bought a new TV and got her IRS refund this week. $T \cdot I$

This time, the implied meanings in ordinary language are different. The first statement can be interpreted as implying that Shirley got her IRS refund and *then* used it to buy a new TV. The second statement can be interpreted as implying that the TV purchase and the IRS refund were unconnected events. A truth-functional interpretation, however, obscures that important difference. From the previous example, we now know that "$I \cdot T$" and "$T \cdot I$" are *logically equivalent*. As these examples illustrate, we should not try to force every ordinary language statement into a truth-functional interpretation.

We can now return to the conditional and connect it to more examples from ordinary language. The truth table for the horseshoe operator defines the truth-functional conditional, also referred to as the *material conditional*. As we have seen, its truth value depends on only the truth and falsity of the antecedent and consequent.

Let's extend our discussion to the relationship of *implication*. The English word "implies" has several meanings, many of which can be illustrated by ordinary language "if ... then ..." statements such as the following:

1. If Sam is a bachelor, then Sam is an unmarried male.
2. If you are exposed to sound that exceeds 140 decibels, then you can suffer hearing loss.
3. If all dolphins are mammals, and Flipper is a dolphin, then Flipper is a mammal.

In example 1, the consequent follows from the antecedent by the definition of the term "bachelor." Thus, the implication is definitional. In example 2, the consequent does *not* follow by definition (as it did in example 1); instead, the consequent is said to follow causally from scientific research. Thus, the implication is empirical. In contrast to the first two examples, in example 3, the consequent follows logically from the antecedent.

The three foregoing examples illustrate some of the different kinds of implication relationships found in ordinary language conditional statements. Nevertheless, there is some general meaning that they all share. That common meaning is the basis for the material conditional, and it can be summed up as follows: First, a conditional statement asserts that *if* the antecedent is true, the consequent is also true. Second, a conditional statement does *not* assert that the antecedent *is* true; it asserts only that *if* the antecedent is true, then so is the consequent. Third, a conditional statement does *not* assert that the consequent *is* true; it asserts only that the consequent is true *if* the antecedent is true. Given this, *if* the antecedent of a conditional statement is true but the consequent is false, then the conditional statement is false. And that is what the truth table for conditional statements illustrates.

In ordinary language, however, the truth of a conditional statement may depend on a special kind of *inferential connection* between the antecedent and consequent. Such a statement should not be translated using the horseshoe operator. Take this example:

> If Boston is in Alaska, then Boston is near the Mexican border.

Most people would rightly consider this statement to be false. After all, Alaska is not near the Mexican border. In fact, Boston is in Massachusetts, and it is not near the Mexican border either. However, if we interpret it truth-functionally by using the horseshoe operator, then the statement is true because the antecedent is false.

Here is another example:

> If Alaska is north of Mexico, then Alaska is a U.S. state.

In this example, both the antecedent and the consequent are true. However, most people would judge the statement to be false based on an error in the inferential connection. In other words, the fact that Alaska is north of Mexico does not automatically make it a U.S. state. After all, Canada is north of Mexico, too. However, if we interpret it truth-functionally by using the horseshoe operator, then the statement is true because both the antecedent and the consequent are true. Once again, we should *not* try to force *every* ordinary language statement into a truth-functional interpretation.

Another kind of conditional statement that is common in ordinary language is called a *counterfactual* conditional. Here are some examples:

- If Lady Gaga were married to the president of the United States, then she would be First Lady.
- If the United States had not entered Vietnam in the 1960s and 1970s, then 50,000 of our soldiers would not have died in combat there.
- If my house were made entirely of paper, then it could not burn.

The examples are called *counterfactuals* because their antecedents are typically contrary to the facts. In order to determine their truth value, we need to investigate the inferential nature of the claims. In the first example, we know that the person married to the current president of the United States is traditionally referred to as the First Lady; therefore this counterfactual is true. In the second example, we accept the inference that had the United States not sent any soldiers into Vietnam in the 1960s and 1970s, then no U.S. soldiers would have died in combat there. Therefore, this counterfactual is also true. The third example is false because a house made of paper certainly could burn. In sum, the first two examples are true but the third is false.

As these examples illustrate, the truth value of counterfactual conditionals is not determined by the truth value of the antecedent and the consequent. However, if we interpret them truth-functionally by using the horseshoe operator, then all three are true because all three antecedents are false. Therefore, counterfactuals should not be translated truth-functionally by using the horseshoe operator.

Much of what we have discussed about conditionals can be applied to biconditionals. (Just as the horseshoe is sometimes called a *material conditional*, the triple bar is sometimes referred to as *material equivalence*.) Again, many statements in ordinary language do not fall under a truth-functional interpretation. In those cases, a truth-functional interpretation would not always assign the truth value that we would ordinarily suppose the statement to have. Here are a few examples:

- The Mississippi River is in Brazil if and only if it is the longest river in the world.
- Al Gore won the Nobel Prize for physics if and only if he discovered a new subatomic particle.

These two examples are false in an ordinary language interpretation. In the first example, the Mississippi River is not in Brazil, and it is not the longest river in the world. In the second example, Al Gore did not win the Nobel Prize for physics (he won the Nobel Peace Prize), and he did not discover a new subatomic particle. However, if the two examples are interpreted truth functionally using the triple bar operator, then they both are true, because in each case both components have the same truth value.

We do not want to force every ordinary language statement into a truth-functional interpretation. Nevertheless, when we are confident that such an interpretation is called for, then truth-functional propositions are a powerful tool for understanding many of the statements and arguments we encounter every day.

Propositions with Assigned Truth Values

A shorter truth table is sometimes possible, provided the simple propositions are assigned specific truth values. For example, suppose the compound proposition "$P \vee \sim S$" has the following truth values assigned: Let P be true and S be false. If the truth values were not assigned, then we would have to create a truth table with four lines. However, with the assigned truth values we need use only one line:

P	S	P $\vee \sim$ S
T	F	$\boxed{T}$ T

The main logical operator controls the final determination of the proposition's truth value. The main operator in this example is the wedge, so it is the final step in the truth table. Since S is false, we place a "T" under the tilde column. We are now ready to determine the truth value of the main operator. Both disjuncts are true, so we place a "T" under the wedge. The box is used to indicate the main operator column. A good grasp of the truth tables for the five logical operators makes the determination of the truth value for this proposition quite easy.

Let's try another example. Suppose the compound proposition "$R \supset (S \cdot P)$" has the following truth values assigned to the simple propositions: Let R be true, S be false, and P be true. Since there are three simple propositions, a full truth table would require eight lines. But given the assigned truth values we need to consider only one line:

$$
\begin{array}{ccc|c}
R & S & P & R \supset (S \cdot P) \\
\hline
T & F & T & \boxed{F} \quad F
\end{array}
$$

The main operator in this example is the horseshoe, so it is the final step in the truth table. Since S is false, we place an "F" under the dot column because at least one of the conjuncts in "$S \cdot P$" is false. We are now ready to determine the truth value of the main operator. The antecedent (R) is true and the consequent $(S \cdot P)$ is false, so we place an "F" under the horseshoe. Once again, the box indicates that this is the main operator column.

These examples illustrate the importance of having a good understanding of the truth tables for the five logical operators.

Now let's see what happens when truth values are *not* assigned to every simple proposition. For example, suppose the compound proposition "$P \cdot Q$" has P assigned as false, but the truth value for Q is unassigned (meaning it could be true or false). Here is the resulting truth table:

$$
\begin{array}{cc|c}
P & Q & P \cdot Q \\
\hline
F & ? & \boxed{F}
\end{array}
$$

We are able to determine that the proposition is false because one of the conjuncts is false. Therefore, in this example the truth value of Q does not matter. Of course, this will not always be the case. For example, what if P were true but the truth value for Q remained unassigned? Here is what we would get:

$$
\begin{array}{cc|c}
P & Q & P \cdot Q \\
\hline
T & ? & ?
\end{array}
$$

One of the conjuncts is true, but the other could be true or false. If Q were true, then the proposition is true. On the other hand, if Q were false, then the proposition is false. Therefore, the truth value of the proposition cannot be determined in this case. The reasoning behind this procedure also underlies the indirect truth table technique, which we will introduce at the end of the chapter.

EXERCISES 7C.2

I. For the following, let *P* be true, *Q* be false, *R* be true, and *S* be false. Determine the truth value of the compound propositions.

1. $P \cdot \sim Q$

Answer:

$$\begin{array}{cc|c} P & Q & P \cdot \sim Q \\ \hline T & F & \boxed{T}\,T \end{array}$$

2. $Q \cdot \sim S$

3. $P \supset Q$

4. $S \vee \sim Q$

⭐ 5. $Q \equiv S$

6. $(Q \vee R) \cdot S$

7. $S \vee (\sim Q \cdot P)$

8. $P \vee (S \vee R)$

⭐ 9. $(Q \supset R) \cdot S$

10. $P \equiv (S \vee R)$

11. $\sim P \vee (\sim S \vee \sim R)$

12. $\sim P \supset (\sim S \supset \sim R)$

⭐ 13. $(R \cdot \sim S) \cdot P$

14. $(R \cdot \sim S) \supset P$

15. $\sim (Q \cdot R) \cdot \sim (S \cdot P)$

16. $(Q \vee R) \cdot (S \vee P)$

⭐ 17. $[\,P \vee (Q \cdot R)\,] \vee \sim S$

18. $[\,P \cdot (Q \cdot R)\,] \equiv \sim S$

19. $\sim [\,P \vee (Q \vee R)\,] \vee \sim (S \vee P)$

20. $\sim [\,P \supset (Q \cdot R)\,] \vee \sim (S \equiv P)$

Video Tutorial 7C2.II
Exercise #17

II. For the following, let *P* be true, *Q* be true, *R* be false, and *S* is unassigned. Determine the truth value of the compound propositions. If the truth value cannot be determined, then explain why.

1. $P \supset \sim Q$

Answer:

$$\begin{array}{cc|c} P & Q & P \supset \sim Q \\ \hline T & T & \boxed{F}\,F \end{array}$$

2. $Q \cdot \sim S$

3. $P \supset Q$

4. $S \vee \sim Q$

⭐ 5. $Q \equiv S$

6. $(Q \vee R) \cdot S$

7. $S \vee (\sim Q \cdot P)$

8. $P \vee (S \vee R)$

⭐ 9. $(Q \supset R) \cdot S$

10. $P \equiv (S \vee R)$

11. $\sim P \vee (\sim S \vee \sim R)$

12. $\sim P \supset (\sim S \supset \sim R)$

⭐ 13. $(R \cdot \sim S) \cdot P$

14. $(R \cdot \sim S) \supset P$

15. $\sim (Q \cdot R) \cdot \sim (S \cdot P)$

16. $(Q \vee R) \cdot (S \vee P)$

⭐ 17. $[\,P \vee (Q \cdot R)\,] \vee \sim S$

18. $[\,P \cdot (Q \cdot R)\,] \equiv \sim S$

19. $\sim [\,P \vee (Q \vee R)\,] \vee \sim (S \vee P)$

20. $\sim [\,P \supset (Q \cdot R)\,] \vee \sim (S \equiv P)$

D. TRUTH TABLES FOR PROPOSITIONS

Truth tables for compound statements and arguments must have a uniform method for displaying work and results. We can start by discussing the following compound proposition:

$$\sim (P \cdot Q) \lor Q$$

Here there are two different simple propositions (P and Q), each of which can be either true or false (two truth values). As we saw earlier, the truth table will have to display four lines ($2 \times 2 = 4$). We first have to fill in those lines for each simple proposition. To complete the truth table, we then need to identify the main operator and a step-by-step method. As we will see in this section, that means identifying what we call the *order of operations*.

Arranging the Truth Values

There is a simple formula to follow to calculate the number of lines for any given proposition: $L = 2^n$. In the formula, L stands for the number of lines in a truth table, 2 represents the number of truth values (true and false), and n stands for the number of different simple propositions in the statement. Therefore, a proposition with three different simple propositions would be $L = 2^3$. Written out, this would be $2 \times 2 \times 2 = 8$ lines. A proposition with four different simple propositions would be $L = 2^4$ or $2 \times 2 \times 2 \times 2 = 16$ lines. By using the formula we can construct the following table:

The Number of Different Simple Propositions	The Number of Lines in the Truth Table
1	2
2	4
3	8
4	16
5	32
6	64

We also discussed how to ensure that you have all the correct arrangements of truth values. You begin with the leftmost column and divide the number of lines in half. Since we have a truth table with four lines, the first two lines under the P will contain T and the last two lines will contain F. The next column, Q, will then alternate one T and one F. More generally, the leftmost column has the first half of the lines designated as T and the second half as F. The next column to the right then cuts this in half, again alternating T's and F's. This continues until the final column before the vertical bar has one T and one F alternating with each other:

P	Q	$\sim (P \cdot Q) \lor Q$
T	T	
T	F	
F	T	
F	F	

The Order of Operations

Order of operations
The order of handling the logical operators within a proposition; it is a step-by-step method of generating a complete truth table.

At this point, we need to know the **order of operations**—the order of handling the logical operators within the proposition. The order of operations is a step-by-step method of generating a complete truth table. *Since the main logical operator controls the final determination of the proposition's truth value, it will be the last step.* The main operator in this example is the wedge. Also, we must determine the truth value of whatever is contained within the parentheses before we can deal with the tilde. Therefore, the *order of operations* for this example is the following: *dot, tilde, wedge*. Let's work through the order of operations in practice.

First, we determine the truth values for each line under the dot:

P	Q	~ (P · Q) ∨ Q
T	T	T
T	F	F
F	T	F
F	F	F

PROFILES IN LOGIC
Early Programmers

The first electronic digital computer, ENIAC (Electronic Numerical Integrator and Computer), was developed during World War II in order to compute "firing tables" for calculating the speed and trajectory of field artillery. Six women were hired to do the programming: Frances Bilas, Betty Jean Jennings, Ruth Lictermann, Kathleen McNulty, Elizabeth Snyder, and Marlyn Wescoff. Their task was to get the computer to model all possible trajectories, which required solving complex equations (called *differential equations*). The team had to create their own programming manuals because none existed.

It soon became apparent that they had to alter the huge computer itself in order to match the program with the machine. Using today's language, they had to create software and hardware at the same time. They had to arrange the computer's complex wires, circuits, cable connections, and vacuum tubes to coordinate the physical steps in the solution with the sequence of equations. Programming ENIAC required understanding both the physical state of the computer *and* logical thinking. As Betty Jennings remarked, it was "a physicalization of *if-then* statements." In fact, the logical operators (negation, conjunction, disjunction, conditional, and biconditional) formed an integral part of programming language. Programmers realized that the truth tables for the logical operators provided a simple but rigorous application for computability, namely the transference of "true" and "false" to "1" and "0" or to "on" and "off" switches. Programs that use these applications follow a flow chart whose path depends on a choice between two possible outcomes in order to move to the next step.

Mathematicians, physicists, and other scientists quickly sought out the ENIAC programmers to help with long-standing problems. Computers have handled problems that it would take many lifetimes to solve without them ever since.

The completed column displays the truth values of the compound proposition "$P \cdot Q$." The next step is the tilde:

P	Q	~	(P · Q)	v	Q
T	T	F	T		
T	F	T	F		
F	T	T	F		
F	F	T	F		

The final step is the wedge:

Main operator
↓

P	Q	~(P · Q)	v	Q
T	T	F T		T
T	F	T F		T
F	T	T F		T
F	F	T F		T

The box indicates that the main operator represents the entire compound proposition. If this proposition were part of an argument (either a premise or a conclusion), then the results of this truth table would help us decide the argument's validity.

Let's work through a longer truth table. The compound proposition "$R \supset (S \vee \sim P)$" has three different simple propositions. Therefore, we calculate that our truth table will have $L = 2^3$ or 8 lines. We must also make sure that the leftmost column has the first half of the lines designated as T and the second half as F. In this example, the first four lines are T and the next four are F. The next column to the right then cuts this in half, again alternating T's and F's, and the third column will then have one T and one F alternating with each other:

R	S	P	R ⊃ (S v ~ P)
T	T	T	
T	T	F	
T	F	T	
T	F	F	
F	T	T	
F	T	F	
F	F	T	
F	F	F	

The next step is to identify the main operator and determine the order of operations. The main operator in this example is the horseshoe, and the order of operations for this example is the following: *tilde, wedge, horseshoe*.

First, we determine the truth values for each line under the tilde:

R	S	P	R ⊃ (S v ~ P)
T	T	T	F
T	T	F	T
T	F	T	F
T	F	F	T
F	T	T	F
F	T	F	T
F	F	T	F
F	F	F	T

The next step is the wedge:

R	S	P	R ⊃ (S v ~ P)
T	T	T	T F
T	T	F	T T
T	F	T	F F
T	F	F	T T
F	T	T	T F
F	T	F	T T
F	F	T	F F
F	F	F	T T

The final step is the horseshoe:

R	S	P	R	⊃ (S v ~ P)
T	T	T	T	T F
T	T	F	T	T T
T	F	T	F	F F
T	F	F	T	T T
F	T	T	T	T F
F	T	F	T	T T
F	F	T	T	F F
F	F	F	T	T T

Constructing truth tables for compound propositions requires a step-by-step approach. It is best to be methodical and not try to do more than one thing at a time. First, calculate the number of lines needed. Second, place the T's and F's under the columns for all the simple propositions in the guide. Third, identify the main operator and the order of operations. Fourth, apply your knowledge of the five operators to fill in the truth values. In the final step, fill in the truth values for the main operator.

Lightboard Video

EXERCISES 7D

Create truth tables for the following compound propositions.

Self-Practice
Questions

1. $P \cdot \sim Q$

Answer:

P	Q	$P \cdot \sim Q$	
T	T	F	F
T	F	T	T
F	T	F	F
F	F	F	T

2. $\sim R \cdot \sim S$

3. $P \supset Q$

4. $S \supset \sim Q$

⭐ 5. $(R \cdot S) \vee Q$

6. $\sim P \vee (\sim S \vee \sim R)$

7. $(R \equiv \sim S) \supset P$

8. $(Q \supset R) \cdot S$

⭐ 9. $\sim (Q \cdot R) \supset P$

10. $P \vee (S \supset R)$

11. $S \cdot (\sim Q \supset R)$

12. $(Q \supset R) \cdot R$

⭐ 13. $P \equiv (\sim S \vee \sim R)$

14. $\sim P \cdot (S \vee R)$

15. $\sim [(Q \cdot R) \cdot \sim (S \vee R)]$

16. $(R \cdot \sim S) \cdot P$

⭐ 17. $\sim [P \supset (Q \vee R)]$

18. $(Q \cdot R) \equiv (Q \vee \sim S)$

19. $[P \vee (Q \cdot R)] \supset S$

20. $\sim [P \vee (Q \vee R)] \vee \sim (S \vee P)$

⭐ 21. $P \supset \sim Q$

22. $Q \cdot \sim S$

23. $P \supset \sim Q$

24. $S \vee \sim Q$

⭐ 25. $Q \equiv S$

26. $(Q \vee R) \cdot S$

27. $S \vee (\sim Q \cdot P)$

28. $P \vee (S \vee R)$

⭐ 29. $(Q \supset R) \cdot \sim S$

30. $P \equiv (S \vee R)$

31. $\sim P \vee (\sim S \vee \sim R)$

32. $\sim P \supset (\sim S \supset \sim R)$

Video Tutorial: 7D
Exercise #9

⭐ 33. $(R \cdot \sim S) \vee P$

34. $(R \cdot \sim S) \supset P$

35. $\sim (Q \cdot R) \cdot \sim (S \cdot P)$

36. $(Q \vee R) \cdot (S \vee P)$

37. $[P \vee (Q \cdot R)] \vee \sim S$

38. $[P \cdot (Q \cdot R)] \equiv \sim S$

39. $\sim [P \vee (Q \vee R)] \vee \sim (S \vee P)$

40. $\sim [P \supset (Q \cdot R)] \vee \sim (S \equiv P)$

E. CONTINGENT AND NONCONTINGENT STATEMENTS

Contingent statements Statements that are neither necessarily true nor necessarily false (they are sometimes true, sometimes false).

Most of the examples of compound statements that we have looked at so far are **contingent statements**: statements that are neither necessarily true nor necessarily false. A truth table for a contingent statement has both true and false results in the main operator column. A simple example is the proposition "$P \vee Q$":

P	Q	P ∨ Q
T	T	T
T	F	T
F	T	T
F	F	F

The truth value for this proposition is *contingent* on (it depends on) the truth values of the component parts. The truth table for any contingent proposition contains both true and false results in the main operator column. However, there are some propositions that are *noncontingent*. In **noncontingent statements**, the truth values in the main operator column *do not* depend on the truth values of the component parts. We will look at two kinds of noncontingent statements: *tautologies* and *self-contradictions*.

Noncontingent statements Statements such that the truth values in the main operator column do not depend on the truth values of the component parts.

Tautology

Consider the following statement: "Horses are carnivorous or horses are not carnivorous." Since this is a disjunction, we know that if one of the disjuncts is true, then the entire statement is true. Therefore, if the first disjunct is true, the second disjunct must be false because it is the negation of the first. But since one of the disjuncts remains true, the disjunction as a whole is true. The only other possibility is that the first disjunct is false. This makes the second disjunct true because it is the negation of the first. Therefore, once again the whole disjunction is true. Since there are no other possibilities, we have shown that the proposition is necessarily true.

This result follows from the logical form of the proposition. If we let *p = horses are carnivorous*, and *~ p = horses are not carnivorous*, then the logical form is "*p* ∨ *~ p*." Here is the truth table:

p	*p* ∨ *~ p*	
T	T	F
F	T	T

The truth table shows that the main operator is true whether *p* is true or false. This type of statement is called a **tautology**—a statement that is necessarily true. Although tautologies are logically true, they are not very useful for conveying information in everyday life. For example, suppose you ask your friend whether she will meet you for dinner tonight and she responds, "Either I will be there or I will not." Her answer is indeed true; in fact, it is necessarily true. However, has she given you any information? Did you learn anything from her response that you did not already know? Tautologies, although necessarily true, are sometimes referred to as "empty truths."

Tautology A statement that is necessarily true.

This is one reason why scientific hypotheses should not be tautologies: They would offer no real information about the world, and they would teach us nothing. A scientific hypothesis that turned out to be a tautology would be obviously true, but trivial. Scientific hypotheses should be statements that could turn out to be either true or false, because only then will we learn something about world.

Self-Contradiction

Another type of noncontingent statement can be illustrated by the following example: "The number 2 is an even number and the number 2 is not an even number." This statement, which is necessarily false, is a **self-contradiction**. We can see this by applying what we have learned about conjunction. If the first conjunct, "The number 2 is an even number," is true, then its negation, the second conjunct, is false. Therefore, the conjunction is false. The only other possibility is that the first conjunct is false. In this case, the second conjunct is true. However, once again the conjunction is false.

Self-contradiction A statement that is necessarily false.

This result follows from the logical form of the proposition. If we let *p = the number 2 is an even number*, and *~ p = the number 2 is not an even number*, then the logical form is "*p · ~ p*." Here is the truth table:

p	*p · ~ p*	
T	F	F
F	F	T

The truth table shows that the main operator is false whether *p* is true or false. This result illustrates the importance of avoiding self-contradictions when we speak or write. If we contradict ourselves, we are saying something that is necessarily false.

EXERCISES 7E

Create truth tables to determine whether each of the following statements is contingent, a tautology, or a self-contradiction.

1. $P \vee (Q \cdot \sim Q)$

Answer: Contingent. The truth table reveals that the main operator has both true and false results.

P Q	P v (Q · ~ Q)
T T	T F F
T F	T F T
F T	F F F
F F	F F T

2. $P \cdot (Q \vee \sim Q)$

3. $P \vee P$

4. $P \cdot P$

★ 5. $(P \vee \sim P) \vee Q$

6. $(P \vee \sim P) \cdot Q$

7. $(R \cdot \sim R) \vee S$

8. $(R \cdot \sim R) \cdot S$

★ 9. $\sim (R \cdot \sim R) \vee \sim (S \vee \sim S)$

10. $\sim (R \vee \sim R) \cdot \sim (S \cdot \sim S)$

11. $P \supset (Q \cdot \sim Q)$

12. $P \cdot (Q \supset \sim Q)$

★ 13. $P \supset P$

14. $\sim P \supset \sim P$

15. $(P \vee \sim P) \supset P$

16. $(P \cdot \sim P) \supset P$

★ 17. $(R \cdot \sim R) \supset (S \vee \sim S)$

18. $(R \vee \sim R) \supset (S \vee \sim S)$

19. $\sim (R \cdot \sim R) \supset \sim (S \cdot \sim S)$

20. $\sim (R \vee \sim R) \supset \sim (S \vee \sim S)$

F. LOGICAL EQUIVALENCE AND CONTRADICTORY, CONSISTENT, AND INCONSISTENT STATEMENTS

In this section, we will compare two or more statements in order to determine whether they are *logically equivalent* with each other, whether they *contradict* each other, whether they are *consistent* with one another, or whether they are *inconsistent*.

Logical Equivalence

Logically equivalent statements Two truth-functional statements that have identical truth tables under the main operator.

To begin our discussion, two truth-functional statements may appear different but have identical columns under the main operator. When this occurs, they are called **logically equivalent statements**. In order to compare two statements, either simple or compound, identical truth values must be plugged in on each line of the respective truth tables. This is done by placing the two statements next to each other so they can share the same guide. The final truth value of each statement is either directly under a simple statement or under the main operator of a compound statement. Once this is completed, we compare the truth tables by looking at the truth values under the main operators.

Let's compare the following: (1) $P \supset Q$; (2) $P \vee Q$.

P	Q	$P \supset Q$	$P \vee Q$
T	T	T	T
T	F	F	T
F	T	T	T
F	F	T	F

Comparing the final results for the main operators reveals that the second and fourth lines are different. Therefore, these are not logically equivalent statements.

Now let's compare two other statements: (1) $\sim (S \cdot H)$; (2) $\sim S \vee \sim H$.

S	H	$\sim (S \cdot H)$		$\sim S \vee \sim H$		
T	T	F	T	F	F	F
T	F	T	F	F	T	T
F	T	T	F	T	T	F
F	F	T	F	T	T	T

The final result for the main operators shows that they are identical; therefore, these are logically equivalent statements.

You might recall the discussion at the end of Section 7B regarding how best to translate the statement "Not both Suzuki and Honda are Japanese-owned companies." The statement was translated as "$\sim (S \cdot H)$" because the word "not" was used to deny the conjunction. The results of the foregoing two truth tables show that "$\sim (S \cdot H)$" and "$\sim S \vee \sim H$" are logically equivalent.

We also looked at the English sentence "Neither Ford nor Chevrolet is a Japanese-owned company" at the end of Section 7B. We saw that the statement can be translated as "$\sim (F \vee C)$." A disjunction is false only when both disjuncts are false. Therefore, a denial of a disjunction is the same as when both disjuncts are denied at the same time. This means that "$\sim (F \vee C)$" and "$\sim F \cdot \sim C$" should be logically equivalent.

We can verify this by creating the appropriate truth tables:

F	C	$\sim (F \vee C)$		$\sim F \cdot \sim C$		
T	T	F	T	F	F	F
T	F	F	T	F	F	T
F	T	F	T	T	F	F
F	F	T	F	T	T	T

Comparing the results for the two main operators shows that they are identical and, therefore, the statements are logically equivalent.

EXERCISES 7F.1

Use truth tables to determine whether any of the pairs of statements are logically equivalent.

1. $\sim (P \cdot Q) \mid \sim P \vee \sim Q$

Answer: Logically equivalent. The truth tables have identical results for the main operators.

P	Q	$\sim (P \cdot Q)$		$\sim P \vee \sim Q$		
T	T	F	T	F	F	F
T	F	T	F	F	T	T
F	T	T	F	T	T	F
F	F	T	F	T	T	T

2. $\sim (P \vee Q) \mid \sim P \cdot \sim Q$

3. $P \vee Q \mid Q \vee P$

4. $P \cdot Q \mid Q \cdot P$

⭐ 5. $P \vee (Q \vee R) \mid (P \vee Q) \vee R$

6. $P \cdot (Q \cdot R) \mid (P \cdot Q) \cdot R$

7. $P \cdot (Q \vee R) \mid (P \cdot Q) \vee (P \cdot R)$

8. $P \vee (Q \cdot R) \mid (P \vee Q) \cdot (P \vee R)$

⭐ 9. $P \mid \sim \sim P$

10. $P \supset Q \mid \sim Q \supset \sim P$

11. $P \supset Q \mid \sim P \vee Q$

12. $P \equiv Q \mid (P \supset Q) \cdot (Q \supset P)$

⭐ 13. $P \equiv Q \mid (P \cdot Q) \vee (\sim P \cdot \sim Q)$

14. $(P \cdot Q) \supset R \mid P \supset (Q \supset R)$

15. $P \mid P \vee P$

16. $P \mid P \cdot P$

⭐ 17. $\sim (P \cdot Q) \mid \sim P \cdot \sim Q$

18. $\sim (P \vee Q) \mid \sim P \vee \sim Q$

19. $(P \cdot Q) \supset R \mid P \vee (Q \supset R)$

20. $(P \cdot Q) \supset R \mid P \supset (Q \cdot R)$

⭐ 21. $P \equiv Q \mid (P \supset Q) \vee (Q \supset P)$

22. $P \equiv Q \mid (P \cdot Q) \cdot (\sim P \cdot \sim Q)$

23. $P \supset Q \mid \sim P \cdot Q$

24. $P \supset Q \mid Q \supset P$

⭐ 25. $P \supset Q \mid \sim Q \vee P$

Contradictory, Consistent, and Inconsistent Statements

Logically equivalent statements have identical truth tables. In contrast, two statements that have opposite truth values under the main operator on every line of their respective truth tables are **contradictory statements**. Consider this pair of statements: (1) "Lincoln was the sixteenth president," and (2) "Lincoln was not the sixteenth president." Translating this pair of statements we get: (1) "*L*," and (2) "~ *L*." Let's compare the truth tables:

Contradictory statements Two statements that have opposite truth values under the main operator on every line of their respective truth tables.

L	L	~L
T	T	F
F	F	T

The results reveal that the two statements have opposite truth values on every line of their respective truth tables; therefore, they are contradictory statements.

"Today is not Friday or tomorrow is Saturday," and "Today is Friday and tomorrow is not Saturday." Are these two compound statements contradictory? To answer this question, the compound statements can be translated. The first is "$\sim F \lor S$," and the second is "$F \cdot \sim S$." We can now complete the truth tables:

F	S	$\sim F \lor S$		$F \cdot \sim S$	
T	T	F	T	F	F
T	F	F	F	T	T
F	T	T	T	F	F
F	F	T	T	F	T

The results reveal that the two compound statements have opposite truth values under the main operator on every line of their respective truth tables; therefore, they are indeed contradictory statements.

Consistent statements have at least one line on their respective truth tables where the main operators are true. For example, suppose that someone claims that "Robert is over 30 years of age," while another person claims that "Robert is over 40 years of age." According to the definition for consistent statements, are these two statements consistent? Can both statements be true at the same time? If Robert is 42 years old, then both statements are true; therefore, they are consistent.

Here is another pair for analysis: (1) $R \lor B$; (2) $R \lor \sim B$. Truth tables reveal the following:

R	B	$R \lor B$	$R \lor \sim B$	
T	T	T	T	F
T	F	T	T	T
F	T	T	F	F
F	F	F	T	T

The truth table comparison shows that the main operators are both *true* for line 1 and line 2. Statements are consistent if there is at least one line on their respective truth tables where both the main operators are true; therefore, these two statements are consistent.

Finally, **inconsistent statements** do not have even one line on their respective truth tables where the main operators are true. (However, inconsistent statements can be false at the same time.) In other words, for two statements to be inconsistent, both statements cannot be true at the same time (but they can both be false). For example, suppose that someone claims that "Frances is over 30 years of age," while another person claims that "Frances is under 20 years of age." Are these two statements inconsistent? If Frances is 42 years old, then the first statement is true and the second is false. On the other hand, if Frances is 19 years old, then the second statement is true and the first is false.

Consistent statements Two (or more) statements that have at least one line on their respective truth tables where the main operators are true.

Inconsistent statements Two (or more) statements that do not have even one line on their respective truth tables where the main operators are true (but they can be false) at the same time.

It might seem that the two statements are contradictory, but that is not the case. To show this, all we need to do is imagine that Frances is 25 years old. In that case, both statements are false; therefore, they cannot be contradictory. The analysis shows that they are inconsistent.

Here is another pair of statements for comparison: (1) "My car ran out of gas and I do not have money," and (2) "My car ran out of gas if and only if I have money." Translating them, we get: (1) $C \cdot \sim M$, and (2) $C \equiv M$. Here are the truth tables:

C	M	C · ~ M		C ≡ M
T	T	F	F	T
T	F	T	T	F
F	T	F	F	F
F	F	F	T	T

This is a set of inconsistent statements because there is no line where the main operators are both true. (Since both statements are false on line 3, they are not contradictory statements.)

Let's work through a longer problem this time. Are the following three statements consistent?

$$P \supset \sim Q$$

$$R \vee Q$$

$$\sim R$$

Here is a completed truth table that displays the three statements side by side:

P	Q	R	P ⊃ ~ Q		R ∨ Q	~ R
T	T	T	F	F	T	F
T	T	F	F	F	T	T
T	F	T	T	T	T	F
T	F	F	T	T	F	T
F	T	T	T	F	T	F
F	T	F	T	F	T	T
F	F	T	T	T	T	F
F	F	F	T	T	F	T

The truth table analysis reveals that in line 6 the main operators are all true. Statements are consistent if there is at least one line on their respective truth tables where the main operators are all true; therefore, the three statements are consistent.

The question of whether or not a set of statements is consistent has practical applications. For example, in a trial the consistency of a witness's statements is crucial. If under cross-examination a witness contradicts himself, then his testimony is inconsistent. Therefore, not all of the witness's statements are true—*at least one* must be false. In more everyday settings the same issue holds true. We expect consistency in the statements made by our relatives, friends, and coworkers. Inconsistency can strain any relationship.

EXERCISES 7F.2

I. Use truth tables to determine whether the following pairs of statements are contradictory, consistent, or inconsistent.

1. $A \vee B \mid {\sim} A \vee B$

Answer: Consistent

A	B	A ∨ B	~A ∨ B
T	T	T	F T
T	F	T	F F
F	T	T	T T
F	F	F	T T

The truth table comparison reveals that in line 1 and line 3 the main operators are both true. Statements are consistent if there is at least one line on their respective truth tables where the main operators are both true; therefore, the two statements are consistent.

2. ${\sim} A \cdot B \mid {\sim} B \vee A$

3. $M \cdot {\sim} M \mid M$

4. $P \supset Q \mid P \cdot {\sim} Q$

5. $T \equiv U \mid T \cdot U$

6. $P \vee Q \mid {\sim} (P \vee Q)$

7. $(Q \supset {\sim} R) \cdot S \mid S \equiv (Q \cdot R)$

8. $Q \vee P \mid {\sim} Q \supset {\sim} P$

9. $C \cdot D \mid {\sim} C \vee {\sim} D$

10. $Q \supset P \mid Q \cdot P$

11. $A \vee B \mid {\sim} A \vee {\sim} B$

12. ${\sim} A \cdot B \mid {\sim} B \cdot A$

13. $M \vee {\sim} M \mid M$

14. $P \supset Q \mid Q \supset P$

15. $T \equiv U \mid T \vee U$

16. $P \vee Q \mid {\sim} (P \cdot Q)$

17. $(Q \supset {\sim} R) \supset S \mid S \equiv (Q \cdot R)$

18. $Q \vee P \mid {\sim} Q \cdot {\sim} P$

19. $C \cdot D \mid {\sim} C \supset {\sim} D$

20. $Q \supset P \mid Q \vee P$

Self-Practice Questions

II. Use truth tables to determine whether the following sets of statements are consistent or inconsistent.

1. $M \cdot \sim N \mid M \mid N \vee P$

Answer:

M	N	P	M · ~N	M	N v P
T	T	T	F F	T	T
T	T	F	F F	T	T
T	F	T	T T	T	T
T	F	F	T T	T	F
F	T	T	F F	F	T
F	T	F	F F	F	T
F	F	T	F T	F	T
F	F	F	F T	F	F

The truth table analysis reveals that in line 3 the main operators are all true. Statements are consistent if there is at least one line on their respective truth tables where the main operators are all true; therefore, the three statements are consistent.

2. $R \equiv U \mid \sim R \cdot U \mid R \vee P$

3. $Q \vee P \mid Q \cdot R \mid \sim P \supset R$

4. $\sim R \supset (Q \supset P) \mid \sim Q \cdot P \mid R \vee \sim Q \mid P \supset R$

⭐ 5. $P \supset \sim Q \mid Q \supset \sim P \mid Q \vee \sim S$

6. $(A \cdot B) \vee C \mid \sim B \cdot A \mid \sim C$

7. $\sim M \vee \sim P \mid \sim M \vee Q \mid P \vee R$

8. $\sim A \supset \sim B \mid \sim A \vee B \mid A \cdot \sim B$

⭐ 9. $R \vee (\sim P \cdot S) \mid Q \vee \sim P \mid Q \supset \sim P$

10. $\sim P \cdot Q \mid \sim P \supset \sim R \mid \sim P \vee (Q \cdot \sim R)$

G. TRUTH TABLES FOR ARGUMENTS

We are ready to apply our knowledge of truth tables to the analysis of arguments. We will start using the symbol "/" (called *slash, forward slash,* or *forward stroke*) for "therefore." (The slash symbol will also be used in Chapters 8 and 9.) Here is an example:

$$\sim (P \cdot Q)$$
$$P \qquad\qquad / Q$$

The argument has two premises: "~ $(P \cdot Q)$," and "P." The conclusion is "Q." If it helps, you can imagine that the slash is the line we have used to separate the premises from the conclusion, but angled to the right. In that sense, it still serves to set off the conclusion from the premises.

Validity

Recall that a *valid argument* is one in which, assuming the premises are true, it is *impossible* for the conclusion to be false. In other words, the conclusion follows necessarily from the premises. An *invalid argument* is one in which, assuming the premises are true, it is *possible* for the conclusion to be false. In other words, the conclusion does *not* follow necessarily from the premises. The first step is to display the argument so we can apply the truth tables for the operators. Here is the basic structure:

P	Q	~ $(P \cdot Q)$	P	/ Q
T	T			
T	F			
F	T			
F	F			

The information is displayed to allow a uniform, methodical application of the truth tables for the operators. The truth table is divided into sections. The first two sections are the premises, and the third is the conclusion (indicated by the slash). We complete the truth table by following the same *order of operations* and the *main logical operator* procedures as before. Here is the finished truth table:

P	Q	~	$(P \cdot Q)$	P	/ Q	
T	T	F	T	T	T	
T	F	T	F	T	F	√
F	T	T	F	F	T	
F	F	T	F	F	F	

The final truth value of each statement is either directly under a simple statement or under the main operator of a compound statement. The question of validity hinges on whether *any* line has true premises and a false conclusion. Since the truth table has revealed all possible cases, we are perfectly situated to decide the question. The second line has true premises and a false conclusion; therefore, the argument is invalid. This result is indicated by the checkmark.

Let's do another one:

$$P \cdot \sim Q$$
$$P \supset \sim S \quad / \sim S$$

This argument contains three simple statements (*P*, *Q*, and *S*); therefore, the truth table will have eight lines. The truth table is completed by following the order of operations and the main logical operator procedures:

P	*Q*	*S*	*P* · ~ *Q*		*P* ⊃ ~ *S*		/ ~ *S*
T	T	T	F	F	F	F	F
T	T	F	F	F	T	T	T
T	F	T	T	T	F	F	F
T	F	F	T	T	T	T	T
F	T	T	F	F	T	F	F
F	T	F	F	F	T	T	T
F	F	T	F	T	T	F	F
F	F	F	F	T	T	T	T

We inspect the truth table to see whether any line has true premises and a false conclusion. Line 4 has both premises true, but the conclusion is true, too. Lines 1, 3, 5, and 7 have false conclusions, but none of those lines has both premises true. No line has both premises true and the conclusion false; therefore, the argument is valid.

A quick method to inspect a completed truth table is to go down the column that displays the final truth values for the conclusion. You need only inspect those lines where the conclusion is false. In those instances, you then need to see if all the premises are true. The truth table method provides a straightforward, mechanical way to show whether an argument using truth-functional operators is valid or invalid.

Analyzing Sufficient and Necessary Conditions in Arguments

We can now use our knowledge of the truth tables for conditional and biconditional statements to further illustrate sufficient and necessary conditions. For example, a parent might say the following conditional statement to a child: "If you eat your spinach, then you will get ice cream." Now, suppose the child does not eat the spinach. The parent will probably feel justified in denying the child the ice cream. Here is the parent's argument:

> If you eat your spinach, then you get ice cream.
> <u>You did not eat your spinach.</u>
> You do not get ice cream.

Most parents think that this is a good argument. But let's see. We can have *S = you eat your spinach*, and *I = you get ice cream*.

$$S \supset I$$
$$\sim S \qquad / \sim I$$

We can construct a complete truth table:

S	I	S⊃I	~S	/~I
T	T	T	F	F
T	F	F	F	T
F	T	T	T	F √
F	F	T	T	T

The results show that it is possible for the premises to be true and the conclusion to be false. Therefore, this is an invalid argument. Logically speaking, the child can get the ice cream even if he or she does not eat the spinach. The reason for this interesting result is that a *sufficient condition* has been given for getting the ice cream: eating the spinach. The first premise sets the sufficient condition. However, since it is an invalid argument, the conclusion could be false even though both premises are true. In other words, it is *not necessary* to eat the spinach to get the ice cream.

Seeing this result might cause smart parents to adjust their argument, since they probably intended to make it necessary to eat the spinach to get the ice cream. This can be accomplished by saying, "If you do not eat your spinach, then you do not get ice cream." Another way of saying the same thing is this: "You will get the ice cream only if you eat your spinach." Now suppose the child does not eat the spinach. The parent will probably feel justified in denying the child the ice cream. This is illustrated in the next argument:

If you do not eat your spinach, then you do not get ice cream.
You did not eat your spinach.
You do not get ice cream.

Here is the translation:

$$\sim S \supset \sim I$$
$$\sim S \qquad /\sim I$$

As before, we can construct a complete truth table:

S	I	~S⊃~I	~S	/~I
T	T	F T F	F	F
T	F	F T T	F	T
F	T	T F F	T	F
F	F	T T T	T	T

Since it is not possible for both premises to be true and the conclusion to be false, the argument is valid. The parent will be relieved.

Since a necessary condition has been established, the child cannot get the ice cream unless he or she eats the spinach. However, a new problem has occurred. Imagine that the child eats the spinach. In that case the parent would, logically speaking, be justified in *not* giving the ice cream. By setting up a *necessary condition*, the parent is stating that eating the spinach is required in order to get the ice cream. However, even if the spinach is eaten, this does not logically guarantee that the ice cream will be received. This follows because a *sufficient condition* has *not* been established. Therefore, to ensure that parents and children are protected both sufficient and necessary conditions should be set together. For example, the parent might say, "You will get ice cream *if and only if* you eat your spinach." The biconditional can be translated as "$S \equiv I$."

Now suppose the child eats the spinach. An argument can be created to capture this possibility:

$$S \equiv I$$
$$S \qquad\qquad /\,I$$

As before, we can construct a complete truth table:

S	I	$S \equiv I$	S	$/\,I$
T	T	T	T	T
T	F	F	T	F
F	T	F	F	T
F	F	T	F	F

The truth table shows that the argument is valid. That takes care of the child's expectations. Now suppose the child does not eat the spinach. An argument can be created to capture this possibility:

$$S \equiv I$$
$$\sim S \qquad\qquad /\sim I$$

We can construct a complete truth table:

S	I	$S \equiv I$	$\sim S$	$/\sim I$
T	T	T	F	F
T	F	F	F	T
F	T	F	T	F
F	F	T	T	T

The truth table shows that the argument is valid. That takes care of the parent's side of the bargain.

Technical Validity

If the conclusion of an argument is a *tautology*, then the conclusion is logically true. As such, the argument is valid because no line of the truth table will have all true premises and a false conclusion. This is an example of a *technically valid argument*. Although valid, this kind of argument comes at a high cost. In that case, the conclusion is trivial—an empty truth that conveys no real information about the world and illuminates nothing.

An argument is also technically valid when at least one of the premises is a *self-contradiction*. No line of the truth table will have all true premises and a false conclusion because the premise with the self-contradiction is logically false. Although the argument is valid, it, too, comes at a high price: the argument is not *sound* (a *sound* argument is one that is *valid* and *has all true premises*).

In a third type of technically valid argument, two premises are *contradictory*. In that case, no line of the truth table will have all true premises and a false conclusion because one of the contradictory premises will be false on every line. However, if we contradict ourselves in the premises, then the argument is not *sound*.

In a fourth type of technically valid argument, two or more premises are *inconsistent*. In that case, all the statements cannot be true at the same time, and at least one premise will be false. (Unlike contradictory premises, two or more inconsistent premises can be false at the same time.) Thus, no line of the truth table will have all true premises and a false conclusion. But once again, the argument will not be *sound*.

Lightboard Video

EXERCISES 7G.1

I. Create truth tables to determine whether the following arguments are valid or invalid.

1. $R \lor S$ $/ R$

Self-Practice
Questions

Answer: Invalid

R	S	R v S	/ R
T	T	T	T
T	F	T	T
F	T	T	F √
F	F	F	F

The argument is invalid; line 3 has the premise true and the conclusion false. This is indicated by the check mark.

2. $R \cdot S$ $/ R$

3. $\sim P \lor \sim S$
   P $/ S$

4. $R \lor \sim S$ $/ S$

 5. $\sim R \lor \sim S$ $/ \sim R$

6. $\sim R \cdot \sim S$ $/ \sim S$

7. $\sim (\sim R \lor \sim S)$
   S $/ R$

8. $\sim (\sim R \cdot \sim S)$
   $\sim S$ $/ \sim R$

9. $\sim (R \lor S)$
   $\sim R$ $/ \sim S$

10. ~(R · S)
     ~R   / ~ S

11. P v (Q v S)   / P

12. (P · Q) v R
     ~ Q   / R

⭐ 13. S v (Q v R)
     ~ Q
     ~ R   / S

14. (S v Q) v R
     Q
     R   / ~ S

15. ~(~ S v Q) · (P v R)
     ~ Q
     ~ P
     ~ R   / ~ S

II. Create truth tables to determine whether the following arguments are valid or invalid.

1. P ⊃ Q
    P   / Q

Answer: Valid

P	Q	P ⊃ Q	P	/ Q
T	T	T	T	T
T	F	F	T	F
F	T	T	F	T
F	F	T	F	F

2. P ⊃ Q
    ~ Q   / ~ P

3. P ⊃ Q
    Q ⊃ R   / P ⊃ R

4. P v Q
    ~ P   / Q

⭐ 5. (P ⊃ Q) · (R ⊃ S)
    P v R   / Q v S

6. P · Q   / P

7. P
    Q   / P · Q

8. P   / P v Q

⭐ 9. R ≡ S   / R

10. (R · S) ⊃ S   / S

11. P ≡ (~ P v ~ S)
     ~ P   / ~ S

12. ~(R ⊃ S)
     ~ R   / ~ S

⭐ 13. ~(R · S)
     ~ R ⊃ P   / ~ S

14. (P v Q) ⊃ S   / P

15. (P · Q) v (R ⊃ P)
     ~ Q v ~ R   / R

16. [S v (Q v R)] ⊃ Q
     ~ Q
     ~ R   / S

⭐ 17. [(S · Q) · R] ⊃ Q
     Q
     R   / ~ S

18. ~(~ S v Q) ⊃ (P v R)
     ~ Q
     ~ P
     ~ R   / ~ S

19. $P \supset Q$
    $Q \supset P$ $/ P \vee Q$

20. $(P \cdot Q) \vee R$
    $\sim Q$ $/ R$

⭐21. $P \supset (Q \vee \sim R)$
    $Q \supset \sim R$ $/ P \supset \sim R$

22. $(P \cdot Q) \equiv (R \supset P)$
    $\sim Q \vee \sim R$ $/ R$

23. $P \supset (\sim P \vee \sim S)$
    $\sim P$ $/ \sim S$

24. $R \supset S$
    $\sim S$ $/ R$

⭐25. $(P \vee Q) \equiv S$ $/ P$

III. First, translate the following arguments using the logical operators. Second, create truth tables to determine whether the arguments are valid or invalid.

1. Either January or February was the coldest month this year. January was clearly not the coldest month. Therefore, February was the coldest month this year.

Answer: *Let J = January was the coldest month this year, and B = February was the coldest month this year.*

J	B	J ∨ B	~J	/ B
T	T	T	F	T
T	F	T	F	F
F	T	T	T	T
F	F	F	T	F

The argument is valid; there is no line where the premises are true and the conclusion is false.

2. Either June or July was the hottest month this year. July was the hottest, so it cannot be June.

3. Either Eddie or Walter is the tallest member of the family. Walter is the tallest, so Eddie is not the tallest.

4. It is not the case that both Judy and Stella booked their flights. Judy did not book her flight; therefore, Stella did not book her flight.

⭐5. Unless we stop interfering in other countries' internal affairs we will find ourselves with more enemies than we can handle. We will stop interfering in other countries' internal affairs. So it is safe to conclude that we will not find ourselves with more enemies than we can handle.

6. It is not the case that both Jim and Mary Lynn are hog farmers. Mary Lynn is not a hog farmer, so Jim cannot be one.

7. It is not the case that either Lee Ann or Johnny is old enough to collect Social Security benefits. Since Lee Ann does not collect Social Security benefits, we can conclude that Johnny does not.

8. If the prosecuting attorney's claims are correct, then the defendant is guilty. The defendant is guilty. Therefore, the prosecuting attorney's claims are correct.

★ 9. If the prosecuting attorney's claims are correct, then the defendant is guilty. The defendant is not guilty. Therefore, the prosecuting attorney's claims are correct.

10. If the prosecuting attorney's claims are correct, then the defendant is guilty. The defendant is not guilty. Therefore, the prosecuting attorney's claims are not correct.

11. If the prosecuting attorney's claims are correct, then the defendant is guilty. The defendant is guilty. Therefore, the prosecuting attorney's claims are not correct.

12. If UFOs exist, then there is life on other planets. UFOs do not exist. Thus, it is not the case that there is life on other planets.

★13. If UFOs exist, then there is life on other planets. UFOs do not exist. Thus, there is life on other planets.

14. If I am the president of the United States, then I live in the White House. I am not the president of the United States. Therefore, I do not live in the White House.

15. If I live in the White House, then I am the president of the United States. I am not the president of the United States. Therefore, I do not live in the White House.

16. If you take 1000 mg of vitamin C every day, then you will not get a cold. You get a cold. Thus, you did not take 1000 mg of vitamin C every day.

★17. If you take 1000 mg of vitamin C every day, then you will not get a cold. You did not get a cold. Thus, you did take 1000 mg of vitamin C every day.

18. If Robert drove south on I-15 from Las Vegas, then Robert got to Los Angeles. Robert did not go south on I-15 from Las Vegas. Therefore, Robert did not get to Los Angeles.

19. If you did not finish the job by Friday, then you did not get the bonus. You finished the job by Friday. Thus, you did get the bonus.

20. If you finished the job by Friday, then you got the bonus. You did not finish the job by Friday. Thus, you did not get the bonus.

Argument Forms

Earlier in the chapter, we defined a *statement form* as a pattern of statement variables and logical operators such that any uniform substitution of statements for the variables results in a statement. Argument form refers to the structure of an argument, not to its content. In propositional logic, an argument form is an arrangement of logical operators and statement variables in which a consistent replacement of the statement variables by statements results in an argument. The result is also called a substitution instance of the argument form. In addition, a deductive argument is *formally valid* by nature of its logical form.

Let's look at an example:

> If you give up cigarettes, then you care about your health. You did give up cigarettes. Therefore, you do care about your health.

Let G = *you give up cigarettes,* and C = *you care about your health.*

$$G \supset C$$
$$G \qquad\qquad / C$$

We can construct a complete truth table:

G	C	G ⊃ C	G	/ C
T	T	T	T	T
T	F	F	T	F
F	T	T	F	T
F	F	T	F	F

Since there is no way to get the conclusion false and both premises true at the same time, the argument is valid. In fact, this argument is a substitution instance of the following valid argument form:

$$p \supset q$$
$$\underline{p \qquad}$$
$$q$$

This argument form is called **modus ponens** ("*modus*" means *method,* and "*ponens*" means *affirming*). This valid argument form is also referred to as *affirming the antecedent.* Any argument whose form is identical to *modus ponens* is valid.

Now let's look at a different argument:

> If you give up cigarettes, then you care about your health. You do care about your health. Therefore, you did give up cigarettes.

Once again, let G = *you give up cigarettes,* and C = *you care about your health.*

$$G \supset C$$
$$C \qquad\qquad / G$$

We can construct a complete truth table:

G	C	G ⊃ C	C	/ G	
T	T	T	T	T	
T	F	F	F	T	
F	T	T	T	F	√
F	F	T	F	F	

Modus ponens A valid argument form (also referred to as *affirming the antecedent*).

The truth table shows that it is possible to get the conclusion false and both premises true at the same time; therefore, the argument is invalid (as indicated by the check mark). This argument is a substitution instance of the following argument form:

$$p \supset q$$
$$\underline{q\qquad}$$
$$p$$

This argument form is referred to as the **fallacy of affirming the consequent**, and it is a formal fallacy. This was illustrated by the truth table analysis of the substitution instance.

Now let's look at another argument:

> If you give up cigarettes, then you care about your health. You do not care about your health. Therefore, you did not give up cigarettes.

Once again, let G = *you give up cigarettes*, and C = *you care about your health.*

$$G \supset C$$
$$\sim C \quad / \sim G$$

We can construct a complete truth table:

G	C	G ⊃ C	∼ C	/ ∼ G
T	T	T	F	F
T	F	F	T	F
F	T	T	F	T
F	F	T	T	T

Since there is no way to get the conclusion false and both premises true at the same time, the argument is valid. In fact, this argument is a substitution instance of the following valid argument form:

$$p \supset q$$
$$\underline{\sim q\qquad}$$
$$\sim p$$

This argument form is called ***modus tollens*** ("modus" means *method*, and "tollens" means *denying*. This valid argument form is also referred to as *denying the consequent*. Any argument whose form is identical to *modus tollens* is valid.

Let's look at one final argument:

> If you give up cigarettes, then you care about your health. You did not give up cigarettes. Therefore, you do not care about your health.

Once again, let *G = you give up cigarettes*, and *C = you care about your health*.

$$G \supset C$$
$$\sim G \qquad / \sim C$$

We can construct a complete truth table:

G	C	G $\supset$ C	$\sim$ G	/ $\sim$ C	
T	T	T	F	F	
T	F	F	F	T	
F	T	T	T	F	√
F	F	T	T	T	

The truth table shows that it is possible to get the conclusion false and both premises true at the same time; therefore, the argument is invalid (as indicated by the check mark). The argument is a substitution instance of the following argument form:

$$p \supset q$$
$$\underline{\sim p}$$
$$\sim q$$

This argument form is referred to as the **fallacy of denying the antecedent**, and it is a formal fallacy. This was illustrated by the truth table analysis of the substitution instance.

The two valid argument forms—*modus ponens* and *modus tollens*—and the two invalid argument forms—the *fallacy of affirming the consequent* and the *fallacy of denying the antecedent*—are developed further in the next chapter.

Fallacy of denying the antecedent An invalid argument form; it is a formal fallacy.

EXERCISES 7G.2

First, translate the arguments from English using logical operators. Next, use truth tables to determine whether the arguments are valid or invalid.

1. If either Barbara or Johnny goes to the party, then Lee Ann will not have to pick up Mary Lynn. Barbara is not going to the party. Lee Ann has to pick up Mary Lynn. Therefore, Johnny is not going to the party.

Answer: Let *B = Barbara goes to the party, J = Johnny goes to the party,* **and** *L = Lee Ann has to pick up Mary Lynn*:

$$(B \lor J) \supset \sim L$$
$$\sim B$$
$$L \qquad / \sim J$$

B	J	L	(B v J) ⊃ ~L	~B	L	/ ~J
T	T	T	T F F	F	T	F
T	T	F	T T T	F	F	F
T	F	T	T F F	F	T	T
T	F	F	T T T	F	F	T
F	T	T	T F F	T	T	F
F	T	F	T T T	T	F	F
F	F	T	F T F	T	T	T
F	F	F	F T T	T	F	T

As the truth table illustrates, there are no lines where all the premises are true and the conclusion is false at the same time; therefore, the argument is valid.

2. Either you take a Breathalyzer test or you get arrested for DUI. You did not take the Breathalyzer test. Therefore, you get arrested for DUI.

3. If animals feel pain or learn from experience, then animals are conscious. Animals do not feel pain. Animals do not learn from experience. Thus, animals are conscious.

4. If animals are not conscious or do not feel pain, then they do not have any rights. Animals do not have any rights. Animals do not feel pain. Thus, animals are not conscious.

⭐ 5. Either you are right or you are wrong. You are not right. Therefore, you are wrong.

6. If either Elvis or the Beatles sold the most records of all time, then I did not win the contest. The Beatles did not sell the most records of all time. Therefore, I won the contest.

7. If X is an even number, then X is divisible by 2. But X is not divisible by 2. Thus, X is not an even number.

8. If X is not an even number, then X is not divisible by 2. But X is divisible by 2. Therefore, X is an even number.

⭐ 9. If Joyce went south on I-15 from Las Vegas, then Joyce got to Los Angeles. Joyce did not go south on I-15 from Las Vegas. Thus, Joyce did not get to Los Angeles.

10. If you did not finish the job by Friday, then you did not get the bonus. You did finish the job by Friday. Therefore, you did get the bonus.

11. If you did finish the job by Friday, then you did get the bonus. You did not finish the job by Friday. Thus, you did not get the bonus.

12. Eddie can vote if, and only if, he is registered. Eddie is registered. Therefore, Eddie can vote.

★13. Eddie can vote if, and only if, he is registered. But Eddie is not registered. Therefore, Eddie cannot vote.

14. Eddie can vote if, and only if, he is registered. Eddie cannot vote. Thus, Eddie is not registered.

15. Linda can think if, and only if, she is conscious. Linda is conscious. Therefore, Linda can think.

H. INDIRECT TRUTH TABLES

A good understanding of the logical operators gives us the ability to analyze truth-functional statements and arguments more quickly—without having to create full-fledged truth tables. Section 7C introduced some of the principles behind the indirect truth table method. When specific truth values are assigned to simple statements, then a short truth table can be constructed.

Thinking Through an Argument

To get started, we can try thinking our way through an argument. This requires a solid grasp of the truth tables for the five logical operators. Let's start with the following argument:

> Stocks will go up in value or we will have a recession.
> <u>We will not have a recession.</u>
> Stocks will go up in value.

If we let S = *stocks will go up in value*, and R = *we will have a recession*, then the translation is this:

$$S \lor R$$
$$\sim R \quad / S$$

One way to begin is by figuring out which truth values for the simple statements are needed to make both premises true at the same time. For example, if the first premise ($S \lor R$) is true, then what can we say about S and R separately? Since this is a disjunction, *at least one* of the disjuncts must be true. We can start by assuming that both S and R are true.

Now if the second premise ($\sim R$) is true, then the simple statement R must be false; there is no other choice. Once we have determined the specific value for R, we must designate the same value for all instances of R throughout the argument. This means that the R in the first premise is false. Recall that under the assumption that the first premise (a disjunction) was true, at least one of the simple statements (S, R) was true. But now we have determined that the only way for the second premise to be true is for R to be false.

When we initially assumed the first premise was true, we did not know whether *S* was true or *R* was true or both were true. But with the analysis of the second premise, we can determine that, in order for the both premises to be true, *S* must be true. Finally, if *S* is true, then the conclusion, *S*, is true. This means that the argument is valid.

We get the same result by starting with the conclusion and temporarily ignoring the premises. However, if you start with the conclusion, then you must determine which truth value will make it false. Once this is determined, the strategy is then to try to get all the premises true. If it can be done, then the argument is invalid.

Now since the conclusion is the simple statement *S*, we must assign it the truth value *false*. Therefore, every occurrence of *S* in the argument is false. Given this, the only way the first premise can be true is if *R* is true. The second premise is ~ *R*. Since *R* has been assigned the truth value *true*, ~ *R* is false. We have shown that if the conclusion is false, then all the premises cannot be true at the same time. The argument is valid.

A Shorter Truth Table

Now that we have thought our way through an argument using logical operators, we are in position to develop a shortcut method of showing validity or invalidity. An *indirect truth table* assigns truth values to the simple statements of an argument in order to determine if an argument is valid or invalid. Here is an example:

$$\sim (P \cdot Q)$$
$$P \qquad\qquad / Q$$

We start by displaying the argument as if we were creating a normal truth table:

P	Q	~ (P · Q)	P	/ Q

The indirect method requires us to look for any possibility of true premises and a false conclusion. Since an indirect truth table looks for the shortest way to decide the possibility of true premises and a false conclusion, it makes sense to assign truth values to any simple statements that allow us to "lock in" one truth value. In this example, since the conclusion is the simple statement *Q*, we can start by assigning *Q* the truth value *false*. The assigned value is placed in the guide on the left side of the truth table:

P	Q	~ (P · Q)	P	/ Q
	F			F

Notice that the *Q* in the conclusion has "F" written under it, but not the *Q* in the first premise. Since the conclusion does not contain any logical operators, we put the truth value directly under the simple statement. However, the *Q* in the first premise is part of a compound statement. Therefore, we will place truth values only under the operators. To do this, we will rely on the guide to assist us.

The next step is to try to get all the premises true at the same time. Since the second premise is the simple statement P, we assign P the truth value *true*. This is added to the information in the truth table:

P	Q	~ (P · Q)	P	/ Q
T	F		T	F

Once again, notice that we placed the truth value for P in the guide and under the P in the second premise. Since the second premise does not contain any logical operators, we put the truth value directly under the simple statement. All the truth values for the simple statements have been assigned; therefore, the truth table can be completed:

P	Q	~ (P · Q)	P	/ Q
T	F	T F	T	F √

The short truth table reveals the possibility of true premises and a false conclusion. Therefore, the argument is invalid. In this example, since the second premise was the simple statement P, we could have started by assigning P the truth value *true*. The next step would have been to assign the simple statement Q in the conclusion the truth value *false*. The resulting truth table would be the same as the earlier one, and it would show that the argument is invalid.

This process has revealed a good strategy for constructing indirect truth tables. Start by assigning truth values to the simple statements, ones that contain no logical operators. But what happens if we get to a point in the assignment of truth values where we have a choice to make? Analysis of the next argument explains the procedure:

$$\sim P \cdot R$$
$$P \vee \sim Q \quad / Q$$

P	Q	R	~P · R	P ∨ ~Q	/ Q
		F		T T	F

The indirect truth table starts by assigning the truth value *false* to the simple statement Q (the conclusion). The negation sign in the second premise is now determined because the guide informs us that Q is false. This information is important. Since the second premise already has a true disjunct, it turns out that no matter what truth value is assigned to P, the second premise is true. This allows us to place a box around the "T" under the wedge in the second premise.

However, there are several possibilities to consider for the first premise. Let's take them one at a time. If P is true, then the first premise is false because the conjunct $\sim P$ is false. Let's see what the truth table would look like for this assignment of truth values:

P	Q	R	~P · R	P ∨ ~Q	/ Q
T	F		F F	T T	F

At this point it would be a mistake to say that we have shown that the argument is valid. Recall that the indirect method requires us to look for *any* possibility of true premises and a false conclusion. We must consider the possibility that *P* is false before we can make a final determination. Assigning the truth value *false* to *P* does not affect the truth value of the second premise, but it does make one of the conjuncts in the first premise true. We can add this possibility to create a second line in the indirect truth table:

P Q R	~P · R	P v ~Q	/ Q
T F	F [F]	[T]T	[F]
F F	T	[T]T	[F]

The truth value of *R* is now crucial for our analysis. It is possible to make the first premise true by assigning *R* the truth value *true*:

P Q R	~P · R	P v ~Q	/ Q
T F	F [F]	[T]T	[F]
F F T	T [T]	[T]T	[F] √

The completed truth table reveals the possibility of true premises and a false conclusion. Therefore, we have shown the argument is invalid. This has been indicated by the check mark to the right of the second line.

Now you can see why this technique is called *indirect truth table*. We purposely assign truth values to the simple statements in order to reveal the possibility of true premises and a false conclusion. A full truth table has every arrangement of truth values. The trade-off is important to recognize. It is less likely that you will get a wrong determination using a full truth table. After all, an indirect truth table considers only a few truth value assignments. Therefore, it is possible to overlook a crucial truth value assignment. *That is why we need to look for any possibility of true premises and a false conclusion.* The indirect truth table method also requires a firm grip on the truth tables for the five logical operators and the flexibility of thinking through possibilities. The full truth table method is more mechanical in nature and proceeds step by step.

Let's look at another example:

$$\sim P \lor Q$$
$$R \supset Q \qquad / P \cdot R$$

Since there are no stand-alone simple statements in either the premises or the conclusion, we cannot quickly assign any truth values. The next strategy is to determine which of the compound statements has the least number of ways it can be true (the premises) or false (the conclusion). The idea is to start with whichever compound statement has the fewest number of ways.

The first premise is a disjunction; therefore, there are three ways it can be true. The second premise is a conditional; it has three ways to be true. Next, we turn to the conclusion to determine the number of ways it can be false. Since the conclusion is a conjunction, there are three ways for it to be false. Since all the compound

statements have the same number of ways, we can choose any of them to start. Let's
try the conclusion:

P	Q	R	~P v Q	R ⊃ Q	/ P · R
T		F	F	T	F
F		T	T T		F
F		F	T T	T	F

The guide on the left lists the three ways that the conclusion can be false. The F's
under the dot in the conclusion are put in a box, because they are the result for the
main operator in all three lines. The assigned truth values for P enable the placement
of truth values under the tilde in the first premise. Given this, we can determine the
truth value for the main operator in two of the three lines. In other words, since the
first premise has at least one disjunct true (the second and third lines), the disjunction
is true for those cases. We note this by placing the final truth values in boxes under
the wedge. At this point, the first line under the wedge cannot be determined because
it might be true or false (depending on the truth value of Q).

The assigned truth values for R determine truth values for the horseshoe in two of
the three lines. In other words, because the antecedent is false on the first and third
lines, the compound statement is true. We note this by placing the final truth values
in boxes under the horseshoe. At this point, the second line under the horseshoe
cannot be determined, because it might be true or false (depending on the truth
value of Q).

Line 3 is enough to show the argument is invalid; but what if we miss that fact? No
problem. When we first start applying the procedure we can easily miss items. The
important thing is to continue on with determining the values for Q. If we finish the
first line and cannot get both premises true, then we are not allowed to make any
final decision. We must proceed to the next line. If we cannot get both premises true
in that line, then again we cannot make any final decision. If none of the three lines
have both premises true and the conclusion false, then the argument is valid.

However, if we get to a line with both premises true and the conclusion false, we
can stop—the argument is invalid. Let's look at the first line. The disjunction in the
first premise is true if Q is true. Let's go ahead and plug in this information:

P	Q	R	~P v Q	R ⊃ Q	/ P · R	
T	T	F	F T	T	F	√
F		T	T T		F	
F		F	T T	T	F	√

Line 1 is complete. As the boxes indicate, both premises are true and the conclusion
is false. Therefore, the indirect truth table shows that the argument is invalid. A check
mark is placed to the right of the line to indicate this result. (A check mark has been
added to indicate that line 3 would have shown the same thing.)

Always remember two points when you construct an indirect truth table for an argument. (1) You have *not* shown that an argument is valid until you have determined that there is no possibility of true premises and a false conclusion. (2) You have shown that an argument is invalid as soon as you have correctly shown that a line contains *all* true premises and a false conclusion.

EXERCISES 7H.1

I. Use the indirect truth table method to determine whether the following arguments are valid or invalid.

1. $(R \cdot Q) \vee S$
   R
   $\sim Q$ $/ \sim S$

2. $(R \vee Q) \cdot S$
   Q
   $\sim R$ $/ S$

Answer for Exercise 1:

R	Q	S	$(R \cdot Q) \vee S$	R	$\sim Q$	$/ \sim S$
T	F	T	F T	T	T	F √

The completed indirect truth table reveals the possibility of true premises and a false conclusion; thus we have shown that the argument is invalid.

3. $(R \cdot Q) \vee S$
   R
   $\sim Q$ $/ S \cdot R$

4. $(P \cdot Q) \vee (R \cdot S)$
   Q
   S
   R $/ P$

★ 5. $[P \vee (Q \vee S)] \supset R$
   $\sim P$
   $\sim Q$
   $\sim S$ $/ \sim R$

6. $(P \vee Q) \cdot (\sim S \cdot Q)$
   $\sim S$
   $\sim Q$ $/ \sim P$

7. $(\sim S \vee \sim Q) \supset \sim R$
   S
   Q $/ R$

8. $R \supset (Q \cdot \sim S)$
   S
   $\sim Q$ $/ \sim R$

★ 9. $\sim (P \vee Q) \vee \sim (R \cdot S)$
   $P \cdot Q$
   R $/ \sim S$

10. $(P \cdot Q) \vee \sim R$
    $\sim P$
    $\sim Q$ $/ R$

11. $(R \vee S) \supset (P \cdot Q)$
    $\sim S$
    $\sim Q$ $/ \sim R$

12. $(R \cdot Q) \lor S$
    R
    Q $/ S \cdot R$

⭐13. $(R \lor Q) \supset \sim S$
    $Q \lor S$ $/ R$

14. $(R \lor S) \supset (P \cdot Q)$
    $\sim S \lor \sim Q$ $/ \sim R$

15. $\sim (R \lor S) \supset (P \lor Q)$
    $\sim S \lor Q$
    $\sim Q \equiv R$ $/ \sim R$

16. $(R \cdot Q) \lor \sim S$
    $R \lor \sim Q$
    $\sim Q \lor \sim S$ $/ \sim S \cdot R$

⭐17. $\sim (\sim R \lor \sim Q) \supset \sim S$
    $Q \supset S$ $/ \sim R \supset S$

18. $(R \lor \sim S) \supset \sim (P \cdot Q)$
    $\sim S \lor \sim Q$ $/ \sim R \cdot P$

19. $\sim [P \lor (Q \lor S)] \supset \sim R$
    $\sim Q \equiv \sim S$ $/ \sim R \supset P$

20. $(Q \lor S) \supset (\sim R \cdot P)$
    $\sim Q \lor S$ $/ \sim Q \supset (S \lor P)$

II. First, translate the arguments from English using logical operators. Next, use indirect truth tables to determine whether the arguments are valid or invalid.

1. If either Barbara or Johnny goes to the party, then Lee Ann will not have to pick up Mary Lynn. Barbara is not going to the party. Lee Ann has to pick up Mary Lynn. Therefore, Johnny is not going to the party.

Answer: Let B = *Barbara goes to the party*, J = *Johnny goes to the party*, and L = *Lee Ann has to pick up Mary Lynn*:

$$(B \lor J) \supset \sim L$$
$$\sim B$$
$$L \qquad / \sim J$$

B	J	L	$(B \lor J) \supset \sim L)$	$\sim B$	L	$/ \sim J$
F	T	T	T $\boxed{F}$ F	$\boxed{T}$	$\boxed{T}$	$\boxed{F}$

The only way for the conclusion to be false is for J to be true. The only way for the third premise to be true is for L to be true. The only way for the second premise to be true is for B to be false. At this point, all the simple statement truth values have been assigned to the guide on the left. Based on the guide, the first premise is false. Since it is impossible to get all the premises true and the conclusion false at the same time, the argument is valid.

2. Either you take a Breathalyzer test or you get arrested for DUI. You did not take the Breathalyzer test. Therefore, you get arrested for DUI.

3. If animals feel pain or learn from experience, then animals are conscious. Animals do not feel pain. Animals do not learn from experience. Thus, animals are not conscious.

4. If animals feel pain or learn from experience, then animals are conscious. Animals do not feel pain. Animals do not learn from experience. Therefore, animals are conscious.

⭐ 5. If animals are not conscious or do not feel pain, then they do not have any rights. Animals do not have any rights. Animals do not feel pain. Thus, animals are not conscious.

6. If animals are not conscious or do not feel pain, then they do not have any rights. Animals are conscious. Animals do feel pain. Therefore, animals have rights.

7. Either you are right or you are wrong. You are not right. Therefore, you are wrong.

8. If either Bill or Gus or Kate committed the crime, then Mike did not do it and Tina did not do it. Bill did not commit the crime. Gus did not commit the crime. Kate did not commit the crime. Thus, Mike did it.

⭐ 9. If either Elvis or the Beatles sold the most records of all time, then I did not win the contest. The Beatles did not sell the most records of all time. Therefore, I won the contest.

10. If I save $1 a day, then I will not be rich in 10 years. If I save $2 a day, then I will not be rich in 10 years. If I save $3 a day, then I will not be rich in 10 years. I will not save $1 a day. I will not save $2 a day. I will not save $3 a day. Therefore, I will not be rich in 10 years.

11. If X is an even number, then X is divisible by 2. But X is not divisible by 2. Thus, X is not an even number.

12. If X is not an even number, then X is not divisible by 2. But X is divisible by 2. Therefore, X is an even number.

⭐13. If Joyce went south on I-15 from Las Vegas, then Joyce got to Los Angeles. Joyce did not go south on I-15 from Las Vegas. Thus, Joyce did not get to Los Angeles.

14. If you did not finish the job by Friday, then you did not get the bonus. You did finish the job by Friday. Therefore, you did get the bonus.

15. If you did finish the job by Friday, then you did get the bonus. You did not finish the job by Friday. Thus, you did not get the bonus.

16. Eddie can vote if, and only if, he is registered. Eddie is registered. Therefore, Eddie can vote.

⭐17. Eddie can vote if, and only if, he is registered. Eddie can vote. Thus, Eddie is registered.

18. Eddie can vote if, and only if, he is registered. But Eddie is not registered. Therefore, Eddie cannot vote.

19. Eddie can vote if, and only if, he is registered. Eddie cannot vote. Thus, Eddie is not registered.

20. Linda can think if, and only if, she is conscious. Linda is conscious. Therefore, Linda can think.

Video Tutorial: 7HI.II
Exercise #6

Using Indirect Truth Tables to Examine Statements for Consistency

Indirect truth tables can be used to determine whether two or more statements are consistent. The procedure draws on the basic strategies behind indirect truth tables but adds one more requirement. If you recall, statements are *consistent* if there is at least one line on their respective truth tables where the main operators are true. This is where the strategy diverges from determining the validity of an argument. In other words, the strategy for analyzing arguments is to look for the possibility of true premises and a false conclusion. However, since examining a set of statements for consistency is not dealing with an argument, there are no premises and a conclusion. Let's work through a simple example:

$$P \vee \sim Q$$

$$\sim P \cdot \sim Q$$

The indirect truth table is constructed as before, except that no slash sign indicating a conclusion is used.

P	Q	$P \vee \sim Q$	$\sim P \cdot \sim Q$

The first step is to determine which of the compound statements has the least number of ways it can be true. The first statement is a disjunction; therefore, there are three ways it can be true. The second statement is a conjunction; there is only one way for it to be true. This narrows the analysis considerably. We lock in the truth values that are needed to get the second statement true:

P	Q	$P \vee \sim Q$	$\sim P \cdot \sim Q$
F	F		T [T]T

We can now go ahead and complete the truth table:

P	Q	$P \vee \sim Q$	$\sim P \cdot \sim Q$
F	F	[T]T	T [T]T

The truth table shows that both statements can be true at the same time; therefore, the statements are consistent.

Let's work through a longer problem this time. Are the following four statements consistent?

$$P \supset \sim Q$$
$$R \vee Q$$
$$\sim R$$
$$Q \supset (P \vee R)$$

The indirect truth table is constructed as before, but this time there are four statements side by side:

P	Q	R	$P \supset \sim Q$	$R \vee Q$	$\sim R$	$Q \supset (P \vee R)$

The first step is to determine which of the statements has the least number of ways it can be true. The first is a conditional; therefore, there are three ways it can be true. The second is a disjunction; there are three ways it can be true. The third is the negation of a simple statement; there is only one way for it to be true. This is where we will start. We lock in the truth value that is needed to get the third statement true:

P	Q	R	P ⊃ ~Q	R ∨ Q	~ R	Q ⊃ (P ∨ R)
		F			T	

The locked-in truth value for R is used to decide the next step. An R appears in the second and fourth statements, so we can look at them. In the fourth statement, the R is part of a disjunction, but the disjunction happens to be the consequent of a conditional. At this point, there are too many possibilities for the fourth statement to be true for us to make any specific determinations. However, the second statement is a disjunction with one of the disjuncts (R) false. Therefore, the only way to get the second statement true is for Q to be true. This information is added to the truth table:

P	Q	R	P ⊃ ~Q	R ∨ Q	~ R	Q ⊃ (P ∨ R)
T	F		F	T	T	

This information helps us decide what we need to do in the first statement. Since Q is true, the consequent of the conditional is false. Therefore, the only way for the first statement to be true is for P to be false. This information is added to the truth table:

P	Q	R	P ⊃ ~Q	R ∨ Q	~ R	Q ⊃ (P ∨ R)
F	T	F	T F	T	T	

The guide is complete. Now all we have to do is use the information in the guide to determine the truth value of the fourth statement. If the fourth statement is true, then the set of statements is consistent. On the other hand, if the fourth statement is false, then the set is inconsistent. Once we make that determination, we are finished because we have narrowed down our search by locking in the truth values for all the simple statements. Here is the final result:

P	Q	R	P ⊃ ~Q	R ∨ Q	~ R	Q ⊃ (P ∨ R)
F	T	F	T F	T	T	F F

The indirect truth table shows that the four statements cannot all be true at the same time. Therefore, the set of statements is inconsistent.

While the process of using indirect truth tables may seem complex at first, it is an efficient way to determine whether an argument is valid or invalid. It is also an efficient way to determine whether sets of statements are consistent or inconsistent. Of course, the technique requires a firm grasp of the truth tables for the five operators. As with most skills, you will become more confident with practice, and applying the technique will go more quickly.

EXERCISES 7H.2

Use indirect truth tables to determine whether the following sets of statements are consistent or inconsistent.

1. $A \vee B \mid \sim A \supset B$

Answer: Consistent. There are three ways to get both statements true, so we can start with any one. Let's try making both A and B true:

A	B	A ∨ B	~A ⊃ B
T	T	[T]	F [T]

We do not have to try the other two possibilities because the truth table shows that both statements can be true at the same time.

2. $M \cdot \sim N \mid M \mid N \vee P$

3. $R \equiv U \mid \sim R \cdot U \mid R \vee P$

4. $\sim (Q \supset \sim R) \cdot S \mid S \supset \sim (Q \cdot R)$

⭐ **5.** $R \vee (\sim P \cdot S) \mid Q \vee \sim P \mid Q \supset \sim P$

6. $\sim R \supset (Q \supset P) \mid \sim Q \cdot P \mid R \vee \sim Q \mid P \supset R$

7. $\sim A \supset \sim B \mid \sim A \vee B \mid A \cdot \sim B$

8. $(A \cdot B) \vee C \mid \sim B \cdot A \mid \sim C$

⭐ **9.** $\sim M \vee \sim P \mid \sim M \vee Q \mid P \vee R$

10. $P \supset \sim Q \mid Q \supset \sim P \mid Q \vee \sim S$

11. $R \vee (S \equiv U) \mid S \vee R$

12. $P \cdot Q \mid \sim P \supset Q$

⭐ **13.** $\sim (Q \supset R) \supset S \mid S \vee (Q \cdot R)$

14. $Q \vee P \mid Q \cdot R \mid \sim P \supset R$

15. $\sim P \cdot Q \mid \sim P \supset \sim R \mid \sim P \vee (Q \cdot \sim R)$

Summary

- Logical operators: Special symbols that are used to translate ordinary language statements.
- The basic components in propositional logic are statements.
- Simple statement: One that does not have any other statement or logical operator as a component.
- Compound statement: A statement that has at least one simple statement and at least one logical operator as components.
- The five logical operator names: tilde, dot, wedge, horseshoe, and triple bar.
- The word "not" and the phrase "it is not the case that" are used to deny the statement that follows them, and we refer to their use as "negation."

- Conjunction: A compound statement that has two distinct statements (called *conjuncts*) connected by the dot symbol.
- Disjunction: A compound statement that has two distinct statements (called *disjuncts*) connected by the wedge symbol.
- Inclusive disjunction: When we assert that *at least one* disjunct is true, and *possibly both* disjuncts are true. Given this, an inclusive disjunction is false when both disjuncts are false, otherwise it is true.
- Exclusive disjunction: When we assert that *at least one* disjunct is true, but *not* both. In other words, we assert that the truth of one *excludes* the truth of the other. Given this, an exclusive disjunction is true when only one of the disjuncts is true, otherwise it is false.
- Conditional statement: In ordinary language, the word "if" typically precedes the antecedent of a conditional statement, and the statement that follows the word "then" is referred to as the consequent.
- Sufficient condition: Whenever one event ensures that another event is realized.
- Necessary condition: Whenever one thing is essential, mandatory, or required in order for another thing to be realized.
- Biconditional: A compound statement made up of two conditionals—one indicated by the word "if" and the other indicated by the phrase "only if."
- Well-formed formula: Any statement letter standing alone, or a compound statement such that an arrangement of operator symbols and statement letters results in a grammatically correct symbolic expression.
- Scope: The statement or statements that a logical operator governs.
- Main operator: The operator that has the entire well-formed formula in its scope.
- Truth-functional proposition: The truth value of any compound proposition using one or more of the five operators is a function of (that is, uniquely determined by) the truth values of its component propositions.
- The truth value of a truth-functional compound proposition is determined by the truth values of its components and the definitions of the logical operators involved. Any truth-functional compound proposition that can be determined in this manner is said to be a truth function.
- A statement variable can stand for any statement, simple or compound.
- Statement form: In propositional logic, an arrangement of logical operators and statement variables such that a uniform substitution of statements for the variables results in a statement.
- Argument form: In propositional logic, an argument form is an arrangement of logical operators and statement variables such that a uniform substitution of statements for the variables results in an argument.
- Substitution instance: A substitution instance of a statement occurs when a uniform substitution of statements for the variables results in a statement. A substitution instance of an argument occurs when a uniform substitution of statements for the variables results in an argument.
- Truth table: An arrangement of truth values for a truth-functional compound proposition that displays for every possible case how the truth value of the proposition is determined by the truth values of its simple components.

- Order of operations: The order of handling the logical operators within a truth-functional proposition; it is a step-by-step method of generating a complete truth table.
- Contingent statements: Statements that are neither necessarily true nor necessarily false (they are sometimes true, sometimes false).
- Noncontingent statements: Statements such that the truth values in the main operator column do not depend on the truth values of the component parts.
- Tautology: A statement that is necessarily true.
- Self-contradiction: A statement that is necessarily false.
- Logically equivalent statements: Two truth-functional statements that have identical truth tables under the main operator.
- Contradictory statements: Two statements that have opposite truth values under the main operator on every line of their respective truth tables.
- Consistent statements: Two (or more) statements that have at least one line on their respective truth tables where the main operators are true.
- Inconsistent statements: Two (or more) statements that do not have even one line on their respective truth tables where the main operators are true (but they can be false) at the same time.
- *Modus ponens*: A valid argument form (also referred to as affirming the antecedent).
- Fallacy of affirming the consequent: An invalid argument form; it is a formal fallacy.
- *Modus tollens*: A valid argument form (also referred to as denying the consequent).
- Fallacy of denying the antecedent: An invalid argument form; it is a formal fallacy.

KEY TERMS

LOGIC CHALLENGE: A CARD PROBLEM

You have not seen a large number of cards. You are told (and we stipulate that this is true) that each card has a number on one of its sides and a letter on the other side. No card has numbers on both sides, and no card has letters on both sides. You are not told how many cards there are, but you are told that the same number might occur on many different cards. The same letter might also occur on many different cards.

Someone else has been allowed to inspect the cards and makes a claim. "I have looked at all the cards and I have discovered a pattern: *If there is a vowel on one side of the card, then there is an even number on the other side.*" The italicized statement could be true or false.

You will be shown four cards. You will only see one side of each card. If you see a letter, then you know there must be a number on the other side. If you see a number, then you know there must be a letter on the other side. Your task is to turn over *only* the cards that have the *possibility* to make the person's italicized statement *false*. The four cards are displayed as follows:

| B | 3 | E | 4 |

Which cards (if any) should you turn over?

Chapter 8

Natural Deduction

Digital homework exercises for this chapter are available in your instructor's online course. For information on how to access these resources, please visit **www.oup.com/he/baronett5e**.

You and your friends are going to catch a movie at a new mall. You approach a place that seems to be still under construction. Someone remarks casually, "If this is not the new mall, then we are in the wrong place." You stop someone and ask for help. It turns out that you are not at the new mall, so the obvious conclusion is that you are in the wrong place. Let's look at the reasoning:

> If this is not the new mall, then we are in the wrong place.
> This is not the new mall.
> We are in the wrong place.

Seeing the argument displayed this way might help you recognize from Chapter 7 that it is an instance of *modus ponens*. But most people would not stop to identify the form because they would recognize immediately that the conclusion follows from the information at hand.

In fact, in many everyday situations, we recognize when reasoning is correct or incorrect, even when we are not sure whether the information is true or false. We may need help to know whether this is the new mall, but we know why it matters. This type of reasoning is *natural*, in the sense that the practical demands of life require that we have some basic forms of reasoning on which we can all rely. We are subject to the practical demands of reasoning on a daily basis. Everyday situations supply us with information that we quickly analyze. But what if the reasoning and the sheer amount of information become more complicated?

We often use basic forms of reasoning without even being aware of them, but even basic reasoning can throw us a curve if we are not careful. Here is an example:

"Would you tell me, please, which way I ought to go from here?" asked Alice.
"That depends a good deal on where you want to get to," said the Cheshire Cat.
"I don't much care where—" said Alice.
"Then it doesn't matter which way you go," said the Cat.
"—so long as I get *somewhere*," Alice added as an explanation.
"Oh, you're sure to do that," said the Cat, "if you only walk long enough."

Lewis Carroll, *Alice's Adventures in Wonderland*

As here, everyday reasoning involves a step-by-step procedure, and it can take care and practice to follow the steps. For example, after adding up the checks you wrote this week, you conclude that you don't have enough money in your checking account to cover everything. You deduce that you had better put some money in the account to ensure you have sufficient funds. In this kind of reasoning, each step follows directly from previous steps. When we get to the final step, we accept that what we have derived is correct, as long as our starting assumptions are correct.

We normally handle everyday arguments without putting them into symbols; in this sense, the reasoning is natural. We can even work our way quite naturally through arguments that involve many steps; but sometimes that gets hard, and we can go astray. In this chapter, we develop a method of proof much like these forms of everyday reasoning called *natural deduction*. Natural deduction is capable of handling complex arguments that go far beyond simple forms of everyday reasoning. This chapter builds on the natural aspect of our reasoning, so that we can recognize and apply the steps.

A. NATURAL DEDUCTION

Natural deduction is a proof procedure by which the conclusion of an argument is validly derived from the premises through the use of rules of inference. The function of **rules of inference** is to *justify* the steps of a proof. A **proof** (also called a *deduction* or a *derivation*) is a sequence of steps in which each step either is a premise or follows from earlier steps in the sequence according to the rules of inference. A justification of a step includes a rule of inference and the prior steps that were used to derive it. This procedure guarantees that each step follows validly from prior steps. A proof ends when the conclusion of the argument has been correctly derived.

There are two types of rules of inference: *implication rules* and *replacement rules*.

Implication rules are *valid argument forms*. When the premises of a valid argument form occur during a proof, then we can validly derive the conclusion of the argument form as a justified step in the proof. (*Modus ponens* and *modus tollens* are two examples of valid argument forms.)

Replacement rules are *pairs of logically equivalent statement forms*. Whenever one pair member of a replacement rule occurs in a proof

---

Natural deduction
A proof procedure by which the conclusion of an argument is validly derived from the premises through the use of rules of inference.

Rules of inference
The function of rules of inference is to justify the steps of a proof.

Proof A sequence of steps (also called a deduction or a derivation) in which each step either is a premise or follows from earlier steps in the sequence according to the rules of inference.

Implication rules
Valid argument forms that are validly applied only to an entire line.

Replacement rules
Pairs of logically equivalent statement forms.

step, then we can validly derive the other pair member as a justified step in the proof. For example, the statement form $\sim (p \cdot q)$ is logically equivalent to $(\sim p \vee \sim q)$.

Both types of rules of inference have the same function—*to ensure the validity of the steps they are used to justify.* A natural deduction proof can begin with any number of premises. Every step of a proof, except the premises, requires justification. Therefore, a proof is valid if each step is either a premise or is validly derived using the rules of inference.

We saw in Chapter 7 how truth tables and the indirect truth table method allow us to determine whether an argument is valid or invalid. However, one drawback with truth tables is that, as the number of simple statements increases, the number of lines needed to complete the truth table can become overwhelming. Of course, the indirect method can reduce the number of lines. However, the flexibility of the indirect method might lead us to overlook an important possibility—and therefore make a wrong determination of an argument.

Natural deduction offers a proof procedure that uses valid argument forms and logically equivalent statement forms. As such, it is a powerful and effective method for proving validity. Of course, the method comes with its own challenges. Mastering the rules of inference takes time, patience, determination, and practice. However, advancing your ability to use natural deduction is no different from learning other skills. For example, learning to talk is a natural part of growing up for most people. But the ability to speak eloquently or in front of a large audience does not

PROFILES IN LOGIC
Gerhard Gentzen

Although he lived only 35 years, Gerhard Gentzen did remarkable work in logic and the foundations of mathematics. Gentzen (1909–45) was interested in the use of *forms of argument*. He understood that logic and mathematics rely on new forms of argument to help prove new theorems. The need for new forms became that much clearer around the turn of the 20th century, when some of the old forms led to some startling paradoxes and contradictions. The entire foundations of logic and mathematics were threatened. After all, if certainty did not exist in mathematical proofs, then perhaps it might not exist at all.

Gentzen developed the system of *natural deduction* to help secure the consistency of a critical branch of mathematics, number theory. Gentzen's system was also adapted for work in logical analysis. Gentzen wanted the term "natural" in logic to mean the same as it does when mathematicians refer to the "natural way of reasoning": We generate rules of argument to derive more theorems. Gentzen's tools allow us to prove the validity of both mathematical and logical arguments. In formal logic proofs, they show how to introduce or eliminate logical operators.

come easily, and it usually requires hard work. Likewise, running is something that most children learn naturally. But the ability to run fast enough to win an Olympic gold medal takes immense training and dedication. Similarly, the ability to reason is a natural process in most humans. However, just as learning to run fast or to talk eloquently takes time, there are levels of abstract reasoning that require dedication and training.

B. IMPLICATION RULES I

Chapter 7 showed that every substitution instance of a valid argument form is valid. Since the implication rules are valid argument forms, they preserve truth. In other words, given true premises, the implication rules yield true conclusions. If you worked on Exercises 7G.1, II, 1–8, then you showed that the eight implication rules are valid. Nevertheless, it will be helpful to discuss their validity in an informal manner. They are referred to as *implication rules* because the premises of the valid argument forms imply their respective conclusions. We will think through the validity of the arguments. This process will add to your understanding of how the implication rules can be used to validly derive steps in a proof.

Modus Ponens (MP)

Modus ponens (MP)

$p \supset q$
p
q

Chapter 7 introduced ***modus ponens*** (**MP**) as part of the discussion of argument form. A conditional statement is false when the antecedent is true and the consequent is false. Given this, whenever a conditional statement is true, and the antecedent of that conditional is also true, then we can conclude that the consequent is true. For example, if it is true that "If the laptop computer that I want is under $500, then I'll buy it," and if it is also true that "the laptop computer that I want is under $500," we can logically conclude that "I'll buy it."

> If the laptop computer that I want is under $500, then I'll buy it.
> The laptop computer that I want is under $500.
> I'll buy it.

If the first premise is true, then we can rule out the possibility that the antecedent is true and the consequent is false. Now, if the second premise is true, then the antecedent of the first premise is true, too. Given this result, the consequent of the first premise is true. If we let p = *the laptop computer that I want is under $500*, and q = *I'll buy it*, we can reveal that the logical form of the argument is *modus ponens*:

Modus Ponens (MP)
$p \supset q$
p
q

The valid argument form *modus ponens* ensures that any uniform **substitution instance** using simple or compound statements results in a valid argument. Here are some examples:

Substitution instance In propositional logic, a substitution instance of an *argument* occurs when a uniform substitution of statements for the variables results in an argument.

Valid Applications of *Modus Ponens* (MP)

1. $R \supset (M \lor N)$	1. $(P \cdot Q) \supset (G \cdot \sim D)$	1. $(K \cdot D) \lor F$
2. R	2. $P \cdot Q$	2. $[(K \cdot D) \lor F] \supset (M \lor C)$
3. $M \lor N$	3. $G \cdot \sim D$	3. $M \lor C$

The third example illustrates an important point regarding all eight implication rules: *The order of the required lines is not important.* However, in order for *modus ponens* to be applied validly, it is necessary that both the conditional statement and the antecedent both appear as *complete separate lines*. If we look once again at the third example we see that it has this form:

$$p$$
$$\frac{p \supset q}{q}$$

Since both the conditional statement and its antecedent appear on separate lines, the necessary requirements for *modus ponens* have been met.

When the implication rule of *modus ponens* is used correctly, the result is a valid argument. However, you must be careful to avoid mistaken applications of *modus ponens*. Here are two examples of misapplications:

Misapplications of *Modus Ponens* (MP)

1. $(L \supset Q) \lor (R \lor S)$		1. $(L \supset Q) \lor (R \lor S)$
2. L	⊘	2. L
3. Q		3. $R \lor S$

A comparison of the three valid applications of *modus ponens* with the two invalid applications pinpoints the problem. In all three valid applications of *modus ponens*, the horseshoe was the main operator of one of the two required lines. However, in both of the misapplications of *modus ponens* the main operator in line 1 is the wedge. This illustrates an important point: *Implication rules are validly applied only to an entire line.* This point will be emphasized in the discussion of each of the eight implication rules. Failure to adhere to this point is the number one cause of mistakes when first learning to use the implication rules.

Learning to use the rules of inference correctly is similar to learning the rules of any game. Some games have rigid rules while others have loose rules. It is quite common for beginners to make mistakes by misapplying the rules. Part of the learning curve of any game is experiencing various situations in which the rules come to play. The examples of misapplications of the rules of inference are not meant to exhaust all the possible mistakes that might be made. However, they will highlight some common errors and you should use them to help understand how each rule should be used correctly. The rules of inference are precise and the examples will show you how to use them properly. The precision is crucial because the function of all the rules of inference is to ensure that each step in a proof is validly derived.

One final note: You may recall from Chapter 7 that the fallacy of affirming the consequent resembles *modus ponens*. Since it is easy to confuse the two forms, you must be careful not to make this mistake when applying *modus ponens*:

The Fallacy of Affirming the Consequent

$$p \supset q$$
$$\underline{q}$$
$$p$$ 🚫

Modus Tollens (MT)

Chapter 7 also introduced ***modus tollens*** (MT). Here is its logical form:

Modus Tollens (MT)

$$p \supset q$$
$$\underline{\sim q}$$
$$\sim p$$

Let's substitute the following statement for the first premise: "If enough people sign up for video streaming on their devices, then the cost of going to the movies has dropped." We let p = *enough people sign up for video streaming on their devices*, and q = *the cost of going to the movies has dropped*. If the first premise is true, then we can rule out the possibility that the antecedent is true and the consequent is false. Now if the second premise, ~ q, is true, then q is false. This means that the consequent, q, in the first premise is false. Therefore, p must be false in order for the first premise to remain true. Given these results, the conclusion, ~ p, is true.

The form of the argument shows that given a conditional statement and the negation of its consequent we can logically derive the negation of the antecedent as a conclusion. Here are some examples of valid applications:

Valid Applications of *Modus Tollens* (MT)

1. $H \supset (T \vee N)$	1. $(G \cdot D) \supset C$	1. $\sim (F \vee D)$
2. $\sim (T \vee N)$	2. $\sim C$	2. $[(T \vee F) \cdot \sim D] \supset (F \vee D)$
3. $\sim H$	3. $\sim (G \cdot D)$	3. $\sim [(T \vee F) \cdot \sim D]$

As with all the implication rules, you must be careful to avoid mistaken applications of *modus tollens*. Here is an example of a misapplication:

Misapplication of *Modus Tollens* (MT)

1. $(L \supset Q) \vee (R \vee S)$
2. $\underline{\sim Q}$ 🚫
3. $\sim L$

In the three examples of valid applications of *modus tollens*, the main operator in one of the required lines is a horseshoe. However, in the example of the misapplication of *modus tollens*, the main operator in line 1 is the wedge. Once again, implication rules are validly applied only to an entire line.

A final note before leaving *modus tollens*: You may recall from Chapter 7 that the fallacy of denying the antecedent resembles *modus tollens*. Since it is easy to confuse the two forms, you must be careful not to make this mistake in applying *modus tollens*:

The Fallacy of Denying the Antecedent

$$p \supset q$$
$$\underline{\sim p} \quad \oslash$$
$$\sim q$$

Hypothetical Syllogism (HS)

The implication rule **hypothetical syllogism (HS)** relies on conditional statements. Hypothetical syllogism has the following logical form:

Hypothetical Syllogism (HS)

$$p \supset q$$
$$\underline{q \supset r}$$
$$p \supset r$$

Hypothetical syllogism (HS)

$p \supset q$
$q \supset r$
$p \supset r$

Let's substitute the following for the first premise: "If I live in Atlanta, then I live in Georgia." Let p = *I live in Atlanta*, and q = *I live in Georgia*. Now if r = *I live in the United States*, then the second premise is, "If I live in Georgia, then I live in the United States." If the first premise is true, then the antecedent cannot be true and the consequent false. The same condition holds for the second premise. The only way for the conclusion to be false is for p to be true and r to be false. However, if r is false, then the q in the second premise must be false as well (because that is the only way to keep the second premise true). But that means that the first premise is false because the antecedent is true and the consequent false. This result is in direct conflict with our assumption that the first premise is true. Therefore, if both premises are true, the conclusion follows necessarily.

The following are examples of valid applications of hypothetical syllogism:

Valid Applications of Hypothetical Syllogism (HS)

1. $H \supset (S \vee N)$	1. $[(G \cdot C) \vee P] \supset \sim S$	1. $(M \vee N) \supset (S \vee Q)$
2. $(S \vee N) \supset \sim R$	2. $\underline{\sim S \supset M}$	2. $(P \vee R) \supset (M \vee N)$
3. $H \supset \sim R$	3. $[(G \cdot C) \vee P] \supset M$	3. $(P \vee R) \supset (S \vee Q)$

Here are two examples of misapplications:

Misapplications of Hypothetical Syllogism (HS)

1. $K \supset (L \vee \sim R)$	1. $(B \vee C) \supset (D \vee E)$
2. $(L \cdot \sim R) \supset M \quad \oslash$	2. $D \supset (F \vee G) \quad \oslash$
3. $K \supset M$	3. $(B \vee C) \supset (F \vee G)$

In the first example, the consequent of the first premise, $L \vee \sim R$, is *not identical* to the antecedent of the second premise, $L \cdot \sim R$. Therefore, the application of hypothetical syllogism is used invalidly. In the second example, only part of the consequent of the first premise, D, occurs as the antecedent of the second premise. Therefore, this is also a misapplication of hypothetical syllogism.

Disjunctive Syllogism (DS)

Disjunctive syllogism (DS)

The implication rule **disjunctive syllogism** (**DS**) has the following two logical forms:

Disjunctive Syllogism (DS)

$p \vee q$	$p \vee q$
$\sim p$	$\sim q$
q	p

$p \vee q$	$p \vee q$
$\sim p$	$\sim q$
q	p

Let's substitute the following for the first premise in the first form: "Either CDs are superior to records or DVDs are superior to film." We let $p = $ *CDs are superior to records*, and $q = $ *DVDs are superior to film*. Since the first premise is a disjunction, we know that if it is true, then at least one of the disjuncts is true. Since the second premise is the negation of p ("CDs are *not* superior to records"), p must be false in order for the second premise to be true. This means that in the first premise, q must be true to ensure that the disjunction is true. Thus, the conclusion, q, follows necessarily from the premises. The same reasoning holds for the second form.

The following are examples of legitimate applications of disjunctive syllogism:

Valid Applications of Disjunctive Syllogism (DS)

1. $(R \supset P) \vee S$	1. $(R \supset P) \vee S$	1. $G \vee [(H \cdot R) \supset S]$	1. $[\sim S \vee (R \supset B)] \vee (P \cdot Q)$
2. $\sim (R \supset P)$	2. $\sim S$	2. $\sim G$	2. $\sim (P \cdot Q)$
3. S	3. $R \supset P$	3. $(H \cdot R) \supset S$	3. $\sim S \vee (R \supset B)$

Here is an example of a misapplication:

Misapplication of Disjunctive Syllogism (DS)

1. $(F \vee G) \vee H$
2. $\sim F$ 🚫
3. H

Disjunctive syllogism is validly applied when there is a negation of the *entire disjunct* of the main operator, not just a part of it. Therefore, the mistake in the example occurs because the negation in the second premise, $\sim F$, is only part of the first disjunct in the first premise, $(F \vee G)$.

Justification: Applying the Rules of Inference

We create proofs using natural deduction by taking the given premises of an argument and deducing whatever is necessary in a step-by-step procedure to prove the conclusion. A complete proof using natural deduction requires a *justification* for each step of the deduction. **Justification** refers to the rule of inference that is applied to every validly derived step in a proof. Here is a simple example:

Justification Refers to the rule of inference that is applied to every validly derived step in a proof.

1. $S \supset P$
2. S / P
3. P 1, 2, MP

The display of the argument follows the pattern introduced in Chapter 7. The conclusion, indicated by the slash mark (/), is for reference. The proof is complete when a justified step in the proof displays the conclusion. In this example, the justification for line 3, *the deduced step*, is set off to the right of the line and spells out its derivation; in this case it was derived from lines 1 and 2 using *modus ponens*. The proof is complete. In addition, the foregoing example illustrates the basic structure related to proof construction. Each line includes a number and a statement, and is either a premise or a derived line with a justification. As you learn to construct proofs, you will need to follow this basic proof structure.

The next example illustrates the use of multiple rules of inference:

1. $\sim R$
2. $P \supset S$
3. $R \vee \sim S$
4. $\sim P \supset Q$ / Q
5. $\sim S$ 1, 3, DS
6. $\sim P$ 2, 5, MT
7. Q 4, 6, MP

In this example, line 5 is derived from lines 1 and 3 (both of which are premises) by disjunctive syllogism. Line 6 is derived from line 2 (a premise) and line 5 (a derived line) by *modus tollens*. Finally, line 7 is derived from line 4 (a premise) and line 6 (a derived line) by *modus ponens*. The process of justifying each line ensures that a rule of inference is validly applied. It also provides a means for checking the proof. Therefore, the correct application of the rules of inference guarantees that lines 5, 6, and 7 have each been validly deduced.

THE FIRST FOUR IMPLICATION RULES	
Modus Ponens (MP)	**Modus Tollens (MT)**
$p \supset q$ p q	$p \supset q$ $\sim q$ $\sim p$
Hypothetical Syllogism (HS)	**Disjunctive Syllogism (DS)**
$p \supset q$ $q \supset r$ $p \supset r$	$p \vee q$ $p \vee q$ $\sim p$ $\sim q$ q p

Lightboard Video

EXERCISES 8B

Self-Practice
Questions

I. The following are examples of what you may encounter in proofs. The last step of each example gives the line numbers needed for its derivation. You are to provide the implication rule that justifies the step.

[1] 1. $P \supset Q$
 2. P / Q
 3. Q 1, 2, _____

Answer: 3. Q 1, 2, MP

[2] 1. $P \supset Q$
 2. $Q \supset R$ / $P \supset R$
 3. $P \supset R$ 1, 2, _____

[3] 1. $R \supset S$
 2. $\sim S$ / $\sim R$
 3. $\sim R$ 1, 2, _____

[4] 1. $(P \cdot Q) \vee (R \supset S)$
 2. $\sim (P \cdot Q)$ / $R \supset S$
 3. $R \supset S$ 1, 2, _____

★ [5] 1. $Q \supset (R \vee S)$
 2. $\sim (R \vee S)$ / $\sim Q$
 3. $\sim Q$ 1, 2, _____

[6] 1. $\sim (R \vee S) \supset (P \supset Q)$
 2. $\sim (R \vee S)$ / $P \supset Q$
 3. $P \supset Q$ 1, 2, _____

[7] 1. $(P \cdot Q) \supset R$
 2. $R \supset \sim P$ / $(P \cdot Q) \supset \sim P$
 3. $(P \cdot Q) \supset \sim P$ 1, 2, _____

[8] 1. $(P \supset Q) \supset (R \supset S)$
 2. $\sim (R \supset S)$ / $\sim (P \supset Q)$
 3. $\sim (P \supset Q)$ 1, 2, _____

★ [9] 1. $(R \supset S) \vee (P \supset Q)$
 2. $\sim (R \supset S)$ / $P \supset Q$
 3. $P \supset Q$ 1, 2, _____

[10] 1. $\sim P \supset Q$
 2. $\sim Q$ / $\sim \sim P$
 3. $\sim \sim P$ 1, 2, _____

[11] 1. $\sim P \supset \sim Q$
 2. $\sim Q \supset \sim R$ / $\sim P \supset \sim R$
 3. $\sim P \supset \sim R$ 1, 2, _____

[12] 1. $(P \cdot R) \supset \sim S$
    2. $(P \cdot R)$ $/ \sim S$
    3. $\sim S$ 1, 2, _____

★ [13] 1. $R \supset (S \vee R)$
    2. $(S \vee R) \supset P$ $/ R \supset P$
    3. $R \supset P$ 1, 2, _____

[14] 1. $R \supset (S \vee R)$
    2. $\sim (S \vee R)$ $/ \sim R$
    3. $\sim R$ 1, 2, _____

[15] 1. $S \vee (P \supset Q)$
    2. $\sim S$ $/ P \supset Q$
    3. $P \supset Q$ 1, 2, _____

II. The following are more examples of what you may encounter in proofs. In these examples the justification (the implication rule) is provided for the last step. However, the step itself is missing. Use the given information to derive the last step of each example.

[1] 1. $(Q \supset S) \vee P$
    2. $\sim (Q \supset S)$
    3.   1, 2, DS

Answer: 3. P 1, 2, DS

[2] 1. $P \supset (Q \vee S)$
    2. P
    3.   1, 2, MP

[3] 1. $(K \vee L) \supset (K \vee N)$
    2. $(K \vee N) \supset (K \vee S)$
    3.   1, 2, HS

[4] 1. $(T \vee R) \supset (Q \vee S)$
    2. $\sim (Q \vee S)$
    3.   1, 2, MT

★ [5] 1. $P \vee (Q \cdot S)$
    2. $\sim P$
    3.   1, 2, DS

[6] 1. $(R \vee S) \supset T$
    2. $\sim T$
    3.   1, 2, MT

[7] 1. $(R \vee \sim T) \supset S$
    2. $R \vee \sim T$
    3.   1, 2, MP

[8]   1. $P \supset (Q \vee \sim R)$
    2. $(Q \vee \sim R) \supset \sim S$
    3.   1, 2, HS

★[9]   1. $(T \supset R) \supset (Q \supset S)$
    2. $\sim (Q \supset S)$
    3   1, 2, MT

[10]   1. $S \supset \sim (\sim R \vee \sim T)$
    2. S
    3.   1, 2, MP

[11]   1. $S \supset \sim (\sim R \vee \sim T)$
    2. $\sim \sim (\sim R \vee \sim T)$
    3.   1, 2, MT

[12]   1. $[\, P \vee (Q \cdot S)\,] \vee (\sim Q \cdot \sim P)$
    2. $\sim [\, P \vee (Q \cdot S)\,]$
    3.   1, 2, DS

★[13]   1. $(P \cdot \sim R) \supset Q$
    2. $\sim Q$
    3.   1, 2, MT

[14]   1. $(P \vee Q) \supset \sim R$
    2. $P \vee Q$
    3.   1, 2, MP

[15]   1. $(Q \cdot S) \vee (\sim Q \vee \sim P)$
    2. $\sim (Q \cdot S)$
    3.   1, 2, DS

III. The following examples contain more than one step for which you are to provide the line numbers needed for the derivation and the implication rule as justification.

[1]   1. $P \supset \sim Q$
    2. $R \supset Q$
    3. P / $\sim R$
    4. $\sim Q$
    5. $\sim R$

Answer:
    4. $\sim Q$ 1, 3, MP
    5. $\sim R$ 2, 4, MT

[2]   1. $\sim S$
    2. $Q \supset (S \vee R)$
    3. Q / R
    4. $S \vee R$
    5. R

[3] 1. $(S \cdot M) \supset Q$
    2. $(Q \vee R) \supset (S \cdot M)$
    3. $P \supset (Q \vee R)$ $/ P \supset Q$
    4. $P \supset (S \cdot M)$
    5. $P \supset Q$

[4] 1. $\sim P$
    2. $Q \vee (P \vee R)$
    3. $P \vee \sim Q$ $/ R$
    4. $\sim Q$
    5. $P \vee R$
    6. R

⭐[5] 1. $R \supset S$
    2. P
    3. $S \supset Q$
    4. $P \supset R$ $/ Q$
    5. $P \supset S$
    6. $P \supset Q$
    7. Q

[6] 1. $S \supset Q$
    2. $\sim R$
    3. S
    4. $Q \supset (R \vee P)$ $/ P$
    5. $S \supset (R \vee P)$
    6. $R \vee P$
    7. P

[7] 1. $\sim Q$
    2. $P \supset Q$
    3. $P \vee (\sim Q \supset R)$ $/ R$
    4. $\sim P$
    5. $\sim Q \supset R$
    6. R

[8] 1. $M \supset \sim Q$
    2. $(P \supset \sim Q) \supset (R \supset \sim L)$
    3. $\sim L \supset S$
    4. $P \supset M$ $/ R \supset S$
    5. $P \supset \sim Q$
    6. $R \supset \sim L$
    7. $R \supset S$

Video Tutorial: 8BIII
Exercise #9

★[9] 1. $R \lor \sim S$
     2. $(P \supset Q) \supset \sim R$
     3. $P \supset L$
     4. $L \supset Q$ / $\sim S$
     5. $P \supset Q$
     6. $\sim R$
     7. $\sim S$

[10] 1. $L \lor \sim S$
     2. $(P \cdot \sim Q) \lor \sim R$
     3. $\sim L$
     4. $(P \cdot \sim Q) \supset S$ / $\sim R$
     5. $\sim S$
     6. $\sim (P \cdot \sim Q)$
     7. $\sim R$

IV. The following examples contain more than one step for which you are to provide the missing derivation. In each case the implication rule and the lines used for the derivation are provided.

[1] 1. $Q \supset R$
     2. $P \supset Q$
     3. $\sim R$ / $\sim P$
     4.   1, 2, HS
     5.   3, 4, MT

Answer:

     4. $P \supset R$ 1, 2, HS
     5. $\sim P$ 3, 4, MT

[2] 1. $Q \supset R$
     2. $P \supset Q$
     3. $\sim R$ / $\sim P$
     4.   1, 3, MT
     5.   2, 4, MT

[3] 1. S
     2. $(P \lor Q) \supset R$
     3. $S \supset \sim R$ / $\sim (P \lor Q)$
     4.   1, 3, MP
     5.   2, 4, MT

[4]   1. $Q \supset R$
      2. $\sim P$
      3. $P \vee Q$ / R
      4.   2, 3, DS
      5.   1, 4, MP

⭐ [5] 1. $P \vee \sim S$
      2. $\sim S \supset (P \supset Q)$
      3. $\sim P$
      4. $(P \supset Q) \supset R$ / R
      5.   1, 3, DS
      6.   2, 5, MP
      7.   4, 6, MP

[6]   1. $P \supset \sim R$
      2. $R \vee S$
      3. $Q \vee P$
      4. $\sim Q$ / S
      5.   3, 4, DS
      6.   1, 5, MP
      7.   2, 6, DS

[7]   1. $(R \supset S) \vee (L \cdot \sim Q)$
      2. $(P \supset Q) \vee \sim M$
      3. $\sim M \supset \sim (R \supset S)$
      4. $\sim (P \supset Q)$ / L · ~ Q
      5.   2, 4, DS
      6.   3, 5, MP
      7.   1, 6, DS

[8]   1. $L \vee R$
      2. $(P \vee Q) \supset S$
      3. $\sim L$
      4. $R \supset (\sim L \supset \sim S)$ / ~ (P ∨ Q)
      5.   1, 3, DS
      6.   4, 5, MP
      7.   3, 6, MP
      8.   2, 7, MT

★ [9]   1. $S \vee (P \vee Q)$
     2. $\sim (Q \supset R)$
     3. $P \supset (Q \supset R)$
     4. $S \supset P$ / Q
     5.   2, 3, MT
     6.   4, 5, MT
     7.   1, 6, DS
     8.   5, 7, DS

[10]   1. $S \vee \sim R$
     2. $\sim L$
     3. $P \supset (Q \supset R)$
     4. $\sim S$
     5. $\sim L \supset P$ / $\sim Q$
     6.   3, 5, HS
     7.   2, 6, MP
     8.   1, 4, DS
     9.   7, 8, MT

C. TACTICS AND STRATEGY

Now that you have seen how each line of a proof is justified by using the first four implication rules, you are ready to use your knowledge to create your own proofs. However, before you plunge in you need to have a few guidelines. Efficient construction of proofs requires that you have an overall goal to keep you focused. You should say, "I need to get here," instead of "I don't much care where," which got Alice off on the wrong foot.

Tactics The use of small-scale maneuvers or devices.

    Tactics is the use of small-scale maneuvers or devices, whereas **strategy** is typically understood as referring to a greater, overall goal. For example, in working through a proof, your strategy might be to isolate as many simple statements as possible, or it might be to reduce, to simplify compound statements. These goals can often be accomplished by employing a variety of tactical moves, such as using *modus ponens* to isolate a statement. The same strategic goal might be accomplished by using *modus tollens* or disjunctive syllogism as a tactical move, enabling you to isolate part of a compound statement.

Strategy Referring to a greater, overall goal.

    It is extremely helpful to have a strategy when employing natural deduction. However, it must be understood that even the best strategies cannot guarantee success. Nevertheless, a well-thought-out strategy, coupled with a firm grasp of the available tactical moves within a proof, will maximize your prospects for successfully completing a proof.

    At first, it is often best to simply plug away at tactical moves until you begin to recognize patterns or begin to see more than one move ahead. In this sense, it is like learning to play checkers or chess. The novice player first learns the moves that are permitted. The initial games are usually devoid of any real strategy. Beginners typically move pieces hoping for some tactical advantage in small areas of the board. Real strategy comes only after you have played enough games to begin to understand long-term goals. It takes time and patience to master offensive and defensive skills, the deployment of deception, the ability to think multiple moves ahead, to recognize traps, and to coordinate numerous tactical maneuvers at the same time—in other words, to have a global strategy.

Applying the First Four Implication Rules

Strategy: Try to locate the conclusion somewhere "inside" the premises. For example, the conclusion might be the antecedent or the consequent of a conditional in one of the premises. On the other hand, the conclusion might occur as a disjunct in a premise. The idea is to "take apart" a proposition by using the rules to isolate what is needed. This overall strategy involves "thinking from the bottom up," in which you first determine what you need, and then find the most efficient way of getting there. Compare this way of thinking to navigating your way through a maze: You can sometimes begin by looking at where the maze ends to help find a path backward to where the maze begins.

Here are some specific tactical moves:

Tactic 1: If what you need to derive is a letter or expression that occurs as the consequent of a conditional in one of the premises, then try *modus ponens* (MP) as part of your proof.

1. E
2. $G \vee \sim H$
3. $E \supset F$
4. F 1, 3, MP

Tactic 2: If what you need to derive contains a letter or expression that occurs as the antecedent of a conditional in one of the premises, then try *modus tollens* (MT) as part of your proof.

1. $\sim L$
2. $M \cdot N$
3. $K \supset L$
4. $\sim K$ 1, 3, MT

Tactic 3: If what you need to derive is a conditional statement, then try to derive it by using hypothetical syllogism (HS) as part of your proof.

1. $\sim F \supset U$
2. S
3. $E \supset \sim F$
4. $E \supset U$ 1, 3, HS

Tactic 4: If what you need to derive is one of the disjuncts in a compound premise, then try using disjunctive syllogism (DS) as part of your proof.

1. ~ (H ⊃ M)
2. ~ S ∨ R
3. (H ⊃ M) ∨ (S · U)
4. S · U   1, 3, DS

The overall strategy and the specific tactics can help at any point in the proof, not just with the conclusion. For instance, it might help you derive a part of the conclusion which you can then use to derive the final conclusion.

Natural deduction proofs allow for creativity because sometimes more than one correct proof is possible for a given problem. The following shows two different but equally correct proofs:

Proof A
1. S ⊃ (P · Q)
2. (P · Q) ⊃ R
3. ~R   / ~S
4. ~ (P · Q)   2, 3, MT
5. ~ S   1, 4, MT

Proof B
1. S ⊃ (P · Q)
2. (P · Q) ⊃ R
3. ~ R   / ~S
4. S ⊃ R   1, 2, HS
5. ~ S   3, 4, MT

Proof A used *modus tollens* twice to derive the conclusion. Proof B first used hypothetical syllogism, then used *modus tollens* to derive the conclusion. Notice also that in Proof A lines 2 and 3 were used first, while Proof B used lines 1 and 2 first. Nevertheless, both proofs correctly derived the conclusion.

When you start creating your own proofs, certain questions naturally arise:

- *How many times can I use a specific rule in a proof?*

You can use a rule as many times as needed (as illustrated in Proof A).

- *How many times can I use a specific line in a proof?*

You can use a line as many times as needed. For example, you might need to derive both parts of a disjunction in order to complete a proof. Of course, each part of the disjunction has to be derived on a separate line with the appropriate justification.

- *What if I derive one part of a disjunction but later on in the proof I need to derive the other part?*

That's fine. You can derive whichever part you need at any point in the proof provided each derivation is correctly justified.

- *What if I derive lines that turn out not to be needed to complete a proof?*

As long as you correctly derive the conclusion—each line of your proof is justified by the rules—it is all right if you derived some lines that turn out to be superfluous.

EXERCISES 8C

I. Use the first four implication rules to complete the proofs. Provide the justification for each step that you derive.

Self-Practice
Questions

[1] 1. $\sim (P \cdot Q)$
     2. $\sim (R \cdot S) \supset (L \cdot \sim Q)$
     3. $(R \cdot S) \supset (P \cdot Q)$ $/ L \cdot \sim Q$

Answer:

     4. $\sim (R \cdot S)$ 1, 3, MT
     5. $L \cdot \sim Q$ 2, 4, MP

[2] 1. $P \supset Q$
     2. $R \supset P$
     3. $\sim Q$ $/ \sim R$

[3] 1. P
     2. $R \supset Q$
     3. $P \supset \sim Q$ $/ \sim R$

[4] 1. $S \supset (P \cdot Q)$
     2. $(P \cdot Q) \supset R$
     3. $\sim R$ $/ \sim S$

⭐[5] 1. $\sim P \supset (Q \vee R)$
     2. $(\sim P \supset \sim S) \supset \sim L$
     3. $(Q \vee R) \supset \sim S$ $/ \sim L$

[6] 1. Q
     2. $L \supset (S \supset P)$
     3. $Q \supset (R \supset S)$
     4. L $/ R \supset P$

[7] 1. $P \supset Q$
     2. $(P \supset R) \supset \sim S$
     3. $Q \supset R$
     4. $(\sim Q \supset \sim P) \supset S$ $/ \sim (\sim Q \supset \sim P)$

[8] 1. $S \supset \sim Q$
     2. $P \supset Q$
     3. $R \supset S$
     4. R $/ \sim P$

⭐[9] 1. $R \vee S$
     2. $\sim (P \vee Q)$
     3. $R \supset (P \vee Q)$
     4. $S \supset (Q \vee R)$ $/ Q \vee R$

[10] 1. $P \lor Q$
      2. $Q \supset \sim R$
      3. $\sim P$
      4. $\sim R \supset \sim S$ $/ \sim S$

[11] 1. $P \supset R$
      2. $\sim S$
      3. $P \lor Q$
      4. $R \supset S$ $/ Q$

[12] 1. $\sim (P \cdot S)$
      2. $\sim R$
      3. $\sim P \supset [P \lor (Q \supset R)]$
      4. $P \supset (P \cdot S)$ $/ \sim Q$

⭐ [13] 1. $P \lor (S \supset Q)$
       2. $\sim Q$
       3. $P \supset Q$
       4. $\sim S \supset R$ $/ R$

[14] 1. $\sim R \lor (P \supset Q)$
      2. $(P \supset Q) \supset (Q \supset \sim R)$
      3. $\sim \sim R$ $/ \sim P$

[15] 1. P
      2. $(Q \supset R) \supset (P \supset Q)$
      3. $P \supset (Q \supset R)$ $/ R$

Video Tutorial: 8C
Exercise #16

[16] 1. $L \lor P$
      2. $\sim S$
      3. $P \supset (Q \cdot R)$
      4. $S \lor (L \supset S)$ $/ Q \cdot R$

⭐ [17] 1. $Q \supset P$
       2. S
       3. $(Q \lor \sim R) \supset \sim P$
       4. $S \supset (Q \lor \sim R)$ $/ \sim R$

[18] 1. $(Q \lor R) \supset \sim P$
      2. $\sim P \supset [P \lor (Q \supset P)]$
      3. $Q \lor R$ $/ R$

[19] 1. $R \supset S$
      2. $(Q \supset S) \supset \sim P$
      3. $\sim P \supset [(Q \supset R) \supset (L \lor \sim S)]$
      4. $Q \supset R$
      5. $\sim L$ $/ \sim R$

[20]   1. $(P \supset S) \supset \sim Q$
    2. $P \supset R$
    3. $(P \supset R) \supset (R \supset Q)$
    4. $(P \supset Q) \supset (R \supset S)$ $/ \sim P$

II. First, translate the following arguments into symbolic form. Second, use the four implication rules to derive the conclusion of each. Letters for the simple statements are provided in parentheses and can be used in the order they are given.

1. Shane is going to the party, or either Rachel or Max is going. Either Rachel is going to the party or Shane is not going to the party. But Rachel is not going to the party. Therefore, Max is going. (S, R, M)

Answer:

    1. $S \vee (R \vee M)$
    2. $R \vee \sim S$
    3. $\sim R$ $/ M$
    4. $\sim S$ 2, 3, DS
    5. $R \vee M$ 1, 4, DS
    6. M 3, 5, DS

2. If I bet red on roulette, then I will win my bet. If I win my bet, then I will stop betting. If I'm feeling lucky, then I bet red on roulette. I'm feeling lucky. It follows that I will stop betting. (R, W, S, L)

3. If Melinda is a comedian, then she is shy. Either Melinda is a comedian, or if she is not shy, then she is famous. Moreover, Melinda is not shy. Consequently, she is famous. (C, S, F)

4. If we continue to fight, then our supply of troops grows thinner. If our supply of troops grows thinner, then either enlistment slows down or more casualties will occur. But we do continue to fight. Also, enlistment does not slow down. This proves that more casualties will occur. (F, S, E, C)

⭐ 5. If my son drinks three sodas, then if he eats some chocolate, then he gets hyper. If he is excited, then my son drinks three sodas. Furthermore, my son is excited, or he either drinks three sodas or he eats some chocolate. But it is not the case that if he eats some chocolate, then he gets hyper. We can conclude that he eats some chocolate. (S, C, H, E)

6. If amino acids were found on Mars, then there is life on Mars, then there is life in the universe outside Earth. Either amino acids were found on Mars or we did not look in the best places. If we did not look in the best places, then if amino acids were found on Mars, then there is life on Mars. But it is not the case that amino acids were found on Mars. Thus, there is life in the universe outside Earth. (A, L, U, P)

7. Either I am going to the movie or I am studying for the exam. If I study for the exam, then I will not fail the course. But I either fail the course or I will graduate on time. I am not going to the movie. Hence, I will graduate on time. (*M, S, F, G*)

8. If there is a recession and the housing sector does not recover, then the national debt will continue growing. Also, the government invests in public projects or the national debt will not continue growing. Either there is a recession and the housing sector does not recover, or the unemployment rate will not go down. But the government is not investing in public projects. This implies that the unemployment rate will not go down. (*R, H, D, P, U*)

⭐ 9. If Suzy buys a new car or a new motorcycle, then she has to take a loan. If Suzy saves half her weekly salary for a year, then if she doesn't go on an expensive vacation, then she will not have to take a loan. Either she goes on an expensive vacation or she saves half her weekly salary for a year. But Suzy does not go on an expensive vacation. Therefore, it is not the case that either Suzy buys a new car or a new motorcycle. (*C, M, L, S, E*)

10. If your aunt is not a lawyer, then she is an accountant. In addition, if your aunt is an accountant, then if she is tired of her job, then she can teach at our college. Your aunt is either looking for new employment or she cannot teach at our college. But your aunt is not a lawyer. Also, she is not looking for new employment. Therefore, she is not tired of her job. (*L, P, J, C, E*)

D. IMPLICATION RULES II

There are four more implication rules to introduce. As with the first four rules, correct application ensures that valid arguments are derived throughout the proofs. Although these were already shown to be valid by the truth table method, we will discuss their validity in an informal manner.

Simplification (Simp)

The implication rule **simplification (Simp)** has the dot as the main operator. There are two logical forms of this rule:

Simplification (Simp)

$$\frac{p \cdot q}{p} \qquad \frac{p \cdot q}{q}$$

Let's substitute the following for the premise in both forms: "Oak trees are deciduous, and pine trees are conifers." Let p = *Oak trees are deciduous*, and q = *pine trees are conifers*. If a conjunction is true, then both conjuncts are true. Therefore, either the right or left conjunct can be validly derived from a conjunction that occurs as the main operator in a premise or a derived line. Since the conclusion is merely one of the two conjuncts, it follows necessarily from the premise or a derived line. The following are examples of valid applications of the rule of simplification:

Valid Applications of Simplification (Simp)

1. $(H \vee D) \cdot (F \vee G)$ 1. $(H \vee D) \cdot (F \vee G)$ 1. $\sim (B \supset D) \cdot Q$ 1. $M \cdot [S \vee (G \supset C)]$
2. $H \vee D$ 2. $F \vee G$ 2. $\sim (B \supset D)$ 2. $S \vee (G \supset C)$

In all four examples, either the right or left conjunct was validly derived.

Here is an example of a misapplication:

Misapplication of Simplification (Simp)

1. $(P \cdot Q) \vee (R \supset S)$
2. P

Since the main operator in line 1 is a wedge, the logical form is $p \vee q$. However, *simplification* can be used only when a conjunction is the main operator, it cannot be used with a disjunction.

Conjunction (Conj)

The implication rule **conjunction (Conj)** can be stated quite simply: Any two true statements can be joined conjunctively with the result being a true statement. Recall that a conjunction is true only when both conjuncts are true. For example, if the statement "June has 30 days" and the statement "Apples are fruit" are both true statements, then it follows that "June has 30 days and apples are fruit." If we let $p = June$ *has 30 days*, and $q = apples$ *are fruit*, then the argument is revealed as an instance of the implication rule conjunction:

Conjunction (Conj)

p

q

$p \cdot q$

Conjunction (Conj)

p

q

$p \cdot q$

If both premises are true, then p and q are true. Therefore, the conjunction of p and q is true. A correct application of the implication rule results in a valid argument. Here are some examples:

Valid Applications of Conjunction (Conj)

1. G 1. $B \supset J$ 1. $S \vee D$
2. $H \vee K$ 2. $L \supset \sim F$ 2. M
3. $G \cdot (H \vee K)$ 3. $(B \supset J) \cdot (L \supset \sim F)$ 3. $(P \cdot Q) \supset R$
                                                    4. $(S \vee D) \cdot M$
                                                    5. $(S \vee D) \cdot [(P \cdot Q) \supset R]$
                                                      6. $M \cdot [(P \cdot Q) \supset R]$
                                                      7. $[(S \vee D) \cdot M] \cdot [(P \cdot Q) \supset R]$

The third example offers an illustration of the various ways that conjunction can be used. For example, lines 4, 5, and 6 were derived by using two premises. However, line 7 was derived from line 4, a derived line, and line 3, a premise.

Here is an example of a misapplication of conjunction:

Misapplication of Conjunction (Conj)

1. S
2. $P \supset R$
3. $S \cdot P$ ⊘

The mistake here is in thinking that conjunction allows you to conjoin part of a line. Like all the implication rules, conjunction has to be applied to an entire line. The rule permits you to conjoin any two complete lines, either premises or derived lines.

Addition (Add)

Addition (Add)

p
___
$p \vee q$

The implication rule **addition (Add)** can be stated this way: Any true statement, either a premise or a derived line, can be joined *disjunctively* with any other statement. The reasoning behind this is that a disjunction is true if at least one of the disjuncts is true. For example, if it is true that "Mt. Everest is the tallest mountain on Earth," then it is also true that "Mt. Everest is the tallest mountain on Earth or butterflies are carnivorous." If we let p = *Mt. Everest is the tallest mountain on Earth*, and q = *butterflies are carnivorous*, we reveal the logical form:

Addition (Add)

$$p$$
$$\overline{p \vee q}$$

If the premise is true, then p is true. Since a disjunction is true if at least one of its disjuncts is true, we can validly deduce $p \vee q$. This means that even if we add (disjunctively) a false statement, such as the one in the example (q = *butterflies are carnivorous*), the resulting derivation $p \vee q$ is true because at least one of the disjuncts is true.

It is important to remember that the *rule of addition can be used only with a disjunction as the main operator* for an entire line. Here are some examples of valid applications:

Valid Applications of Addition (Add)

1. S
2. $S \vee (Q \cdot R)$

1. R
2. $R \vee (Q \supset T)$

1. $M \supset N$
2. $(M \supset N) \vee (Q \cdot \sim P)$

1. $\sim D \cdot T$
2. $(\sim D \cdot T) \vee [(P \supset R) \cdot S]$

In all four examples the entire first line was used for the application of addition. If only part of a line is used, then the result is a misapplication. Here is an example:

Misapplication of Addition (Add)

1. $(P \cdot Q) \supset (R \cdot S)$
2. $(P \cdot Q) \vee T$ ⊘

The mistake occurs because only part of line 1 was used (the antecedent). For this example, the only way to correctly apply the rule of addition to line 1 is to derive a *disjunction* with $(P \cdot Q) \supset (R \cdot S)$ as the first disjunct. For example, we could validly derive the following using addition: $[(P \cdot Q) \supset (R \cdot S)] \vee \sim D$.

Here is another example of a mistake in applying the rule:

Misapplication of Addition (Add)

1. $P \supset (\sim Q \vee S)$

2. $R \vee D$ 🚫

The rule of addition *does not* allow you to just add anything you wish from nothing. It allows you to create a disjunction *only with an already established line*.

Constructive Dilemma (CD)

The implication rule **constructive dilemma (CD)** is complex because it combines three different logical operators: the horseshoe, the dot, and the wedge. Although the rule can be difficult to grasp at first, working through an example should help you to better understand the logic behind it. First, let's look at the logical form:

Constructive dilemma (CD)

$(p \supset q) \cdot (r \supset s)$

$p \vee r$

$q \vee s$

Constructive Dilemma (CD)

$(p \supset q) \cdot (r \supset s)$

$p \vee r$

$q \vee s$

Let's substitute the following for the first premise:

If I live in Hawaii, then I surf, *and* if I live in Colorado, then I ski.

Let p = *I live in Hawaii*, q = *I surf*, r = *I live in Colorado*, and s = *I ski*. Substituting for the letters in the argument form for constructive dilemma, the second premise is "I live in Hawaii or I live in Colorado." The conclusion is "I surf or I ski." The main operator of the first premise is the dot. Therefore, if the first premise is true, then both conjuncts are true. Since both conjuncts are conditional statements, the antecedents cannot be true and consequents false.

Now, if the second premise is true, then *at least one* of the disjuncts, p or r, is true. This means that *at least one* of the following must be true: "I live in Hawaii," or "I live in Colorado." Given this, *at least one* of the antecedents in the first premise is true (p or r). Since we previously eliminated the possibility of true antecedent and false consequent in both conditionals of the first premise, we now know that *at least one* of q or s must be true. In other words, *at least one* of the following must be true: "I surf," or "I ski." This analysis shows that if the premises are true, then the conclusion is true, because it is a disjunction with *at least one* true disjunct (q or s).

The following are examples of valid applications of constructive dilemma:

Valid Applications of Constructive Dilemma (CD)

1. $(S \supset Q) \cdot (M \supset N)$ 1. $[\sim G \supset (P \cdot R)] \cdot [\sim D \supset (H \cdot F)]$

2. $S \vee M$ 2. $\sim G \vee \sim D$

3. $Q \vee N$ 3. $(P \cdot R) \vee (H \cdot F)$

Here are two examples of misapplications:

Misapplications of Constructive Dilemma (CD)

1. $(S \supset \sim P) \lor (Q \supset \sim R)$	1. $(S \supset M) \cdot [(F \cdot G) \supset H]$
2. $S \lor Q$	2. $S \lor F$
3. $\sim P \lor \sim R$ ⊘	3. $M \lor H$ ⊘

In the first example of a misapplication, the main operator in premise 1 is the wedge. However, for constructive dilemma to work correctly the main operator must be a dot. In the second example, the statement, $F \cdot G$, is an antecedent, but premise 2 only has F as the second disjunct. But in order for constructive dilemma to be used correctly, the second disjunct in premise 2 has to be the entire antecedent, $F \cdot G$. Since this is not the case, this is a misapplication of constructive dilemma.

THE EIGHT IMPLICATION RULES	
Modus Ponens (MP)	*Modus Tollens* (MT)
$p \supset q$ $\underline{p}$ q	$p \supset q$ $\underline{\sim q}$ $\sim p$
Hypothetical Syllogism (HS)	**Disjunctive Syllogism (DS)**
$p \supset q$ $\underline{q \supset r}$ $p \supset r$	$p \lor q$ $p \lor q$ $\underline{\sim p}$ $\underline{\sim q}$ q p
Simplification (Simp)	**Conjunction (Conj)**
$\underline{p \cdot q}$ $\underline{p \cdot q}$ q p	p $\underline{q}$ $p \cdot q$
Addition (Add)	**Constructive Dilemma (CD)**
$\underline{p}$ $p \lor q$	$(p \supset q) \cdot (r \supset s)$ $\underline{p \lor r}$ $q \lor s$

Since we added four more implication rules to the original set, we need to add to our strategy and tactics guide:

Applying the Second Four Implication Rules

Strategy: We can continue employing the global strategy of trying to locate the conclusion somewhere "inside" the premises. Here are some specific tactical moves associated with the second four implication rules:

Tactic 5: If what you need to derive is a letter or expression that occurs as a conjunct in a premise, then try simplification (Simp) as part of your proof.

1. $R \lor \sim S$
2. $(E \supset \sim F) \cdot (S \supset \sim U)$
3. $\sim F \cdot R$
4. $S \supset \sim U$ 2, Simp

Tactic 6: If what you need to derive is a conjunction, then first, identify and obtain the individual conjuncts, and second, use conjunction (Conj) as part of your proof.

    1. $M \supset \sim N$
    2. $S \cdot (U \vee N)$
    3. $R \vee S$
    4. $(R \vee S) \cdot (M \supset \sim N)$ 1, 3, Conj

Tactic 7: If what you need to derive has a letter or expression that does *not* occur in *any* of the premises, then you have to use addition (Add) to introduce the letter or expression you need as part of your proof.

    1. $M \vee L$
    2. $E \supset \sim F$
    3. $L \cdot H$
    4. $(E \supset \sim F) \vee (G \cdot S)$ 2, Add

Tactic 8: If what you need to derive is a disjunction, then try applying constructive dilemma (CD) as part of your proof.

    1. $(E \supset \sim F) \cdot (S \supset \sim U)$
    2. $R \supset (M \vee S)$
    3. $E \vee S$
    4. $\sim F \vee \sim U$ 1, 3, CD

    As with the first set of implication rules, remember that these specific tactics can help at any point in the proof, not just with the final conclusion.

EXERCISES 8D

    I. The following are more examples of what you may encounter in proofs. The last step of each example gives the line numbers needed for its derivation. You are to provide the implication rule that justifies the step. This will give you practice using the second set of four implication rules.

Self-Practice
Questions

    [1] 1. $(P \supset Q) \cdot (R \supset S)$
        2. $P \vee R$ $/ Q \vee S$
        3. $Q \vee S$ 1, 2, _____

Answer: 3. $Q \vee S$ 1, 2, CD

    [2] 1. $(P \supset R) \cdot (Q \supset R)$ $/ P \supset R$
        2. $P \supset R$ 1, _____

    [3] 1. $T \vee U$
        2. $\sim P$ $/ (T \vee U) \cdot \sim P$
        3. $(T \vee U) \cdot \sim P$ 1, 2, _____

    [4] 1. R $/ R \vee (P \cdot \sim Q)$
        2. $R \vee (P \cdot \sim Q)$ 1, _____

⭐[5]   1. ~ P
     2. T ⊃ U   / ~ P · (T ⊃ U)
     3. ~ P · (T ⊃ U)   1, 2, _____

[6]   1. ~ (P ∨ Q) · R   / ~ (P ∨ Q)
     2. ~ (P ∨ Q)   1, _____

[7]   1. (~ P ⊃ Q) · (~ R ⊃ S)
     2. ~ P ∨ ~ R   / Q ∨ S
     3. Q ∨ S   1, 2, _____

[8]   1. P   / P ∨ ~ Q
     2. P ∨ ~ Q   1, _____

⭐[9]   1. P
     2. Q   / P · Q
     3. P · Q   1, 2, _____

[10]   1. (S ∨ P) · M   / S ∨ P
     2. S ∨ P   1, _____

[11]   1. [(P · R) ⊃ ~ S] · [(P ∨ R) ⊃ ~ T]
     2. (P · R) ∨ (P ∨ R)   / ~ S ∨ ~ T
     3. ~ S ∨ ~ T   1, 2, _____

[12]   1. P ⊃ Q   / (P ⊃ Q) ∨ ~ (R ∨ S)
     2. (P ⊃ Q) ∨ ~ (R ∨ S)   1, _____

⭐[13]   1. P
     2. (R ⊃ S) ∨ Q   / P · [(R ⊃ S) ∨ Q]
     3. P · [(R ⊃ S) ∨ Q]   1, 2, _____

[14]   1. (~ P ⊃ Q) · (~ R ⊃ S)   / ~ P ⊃ Q
     2. ~ P ⊃ Q   1, _____

[15]   1. (S ⊃ P) · [R ⊃ (~ Q · L)]
     2. S ∨ R   / P ∨ (~ Q · L)
     3. P ∨ (~ Q · L)   1, 2, _____

II. The following are more examples of what you may encounter in proofs. In these examples the justification (the implication rule) is provided for the last step. However, the step itself is missing. Use the given information to derive the last step of each example. This will give you practice using the second set of four implication rules.

[1]   1. (S ⊃ T) · (P ⊃ Q)
     2. S ∨ P
     3.   1, 2, CD

Answer: 3. T ∨ Q   1, 2, CD

[2] 1. $(M \supset P) \cdot K$
   2.   1, Simp

[3] 1. $P \vee Q$
   2. $S \vee T$
   3.   1, 2, Conj

[4] 1. $\sim (S \vee T)$
   2.   1, Add

⭐ [5] 1. $P \cdot (Q \supset R)$
   2.   1, Simp

[6] 1. $(R \vee S) \cdot (P \supset Q)$
   2. $S \vee Q$
   3.   1, 2, Conj

[7] 1. $[P \supset (R \vee L)] \cdot [S \supset (Q \vee M)]$
   2. $P \vee S$
   3.   1, 2, CD

[8] 1. $\sim S$
   2.   1, Add

⭐ [9] 1. $P \supset Q$
   2. $R \vee S$
   3.   1, 2, Conj

[10] 1. $[P \vee (\sim R \vee \sim S)] \cdot (Q \supset R)$
    2.   1, Simp

[11] 1. $(\sim R \supset \sim S) \cdot (\sim P \supset \sim Q)$
    2. $\sim R \vee P$
    3.   1, 2, CD

[12] 1. $(S \supset \sim Q)$
    2. $\sim (\sim P \cdot \sim Q)$
    3.   1, 2, Conj

⭐[13] 1. $(\sim P \vee \sim S) \cdot (\sim L \supset \sim R)$
    2.   1, Simp

[14] 1. $P \supset \sim (\sim S \vee \sim L)$
    2.   1, Add

[15] 1. $[\sim L \supset (\sim Q \vee R)] \supset \sim S$
    2. $P \supset \sim Q$
    3.   1, 2, Conj

III. **Use the eight implication rules to complete the proofs. Provide the justification for each step that you derive.**

[1] 1. $Q \supset (P \lor R)$
   2. $Q \cdot S$ / $P \lor R$

Answer:

   1. $Q \supset (P \lor R)$
   2. $Q \cdot S$ / $P \lor R$
   3. Q 2, Simp
   4. $P \lor R$ 1, 3, MP

[2] 1. $R \supset (P \lor Q)$
   2. $S \lor {\sim} (P \lor Q)$
   3. ${\sim} S$ / ${\sim} R$

[3] 1. $(M \supset P) \cdot (S \lor Q)$
   2. $R \supset M$ / $R \supset P$

[4] 1. $[(M \cdot R) \lor S] \supset (P \lor Q)$
   2. M
   3. R / $P \lor Q$

⭐ [5] 1. P
   2. $(P \lor Q) \supset R$
   3. $R \supset S$ / S

[6] 1. $P \lor (M \lor R)$
   2. $M \supset S$
   3. $R \supset Q$
   4. ${\sim} P$ / $S \lor Q$

[7] 1. $(M \lor {\sim} P) \supset (Q \lor {\sim} S)$
   2. $M \cdot {\sim} R$ / $Q \lor {\sim} S$

[8] 1. $P \cdot R$
   2. $(P \supset Q) \cdot (R \supset S)$ / $Q \lor S$

⭐ [9] 1. $P \cdot (S \lor Q)$
   2. $(P \lor R) \supset M$ / M

[10] 1. ${\sim} (Q \cdot R)$
   2. $P \lor S$
   3. $[P \supset (Q \cdot R)] \cdot (S \supset L)$
   4. S / L

[11] 1. $(M \lor Q) \supset {\sim} P$
   2. M
   3. $P \lor S$ / $S \cdot (M \lor Q)$

[12] 1. $\sim P \cdot D$
    2. $P \lor (Q \cdot R)$
    3. $P \lor (S \cdot L)$ / $Q \cdot S$

★ [13] 1. $(P \supset Q) \cdot (R \supset S)$
    2. $P \lor L$
    3. $(L \supset M) \cdot (N \supset K)$ / $Q \lor M$

[14] 1. $(P \lor R) \supset S$
    2. $P \cdot Q$ / $P \cdot S$

[15] 1. $R \lor (P \lor S)$
    2. $\sim R$
    3. $P \supset Q$
    4. $\sim R \supset (S \supset L)$ / $Q \lor L$

[16] 1. $Q \supset S$
    2. $\sim R \cdot P$
    3. $P \supset Q$
    4. P / $S \cdot \sim R$

★ [17] 1. $S \lor P$
    2. $(R \lor S) \supset L$
    3. $(P \lor Q) \supset R$
    4. $\sim S$ / L

[18] 1. $(P \cdot Q) \supset R$
    2. $Q \cdot \sim S$
    3. $Q \supset (P \cdot S)$ / R

[19] 1. $(R \lor S) \lor (\sim L \cdot M)$
    2. $(P \cdot Q) \supset \sim (R \lor S)$
    3. $\sim L$
    4. $(\sim L \lor M) \supset (P \cdot Q)$ / $(\sim L \cdot M) \cdot \sim L$

[20] 1. $N \supset \sim L$
    2. $\sim P \cdot K$
    3. $(\sim P \lor Q) \supset (\sim R \supset S)$
    4. $\sim L \supset M$
    5. $N \lor \sim R$ / $\sim R \supset S$

★ [21] 1. $R \supset P$
    2. $(Q \cdot \sim R) \supset (S \cdot \sim R)$
    3. $\sim P$
    4. $P \lor Q$ / S

[22] 1. $R \supset S$
    2. $P \supset \sim Q$
    3. $\sim Q \supset R$
    4. $P \cdot Q$ / $R \cdot S$

[23] 1. $(R \lor Q) \supset [P \supset (S \equiv L)]$
    2. $(P \lor Q) \supset R$
    3. $P \cdot S$ / $S \equiv L$

[24] 1. $P \lor (Q \supset R)$
    2. $(S \lor L) \supset (Q \cdot M)$
    3. $Q \supset \sim P$
    4. $S \cdot N$ / R

★[25] 1. $(M \lor N) \supset (P \cdot K)$
    2. $(P \lor \sim Q) \supset [(R \supset L) \cdot S]$
    3. M / $P \cdot (R \supset L)$

[26] 1. $R \supset \sim S$
    2. $(\sim Q \cdot \sim S) \supset L$
    3. P
    4. $P \supset \sim Q$
    5. $(R \cdot L) \supset M$
    6. R / M

[27] 1. $\sim P \cdot (N \supset L)$
    2. $\sim Q \cdot (\sim K \equiv J)$
    3. $(\sim P \cdot \sim Q) \supset [(\sim P \lor R) \supset (S \cdot M)]$ / $S \cdot \sim Q$

[28] 1. $(Q \cdot R) \lor \sim P$
    2. $R \supset S$
    3. $[\sim P \cdot \sim (Q \cdot R)] \supset (L \supset \sim Q)$
    4. $\sim (Q \cdot R) \supset (\sim Q \supset R)$
    5. $\sim (Q \cdot R) \cdot \sim M$ / $L \supset S$

★[29] 1. $P \cdot \sim Q$
    2. $(P \lor \sim R) \supset (\sim S \cdot M)$
    3. $(\sim S \cdot P) \supset (P \supset N)$ / N

[30] 1. $\sim P \supset Q$
    2. $R \cdot (S \supset L)$
    3. $(Q \cdot \sim M) \supset (R \supset \sim L)$
    4. $\sim P \cdot \sim K$
    5. $\sim P \supset \sim M$ / $\sim L$

IV. First, translate the following arguments into symbolic form. Second, use the eight implication rules to derive the conclusion of each. Letters for the simple statements are provided in parentheses and can be used in the order given.

1. If Samantha got a transfer, then if her company has a branch in Colorado, then Samantha lives in Denver. Either Samantha lives in Denver or she got a transfer. But Samantha does not live in Denver. It follows that her company does not have a branch in Colorado. (*S, C, D*)

Answer:

[1]   1. $S \supset (C \supset D)$
2. $D \lor S$
3. $\sim D$ $/ \sim C$
4. S 2, 3, DS
5. $C \supset D$ 1, 4, MP
6. $\sim C$ 3, 5, MT

2. Credit card fees continue to go up. If credit card fees continue to go up, then if customers stop making payments on their cards, then either credit card companies lose customers or the companies lower the fees. However, it is not the case that either credit card companies lose customers or the companies lower the fees. Therefore, either customers do not stop making payments on their cards or the companies lower the fees. (F, S, L, W)

3. If 3D movies are making large profits, then movie companies are producing what people want to see and the movie companies are creating jobs. Either movie ticket sales are going up or it is not the case that movie companies are producing what people want to see and the movie companies are creating jobs. But movie ticket sales are not going up. If 3D movies are not making large profits and movie ticket sales are not going up, then Hollywood will start making different kinds of movies and movie companies will start being more creative. Thus, Hollywood will start making different kinds of movies. (P, M, J, S, H, C)

4. Paris has many art museums, and they are not expensive to visit. However, if Paris has many art museums, then either they are expensive to visit or they get large crowds. Furthermore, if they are expensive to visit or they get large crowds, then they are not worth seeing. Therefore, either they are not worth seeing or they are not expensive to visit. (A, E, L, W)

5. Baseball is not the most popular sport or hockey is not the most popular sport. If advertisers continue to pay high costs for television commercial time, then the advertisers expect to see an increase in sales. If baseball is not the most popular sport, then the number of baseball fans is small, and if hockey is not the most popular sport, then hockey is not appealing to advertisers. If the number of baseball fans is small or hockey is not appealing to advertisers, then the advertisers cannot expect to see an increase in sales. Therefore, advertisers will not continue to pay high costs for television commercial time. (B, H, P, S, F, A)

6. Cell phones are expensive, but they do not break down quickly. If cell phones are made cheaply, then they break down quickly. If cell phones are worth the added cost, then they have a high resale value. If cell phones are expensive, then either they are made cheaply or they are worth the added cost. It follows that either cell phones break down quickly or they have a high resale value. (E, B, C, A, H)

Video Tutorial 8DIV
Exercise #7

7. If exercise is important for health, then you should have a regular exercise routine. Staying healthy saves you money. If staying healthy saves you money, then you can afford good exercise equipment. If you can afford good exercise equipment, then you will use the equipment. So either you will use the equipment or you should have a regular exercise routine. (*E, R, H, A, U*)

8. If natural disasters will continue to increase, then the country's infrastructure will deteriorate and costs for repairing the damage will slow the economy. If global warming is affecting the world's weather, then natural disasters will continue to increase. If the country's infrastructure will deteriorate and costs for repairing the damage will slow the economy, then we must find alternative sources of energy. Thus, if global warming is affecting the world's weather, then we must find alternative sources of energy. (*N, I, R, G, A*)

★ 9. If social networking is a global phenomenon, then it is able to connect people with diverse backgrounds. If people can better understand different cultures, then the social networking folks will not stereotype different cultures. Social networking is a global phenomenon. If social networking is able to connect people with diverse backgrounds, then people can better understand different cultures. Therefore, the social networking folks will not stereotype different cultures. (*G, C, U, S*)

10. If both government corruption and corporate corruption can be eliminated, then the economy will not stagnate. If dishonest people are elected, then the economy will stagnate. Furthermore, both government corruption and corporate corruption can be eliminated. Thus, government corruption can be eliminated and dishonest people are not elected. (*G, C, E, D*)

E. REPLACEMENT RULES I

The implication rules are valid argument forms, but the replacement rules are pairs of logically equivalent statement forms (they have identical truth tables). According to the **principle of replacement**, logically equivalent expressions may replace each other within the context of a proof. The ten replacement rules were shown to be logically equivalent statement forms by you in Exercises 7F.1, 1–16. Unlike the eight implication rules that are restricted to entire lines of a proof, replacement rules have no such restriction. They can be used either for an entire line or part of a line.

Principle of replacement
Logically equivalent expressions may replace each other within the context of a proof.

De Morgan (DM)

De Morgan (DM), a replacement rule with two sets of logically equivalent statement forms, is named after the logician Augustus De Morgan:

De Morgan (DM)
$\sim (p \cdot q) :: \sim p \lor \sim q$
$\sim (p \lor q) :: \sim p \cdot \sim q$

De Morgan (DM)
$$\sim (p \cdot q) :: \sim p \lor \sim q$$
$$\sim (p \lor q) :: \sim p \cdot \sim q$$

The new symbol "::" is used in all the replacement rules; it means *is logically equivalent to*. *De Morgan replacement rules can be used validly only with conjunction or disjunction.* Let's examine the first pair. We can use the statement "It is not the case that both Judy likes riding roller coasters and Eddie likes riding roller coasters" as a substitution for the left side of the first pair: $\sim (p \cdot q)$. The original statement is logically equivalent to this statement: "Either Judy does not like riding roller coasters or Eddie does not like riding roller coasters." The original statement and the second statement express the same proposition: that *at least one* of the two people mentioned does not like to ride roller coasters.

The second pair of De Morgan can be understood in a similar manner. For example, the statement "It is not the case that either Judy or Eddie likes riding roller coasters" is logically equivalent to "Judy and Eddie do not like riding roller coasters." These two statements express the same proposition: that both of the people mentioned do not like to ride roller coasters.

The replacement rules offer some flexibility. For example, the pairs of statement forms that make up the replacement rules can be used in either direction. In other words, if a left member of a pair occurs in a proof, then it can be replaced by the right

PROFILES IN LOGIC
Augustus De Morgan

When asked how old he was, Augustus De Morgan (1806–71), ever the mathematician, once remarked, "I was x years old in the year x-squared." (De Morgan was 43 years old in the year 1849.) One of De Morgan's main interests was in the problem of transforming thoughts into symbols. Although trained as a mathematician, De Morgan read widely in many other fields. From years of intense studies, De Morgan realized that all scientific and mathematical fields advanced only when they had a robust system of symbols.

De Morgan is also credited with establishing a mathematical basis for understanding Aristotelian categorical syllogisms. For example, from the premises "Some D are J" and "Some D are N," we cannot validly conclude that "Some J are N." However, De Morgan showed, from the premises "Most D are J" and "Most D are N," we can validly conclude that "Some J are N." In fact, De Morgan provides a mathematical formula for this problem. Let the number of D's = x, the number of D's that are J's = y, and the number of D's that are N's = z. From this we can conclude that *at least* $(y + z) - x$ J's are N's.

De Morgan recognized what had hindered the development of logic from Aristotle's time—the lack of a system of logical symbols. De Morgan argued that logic and mathematics should be studied together so that the disciplines can learn from each other. When he taught mathematics, he always included logical training as part of the curriculum.

member. Likewise, if a right member of a pair occurs in a proof, then it can be replaced by the left member.

Here is an example of a valid application of the rule:

Valid Application of De Morgan (DM)

1. $\sim (A \cdot B) \supset C$
2. $\sim A \cdot M$ / C
3. $\sim A$ 2, Simp
4. $\sim A \vee \sim B$ 3, Add
5. $\sim (A \cdot B)$ 4, DM
6. C 1, 5, MP

The strategy used for the proof was to try to derive the antecedent of line 1 in order to be able to use *modus ponens* to derive the conclusion. The first step was to isolate $\sim A$. Next, the rule of addition was used. The application of De Morgan allowed the valid derivation of the antecedent of the first premise.

The next two examples show misapplications:

Misapplications of De Morgan (DM)

1. $\sim (A \cdot B)$ 1. $\sim C \vee \sim D$
2. $\sim A \cdot \sim B$ 🚫   2. $\sim (C \vee D)$ 🚫

The two misapplications *do not result in logically equivalent statements.* This point is crucial, because the misapplications *do not yield valid inferences.* The proof procedure of natural deduction requires that every step of a proof is a valid derivation. But in both misapplication examples, line 2 *does not validly follow* from line 1. (You might want to try constructing truth tables to verify that the derivations in each example are not logically equivalent to the original statements.)

Double Negation (DN)

Double negation
(DN)
$p :: \sim \sim p$

The replacement rule **double negation (DN)** justifies the introduction or elimination of pairs of negation signs, because the replacements result in valid derivations. This line of reasoning is revealed in the following form:

Double Negation (DN)

$$p :: \sim \sim p$$

For example, the contradiction of the statement "Golf is a sport" is the statement "It is not the case that golf is a sport." Following the same procedure, the contradiction of "It is not the case that golf is a sport" can be written as "It is not the case that it is not the case that golf is a sport." This means that the statement "Golf is a sport" is logically equivalent to the statement "It is not the case that it is not the case that golf is a sport."

Here are two examples of valid applications:

Valid Applications of Double Negation (DN)

1. $(Q \lor R) \supset \sim P$		1. $P \supset Q$	
2. P	$/ \sim (Q \lor R)$	2. R	
3. $\sim\sim P$	2, DN	3. $\sim P \supset \sim R$	$/ Q$
4. $\sim (Q \lor R)$	1, 3, MT	4. $\sim\sim R$	2, DN
		5. $\sim\sim P$	3, 4, MT
		6. P	5, DN
		7. Q	1, 6, MP

In the first example, the tactical move was to apply double negation to P in order to derive the negation of the consequent of the first premise. In turn, this allowed *modus tollens* to be used to derive the conclusion.

In the second example, a similar strategy was employed. Since line 2 is the negation of the consequent in line 3, double negation was used to derive $\sim\sim R$ from its logically equivalent pair member R. Double negation was then used a second time in line 6 to derive P from its logically equivalent pair member $\sim\sim P$. This example clearly illustrates what was stated earlier: replacement rules can be applied *left to right* or *right to left*.

The next example illustrates a misapplication:

Misapplication of Double Negation (DN)

1. $\underline{Q \lor R}$
2. $\sim (\sim Q \lor \sim R)$ 🚫

Line 2 is a misapplication of double negation. We can show that $\sim (\sim Q \lor \sim R)$ is *not* logically equivalent to $Q \lor R$. If we apply De Morgan (DM) to line 2, then we get $\sim\sim Q \cdot \sim\sim R$. We can then apply double negation (DN) two times. When we apply DN to the left conjunct we get $Q \cdot \sim\sim R$. When we then apply DN to the right conjunct we get $Q \cdot R$. Of course, $Q \cdot R$ is *not* logically equivalent to $Q \lor R$.

Commutation (Com)

The principle behind **commutation (Com)** can be easily illustrated. For example, it should be clear that the following two disjunctive statements are logically equivalent:

1. Either digital music is better than analog music or plasma TVs are expensive items.
2. Either plasma TVs are expensive items or digital music is better than analog music.

The same can be said for the following two conjunctive statements:

3. Digital music is better than analog music, and plasma TVs are expensive items.
4. Plasma TVs are expensive items, and digital music is better than analog music.

Commutation (Com)

$p \lor q :: q \lor p$
$p \cdot q :: q \cdot p$

It should be obvious that the order of the disjuncts in the first set and the order of the conjuncts in the second set does not affect the truth value of the compound statements. (Once again, truth tables can verify these claims.) The examples illustrate the forms of the rule:

Commutation (Com)

$$p \vee q :: q \vee p$$
$$p \cdot q :: q \cdot p$$

The two pairs of logically equivalent statement forms illustrate that commutation can be used only with disjunction or conjunction. Here are two examples of valid applications:

Valid Applications of Commutation (Com)

1. $(M \cdot N) \supset (P \vee Q)$		1. $(S \vee P) \supset (R \cdot Q)$	
2. $S \cdot (N \cdot M)$	/ $P \vee Q$	2. $\sim Q$	/ $\sim S \cdot \sim P$
3. $N \cdot M$	2, Simp	3. $\sim Q \vee \sim R$	2, Add
4. $M \cdot N$	3, Com	4. $\sim R \vee \sim Q$	3, Com
5. $P \vee Q$	1, 4, MP	5. $\sim (R \cdot Q)$	4, DM
		6. $\sim (S \vee P)$	1, 5, MT
		7. $\sim S \cdot \sim P$	6, DM

In the first example, the strategy was to recognize that the $N \cdot M$ in line 2 could eventually be used to get the antecedent of the first premise. The first tactical move applied simplification (Simp) to line 2. The second tactical move applied commutation (Com) to line 3. That step is a valid inference because lines 3 and 4 are logically equivalent. The final step used *modus ponens* (MP) to derive the conclusion.

In the second example, the strategy was to recognize that addition (Add) could be used on the second premise to get Q and R in position to use commutation (Com). Once this was accomplished, De Morgan (DM) and *modus tollens* (MT) were used in order to derive the conclusion.

The next example shows a misapplication:

Misapplication of Commutation (Com)

1. $M \supset (P \vee Q)$
2. $(P \vee Q) \supset M$ 🚫

This example attempted to apply commutation to a conditional. However, commutation can be used validly only with disjunction or conjunction. Therefore, the derivation is invalid. (You might want to try constructing a truth table to verify that the derivation in line 2 of the misapplication example is not logically equivalent to the statement in line 1.)

Association (Assoc)

Association (Assoc)
$p \vee (q \vee r) :: (p \vee q) \vee r$
$p \cdot (q \cdot r) :: (p \cdot q) \cdot r$

Association (Assoc) allows the use of parentheses to group the component parts of certain complex truth-functional statements in different ways without affecting the truth value. The following two pairs of logically equivalent statement forms show the logical form of the rule:

Association (Assoc)

$$p \vee (q \vee r) :: (p \vee q) \vee r$$
$$p \cdot (q \cdot r) :: (p \cdot q) \cdot r$$

As an example, suppose we let p = *Walter will vote in the next election*, q = *Sandy will vote in the next election*, and r = *Judy will vote in the next election*. If we join these three statements and create disjunctions, we get the following:

> Either Walter will vote in the next election or Sandy will vote in the next election or Judy will vote in the next election.

When parentheses are used to group the first two simple statements together, then the second occurrence of the wedge becomes the main operator: $(p \vee q) \vee r$. On the other hand, if we use parentheses to group the second and third simple statements together, then the first occurrence of the wedge becomes the main operator: $p \vee (q \vee r)$. These different groupings have no effect on the truth value of the complex statement. As with all the replacement rules, you can consult the truth tables for these logically equivalent statement forms from Chapter 7. The truth tables demonstrate that the rules are replacing a statement of one form for a statement of a logically equivalent form.

Here are two examples of valid applications:

Valid Applications of Association (Assoc)

1. $(P \vee Q) \supset S$		1. $(M \cdot \sim Q) \supset \sim S$	
2. $\sim M$		2. $M \cdot (\sim Q \cdot R)$	$/ \sim S$
3. $(M \vee P) \vee Q$	$/ S$	3. $(M \cdot \sim Q) \cdot R$	2, Assoc
4. $M \vee (P \vee Q)$	3, Assoc	4. $M \cdot \sim Q$	3, Simp
5. $P \vee Q$	2, 4, DS	5. $\sim S$	1, 4, MP
6. S	1, 5, MP		

In the first example, line 4 is validly derived from line 3. This step is justified because it uses association correctly. The overall strategy of the proof involved separating the M from the P. In turn, the $\sim M$ in line 2 was used in the application of disjunctive syllogism.

In the second example, the strategy was to try to derive the antecedent of line 1. This required two tactical moves. First, association validly replaced the grouping in line 2. Second, simplification validly isolated $M \cdot \sim Q$ (the antecedent of the first premise).

A word of caution: Association yields a valid derivation only when the affected logical operators in the two statements are either both disjunctions or else both conjunctions. The next two examples show misapplications:

Misapplications of Association (Assoc)

1. $(P \cdot \sim Q) \vee R$		1. $P \cdot (\sim Q \vee R)$	
2. $P \cdot (\sim Q \vee R)$	⊘	2. $(P \cdot \sim Q) \vee R$	⊘

These two examples did not heed the caution. A mixture of conjunction and disjunction was used, resulting in invalid derivations. The two misapplications do not result in logically equivalent statements. This point is crucial because the misapplications do not yield valid inferences. (You might want to try constructing truth tables to verify that in both examples the derivations are not logically equivalent to the original statements.)

Distribution (Dist)

The replacement rule **distribution (Dist)** can be illustrated by analyzing the following statement:

Motorcycles are loud, and either trucks or buses get poor gas mileage.

If we let p = *Motorcycles are loud*, q = *trucks get poor gas mileage*, and r = *buses get poor gas mileage*, we get $p \cdot (q \vee r)$. Since the main operator is a conjunction, if the compound statement is true, then both conjuncts are true. This means that p is true, and *at least one* of the disjuncts, q or r, is true. Given this, the following disjunction is true:

Motorcycles are loud and trucks get poor gas mileage, or motorcycles are loud and buses get poor gas mileage.

The logical form of this compound statement is $(p \cdot q) \vee (p \cdot r)$. Therefore, if $p \cdot (q \vee r)$ is true, then $(p \cdot q) \vee (p \cdot r)$ is true. This result is the first pair of the following logically equivalent statement forms:

Distribution (Dist)

$$p \cdot (q \vee r) :: (p \cdot q) \vee (p \cdot r)$$
$$p \vee (q \cdot r) :: (p \vee q) \cdot (p \vee r)$$

The second pair of statement forms can be understood in a similar manner. Consider the complex statement, "Motorcycles are loud or both trucks and buses get poor gas mileage." If we let p = *Motorcycles are loud*, q = *trucks get poor gas mileage*, and r = *buses get poor gas mileage*, we get $p \vee (q \cdot r)$. Since the main operator is the wedge, the compound statement is true if at least one of the disjuncts is true. Therefore, if the first disjunct, p, is true, then $(p \vee q)$ is true and $(p \vee r)$ is true. On the other hand, if the second disjunct is true, then both q and r are true. Therefore, once again, $(p \vee q)$ is true and $(p \vee r)$ is true.

Here are two examples of valid applications:

Valid Applications of Distribution (Dist)

1. $\sim (M \cdot N)$			1. $\sim C$	
2. $M \cdot (N \vee P)$	/ $M \cdot P$		2. $A \vee (C \cdot D)$	/ A
3. $(M \cdot N) \vee (M \cdot P)$	2, Dist		3. $(A \vee C) \cdot (A \vee D)$	2, Dist
4. $M \cdot P$	1, 3, DS		4. $A \vee C$	3, Simp
			5. A	1, 4, DS

In the first example, the strategy was to try to get the M and N of the second premise together. Distribution justified the derivation in line 3. This produced a disjunction to which disjunctive syllogism was applied. In the second example, the strategy was to isolate A. A tactical move placed the A and C together in such a way that the $\sim C$

in the first line was used. Therefore, distribution was a key tactical move in completing the proof.

A word of caution: Distribution can be used *only with conjunction and disjunction.* The next three examples illustrate misapplications:

Misapplications of Distribution (Dist)

1. $B \vee (C \cdot D)$
2. $(B \vee C) \vee (B \vee D)$ 🚫

1. $(M \cdot N) \vee (M \cdot P)$
2. $M \cdot (N \cdot P)$ 🚫

1. $P \cdot (Q \supset R)$
2. $(P \cdot Q) \supset (P \cdot R)$ 🚫

In the first example, an attempt was made to use distribution on line 1, where the main operator is a wedge. However, the mistake occurs because the main operator in line 2 (the derived line) is a wedge. In order to use distribution correctly on line 1, the result would have to be a dot as the main operator: $(B \vee C) \cdot (B \vee D)$. Therefore, the mistake resulted in a misapplication.

In the second example, a correct application of distribution would have given this result for line 2: $M \cdot (N \vee P)$. However, the mistake occurred because the derived line used a dot in the second conjunct: $(N \cdot P)$. This was a misapplication of distribution. In the third example of a misapplication, an attempt was made to use distribution on line 1, where the operator inside the parentheses is a *horseshoe.* However, distribution can be used only with conjunction and disjunction. You might want to try constructing truth tables to verify that the derivations in these three examples are *not logically equivalent* to the original statements.

THE FIRST FIVE REPLACEMENT RULES	
De Morgan (DM)	**Double Negation (DN)**
$\sim(p \cdot q) :: (\sim p \vee \sim q)$ $\sim(p \vee q) :: (\sim p \cdot \sim q)$	$p :: \sim\sim p$
Commutation (Com)	**Association (Assoc)**
$p \vee q :: q \vee p$ $p \cdot q :: q \cdot p$	$p \vee (q \vee r) :: (p \vee q) \vee r$ $p \cdot (q \cdot r) :: (p \cdot q) \cdot r$
Distribution (Dist)	
$p \cdot (q \vee r) :: (p \cdot q) \vee (p \cdot r)$ $p \vee (q \cdot r) :: (p \vee q) \cdot (p \vee r)$	

We can now add the first five replacement rules to our strategy and tactics guide:

Applying the First Five Replacement Rules

Strategy: We continue employing the global strategy of trying to locate the conclusion somewhere "inside" the premises. However, we can now add to our overall strategy. You can apply a replacement rule whenever you need to "exchange" one proposition with one that is logically equivalent. For example, by correctly applying either De Morgan (DM) or distribution (Dist) you can derive a disjunction, and then use disjunctive syllogism (DS) to derive the conclusion. At other times, you might need to use either De Morgan (DM) or distribution (Dist) to derive a conjunction, and then use simplification (Simp) to derive the conclusion.

Here are some specific tactical moves associated with the first five replacement rules:

Tactic 9: Try using conjunction (Conj) to establish the basis for De Morgan (DM).

1. $\sim G$
2. $\sim H$
3. $\sim G \cdot \sim H$ 1, 2, Conj
4. $\sim (G \vee H)$ 3, DM

Tactic 10: Try using addition (Add) to establish the basis for De Morgan (DM).1

1. $\sim K$
2. $\sim K \vee \sim L$ 1, Add
3. $\sim (K \cdot L)$ 2, DM

Tactic 11: Try using constructive dilemma (CD) to establish the basis for De Morgan (DM).

1. $(E \supset \sim F) \cdot (S \supset \sim U)$
2. $E \vee S$
3. $\sim F \vee \sim U$ 1, 2, CD
4. $\sim (F \cdot U)$ 3, DM

Tactic 12: Try using distribution (Dist) to establish the basis for simplification (Simp).

1. $M \vee (N \cdot O)$ 1. $(H \cdot K) \vee (H \cdot L)$
2. $(M \vee N) \cdot (M \vee O)$ 1, Dist   2. $H \cdot (K \vee L)$ 1, Dist
3. $M \vee N$ 2, Simp   3. H 2, Simp

Tactic 13: Try using distribution (Dist) to establish the basis for disjunctive syllogism (DS).

1. $M \cdot (N \vee O)$ 1. $(H \vee K) \cdot (H \vee L)$
2. $\sim (M \cdot N)$ 2. $\sim H$
3. $(M \cdot N) \vee (M \cdot O)$ 1, Dist   3. $H \vee (K \cdot L)$ 1, Dist
4. $M \cdot O$ 2, 3, DS   4. $K \cdot L$ 2, 3, DS

Tactic 14: Try using commutation (Com) to establish the basis for *modus ponens* (MP).

1. $(E \vee F) \supset (G \cdot H)$
2. $F \vee E$
3. $E \vee F$ 2, Com
4. $G \cdot H$ 1, 3, MP

Tactic 15: Try using commutation (Com) to establish the basis for disjunctive syllogism (DS).

1. $(S \cdot U) \vee W$
2. $\sim (U \cdot S)$
3. $\sim (S \cdot U)$ 2, Com
4. W 1, 3, DS

As we saw with the implication rules, these specific tactics can help at any point in the proof, not just with the final conclusion.

EXERCISES 8E

I. The following are examples of what you might encounter in proofs. The last step of each example gives the number of the step needed for its derivation. You are to provide the justification (the replacement rule) in the space provided. This will give you practice using the first five replacement rules.

Lightboard Video

Self-Practice Questions

[1] 1. ~ (S · R)
     2. ~ S v ~ R   1, _____

Answer: 2. ~ S v ~ R   1, DM

[2] 1. S v P
     2. P v S   1, _____

[3] 1. R v (S v P)
     2. (R v S) v P   1, _____

[4] 1. P · (S v Q)
     2. (P · S) v (P · Q)   1, _____

★ [5] 1. S
       2. ~ ~ S   1, _____

[6] 1. ~ P v ~ Q
     2. ~ (P · Q)   1, _____

[7] 1. P v (Q · R)
     2. (Q · R) v P   1, _____

[8] 1. (P v Q) v R
     2. P v (Q v R)   1, _____

★ [9] 1. (P · Q) v (P · R)
       2. P · (Q v R)   1, _____

[10] 1. ~ ~ Q
      2. Q   1, _____

[11] 1. ~ (~ Q v R)
      2. ~ ~ Q · ~ R   1, _____

[12] 1. (P v Q) · (P v R)
      2. P v (Q · R)   1, _____

★ [13] 1. (S · Q) · R
        2. S · (Q · R)   1, _____

[14] 1. ~ [(P · Q) v (R · S)]
      2. ~ (P · Q) · ~ (R · S)   1, _____

[15] 1. [(P · Q) v (R · S)] · [(L · M) v (N · K)]
      2. [(L · M) v (N · K)] · [(P · Q) v (R · S)]   1, _____

II. The following are more examples of what you might encounter in proofs. In these examples the justification (the replacement rule) is provided for the last line; however, the line itself is missing. Use the given information to derive the last line of each example. This will give you more practice using the first five replacement rules.

[1] 1. $S \cdot R$
    2.   1, Com

Answer: 2. $R \cdot S$ 1, Com

[2] 1. $(S \vee P) \cdot (S \vee Q)$
    2.   1, Dist

[3] 1. $\sim \sim Q$
    2.   1, DN

[4] 1. $(R \cdot S) \cdot P$
    2.   1, Assoc

⭐ [5] 1. $\sim P \cdot \sim Q$
    2.   1, DM

[6] 1. $\sim \sim (P \cdot R)$
    2.   1, DN

[7] 1. $P \cdot Q$
    2.   1, Com

[8] 1. $P \vee (Q \cdot R)$
    2.   1, Dist

⭐ [9] 1. $(R \vee S) \vee (P \supset Q)$
    2.   1, Assoc

[10] 1. $\sim (\sim P \vee \sim Q)$
    2.   1, DM

[11] 1. $P \cdot [\,(S \supset R) \vee (Q \supset L)\,]$
    2.   1, Dist

[12] 1. $\sim [\,(\sim P \cdot \sim Q) \vee (\sim R \cdot \sim S)\,]$
    2.   1, DM

⭐ [13] 1. $[\,R \supset (P \cdot Q)\,] \vee (L \vee M)$
    2.   1, Assoc

[14] 1. $[\,(S \vee R) \supset Q\,] \vee \sim [\,(\sim P \vee L) \supset K\,]$
    2.   1, Com

[15] 1. $S \vee [\,P \cdot (Q \supset M)\,]$
    2.   1, Dist

III. Use the eight implication rules and the five replacement rules to complete the proofs. Provide the justification for each step that you derive.

[1] 1. ~ (S · L)
     2. (Q · R) ⊃ (M ≡ N)
     3. P ⊃ (Q · R)
     4. (M ≡ N) ⊃ (S · L)   / ~ P

Answer:

     5. ~ (M ≡ N)   1, 4, MT
     6. ~ (Q · R)   2, 5, MT
     7. ~ P   3, 6, MT

[2] 1. ~ S
     2. R ⊃ (S v Q)
     3. R · L   / Q

[3] 1. ~ (~ P v ~ Q)
     2. (P · Q) ⊃ (R v S)   / R v S

[4] 1. S ⊃ (L v M)
     2. (P · Q) ⊃ ~ R
     3. (S v P) · (S v Q)   / (L v M) v ~ R

⭐ [5] 1. P ⊃ (Q · R)
     2. ~ Q · S   / ~ P

[6] 1. (P v Q) ⊃ ~ (R ≡ S)
     2. R ≡ S   / ~ P

[7] 1. [S ⊃ (L · M)] · [P ⊃ (M · Q)]
     2. S v P   / M

[8] 1. P ⊃ (Q · R)
     2. P · (S v R)
     3. L ⊃ (M ≡ P)   / (Q · R) v (M ≡ P)

⭐ [9] 1. ~ (P · Q)
     2. (~ P v ~ Q) ⊃ (R · S)
     3. (R v ~ Q) ⊃ ~ T   / ~ T

[10] 1. P · Q
      2. (P v R) ⊃ (S · L)
      3. (S · L) ⊃ (R v S)   / R v S

[11] 1. (P v Q) v ~ R
      2. [(P v Q) ⊃ Q] · (~ R ⊃ S)
      3. ~ P   / Q v (S · ~ R)

[12] 1. P · ~ Q
      2. R ⊃ Q   / ~ R · P

★[13] 1. ~P
     2. Q ∨ (R · P)   / Q

[14] 1. S ⊃ (Q · M)
     2. S ∨ (P · L)
     3. P ⊃ (Q · R)   / Q · (M ∨ R)

[15] 1. P
     2. (R ∨ Q) · S
     3. P ⊃ (L ≡ M)
     4. (L ≡ M) ⊃ ~(S · R)   / S · Q

[16] 1. P ⊃ ~Q
     2. (P · R) ∨ (P · S)
     3. L ∨ Q   / L

★[17] 1. P ∨ Q
     2. (R · S) · L   / [(L · R) · P] ∨ [(L · R) · Q]

[18] 1. (P ∨ Q) ⊃ ~R
     2. S · R   / ~P

[19] 1. P
     2. Q ∨ (R ∨ S)
     3. R ⊃ ~P   / Q ∨ S

[20] 1. ~R
     2. (Q ⊃ R) · (S ⊃ L)
     3. Q   / ~M ∨ L

★[21] 1. P ⊃ ~~R
     2. P · ~(S · R)   / ~S

[22] 1. ~P · Q
     2. ~(~P · ~R)
     3. (R ∨ S) ⊃ ~(L ∨ M)   / ~(M ∨ L)

[23] 1. ~P
     2. (Q ∨ ~R) ⊃ (P · S)   / R

[24] 1. ~P
     2. (P · Q) ∨ (R · S)   / ~(P ∨ ~R)

★[25] 1. ~(P · Q)
     2. R
     3. [S ⊃ (P · Q)] · (R ⊃ L)
     4. S ∨ R   / ~P ∨ (~Q · L)

[26] 1. P ∨ (Q ⊃ R)
     2. P ⊃ R
     3. ~Q ⊃ S
     4. ~R   / S ∨ K

[27]   1. $(P \vee Q) \supset R$
    2. $\sim R$
    3. $\sim S \supset (Q \vee R)$ / S

[28]   1. $P \supset Q$
    2. $R \vee P$
    3. $S \supset (L \vee \sim R)$
    4. $S \cdot \sim L$ / $Q \vee M$

★ [29]   1. $P \supset \sim Q$
    2. $P \cdot (R \vee Q)$
    3. $R \supset S$ / S

[30]   1. $P \supset Q$
    2. $\sim (L \vee \sim P)$
    3. $L \vee S$ / $Q \cdot S$

[31]   1. $(Q \vee S) \supset \sim P$
    2. $Q \vee (R \cdot S)$
    3. $(Q \vee R) \supset \sim L$
    4. $K \supset (L \vee P)$ / $\sim K$

[32]   1. $(P \vee Q) \supset \sim R$
    2. $P \cdot (S \vee R)$
    3. $(N \cdot M) \cdot L$ / $N \cdot S$

★[33]   1. $\sim (J \equiv M) \cdot R$
    2. $[S \supset (L \cdot M)] \vee (N \cdot J)$
    3. $[S \supset (L \cdot M)] \supset (J \equiv M)$ / $(J \vee K) \cdot (R \vee \sim H)$

[34]   1. $\sim [(\sim P \vee \sim Q) \vee (R \vee \sim S)]$
    2. $P \supset (R \vee L)$ / L

[35]   1. $(R \cdot M) \supset L$
    2. $(\sim M \vee Q) \supset \sim (R \cdot S)$
    3. $R \cdot \sim L$ / $\sim (L \vee S)$

**IV. First, translate the following arguments into symbolic form. Second, use the
eight implication rules and the five replacement rules to derive the conclusion of
each. Letters for the simple statements are provided in parentheses and can be
used in the order given.**

1. Maggie is single. Since it is not the case that Maggie is divorced and she is single,
   we can conclude that Maggie is not divorced. (*S, D*)

Answer:

[1]   1. S
    2. $\sim (D \cdot S)$ / $\sim D$
    3. $\sim D \vee \sim S$ 2, DM
    4. $\sim \sim S$ 1, DN
    5. $\sim D$ 3, 4, DS

2. If you do not change the oil in your car regularly, then if you take your car in for required maintenance, then any car repairs will be covered by the warranty, and it is not the case that if you did take your car in for required maintenance, then any car repairs are covered by the warranty. Therefore, you did change the oil in your car regularly. (*O, M, W*)

3. Humans are not by nature competitive but they are cooperative. If humans are cooperative, then either they can work together peacefully or they are by nature competitive. We can infer that humans can work together peacefully. (*C, O, P*)

4. If you have a good retirement plan, then you do not need to worry about inflation. You either have a good retirement plan or you make wise investments or else you plan to work for a long time. If you either make wise investments or you plan to work for a long time, then you do not need to borrow money later in life. Therefore, it is not the case that you need to worry about inflation and you need to borrow money later in life. (*R, I, W, L, B*)

⭐ 5. Accidents are not avoidable and long-term health care is often required, or else accidents are not avoidable and first aid is sometimes available. But first aid is sometimes not available. Therefore, long-term health care is often required. (*A, L, F*)

6. If it did not snow last night, then we can go hiking. If we get visitors, then we cannot paint the spare bedroom this weekend. It is not the case that we do not get visitors, and it snowed last night. Therefore, either we can go hiking or we cannot paint the spare bedroom this weekend. (*S, H, V, P*)

7. If either scandals are rampant in politics or incompetence is rewarded at election time, then the government is not effective. Either the government is effective but scandals are rampant in politics, or else government is effective and there are barely enough competent people to run things. We can conclude that there are barely enough competent people to run things. (*S, I, E, C*)

8. If the results of your experiment are not replicable, then the results are not accepted by scientists. If it is not the case that both the results are accepted by scientists and there is any evidence of experimental error, then the results are accepted by scientists. But there is not any evidence of experimental error. Therefore, the results of your experiment are replicable. (*R, A, E*)

⭐ 9. If your novel is well written, then your book will get good reviews and it might be made into a movie. Your novel is well written and it is pulp fiction, or else your novel is well written and it is soon forgotten by the reading public. We can conclude that your novel is well written and it might be made into a movie. (*N, R, M, P, F*)

10. If it is not the case that she is either a citizen or a permanent resident, then she still has certain basic rights. If she is currently applying for asylum and she has not overstayed her visa, then she is not a permanent resident and she is not a citizen. Moreover, she is currently applying for asylum and she has not overstayed her visa. Therefore, she still has certain basic rights. (*C, P, R, A, V*)

F. REPLACEMENT RULES II

There are five additional replacement rules for us to consider. As with the first five sets, a correct application ensures that derivations will be valid arguments.

Transposition (Trans)

One way to see how **transposition (Trans)** functions is to recall the discussion of necessary and sufficient conditions. For example, the statement "If you get at least a 90 on the exam, then you get an A" is logically equivalent to the statement "If you did not get an A, then you did not get at least a 90 on the exam." The logical form of this set of statements is captured by the replacement rule:

Transposition (Trans)

$$p \supset q :: \sim q \supset \sim p$$

Here are two examples of valid applications of the rule:

Valid Applications of Transposition (Trans)

1. $S \supset \sim Q$		1. $S \cdot \sim M$	
2. $P \supset Q$	$/ S \supset \sim P$	2. $(P \vee R) \supset M$	$/ \sim P \cdot \sim R$
3. $\sim Q \supset \sim P$	2, Trans	3. $\sim M \supset \sim (P \vee R)$	2, Trans
4. $S \supset \sim P$	1, 3, HS	4. $\sim M$	1, Simp
		5. $\sim (P \vee R)$	3, 4, MP
		6. $\sim P \cdot \sim R$	5, DM

In the first example, transposition was used tactically on line 2 to derive $\sim Q$ as an antecedent of a conditional statement. This created the opportunity to apply hypothetical syllogism to validly derive the conclusion.

In the second example, the strategy was to recognize that $\sim M$ could be derived on a separate line. Given this, the tactical move of transposition on line 2 set up $\sim M$ as the antecedent of a conditional. Once that was achieved the final result was within reach.

The next example shows a misapplication:

Misapplication of Transposition (Trans)

1. $\sim P \supset \sim Q$	
2. $P \supset Q$	🚫

The mistake occurs because the negation signs were eliminated without transposing the antecedent and consequent. (You might want to try constructing a truth table to verify that the derivation in line 2 is not logically equivalent to the statement in line 1.)

Material Implication (Impl)

Material implication (Impl) can be illustrated by the following two statements:

1. If you get fewer than 60 points, then you fail the exam.
2. Either you do not get fewer than 60 points or you fail the exam.

Transposition (Trans)
$p \supset q :: \sim q \supset \sim p$

Material implication (Impl)
$p \supset q :: \sim p \vee q$

Truth tables can verify that these are logically equivalent statements. The logical form of this set of statements is captured by the replacement rule:

Material Implication (Impl)

$$p \supset q :: \sim p \vee q$$

Here are two examples of valid applications of the rule:

Valid Applications of Material Implication (Impl)

1. $\sim R$	$/ (R \supset S) \vee P$	1. B	
2. $\sim R \vee S$	1, Add	2. $(B \supset C) \vee D$	$/ C \vee D$
3. $R \supset S$	2, Impl	3. $(\sim B \vee C) \vee D$	2, Impl
4. $(R \supset S) \vee P$	3, Add	4. $\sim B \vee (C \vee D)$	3, Assoc
		5. $\sim \sim B$	1, DN
		6. $C \vee D$	4, 5, DS

In the first example, material implication allowed the derivation of a conditional statement in line 3. This change was needed in order to get the statement into the same form as appears in the conclusion.

In the second example, the overall strategy was to ensure that C could be joined with D in a disjunction, as indicated by the conclusion. Since material implication allows the derivation of a disjunction from a conditional statement, the tactical move in line 3 helped to eventually derive the conclusion.

The next two examples are misapplications:

Misapplications of Material Implication (Impl)

1. $S \supset R$	1. $\sim D \vee G$
2. $\sim S \cdot R$ 🚫	2. $\sim (D \supset G)$ 🚫

In the first example, the mistake occurs from using a dot instead of a wedge. In the second example, the mistake occurs from the incorrect placement of the tilde. (You might want to try constructing truth tables to verify that the derivations in both examples are not logically equivalent to the original statements.)

Material Equivalence (Equiv)

Material equivalence (Equiv)
$p \equiv q :: (p \supset q) \cdot (q \supset p)$
$p \equiv q :: (p \cdot q) \vee (\sim p \cdot \sim q)$

In Chapter 7, the truth table for **material equivalence (Equiv)** revealed that $p \equiv q$ is true when p and q are both true and when p and q are both false. With this in mind, let's look at the two forms for the replacement rule:

Material Equivalence (Equiv)

$$p \equiv q :: (p \supset q) \cdot (q \supset p)$$
$$p \equiv q :: (p \cdot q) \vee (\sim p \cdot \sim q)$$

For the first pair, if p and q are both true, then $p \supset q$ and $q \supset p$ are true, because in both instances the antecedent and consequent are true. Likewise, if p and q are both false, then $p \supset q$ and $q \supset p$ are once again true, because in both instances the antecedent and the consequent are false. Also, if p is true and q is false, then $p \supset q$ is false. In that case, the conjunction is false. Likewise, if p is false and q is true, then $q \supset p$ is false. In that case, too, the conjunction is false. Therefore, $p \equiv q$ is logically equivalent to $(p \supset q) \cdot (q \supset p)$.

For the second pair, if p and q are both true, then $p \cdot q$ is true; therefore, the disjunction $(p \cdot q) \vee (\sim p \cdot \sim q)$ is true. If p and q are both false, then $\sim p \cdot \sim q$ is true; therefore, the disjunction $(p \cdot q) \vee (\sim p \cdot \sim q)$ is again true. Now, if p is true and q is false, then $p \cdot q$ and $\sim p \cdot \sim q$ are both false. In that case, the disjunction is false. Likewise, if p is false and q is true, then $p \cdot q$ and $\sim p \cdot \sim q$ are both false. In that case, too, the disjunction is false. Therefore, $p \equiv q$ is logically equivalent to $(p \cdot q) \vee (\sim p \cdot \sim q)$.

Here are two examples of valid applications:

Valid Applications of Material Equivalence (Equiv)

1. $\sim S$			1. $C \equiv D$	
2. $(\sim Q \vee \sim R) \supset S$	/ $Q \equiv R$		2. $(C \cdot D) \supset \sim P$	/ $\sim C$
3. $\sim (\sim Q \vee \sim R)$	1, 2, MT		3. P	
4. $\sim\sim Q \cdot \sim\sim R$	3, DM		4. $(C \cdot D) \vee (\sim C \cdot \sim D)$	1, Equiv
5. $Q \cdot \sim\sim R$	4, DN		5. $\sim\sim P \supset \sim (C \cdot D)$	2, Trans
6. $Q \cdot R$	5, DN		6. $P \supset \sim (C \cdot D)$	5, DN
7. $(Q \cdot R) \vee (\sim Q \cdot \sim R)$	6, Add		7. $\sim (C \cdot D)$	3, 6, MP
8. $Q \equiv R$	7, Equiv		8. $\sim C \cdot \sim D$	4, 7, DS
			9. $\sim C$	8, Simp

In the first example, since the conclusion is $Q \equiv R$, the overall strategy was to derive one of the two logically equivalent pairs. That means that if $Q \cdot R$ is isolated, then addition can be used to derive the necessary part. Therefore, rather than use material equivalence as a tactical move within the body of the proof, it was used to derive the final step.

The next two examples are misapplications:

Misapplications of Material Equivalence (Equiv)

1. $G \equiv H$		1. $(M \supset Q) \vee (Q \supset M)$
2. $(G \cdot H) \cdot (\sim G \cdot \sim H)$ ⊘		2. $M \equiv Q$ ⊘

In the first example, the mistake in line 2 was making the main operator a dot instead of a wedge. In the second example, line 1 has a wedge as the main operator. But in order for the rule to be applied correctly, there has to be a dot as the main operator. (You might want to try constructing truth tables to verify that the derivations in both examples are not logically equivalent to the original statements.)

Exportation (Exp)

Consider the following statement: "If it snows this afternoon and we buy a sled, then we can go sledding." This is logically equivalent to the statement "If it snows this afternoon, then if we buy a sled, then we can go sledding." The logical form of this set of statements is captured by the replacement rule:

Exportation (Exp)

$$(p \cdot q) \supset r :: p \supset (q \supset r)$$

Here are two examples of valid applications:

Valid Applications of Exportation (Exp)

1. Q		1. G	
2. $(Q \cdot R) \supset S$	/ $\sim R \vee S$	2. $H \supset (K \supset \sim G)$	/ $\sim H \vee \sim K$
3. $Q \supset (R \supset S)$	2, Exp	3. $(H \cdot K) \supset \sim G$	2, Exp
4. $R \supset S$	1, 3, MP	4. $\sim \sim G$	1, DN
5. $\sim R \vee S$	4, Impl	5. $\sim (H \cdot K)$	3, 4, MT
		6. $\sim H \vee \sim K$	5, DM

Exportation (Exp)
$(p \cdot q) \supset r :: p \supset (q \supset r)$

In the first example, **exportation (Exp)** was used tactically to derive a conditional statement with Q as the antecedent. This led to the eventual derivation of the conclusion. In the second example, exportation was used tactically to derive a conditional statement with $\sim G$ as the consequent. Once again, this led to the eventual derivation of the conclusion.

The next two examples are misapplications:

Misapplications of Exportation (Exp)

1. $Q \supset (R \supset S)$		1. $(D \cdot G) \supset H$	
2. $Q \supset (R \cdot S)$ ⊘		2. $(D \supset G) \supset H$ ⊘

There are two mistakes in the first example. They can be illustrated by comparing line 2 with a *correct* application: $(Q \cdot R) \supset S$. In other words, one mistake placed the dot between the R and S, and the second was the misplacement of the horseshoe. (You might want to try constructing truth tables to verify that the derivations in both examples are not logically equivalent to the original statements.)

Tautology (Taut)

Tautology (Taut)
$p :: p \vee p$
$p :: p \cdot p$

A tautology is a statement that is necessarily true. The principle behind the replacement rule **tautology (Taut)** can be illustrated by considering the following statement: "August has 31 days." If this statement is true, then the *disjunction* "August has 31 days or August has 31 days" is true. The truth tables for these statements are identical, so they are logically equivalent statements.

Similarly, if the statement "August has 31 days" is true, then the *conjunction* "August has 31 days and August has 31 days" is true. Once again, the truth tables for these statements are identical, so they are logically equivalent statements.

Here are the forms for the rule:

Tautology (Taut)
$$p :: p \vee p$$
$$p :: p \cdot p$$

Here are two examples of valid applications:

Valid Applications of Tautology (Taut)

1. $(Q \supset S) \cdot (R \supset S)$			1. $P \supset R$	
2. $Q \vee R$	/ S		2. $P \vee (Q \cdot P)$	/ R
3. $S \vee S$	1, 2, CD		3. $(P \vee Q) \cdot (P \vee P)$	2, Dist
4. S	3, Taut		4. $P \vee P$	3, Simp
			5. P	4, Taut
			6. R	1, 5, MP

In the first example, tautology was used to derive the final step of the proof. In the second example, tautology was used as a tactical move to isolate P in order for *modus ponens* to be applied to derive the conclusion.

The next example is a misapplication:

Misapplication of Tautology (Taut)

1. $S \supset (Q \vee S)$
2. $S \supset Q$

The mistake occurs because the two instances of S are not directly connected with each other with either a disjunction or a conjunction as the main operator. (You might want to try constructing a truth table to verify that line 2 is not logically equivalent to line 1.)

THE TEN REPLACEMENT RULES	
De Morgan (DM)	**Double Negation (DN)**
$\sim(p \cdot q) :: \sim p \vee \sim q$ $\sim(p \vee q) :: \sim p \cdot \sim q$	$p :: \sim\sim p$
Commutation (Com)	**Association (Assoc)**
$p \vee q :: q \vee p$ $p \cdot q :: q \cdot p$	$p \vee (q \vee r) :: (p \vee q) \vee r$ $p \cdot (q \cdot r) :: (p \cdot q) \cdot r$
Distribution (Dist)	**Transposition (Trans)**
$p \cdot (q \vee r) :: (p \cdot q) \vee (p \cdot r)$ $p \vee (q \cdot r) :: (p \vee q) \cdot (p \vee r)$	$p \supset q :: \sim q \supset \sim p$
Material Implication (Impl)	**Material Equivalence (Equiv)**
$p \supset q :: \sim p \vee q$	$p \equiv q :: (p \supset q) \cdot (q \supset p)$ $p \equiv q :: (p \cdot q) \vee (\sim p \cdot \sim q)$
Exportation (Exp)	**Tautology (Taut)**
$(p \cdot q) \supset r :: p \supset (q \supset r)$	$p :: p \vee p$ $p :: p \cdot p$

We can now add the second five replacement rules to our strategy and tactics guide:

Applying the Second Five Replacement Rules

Strategy: We continue employing the global strategy of trying to locate the conclusion somewhere "inside" the premises, and applying a replacement rule whenever we need to "exchange" one proposition with one that is logically equivalent. Here are some specific tactical moves associated with the second five replacement rules:

Tactic 16: Try using transposition (Trans) to establish the basis for hypothetical syllogism (HS).

1. $E \supset {\sim} F$
2. $U \supset F$
3. ${\sim} F \supset {\sim} U$ 2, Trans
4. $E \supset {\sim} U$ 1, 3, HS

Tactic 17: Try using material implication (Impl) to establish the basis for distribution (Dist).

1. $E \supset ({\sim} F \cdot G)$
2. ${\sim} E \vee ({\sim} F \cdot G)$ 1, Impl
3. $({\sim} E \vee {\sim} F) \cdot ({\sim} E \vee G)$ 2, Dist

Tactic 18: Try using material implication (Impl) to establish the basis for hypothetical syllogism (HS).

1. ${\sim} H \vee K$
2. ${\sim} K \vee G$
3. $H \supset K$ 1, Impl
4. $K \supset G$ 2, Impl
5. $H \supset G$ 3, 4, HS

Tactic 19: Try using exportation (Exp) to establish the basis for *modus ponens* (MP).

1. R
2. $(R \cdot S) \supset U$
3. $R \supset (S \supset U)$ 2, Exp
4. $S \supset U$ 1, 3, MP

Tactic 20: Try using exportation (Exp) to establish the basis for *modus tollens* (MT).

1. $E \supset (F \supset G)$
2. ${\sim} G$
3. $(E \cdot F) \supset G$ 1, Exp
4. ${\sim}(E \cdot F)$ 2, 3, MT

Tactic 21: Try using material equivalence (Equiv) to establish the basis for simplification (Simp).

1. $K \equiv L$
2. $(K \supset L) \cdot (L \supset K)$ 1, Equiv
3. $K \supset L$ 2, Simp

Tactic 22: Try using material equivalence (Equiv) to establish the basis for disjunctive syllogism (DS).

1. $K \equiv L$
2. ${\sim}(K \cdot L)$
3. $(K \cdot L) \vee ({\sim} K \cdot {\sim} L)$ 1, Equiv
4. ${\sim} K \cdot {\sim} L$ 2, 3, DS

As we saw with the first five replacement rules, these specific tactics can help at any point in the proof, not just with the final conclusion.

EXERCISES 8F

I. The following are examples of what you may encounter in proofs. The last step of each example gives the line number needed for its derivation. You are to provide the replacement rule that justifies the step. This will give you practice using the second group of replacement rules.

Self-Practice
Questions

[1] 1. $R \supset S$
2. $\sim S \supset \sim R$ 1, _____

Answer: 2. $\sim S \supset \sim R$ 1, Trans

[2] 1. $(S \cdot R) \supset Q$
2. $S \supset (R \supset Q)$ 1, _____

[3] 1. $P \supset Q$
2. $\sim P \vee Q$ 1, _____

[4] 1. R
2. $R \vee R$ 1, _____

★ [5] 1. $R \equiv S$
2. $(R \supset S) \cdot (S \supset R)$ 1, _____

[6] 1. $\sim P \supset \sim Q$
2. $Q \supset P$ 1, _____

[7] 1. $(P \cdot Q) \vee (\sim P \cdot \sim Q)$
2. $P \equiv Q$ 1, _____

[8] 1. $P \supset (Q \supset R)$
2. $(P \cdot Q) \supset R$ 1, _____

★ [9] 1. $\sim P \vee Q$
2. $P \supset Q$ 1, _____

[10] 1. $P \cdot P$
2. P 1, _____

[11] 1. $[(P \vee Q) \cdot R] \supset (S \vee L)$
2. $(P \vee Q) \supset [R \supset (S \vee L)]$ 1, _____

[12] 1. $(P \cdot Q) \supset R$
2. $\sim R \supset \sim (P \cdot Q)$ 1, _____

★ [13] 1. $(S \vee L) \equiv (Q \vee K)$
2. $[(S \vee L) \cdot (Q \vee K)] \vee [\sim (S \vee L) \cdot \sim (Q \vee K)]$ 1, _____

[14] 1. $(M \cdot \sim P) \vee (M \cdot \sim P)$
2. $M \cdot \sim P$ 1, _____

[15] 1. $\sim [P \vee (Q \cdot R)] \vee (S \cdot L)$
2. $[P \vee (Q \cdot R)] \supset (S \cdot L)$ 1, _____

II. The following are more examples of what you may encounter in proofs. In these examples the justification (the replacement rule) is provided for the last step. However, the step itself is missing. Use the given information to derive the last step of each example. This will give you more practice using the second group of replacement rules.

[1] 1. $\sim S \supset \sim R$
    2.   1, Trans

Answer: 2. $R \supset S$ 1, Trans

[2] 1. $(R \cdot S) \vee (\sim R \cdot \sim S)$
    2.   1, Equiv

[3] 1. $Q \cdot Q$
    2.   1, Taut

[4] 1. $R \supset (S \supset P)$
    2.   1, Exp

★ [5] 1. $\sim S \vee P$
    2.   1, Impl

[6] 1. $[(P \vee Q) \supset (S \vee R)] \cdot [(S \vee R) \supset (P \vee Q)]$
    2.   1, Equiv

[7] 1. $(S \vee S) \cdot (S \vee S)$
    2.   1, Taut

[8] 1. $\sim [(Q \vee L) \cdot \sim K] \vee (M \supset P)$
    2.   1, Impl

★ [9] 1. $(R \vee K) \equiv (Q \vee S)$
    2.   1, Equiv

[10] 1. $\sim (P \cdot Q) \supset \sim (S \vee Q)$
    2.   1, Trans

III. Complete the following proofs. Provide the justification for each step that you derive. Note: Each proof will require you to use *one implication rule* and *one replacement rule* to complete the proof.

[1] 1. $(\sim T \vee \sim R) \supset S$
    2. $\sim (T \cdot R)$ / S

Answer:
    3. $\sim T \vee \sim R$ 2, DM
    4. S 1, 3, MP

[2] 1. $S \supset P$
    2. $\sim P \vee (R \cdot Q)$ / $S \supset (R \cdot Q)$

[3] 1. $T \vee S$
    2. $\sim \sim R$ / $(T \vee S) \cdot R$

[4] 1. $(\sim T \supset S) \cdot (R \supset P)$
    2. $T \supset R$ / $S \vee P$

⭐ [5] 1. $S \supset (P \supset Q)$
    2. $\sim Q$ / $\sim (S \cdot P)$

[6] 1. $(T \vee Q) \vee S$
    2. $\sim T$ / $Q \vee S$

[7] 1. $S \vee (T \cdot R)$ / $S \vee T$

[8] 1. $S \vee S$ / $S \vee T$

⭐ [9] 1. $P \equiv S$ / $P \supset S$

[10] 1. $\sim T \supset \sim P$
     2. $T \supset S$ / $P \supset S$

[11] 1. $\sim (T \vee S) \supset (P \vee Q)$
     2. $\sim T \cdot \sim S$ / $P \vee Q$

[12] 1. $R \vee (P \vee S)$
     2. $\sim S$ / $R \vee P$

⭐[13] 1. $(S \cdot T) \cdot R$ / S

[14] 1. $T \cdot (S \vee R)$
     2. $\sim (T \cdot S)$ / $T \cdot R$

[15] 1. $(R \cdot P) \vee (\sim R \cdot \sim P)$
     2. $(R \equiv P) \supset T$ / T

IV. Use all the rules of inference (eight implication rules and ten replacement rules) to complete the proofs. Provide the justification for each step that you derive.

[1] 1. $(S \vee \sim P) \vee R$
    2. $\sim S$ / $P \supset R$

Answer:

    3. $S \vee (\sim P \vee R)$ 1, Assoc
    4. $\sim P \vee R$ 2, 3, DS
    5. $P \supset R$ 4, Impl

[2] 1. $\sim P$
    2. $(Q \vee P) \vee R$ / $Q \vee R$

[3] 1. $\sim (P \cdot P)$ / $P \supset Q$

[4] 1. $Q \vee R$
    2. $[\, Q \supset (S \cdot P) \,] \cdot [\, R \supset (P \cdot L) \,]$ / P

⭐ [5] 1. $\sim Q \supset \sim P$
    2. $(P \cdot R) \supset S$
    3. P / $Q \vee S$

[6]   1. $P \supset Q$
    2. $(R \cdot S) \supset P$
    3. R / $S \supset Q$

[7]   1. $P \lor (T \cdot R)$
    2. $S \supset \sim (P \lor T)$ / $\sim S$

[8]   1. $\sim (S \lor Q)$ / $\sim P \supset \sim S$

⭐[9]   1. $\sim P \cdot Q$
    2. $Q \supset (R \supset P)$ / $\sim R$

[10]   1. $\sim P$
     2. $\sim Q \supset P$
     3. $\sim Q \lor (\sim P \supset R)$ / $R \lor S$

[11]   1. $P \lor Q$
     2. $(Q \supset R) \cdot (T \supset A)$
     3. $(P \supset B) \cdot (C \supset D)$ / $B \lor R$

[12]   1. $P \supset (\sim Q \cdot R)$
     2. $R \supset Q$ / $\sim P$

⭐[13]   1. $[P \supset (Q \cdot R)] \cdot [S \supset (L \cdot Q)]$
     2. $P \cdot R$ / $Q \cdot (R \lor L)$

[14]   1. $\sim P \supset (Q \lor R)$ / $(\sim P \cdot \sim Q) \supset R$

[15]   1. $P \supset (Q \cdot R)$
     2. $Q \supset \sim R$ / $P \supset S$

[16]   1. $T \supset (R \cdot S)$
     2. $R \supset (S \supset P)$ / $(P \lor \sim T) \lor Q$

⭐[17]   1. $\sim (P \cdot Q) \supset (R \lor S)$
     2. $\sim P \lor \sim Q$
     3. T / $(T \cdot R) \lor (T \cdot S)$

[18]   1. $\sim (P \cdot Q)$
     2. $(P \cdot Q) \lor (R \cdot S)$ / $Q \lor S$

[19]   1. $P \supset (Q \lor R)$
     2. $S \supset \sim (Q \lor R)$ / $\sim (P \cdot S)$

[20]   1. $T \lor S$
     2. $\sim T$
     3. $(S \lor S) \supset (\sim P \lor R)$ / $\sim R \supset \sim P$

⭐[21]   1. $(P \lor Q) \lor \sim R$
     2. $[(P \lor Q) \supset Q] \cdot (\sim R \supset S)$
     3. $\sim P$ / $Q \lor (S \cdot \sim R)$

[22]   1. $(\sim P \lor Q) \supset R$
     2. $(S \lor R) \supset P$
     3. $P \supset Q$ / Q

▷
Video Tutorial: 8FIV
Exercise #8

[23] 1. $P \supset Q$
    2. $R \supset (S \supset P)$
    3. $Q \supset {\sim} P$ / ${\sim} R \lor {\sim} S$

[24] 1. ${\sim} Q$
    2. $R \supset Q$
    3. ${\sim} S \supset M$
    4. $R \lor (S \supset Q)$ / $M \lor K$

★[25] 1. ${\sim} P \supset Q$
    2. ${\sim} R \supset {\sim} ({\sim} S \lor P)$
    3. $Q \supset {\sim} S$ / R

[26] 1. ${\sim} P$
    2. $(Q \supset P) \cdot (S \supset L)$
    3. Q / $M \supset L$

[27] 1. $T \equiv R$
    2. $({\sim} R \supset {\sim} T) \supset (P \cdot {\sim} S)$ / ${\sim} S \lor T$

[28] 1. $P \supset (Q \lor R)$
    2. $(S \lor T) \supset R$
    3. ${\sim} Q \cdot {\sim} R$ / ${\sim} P \cdot {\sim} (S \lor T)$

★[29] 1. ${\sim} R \lor {\sim} S$
    2. $P \lor [Q \lor (R \cdot S)]$
    3. $L \supset {\sim} P$ / $L \supset Q$

[30] 1. $(P \cdot Q) \supset R$
    2. P
    3. ${\sim} Q \lor S$ / ${\sim} Q \lor (R \cdot S)$

[31] 1. $(P \lor Q) \supset S$
    2. $R \lor (P \lor Q)$
    3. ${\sim} R$
    4. ${\sim} T \supset R$ / $S \equiv T$

[32] 1. ${\sim} P \supset (Q \lor R)$
    2. $(S \lor Q) \supset R$
    3. ${\sim} R$ / P

★[33] 1. $S \supset Q$
    2. $R \cdot S$
    3. $Q \supset (L \lor {\sim} R)$ / L

[34] 1. $C \supset F$
    2. $A \supset B$
    3. ${\sim} F \cdot A$
    4. ${\sim} C \supset (B \supset D)$ / $B \cdot D$

[35]   1. ~ P ∨ Q
    2. R · (S ∨ P)
    3. ~ S   / Q

[36]   1. P ∨ Q
    2. [P ⊃ (R · S)] · (Q ⊃ L)
    3. ~ (R · S)
    4. Q   / ~ R ∨ (~ S · L)

★[37]   1. Q ∨ (P ⊃ S)
    2. S ≡ (R · T)
    3. P · ~ Q   / P · R

[38]   1. P ⊃ (R ∨ S)
    2. ~ [(~ P ∨ ~ Q) ∨ (R ∨ ~ L)]   / S

[39]   1. (Q ∨ S) ⊃ ~ P
    2. Q ∨ (R · S)
    3. (Q ∨ R) ⊃ ~ L
    4. K ⊃ (L ∨ P)   / ~ K

[40]   1. R
    2. ~ (P · ~ Q)
    3. P ∨ S
    4. ~ (R · S)   / Q

★[41]   1. P ∨ R
    2. ~ P ∨ (Q · R)
    3. R ⊃ (Q · S)   / Q · S

[42]   1. ~ S
    2. ~ P ⊃ ~ Q
    3. Q · (R ∨ S)   / P · R

[43]   1. Q · S
    2. (Q · ~ P) ⊃ ~ R
    3. Q ⊃ ~ P
    4. (S · T) ⊃ (P ∨ R)   / ~ T

[44]   1. ~ P ∨ Q
    2. (P ∨ R) · S
    3. ~ (R ∨ L)   / Q

★[45]   1. P ⊃ Q
    2. Q ⊃ ~ (R ∨ P)
    3. ~ S ⊃ Q
    4. S ⊃ (M ⊃ L)
    5. R
    6. M ∨ P   / L

[46] 1. $\sim S \supset (N \supset T)$
      2. $\sim S \cdot (R \supset S)$
      3. $(\sim M \cdot \sim N) \supset (\sim O \lor \sim P)$
      4. $(Q \lor \sim R) \supset \sim M$
      5. $(\sim R \cdot \sim S) \supset (\sim \sim O \cdot \sim T)$ $/ \sim P$
[47] 1. $\sim A \cdot \sim B$
      2. $\sim D \supset A$
      3. $M \supset [(N \lor O) \supset P]$
      4. $Q \supset (S \lor T)$
      5. $(\sim Q \lor R) \supset (M \cdot N)$
      6. $\sim D \lor \sim (S \lor T)$ $/ P \cdot \sim B$
[48] 1. $(\sim Q \lor \sim S) \supset T$
      2. $(M \lor N) \supset [(O \lor P) \supset (\sim Q \cdot R)]$ $/ M \supset (O \supset T)$
★[49] 1. $\sim (S \supset Q)$
      2. $(M \cdot N) \supset (O \lor P)$
      3. $\sim [O \lor (N \cdot P)]$
      4. $N \equiv \sim (Q \cdot R)$ $/ \sim (M \lor Q)$
[50] 1. $\sim (R \lor S)$
      2. $\sim (M \cdot N) \lor \sim (O \cdot P)$
      3. $\sim (O \cdot M) \supset S$
      4. $(Q \cdot R) \equiv \sim P$ $/ \sim (N \cdot T)$
[51] 1. $G \supset H$
      2. $D \equiv (G \lor H)$
      3. $H \equiv K$ $/ D \equiv K$

V. First, translate the following arguments into symbolic form. Second, use the implication rules and the replacement rules to derive the conclusion of each. Letters for the simple statements are provided in parentheses and can be used in the order given.

1. Science will eventually come to an end. If science comes to an end and metaphysical speculation runs rampant, then intellectual progress will end. However, it is not the case that either intellectual progress will end or we stop seeking epistemological answers. Therefore, metaphysical speculation will not run rampant. (S, M, I, E)

Answer:

   1. S
   2. $(S \cdot M) \supset I$
   3. $\sim (I \lor E)$ $/ \sim M$
   4. $\sim I \cdot \sim E$ 3, DM
   5. $\sim I$ 4, Simp
   6. $\sim (S \cdot M)$ 2, 5, MT
   7. $\sim S \lor \sim M$ 6, DM
   8. $\sim \sim S$ 1, DN
   9. $\sim M$ 7, 8, DS

2. Either dolphins or chimpanzees are sentient beings. If chimpanzees can solve complex problems, then chimpanzees are sentient beings. If dolphins can learn a language, then dolphins are sentient beings. Chimpanzees can solve complex problems, and dolphins can learn a language. So, we must conclude that both chimpanzees and dolphins are sentient beings. (*D, C, S, L*)

3. If sports continue to dominate our culture, then it is not the case that either we will mature as a society or we will lose touch with reality. We will mature as a society, or we will both decline as a world power and we will lose touch with reality. Therefore, sports will not continue to dominate our culture. (*S, M, L, D*)

4. If people know how to read and they are interested in the history of ideas, then they will discover new truths. If people do not know how to read, then they cannot access the wisdom of thousands of years. But people can access the wisdom of thousands of years. Thus, if they are interested in the history of ideas, then they will discover new truths. (*R, H, D, W*)

⭐ 5. That movie will not win the Academy Award for Best Picture. Therefore, if the governor of our state is not impeached, then that movie will not win the Academy Award for Best Picture. (*M, G*)

6. If the world's population continues to grow, then if birth control measures are made available in every country, then the world's population will not continue to grow. Hence, if the world's population continues to grow, then birth control measures are not made available in every country. (*P, B*)

7. Either my roommate did not pay his phone bill or he did not pay this month's rent, or else he got a part-time job. If it is not the case that my roommate pays his phone bill and he pays this month's rent, then he moves out. But he did not move out. It follows that he got a part-time job. (*P, R, J, M*)

8. Either it is not the case that if the thief entered through the basement door, then she picked the lock, or else the door was not locked. If the thief entered through the basement door, then she picked the lock, if and only if the door was locked. This suggests that it is not the case that if the thief entered through the basement door, then she picked the lock. (*B, P, L*)

⭐ 9. If there is a raging fire in the attic, then there is a constant supply of oxygen to the room. If there is a raging fire in the attic, then a window must have been left open. Thus, if there is a raging fire in the attic, then a window must have been left open and there is a constant supply of oxygen to the room. (*F, O, W*)

10. Either we do not get a new furnace or else we repair the roof or we spend the money to overhaul the car's engine. If we sell the house, then it is not the case that if we do get a new furnace, then we repair the roof. However, we did not spend the money to overhaul the car's engine. Therefore, we did not sell the house. (*F, R, C, S*)

11. If all languages have a common origin, then there are grammatical similarities among languages and common root words among all languages. If there are grammatical similarities among languages, then if there are some distinct dialects, then there are not common root words among all languages. This implies that if all languages have a common origin, then there are not some distinct dialects. (*O, G, R, D*)

12. Either the administration does not cut the budget for social services or the administration reduces the defense budget. If the administration does cut the budget for social services, then it lowers the tax rate. Thus, if the administration does cut the budget for social services, then it lowers the tax rate and it reduces the defense budget. (*S, D, T*)

⭐ 13. It is not the case that either humans are always healthy or humans stay young forever. If humans are immortal, then it is not the case that either humans do not stay young forever or humans are always healthy. We can conclude that humans are not immortal. (*H, Y, I*)

14. If you get malaria, then you can get very sick and you can die. Therefore, if you get malaria, then you can die. (*M, S, D*)

15. It is not the case that either witchcraft is real or astrology is considered a science. If the majority of people are not superstitious or they believe things without evidence, then astrology is considered a science. It follows that people are superstitious. (*W, A, S, E*)

G. CONDITIONAL PROOF

The proof procedure we have been using is capable of handling most valid arguments. However, additional proof procedure methods are available. **Conditional proof (CP)** is a strategic method that starts by assuming the antecedent of a conditional statement on a separate line and then proceeds to derive the consequent on a separate line. As you will see, conditional proof is a technique for building a conditional statement, and it is used in conjunction with the rules of inference. Consider this example:

1. Q
2. $P \supset (Q \supset R)$ $/ P \supset R$

Notice that the conclusion is a conditional statement. The conditional proof procedure is displayed in a special way to distinguish its role in a natural deduction proof. The first step is to assume the antecedent of the conclusion (or any line in a proof that you wish to derive):

1. Q
2. $P \supset (Q \supset R)$ $/ P \supset R$
   > 3. P *Assumption (CP)*

Conditional proof (CP) A method that starts by assuming the antecedent of a conditional statement on a separate line and then proceeds to validly derive the consequent on a separate line.

Note that line 3 is indented. It is shown this way because it was *not* derived from any other line—it was *not validly deduced*. On the contrary, we are *assuming* the truth of line 3. This is also why this line is justified as *Assumption (CP)*. All of our proofs to this point have contained lines that were either given premises or statements derived from previous lines, which, in turn, were justified by the implication rules or replacement rules. This procedure and requirement ensured that each line in a derived proof is a valid argument. However, in the foregoing example, line 3 has not been proven. It is therefore an *assumption* on our part, and is justified as such.

We now have the opportunity to explore the consequences of our assumption. We can ask, "If *P*, then what follows?" At this point, we are free to use the implication rules and the replacement rules, as long as we acknowledge that any derivations that rely on line 3 are the result of the assumption. Therefore, we will have to keep indenting any lines that rely on line 3. The next steps in the proof are as follows:

1. *Q*
2. *P* ⊃ (*Q* ⊃ *R*)   / *P* ⊃ *R*
    3. *P*   Assumption (CP)
    4. *Q* ⊃ *R*   2, 3, MP
    5. *R*   1, 4, MP

PROFILES IN LOGIC
Augusta Ada Byron

Ada Byron (1815–52) was the daughter of the poet Lord Byron, but she never got to know her father. Her parents separated when Ada was only a month old. When she was 18, she met Charles Babbage, the inventor of the "analytical engine," an elaborate calculating machine. Ada Byron worked with Babbage for the next 10 years, trying to solve the complex problems associated with what we now call computer programming. How can we get a machine to do complex mathematical calculations and analysis? A major problem for Babbage was to get a machine to calculate Bernoulli numbers (special sequences of rational numbers). Ada Byron's work on this difficult problem culminated in her breakthrough—the first computer program ever. What she created was an *algorithm*, a series of steps that achieve a final result. The analytic engine could do its calculations step by step, and so can modern computers.

But Ada Byron envisioned machines that could do far more than just calculate numbers. She wrote of a machine that could "compose elaborate and scientific pieces of music of any degree of complexity or extent." In the late 1970s, the United States Department of Defense began work on a programming language capable of integrating many complex embedded computer applications. The successful program bears the name *Ada*, in recognition of Ada Byron's achievements.

At this point, we have all the necessary ingredients to complete our proof. We started out by assuming P (the antecedent of the conclusion) and from this we derived R (the consequent of the conclusion). The next line in the proof combines these results.

1. Q
2. $P \supset (Q \supset R)$ $/ P \supset R$
      3. P Assumption (CP)
      4. $Q \supset R$ 2, 3, MP
      5. R 1, 4, MP
6. $P \supset R$ 3–5, CP

Our proof is now complete. Line 6 is a *conditional statement* and it has been derived by a sequence of steps from line 3 through line 5. Note the difference in notation for the lines of the proof. Whereas line 4 uses a *comma*, line 6 uses a *dash*. The dash indicates that the *entire CP sequence* was used to derive the step.

Line 6 ends the conditional proof sequence, and the result is *discharged*, meaning that it no longer needs to be indented. The conditional proof sequence starts with an assumption, and the final result of the *CP* sequence is a conditional statement. This is why line 6 must be justified by listing the entire sequence. What the proof shows is that the conclusion can be validly derived from the original premises.

There are even some arguments that have conclusions that cannot be derived by the rules alone; these arguments need further techniques, one of which is conditional proof. This is illustrated by the following:

$P \supset \sim Q$ $/ P \supset (P \cdot \sim Q)$

Here is the conditional proof:

1. $P \supset \sim Q$ $/ P \supset (P \cdot \sim Q)$
      2. P Assumption (CP)
      3. $\sim Q$ 1, 2, MP
      4. $P \cdot \sim Q$ 2, 3, Conj
5. $P \supset (P \cdot \sim Q)$ 2–4, CP

Conditional proof can be used in a variety of ways. For example, it is possible to have a conditional proof *within* another conditional proof. The following example illustrates this point.

1. $\sim P \supset Q$
2. $\sim R \vee [\sim P \supset (\sim Q \vee \sim U)]$ $/ R \supset (U \supset P)$

The antecedent of the main operator in the conclusion is R. We can start a *CP* by assuming R. In fact, the second premise is a disjunction that has $\sim R$ as the first disjunct. However, if we use material implication (Impl) on the second premise, then we can derive another conditional with R as the antecedent.

Now, if we start the *CP*, and somewhere within the indented lines we use material implication on premise 2, we cannot use that result outside the *CP*. *Since every line in a CP sequence is based on an assumption, it is not valid outside that assumption.* Therefore, as a general strategy when using *CP*, look to see if you need to use the implication rules and the replacement rules on the given premises before you start the *CP* sequence. This strategy is illustrated by line 3 in the following display. Line 4 starts the *CP* sequence:

1. ~ P ⊃ Q
2. ~ R ∨ [~ P ⊃ (~ Q ∨ ~ U)]   / R ⊃ (U ⊃ P)
3. R ⊃ [~ P ⊃ (~ Q ∨ ~ U)]   2, Impl
> 4. R   *Assumption (CP)*
> 5. ~ P ⊃ (~ Q ∨ ~ U)   3, 4, MP

At this point, we need to survey what we have and where we are going. The conclusion is a conditional statement. The antecedent is *R*, but the consequent happens to be a conditional statement as well. Line 4 provides the antecedent of the conclusion. Several options are available. We can try a second use of *CP*. This gives us two further choices: We can start by assuming either *U* or ~ *P*. Let's think ahead a few steps. If we start with *U*, then we will probably have to add *Q* somewhere along the line in order to isolate *P*. However, if we start with ~ *P*, then we can immediately get ~ *Q* ∨ ~ *U* from line 5. Perhaps transposition (Trans) can then come into play. Let's try ~ *P* and see how far we can get:

1. ~ P ⊃ Q
2. ~ R ∨ [~ P ⊃ (~ Q ∨ ~ U)]   / R ⊃ (U ⊃ P)
3. R ⊃ [~ P ⊃ (~ Q ∨ ~ U)]   2, Impl
> 4. R   *Assumption (CP)*
> 5. ~ P ⊃ (~ Q ∨ ~ U)   3, 4, MP
>> 6. ~ P   *Assumption (CP)*
>> 7. ~ Q ∨ ~ U   5, 6, MP
>> 8. Q   1, 6, MP
>> 9. ~ ~ Q   8, DN
>> 10. ~ U   7, 9, DS

We are getting close to the consequent of the conclusion, so we can now discharge the second assumption:

1. ~ P ⊃ Q
2. ~ R ∨ [~ P ⊃ (~ Q ∨ ~ U)]   / R ⊃ (U ⊃ P)
3. R ⊃ [~ P ⊃ (~ Q ∨ ~ U)]   2, Impl
> 4. R   *Assumption (CP)*
> 5. ~ P ⊃ (~ Q ∨ ~ U)   3, 4, MP
>> 6. ~ P   *Assumption (CP)*
>> 7. ~ Q ∨ ~ U   5, 6, MP
>> 8. Q   1, 6, MP
>> 9. ~ ~ Q   8, DN
>> 10. ~ U   7, 9, DS
> 11. ~ P ⊃ ~ U   6–10, CP

Using transposition (Trans) on line 11 gives the desired consequent and makes it possible to complete the proof.

1. $\sim P \supset Q$
2. $\sim R \vee [\sim P \supset (\sim Q \vee \sim U)]$ $/ R \supset (U \supset P)$
3. $R \supset [\sim P \supset (\sim Q \vee \sim U)]$ 2, Impl
     4. R *Assumption (CP)*
     5. $\sim P \supset (\sim Q \vee \sim U)$ 3, 4, MP
       6. $\sim P$ *Assumption (CP)*
       7. $\sim Q \vee \sim U$ 5, 6, MP
       8. Q 1, 6, MP
       9. $\sim \sim Q$ 8, DN
       10. $\sim U$ 7, 9, DS
     11. $\sim P \supset \sim U$ 6–10, CP
     12. $U \supset P$ 11, Trans
13. $R \supset (U \supset P)$ 4–12, CP

Line 4 started one conditional proof sequence. But before it was completed, another conditional proof sequence began with line 6. Note that *both* lines have been justified: *Assumption (CP)*.

In addition to showing an assumption, the use of indentation with conditional proofs lets us know that no line within the *CP* sequence can be used outside the sequence, meaning you cannot use any line within the sequence 6–10 after line 11. Also, if the proof were longer, you could not use any line within the sequence 4–12 after line 13. This requirement should make sense, if we think about what *CP* does. Since every line in a *CP* sequence is based on an assumption, the lines are not valid outside that assumption. This is why every *CP* sequence must end with a conditional statement. Once the *CP* is completed, we can use the discharged conditional statement, because its validity is based on a series of steps that have been carefully contained within the rules of the natural deduction proof procedure. (Of course, you can discharge more than one line from a *CP* sequence. For example, line 11, $\sim P \supset \sim U$, was discharged and justified as 6–10, CP. If needed in a proof, we could have also discharged a new line; for example, $\sim P \supset Q$ would be justified as 6–8, CP.)

Another way to use conditional proof is to have more than one *CP* sequence within a proof, but with each sequence separate, as in the following example:

1. $(\sim R \vee \sim Q) \cdot (R \vee P)$
2. $P \supset \sim S$
3. $Q \vee S$ $/ P \equiv Q$

If we apply material equivalence, then we can see that the conclusion is logically equivalent to $(P \supset Q) \cdot (Q \supset P)$. Since the conclusion is the *conjunction* of two *conditionals*, we might try assuming the antecedent of each one to see what we can derive. Of course, before we start *CP*, we should consider whether the given premises could offer us any interesting results.

We can start the proof as follows:

1. $(\sim R \vee \sim Q) \cdot (R \vee P)$
2. $P \supset \sim S$
3. $Q \vee S$ / $P \equiv Q$
4. $\sim R \vee \sim Q$ 1, Simp
5. $R \vee P$ 1, Simp
    6. P Assumption (CP)
    7. $\sim S$ 2, 6, MP
    8. Q 3, 7, DS
9. $P \supset Q$ 6–8, CP

At this point in our proof we have deduced the first part of the conjunction: $(P \supset Q) \cdot (Q \supset P)$. We now need to derive the second part.

1. $(\sim R \vee \sim Q) \cdot (R \vee P)$
2. $P \supset \sim S$
3. $Q \vee S$ / $P \equiv Q$
4. $\sim R \vee \sim Q$ 1, Simp
5. $R \vee P$ 1, Simp
    6. P Assumption (CP)
    7. $\sim S$ 2, 6, MP
    8. Q 3, 7, DS
9. $P \supset Q$ 6–8, CP
    10. Q Assumption (CP)
    11. $\sim \sim Q$ 10, DN
    12. $\sim R$ 4, 11 DS
    13. P 5, 12 DS
14. $Q \supset P$ 10–13, CP
15. $(P \supset Q) \cdot (Q \supset P)$ 9, 14, Conj
16. $P \equiv Q$ 15, Equiv

As before, we must ensure that any individual line within the two CP sequences (6–8, and 10–13) are not used anywhere outside of the CP sequences. In addition, each discharged step (line 9 and line 14) is correctly formulated to be the result of a CP sequence, namely, a conditional statement.

EXERCISES 8G

I. **Apply conditional proof (CP) to the following arguments. Use the implication rules and the replacement rules.**

[1] 1. $P \supset Q$ $/ P \supset (S \supset Q)$

Lightboard Video

Answer:

   1. $P \supset Q$ $/ P \supset (S \supset Q)$
      2. P *Assumption (CP)*
      3. Q 1, 2, MP
      4. $Q \vee \sim S$ 3, Add
      5. $\sim S \vee Q$ 4, Com
      6. $S \supset Q$ 5, Impl
   7. $P \supset (S \supset Q)$ 2–6, CP

Self-Practice Questions

[2] 1. $U \supset \sim Q$ $/ (P \cdot R) \supset \sim (U \cdot Q)$

[3] 1. $P \vee Q$
    2. $R \supset \sim Q$ $/ R \supset P$

[4] 1. $R \supset \sim S$
    2. $(\sim S \vee P) \supset \sim Q$ $/ R \supset \sim Q$

★[5] 1. $(P \cdot Q) \supset S$
    2. $P \supset Q$ $/ P \supset S$

[6] 1. $P \supset (\sim Q \cdot \sim R)$ $/ \sim P \vee \sim R$

[7] 1. $P \supset Q$
    2. $P \supset R$ $/ P \supset [(Q \cdot R) \vee \sim S]$

[8] 1. $\sim P$
    2. $(Q \vee R) \supset S$
    3. $L \supset (\sim P \supset \sim S)$ $/ L \supset \sim (Q \vee R)$

★[9] 1. $P \supset (Q \cdot R)$
    2. $S \supset (Q \cdot T)$ $/ (S \vee P) \supset Q$

[10] 1. Q
     2. $P \supset [\sim Q \vee (R \supset S)]$ $/ (P \cdot R) \supset S$

Video Tutorial: 8GI
Exercise #9

[11] 1. $\sim P$
     2. $Q \supset R$
     3. $R \supset S$ $/ Q \supset (S \cdot \sim P)$

[12] 1. $(P \vee Q) \supset S$ $/ \sim S \supset [(R \vee \sim P) \cdot (R \vee \sim Q)]$

★[13] 1. $[(P \vee Q) \vee R] \supset (S \vee L)$
     2. $(S \vee L) \supset (M \vee K)$ $/ Q \supset (M \vee K)$

[14] 1. $P \supset (Q \cdot R)$ $/ (S \supset P) \supset (S \supset R)$

[15] 1. $(P \vee Q) \supset R$
      2. $L \supset (S \cdot P)$ $/ L \supset R$

[16] 1. $(P \cdot Q) \vee (R \cdot S)$
      2. $R \supset L$ $/ \sim P \supset L$

⭐[17] 1. $Q \supset \sim P$
      2. $\sim P \vee (Q \vee R)$ $/ P \supset (R \vee \sim S)$

[18] 1. P
      2. $(P \vee P) \supset [Q \supset \sim (R \vee S)]$ $/ Q \supset \sim S$

[19] 1. $(P \vee \sim Q) \vee R$
      2. $\sim Q \supset \sim S$ $/ \sim R \supset (S \supset P)$

[20] 1. $\sim P$
      2. $Q \supset (R \supset P)$
      3. $\sim R \supset (S \vee P)$ $/ Q \supset S$

⭐[21] 1. $[(A \cdot B) \cdot C] \supset D$ $/ A \supset [B \supset (C \supset D)]$

[22] 1. $(P \vee Q) \supset R$
      2. $S \supset (P \cdot K)$ $/ \sim R \supset \sim S$

[23] 1. $P \supset (Q \vee R)$
      2. $\sim Q \supset (R \supset \sim P)$ $/ P \supset (P \supset Q)$

[24] 1. $P \supset Q$ $/ \sim (Q \vee S) \supset \sim P$

⭐[25] 1. $(P \vee Q) \supset (R \cdot S)$
      2. $(R \vee \sim L) \supset [M \cdot (K \vee N)]$ $/ P \supset [R \cdot (K \vee N)]$

[26] 1. $\sim (P \cdot \sim Q)$
      2. $\sim P \supset \sim R$
      3. $(R \cdot Q) \supset S$ $/ R \supset S$

[27] 1. P
      2. $Q \cdot R$
      3. $S \supset [\sim R \vee (P \supset \sim L)]$ $/ S \supset \sim L$

[28] 1. $P \supset (Q \cdot R)$
      2. $S \supset (\sim Q \cdot R)$ $/ P \supset \sim S$

⭐[29] 1. $R \supset \sim U$
      2. $P \supset (Q \vee R)$
      3. $(Q \supset S) \cdot (S \supset T)$ $/ P \supset (\sim U \vee T)$

[30] 1. $\sim P \supset Q$
      2. $\sim (Q \cdot \sim S)$
      3. $R \supset (P \supset S)$ $/ R \supset S$

[31] 1. ~ P ∨ (Q ⊃ R)
      2. P
      3. ~ Q ⊃ S   / ~ S ⊃ R

[32] 1. D ⊃ E
      2. E ⊃ F
      3. A ⊃ [C ∨ (D · ~ B)]   / A ⊃ (C ∨ F)

★[33] 1. P ⊃ Q
      2. (P · Q) ≡ S   / P ≡ S

[34] 1. P · Q
      2. P ⊃ ~ (R · S)
      3. Q ⊃ (R ∨ S)   / R ≡ ~ S

[35] 1. ~ (C ≡ D)   / C ≡ ~ D

[36] 1. B ≡ (C ∨ D)
      2. (H ⊃ B) ⊃ (G ≡ ~ G)
      3. (H ∨ C) ≡ D   / H ≡ (B ∨ G)

[37] 1. ~ P ⊃ (R ⊃ ~ T)
      2. U ⊃ (~ Q ⊃ ~ R)
      3. ~ Q · T   / ~ R ∨ (~ U · P)

II. First, translate the following arguments into symbolic form. Second, use the implication rules, the replacement rules, and conditional proof to derive the conclusion of each. Letters for the simple statements are provided in parentheses and can be used in the order given.

1. If you travel to other countries, then you can learn another language. In addition, if you travel to other countries, then you can test your ability to adapt. So if you travel to other countries, then you can test your ability to adapt and you can learn another language. (C, L, A)

Answer:

[1] 1. C ⊃ L
     2. C ⊃ A   / C ⊃ (A · L)
         | 3. C   *Assumption (CP)*
         | 4. A   2, 3, MP
         | 5. L   1, 3, MP
         | 6. A · L   4, 5, Conj
     7. C ⊃ (A · L)   3–6, CP

2. If animals are conscious, then they are self-aware and they can feel pain. If animals can feel pain and they are conscious, then they have certain rights. It follows that if animals are conscious, then they have certain rights. (C, S, P, R)

3. If call center representatives are rude, then they are not trained correctly. If call center representatives are rude, then if they are not trained correctly, then customers have a right to complain. So, if call center representatives are rude, then customers have a right to complain. (R, T, C)

4. If either your credit card information is stolen or your e-mail is hacked, then identity theft can occur. If either legal issues arise or monetary loses occur, then you are a victim of fraud and your credit card information is stolen. Therefore, if legal issues arise, then identity theft can occur. (*C, E, I, L, M, F*)

⭐ 5. If a movie has a low budget, then it can still win the Academy Award for Best Picture. If a movie stars an unknown actor, then if the producer is just starting out in show business, then a movie has a low budget. Therefore, if a movie stars an unknown actor, then if the producer is just starting out in show business, then it can still win the Academy Award for Best Picture. (*L, A, U, P*)

H. INDIRECT PROOF

Indirect proof (IP) A method that starts by assuming the negation of the required statement and then validly deriving a contradiction on a subsequent line.

Indirect proof (IP) can be used to derive either the conclusion of an argument or an intermediate line in a proof sequence. The technique starts by assuming the *negation* of the statement to be derived, and then deriving a contradiction on a subsequent line. The indirect proof sequence is then discharged by negating the *assumed* statement. The reasoning behind the procedure is straightforward: If in the context of a proof the negation of a statement leads to an absurdity—a *contradiction*—then we have *indirectly* established the truth of the original statement. (That is why the procedure is sometimes called "*reductio ad absurdum*," which means reduction to the absurd.)

The indirect proof method needs to be displayed in a special way to distinguish its role in a natural deduction proof. The display is similar to that of conditional proof, in that the indirect proof sequence starts with an assumption. The following illustrates the method of indirect proof:

$$
\begin{array}{lll}
1. & \sim M \supset \sim N & \\
2. & (\sim L \cdot \sim M) \supset N & \quad / \, L \vee M \\
& \quad 3. \sim (L \vee M) & \text{Assumption (IP)} \\
& \quad 4. \sim L \cdot \sim M & \text{3, DM} \\
& \quad 5. \, N & \text{2, 4, MP} \\
& \quad 6. \sim M & \text{4, Simp} \\
& \quad 7. \sim N & \text{1, 6, MP} \\
& \quad 8. \, N \cdot \sim N & \text{5, 7, Conj} \\
& \quad 9. \sim\sim (L \vee M) & \text{3–8, IP} \\
& \quad 10. \; L \vee M & \text{9, DN}
\end{array}
$$

Line 3 begins the sequence; it is indented and justified as *Assumption (IP)*. Line 8 displays the goal of all *IP* sequences, which is to *derive a contradiction*. Line 9 discharges the *IP* sequence by negating the assumption that started the sequence: line 3. The final result is the statement that we wished to prove. As with *CP*, we cannot use any line within an *IP* sequence outside that sequence as part of our overall proof.

The method of indirect proof relies on a simple and clear principle: If two lines in a proof are contradictory statements, then one of them is false. In addition, we can easily show why we should avoid contradictions. Quite simply, *anything follows from a contradiction.* Consider these two proofs:

1. *P*		1. *P*		
2. ~ *P*	/ *Q*	2. ~ *P*	/ ~ *Q*	
3. *P* v *Q*	1, Add	3. *P* v ~ *Q*	1, Add	
4. *Q*	2, 3, DS	4. ~ *Q*	2, 3, DS	

As illustrated by the two proofs, you can derive anything from a contradiction. However, whenever a set of statements implies a contradiction, not all of the statements can be true. Thus, the method of indirect proof allows us to show the following: If a set of premises are assumed to be true, and the *negation of the conclusion leads to a contradiction*, then it follows that the negation of the conclusion must be false. Thus, the original conclusion must be true.

Here is another example of how indirect proof can be used:

1. *D* ⊃ *C*		
2. *A* v (*B* · *C*)		
3. *A* ⊃ *D*	/ *C*	
4. ~ *C*	Assumption (IP)	
5. ~ *D*	1, 4, MT	
6. ~ *A*	3, 5, MT	
7. *B* · *C*	2, 6, DS	
8. *C*	7, Simp	
9. ~ *C* · *C*	4, 8, Conj	
10. ~ ~ *C*	4–9, IP	
11. *C*	10, DN	

Line 4 begins the indirect proof sequence; it is indented and justified as *Assumption (IP)*. Line 9 is the contradiction derived in the *IP* sequence. Line 10 discharges the *IP* sequence by negating the assumption that started the sequence: line 4.

The methods of indirect proof and conditional proof can *both* be used in a proof. Here is an example:

1. ~ (*P* · ~ *Q*) v (*P* ⊃ *R*)	/ *P* ⊃ (*Q* v *R*)	
2. *P*	Assumption (CP)	
3. ~ (*Q* v *R*)	Assumption (IP)	
4. ~ *Q* · ~ *R*	3, DM	
5. ~ *Q*	4, Simp	
6. *P* · ~ *Q*	2, 5, Conj	
7. ~ ~ (*P* · ~ *Q*)	6, DN	
8. *P* ⊃ *R*	1, 7, DS	
9. *R*	2, 8, MP	
10. ~ *R*	4, Simp	
11. *R* · ~ *R*	9, 10, Conj	
12. ~ ~ (*Q* v *R*)	3–11, IP	
13. *Q* v *R*	12, DN	
14. *P* ⊃ (*Q* v *R*)	2–13, CP	

Line 2 started a *CP* sequence by assuming the antecedent of the conclusion. This means that if we were able to derive the consequent of the conditional in the conclusion, then we could discharge the *CP*. At that point in the proof, an indirect proof sequence was started by negating the consequent in the conclusion. The overall strategy was to try to derive a contradiction; this would establish the truth of the original statement. Once this was accomplished, the *IP* sequence was discharged. The final step of the proof discharged the *CP* sequence. As the proof illustrates, each sequence of *IP* and *CP* has been correctly discharged, and no line within either sequence has been used outside that sequence. The proof shows that the conclusion follows from the premises.

EXERCISES 8H

Self-Practice
Questions

I. Apply indirect proof to the following arguments. Use the implication rules and the replacement rules. You can also use conditional proof, if needed.

[1] 1. $P \supset \sim (P \vee Q)$ / $\sim P$

Answer:

1.	$P \supset \sim (P \vee Q)$	/ $\sim P$
2.	P	*Assumption (IP)*
3.	$\sim (P \vee Q)$	1, 2, MP
4.	$\sim P \cdot \sim Q$	3, DM
5.	$\sim P$	4, Simp
6.	$P \cdot \sim P$	2, 5, Conj
7.	$\sim P$	2–6, IP

[2] 1. P / $Q \vee \sim Q$

[3] 1. $P \supset (Q \cdot S)$
     2. $\sim S$ / $\sim P$

[4] 1. $P \supset Q$
     2. $R \supset P$
     3. $\sim Q$ / $\sim R$

★ [5] 1. $\sim Q \vee P$
      2. $\sim (P \vee S)$ / $\sim Q$

[6] 1. $(Q \supset Q) \supset S$ / S

[7] 1. $P \vee (\sim P \supset Q)$
     2. $\sim Q$ / P

[8] 1. $P \supset Q$
     2. $P \vee (Q \cdot S)$ / Q

⭐[9] 1. $[P \supset (Q \cdot R)] \cdot (S \supset L)$
　　　2. S　　　　　　　　　　/ L

[10] 1. $(P \lor \sim P) \supset \sim Q$
　　　2. $R \supset Q$　　　　　　/ $\sim R$

[11] 1. $(R \lor S) \supset (\sim P \cdot \sim Q)$
　　　2. P　　　　　　　　　/ $\sim R$

[12] 1. $R \lor S$
　　　2. $Q \supset \sim R$
　　　3. $P \supset Q$
　　　4. $\sim S$　　　　　　　/ $\sim P$

⭐[13] 1. $\sim P \supset \sim (Q \lor \sim P)$　/ P

[14] 1. $P \lor (Q \cdot P)$
　　　2. $P \supset R$　　　　　　/ R

[15] 1. $S \supset \sim (\sim Q \lor P)$
　　　2. $Q \equiv P$　　　　　　/ $\sim S$

[16] 1. $P \lor Q$
　　　2. $(S \lor Q) \supset P$　　/ P

⭐[17] 1. $\sim P \cdot \sim T$
　　　2. $\sim (P \cdot \sim Q) \supset R$　/ $R \lor T$

[18] 1. $P \lor \sim (Q \cdot S)$　　/ $Q \supset (S \supset P)$

[19] 1. $Q \supset \sim R$
　　　2. $P \lor Q$
　　　3. $\sim P \supset (Q \supset R)$　/ P

[20] 1. $(\sim Q \supset \sim S) \cdot (\sim S \supset S)$　/ Q

⭐[21] 1. $P \supset (\sim P \equiv \sim Q)$
　　　2. $\sim P \lor \sim Q$　　　/ $\sim P$

[22] 1. $A \supset B$
　　　2. $A \supset C$
　　　3. $\sim B \lor \sim C$　　　/ $\sim A$

[23] 1. $(P \lor Q) \supset (L \cdot \sim M)$
　　　2. $\sim L \lor M$　　　　　/ $\sim (P \cdot K)$

[24] 1. $\sim P \supset Q$
　　　2. $\sim R \supset (\sim P \cdot \sim S)$
　　　3. $\sim S \supset \sim Q$　　　/ R

⭐[25] 1. $P \supset Q$
　　　2. $(R \cdot S) \lor L$
　　　3. $L \supset \sim Q$　　　/ $(\sim S \lor R) \supset \sim P$

[26] 1. $(P \vee Q) \supset R$
      2. $\sim S \supset (Q \vee R)$
      3. $\sim R$ / S

[27] 1. $(\sim D \vee E) \supset (A \cdot C)$
      2. $(A \vee B) \supset (C \supset D)$ / D

[28] 1. $(P \equiv \sim Q) \equiv R$
      2. $(P \vee S) \supset (R \cdot \sim Q)$
      3. $P \equiv \sim S$
      4. $R \supset \sim P$ / $\sim P$

⭐[29] 1. $P \supset Q$
      2. $\sim R \supset (P \cdot S)$
      3. $S \supset \sim Q$ / R

[30] 1. $(P \cdot Q) \vee (R \cdot S)$ / $Q \vee S$

[31] 1. $\sim P \supset \sim (Q \supset P)$
      2. $\sim R \supset (\sim P \supset \sim Q)$ / $R \vee P$

[32] 1. $P \supset Q$ / $Q \supset [P \supset (P \cdot Q)]$

⭐[33] 1. $(P \supset Q) \supset \sim (S \supset R)$
      2. $\sim (P \vee T)$ / S

[34] 1. $S \supset [(R \vee T) \supset (U \cdot \sim L)]$
      2. $H \supset [(K \vee L) \supset (M \cdot R)]$ / $(H \cdot S) \supset \sim L$

[35] 1. $G \supset (E \cdot F)$
      2. $A \supset B$
      3. $A \vee G$
      4. $(B \vee C) \supset D$ / $D \vee E$

[36] 1. $D \supset \sim (E \vee \sim E)$
      2. $A \supset [(B \vee \sim B) \supset (C \vee D)]$ / $A \supset C$

⭐[37] 1. $P \supset (Q \cdot S)$
      2. $Q \supset (R \vee \sim S)$
      3. $P \vee (Q \supset R)$ / $Q \supset R$

[38] 1. $C \supset \{[D \supset (E \supset D] \supset (F \cdot \sim F)\}$
      2. $A \supset [(B \supset B) \supset C]$ / $\sim A$

[39] 1. $N \supset (K \vee \sim L)$
      2. $M \supset (N \cdot L)$
      3. $M \vee (N \supset K)$ / $\sim K \supset \sim N$

[40] 1. $R \supset S$
      2. $R \vee U$
      3. $U \supset (Q \cdot M)$
      4. $(S \vee H) \supset P$ / $\sim P \supset Q$

[41] 1. $(S \cdot N) \supset \sim E$
  2. $S \vee L$
  3. N
  4. K
  5. $L \supset M$
  6. $(M \cdot K) \supset R$
  7. $R \supset \sim E$ $/ \sim E$

[42] 1. $G \supset (H \cdot K)$ $/ (G \supset H) \cdot (G \supset K)$

[43] 1. $\sim M$
  2. $K \equiv (M \vee L)$ $/ K \equiv L$

[44] 1. $[D \supset \sim (G \cdot \sim H)] \supset \sim C$
  2. $\sim (D \cdot U) \supset C$ $/ D \cdot (G \vee U)$

★[45] 1. $K \supset (L \vee M)$
  2. $H \supset (G \vee K)$
  3. $(M \vee F) \supset \sim (H \cdot K)$
  4. $(G \cdot H) \supset (K \cdot L)$ $/ H \supset [K \cdot (L \cdot \sim M)]$

[46] 1. $(N \cdot \sim G) \supset L$
  2. $C \supset (N \cdot \sim G)$
  3. $H \supset (C \vee B)$
  4. $B \supset N$
  5. $(B \cdot G) \supset K$
  6. $\sim K$ $/ H \supset (L \cdot \sim G)$

II. First, translate the following arguments into symbolic form. Second, use the implication rules, the replacement rules, and indirect proof to derive the conclusion of each. Letters for the simple statements are provided in parentheses and can be used in the order given.

 1. My car is not fuel-efficient and it is not reliable. Consequently, my car is fuel-efficient if and only if it is reliable. (F, R)

Answer:

[1] 1. $\sim F \cdot \sim R$ $/ F \equiv R$
   2. $\sim (F \equiv R)$ *Assumption (IP)*
   3. $\sim [(F \cdot R) \vee (\sim F \cdot \sim R)]$ 2, Equiv
   4. $\sim (F \cdot R) \cdot \sim (\sim F \cdot \sim R)$ 3, DM
   5. $\sim (\sim F \cdot \sim R)$ 4, Simp
   6. $(\sim F \cdot \sim R) \cdot \sim (\sim F \cdot \sim R)$ 1, 5, Conj
   7. $\sim \sim (F \equiv R)$ 2–6, IP
   8. $F \equiv R$ 7, DN

2. If she finished her term paper on time, then she does not have to work on it over spring break. Either she does have to work on it over spring break or she did not finish her term paper on time and she gets a lower grade. Therefore, she did not finish her term paper on time. (*F, S, L*)

3. If the murder happened in the hotel room, then there are bloodstains somewhere in the room. It follows that it is not the case that the murder happened in the hotel room and there are not bloodstains somewhere in the room. (*M, B*)

4. If criminals are not put on trial, then they are likely to commit worse crimes. If criminals are put on trial and they are acquitted, then they are likely to commit worse crimes. Since criminals are acquitted, we can conclude that criminals are likely to commit worse crimes. (*T, W, A*)

⭐ 5. It is not the case that Sam did not get the job offer and he is still working at the factory. If Sam did not get the job offer, then he is still working at the factory. We can infer that Sam did get the job offer. (*J, F*)

I. PROVING LOGICAL TRUTHS

Logical truth A statement that is necessarily true; a tautology.

A **logical truth** is a statement that is necessarily true; in other words, it is a tautology. An argument that has a tautology as its conclusion is valid no matter what premises are given. In fact, we can use natural deduction to prove logical truths *without using any given premises*. Logical truths can be derived by using either conditional proof (CP) or indirect proof (IP).

We start by writing the statement to be proved as the conclusion of an argument, but since there are no given premises, we must begin with an indented first line, and use either CP or IP. The indented sequence will eventually be discharged, and the final line of the proof will be the logical truth that was displayed at the beginning as the conclusion.

The following logical truth is proven by using the *conditional proof* (CP) method:

$$/ [(P \lor Q) \cdot \sim P] \supset Q$$

1. $(P \lor Q) \cdot \sim$	$\sim P$ Assumption (CP)
2. $P \lor Q$	1, Simp
3. $\sim P$	1, Simp
4. Q	2, 3, DS
5. $[(P \lor Q) \cdot \sim P] \supset Q$	1–4, CP

If you recall, the conditional proof method permits the assumption of any statement at any time in a proof. This is what we did in line 1, which we indented and justified as *Assumption (CP)*. Based on this single assumption, we were able to deduce the consequent of the conclusion to be proved. At this point, we merely needed to discharge the indented sequence in the normal way by having the assumption in line 1 become the antecedent of a conditional statement. The proof is complete and we have proven a logical truth without using any given premises.

The same logical truth can also be proven by using the *indirect proof* (IP) method:

/ [(P ∨ Q) · ~ P] ⊃ Q

1. ~ {[(P ∨ Q) · ~ P] ⊃ Q}	Assumption (IP)
2. ~ {~ [(P ∨ Q) · ~ P] ∨ Q}	1, Impl
3. ~ ~ [(P ∨ Q) · ~ P] · ~ Q	2, DM
4. [(P ∨ Q) · ~ P] · ~ Q	3, DN
5. (P ∨ Q) · ~ P	4, Simp
6. P ∨ Q	5, Simp
7. ~ P	5, Simp
8. Q	6, 7, DS
9. ~ Q	4, Simp
10. Q · ~ Q	8, 9, Conj
11. ~ ~ {[(P ∨ Q) · ~ P] ⊃ Q}	1–10, IP
12. [(P ∨ Q) · ~ P] ⊃ Q	11, DN

The indirect proof method permits the assumption of the negation of any statement at any time in a proof. In this case, we wanted to derive a contradiction from the negation of the conclusion. This is what we did in line 1, which we indented and justified as *Assumption (IP)*. Based on this assumption, we were able to deduce a contradiction, which is displayed in line 10. At this point, we discharged the indented sequence in the normal way by negating the assumption in line 1. The proof is complete and once again we have proven a logical truth without using any given premises.

If a logical truth has a biconditional as the main connective, then you can use more than one indented sequence. For example:

/ [S · (R ⊃ S)] ≡ S

1. S · (R ⊃ S)	Assumption (CP)
2. S	1, Simp
3. [S · (R ⊃ S)] ⊃ S	1–2, CP
4. S	Assumption (CP)
5. S ∨ ~ R	4, Add
6. ~ R ∨ S	5, Com
7. R ⊃ S	6, Impl
8. S · (R ⊃ S)	4, 7, Conj
9. S ⊃ [S · (R ⊃ S)]	4–8, CP
10. {[S · (R ⊃ S)] ⊃ S} · {S ⊃ [S · (R ⊃ S)]}	3, 9, Conj
11. [S · (R ⊃ S)] ≡ S	10, Equiv

The use of the conditional proof method in this example relied on our knowledge of the replacement rule *material equivalence* (Equiv). Our strategy was to derive two conditional statements so we could apply the replacement rule. Thus, we started one CP at line 1 and another at line 4. In both instances, we indented and justified the lines as *Assumption (CP)* and we were able to deduce the consequent that we needed. We discharged each indented sequence when we derived the appropriate consequent and the completed proof was constructed without any given premises.

It sometimes helps to have one indented sequence within another indented sequence in order to derive the final conclusion, as the following proof illustrates.

	/ $[(P \supset Q) \cdot (P \supset S)] \supset [P \supset (Q \cdot S)]$
1. $(P \supset Q) \cdot (P \supset S)$	Assumption (CP)
2. P	Assumption (CP)
3. $P \supset Q$	1, Simp
4. Q	2, 3, MP
5. $P \supset S$	1, Simp
6. S	2, 5, MP
7. $Q \cdot S$	4, 6, Conj
8. $P \supset (Q \cdot S)$	2–7, CP
9. $[(P \supset Q) \cdot (P \supset S)] \supset [P \supset (Q \cdot S)]$	1–8, CP

The strategy was to start each sequence by assuming the antecedent of each conditional statement that was to be derived (lines 1 and 2). We indented and justified the lines as *Assumption (CP)* and we were able to deduce the consequent that we needed. We discharged each indented sequence when we derived the appropriate consequent. Once again, the completed proof was constructed without any given premises.

EXERCISES 8I

Construct proofs for the following logical truths.

1. $/(P \vee {\sim}P) \vee Q$

Answer:

1. P	Assumption (CP)
2. $P \vee Q$	1, Add
3. $P \supset (P \vee Q)$	1–2, CP
4. ${\sim}P \vee (P \vee Q)$	3, Impl
5. $({\sim}P \vee P) \vee Q$	4, Assoc
6. $(P \vee {\sim}P) \vee Q$	5, Com

2. $/ (P \cdot {\sim}P) \supset P$

3. $/ {\sim}P \supset {\sim}P$

4. $/ (R \cdot {\sim}R) \supset (S \vee {\sim}S)$

★ 5. $/ {\sim}[(S \supset {\sim}S) \cdot ({\sim}S \supset S)]$

6. $/ Q \supset [(Q \supset R) \supset R]$

7. $/ [(P \vee Q) \cdot {\sim}P] \supset Q$

8. $/ {\sim}(R \cdot {\sim}R) \vee {\sim}(S \vee {\sim}S)$

★ 9. $/ [{\sim}(L \cdot {\sim}M) \cdot {\sim}M] \supset {\sim}L$

10. $/ \sim(R \cdot \sim R) \supset \sim(S \cdot \sim S)$

11. $/ (K \supset L) \supset [(K \cdot M) \supset (L \cdot M)]$

12. $/ [(P \supset Q) \cdot (P \supset R)] \supset [P \supset (Q \cdot R)]$

⭐ 13. $/ (R \vee \sim R) \supset (S \vee \sim S)$

14. $/ (R \supset S) \supset [(R \supset \sim S) \supset \sim R]$

15. $/ \sim(R \vee \sim R) \supset \sim(S \vee \sim S)$

16. $/ (P \equiv Q) \vee \sim(P \equiv Q)$

⭐ 17. $/ [K \supset (L \supset M)] \supset [(K \supset L) \supset (K \supset M)]$

18. $/ S \equiv [S \vee (R \cdot \sim R)]$

19. $/ S \equiv [S \cdot (R \supset S)]$

20. $/ (K \supset L) \vee (\sim L \supset K)$

21. $/ [(B \cdot \sim C) \vee (D \cdot \sim G)] \vee [(C \cdot G) \vee (\sim B \vee \sim D)]$

22. $/ (G \equiv K) \equiv [(G \cdot K) \vee (\sim G \cdot \sim K)]$

Video Tutorial: 81
Exercise #17

Summary

Study Materials

- Natural deduction: A proof procedure by which the conclusion of an argument is validly derived from the premises through the use of rules of inference.
- There are two types of rules of inference: implication rules and replacement rules. The function of rules of inference is to justify the steps of a proof.
- Proof: A sequence of steps in which each step either is a premise or follows from earlier steps in the sequence according to the rules of inference.
- Implication rules are valid argument forms. They are validly applied only to an entire line.
- Replacement rules: Pairs of logically equivalent statement forms.
- *Modus ponens* (MP): A rule of inference (implication rule).
- Substitution instance: In propositional logic, a substitution instance of an *argument* occurs when a uniform substitution of statements for the variables results in an argument.
- *Modus tollens* (MT): A rule of inference (implication rule).
- Hypothetical syllogism (HS): A rule of inference (implication rule).
- Disjunctive syllogism (DS): A rule of inference (implication rule).
- Justification: Refers to the rule of inference that is applied to every validly derived step in a proof.
- Tactics: The use of small-scale maneuvers or devices.
- Strategy: Typically understood as referring to a greater, overall goal.
- Simplification (Simp): A rule of inference (implication rule).

- Conjunction (Conj): A rule of inference (implication rule).
- Addition (Add): A rule of inference (implication rule).
- Constructive dilemma (CD): A rule of inference (implication rule).
- Principle of replacement: Logically equivalent expressions may replace each other within the context of a proof.
- De Morgan (DM): A rule of inference (replacement rule).
- Double negation (DN): A rule of inference (replacement rule).
- Commutation (Com): A rule of inference (replacement rule).
- Association (Assoc): A rule of inference (replacement rule).
- Distribution (Dist): A rule of inference (replacement rule).
- Transposition (Trans): A rule of inference (replacement rule).
- Material implication (Impl): A rule of inference (replacement rule).
- Material equivalence (Equiv): A rule of inference (replacement rule).
- Exportation (Exp): A rule of inference (replacement rule).
- Tautology (Taut): A rule of inference (replacement rule).
- Conditional proof (CP): A method that starts by assuming the antecedent of a conditional statement on a separate line and then proceeds to validly derive the consequent on a separate line.
- When the result of a conditional proof sequence is discharged it no longer needs to be indented.
- Indirect proof (IP): A method that starts by assuming the negation of the required statement and then validly deriving a contradiction on a subsequent line.
- Logical truth: A statement that is necessarily true; a tautology.

KEY TERMS

LOGIC CHALLENGE: THE TRUTH

Three of your friends, Wayne, Eric, and Will, want to know what you have learned in your logic class, so you think of a demonstration. You will leave the room and they are to choose among themselves whether to be a *truth-teller* or a *liar*. Every statement a truth-teller makes is *true*, and every statement a liar makes is *false*. You leave the room and then after a short while return. You then ask Wayne this question: "Are you a truth-teller or a liar?" Before he answers, you tell him that he is to whisper the answer to Eric. After hearing the answer, Eric announces this: "Wayne said that he is a truth-teller. He is indeed a truth-teller, and so am I." Upon hearing this, Will says the following: "Don't believe Eric, he is a liar. I am a truth-teller."

Use your reasoning abilities to determine who is a truth-teller and who is a liar.

Chapter 9

Predicate Logic

A. *Translating Ordinary Language*
B. *Four New Rules of Inference*
C. *Change of Quantifier (CQ)*
D. *Conditional and Indirect Proof*
E. *Demonstrating Invalidity*
F. *Relational Predicates*
G. *Identity*

Digital homework exercises for this chapter are available in your instructor's online course. For information on how to access these resources, please visit **www.oup.com/he/baronett5e.**

In the course of a semester, you encounter a dizzying number of new faces and things to learn. You are still probably trying to sort them out. To help, it is only natural to ask what the members of a group share. What are their common characteristics—or do the members of a group instead display significant differences? The results can be humorous:

> Dogs come when they're called. Cats take a message and get back to you.
>
> Mary Bly, quoted in *Boundaries—Where You End and I Begin* by Anne Katherine

Or serious:

> Great minds discuss ideas; average minds discuss events; small minds discuss people.

When statements like these are strung together, they sometimes form an argument. This chapter introduces a new tool for analyzing complex arguments, the symbolic system called *predicate logic*.

We have examined many types of statements and arguments. For example, categorical logic analyzes arguments using Venn diagrams and rules. The basic components of categorical syllogisms are *class terms*, and validity is determined by arrangement of the terms within an argument. For example:

> All computers are inorganic objects. Some computers are conscious beings. Therefore, some inorganic objects are conscious beings.

On the other hand, propositional logic analyzes arguments using truth tables and natural deduction. The basic components are *statements*, and validity is determined by arrangement of the statements within an argument. Here is an example:

> If toxic waste is not properly secured, then it poses a health hazard. Nuclear power plants and petroleum refineries produce toxic waste. Nuclear power plants and petroleum refineries do not always properly secure their toxic waste. Therefore, nuclear power plants and petroleum refineries pose health hazards.

In this chapter, we take one more step. Many arguments combine the distinctive features of both categorical *and* propositional logic. For example:

> A person can be elected president of the United States if and only if that person is a natural born citizen of the United States, a resident for 14 years, and at least 35 years of age. Abraham Lincoln was the sixteenth president of the United States. Therefore, Abraham Lincoln was a natural born citizen of the United States, a resident for 14 years, and at least 35 years of age when he was elected president.

The validity of these arguments cannot easily be determined by the individual methods of categorical or propositional logic. A new method of proof is needed. As we saw earlier, George Boole began connecting some features of categorical logic with features of propositional logic. A key idea is the modern interpretation of universal categorical statements as conditional statements. For example, "All cheetahs are mammals" can be interpreted as follows: *For any object, if that object is a cheetah, then it is a mammal.* This kind of interpretation accomplishes two things. First, it eliminates existential import, because a conditional statement makes no existence claim. (A proposition has existential import if it presupposes the existence of certain kinds of objects.) Second, it places validity nearer to the modern idea of logical form.

Gottlob Frege, a German mathematician, philosopher, and logician, took the decisive step in connecting categorical logic with propositional logic in the late 19th century. Frege demonstrated clearly how the special features of the two logics could be combined, using quantifiers, as **predicate logic**.

Predicate logic is flexible. It enables us to analyze arguments about individuals (for example, *Socrates*), properties of individuals (*Socrates was a Greek philosopher*), and relations between individuals (*Socrates was the teacher of Plato*). Predicate logic is also capable of expressing complex and precise language in a formal manner. In fact, some of the basic principles of predicate logic are used in computer programming and mathematics. The principles have even been adapted to artificial intelligence programs. Predicate logic has advanced through rigorous analysis of symbol arrangement and through the development of special rules. Of course, the main concern is still the same as the other areas of logic—the validity of arguments.

Predicate logic
Integrates many of the features of categorical and propositional logic. It combines the symbols associated with propositional logic with special symbols that are used to translate predicates.

A. TRANSLATING ORDINARY LANGUAGE

Our study of predicate logic begins by establishing a foundation for correct translations of ordinary language statements. We start by introducing techniques for translating *singular statements*, *universal statements*, and *particular statements*. We give special attention to the meaning of ordinary language statements.

Singular Statements

You may recall from Chapter 5 that a singular statement, or singular proposition, is about a specific person, place, time, or object. We use it to distinguish individuals from the characteristics that are asserted of them. Since *predicates* are the fundamental unit in predicate logic, uppercase letters $(A, B, C, \ldots, X, Y, Z)$, called **predicate symbols** are used. For example, in the statement "Abraham Lincoln was a lawyer," the subject is "Abraham Lincoln" and the predicate is "was a lawyer." Here are some more examples of ordinary language predicates:

Predicate symbols
Predicates are the fundamental units in predicate logic. Uppercase letters are used to symbolize the units.

"is an athlete"
"is a bachelor"
"was a Congressperson"
"is a state"

The *subject* of a singular statement is translated using lowercase letters $(a, b, c, \ldots, u, v, w)$. These lowercase letters, called **individual constants**, act as names of individuals. (Notice that the lowercase letters for individual constants stop at the letter w. That's because the lowercase letters x, y, and z play a special role in predicate logic, which will be explained soon.)

Individual constants
The subject of a singular statement is translated using lowercase letters. The lowercase letters act as names of individuals.

The system used for translating singular statements puts the capital letter first (the symbol designating the characteristic predicated), followed by a lowercase letter (the symbol denoting the individual). For example, "Abraham Lincoln was a lawyer" can be translated as *La*.

PROFILES IN LOGIC
Gottlob Frege

Gottlob Frege (1848–1925) was one of the most original and influential modern thinkers. For Frege, "every mathematician must be a philosopher, and every philosopher must be a mathematician," and his monumental attempt to reduce mathematics to logic connected the two fields forever. Frege believed in the *a priori* nature of mathematics and logic, which meant that both fields could be developed by reason alone. Ironically, his work led to the discovery of logical and mathematical paradoxes that revolutionized the foundations of mathematics.

Frege developed the logic of quantifiers, the distinction between constants and variables, and the first modern clarification of sense and reference. For example, the term "dog" refers to all sorts of four-legged friends, but its sense, or meaning, is not the same as any of them—or even all of them taken together. And those are just a few of his original insights. In fact, the important and influential field of mathematical logic can be traced to Frege's pioneering work.

Here are some more translations:

Statement in English	Symbolic Translation
Arnold Schwarzenegger was a governor.	*Ga*
Maria Sharapova is an athlete.	*Am*
The Arctic Circle is not warm.	*~Wa*
Nevada is a desert.	*Dn*

Predicate logic offers a powerful way of capturing ordinary language into precise statement and argument analysis. For example, the singular statement "Mahershala Ali won the Academy Award for Best Actor in a Supporting Role in 2017" asserts that one individual person has a specific characteristic. In this statement, the subject "Mahershala Ali," denotes a particular individual. The predicate "won the Academy Award for Best Actor in a Supporting Role in 2017" designates a specific characteristic. It is possible for the same subject and predicate to occur in a variety of singular statements. Some of these assertions will be true, and some will be false. For example, "Mahershala Ali won the Academy Award for Best Director in 2017" is a false statement. The statement contains the same subject as the earlier statement, but it contains a different predicate. The statement "Jack Nicholson won the Academy Award for Best Actor in a Supporting Role in 2017" is false. The statement contains the same predicate as the earlier example, but it contains a different subject.

More complex statements can be translated by using the basic apparatus of propositional logic. Here are some examples:

Statement in English	Symbolic Translation
Carly is either a fashion designer or a dancer.	*Fc* v *Dc*
If Shane is an honor student, then he is bright.	*Hs* ⊃ *Bs*
Jill can get the job if and only if she is honest and loyal.	*Jb* ≡ (*Hb* · *Lb*)
John will win the contest only if he does not panic.	*Cj* ⊃ *~Pj*

Universal Statements

Universal statements either affirm or deny that every member of a subject class is a member of a predicate class. This is accomplished by translating the universal statements in the following way:

Universal Statement Form	Boolean Interpretation
All S are P.	*If anything is an S, then it is a P.*
No S are P.	*If anything is an S, then it is not a P.*

The interpretations can be translated using the horseshoe. However, we need a new symbol to capture the idea that universal statements assert something about *every member of the subject class*. That symbol is called the **universal quantifier**. This is where the three lowercase letters *x*, *y*, and *z* come into play. When one of the letters is placed within parentheses—for example, (*x*)— it gets translated as "for any *x*." The three designated lowercase letters are called **individual variables**.

Universal quantifier
The symbol used to capture the idea that universal statements assert something about every member of the subject class.

Individual variables
The three lowercase letters *x*, *y*, and *z*.

We can now complete the translation of the two universal statement forms:

Statement Form	Symbolic Translation	Verbal Meaning
All S are P.	$(x)(Sx \supset Px)$	For any x, if x is an S, then x is a P.
No S are P.	$(x)(Sx \supset \sim Px)$	For any x, if x is an S, then x is not a P.

Using this information, let's do a simple translation:

All humans are moral agents. $(x)(Hx \supset Mx)$

In the symbolic translation $(x)(Sx \supset Px)$, both S and P are predicates. This is illustrated by the verbal meaning. When we say, "For any x, if x is an S, then x is a P," the capital letters in both the antecedent and the consequent are both predicates. Here are some additional examples:

Statement in English	Symbolic Translation
No humans are moral agents.	$(x)(Hx \supset \sim Mx)$
All alcoholic drinks are depressants.	$(x)(Ax \supset Dx)$
No French fries are healthy foods.	$(x)(Fx \supset \sim Hx)$
All magazines are glossy publications.	$(x)(Mx \supset Gx)$
No millionaires are tax evaders.	$(x)(Mx \supset \sim Tx)$

Bound variables
Variables governed by a quantifier.

Statement function
A pattern for a statement. It does not make any universal or particular assertion about anything, and it has no truth value.

Free variables
Variables that are not governed by any quantifier.

Let's look at the first example: $(x)(Hx \supset \sim Mx)$. The variables in this statement are **bound variables**, meaning that they are governed by a quantifier. (A variable is bound when it lies within the scope of the quantifier.) But what happens when we remove the quantifier? The result is $Hx \supset \sim Mx$. This is a **statement function**; it does not make any universal or particular assertion about anything, and it has no truth value. In other words, it is merely a pattern for a statement. The variables in statement functions are **free variables**, meaning that they are not governed by any quantifier.

The placement of a quantifier is important. For example:

$(x)(Rx \supset Fx)$
$(x)Rx \supset Fx$

In the first example, the quantifier governs everything in parentheses. Therefore, both variables are bound. However, in the second example, the quantifier governs only Rx, making it a bound variable. Fx, however, is a free variable. There is a simple rule to follow: A quantifier governs only the expression immediately following it.

Particular Statements

Particular statements either affirm or deny that at least one member of a subject class is a member of a predicate class. (If you worked through categorical logic in Chapters 5 and 6, then you know that particular statements involve existential import.) Boolean translations are accomplished in the following way:

Universal Statement Form	Boolean Interpretation
Some S are P.	At least one thing is an S and it is also a P.
Some S are not P.	At least one thing is an S and it is not a P.

Notice that while the translations for universal statements are conditional statements, the translations for particular statements are conjunctions. Therefore, the symbolic translations use the dot. However, we need a new symbol to capture the idea of existence. The **existential quantifier** is formed by putting a backward E in front of a variable, and then placing them both in parentheses: $(\exists x)$. This gets translated as "there exists an x such that." We then combine the existential quantifier with the dot symbol to translate particular statements.

Existential quantifier Formed by putting a backward E in front of a variable, and then placing them both in parentheses.

Statement Form	Translation	Verbal Meaning
Some S are P.	$(\exists x)(Sx \cdot Px)$	*There exists an x such that x is an S and x is a P.*
Some S are not P.	$(\exists x)(Sx \cdot {\sim}Px)$	*There exists an x such that x is an S and x is not a P.*

Using this information, let's do a simple translation:

Some battleships are monstrosities.　　$(\exists x)(Bx \cdot Mx)$

The translation can be read in the following way: Something exists that is both a battleship and a monstrosity. Here are some additional examples:

Statement in English	Symbolic Translation
Some birds are not flyers.	$(\exists x)(Bx \cdot {\sim}Fx)$
Some hermits are introverts.	$(\exists x)(Hx \cdot Ix)$
Some sweeteners are addictive products.	$(\exists x)(Sx \cdot Ax)$
Some divers are not fearless people.	$(\exists x)(Dx \cdot {\sim}Fx)$

Summary of Predicate Logic Symbols	
A–Z	predicate symbols
a–w	individual constants
$x, y,$ and z	individual variables
$(x), (y), (z)$	universal quantifiers
$(\exists x), (\exists y), (\exists z)$	existential quantifiers

Paying Attention to Meaning

Some statements in ordinary language are more complex than the statements we have been examining. For example, consider this statement:

All thoroughbreds are either brown or gray.

Symbolizing this statement requires a close examination of the statement's meaning. We can interpret the statement as expressing the following: *If anything is a thoroughbred, then either it is brown or it is gray.* If we let T = thoroughbred, B = brown, and G = gray, then we get this translation:

All thoroughbreds are either brown or gray.　　$(x)[Tx \supset (Bx \lor Gx)]$

Here is another statement that requires careful consideration:

Thoroughbreds and mules are quadrupeds.

Even though the word "and" appears in the statement, the statement is *not* asserting that anything is *both* a thoroughbred and a mule. Instead, the meaning of the statement is this: *If anything is either a thoroughbred or a mule, then that individual is a quadruped.* Therefore, if we let *T* = thoroughbreds, *M* = mules, *Q* = quadrupeds, we get this translation:

Thoroughbreds and mules are quadrupeds. $(x)[(Tx \lor Mx) \supset Qx]$

Here are some more examples of translations:

1. There are plastic bags. $(\exists x)(Bx \cdot Px)$
2. There are cloth bags. $(\exists x)(Bx \cdot Cx)$
3. UFOs exist. $(\exists x)Ux$

Notice that the statement in example 3 merely asserts that a class of objects exists. Therefore, it can be translated by using one predicate and an existential quantifier.

In predicate logic, the **domain of discourse** is the set of individuals over which a quantifier ranges. A domain (or *universe*) of discourse can be *restricted* (specified) or *unrestricted*. For example, if we restrict the domain of discourse to humans, we get this translation:

4. Everyone is good. $(x)Gx$

However, if the domain of discourse is unrestricted, then the translation of the statement is different:

5. Everyone is good. $(x)(Hx \supset Gx)$

The domain of discourse is specified within the translation itself. The translation can be read as follows: For any *x*, if *x* is a human, then *x* is good. Here are some more examples of translations using unrestricted domains:

6. Termites are insects. $(x)(Tx \supset Ix)$
7. Termites are eating your house. $(\exists x)(Tx \cdot Ex)$
8. Children are not judgmental. $(x)(Cx \supset \sim Jx)$
9. Some children are starving. $(\exists x)(Cx \cdot Sx)$

The statement in example 6 asserts something of the entire class of termites. Therefore, it is translated by using a universal quantifier. In contrast, the statement in example 7 asserts something about only some termites. Therefore, it is translated by using an existential quantifier. Here are two more examples:

10. Only guests are welcome. $(x)(Wx \supset Gx)$
11. None but the brave are lonely. $(x)(Lx \supset Bx)$

The statement in example 10 uses the word "only." You might recognize this as an *exclusive* proposition. When this kind of statement gets translated as a conditional statement the class term after the word "only" becomes the consequent. In other words, persons are welcome only if they are guests.

The statement in example 11 uses the words "none but." This, too, is an *exclusive* proposition. When it gets translated as a conditional statement the class term after

---

Domain of discourse

The set of individuals over which a quantifier ranges.

the words "none but" becomes the consequent. In other words, persons are lonely only if they are brave.

Here are two other examples:

12. Not one student failed the midterm exam. $\sim(\exists x)(Sx \cdot Fx)$ or $(x)(Sx \supset \sim Fx)$

13. It is not the case that every student graduates. $\sim(x)(Sx \supset Gx)$ or $(\exists x)(Sx \cdot \sim Gx)$

The statements in examples 12 and 13 can be translated by using either a universal or existential quantifier. This illustrates an important point: A universal statement is equivalent to a negated existential statement, and an existential statement is equivalent to a negated universal statement. In other words, the universal translation of example 12 can be read this way: *No students failed the midterm exam.* This is equivalent to the original statement: *Not one student failed the midterm exam.*

Here are a few examples to illustrate how the logical operators of propositional logic can be combined to form compound arrangements of universal and particular statements:

14. If some Academy Award movies are films not worth watching, then all movies are films capable of disappointing audiences. $(\exists x)(Ax \cdot \sim Wx) \supset (x)(Mx \supset Dx)$

15. If all science fiction writers are philosophers, then some philosophers are famous. $(x)(Sx \supset Px) \supset (\exists x)(Px \cdot Fx)$

EXERCISES 9A

Translate the following statements into symbolic form. You can use the predicate letters that are provided.

Self-Practice
Questions

1. Ginger is a spice. (G, S)
Answer: $(x)\,(Gx \supset Sx)$

2. Curry chicken is pungent. (C, P)

3. Rabbits are sexually active. (R, S)

4. Sir Lancelot was a member of the Round Table. (R)

⭐ **5.** Steve McQueen is an Academy Award winner. (A)

6. Only if Pam runs the mile under 4 minutes will she qualify. (M, Q)

7. The Taj Mahal is one of the Seven Wonders of the Modern World. (S)

8. Diamonds are the hardest substance on Earth. (D, H)

⭐ **9.** Used cars are good if and only if they were well maintained and have low mileage. (U, G, M, L)

10. Broiled salmon tastes good. (S, G)

Video Tutorial: 9A
Exercise #9

11. Textbooks are my friends. (*T*, *F*)

12. Pittsburgh is cold only if it has a bad winter. (*C*, *W*)

⭐ **13.** Cell phones are not universally admired products. (*C*, *U*)

14. Susan will pass the exam only if she is well prepared. (*E*, *W*)

15. Only if Fidelix gets here by 8:00 PM will he be admitted. (*G*, *A*)

16. All deciduous trees are colorful trees during autumn. (*D*, *C*)

⭐ **17.** No coconuts are pink fruit. (*C*, *P*)

18. Some short stories are not about people. (*S*, *P*)

19. If anything is alive, then it is aware of its environment. (*A*, *E*)

20. Every volcano is a dangerous thing. (*V*, *D*)

⭐ **21.** Labyrinths are amazing structures. (*L*, *A*)

22. Not even one student showed up for the pep rally. (*S*, *P*)

23. Only registered voters are allowed to vote. (*R*, *V*)

24. Every DUI citation is a serious offense. (*D*, *S*)

⭐ **25.** Basketball players are not comfortable in bunk beds. (*B*, *C*)

26. No MP3 players are good birthday gifts. (*M*, *B*)

27. All knitted underwear is warm and comfortable. (*K*, *W*, *C*)

28. No knitted underwear is a bikini substitute. (*K*, *B*)

⭐ **29.** Some SUVs are not environmentally friendly vehicles. (*S*, *E*)

30. Some buses are not comfortable transportation. (*B*, *C*)

31. Whales are a protected species. (*W*, *P*)

32. No movie ratings are accurate pieces of information. (*M*, *A*)

⭐ **33.** Fanatics never compromise. (*F*, *C*)

34. Only graduates can participate in the commencement. (*G*, *P*)

35. A person is medically dead if and only if there is not any detectable brain stem activity. (*P*, *D*, *B*)

36. Not one representative returned my call. (*R*, *C*)

⭐ **37.** All whole numbers are either even or odd. (*W*, *E*, *O*)

38. Anything that is either sweet or crunchy is tasty. (*S*, *C*, *T*)

39. None but qualified staff members are permitted to enter the work area. (*Q*, *P*)

40. Some hurricanes are violent. (*H*, *V*)

⭐ **41.** If some TV shows are worth watching, then every TV show is informative. (*T*, *W*, *I*)

42. No pessimists are happy. (*P, H*)

43. Tom is sleeping if and only if Jerry is awake. (*S, A*)

44. Nothing bad lasts forever. (*B, L*)

⭐ 45. Everything that is alive is mortal. (*A, M*)

46. Only pleasant people are happy people. (*P, H*)

47. Both Plato and Socrates were philosophers. (*P*)

48. If Sue is not late for class, then she will not miss the exam. (*C, E*)

⭐ 49. Whenever both Tim and Sarah are at the meetings, then neither Frank nor Rachel is at the meetings. (*M*)

50. Isaac Newton was either a scientist or a mathematician, or else he was both. (*S, M*)

51. None but cats are predators. (*C, P*)

52. Whenever Jacqueline smokes she coughs. (*S, C*)

⭐ 53. If Paul is not a poker player, then he is not a gambler. (*P, G*)

54. Neither motorcycles nor mopeds are stable vehicles. (*M, P, S*)

55. Whenever Jake is late for supper, then he cries. (*S, C*)

56. If Chris goes to the party, then he will have fun. (*P, F*)

⭐ 57. Both Shane and Agatha are dancers, but neither one is a professional. (*D, P*)

58. Everything is expensive. (*E*)

59. All animals can think. (*A, T*)

60. It is not the case that birds are either mammals or crustaceans. (*B, M, C*)

B. FOUR NEW RULES OF INFERENCE

The translations from ordinary language provide experience with using the symbols of predicate logic. In addition, we have been able to use the logical operators of propositional logic. However, in order to construct proofs in predicate logic, a few additional rules are needed.

Two of these new rules remove quantifiers, and two introduce quantifiers. One of the rules that remove quantifiers is for universal quantifiers, and the other is for existential quantifiers. These are generally used at the beginning of a sequence of steps. On the other hand, one of the rules that introduce quantifiers is for universal quantifiers, and the other is for existential quantifiers. These are generally used at the end of a sequence of steps.

Universal Instantiation (UI)

Some arguments in ordinary language are obviously valid, but they cannot be proven with just the rules of inference that were introduced in Chapter 8. Here is an example:

Steven Hawking was a physicist. All physicists are logical thinkers. Therefore, Steven Hawking was a logical thinker.

Symbolizing the argument reveals why we don't yet have the means to prove its validity:

1. Ps
2. $(x)(Px \supset Lx)$ $/ Ls$

The rules of inference that we have so far cannot be applied to derive the conclusion. For example, we cannot apply *modus ponens* to lines 1 and 2, because the rule requires a conditional statement. Line 2 is *not* a conditional; it is a *universally quantified statement*. What we need is something that allows us to remove the universal quantifier, and derive $Ps \supset Ls$. If we can derive this step, then *modus ponens* can be applied (with premise 1). The sequence will end with a valid derivation of the conclusion.

In order to understand the process involved, we need to look at a few simple examples. Let's use the quantified statement in the foregoing argument:

$$(x)(Px \supset Lx)$$

If we remove the universal quantifier, then we get a statement function with two free occurrences of the *x*-variable:

$$Px \supset Lx$$

Instantiation When instantiation is applied to a quantified statement, the quantifier is removed, and every variable that was bound by the quantifier is replaced by the same instantial letter.

If we replace the *x*-variable with the constant *s*, then we get an *instance* of the original quantified statement:

$$Ps \supset Ls$$

The process is called **instantiation**, and the *s* that is introduced is called the **instantial letter**. When instantiation is applied to a quantified statement, the quantifier is removed, and *every variable that was bound by the quantifier* is replaced by the same instantial letter. A substitution instance of a statement function can be validly deduced from the universally quantified statement by the rule of **universal instantiation (UI)**.

We can now complete the proof of the argument:

Instantial letter
The letter (either a variable or a constant) that is introduced by universal instantiation or existential instantiation.

1. Ps
2. $(x)(Px \supset Lx)$ $/ Ls$
3. $Ps \supset Ls$ 2, UI
4. Ls 1, 3, MP

Universal instantiation (UI)
The rule by which we can validly deduce the substitution instance of a statement function from a universally quantified statement.

As always, we have to be careful not to misapply the process of instantiation. Here are some examples:

Misapplications of UI

Original quantified statement: $(x)(Px \supset Lx)$

Misapplications:

A. $(x)(Ps \supset Ls)$ ⊘

B. $Ps \supset Lr$ ⊘

C. $Ps \supset Lx$ ⊘

The mistake in A is the result of not removing the universal quantifier. The mistake in B is the result of not replacing every variable that was bound by the quantifier by the same instantial constant. The mistake in C is the result of not replacing the second bound *x*-variable by the instantial letter.

Universal Generalization (UG)

We saw how a rule provided for the removal of a quantifier. Now we can look at a rule that provides the introduction of a quantifier. Consider this argument:

> All private universities are self-funded institutions. All self-funded institutions are taxed. Therefore, all private universities are taxed.

The argument can be translated and symbolized as follows:

1. $(x)(Px \supset Sx)$
2. $(x)(Sx \supset Tx)$ $/ (x)(Px \supset Tx)$

Both the premises and the conclusion are universally quantified statements. We might anticipate an application of hypothetical syllogism during the proof sequence. However, we must first remove the universal quantifier from both premises—and that requires a new strategy.

Let's start with the first premise. Since it is a universally quantified statement, we could begin by listing applications of UI. For example:

$$Pa \supset Sa$$
$$Pb \supset Sb$$
$$Pc \supset Sc$$
$$\ldots \text{and so on.}$$

In other words, *any* arbitrarily selected individual can be substituted uniformly in the statement function that results from removing the universal quantifier. We can therefore substitute a *variable* instead of a constant. The same reasoning applies to the second premise as well.

Based on this reasoning, we can now introduce a new rule. **Universal generalization (UG)** holds that you can validly deduce the universal quantification of a statement function from a substitution instance only when the instantial letter is a variable. Here is the completed proof that incorporates the new rule:

1. $(x)(Px \supset Sx)$
2. $(x)(Sx \supset Tx)$ $/ (x)(Px \supset Tx)$
3. $Py \supset Sy$ 1, UI
4. $Sy \supset Ty$ 2, UI
5. $Py \supset Ty$ 3, 4, HS
6. $(x)(Px \supset Tx)$ 5, UG

Universal generalization (UG) The rule by which we can validly deduce the universal quantification of a statement function from a substitution instance with respect to the name of any arbitrarily selected individual (subject to restrictions).

Notice that in the move from line 5 to line 6 every instance of *y* was replaced by *x*. For universal generalization, every occurrence of the instantial letter must be replaced with the variable in the quantifier. As always, we have to be careful not to misapply the rule. Here are some examples:

Misapplications of UG

A. 1. $My \supset Ry$
    2. $(x)(Mx \supset Ry)$ 🚫

B. 1. $Md \supset Rd$
    2. $(x)(Mx \supset Rx)$ 🚫

The mistake in A is the result of *not* replacing *every* instance of *y* with *x*. The mistake in B is the result of the instantial letter in line 1 being a constant (*d*) instead of a variable.

Existential Generalization (EG)

We saw how UG provided for the introduction of a universal quantifier. Now we can look at a rule that provides for the introduction of an existential quantifier. Consider this argument:

> All carbon-based organisms are mortal creatures. Will Smith is a carbon-based organism. Therefore, there is at least one mortal creature.

The argument can be translated and symbolized as follows:

1. $(x)(Cx \supset Mx)$
2. Cw / $(\exists x)Mx$

This looks like a perfect setup for *modus ponens*. If we apply UI to line 1, then we can easily derive the conclusion:

1. $(x)(Cx \supset Mx)$
2. Cw / $(\exists x)Mx$
3. $Cw \supset Mw$ 1, UI
4. Mw 2, 3, MP
5. $(\exists x)Mx$ 4, EG

The deduction of *Mw* on line 4 reveals an instance of at least one mortal creature (in this instance, Will Smith). This result provides the rationale for deriving the conclusion, which states that there is at least one mortal creature.

Existential generalization (EG) is a rule that permits us to existentially generalize an instance of a quantified formula, and it proceeds just that way. It can also be applied to a variable as well as a constant. Here is an example:

1. $(x)(Cx \supset Mx)$
2. $(x)Cx$ / $(\exists x)Mx$
3. $Cy \supset My$ 1, UI
4. Cy 2, UI
5. My 3, 4, MP
6. $(\exists x)Mx$ 5, EG

According to line 5, any arbitrary individual is an *M*; therefore, we can validly deduce that at least one thing is an *M*. Of course, we presuppose a basic, but reasonable, assumption of predicate logic: *At least one thing exists in the universe.* Without this assumption, even the instantiation in line 4 would be impossible.

For universal generalization (UG) *every* occurrence of the instantial letter must be replaced with the quantifier variable. However, for existential generalization (EG) *at*

Existential generalization (EG) The rule that permits the valid introduction of an existential quantifier from either a constant or a variable.

least one of the instantial letters must be replaced with the quantifier variable. Given this, the following are all correct applications of EG:

1. $Mx \cdot Rx$ 1. $Mx \cdot Rx$ 1. $Ma \cdot Ra$ 1. $Ma \cdot Ra$
2. $(\exists x)(Mx \cdot Rx)$ 2. $(\exists y)(My \cdot Rx)$ 2. $(\exists x)(Mx \cdot Rx)$ 2. $(\exists x)(Mx \cdot Ra)$

As always, we have to be careful not to misapply the rule. Here are some examples:

Misapplications of EG

A. 1. $\underline{Mx \cdot Rx}$ B. 1. $\underline{Ma \cdot Ra}$
    2. $(\exists y)My \cdot Rx$ ⊘   2. $(\exists y)My \cdot Ra$ ⊘

The mistake in both A and B is the result of the existential quantifier not being applied to the entire line.

We have seen two kinds of generalization: universal and existential. Universal generalization requires that *every* occurrence of the instantial letter must be replaced with the quantifier variable. On the other hand, existential generalization requires only that *at least one* of the instantial letters must be replaced with the quantifier variable.

Existential Instantiation (EI)

We saw how UI provided for the removal of a universal quantifier. Now we can look at a rule that provides the removal of an existential quantifier. Consider this argument:

> All breakfast cereals are rich in fiber. Some breakfast cereals are kids' foods. Therefore, some kids' foods are rich in fiber.

The argument can be translated as follows:

1. $(x)(Bx \supset Rx)$
2. $(\exists x)(Bx \cdot Kx)$ / $(\exists x)(Kx \cdot Rx)$

The beginning strategy is to remove the quantifiers in both premises. You already know that UI can be applied to line 1. We can interpret line 2 as stating that there exists something that is both a B and a K. **Existential instantiation (EI)** is a rule that permits giving a *name* to the thing that exists. The name can then be represented by a constant. For example, we can replace the x-variable in line 2 with the instantial letter c. This creates the next step in the proof:

Existential instantiation (EI) The rule that permits giving a name to a thing that exists. The name can then be represented by a constant.

1. $(x)(Bx \supset Rx)$
2. $(\exists x)(Bx \cdot Kx)$ / $(\exists x)(Kx \cdot Rx)$
3. $Bc \cdot Kc$ 2, EI

At this point we can apply UI to line 1:

1. $(x)(Bx \supset Rx)$
2. $(\exists x)(Bx \cdot Kx)$ / $(\exists x)(Kx \cdot Rx)$
3. $Bc \cdot Kc$ 2, EI
4. $Bc \supset Rc$ 1, UI

We applied EI to line 2 before we applied UI to line 1, because there are certain restrictions to EI. The restrictions ensure that we do not create an invalid step in the proof. For example, if we use UI before EI, then we derive $Bc \supset Rc$. If we do this, then we cannot use the same constant c, for EI. Here is the reason: If UI establishes the constant c before EI, then we are *not* justified in assuming the thing that is a B and a K (from the existential quantifier) has the same name as the thing instantiated by UI. We have to assign the EI instantiation a different name. However, by applying EI first and establishing a name, we are justified in giving the UI instantiation the same name, because the universal quantifier can be instantiated to *any* arbitrary individual, including the one named by the EI. (In addition, the existential name cannot occur in the line that indicates the conclusion to be derived.) Having established this restriction on EI, we can complete the proof:

1. $(x)(Bx \supset Rx)$
2. $(\exists x)(Bx \cdot Kx)$ / $(\exists x)(Kx \cdot Rx)$
3. $Bc \cdot Kc$ 2, EI
4. $Bc \supset Rc$ 1, UI
5. Bc 3, Simp
6. Rc 4, 5, MP
7. Kc 3, Simp
8. $Kc \cdot Rc$ 6, 7, Conj
9. $(\exists x)(Kx \cdot Rx)$ 8, EG

As always, we have to be careful not to misapply the rule. Here are some examples:

Misapplications of EI

A.   1. Fd
    2. $(\exists y)My$
    3. Md 🚫

B.   1. $(\exists y)My$
    2. $(\exists x)Px$
    3. Mc
    4. Pc 🚫

The mistake in A is the result of using the instantial letter d that appeared earlier in the proof sequence in line 1. A similar mistake occurs in B. The instantial letter c is validly derived on line 3. However, its use on line 4 violates the restriction that prohibits using an instantial letter that appeared earlier in the proof sequence.

Summary of the Four Rules

We can now summarize the four new rules of inference. This will require the introduction of a few new symbols: $\mathcal{S}x$, $\mathcal{S}y$, and $\mathcal{S}a$. The first two symbols are used to represent *any statement function* (any symbolic arrangement containing individual *variables*). The third symbol is used to represent *any statement* (any symbolic arrangement containing individual *constants*). Here are the four predicate logic rules:

Universal Instantiation (UI)	
$\dfrac{(x)Sx}{Sy}$ $\dfrac{(x)Sx}{Sa}$	
Universal Generalization (UG)	**Not Permitted**
$\dfrac{Sy}{(x)Sx}$	$\dfrac{Sa}{(x)Sx}$
Existential Instantiation (EI)	**Not Permitted**
$\dfrac{(\exists x)Sx}{Sa}$	$\dfrac{(\exists x)Sx}{Sy}$

Restriction: The existential name (a) cannot be a name that appears in any previous line of the proof, and it cannot appear in the line that indicates the conclusion to be derived.

Existential Generalization (EG)	
$\dfrac{Sa}{(\exists x)Sx}$ $\dfrac{Sy}{(\exists x)Sx}$	

Tactics and Strategy

The most important thing to remember when doing proofs in predicate logic is not to misapply the rules. The four new rules of inference mesh smoothly with the previous rules of inference in Chapter 8. Therefore, your familiarity with the previous rules should help you create proofs in predicate logic.

One more basic principle needs to be reinforced. The four new rules are similar to the eight implication rules in an important way: *They can be applied only to an entire line of a proof (either a premise or a derived line).* Let's look at how this affects strategy in a proof. Consider this argument:

1. $Pg \cdot Rg$
2. $(\exists x)Px \supset (x)(Rx \supset Sx)$ / Sg

One strategic goal is to instantiate the information in line 2. However, line 2 is a conditional statement. In other words, the entire line is governed neither by the existential quantifier nor the universal quantifier. In fact, the existential quantifier governs only the antecedent, while the universal quantifier governs only the consequent. Therefore, we cannot apply either EI or UI to line 2.

Line 1 provides the means to solve our problem. The first step is to derive Pg on a separate line by simplification. Next, we can apply EG to derive the consequent of line 2. From there, the proof will proceed smoothly.

1. $Pg \cdot Rg$
2. $(\exists x)Px \supset (x)(Rx \supset Sx)$ / Sg
3. Pg 1, Simp
4. $(\exists x)Px$ 2, EG
5. $(x)(Rx \supset Sx)$ 2, 4, MP
6. $Rg \supset Sg$ 5, UI
7. Rg 1, Simp
8. Sg 6, 7, MP

The following strategy and tactics guide can be used with the four new rules of inference for predicate logic:

STRATEGIES AND TACTICS

Strategy 1: Look at the conclusion.

Tactical moves—
    A. If you need to perform universal generalization (UG) on the last line of the proof, try using universal instantiation (UI) on the premises to instantiate a variable. (UG can be used only on a variable, not on a constant.)
    B. If you need to perform existential generalization (EG) on the last line of the proof, try using both UI and EI on the premises. (Be sure to use EI first.)

Strategy 2: Look at the premises.

Tactical moves—
    A. If the premises have universal quantifiers, then try using universal instantiation (UI). Determine whether you need to instantiate a variable or a constant. (You may instantiate the same variable for more than one premise.)
    B. If the premises have more than one existential quantifier, try using existential instantiation (EI). (Make sure not to instantiate a letter that occurs earlier in the proof.)

Strategy 3: Remember that the four predicate logic rules can be applied only to an entire line in a proof (either a premise or a derived line).

Tactical moves—
    A. Try using simplification to separate two conjuncts. You can then use either EI or UI to instantiate whatever you need.
    B. Try deriving the antecedent of a conditional on a separate line, and then derive the consequent by *modus ponens*. You can then use either EI or UI to instantiate whatever you need.

EXERCISES 9B

Lightboard Video

Self-Practice
Questions

I. **The proofs for the following arguments have been given. Choose the correct rule for the missing justifications.**

[1] 1. $(y)(Py \supset Sy)$
    2. $(\exists y)(Py \cdot Ty)$ / $(\exists y)(Ty \cdot Sy)$
    3. $Pa \cdot Ta$ 2,
    4. Pa 3, Simp
    5. $Pa \supset Sa$ 1,
    6. Sa 4, 5, MP
    7. Ta 3, Simp
    8. $Ta \cdot Sa$ 6, 7, Conj
    9. $(\exists y)(Ty \cdot Sy)$ 8,

Answer:
    The justification for line 3: **EI**
    The justification for line 5: **UI**
    The justification for line 9: **EG**

[2] 1. $(x)(Nx \supset Mx)$
    2. $(x)(Mx \supset Ox)$
    3. Na / Oa
    4. $Na \supset Ma$ 1,
    5. $Ma \supset Oa$ 2,
    6. $Na \supset Oa$ 4, 5, HS
    7. Oa 3, 6, MP

[3] 1. $(\exists x)(Px \cdot Qx)$
    2. $(x)(Px \supset Rx)$ / $(\exists x)(Qx \cdot Rx)$
    3. $Pa \cdot Qa$ 1,
    4. $Pa \supset Ra$ 2,
    5. Pa 3, Simp
    6. Ra 4, 5, MP
    7. Qa 3, Simp
    8. $Qa \cdot Ra$ 6, 7, Conj
    9. $(\exists x)(Qx \cdot Rx)$ 8,

II. In the following proofs the correct justification has been given for the rule. You are to supply the missing information in the line.

[1] 1. $(x)(Kx \supset \sim Sx)$
    2. $(\exists x)(Sx \cdot Wx)$ / $(\exists x)(Wx \cdot \sim Kx)$
    3.   2, EI
    4.   1, UI
    5. Sa 3, Simp
    6. $\sim \sim Sa$ 5, DN
    7. $\sim Ka$ 4, 6, MT
    8. Wa 3, Simp
    9. $Wa \cdot \sim Ka$ 7, 8, Conj
    10.   9, EG

Answer:
    The information in line 3: $Sa \cdot Wa$
    The information in line 4: $Ka \supset \sim Sa$
    The information in line 10: $(\exists x)(Wx \cdot \sim Kx)$

[2] 1. $(\exists x)(Px \cdot Qx)$
    2. $(\exists x)(Rx \cdot Sx)$
    3. $[(\exists x) Px \cdot (\exists x) Rx] \supset Ta$ / Ta
    4.   1, EI
    5.   2, EI
    6. Pa 4, Simp
    7. Rb 5, Simp
    8.   6, EG
    9.   7, EG
    10. $(\exists x) Px \cdot (\exists x) Rx$ 8, 9, Conj
    11. Ta 3, 10, MP

III. Use the rules of inference to derive the conclusion of each argument.

[1] 1. $(x)(Sx \supset Tx)$
     2. $(x)(Tx \supset \sim Ux)$ / $(x)(Sx \supset \sim Ux)$

Answer:

3. $Sx \supset Tx$ 1, UI
4. $Tx \supset \sim Ux$ 2, UI
5. $Sx \supset \sim Ux$ 3, 4, HS
6. $(x)(Sx \supset \sim Ux)$ 5, UG

[2] 1. $(\exists x)\, Gx \supset (x)\, Hx$
     2. Ga / Ha

[3] 1. Ta
     2. $(x)\,(Sx \supset \sim Tx)$ / $\sim Sa$

[4] 1. $(x)\,(Px \supset \sim Qx)$
     2. Qa / $\sim Pa$

★ [5] 1. $(\exists x)\, Hx$
       2. $(x)(Hx \supset Px)$ / $(\exists x)(Hx \cdot Px)$

Video Tutorial: 9BIII
Exercise #5

[6] 1. $Fa \cdot \sim Ga$
     2. $(x)\,[Fx \supset (Gx \vee Hx)]$ / Ha

[7] 1. $(x)\,(Sx \supset Tx)$
     2. $(x)\,(Tx \supset Px)$
     3. Sa / $(\exists x)\, Px$

[8] 1. $(x)[(Fx \vee Gx) \supset Hx]$
     2. $\sim Ha$ / $(\exists x) \sim Gx$

★ [9] 1. $(x)(Ux \supset Sx)$
       2. $(\exists x)(Ux \cdot Tx)$ / $(\exists x)(Tx \cdot Sx)$

[10] 1. $(\exists x)(Fx \cdot \sim Gx)$
      2. $(x)(Hx \supset Gx)$ / $(\exists x)(Fx \cdot \sim Hx)$

[11] 1. $Ha \vee Hb$
      2. $(x)(\sim Cx \supset \sim Hx)$ / $Ca \vee Cb$

[12] 1. $(x)\,[(Fx \vee Gx) \supset Hx]$
      2. $(\exists x)\, Fx$
      3. $(x)\, Lx \supset \sim (\exists x)\, Hx$ / $\sim (x)\, Lx$

★[13] 1. $(\exists x)\,(Px \cdot Qx)$
       2. $(x)\,(Px \supset Rx)$ / $(\exists x)\,(Qx \cdot Rx)$

[14] 1. $(x)\,[(Fx \cdot Gx) \supset Hx]$
     2. $(\exists x)\,Fx$
     3. $(x)\,Gx$ $/\,(\exists x)\,Hx$

[15] 1. $(\exists x)(Tx \cdot \sim Mx)$
     2. $(x)[Tx \supset (Rx \vee Mx)]$ $/\,(\exists x)\,Rx$

[16] 1. $(\exists x)\,(Sx \cdot Tx)$
     2. $(x)\,(Px \supset \sim Sx)$ $/\,(\exists x)\,(Tx \cdot \sim Px)$

⭐[17] 1. $(x)\,[\sim (Fx \vee Gx) \supset Hx]$
     2. $(x)\,(Hx \supset Lx)$
     3. $(x) \sim Fx$ $/\,(x)\,(Gx \vee Lx)$

[18] 1. $(\exists x)\,Px \supset (\exists x)\,Kx$
     2. $(\exists x)\,Mx \supset (x)\,Nx$
     3. $Mc \cdot Pc$ $/\,(\exists x)\,(Nx \cdot Kx)$

[19] 1. $(x)\,(Lx \supset Fx)$
     2. $(\exists x)(Lx \cdot \sim Hx)$
     3. $(x)\,[(Fx \cdot \sim Gx) \supset Hx]$ $/\,(\exists x)\,Gx$

[20] 1. $Ha \cdot \sim Hb$
     2. $Fa \cdot Fb$
     3. $(x)\,[Fx \supset (Gx \equiv Hx)]$ $/\,Ga \cdot \sim Gb$

IV. First, translate the following arguments. Second, use the rules of inference to derive the conclusion of each argument.

1. If something is heavy, then it is not glass. If something is fragile, then it is glass. Therefore, if something is heavy, then it is not fragile. (H, G, F)

    1. $(x)\,(Hx \supset \sim Gx)$
       $(x)\,(Fx \supset Gx)$ $/\,(x)\,(Hx \supset \sim Fx)$

Answer:

    1. $(x)\,(Hx \supset \sim Gx)$
    2. $(x)\,(Fx \supset Gx)$ $/\,(x)\,(Hx \supset \sim Fx)$
    3. $Hy \supset \sim Gy$ 1, UI
    4. $Fy \supset Gy$ 2, UI
    5. $\sim Gy \supset \sim Fy$ 4, Trans
    6. $Hy \supset \sim Fy$ 3, 5, HS
    7. $(x)\,(Hx \supset \sim Fx)$ 6, UG

2. Either Anna is a graduate or Ben is a graduate. Those who are not finished are not graduates. Thus, either Anna is finished or Ben is finished. (G, F)

3. Some boxers are dancers. All boxers are courageous. Consequently, some dancers are courageous. (B, D, C)

4. Something is fearless. Everything that is fearless is both strong and disciplined. It follows that something is both strong and disciplined. (*F, S, D*)

★ 5. Nothing is rare. Everything is either beautiful or expensive if and only if it is rare. Therefore, something is expensive if and only if it is beautiful. (*R, B, E*)

C. CHANGE OF QUANTIFIER (CQ)

The four new rules of inference allow us to prove the validity of many different types of arguments. However, there are still some arguments that require us to generate an additional rule of inference. Here is an example:

> Either some hallucinations are illusions, or else some visions are ghosts. However, it is not the case that there are any ghosts. Therefore, there are some illusions.

Translating the argument reveals the difficulty:

1. $(\exists x)(Hx \cdot Ix) \lor (\exists x)(Vx \cdot Gx)$
2. $\sim (\exists x) Gx$ / $(\exists x) Ix$

The second premise has a tilde in front of the existential quantifier. However, we cannot instantiate the statement until the tilde is removed. Once the tilde is removed, we can then use instantiation to help derive the conclusion. A new rule, called **change of quantifier (CQ)**, allows the removal or introduction of negation signs. The rule is a set of four logical equivalences, and their function is similar to replacement rules in that they can be applied to part of a line or to an entire line. We can use a symbol introduced earlier, $\overline{S}x$, to help generalize the logical equivalences.

Change of quantifier (CQ) The rule allows the removal or introduction of negation signs. (The rule is a set of four logical equivalences.)

CHANGE OF QUANTIFIER (CQ)
$(x)\overline{S}x :: \sim (\exists x) \sim \overline{S}x$
$\sim (x)\overline{S}x :: (\exists x) \sim \overline{S}x$
$(\exists x)\overline{S}x :: \sim (x) \sim \overline{S}x$
$\sim (\exists x)\overline{S}x :: (x) \sim \overline{S}x$

The following set of statements can help you understand the four logical equivalences. A careful look will allow you to recognize that the statements in each pair are equivalent in meaning.

Everything is alive.

It is not the case that everything is alive.

Something is alive.

It is not the case that something is alive.

It is not the case that something is not alive.

Something is not alive.

It is not the case that everything is not alive.

Everything is not alive.

Armed with this new rule, we can now complete the proof:

1. $(\exists x)(Hx \cdot Ix) \vee (\exists x)(Vx \cdot Gx)$
2. $\sim (\exists x) Gx$ / $(\exists x) Ix$
3. $(x) \sim Gx$ 2, CQ
4. $\sim Gx$ 3, UI
5. $\sim Gx \vee \sim Vx$ 4, Add
6. $\sim Vx \vee \sim Gx$ 5, Com
7. $\sim (Vx \cdot Gx)$ 6, DM
8. $(x) \sim (Vx \cdot Gx)$ 7, UG
9. $\sim (\exists x)(Vx \cdot Gx)$ 8, CQ
10. $(\exists x)(Hx \cdot Ix)$ 1, 9, DS
11. $Ha \cdot Ia$ 10, EI
12. Ia 11, Simp
13. $(\exists x) Ix$ 12, EG

As indicated by the proof, we needed to apply the rule at two separate steps in the sequence. The first application occurred on line 3, and it used the fourth pair of logical equivalences. The second application occurred on line 9, and it also used the fourth pair of logical equivalences.

A few more examples will illustrate further applications of the rule:

1. $\sim Ca$
2. $(\exists x)(Ax \vee Bx) \supset (x) Cx$ / $(x) \sim (Ax \vee Bx)$
3. $(\exists x) \sim Cx$ 1, EG
4. $\sim (x) Cx$ 3, CQ
5. $\sim (\exists x)(Ax \vee Bx)$ 2, 4, MT
6. $(x) \sim (Ax \vee Bx)$ 5, CQ

The change of quantifier rule was applied twice in the proof sequence. The first application occurred on line 4, and it used the second pair of logical equivalences. The second application occurred on line 6, and it used the fourth pair of logical equivalences. Here is another example:

1. $(x) \sim Bx \supset (x) \sim Cx$
2. $(\exists x)(Ax \cdot Dx) \supset \sim (\exists x) Bx$ / $(\exists x)(Ax \cdot Dx) \supset \sim (\exists x) Cx$
3. $(\exists x)(Ax \cdot Dx) \supset (x) \sim Bx$ 2, CQ
4. $(\exists x)(Ax \cdot Dx) \supset (x) \sim Cx$ 1, 3, HS
5. $(\exists x)(Ax \cdot Dx) \supset \sim (\exists x) Cx$ 4, CQ

The change of quantifier rule was applied twice in the proof sequence. The first application occurred on line 3, and it used the fourth pair of logical equivalences. However, notice that the rule was applied only to the consequent of line 2. This illustrates that the rule can be applied to part of a line. The second application occurred in line 5, and it also used the fourth pair of logical equivalences. Once again, the rule was applied only to the consequent of line 4.

EXERCISES 9C

I. For each of the following, use the change of quantifier rule. This will give you practice using the pairs of logical equivalences.

1. $\sim (\exists x)\,(Tx \cdot Rx)$

Answer: $(x) \sim (Tx \cdot Rx)$

2. $\sim (x)\,(Px \supset \,\sim Sx)$

3. $\sim (\exists x) \sim (Jx \cdot \,\sim Kx)$

4. $\sim (x) \sim (Dx \supset Gx)$

⭐ 5. $(x) \sim (Px \supset Qx)$

6. $(\exists x) \sim (Px \cdot Qx)$

7. $\sim (x)\,(Px \supset \,\sim Qx)$

8. $(\exists x)\,(Px \cdot Qx)$

⭐ 9. $(x) \sim (Px \supset Qx)$

10. $\sim (\exists x) \sim (Jx \cdot \,\sim Kx)$

II. Use the change of quantifier rule and the other rules of inference to construct proofs for the following arguments.

[1] 1. $\sim (x)\,Fx$
    2. $(x)\,Gx \supset (x)\,Fx$ / $(\exists x) \sim Gx$

Answer:

    1. $\sim (x)\,Fx$
    2. $(x)\,Gx \supset (x)\,Fx$ / $(\exists x) \sim Gx$
    3. $\sim (x)\,Gx$ 1, 2, MT
    4. $(\exists x) \sim Gx$ 3, CQ

[2] 1. $\sim (\exists x)\,Dx$ / $Da \supset Ga$

[3] 1. $(x) \sim Gx$
    2. $(x)\,Fx \supset (\exists x)\,Gx$ / $(\exists x) \sim Fx$

[4] 1. $(\exists x)\,Gx \supset (x)\,Fx$
    2. $Ga \vee (x) \sim Hx$
    3. $\sim (x)\,Fx \vee (\exists x) \sim Fx$ / $\sim Hb$

⭐ [5] 1. $\sim (\exists x)\,Gx$
    2. $(\exists x)\,Fx \vee (\exists x)\,(Gx \cdot Hx)$ / $(\exists x)\,Fx$

[6] 1. $(y)\,[\,(\sim By \vee Cy) \supset Dy\,]$
    2. $\sim (x)\,(Ax \vee Bx)$ / $(\exists z)\,Dz$

[7] 1. $\sim (x)\,Fx$
    2. $Ga \equiv Hb$
    3. $(\exists x) \sim Fx \supset \,\sim (\exists x)\,Gx$ / $\sim Hb$

Video Tutorial: 9CII
Exercise #5

[8] 1. $(\exists y)(\sim By \lor \sim Ay)$
 2. $(x)[(Ax \lor Bx) \supset Cx]$
 3. $(\exists z) \sim (Dz \lor \sim Bz)$ / $(\exists x) Cx$

⭐ [9] 1. $\sim (x) Gx$
 2. $(x)(Fx \supset Gx)$
 3. $\sim (x) Hx \lor (x) Fx$ / $(\exists x) \sim Hx$

[10] 1. $(\exists x)(Cx \cdot \sim Bx)$
 2. $(x)(\sim Dx \lor Ax)$
 3. $(x)(Ax \supset Bx)$ / $(\exists x)(Cx \cdot \sim Dx)$

[11] 1. $(x)[(Hx \lor Lx) \supset Mx]$
 2. $(x)[Fx \supset (Gx \lor Hx)]$ / $(x)[(Fx \cdot \sim Gx) \supset Mx]$

[12] 1. $\sim (\exists x)(Fx \cdot \sim Gx)$
 2. $\sim (\exists x)(Gx \cdot \sim Hx)$ / $(x)(Fx \supset Hx)$

⭐[13] 1. $\sim (\exists x) Lx$
 2. $(\exists y) My$
 3. $(x)[(Kx \supset \sim Mx) \lor La]$ / $\sim (y) Ky$

[14] 1. $\sim (\exists x) Dx$
 2. $(\exists x)(Bx \cdot Cx) \lor (\exists x)(Fx \cdot Dx)$ / $(\exists x) Cx$

[15] 1. $(\exists x) \sim Hx \supset (\exists x) Gx$
 2. $\sim [(x) Fx \supset (\exists x) Gx]$
 3. $(x)[(Fx \cdot Hx) \supset La]$ / La

[16] 1. $\sim (\exists x)(Hx \cdot \sim Kx)$
 2. $\sim (\exists x)(Cx \cdot \sim Gx)$
 3. $(x)(Dx \supset Kx) \supset (\exists x)(Dx \cdot Cx)$
 4. $(x)(Dx \supset Hx)$ / $(\exists x)(Dx \cdot Gx)$

⭐[17] 1. $\sim (\exists x) Cx$
 2. $(\exists x)(Dx \cdot \sim Gx) \supset (x)(Hx \lor Cx)$
 3. $\sim (x)(\sim Gx \supset Hx)$ / $\sim (x) Dy$

[18] 1. $(x)[Sx \supset (Mx \cdot Lx)]$
 2. $(\exists x)(Mx \cdot Dx) \lor (\exists x)(Mx \cdot Sx)$
 3. $\sim (\exists x)[Mx \cdot (Kx \lor Lx)]$ / $(\exists x)(Dx \cdot \sim Kx)$

[19] 1. $\sim (\exists x)[(Hx \cdot Dx) \cdot Kx]$
 2. $\sim (\exists x)[(Hx \cdot \sim Lx) \cdot Gx]$
 3. $(x)[Hx \supset (Dx \lor \sim Lx)]$ / $\sim (\exists x)[Hx \cdot (Kx \cdot Gx)]$

III. First, translate the following arguments. Second, use the change of quantifier rules and the other rules of inference to derive the conclusion of each argument.

 1. It is not true that something is sweet. Therefore, if something is sweet, then it is artificial. (S, A)

Answer:

[1]   1. $\sim (\exists x)\, Sx$ / $(x)\,(Sx \supset Ax)$
      2. $(x) \sim Sx$ 1, CQ
      3. $\sim Sx$ 2, UI
      4. $\sim Sx \lor Ax$ 3, Add
      5. $Sx \supset Ax$ 4, Impl
      6. $(x)\,(Sx \supset Ax)$ 5, UG

2. If something is either concrete or steel, then everything is heavy. But something is not heavy. We can conclude that it is false that something is concrete. (*C, S, H*)

3. Not everything is either not a tragedy, or it is a joke. It is not true that some stories are not jokes. Thus, something is not a story. (*T, J, S*)

4. Not all clowns are funny. It is false that some mimes are not funny. Therefore, something is not a mime. (*C, F, M*)

⭐ 5. It is false that something is either an herb or a garnish. If anything is both a fragrance and not a garnish, then something is an herb. Therefore, something is not a fragrance. (*H, G, F*)

D. CONDITIONAL AND INDIRECT PROOF

We saw in Chapter 8 that some arguments in propositional logic can be proven valid by conditional proof or indirect proof. The two methods can also be used with arguments containing quantifiers.

Conditional Proof (CP)

A conditional proof (CP) sequence in predicate logic uses the same indenting technique as in propositional logic. Also, the process of discharging a CP sequence remains the same. However, some special features can arise within both a predicate logic conditional proof and a predicate logic indirect proof. We can get started by looking at a valid argument that uses quantifiers:

1. $(x)\,(Ax \supset Bx)$ / $(\exists x)\,(Ax \cdot Cx) \supset (\exists x)\, Bx$

Since the conclusion is a conditional statement, we can assume the antecedent in the first line of a conditional sequence. Once this is done, we can use any of the instantiation or generalization rules within the indented sequence. When the desired line is derived, it is discharged as a conditional statement in which the first line of the CP sequence is the antecedent, and the last line of the CP sequence is the consequent. Here is the completed proof:

1. $(x)\,(Ax \supset Bx)$ / $(\exists x)\,(Ax \cdot Cx) \supset (\exists x)\, Bx$
   2. $(\exists x)\,(Ax \cdot Cx)$ Assumption (CP)
   3. $Ag \cdot Cg$ 2, EI
   4. Ag 3, Simp
   5. $Ag \supset Bg$ 1, UI
   6. Bg 4, 5, MP
   7. $(\exists x)\, Bx$ 6, EG
8. $(\exists x)\,(Ax \cdot Cx) \supset (\exists x)\, Bx$ 2–7, CP

Our proof is done, but sometimes a new restriction to universal generalization (UG) is needed if we are to avoid invalid deductions.

Universal Generalization (UG)

$$\frac{\mathcal{S}y}{(x)\mathcal{S}x}$$

Restriction: Universal generalization cannot be used within an indented proof sequence, if the instantial variable is free in the first line of that sequence.

Let's look at a proof that obeys the restriction:

1. $(x) (Cx \supset Dx)$ / $(x) Cx \supset (x) Dx$
> 2. $(x) Cx$ *Assumption (CP)*
> 3. Cx 2, UI
> 4. $Cx \supset Dx$ 1, UI
> 5. Dx 3, 4, MP
> 6. $(x) Dx$ 5, UG

7. $(x) Cx \supset (x) Dx$ 2–6, CP

In the proof, the variable x is bound by a universal quantifier in line 2 (the first line of the indented sequence). Therefore, when UI is applied to line 2, we validly derive an *arbitrarily selected individual* in line 3. When Dx is subsequently derived in line 5, the result is based on the arbitrarily selected individuals in both lines 3 and 4. Therefore, UG is applied correctly.

But what happens if we start a CP assumption with a free variable? In that case, the free variable *does not name an arbitrary individual*, because a free variable *names an individual that is assumed to have a particular property*. Therefore, we cannot bind that variable using universal generalization. Let's look at an example that fails to obey the restriction:

1. $(x) Cx \supset (x) Dx$ / $(x) (Cx \supset Dx)$
> 2. Cx *Assumption (CP)*
> 3. $(x) Cx$ 2, UG (**Misapplication:** x is free in line 2) 🚫
> 4. $(x) Dx$ 1, 3, MP
> 5. Dx 4, UI

6. $Cx \supset Dx$ 2–5, CP
7. $(x) (Cx \supset Dx)$ 6, UG

In the first line of the CP sequence (line 2), the variable x is free. Since it was not derived by UI, it is not an arbitrarily selected individual. Therefore, line 3 is invalidly derived because it fails to conform to the restriction on UG. To understand why the restriction on UG is needed, we can look closely at the defective sequence above. Let's imagine that in line 1, Cx stands for "x is a cat," and Dx stands for "x is a dog." Given this, line 1 is "If everything is a cat, then everything is a dog." Since the antecedent "everything is a cat" is false, the conditional is true, so line 1 (the premise) is true. However, line 7 (the conclusion) is now "For any x, if x is a cat, then x is a dog," or simply "All cats are dogs." The conclusion is false; therefore, the argument is invalid. This results from the violation of the restriction on UG in line 3.

Indirect Proof (IP)

An indirect proof (IP) sequence in predicate logic uses the same indenting technique that was established in propositional logic. Also, the process of discharging an IP sequence remains the same. However, the restriction for using universal generalization (UG) regarding free variables applies equally to an indirect proof sequence.

We can get started by looking at an argument that uses quantifiers:

1. $(\exists x)\ Fx$
2. $(x)\ (Fx \supset Gx)$ / $(\exists x)\ Gx$
   > 3. $\sim (\exists x)\ Gx$ Assumption (IP)
   > 4. $(x) \sim Gx$ 3, CQ
   > 5. Fa 1, EI
   > 6. $Fa \supset Ga$ 2, UI
   > 7. Ga 5, 6, MP
   > 8. $\sim Ga$ 4, UI
   > 9. $Ga \cdot \sim Ga$ 7, 8, Conj
10. $\sim\sim (\exists x)\ Gx$ 3–9, IP
11. $(\exists x)\ Gx$ 10, DN

The indirect proof sequence begins on line 3 by negating the conclusion. We can apply the same strategy for all indirect proofs: Try to derive a contradiction, and then discharge the IP sequence by negating the assumption. Line 3 has a negation in front of the existential quantifier. Therefore, we have to apply the change of quantifier rule to line 3 before we can begin an instantiation. Once the basic groundwork is in place, the proof can be completed.

In predicate logic, the two techniques of CP and IP can be combined in one proof, as long as we use the rules of inference properly. Here is an example:

1. $(x)\ [Gx \supset (Fx \cdot Hx)]$ / $(\exists x)\ (Fx \vee Gx) \supset (\exists x)\ Fx$
   > 2. $(\exists x)\ (Fx \vee Gx)$ Assumption (CP)
   >> 3. $\sim (\exists x)\ Fx$ Assumption (IP)
   >> 4. $(x) \sim Fx$ 3, CQ
   >> 5. $Fa \vee Ga$ 2, EI
   >> 6. $\sim Fa$ 4, UI
   >> 7. Ga 5, 6, DS
   >> 8. $Ga \supset (Fa \cdot Ha)$ 1, UI
   >> 9. $Fa \cdot Ha$ 7, 8, MP
   >> 10. Fa 9, Simp
   >> 11. $Fa \cdot \sim Fa$ 6, 10, Conj
   > 12. $\sim\sim (\exists x)\ Fx$ 3–11, IP
   > 13. $(\exists x)\ Fx$ 12, DN
14. $(\exists x)\ (Fx \vee Gx) \supset (\exists x)\ Fx$ 2–13, CP

The overall strategy is to start with a CP sequence by assuming the antecedent of the conditional statement that we want to derive. The goal of this strategy is to validly derive the consequent of the conditional, and then discharge the CP sequence. In order to derive the consequent, we use an IP sequence as a tactic to derive a contradiction within the IP sequence. This provides the means to derive the consequent within the CP sequence.

EXERCISES 9D

I. Use either *conditional proof* or *indirect proof* to derive the conclusions of the following arguments.

[1] 1. $(\exists x)\,(Sx \lor Px\,) \supset (x)\,Tx$
    $(\exists x)\,Qx \supset (\exists x)\,(Rx \cdot Sx)$ $/\,(x)(Qx \supset Tx)$

Answer:

1. $(\exists x)\,(Sx \lor Px\,) \supset (x)\,Tx$
2. $(\exists x)\,Qx \supset (\exists x)\,(Rx \cdot Sx)$ $/\,(x)(Qx \supset Tx)$
    3. Qx Assumption (CP)
    4. $(\exists x)\,Qx$ 3, EG
    5. $(\exists x)\,(Rx \cdot Sx)$ 2, 4, MP
    6. $Rb \cdot Sb$ 5, EI
    7. Sb 6, Simp
    8. $Sb \lor Pb$ 7, Add
    9. $(\exists x)\,(Sx \lor Px)$ 8, EG
    10. $(x)\,Tx$ 1, 9, MP
    11. Tx 10, UI
  12. $Qx \supset Tx$ 3–11, CP
  13. $(x)(Qx \supset Tx)$ 12, UG

[2] 1. $(x)\,(Fx \supset Gx)$ $/\,(x)\,Fx \supset (x)\,Gx$

[3] 1. $(x)\,(Bx \supset Cx)$ $/\,{\sim}\,(x)\,Cx \supset {\sim}\,(x)\,Bx$

[4] 1. $(x)\,{\sim}\,Dx$
    2. ${\sim}\,(\exists x)\,Bx \supset (\exists x)\,(Cx \cdot Dx)$ $/\,(\exists x)\,Bx$

⭐ [5] 1. $(x)\,(Fx \supset Hx)$
    2. $(x)\,(Fx \supset Gx)$ $/\,(x)\,[Fx \supset (Gx \cdot Hx)]$

[6] 1. $(x)\,Hx \lor (x)\,Kx$ $/\,(x)\,({\sim}\,Hx \supset Kx)$

[7] 1. $(x)\,(Bx \supset Dx)$
    2. $(x)\,(Bx \supset Cx)$ $/\,(x)\,[Bx \supset (Cx \cdot Dx)]$

[8] 1. $(\exists x)\,Fx$
    2. $(x)\,(Fx \supset Gx)$ $/\,(\exists x)\,Gx$

⭐ [9]   1. ~ (∃y) Ky ⊃ ~ (∃z) Mz
        2. (∃x) [Hx ⊃ (y) ~ Ky]   / (x) Hx ⊃ (z) ~ Mz

[10]   1. (x) [Sx ∨ (Bx · ~ Fx)]
       2. (x) Fx   / (x)(Cx ⊃ Sx)

[11]   1. (x) [(Hx ∨ Lx) ⊃ Mx]
       2. (x) [(Fx ∨ Gx) ⊃ Hx]   / (x) (Fx ⊃ Mx)

[12]   1. (y) Ly
       2. (x) (Lx ⊃ ~ Mx)   / (z) ~ Mz

⭐ [13] 1. (x) [Gx ⊃ (Hx · Lx)]   / (x) (Fx ⊃ Gx) ⊃ (x) (Fx ⊃ Lx)

[14]   1. ~ (∃x) Lx ⊃ (∃x) Mx
       2. (x) (Lx ⊃ Mx)   / ~ (x) ~ Mx

[15]   1. (∃x) Hx ⊃ (∃x) (Gx · Lx)
       2. (x)(Fx ⊃ Hx)   / (∃x) Fx ⊃ (∃x) Gx

[16]   1. (∃x) Dx ⊃ (x) Fx
       2. (∃x) Bx ⊃ (∃x) (Cx · Dx)   / (x) (Bx ⊃ Fx)

⭐ [17] 1. (∃x) (Dx ∨ Mx) ⊃ (x) Fx
       2. (∃x) Bx ⊃ (∃x) (Cx · Dx)   / (x) (Bx ⊃ Fx)

[18]   1. La ∨ Lb
       2. (x) (Lx ⊃ Mx)   / (∃x) Mx

[19]   1. (x) [(Hx ∨ Lx) ⊃ Mx]
       2. (x) [Fx ⊃ (Gx ∨ Hx)]   / (x) [(Fx · ~ Gx) ⊃ Mx]

[20]   1. (x) [Bx ≡ (y) Cy]   / (x) Bx ∨ (x) ~ Bx

⭐ [21] 1. ~ (∃x)(Kx · ~ Px)
       2. (∃x)Gx ⊃ (x)(Hx ⊃ Kx)
       3. (∃x)Lx ⊃ (x)(Px ⊃ ~ Hx)   / (∃x)(Gx · Lx) ⊃ ~ (∃x)Hx

[22]   / (∃x)(Ca · Dx) ≡ [Ca · (∃x)Dx]

[23]   1. (x)[(Cx · Dx) ⊃ Jx]
       2. (x)[Gx ∨ (Bx · ~ Rx)]
       3. (x){Bx ⊃ [Hx ∨ (Jx ⊃ Rx)]}
       4. ~ (∃x)[(Bx · Cx) · (Dx ≡ Gx)]   / (x)[Cx ⊃ (Gx ∨ Hx)]

**II. First, translate the following arguments. Second, use either *conditional proof*
or *indirect proof* to derive the conclusions of each argument.**

1. Either Anabelle is a cat or Bob is a cat. All cats are mammals. Therefore, there
    is a mammal. (*C, M*)

Answer:

1. $Ca \lor Cb$
2. $(x)\,(Cx \supset Mx)$ $/\,(\exists x)\,Mx$
   > 3. $\sim (\exists x)\,Mx$ *Assumption (IP)*
   > 4. $(x)\sim Mx$ 3, CQ
   > 5. $Ca \supset Ma$ 2, UI
   > 6. $Cb \supset Mb$ 2, UI
   > 7. $(Ca \supset Ma) \cdot (Cb \supset Mb)$ 5, 6, Conj
   > 8. $Ma \lor Mb$ 1, 7, CD
   > 9. $\sim Ma$ 4, UI
   > 10. Mb 8, 9, DS
   > 11. $\sim Mb$ 4, UI
   > 12. $Mb \cdot \sim Mb$ 10, 11, Conj
13. $\sim\sim (\exists x)\,Mx$ 3–12, IP
14. $(\exists x)\,Mx$ 13, DN

2. All beagles are canines. Also, all puppies are animals. It follows that all beagle puppies are canines and animals. (B, C, P, A)

3. Everything is fragile. Everything is either sweet, or else bitter and not fragile. Therefore, something is either cold or sweet. (F, S, B, C)

4. There is something that is either not tired or hungry only if everything is jolly. Everything is tired or grouchy only if miserable. Therefore, everything is miserable or everything is jolly. (T, H, J, G, M)

⭐ 5. All UFOs are spaceships. There is a spaceship only if there is an alien. We can conclude that there is a UFO only if there is an alien. (U, S, A)

E. DEMONSTRATING INVALIDITY

There are two methods for demonstrating invalidity in predicate logic. However, neither of the methods is mechanical in the way that a complete truth table or a Venn diagram can be when used to determine the invalidity of an argument. One of the methods we can use draws on the ability to create *counterexamples*. The second method is called the *finite universe method*. It consists in creating models using increasing numbers of individuals in order to show an argument is invalid.

Counterexample Method

Introduced in Chapter 1, a counterexample to an argument is a substitution instance of an argument form that has actually true premises and a false conclusion. A good way to create a counterexample is to use widely familiar objects because the idea is to create statements whose truth value is readily acceptable. Thinking of counterexamples challenges our creativity, but it is rewarding when you think of a good example. As with most skills, practice makes it easier because the training strengthens our ability to think through a problem.

Here is an example using quantifiers:

1. $(x)(Fx \supset Gx)$
2. $(\exists x)(Hx \cdot \sim Gx)$ $/ (\exists x)(Fx \cdot \sim Hx)$

One way to begin thinking about the argument is to notice that it refers to three different groups of objects. Next, we can translate the statements into English to get a feel for them. For example, the first premise can be translated as "Every F is a G." If the first premise is true, then the F group is included in the G group (or else we can say that F is a subset of G). The second premise can be translated as "There is at least one H that is not a G." If the second premise is true, then at least one member of the H group is not included in the G group. Finally, the conclusion can be translated as "There is at least one F that is not an H." At this point we have to change our thinking process a bit because our goal is for the conclusion to be false and the premises to be true. In other words, if the conclusion is false, then it *is not the case that* at least one member of the F group is *not included* in the H group. If the conclusion is false, then *all* the members of F *are* members of H.

Now that we have the pieces drawn out, we can begin putting them together to create a counterexample. Since we want the conclusion to be a false statement, we need to have *every member of F be a member of H*. Here is one possibility: If we let $F =$ *children*, and $H =$ *humans*, then we get "Some children are not humans." This is obviously false, because every child is a human. In addition, we now need only to think of something to fit the G group. Let's see what we have so far:

All children are _____.
Some humans are not _____.
Therefore, some children are not humans.

We need something that will make both premises true. There are several things that can fit, but here we offer just one solution: let $G =$ *persons under 21 years of age*.

All children are persons under 21 years of age.
Some humans are not persons under 21 years of age.
Therefore, some children are not humans.

The premises are true, and the conclusion is false. Therefore, the counterexample to the original argument shows that it is invalid.

Let's try another example that may seem plausible, but is it? To find out, we again look for a counterexample:

1. $(x)(Dx \supset Kx)$
2. $\sim Da$ $/ \sim Ka$

This example has a singular statement in the second premise and in the conclusion. When this occurs we should think of an individual who is well known. This way, the truth value of the statements we create will be obvious. For example, the first premise can be translated as "Every D is a K." In other words, if the first premise is true, then the D group is included in the K group. The second premise can be translated as "*a* is not a *D*." Thus, if the second premise is true, then the individual *a* is not a member of *D*. Finally, the conclusion can be translated as "*a* is not a *K*." Recall that our goal is for the conclusion to be false and the premises to be true. If the conclusion is false, then the individual *a* is a member of the *K* group. Here is one substitution instance:

> All United States senators are humans.
> Jon Stewart is not a United States senator.
> Therefore, Jon Stewart is not a human.

The premises are true, and the conclusion is false. Therefore, the counterexample to the original argument shows that it is invalid.

The counterexample method works well with simple invalid predicate logic arguments. However, as arguments get more complex, the method can become quite challenging. The next method for showing invalidity can handle the complex cases.

Finite Universe Method

A valid argument that uses quantifiers is valid for any number of individuals, with just one stipulation: There is at least one individual in the universe. In order to show that an argument that uses quantifiers is invalid, a model containing at least one individual needs to reveal the possibility of true premises and a false conclusion. If an argument using quantifiers is invalid, it is always possible to create such a model. This is referred to as the **finite universe method**, or *possible universe method*, of showing invalidity.

We first establish a set of individuals that are said to exist in the possible universe of the given model. We then use the indirect truth table method to determine invalidity. However, before we get to arguments, we need to develop a few basic building blocks.

Let's imagine a universe that contains only one individual. Imagine further that this individual is bald. If we assign the letter *a* to this individual, then we get *Ba*. An interesting thing occurs: The existential statement "Something is bald" and the universal statement "Everything is bald" are equivalent. In other words, in this universe containing one individual, $(\exists x)\, Bx$ is equivalent to $(x)\, Bx$. We can formalize the results as follows:

> (*x*) *Bx* is *conditionally equivalent* to *Ba*
> (∃*x*) *Bx* is *conditionally equivalent* to *Ba*

We use the expression "conditionally equivalent" because the equivalence is in *this* possible universe. In other words, it is not unconditionally equivalent. We will assign the symbol "-CE-" to the expression "conditionally equivalent."

Now what happens in a universe containing two individuals? Let's assign the letter *a* to one individual, and the letter *b* to the other individual. In this universe, the universal statement "Everything is bald" can be symbolized as follows:

$$(x)\ Bx \text{ -CE- } Ba \cdot Bb$$

In a universe containing two individuals, if *everything is bald*, then both individuals are bald. This result is symbolized by using a *conjunction*. However, in the universe containing two individuals, the existential statement "Something is bald" gets symbolized differently:

Finite universe method The method of demonstrating invalidity that assumes a universe, containing at least one individual, to show the possibility of true premises and a false conclusion.

$$(\exists x)\ Bx \text{ -CE- } Ba \lor Bb$$

In the universe containing two individuals, if *something is bald*, then *at least one* individual is bald. This result is symbolized by a *disjunction*. The general thrust of the procedure should now be clear: As the number of individuals in the possible universe increases, they are joined by a *conjunction* for a universal statement. However, they are joined by a *disjunction* for an existential statement.

Let's extend this idea even further. Suppose we have a universe containing three individuals, and we have the statement $(x)(Fx \supset Gx)$. These are the results:

$$(x)(Fx \supset Gx) \text{ -CE- } [(Fa \supset Ga) \cdot (Fb \supset Gb) \cdot (Fc \supset Gc)]$$

In this universe, the statement $(\exists x)\ (Fx \cdot Gx)$ has this result:

$$(\exists x)\ (Fx \cdot Gx) \text{ -CE- } [(Fa \cdot Ga) \lor (Fb \cdot Gb) \lor (Fc \cdot Gc)]$$

Indirect Truth Tables

We are now in position to show the invalidity of an argument. The following example will illustrate the procedure:

$(x)\ (Hx \supset Mx)$
$(x)\ (Rx \supset Mx) \quad / (x)\ (Rx \supset Hx)$

We can try a universe containing one individual, represented by the letter a:

$Ha \supset Ma$
$Ra \supset Ma \quad / Ra \supset Ha$

The first step is to determine whether to start with a premise or with the conclusion. Recall that the most efficient way to proceed is to start with whatever has the least number of possible cases. For this example, since the conclusion is a conditional statement, there is only one way for the conclusion to be false—when the antecedent is true and the consequent is false. We assign the appropriate truth values to the guide on the left:

Ha	Ma	Ra	Ha ⊃ Ma	Ra ⊃ Ma	/ Ra ⊃ Ha
F		T	T		F

The assignment of truth values makes the first premise true because the antecedent is false. Now if *Ma* is true, then the second premise is true. We add this information to complete the truth table:

Ha	Ma	Ra	Ha ⊃ Ma	Ra ⊃ Ma	/ Ra ⊃ Ha	
F	T	T	T	T	F	√

The assignment of truth values in a universe containing one individual reveals the possibility of true premises and a false conclusion. Therefore, the argument is invalid. This result has been indicated by the check mark to the right of the line.

Let's try an argument with a universal statement in the premise and an existential statement in the conclusion:

$(x)\,(Cx \supset Dx)$ $/\,(\exists x)\,(Cx \cdot Dx)$

We can try a universe containing one individual:

Ca	Da	Ca ⊃ Da	/ Ca · Da
F	T	T	F √

The assignment of truth values shows that the argument is invalid. But what if a universe containing one individual does not show that an argument is invalid? In that case, we must try a universe containing two individuals. Here is an example:

All fanatics are dangerous people. There is at least one fanatic. Therefore, everything is dangerous.

We can translate it and get the following:

$(x)\,(Fx \supset Dx)$
$(\exists x)\,Fx$ $/\,(x)\,Dx$

We first try a universe containing one individual:

Fa	Da	Fa ⊃ Da	Fa	/ Da
T	F	F	T	F

The conclusion is false when Da is false. The second premise is true when Fa is true. However, these assignments make the first premise false. Therefore, this universe is not sufficient to show the argument is invalid. We must next try a universe containing two individuals:

Fa	Da	Fb	Db	(Fa ⊃ Da) · (Fb ⊃ Db)	Fa v Fb	/ Da · Db
T	T	F	F	T T T	T	F √

The truth table shows the possibility of true premises and a false conclusion. Therefore, the argument is invalid. The finite universe method can be summed up in three steps:

1. Try a universe containing one individual. If the argument is shown to be invalid, you are finished. Otherwise, go to step 2.
2. Try a universe containing two individuals. If the argument is shown to be invalid, you are finished. Otherwise, go to step 3.
3. Try a universe containing three individuals. If the argument is still not shown to be invalid, then go back and check your work for any simple mistakes. Going beyond a universe containing three individuals can make the indirect truth tables difficult to manage. If you suspect that the argument is valid, then try proving its validity using the rules of inference.

EXERCISES 9E

Self-Practice
Questions

I. Use the *counterexample* method to show the invalidity of the following arguments.

[1]   1. $(x) (Cx \supset Dx)$
      2. $(\exists x) Cx$ / $(x) Dx$

Answer:

> Every puppy is a dog.
> There is a puppy.
> Therefore, everything is a dog.

[2]   1. $(x) (Dx \supset Fx)$ / $(\exists x) Dx \supset (x) Fx$

[3]   1. $(x) (Fx \supset \sim Hx)$
      2. $(\exists x) Gx$
      3. $(\exists x) Fx$ / $(\exists x) (Gx \cdot \sim Hx)$

[4]   1. $(\exists x) Lx$ / $(x) Lx$

★ [5]   1. $(\exists x) (Gx \cdot Hx)$ / $(x) (Gx \supset Hx)$

[6]   1. $(x) (Dx \supset \sim Lx)$
      2. $(x) (Dx \supset Gx)$ / $(x) (Lx \supset \sim Gx)$

[7]   1. $(x) (Bx \supset Cx)$
      2. $(x) (Bx \supset Dx)$ / $(x) (Cx \supset Dx)$

[8]   1. $(\exists x) (Fx \cdot Gx)$
      2. $(\exists x) (Hx \cdot \sim Gx)$ / $(\exists x) (Fx \cdot \sim Hx)$

★ [9]   1. $(x) (Fx \supset Gx)$ / $(x) Fx \lor (x) Gx$

[10]   1. $(\exists x) Lx$
      2. $(\exists x) Dx$ / $(\exists x) (Lx \cdot Dx)$

II. Use the *finite universe method* to show the invalidity of the following arguments.

[1]   1. $(x) (Px \supset \sim Qx)$
      2. $(x) (Qx \supset \sim Rx)$ / $(x) (Px \supset \sim Rx)$

Answer:

A universe containing one individual:

> $Pa \supset \sim Qa$
> $Qa \supset \sim Ra$ / $Pa \supset \sim Ra$

The following truth value assignments show the argument is invalid:

Pa	Qa	Ra	$Pa \supset \sim Qa$	$Qa \supset \sim Ra$	/ $Pa \supset \sim Ra$
T	F	T	T T	T F	F F √

[2] 1. $(x) (Dx \lor Fx)$
　　 2. $(x) Dx$ 　　　　　　　$/ (x) \sim Fx$

[3] 1. $(\exists x) (Px \cdot \sim Qx)$
　　 2. $(x) (Rx \supset \sim Qx)$ 　　　$/ (x) (Rx \supset Px)$

[4] 1. $(x) (Fx \supset Hx)$
　　 2. $(x) \sim Fx$ 　　　　　$/ (x) \sim Hx$

★ [5] 1. $(x) (Lx \supset Mx)$
　　 2. $(x) Mx$ 　　　　　　$/ (x) Lx$

[6] 1. $(x) (Gx \lor Hx)$ 　　　$/ (x) Gx$

[7] 1. $(x) (Dx \supset Gx)$
　　 2. $(\exists x) Gx$ 　　　　　$/ (x) Dx$

[8] 1. $(x) (Cx \supset \sim Dx)$ 　　$/ (x) (Dx \supset Cx)$

★ [9] 1. $(x) (Hx \supset Fx)$
　　 2. $(x) (Fx \supset Gx)$ 　　　$/ (x) (Gx \supset Hx)$

[10] 1. $\sim (x) Fx \supset (\exists y) Gy$ 　$/ (x) Fx \supset (\exists y) Gy$

[11] 1. $(\exists x) (Fx \cdot \sim Dx)$
　　 2. $(\exists x) (Cx \cdot Dx)$ 　　　$/ (x) (Fx \supset \sim Cx)$

[12] 1. $\sim (x) (Mx \supset Kx)$ 　　$/ (x) Mx \supset (x) Kx$

★[13] 1. $(\exists x) (Gx \cdot Lx)$
　　 2. $(\exists x) (Gx \cdot Hx)$ 　　　$/ (x) (Lx \supset Hx)$

[14] 1. Ga
　　 2. $(x) (Lx \supset Gx)$ 　　　$/ La$

[15] 1. $(\exists x) (Gx \cdot \sim Dx)$
　　 2. $(\exists x) (Hx \cdot \sim Fx)$
　　 3. $(\exists x) (Dx \cdot Hx)$ 　　$/ (\exists x) (Gx \cdot Hx)$

Video Tutorial: 9EII
Exercise #9

III. First, translate the following arguments. Second, use the *finite universe* method to show they are invalid.

1. All diamonds are carbon. Graphite is carbon. Thus, diamonds are graphite. (D, C, G)

Translation:

　　 1. $(x) (Dx \supset Cx)$
　　 2. $(x) (Gx \supset Cx)$ 　　　$/ (x) (Dx \supset Gx)$

A universe containing one individual:

　　 1. $Da \supset Ca$
　　 2. $Ga \supset Ca$ 　　　　$/ Da \supset Ga$

Da	Ca	Ga	Da ⊃ Ca	Ga ⊃ Ca	/ Da ⊃ Ga
T	T	F	**T**	**T**	**F** √

2. All horses are mammals. Some horses are pets. Therefore, all pets are mammals. (*H, M, P*)

3. All problem-solvers and all thinkers have minds. Computers are problem-solvers. Thus, computers are thinkers. (*P, T, M, C*)

4. Every dancer and every singer is right-brained. There is at least one singer. Thus, everyone is right-brained. (*D, S, R*)

⭐ 5. Some CEOs are not people blindly devoted to profits. Some women are CEOs. Therefore, some people blindly devoted to profits are not women. (*C, B, W*)

F. RELATIONAL PREDICATES

Monadic predicate
A one-place predicate that assigns a characteristic to an individual.

The system of predicate logic developed thus far is capable of handling many kinds of statements and arguments. So far, however, we have been using **monadic predicates**, such as *Fx*, *Gy*, and *Hz*. These are one-place predicates that assign a characteristic to an individual. But we know that ordinary language is extremely complex. For example, consider this argument:

> Saul is older than Pablo. In addition, Pablo is older than Chang. Of course, it is true of anything that if one thing is older than a second thing, and the second thing is older than a third thing, then the first thing is older than the third thing. It follows that Saul is older than Chang.

Relational predicate
Establishes a connection between individuals.

An essential part of the argument is the phrase "is older than." A translation of this phrase requires a **relational predicate**, which establishes a connection between individuals. For example, a binary relation connects two individuals, such as the phrase "is older than." As you can imagine, relations can exist between three or more individuals. However, we will concentrate on binary relations.

A translation of an ordinary language statement that uses relational predicates often provides a guide to the symbols. These guides are written in a special way, and they are used to help understand the translation. For example, the phrase "is older than" can be translated as *Oxy*. This is read as "*x* is older than *y*." A complete guide to the translation of the earlier argument is written in this style:

Oxy: *x* is older than *y*; *s*: Saul; *p*: Pablo; *c*: Chang

We can now translate the argument:

Osp
Opc
(*x*) (*y*) (*z*) [(*Oxy* · *Oyz*) ⊃ *Oxz*]   / *Osc*

We will defer the proof of the argument until the next section. For now, we will concentrate on translating ordinary language using relational predicates.

Translations

Translating ordinary language using relational predicates requires paying close attention to the placement of the logical symbols. Here are some examples that involve relations among specifically named individuals:

1. Kelly is married to Rick.   *Mkr*
2. Peter is the father of Helen.   *Fph*
3. Kris loves Morgan.   *Lkm*

These three examples illustrate some general features of relations. The first is an example of a **symmetrical relationship**. In other words, if Kelly is married to Rick, then Rick is married to Kelly. If we let *Mxy*: *x* is married to *y*, then the form of the symmetrical relationship is as follows:

$$(x)\,(y)\,(Mxy \supset Myx)$$

The second example illustrates an **asymmetrical relationship**. In other words, if Peter is the father of Helen, then Helen is *not* the father of Peter. If we let *Fxy*: *x* is the father of *y*, then the form of the asymmetrical relationship is as follows:

$$(x)\,(y)\,(Fxy \supset {\sim} Fyx)$$

A **nonsymmetrical relationship** is neither symmetrical nor asymmetrical. The third example is an illustration of a nonsymmetrical relationship. If Kris loves Morgan, then Morgan may or may not love Kris. (Since both outcomes are possible, the form of the relationship would have to include both possibilities. Given this, it is generally not useful to create a form of the nonsymmetrical relationship.)

Here is another example of an ordinary language statement that uses specifically named individuals:

> If the Eiffel Tower is taller than the Washington Monument, and the Washington Monument is taller than the Lincoln Memorial, then the Eiffel Tower is taller than the Lincoln Memorial.

This example is an illustration of a **transitive relationship**. In general terms, if A is taller than B, and B is taller than C, then A is taller than C. If we let *Txy*: *x* is taller than *y*, then the form of the transitive relationship is as follows:

$$(x)\,(y)\,(z)\,[(Txy \cdot Tyz) \supset Txz]$$

Of course, not all relations are transitive. For example, "the mother of" is an **intransitive relationship**. In general terms, if A is the mother of B, and B is the mother of C, then A is *not* the mother of C. If we let *Mxy*: *x* is the mother of *y*, then the form of the intransitive relationship is as follows:

$$(x)\,(y)\,(z)\,[(Mxy \cdot Myz) \supset {\sim} Mxz]$$

A **nontransitive relationship** is neither transitive nor intransitive. Here is an example:

> Kris loves Morgan and Morgan loves Terry.

This illustrates a nontransitive relationship. If Kris loves Morgan and Morgan loves Terry, then Kris may or may not love Terry. (Since both outcomes are possible, the form of the relationship would have to include both possibilities. Given this, it is generally not useful to create a form of the nontransitive relationship.)

We can now examine some translations of ordinary language statements that do not use specifically named individuals. Here is an example:

> Someone helps everyone.

Symmetrical relationship Illustrated by the following: If A is married to B, then B is married to A.

Asymmetrical relationship Illustrated by the following: If A is the father of B, then B is not the father of A.

Nonsymmetrical relationship When a relationship is neither symmetrical nor asymmetrical, then it is nonsymmetrical. Illustrated by the following: If Kris loves Morgan, then Morgan may or may not love Kris.

Transitive relationship Illustrated by the following: If A is taller than B, and B is taller than C, then A is taller than C.

Intransitive relationship Illustrated by the following: If A is the mother of B, and B is the mother of C, then A is not the mother of C.

Nontransitive relationship Illustrated by the following: If Kris loves Morgan and Morgan loves Terry, then Kris may or may not love Terry.

Although it is a short sentence, there is a lot of logical information that has to be unpacked. The translation will include an existential quantifier (for "someone") and a universal quantifier (for "everyone"). Let's begin the translation by rephrasing the statement using some symbols:

There is an *x* such that *x* is a person, and for every *y*, if *y* is a person, then *x* helps *y*.

The rephrased statement is a blueprint for the construction of the final translation:

$$(\exists x)\ [Px \cdot (y)\ (Py \supset Hxy)]$$

The translation keeps all the logical symbols in order and captures the relations in the English sentence. Here is another example:

Everyone flatters someone.

You probably already realized that the translation will include a universal quantifier (for "everyone") and an existential quantifier (for "someone"). Once again, it helps to begin the translation by rephrasing the statement:

For any *x*, if *x* is a person, *then* there is a *y* such that *y* is a person and *x* flatters *y*.

The rephrased statement is the basis for the final translation:

$$(x)\ [Px \supset (\exists y)(Py \cdot Fxy)]$$

Let's look at another example:

No one cheats everyone.

The translation will have two universal quantifiers (one for "no one" and one for "everyone"). We can begin the translation by rephrasing the statement:

For every *x*, if *x* is a person, then it is not true that for every *y*, if *y* is a person, *x* cheats *y*.

The rephrased statement is the basis for the translation:

$$(x)\ [Px \supset \sim (y)(Py \supset Cxy)]$$

There is an alternate translation that is logically equivalent to the one above. In order to construct the alternative translation, the original statement needs to be rephrased in a different way:

It is not the case that there is an *x* such that *x* is a person, and for every *y*, if *y* is a person, then *x* cheats *y*.

The rephrased statement is the basis for the following translation:

$$\sim (\exists x)\ [Px \cdot (y)\ (Py \supset Cxy)]$$

One more example will illustrate another kind of translation that is possible using relational predicates:

No one influences anyone.

Once again, we begin the translation by rephrasing the statement:

For any *x*, if *x* is a person, then for any *y*, if *y* is a person, *x* does not influence *y*.

The translation has two universal quantifiers:

$$(x) [Px \supset (y)(Py \supset \sim Ixy)]$$

There is an alternate translation that is logically equivalent to the one above. Once again, in order to construct the alternative translation, the original statement needs to be rephrased in a different way:

> It is not the case that there is an x such that x is a person, and there is a y such that y is a person, and x influences y.

The translation has two existential quantifiers:

$$\sim (\exists x) [Px \cdot (\exists y) (Py \cdot Ixy)]$$

The following is a summary of some of the examples presented. You can use it as a guide to help with translations.

English Statement	Translation
Kelly is married to Rick.	Mkr
Peter is the father of Helen.	Fph
Kris loves Morgan.	Lkm
Someone helps everyone.	$(\exists x) [Px \cdot (y) (Py \supset Hxy)]$
Everyone flatters someone.	$(x) [Px \supset (\exists y)(Py \cdot Fxy)]$
No one cheats everyone.	$(x) [Px \supset \sim (y)(Py \supset Cxy)]$
	or
	$\sim (\exists x) [Px \cdot (y) (Py \supset Cxy)]$
No one influences anyone.	$(x) [Px \supset (y)(Py \supset \sim Ixy)]$
	or
	$\sim (\exists x) [Px \cdot (\exists y) (Py \cdot Ixy)]$

EXERCISES 9F.1

Translate the following statements into symbolic form.

Self-Practice
Questions

1. Every play by William Shakespeare is either a tragedy or a history.
   (Pxy: x is a play by y; Tx: x is a tragedy; Hx: x is a history; s: William Shakespeare)

Answer: $(x) [Pxs \supset (Tx \vee Hx)]$

2. No one in this city is a relative of George Washington.
   (Cx: x is in this city; Rxy: x is a relative of y; w: George Washington)

3. Sam cannot jump higher than everyone on the team.
   (Fxy: x can jump higher than y; Tx: x is on the team; s: Sam)

4. Some strange disease killed Leo.
   (Kxy: x killed y; Sx: x is strange; Dx: x is a disease; l: Leo)

⭐ 5. Something destroyed everything.
   (Dxy: x destroyed y)

6. There is a barber who shaves all those barbers who do not shave themselves.(*Bx*: *x* is a barber; *Sxy*: *x* shaves *y*)

7. Anyone older than Florence is older than Ralph.
(*Oxy*: *x* is older than *y*; *f*: Florence; *r*: Ralph)

8. If anyone fails the exam, then everyone will blame someone.
(*Fx*: *x* fails the exam; *Bxy*: *x* will blame *y*)

⭐ 9. Anyone who reads Tolstoy reads Dostoevsky.
(*Rxy*: *x* reads *y*; *t*: Tolstoy; *d*: Dostoevsky)

10. No one is smarter than Isaac.
(*Sxy*: *x* is smarter than *y*; *i*: Isaac)

11. Jane is taller than Lester.
(*Txy*: *x* is taller than *y*; *j*: Jane; *l*: Lester)

12. No one is a sister of everyone.
(*Sxy*: *x* is a sister of *y*)

⭐ 13. Everyone is a child of someone.
(*Cxy*: *x* is a child of *y*)

14. Sharon has at least one brother.
(*Bxy*: *x* is a brother of *y*; *s*: Sharon)

15. Steve has no living relatives.
(*Lx*: *x* is living; *Rxy*: *x* is a relative of *y*; *s*: Steve)

16. Someone is the uncle of every United States senator.
(*Sx*: *x* is a United States senator; *Uxy*: *x* is the uncle of *y*)

⭐ 17. Every grandparent is the parent of a parent of someone.
(*Gx*: *x* is a grandparent; *Pxy*: *x* is a parent of *y*)

18. No one ate anything.
(*Axy*: *x* ate *y*)

19. Anyone who is not faster than Mabel is not faster than Sophie.
(*Wxy*: *x* is faster than *y*; *m*: Mabel; *s*: Sophie)

20. Every retired steelworker lives on some fixed income.
(*Rx*: *x* is retired; *Sx*: *x* is a steelworker; *Lxy*: *x* lives on *y*; *Fy*: *y* is a fixed income)

Proofs

The inference rules that have been introduced can be used with relational predicates. However, in a few special situations, the relational predicates and overlapping quantifiers place restrictions on some of the rules. But before we get to the restrictions, let's take a look at a straightforward proof. The example is the argument that was introduced earlier, only now applied to relational predicates. Here is the argument:

Saul is older than Pablo. In addition, Pablo is older than Chang. Of course, it is true of anything that if one thing is older than a second thing, and the second thing is older than a third thing, then the first thing is older than the third thing. It follows that Saul is older than Chang.

1. Osp
2. Opc
3. $(x) (y) (z) [(Oxy \cdot Oyz) \supset Oxz]$ / Osc
4. $(y) (z) [(Osy \cdot Oyz) \supset Osz]$ 3, UI
5. $(z) [(Osp \cdot Opz) \supset Osz]$ 4, UI
6. $(Osp \cdot Opc) \supset Osc$ 5, UI
7. $Osp \cdot Opc$ 1, 2, Conj
8. Osc 6, 7, MP

Notice that in lines 4, 5, and 6, each time UI was applied, the leftmost quantifier was eliminated: line 4 eliminated (x); line 5 eliminated (y); finally, line 6 eliminated (z). The proof sequence applied the rules of inference to premises with relational predicates and overlapping quantifiers. No restrictions were placed on the rules in the proof.

A New Restriction

The next example shows how instantiation and generalization can proceed with overlapping quantifiers.

1. $(\exists x) (y) (Axy \supset Bxy)$
2. $(x) (y) Axy$ / $(\exists x) (y) Bxy$
3. $(y) (Acy \supset Bcy)$ 1, EI
4. $(y) Acy$ 2, UI
5. $Acy \supset Bcy$ 3, UI
6. Acy 4, UI
7. Bcy 5, 6, MP
8. $(y) Bcy$ 7, UG
9. $(\exists x) (y) Bxy$ 8, EG

The proof followed the normal way of using instantiation by applying EI to line 1 before applying UI. The important step for us to examine occurs in line 8. The instantial variable y in line 8 was derived from line 3. The crucial aspect of line 3 is that the instantial variable y *is not free* in line 3. We can formalize this discussion as an additional restriction placed on UG:

Universal Generalization (UG)

$$\frac{\mathcal{S}y}{(x)\mathcal{S}x}$$

Restriction 1: Universal generalization cannot be used within an indented proof sequence, if the instantial variable is free in the first line of the sequence.

Restriction 2: Universal generalization cannot be used if the instantial variable y is free in any line that was obtained by existential instantiation (EI).

Restriction 1 was introduced earlier in the chapter in section D. Here is an example of a violation of restriction 2:

1. $(x)\ (\exists x)\ Bxy$
2. $(\exists x)\ Bxy$ 1, UI
3. Bxa 2, EI
4. $(x)\ Bxa$ 3, UG **[Misapplication]** ⊘
5. $(x)\ (\exists x)\ Bxy$ 4, EG

The derivation in line 4 is invalid because it contains the name "*a*" that was introduced by existential instantiation in line 3, but *x* is free in line 3. Let's look closely at the defective sequence above to see why restriction 2 is needed. In line 1, $(x)\ (\exists x)$ *Bxy*, the assertion is that for every *x* in the universe there exists some *y* that stands in relation *B* to *x*. However, we *cannot* interpret line 1 as asserting that there exists only *one* thing that stands in relation *B* to *every x* in the universe. In other words, each *x* may have a different thing related to it. In line 2, one *x* has been selected, and line 3 gives a name (*a*) to the thing related to *x*. Line 4 then concludes that *everything* in the universe stands in relation *B* to *a*. However, as we said above, we *cannot* interpret line 1 as asserting that there exists only *one* thing that stands in relation *B* to *every x* in the universe. Adhering to restriction 2 allows us to avoid such mistakes.

Universal instantiation (UI) is applied in the same manner as before. However, you must be careful not to violate the basic technique when applying it to certain relations. For example, here is how UI works without any relations involved:

1. $(x)\ (Fx \supset Hx)$
2. $Fy \supset Hy$ 1, UI

The important thing to notice is that the instantial variable *y* is free in line 2. The same kind of result needs to follow when you apply UI to a relation. Here is an example of a correct application of UI:

1. $(x)\ (\exists y)\ Gxy$
2. $(\exists y)\ Gxy$ 1, UI Valid: The instantial variable *x* is free in line 2.

Here is an example of a *misapplication* of UI:

1. $(x)\ (\exists y)\ Gxy$
2. $(\exists y)\ Gyy$ 1, UI **Misapplication:** The instantial variable *y* is not ⊘
                   free in line 2; it's bound by the existential quantifier.

Change of Quantifier

We apply the change of quantifier rule to overlapping quantifiers step by step. The following example illustrates the correct technique:

1. $\sim (\exists x)\ (y)\ Gxy$
2. $(x) \sim (y)\ Gxy$ 1, CQ
3. $(x)\ (\exists y) \sim Gxy$ 2, CQ

The first application of the rule moved the tilde and switched the existential quantifier to a universal quantifier. The second application moved the tilde and switched the universal quantifier to an existential quantifier.

Conditional Proof and Indirect Proof

The next example illustrates how the conditional proof method can be applied in essentially the same manner as before. The addition of relational predicates and over-lapping quantifiers do not affect the method, as long as the rules of inference and restrictions are followed.

1. $(x) [(y) Fxy \supset Ga]$ $/ (x) (y) Fxy \supset Ga$
   - 2. $(x) (y) Fxy$ Assumption (CP)
   - 3. $(y) Fby \supset Ga$ 1, UI
   - 4. $(y) Fby$ 2, UI
   - 5. Ga 3, 4, MP
6. $(x) (y) Fxy \supset Ga$ 2–5, CP

The next example illustrates how the indirect proof method can be applied. Once again, the addition of relational predicates and overlapping quantifiers do not affect the method, as long as the rules of inference and restrictions are followed.

1. $(x) [(Fx \cdot Gx) \supset Hax]$
2. $(x) (Fx \supset \sim Hxx)$
3. Fa _____ $/ \sim Ga$
   - 4. Ga Assumption (IP)
   - 5. $(Fa \cdot Ga) \supset Haa$ 1, UI
   - 6. $Fa \cdot Ga$ 3, 4, Conj
   - 7. Haa 5, 6, MP
   - 8. $Fa \supset \sim Haa$ 2, UI
   - 9. $\sim Haa$ 3, 8, MP
   - 10. $Haa \cdot \sim Haa$ 7, 9, Conj
11. $\sim Ga$ 4–10, IP

EXERCISES 9F.2

Use the rules of inference to derive the conclusions of the following arguments. You can use conditional proof or indirect proof.

[1] 1. $(\exists x) [Lx \cdot (y) (My \supset Pxy)]$ $/ (\exists x) [Lx \cdot (Mb \supset Pxb)]$

Answer:

1. $(\exists x) [Lx \cdot (y) (My \supset Pxy)]$ $/ (\exists x) [Lx \cdot (Mb \supset Pxb)]$
2. $La \cdot (y) (My \supset Pay)$ 1, EI
3. La 2, Simp
4. $(y) (My \supset Pay)$ 2, Simp
5. $Mb \supset Pab$ 4, UI
6. $La \cdot (Mb \supset Pab)$ 3, 5, Conj
7. $(\exists x) [Lx \cdot (Mb \supset Pxb)]$ 6, EG

[2]   1. (x) $(Fax \lor Fxa)$ / Faa

[3]   1. (x) $[Fx \supset (y) Hxy]$
       2. Fa / $(y) Hay$

[4]   1. (x) (y) $(Fxy \supset Fyx)$
       2. Fab / Fba

★ [5]   1. (x) (y) $(Fxy \supset \sim Fyx)$
       2. Fba / $\sim Fab$

Video Tutorial: 9
FII Exercise #5

[6]   1. $(\exists x)$ (y) $\sim Gxy$
       2. (x) $(\exists y)$ $Fxy \supset (x)$ $(\exists y)$ Gxy / $(\exists x)$ (y) $\sim Fxy$

[7]   1. (x) $(\exists y)$ $\sim Mxy$
       2. (x) (y) $(Lx \supset Mxy)$ / $(\exists x)$ $\sim Lx$

[8]   1. $(\exists x)$ $[Fx \cdot (y) (Fy \supset Gyx)]$ / $(\exists x)$ $(Fx \cdot Gxx)$

★ [9]   1. $\sim (\exists x)$ $[Fx \cdot (\exists y) (Fy \cdot Bxy)]$ / (x) $[Fx \supset (y) (Fy \supset \sim Bxy)]$

[10] 1. $(\exists x)$ $[Mx \cdot (y) (My \supset Pxy)]$ / $(\exists x)$ Pxx

[11] 1. $(\exists x)$ (y) Cxy
       2. (x) $(\exists y)$ $(Cxy \supset Dxy)$ / $(\exists x)$ $(\exists y)$ Dxy

[12] 1. (x) $[Fx \supset (y) (Gy \supset Hxy)]$
       2. $Fa \cdot \sim Hab$ / $\sim Gb$

★ [13] 1. (x) $(\exists y)$ $(Mx \cdot Py)$ / (x) Mx

[14] 1. $(\exists x)$ $Lx \supset \sim (\exists y)$ Py
       2. (x) $(Lx \supset Mx)$ / (x) $[(\exists y) Ly \supset \sim Px]$

[15] 1. $(La \cdot Ma) \cdot \sim Pab$
       2. (x) $\{(Lx \cdot Mx) \supset (y) [(\sim Ly \cdot My) \supset Pxy]\}$
                                                                    / $Mb \supset Lb$

[16] 1. $(\exists x)$ (y) $\sim Mxy$
       2. (x) $(\exists y)$ $Lxy \supset (x)$ $(\exists y)$ Mxy / $(\exists x)$ (y) $\sim Lxy$

★ [17] 1. Fa / (x) $[(Gx \cdot Hxa) \supset (\exists y) (Fy \cdot Hxy)]$

[18] 1. $(\exists x)$ $Fx \supset (\exists y)$ Gy
       2. $(\exists x)$ $\{Fx \cdot (y) [(Gy \lor Hy) \supset Lxy]\}$ / $(\exists x)$ $(\exists y)$ Lxy

[19] 1. $(\exists x)$ $\{Fx \cdot (y) [(Fy \cdot Dxy) \supset Hxy]\}$
       2. (x) $[Fx \supset (\exists y) (Fy \cdot Dxy)]$ / $(\exists x)$ $(\exists y)$ $[(Fx \cdot Fy) \supset Hxy]$

[20] 1. $(\exists x)$ Fx / $\sim (\exists x)$ $\{Fx \cdot (y) [Fy \supset (Hxy \equiv \sim Hyy)]\}$

G. IDENTITY

There is a special kind of relation that occurs in ordinary language that can be illustrated by the following argument:

> Lewis Carroll wrote *Alice's Adventures in Wonderland*. But Lewis Carroll is Charles Lutwidge Dodgson. Therefore, Charles Lutwidge Dodgson wrote *Alice's Adventures in Wonderland*.

The argument involves *identity*. The **identity relation** is sometimes defined as a binary relation that holds between a thing and itself. In this example, the conclusion indicates an identity between the person who is Lewis Carroll and the person who is Charles Lutwidge Dodgson. We will use the identity symbol "=" to translate statements involving the identity relation. For example:

> Lewis Carroll is Charles Lutwidge Dodgson. $l = c$

Identity relation A binary relation that holds between a thing and itself.

The translation is quite short compared to the statement in English. However, this will not always be the case. Many ordinary language statements that use identity relations require long arrangements of symbols. This is necessary in order to spell out the details. Several kinds of identity relations need to be explored, so let's get started.

Simple Identity Statements

An assertion that one named individual is identical to another named individual is common in ordinary language. The Lewis Carroll–Charles Lutwidge Dodgson identity relation is one example. In this case, the assertion is that the name "Lewis Carroll" and the name "Charles Lutwidge Dodgson" *designate the same person*. Here are some more examples:

Istanbul is Constantinople.	$i = c$
Bono is Paul Hewson.	$b = p$
The Mississippi River is Old Man River.	$m = o$
Mount Everest is Sagarmatha.	$e = s$

We can modify the identity symbol to translate a negated identity statement. Here is the technique:

Brad Pitt is not Angelina Jolie.	$b \neq a$
Mount Everest is not K2.	$e \neq k$
Muhammad Ali is not Will Smith.	$m \neq w$

The symbol "≠" is a shorthand way of writing the negation of an identity. For example, instead of writing $\sim (a = b)$, we can simply write $a \neq b$. There are many kinds of ordinary language statements that require more elaborate arrangements. We will examine some of the most common types.

"Only"

Recall that statements with the word "only" can be rewritten as straightforward categorical statements. Here is an example:

Original: Only government-issued IDs are valid documents.
Rewritten: All valid documents are government-issued IDs.

In the example, the term that follows "only" is a plural noun ("government-issued IDs"). However, there are many examples in ordinary language where the word or words following "only" designate an individual. These kinds of statements require a more complex translation. Here is an example:

Only John F. Kennedy was a Catholic U.S. president.

If we unpack the statement's meaning, two things are clear: first, that John F. Kennedy was a Catholic U.S. president; and second, that *if anyone* was a Catholic U.S. president, then that person is John F. Kennedy. The translation needs to capture these two points. If we let Cx: x was a Catholic, Ux: x was a U.S. president, and j: John F. Kennedy, then the translation is the following:

Only John F. Kennedy was a Catholic U.S. president. $Cj \cdot Uj \cdot (x)\,[(Cx \cdot Ux) \supset x=j]$

The translation can be read this way: John F. Kennedy was a Catholic U.S. president, and if anyone was a Catholic U.S. president, then that person is identical to John F. Kennedy. The translation uses the dot, the horseshoe, the identity sign, and a universal quantifier.

As illustrated in the translation, parentheses are used a bit differently when translating identity relations. For example, there are some cases where we will be able to write the following: $Fs \cdot Hs \cdot Fr \cdot Hr$. Normally, we must separate the three dots by using parentheses. The same modification to the use of parentheses holds for a string of disjunctions. In addition, instead of writing $(x=j) \cdot (f=h) \cdot (x=y)$, we can simplify it to $x=j \cdot f=h \cdot x=y$. Finally, instead of $Gx \supset (x=j)$, we can write $Gx \supset x=j$.

"The Only"

Statements with the phrase "the only" can be rewritten as categorical statements. Here is an example:

Original: The only students in the course are seniors.
Rewritten: All students in the course are seniors.

In the example, the term that follows "the only" is a plural noun ("students"). However, if the ordinary language statement designates an individual, then the translation is more complex. Here is an example that requires careful analysis before attempting a translation:

The only student who passed the driver's exam is Mary.

The translation has to capture the following two points: Mary did not fail the driver's exam; all the other students did fail. If we let Sx: x is a student, Px: x passed the driver's exam, and m: Mary, then the translation is the following:

$$Sm \cdot Pm \cdot (x)\,[(Sx \cdot Px) \supset x = m]$$

The translation can be read this way: Mary is a student and Mary passed the driver's exam, and if any student passed the driver's exam, then that student is Mary. This has the same meaning as the original statement.

"No ... Except"

Some statements that use the phrase "No ... except" are similar to those that use "the only." Here is an example:

No employee except George is late for work.

The translation has to capture the following points: George is late for work; no other employee is late for work. If we let Ex: x is an employee, Lx: x is late for work, and g: George, then the translation is the following:

$$Eg \cdot Lg \cdot (x)\,[(Ex \cdot Lx) \supset x = g]$$

The translation can be read this way: George is an employee and George is late for work, and if any employee is late for work, then that employee is George. This has the same meaning as the original statement.

"All Except"

Statements that use the phrase "All except" are similar to ones that use "No ... except" and "the only," but there is a slight difference. Here is an example:

All the states except Hawaii are located in North America.

The translation has to capture the following points: Hawaii is not located in North America; all the other states are located in North America. If we let Sx: x is a state, Lx: x is located in North America, and h: Hawaii, then the translation is the following:

$$Sh \cdot \sim Lh \cdot (x)\,[(Sx \cdot x \neq h) \supset Lx\,]$$

The translation can be read this way: Hawaii is a state and Hawaii is not located in North America, and if any state is not identical to Hawaii, then that state is located in North America. This has the same meaning as the original statement.

Here is another example:

All the reindeers except Rudolph are allowed to join in reindeer games.

If we let Rx: x is a reindeer, Ax: x is allowed to join in reindeer games, and r: Rudolph, then the translation is the following:

$$Rr \cdot \sim Ar \cdot (x)\,[(Rx \cdot x \neq r) \supset Ax]$$

The translation can be read this way: Rudolph is a reindeer and Rudolph is not allowed to join in reindeer games, and if any reindeer is not identical to Rudolph, then that reindeer is allowed to join in reindeer games. This has the same meaning as the original statement.

Superlatives

There are some statements that contain *superlatives* (a form of an adjective used to indicate the greatest degree of the quality described by the adjective). Here are some common examples of superlatives: *fastest, tallest, oldest, lightest,* and *warmest.* If you say "Death Valley is the hottest place on Earth," then you are claiming that no other place on Earth is hotter than Death Valley. If we let Px: x is a place on Earth, Hxy: x is hotter than y, and d: Death Valley, then the translation is the following:

$$Pd \cdot (x) \, [(Px \cdot x \neq d) \supset Hdx]$$

The translation can be read this way: Death Valley is a place on Earth, and if anything is a place on Earth and not identical to Death Valley, then Death Valley is hotter than it.

Here is another example:

Burj Khalifa is the tallest structure in the world.

If we let Sx: x is a structure in the world, Txy: x is taller than y, and b: Burj Khalifa, then the translation is the following:

$$Sb \cdot (x) \, [(Sx \cdot x \neq b) \supset Tbx]$$

The translation can be read this way: Burj Khalifa is a structure in the world, and if anything is a structure in the world and not identical to Burj Khalifa, then Burj Khalifa is taller than it.

"At Most"

Some ordinary language statements that use the phrase "at most" can be translated without using numerals. Here is an example:

There is at most one president.

Notice that the statement does not assert that there really are any objects that have the property of being a president. The statement asserts only that *if* any objects have that property, then the maximum number of objects is one. The translation will thus include universal quantifiers and the horseshoe. If we let Px: x is a president, then the translation is the following:

$$(x) \, (y) \, [(Px \cdot Py) \supset x = y]$$

It may seem odd that the translation uses two universal quantifiers to translate the phrase "at most one." The idea behind the translation is that if there are two items, then they are identical. The translation can be read this way: For any x and any y, if x is a president, and y is a president, then x is identical to y.

Following this principle, the phrase "at most two" would get translated by using three universal quantifiers. Here is an example:

There are at most two unicorns.

If we let Ux: x is a unicorn, then the translation is the following:

$$(x)\,(y)\,(z)\,[(Ux \cdot Uy \cdot Uz) \supset (x=y \vee x=z \vee y=z)]$$

The translation can be read this way: For any x, any y, and any z, if x is a unicorn, and y is a unicorn, and z is a unicorn, then either x is identical to y, or x is identical to z, or y is identical to z.

"At Least"

Ordinary language statements that use the phrase "at least" can also be translated without using numerals. Here is an example:

There is at least one honest politician.

Statements that use the phrase "at least" assert that the objects having the property in question actually exist. Their translation will include existential quantifiers. However, the translations will use a number of quantifiers equal to the number of objects mentioned in the original statement. Therefore, if we let Hx: x is honest, and Px: x is a politician, then the translation is the following:

$$(\exists x)\,(Hx \cdot Px)$$

We can now translate the statement "There are at least two honest politicians." As before, let Hx: x is honest, and Px: x is a politician:

$$(\exists x)\,(\exists y)\,(Hx \cdot Px \cdot Hy \cdot Py \cdot x \neq y)$$

The translation has to ensure that the two objects are distinct. Therefore, the equal sign with a slash through it is used to indicate that x and y are not identical. The translation can be read this way: There exists an x and there exists a y such that x is an honest politician and y is an honest politician, and x is not identical to y. This has the same meaning as the original statement.

"Exactly"

Ordinary language statements that use the word "exactly" can often be translated as a combination of "at least" and "at most." Here is an example:

There is exactly one pizza in the oven.

The statement is actually asserting two things: There is *at least* one pizza in the oven, and there is *at most* one pizza in the oven. The translation will therefore include both an existential quantifier and a universal quantifier. If we let Px: x is a pizza, and Ox: x is in the oven, then the translation is the following:

$$(\exists x)\,\{Px \cdot Ox \cdot (y)\,[(Py \cdot Oy) \supset x=y]\}$$

We can now translate the statement "There are exactly two pizzas in the oven." As before, let Px: x is a pizza, and Ox: x is in the oven:

$$(\exists x)\,(\exists y)\,\{Px \cdot Ox \cdot Py \cdot Oy \cdot x \neq y \cdot (z)\,[(Pz \cdot Oz) \supset (z = x \vee z = y)]\}$$

The translation has to ensure that the two objects are distinct. In other words, there are *at least* two pizzas. Therefore, the equal sign with a slash through it is used to indicate that x and y are not identical. In addition, the translation has to ensure that there are *at most* two pizzas. The universal quantifier was used for this purpose. The translation can be read this way: There exists an x and there exists a y such that x is a pizza in the oven and y is a pizza in the oven, and x is not identical to y, and for any z, if z is a pizza in the oven, then either z is identical to x or z is identical to y. This has the same meaning as the original statement.

Definite Descriptions

Definite description
Describes an individual person, place, or thing.

Sometimes we refer to a person by *name* (for example, "Matt Groening") and sometimes we refer to the same person by a *description* (for example, "the creator of *The Simpsons*"). This type of description is called a **definite description** because it describes an individual person, place, or thing. Definite descriptions are found in ordinary language. For example, "Matt Groening is the creator of *The Simpsons*." In this example, the statement asserts that one, and only one, person is the creator of *The Simpsons*.

A translation of a statement with a definite description needs to accomplish several tasks. Let's examine these tasks by way of the example:

Matt Groening is the creator of *The Simpsons*.

The translation has to show that *exactly one* person created *The Simpsons*. In order to do this, the translation must show two things: *At least one* person created *The Simpsons*, and *at most one* person created *The Simpsons*. If we let Cxs: x created *The Simpsons*, and m: Matt Groening, then the translation is the following:

$$(\exists x)\,[Cxs \cdot (y)\,(Cys \supset y = x) \cdot x = m\,]$$

The translation can be read this way: There exists an x such that x is the creator of *The Simpsons*, and for any y, if y is the creator of *The Simpsons*, then y is identical to x, and x is identical to m. This has the same meaning as the original statement.

Here is another example:

Shane's mother adores him.

Of course, the sentence does not bother to mention that *exactly one* person is Shane's mother, but the translation has to show just that. In other words, *at least one* person is Shane's mother, and *at most one* person is Shane's mother. If we let Mxs: x is the mother of Shane, and Axs: x adores Shane, then the translation is the following:

$$(\exists x)\,[Mxs \cdot (y)\,(Mys \supset y = x) \cdot Axs]$$

The translation can be read this way: There exists an *x* such that *x* is the mother of Shane, and for any *y*, if *y* is the mother of Shane, then *y* is identical to *x*, and *x* adores Shane. This has the same meaning as the original statement.

Here is another example:

The present king of the United States is tall.

The sentence can be interpreted to mean that there is one and only one present king of the United States and he is tall. Let's explore this interpretation: let *Pxu*: *x* is the present king of the United States, *Tx*: *x* is tall.

$$(\exists x)\, [Pxu \cdot (y)\, (Pyu \supset y = x) \cdot Tx]$$

PROFILES IN LOGIC
Bertrand Russell

It is hard to imagine a philosopher with as long and interesting a life as Bertrand Russell (1872–1970). His influence stretched from logic and philosophy to literature and social issues.

Russell collaborated with Alfred Whitehead in the monumental *Principia Mathematica*, in which they tried to reduce mathematics to formal logic. They thought that all *mathematical truths* could be translated into *logical truths*, and all *mathematical proofs* could be translated as *logical proofs*. Russell was also instrumental in clarifying the basics of predicate logic. He firmly believed that by using logic, philosophers could reveal the *logical form* of ordinary language statements. This would go a long way in resolving many problems caused by the ambiguity and vagueness of ordinary language.

However, Russell's writing was not limited to technical aspects of logic and philosophy. He wrote many successful books that popularized philosophical thinking, with a gift for explaining difficult subjects in clear language. He was awarded the Nobel Prize for Literature in 1950, "in recognition of his varied and significant writings in which he champions humanitarian ideals and freedom of thought."

Russell was not one to hide away in academia. He fought passionately for many social causes throughout his life and was imprisoned for 5 months in 1918 as a result of antiwar protests. Forty-three years later, in 1961, he was again imprisoned for participating in antinuclear protests.

Russell believed that education was essential for social progress: "Education is the key to the new world." We need to understand nature and each other. He was highly critical of superstitious beliefs of any kind. If we rely on evidence instead of superstitions, then we can make social progress: "It is undesirable to believe a proposition when there is no ground whatever for supposing it true."

Russell summed up his life in this statement: "Three passions, simple but overwhelmingly strong, have governed my life: the longing for love, the search for knowledge, and unbearable pity for the suffering of mankind."

This type of statement has important historical significance. The interest of logicians has focused on the truth value of such statements. The philosopher Bertrand Russell proposed one solution: A statement containing a definite description asserts that a specific object exists, and there is only one such object, and the object has the particular characteristic. Under Russell's solution, the foregoing statement is false.

SUMMARY OF IDENTITY TRANSLATIONS	
Simple Identity Statement	
Michelle Obama is Michelle LaVaughn Robinson.	$m = r$
Only	
Only John F. Kennedy was a Catholic U.S. president.	$Cj \cdot Uj \cdot (x)\,[(Cx \cdot Ux) \supset x = j]$
The Only	
The only student who passed the driver's exam is Mary.	$Sm \cdot Pm \cdot (x)\,[(Sx \cdot Px) \supset x = m]$
No . . . Except	
No employee except George is late for work.	$Eg \cdot Lg \cdot (x)\,[(Ex \cdot Lx) \supset x = g]$
All Except	
All the states except Hawaii are located in North America.	$Sh \cdot {\sim} Lh \cdot (x)\,[(Sx \cdot x \neq h) \supset Lx]$
Superlatives	
Death Valley is the hottest place on Earth.	$Pd \cdot (x)\,[(Px \cdot x \neq d) \supset Hdx]$
At Most	
There are at most two unicorns.	$(x)\,(y)\,(z)\,[(Ux \cdot Uy \cdot Uz) \supset (x = y \vee x = z \vee y = z)]$
At Least	
There are at least two honest politicians.	$(\exists x)\,(\exists y)\,(Hx \cdot Px \cdot Hy \cdot Py \cdot x \neq y)$
Exactly	
There are exactly two pizzas in the oven.	$(\exists x)\,(\exists y)\,\{Px \cdot Ox \cdot Py \cdot Oy \cdot x \neq y \cdot (z)\,[(Pz \cdot Oz) \supset (z = x \vee z = y)]\}$
Definite Descriptions	
Shane's mother adores him.	$(\exists x)\,[Mxs \cdot (y)\,(Mys \supset y = x) \cdot Axs\,]$

EXERCISES 9G.1

Translate the following statements into symbolic form.

1. Stephanie Kwolek invented Kevlar.
    (Ixk: x invented Kevlar; s: Stephanie Kwolek)
    Answer: $(\exists x)\,[Ixk \cdot (y)\,(Iyk \supset y = x) \cdot x = s]$

2. There is at most one moon orbiting around Earth.
    (Mx: x is a moon; Ox: x is orbiting around Earth)

3. There is exactly one happy professor.
    (Hx: x is happy; Px: x is a professor)

4. Only Tammy is the editor of the *Daily Scoop*.
    (Ex: x is the editor of the *Daily Scoop*; t: Tammy)

⭐ 5. Joseph Conrad is Jozef Teodor Konrad Korzeniowski.
    (c, k)

6. The only child in the playground is Stella.
   (*Cx*: *x* is a child; *Px*: *x* is in the playground; *s*: Stella)

7. All patients except Lou hate medicine.
   (*Px*: *x* is a patient; *Hx*: *x* hates medicine; *l*: Lou)

8. Antarctica is the coldest continent on Earth.
   (*Px*: *x* is a place on Earth; *Cxy*: *x* is colder than *y*; *a*: Antarctica)

⭐ 9. There is at least one famous scientist.
   (*Fx*: *x* is famous; *Sx*: *x* is a scientist)

10. No president except James Buchanan was a bachelor.
    (*Px*: *x* is a president; *Bx*: *x* is a bachelor; *j*: James Buchanan)

11. George Eliot is Mary Ann Evans.
    (*g*, *m*)

12. All states except Hawaii get snow.
    (*Sx*: *x* is a state; *Wx*: *x* gets snow; *h*: Hawaii)

⭐ 13. There are at least two pirates.
    (*Px*: *x* is a pirate)

14. The youngest Nobel laureate is Lawrence Bragg.
    (*Nx*: *x* is a Nobel laureate; *Yxz*: *x* is younger than *z*; *b*: Lawrence Bragg)

15. Only Egypt has the Sphinx.
    (*Sx*: *x* has the Sphinx; *e*: Egypt)

16. Alexander Fleming discovered penicillin.
    (*Cxp*: *x* discovered penicillin; *f*: Alexander Fleming)

⭐ 17. The only villain in the movie was Krutox.
    (*Vx*: *x* is a villain; *Mx*: *x* is in the movie; *k*: Krutox)

18. No planet in our solar system except Earth is habitable.
    (*Px*: *x* is a planet; *Sx*: *x* is in our solar system; *Hx*: *x* is habitable; *e*: Earth)

19. There are exactly two senators from California.
    (*Sx*: *x* is a senator; *Cx*: *x* is from California)

20. There are at most two senators from New York.
    (*Sx*: *x* is a senator; *Nx*: *x* is from New York)

▷

Video Tutorial: 9G
Exercise #13

Proofs

We know how to translate identity statements. However, a special kind of identity relation needs to be developed in order to construct some proofs. The idea that *anything is identical to itself* is expressed by the **reflexive property**. This idea can be symbolized as follows:

$$(x)\ Ixx$$

Reflexive property
The idea that *anything is identical to itself* is expressed by the reflexive property.

The statement can be read as "For any x, x is identical to itself." Not all relations are reflexive. For example, *nothing can be taller than itself.* This is an example of an **irreflexive relationship**; it can be symbolized as follows:

$$(x) \sim Txx$$

The statement can be read as "For any x, x is not taller than itself." A **nonreflexive relationship** is neither reflexive nor irreflexive. For example, if a person loves someone else, but does not love himself, then the relation is not reflexive. On the other hand, if a person loves someone else, and loves herself, then the relation is not irreflexive.

Irreflexive relationship
An example of an irreflexive relationship is expressed by the statement "Nothing can be taller than itself."

Nonreflexive relationship A relationship that is neither reflexive nor irreflexive.

We can now generate three special rules for proofs using the identity relation (Id).

1. Premise   2. $\Phi = \Psi :: \Psi = \Phi$ 3. $\mathbb{S}\Phi$
   $\Phi = \Phi$ $\underline{\Phi = \Psi}$
                                                                   $\mathbb{S}\Psi$

The identity rules require the introduction of two new symbols: Φ and Ψ. These symbols are used to represent either individual *variables* or individual *constants*.

Rule 1 expresses the *reflexive* property (*anything is identical to itself*). This rule permits the insertion of a self-identity on any line of a proof after a premise.

Rule 2 is a replacement rule. It is a special case of a *symmetrical* relationship used for the identity relation. Rule 2 permits the replacement of $a = b$ with $b = a$, or $a \neq b$ with $b \neq a$.

Finally, Rule 3 is a special case of the *transitive* property. Rule 3 allows us to infer from $a = b$, and $b = c$, that $a = c$.

Let's look at a simple argument that illustrates the *first rule* for identity.

> Anything that is identical to Moby Dick is a whale. It follows that Moby Dick is a whale.

If we let Wx: x is a whale, and m: Moby Dick, then we can translate the argument:

$(x) (x = m \supset Wx)$ / Wm

Here is the completed proof:

1. $(x) (x = m \supset Wx)$ / Wm
2. $m = m \supset Wm$ 1, UI
3. $m = m$ Id
4. Wm 2, 3, MP

Identity Rule 1 permits the insertion of a self-identity on any line of a proof after a premise. Since the rule is applied directly into the proof, no other line number is needed. However, the other two identity rules require reference to a line or lines. Let's examine an argument that illustrates the *second rule* for identity:

> Louisiana is part of the contiguous 48 states. The only island state is Hawaii. Hawaii is not Louisiana. Thus, there is a part of the contiguous 48 states that is not an island state.

If we let *Cx*: *x* is part of the contiguous 48 states, *Sx*: *x* is an island state, *l*: Louisiana, and *h*: Hawaii, then we can translate the argument.

1. *Cl*
2. *Sh* · (*x*)(*Sx* ⊃ *x* = *h*)
3. *h* ≠ *l*   / (∃*x*)(*Cx* · ~ *Sx*)
4. (*x*)(*Sx* ⊃ *x* = *h*)   2, Simp
5. *Sl* ⊃ *l* = *h*   4, UI
6. *l* ≠ *h*   3, Id
7. ~*Sl*   5, 6, MT
8. *Cl* · ~*Sl*   1, 7, Conj
9. (∃*x*)(*Cx* · ~ *Sx*)   8, EG

We used the *second identity rule* to justify line 6. Recall that since *l* ≠ *h* can be used as an abbreviation for ~ (*l* = *h*), we are, therefore justified in deriving line 7.

We can use the identity rules in a conditional proof or an indirect proof. Here is an example that illustrates the *third rule* for identity:

1. ~ (*Cb* ⊃ *Db*)
2. *Ca* ⊃ *Da*   / ~ (*a* = *b*)
    3. *a* = *b*   Assumption (*IP*)
    4. *Cb* ⊃ *Db*   2, 3, Id
    5. ~ (*Cb* ⊃ *Db*) · (*Cb* ⊃ *Db*)   1, 4, Conj
6. ~ (*a* = *b*)   3–5, IP

The justification for line 4 includes a reference to both line 2 and line 3 because it applied the third identity rule. The basic techniques of indirect proof are the same for proofs using the identity rules. Therefore, the IP sequence is discharged in the usual way.

EXERCISES 9G.2

Use the rules of inference to derive the conclusions of the following arguments. You can use conditional proof or indirect proof.

[1] 1. *Fa*
    2. (*y*) (*Fy* ⊃ *Gy*)
    3. *a* = *b*   / *Gb*

Answer:

    1. *Fa*
    2. (*y*) (*Fy* ⊃ *Gy*)
    3. *a* = *b*   / *Gb*
    4. *Fa* ⊃ *Ga*   2, UI
    5. *Ga*   1, 4, MP
    6. *Gb*   3, 5, Id

[2] 1. Ha
   2. $\sim Hb$ / $\sim (a = b)$

[3] 1. Hc
   2. $a = b \supset c = d$
   3. $b = a$ / Hd

[4] 1. $(x) (x = a)$
   2. $(\exists x) (x = b)$ / $b = a$

⭐ [5] 1. Fb
   2. $(x) (Fa \supset x \neq a)$ / $a \neq b$

[6] 1. $(x) (x = a)$
   2. Da / $Db \cdot Dc$

[7] 1. $Ha \cdot Hb$
   2. $(x) (Hx \supset \sim Lxx)$
   3. Lab / $\sim (a = b)$

[8] 1. $Fc \cdot Gca$
   2. $(\exists x) \{(Fx \cdot Gxa) \cdot (y) [(Fy \cdot Gya) \supset y = x] \cdot Hxb\}$ / Hcb

⭐ [9] 1. $\sim Lb$
   2. $(x) [Hx \supset (Lx \cdot x = b)]$ / $\sim Ha$

[10] 1. Ca
    2. $(x) (Cx \supset (\exists y) Dyx)$
    3. $(y) \sim Dyb$ / $\sim (a = b)$

[11] 1. $(x) (x = b \supset Gx)$
    2. $(x) (Fx \supset x = a)$
    3. $a = b$ / $(x) (Fx \supset Gx)$

[12] 1. $(\exists x) (Cx \cdot Dx)$
    2. $(x) (Cx \supset x = a)$
    3. $(x) (Dx \supset x = b)$ / $a = b$

⭐[13] 1. $(Fb \cdot Gab) \cdot (x) [(Fx \cdot Gax) \supset x = b]$
    2. $(\exists x) [(Fx \cdot Gax) \cdot Hx]$ / Hb

[14] 1. $Ca \cdot Fb$
    2. $(x) (Cx \supset Dx)$
    3. $(x) (Fx \supset Gx)$
    4. $b = a$ / $Db \cdot Ga$

[15] 1. $(\exists x) (y) (Hxy \cdot x = a)$
    2. $(x) (\exists y) (Hxy \supset x = y)$ / Haa

[16] 1. $(x) (Gx \supset Hx)$
    2. $Fa \cdot \sim Hb$
    3. $(x) (Fx \supset Gx)$ / $\sim (a = b)$

⭐[17] 1. $(Fb \cdot Hab) \cdot (x) [(Fx \cdot Hax) \supset x = b]$
　　　　2. $(\exists x) \{(Fx \cdot Gx) \cdot (y) [(Fy \cdot Gy) \supset y = x] \cdot Hax\}$　　　$/ (\exists x) \{(Fx \cdot Gx) \cdot (y) [(Fy \cdot Gy) \supset y = x] \cdot x = b\}$

[18] 1. $\sim (x) \sim (Hx \cdot Lx)$
　　　2. $(y) [\sim (y = a) \supset \sim Hy]$
　　　3. $(z) [\sim (z = b) \supset \sim Lz]$　　　　　$/ a = b$

[19] 1. $(Da \cdot \sim Ha) \cdot (x) [(Dx \cdot x \neq a) \supset Hx]$
　　　2. $(Db \cdot \sim Lb) \cdot (x) [(Dx \cdot x \neq b) \supset Lx]$
　　　3. $a \neq b$　　　　　　　　　　　　　　　　$/ La \cdot Hb$

[20] 1. $(\exists x) (y) [(\sim Hxy \supset x = y) \cdot Lx]$　　$/ (x) \{\sim Lx \supset (\exists y) [\sim (y = x) \cdot Hyx]\}$

⭐[21] 1. $Cj \cdot Uj \cdot (x) [(Cx \cdot Ux) \supset x = j]$
　　　　2. Aj　　　　　　　　　　　　　　　　　$/ (x) [(Cx \cdot Ux) \supset Ax]$

[22] 1. $(\exists x)(Fx \cdot Gx \cdot \sim Rx)$
　　　2. $Fm \cdot Gm \cdot (x)[(Fx \cdot Gx) \supset x = m]$
　　　3. $Fh \cdot Rh$　　　　　　　　　　　　　　$/ h \neq m$

[23] 1. $(x)(y)(Lxy \supset \sim Lyx)$
　　　2. $Hb \cdot (x)[(Hx \cdot x \neq b) \supset Lbx]$
　　　3. $(\exists x)\{Hx \cdot (y)[(Hy \cdot y \neq x) \supset Lxy] \cdot Kx\}$　$/ Kb$

[24] 1. $Gj \cdot Kj \cdot (x)[(Gx \cdot Kx) \supset x = j]$
　　　2. $Gr \cdot \sim Kr \cdot (x)[(Gx \cdot x \neq r) \supset Kx]$　　$/ (\exists x) (\exists y) \{(Gx \cdot Gy \cdot x \neq y) \cdot (z)[(Gz \supset$
　　　　　　　　　　　　　　　　　　　　　　　$(z = x \vee z = y)]\}$

⭐[25] 1. $(\exists x) (Hx \cdot \sim Gx)$
　　　　2. $(\exists x) (\exists y) (Gx \cdot Kx \cdot Gy \cdot Ky \cdot x \neq y)$
　　　　3. $(x) (y) (z) [(Kx \cdot Ky \cdot Kz) \supset$　　　$/ \sim (x)(Hx \supset Kx)$
　　　　　　$(x = y \vee x = z \vee y = z)]$

[26] 1. $(\exists x)(\exists y)(Gx \cdot Ox \cdot Gy \cdot Oy \cdot x \neq y)$
　　　2. $(x)(y)(z)[(Px \cdot Ox \cdot Py \cdot Oy \cdot Pz \cdot Oz) \supset (x = y \vee x = z \vee y = z]$
　　　3. $(x)(Gx \supset Px)$　　　　　　　　$/ (\exists x)(\exists y)\{(Px \cdot Ox \cdot Py \cdot Oy \cdot x \neq y \cdot (z)[(Pz \cdot Oz) \supset (z = x \vee z = y)]\}$

[27] 1. $(x)\{Mx \supset [Lx \equiv (\sim Hx \cdot \sim Kx)]\}$
　　　2. $Mn \cdot Hn \cdot (x)[(Mx \cdot Hx) \supset x = n]$
　　　3. $Mc \cdot \sim Kc \cdot Mn \cdot \sim Kn \cdot (x)[(Mx \cdot x \neq c \cdot x \neq n) \supset Kx]$
　　　4. $c \neq n$　　　　　　　　　$/ (\exists x)\{Mx \cdot Lx \cdot (y)[(My \cdot Ly) \supset y = x]\}$

[28] 1. $(x)\{Dx \supset [\sim (Hx \vee Gx) \equiv Kx]\}$
　　　2. $Da \cdot \sim Ga \cdot Db \cdot \sim Gb \cdot (x)[(Dx \cdot x \neq a \cdot x \neq b) \supset Gx]$
　　　3. $Hb \cdot (x)[(Dx \cdot Hx) \supset x = b]$
　　　4. $a \neq b$　　　　　　　　　　$/ (\exists x)\{Dx \cdot Kx \cdot (y)[(Dy \cdot Ky) \supset y = x]\}$

Summary

- Predicate logic: Integrates many of the features of categorical and propositional logic. It combines the symbols associated with propositional logic with special symbols that are used to translate predicates.
- Predicates: The fundamental units in predicate logic. Uppercase letters, called "predicate symbols," are used to symbolize the units.
- The subject of a singular statement is translated using lowercase letters. The lowercase letters, called "individual constants," act as names of individuals.
- Universal quantifier: The symbol that is used to capture the idea that universal statements assert something about every member of the subject class.
- The three lowercase letters x, y, and z, are individual variables.
- Bound variables: Variables governed by a quantifier.
- Statement function: An expression that does not make any universal or particular assertion about anything; therefore, it has no truth value. Statement functions are simply patterns for a statement.
- Free variables: The variables in statement functions; they are not governed by any quantifier.
- Existential quantifier: Formed by putting a backward E in front of a variable, and then placing them both in parentheses.
- Domain of discourse: The set of individuals over which a quantifier ranges.
- When instantiation is applied to a quantified statement, the quantifier is removed, and every variable that was bound by the quantifier is replaced by the same instantial letter.
- Universal instantiation (UI): The rule by which we can validly deduce the substitution instance of a statement function from a universally quantified statement.
- Universal generalization (UG): The rule by which we can validly deduce the universal quantification of a statement function from a substitution instance with respect to the name of any arbitrarily selected individual (subject to restrictions).
- Existential generalization (EG): The rule that permits the valid introduction of an existential quantifier from either a constant or a variable.
- Existential instantiation (EI): The rule that permits giving a name to a thing that exists. The name can then be represented by a constant.
- The four new rules of predicate logic are similar to the eight implication rules, in that they can be applied only to an entire line of a proof (either a premise or a derived line).
- Change of quantifier (CQ): The rule that allows the removal or introduction of negation signs. The rule is a set of four logical equivalences.
- Universal generalization cannot be used within an indented proof sequence if the instantial variable is free in the first line of the sequence.
- A counterexample to an argument is a substitution instance of an argument form that has actually true premises and a false conclusion.

- The finite universe method of demonstrating invalidity assumes a universe, containing at least one individual, to show the possibility of true premises and a false conclusion.
- Monadic predicate: A one-place predicate that assigns a characteristic to an individual.
- Relational predicate: Establishes a connection between individuals.
- Symmetrical relationship: Can be illustrated by the following: If A is married to B, then B is married to A.
- Asymmetrical relationship: Can be illustrated by the following. If A is the father of B, then B is *not* the father of A.
- Nonsymmetrical relationship: When a relationship is neither symmetrical nor asymmetrical. For example: If Kris loves Morgan, then Morgan may or may not love Kris.
- Transitive relationship: Can be illustrated by the following: If A is taller than B, and B is taller than C, then A is taller than C.
- Intransitive relationship: Can be illustrated by the following: If A is the mother of B, and B is the mother of C, then A is *not* the mother of C.
- Nontransitive relationship: Can be illustrated by the following: If Kris loves Morgan and Morgan loves Terry, then Kris may or may not love Terry.
- Identity relation: A binary relation that holds between a thing and itself.
- Definite description: Describes an individual person, place, or thing.
- Reflexive property: The idea that *anything is identical to itself.*
- Irreflexive relationship: Can be illustrated by the following expression: "Nothing can be taller than itself."
- Nonreflexive relationship: A relationship that is neither reflexive nor irreflexive.

KEY TERMS

asymmetrical
  relationship   509
bound variables   476
change of quantifier
  (CQ)   492
definite description   522
domain of discourse   478
existential generalization
  (EG)   484
existential instantiation
  (EI)   485
existential quantifier   477
finite universe
  method   503
free variables   476
identity relation   517

individual constants   474
individual variables   475
instantial letter   482
instantiation   482
intransitive
  relationship   509
irreflexive
  relationship   526
monadic predicate   508
nonreflexive
  relationship   526
nonsymmetrical
  relationship   509
nontransitive
  relationship   509
predicate logic   473

predicate symbols   474
reflexive property   525
relational predicate   508
statement function   476
symmetrical
  relationship   509
transitive
  relationship   509
universal generalization
  (UG)   483
universal instantiation
  (UI)   482
universal quantifier   475

LOGIC CHALLENGE: YOUR NAME AND AGE, PLEASE

Three friends are riding home on a bus when they notice someone they haven't seen for many years. Raul says, "Look, there's *Mary*. She is our age, 26." Renee responds, "Actually, her name is *Marcie*. She is 2 years younger than us." Rachel laughs and says, "Her name is *not Mary*. She is 2 years older than us."

It turns out that Raul, Renee, and Rachel have each made *one true* and *one false* statement regarding the person in question. If so, determine the correct name and age of the person referred to by the three friends.

PART IV

INDUCTIVE LOGIC

Chapter 10

Analogical Arguments

    A. *The Framework of Analogical Arguments*
    B. *Analyzing Analogical Arguments*
    C. *Strategies of Evaluation*

Digital homework exercises for this chapter are available in your instructor's online course. For information on how to access these resources, please visit **www.oup.com/ he/baronett5e.**

A good analogy opens up new ways of thinking. It offers us an unexpected connection between things that arouse our imagination.

> A nation wearing atomic armor is like a knight whose armor has grown so heavy he is immobilized; he can hardly walk, hardly sit his horse, hardly think, hardly breathe. The H-bomb is an extremely effective deterrent to war, but it has little virtue as a weapon of war, because it would leave the world uninhabitable.   E. B. White, "Sootfall and Fallout"

Analogy To draw an analogy is simply to indicate that there are similarities between two or more things.

To draw an **analogy** is simply to indicate that there are similarities between two or more things. You might be more inclined to buy a particular car if you had good experience with a similar model. On the other hand, you might decide *not* to buy that model because of the poor performance of the last car you owned. In each case, we reason that, because two cars share some relevant characteristics, they might also share others.

Analogical reasoning One of the most fundamental tools used in creating an argument. It can be analyzed as a type of inductive argument— it is a matter of probability, based on experience, and it can be quite persuasive.

Analogical reasoning is one of the most fundamental tools used in creating an argument, and it can be quite persuasive. It can be analyzed as a type of inductive argument: It is a matter of probability, based on experience. For example, another car of the same model may not perform the same as yours. However, if an analogical argument is strong, then the probability that the conclusion is true is high.

Analogical reasoning plays a major part in legal decisions. Suppose a court has ruled that college students may not be restrained from speaking out about cuts in scholarships. A different court may conclude, by analogical reasoning, that the same group cannot be stopped from holding a peaceful rally because a rally is similar to speaking. An argument from an older legal decision, like this one, is said to appeal to *precedent*. When spelled out in detail, the analogy will identify those respects in which the older decision and the current one are alike. (We will return to legal arguments in the next chapter.) This chapter explores how analogical arguments work and how they can be evaluated.

A. THE FRAMEWORK OF ANALOGICAL ARGUMENTS

We know that ordinary language arguments often require rewriting, and that in turn requires a close reading to determine the premises and conclusion. We will construct a general framework that can guide our analysis and evaluation of analogical reasoning.

Every analogical argument has three defining features. First, it must refer to characteristics that two (or more) things have in common. Second, it must identify a new characteristic in one of the things being compared. Finally, it concludes that the other thing in the comparison probably has the new characteristic as well. (In analogical arguments, the things being compared are also referred to as *analogues*.) The framework for an **analogical argument** translates these features into premises and a conclusion:

> **Analogical argument** The argument lists the characteristics that two (or more) things have in common and concludes that the things being compared probably have some other characteristic in common.

ANALOGICAL ARGUMENTS: A FRAMEWORK

Premise 1: X and Y have characteristics a, b, c . . . in common.
Premise 2: X has characteristic k.
Therefore, *probably* Y has characteristic k.

Example 1

A father buys his son, Mike, a shirt that (naturally) the son does not like. The father justifies his decision:

> I bought the shirt for you because your friend Steve has one like it, and you guys wear your hair the same, wear the same kind of pants and shoes, and like the same music and television programs. Since Steve must like his shirt, I thought that you would like the shirt, too.

If we let S = *Steve*, M = *Mike*, a = *you guys wear your hair the same*, b = *wear the same kind of pants*, c = *shoes*, d = *the same music*, e = *television programs*, and f = *the shirt*, then the father's analogical reasoning can be displayed as follows:

> Premise 1: S and M have a, b, c, d, and e in common.
> Premise 2: S likes f.
> Therefore, *probably* M will like f.

The force of an analogical argument works through the two premises, and each plays a specific role. Premise 1 takes two different objects (in this case, people) and shows how they are similar by listing certain characteristics that the two objects have in common. If premise 1 does its job effectively, then we should begin to see that the two objects share certain characteristics:

Premise 1

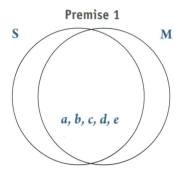

The circles represent the two people referred to in the argument (Steve and Mike). The lowercase letters stand for the five characteristics that they have in common, and these are placed in the area where the two circles overlap.

At this point, premise 2 is introduced to make a claim regarding one of the two objects: S has a new characteristic that was not listed in premise 1. In other words, the two premises work together. Premise 1 shows that S and M have several characteristics in common (*a*, *b*, *c*, *d*, and *e*). Premise 2 points out that S has an additional characteristic, namely *f*, which is somewhere in the S circle. The conclusion is that M very probably has characteristic *f*, too.

Premise 1, if effective, persuades us that S and M share certain characteristics. Premise 2 places the *f* inside S, as a matter of objective fact. The conclusion asserts that *f* should be applied to M as well. The goal is for us to accept this picture:

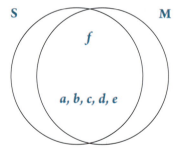

According to the picture, the conclusion is true. However, we can show that it is *possible* for the conclusion to be false because *f* could actually be placed in at least two different locations:

What Premise 2 Really Says

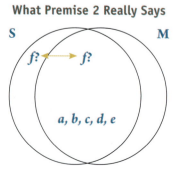

Always remember that an analogical argument does *not* claim that S and M are identical, but only that they are similar. Premise 2 merely states that *f* is in S, but it is possible that characteristic *f* is not in M. Given this, the conclusion might be false, even if the premises are assumed to be true, as indicated by the next picture:

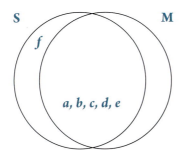

In sum, an analogical argument can claim, at best, only that it is *probable* that *f* is in M, and this probability rests heavily on the first premise and its relevance to the conclusion. *The way to assess the strength of an analogical argument is to determine the degree of support that the first premise provides for the conclusion*, as we will see in the rest of this chapter. For now, though, we will continue applying the general framework to reveal the reasoning behind analogical arguments.

Example 2

Analogical arguments can be about people, places, times, and animate or inanimate objects. Let's look at an example involving defective tires.

> *Premise 1*: The steel-belted tires that have been involved in blowouts (T) and the steel-belted tires on your automobile (Y) have the following attributes in common: *a*, same size; *b*, same tread design; *c*, same manufacturer; *d*, same place of manufacture; *e*, on same type of vehicle; and *f*, same recommended tire pressure.
> *Premise 2*: The steel-belted tires involved in blowouts (T) have been determined to be *g*, defective.
> *Conclusion*: Therefore, *probably* the steel-belted tires on your automobile (Y) are *g*, defective.

First, we use the framework for analogical arguments to extract the relevant information:

> Premise 1: T and Y have *a, b, c, d, e,* and *f,* in common.
> Premise 2: T has *g.*
> Therefore, *probably* Y has *g.*

The force of the analogical argument works through the two premises. The idea is to get us to agree that the two things being compared share several characteristics. The first premise can be depicted as follows:

Premise 1

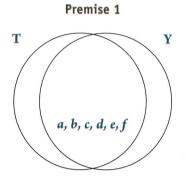

Premise 2 introduces a new characteristic attached to T. As in our earlier example, we can actually draw two different pictures of the argument:

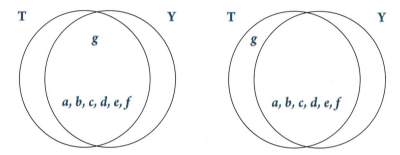

Premise 1, if effective, persuades us that T and Y share certain characteristics. Premise 2 places the *g* inside T (objective fact). However, it is possible for the conclusion to be false, even if the premises are assumed to be true. Since premise 2 merely states that *g* is in T, it could turn out that *g* is not in Y. How likely is it that *g* is in Y? In other words, how strong is the analogical argument? The rest of this chapter will concentrate on specific techniques for determining the strength of analogical arguments.

EXERCISES 10A

Self-Practice
Questions

Reveal the framework of the analogical argument in each example by determining what would go in the premises and the conclusion.

1. We know that humans are capable of highly abstract thinking by their ability to understand and use complex concepts. Recent research on dolphins has revealed that dolphins have brains almost identical in size to humans. Dolphins have a body size nearly identical to humans. Experiments have shown that dolphins can understand verbal commands and sign language instructions, which humans can do quite easily. Like humans, dolphins have a strong sense of self-identity, because it has been shown that dolphins can recognize themselves in mirrors and when shown their image on a TV screen. Therefore, it is highly probable that dolphins are capable of highly abstract thinking.

Answer:

> *Premise 1:* X, humans, and Y, dolphins, have the following attributes in common: *a*, dolphins have brains almost identical in size to humans; *b*, dolphins have a body size nearly identical to humans; *c*, dolphins can understand verbal commands and sign language instructions, which humans can do quite easily; *d*, like humans, dolphins have a strong sense of self-identity, because it has been shown that dolphins can recognize themselves in mirrors and when shown their image on a TV screen.
>
> *Premise 2:* We know that X, humans, are *e*, capable of highly abstract thinking by their ability to understand and use complex concepts.
>
> *Conclusion:* Therefore, it is highly probable that Y, dolphins, are *e*, capable of highly abstract thinking.

The structure of the argument can now be displayed:

> X and Y have *a, b, c,* and *d* in common.
> <u>X has *e*.</u>
> Therefore, *probably* Y has *e*.

2. Chimpanzees are certainly capable of feeling pain. They will avoid negative feedback (electrical shocks) in a laboratory setting when given the opportunity to do so. When one chimpanzee is injured, others will recognize the pain behavior and try to comfort and help the injured member of the group. Chimpanzees that have been given pain-relief medicine soon after an injury connect the medicine to the relief from pain, because when injured again they will give the sign for the medicine. Humans display all of these behaviors as well. There are legal and ethical constraints that protect humans from experimentation without their consent. Therefore, chimpanzees should be afforded the same protections.

3. Bitcoin was created in 2009 by Satoshi Nakamoto (almost certainly a false name) in order to be anonymous currency, easy to use, self-regulating and free from any central authority. Instead of relying on a government or bank issuer, the bitcoin system is entirely powered by users, transferred via unique, anonymous IDs. One way to look at it is to think of bitcoin as being similar to vintage baseball cards and comic books. There are a finite number of these items in existence. Furthermore, as interest in owning them rises, the amount someone would pay for them goes up. In addition, these items are not quite legal tender for all debts, public and private. Also, if there is a perceived value, then a card, comic, or bitcoin can be used to "buy" some goods. Since vintage baseball cards and comic books have no real-world value other than what people agree to, it follows that bitcoin have no real-world value other than what people agree to.

> Adapted from Devin Coldewey, "Bitcoin: The Internet's Secret Currency
> Makes Its First Public Appearances," *NBC News*

4. England and Japan have much lower overall crime rates than the United States. The United States has 20 times more homicides than England and 30 times more than Japan. All three countries have large populations, are highly industrialized, and are in the top five in terms of economic strength among the world's countries. In addition, all three countries are democracies, have separate branches of government, and a large prison system. But England and Japan have strict gun control legislation. If the United States wants to lower its homicide rate, then it has to pass strict gun control legislation.

Video Tutorial: 10A
Exercise #5

★ 5. I am a junior at Lincoln Heights High School. My parents make me do all the housework, like taking out the trash, laundry, dishes, vacuuming, washing the car, and cleaning up the rooms. My kid brother, who is in fifth grade, doesn't have to do anything. But he eats the same food as me, has his own bedroom like me, and gets the same amount of allowance as me. If I have to do so much work, then he should, too.

6. The recent unearthing of some bones in central China has been the source of much controversy. Some experts are claiming that it is the oldest evidence of a human ever discovered, because it predates the next earliest fossil by 20,000 years. The experts claim that the cranial area is the same as the earliest agreed upon fossil of a human. The jawbone matches human fossils of a later date. Crude tools were found near the bones. The teeth match the later human fossils. If the oldest recognized bones have been declared to be human, then these must be human as well.

7. The government gives billions of dollars to big farming companies *not* to grow crops, in order to keep prices stable. Thus consumers are protected—at least so say the farmers. I run a business. I have a small area where I raise worms. Like big businesses, I too have expenses. I pay for help, buy equipment, purchase supplies, suffer losses, pay taxes, pay utilities, and am subject to the laws of supply and demand. If they can get money for not growing crops, then I would be more than willing to get money from the government, so I can stop growing those slimy worms!

Video Tutorial: 10A
Exercise #8

8. A computer program developed by professors at Carnegie-Mellon University beat Garry Kasparov when he was the world chess champion. Computer programs are used to help diagnose diseases and predict economic trends, the winners in horse races, and other sports. They can calculate and analyze, in a few seconds, problems that no human could do in a lifetime. Advanced computer programs have demonstrated the ability to learn from experience and adapt to new situations. They can understand language and communicate concepts and ideas. Any human who can do these things is considered to possess consciousness. Some computer programs should be given the same designation.

★ 9. Fruit has many attributes that are good for your health. Fruit provides energy, roughage, sugars, citric acid, vitamins, and minerals. The new candy bar, Chocolate Peanut Gooies, provides energy, roughage, sugar, citric acid, vitamins, and minerals. How can it not be good for your health too?

10. *Planet X24: Our Last Hope*, the new movie by director Billy Kuberg, has just been released. It's his fourth sci-fi film. His other three had newcomers in the starring roles, were based on novels by Joel Francis Hitchmann, opened in the summer, and had huge marketing tie-ins. This new movie has an unknown actor in the lead role, is based on a novel by Joel Francis Hitchmann, is opening in the summer, and has huge marketing tie-ins. Each of Kuberg's first three sci-fi films grossed over $550 million. I predict this new film will gross about the same amount.

11. I already ate apples, oranges, peaches, and cherries from her fruit stand, and I enjoyed all of them. I am going to try her pears. I am sure I will enjoy them.

12. I took Philosophy 101, 102, 103, and 104 and got an A in each course. I am going to take Philosophy 105, so I expect to get an A in that course as well.

⭐ 13. Evidence indicates that adding fertilizer helps fruit trees and vegetable plants to grow better. Seaweed is a plant. Therefore, adding fertilizer should help seaweed grow better.

▷

Video Tutorial: 10A
Exercise #13

14. "Being a four-star commander in a combat theater is like being a combination of Bill Gates and Jay-Z, with enormous firepower added," said Thomas E. Ricks, the author of "The Generals." The commanders who lead the nation's military services and those who oversee troops around the world enjoy an array of perquisites befitting a billionaire, including executive jets, palatial homes, drivers, security guards and aides to carry their bags, press their uniforms and track their schedules in 10-minute increments. Their food is prepared by gourmet chefs. If they want music with their dinner parties, their staff can summon a string quartet or a choir. Many people claim that perhaps there is something about a sense of entitlement and of having great power that skews the judgment of rich and famous civilians, and this tends to become corrosive over time upon how they live their life. If so, then this may be true of military commanders.

Adapted from Rajiv Chandrasekaran and Greg Jaffe, "Petraeus Scandal Puts
Four-Star General Lifestyle Under Scrutiny," *The Washington Post*

15. A study by U.S. and Korean researchers, including Harvard Business School's Jordan Siegel, found that if you operate in a sexist country full of educated, talented women, it makes good business sense to tap them for management roles. . . . It's depressing how governments don't realize that failing to harness half of populations holds back growth. Planes that need two engines to fly don't take off when one isn't working, so why do nations think they can thrive in our madly competitive world with one engine?

William Pesek, "Sexism That Irks Goldman Is Boon for Savvy CEOs"

16. You expect far too much of a first sentence. Think of it as analogous to a good country breakfast: what we want is something simple, but nourishing to the imagination. Hold the philosophy; hold the adjectives; just give us a plain subject and verb and perhaps a wholesome, nonfattening adverb or two.

Larry McMurtry, *Some Can Whistle*

17. Many orthodox people speak as though it were the business of sceptics to disprove received dogmas rather than of dogmatists to prove them. This is, of course, a mistake. If I were to suggest that between the Earth and Mars there is a china teapot revolving about the sun in an elliptical orbit, nobody would be able to disprove my assertion provided I were careful to add that the teapot is too small to be revealed even by our most powerful telescopes. But if I were to go on to say that, since my assertion cannot be disproved, it is an intolerable presumption on the part of human reason to doubt it, I should rightly be thought to be talking nonsense. If, however, the existence of such a teapot were affirmed in ancient books, taught as the sacred truth every Sunday, and instilled into the minds of children at school, hesitation to believe in its existence would become a mark of eccentricity and entitle the doubter to the attentions of the psychiatrist in an enlightened age or of the Inquisitor in an earlier time. It is customary to suppose that, if a belief is widespread, there must be something reasonable about it. I do not think this view can be held by anyone who has studied history.   Bertrand Russell, "Is There a God?"

18. Students should be allowed to look at their textbooks during examinations. After all, surgeons have X-rays to guide them during an operation, lawyers have briefs to guide them during a trial, carpenters have blueprints to guide them when they are building a house. Why, then, shouldn't students be allowed to look at their textbooks during an examination?   Max Shulman, "Love Is a Fallacy"

19. Like other colonial peoples, adolescents are economically dependent on the dominant society, and appear in its accounts as the beneficiaries of its philanthropy. Like them also, adolescents are partly dependent because of their immature stage of development, but even more because of restrictions placed upon them by the dominant society. . . . Nevertheless, "teen-agers" do have money. . . . They scrounge it from home or earn it at odd times, and this, too, contributes to their colonial status. The "teen-age" market is big business. We all share an economic interest in the dependency of the "teen-ager." The school is interested in keeping him off the streets and in custody. Labor is interested in keeping him off the labor market. Business and industry are interested in seeing that his tastes become fads and in selling him specialized junk that a more mature taste would reject. Like a dependent native, the "teen-ager" is encouraged to be economically irresponsible because his sources of income are undependable and do not derive from his personal qualities.   Edgar Z. Friedenberg, *Coming of Age in America*

B. ANALYZING ANALOGICAL ARGUMENTS

Four criteria can be used to analyze the strength of an analogical argument. Each involves looking specifically at the first premise. We look at the *number of things* referred to in the premise, the *variety* of those things, the *number of characteristics* claimed to be similar, and the *relevance* of those characteristics.

First, the strength of an analogical argument is related to the *number of things* referred to in the first premise. A large number of examples of the same kind, with the same item, will serve to establish the conclusion with a much higher degree of probability than if the conclusion were based on one instance alone. In example 1 before, if the father had compared his son to a number of friends rather than just to Steve, and if all the friends had worn the same shirt, then this would increase the probability that the conclusion is true. In example 2 before, presumably an adequate number of instances of defective tires have been examined to make the conclusion probably true.

There is rarely a simple numerical ratio between the number of instances and the probability of the conclusion. For example, if one analogical argument refers to two instances, and a second refers to ten instances, we *cannot* claim that the conclusion in the second is exactly five times as probable as the first.

Second, the strength of an analogical argument is related to the *variety of things* referred to in the first premise. In example 1, if the father could show that a lot of people of different ages seem to be wearing the shirt in question, then this would seem to make the shirt desirable to more people, and it might raise the probability that Mike would like the shirt. In example 2, if it can be shown that defective tires were made in many locations and at different times, then this variety in the place and time of manufacture would increase the likelihood that defective tires are on your automobile. This additional evidence would increase the probability that the conclusion is true.

Third, the strength of an analogical argument is related to the *number of character-istics* that are claimed to be similar between the things being compared. All things being equal, the greater the number of characteristics listed in the first premise the more probable the conclusion will be. In example 1, premise 1 lists five characteristics. Example 2 lists six characteristics in its first premise. This does not mean that the conclusion of the second argument is 20% more likely to be true. There is no simple mathematical formula for judging the probability of the conclusion based on the number of characteristics in the first premise.

Fourth, the strength of an analogical argument is related to the *relevance of the characteristics* referred to in the first premise. Some characteristics may have no real bearing on the analogy, and the weight of each characteristic has to be determined on its own merits. In fact, relevance is the single most important criterion on which to judge the strength of an analogical argument. An argument based on a single *relevant* characteristic between two things will be far more convincing than an argument based on ten *irrelevant* characteristics between ten things. However, determining relevance is not always easy. This is why it is important to make arguments by anal-ogy strong enough to withstand scrutiny.

The relevance of any particular characteristic in the premises depends on how it is related to the conclusion of an argument. Take, for example, the color of a car:

A. My Ford Fusion Hybrid and your Hummer are the same color. My vehicle aver-ages 40 miles per gallon of gasoline. Therefore, your vehicle will probably average 40 miles per gallon of gasoline.

B. My Toyota Camry and your Hyundai Sonata are the same color. My daughter likes the color of my car. Therefore, my daughter will probably like the color of your car, too.

In A, the characteristic that the two vehicles have in common (the color) is not relevant to gas mileage, so it does not offer support for the conclusion. However, in B, the characteristic that the two cars have in common (the color) *is* relevant to whether the daughter will like the color, so it does offer support for the conclusion.

Relevance is often the most crucial factor, even when the things being compared have several things in common. Here are two more examples:

> **C.** My sister's Chevrolet Volt Hybrid and her boyfriend's Dodge Ram pickup truck are the same color, they were both bought on the same day, and they have the same kind of financing deal. My sister's car averages 50 miles per gallon of gasoline. Therefore, her boyfriend's truck will probably average 50 miles per gallon of gasoline.
>
> **D.** My father's Toyota Prius and my mother's Honda Civic Hybrid have the same engine size. My father's car averages 48 miles per gallon of gasoline. Therefore, my mother's car will probably average 48 miles per gallon of gasoline.

In C, three characteristics are listed in the first premise, while only one characteristic is referred to in the first premise of D. But since none of the three characteristics in C are relevant to gas mileage, together they offer no support for the conclusion. However, in D, the single characteristic referred to in the first premise is relevant to gas mileage, so by itself it offers some support for the conclusion.

Of course, in another argument engine size may not be relevant. This is why we must be careful to assess each characteristic in its relationship to a particular argument. Note, too, that some characteristics might be relevant and others might not. Again, each characteristic has to be evaluated in relation to the argument in which it appears.

Criteria for Analyzing Analogical Arguments

1. The strength of an analogical argument is related to the *number of things* referred to in the first premise. A large number of examples of the same kind, with the same item, establish the conclusion with a much higher degree of probability than would be the case if the conclusion were based on one instance alone.
2. The strength of an analogical argument is related to the *variety of things* referred to in the first premise. If the first premise shows some variety among the things being compared, then it might make the conclusion more likely.
3. The strength of an analogical argument is related to the *number of characteristics* that are claimed to be similar between the things being compared. All things being equal, the greater the number of characteristics listed in the first premise, the more probable the conclusion.
4. The strength of an analogical argument is related to the *relevance of the characteristics* referred to in the first premise. These characteristics must carry weight when it comes to deciding the probability of the conclusion.

EXERCISES 10B

I. You have already revealed the framework of the analogical arguments in Exercises 10A. Now analyze those same arguments by applying the four criteria for the strength of the argument: (a) Determine the number of things referred to in the first premise; (b) assess the variety of things referred to in the first premise; (c) list the number of characteristics that are claimed to be similar between the things being compared; (d) determine the relevance of the characteristics.

Refer back to Exercises 10A for the exercises. The first exercise and a solution are provided here:

Self-Practice
Questions

1. We know that humans are capable of highly abstract thinking by their ability to understand and use complex concepts. Recent research on dolphins has revealed that dolphins have brains almost identical in size to humans. Dolphins have a body size nearly identical to humans. Experiments have shown that dolphins can understand verbal commands and sign language instructions, which humans can do quite easily. Like humans, dolphins have a strong sense of self-identity, because it has been shown that dolphins can recognize themselves in mirrors and when shown their image on a TV screen. Therefore, it is highly probable that dolphins are capable of highly abstract thinking.

Answer:

1. (a) *Number of entities:* Dolphins and humans (we are not told how many dolphins were studied).

   (b) *Variety of instances:* We are not given specific information on the age, sex, or species of the dolphins studied.

   (c) *Number of characteristics:* Brain size; body size; ability to understand verbal commands; ability to understand sign language; strong sense of self-identity.

   (d) *Relevancy:* Of all the characteristics referred to, body size seems the least relevant to the question of highly abstract thinking.

Video Tutorial: 10B
Exercise #8

II. For the following argument by analogy, consider alternative scenarios. For each of these, decide whether it *strengthens, weakens,* or *is irrelevant to* the original argument. Do each one independently of the others.

Imagine that an auto mechanic says the following:

> Your car has ABS brakes manufactured by Skidmore Brake Company. Unfortunately, that company is no longer in business. Research has shown that the brakes made by that company failed to work in at least 1000 cases. The brakes failed in cars, trucks, and SUVs. Therefore, I recommend that you replace your ABS brake system.

1. What if there had been only ten recorded cases of brake failure with those particular brakes?

Answer: Weakens the argument. The number of entities in the premises is now decreased substantially.

2. What if the recorded cases of failure had all been in cars and you have a truck?

3. What if the majority of the recorded cases of brake failure involved red cars, but your car is blue?

4. What if none of the recorded cases of failure involved SUVs, and you have an SUV?

★ 5. What if the brakes in your car are only 1 month old?

C. STRATEGIES OF EVALUATION

Three strategies can further help determine the strength of analogical arguments. We look in turn at *disanalogies, counteranalogies,* and the *unintended consequences* of analogies.

Disanalogies

The first strategy involves the obvious fact that any two distinct things have differences between them. These differences can be exploited and, if significant, can severely weaken any analogical argument. To point out differences between two things is to reveal **disanalogies**.

As we saw earlier, the function of premise 1 of an analogical argument is to point out similarities between the two things. Disanalogies can affect the degree of overlap between the two things in question by acknowledging significant and relevant differences between them. If effective, this strategy lowers the probability that the characteristic attached to the thing referred to in premise 2 is also attached to the thing referred to in the conclusion. In example 1, the son Mike could point out differences between himself and Steve. These differences might include the following: *p*, the color of shirts they wear; *q*, the logos (or lack of logos) on the shirts they typically wear; *r*, the food they like; and *v*, the movies they like. Pointing out the disanalogies (differences) deemphasizes the overlap between the two, as illustrated here:

> **Disanalogies** To point out differences between two things.

Disanalogies and Overlap

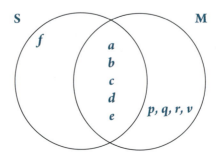

Notice that the strategy of pointing out disanalogies does not directly affect the original characteristics (*a* through *e*) listed in premise 1. Those characteristics remain in the area where S and M overlap. Rather, the new picture reveals that, *if* we can effectively point out relevant differences between S and M, then even if Steve likes his shirt, *f*, the probability, according to our new picture, is that *f* is *not* in M (Mike does not like the shirt). If we look back at the overlap *without* disanalogies, we can see how disanalogies can reduce the likelihood that the conclusion is true.

Overlap Without Disanalogies

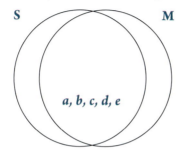

PROFILES IN LOGIC
David Hume

The ideas of David Hume (1711–76) echo throughout modern philosophy, but one of his most memorable contributions to logic concerns reasoning by analogy. In his *Dialogues Concerning Natural Religion*, Hume dissects a famous analogical argument. The *design argument*—which many people still use today—starts with the idea that objects like watches could not have randomly assembled themselves. Anything so orderly and intricate had to be designed and built for a specific purpose by an intelligent creature. In the same way, observation of the universe reveals an orderly design and purpose. It follows by analogy that it was designed and built for a specific purpose by an intelligent creature, namely God.

Hume provides several criticisms of the design argument. First, he points out, watches and other man-made objects are very different from much of the universe,

which in fact exhibits great disorder and randomness. These flaws in the analogy (relevant disanalogies) weaken the analogical argument.

Second, Hume offered a counteranalogy. He points out that some forms of animal life and vegetation do reveal order, but they are still the result of natural processes without any intentional intelligent design or purpose.

Third, Hume notes, the argument by design has unintended consequences. Since we human designers of watches are finite creatures, then probably God is finite; since we are imperfect, then perhaps God is imperfect; since groups of designers and builders create watches, then many gods were needed to create our universe. Since humans can create imperfect products, perhaps our universe "is a botched creation of an inferior deity who afterwards abandoned it, ashamed of the poor quality of the product."

Counteranalogy

Counteranalogy
A new, competing argument—one that compares the thing in question to something else.

A second type of evaluation relies on a **counteranalogy**—a new, competing argument—one that compares the thing in question to *something else*. This new argument may lead to a conclusion that contradicts the conclusion of the original argument. In example 1, for instance, suppose that Mike's mother insists she predicted all along that Mike would *not* like the shirt his father bought. Her reasoning might run like this:

> Mike (M) is more like Nick (N) because they both wear the same kind of pants (*a*); like the same music (*b*); like the same television programs (*c*); like the same colors (*d*); wear the same kinds of logos (*e*); like the same kinds of food (*f*); and like the same movies (*g*). Nick does *not* like that kind of shirt (*h*); therefore, probably Mike will not like it.

This completely new, competing analogical argument is pictured here:

The Counteranalogy

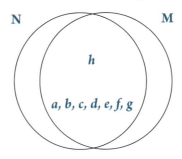

A counteranalogy, appropriately enough, *counters* the original analogical argument. In fact, there is no limit to the number of counteranalogies we can create from a given analogy. Of course, we are still faced with the prospect of weighing, judging, and evaluating the competing strengths of two analogies. And all the counteranalogies, as well as the original analogy, are subject to disanalogies as well.

Unintended Consequences

Unintended consequences
If you can show that something unacceptable to a person presenting an analogy follows from that analogy, then you put that person in a difficult position.

The third strategy of evaluating an analogy is the discovery of **unintended consequences**: If you can show that something unacceptable to a person presenting an analogy follows from that analogy, then you put that person in a difficult position. We say that the person has "painted himself into a corner." The discovery forces the person either to accept the unintended consequence or to weaken the original analogy. For example, suppose Mike says the following:

> O.K., Dad, you are correct; Steve and I are very much alike. But since Steve likes smoking cigarettes, you won't mind if I start smoking, too, right?

The father might respond by saying the following:

> Steve's parents don't seem to care what he does, but I care what you do. Besides, Steve's parents are rich and can give him more spending money than we can give you. Also, Steve doesn't seem too interested in personal grooming and the odor

associated with smoking cigarettes, but you are very particular about the scent you give off. Therefore, I do mind if you smoke.

Mike's father sounds reasonable, but he is really pointing out disanalogies. He is thus effectively weakening his own original analogical argument by admitting there are relevant differences between Steve and Mike.

Combining Strategies

Let's see how disanalogies, counteranalogies, and unintended consequences can affect our analysis of a more extended analogical argument—the kind that appear in the media nearly everyday. Suppose a political commentator makes the following argument:

> The United States has the right to defeat and to destroy the Islamic State of Iraq and Syria (ISIS). If your neighbors threatened your property, stockpiled dangerous weapons, disparaged our form of government and our social customs, threatened our very way of life, and killed innocent people, then our government is justified in going into their house and stopping them—by force, if necessary. The ISIS terrorists have threatened several countries, stockpiled dangerous weapons, disparaged our form of government and our social customs, threatened our very way of life, and killed innocent people, including some of our citizens. Therefore, we are justified in going into Syria and eliminating ISIS by force.

Let X = *a family living in the United States*, I = *Islamic State of Iraq and Syria*, a = *threatened their neighbor's property*, b = *stockpiled dangerous weapons*, c = *disparaged our form of government*, d = *disparaged our social customs*, e = *threatened our very way of life*, f = *killed innocent people*, and g = *we would feel justified in going in and stopping them by force*. We can then reconstruct the argument:

> X and I have *a, b, c, d, e*, and *f* in common.
> <u>In the case of X, *g*.</u>
> Therefore, in the case of I, *probably g*.

We can now draw the analogical argument:

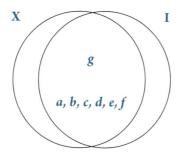

On the same TV program, another talking head might respond by saying this:

> You are comparing apples to oranges. A family living in the United States is subject to the laws of this country; this is not the case with foreign countries. We have no right to impose, nor can we enforce, our laws on another country.

> A threat by one U.S. citizen on another is grounds for immediate action by our government, so if your neighbor threatens your property, you are afforded the protection of our government. Although a threat or an action by a terrorist group should cause us to be ready for any eventuality, it does not give us the right to invade a sovereign nation such as Syria.

This commentator is pointing out differences and is using disanalogies to weaken the original analogy. Of course, we should pay close attention to the relevance of the characteristics in both the original analogy and the disanalogy to see how much weight we should give to each. We can then determine for ourselves the strength of the original analogy.

A different commentator might respond like this:

> Syria is more like Vietnam when we first got involved. Vietnam was a divided country, at war with itself, with one side asking for our help and the other side telling us to keep out. North Vietnam received military and financial assistance from the Soviet Union, while Russia has argued that we have no right to invade Syria today. We suffered too many deaths and wounded in Vietnam. We already know how costly the war in Iraq has been, and any invasion of Syria will result in many more deaths and wounded. We stayed too long in Vietnam and Iraq and, in the end, the results were not what we had hoped for. This will happen again in Syria. Many people felt that we should not have gone into Vietnam in the first place. Therefore, we are not justified in invading Syria.

This commentator is using a counteranalogy to show that a completely different conclusion can be reached. As we have seen, a counteranalogy is subject to the three strategies of evaluation: (1) its strength can be questioned by pointing out disanalogies between Vietnam and Syria; (2) unintended consequences of the analogy might be discovered; and (3) a new counteranalogy could also be constructed.

A final commentator might have this to say:

> I agree that we are justified in invading Syria to eliminate ISIS by force. Of course, this means that countries such as Russia and China will not join in any coalition to help us defeat ISIS. Some countries may even sever economic and diplomatic ties with us, as they have forcefully repeated. In turn, this will make our economy suffer. But that's the price we have to be willing to pay for protecting ourselves.

This illustrates the strategy of pointing out some unintended consequences of the analogy. Of course the original talking head might find these results acceptable; but if the last commentator is wise enough, and knows the opponent well, then she is sure to think of consequences that she knows her opponent will find unacceptable.

STRATEGIES FOR EVALUATING ANALOGICAL ARGUMENTS
Disanalogy: To point out the *differences* between the two (or more) things referred to in the first premise of an analogical argument.
Counteranalogy: To create a completely new, competing, analogical argument.
Unintended consequences of an analogy: To point to something that is a direct result of the original analogy, but that is unacceptable to the person presenting that analogy.

EXERCISES 10C

You revealed the framework of the analogical arguments in Exercises 10A. Next, you analyzed those arguments in Exercises 10B. Now, you are in position to conclude your evaluation of those arguments by using the three strategies illustrated in this section: (a) point out any relevant disanalogies between the things being compared; (b) construct a counteranalogy; and (c) determine any unintended consequences of the analogy.

Self-Practice Questions

Refer back to Exercises 10A for the exercises. The first exercise and a solution are provided here:

1. We know that humans are capable of highly abstract thinking by their ability to understand and use complex concepts. Recent research on dolphins has revealed that dolphins have brains almost identical in size to humans. Dolphins have a body size nearly identical to humans. Experiments have shown that dolphins can understand verbal commands and sign language instructions, which humans can do quite easily. Like humans, dolphins have a strong sense of self-identity, because it has been shown that dolphins can recognize themselves in mirrors and when shown their image on a TV screen. Therefore, it is highly probable that dolphins are capable of highly abstract thinking.

Answer:

(a) *Disanalogies:* Humans display complex speech patterns and can create completely new forms. Mathematical skills, which are taken as a hallmark of abstract thinking, are not mentioned as one of the dolphins' abilities; poetry, art, music and other aesthetic abilities have not been shown to exist in dolphins.

Video Tutorial: 10C
Exercise #8

(b) *Counteranalogy:* Dolphins are more like dogs. They both have highly sensitive senses of smell; they both have extraordinary sensitivity to sounds that humans cannot detect; they both can learn to react correctly to certain signs or verbal commands; they both seem to bond well with humans; they both are able to learn tricks of performance. Since there is no evidence that dogs are capable of highly abstract thinking, dolphins probably do not have that ability either.

(c) *Unintended consequences:* If dolphins are capable of highly abstract thinking, then perhaps they should be afforded rights similar to humans. They should not be kept and raised in captivity and be subject to experiments like those mentioned in the article. The researchers should obtain informed consent agreements from the dolphins before embarking on any further experiments.

Summary

Study Materials

- To draw an analogy is simply to indicate that there are similarities between two or more things.
- Analogical reasoning is one of the most fundamental tools used in creating an argument. It can be analyzed as a type of inductive argument—it is a matter of probability, based on experience, and it can be quite persuasive.

- An analogical argument is analyzed by revealing the general framework of the argument. The argument lists the characteristics that two (or more) things have in common and concludes that the things being compared probably have some other characteristic in common.
- If an analogical argument is strong, then it raises the probability that the conclusion is true.
- Four criteria are used to analyze the first premise of an analogical argument: (*a*) the strength of an analogical argument is related to the number of things referred to in the first premise. (*b*) The strength of an analogical argument is related to the variety of things referred to in the first premise. (*c*) The strength of an analogical argument is related to the number of characteristics that are claimed to be similar between the things being compared. (*d*) The strength of an analogical argument is related to the relevance of the characteristics referred to in the first premise.
- Disanalogies: To point out differences between two things.
- Counteranalogy: A new, competing argument—one that compares the thing in question to something else.
- Unintended consequences: If you can show that something unacceptable to a person presenting an analogy follows from that analogy, then you put that person in a difficult position.

KEY TERMS

LOGIC CHALLENGE: BEAT THE CHEAT

While walking downtown, you come across a very excited group of people. They have gathered around a loud man who is challenging them to a bet. You watch as the man holds up two cards; one is blank, and the other has an X written on it. He then quickly places them face down on a small table and shuffles their positions many times. He is willing to bet $10 that no one can locate the card with the X. Another man steps forward and puts $10 down on the table and chooses one of the cards. He turns it over, reveals that it is blank, and promptly loses $10. Three other people try and they each fail, too.

By now you are convinced that the game is a scam. The man is obviously palming or hiding the card with the X and putting two blank cards down on the table. Suddenly, you realize that you can beat the cheat. You ask the crowd how many people lost $10, and then you challenge the cheat to bet that amount for one game.

You win the bet and return everyone's lost $10. How did you do it?

Chapter 11

Legal Arguments

Digital homework exercises for this chapter are available in your instructor's online course. For information on how to access these resources, please visit **www.oup.com/he/baronett5e.**

You have probably seen the old image of *Justice* wearing a blindfold and holding a balancing scale. The image is meant to evoke an ideal. Justice, it says, has nothing to do with stereotypes or emotional appeals. The law should be blind to any sort of prejudice. Yet legal debates often involve politically and emotionally charged issues, such as gay marriage, crime, or abortion. When civil rights protesters were met with violence, the courts were called to decide legal arguments. When fears of terrorism led to imprisonment without trial and, some say, even torture, the courts again had to decide what must be done. And when citizens then protest court decisions, they are exercising a right protected by law.

In fact, disputes like these help explain the ideal of blind justice. The process of making legal decisions has evolved to emphasize rationality and impartiality, which we depend on for our everyday safety, security, and well-being. Although legal debates often involve emotional issues, legal discourse has evolved patterns and conventions that we can recognize. Legal arguments can be understood once you are able to grasp the underlying logic, and our reasoning skills can complement our understanding of the practical demands of the law.

This chapter looks at the logical foundation of legal arguments. We will explore the use of *conditional statements, sufficient and necessary conditions, disjunction, conjunction*, and the role of *analogies*. We will see how inductive analysis helps explain legal reasoning.

A. DEDUCTIVE AND INDUCTIVE REASONING

The logical basis of legal arguments has a long history. According to Aristotle, writing in the 4th century BCE, "The law is reason free from passion." The defining documents of the United States describe the rights of citizens, and the duties and responsibilities of government. The Constitution spells out in detail guidelines for many legal issues and their remedies in Amendment 5:

> No person shall be held to answer for a capital, or otherwise infamous crime, unless on a presentment or indictment of a Grand Jury, except in cases arising in the land or naval forces, or in the Militia, when in actual service in time of War or public danger; nor shall any person be subject for the same offense to be twice put in jeopardy of life or limb; nor shall be compelled in any criminal case to be a witness against himself, nor be deprived of life, liberty, or property, without due process of law; nor shall private property be taken for public use, without just compensation.

Legislative bodies usually enact laws, which then get expressed in formal documents. Federal laws are also referred to as *statutes*. In charging individuals with crimes, for example, federal prosecutors must make a judgment that a statute is applicable to the case at hand. An average reader may not find that judgment so easy. Take this example:

Crimes and Criminal Procedure
US Code—Section 111: Assaulting, resisting, or impeding certain officers or employees.
   (a) In General—Whoever
      (1) forcibly assaults, resists, opposes, impedes, intimidates, or interferes with any person designated in section 1114 of this title while engaged in or on account of the performance of official duties; or . . .

And that's just the first clause. Fortunately, the ability to recognize a few basics will let you engage in reasoned debates about the meaning and intent of laws like these. **Appellate courts** are courts of appeal that review the decisions of lower courts. Legal briefs to these courts may also look complicated, but they, too, rely on the same kind of reasoning.

Appellate courts
Courts of appeal that review the decisions of lower courts.

In law, the term "deductive reasoning" generally means going from the *general* to the *specific*—that is, from the statement of a *rule* to its application to a particular legal case. Although this definition is too narrow to capture all the varieties of deductive reasoning in logic, for legal purposes it serves the intended goal. On the other hand, many law textbooks define "inductive reasoning" as the process of going from the *specific* to the *general*. It comes into play whenever we move from a *specific case* or legal opinion to a *general rule*. Again, although this legal use, too, is narrow, it is a legitimate part of the larger class of inductive reasoning in logic.

B. CONDITIONAL STATEMENTS

Conditional statements play a major role in *legal reasoning*, which is also referred to as **rule-based reasoning**. Once you recognize a conditional statement, you have a powerful tool for assessing the strengths or weaknesses of the legal argument quickly and precisely. (Conditional statements were introduced in Chapter 1 and further developed in Chapter 7.)

When legal terminology contains the words "if" or "only if," then the application of sufficient and necessary conditions can often assist in unraveling the legal issues. Let's work through some examples to sharpen our skills:

> A judge may admit evidence of a prior conviction, if it falls within either of two categories.

Although we do not yet know the "two categories" mentioned in the statement, the key word is "if"; it alerts us that we are dealing with a conditional statement. Since the "if" always precedes the antecedent, it must be placed first when we reconstruct the given sentence. In our example, we could rewrite the sentence as follows:

> If evidence of a prior conviction falls within either of two categories, then it may be admitted.

Here is another example:

> If the judge has refused to admit into evidence a piece of evidence, that information cannot be considered when deciding a case.

Although the word "then" is absent, you should recognize that this is a conditional statement. We can easily reconstruct the sentence by placing the word "then" in the appropriate place.

In examples of rule-based legal reasoning, you should pay attention to the possibility of the existence of conditional statements. We already know that the word "if" is a good indicator. We also know that certain statements in ordinary language can be translated into a conditional statement using the word "if." The phrases *every time, whenever, all cases where, given that*, and *in the event of* all indicate a conditional statement. If we encounter, say, the statement "*Whenever* the judge has refused to admit into evidence a piece of evidence, that information cannot be considered when deciding a case," we can recognize this as an instance of a conditional statement.

C. SUFFICIENT AND NECESSARY CONDITIONS

Before we see how conditional statements relate to legal concerns, we need to review two kinds of conditions. A **sufficient condition** occurs whenever one event ensures that another event is realized. Another way of saying that something is a sufficient condition is to think of the phrases "is enough for" or "it guarantees." Now suppose that the law of the state in which you are driving states that anyone caught driving with a blood alcohol level above 0.08% will be subject to a citation for *driving while*

Rule-based reasoning
Legal reasoning is also referred to as "rule-based reasoning."

Sufficient condition
Whenever one event ensures that another event is realized.

intoxicated (DWI) or, in some states, *driving under the influence* (DUI). If you are stopped by the police and agree to take a breath-analyzer test, then the following indicates a sufficient condition.

If your blood alcohol level exceeds 0.08%, then you are cited for DWI.

In other words, anyone caught driving with a blood alcohol level above 0.08% has met a *sufficient condition* for being issued a citation for DWI. Compare these results with a new case:

If you are cited for DWI, then your blood alcohol level exceeds 0.08%.

Even though it might be true that you were cited for a DWI, this is *not sufficient* information to determine that your blood alcohol level exceeds 0.08%. You might have refused to take a breath-analyzer test, so your blood alcohol level was not determined. Or you might have been given a variety of field sobriety tests, such as walking a straight line and turning, standing on one foot, or closing your eyes and touching the tip of your nose. If, in the officer's opinion, you failed the field sobriety test, then you may have been cited for DWI.

PROFILES IN LOGIC
Cesare Beccaria

Cesare Beccaria (1738–94) wrote a short but influential book, *On Crimes and Punishments*, to provide a clear foundation for the criminal justice system. Theoretical justifications for the punishment of criminals have a long history: *retribution* (revenge, or "an eye for an eye"); *rehabilitation* (reforming the offender into a productive member of society); *incapacitation* (simply removing the offender from society); and *deterrence* (discouraging others from committing crimes). Since Beccaria thought that the only justification for punishment was to create a better society, he advocated deterrence as the fundamental justification for punishment.

For Beccaria, two basic principles must be rigorously followed for deterrence to work effectively—*certainty* and *celerity*. "Certainty" means that everyone in the society must see that laws will be strictly enforced and that punishment will be consistent. In other words, identical punishments must follow identical crimes. For that reason,

Beccaria argued, judges should not have the power to alter any punishment. "Celerity" means that punishment should occur swiftly. People need to connect a specific punishment to a specific crime (*certainty*)—and to connect it immediately (*celerity*). "A punishment may not be an act of violence, of one, or of many, against a private member of society; it should be public, immediate, and necessary, the least possible in the case given, proportioned to the crime, and determined by the laws."

Beccaria argued that the most damaging crimes are committed by those who have gained the greatest benefits from society. In today's terms, this means that white-collar crimes are the most damaging. In support of this idea, Beccaria argued that most people are not likely to imitate violent crimes. However, seeing wealthy criminals abusing their positions in society for personal gain, and often getting light punishment for it, tears the fabric of society.

On the other hand, a **necessary condition** means that one thing is *essential, man-datory,* or *required* in order for another thing to be realized. Here is a simple example of a necessary condition:

> If you are allowed to vote in the presidential election, then you are at least 18 years old.

Necessary condition
Whenever one thing is *essential, mandatory,* or *required* in order for another thing to be realized.

According to the law, you must be at least 18 years of age in order to be able to vote in a presidential election. Therefore, being at least 18 years of age is a *necessary condition* to vote. In other words, if you are *not* at least 18 years of age, then you are *not* allowed to vote in the presidential election. Compare the foregoing results with a new example:

> If you are not allowed to vote in the presidential election, then you are not at least 18 years old.

Even if you are *not* allowed to vote in the presidential election, we *cannot* say for sure that you are *not* at least 18 years old. There are many other reasons why you might not be allowed to vote as well. Perhaps you missed the deadline for registering, or you were convicted of a certain felony.

D. DISJUNCTION AND CONJUNCTION

The legal use of *disjunction* is illustrated by an "either/or" test, in which at least one component must be satisfied. Here is one possible example:

> A lawyer is not permitted to get a contingent fee in child custody cases or divorce cases.

If we let C = *child custody cases*, and D = *divorce cases*, then we can write:

> A lawyer is *not* permitted to get a contingent fee for C *or* D.

C or D is a *sufficient* condition for the lawyer *not* to be allowed to get a contingent fee. Thus, the rule sets the condition that a particular result will occur *if* a case falls within one of two possibilities. The word "if" is essential here. It alerts us that we are dealing with sufficient conditions and a conditional statement. If we let "L" stand for the phrase "A lawyer is *not* permitted to get a contingent fee," we then reconstruct the statement:

> If (C or D), then L.

This is a compound statement and it contains three simple statements (represented by the letters "C," "D," and "L"). We can now picture the rule:

This picture can also be interpreted as indicating that we have an *exclusive* disjunction (where C and D cannot both occur at the same time), because C and D do not overlap. (As an exercise in legal thinking, do you think that this is correct when it comes to our hypothetical lawyer? Does the rule clearly indicate that we are dealing with exclusive disjunction? Why or why not?)

On the other hand, a *rule* containing a *conjunction* specifies a test for *necessary conditions* that must be met for the rule to apply. Suppose a rule defines "burglary" as having five components, *all of which must be met* for a case to fall under the definition. If even one of the five parts is not met, then the burglary rule should not be applied. Necessary conditions and conjunctions specify logical, and in this case legal, commitments that are specific and comprehensive.

E. ANALYZING A COMPLEX RULE

We now have the logical tools to analyze a complex legal rule. For example, Rule 609(a) of the Federal Rules of Evidence deals with questioning the character of a witness for truthfulness. We will paraphrase the rule to highlight the grounds for the possible impeachment of a witness by evidence of a conviction of a crime:

> Evidence that a witness has been convicted of a crime shall be admitted if either (1) the crime was punishable by death or imprisonment in excess of one year under the law under which he/she was convicted, and its **probative value** of admitting this evidence outweighs its **prejudicial effect** to the accused, or (2) that establishing the elements of the crime required proof or admission of an act of dishonesty or false statement by the witness, regardless of punishment.

Probative value
Evidence that can be used during a trial to advance the facts of the case.

Prejudicial effect
Evidence that might cause some jurors to be negatively biased toward a defendant.

The term "probative value" refers to evidence that can be used during a trial to advance the facts of the case. The term "prejudicial effect" describes evidence that might cause some jurors to be negatively biased toward a defendant. For example, the defendant might belong to a religious group that is not popular.

A complete analysis will, of necessity, take many steps. However, at the end we will have revealed the logic behind this complex rule. We start by highlighting in italics all the logical operators at work:

> Evidence that a witness has been convicted of a crime shall be admitted *if* either (1) the crime was punishable by death *or* imprisonment in excess of one year under the law under which he/she was convicted, *and* its probative value of admitting this evidence outweighs its prejudicial effect to the accused, *or* (2) that establishing the elements of the crime required proof *or* admission of an act of dishonesty *or* false statement by the witness, regardless of punishment.

We can use the logical operators to outline the rule:

> Evidence that a witness has been convicted of a crime shall be admitted (E) *if* it meets *either* criterion A *or* B:
>
> **Criterion A:** The evidence shall be admitted *if* both A1 *and* A2 are true:
>   A1. The prior conviction was punishable by either a or b:
>   a. Death

b. Imprisonment in excess of one year
A2.   Its probative value outweighs its prejudicial effect.

Criterion B: The evidence shall be admitted *if* it involved either of the following:
B1.   Establishing the elements of the crime required *proof* of either a or b, as follows:
a. An act of dishonesty by the witness
b. A false statement by the witness
B2.   Establishing the elements of the crime required an *admission* of either a or b:
a. An act of dishonesty by the witness
b. A false statement by the witness

Given this, the overall logical structure of this rule is simple: If either A or B, then E. From this basic structure we can recognize that this rule designates both A and B as *sufficient conditions* for E. This means that the antecedent of the conditional statement will be satisfied if either A or B is true.

Our next step is to analyze both A and B into their components. Criterion A is very complex, but we can see that three logical operators are involved (*if; and; or*). We are told that A is realized whenever two further conditions are true at the same time: A1 and A2. Thus, *if* both A1 *and* A2 are true, then A will be true (we already know that if A is true, then E will be true).

On closer inspection, we see that A1 is itself complex: It contains "or." This tells us that A1 can be realized in either of two ways—when either A1a is true or A1b is true. A2 is a bit more complicated, because it asks us to gauge the relative value of two things. We are told that the court must be able to determine that A2a, the probative value, outweighs A2b, the prejudicial effect. Of course, we would need to know the facts of the case before we could determine the actual value of each component; a judge would have to decide. However, we can still understand the logic behind this requirement. In order for A2 to hold, A2a must be greater than A2b.

We can now combine our analysis into one result for criterion A:

If [(A1a, the prior conviction was punishable by death, *or* A1b, by imprisonment in excess of one year), *and* (A2a, its probative value outweighs A2b, its prejudicial effect)], *then* E, evidence of a prior conviction shall be admitted.

As we have outlined, we must acknowledge that E can be realized even if A does not occur, because the rule asserts that B is sufficient to bring about E. As before, let E = *evidence of a prior conviction shall be admitted.* We notice that B can be realized if either B1 or B2 is the case. So either B1 or B2 is sufficient for B to occur. However, for a complete analysis we need to explore B1 and B2. It turns out that B1 can occur if either B1a is the case (*proof* of an act of dishonesty by the witness), *or* B1b is the case (*proof* of a false statement by the witness). Similarly, B2 can occur if either B2a is the case (*admission* of an act of dishonesty by the witness), *or* B2b is the case (*admission* of a false statement by the witness). This analysis results in the following conditional statement:

If [(B1a, *proof* of an act of dishonesty by the witness, *or* B1b, *proof* of a false statement by the witness), *or* (B2a, *admission* of an act of dishonesty by the witness, *or* B2b, *admission* of a false statement by the witness)], *then* E, evidence of a prior conviction shall be admitted.

Our analysis of a complex rule is complete. It has revealed the existence of sufficient and necessary conditions, the use of conjunction, disjunction, and conditional statements. It has shown what must occur in order for the rule to be applied. Taking apart legal rules this way allows us to see how the rules work by showing the logical foundation of the legal reasoning. We can then see both the strengths and weaknesses of a legal position by asking whether the facts at hand fit the rule. As we move back and forth between the statements and the logical operators, we become more sensitive to the subtleties of legal language and its logical structure.

EXERCISES 11E

Self-Practice
Questions

For each exercise you are to explain the logical apparatus used in a particular rule of evidence. Follow the method of analysis that we did for Rule 609(a) of the Federal Rules of Evidence. Highlight any logical operators when available. Rewrite and reconstruct the statements whenever necessary in order to reveal the logic of the rule. (All the exercises are adapted from the Federal Rules of Evidence.)

1. RULE 603. OATH OR AFFIRMATION

Before testifying, every witness shall be required to declare that the witness will testify truthfully, by oath or affirmation administered in a form calculated to awaken the witness' conscience and impress the witness' mind with the duty to do so.

Answer:

Highlight logical operators:

Before testifying, every witness shall be required to declare that the witness will testify truthfully, by oath **or** affirmation administered in a form calculated to awaken the witness' conscience **and** impress the witness' mind with the duty to do so.

Reconstruct the statements in order to reveal the logic of the rule:

If (T) testifying, then either (O) a witness shall be required to declare that the witness will testify truthfully by oath or (A) a witness shall be required to declare that the witness will testify truthfully by affirmation, and (C) administered in a form calculated to awaken the witness' conscience and (D) administered in a form calculated to impress the witness' mind with the duty to do so.

If T, then (O or A) and (C and D)

2. RULE 605. COMPETENCY OF JUDGE AS WITNESS

The judge presiding at the trial may not testify in that trial as a witness.

3. RULE 606(A). COMPETENCY OF JUROR AS WITNESS—AT THE TRIAL.

A member of the jury may not testify as a witness before that jury in the trial of the case in which the juror is sitting. If the juror is called so to testify, the opposing party shall be afforded an opportunity to object out of the presence of the jury.

4. RULE 606(B). COMPETENCY OF JUROR AS WITNESS—INQUIRY INTO VALIDITY OF VERDICT OR INDICTMENT.

Upon an inquiry into the validity of a verdict or **indictment** (a formal accusation presented by a grand jury), a juror may not testify as to any matter or statement occurring during the course of the jury's deliberations or to the effect of anything upon that or any other juror's mind or emotions as influencing the juror to assent to or dissent from the verdict or indictment or concerning the juror's mental processes in connection therewith. But a juror may testify about (1) whether extraneous prejudicial information was improperly brought to the jury's attention, (2) whether any outside influence was improperly brought to bear upon any juror, or (3) whether there was a mistake in entering the verdict onto the verdict form. A juror's **affidavit** (a written statement signed before an authorized official), or evidence of any statement by the juror may not be received on a matter about which the juror would be precluded from testifying.

> **Indictment** A formal accusation presented by a grand jury.

> **Affidavit** A written statement signed before an authorized official.

★ 5. RULE 608(A). EVIDENCE OF CHARACTER AND CONDUCT OF WITNESS— OPINION AND REPUTATION EVIDENCE OF CHARACTER.

The credibility of a witness may be attacked or supported by evidence in the form of opinion or reputation, but subject to these limitations: (1) the evidence may refer only to character for truthfulness or untruthfulness, and (2) evidence of truthful character is admissible only after the character of the witness for truthfulness has been attacked by opinion or reputation evidence or otherwise.

> ▷
>
> Video Tutorial: 11E
> Exercise #5

6. RULE 608(B). EVIDENCE OF CHARACTER AND CONDUCT OF WITNESS— SPECIFIC INSTANCES OF CONDUCT.

Specific instances of the conduct of a witness, for the purpose of attacking or supporting the witness' character for truthfulness, other than conviction of crime as provided in Rule 609, may not be proved by extrinsic evidence. They may, however, in the discretion of the court, if probative of truthfulness or untruthfulness, be inquired into on cross-examination of the witness (1) concerning the witness' character for truthfulness or untruthfulness, or (2) concerning the character for truthfulness or untruthfulness of another witness as to which character the witness being cross-examined has testified. The giving of testimony, whether by an accused or by any other witness, does not operate as a waiver of the accused's or the witness' privilege against self-incrimination when examined with respect to matters that relate only to character for truthfulness.

7. RULE 609(B). IMPEACHMENT BY EVIDENCE OF CONVICTION OF CRIME—TIME LIMIT.

Evidence of a conviction under this rule is not admissible if a period of more than 10 years has elapsed since the date of the conviction or of the release of the witness from the confinement imposed for that conviction, whichever is the later date, unless the court determines, in the interests of justice, that the probative value of the conviction supported by specific facts and circumstances substantially outweighs its prejudicial effect. However, evidence of a conviction more than 10 years old as calculated herein, is not admissible unless the proponent gives to the adverse party sufficient advance written notice of intent to use such evidence to provide the adverse party with a fair opportunity to contest the use of such evidence.

8. RULE 609(C). IMPEACHMENT BY EVIDENCE OF CONVICTION OF CRIME—EFFECT OF PARDON, ANNULMENT, OR CERTIFICATE OF REHABILITATION.

Evidence of a conviction is not admissible under this rule if (1) the conviction has been the subject of a pardon, annulment, certificate of rehabilitation, or other equivalent procedure based on a finding of the rehabilitation of the person convicted, and that person has not been convicted of a subsequent crime which was punishable by death or imprisonment in excess of one year, or (2) the conviction has been the subject of a pardon, annulment, or other equivalent procedure based on a finding of innocence.

★ 9. RULE 609(D). IMPEACHMENT BY EVIDENCE OF CONVICTION OF CRIME—JUVENILE ADJUDICATIONS.

Evidence of juvenile adjudications is generally not admissible under this rule. The court may, however, in a criminal case allow evidence of a juvenile adjudication of a witness other than the accused if conviction of the offense would be admissible to attack the credibility of an adult and the court is satisfied that admission in evidence is necessary for a fair determination of the issue of guilt or innocence.

10. RULE 609(E). IMPEACHMENT BY EVIDENCE OF CONVICTION OF CRIME—PENDENCY OF APPEAL.

The pendency of an appeal therefrom does not render evidence of a conviction inadmissible. Evidence of the pendency of an appeal is admissible.

11. RULE 610. RELIGIOUS BELIEFS OR OPINIONS

Evidence of the beliefs or opinions of a witness on matters of religion is not admissible for the purpose of showing that by reason of their nature the witness' credibility is impaired or enhanced.

12. RULE 611(A). MODE AND ORDER OF INTERROGATION AND PRESENTATION—CONTROL BY COURT.

The court shall exercise reasonable control over the mode and order of interrogating witnesses and presenting evidence so as to (1) make the interrogation

Video Tutorial: 11E
Exercise #11

and presentation effective for the ascertainment of the truth, (2) avoid need-less consumption of time, and (3) protect witnesses from harassment or undue embarrassment.

⭐ 13. RULE 611(B). MODE AND ORDER OF INTERROGATION AND PRESENTATION—SCOPE OF CROSS-EXAMINATION.

Cross-examination should be limited to the subject matter of the direct exam-ination and matters affecting the credibility of the witness. The court may, in the exercise of discretion, permit inquiry into additional matters as if on direct examination.

14. RULE 611(C). MODE AND ORDER OF INTERROGATION AND PRESENTATION—LEADING QUESTIONS.

Leading questions should not be used on the direct examination of a witness except as may be necessary to develop the witness' testimony. Ordinarily leading questions should be permitted on cross-examination. When a party calls a hostile witness, an adverse party, or a witness identified with an adverse party, interrogation may be by leading questions.

15. RULE 612. WRITING USED TO REFRESH MEMORY

Except as otherwise provided in criminal proceedings by section 3500 of title 18, United States Code, if a witness uses a writing to refresh memory for the purpose of testifying, either (1) while testifying, or (2) before testifying, if the court in its discretion determines it is necessary in the interests of justice, an adverse party is entitled to have the writing produced at the hearing, to inspect it, to cross-examine the witness thereon, and to introduce in evidence those portions which relate to the testimony of the witness.

16. RULE 613(A). PRIOR STATEMENTS OF WITNESSES—EXAMINING WITNESS CONCERNING PRIOR STATEMENT.

In examining a witness concerning a prior statement made by the witness, whether written or not, the statement need not be shown nor its contents disclosed to the witness at that time, but on request the same shall be shown or disclosed to oppos-ing counsel.

⭐ 17. RULE 613(B). PRIOR STATEMENTS OF WITNESSES—EXTRINSIC EVIDENCE OF PRIOR INCONSISTENT STATEMENT OF WITNESS.

Extrinsic evidence of a prior inconsistent statement by a witness is not admissible unless the witness is afforded an opportunity to explain or deny the same and the opposite party is afforded an opportunity to interrogate the witness thereon, or the interests of justice otherwise require. This provision does not apply to admissions of a party-opponent as defined in rule 801(d)(2).

18. RULE 614(A). CALLING AND INTERROGATION OF WITNESSES BY COURT—CALLING BY COURT.

The court may, on its own motion or at the suggestion of a party, call witnesses, and all parties are entitled to cross-examine witnesses thus called.

19. RULE 614(B). CALLING AND INTERROGATION OF WITNESSES BY COURT—INTERROGATION BY COURT.

The court may interrogate witnesses, whether called by itself or by a party.

20. RULE 614(C). CALLING AND INTERROGATION OF WITNESSES BY COURT—OBJECTIONS.

Objections to the calling of witnesses by the court or to interrogation by it may be made at the time or at the next available opportunity when the jury is not present.

⭐ 21. RULE 615. EXCLUSION OF WITNESSES

At the request of a party the court shall order witnesses excluded so that they cannot hear the testimony of other witnesses, and it may make the order of its own motion. This rule does not authorize exclusion of (1) a party who is a natural person, or (2) an officer or employee of a party which is not a natural person designated as its representative by its attorney, or (3) a person whose presence is shown by a party to be essential to the presentation of the party's cause, or (4) a person authorized by statute to be present.

F. ANALOGIES

Precedent A judicial decision that can be applied to later cases.

Legal reasoning probably could not work without using analogies. It relies on **precedent** (a judicial decision that can be applied to later cases), and the use of similar cases. Lawyers' arguments and judges' written opinions usually contain reasoning by analogy as an essential component. (Chapter 10 introduced analogical reasoning.)

Once you know where and how a legal argument uses analogies, you gain a foothold to start your analysis of the case at hand. You should always look for the logical components involved in legal reasoning, because the more you begin to see them, the more quickly you can apply them.

Rules of law The legal principles that have been applied to historical cases.

Analogical reasoning is one of the most fundamental tools used in the legal profession. Lawyers try to find **rules of law**, or legal principles that have been applied to historical cases. Along with this, the lawyers must show that the facts of the current case are sufficiently similar to the precedent. Because they share relevant characteristics, they should share the same legal outcome. Therefore, the lawyers argue, the judge should make the same decision as laid down in the precedent.

A rational decision will choose a course of action that has the highest probability of being correct. If an analogical argument is strong, then it raises the probability that the conclusion is true. For example, once a court has decided that members of a group may not be restrained from *speaking*, another court is likely to conclude, by analogical reasoning, that the same group cannot be stopped from *parading*. In other words, the court holds that parading and speaking share relevant characteristics. Arguments like this, from precedent, will identify those respects in which the older cases and the current case are closely alike.

Knowing how to reconstruct the analogy's structure allows you to uncover the mechanisms at work in legal reasoning. Let's imagine that lawyers are arguing a case about that parade, which we will designate as case A. One of the lawyers might argue that case B, a case previously decided by the courts about free speech, and case A, the present case, have many points in common. She would have to illustrate clearly the common points to the court by referring to the facts in A and B. She then shows that case B has already been decided by having rule Z applied to it. She then concludes that rule Z should be applied to the present case A. Therefore, she has argued by analogy that case B should be used as a precedent in deciding case A.

However, the argument is strong only if cases A and B are judged to be similar enough for the rule to apply. Of course, an opposing lawyer will try to show that cases A and B contain substantial differences. He will argue that rule Z *should not* be applied to the present case, because the two cases are *not* similar enough for the rule to be applied. He must point out relevant differences (disanalogies) between case authority (the prior case) and the case being currently adjudicated in order to justify a different result.

Of course, it is not always easy to identify the *relevant* characteristics in a particular legal case. Ultimately, a judge (or an appeals court) will have to decide what kinds of similarities and differences are legally significant. A lawyer argues that significant relevant *similarities* exist, and the opposing lawyer argues that significant relevant *differences* exist. Even then, however, there still remain the *logical* issues regarding the uses of analogies. We can engage in a logical assessment of the legal analogies and offer a reasonable, informed opinion.

Let's examine a fictional case, *Judy B. v. Quickoilz*:

> Judy B. had the oil in her car changed at a company called Quickoilz. While driving home, the oil light came on and the engine temperature gauge began to rapidly rise. She quickly stopped the car, looked underneath, and saw that the screw in the oil pan was missing. All the oil had been lost and the car was overheating. She lived in a rural area outside Las Vegas, and it was 117 degrees outside. She had a baby with her, and instead of trying to walk the five miles to her home, with no water, she decided to keep driving the car. She managed to get the car to within 100 yards of her house before the engine seized up. The engine was ruined, so she sued Quickoilz.

Judy B. is the **plaintiff**, or person initiating the lawsuit, and Quickoilz is the defendant in the case. During the hearing, Judy's lawyer argues that Quickoilz is fully responsible for the damage to the engine, since they must have improperly replaced the oil pan screw. Therefore, Quickoilz should be required to pay the entire bill for a new engine replacement.

Plaintiff The person who initiates a lawsuit.

Quickoilz's lawyer argues that Judy B. is ultimately responsible for the engine failure. He claims that if she had turned off the car as soon as the oil light came on and the temperature gauge began rising, then the engine would not have been damaged. Since she willingly and knowingly kept driving, she assumed responsibility for the consequences. Quickoilz's lawyer then cites a rule of law, which we shall call "AR-1: Assumption of Risk":

> A plaintiff has voluntarily accepted or exposed him or herself to a risk of damage, injury, or loss, whenever he or she understands that the condition or situation is clearly dangerous, but nevertheless makes the decision to act. In all such cases, the defendant in the case may raise the issue of the plaintiff's knowledge and appreciation of the danger as an affirmative defense. If successful, the application of the assumption of risk as an affirmative defense shall result in either a reduction or complete elimination of the damages assessed against the defendant.

Quickoilz's lawyer then refers the court to a past case, *The Spyder v. Kaufman Brothers*:

> A man calling himself *The Spyder* attempted to climb to the top of a fifty-story office building owned by the Kaufman brothers. The plaintiff did this without the permission of the owners of the building. He managed to get thirty feet off the ground when he stepped on a ledge that collapsed under him. He fell to the ground and broke his pelvis. He sued the building's owners for damages, and argued that they were responsible for letting a defective ledge go unrepaired.

The defendant's lawyer argued that Rule AR-1 should be applied because the man had voluntarily accepted and exposed himself to a risk of injury; he clearly understood that the situation was dangerous, but nevertheless he made the decision to climb the building. The court agreed with the defendant's argument that Rule AR-1 was applicable to this case and found in favor of the defendant.

Quickoilz's lawyer then argues that *The Spyder v. Kaufman Brothers* case should be applied to the present case. Applying the language of Rule AR-1, "Judy B. voluntarily accepted and exposed herself to damage or loss; she clearly understood that the situation was dangerous, but nevertheless she made the decision to drive the car." Therefore, since she voluntarily assumed the risk, she bears responsibility for the engine damage. Thus, Rule AR-1 is applicable, and the court should decide in favor of the defendant.

In response, the plaintiff's lawyer argues that Judy B. was caught in a dilemma—a decision that had to be made between two choices, either of which would lead to an unwanted result.

> *The Spyder v. Kaufman Brothers* does *not* apply to the present case, because the facts of the two cases are substantially different. In *The Spyder v. Kaufman Brothers* the plaintiff voluntarily placed himself in the dangerous situation. But Judy B.'s decision was not made voluntarily. It was the defendant's negligence that put her between a rock and a hard place. She could either keep driving the car and expose the engine to damage, or walk in 117 degrees heat with no water and expose herself and her baby to serious physical harm. Her decision was *not*

voluntary, because she was caught in a dilemma not of her own making. The two choices were forced on her by Quickoilz's negligence; they were not initiated by Judy B.

The plaintiff's lawyer then refers the court to another past case, which we will call *Elsa W. v. Ian R.*:

Elsa W. jumped in front of a swerving car in order to get her child out of harm's way. The parent was injured and sued the driver to recover medical bills. The defendant in the case, Ian R., invoked AR-1 (the assumption of risk rule as described above), claiming that the parent voluntarily chose the action that led to the injury. The court rejected the defendant's argument that the parent had voluntarily assumed the risk, and held instead that the action of the driver forced the parent to save the child, as any parent would naturally do; therefore, the parent's actions were not voluntary.

Judy B.'s lawyer argues that the court's decision in *Elsa W. v. Ian R.* should be used in the present case. Rule AR-1 is not applicable to this case; therefore, the court should decide in favor of the plaintiff.

Both the defendant and the plaintiff use analogical reasoning. Both sides refer to a rule of law, and both sides cite cases that could be used as precedent. Let's diagram the arguments:

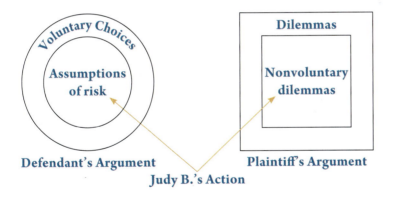

The defendant's argument is illustrated by the large circle representing the class of human actions called "voluntary choices" and the smaller circle representing the class of human actions called "assumptions of risk." We can see that every instance of an assumption of risk falls within the larger class of voluntary choices. This follows because many everyday voluntary choices assume *no* risk—such as which book to read or what to have for dinner. So, although every assumption of risk is also a voluntary choice, not every voluntary choice is an assumption of risk. The defendant concludes that Judy B.'s action should be placed inside the class of "assumptions of risk."

Judy B.'s lawyer has argued that her decision was not voluntary. This is seen in the right side of the diagram, which illustrates the difference between *assumption of risk* (which requires a *voluntary choice*), and a *dilemma* forced upon the plaintiff (which absolves her of voluntary choice).

The plaintiff's argument is illustrated by the large rectangle representing the class of situations called "dilemmas" and the smaller rectangle representing the class of situations called "nonvoluntary dilemmas." We can see that every instance of a nonvoluntary dilemma falls within the larger class of dilemmas. Many dilemmas are self-imposed—for example, asking two people out on a date at the same time. Whoever you choose, someone will be hurt by your action. So, although every nonvoluntary dilemma is a dilemma, not every dilemma is a nonvoluntary dilemma. The plaintiff concludes that Judy B.'s action should be placed inside the class of "nonvoluntary dilemmas."

G. THE ROLE OF PRECEDENT

State and federal appeals courts, state supreme courts, and the Supreme Court of the United States all render decisions and opinions that we can analyze with our logical tools. We look for instances of analogical reasoning, sufficient and necessary conditions, and logical operators such as conjunction, disjunction, negation, and conditional statements.

The use of a prior court decision as a precedent can be understood as a species of analogical reasoning. Arguing that a prior case should be applied to a present case requires pointing out the relevant similarities of the two cases. The legal use of analogical reasoning is subject to all the same constraints as in everyday use. It can be analyzed and evaluated for its strengths and weaknesses using the criteria for judging analogical arguments.

We will look next at an actual U.S. Supreme Court decision. The case involved an Oregon jury that determined that Honda had to pay $5 million to plaintiffs who had suffered injuries while driving an ATV. That sounds like a lot of money, but there were horrible injuries. The case raised important legal questions: Are "punitive damages" in the millions crucial to protecting consumers? Is there such a thing as "excessive damages"? It was up to the Supreme Court to decide. First, we provide a summary of the case. This is not an official part of either the actual court opinion or the dissenting opinion. It is the abstract, or *syllabus*, offered by the court's Reporter of Decisions. It names the justice who wrote the opinion of court, as well as those who joined the opinion. It also mentions who wrote the dissenting opinion and who joined in the dissent.

Second, we give the opening sections of the Opinion of the Court. This introduces the court's reasoning, along with important legal and historical background.

Third, we leave an edited version of the remainder of the Opinion of the Court to the exercises, so that you can practice applying what you know. Each exercise contains only part of a complex court opinion. However, when you are finished, you will have analyzed the entire decision.

Fourth, the dissenting opinion provides the material for another set of exercises. You will see the entire legal procedure as it unfolds. Since the dissenting opinion offers criticism of the opinion, you will see how courts wrestle with difficult decisions.

SUPREME COURT OF THE UNITED STATES

HONDA MOTOR CO., LTD. V. OBERG
Argued April 20, 1994—Decided June 24, 1994

Syllabus

After finding petitioner Honda Motor Co., Ltd., liable for injuries that respondent Oberg received while driving a three-wheeled all-terrain-vehicle manufactured and sold by Honda, an Oregon jury awarded Oberg $5 million in punitive damages, over five times the amount of his compensatory damages award. In affirming, both the Oregon State Court of Appeals and the Oregon State Supreme Court rejected Honda's argument that the punitive damages award violated due process because it was excessive and because Oregon courts have no power to correct excessive verdicts under a 1910 Amendment to the State Constitution, which prohibits judicial review of the amount of punitive damages awarded by a jury "unless the court can affirmatively say there is no evidence to support the verdict."

The decision of Supreme Court of the United States: "The judgment is reversed, and the case is remanded to the Oregon Supreme Court for further proceedings not inconsistent with this opinion. *It is so ordered.*"

Justice *Stevens, J.*, delivered the opinion of the Court, in which *Blackmun, O'Connor, Scalia, Kennedy, Souter,* and *Thomas, J.J.*, joined. *Scalia, J.*, filed a concurring opinion. Justice *Ginsburg, J.*, filed a dissenting opinion, in which *Rehnquist, C. J.*, joined.

OPINION OF THE COURT

An amendment to the Oregon Constitution prohibits judicial review of the amount of punitive damages awarded by a jury, "unless the court can affirmatively say there is no evidence to support the verdict." The question presented is whether that prohibition is consistent with the Due Process Clause of the Fourteenth Amendment. We hold that it is not.

Petitioner Honda Motor Co. manufactured and sold the three-wheeled all-terrain vehicle that overturned while respondent was driving it, causing him severe and permanent injuries. Respondent brought suit alleging that petitioner knew or should have known that the vehicle had an inherently and unreasonably dangerous design. The jury found petitioner liable and awarded respondent $919,390.39 in compensatory damages and punitive damages of $5 million. The compensatory damages, however, were reduced by 20% to $735,512.31, because respondent's own negligence contributed to the accident. On appeal, relying on our then recent decision in *Pacific Mut. Life Ins. Co.* v. *Haslip*, 499 U. S. 1 (1991), petitioner argued that the award of punitive damages violated the Due Process Clause of the Fourteenth Amendment, because the punitive damages were excessive and because Oregon courts lacked the power to correct excessive verdicts.

The Oregon Court of Appeals affirmed, as did the Oregon Supreme Court. The latter court relied heavily on the fact that the Oregon statute governing the award of punitive damages in product liability actions and the jury instructions in this case contain substantive criteria that provide at least as much guidance to the factfinders as the Alabama statute and jury instructions that we upheld in *Haslip*. The Oregon Supreme Court also noted that Oregon law provides an additional protection by requiring the plaintiff to prove entitlement to punitive damages by clear and convincing evidence rather than a mere preponderance.

Recognizing that other state courts had interpreted *Haslip* as including a "clear constitutional mandate for meaningful judicial scrutiny of punitive damage awards," the Court nevertheless declined to "interpret *Haslip* to hold that an award of punitive damages, to comport with the requirements of the Due Process Clause, always must be subject to a form of postverdict or appellate review that includes the possibility of remittitur." It also noted that trial and appellate courts were "not entirely powerless" because a judgment may be vacated if "there is no evidence to support the jury's decision," and because "appellate review is available to test the sufficiency of the jury instructions."

We granted *certiorari*, to consider whether Oregon's limited judicial review of the size of punitive damage awards is consistent with our decision in *Haslip*. Our recent cases have recognized that the Constitution imposes a substantive limit on the size of punitive damage awards. *Pacific Mut. Life Ins. Co. v. Haslip; TXO Production Corp. v. Alliance Resources, Corp.* Although they fail to "draw a mathematical bright line between the constitutionally acceptable and the constitutionally unacceptable," a majority of the Justices agreed that the Due Process Clause imposes a limit on punitive damage awards. A plurality assented to the proposition that "grossly excessive" punitive damages would violate due process, while Justice O'Connor, who dissented because she favored more rigorous standards, noted that "it is thus common ground that an award may be so excessive as to violate due process." In the case before us today we are not directly concerned with the character of the standard that will identify unconstitutionally excessive awards; rather we are confronted with the question of what procedures are necessary to ensure that punitive damages are not imposed in an arbitrary manner. More specifically, the question is whether the Due Process Clause requires judicial review of the amount of punitive damage awards.

The opinions in both *Haslip* and *TXO* strongly emphasized the importance of the procedural component of the Due Process Clause. In *Haslip*, the Court held that the common law method of assessing punitive damages did not violate procedural due process. In so holding, the Court stressed the availability of both "meaningful and adequate review by the trial court" and subsequent appellate review. Similarly, in *TXO*, the plurality opinion found that the fact that the "award was reviewed and upheld by the trial judge" and unanimously affirmed on appeal gave rise "to a strong presumption of validity." Concurring in the judgment, Justice Scalia (joined by Justice Thomas) considered it sufficient that traditional common law procedures were followed. In particular, he noted that "'procedural due process' requires judicial review of punitive damages awards for reasonableness. . . ."

All of those opinions suggest that our analysis in this case should focus on Oregon's departure from traditional procedures. We therefore first contrast the relevant common law practice with Oregon's procedure, which that State's Supreme Court once described as "a system of trial by jury in which the judge is reduced to the status of a mere monitor." We then examine the constitutional implications of Oregon's deviation from established common law procedures.

Judicial review of the size of punitive damage awards has been a safeguard against excessive verdicts for as long as punitive damages have been awarded. One of the earliest reported cases involving exemplary damages, *Huckle v. Money*, (1763), arose out of King George III's attempt to punish the publishers of the allegedly seditious *North Briton*, No. 45. The King's agents arrested the plaintiff, a journeyman printer, in his home and detained him for six hours. Although the defendants treated the plaintiff rather well, feeding him "beef steaks and beer, so that he suffered very little or no damages," the jury awarded him £300, an enormous sum almost three hundred times the plaintiff's weekly wage.

The defendant's lawyer requested a new trial, arguing that the jury's award was excessive. Plaintiff's counsel, on the other hand, argued that "in cases of tort . . . the Court will never interpose in setting aside verdicts for excessive damages." While the court denied the motion for new trial, the Chief Justice explicitly rejected plaintiff's absolute rule against review of damages amounts. Instead, he noted that when the damages are "outrageous" and "all mankind at first blush must think so," a court may grant a new trial "for excessive damages." In accord with his view that the amount of an award was relevant to the motion for a new trial, the Chief Justice noted that "[u]pon the whole, I am of opinion the damages are not excessive."

Subsequent English cases, while generally deferring to the jury's determination of damages, steadfastly upheld the court's power to order new trials solely on the basis that the damages were too high. *Fabrigas v. Mostyn*, (1773): Damages "may be so monstrous and excessive, as to be in themselves an evidence of passion or partiality in the jury"; *Sharpe v. Brice*, (1774): "It has never been laid down, that the Court will not grant a new trial for excessive damages in any cases of tort"; *Leith v. Pope*, (1779): "[I]n cases of tort the Court will not interpose on account of the largeness of damages, unless they are so flagrantly excessive as to afford an internal evidence of the prejudice and partiality of the jury"; *Hewlett v. Cruchley*, (1813): "[I]t is now well acknowledged in all the Courts of *Westminster-hall*, that whether in actions for criminal conversation, malicious prosecutions, words, or any other matter, if the damages are clearly too large, the Courts will send the inquiry to another jury."

EXERCISES 11G

I. The following passages are from the *Opinion of the Court*. They continue the Court's opinion and lay out the reasons for the majority decision. Some of the passages have been edited to simplify the task at hand. In many instances we have omitted reference to case numbers (e.g., *Hurtado v. California*, 110 U.S. 516, 538 is reduced to *Hurtado v. California*). On the one hand, we have tried to keep as much of the legal arguments and apparatus intact; on the other hand, we tried to emphasize the logic at play.

Self-Practice
Questions

Your job is to describe the reasoning involved in each passage. You can do this by illustrating the logic involved. You should look for uses of logical operators such as conjunction, disjunction, negation, and conditional statements; sufficient and necessary conditions; and the analogical reasoning involved in the Court's arguments.

1. Respondent calls to our attention the case of *Beardmore v. Carrington*, in which the court asserted that "there is not one single case, (that is law), in all the books to be found, where the Court has granted a new trial for excessive damages in actions for torts." Respondent would infer from that statement that 18th century common law did not provide for judicial review of damages.

Respondent's argument overlooks several crucial facts. First, the *Beardmore* case antedates all but one of the cases cited in the previous paragraph. Even if respondent's interpretation of the case were correct, it would be an interpretation the English courts rejected soon thereafter.

Answer:

Three items can be used to get started: first, the passage uses analogical reasoning (*Beardmore v. Carrington*); second, it uses the logical operators "not" and "if"; third, it contains the word "infer."

The respondent argued that the case of *Beardmore v. Carrington* offers a precedent for the court not to grant a new trial. The court in *Beardmore* asserted that "there is **not** one single case, (that is law), in all the books to be found, where the Court has granted *a new trial* for excessive damages in actions for torts." However, in its opinion the U.S. Supreme Court argued that the respondent's inference "that 18th century common law did **not** provide for *judicial review of damages*" was faulty. The opinion pointed out that the "respondent's *argument overlooks several crucial facts*": First, *Beardmore* came before (antedates) *all but one of the cases* cited. Second, "even **if** respondent's interpretation of the case were correct, [then] it would be an interpretation the English courts rejected soon thereafter." In other words, although the respondent's interpretation of the court's assertion in *Beardmore* might be correct, the assertion was rejected by later courts.

2. Second, *Beardmore* itself cites at least one case which it concedes granted a new trial for excessive damages, *Chambers v. Robinson*, although it characterizes the case as wrongly decided.

3. Third, to say that "there is not one single case . . . in all the books" is to say very little, because then, much more so than now, only a small proportion of decided cases was reported. For example, the year *Beardmore* was decided only 16 Common Pleas cases are recorded in the standard reporter.

4. Finally, the argument respondent would draw, that 18th century English common law did not permit a judge to order new trials for excessive damages, is explicitly rejected by *Beardmore* itself, which cautioned against that very argument: "We desire to be understood that this Court does not say, or lay down any rule that there never can happen a case of such excessive damages in tort where the Court may not grant a new trial."

⭐ 5. Common law courts in the United States followed their English predecessors in providing judicial review of the size of damage awards. They too emphasized the deference ordinarily afforded jury verdicts, but they recognized that juries sometimes awarded damages so high as to require correction. In 1822, Justice Story ordered a new trial unless the plaintiff agreed to a reduction in his damages. In explaining his ruling, he noted: "As to the question of excessive damages, I agree, that the court may grant a new trial for excessive damages. . . . It is indeed an exercise of discretion full of delicacy and difficulty. But if it

Video Tutorial: 11G
Exercise #5

should clearly appear that the jury have committed a gross error, or have acted from improper motives, or have given damages excessive in relation to the person or the injury, it is as much the duty of the court to interfere, to prevent the wrong, as in any other case." *Blunt v. Little.*

6. In the 19th century, both before and after the ratification of the Fourteenth Amendment, many American courts reviewed damages for "partiality" or "passion and prejudice." Nevertheless, because of the difficulty of probing juror reasoning, passion and prejudice review was, in fact, review of the amount of awards. Judges would infer passion, prejudice, or partiality from the size of the award. *Taylor v. Giger*: "In actions of tort . . . a new trial ought not to be granted for excessiveness of damages, unless the damages found are so enormous as to shew that the jury were under some improper influence, or were led astray by the violence of prejudice or passion."

7. Nineteenth-century treatises similarly recognized judges' authority to award new trials on the basis of the size of damage awards. "[E]ven in personal torts, where the jury find *outrageous damages*, clearly evincing partiality, prejudice and passion, the court will interfere for the relief of the defendant, and order a new trial"); "The court again holds itself at liberty to set aside verdicts and grant new trials . . . whenever the damages are so excessive as to create the belief that the jury have been misled either by passion, prejudice, or ignorance"); When punitive damages are submitted to the jury, "the amount which they may think proper to allow will be accepted by the court, unless so exorbitant as to indicate that they have been influenced by passion, prejudice or a perverted judgment."

8. Modern practice is consistent with these earlier authorities. In the federal courts and in every State, except Oregon, judges review the size of damage awards. See *Dagnello v. Long Island R. Co.*, citing cases from all 50 States except Alaska, Maryland, and Oregon.

9. There is a dramatic difference between the judicial review of punitive damages awards under the common law and the scope of review available in Oregon. An Oregon trial judge, or an Oregon Appellate Court, may order a new trial if the jury was not properly instructed, if error occurred during the trial, or if there is no evidence to support any punitive damages at all. But if the defendant's only basis for relief is the *amount* of punitive damages the jury awarded, Oregon provides no procedure for reducing or setting aside that award. This has been the law in Oregon at least since 1949 when the State Supreme Court announced its opinion in *Van Lom v. Schneiderman*, definitively construing the 1910 amendment to the Oregon Constitution. In that case the court held that it had no power to reduce or set aside an award of both compensatory and punitive damages that was admittedly excessive.

10. Respondent argues that Oregon's procedures do not deviate from common law practice, because Oregon judges have the power to examine the size of

the award to determine whether the jury was influenced by passion and prejudice. This is simply incorrect. The earliest Oregon cases interpreting the 1910
amendment squarely held that Oregon courts lack precisely that power. No
Oregon court for more than half a century has inferred passion and prejudice
from the size of a damages award, and no court in more than a decade has even
hinted that courts might possess the power to do so.

11. Finally, if Oregon courts could evaluate the excessiveness of punitive damage
awards through passion and prejudice review, the Oregon Supreme Court
would have mentioned that power in this very case. Petitioner argued that
Oregon procedures were unconstitutional precisely because they failed to
provide judicial review of the size of punitive damage awards.

12. Respondent also argues that Oregon provides adequate review, because the
trial judge can overturn a punitive damage award if there is no substantial
evidence to support an award of punitive damages. This argument is uncon-
vincing, because the review provided by Oregon courts ensures only that there
is evidence to support *some* punitive damages, not that there is evidence to
support the amount actually awarded. While Oregon's judicial review ensures
that punitive damages are not awarded against defendants entirely innocent
of conduct warranting exemplary damages, Oregon, unlike the common law,
provides no assurance that those whose conduct is sanctionable by punitive
damages are not subjected to punitive damages of arbitrary amounts. What we
are concerned with is the possibility that a guilty defendant may be unjustly
punished; evidence of guilt warranting some punishment is not a substitute
for evidence providing at least a rational basis for the particular deprivation
of property imposed by the State to deter future wrongdoing.

13. Oregon's abrogation of a well-established common law protection against
arbitrary deprivations of property raises a presumption that its procedures
violate the Due Process Clause. As this Court has stated from its first Due
Process cases, traditional practice provides a touchstone for constitutional
analysis. Because the basic procedural protections of the common law have
been regarded as so fundamental, very few cases have arisen in which a party
has complained of their denial. In fact, most of our Due Process decisions
involve arguments that traditional procedures provide too little protection
and that additional safeguards are necessary to ensure compliance with the
Constitution. Nevertheless, there are a handful of cases in which a party has
been deprived of liberty or property without the safeguards of common law
procedure. When the absent procedures would have provided protection
against arbitrary and inaccurate adjudication, this Court has not hesitated to
find the proceedings violative of Due Process.

14. Of course, not all deviations from established procedures result in constitutional infirmity. As the Court noted in *Hurtado*, to hold all procedural change
unconstitutional "would be to deny every quality of the law but its age, and to

render it incapable of progress or improvement." A review of the cases, however, suggests that the case before us is unlike those in which abrogations of common law procedures have been upheld.

In *Hurtado*, for example, examination by a neutral magistrate provided criminal defendants with nearly the same protection as the abrogated common law grand jury procedure. Oregon, by contrast, has provided no similar substitute for the protection provided by judicial review of the amount awarded by the jury in punitive damages. . . . If anything, the rise of large, interstate and multinational corporations has aggravated the problem of arbitrary awards and potentially biased juries.

15. Punitive damages pose an acute danger of arbitrary deprivation of property. Jury instructions typically leave the jury with wide discretion in choosing amounts, and the presentation of evidence of a defendant's net worth creates the potential that juries will use their verdicts to express biases against big businesses, particularly those without strong local presences. Judicial review of the amount awarded was one of the few procedural safeguards which the common law provided against that danger. Oregon has removed that safeguard without providing any substitute procedure and without any indication that the danger of arbitrary awards has in any way subsided over time. For these reasons, we hold that Oregon's denial of judicial review of the size of punitive damage awards violates the Due Process Clause of the Fourteenth Amendment.

16. Respondent argues that Oregon has provided other safeguards against arbitrary awards and that, in any event, the exercise of this unreviewable power by the jury is consistent with the jury's historic role in our judicial system.

Respondent points to four safeguards provided in the Oregon courts: the limitation of punitive damages to the amount specified in the complaint, the clear and convincing standard of proof, pre-verdict determination of maximum allowable punitive damages, and detailed jury instructions.

⭐17. The first, limitation of punitive damages to the amount specified, is hardly a constraint at all, because there is no limit to the amount the plaintiff can request, and it is unclear whether an award exceeding the amount requested could be set aside. See *Tenold v. Weyerhaeuser Co:* Oregon Constitution bars court from examining jury award to ensure compliance with $500,000 statutory limit on noneconomic damages.

18. The second safeguard, the clear and convincing standard of proof, is an important check against unwarranted imposition of punitive damages, but, like the "no substantial evidence" review discussed above, it provides no assurance that those whose conduct is sanctionable by punitive damages are not subjected to punitive damages of arbitrary amounts.

19. Regarding the third purported constraint, respondent cites no cases to support the idea that Oregon courts do or can set maximum punitive damage awards

in advance of the verdict. Nor are we aware of any court which implements that procedure.

20. Respondent's final safeguard, proper jury instruction, is a well-established and, of course, important check against excessive awards. The problem that concerns us, however, is the possibility that a jury will not follow those instructions and may return a lawless, biased, or arbitrary verdict.

In support of his argument that there is a historic basis for making the jury the final arbiter of the amount of punitive damages, respondent calls our attention to early civil and criminal cases in which the jury was allowed to judge the law as well as the facts. As we have already explained, in civil cases, the jury's discretion to determine the amount of damages was constrained by judicial review. The criminal cases do establish—as does our practice today—that a jury's arbitrary decision to acquit a defendant charged with a crime is completely unreviewable. There is, however, a vast difference between arbitrary grants of freedom and arbitrary deprivations of liberty or property. The Due Process Clause has nothing to say about the former, but its whole purpose is to prevent the latter. A decision to punish a tortfeasor by means of an exaction of exemplary damages is an exercise of state power that must comply with the Due Process Clause of the Fourteenth Amendment. The common law practice, the procedures applied by every other State, the strong presumption favoring judicial review that we have applied in other areas of the law, and elementary considerations of justice, all support the conclusion that such a decision should not be committed to the unreviewable discretion of a jury.

II. The next set of passages is from the *footnotes* to the *Opinion of the Court*. They offer additional examples of the majority's decision-making process. Once again, you are to describe the reasoning involved in each passage. Illustrate the logical apparatus involved (the uses of logical operators), and the analogical reasoning that constitutes the Supreme Court's arguments.

1. The jury instructions in the original Oregon trial, in relevant part, read: "Punitive damages may be awarded to the plaintiff in addition to general damages to punish wrongdoers and to discourage wanton misconduct. In order for plaintiff to recover punitive damages against the defendant[s], the plaintiff must prove by clear and convincing evidence that defendant[s have] shown wanton disregard for the health, safety, and welfare of others.... If you decide this issue against the defendant[s], you may award punitive damages, although you are not required to do so, because punitive damages are discretionary. In the exercise of that discretion, you shall consider evidence, if any, of the following: First, the likelihood at the time of the sale [of the three-wheeled vehicle] that serious harm would arise from defendants' misconduct. Second, the degree of the defendants' awareness of that likelihood. Third, the duration of the misconduct. Fourth, the attitude and conduct of the defendant[s] upon notice of the alleged condition of the vehicle. Fifth, the financial condition of

the defendant[s]. And the amount of punitive damages may not exceed the sum of $5 million."

Answer:

The passage presents a series of rules that must be followed for two issues: (1) "In order for plaintiff to recover punitive damages against the defendant," and (2) the jury's exercise of discretion if they decide against the defendant.

(A) In order for plaintiff to recover punitive damages against the defendant[s], (B) the plaintiff must prove by clear and convincing evidence that defendant[s have] shown wanton disregard for the health, safety, and welfare of others. . . . **If** (C) you decide this issue against the defendant[s], [**then**] (D) you may award punitive damages, although you are **not** required to do so, **because** punitive damages are discretionary. In the exercise of that discretion, you shall consider evidence, **if** any, of the following: (E) First, the likelihood at the time of the sale [of the three-wheeled vehicle] that serious harm would arise from defendants' misconduct. (F) Second, the degree of the defendants' awareness of that likelihood. (G) Third, the duration of the misconduct. (H) Fourth, the attitude and conduct of the defendant[s] upon notice of the alleged condition of the vehicle. (I) Fifth, the financial condition of the defendant[s]. **And** (J) the amount of punitive damages may not exceed the sum of $5 million.

> A only if B.
> If C, then (D or not D).
> If C, then [(E or F or G or H or I) and J].

2. As in many early cases, it is unclear whether this case (*Fabrigas v. Mostyn*) specifically concerns punitive damages or merely ordinary compensatory damages. Since there is no suggestion that different standards of judicial review were applied for punitive and compensatory damages before the twentieth century, no effort has been made to separate out the two classes of case.

3. The amended Article VII, §3, of the Oregon Constitution provides: "In actions at law, where the value in controversy shall exceed twenty dollars, the right of trial by jury shall be preserved, and no fact tried by a jury shall be otherwise re-examined in any court of this State, unless the court can affirmatively say there is no evidence to support the verdict."

4. The Oregon Supreme Court in *Van Lom v. Schneiderman* stated the following: "The court is of the opinion that the verdict of $10,000.00 is excessive. Some members of the court think that only the award of punitive damages is excessive; others that both the awards of compensatory and punitive damages are excessive. Since a majority are of the opinion that this court has no power to disturb the verdict, it is not deemed necessary to discuss the grounds for these divergent views."

⭐ 5. The Oregon Supreme Court in *Van Lom v. Schneiderman* stated the following: "The guaranty of the right to jury trial in suits at common law, incorporated in the Bill of Rights as one of the first ten amendments of the Constitution of the United States, was interpreted by the Supreme Court of the United States to refer to jury trial as it had been theretofore known in England; and so it is that the federal judges, like the English judges, have always exercised the prerogative of granting a new trial when the verdict was clearly against the weight of the evidence, whether it be because excessive damages were awarded or for any other reason."

6. Respondent cites as support for its argument *Chicago, R. I. & P. R. Co. v. Cole*. In that case, the Court upheld a provision of the Oklahoma Constitution providing that "the defense of contributory negligence . . . shall . . . be left to the jury." *Chicago, R. I.* provides little support for respondent's case. Justice Holmes' reasoning relied on the fact that a State could completely abolish the defense of contributory negligence. This case, however, is different, because the *TXO* and *Haslip* opinions establish that States cannot abolish limits on the award of punitive damages.

7. Respondent also argues that empirical evidence supports the effectiveness of these safeguards. It points to the analysis of an *amicus* showing that the average punitive damage award in a products liability case in Oregon is less than the national average. While we welcome respondent's introduction of empirical evidence on the effectiveness of Oregon's legal rules, its statistics are undermined by the fact that the Oregon average is computed from only two punitive damage awards. It is well known that one cannot draw valid statistical arguments from such a small number of observations.

   Empirical evidence, in fact, supports the importance of judicial review of the size of punitive damage awards. The most exhaustive study of punitive damages establishes that over half of punitive damage awards were appealed, and that more than half of those appealed resulted in reductions or reversals of the punitive damages. In over 10 percent of the cases appealed, the judge found the damages to be excessive.

8. Judicial deference to jury verdicts may have been stronger in 18th century America than in England, and judges' power to order new trials for excessive damages more contested. Nevertheless, because this case concerns the Due Process Clause of the Fourteenth Amendment, 19th century American practice is the "crucial time for present purposes." As demonstrated above, by the time the Fourteenth Amendment was ratified in 1868, the power of judges to order new trials for excessive damages was well established in American courts. In addition, the idea that jurors can find law as well as fact is not inconsistent with judicial review for excessive damages.

III. The next set of passages is from the *dissenting opinion* by Justice Ginsberg. They offer examples of the reasons for dissenting from the majority opinion. Once again, some of the passages have been edited to simplify the task at hand. As before, you are to describe the reasoning involved in each passage.

Illustrate the logical apparatus involved (the uses of logical operators) and the analogical reasoning that constitutes the dissenting opinion.

1. Where the factfinder is a jury, its decision is subject to judicial review to this extent: The trial court, or an appellate court, may nullify the verdict if reversible error occurred during the trial, if the jury was improperly or inadequately instructed, or if there is no evidence to support the verdict. Absent trial error, and if there is evidence to support the award of punitive damages, however, Oregon's Constitution, Article VII, §3, provides that a properly instructed jury's verdict shall not be reexamined. Oregon's procedures, I conclude, are adequate to pass the Constitution's due process threshold. I therefore dissent from the Court's judgment upsetting Oregon's disposition in this case.

Answer:

(A) Where the factfinder is a jury, its decision is subject to judicial review to this extent: (B) The trial court, **or** an appellate court, may nullify the verdict **if** (C) reversible error occurred during the trial, **if** (D) the jury was improperly **or** inadequately instructed, **or if** (E) there is no evidence to support the verdict. (F) Absent trial error, **and if** (G) there is evidence to support the award of punitive damages, however, [**then**] (H) Oregon's Constitution, Article VII, §3, provides that a properly instructed jury's verdict shall **not** be reexamined. (I) Oregon's procedures, I **conclude**, are adequate to pass the Constitution's due process threshold. (J) I **therefore** dissent from the Court's judgment upsetting Oregon's disposition in this case.

> If A, then [if (C or D or E), then B].
> If (F and G), then H.
> Therefore I.
> Therefore J.

2. To assess the constitutionality of Oregon's scheme, I turn first to this Court's recent opinions in *Haslip*, and *TXO*. The Court upheld punitive damage awards in both cases, but indicated that due process imposes an outer limit on remedies of this type. Significantly, neither decision declared any specific procedures or substantive criteria essential to satisfy due process. In *Haslip*, the Court expressed concerns about "unlimited jury discretion, or unlimited judicial discretion for that matter, in the fixing of punitive damages," but refused to "draw a mathematical bright line between the constitutionally acceptable and the constitutionally unacceptable. . . ." And in *TXO*, a majority agreed that a punitive damage award may be so grossly excessive as to violate the Due Process Clause. In the plurality's view, however, "a judgment that is a product" of "fair procedures . . . is entitled to a strong presumption of validity."

3. The procedures Oregon's courts followed in this case satisfy the due process limits indicated in *Haslip* and *TXO*; the jurors were adequately guided by the trial court's instructions, and Honda has not maintained, in its full presentation

to this Court, that the award in question was "so 'grossly excessive' as to violate the Federal Constitution."

4. Several preverdict mechanisms channeled the jury's discretion more tightly in this case than in either *Haslip* or *TXO*. First, providing at least some protection against unguided, utterly arbitrary jury awards, respondent Oberg was permitted to recover no more than the amounts specified in the complaint, $919,390.39 in compensatory damages and $5 million in punitive damages. The trial court properly instructed the jury on this damage cap. No provision of Oregon law appears to preclude the defendant from seeking an instruction setting a lower cap, if the evidence at trial cannot support an award in the amount demanded. Additionally, if the trial judge relates the incorrect maximum amount, a defendant who timely objects may gain modification or nullification of the verdict.

★ 5. Second, Oberg was not allowed to introduce evidence regarding Honda's wealth until he "presented evidence sufficient to justify to the court a prima facie claim of punitive damages. During the course of trial, evidence of the defendant's ability to pay shall not be admitted unless and until the party entitled to recover establishes a prima facie right to recover [punitive damages]." This evidentiary rule is designed to lessen the risk "that juries will use their verdicts to express biases against big businesses," to take into account "[t]he total deterrent effect of other punishment imposed upon the defendant as a result of the misconduct."

6. Third, and more significant, as the trial court instructed the jury, Honda could not be found liable for punitive damages unless Oberg established by "clear and convincing evidence" that Honda "show[ed] wanton disregard for the health, safety and welfare of others." [Governing product liability actions, see §41.315(1): "Except as otherwise specifically provided by law, a claim for punitive damages shall be established by clear and convincing evidence."] "[T]he clear and convincing evidence requirement," which is considerably more rigorous than the standards applied by Alabama in *Haslip* and West Virginia in *TXO*, "constrain[s] the jury's discretion, limiting punitive damages to the more egregious cases." Nothing in Oregon law appears to preclude a new trial order if the trial judge, informed by the jury's verdict, determines that his charge did not adequately explain what the "clear and convincing" standard means.

7. Fourth, and perhaps most important, in product liability cases, Oregon requires that punitive damages, if any, be awarded based on seven substantive criteria: "(a) The likelihood at the time that serious harm would arise from the defendant's misconduct; (b) [t]he degree of the defendant's awareness of that likelihood; (c) [t]he profitability of the defendant's misconduct; (d) [t]he duration of the misconduct and any concealment of it; (e) [t]he attitude and conduct of the defendant upon discovery of the misconduct; (f) [t]he financial condition of the defendant; and (g) [t]he total deterrent effect of

other punishment imposed upon the defendant as a result of the misconduct, including, but not limited to, punitive damage awards to persons in situations similar to the claimant's and the severity of criminal penalties to which the defendant has been or may be subjected."

8. These substantive criteria (*a* through *g* in question 7), and the precise instructions detailing them, gave the jurors "adequate guidance" in making their award far more guidance than their counterparts in *Haslip* and *TXO* received. In *Haslip*, for example, the jury was told only the purpose of punitive damages (punishment and deterrence) and that an award was discretionary, not compulsory. We deemed those instructions, notable for their generality, constitutionally sufficient.

9. The Court's opinion in *Haslip* went on to describe the checks Alabama places on the jury's discretion *postverdict*—through excessiveness review by the trial court, and appellate review, which tests the award against specific substantive criteria. While postverdict review of that character is not available in Oregon, the seven factors against which Alabama's Supreme Court tests punitive awards strongly resemble the statutory criteria Oregon's juries are instructed to apply. And this Court has often acknowledged, and generally respected, the presumption that juries follow the instructions they are given. As the Supreme Court of Oregon observed, *Haslip* "determined only that the Alabama procedure, as a whole and in its net effect, did not violate the Due Process Clause."

10. The Oregon court also observed, correctly, that the Due Process Clause does not require States to subject punitive damage awards to a form of postverdict review "that includes the possibility of remittitur." Because Oregon requires the factfinder to apply objective criteria, moreover, its procedures are perhaps more likely to prompt rational and fair punitive damage decisions than are the *post hoc* checks employed in jurisdictions following Alabama's pattern.

11. The Supreme Court of Oregon's conclusions are buttressed by the availability of at least some postverdict judicial review of punitive damage awards. Oregon's courts ensure that there is evidence to support the verdict: "If there is no evidence to support the jury's decision—in this context, no evidence that the statutory prerequisites for the award of punitive damages were met—then the trial court or the appellate courts can intervene to vacate the award."

12. The State's courts have shown no reluctance to strike punitive damage awards in cases where punitive liability is not established, so that defendant qualifies for judgment on that issue as a matter of law. In addition, punitive damage awards may be set aside because of flaws in jury instructions. See *Honeywell v. Sterling Furniture Co*: setting aside punitive damage award because it was prejudicial error to instruct jury that a portion of any award would be used to pay plaintiff's attorney fees and that another portion would go to State's common injury fund. As the Court acknowledges, "proper jury instructio[n] is a well established and, of course, important check against excessive awards."

⭐13. In short, Oregon has enacted legal standards confining punitive damage awards in product liability cases. These state standards are judicially enforced by means of comparatively comprehensive preverdict procedures but markedly limited postverdict review, for Oregon has elected to make fact-finding, once supporting evidence is produced, the province of the jury.... The Court today invalidates this choice, largely because it concludes that English and early American courts generally provided judicial review of the size of punitive damage awards. The Court's account of the relevant history is not compelling.

14. I am not as confident as the Court about either the clarity of early American common law, or its import. Tellingly, the Court barely acknowledges the large authority exercised by American juries in the 18th and 19th centuries. In the early years of our Nation, juries "usually possessed the power to determine both law and fact." *Georgia v. Brailsford*: Chief Justice John Jay, trying a case in which State was party, instructed jury it had authority "to determine the law as well as the fact in controversy." And at the time trial by jury was recognized as the constitutional right of parties "[i]n [s]uits at common law," U.S. Constitution, Amendment 7, the assessment of "uncertain damages" was regarded, generally, as exclusively a jury function.

15. More revealing, the Court notably contracts the scope of its inquiry. It asks: Did common law judges claim the power to overturn jury verdicts they viewed as excessive? But full and fair historical inquiry ought to be wider. The Court should inspect, comprehensively and comparatively, the procedures employed—at trial *and* on appeal—to fix the amount of punitive damages. Evaluated in this manner, Oregon's scheme affords defendants like Honda *more* procedural safeguards than 19th century law provided.

16. Oregon instructs juries to decide punitive damage issues based on seven substantive factors and a clear and convincing evidence standard. When the Fourteenth Amendment was adopted in 1868, in contrast (see *Haslip*), "no particular procedures were deemed necessary to circumscribe a jury's discretion regarding the award of [punitive] damages, or their amount." The responsibility entrusted to the jury surely was not guided by instructions of the kind Oregon has enacted.

⭐17. Furthermore, common law courts reviewed punitive damage verdicts extremely deferentially, if at all. See *Day v. Woodworth*: assessment of "exemplary, punitive, or vindictive damages ... has been always left to the discretion of the jury, as the degree of punishment to be thus inflicted must depend on the peculiar circumstances of each case"; *Missouri Pacific R. Co. v. Humes*: "[t]he discretion of the jury in such cases is not controlled by any very definite rules"; *Barry v. Edmunds*: in "actions for torts where no precise rule of law fixes the recoverable damages, it is the peculiar function of the jury to determine the amount by their verdict." True, 19th century judges occasionally asserted that they had authority to overturn damage awards upon concluding, from the size of an award, that the jury's decision must have been based on "partiality" or "passion and prejudice." But courts rarely *exercised* this authority.

18. Because Oregon's procedures assure "adequate guidance from the court when the case is tried to a jury," (*Haslip*), this Court has no cause to disturb the judgment in this instance, for Honda presses here only a *procedural* due process claim. True, in a footnote to its petition for *certiorari*, not repeated in its briefs, Honda attributed to this Court an "assumption that procedural due process requires [judicial] review of *both* federal substantive due process and state law excessiveness challenges to the size of an award." But the assertion regarding "state law excessiveness challenges" is extraordinary, for this Court has never held that the Due Process Clause requires a State's courts to police jury fact-findings to ensure their conformity with state law. And, as earlier observed, the plurality opinion in *TXO* disavowed the suggestion that a defendant has a federal due process right to a correct determination under state law of the "reasonableness" of a punitive damages award.

19. Honda further asserted in its *certiorari* petition footnote: "Surely . . . due process (not to mention Supremacy Clause principles) requires, at a minimum, that state courts entertain and pass on the federal law contention that a particular punitive verdict is so grossly excessive as to violate substantive due process. Oregon's refusal to provide even that limited form of review is particularly indefensible." But Honda points to no definitive Oregon pronouncement postdating this Court's precedent setting decisions in *Haslip* and *TXO* demonstrating the hypothesized refusal to pass on a federal law contention.

20. It may be that Oregon's procedures guide juries so well that the "grossly excessive" verdict Honda projects in its *certiorari* petition footnote never materializes. [Between 1965 and the present, awards of punitive damages in Oregon have been reported in only two products liability cases, including this one.] If, however, in some future case, a plea is plausibly made that a particular punitive damage award is not merely excessive, but "so 'grossly excessive' as to violate the Federal Constitution," *TXO*, and Oregon's judiciary nevertheless insists that it is powerless to consider the plea, this Court might have cause to grant review. No such case is before us today, nor does Honda, in this Court, maintain otherwise (size of award against Honda does not appear to be out of line with awards upheld in *Haslip* and *TXO*).

21. To summarize: Oregon's procedures adequately guide the jury charged with the responsibility to determine a plaintiff's qualification for, and the amount of, punitive damages, and on that account do not deny defendants procedural due process; Oregon's Supreme Court correctly refused to rule that "an award of punitive damages, to comport with the requirements of the Due Process Clause, *always* must be subject to a form of postverdict or appellate review" for excessiveness; the verdict in this particular case, considered in light of this Court's decisions in *Haslip* and *TXO*, hardly appears "so 'grossly excessive' as to

violate the substantive component of the Due Process Clause," *TXO*. Accordingly, the Court's procedural directive to the state court is neither necessary nor proper. The Supreme Court of Oregon has not refused to enforce federal law, and I would affirm its judgment.

IV. The next set of passages is from the *footnotes* to the *dissenting opinion*. They offer additional examples of the dissenting opinion's decision-making process. Once again, you are to describe the reasoning involved in each passage. Illustrate the logical apparatus involved (the uses of logical operators) and the analogical reasoning that constitutes the Supreme Court's arguments.

1. The *Haslip* jury was told that it could award punitive damages if "reasonably satisfied from the evidence" that the defendant committed fraud.

Answer:

(A) The *Haslip* jury was told that it could award punitive damages **if** (B) "reasonably satisfied from the evidence" that the defendant committed fraud.

If B, then A.

No argument is put forward in this passage. The statement is meant to help clarify the facts of the case.

2. The trial court in the Oregon case instructed the jury as follows: "Punitive damages: If you have found that plaintiff is entitled to general damages, you must then consider whether to award punitive damages. Punitive damages may be awarded to the plaintiff in addition to general damages to punish wrongdoers and to discourage wanton misconduct."

3. The trial judge did not instruct the jury on the following factors: (1) The "profitability of [Honda's] misconduct," or (2) the "total deterrent effect of other punishment" to which Honda was subject. Honda objected to an instruction on factor (1), which it argued was phrased "to assume the existence of misconduct," and expressly waived an instruction on factor (2), on the ground that it had not previously been subject to punitive damages. In its argument before the Supreme Court of Oregon, Honda did not contend that the trial court failed to instruct the jury concerning the criteria, or "that the jury did not properly apply those criteria."

4. The trial judge in *Haslip* instructed the jury as follows:
   "Now, if you find that fraud was perpetrated then in addition to compensatory damages you may in your discretion, when I use the word discretion, I say you don't have to even find fraud, you wouldn't have to, but you may, the law says you may award an amount of money known as punitive damages.
   "This amount of money is awarded to the plaintiff but it is not to compensate the plaintiff for any injury. It is to punish the defendant. Punitive means to punish or it is also called exemplary damages, which means to make an example. So, if you feel or not feel, but if you are reasonably satisfied from the

evidence that the plaintiff[s] . . . ha[ve] had a fraud perpetrated upon them and as a direct result they were injured [then] in addition to compensatory damages you may in your discretion award punitive damages. . . .

"Should you award punitive damages, in fixing the amount, you must take into consideration the character and the degree of the wrong as shown by the evidence and necessity of preventing similar wrong."

Summary

Study Materials

- Legal arguments can be appreciated and understood when you are able to grasp the underlying logic. Legal discourse has evolved patterns and conventions that we can recognize and apply to specific legal cases.
- Appellate courts: Courts of appeal that review the decisions of lower courts.
- A rule that specifies a test with mandatory elements lists all the necessary conditions that must be met in order for the rule to be applicable.
- In law, the term "deductive reasoning" generally means as going from the *general* to the *specific*—that is, from the statement of a *rule* to its application to a particular legal case.
- Many law textbooks define "inductive reasoning" as the process of going from the *specific* to the *general*. It comes into play whenever we move from a specific case or legal opinion to a general rule.
- Legal reasoning is also called "rule-based reasoning."
- Sufficient condition: Whenever one event ensures that another event is realized.
- Necessary condition: Whenever one thing is *essential, mandatory,* or *required* in order for another thing to be realized.
- Probative value: Evidence that can be used during a trial to advance the facts of the case.
- Prejudicial effect: Evidence that might cause some jurors to be negatively biased toward a defendant.
- Indictment: A formal accusation presented by a grand jury.
- Affidavit: A written statement signed before an authorized official.
- Legal reasoning, relying as it does on precedent (a judicial decision that can be applied to later cases) and similar cases, often relies on analogies.
- Rules of law: The legal principles that have been applied to historical cases.
- Plaintiff: The person who initiates a lawsuit.

LOGIC CHALLENGE: A GUILTY PROBLEM

Imagine that you are a private investigator specializing in determining the truth value of suspects' statements to the police. You are shown a videotape of four suspects accused of robbing a quick-loan store. The four suspects happen to know each other. When you view the videotape, you are allowed to hear each suspect make only one statement.

> *Alice:* Benny did it.
> *Benny:* David did it.
> *Connie:* I did not do it.
> *David:* What Benny said about me is false.

Assume that only one person did it and only one of the four statements is true. If so, determine the following two things:

1. Who committed the crime?

2. Which one of the statements is true?

Chapter 12

Moral Arguments

Digital homework exercises for this chapter are available in your instructor's online course. For information on how to access these resources, please visit **www.oup.com/ he/baronett5e**.

On a gut level, moral arguments are about right and wrong, and they can quickly become demanding, commanding, and heated. "Thou shalt not kill." "Abortion is wrong." However, value judgments enter a lot of what we do and say—and so does the word "should." "You should remember to wash your hands before eating." "I should really be studying for that test tomorrow." "I should never have bought that stupid car."

To make things more complicated, some arguments rely solely on *factual claims* for support, some arguments rely solely on *value judgments* for support, and some arguments rely on a mixture of the two. "You take one more step, and you're in deep trouble." "You should stop lying, because you will quickly lose your credibility." "Without affordable health care, thousands of Americans will die." Where exactly do the factual claims end and the value judgments begin?

Since logic is the systematic use of methods and principles to analyze, evaluate, and construct arguments, logic provides many skills that you can apply to moral reasoning. For example, you can reconstruct someone's moral argument, adding missing premises if needed. You can also use analogical reasoning or evaluate a moral argument for inconsistencies.

As usual, the first step in analyzing an argument is clarifying the premises and conclusion. Imagine that you want to take a vacation to Los Angeles from your home in New York. You discuss it with two friends, who offer their advice. One friend mentions the fact that you can fly from the East Coast of the United States to the West Coast nonstop in about 6 hours. He then adds another piece of information by citing the fact that it would take about 4 days to drive the same distance across the

United States (factoring in time needed to eat and sleep). From this, he concludes that you *should* fly rather than drive to Los Angeles. Here is the argument:

> You can fly from New York to Los Angeles in about 6 hours. It takes about 4 days to drive the same distance. You *should* fly rather than drive.

However, the second friend might agree with the two premises just described, but she comes to the opposite conclusion—that you *should* drive instead of fly.

> You can fly from New York to Los Angeles in about 6 hours. It takes about 4 days to drive the same distance. You *should* drive rather than fly.

Can these differences be explained by just the facts involved? Obviously, both arguments use the same factual claims in the premises. However, the word "should" appears in both conclusions, but it is found nowhere in the premises. What is the justification for its introduction? The exploration of the difference between facts and values, as well as words such as "should" and "ought," starts our discussion of moral arguments. Let's begin.

A. VALUE JUDGMENTS

Value judgment A claim that a particular human action or object has some degree of importance, worth, or desirability.

A **value judgment** is a claim that a particular human action or object has some degree of importance, worth, or desirability. Let's see how value judgments enter into our discussion of your travel plans.

Justifying "Should"

Justifying the use of the word "should" in the conclusion of both arguments requires an introduction of new information in the premises. Since both arguments are missing this important ingredient, we can treat them as enthymemes (Chapter 1 introduced enthymemes and missing information). For the first argument, a possible implied premise is that *you probably want to make the trip as quickly as possible*. Adding this as a new premise would make the first argument strong. On the other hand, for the second argument, a possible implied premise is that *you probably want to see as much of the country as possible*. Adding this new information would make the second argument strong.

Both argument reconstructions deliberately supplied a premise designed to make each argument strong. When you have the time to reflect more thoroughly about the available options, then you might decide that you do want to see as much of the country as possible. In that case, the added premise in the first argument would be false, so the argument would not be cogent. However, the added premise in the second argument would be true, so that would yield a cogent argument.

In these two examples, the word "should" in the conclusion was justified as following from a *desired goal*. The intent of each argument was to offer good reasons why you should choose one method of transportation over another. The evaluation of the arguments hinged on how well the arguments match the intended goal. Notice that *if* you had decided that you wanted to make the trip as quickly as possible, then the added premise in the first argument would be true and the argument would be cogent.

It would also follow that the added premise in the second argument would be false and the argument would not be cogent.

But what happens if we eliminate the intended goal of the trip? What if, instead, you and your friends were just talking about travel in general? Now suppose that one of your friends remarked that he hated driving long distances, while another friend remarked that she loved taking long road trips. These would be instances of value judgments.

Types of Value Judgments

There are many types of value judgments. For example, moral value judgments place emphasis on human actions or behaviors by asserting that they are *good, bad, right,* or *wrong*. Here are some examples of moral claims:

1. Murder is wrong.
2. You should always tell the truth.
3. Torturing prisoners is an immoral act.
4. Extracting information by torture in order to save lives is the morally right thing to do.

A second type of value judgment concerns matters of personal taste or value. For example, one person might say "Anchovies taste great" while another might say "Anchovies taste terrible." *Neither of these two statements asserts any facts about anchovies.* At best, they are an assertion of a person's feelings about the taste of anchovies. Examine the following three sentences:

5. Anchovies taste great.
6. Anchovies taste terrible.
7. Anchovies are small fish belonging to the herring family.

Sentence 7 is the only one of the three that *asserts something factual* about anchovies. If they are members of the herring family, then the statement is true; otherwise the statement is false. The first two sentences may appear to assert something about anchovies, but they do not. If you hate the taste of anchovies you might imagine that everyone else does too, and are amazed that anyone would find the taste desirable. On the other hand, if you love the taste of a certain kind of ice cream you might be surprised that other people do not share your personal value judgment. We would like our personal value judgments to be *universally shared* and are often surprised when they are not. So, for example, when you introduce your favorite ice cream to a friend and she says that "it is just OK," you might ask her to take another bite, hoping that she will change her mind and agree with your value judgment.

Another way of describing the set of three sentences regarding anchovies is to label the first two *subjective* and the third *objective*. In other words, the first two sentences *refer to the person* making the claim about anchovies and are, therefore, *subjective* claims. As such, these claims can be rewritten to bring out this point:

8. Anchovies taste great *to me*.
9. Anchovies taste terrible *to me*.

Now, these two statements can be considered either true or false, but their truth value cannot be determined by an examination of the facts concerning anchovies. These *subjective* statements are true if the persons uttering the statements are accurately describing how anchovies taste *to them*, otherwise they are false. Contrast those two statements with the third statement whose *objective* truth value can be determined by the facts concerning anchovies.

Now look closely at the next statement:

> Killing another human being is always wrong.

It is fair to say that when most people make this claim they intend it to be an objective assertion. It is not likely that they would think that it was comparable to the assertions regarding the taste of anchovies. Nevertheless, it is a value judgment; more specifically, a *moral value judgment*. It is typically used in the following way:

> You *should not* kill a human being.

Here we have another instance of the word "should." It is being used as a directive for how you *ought to* act toward other humans. When the words *should* and *ought* are used in a moral setting, the resulting statements are also referred to as *prescriptive* or *normative*. **Prescriptive statements** offer advice. In a medical setting, a physician may prescribe medicine or a course of treatment. In a moral setting, advice may be offered either by specifying a particular action that ought to be performed or by providing general moral rules, principles, or guidelines that should be followed.

Normative statements establish standards for correct moral behavior, determining norms or rules of conduct. Given this, we can see that the statement "You *should not* kill a human being" has a different function than the earlier example "You *should* drive across the United States." There, the emphasis was not in any way connected to a moral decision. Therefore, different types of value judgments play decidedly different roles in the construction and analysis of arguments. Since we are interested in moral reasoning we need to explore how moral value judgments function in the construction, analysis, and evaluation of moral arguments.

Prescriptive statement A statement that offers advice either by specifying a particular action that ought to be performed or by providing general moral rules, principles, or guidelines that should be followed.

Normative statement A statement that establishes standards for correct moral behavior, determining norms or rules of conduct.

Taste and Value

Let's imagine that someone is trying to persuade you that incest is morally wrong. She might resort to empirical research that indicates nearly all cultures view incest as morally wrong. This evidence is then used to conclude that "You should not commit incest." Now compare this result with the following scenario. Imagine that someone is trying to persuade you that anchovies taste terrible. She might resort to surveys that show that most people do not like the taste of anchovies. This evidence is then used to conclude that "You should not like anchovies."

Most people agree that there is a substantial difference between the incest and anchovies examples, because they believe there is a fundamental difference between a moral value judgment and one involving personal taste. Of course, both arguments are classified as value judgments, and both arguments have the word "should" in the conclusion. But suppose a close friend claims that the two cases are *not* fundamentally different; in other words, he thinks that *all value judgments are the same.* In fact, he believes that since empirical evidence is irrelevant in the anchovy argument, then it is also irrelevant in the incest argument. Therefore, we need to think seriously about two questions:

    A. Are the two uses of "should" really that different?
    B. If so, in what fundamental ways are they different?

We can start out by assessing the use of the empirical data. In the anchovy example, no matter if you were the only person on earth who liked the taste of anchovies, we would think it foolish for anyone to claim that *you should not like them.* Since personal taste concerning foods is subjective, any supposed "objective" evidence regarding other humans is actually just a tally of their personal tastes.

On the other hand, the use of empirical data regarding cultural attitudes toward incest seems to appeal to an *objective fact* and not just a tally of personal feelings. Those holding this position argue that there are "moral facts" that support moral beliefs. The challenge is then to determine the "objective" nature of certain moral judgments. In other words, if they are objective, then how do we come to that determination? To help us gain insight into the nature and complexity of moral claims, we need to look at some moral theories, the subject of the next section.

EXERCISES 12A

Determine whether the following statements are factual claims or value claims. If a statement makes a value claim, then determine if it is a moral value claim or a personal value claim.

Self-Practice
Questions

    1. Capital punishment is wrong.
Answer: Moral value claim

    2. Your answer to the homework problem is wrong.

    3. Pizza is the most delicious kind of food on the planet.

    4. Euthanasia is an acceptable act.

⭐ 5. The movie *Inception* won four Academy Awards.

    6. The movie *Inception* was confusing and difficult to follow.

    7. Venison is deer meat.

    8. Eating meat is wrong.

⭐ 9. Air travel is boring.

    10. Air travel is the safest way to travel.

    11. Anyone afraid of flying is irrational.

Video Tutorial: 12A
Exercise #11

12. Tax evasion is a criminal offense.

⭐13. Not paying taxes is a justified form of protest.

14. Giving big corporations tax breaks is welfare for millionaires.

15. Microsoft employs the most workers of any software company in the United States.

B. MORAL THEORIES

There are many different kinds of moral theories. We can distinguish *normative ethical theories* from *meta-ethical theories*. Normative ethical theories focus on what is right and wrong. They concentrate directly on clarifying criteria for judging how we ought to act or the kind of person we should be. In contrast, meta-ethical theories focus on the nature of moral judgments through an analysis of moral language. In other words, a meta-ethical theory is not directly concerned with articulating which actions are right or wrong; instead, the focus is on what it means to say that an action is right or wrong. The focus is thus on the logical analysis of moral concepts and how they are used.

Some ethical theories offer ways of determining whether a human action is morally right or wrong by placing emphasis on the outcome of the action. These theories look to the ultimate consequences of our actions as the focal point for moral deliberations. On the other hand, some theories reject any consideration of the outcome of an action and instead hold that moral acts are right or wrong in themselves. In addition, some moral theories try to combine these two types of approaches. There are even theories that hold that *all* moral judgments are relative to individuals, cultures, and societies. Although there are numerous normative and meta-ethical theories, we will examine only a few in this section.

Emotivism

Consider the following claims:

- Murder is morally wrong.
- You ought always to tell the truth.
- You ought not to steal.

To most people, these seem like perfectly understandable and meaningful *moral statements*. It would be easy to take a survey and get people's responses to each statement. But it is unlikely that you will find many people who say that they do not understand the statements at all. Now compare the three foregoing claims with three different statements:

- Harrisburg is the capital of Pennsylvania.
- The Eiffel Tower is in Paris, France.
- Mount Everest is the fourth tallest mountain in the world.

Once again, most people would think these to be perfectly understandable and meaningful *factual statements*. Also, it would be easy to take a survey and get people's responses to each of these statements. And again, it is unlikely that you will find many people who say that they do not understand the statements at all. Now suppose we ask people how they would *verify* the truth or falsity of the *factual* statements. It should be an easy task, because each of the statements refers to objective facts about the world. Therefore, appropriate and uncontroversial empirical support would be readily available.

But suppose we ask people how they would *verify* the truth or falsity of the *moral statements*. This would not be as easy, because it is not obvious that each of the moral statements refers to any kind of objective facts about the world. Therefore, appropriate and uncontroversial empirical support would not be readily available.

Difficulties such as these are addressed by **emotivism**, a theory that asserts that moral value judgments are merely expressions of our attitudes or emotions. Emotivism thus bypasses the problem of objectively verifying the truth or falsity of moral value judgments. If a moral judgment is an expression of one's personal emotions, then it is not an assertion of fact in the objective sense. Supporters of emotivism often point out that we currently have no reliable means of verifying the accuracy of anyone's subjective statements. The important thing to remember is that emotivism rejects any notion that moral value judgments are in any way descriptions of objective moral facts. Therefore, moral value judgments are no different from other personal value judgments, for example, expressions of taste, such as the utterance "Apples taste delicious (*to me*)."

Thus, for emotivism, moral statements are nothing but expressions of what we personally like and dislike, or of what we approve and disapprove of. As such, they can be used to persuade others to have the same moral feelings that we have. So, according to emotivism, when you say "Murder is wrong," you are not referring to anything objective; this and all other moral value judgments assert nothing factual about the world.

However, emotivism raises some important practical considerations. How do we talk about related moral and legal issues, such as blame, responsibility, and praise? How do we decide when there is a legitimate moral dispute? Since emotivism holds that moral judgments are merely pronouncements of personal taste, then a dispute about a case of child negligence, for example, would be reduced to assertions about each individual's personal feelings. If emotivism is correct, there would be no objective moral aspect to consider in the case.

Consequentialism

Consequentialism refers to a *class* of moral theories in which the moral value of any human action or behavior is determined exclusively by its outcomes. In other words, consequentialist theories hold that a human action is judged morally right or wrong, good or bad, solely on the end result of the action. Similarly, people are judged to be morally good or bad strictly by the consequences of their actions.

Emotivism A theory that asserts that moral value judgments are merely expressions of our attitudes or emotions.

Consequentialism A class of moral theories in which the moral value of any human action or behavior is determined exclusively by its outcomes.

Teleology The philosophical belief that the value of an action or object can be determined by looking at the purpose or the end of the action or object.

Consequentialist theories are based on **teleology**, the philosophical belief that the value of an action or object can be determined by looking at the purpose or the end of the action or object. (The term "teleology" comes from "*telos*," meaning *end*, so it is the study of the end, purpose, or design of an object or human action.) We will look at two consequentialist theories: *egoism* and *utilitarianism*.

Egoism

Egoism The basic principle that everyone should act in order to maximize his or her own individual pleasure or happiness.

As the name indicates, **egoism** is the basic principle that everyone should act in order to maximize his or her own individual pleasure or happiness. Egoism reduces the moral value of an act to the outcome of its consequences to one person, the acting agent. (Since "ego" means *the self*, the moral theory is really just *self-ism*.) Egoism's moral directive is quite simple: *All humans ought to pursue their own personal pleasure.*

It is interesting to consider whether an unintended, but potentially positive consequence of egoism is possible. If everyone consistently followed the directive of egoism, could this increase the overall happiness of society as a whole? Some argue that since we cannot know with certainty how our actions will affect other people, we should not even attempt to consider them. By consistently pursuing our own pleasure or happiness, we are doing our best to maximize the overall happiness of society. As evidence for this position, quite often the best intentions go in vain. As a consequence, if we give up the chance to pursue our own pleasure, then we risk the possibility that no happiness will be achieved. How often has it happened that a seemingly good deed has failed to achieve its goal? (There is a popular paraphrase of a line in Robert Burns's poem "To a Mouse": "The best laid plans of mice and men often go astray.") Therefore, we *ought* always to pursue our own happiness.

Of course, since we cannot know precisely all the future consequences of our actions, we cannot be certain that our own pursuit of pleasure or happiness will end in a good result. An action may result in a short-term pleasure, but if repeated often enough, it might lead to long-term unhappiness and pain. Think of alcohol and drug addiction.

These considerations point to two challenges to most ethical theories. First, how do we *define* what would be *happiness* or *pleasure* for everyone (or for egoism, my own happiness or pleasure)? And second, how do we *measure* or quantify amounts or degrees of *happiness* or *pleasure*? For example, is the happiness or the pleasure of a child comparable to that of an adult? In other words, the challenge is to develop measuring devices, scales, or charts that we can consult to determine the level, degree, or extent of happiness or pleasure in an individual (for egoism), or for society as a whole, or even between cultures.

Utilitarianism

Another specific and important example of a consequentialist moral theory (and therefore, teleological) is *utilitarianism*. Although there are many varieties of utilitarianism, they all agree on a few fundamental principles. The most important principle for

utilitarianism can be summed up in the famous dictum "the greatest good for the greatest number." Any action or human behavior is to be judged by its outcomes—specifically, whether it brought about the greatest good to the greatest number of people. (The name *utilitarianism* is derived from the term "utility," which means *usefulness*.) Since utilitarianism is a moral theory, it concentrates on the usefulness of human actions and behaviors and asks how they affect the overall good or happiness of a society. (Compare this with the term "public utilities," which typically refers to organizations that supply water or electricity, which are useful and beneficial to society.)

Utilitarianism (like egoism, for that matter) is grounded on the psychological assumption that the great driving force of human behavior is the *avoidance of pain* and the *seeking of pleasure*. So, from the psychological evidence supporting this view of human nature, utilitarianism derives its moral directive: *All humans ought to act in order to maximize the greatest pleasure or happiness for the greatest number of people.*

According to utilitarianism, every human action demonstrates **universalizability**, meaning that the same principles hold for all people at all times. More simply, "What if everyone did that?" The underlying sentiment is utilitarian because it appeals to the outcome of our actions. Generally speaking, the question is mostly used in a rhetorical way, in that it appeals to the possible *negative* effects of certain actions. For example, you throw a piece of litter on the ground and are asked, "What would happen if everyone littered?" Since the end result of everyone performing that action would be an unwanted situation, we are then instructed not to litter.

Jeremy Bentham, one of the foremost defenders of utilitarianism, thought that we could measure or quantify the results of our actions. Bentham counseled us to do the following:

1. Determine the possible actions available to you in any given situation.
2. List all the people your action will affect. (Be sure to include yourself in the list.)
3. Calculate the total amount of pleasure derived as the outcome of each possible action.
4. Calculate the total amount of pain derived as the outcome of each possible action.
5. Subtract the amount of pain from the amount of pleasure derived as the outcome of each possible action.
6. You ought to choose the action whose outcome results in the greatest amount of pleasure.

However, the same challenges associated with consequentialist theories are relevant to Bentham's six-step procedure. First, we need clear definitions of "happiness" and "pleasure," definitions that cut across individuals, cultures, and societies. Second, we need to develop ways to *measure* or *quantify* the amount of pleasure and pain as a result of our possible actions.

Nevertheless, many people do try to apply Bentham's ideas, even if they are not familiar with the specifics of his theory. People often attempt to weigh the pros and cons of their actions. We sometimes try to gauge the extent of the pain and pleasure that will result, even though we do not have a clear-cut system of quantifying them. We often use our decidedly nonquantitative "calculations" to justify our actions, and we do often try to maximize the greatest happiness for the greatest number.

Deontology

Deontology The theory that duty to others is the first and foremost moral consideration.

A deontological moral theory is radically different from a consequentialist theory. We know that consequentialist theories emphasize the results of our actions. A deontological theory rejects any emphasis on the results or outcomes of an action, and instead recognizes the *role of duty*. **Deontology** holds that duty to others is the first and foremost moral consideration, and it lays the groundwork for discovering those duties. (The root word "deon" means *duty* or *obligation*, so *deontology* is the study of duties.)

Categorical imperative The basic idea is that your actions or behavior toward others should always be such that you would want everyone to act in the same manner.

An important distinction for deontology is that performing a particular duty does not have to have any immediate positive consequence. In this sense, a recognized duty (for example, telling the truth) is an instance of what Immanuel Kant called a **categorical imperative**. The basic idea is that your actions or behavior toward others should always be such that *you would want everyone to act in the same manner*. In this context, "categorical" means *absolute* and *unconditional*, and "imperative" means

PROFILES IN LOGIC
Jeremy Bentham

Happiness, for Jeremy Bentham (1748–1832), is achieved by maximizing pleasure and minimizing pain. Bentham was influenced by the social upheavals of the Industrial Revolution. Although qualified to practice law, he chose not to; instead, he tried to influence society by his writings. His *Introduction to the Principles of Morals and Legislation* contains the details of "the greatest happiness principle."

Bentham's thinking combined the clarification of concepts with rigorous deductive argument. He chose reason over tradition, and rationality over authority. He also championed a scientific description of human nature. His emphasis on "pleasure and pain" as the prime motivations for human behavior

anticipated the modern approach to modifying that behavior, through *positive* and *negative feedback*—in other words, rewards and punishment. "Nature has placed mankind under the governance of two sovereign masters, *pain* and *pleasure*. It is for them alone to point out what we ought to do, as well as to determine what we shall do."

Upon his death, Bentham had tens of thousands of unpublished pages of material that he hoped would eventually be published. He left the bulk of his considerable fortune to help support University College, London. According to his instructions, his body was to be preserved and displayed sitting in a chair. In fact, you can visit Bentham at the university today.

command or *obligation*. In other words, a categorical imperative is an absolute and universal moral law. For example, telling the truth would be a categorical imperative, because it is something that each individual would want everyone to do. However, even if it is a universal moral law to always tell the truth, we cannot expect that good consequences will result every time we apply the moral law. This is illustrated by the saying "the truth often hurts." Therefore, a deontological theory is quite different from a consequentialist moral theory that is based on the outcomes of our actions.

Deontology and consequentialism can also be distinguished by exploring two moral uses of the word "ought." Consequentialist theories rely on a *conditional ought*. For example, the statement "You ought to tell the truth" would be correct only if this would result in the best possible outcome in a given situation. Therefore, consequentialist theories place *conditions* on the use of *ought*. On the other hand, deontological theories rely on an *unconditional ought*. For example, the statement "You ought to tell the truth" would *always* be applicable, *with no exceptions no matter what the outcome*. For deontology, all moral rules are universal, they have no exceptions, and they are absolutely binding to all people. In other words, it is your unconditional duty to always tell the truth.

Relativism

Relativism makes two claims:

1. All moral value judgments are determined by a society's beliefs toward actions or behavior.
2. There are no objective or universal moral value judgments.

This means that all moral judgments are *intersubjective*. For example, the statement "Stealing is wrong" means that the community in general disapproves of stealing. Moral judgments are therefore reduced to a society's attitudes toward a particular behavior.

Adherents of relativism point to profound cultural and ethical differences among societies. For example, some cultures developed in the difficult terrain of the arctic. Those people survived the yearlong harsh conditions and became meat eaters, simply because there was no vegetation. By the relativist light, it would be absurd to expect them to be vegetarians and to hold that they are somehow morally deficient. Similarly, some nomadic cultures found it impossible to raise too many children at the same time, or to raise children who would not be able to quickly survive on their own. Consequently, infanticide was a regularly practiced way of life. Again, the relativist concludes that we cannot judge their actions and behaviors by our ethical standards that were developed over centuries in far different environments and under completely different circumstances.

Relativists also point out that most people's moral beliefs were conditioned by some combination of their immediate family and the society in which they were raised. Therefore, your individual moral beliefs are determined for the most part by where and when you were raised, just like the language you learned. In addition, relativists emphasize the difficult (and they think impossible) problem of judging between two competing moral systems. Relativists point out that every set of moral beliefs is judged by its adherents to be superior to all other sets of moral beliefs. Thus, relativists

Relativism First, all moral value judgments are determined by a society's beliefs toward actions or behavior. Second, there are no objective or universal moral value judgments.

stress the point that there are no objective criteria that we could apply to decide which moral system is "correct."

Contrasting Moral Theories

The many different moral theories can be illustrated by analyzing a hypothetical situation. A large cruise ship sinks and twenty people manage to make it to a small lifeboat. However, there are only enough provisions to keep ten people alive for at most a few days. Also, the lifeboat will capsize if all twenty people are allowed to enter it. The officer in charge decides that ten adult males will have to swim away from the lifeboat in order to give the remaining ten people a chance to survive.

A consequentialist might agree that the decision was morally justified based on a calculation of the best possible outcome for the most people. On the other hand, a deontologist might disagree with the decision. The deontologist could invoke the categorical imperative that our actions or decisions should never purposely or consciously harm innocent people. Finally, a relativist would argue that there is no one right answer.

EXERCISES 12B

Self-Practice
Questions

Answer "true" or "false" to the following statements.

1. A utilitarian argument for capital punishment might be that it benefits society by eliminating dangerous individuals.

Answer: True

2. Every moral theory is based on the determination of how a person's act either produces pleasure or avoids pain.

3. An ethical theory is teleological if it relies on the belief that the value of an action or object can be determined by looking at the purpose or the end of the action or object.

4. The fact that pleasure, pain, and happiness are different for each person is a problem for deontological theories.

⭐ 5. Consequentialist moral theories are based on our duties to others.

6. Deontological theories hold that duty to others is the first and foremost moral consideration.

7. Utilitarianism holds that moral values are relative to individuals and cultures; therefore, there can be no universal moral principles.

8. Emotivism asserts that moral value judgments are merely expressions of our attitudes or emotions.

⭐ 9. A categorical imperative is a rule relative to a particular culture or religion.

10. Egoism holds that everyone should act in order to maximize his or her own individual pleasure or happiness.

Video Tutorial: 12B
Exercise #9

11. Emotivism holds that all moral value judgments are merely expressions of our feelings about certain human behaviors.

12. Relativism holds that the same principles hold for all people at all times.

⭐13. A criticism of utilitarianism is that we can never know all the consequences of our actions.

14. A criticism of deontology is that we do not have a way to measure pleasure and pain.

15. An important factor for teleological moral theories is the motive behind a particular act or behavior.

C. THE NATURALISTIC FALLACY

As we saw earlier, some moral theories use facts about human nature as the basis for moral value judgments. They rely on psychological and biological evidence to argue that human behavior can be reduced to two forces: the desire for pleasure (or happiness) and the avoidance of pain. The basic principle for all *naturalistic*

PROFILES IN LOGIC
G. E. Moore

G. E. Moore (1873–1958), a British philosopher, preferred to use the initials "G. E." instead of his given names "George Edward." Moore was a well-respected teacher at the University of Cambridge who treated his students "as responsible thinkers."

Moore's approach to philosophical problems is often called "common sense realism," by which he hoped to refute skepticism. For example, Moore argued that a statement such as "The earth has existed for many years before I was born" is a truism that he knows for certain. But Moore argues that we must be careful to separate the *truism* from the subsequent *analysis of the truism*.

One of Moore's major contributions is his influential work in the area of ethics.

For Moore, the property of *goodness* is simple, and it cannot be analyzed by nonmoral terms. In other words, the property cannot be analyzed by empirical research. For example, Moore held that we cannot define "goodness" in terms of pleasure or the evolution of certain human habits, traits, or desires. Any attempt to apply scientific results to moral arguments falls prey to the "naturalistic fallacy." However, Moore argued that we can avoid the naturalistic fallacy by accepting that ethical questions must be answered by invoking ethical beliefs. Any ethical question—for example, Should we use human embryos for stem cell research?—can be answered only by the application of ethical concepts.

Naturalistic moral principle Since it is natural for humans to desire pleasure (or happiness) and to avoid pain, human behavior ought to be directed to these two ends.

Naturalistic fallacy Value judgments cannot be logically derived from statements of fact.

moral theories, such as egoism and utilitarianism, is captured by the **naturalistic moral principle**:

> Since it is *natural* for humans to desire pleasure (or happiness) and to avoid pain, we can conclude that human behavior *ought* to be directed to these two ends.

The argument has been criticized for falling prey to the **naturalistic fallacy**: *Value judgments cannot be logically derived from statements of fact*. This line of criticism (also known as the "is-ought" distinction) was originally presented by David Hume, but the name *naturalistic fallacy* was coined by G. E. Moore. The criticism begins by drawing a line between factual statements and value judgments. On one side of the line are the factual statements, and on the other side of the line are value judgments. In other words, an ethical pronouncement that you *ought to do* something *cannot* be logically deduced from statements that assert only *what is the case*.

The fallacious use of the naturalistic moral principle can be illustrated by a few examples. We know that *factual statements* assert that something is or is not the case, and they are decided by empirical investigations. For example, we could gather data about human eating habits and determine the following fact: Most humans get pleasure from eating ice cream. Since we have discovered a fact about humans, we can apply the naturalistic moral principle to create this argument:

> It *is* true that most humans get pleasure from eating ice cream. Therefore, humans *ought* to eat ice cream.

Our data gathering about human eating habits might also reveal this fact: Most humans do not like the taste of anchovies. Once again, if we have discovered a fact about humans, then we can apply the naturalistic moral principle:

> It *is* the case that most humans do not like the taste of anchovies. Therefore, humans *ought not* to eat anchovies.

Once we recognize that these are two instances of the *naturalistic fallacy*, then we can assert that the "ought" in the two conclusions does not follow logically from the "is" in the premises. To avoid the fallacy, the factual premise (the "is") has to be combined with a *moral principle* in order to derive the ethical "ought" in the conclusion. This is the subject of the next section.

D. THE STRUCTURE OF MORAL ARGUMENTS

Moral arguments generally have conclusions that assert some moral position or action, such as "You ought to do X" or "It is wrong to do Y." In its simplest form, these are the requirements for a moral argument:

1. There is at least one premise describing a particular situation where a decision to act will be made by someone (this is a nonmoral statement).
2. There is at least one premise that supplies a moral rule, principle, or command.
3. The conclusion asserts that a specific action should be performed.

Of course, not all moral arguments come in complete packages. Some have missing premises or conclusions, but these are generally easily filled in by those familiar with the context in which the moral argument occurs. The moral premise is necessary for two reasons:

1. It fills in the gap described by the "is-ought" problem.
2. It supplies the general moral rule or principle needed to derive a specific moral action or behavior. In other words, it provides the moral grounds for *why you ought to do X.*

In order to see how the moral and nonmoral premises work, consider these four arguments:

A. Some prisoners of war have been tortured while in U.S. custody. Therefore, the United States should stop torturing prisoners of war.

B. Some prisoners of war have been tortured while in U.S. custody. Therefore, the United States should not stop torturing prisoners of war.

C. Some prisoners of war have been tortured while in U.S. custody. The United States has signed an agreement to abide by the Geneva Convention. The United States is violating the Geneva Convention, which prohibits the torture of prisoners of war. Therefore, the United States should stop torturing prisoners of war.

D. Some prisoners of war have been tortured while in U.S. custody. The United States is gaining valuable information from the torture of prisoners of war. Anything the United States can do to fight the war on terror should be permitted. Therefore, the United States should not stop torturing prisoners of war.

In arguments A and B the single nonmoral premise describes a reported fact about U.S. treatment of prisoners of war. It is easily seen that neither the conclusion in argument A, nor the conclusion in B, follows from the single premise. However, arguments C and D have premises that attempt to provide the necessary moral justification for their respective conclusions. As with most moral arguments, the moral premises are generally the point of departure for further argumentation and analysis. Nevertheless, many times nonmoral issues drive the force of analysis. For example:

Our mother has been in a coma for several months and is being kept alive by life-sustaining equipment. The attending physician's opinion is that the coma is irreversible. There appears to be little or no brain activity in our mother. Therefore, we should ask the physician to take our mother off the life-sustaining equipment.

It is possible that other relatives might disagree with the conclusion for a variety of moral and nonmoral reasons. For example, they might point out that the physician cannot be certain that the patient will never come out of the coma. They might argue that little or no brain activity is a measure of what is occurring in the patient's brain, but not in her mind. Also, the equipment to measure brain activity is only our best guide today as to what is happening in a person's brain. They might point out that more powerful equipment will be developed in the future that will give us a better picture of what is occurring in the brain. In other words, the argument against taking the patient off the life-sustaining equipment may be over the factual or empirical nature of the status of the coma, and not a moral debate over "pulling the plug." In fact, it is possible that all the relatives will agree to the decision to let the mother die if they can agree on the nature and extent of the coma.

When starting to analyze moral arguments it often helps to see them as deductive. This simplifies the logical analysis into *valid, invalid, sound,* and *unsound.* For example, many moral arguments have this structure:

> X is Y.
> <u>Anything Y is morally wrong.</u>
> X is morally wrong.

For example, let X = *killing an innocent human,* and Y = *murder*:

> Killing an innocent human is murder.
> <u>Murder is morally wrong.</u>
> Killing an innocent human is morally wrong.

To see another example, this time let X = *stealing,* and Y = *taking other people's property without their consent*:

> Stealing is taking other people's property without their consent.
> <u>Taking other people's property without their consent is morally wrong.</u>
> Stealing is morally wrong.

Since both examples result in valid arguments, the remaining question is one of soundness. The first premise in both arguments is considered by most people to be merely definitional. One premise defines "killing," and the other defines "stealing." As such, their truth value would probably not be debated. But in order to determine soundness, we must be able to decide the truth value of the second premise of each argument. Here is where we run into problems. The second premise of each of the two arguments is a moral value judgment. We already discussed the problems with determining the truth value of this kind of statement. The statement is not merely definitional; nor does it seem to assert a fact of the world. Therefore, the soundness issue will usually be a difficult hurdle to overcome.

So, should we treat some moral arguments as deductive? One reason to do this is that many people feel strongly that moral rules or principles are universal. Hence, the logical intent of an argument using a general moral rule as a premise must be to have the moral action prescribed in the conclusion to follow with necessity. And this indeed is how many people perceive or intend their moral arguments to be interpreted.

Of course, we can also classify some moral arguments as inductive, instead of deductive. Let's see how the logical analysis and evaluation would proceed. For example, suppose you come across a research survey that asked a large number of Christians, chosen at random, to state their beliefs concerning several social issues. You might read the following statistic: "Ninety percent of Christians believe that stem cell research is morally wrong." Now, perhaps you know someone who is a Christian; if so, you might create this argument:

> **E.** Ninety percent of Christians believe that stem cell research is morally wrong. Gerry is a Christian. Therefore, Gerry *probably* believes that stem cell research is wrong.

This is a straightforward inductive argument. If the premises are assumed to be true, then we can classify it as a strong argument. In addition, if the research was well conducted and we have reason to believe that the evidence in the first premise is factually true, then we can also classify the argument as cogent. But now look at the next argument:

> **F.** Ninety percent of Christians believe that stem cell research is morally wrong. Gerry is a Christian. Therefore, Gerry *ought* to believe that stem cell research is wrong.

This is a not a straightforward inductive argument. The "ought" in the conclusion of argument F is quite different from the word "probably" in the conclusion of argument E. The conclusion of E merely asserts that a high statistical probability can be attached to the claim that "Gerry believes that stem cell research is wrong." Of course, the conclusion does not follow necessarily, but that is not a requirement of a strong inductive argument. The premises in argument E, if true, do provide strong statistical evidence for the conclusion.

On the other hand, the conclusion of F does *not* assert anything about a statistical probability that can be attached to the claim that "Gerry believes that stem cell research is wrong." Instead, the conclusion of F offers a *moral prescription* of what Gerry *ought* to do. Here again we see an *ought statement* derived from an *is statement*. But perhaps the argument is missing some key information, and we can provide the missing moral link:

> **G.** Ninety percent of Christians believe that stem cell research is morally wrong. Gerry is a Christian. Every Christian ought to believe what the vast majority of Christians believe. Therefore, Gerry *ought* to believe that stem cell research is wrong.

The added premise seems to fill in the missing gap between the "is" in the premises and the "ought" in the conclusion. However, now the argument is no longer inductive, it is deductive. Thus, we are back to determining its validity and soundness.

Let's add one more twist to the argument. Suppose we change the conclusion:

> **H.** Ninety percent of Christians believe that stem cell research is morally wrong. Gerry is a Christian. Every Christian ought to believe what the vast majority of Christians believe. Therefore, Gerry *probably ought* to believe that stem cell research is wrong.

This would have the appearance of making the argument inductive once again. Nevertheless, there is something odd about the phrase "probably ought." Moral prescriptions about what we ought to do are not generally couched in terms of what we *probably ought to do*, but rather of what we *ought to do*, with no added qualifications.

You can apply the discussion thus far to two last examples, to deepen your understanding:

I. Seventy-five percent of Americans believe that abortions are sometimes morally justified. Maxine is an American. Therefore, Maxine *probably* believes that abortions are sometimes morally justified.

J. Seventy-five percent of Americans believe that abortions are sometimes morally justified. Maxine is an American. Therefore, Maxine *ought* to believe that abortions are sometimes morally justified.

E. ANALOGIES AND MORAL ARGUMENTS

Analogies are often used in moral arguments as a way to support a moral prescription in the conclusion. Like all analogical reasoning, the premises of an analogical moral argument try to link two or more situations that call for a moral decision or determination to be made. The idea is to persuade others that they should (or should not) perform a certain action (or hold a certain belief), because the present case is similar to a previously determined moral situation. Thus, analogical moral arguments are attempts to point out that our moral actions (or beliefs) should be consistent. The following is an analogical moral argument:

> You believe that every human embryo or fetus is a human being. You believe that abortion is wrong, because it is the murder of an innocent human being. Yet you also believe that abortion is morally permissible in cases of rape and incest. But a human embryo or fetus conceived by an act of rape or incest is no less an innocent human being than one conceived by an act of consensual sex. Therefore, you *ought* to believe that abortion is *not* morally permissible in cases of rape and incest.

The point of the premises is to force someone into recognizing the inconsistency of holding (1) that *every* human embryo or fetus is a human being and (2) that an embryo or fetus conceived by incest or rape is *not* an innocent human being. In other words, people who hold (1) and (2) would need to explain why and how a fetus conceived by rape or incest is different from a fetus that was conceived through consensual sex. They would have to explain how the act of conception in the case of rape or incest causes the resulting fetus to be excluded from the class of innocent human beings.

Let's look at another example of an analogical moral argument:

> You told me that you think that using marijuana is morally wrong, not because it is illegal, but because it is addictive and physically harmful after long-term use. But you regularly drink alcohol, even though you are aware of studies that show that it is addictive and physically harmful after long-term use. Therefore, you *ought* not to drink alcohol, because it is morally wrong.

As in the previous example, the intent of the premises is to force others into recognizing that they hold inconsistent positions. (1) They believe that using marijuana is morally wrong, because it is addictive and physically harmful after long-term use. (2) They regularly drink alcohol, even though they are aware of studies that show that it is addictive and physically harmful after long-term use. Hence, they would have to explain how regularly drinking alcohol is different from using marijuana in order to justify its continued use on moral grounds. Furthermore, the first premise precludes them from replying that the illegality of marijuana is the relevant moral difference.

In sum, we can reconstruct, analyze, and evaluate analogical moral arguments by using the same techniques as for nonmoral analogical arguments. We can evaluate the strengths and weaknesses of analogical moral arguments by assessing the relevant instances in the premises. We can also apply the familiar techniques of looking for disanalogies, counteranalogies, and any unintended consequences of the analogy. These logical analysis techniques allow us to understand how analogical moral arguments function—and how they can be evaluated for degrees of strength.

EXERCISES 12E

I. Discuss the following moral issues in light of the ideas put forward in this chapter. Use the moral theories described in this chapter to construct arguments regarding the following issues. Choose a moral theory and construct an argument by applying it to an issue. Then take a different moral theory and apply it to a different issue. Discuss the strength of the arguments you construct in light of the discussions regarding each particular theory you use. Try to use each moral theory at least twice.

Self-Practice
Questions

1. downloading music illegally	7. welfare	⭐ 13. freedom of speech
2. gambling	8. giving to charities	14. smokers' rights
3. state-run lotteries	⭐ 9. animal rights	15. prostitution
4. rehabilitation of criminals	10. abortion	16. cheating on exams
⭐ 5. stealing	11. capital punishment	⭐ 17. birth control
6. murder	12. affirmative action	18. telemarketing

Answer to #1: downloading music illegally

Your answers will depend on the particular moral theory you choose for each issue. Here is an example that applies *utilitarianism*:

ARGUMENT: *Downloading music illegally* denies artists (music composers, lyricists, and musicians) a fair share of any royalties for their original work. It also reduces the sales of the companies that produced and marketed the music. Without royalties, artists lose incentive to create new music, and without sales, music companies cannot afford to produce new music. The immediate pleasure derived from those listening to illegally downloaded music does not outweigh the pain of the artists and company employees who will not be able to survive a continued economic loss. The long-term effect is that artists and music companies will no longer produce new music.

DISCUSSION OF THE ARGUMENT: Not everyone downloads music illegally. Enough people are willing to buy music to ensure that artists get some royalties and to keep music companies in business. Also, with the explosion of the Internet, some artists now self-publish their work or even offer it for free. The idea is to gain a following of loyal fans willing to pay a small fee directly to the artist, instead of buying music from a company at a higher cost. In some cases this income will match the artist's royalty derived from a contract in which the music company keeps the lion's share of the profits.

II. The following passages are taken from various sources. Identify the moral arguments in each passage, and use any of the theories discussed in this chapter in your analysis of the arguments.

1. But across action sports, where individuality is prized, many are uncomfortable with rules or restrictions. "I respect that everyone should wear a helmet, like I wear a helmet," professional snowboarder Keir Dillon says. "But I don't think it should be mandated. For me, I always get worried about mandating or having governing bodies over our sport."

   Matt Higgins, "Head Games"

Answer:

ARGUMENT: I respect that everyone should wear a helmet, like I wear a helmet. [However,] I always get worried about mandating or having governing bodies over our sport. [Therefore,] I don't think it [wearing a helmet] should be mandated.

DISCUSSION: The basic principle of *egoism* is that everyone should act in order to maximize his or her own individual pleasure or happiness. Although wearing a helmet reduces the likelihood of injuries, individual riders should have the freedom to choose for themselves. The governing bodies of the sport can strongly *suggest* that riders use helmets, and they can provide data regarding the severity of accidents to riders who do not wear helmets, but they should not mandate their use.

2. With over 1 billion people, China should have a greater voice on the issue of world peace. Norway is only a small country, but it must be in the minority concerning the conception of freedom and democracy. Hence, the selection of the "Nobel Peace Prize" should be open to the people in the world.

   Ed Flanagan, "Big PR Goof? China's Confusing Confucius Prize," *NBC News*

3. "Never did get you for stealing that money?"
   "I didn't consider it stealing."
   "It didn't belong to you."
   "I needed a road stake. Like that bank in New Mexico. I needed a road stake, and there it was. I never robbed no citizen or took a man's watch!"
   "It's all stealing."

   From the screenplay of the 1969 movie *True Grit*

4. While most people took Internet access for granted as a constant, the suddenness of Egypt's Internet shutdown raises the question: Is access to the Internet a human right? "There are certain technological advances that are such leaps forward in human evolution that they do, in fact, become human rights.

Video Tutorial: 12EII
Exercise #4

Vaccines, for example. Potable water. I believe the Internet has become one as well," said John Addis.   Wilson Rothman, "Is Internet Access a Human Right?" *Technolog*

⭐ 5. The nation's underlying divides are still ideological, but we rarely fight them honestly as philosophical differences. We just accuse the other side of corruption. Politics is no longer a debate; it's an attempt to destroy lives through accusation.   David Brooks, "We All, Again, Just Made Fools of Ourselves," *The New York Times*

6. It is frequently stated that illicit drugs are "bad, dangerous, destructive," or "addictive," and that society has an obligation to keep them from the public. But nowhere can be found reliable, objective scientific evidence that they are any more harmful than other substances and activities that are legal. In view of the enormous expense, the carnage and the obvious futility of the "drug war," resulting in massive criminalization of society, it is high time to examine the supposed justification for keeping certain substances illegal.

Benson B. Roe, M.D., "Why We Should Legalize Drugs"

7. The violent behavior caused by drugs won't magically stop because the drugs are legal. Legal PCP isn't going to make a person less violent than illegally purchased PCP. So, crimes committed because of drugs will increase as the number of drug users will increase with the legalization of drugs. The psychopathic behavior that drugs cause will not somehow magically stop because drugs are legal.   Carolyn C. Gargaro, "Drugs"

8. And yet, while young men's failures in life are not penalizing them in the bedroom, their sexual success may, ironically, be hindering their drive to achieve in life. Don't forget your Freud: Civilization is built on blocked, redirected, and channeled sexual impulse, because men will work for sex. Today's young men, however, seldom have to. As the authors of last year's book *Sex at Dawn: The Prehistoric Origins of Modern Sexuality* put it, "Societies in which women have lots of autonomy and authority tend to be decidedly male-friendly, relaxed, tolerant, and plenty sexy." They're right. But then try getting men to do anything.   Mark Regnerus, "Sex Is Cheap," *Slate*

⭐ 9. "It's interesting because different cultures have different views on concussions and different views on identifying concussions, or even what the symptoms are that may suggest concussion," Dr. Ruben Echemendia recently told reporters. "So we know from our research, for example, that the reporting of symptoms varies by language of origin." Echemendia's group has determined that players from different nationalities and cultural backgrounds report concussions in different manners. Different cultures also put more or less importance around different symptoms, Echemendia explained. One culture may not consider a headache to be important and won't report it, but they will report dizziness. Meanwhile, headaches can be one of the indicators for post-concussion syndrome.

Pierre LeBrun, "National Hockey League Has Unique Off-Ice Concussion Foe"

10. The list of growing jobs is heavy on nurturing professions, in which women, ironically, seem to benefit from old stereotypes and habits. Theoretically, there is no reason men should not be qualified. But they have proved remarkably unable to adapt. Over the course of the past century, feminism has pushed women to do things once considered against their nature—first enter the workforce as singles, then continue to work while married, then work even with small children at home. Many professions that started out as the province of men are now filled mostly with women—secretary and teacher come to mind. Yet I'm not aware of any that have gone the opposite way. Nursing schools have tried hard to recruit men in the past few years, with minimal success. Teaching schools, eager to recruit male role models, are having a similarly hard time. The range of acceptable masculine roles has changed comparatively little, and has perhaps even narrowed as men have shied from some careers women have entered. And with each passing day, they lag further behind.

Hanna Rosin, "The End of Men," *Atlantic*

11. Let me make my somewhat seditious proposal explicit: We should not call ourselves "atheists." We should not call ourselves "secularists." We should not call ourselves "humanists," or "secular humanists," or "naturalists," or "skeptics," or "anti-theists," or "rationalists," or "freethinkers," or "brights." We should not call ourselves anything. We should go under the radar—for the rest of our lives. And while there, we should be decent, responsible people who destroy bad ideas wherever we find them. Now, it just so happens that religion has more than its fair share of bad ideas. And it remains the only system of thought, where the process of maintaining bad ideas in perpetual immunity from criticism is considered a sacred act. This is the act of faith. And I remain convinced that religious faith is one of the most perverse misuses of intelligence we have ever devised. So we will, inevitably, continue to criticize religious thinking. But we should not define ourselves and name ourselves in opposition to such thinking. So what does this all mean in practical terms? Well, rather than declare ourselves "atheists" in opposition to all religion, I think we should do nothing more than advocate reason and intellectual honesty—and where this advocacy causes us to collide with religion, as it inevitably will, we should observe that the points of impact are always with specific religious beliefs—not with religion in general. There is no religion in general.

Sam Harris, "The Problem with Atheism," *Washington Post*

12. *Lotteries Bilk the Poor*: Last week, the Mega Millions lotto paid what was described in media reports as a "$380 million" jackpot. Actually the number reflects an annuity that pays $380 million over 26 years. The present value of the annuity, the only figure that matters, is $240 million—heady enough. Any money sum can be made to appear to roughly twice as great by expressing the number as a long-term annuity. If your employer offered you $50,000 this year, or $80,000 conveyed as one payment of $3,000 annually for each of the

next 26 years—the same proportion as the Mega Millions markup—which would you choose? The media should not sensationalize lottery numbers by using the phony figures the lotto companies promote. But that's the least of the problems with lotteries, whose financial structure—spectacularly low chances of winning for players, combined with riches for those administering the lottos—make them, as a wag once said, "a tax on the stupid." As TMQ wrote two years ago of state-sponsored lotteries, "There is almost no chance you will win, while total assurance you will lose the average of $190 annually that Americans throw away on government-run roulette. Worse, public lotteries, with their glitzy false promises of instant wealth, are a tax on poverty—as David Brooks of *The New York Times* has noted, households with an income of less than $13,000 spend an average of $645 annually on scratch-off tickets, meaning the poor are the main group throwing away cash at government lotto sites." Government, which ought to aid the poor, instead cynically markets lottos to the poor—with false promises of instant wealth, plus a high concentration of lotto sales outlets in low-income neighborhoods. The goal of this cynicism? Wealth for lotto companies and kickbacks—excuse me, consulting fees—for the politicians and government bureaucrats involved.

Gregg Easterbrook, "The Next Step"

Summary

Study Materials

- Some arguments rely solely on factual claims for support, some arguments rely solely on value judgments for support, and some arguments rely on a mixture of the two.
- Value judgment: A claim that a particular human action or object has some degree of importance, worth, or desirability.
- Prescriptive statement: In a moral setting, a statement that offers advice either by specifying a particular action that ought to be performed or by providing general moral rules, principles, or guidelines that should be followed.
- Normative statement: A statement that establishes standards for correct moral behavior, determining norms or rules of conduct.
- Emotivism: A theory that asserts that moral value judgments are merely expressions of our attitudes or emotions.
- Consequentialism: A class of moral theories in which the moral value of any human action or behavior is determined exclusively by its outcomes.
- Teleology: The philosophical belief that the value of an action or object can be determined by looking at the purpose or the end of the action or object.
- Egoism: The basic principle that everyone should act in order to maximize his or her own individual pleasure or happiness.
- The most important principle for utilitarianism can be summed up in the famous dictum "the greatest good for the greatest number."

- According to utilitarianism, every human action demonstrates "universalizability," meaning that the same principles hold for all people at all times.
- Deontology: The theory that duty to others is the first and foremost moral consideration; it lays the groundwork for discovering those duties.
- The basic idea of a categorical imperative is that your actions or behavior toward others should always be such that you would want everyone to act in the same manner.
- Relativism makes two claims: First, all moral value judgments are determined by a society's beliefs toward actions or behavior. Second, there are no objective or universal moral value judgments.
- Naturalistic moral principle: Since it is natural for humans to desire pleasure (or happiness) and to avoid pain, human behavior ought to be directed to these two ends.
- Naturalistic fallacy: Value judgments cannot be logically derived from statements of fact.

KEY TERMS

LOGIC CHALLENGE: DANGEROUS CARGO

You own a small resort on a tropical island where the only way on and off is by boat. Three of your guests, Leo, Aries, and Aquarius, had a bad weekend and they are standing by the boat dock with their luggage demanding to get off the island as quickly as possible. Leo, Aries, and Aquarius are all relatives who came together in one car, which is parked on the mainland. Over the last few days, old childhood squabbles surfaced, which threaten to escalate into violence.

To make things worse, a further difficulty arises. Your large boat is broken, and the small boat can hold only you and one passenger. As soon as the three guests hear this, they make more demands. Leo says, "Don't leave me alone either here or at the car with Aries." Upon hearing this, Aquarius says, "Well, you'd better not leave me alone either here or at the car with Leo." How can you get the three relatives to their car while meeting their demands?

Chapter 13

Statistical Arguments and Probability

A. Samples and Populations
B. Statistical Averages
C. Standard Deviation
D. What If the Results Are Skewed?
E. The Misuse of Statistics
F. Probability Theories
G. Probability Calculus
H. True Odds in Games of Chance
I. Bayesian Theory

Digital homework exercises for this chapter are available in your instructor's online course. For information on how to access these resources, please visit **www.oup.com/he/baronett5e**.

Television commercials are fond of claims like this:

- Four out of five dentists recommend the ingredient found in our toothpaste.
- Our diet cola has 30% fewer calories.
- Get up to 70% off our previously low prices on selected items.
- American children watch an average of five hours of television a day. That means that they have watched an average of 5000 hours of television before entering first grade. Our *Early Reading Program* DVDs are fun and educational at the same time. So why not let your child's television viewing help prepare them for their first days in school? Don't let your children fall behind. Give them the right head start.

After the commercials end, a short news update might announce this: "A recent survey reveals that the incumbent mayor, who is running for reelection and who is being investigated for alleged ties to a securities fraud scandal, trails his opponent: 34% of those surveyed said they will vote for the mayor; 62% said they will vote for his opponent; and 4% said that they haven't made up their minds."

Evaluating arguments that rely on statistical evidence requires us to interpret correctly the statistical evidence as it is presented. However, in many everyday arguments the words "average" and "percentage" are ambiguous because we are not told how the average or percentage was derived. (Chapter 4 examined the *fallacy of misleading precision.*) Information as to how statistical figures are computed is just as crucial for evaluating many statistical arguments. This chapter supplies the tools we need to make those evaluations and then introduces probability.

A. SAMPLES AND POPULATIONS

Suppose a criminal justice researcher wants to know the conviction rate in felony cases in the state where she teaches. She compiles this statistic: 70% of a sample of defendants in criminal cases were found guilty. Let's look at how this statistic might be used in an argument:

> Seventy percent of a *sample* of defendants in criminal cases were found guilty. Therefore, probably 70% of *all* defendants in criminal cases are found guilty.

But how was the sample gathered? How large was the sample? Was it a random sample? Is there any evidence that the sample is not representative of the population of all defendants? Our answers to these questions will help determine the strength of the argument. Therefore, we need to know as much as we can about the research that was conducted.

Population Any group of objects, not just human populations.

Sample A subset of a population.

Representative sample A sample that accurately reflects the characteristics of the population as a whole.

Population refers to any group of objects, not just a human population. A **sample** is a subset, or part, of a population. If the population in question is the student body of a large university (say, 10,000 students), then a sample would be any portion of that population. A **representative sample** accurately reflects the characteristics of the population as a whole. Let's see what that takes.

Imagine that a senior class in sociology is told to determine the student population's opinion on a proposed tuition increase. Two members of this class decide to work together. They each interview two students in their remaining three classes that day, for a total of twelve students. They discover that ten students are opposed to the tuition increase. Armed with this data, they make a bold generalization:

> Eighty-three percent of a *sample* of students is opposed to a tuition increase. Therefore, probably 83% of the student *population* of 10,000 is opposed to a tuition increase.

The teacher analyzes the students' argument by asking a few simple questions. *What exactly is the sample?* Here we need to specify the details of the study. In this case, each researcher interviewed two students in their remaining three classes that day, for a total of twelve students. *What is claimed to be true of the sample?* Ten students (out of the twelve studied) are opposed to the tuition increase. *What is the population?* In this case it is 10,000 students. *What did the researchers conclude?* Probably 83% of the student *population* of 10,000 is opposed to a tuition increase.

The teacher points out that they have based their generalization on a small sample. A sample size of twelve, relative to a student body of 10,000, is small and extremely unlikely to be representative of the population. This is an example of the *fallacy of hasty generalization* (see Chapter 4). There is no simple formula for calculating the ratio of sample size to population to ensure a representative sample. However, when a sample size is small relative to the size of the population, other factors (which we will soon discuss) can help ensure that a representative sample has been achieved. Without the necessary equipment to strengthen it, however, a small sample weakens the argument.

Our intrepid students go back to work and this time they gather a large sample. They begin polling more students in their classes, and they poll students from their dormitory. Their sample size swells to over 300 students. Analyzing the data prompts them to make a new argument:

> Seventy-six percent of a *sample* of 300 students is opposed to a tuition increase. Therefore, probably 76% of the student *population* is opposed to a tuition increase.

Their teacher does not question the sample size, but does inquire into which students were polled. The researchers admit that the vast majority of those polled in their upper-level classes are probably either juniors or seniors. Also, they live in a dorm reserved for juniors and seniors. These admissions weaken the argument, because the sample is not representative of all students: It is *biased* toward juniors and seniors. This is an example of the *fallacy of biased sample* (see Chapter 4) because both freshmen and sophomores are underrepresented in the sample. If the researchers had restricted their conclusion to juniors and seniors, then their argument would be stronger. Since the researchers wanted to make a generalization about the entire student population, their sample was biased because it excluded certain subsets of that population.

The researchers go back to work and supplement their data by polling an appropriate number of freshmen and sophomores. Their new data yields a new argument:

> Seventy-two percent of a *sample* of 500 students is opposed to a tuition increase. Therefore, probably 72% of the student *population* is opposed to a tuition increase.

The teacher remarks that both the sample size and the distribution of students' year in school strengthen the argument. However, this is not a *random sample*. The researchers polled only students they had easy access to. To get a **random sample**, you must ensure that *every member of the population has an equal chance of getting in*. A random sample strengthens the likelihood that the sample represents the population.

Random sample
A sample in which every member of the population has an equal chance of getting in.

EXERCISES 13A

For the following passages, first identify the *sample* and *population* in the passages. Next, discuss whether the sample is representative of the population referred to in the conclusion. Analyze for sample size, potential bias, and randomness. Determine how your answers to these questions affect the strength of the arguments.

Self-Practice Questions

1. I am never going to buy another Hinckley car again. I had one and so did my sister. Both our cars were constantly in the shop. They had electrical and

carburetor problems that caused them to stall all the time with no warning. Then we would have to get them towed, because they wouldn't start again. I am sure that all Hinckley cars have the same kinds of problems; that's why I won't buy one no matter what the price.

Answer:

Sample: Two Hinckley cars.

Population: All Hinckley cars.

Sample size: Two cars are a very small sample when we are discussing potentially millions of cars. This reduces the likelihood that the sample is representative of the population.

Potential bias: The sample excludes any cars that other owners might praise. It doesn't allow for the possibility of evidence that would go against its claims. This reduces the likelihood that the sample is representative of the population.

Randomness: This is not a random sample because not every Hinckley car had an equal chance of getting into the sample. This reduces the likelihood that the sample is representative of the population.

2. For 1 year, a veterinarian kept track of all the dogs brought in to her clinic for testing after they had bitten someone. Out of 132 dogs brought in, pit bulls accounted for 67% of all attacks resulting in bite wounds to people. The veterinarian concluded that pit bulls are twice as likely to bite someone as all other dog breeds combined anywhere in the United States.

3. A study of psychiatric outpatients at a major hospital in Chicago showed that patients given counseling, plus some form of drug therapy, stayed in the program only one-third as long as those given just counseling. For 3 years the researchers followed 1600 patients; half were given only counseling and the other half were given counseling and drug treatment. The group given counseling and drugs felt confident that they could now cope with their problems and left the program, while the group given just counseling stayed in the program three times longer. The researchers argue that these results should obtain no matter where a similar program was implemented.

4. There have been over 4000 UFO sightings around the world in the past five years. Our analysis of these cases shows that 78% of the sightings have never been adequately explained by any government agency in any country where the sightings occurred. The number of sightings that appear to be hoaxes, or where the credibility of the eyewitnesses is under question, is insignificant. Given this information, we can confidently say that UFOs are real and the sightings are unequivocally of extraterrestrial spaceships manned by organisms far more advanced than earthlings.

★ 5. A random study of 6000 urban public high school seniors throughout the United States has confirmed what many have long suspected. The students were given the same verbal, mathematical, perceptual, and manual dexterity test that was given 20 years ago to high school seniors. The Bincaid-Forbush test had not been used for over 15 years, so the researchers thought that it could be a good way of comparing the results of the preceding generation (many of whom are probably the parents of today's seniors) with the current crop of students. As expected, verbal and math scores have declined by 20% in today's students.

Surprisingly, the perceptual and manual dexterity scores of today's students are 34% higher than their parents' generation. The researchers speculate that the rise of computers and arcade video games can explain both results. They hypothesize that verbal and math skills have deteriorated because video games require very little reading or calculating. However, these games require superior perceptual and manual dexterity skills, and thus give today's students much more exposure to this kind of skill development.

6. I have closely examined ninety-three wars that took place within the last 200 years. I use the word "war" to include both external conflicts (between two or more countries) and internal or civil wars. In 84% of those cases the wars were precipitated by a recent change in the government. Specifically, those 84% occurred soon after a conservative leader of that country took over from someone who was more liberal. The terms "conservative" and "liberal" are applied after examining and rating the leader on a scale from one to ten for variables related to economic beliefs, religious pronouncements, social welfare programs, military buildup, judicial appointments, immigration laws, and the treatment of criminals. From these results, we can safely conclude that approximately four out of every five future wars around the world will occur after a conservative leader replaces a liberal leader.

7. Eight out of ten people surveyed chose Slacker Soda over the next four most popular brands of soft drink. It is clear that America has spoken. Eighty percent of all Americans can't be wrong. Don't you think that you should start drinking Slacker Soda?

8. Research on people's dreams shows that they are not visions of the future. A group of psychologists monitored thirty volunteers for 1 year. The volunteers were told to keep a daily log only of the dreams they could clearly recall. They were also told to record anything that happened within a few days of the dream that they felt corresponded to the dream (to determine if they thought the dream was a premonition). On average, the volunteers recorded three dreams a night. In 1 year the researchers had over 25,000 dreams to analyze. They found that less than 1% of the dreams could be accurately correlated with a subsequent event in the dreamer's life (and these were usually trivial events). They concluded that humans' dreams do not come from the future, they do not offer a glimpse of some inevitable occurrence, nor do they act as a warning so we can avoid unpleasant events.

⭐ 9. From 1903 to 2008, whenever the American League won the World Series, cigarette sales rose 20% over the previous year. But when the National League won the World Series, liquor sales rose 25% for the next year. Stock buyers pay heed! Watch who wins the World Series, and then buy or sell accordingly.

10. A study of college majors has revealed some interesting results. The study looked at more than 20,000 students who were accepted to U.S. law schools and medical schools for the past 20 years. The highest *percentage* of any major to be accepted to both law and medical schools was philosophy majors. The researchers speculate that this can be partially explained by the fact that philosophy majors have to take numerous logic courses and to write critical papers using logical reasoning. Since both the LSAT and MCAT (the law school and medical school standardized tests required of all applicants) have a *logical reasoning* section, philosophy majors are better prepared and tend to score higher on that section. The researchers encourage those planning to apply to law or medical school to take as many philosophy courses as they can.

B. STATISTICAL AVERAGES

Imagine that in class one day, your instructor tells you that a slide will appear on screen, showing a room with people whose average age is 45. Now, if you are around 20 years of age, you might anticipate that the people on the slide will look somewhat like your parents. To your surprise, you see five very young children and six people who look to be your grandparents' age. To you, none of the people appear even close to 45 years of age; everyone is either much too young or much too old. One of your classmates is equally puzzled and complains to the teacher: The class was misled. You were told that the average age in the slide would be 45, so it should depict a middle-aged person, right? Yet not even one person looks middle-aged.

The average age given was correct. Your teacher lists the ages of the people in the picture:

The Ages of the Five Younger People	The Ages of the Six Older People
5	76
5	77
4	78
3	79
2	80
	86

Mean A statistical average that is determined by adding the numerical values in the data concerning the examined objects, then dividing by the number of objects that were measured.

If we add the ages in the first column, we get 19. The second column adds up to 476. Together they add up to 495, which is the total age of the eleven people. We now divide the *total age* by the *number of people* to get the *average age*; this gives us $495 \div 11 = 45$. The average age of the eleven people in the slide is indeed 45.

This type of statistical average, called the *mean*, is one way to describe a set of data. The **mean** is determined by adding the numerical values in the data for the objects examined, then dividing by the number of objects. When newspapers, magazines, and other nontechnical sources refer to the "average" of a set of numerical data, they usually intend the *mean*. You have probably run into claims like these (whether or not they are true):

- The average yearly salary of a National Basketball Association (NBA) player is $5 million.
- The top ten movie stars average $20 million per movie.
- High school teachers in the United States average $30,000 a year.
- The top fifteen corporation CEOs in the United States averaged $50 million in stock compensation last year.
- The average yearly income for U.S. teenagers is $2000.

Since calculating the mean uses simple arithmetic (adding and dividing), it is normally the first kind of average that we are taught in school. (In fact, it is also referred to as the *arithmetical mean*.) As we saw in the slide example, the *mean* can be psychologically misleading, even when it is perfectly accurate. If you, too, felt misled, you can appreciate how easily statistics can be used to manipulate our ideas. For most people, "average" easily calls up an *image* rather than data. And the image that you have of a 45-year-old depends partly on your own age. A teenager's conception of someone who is 45 will surely differ from the perspective of a person who really is 45. People around 85 years of age will probably envision someone who is 45 as quite young. Very young children may not have a clear picture of a 45-year-old at all.

To see this more fully, imagine that your teacher promises another slide, and it, too, will have eleven people whose average age is 45. At this point, you might try to avoid picturing in your mind what the people will look like, since your first guess was way off the mark. As soon as the slide appears, however, you see that all of the people look around the same age and not unlike your parents. Your teacher lists the ages of the people in the new picture:

The Ages of the Eleven People in the Second Slide

41	46
42	47
43	47
43	47
44	47
	48

To calculate the mean of this second set of values, we once again add all eleven ages, and once again the result is 495. We now divide 495 by the total number of people to get 495 ÷ 11 = 45. Sure enough, the mean age of the eleven people in the second slide is 45. As far as this one "average" is concerned, there is no difference between the two sets of people on the two slides. Of course, there is still a great gap between the ages of the younger and older people in the first slide, while the people in the second slide differ very little in age. That is why knowing the *mean* can tell us only so much.

Median A statistical average that is determined by locating the value that separates the entire set of data in half.

Fortunately, additional kinds of *average* can add to our understanding of the data. The **median**, for one, is determined by locating the value that breaks the entire set of data in half. In other words, 50% of the data is above the median, and 50% is below it. For the people in the first slide, the *median* age is 76. Exactly five values are smaller than 76 (5, 5, 4, 3, 2), and exactly five values are greater than 76 (77, 78, 79, 80, 86). In contrast, for the people in the second slide, the *median* age is 46. You can easily check for yourself that half the values are smaller than 46 (41, 42, 43, 43, 44), and half are larger (47, 47, 47, 47, 48).

Let's put what we know about the ages of the two sets of people together:

Slide 1: Mean = 45; Median = 76
Slide 2: Mean = 45; Median = 46

Having information about the median age often greatly expands our understanding. To see why, suppose you discuss what happened in class with your roommates later that night. If you give them only the *mean* age (45), then they would have no way to differentiate between the two groups of people. However, let's see what happens when you provide them with the *median* age of the groups. Since the median age is 76 for the people on slide 1, half are older than 76 and half younger than 76. Thus, the younger people must be very young in order for the mean age to be 45. Although your roommates would not know the exact ages of the eleven people involved, they can correctly infer that the slide includes children.

However, the results for slide 2 are not as informative. If you tell your roommates that the mean is 45 and the median is 46, then what can they conclude? Remember, they did not see the slides, and you did not tell them what you saw. Can they conclude that all the people are in their 40s? No, they could not do this. The ages might be clustered in the 40s, or they might instead be more like the ages in the first slide—sharply divided between older people and children. Take the following set of numbers:

1, 2, 3, 4, 5, 46, 84, 86, 87, 88, 89

Here, the numbers again total 495, and the *mean* is again 495 ÷ 11 = 45. But what about the median age? Well, since there are exactly five values smaller than 46 (1, 2, 3, 4, 5) and exactly five values larger than 46 (84, 86, 87, 88, 89), the median is exactly the same as for slide 2.

For an odd number of items like these, it is easy to find the median; you simply find the number in the middle of the set. However, an even number of items requires two more quick steps. Suppose a data set consists of these six numbers:

8, 11, 17, 33, 36, 40

The first step is to locate the *two values* that together make up the middle of the set. Here 17 and 33 make up the middle, because there are two values to the left of them (8, 11) and two to the right (36, 40). The second step is to *add* the two middle values; in this case we get 17 + 33 = 50. The final step is to *divide* this number by two (the number of items we added together). The result is 50 ÷ 2 = 25. Hence, the median for these six numbers is 25. (For practice, how does the median compare to the mean for those six numbers?)

There is one more type of average that you should know. The **mode** is the value that occurs most. For example, for slide 1 the mode is 5, because that value occurs twice and no other value occurs more than once. For slide 2 the mode is 47, because it occurs four times (43 occurs twice, but this time it is not the mode).

Mode A statistical average that is determined by locating the value that occurs most.

If two values have the same number of instances, then we call the data *bimodal*, like this set:

4, 6, 10, 10, 22, 35, 35, 56

The numbers 10 and 35 each occur twice, and all the other values occur only once. In much the same way, if three different values occur the most, the set is *trimodal*. Let's look at all three measures of average age for the two slides:

Slide 1: Mean = 45; Median = 76; Mode = 5
Slide 2: Mean = 45; Median = 46; Mode = 47

Once again, let's see how the new information regarding the *mode* affects your room-mates' understanding. (Remember: They do not have access to the slides or to the actual ages for each group.) Your roommates were able to infer from the mean and median that group 1 had five very young children; in fact, from the mode, they can infer that *at least two* are 5 years old. However, your roommates could not infer very much before about group 2. Now, thanks to the mode, they know that *at least two* are 47 years old. They can begin to suspect that the ages are somewhat close together.

Unfortunately, they cannot know just *how* close. Knowing the mean, median, and mode still often gives a limited picture. To understand the *amount of diversity* within a group, we need a more powerful statistical tool, as we will see in the next section.

EXERCISES 13B

I. Determine the *mean*, *median*, and *mode* for the following sets of values:

1. [2, 3, 4, 4, 8, 10]

Answer: Mean: 5.17; Median: 4; Mode: 4

Self-Practice Questions

2. [3, 5, 7, 9, 11, 11, 11]

3. [1, 2, 3, 3, 5, 7, 11, 13, 13]

4. [10, 20, 30, 40]

⭐ 5. [100, 110, 200, 200, 210, 300]

II. Determine the *mean*, *median*, and *mode* for the following sets of incomes:

1. [$6,000, $42,000, $42,000, $120,000]

Answer: Mean: $52,500; Median: $42,000; Mode: $42,000

2. [$100,000, $100,000, $100,000, $3 million, $5 million]

3. [$10, $10, $10, $10]

4. [$7, $77, $777, $7777]

⭐ 5. [50 cents, $1, $1000, $1000, $4000]

III. Determine the *mean, median,* and *mode* for the following sets of grade point averages (GPAs):

Video Tutorial: 13BII
Exercise #5

1. [2.14, 2.49, 3.26, 3.26, 3.78, 3.99]

Answer: Mean: 3.15; Median: 3.26; Mode: 3.26

2. [1.88, 2.03, 2.56, 2.89, 3.64, 3.89]

3. [3.25, 3.25, 3.25, 3.75, 3.75]

4. [1.00, 2.00, 3.00, 4.00]

⭐ 5. [2.86, 2.96, 3.16, 3.16, 3.26, 3.36]

IV. Determine the *mean, median,* and *mode* for the following sets of heights (in inches):

1. [37″, 45″, 48″, 67″, 67″, 78″, 86″]

Answer: Mean: 61.14″; Median: 67″; Mode: 67″

2. [38″, 40″, 44″, 45″, 49″, 52″]

3. [23″, 27″, 27″, 27″, 29″, 29″]

4. [30″, 31″, 32″, 33″, 34″, 35″, 36″]

⭐ 5. [24″, 27″, 28″, 74″, 74″, 80″, 80″]

C. STANDARD DEVIATION

Standard deviation
A measure of the amount of diversity in a set of numerical values.

The **standard deviation** is a measure of the *amount of diversity* in a set of numerical values. Consider a bell-shaped, or *normal*, curve. Although the numerical values are spread throughout the curve, the majority of the values are clustered around the *mean*:

A Bell Curve

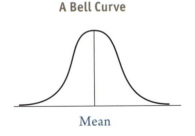

Mean

We call that spread or clustering the *distribution*. Let's see how to interpret the standard deviation to understand that distribution for a normal curve.

Dividing the Curve

As you can see, an equal number of values are found on both sides of the mean; this gives the curve its bell shape. Statisticians have developed a way of dividing the area under the curve into equal parts:

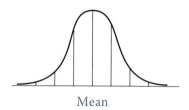

Mean

The areas to the *right* of the mean represent values that are *larger* than the mean, and the areas to the *left* represent values that are *smaller* than the mean. Each of the areas constitutes one standard deviation from the mean. Thus, the area directly to the right of the mean is designated as +1 SD (standard deviation), the next area to the right is +2 SD, and the third area is +3 SD. Similarly, the area directly to the left of the mean is designated as –1 SD, the next area to the left is –2 SD, and the third area is –3 SD:

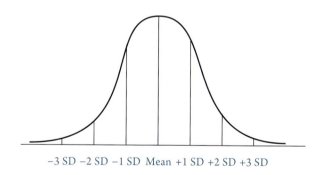

–3 SD –2 SD –1 SD Mean +1 SD +2 SD +3 SD

If you look closely, you can observe that area from +1 SD to –1 SD makes up the largest portion of the bell curve. In fact, this area contains approximately 68% of all the data. This means that approximately 34% of the data is in the +1 SD area, and approximately 34% is in the –1 SD area. The next two areas, +2 SD and –2 SD, each contain approximately 13.5% of the data, for a total of 27%. Therefore, the four areas from +2 SD to –2 SD contain approximately 95% of all the data. The +3 SD and the –3 SD areas each contain approximately 2.3% of the data, for a total of 4.6%. The grand total of all six areas is *approximately* 99.6%. The remaining 0.4% lie at the extreme ends:

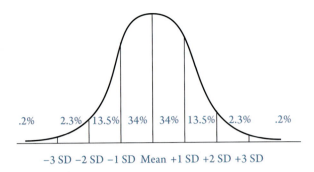

.2%   2.3% 13.5% 34%   34% 13.5%   2.3%   .2%

−3 SD −2 SD −1 SD Mean +1 SD +2 SD +3 SD

Apparently, a bell curve has few values indeed at the extremes. We can see this easily by adding color, to illustrate the total area captured by each SD:

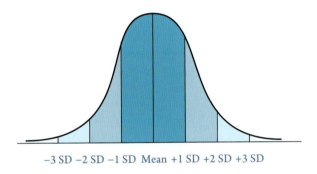

−3 SD −2 SD −1 SD Mean +1 SD +2 SD +3 SD

The two dark areas contain the data for +1 SD and −1 SD; the next two areas contain the data for +2 SD and −2 SD; the next two areas contain the data for +3 SD and −3 SD; and the two small areas at each end of the curve contain the fewest members—the extreme limits.

The Size of the Standard Deviation

Another way to look at the diversity is to ask how far from the mean we need to go to get a given percentage of the values. For example, you take a test for which the possible scores range anywhere from 0 to 100 (in whole numbers). You learn later that a graph of the scores takes the form of a normal curve, so the scores are spread equally on both sides of the mean. Let's imagine that the mean score was 50. You would then know that approximately 34% of the scores were within +1 SD from the mean, and approximately 34% of the scores were within −1 SD from the mean. Therefore, approximately 68% of all the scores fell with these two areas. *But how far from the mean do we have to go to get that 68%?*

The answer lies in the *size* of the standard deviation—in our picture, the width of each vertical slice in the bell curve. Suppose you are told that the standard deviation was 15 points. This tells us how far we have to go from the mean to get each area of the curve. *The larger the size of the standard deviation, the larger the diversity; the smaller the size of the standard deviation, the smaller the diversity.*

In our example, the mean was 50, and to get the value for +1 SD, you simply *add* 15 points to the mean: 50 + 15 = 65. To get the value for −1 SD you must *subtract* 15 points from the mean: 50 − 15 = 35. Therefore, approximately 68% of the scores fell within the range of 35–65.

The range of scores in the next two areas is calculated in much the same way. Since the standard deviation is 15, to get +2 SD means that we have to go 15 × 2 = 30 points away from the mean. This time, you *add* 30 to the mean: 50 + 30 = 80. To get the value for −2 SD you must *subtract* 30 points from the mean: 50 − 30 = 20. Therefore, approximately 95% of the scores fell within the range of 20–80.

What about the range of scores in the 3 SD range? To get +3 SD, we have to go 15 × 3 = 45 points away from the mean: 50 + 45 = 95. To get −3 SD, we have to subtract 45 points from the mean: 50 − 45 = 5. We now know that approximately 99.6% of the scores fell within the range of 5–95. If you scored 100, you were very special.

Let's compare these results with another example. Suppose the same test is given to another class. A graph of the scores once again takes the form of a normal curve, with a mean of 50. But now suppose that the standard deviation for the second group was 3. Since *the smaller the size of the standard deviation, the smaller the diversity*, you can immediately infer that the second class has very little difference in its scores. In that group, you would have been very special if you had come even close to 100.

We can calculate the SD ranges to verify our inference. To get the value for +1 SD, you *add* 3 to the mean: 50 + 3 = 53. To get the value for −1 SD, you *subtract* 3 points from the mean: 50 − 3 = 47. Therefore, approximately 68% of the scores fell within the range of 47–53. This means that 68% of the scores were separated by only 6 points (47–53). Compare this to your own class, in which 68% of the scores were separated by 30 points (35–65).

The range of scores in the next two areas is easily calculated. To get the value for +2 SD, you *add* 6 to the mean: 50 + 6 = 56. To get the value for −2 SD, you *subtract* 6 points from the mean: 50 − 6 = 44. Therefore, approximately 95% of the scores fell within the range of 44–56. This means that 95% of the scores were separated by only 12 points (44–56). In contrast, in your class, 95% of the scores were separated by 60 points (20–80).

Finally, let's determine the range of scores in the 3 SD area. To get the value for +3 SD, you *add* 9 to the mean: 50 + 9 = 59. To get the value for −3 SD you *subtract* 9 points from the mean: 50 − 9 = 41. Therefore, approximately 99.6% of the scores fell within the range of 41–59. This means that 99.6% of the scores were separated by only 18 points (41–59). Again, compare this to your class, in which 99.6% of the scores were separated by 90 points (5–95).

The graph of the second group is a normal curve, but its shape has to reflect its lack of diversity. It must show that scores are relatively close to the mean. That means the curve is very narrow, *because the size of the deviation is small:*

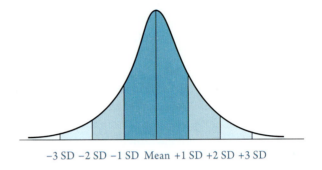

−3 SD −2 SD −1 SD Mean +1 SD +2 SD +3 SD

Since the range of scores for each SD was quite small, the sides of the curve slope down very sharply from the top—once again indicating the small diversity in the group.

How to Calculate the Standard Deviation

In real-life research, the amount of data can be enormous, but computers can do the calculations quickly, efficiently, and with little chance of error. (Handheld calculators programmed to do statistical calculations can handle smaller data sets.) Still, finding the standard deviation has just six steps. Let's do a simple calculation ourselves to see how it works. We will use the following small set of values as our reference.

[1, 3, 8, 17, 22, 33, 42]

STEP 1: Calculate the mean value. The sum of the seven numbers in our set is 126. We divide this by the number of items in the set to get the mean: 126 ÷ 7 = 18.

STEP 2: Calculate the difference between each value in the set and the mean value. A value that is smaller than the mean will result in a negative difference; a value greater than the mean will result in a positive difference; a value that is identical to the mean will result in a 0. Here are the results for our set (the boldface numbers are the values in our data set):

1 − 18 = −17	**17** − 18 = −1	**42** − 18 = 24
3 − 18 = −15	**22** − 18 = 4	
8 − 18 = −10	**33** − 18 = 15	

STEP 3: Multiply each difference by itself. This means that we are *squaring the differences.*

Why is squaring necessary to get the amount of variation? Why not just add the differences? To see why, take a worst-case scenario. Suppose that there were only four values in a set of data, and the mean was 20. If the values of the four members of the set were 18, 19, 21, and 22, then the differences would be –2, –1, 1, and 2. Adding these four numbers gives us a result of 0—but there is some small variation nonetheless. To get a meaningful result, we must change a negative value into a positive value by squaring, so all the results will be positive numbers.

In our problem, squaring the differences (–17, –15, –10, –1, 4, 15, 24) gives 289, 225, 100, 1, 16, 225, and 576.

STEP 4: Add the results of the squaring process in step 3. The sum of the seven numbers (289, 225, 100, 1, 16, 225, 576) is 1432.

STEP 5: Divide the result of step 4 by *one fewer* than the number of members in the set. This gives us the following result: 1432 ÷ 6 = 238.7. This result is called the *total variance*.

STEP 6: The square root of the total variance is the standard deviation. The square root of 238.7 is 15.4. Therefore, the set of values [1, 3, 8, 17, 22, 33, 42] has a standard deviation of 15.4.

THE SIX STEPS TO THE STANDARD DEVIATION

Step 1: Calculate the mean value.
Step 2: Calculate the difference between each value in the set and the mean value.
Step 3: Multiply each difference by itself (square each difference).
Step 4: Add the results of the squaring process in step 3.
Step 5: Divide the result of step 4 by one fewer than the number of members in the set.
Step 6: The square root of the total variance is the standard deviation.

EXERCISES 13C

Since you have already calculated the mean value of each set of data in Exercises 13B, you have already finished step 1 of calculating the standard deviation. Now perform steps 2–6 and determine the standard deviation for each set of data. Refer back to Exercises 13B for the exercises. The first exercise and a solution are provided here:

Self-Practice
Questions

  I. 1. [2, 3, 4, 4, 8, 10]
Answer: The standard deviation is 3.13.

            Step 1: 5.17
            Step 2: 2 – 5.17 = –3.17   4 – 5.17 = –1.17
                     3 – 5.17 = –2.17   8 – 5.17 = 2.83
                     4 – 5.17 = –1.17   10 – 5.17 = 4.83
            Step 3: 10.05; 4.71; 1.37; 1.37; 8.01; 23.33
            Step 4: 48.84
            Step 5: 9.77
            Step 6: 3.13

Video Tutorial: 13CII
Exercise #5

D. WHAT IF THE RESULTS ARE SKEWED?

So far we have looked at normal curves. While real-life data do not always fit perfectly bell-shaped curves, the same basic principles apply in calculating the standard deviation. The problem lies in interpreting and applying the unexpected results.

Many measurements involve "objective" criteria for some "naturally occurring" phenomenon. For example, you can measure the height of every student in class and determine the mean, median, mode, and standard deviation. A ruler or tape measure is equally objective, whether it is in inches or centimeters. But not all measuring devices are objective—especially when it comes to human capabilities. For example, many people have challenged whether I.Q. exams truly measure intelligence. Perhaps intelligence is not even quantifiable or not just one simple thing. For many children, the results of some verbal and mathematical I.Q. exams give substantially different results from tests that do not rely on the same verbal skills.

At least some physical skills lend themselves to objective measurement. For example, we can measure the amount of time it takes each class member to run 100 yards, to swim 50 meters, or to throw a baseball. We can measure how much weight each student can lift, or even many types of hand and finger dexterity. We can then determine the amount of variation.

However, when it comes to nonphysical skills, things can get more difficult. Teachers try very hard to create tests that will accurately determine the level of understanding. But we all know from experience that something can go very wrong. For example, suppose a teacher decides on the following scale for determining grades on an upcoming exam:

A: 90–100
B: 80–89
C: 70–79
D: 60–69
F: 0–59

After the exam, the teacher calculates the mean and the standard deviation. Here is one possible distribution of grades:

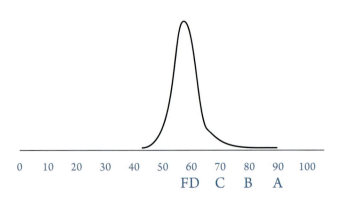

The mean appears to be around 58, and we can see that most of the class got an F. Only a very small percentage of the class received an A, B, or C grade. (F and D are right next to each other at the bottom of the graph, because 59 starts the F range and 60 is the lowest possible score for a D.)

If the class results reflected a normal curve, the *mean* would instead be somewhere over the C range. There would then be a smaller number of D and B grades, followed by an even smaller number of F and A grades. The actual results lean far to the left of what we had anticipated, and they are said to be *skewed*. How should we understand the outcome? On one hand, the students might interpret the graph to mean that the exam was *too hard*. On the other hand, the teacher might conclude that the class had not prepared adequately for the exam. Either way, the teacher might decide to *curve* the results of the exam by simply sliding the existing curve to the right:

This places the mean over the C range. The teacher can then adjust the original grading scale to get an appropriate number of A, B, D, and F grades.

What if, however, the results of the exam had produced this graph?

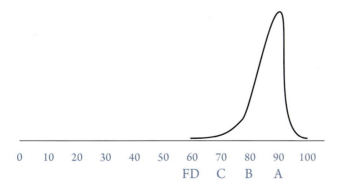

Here the mean appears to be around 91, and we can see that most of the class got an A. Only a very small percentage received an F, D, or C. If we expected a normal curve, we instead find a curve that is *skewed* far to the right. On one hand, the students might explain the results as the outcome of their having studied diligently for the exam. On the other hand, the teacher might conclude that the test was *too easy*. This time, the teacher might decide to curve the results by sliding the existing curve to the left:

Distribution of Grades after the "Curve"   Original Distribution of Grades

| 0 | 10 | 20 | 30 | 40 | 50 | 60 | 70 | 80 | 90 | 100 |

FD   C   B   A

This movement of the curve places the mean over the C range. The teacher can then easily adjust the original grading scale to get an appropriate number of A, B, D, and F grades.

As you can see, data analysis often leads to new questions—and disagreement about the answers. In our two examples, did the original results accurately measure what the class knew? Have the new curves produced more accurate pictures? How can we best decide?

These kinds of questions need to be asked and debated whenever we have to interpret complex statistical data. Social policy, such as federal funding for early childhood education, often depends on the results of statistical studies. For some administrations, statistical data justified an increase in the amount of money for preschools. Other administrations have used statistical data to justify a decrease in the amount of money available. They relied on different data as well as different interpretations of that data.

E. THE MISUSE OF STATISTICS

Statistics can mislead us either intentionally or unintentionally. Statements containing quantitative terms are often interpreted differently than those containing qualitative terms. For example:

1. The latest album by the Green Biscuits is number one in sales this year.
2. The latest album by the Green Biscuits is the best album this year.

Most people would accept statement 1 at face value because they assume that the statistics were compiled objectively and accurately. However, the word "best" in statement 2 is vague. Even when an album wins awards people often argue about the subjective nature of the voting process.

As explained in Chapter 4, the fallacy of misleading precision occurs when a claim appears to be statistically significant but is not. Statistics can be accurate, but they can also be easily misinterpreted. For example, suppose you read the following:

> Since we began advertising on the Internet, sales of our Premium Widgets have increased 400% over the first quarter. Stock options will be offered only for a limited time, so this might be your best chance to invest in our growing company.

Put your checkbook away. More information is needed to evaluate the claim. For example, suppose we find that the company sold a total of two Premium Widgets during the first quarter (at $10 each), and the company lost a million dollars. A 400% increase in sales means that they sold eight Premium Widgets during the second quarter (for a whopping $80 in sales), and they still lost a lot of money. The statistics are accurate, but if you misinterpret the information, then you might make a bad investment.

Statistics can mislead in other ways as well. In the article "Skipping Breakfast and Heart Disease: Not So Simple," author Madelyn Fernstrom raises some important questions concerning a large research study. The researchers examined surveys designed to estimate food intake of 26,902 male health professionals from 1992 to 2008 (16 years). At the start of the surveys, the subjects were between 45 and 82 years old.

The researchers determined that men who skipped breakfast had a 27% higher risk of heart attack or death from coronary heart disease than those who ate breakfast. After reading this statistic, it may be tempting to conclude two things: (1) Males who regularly skip breakfast are increasing their risk of heart disease, and (2) eating breakfast can lower the risk of heart disease in males. But before we accept these conclusions we should carefully analyze the information in the study.

Several key problems stand out that reduce the generalizability of the findings:

- The study used only male subjects who were health professionals.
  Weakness: This is not representative of all occupations.

- The subjects were between 45 and 82 years old.
  Weakness: This is not representative of all age categories.

- Only 3400 of the more than 26,000 were self-reported breakfast skippers.
  Weakness: Only approximately 13% of the subjects were self-reported breakfast skippers.

- The subjects were asked only once, at the start of the study, if they were breakfast eaters.
  Weakness: It assumes that the subjects' eating habits did not change over the 16-year study period.

As Fernstrom correctly points out, "It's important to note that simply grabbing breakfast—any breakfast at all, even if it's something unhealthy like a doughnut—is not enough to protect your heart health." In addition, breakfast may be one factor in maintaining a healthy heart, but there are many others of equal importance, such as exercise, smoking, alcohol intake, and the kinds of food eaten, to name only a few.

Fernstrom adds, "The important health message is that it's not just when you eat, but *what* you eat. . . . Grabbing a high calorie, low nutrient breakfast, on the other hand, is not a health plus."

EXERCISES 13E

Self-Practice
Questions

Analyze the statistical reasoning in each passage.

1. In general, however, the financial odds still greatly favor a person with a college degree. The Bureau of Labor Statistics estimates that median weekly earnings for a person with a bachelor's degree was $1,025 in 2009, compared with just $626 for those with only a high school diploma.

   Allison Linn, "Is It Worth It to Go to College?"

Answer:

Since the Bureau of Labor Statistics has access to large amounts of data, we can assume that the size of the data set is adequate. The *median* weekly income for persons with a bachelor's degree was $1025 (in 2009); therefore we know that 50% of that data set made more than that amount and 50% made less. For those with only a high school diploma, 50% of that data set made more than $626 a week and 50% made less.

   On the surface, the difference between $1025 and $626 is substantial. However, we are not told either the *mean* or the *standard deviation* in the two sets of data. Without that information, we cannot determine the amount of diversity in the sets. In addition, people with bachelor's degrees in engineering and computer science average three to four times the yearly salary of many social science majors. The article does not distinguish between majors. It therefore may misleadingly suggest that any kind of bachelor's degree puts you in a position to make substantially more than a person with only a high school diploma.

2. A study finds that Best Actress Oscar winners have a 63% chance of their marriages ending sooner than nonwinners. The median marriage duration was 4.30 years; 9.51 for nonwinners.   Ken McGuffin, "The Oscar Curse?"

3. Reuters Legal compiled a tally of reported decisions in which judges granted a new trial, denied a request for a new trial, or overturned a verdict, in whole or in part, because of juror actions related to the Internet. The data show that since 1999 at least 90 verdicts have been the subject of challenges, because of alleged Internet-related juror misconduct. More than half of the cases occurred in the last two years. Judges granted new trials or overturned verdicts in 28 criminal and civil cases—21 since January 2009. In three-quarters of the cases in which judges declined to declare mistrials, they nevertheless found Internet-related misconduct on the part of jurors. These figures do not include the many incidents that escape judicial notice.

   "As Jurors Go Online, U.S. Trials Go Off Track," Reuters

Video Tutorial: 13E
Exercise #3

4. Alberto Contador might face a one-year doping suspension and be stripped of his 2010 Tour de France title. . . . Contador, whose sample contained 50 picograms (trillionths of a gram) of a banned substance, is being diagnosed as a little bit pregnant in a context where there shouldn't be any ambiguity. When Contador offered the explanation that he had consumed tainted beef purchased in Spain, . . . statistics about Clenbuterol contamination in the food and water supply were debated. One authority didn't swallow the steak story. Christiane Ayotte, longtime director of the WADA-accredited lab in Montreal, was blunt with reporters in an informal media briefing in mid-October. "You'll never find a ton of [Clenbuterol] because the doses are really small," Ayotte said then, calling the beef excuse implausible. "Most of the samples are below 1 nanogram—a billionth of a gram."

Bonnie D. Ford, "Why Contador Case Sets Bad Precedent"

⭐ 5. It's possible to see procrastination as the quintessential modern problem. It's also a surprisingly costly one. Each year, Americans waste hundreds of millions of dollars because they don't file their taxes on time. The Harvard economist David Laibson has shown that American workers have forgone huge amounts of money in matching 401(k) contributions because they never got around to signing up for a retirement plan. Seventy percent of patients suffering from glaucoma risk blindness because they don't use their eyedrops regularly. Procrastination also inflicts major costs on businesses and governments. The recent crisis of the euro was exacerbated by the German government's dithering, and the decline of the American auto industry, exemplified by the bankruptcy of General Motors was due in part to executives' penchant for delaying tough decisions.

James Surowiecki, "Later: What Does Procrastination Tell Us About Ourselves?"

6. Another argument for Zenyatta is that she brought more mainstream coverage to the Sport. . . . The numbers simply do not support that. In 2004, Smarty Jones was attempting to join Seattle Slew as the only undefeated Triple Crown winners in history; a record crowd of 120,139 showed up to see his Belmont. Compare that to the 72,739 who came to Churchill Downs on Nov. 6 to see if Zenyatta would retire undefeated. . . . A search of news archives shows far more was written about Smarty Jones throughout the course of 2004 than Zenyatta in 2010: 7,350 articles for Smarty Jones; 2,260 articles for Zenyatta.

Amanda Duckworth, "Facts vs. Feelings"

7. There's been a lot of misinformation thrown around during Michigan's rather hastily arranged price tag debate. The governor cited research offered up by a group called the Coalition for Retail Pricing Modernization saying price tag application cost Michigan stores $2.2 billion annually. The governor cited the cost as a cause of Michigan's downtrodden economy. The questionable research extrapolates from a 2007 economics paper, which found that prices in an area of New York that then required price tags were about 10 percent

higher than stores in nearby New Jersey, which didn't. It ignored other factors which make New York stores pricier. Then, the group calculated 10 percent of Michigan store sales to arrive at the $2.2 billion. The back-of-the-envelope calculation was cited by the governor in his arguments, but derided by consumer advocates. "The true cost of placing price stickers on Michigan groceries is a small fraction of $2 billion," said Edgar Dworsky.

Bob Sullivan, "Another Nail in the Coffin of Price Tags"

8. A neuroanalytics company that specializes in measuring emotional responses and degree of attention looked at how people responded to six related terms: "climate crisis," "environmental destruction," "environmental collapse," "weather destabilization," "global warming" and "climate change." The researchers compared three groups of people who were distinguished by their political affiliation: 40 Republicans, 40 Democrats and 40 independents, for a total of 120 participants. The researchers measured the "emotional intensity" of the subjects responses to audio recordings that inserted one of the six terms listed above; for example, they might hear the following: "Sea levels will rise dramatically, to the point that many coastal cities will be submerged, as a result of global warming." The "emotional intensity" level was rated on a scale of zero to five (five being the strongest) by measuring electrical activity of the participants' brains and skin. The study found a 60% greater emotional response to the term "climate crisis" than to "climate change" among Democrats, a tripling in emotional response among Republicans, and it elicited the greatest emotional response among independents. Some advocacy groups are using these results to push for TV networks to start using the term "climate crisis" in their reporting.

Adapted from Jeff Berardelli, "Does the Term 'Climate Change'
Need a Makeover? Some Think So—Here's Why," CBS Interactive Inc.

9. Scientists wanted to study the effects of coal- and oil-fired power plants on the health of nearby communities. Researchers from the University of California, Berkeley, compared the rate of preterm births before and after eight power plants closed between 2001 and 2011 in California. According to the World Health Organization, preterm birth is the leading cause of death among newborns, and preterm babies also face heightened risk of disability and illness. The results of the study showed that the preterm births, defined as those that occur before 37 weeks of pregnancy, accounted for 7% of all births before the plants closed. However, the rate dropped to 5.1% in the year afterward among populations in neighboring areas.

Adapted from "Shuttering Coal and Oil Power Plants Boosts Fertility,
Babies' Health," CBS Interactive Inc.

10. Researchers studied three states that expanded Medicaid eligibility for adults since the year 2000—New York, Maine and Arizona, and compared them to neighboring states that did not expand eligibility—Pennsylvania, New

Hampshire, Nevada and New Mexico. Adults between the ages of 20 and 64 years old were studied for five years before and after the expansion, using data from the U.S. Centers for Disease Control and Prevention. The results showed that Medicaid expansions were associated with a reduction in mortality from all causes, by 19.6 deaths per 100,000 adults, for a 6% decrease compared to the states without expansions. Also, the mortality declines were greatest among adults between ages 35–64, minorities, and residents of poor counties. It appears that state expansions of Medicaid coverage to adults can be effective at improving both access to care and health for low-income Americans.

Adapted from Lewis Krauskopf, "Expanding Medicaid Cuts Death Rates," *Reuters*.

F. PROBABILITY THEORIES

Statements and arguments that include the word "probability" also play a large part in conversations, material, and other media. On any given day you might read these items:

- The probability of winning the Grand Prize in the Powerball Lottery is 1 in 195,249,054.   www.powerball.com

- The probability of a large earthquake on the San Andreas Fault in the next 30 years is about 21%, or about 1 out of 5.   U.S. Geological Survey

- Strictly speaking, the probability of doomsday isn't any higher than it is on any normal Wednesday, but there's been a fair bit of kerfuffle and hullabaloo over the CERN Large Hadron Collider (LHC) and whether it will create a black hole that will destroy the entire planet.

  Matt Blum, "The Large Hadron Collider Will Not Destroy
  the World Tomorrow, or Ever"

Evaluating statements and arguments that rely on probabilities requires that we accurately interpret the information. However, like the term "average," the term "probability" is ambiguous, and we need to know exactly how the word is being used. Three theories can help provide some clarity.

A Priori Theory

Sometimes we can determine whether something is true or false without having any experience of the things involved. Our knowledge is then said to be *a priori*. For example, the statement "All bachelors are unmarried males" is true by definition, even if we have never actually seen a bachelor. Similarly, we know *a priori* that "all unicorns have one horn."

The ***a priori*** **theory of probability** ascribes to a simple event a fraction between 0 and 1; the denominator of this fraction is the number of equally possible, or **equiprobable,** outcomes, and the numerator is the number of outcomes in which the event in

A priori theory of probability Ascribes to a simple event a fraction between 0 and 1.

Equiprobable When each of the possible outcomes has an equal probability of occurring.

question occurs. Probability calculations using the *a priori*, or *classical*, theory rely on two major assumptions:

1. All possible outcomes of a given situation can be determined.
2. Each possible outcome has an equal probability of occurring.

Consider a coin toss. We can quickly calculate the probability of the coin coming up heads (or tails) because we assume two things: There are just two possible outcomes, heads or tails; and each of these two possible outcomes has an equal probability of occurring. We can state that probability as a fraction by making the number of desired, or *positive*, outcomes the numerator and the number of *all* possible outcomes the denominator. Thus, the probability of heads is ½ (or 50%, or 0.5, or 50-50), because there is just one positive outcome (heads) and just two possible outcomes (heads and tails).

It is not surprising that the *a priori* theory originated with games of chance. Coin tosses, dice, and lotteries are all subject to *a priori* calculations. The assumption of equiprobable outcomes is really the assumption of randomness. This does not mean that any actual coin, dice, or lottery is perfectly random. Rather, our calculations are based on *a priori* assumptions.

PROFILES IN LOGIC
Blaise Pascal

Blaise Pascal (1623–62) achieved much in a short life. In science, he became convinced that a vacuum exists, an idea not generally accepted at the time. In mathematics, Pascal did crucial work on many topics, including conic sections (such as circles and ellipses, the orbit of the planets). Have you ever seen a triangle like this one, where we obtain a number in each new row by adding the pairs of numbers above it?

            1
          1   1
        1   2   1
      1   3   3   1
    1   4   6   4   1
  1   5 10 10   5   1

This arithmetical triangle simplifies a remarkable range of calculations, from algebra to statistics, and today it is called *Pascal's triangle*. In probability, he laid the very

foundations, in letters to and from Pierre Fermat, of *a priori* probability. The foundation of probability is built on the solutions to two related questions: (1) How often can we expect two sixes to appear when we throw a pair of dice? (2) What odds should someone give that will ensure a minimum profit in dice games?

Pascal's most famous work, however, is in philosophy, and it is also his most personal. His *Pensées* recounts his thoughts on human suffering—but here, too, he tries to ground all-too-human questions in mathematics and logic. In this book, Pascal manages to use his insights into probability theory as a basis for religious belief. He derived a betting proposition that has come to be known as *Pascal's wager*: If God exists and you believe, he argued, then you win everything. If God exists and you don't believe, then you lose everything. Pascal concludes that part of the human predicament is that we are *compelled to gamble*.

Take a single event, like a single toss. (We return to combinations of events, or *compound* events, later in the chapter.) Dice usually come in pairs (one of a pair of dice is called a *die*), and we can ask, "What is the probability of a die coming up 4 on any toss?" Assuming that all outcomes are equiprobable ensures that it is a fair game, governed by randomness. We also assume that the die has six sides, that only one of the numerals (1, 2, 3, 4, 5, or 6) occurs on each of the six faces, and that landing on an edge will not count as a legitimate outcome. With those assumptions, the one positive outcome (4) becomes the numerator, and all the possible outcomes become the denominator, giving us the fraction $\frac{1}{6}$. What is the probability that an even number will come up on any toss of the die? There are three positive outcomes (2, 4, and 6), and so the probability of an even number coming up is $\frac{3}{6}$, or $\frac{1}{2}$.

Relative Frequency Theory

The **relative frequency theory of probability** relies on direct observation of events. According to this theory, probabilities can be computed by dividing the number of favorable cases by the total number of observed cases.

Actuarial tables rely on relative frequency theory. Although insurance schemes go back at least 2000 years, the probability methods needed were developed only after the year 1650. Companies that offered insurance for ships bringing goods to a country needed to know how many ships successfully returned to port. Accurate empirical research was necessary to determine the number of ships leaving port, the number of ships arriving safely back, as well as the amount of goods successfully imported. Over time, adequate information enabled insurers to charge just enough for insurance to make it affordable to shipping companies, as well as guaranteeing a profit to the insurance company. Charging too much for insurance would scare away potential customers, while charging too little would mean that the insurance company would not have enough money to pay off claims.

Direct observation is especially important when we cannot know *a priori* all the possible positive and negative outcomes. For example, to know the probability that a 20-year-old female will live to age 65 requires thousands of observations of 20-year-old females to see how many actually live to age 65. Researchers might track 10,000 20-year-old females for the next 45 years to see how many were still alive. On the other hand, the researchers might go back 45 years and get a list of 10,000 females who were 20 years old at that time. They then would need to find out how many of those 10,000 females were still alive today.

The total number of observed cases (10,000) becomes the denominator of a fraction, while the positive outcomes (those actually living to age 65) becomes the numerator. Therefore, if 9200 females were still alive at age 65, the fraction would be $\frac{9200}{10,000}$. This can be reduced to $\frac{92}{100}$, which means that there is a 92% chance that a 20-year-old female will live to age 65, according to the historical data. The frequency of a 20-year-old female living to age 65 is *relative* to the set of observed

Relative frequency theory of probability
The theory that some probabilities can be computed by dividing the number of favorable cases by the total number of observed cases.

cases, which explains the name *relative frequency theory*. Here is the formula for this method:

$$Pr(A) = p \, / \, tn$$

The formula tells us that the probability of an event, *Pr (A),* is equal to the number of positive outcomes, *p,* divided by the total number of observed cases, *tn.*

It is important not to misapply probability calculations. An insurance company that issues a policy to a 20-year-old female is not predicting that this particular individual has a 92% chance of living to age 65. This individual is considered a member of the class of 20-year-old females, so her probability of living to age 65 is relative to the probability regarding the entire class, which in this case is 92%. The insurance company is not only insuring this one particular 20-year-old female, they hope to insure thousands. The monthly premium the insurance company charges each female is calculated to guarantee the company will have enough to pay off the 8% of the females who will die before age 65, plus ensure the company a profit.

Subjectivist Theory

Sometimes neither *a priori* nor relative frequency methods work. For example, in a race with ten horses, *a priori* calculations would tell us that the favorite should win only 10% of the time. (The favorite is the horse that has the most money bet on it.) Clearly this is not the case, because extensive research shows that favorites in horse races win approximately ⅓ of the time. Professional sports gamblers also cannot rely so simply on statistical, historical data. A team's won-loss record is certainly relevant to predicting how the team will do in the future. However, the number of variables affecting the outcome of a sporting event is immense. The team playing this year is not identical to last year's team. Players come and go, get older, and get injured. The horses in the Kentucky Derby probably have never all raced together before—and never in the Kentucky Derby. (Horses get only one chance to run in the Kentucky Derby—when they are 3 years old.) To calculate the odds, we must interpret the historical data subjectively.

Subjectivist theory of probability
The theory that some probability determinations are based on the lack of total knowledge regarding an event.

The **subjectivist theory of probability** is based on a lack of total knowledge regarding an event. However, this does not mean that the probability calculations are mere guesses. They often rely on relative frequency data. Professional gamblers and professional stock market investors rely on years of experience to sift and to weigh the pertinent information. They need that experience to cope with not only the mounds of data, but also with their partial ignorance (lack of total knowledge).

As indicated earlier, evidence shows that the favorite wins approximately ⅓ of the time (33%) in horse races. Is it therefore wise to bet the favorite in every race? Wouldn't you be assured of picking the winner 33% of the time? The answer to the second question is "yes," but the answer to the first question is "no." Although this system will ensure that you will have a winning ticket ⅓ of the time, you also have a losing ticket ⅔ of the time. In addition, the favorite has the most money bet on it, so the payoff is the smallest of all the potential payoffs. You would need to get 2:1 odds *just to break even*, but favorites pay far less than that, on average. For example, suppose you make a $2 bet on the favorite in nine races. You will have invested a total of $18. Since favorites pay approximately $4 to win, and since you will win only ⅓ of the time (or three races), you will get back around $12. Therefore, you will lose approximately $6 for each $18 invested.

Sometimes we use probability calculations to refer to events, but they can be used to refer to our statements as well. In a sense, two different situations are occurring at the same time. For example, suppose I draw a marble at random from a jar containing five red, five black, and five green marbles, and I ask you to guess the color. Let's imagine that the marble has already been picked and I can see that it is red, but you cannot see it. From my perspective, the probability of its being red is 1, because I have total knowledge of the outcome. From your perspective, all three colors have equal probability (⅓), because you lack certain information. If you say "The marble is red," then your *statement* has a ⅓ chance of being true, from your perspective. From my perspective, your statement *is* true. Therefore, probability is intimately connected to the availability of relevant information regarding an event.

G. PROBABILITY CALCULUS

Probability calculus refers to the rules for calculating the probability of compound events from the probability of simple events. The results can be displayed as fractions, percentages, ratios, or a decimal between 0 and 1.

For example, what is the probability that the next toss of a coin will come up either heads or tails? (We already stipulated that landing on edge will not count as a legitimate outcome.) Since there are two positive outcomes (heads or tails), and two possible outcomes (heads or tails), the fraction is ²⁄₁ or just 1. This corresponds to the notion of a *tautology*, a statement that is necessarily true. (In contrast, a contingent statement is neither necessarily true nor necessarily false.) At the opposite end of the probability spectrum is the probability that the coin will come up *both* heads and tails at the same time. Since the positive outcomes are 0, the fraction is ⁰⁄₂, or just 0. This corresponds to the notion of a *self-contradiction*, another kind of noncontingent statement. However, most of our examples will be about contingent events.

Conjunction Methods

When we need to calculate the probability of two or more events occurring together (*A and B*), we rely on one of two conjunction methods: the *restricted* or the *general*. Each conjunction method provides a formula for a simple calculation of joint occurrences.

The **restricted conjunction method** is used when two or more events are *independent of each other*: The occurrence of one event has no bearing whatsoever on the occurrence or nonoccurrence of the other event. For example, tails on one toss of the coin has no effect on the probability of tails (or heads, for that matter) occurring on

Probability calculus
The rules for calculating the probability of compound events from the probability of simple events. The results can be displayed as fractions, percentages, ratios, or a decimal between 0 and 1.

Restricted conjunction method
The method that is used in situations dealing with two or more independent events, where the occurrence of one event has no bearing whatsoever on the occurrence or nonoccurrence of the other event.

the next toss; these are independent events. Here is the formula for the probability of occurrence of two independent events:

$$Pr(A \text{ and } B) = Pr(A) \times Pr(B)$$

Why must we multiply the probability of the first occurrence (A) times the probability of the second occurrence (B)? The coin toss example provides the justification. Suppose a coin is tossed two times. *A priori* assumptions allow us to list all the possible outcomes:

Toss 1	Toss 2
Heads	Heads
Tails	Tails
Heads	Tails
Tails	Heads

Of course, these four possible combinations can go in any order. According to the list, the conjunction *tails and tails* occurs once. Since there are four possible outcomes, the probability is ¼ for the occurrence of *tails and tails*. The formula should give the identical results. The formula shows that the probability of *tails and tails, Pr (A and B)*, is equal to the probability of tails (toss 1) *times* the probability of tails (toss 2). Since the probability of the positive outcome tails is ½ for each independent event, we multiply ½ × ½ to get the *Pr (A and B)* = ¼, which is identical to the result in the list of possible outcomes.

What is the probability that 4 will come up in two successive throws of a die? The restricted conjunction formula gives this result:

$$Pr(A \text{ and } B) = \tfrac{1}{6} \times \tfrac{1}{6}$$

Under the *a priori* assumption of equiprobable outcomes, the probability of each independent occurrence of 4 is calculated as ⅙. Therefore, the final determination that 4 will come up in any two successive throws of the die is ⅙ × ⅙ = 1⁄36. This can be verified by listing all the possible outcomes. The list might start with the possibility that the first toss will be 1. Six possibilities are conjoined with this result (since any of the six numbers could come up in the second toss). Since the same number of possibilities can be conjoined with any of the six numbers occurring on the first toss, there would be thirty-six total possible outcomes, of which only one would correspond to the joint occurrence of *4 and 4*. This result, 1⁄36, matches the result from our formula. Although both methods are reliable, the formula is obviously more efficient and convenient than generating lists of possibilities.

The **general conjunction method** facilitates the calculation of the probability of two (or more) events occurring together, regardless of whether the events are independent. Two (or more) events are *not* independent when the occurrence of one event affects the probability of the other event. In these cases, the probability of subsequent events is dependent on prior events. For example, if a jar contains ten marbles, five red and five black, then what is the probability of picking two red ones in succession

General conjunction method The method that is used for calculating the probability of two or more events occurring together, regardless of whether the events are independent.

if we do not put the first marble back into the jar? Since we are reducing the number of marbles from ten to nine, the probability of picking a second red marble becomes dependent on our first pick.

Given the jar of marbles, the probability that the first marble picked will be red is $5/10$, or $1/2$. However, if the first marble is red and is not put back into the jar, then there will be only nine marbles left, four of which will be red. So, now, the probability that the second marble picked will be red changes to $4/9$. Here is the formula for the general conjunction method:

$$Pr\,(A\;and\;B) = Pr\,(A\,) \times Pr\,(B,\,if\,A)$$

With this formula, it is easy to compute the probability that two red marbles will be picked in succession. The probability that the first marble picked will be red, $Pr\,(A)$, is $1/2$. The probability that the second marble picked will be red, $Pr\,(B,\,if\,A)$, is $4/9$. This is a **conditional probability**, the probability that one event will occur given the knowledge that another event has already occurred. We can read the notation $Pr\,(B,\,if\,A)$ as the *probability of B given A*. Therefore, the probability that two red marbles will be picked in succession, under these conditions, is $1/2 \times 4/9 = 4/18$, or $2/9$:

$$Pr\,(A\;and\;B) = \tfrac{1}{2} \times \tfrac{4}{9}$$

What is the probability that the first three marbles picked from our jar will all be red? If the first two marbles are red, then eight marbles are left in the jar, of which three are red. The formula gives these results:

$$Pr\,(A\;and\;B\;and\;C) = \tfrac{1}{2} \times \tfrac{4}{9} \times \tfrac{3}{8}$$

Therefore, the probability that three red marbles will be picked in succession, under these conditions, is $1/2 \times 4/9 \times 3/8 = 12/144$, or $1/12$.

> **Conditional probability** The calculation of the probability that one event will occur given the knowledge that another event has already occurred.

Disjunction Methods

When we need to calculate the probability that either one of two or more events will occur (*A or B*), we rely on one of two disjunction methods: the *restricted* or the *general*. Each disjunction method provides a formula for easy calculation of either one of two independent events.

There are two requirements for using the **restricted disjunction method**: (1) the situation must involve two or more events that are independent of each other, and (2) the events must be **mutually exclusive** (if one event occurs, then the other cannot). Here is the formula:

$$Pr\,(A\;or\;B) = Pr\,(A) + Pr\,(B)$$

Suppose five green marbles are added to the jar already containing five red and five black marbles. The formula can be used to compute the probability of picking *either a red or a black marble*. The probability of picking red, $Pr\,A$, is $5/15$, or $1/3$. The probability of picking black is the same, $5/15$, or $1/3$. Therefore, we get this result:

$$Pr\,(A\;or\;B) = \tfrac{1}{3} + \tfrac{1}{3}$$

> **Restricted disjunction method** The method that is used to calculate probability when two (or more) events are independent of each other, and the events are mutually exclusive.

> **Mutually exclusive** Two events, such that if one event occurs, then the other cannot.

So the probability of picking *either a red or a black* marble is $\frac{1}{3} + \frac{1}{3} = \frac{2}{3}$. What is the probability of picking *a red or black or green* marble? Since we get $\frac{1}{3} + \frac{1}{3} + \frac{1}{3} = 1$, it is a *certainty* that you will pick one of the three colored marbles.

What is the probability that you will throw *either a 4 or an odd number*, if you throw one die? The formula gives this result:

$$Pr\,(A\ or\ B) = \frac{1}{6} + \frac{1}{2}$$

The probability of throwing a 4, $Pr\,(A)$, is $\frac{1}{6}$ for a six-sided die, and the probability of throwing an odd number is $\frac{1}{2}$. Therefore, the probability that you will throw *either a 4 or an odd number* is $\frac{1}{6} + \frac{1}{2} = \frac{1}{6} + \frac{3}{6} = \frac{4}{6}$, or $\frac{2}{3}$.

General disjunction method The method that is used for calculating the probability of occurrence of two or more events that are not mutually exclusive.

The **general disjunction method** is used when two or more events are not mutually exclusive. Here is the formula:

$$Pr\,(A\ or\ B) = [Pr\,(A) + Pr\,(B)] - [Pr\,(A) \times Pr\,(B)]$$

The formula is complex, but it works. For example, suppose we wanted to compute the probability that tails will come up in either of the first two tosses of a coin. Since these are independent events, the probability of tails coming up on the first toss, $Pr\,(A)$, is $\frac{1}{2}$; the same probability, $\frac{1}{2}$, exists for the second toss, $Pr\,(B)$. But these are *not* mutually exclusive events. The *restricted disjunction formula* would give this result:

$$Pr\,(A\ or\ B) = \frac{1}{2} + \frac{1}{2}$$

This would mean that the probability of a tails coming up in either of the first two tosses would be $\frac{1}{2} + \frac{1}{2} = 1$. But surely this cannot be correct. Let's look once again at the list of possibilities for tossing a coin two times:

Toss 1	Toss 2
Heads	Heads
Tails	Tails
Heads	Tails
Tails	Heads

The list yields four possibilities, three of which contain at least one tails coming up. This means that the probability of tails coming up in either of the first two tosses is $\frac{3}{4}$. The *general disjunction formula* should give the same result:

$$Pr\,(A\ or\ B) = \left[\frac{1}{2} + \frac{1}{2}\right] - \left[\frac{1}{2} \times \frac{1}{2}\right]$$

The fractions in the first set of brackets *add up* to 1. The *product* of the fractions in the second set of brackets is $\frac{1}{4}$. Therefore, the probability of getting tails in either of two tosses is $1 - \frac{1}{4} = \frac{3}{4}$. The complexity of the general disjunction formula pays off.

Suppose we pick from our jar of five red, five black, and five green marbles. What is the probability of getting a black marble in either of two picks—provided we return the first marble picked back to the jar? The formula gives this result:

$$Pr\,(A\ or\ B) = \left[\frac{1}{3} + \frac{1}{3}\right] - \left[\frac{1}{3} \times \frac{1}{3}\right]$$

The first set of brackets gives $\frac{1}{3} + \frac{1}{3} = \frac{2}{3}$. The second set of brackets gives $\frac{1}{3} \times \frac{1}{3} = \frac{1}{9}$. We can change $\frac{2}{3}$ into $\frac{6}{9}$ to allow the subtraction of the second bracket. Our final result is $\frac{6}{9} - \frac{1}{9} = \frac{5}{9}$. This is the probability of getting a black marble in either of two picks from the jar.

Negation Method

Once we know the probability of the occurrence of an event, we can easily calculate the probability of the event *not* occurring. Here is the **negation method** formula:

$$Pr\,(\sim A) = 1 - Pr\,(A)$$

For example, as we saw earlier with the restricted conjunction method, the probability of getting two tails in successive tosses of a coin is $\frac{1}{4}$. Using this information, the negation formula allows us to calculate the probability that two tails in succession will not occur:

$$Pr\,(\sim A) = 1 - \tfrac{1}{4}$$

Therefore, the probability that two tails will not occur in succession is $1 - \frac{1}{4} = \frac{3}{4}$.

The general disjunction method calculations showed that the probability of tails coming up in either of the first two coin tosses is $\frac{3}{4}$. Applying this information to the negation formula lets us calculate the probability that tails will *not* come up in either of the first two tosses:

$$Pr\,(\sim A) = 1 - \tfrac{3}{4}$$

Therefore, the probability that tails will *not* occur in either of the first two tosses is $1 - \frac{3}{4} = \frac{1}{4}$. This agrees with the list of possibilities, because the only way at least one tails will *not* come up in two successive tosses is if two heads come up. The probability of that happening is $\frac{1}{4}$.

> **Negation method**
> The method that is used once the probability of an event occurring is known; it is then easy to calculate the probability of the event not occurring.

EXERCISES 13G

1. A deck of fifty-two playing cards containing two red queens and two black queens is thoroughly shuffled. Determine the probability of picking one card at random and getting a black queen.

Answer: $\frac{2}{52} = \frac{1}{26}$. There are two black queens and fifty-two cards.

2. Determine the probability of picking one card at random and getting any queen.

3. Determine the probability of picking two cards at random (without replacing the first one picked) and getting any two queens.

4. Determine the probability of picking two cards at random (without replacing the first one picked) and getting both black queens.

⭐ 5. Determine the probability that two people randomly chosen will both be born on Monday.

Self-Practice Questions

6. Determine the probability that four people randomly chosen will all be born on the same day of the week.

7. Determine the probability that two people randomly chosen will both be born in the same month of the year.

8. Determine the probability that four people randomly chosen will all be born in the same month of the year.

⭐ 9. Determine the probability that two people randomly chosen will both have their Social Security numbers end with an odd number.

10. Determine the probability that four people randomly chosen will all have their Social Security numbers end with an odd number.

11. Imagine that there are two identical-looking opaque jars, but one contains a red marble and the other contains a black marble. Suppose you are allowed to pick a marble from any jar you wish. You record the results (red or black marble picked), replace the marble, and have the jars' positions randomly mixed again. The procedure is repeated until you have picked three times. Determine the probability that you will pick the red marble *at least once*.

12. Imagine a box of fifteen CDs contains these types of music: four jazz CDs, four classical CDs, three rap CDs, three reggae CDs, one disco CD. If two CDs are drawn, but the first CD is *not* put back into the box before the second is picked, determine the probability that both CDs will be jazz.

⭐13. From the information give in #12, if two CDs are drawn, but the first CD *is* put back into the box before the second is picked, determine the probability that both CDs will be jazz.

14. From the information given in #12, if two CDs are drawn, but the first CD is *not* put back into the box before the second is picked, determine the probability that *neither* CD will be jazz.

15. From the information given in #12, if two CDs are drawn, but the first CD *is* put back into the box before the second is picked, determine the probability that *neither* CD will be jazz.

16. If you know only that George Washington was born in February, what is the probability that, if given one guess, you will correctly pick the day of the week he was born? What if he was born in a leap year?

⭐17. In a normal deck of fifty-two playing cards there are four aces: two red and two black. What is the probability that a single card chosen at random will be a red ace? That it will be any ace at all?

18. What is the probability that the ages of two people, chosen at random, will both be even numbers?

19. What is the probability that the ages of five people, chosen at random, will all be even numbers?

20. Without looking up their actual birth dates, calculate the probability that Abraham Lincoln and John Kennedy were both born in leap years.

⭐21. Without looking up their actual birth dates, calculate the probability that Abraham Lincoln, John Kennedy, Ronald Reagan, and George W. Bush were all born in leap years.

22. Imagine that there is an opaque jar that contains two red marbles and three black marbles, and you are going to reach in and pick one of the marbles. Determine the probability that you will pick a red marble in the first try.

23. Imagine that there is an opaque jar that contains two red marbles and three black marbles and you are going to reach in and pick one of the marbles. If you pick a marble, but do not replace it, then determine the probability that you will pick both red marbles in the first two picks.

24. Suppose there are two indistinguishable envelopes, one containing a $1 bill, and the other a $100 bill. You pick one envelope, its contents are revealed to you, and the money is replaced. You do this again two more times, for a total of three picks. What is the probability that you will pick the envelope with the $100 bill at least once?

⭐25. Suppose you have a drawer of socks in these colors and amounts:

three black socks
four white socks
four brown socks
three orange socks
one red sock

If you draw two socks in succession, without replacing the first before the second draw, then what is the probability that both socks will be brown?

H. TRUE ODDS IN GAMES OF CHANCE

In a "fair" game of chance, the payoff odds of winning guarantee that, in the long run, the gambler will break even. The ability to calculate true odds will allow you to determine whether you are playing a fair game or whether the odds are stacked against you. We know that a coin toss has an equal probability of coming up heads or tails, so each has a probability of $\frac{1}{2}$. If you bet $1 on each toss of the coin, you will *win* the same number of times that you will *lose*, in the long run. Since there are one out of two chances of winning, one out of two chances of losing, true odds for this game are one-to-one, written as 1:1. So for every dollar you bet, you will get $1, if you win. If you lose, then your dollar is taken away.

As we calculated earlier, the probability of 4 coming up on one toss of a die is $\frac{1}{6}$. Using the negation formula, we determine the probability that 4 will *not* come up as $\frac{5}{6}$. Therefore, if you bet that 4 will come up, you must *receive* odds of 5:1 to ensure a fair bet. On the other hand, if you bet that 4 will *not* come up then you must be willing to *give* 5:1 odds.

Most casino games do not provide true odds. This should not be surprising, since casinos would not survive if there were an equal chance of winning or losing on their games. To ensure a winning margin, casino games offer odds stacked in their favor, odds designed to guarantee that the casino will win, in the long run. For example, the majority of American roulette wheels contain eighteen red numbers and eighteen black numbers, arranged from 1 to 36. In addition, there are two green numbers, 0 and 00. Since there are a total of thirty-eight possible outcomes, the probability of red coming up is $^{18}/_{38}$. The probability that red will *not* come up is, therefore, $^{20}/_{38}$ (eighteen black numbers plus two green numbers). As we can see, if you bet red, the odds are slightly against your winning. However, the casino will only offer you 1:1 odds for this bet (meaning that you will get a dollar back for each dollar you bet). After thousands of such bets the casino is virtually guaranteed to come out ahead.

If you decide to place your bet on your lucky number, what will happen? The casino is willing to give you 35:1 odds for this bet. But since there are thirty-eight numbers, the odds are once again not true. Odds have to deviate only slightly away from true odds to provide the casino with a winning margin, especially with millions of bets taken annually.

I. BAYESIAN THEORY

A major advance in probability theory and method came when Thomas Bayes was able to unite much of the probability calculus and the relative frequency theory into a method for calculating conditional probability. Bayes's ideas proved so useful that they have been applied to everything from risk assessment and hypothesis testing to the probability of false positives in disease testing. Bayes's theory is also used extensively in judging the predictive ability of exams and other measures. For example, formulas are available to determine whether the SAT is a useful predictor of success in college.

In fact, a single conditional probability formula combines the restricted disjunction method, the general conjunction method, the negation method, and the relative frequency theory. The general conjunction method already introduced the idea of conditional probability. It allowed us to calculate the probability of one event occurring *if another event occurred first*. What Bayes's theory does is to expand this basic conditional to include relative frequency. Here is the formula we will be using:

$$Pr(A, if B) = \frac{Pr(B, if A) \times Pr(A)}{Pr(B)}$$

This formula allows us to calculate the conditional probability of two mutually exclusive and exhaustive events. As defined earlier, "*mutually exclusive*" means two events, such that if one event occurs, then the other cannot; "*exhaustive*" means there are no other possibilities. For example, consider this problem:

> A teacher calculates that 80% of the students who passed had perfect attendance. Meanwhile 10% of students who did *not* pass had perfect attendance. Of the total number of students in all her classes, 75% passed the courses. What is the correct interpretation of the data? Is perfect attendance a good predictor of passing the courses?

This problem fulfills the requirements we have set forth. There are two possibilities for each event: (1) passing or not passing, and (2) perfect attendance or not perfect attendance. Together, they form a set of mutually exclusive and exhaustive events (a student cannot both pass and not pass, and a student cannot both have perfect attendance and not have perfect attendance).

If A = *passing the course* and B = *perfect attendance*, we can use the data to fill in the formula. We want to determine the probability of passing, *if perfect attendance is achieved*, which is written *Pr (A, if B)*. Suppose this data is provided:

(1) The probability of perfect attendance, if they passed the course, is 80%, or 0.80, which can be written as *Pr (B, if A) = 0.80*
(2) The probability of perfect attendance, if they did *not* pass the course, is 10%, or 0.10, which can be written as *Pr (B, if ~A) = 0.10*
(3) The probability of passing the course is 75%, or 0.75, which can be written as *Pr (A) = 0.75*

This information can now be applied directly to the general formula:

$$Pr\ (A, if\ B) = \frac{(0.80 \times 0.75)}{Pr\ (B)}$$

$$= \frac{0.60}{Pr\ (B)}$$

A new formula is needed to calculate the *Pr (B)*, one that allows us to calculate the *total probability*:

$$Pr\ (B) = [Pr\ (B, if\ A] \times Pr\ (A)] + [Pr\ (B, if \sim A) \times Pr\ (\sim A)]$$

This formula can be interpreted by using information from the example. The probability of B (*perfect attendance*) is defined through a set of conditional relationships. The left set of brackets relates B to A (*passing*), while the right set of brackets relates B to ~A (*not passing*). Since A and ~A are mutually exclusive, the *total probability* of B (*perfect attendance*) can be calculated by determining the complete relationship with A and ~A. Since *Pr (A) = 0.75*, the negation formula can be used to calculate that *Pr (~A) = 0.25*. Placing this information into the formula gives us *Pr (B)*:

$$Pr\ (B) = (0.80 \times 0.75) + (0.10 \times 0.25)$$
$$Pr\ (B) = 0.60 + 0.025$$
$$Pr\ (B) = 0.625$$

Adding this information to the previous calculations gives this result:

$$Pr\ (A, if\ B) = \frac{0.60}{0.625}$$
$$Pr\ (A, if\ B) = 0.96$$

Therefore, perfect attendance is a strong measure for predicting who will pass the course.

EXERCISES 13I

Use the discussion in this section and apply the Bayes's formula to the following situations.

1. Shane conducted a survey of his friends. The results showed that 60% own a video game console and 40% own a laptop computer; but interestingly, none of his friends own both items. He also found out that 20% of the video game console owners have Twitter accounts, but that 70% of the laptop owners have Twitter accounts. Using all the information given, calculate the probability that a friend who has a Twitter account is a laptop owner.

Answer:

$Pr = prbability; \; L = laptop; \; T = Twitter \; account; \; V = video \; game \; console:$

$$Pr\,(L, if\,T) = \frac{Pr\,(L) \times Pr\,(T, if\,L)}{[Pr\,(L) \times Pr\,(T, if\,L)] + [Pr\,(V) \times Pr\,(T, if\,V)]}$$

$$= \frac{0.4 \times 0.7}{(0.4 \times 0.7) + (0.6 \times 0.2)}$$

$$= \frac{0.28}{0.28 + 0.12}$$

$$= \frac{0.28}{0.4}$$

$$= .7$$

2. Frances is supposed to arrive at work by 9:00 AM. She leaves for work at 8:00 AM 40% of the time, but she leaves for work at 8:30 AM 60% of the time. On the days she leaves for work at 8:00 AM, she arrives by 9:00 AM 70% of the time. But for the days she leaves for work at 8:30 AM, she arrives by 9:00 AM 30% of the time. If she arrived at work by 9:00 AM today, then what is the probability that she left for work at 8:00 AM?

3. A student has a number of books that she purchased for her classes: 70% of her books cost under $100, and 30% of her books cost $100 or more. Of the books that cost under $100, 10% are hardbacks and 90% are paperbacks. Of the books that cost $100 or more, 80% are hardbacks and 20% are paperbacks. She recently loaned one of her hardback books to a friend. Using all the information given, calculate the probability that the book she loaned to her friend cost under $100.

4. Carly took her car to a garage for inspection, and the mechanic said that her engine needed some major work. The mechanic said that if she did the repairs, then there was a 25% probability that the engine will break down within the next 25,000 miles. But if she did not do the repairs, then there was a 67%

probability that the engine will break down within the next 25,000 miles. If it is as likely as not that Carly did the repairs, then suppose Carly's car engine did break down within the next 25,000 miles. Calculate the probability that she did the repairs.

⭐ 5. Imagine that a researcher gathers data on a new test for high school seniors, the Multiphasic Aptitude Diagnostic Test (MADT). He wants to determine whether scoring above 1200 on the MADT is a good predictor of graduating college with a GPA greater than 3.5. He calculates that 70% of the students who graduated with a GPA greater than 3.5 scored above 1200 on the MADT. The data also indicate that 15% of students who did *not* graduate with a GPA greater than 3.5 scored above 1200 on the MADT. The percentage of students who graduated with a GPA greater than 3.5 was 20%. What is the correct interpretation of the data? Is scoring above 1200 on the MADT a good predictor of graduating college with a GPA greater than 3.5?

Summary

Study Materials

- Evaluating arguments that rely on statistical evidence requires that we can correctly interpret the statistical evidence as it is presented.
- Population: Any group of objects, not just human populations.
- Sample: A subset of a population.
- Representative sample: A sample that accurately reflects the characteristics of the population as a whole.
- Random sample: A sample in which every member of the population has an equal chance of getting in.
- Mean: A statistical average that is determined by adding the numerical values in the data concerning the examined objects, then dividing by the number of objects that were measured.
- Median: A statistical average that is determined by locating the value that separates the entire set of data in half.
- Mode: A statistical average that is determined by locating the value that occurs most.
- Standard deviation: A measure of the amount of diversity in a set of numerical values.
- Probability calculations using the *a priori* theory rely on hypothetical reasoning based on two major assumptions. The first is that all the possible outcomes can be determined, and the second is that each of the possible outcomes has an equal probability of occurring (equiprobable).
- In the relative frequency theory, some probabilities can be computed by dividing the number of favorable cases by the total number of observed cases.

- Reliance on statistical, historical data is not the same as relative frequency applications. Calculations of this kind fall under the subjective theory of probability, where determinations are based on the lack of total knowledge regarding an event.
- Probability calculus: The rules for calculating the probability of compound events from the probability of simple events. The results can be displayed as fractions, percentages, ratios, or a decimal between 0 and 1.
- The restricted conjunction method is used in situations dealing with two or more independent events, where the occurrence of one event has no bearing whatsoever on the occurrence or nonoccurrence of the other event.
- The general conjunction method is used for calculating the probability of two or more events occurring together, regardless of whether the events are independent.
- Conditional probability: The calculation of the probability that one event will occur given the knowledge that another event has already occurred. For example, *Pr (B, if A)* is read as the *probability of B given A*.
- The restricted disjunction method is used to calculate the probability when two (or more) events are independent of each other, and the events are mutually exclusive (if one event occurs, then the other cannot).
- The general disjunction method is used for calculating the probability of occurrence of two or more events that are not mutually exclusive.
- The negation method is used once the probability of an event occurring is known; it is then easy to calculate the probability of the event not occurring.

KEY TERMS

a priori **theory of**
   probability   633
conditional
   probability   639
equiprobable   633
general conjunction
   method   638
general disjunction
   method   640
mean   616

median   618
mode   619
mutually exclusive   639
negation method   641
population   612
probability calculus   637
random sample   613
relative frequency
   theory of
   probability   635

representative
   sample   612
restricted conjunction
   method   637
restricted disjunction
   method   639
sample   612
standard deviation   620
subjectivist theory of
   probability   636

LOGIC CHALLENGE: THE SECOND CHILD

You are at a playground and happen to strike up a conversation with a stranger. You are told that he is there to watch his daughter play basketball. When you ask if he has any other children, he tells you that he has one more child. What is the probability that the second child is a female?

Chapter 14

Causality and Scientific Arguments

A. *Sufficient and Necessary Conditions*
B. *Causality*
C. *Mill's Methods*
D. *Limitations of Mill's Methods*
E. *Theoretical and Experimental Science*
F. *Inference to the Best Explanation*
G. *Hypothesis Testing, Experiments, and Predictions*
H. *Science and Superstition*

Digital homework exercises for this chapter are available in your instructor's online course. For information on how to access these resources, please visit **www.oup.com/he/baronett5e.**

Medical research has uncovered the cause of many diseases and how to treat them. In fact, the news is filled with the latest discoveries—but not all the claims you meet are unambiguous or true. Here are some items that you might have come across:

> Electronic cigarettes, which are increasingly used worldwide, are said to be unsafe and pose health risks, a new study suggests.
>
> "Electronic Cigarettes Pose Health Risks," Bernama.com

> It might be the potlucks, it might be those long hours sitting in pews, but whatever the cause, a new study presented this week shows a link between religious activity and weight gain.
>
> Diane Mapes, "Praise the Lard? Religion Linked to Obesity in Young Adults," Msnbc.com

> Girls, but not boys, who walk or bike to school instead of getting a ride perform better in tests of verbal and math skills, according to a new study of teens living in Spanish cities. And the longer the commute, the higher the test scores.
>
> "Girls Who Walk, Bike to School Do Better in Tests," Reuters

> A new report from British scientists suggests that long-term, low-dose aspirin use may modestly reduce the risk of dying of certain cancers, though experts warn the study isn't strong enough to recommend healthy people start taking a pill that can cause bleeding and other problems.
>
> "Aspirin May Cut Cancer Deaths, but Caution Urged," Associated Press

The search for causes is a large part of science, medicine, as well as everyday life. Cause-effect relationships are at the heart of physics, chemistry, biology, and many other fields. In everyday life you might look for reasons as to why your car is stalling in traffic, why your computer suddenly stopped working, or why your stomach is aching. We begin by discussing cause-effect relationships. We will see how John Stuart Mill developed basic principles of causality and scientific investigation. The rest of the chapter will focus on scientific theories and hypotheses, how they are tested in experiments, how they differ from superstition—and why they provide the best, and generally most reliable, way to understand the physical world.

A. SUFFICIENT AND NECESSARY CONDITIONS

The word "cause" has several meanings, and in everyday situations the possibility of ambiguity arises. For example, parents often tell their children that they must take vitamins because vitamins will help them grow. The claim is not that vitamins alone will cause children to grow; it is that vitamins are a *necessary condition* for children's growth. In another situation a child might complain of a stomachache. The parent could suggest that the child stop drinking so much soda. Of course, the parent could also give the child some medicine to ease the pain. The parent relies on an understanding that several methods of reducing or eliminating the stomachache are possible. In other words, the parent is offering a *sufficient condition* to bring about a desired effect. A basic knowledge of sufficient and necessary conditions can help in the overall understanding of scientific arguments. To begin our discussion, consider this statement:

> If you live in New Jersey, then you live in the United States.

Sufficient condition
Whenever one event ensures that another event is realized.

A **sufficient condition** occurs whenever one event ensures that another event is realized. Another way of saying that something is a sufficient condition is to think of the phrases "is enough for" or "it guarantees." In the foregoing statement, living in New Jersey is *sufficient* for living in the United States. Of course, if you live in any of the other forty-nine states, then you also live in the United States. Nevertheless, living in New Jersey is sufficient (is enough) to guarantee that you live in the United States.

Necessary condition
Whenever one thing is *essential, mandatory,* or *required* in order for another thing to be realized.

On the other hand, a **necessary condition** means that one thing is *essential, mandatory,* or *required* in order for another thing to be realized. Given this, in the foregoing statement, living in the United States is necessary for living in New Jersey. In other words, if you *do not* live in the United States, then you *do not* live in New Jersey.

These ideas can also be expressed in the following ways:

> *Sufficient condition:* If you live in New Jersey, then you live in the United States.
> *Necessary condition:* If you do not live in the United States, then you do not live in New Jersey.

Here are some more examples of sufficient and necessary conditions:

> *Sufficient condition:* If you have a gerbil for a pet, then you have an animal for a pet.
> *Necessary condition:* If you do not have an animal for a pet, then you do not have a gerbil for a pet.

Sufficient condition: If there is a fire in the room, then there is oxygen in the room.
Necessary condition: If there is no oxygen in the room, then there is not a fire in the room.

There are instances where *both* sufficient and necessary conditions are present. For example, the ideal gas law holds that as the pressure of a gas rises (or falls), so does its temperature. In other words, the rising (or falling) pressure is both a sufficient and a necessary condition for the rising (or falling) temperature of the gas. Here is another example:

A. If today is Friday, then tomorrow is Saturday.
B. If today is not Friday, then tomorrow is not Saturday.

Upon analysis, we see that today's being Friday is *both* sufficient and necessary for tomorrow being Saturday. The days of the week follow each other in a standard, accepted, and stipulated pattern. Therefore, if today is Friday, then of course tomorrow must be Saturday. In addition, if today is not Friday, then tomorrow cannot possibly be Saturday.

Let's analyze two more statements:

C. If today is Friday, then I am six feet tall.
D. If today is not Friday, then I am not six feet tall.

Upon analysis we see that today's being Friday is *neither* sufficient *nor* necessary for my being six feet tall. These results should not be surprising if we look at the relationship between the things talked about in C and D. There is no connection between the two that would make the truth or falsity of one somehow dependent on the other.

Let's examine a situation that has several sufficient and necessary ingredients. Universities and colleges have specific requirements that must be met in order to get a bachelor's degree, so let's consider a hypothetical situation where the following four requirements need to be fulfilled:

1. A recognized major
2. A recognized minor (must be different from the major)
3. An overall grade point average (GPA) of at least 2.00
4. A passing grade in at least 125 credits

Furthermore, the university stipulates that each of these four requirements is *necessary* (you cannot get a bachelor's degree unless you fulfill all four requirements). The university also lists the options that are available to satisfy each of the four requirements. For example, the university lists twenty recognized majors, such as psychology, history, physics, economics, and English. Therefore, majoring in psychology is sufficient to fulfill requirement 1. The university also lists the recognized minors (we can use the same list as the majors for our purposes). Therefore, minoring in history is sufficient to fulfill requirement 2. An overall GPA of 2.75 (or higher) is sufficient to fulfill requirement 3. Finally, a total of 128 credits with a passing grade is sufficient to fulfill requirement 4. This combination of fulfilled requirements is referred to as a *set of necessary and sufficient conditions* (in this example, to get a bachelor's degree). The following diagram provides an illustration of the relationship between the sufficient and necessary conditions in this example:

Sufficient Conditions	Psychology	Psychology	2.00	125	
	History	History	2.50	126	
	Physics	Physics	3.23	130	
	Economics	Economics	3.40	132	
	(Etc.)	(Etc.)	(Etc.)	(Etc.)	
Necessary Conditions	Major +	Minor +	Minimum 2.00 GPA +	Minimum 125 credits =	Bachelor's degree

EXERCISES 14A

Self-Practice
Questions

I. In each exercise, determine whether the intended *sufficient condition* does in fact guarantee that the other event is realized.

1. If Ed is a bachelor, then Ed is an adult male.

Answer: Sufficient condition. A bachelor is defined as being an unmarried adult male. Given this, if Ed is a bachelor, then Ed is an adult male.

2. If Ed is an adult male, then Ed is a bachelor.

3. If there is oxygen in the room, then there is a fire in the room.

4. If there is a fire in the room, then there is oxygen in the room.

⭐ 5. If this is the month of June, then this month has exactly 30 days.

6. If this month has exactly 30 days, then this is the month of June.

7. If I live in the White House, then I am the president of the United States.

8. If I am the president of the United States, then I live in the White House.

⭐ 9. If I have exactly 100 pennies, then I have at least the equivalent of $1.

10. If I have at least the equivalent of $1, then I have exactly 100 pennies.

11. If I am over 21 years of age, then I am over 10 years of age.

12. If I am over 10 years of age, then I am over 21 years of age.

⭐13. If I am eating a banana, then I am eating a fruit.

14. If I am eating a fruit, then I am eating a banana.

15. If I hurt a human, then I hurt a mammal.

16. If I hurt a mammal, then I hurt a human.

II. In each exercise, determine whether the intended *necessary condition* is in fact required in order for the other event to be realized.

1. If Ed is not an adult male, then Ed is not a bachelor.

Answer: Necessary condition. A bachelor is defined as being an unmarried adult male. Given this, if Ed is *not* an adult male, then Ed is *not* a bachelor.

2. If Ed is a not a bachelor, then Ed is not an adult male.

3. If there is not a fire in the room, then there is not oxygen in the room.

4. If there is not oxygen in the room, then there is not a fire in the room.

⭐ 5. If this month does not have exactly 30 days, then this is not the month of June.

6. If this is not the month of June, then this month does not have exactly 30 days.

7. If I am not the president of the United States, then I do not live in the White House.

8. If I do not live in the White House, then I am not the president of the United States.

⭐ 9. If I do not have at least the equivalent of $1, then I do not have exactly 100 pennies.

10. If I do not have exactly 100 pennies, then I do not have at least the equivalent of $1.

11. If I am not over 10 years of age, then I am not over 21 years of age.

12. If I am not over 21 years of age, then I am not over 10 years of age.

⭐13. If I am not eating a fruit, then I am not eating a banana.

14. If I am not eating a banana, then I am not eating a fruit.

15. If I do not hurt a mammal, then I do not hurt a human.

16. If I do not hurt a human, then I do not hurt a mammal.

B. CAUSALITY

A *cause* is a set of conditions that bring about an effect. For example, imagine that a window in your house breaks. If we saw a rock hit the window, we probably would claim that the rock was *the cause* of the broken window. For practical purposes, for assigning blame perhaps, this is a normal claim to make. However, for a deeper understanding of causality, we need to consider some alternatives.

If we take the same rock and strike a similar window, we would expect to get similar results. That already tells us something about what we expect of a cause-effect relationship: *same cause, same effect*. However, if we throw the rock so that it barely grazes the window, then the window might not break. Alternatively, we could keep the rock the same and the angle at which it strikes the window the same, but change the velocity with which it strikes the window. In other words, we throw the rock more softly. Again, it might not break the window. The weight of the rock, the angle of incidence, and the velocity are all parts of the event, and all of them can vary. In a scientific experiment, they are the *variables*.

Causal network A set of conditions that bring about an effect.

What we originally called *the cause* (the rock) has evolved into a **causal network**, a *set of conditions* that bring about an effect. By changing the parts of the event, the variables, we can achieve different results. For example, by varying the velocity of the rock, or by varying the angle of incidence of the rock, or by using rocks of various densities, we can discover the set of conditions that are involved in cause-effect relationships. This holds for the window itself, which is surely part of the event. By conducting experiments, we can find the necessary range of glass density and strength needed to bring about a desired effect—if it is our house, to keep the window from breaking. However, we must be sure to eliminate factors that are *not* necessary for the effect to have happened, such as the time of day, the color of the window frame, or the color of the rock. This is how we establish the set of *necessary and sufficient conditions* that constitute the cause of the event in question.

Normal state The historical information regarding an object.

Abnormal state A drastic change in the normal state regarding an object.

We single out the rock as the cause because we are able to establish the **normal state** of a system. If the window has been in an unbroken state for some time, then that is its normal state. As soon as it breaks, an **abnormal state** is established. Any change from the normal state requires explanation, typically a causal one.

Precipitating cause The object or event directly involved in bringing about an effect.

A **precipitating cause** is the object or event directly involved in bringing about an effect. In our example, it would be safe to call the rock the precipitating cause of the broken window. We then add to the precipitating cause the causal network in order to have a complete scientific explanation of the cause-effect relationship.

Remote cause Something that is connected to the precipitating cause by a chain of events.

On the other hand, a **remote cause** is something that is connected to the precipitating cause by a chain of events. We can trace the chain of events back in time depending on our needs. For example, we might not be interested in determining how the rock came to hit the window if we are scientists or engineers developing stronger windows. However, we may very much want to know the remote cause in order to assign blame and recover the cost of repairs. Let's imagine that some children had been playing baseball. Without thinking, and for no real reason other than curiosity and a dare from another player, the pitcher picked up a rock and tossed it at the batter. The batter hit the rock, which then hit the window. If we were interested in assigning blame for legal purposes, we could charge the batter, the pitcher, and perhaps the player who instigated the dare.

A legal test to determine the cause of an event is not the same as a scientific one. For scientific purposes, to determine the *physical cause* of the broken window, we need consider only the precipitating cause and the causal network, not the remote causes. Of course, a trial often calls on scientific testimony. However, for legal purposes, the remote causes would probably be emphasized—in our example, the chain of events that led to the rock hitting the window. In a trial, too, we would have to show that we suffered a loss (the broken window). A scientific investigation would focus simply on what happened when the rock hit the window.

These same issues appear in other cases. If someone is found dead under suspicious circumstances, the police will probably have an autopsy performed. The medical expert performing the autopsy seeks the physical cause of death—the precipitating cause and its effects on the body. So far, there need be no legal or moral issues involved. However, if it is determined that death was by poison, then the police will have to investigate if it was self-administered or was left by someone else. They will also ask if the poison was administered accidentally or deliberately. If there is evidence of a crime, then the police and district attorney will look for the remote causes of the death.

C. MILL'S METHODS

Is there a best way to discover causes? And if we found the right method, would it be what we call science? Many scientists and philosophers have suggested what they thought would be the most efficient and reliable way to conduct experiments. John Stuart Mill proposed one influential program in his book *A System of Logic*. We will look at five methods of experimental inquiry (also called "canons," which means general principles) that are discussed in Mill's book. They are the *method of agreement*, the *method of difference*, the *joint method of agreement and difference*, the *method of residues*, and the *method of concomitant variations*. As you will see, Mill's principles are the basis for many of the causal inductive arguments people make in everyday life.

Method of Agreement

The **method of agreement** looks at two or more instances of an event to see what they have in common. For example, if four people eat at a restaurant, but only three get food poisoning, then the method of agreement tells us to investigate what the three instances have in common. We can create a chart to display the data:

Method of agreement The method that looks at two or more instances of an event to see what they have in common.

Instances of the **Effect**	Possible Causes							
	Fish	Spaghetti	Ham	Bread	Appetizer	Soda	Beer	Wine
John: Food poisoning		√		√	√		√	
Robert: Food poisoning	√				√	√		
Christina: Food poisoning			√	√	√			√

The check marks indicate when a condition has been met. A blank space under an item indicates that a condition has not been met. For example, the chart indicates that John had the spaghetti, bread, appetizer, and beer. We also know from the chart that he did *not* have fish, ham, soda, or wine. We see that all three cases of food poisoning have just one thing in common: the appetizer. Therefore, of the eight conditions under investigation, the appetizer is the probable cause of the food poisoning.

Whenever a series of similar, but unexplained events occur, we are likely to wonder what they have in common. However, the method of agreement does not provide conclusive proof that we have found the cause. It can offer only partial, tentative inductive evidence. For example, the three people who came down with food poisoning might have had other features in common, and we simply overlooked them. All three victims might have had water (tap or bottled), or they might have grabbed a mint at the cash register before leaving. Maybe the three ate something even before going to the restaurant. Or perhaps their utensils were not washed properly.

The method of agreement may also run into trouble because it depends on how we decide to list things. Consider the possibility that two *different* items on our chart caused the food poisoning. For example, what if both the fish and the bread were contaminated, but not the appetizer? Could this explain why the three got sick? Since Robert ate the fish, this explains one instance. And since John and Christina both ate the bread, this would explain the remaining two instances of food poisoning. This is why experimental data can offer evidence to support a claim that something is a cause, but still leave a measure of uncertainty.

Let's look at another example. Suppose a mechanic has four cars towed to her garage in less than 1 hour, and the car owners all complain that their car just began sputtering and then stalled. Once again, we can draw a chart to see the results:

Instances of the **Effect**	Possible Causes				
	Spark Plugs	Generator	Water in Gasoline	Alternator	Carburetor
Car 1: Stopped running	√		√		
Car 2: Stopped running			√		
Car 3: Stopped running	√		√		
Car 4: Stopped running			√		

We can now interpret the results. In two instances, the spark plugs had to be replaced (car 1 and car 3). There were no instances in which the generator, alternator, or carburetor showed signs of being defective. But in all four cases water was found in the gasoline. The mechanic can use this information to do follow-up research. For example, she might find that all four drivers had recently bought gas from the same nearby gas station. She could then refill the tanks with good gas and see the result. The mechanic could also replace the two sets of old spark plugs to see if the cars start. Here the method of agreement adds something to our investigation: It allows the mechanic to follow up on the initial results. It helps narrow the search, once we have the right background information to know which of the hundreds of possible variables are relevant. However, if an event is truly novel, then background knowledge will not be much help.

Method of difference
The method that looks for what all the instances of an event do not have in common.

Method of Difference

The **method of difference** looks instead for what all the instances of an event do *not* have in common. If they have everything in common except one item, then that item is a likely cause.

Let's examine that unfortunate group of diners at a different meal. This time we need to investigate all four people to locate the *difference* between the three who got food poisoning and the one person who did not get it. We are really looking at the *absence* of food poisoning. Once again, we can create a chart to display the data:

Instances of the **Effect**	Possible Causes			
	Hamburger	French Fries	Tea	Pie
John: Food poisoning	√	√	√	√
Robert: Food poisoning	√	√	√	√
Christina: Food poisoning	√	√	√	√
Kristin: No food poisoning	√		√	√

We look for a single condition that was present when the effect occurred and that was absent when the effect did not occur. We see that there is only one circumstance that differentiates Kristin, who does not have food poisoning, from the three other people—the French fries. We conclude that, of the four circumstances under investigation, the French fries are the probable cause of the food poisoning.

The method identifies a *sufficient condition* as the probable cause. However, it still does not provide conclusive proof. Once again, we might have disregarded or overlooked other variables that differ among the four people. Those other possibilities have still not been ruled out.

Joint Method of Agreement and Difference

The **joint method of agreement and difference** combines our first two approaches. If two or more instances of an event have only one thing in common, while the instances in which it does *not* occur all share the absence of that thing, then the item is a likely cause.

Adding the results of the method of agreement and the method of difference into one analysis strengthens our claim. We can highlight the results to illustrate how each method is to be applied:

Joint method of agreement and difference If two or more instances of an event have only one thing in common, while the instances in which it *does* not occur all share the absence of that thing, then the item is a likely cause.

Instances of the **Effect**	Possible Causes							
	Fish	Spaghetti	Ham	Bread	Appetizer	Soda	Beer	Wine
John: Food poisoning		√		√	√		√	
Robert: Food poisoning	√				√	√		
Christina: Food poisoning			√	√	√			√
Kristin: No food poisoning	√			√				√

The three white rows (John, Robert, and Christina) show the results of the method of agreement, while the shaded row (Kristin) shows the results of the method of difference. First, *the effect must always be present when the cause is present.* In each instance in white, the cause, the appetizer, is present. Second, *the effect must always be absent when the cause is absent.* The shaded box shows that food poisoning is absent when the cause, the appetizer, is absent.

Our conclusion has a higher probability of being correct than if we had used either of the first two methods alone. The method of agreement by itself could not rule out the possibility that two different items listed on our chart caused the food poisoning. Perhaps both the fish and the bread were contaminated, but not the appetizer. The joint method eliminates this possibility. In the shaded row, Kristin ate the fish and the bread and did not get food poisoning. Therefore, neither of those items could be a cause of the illness.

The joint method allows us to assert that the appetizer was a *sufficient condition* for food poisoning. The joint method also allows us to assert that the appetizer was a *necessary condition*.

The same principles apply to our example of stalled cars:

Instances of the **Effect**	Possible Causes				
	Spark Plugs	Generator	Water in Gasoline	Alternator	Carburetor
Car 1: Stopped running	√		√		
Car 2: Stopped running			√		
Car 3: Stopped running	√		√		
Car 4: Stopped running			√		
Car 5: Did not stop running					

Again, the four white rows show the results of the method of agreement, while the shaded row shows the results of the method of difference. First, *the method of agreement requires that the effect must always be present when the cause is present.* In each case in white, the cause, water in the gasoline, is present whenever the car stopped running. Second, *the method of difference requires that the effect must always be absent when the cause is absent.* In the shaded row, the effect (the car stopping) is absent when the cause, water in the gasoline, is absent.

Again our conclusion has a higher probability than with each of the first two methods considered alone. The joint method allows us to assert that water in the gasoline was probably both a *sufficient condition* and a *necessary condition* for the effect.

Method of Residues

Method of residues
The method that subtracts from a complex set of events those parts that already have known causes.

The **method of residues** subtracts from a complex set of events those parts that already have known causes. Whatever remains (the "residue") is a likely cause of the remaining effect.

Suppose your roommate returns from a party with a stomachache, headache, and a rash. You piece together the food and drinks that your roommate consumed and form this list: hot dogs, pizza, chips, pretzels, macadamia nuts, and soda. Soda always gives him a headache, so that explains one symptom. He sometimes gets a stomachache from hot dogs, so that could account for another symptom. He does not remember ever having had a reaction to pizza, chips, or pretzels. That leaves just two things—the nuts and the rash. Sure enough, this was the first time he had eaten macadamia nuts, so the rash was probably caused by an allergic reaction to them. He plans on visiting the campus medical clinic to get tested for allergies to verify his conclusion.

We can again follow the reasoning by drawing a chart:

Symptoms	Possible Causes of the Symptoms					
	Hot Dogs	Pizza	Chips	Pretzels	Macadamia Nuts	Soda
Stomachache	√	x	x	x	x	x
Headache	x	x	x	x	x	√
Rash	x	x	x	x	√	x

However, we need to interpret this chart differently from the previous examples. With the method of residues, we are actively drawing on our background knowledge. For example, we concluded from past experience that hot dogs were the probable cause of the stomachache, so we placed a check mark to indicate that cause-effect relationship. Similarly, the two x's in the hot dogs column indicate that hot dogs had not been connected before to either a headache or rash.

We also concluded from past experience that soda was the probable cause of the headache, so we placed a check mark to indicate a causal connection. The two x's in the soda column indicate that soda has not been connected previously to either a stomachache or rash. In the columns for pizza, chips, and pretzels we find only x's because they have not been connected before to any of the symptoms.

The method of residues tells us to subtract from a complex set of events those parts that are already understood. We have done just that for the stomachache and headache. We also eliminate items that have no previous connection to any of the symptoms. Whatever remains, we conclude, is the most likely cause of the remaining effect. In this case, the macadamia nuts are the probable cause of the rash. We placed the check mark in a shaded box to indicate that this causal connection is newly discovered.

Method of Concomitant Variations

The **method of concomitant variations** looks for two factors that vary together. If a variation of one part of an event accompanies a variation in another part of the event, then the two parts are probably causally connected. (The word "concomitant" means *accompanying*.)

This method looks for a **correlation**, or correspondence between two sets of objects, events, or data. For example, suppose a car company wants to determine the speed at which a particular car gets the best gas mileage. Many automatic transmissions have three gears that shift up and down, depending on the car's speed and the engine's revolutions per minute (RPM). In a simple experiment, a test car is equipped with a special one-gallon gasoline tank. The car will go around a test track and maintain a fixed speed until it uses up that single gallon of gasoline. The number of miles traveled will determine the car's mileage at that speed, in miles per gallon (MPG). The engineers then repeat the test run at different speeds to see which gives the best mileage.

Method of concomitant variations The method that looks for two factors that vary together.

Correlation A correspondence between two sets of objects, events, or data.

This example involves isolating one variable, *speed*. The engineers thus make sure to keep tire size, tire pressure, the weather, road conditions, and other factors constant throughout the experiment, in order to see how speed affects the gas mileage of this one car model. Of course, many variables affect gas mileage, and the same method could test for those as well. The engineers could increase or decrease the tire size, for example, while keeping other variables constant. Regardless, in each case they are looking for a *correlation*—between a given variable and gas mileage.

Focusing for now on speed and mileage, suppose we make a chart of the results for the company's most popular subcompact car:

	Miles per Hour (MPH)								
	0	10	20	30	40	50	60	70	80
Miles per gallon of gasoline (MPG)	0	12	18	25	35	37	29	25	21

The first column indicates the worst possible driving situation, just sitting with the car idling. When the gallon of gasoline is used up, the car will have traveled exactly 0 miles at 0 MPH, so its MPG will also be 0. You can see that the MPG increases steadily until it reaches its peak at 37 MPG, when the car's speed is 50 MPH. It then decreases steadily for speeds over 50 MPH.

The method of concomitant variations looks for correlations, but the correlation can be either positive or negative. In other words, the two variables must change together, but they may change in the same direction or in opposite directions. In this example, in the range from 0 to 50 MPH we observe a positive correlation between speed and MPG. From 50 to 80 MPH, we see a negative correlation.

Once the method has found a correlation, it can help reveal a cause-effect relationship. Here we observe a complex relationship between speed and gas mileage, but why? Perhaps the explanation lies in the car's three gears. Because the lowest two gears are used to accelerate from a standing position, a lower MPG is found from 10 to 40 MPH. The engine needs the most power to get moving, so it consumes a lot of gasoline. If you ever rode a ten-speed bicycle, you know that when you start out at the lowest gears, you need a lot of energy to turn the pedals. As your speed increases, and you shift through higher gears, the power needed to turn the pedals decreases, and you reach a "sweet spot." The same principle holds true for cars, too. With the results in hand, the engineers can do further tests to confirm that causal relationship.

All cars have a "sweet spot," the speed at which the car runs most efficiently, which varies considerably from car to car, especially with engine size and car weight. The "sweet spot" typically occurs soon after the car shifts into its highest gear. After that, further acceleration will usually cause a decrease in MPG. We can see just that in the chart for the range from 50 to 80 MPH.

As we can already see, the method of concomitant variations has its limits. It can point to a causal relationship, but that still leaves work to be done to discover why. The results can even be misleading, because neither variable may prove to be the cause of the other. A basic principle of science holds that *every cause-effect relationship is a case of correlation, but not every correlation is a cause-effect relationship.* In other words, causality requires correlation, but correlation does not require causality. For example, there is a high correlation between Sundays and Mondays: One always follows directly after the other. But Sundays do not cause Mondays to occur. There is a high correlation between a person's weight and pants size. But your weight does not cause your pants size to be what it is, nor does your pants size cause you to weigh a certain amount. Of course, the *reason* you buy a certain pants size is your weight. Nevertheless there is no direct cause-effect relationship between your weight and the pants.

EXERCISES 14C

Self-Practice
Questions

I. Answer "true" or "false" to the following:

1. A causal network is the degree of probability that we assign to an event occurring.

Answer: False

2. A remote cause is something that is connected to the precipitating cause by a chain of events.

3. A correlation by itself is not a sufficient condition for making a causal claim.

4. The method of residues tells us that if two or more instances in which an event occurs have only one thing in common, while the two or more instances in which it does not occur all have the absence of that thing, then the item in which the two sets of instances differ is causally connected to the event.

5. The method of agreement tells us that if all the instances in which the event under investigation occurs, and an instance in which it does not occur, have everything in common except one item, then that item is causally connected to the event.

6. The method of difference looks for what all the instances of an event do not have in common.

7. The method of concomitant variations tells us that if you subtract from any complex set of events those parts that are already understood to be the effects of known causes, then what remains is causally connected to the remaining effect.

8. The joint method of agreement and difference tells us that a variation of one part of an event accompanies a variation in another part of the event, either in direct or inverse proportion, then the two parts are causally connected.

9. Since the word "cause" has several meanings, when it is used in everyday situations the possibility of ambiguity arises.

10. Mill's methods do not provide conclusive proof of causality.

II. Determine which of Mill's methods matches the descriptions that follow:

1. If you subtract from any complex set of events those parts that are already understood to be the effects of known causes, then what remains is causally connected to the remaining effect.

Answer: The method of residues

2. If all the instances in which the event under investigation occurs, and an instance in which it does not occur, have everything in common except one item, then that item is causally connected to the event.

3. If a variation of one part of an event accompanies a variation in another part of the event, either in direct or inverse proportion, then the two parts are causally connected.

4. If two or more instances of an event under investigation have only one thing in common, then the circumstance in which all the instances agree is causally connected to the given event.

⭐ 5. If two or more instances in which an event occurs have only one thing in common, while the two or more instances in which it does not occur all have the absence of that thing, then the item in which the two sets of instances differ is causally connected to the event.

III. For each of the following cases, do three things. First, construct a chart based on the information given for each case. Second, determine which of Mill's methods apply to each case. Third, determine the conclusion that can be derived from the method.

1. Tom and Marsha both bought new cars. They chose the same make and model, with the same size engine, automatic transmission, and same tire size. They both buy the same octane gas at the same gas station. Tom drives his car exclusively in the city, while Marsha does mainly highway driving. However, when they compared gas mileage, Marsha's car averages 35 miles per gallon (MPG), but Tom's car averages only 26 MPG.

Answer:

The **Effect**	Possible Causes								
	Make	Model	Engine Size	Automatic Transmission	Tire Size	Gas Station	Gas Octane	City Driving	Highway Driving
Tom: 26 MPG	√	√	√	√	√	√	√	√	
Marsha: 35 MPG	√	√	√	√	√	√	√		√

The chart displays the *method of difference.* We can conclude that city driving is the probable cause of Tom's car averaging 26 MPG, and highway driving is the probable cause of Marsha's car averaging 35 MPG.

2. A student majoring in physics wanted to see if a relationship exists between height above or below sea level and the boiling point of water. Her experiments result in the following data: At sea level, water boils at approximately

212° F; at 500 feet above sea level, water boils at approximately 211° F; at 1000 feet above sea level, water boils at approximately 210° F; at 500 feet below sea level, water boils at approximately 213° F; and at 1000 feet below sea level, water boils at approximately 214° F.

3. Lois received at least a score of 90 on all four math exams this semester. She tried to determine why she did so well. She had different meals the night before the exams; she studied a different number of hours; two times she studied with friends and two times she didn't. The only thing that she remembered doing before all four exams was getting at least 8 hours of sleep the night before.

4. Judy's electric bill averaged $200 a month for 3 months. She noticed that she used the air conditioner in the bedroom all night. For the next 2 months she decided to try to sleep without using the air conditioner. The electric bill for those 2 months averaged $75 a month.

⭐ 5. Suzie had $250 in her wallet on Friday afternoon. By Sunday night she had only $10 left. She recalled spending $60 on a dinner and a date Friday night. Then she spent $70 on groceries, $40 on gas for her car, and lent $50 to a friend. She didn't recall spending any more money, so the only thing she could think of was that she must have lost $20 somewhere.

6. Frank's three dogs suddenly started having fleas. They get baths at different times, and he uses different dog shampoos on them since they have very different hair types. They eat different kinds of food and like different doggie snacks. But last week a neighbor's dog got into the backyard and all three dogs played with it. The flea problem occurred soon after.

7. Two students who share the same dorm room received coupons in the mail for a free meal at a restaurant that recently opened near campus. However, the two students across the hall in the same dorm did not get any coupons. All four are juniors, they all have cafeteria passes, and they have lived in the same dorm for two years. The two students who received coupons in the mail remember participating in a survey at the student union the previous month. The other two students did not fill out the survey forms.

8. Linda's house was quite hot in the summer. She tried adding insulation to the attic, and it helped some the next summer. She added sunscreens to the windows, and that helped too. She planted six large shade trees, and the house was even somewhat cooler. She added aluminum siding to the house, but it didn't get any cooler.

⭐ 9. Two tomato plants were started from the same batch of seeds. They were all placed in the same kind of soil, given the same watering schedule and same amount of water, and had the same access to sun. Only one of the plants was sprayed with a fertilizer once a week; the other plant never received the fertilizer. The plant that received the fertilizer produced twice as many pounds of tomatoes as the nonfertilized plant.

10. After Luke washes his T-shirts, it takes them 25 minutes to dry in a heavy-duty dryer. Whenever he adds his underwear and socks to the T-shirts load, it takes 50 minutes to dry. If he adds his jeans to the underwear, socks, and T-shirts load, it takes an hour and a half to dry.

11. Marcie heard a buzzing sound that sounded like it came from an electronic source. She switched off the TV, but the sound did not go away. She turned off her computer, but the sound persisted. She switched off the lights in the room, but she still heard the sound. She decided that the sound must be coming from the next-door apartment.

Video Tutorial: 14CIII
Exercise #12

12. Chris noticed that for the entire spring semester she had a backache on Tuesdays and Thursdays, but not on the other three school days. On all 5 days she walked the same route to school and back home, and she spent the same amount of hours on campus. She ate similar meals each day and did similar exercise routines. She got the same amount of sleep each night and slept in the same bed each night. But she did note that on Tuesdays and Thursdays she had to carry four heavy textbooks in her backpack instead of only two small books on the other 3 school days.

★13. TreShawn boiled an egg for 3 minutes. Opening it, he found that it was quite runny. He tried boiling another egg for 4 minutes; it was a little thicker, but still not what he wanted. He boiled another egg for 5 minutes, and it was exactly what he wanted. He then decided to try to get a hard-boiled egg. After adding an additional minute of boiling to each subsequent egg, he determined that the hard-boiled egg he liked took 10 minutes of boiling.

14. Leslie wanted to try to spend less money, so she gathered information about her spending habits. According to her bank records she averaged ten ATM withdraws amounting to $200 a month. She decided to keep the ATM card at home except for Saturdays. For the next 3 months she averaged four withdrawals amounting to $80 a month.

15. Five friends (let's call them *1, 2, 3, 4,* and *5*) each lost approximately six pounds in the last month. Friends *2, 4,* and *5* eat meat; friends *1* and *3* are vegetarians; *1, 3, 4,* and *5* drink coffee regularly; *2* drinks nothing but tea; *2, 3,* and *5* work full time; *1* and *4* work part time; *1, 3, 4,* and *5* take night classes; *2* does not take any classes. They have all been meeting three times a week at a gym where they do intense aerobic routines.

D. LIMITATIONS OF MILL'S METHODS

Mill's basic principles can be adapted to a variety of settings in both science and everyday life. In fact, we shall see how they help understand the process of science. However, the methods all have their limitations, especially if they are applied in a simplistic way. Suppose a person woke up three mornings in a row with a terrible hangover. He carefully lists what he had the three previous nights: gin and tonic water, vodka and tonic water, and whisky and tonic water. Applying the method of agreement, he concludes that the tonic water caused the hangovers.

Similar mistakes can be made using the method of difference. For example, suppose someone drove to work each day for a year; but with the price of gas getting so high, she decided to start walking to work to save some money. At the end of the workday the manager announces that, because of the economic downturn, everyone will have to take a 10% pay cut. On the way home she reconstructs the evidence. For 1 year, she drove her car to work, and each day there was no pay cut. She walked to work for 1 day, and her pay was cut 10%. She concludes that walking to work caused the pay cut. (For a related discussion, see the *false cause fallacies* section in Chapter 4.)

Although Mill's methods do not provide conclusive proof of causality, they are helpful in discovering correlations and potential causes. However, they still rely heavily on background knowledge in order to get started. Experimenters must list what they think are *relevant* similarities or differences among sets of objects or events. The methods are thus not very helpful in discovering new cause-effect relationships. After all, if we have never encountered a factor before, or have never seen it as a cause, we can easily overlook or reject it. Finally, Mill's methods can show only a correlation, but correlation does not guarantee causation. At best, a correlation reveals a probable case of causality. Mill's methods can help reveal a *necessary* ingredient in causation (a *correlation*), but they do not by themselves provide *sufficient* evidence of causation.

The ability to discover causes is a powerful tool. When we know how part of the world works, we can often create things that will benefit us, such as vaccines, antibiotics, and cures for diseases. Discovering the cause of malaria enabled scientists to create drugs to fight the disease. Scientists are trying other new approaches as well:

> Scientists working on malaria have found a way of genetically manipulating large populations of mosquitoes that could dramatically reduce the spread of the deadly disease . . . making genetic changes to a few mosquitoes and then allowing them to breed; genetic alterations could spread through large mosquito populations in just a few generations.
>
> Kate Kelland, "Scientists Tweak Mosquito Genes to Fight Malaria," Reuters

Knowing that certain types of mosquitoes carry the disease to humans has not yet enabled us to eradicate the disease. A complex, worldwide problem like malaria requires a multipronged solution. However, without knowing the cause, we could not even think of rational ways to combat the disease.

Discovering causes also expands our ability to predict correctly the future. If we know what causes things to break, collapse, or burn, then we can often predict their life span. Although we cannot predict with perfect accuracy when any water heater will break, for example, we can use statistical data on similar models to predict the average life expectancy. This information helps you determine when to purchase a new water heater.

Similarly, physicians can often predict with great accuracy how a disease will run its course. This knowledge allows decisive action by targeting the cause and administering potential remedies. Of course, many phenomena are very complex, and our knowledge of the underlying causes may not yet allow accurate predictions. This is especially true for many social issues, such as poverty, crime, and domestic and international conflicts:

> Predictions usually deal with events—who will win an election, whether or not a country will go to war, the specification of a new invention; they center on decisions. Yet such predictions, while possible, cannot be formalized, i.e., made subject to rules. The prediction of events is inherently difficult. Events are the intersect of social vectors (interests, forces, pressures, and the like). While one can to some extent assess the strength of these vectors individually, one would need a "social physics" to predict the exact crosspoints where decisions and forces combine. . . . Forecasting is possible where there are regularities and recurrences of phenomena (these are rare), of where there are persisting trends whose direction, if not an exact trajectory, can be plotted with statistical time-series or be formulated as historical tendencies. Necessarily, therefore, one deals with probabilities and an array of possible projections. But the limitations of forecasting are also evident. The further one reaches ahead in time with a set of forecasts, the greater the margin for error, since the fan of the projections widens.
>
> Daniel Bell, *The Coming of the Post-Industrial Society*

As we saw, Mill's methods can only reveal evidence of probable causes; they provide no real explanatory power. Discovering instances of causation is an important step in

PROFILES IN LOGIC
John Stuart Mill

John Stuart Mill (1806–73) believed that the advance of knowledge went hand in hand with advances in human freedom and equality. For Mill, logic played a crucial role in that advancement. Deductive logic tells us if our reasoning is correct, and inductive logic is our best guide to discovering new truths. Since our inductive inferences are a combination of our current experiences and our memory, the conclusions do not follow with necessity. Although our inductive reasoning is subject to error, Mill argued that a scientific approach to knowledge, however fallible, is superior to superstitious beliefs that direct observation shows to be false.

Mill argued that our ability to recognize patterns existing in nature is the foundation of our discovering the "laws of nature," which in turn are shown to be accurate through our ability to explain and predict. Science advances by assuming that *causes* exist and that we can discover them.

Mill believed that we will find the best ways to live by carefully observing the way the world is. "Few human creatures would consent to be changed into any other lower animals, for a promise of the fullest allowance of a beast's pleasures; no intelligent human being would consent to be a fool, no instructed person would be an ignoramus, no person of feeling and conscience would be selfish and base, even though they should be persuaded that the fool, the dunce, or the rascal is better satisfied with his lot than they are with theirs."

understanding the world—but it is only part of what we need. We also need to understand *how* and *why* particular instances of causation function as they do. Answers to these questions take us beyond being able to identify cause-effect relationships. We must develop theories and hypotheses—the basis of scientific reasoning.

E. THEORETICAL AND EXPERIMENTAL SCIENCE

We sometimes need an explanation that not only captures certain facts, but also gives us a way of discovering new ones. This is what a good **hypothesis** does. It provides an explanation for known facts and a way to test our explanation. In addition, a good hypothesis can foster new technologies, which in turn create new ways of exploring the world. These inventions allow us to make more precise observations and to discover new facts.

> **Hypothesis** Provides an explanation for known facts and a way to test an explanation.

The interplay of science and technology is a complex process, but it follows a repeating pattern:

Facts ⟶ Hypothesis ⟶ Technology ⟶ New facts ⟶ New hypothesis. . . .

For example, the creation of better and stronger telescope lenses allowed Galileo to see clearly the surface of our moon, and to discover some moons of Jupiter. The new information that Galileo gathered by using the improved telescopes helped refute the then generally accepted view of the universe and Earth's place in it. More recently, advances in artificial intelligence and animal sensation provide new information that can lead to new hypotheses about the nature of consciousness. For example, evidence about the nervous systems of certain animals can be used to discuss the theoretical frameworks that argue for or against animal consciousness.

There are two aspects of science—*theoretical* and *experimental*—and each has an important role to play in our knowledge of the physical world. **Theoretical science** proposes explanations for observations of natural phenomena, while **experimental science** tests those explanations. Both theoretical science and experimental science are involved in the development of new inventions and technologies that may allow us to gather new data and new facts about the physical world.

> **Theoretical science** Proposes explanations for natural phenomena.
>
> **Experimental science** Tests the explanations proposed by theoretical science.

The impact of experimental science and theoretical science that occurred during Galileo's time can be seen throughout the ensuing centuries. For example, recent advances in technology are forcing us to rethink our theories of mind and consciousness; this is especially true in the role that genetics plays in human behavior. We are achieving greater insight into the physiology and chemistry of the brain thanks to such advancements as magnetic resonance imaging (MRI) and computerized axial tomography (CAT) scans. These reveal structures and processes never before seen, which forces us to create new hypotheses of the mind.

Theoretical science, in turn, can have sweeping consequences as well. The *theoretical* breakthrough regarding the structure of DNA, made by James Watson and Francis Crick, provided *experimental* scientists with clues about where to look, what to look for, and what could be predicted based on consequences of the theoretical work. The early 20th century saw the rise of Albert Einstein's theories of space-time, as well as quantum theory (the physics of subatomic particles). These theories led to many unexpected and unique predictions about the world. When experimental results verified both Einstein's theories and quantum physics, they opened new horizons for understanding the world and our place in it.

Chapter 2 explained how theoretical definitions assign a meaning to a term and assist in understanding how a term fits into a general theory. A theory is scientific if it generates hypotheses that can be tested. A theory that produces untestable hypotheses is not a scientific theory. A fruitful scientific theory is one that generates multiple *confirmed* hypotheses. In contrast, a theory that repeatedly generates *refuted* hypotheses is not useful. The words "confirmed" and "refuted" are not identical to "true" and "false" when they are used to describe hypotheses. Instead, they mean that we have some evidence that *supports* one hypothesis and *denies* the other hypothesis.

An important factor for any scientific theory is its ability to let the physical world decide. Experiments are ways of letting the physical world answer unambiguously "yes" or "no" to our hypotheses. A successful scientific theory also provides fertile ground for invention and experimentation. For example, recently the most precise measurements of an electron ever made suggest that it's nearly perfectly spherical. The laser experiments conducted by researchers at Imperial College London took ten years to design and complete. One of the researchers made the point well:

> We're really pleased that we've been able to improve our knowledge of one of the basic building blocks of matter. It's been a very difficult measurement to make, but this knowledge will let us improve our theories of fundamental physics. People are often surprised to hear that our theories of physics aren't "finished," but in truth they get constantly refined and improved by making ever more accurate measurements.   ScienceDaily.com

A scientific theory functions like an abstract tool. Physical tools often come with manuals that tell you how to operate the tool safely and effectively. The manuals speak in general terms to let you know which tasks are appropriate. Physical tools can be useful for some tasks and useless for others. For example, a hammer is good for driving nails into wood, but it's not good for delicate brain surgery. Through trial and error we learn the limits of tools. Just as we do not expect any physical tool to solve all our problems, we should not expect a scientific theory to answer every possible question.

Abduction The process that occurs when we infer explanations for certain facts.

Inference to the best explanation Reasoning from the premise that a hypothesis would explain certain facts to the conclusion that the hypothesis is the best explanation for those facts.

F. INFERENCE TO THE BEST EXPLANATION

The logician Charles S. Peirce argued that it is a common human trait to infer explanations for our experience, especially for events with recurring patterns. He called this process **abduction**. But what happens when people infer different explanations for the same facts? How do we decide which explanation is correct? In **inference to the best explanation**, we reason from the premise that a hypothesis would explain certain facts to the conclusion that the hypothesis is the best explanation for those facts. For scientists, the term "best explanation" means *the most plausible explanation* based on our *background knowledge*, which is everything we know to be true. It includes all facts and hypotheses that have already been confirmed or refuted through observation and experiment. Science is an interrelated set of elements, all of which support each other in the quest to understand the physical world. Together, they make up the scientific method.

Peirce's ideas apply to a recent tragedy. Many explanations for the earthquake and the devastating tsunami that struck Japan in 2011 have been proposed. Here are three:

- The disasters are God's way of punishing the Japanese for their attack on Pearl Harbor.
- The Japanese built the nuclear plants too close to the ocean.
- Japan is located on the Pacific "rim of fire," which is one of the world's major geological fault lines. It has a long history of powerful earthquakes and massive tsunamis, and similar disasters have been documented for centuries.

The first hypothesis does nothing to explain the dozens of earthquakes and tsunamis that have occurred in the same places in Japan going back several centuries—long before the attack on Pearl Harbor. The second hypothesis might help explain why the nuclear power plants were damaged by the earthquake and tsunami. They were built too close to the ocean. However, it does nothing to explain the cause of the earthquake and the tsunami. The third hypothesis provides a causal explanation based on historical data, contemporary knowledge of the causes of earthquakes and tsunamis, and their probability.

In cases like this, perhaps we can pay attention to Peirce's advice: "Facts cannot be explained by a hypothesis more extraordinary than these facts themselves; and of various hypotheses the least extraordinary must be adopted" (quoted in *The Play of Musement* by Thomas Sebeok).

Let's look at another example. Suppose there was no snow in your yard when you went to sleep, but when you woke up there was snow in the yard. This is a fact, and one explanation is that it snowed last night. A second explanation is that your friends have executed an elaborate prank by placing artificial snow in your yard. How do we decide which explanation is best? We had better gather more evidence.

The idea is to force the explanation to predict something else that we do not know yet. For example, we might look around the neighborhood to see if there is snow anywhere besides your yard. If there is snow everywhere in the neighborhood, then it is unlikely that your friends would have been able to get hold of that much artificial snow. If snow is everywhere in the neighborhood, then we say that the snow hypothesis has been *confirmed* and the prank hypothesis has been *refuted*. Gathering additional evidence is an ongoing process. Only in exceptional cases can a single confirmation or refutation establish a definitive answer. Instead, the accumulation of evidence after repeated experiments points us in the right direction.

To see why we cannot determine the best explanation based solely on what we already know, take the two hypotheses to explain the snow in your yard. The reasoning might go as follows:

- If it snowed last night, then there is snow in your yard. There is snow in your yard. Therefore, it snowed last night.
- If your friends played a prank on you last night, then there is snow in your yard. There is snow in your yard. Therefore, your friends played a prank on you last night.

Both arguments commit the fallacy of affirming the consequent; they are, therefore, both invalid. This is why we need evidence that goes beyond the known facts. We need to think of things that we can do that will allow us to gather new facts, and this additional information will help us decide which explanation is better.

The same process can be seen in a criminal trial. The prosecution needs to gather important and relevant incriminating evidence in order to convince the jury of the guilt of the defendant. But what determines guilt "beyond a reasonable doubt"? It may take several additional pieces of evidence. Of course, the defense will do its best to discredit the prosecution's evidence.

In biology, Charles Darwin's reasoning was partly based on his inference that, although natural selection was not the only explanation for the diversity of species, as far as he could determine, it was the best explanation. In fiction, Sherlock Holmes remarked, "Once you eliminate the impossible, whatever remains, no matter how improbable, must be the truth." The private detective started his reasoning process with a set of facts. Next, he devised various hypotheses—his possible suspects.

PROFILES IN LOGIC
Charles S. Peirce

Charles S. Peirce (1839–1914) is considered by some to be the greatest American philosopher-mathematician. He did outstanding work in both logic and mathematics, creating many of the notations used today. According to Peirce, the conclusions of mathematics follow by necessity, but logic is broader still, because it investigates any and all kinds of arguments.

In philosophy he founded *pragmatism*, the application of scientific methods and results to philosophical problems. Peirce coined the term "abduction" to an all-encompassing activity—generating hypotheses in order to explain facts and to deduce predictions. Deduction and induction alone, he believed, are not sufficient to complete logic.

Peirce stressed the use of truth tables as a way to reveal the logic behind truth-functional operators. Although it took the work of others, most notably the philosopher Ludwig Wittgenstein (1889–1951), before truth tables were fully accepted, this system became the perfect tool for something else as well: It helped in creating computers. The system of truth values (true and false) is a foundation of computer languages and hardware applications.

Holmes's subsequent investigations and research led him to a series of new facts that, one by one, allowed him to eliminate hypotheses until one remained—the best explanation. (Holmes referred to his method as "deduction," but he repeatedly used the process of abduction.)

Our hypotheses are only as good as our imagination. We might fail to think of the correct hypothesis. In this sense, abduction has many of the drawbacks that we saw with Mill's methods. Whether we hit on the correct hypothesis often depends on our background knowledge and our imagination. This is why breakthroughs in science and other fields often take so long. It sometimes takes several generations for someone to think of the correct hypothesis or to devise a new way of gathering evidence—a novel experiment—that will point us in the right direction.

G. HYPOTHESIS TESTING, EXPERIMENTS, AND PREDICTIONS

Hypotheses are sometimes easy to propose but difficult to test. Exploring this idea will allow us to see how experiments and predictions help us understand the world. This, in turn, will enable us to analyze scientific reasoning in greater detail.

Controlled Experiments

The best way to test a hypothesis is with a **controlled experiment**—an experiment in which multiple experimental setups differ by only one variable. You might have recognized that the principle behind this kind of research is Mill's method of difference. In fact, many of Mill's methods have been adapted for modern scientific research. This should not be surprising, since we know that the methods are useful for revealing instances of correlation and uncovering potential causes.

In everyday life, many variables affect the outcome of a given situation, often making strong cause-effect claims very difficult. But a laboratory setting can reduce the number of variables. For example, suppose we want to see the effect of a new fertilizer on plant growth. The idea is to make things as similar as possible—except for one variable. The researchers need to control the plant seeds, growing areas, soil, amount of water, and available sunlight, making sure that these items are as similar as possible for every plant in the experiment. One group of plants, the **experimental group**, is given a precise amount of a fertilizer, which the other group, the **control group**, does not get. At the end of the experiment, the plants in the two groups are compared. Any statistical difference between the groups—for example, size or crop yield—might then be ascribed to the fertilizer. Further tests must then replicate all the experimental factors. These *repeated trials* are necessary before the effects of the fertilizer, positive or negative, can be accepted as definitive.

Through this painstaking attention to detail and methodical procedure, controlled laboratory experiments help scientists to uncover causal relationships. A scientific theory must stand up to the severest testing we can devise. It must provide coherent and effective explanations. It must provide correct predictions repeatedly, and help

Controlled experiment One in which multiple experimental setups differ by only one variable.

Experimental group The group that gets the variable being tested.

Control group The group in which the variable being tested is withheld.

us to discover new facts about the world. When opponents of Darwin's theory of evolution by natural selection call it "only a theory," they ignore what a theory means in science. They ignore how much it predicts, the repeated success of its predictions, and the breadth of causal relationships that it has helped biologists to discover.

Determining Causality

Of course, many things can affect the results of an experiment, forcing scientists to go to great lengths to ensure that nothing disrupts the experimental setting. In addition, since a controlled experiment is by definition "artificial," the results may not match real life. For example, quite often laboratory experiments that test new drugs are conducted on animals whose physiology does not match that of humans. Consequently, positive (or negative) results with the laboratory animals may not match what we would find if the drug were given to humans. This is why taking the results of controlled laboratory experiments and proclaiming that similar connections exist in the outside world is so problematic. Most scientists candidly admit that their promising lab results may not fit the world at large. Unfortunately, popularized versions of laboratory results are sometimes disseminated mistakenly to the public. This is why we often see claims that a cure for a disease has been found, or that scientists have isolated the cause of a disease, only to be disappointed later on.

In understanding the complex nature of causality, we can point to five criteria:

CRITERIA FOR DETERMINING CAUSALITY
1. There should be a *correlation* between the *cause* and the *effect*.
2. The cause should precede the effect.
3. The cause should be in the *proximity* of the effect.
4. A set of *sufficient* and *necessary* conditions should exist.
5. *Alternative explanations* should be ruled out.

None of the five criteria alone is sufficient to establish a cause-effect relationship. Instead, it is the weight of the answers to all five criteria that together support our determination of a cause-effect relationship.

As we saw earlier, a correlation alone cannot establish a causal relationship. For example, there is a strong correlation between a barometer falling and a storm. There is also a strong correlation between people putting on swimsuits and getting wet. In neither case do we have a causal relationship.

The second criterion cautions us to consider the time lag between the cause and the effect. The longer the time between the cause and the effect, the more the situation can be interrupted by other variables that might have brought about the effect. This same note of caution is realized in the third criterion. The greater the spatial distance between the cause and the effect, the greater the chance of other variables interfering.

The fourth criterion derives its meaning from the results of our discussion of sufficient and necessary conditions. In other words, the criterion requires that a claim that "X caused Y" must be backed by two things: (1) X was *sufficient* to bring about Y; and (2) X was *necessary* for Y (without X, Y would *not* have occurred).

The fifth criterion, the ability to rule out plausible alternative explanations, is the glue that unifies the set. Any causal claim can be challenged by suggestions of alternative potential causes. (We saw this earlier in the example of the two competing hypotheses for the snow in your yard.) Therefore, a strong causal claim should be backed up by evidence that confirms the hypothesis, and evidence that refutes (or disconfirms) rival, alternative causal claims.

Each of these five criteria has its place in science. They can also help us see how scientific explanations are vastly different from superstitious beliefs.

H. SCIENCE AND SUPERSTITION

Even in science, a causal hypothesis is often extremely difficult to test directly. Although it may say something about the world that is either true or false (for example, "The disease was caused by a parasite"), we cannot simply look at a hypothesis and directly determine its truth or falsity. We must force the hypothesis to do something—to put itself out on a limb, so to speak. This is accomplished by getting the hypothesis to make a *prediction*.

The Need for a Fair Test

A proposed experiment is simply another way of asking the question "What if we do this?" For example, if your car does not start, someone might suggest that you have a dead battery. Although the suggestion (which is a hypothesis or conjecture) is either true or false, we cannot discover the answer by looking at the battery. What we can do is propose a simple experiment: What if we try the headlights? The person who hypothesized that we have a dead battery would be forced to predict that the headlights would not work (in most cars the headlights need power from the battery). If the headlights come on as normal, then the prediction is false, and we would have evidence to refute the hypothesis. However, if the headlights do not come on as normal, then the prediction is true and we would have evidence to support (confirm) the hypothesis.

We can try different experiments in order to get different predictions. For example, if we disconnect the battery, take it to a garage, and hook it up to a battery tester (the experiment), the dead-battery hypothesis would predict that the battery would have little or no power. Again, this prediction is either true or false, and the results can be used to confirm or disconfirm the hypothesis. Another possible experiment would be to try to start the car using jumper cables that are attached to another car's battery. If the dead-battery hypothesis is correct, the car should then start. The truth or falsity of this prediction will again be the indirect evidence that confirms or refutes the hypothesis.

Predictions are crucial to our understanding of the truth of hypotheses. In fact, even a hypothesis that does not make an explicit causal claim should be tested. Since predictions are generally specific statements that are testable, they provide the means for determining, *indirectly*, the truth or falsity of the hypothesis. After an experiment is completed, we can take the truth value of the prediction and trace it back to its source, the hypothesis. Therefore, the fate of the hypothesis rests on the fate of the prediction.

When considering scientific results, we must make decisions about the relevance of the available evidence. We need to have criteria that will eliminate evidence that is misleading or irrelevant. These criteria must also help us to decide how much weight to give each piece of evidence. This is required if we are to judge accurately the strength of a causal argument. Here are three requirements for acceptable predictions that ensure that a fair test of a causal hypothesis has been conducted:

REQUIREMENTS FOR A FAIR TEST OF A CAUSAL HYPOTHESIS

1. The prediction should be *verifiable*.
2. The prediction should *not* be *trivial*.
3. The prediction should have a *logical connection* to the hypothesis.

Verifiable Predictions

Verifiable prediction
A prediction that, if true, must include an observable event.

A **verifiable prediction** is a prediction that, if it is true, includes an observable event. Suppose there is a house where all the people living there got sick for no apparent reason. Two causal hypotheses are put forward:

> **Hypothesis 1:** A high degree of radioactivity in the house is causing the illness.
> **Hypothesis 2:** A disease-causing ghost is haunting this house.

The two hypotheses are statements that could be either true or false. Also, neither hypothesis can be tested directly by simply looking around the house, because both of the conjectured entities are things that are invisible to the unaided human eye (radioactivity and ghosts). But are both hypotheses equally testable and verifiable?

An advocate of hypothesis 1 might predict that if we take a Geiger counter and go around the house (the experiment), then we will find a high reading of radioactivity. If the Geiger counter is operating correctly, and we do get a high reading, then we can safely say that the prediction is true; therefore, the hypothesis has some evidence to support, or to confirm it. However, if there is no sign of radioactivity, then the prediction is false, and we would have evidence to refute the hypothesis. A verifiable prediction does not have to be true, only verifiable. In other words, there must be a method for deciding, clearly and objectively, the truth or falsity of the prediction.

We would accept the evidence for or against hypothesis 1 because Geiger counters are an established source of scientific evidence. Their reliability has been repeatedly confirmed. Geiger counters provide one source of empirical evidence in the complex field of subatomic particles and quantum physics. We understand how Geiger counters work, and we trust them to be a good source of objective evidence. There is also a well-established theoretical framework that secures their place in the scientific community.

Let's turn now to hypothesis 2. What would function as a device that is comparable to the Geiger counter? Short of a *Ghostbusters*-type gadget, there seems to be no comparable method of gathering evidence for the ghost hypothesis. A ghost hypothesis defender might say "But of course the ghost is invisible, so it is impossible to detect." Yet exactly the same challenge confronted hypothesis 1, since we cannot see radioactivity either. Nevertheless, we are able to gather indirect physical evidence to decide if the radioactivity is actually there. In addition, although radioactivity is invisible, we know that it is a part of the physical world and is therefore subject to detection.

Our knowledge of the physical reality of radioactivity also allows us to determine how it causes illness. We have learned how radioactivity affects human tissue and alters human cells, often leading to tragic results. The ghost hypothesis provides no comparable understanding. For example, if ghosts are not only invisible, but also immaterial (not part of the physical world), as many ghost hypotheses allege, then it would be extremely difficult to explain how ghosts could physically affect us. Quite often ghost stories are filled with inconsistencies. For example, a movie might depict a ghost walking unimpeded through doors or walls, but in the next instant the ghost is seen climbing stairs. If the ghost is truly immaterial, then it should not be able to interact with any material objects.

We can assert, then, that a prediction does not meet the first requirement whenever there is no acceptable method to check objectively the truth value of the prediction. Therefore, we need not accept as evidence someone's subjective claim that he can see ghosts.

Nontrivial Predictions

The first requirement for a fair test of a causal hypothesis turns on predictions of future observations and future experiments. The second requirement turns on what we already know and wish to explain. A **nontrivial prediction** requires reference to background knowledge, which is everything we know to be true. Of course, background knowledge changes over time. Therefore, to decide if a prediction satisfies the second requirement, it is necessary to judge it in the light of what we know at the time it is put forth.

Suppose I claim to have the power to see the future (hypothesis). Of course, my claim is either true or false. Now, having understood and accepted the first requirement for a fair test of a hypothesis, you correctly ask me to provide some evidence. That is easy enough for me to do. If all you want is a prediction that is verifiable, then I predict that tomorrow the sun will come up. If you have only the first requirement to use, then you are forced to accept my prediction as being a fair test of the hypothesis. Therefore, the claim that I have the power to see the future will most probably turn out to be true. However, this should *not* be acceptable. We want to avoid situations such as this; we want to be able to eliminate predictions like this one, ones that are highly likely to be true. This is just what the second requirement effectively does. It provides a way of handling predictions that should *not* be used as evidence. A prediction which is likely to be true whether or not the hypothesis is true *does not* provide a good test of the hypothesis. Without the second requirement, we would be forced to accept almost anything as evidence, as long as it is merely verifiable (as long as it

> **Nontrivial prediction** A prediction that requires reference to background knowledge, which is everything we know to be true.

satisfied the first requirement). Although the first requirement is a necessary condition, by itself it is not a sufficient condition to ensure a fair test of a hypothesis.

Let's get back to the hypothesis that I have the power to see the future. The second requirement for predictions allows us to eliminate predictions that we consider trivial, and hence carry no weight. This new requirement forces me to revise my original prediction ("The sun will come up tomorrow") because as it stands, even if it turns out true (which is a near certainty), it will carry no weight in support of my hypothesis. Accepting this criticism now forces me to be more specific. I offer this prediction as evidence of my power to see the future:

> Tomorrow, at exactly 1:35 PM, it will start raining on the steps of the U.S. Capitol building. Then it will stop raining at exactly 1:57 PM. But it will rain only on the steps of the Capitol building; it will not rain anywhere else in Washington, D.C.

Would you accept this as a good test? Is this prediction trivial? What we know about the weather should lead us to say that the prediction, being so specific about something that is as unpredictable as the weather in a specific part of a city, is nontrivial. This is all that the second requirement asks of a prediction. Furthermore, the prediction meets the first requirement, because it is easily verifiable. Therefore, according to the first two requirements, this would be a fair test of the hypothesis. Of course, when my prediction turns out to be false, then you would have good evidence that refutes my hypothesis.

The history of Halley's Comet illustrates the principles we have been describing. Applying part of Isaac Newton's theories, Edmund Halley hypothesized that comets reappear in regular cycles. In 1705, Halley predicted that a comet would appear in the year 1758 in a precise location of the sky. In order to judge whether his prediction was trivial, we have to consider not what we know to be true today, but rather what the background knowledge was in 1705. Halley's hypothesis was not yet part of what was known to be true. Therefore, his prediction was considered, at that time, unlikely to be true.

If Halley had predicted that a comet would appear *somewhere* in the sky *sometime* in the 1750s, this would have been a trivial prediction, because many comets had been observed throughout recorded history. The phrase "*somewhere* in the sky," is vague, and the range of dates—"*sometime* in the 1750s"—is too long to offer any precision to the prediction. Therefore, when Halley's specific, and unlikely, prediction did in fact turn out to be true (in the location and time predicted), scientists had good justification for claiming that his hypothesis was also true (based on the confirming evidence).

Halley's hypothesis then became part of the background knowledge, something scientists knew to be true. Therefore, after 1758, if anyone predicted that Halley's Comet would reappear in another 76 years, this would have been considered likely to be true. Therefore, future predictions regarding the return of Halley's Comet do not carry the same weight as the initial one. Each correct prediction confirms the hypothesis to some extent, but the weight diminishes with each subsequent confirmation. When background knowledge changes, then our decisions regarding the second requirement often change as well.

Connecting the Hypothesis and Prediction

The third requirement for an acceptable prediction ensures that there is a connection between the hypothesis and the prediction. This is necessary because we want to use the prediction's truth value as evidence to confirm or refute the hypothesis. We therefore need a direct link.

To derive a prediction from a hypothesis, we must first develop an experiment that will test the hypothesis. We cannot simply take a hypothesis and deduce a prediction straight away. For example, Halley's hypothesis simply stated that comets, like planets, orbit the sun. From this claim nothing much can be predicted. However, Halley consulted the information about comets that had been gathered over many centuries. He noticed a pattern: A comet appeared in a specific place in the sky in 1682, 1606, and 1530. Halley conjectured that they were instances of the same comet. In other words, from the available data and his hypothesis that comets return, he was able to calculate the next return of the comet. This process enabled Halley to make a specific prediction. Of course, the prediction could have turned out to be false. However, when the prediction turned out to be true, then the truth value could be transferred back to the hypothesis as confirmation. (Unfortunately, Halley did not live long enough to see his hypothesis confirmed.)

Putting It All Together

What separates scientific theories from nonscientific ones is that scientific theories generate hypotheses that can be tested. In addition, a useful scientific theory is one that generates multiple *confirmed* hypotheses. In contrast, a theory that repeatedly generates *refuted* hypotheses is not useful. As mentioned earlier, the terms "confirmed" and "refuted" are used to describe hypotheses. "Confirmed" means we have evidence that *supports* a hypothesis; "refuted" (or "disconfirmed") means we have evidence that *denies* a hypothesis.

The ideas we have been exploring can be illustrated by looking at a famous example from biology. The modern concept of "inheritance" (the characteristics transmitted from parents to their offspring) derives in large part from the work of Gregor Mendel in the 19th century. Mendel's theoretical framework included several general principles that he defined as follows:

- "Factor" means the hereditary unit in which a characteristic (trait) is transmitted from one generation to the next.
- "The first principle of inheritance" means that each individual inherits two factors, one from each parent.
- "The second principle of inheritance" means that the factors are inherited randomly from each parent.
- "The third principle of inheritance" means that if two traits are inherited that cannot both be displayed, then the trait that is displayed is called "dominant" and the other is called "recessive."

Mendel knew that until he conducted experiments and tested specific hypotheses, he couldn't know for sure if his theory was useful. He also knew that he needed to conduct experiments that provided clear and precise results. Mendel chose pea plants. He started with two types, one in which the offspring were *all tall*, and the other in which the offspring were *all short*. These were referred to as "true-breeding" plants, meaning that the parents *always* pass down a specific characteristic or trait to their offspring. In the case of these two types of pea plants the outward appearance of height was easily determined.

Mendel was able to cross-pollinate the two types of true-breeding plants (for experimental purposes these are referred to as the *first generation*). Mendel already knew that the offspring (the *second generation*) consistently revealed the following: They were all tall pea plants. Let's apply Mendel's ideas and see why this happens. According to Mendel's first principle of inheritance, each individual inherits two factors, one from each parent. For simplicity we can use the capital letter "T" to stand for the tall trait, and the lowercase letter "s" to stand for the short trait. We can then diagram the *first generation* like this:

First generation   T T   s s

Since the second principle of inheritance holds that the factors are inherited randomly from each parent, we can diagram this as follows:

First generation   T T   s s

According to Mendel's theory, the second generation looks like this:

Second generation   T s   T s   T s   T s

We now apply Mendel's third principle of inheritance: if two traits are inherited that cannot both be displayed, then the trait that is displayed is called "dominant" and the other is called "recessive." At first glance, since the second generation pea plants were all tall, this would seem to support Mendel's ideas. However, Mendel could *not* use this as confirming evidence because doing so would violate the second requirement for a fair test (the results were something that Mendel already knew would happen).

The next step is crucial. Mendel decided to cross-pollinate members of the second generation. He had never done this, so he did not know what would happen. However, using his theory he *hypothesized* that what would occur: He *predicted* that the third generation would have a ratio of three tall plants to every one short plant (3:1). Let's diagram the experimental setup, apply Mendel's principles, and see whether his prediction was true or false.

Second generation   T s   T s

According to Mendel's hypothesis, the third generation *should* look like this:

Third generation   T s   T T   s s   s T

Applying his third principle, the ratio is 3:1. Since three offspring will have a "T" they will be tall (dominance); the remaining one will be short (the "s s" one). The *predicted* results matched the results of the experiment. This satisfies all three requirements for a fair test: (1) The prediction was *verifiable* (the results were clearly observable); (2) The prediction was *nontrivial* (since Mendel had not performed the experiment before and he did not know what the results would be); (3) There is a clear *connection between the hypothesis and the prediction* (the prediction was based on applying the principles of inheritance to a specific experiment).

Unfortunately, Mendel's theory of inheritance was not fully accepted at the time because it failed to correctly predict outcomes for some inherited traits in humans; thus it was abandoned. However, several decades later scientists realized that Mendel's theory was indeed useful for explaining and predicting many kinds of inheritance problems, but of course not all. In fact, Mendel's theory offers a simple and accurate explanation for why some diseases reappear after a few generations. In many cases the theory can accurately predict the probability that a child will inherit a disease based on the genetic profile of the parents.

Over time we learn where a theory works, and where it doesn't. We are able to learn something about the world because the hypotheses it generates are testable, which is why experimentation is so important. Scientific experiments and repeated testing under strict controls provide the best method for determining the success, failure, or limitations of a theory. We learn from success, but also from failure.

Science and Superstition

These examples illustrate the vast difference between science and superstition. Our knowledge of the world has allowed us to shed some beliefs that were based on a general lack of understanding of the physical world. For example, although we do not yet know everything about human diseases, we do know enough to say that they are caused by physical processes.

Of course, some individuals refuse to accept medical and scientific advances. These people often stubbornly refuse to allow medical treatment for their children, for example. The result is that sometimes society has to step in and provide the medical assistance that might cure the disease, or at least reduce the symptoms, and needless pain and suffering. Still others refuse to accept evolution or global warming. Their beliefs have practical and political consequences.

Evolutionary theory faces an ongoing battle. Based on the standards that we have been discussing in this chapter, there should be no question that evolutionary theory is scientific. It is highly testable, it has been tested repeatedly, and it has been tremendously successful and fruitful in explaining a large part of the world. Neither creationism nor "intelligent design" can make the same claims. They do not generate testable hypotheses, and they are not fruitful in explaining anything new about the physical world. They do not meet the basic criteria for a scientific theory as set forth in this chapter.

Physical tools and inventions are usually put through rigorous tests in order to learn the conditions under which they are likely to fail. When, how, and why they fail unlocks part of nature's secrets. This knowledge provides the basis for improving our inventions. The same holds for scientific theories. Our scientific knowledge of the world advances by confronting our theories with new problems. If the theory fails, then we can improve it. However, a nonscientific theory insulates itself from failure—it does not help us learn anything new about the world.

Applying the criteria for testing hypotheses can help expose false beliefs. For example, some people have claimed to be able to perform *mental telepathy*, the act of sending and receiving thoughts. A few believers have accepted the challenge of displaying their "powers" in controlled scientific experiments. One simple test is to place two people in separate rooms and show one of them a series of cards. The cards might be pictures of animals, they might have numbers written on them, or they can be ordinary playing cards. If experimental subjects can perform mental telepathy, then they should score higher on their responses than non-telepathists.

Suppose you were told that someone in another room is going to turn over a random series of ten cards. Your job is to guess what is written on each card. You are told that each card has one number written on it. To make it easy, the numbers run from 1 to 10, and no number occurs twice. Using simple probability, we can see that you should guess correctly approximately 10% of the time. Repeated experiments have shown this to be the case.

The self-proclaimed mental telepathists who agreed to be tested under strict experimental conditions scored no higher than other subjects. When confronted with the results, some subjects refused to accept the outcome. They resorted to *ad hoc* rescue of their belief (*ad hoc* means *for this specific purpose*), which is an attempt to save a belief that has been confronted with refuting evidence. For example, subjects might say that skeptics (like the experimenters) give off "negative waves" that interfere with the positive telepathic waves—in other words, that there is something about a scientific experiment that causes the failure. And, yes, there is indeed something about a well-controlled scientific experiment: It reveals the truth.

A rational and scientific approach can reveal the utter foolishness of many nonscientific beliefs. For example, based on his cryptic calculations and reading of the Bible, Harold Camping predicted that the "rapture" would occur on May 21, 2011. We were told that all good Christians would ascend to heaven that day, while everyone else would be left behind to suffer until the end of the world. Camping predicted that God would completely destroy Earth (and presumably the entire universe) after 5 months, on October 21, 2011. Needless to say, Camping was wrong.

Camping had a history of failed predictions about the end of the world. He previously predicted that it would occur on May 21, 1988. When that day came and went he then predicted that it would end on September 7, 1994. After each of his first two failed predictions, Camping resorted to *ad hoc* rescue. He proclaimed that he had miscalculated, but that his basic system was correct. It just needed some fine-tuning. (To be fair, Camping was not the only one to fail miserably in his predictions; failed predictions of the end of the world litter the pages of history.)

Although Camping's system of calculations and predictions based on his interpretations of the Bible are scientifically bankrupt, they are not economic failures. His Family Radio and ministry have generated more than $100 million in donations, some of it from people who sold everything they had because of their fervent belief in Camping's predictions. This is an example in which an understanding of sound reasoning and sound claims can have enormous practical consequences.

The Allure of Superstition

The allure of superstitions and their psychological hold on humans are not difficult to understand. Here is one explanation of why superstitions are so easily formed, and why they are so difficult to remove:

> It was in 1947 that a dozen pigeons gave researchers at the University of Indiana what was to prove the most fundamental insight into the roots of superstition and magic—even, many would argue, of religion itself. These birds were put on restricted rations, so that before long their body weight had fallen by 25% and they were permanently hungry. When each bird had, in the words of Professor Burrhus Frederic [B.F.] Skinner, been "brought to a stable state of hunger," it found itself spending several minutes every day in a special cage. At one end of the cage was an automatic food hopper, linked to a timer so that it would swing into place every 15 seconds, and remain in place for five seconds before disappearing.
>
> Crucial to the set-up was the fact that, no matter what the pigeon did, the food came and went at set intervals. For the purpose of the experiment was to observe what affect its comings and goings had on the pigeons. And, sad to say, it made them—and, by extension, us—look somewhat foolish.
>
> Before long, one of the pigeons had begun making strange counterclockwise turns in the intervals between the hopper's arrivals. Others indulged in repetitive head movements, while two birds developed a complicated pendulum motion of the head and body. By the end of the experiment, six of the eight subjects were performing elaborate routines, clearly with the intention of hastening the return of the food. In each case, the routine grew out of some action that the bird had just happened to be performing when the hopper appeared.
>
> Describing what is now regarded as a classic experiment, Skinner was in no doubt as to the mechanism involved: "The bird behaves as if there were a causal relation between its behavior and the presentation of food, although such a relation is lacking." . . . "The experiment," he said, "might be said to demonstrate a sort of superstition."   David Newnham, "Hostages to Fortune," *Guardian*

It is the interplay of theories, hypotheses, data, experiments, and predictions that establishes authentic scientific understanding of the world. We cannot deduce a prediction only from a hypothesis; we cannot make a prediction only from data; and we cannot get a prediction only from an experiment. A scientific prediction is the offspring of hypotheses, data, and experiments; it is a direct logical consequence that may or may not actually fit the real world. If the prediction turns out to be true, then the hypothesis is confirmed (to some degree). If the prediction turns out to be false, then the hypothesis is refuted.

Notice that in this process we transfer the truth value to the hypothesis. (It is said to be *confirmed* or *refuted*.) But what about the experiment's role in the process? Could something have gone wrong with the experimental setup? These are very important questions. If the prediction is a product of the hypothesis, data, and the experiment, then why is the hypothesis saddled with the results? Part of the answer lies in our ability to check directly the experimental setup and the data. This is another reason that the results of a single experiment are never taken as a final proof. Scientific experiments must be repeated and the results must be replicated. It is the cumulative aspect of scientific research in the light of repeated and rigorous testing over long periods of time and under varying conditions that makes science our best guide to understanding the physical world.

It is important to remember that the application of the scientific method attempts to confirm or refute a hypothesis. As such, this process should always be considered partial and tentative. The weight we give to a confirmation or refutation is never all or nothing. We must accumulate evidence over a long time. If we make mistakes, they will be revealed by the results of repeated experiments.

EXERCISES 14H

Self-Practice
Questions

I. Answer "true" or "false" to the following:

1. Inference to the best explanation produces a valid argument.

Answer: False

2. Theoretical science proposes explanations for observations of natural phenomena.

3. The process of abduction occurs when we control all the variables in an experimental setting.

4. A control group is the group that gets the variable being tested.

⭐ 5. The results of experiments are used to confirm (support) or disconfirm (refute) a hypothesis.

6. A controlled experiment is one in which multiple experimental setups differ by only one variable.

7. A prediction must be unlikely to be true based on our background knowledge.

8. The experimental group is the group in which the variable being tested is withheld.

⭐ 9. Each of the five criteria for establishing causality is a sufficient condition for supporting a causal claim.

10. A verifiable prediction must be true.

II. **Create two different hypotheses to explain the circumstances in each of the following situations. For each hypothesis, think of an experiment that would result in additional evidence that could be used to either confirm or refute the hypothesis.** (*Note:* **It is often possible to devise a single experiment to test more than one hypothesis at the same time, but it is not required.**)

1. You come home to find that the lights in your apartment do not work. You then determine that nothing that requires electricity works in your apartment.

Answer:

> *Hypothesis 1:* The circuit breaker in your fuse box tripped off.
> *Experiment 1:* Check the fuse box settings.
> *Hypothesis 2:* There is no electricity in other apartments on your floor due to a main circuit malfunction.
> *Experiment 2:* Call the building superintendent to see if other apartments are affected.

2. A credit card company calls to tell you that your payment is overdue. However, you know that you sent them a check by mail more than a week ago.

3. You turn the key in the ignition of your car and the car does not start. In fact, there is just a small clicking sound when you turn the key.

4. After washing your clothes at the laundromat, you place everything in a dryer and put in enough money for 1 hour of drying time. You return in 1 hour to find that your clothes are still as wet as when you first put them in the dryer.

⭐ 5. You go away for a 2-week vacation and ask your friend to water your houseplants. When you return you see that the plants are dying.

Video Tutorial: 14HII
Exercise #5

6. You are a salesclerk in a clothing store. A customer comes in and complains that you did not give her the correct change when she purchased a few items less than half an hour ago.

7. You are driving your car when suddenly you notice that the gas gauge is almost at empty. However, you know that you just filled up the gas tank yesterday and you have not driven the car since then.

8. You had a soft-boiled egg and a coffee with milk, but no sugar, for breakfast; then you had a cheeseburger and yogurt shake for lunch. On your way home your stomach begins to ache.

⭐ 9. You are using your cell phone to talk to your mother when the connection suddenly ends. You try dialing your mother's number, but you cannot get a dial tone on the phone.

10. Arrangements have been made for you to meet your friend at a certain movie theater. Before leaving your house, you verified the time and place, and your friend said that he was taking a taxi to meet you. The movie is about to start in 5 minutes and your friend has not arrived. Neither one of you has a cell phone.

III. Analyze the following case studies by picking out the hypothesis, experiment, and prediction. Does the evidence offered in the case study confirm or disconfirm the hypothesis? How much weight would you give to the evidence? If a causal claim is being put forward, then analyze the strength of the argument by checking for any reasonable alternative explanations or other possible facts which, if uncovered, would weaken the causal claim.

1. There have been reports from around the world of some extraordinary "operations." It seems that people with cancerous tumors have been "cured" without any incisions made. When captured on film, the "doctor" seems to be pressing on the patient's body where the tumor is located. Suddenly, blood begins to ooze and the tumor appears to be removed. When cleaned, the patient shows no sign of having been cut. Skeptical researchers did some checking. They performed two simple experiments. First, they tested the material supposedly taken from the patient's body. The patients and their "doctors" claimed that they were cancerous tumors. Results of laboratory analysis showed that the material and blood were from a pig. The second experiment was to take the patients back to the clinic or hospital where the tumors were first noticed, and where records and X-rays were available, in order to see if the tumors had been removed. In all cases, the tumors were exactly where they had originally been; none had been removed.

Answer:

Hypothesis: Cancerous tumors can be physically removed by "surgery," but without any incision.
Experiment: There are two experiments. (A) Test the material (supposedly) taken from the patient to determine its composition. (B) Check the patients to see if the tumors had been removed.
Prediction: The "doctors" and the believing patients (those putting forth the hypothesis) should predict the following: (a) the material will be human cancerous tissue; (b) the tumors will no longer be in the patient.
Confirm/Disconfirm: Since both predictions were false, the evidence gathered from the experiments disconfirms the hypothesis. The evidence carries a lot of weight, because the scientific results are objective and can be accepted as a clear refutation of the hypothesis.
Alternative Explanations: A reasonable explanation is that the "doctors" were scam artists or sleight-of-hand tricksters preying on desperate people.

2. Recently, some physiological psychologists have hypothesized that something in the blood of schizophrenics causes their abnormal behavior. In order to test their conjecture they took some blood from a patient who had been receiving treatment for acute schizophrenia. The researchers then took two groups of spiders that regularly spin uniformly geometrical webs. One group of spiders was given a small injection of the blood, while the other group was left untouched. For the next 2 weeks, the spiders given the blood produced bizarre,

asymmetrical webs, which one researcher called *surreal*. The other group spun their normal webs. The researchers are claiming that this supports their contention that there is some, as yet unknown, factor in the schizophrenic's blood that caused the spider's unusual behavior, and is causing the abnormal behavior in the human subject.

3. I decided to revisit the "executive monkey syndrome" hypothesis. Many years ago some researchers stumbled onto what they thought was evidence that the psychological pressure of "command decisions" caused illness. They restrained two monkeys in chairs. One monkey was provided with a button that, if pressed at the right time, would stop an electrical shock given to both monkeys at the same time. This was the "executive monkey." The other monkey had no way to stop the shock. The executive monkey learned quickly that it could stop the shock from occurring, and it seemed preoccupied with timing the button pressing. This went on for some weeks. Once the experiment was completed, autopsies on the two monkeys revealed that the "executive" had stomach ulcers while the other monkey had none. However, subsequent research has failed to duplicate these results.

4. If you bought a condo in the wrong tower, you were unlucky. It has been revealed that tenants living in one of the two *Sublime Inn* towers are suffering from a mysterious disease. It is believed that the disease is linked to a fungus growing in the air-conditioning system of the tower. The towers are both 5 years old and were built by the same contractor, yet there is no sign of the fungus in the other tower. Engineers, medical personnel, and others are looking for any other difference between the two towers, or between the tenants themselves, that could explain what is happening.

5. Joe's car would not start. He wondered why. His friend said the battery was dead. Joe replaced the battery. The car started. The friend said that this proved he was right.

6. "The garlic is what does it," says Ralph. He was referring to his dog, Balboa, now 14 years of age. "I started mixing a clove of garlic into his dog food ever since he was a puppy. There were six puppies in the litter when he was born. I've kept track of Balboa's sisters and brothers and all of them died before they were 10 years old. He's the last one left. The garlic's what has done it."

7. Pete was videotaping his sister Nancy while she was walking toward the line of people waiting to go on a roller-coaster ride. Nancy fell hard on the concrete and broke her arm. After getting the arm set and placed in a cast, Pete watched the video to see if he could determine why Nancy fell. Nancy maintained that someone had pushed her from behind. However, when Pete replayed the video recording of the event, he could not see anyone near her. The next day he decided to go back to the park to see if he could find something that might have made Nancy trip and fall. Using the video as a guide, he located the spot

where she fell; however, he could not find a hole in the ground or any uneven surface that might have caused her to fall. Pete concluded that Nancy must have lost her balance as she was walking.

Video Tutorial: 14HIII
Exercise #8

8. The study of twins separated at birth confirms that genetics controls your destiny. Researchers tracked down a set of twins, now 25 years old, and checked for similarities. Both males eat the same brand of cereal, smoke the same brand of cigarettes, have each married a nurse, work as auto mechanics, and are registered Democrats, and yet neither twin has ever come in contact with the other. The only possible cause of these remarkable similarities is that they have identical genetic makeup.

★ 9. For the past 2 weeks, every time Becky's cat, Melanie, sat on her lap, Becky started sneezing uncontrollably. Thinking that she was becoming allergic to her cat, Becky tried an experiment. She gave the cat to her neighbor for a day; during that time, she did not sneeze. As soon as the cat returned and sat on Becky's lap, she began sneezing. Becky started taking some over-the-counter allergy medicine, and the sneezing stopped. What Becky did not know was that the bottle of a new kind of flea powder her husband started using a few weeks earlier had broken, and so he bought the powder they had always used before. Becky continues to take the allergy medicine.

10. The "illusion of causality" is a cognitive bias that makes some people believe a causal relationship exists between two events simply because one happened after the other. Although there is considerable long-term evidence that vaccinating children does not cause autism, some people continue to believe that it does and thus refuse to vaccinate their children. It has been conjectured that perhaps exposing people to more information might make parents more likely to vaccinate their kids. Scientists at Dartmouth conducted a randomized trial of different approaches to influencing attitudes about vaccines among parents. The study's 1,759 participants were split into groups, and each group was presented with different information about why vaccines are important, such as why the diseases that a measles, mumps, and rubella vaccine could prevent are worth avoiding, to images of children stricken with those diseases, and a heartfelt story about an infant who nearly died of a case of measles. None of these efforts made parents more likely to vaccinate their kids. The results provide some evidence that simply exposing people to more information doesn't help remove the causal illusion.

Adapted from Christie Aschwanden, "Your Brain Is Primed to Reach
False Conclusions," *ABC News*

11. Researchers conjectured that turning off cameras designed to catch motorists running red lights would probably result in a rise in car crashes. Some cities continue to add cameras at intersections with traffic signals, but others have ended their red-light camera programs. Researchers compared trends in annual crash rates in 14 cities that had ended their camera programs with

those in 29 cities in the same regions that continued their camera programs. They found that, after adjusting for other factors, red-light-running crashes went up 30 percent in those that had ended their camera programs. A second part of the study compared fatal red-light-running crashes in 57 cities with camera programs to 33 cities that haven't introduced cameras, finding that the rate of such crashes was 21 percent lower in cities with cameras. The rate of all types of crashes at intersections with traffic signals was 14 percent lower when cameras were present.

Adapted from "Turning Off Red-light Cameras Can Be Deadly," The Associated Press

12. It has become clear that repetitive blows to the head in high-impact contact sports such as football, ice hockey, mixed martial arts and boxing place athletes at risk of permanent brain damage. If a child who plays football is subjected to advanced radiological and neurocognitive studies during the season and several months after the season, there is evidence of brain damage at the cellular level of brain functioning, even if there were no documented concussions or reported symptoms. If that child continues to play over many seasons, these cellular injuries accumulate to cause irreversible brain damage. Depending on the severity of the condition, that child has a risk of manifesting symptoms of Chronic Traumatic Encephalopathy (CTE) such as major depression, memory loss, suicidal thoughts and actions, loss of intelligence as well as dementia later in life. We should at least wait for our children to grow up, be provided with the information and education on the risk of play, and let them make their own decisions. No adult, not a parent or a coach, should be allowed to make this potentially life-altering decision for a child.

Adapted from Bennet Omalu, "Don't Let Kids Play Football," The New York Times

★13. Although doctors have long known that stress is harmful to the heart, new research supports a causal connection to activity in certain areas of the brain. Researchers tracked the health of nearly 300 people for an average of about four years. During that time, 22 were diagnosed with a heart attack, chest pain, and heart failure. Brain scans showed that elevated levels of activity in the amygdala (a small region of the brain closely tied to stress) led to the blood vessels lighting up, and that led to more chest pain and heart attacks. These people also developed heart problems sooner than people with lower levels of activity in the amygdala. The results provide insight into how stress can lead to cardiovascular disease, and support the idea that heightened activity in a key part of the brain may explain why stress boosts people's odds for heart disease.

Adapted from "Here's How Stress in Your Brain May Cause Heart Troubles," HealthDay

14. During the 20th century, industrialized nations added 30 years to life expectancy. These gains were the result of efficient sanitation, cleaner water, the development of vaccinations, a reliable supply of food, and the development of electricity and refrigeration to keep food fresh. However, evidence now shows that in the 21st century this trend may not continue. Since more people are

living longer, future gains in life expectancy will have to come from preventing and treating the chronic diseases associated with old age, such as heart disease, cancer, diabetes, strokes and dementia. But many elements of 21st century society work against this. For example, we often eat unhealthy foods and drinks which contribute to obesity, diabetes and heart disease. We also don't get enough exercise, which results in many Americans becoming obese. Therefore, many of us will most likely live shorter, sicklier lives.

Adapted from Steve Vernon, "It's Getting Harder to Live Longer in the U.S.," *Moneywatch*

15. Researchers wanted to study the psychology behind certain kinds of cereal purchases. They hypothesized that the marketing strategy of having cartoon characters lock eyes with children may influence their connection with a brand, fostering loyalty and inspiring their interest in the products. The researchers polled 63 college-aged individuals who were randomly shown a box of Trix cereal that had the rabbit either gazing straight at the viewer, or else looking down. The individuals were then asked to rate their feelings of trust and connection to the brand. They found that the eye contact increased positive feelings towards the product, and made them more likely to want it. After the experiment was completed one of the researchers said, "If you are a parent who does not want your kids to go 'cuckoo for Cocoa Puffs,' avoid taking them down the cereal aisle."

Adapted from Ryan Jaslow, "Cereal Box Characters are Staring at Your Children," *CBS News*

16. Scientists wondered if a person could experience a state of unconsciousness without entering into a deep sleep; in other words, if it was possible to turn someone's consciousness on and off like a light switch. Researchers implanted electrodes in the brain of a 54-year-old woman with epilepsy. They were looking to identify the site of the woman's seizures, using electrical stimulation on the region of the brain called the "claustrum," a thin layer of neurons attached to the neocortex center of the brain. It was found that stimulating this area of the brain disrupted normal consciousness, but once the electrodes were shut off, the woman returned to a normal state of consciousness and had no memory of what had just occurred. Though the woman was unresponsive while in this state, the brain stimulation caused only a minor change to her motor and language abilities. Additionally, stimulating the claustrum did not cause a seizure. The results indicate that this region of the brain might be a gateway to consciousness. The researchers caution that the findings are only a first step, but that it may help provide a new way to treat epilepsy and possibly also patients in a coma or with schizophrenia or other disorders.

Adapted from Jessica Firger, "Brain Study Switches a Woman's Consciousness On and Off," *CBS News*

17. Is it possible that dolphins use complex nonlinear mathematics when hunting? Scientists wanted to find out. Since observations showed dolphins blowing multiple tiny bubbles around prey as they hunted, it was thought perhaps the

dolphins have a type of sonar that can do what human sonar cannot. Researchers used computer programs to model the types of echolocation pulses that dolphins emit and processed them using nonlinear mathematics instead of the standard way of processing sonar returns. The math involved is complex. Essentially it relies upon sending out pulses that vary in amplitude. The first may have a value of 1, while the second is one-third that amplitude. If the dolphin remembers what the ratios of the two pulses were, and can multiply the second echo by that and add the echoes together, it can make the fish "visible" to its sonar. The modeling technique worked, and could explain how dolphins achieve hunting success with bubbles. If replicated, the sonar model may prove to be a huge benefit to humans. It might be able to detect covert circuitry, such as bugging devices hidden in walls, stones or foliage. It could also dramatically improve detection of sea mines.

Adapted from Jennifer Viegas, "Dolphins Appear to Do Nonlinear
Mathematics," Discovery Channel

18. People who have an amazing ability to recall specific events have what is called "highly superior autobiographical memory," or HSAM. It was speculated that perhaps this ability makes them less susceptible to being manipulated by false memories than the rest of us. A study tested 20 super-memory people and 38 age- and sex-matched people with normal memory powers on three different tests known to elicit false memories. All of the subjects were asked to read about United Flight 93 of Sept. 11, 2001. Part of what they read stated that "video footage of the plane crashing" was taken by somebody on the ground. In fact, no such video exists. Yet after reading the material, 20 percent of HSAM people and 29 percent of the other group indicated they had indeed seen the video. In a later interview, 10 percent of HSAM people stuck to their stories. Of the total number of fake details about the crash planted in their minds, there was no significant difference in false memory between HSAM and normal memory participants. Our brains construct memories from individual bits of information, and then piece those bits together to reassemble it when we remember something. But new information is constantly mixing with old and can become incorporated in the reassembled memory.

Adapted from Brian Alexander, "Even People with Super Recall
Tripped Up by False Memories," NBCnews.com

19. Fire investigators suspected that titanium alloy golf clubs were the cause of at least two blazes on southern California area golf courses which spread to nearby homes. The idea was that the golf clubs struck rocks next to dry vegetation causing the vegetation to burst into flames. To test this idea, scientists re-created the conditions on the days of the fires in a laboratory. By using high-speed cameras and electron microscopes the scientists found that, when hit upon a rock, golf clubs containing titanium can produce sparks of up to 3000 degrees that will burn for more than a second. Since titanium reacts violently with both oxygen and nitrogen in the air, this allows the spark enough time

to ignite nearby foliage. In contrast, when standard stainless steel clubs were used, there was no reaction.

Adapted from "Titanium Clubs Behind Two Blazes," Associated Press

20. If a mouse could cough, could we detect it? If so, can we use that to test the effectiveness of cough suppressants? Scientists at Guangzhou Medical College in China exposed 40 mice to fine mists of capsaicin, the molecule that makes chili peppers spicy. The mice were placed in a machine that measures changes in body volume to detect when air moved in and out, and listened with mini-microphones. Although the mice made a variety of sounds, the scientists identified explosive noises that coincided with one would expect with coughs. When given cough suppressants such as codeine, mouse coughing dropped dramatically.

Adapted from Charles Choi, "Did You Hear Something? Mice Can Cough," science.nbcnews.com

Study Materials

Summary

- The word "cause" has several meanings, and in everyday situations the possibility of ambiguity arises.
- Sufficient condition: Whenever one event ensures that another event is realized.
- Necessary condition: Whenever one thing is *essential, mandatory,* or *required* in order for another thing to be realized.
- Causal network: A set of conditions that bring about an effect.
- Normal state: The historical information regarding an object.
- Abnormal state: A drastic change in the normal state. Any change from the normal state requires an explanation, typically a causal one.
- Precipitating cause: The object or event directly involved in bringing about an effect.
- Remote cause: Something that is connected to the precipitating cause by a chain of events.
- Method of agreement: The method that looks at two or more instances of an event to see what they have in common.
- Method of difference: The method that looks for what all the instances of an event do not have in common.
- Joint method of agreement and difference: If two or more instances of an event have only one thing in common, while the instances in which it does *not* occur all share the absence of that thing, then the item is a likely cause.
- Method of residues: The method that subtracts from a complex set of events those parts that already have known causes.
- Method of concomitant variations: The method that looks for two factors that vary together.

- Correlation: A correspondence between two sets of objects, events, or data.
- Although Mill's methods do not provide conclusive proof of causality, the five methods are helpful in discovering correlations and potential causes.
- A good hypothesis provides an explanation for known facts and a way to test an explanation.
- Theoretical science proposes explanations for natural phenomena, while experimental science tests those explanations.
- The process of abduction occurs when we infer explanations for certain facts.
- Inference to the best explanation: Reasoning from the premise that a hypothesis would explain certain facts to the conclusion that the hypothesis is the best explanation for those facts.
- Controlled experiment: One in which multiple experimental setups differ by only one variable.
- Experimental group: The group that gets the variable being tested.
- Control group: The group in which the variable being tested is withheld.
- Five criteria need to be considered to fully appreciate the complexity of causality: (1) There should be a correlation between the cause and the effect. (2) The cause should precede the effect. (3) The cause should be in the proximity of the effect. (4) A set of necessary and sufficient conditions should exist. (5) Alternative explanations should be ruled out.
- The weight of our answers to all five criteria together establishes the grounds for a satisfactory cause-effect relationship.
- We can test a hypothesis by getting it to make a prediction. Predictions are either true or false; the results are used to confirm (support) or disconfirm (refute) the hypothesis.
- Three requirements ensure a fair test of the causal hypothesis: (1) The prediction should be something that is verifiable. (2) The prediction should be unlikely to be true based on our background knowledge. (3) There should be a connection between the hypothesis and the prediction.
- Verifiable prediction: A prediction that, if true, must include an observable event.
- Nontrivial prediction: A prediction that requires reference to background knowledge, which is everything we know to be true.
- The weight we give to a confirmation or refutation is never all-or-nothing. We need to accumulate evidence over a long time.

KEY TERMS

LOGIC CHALLENGE: THE SCALE AND THE COINS

You are given ten large canvas bags of identical-looking coins. Nine of the bags contain coins that weigh 1 ounce each, and one bag contains coins that weigh 1.1 ounces each. Because of the small difference in weight, you cannot distinguish the 1-ounce coin from the 1.1-ounce coin just by holding them in your hands. And since they look identical in shape and size, they cannot be distinguished that way either.

You are given a scale. You can place on the scale as much or as little of the contents of the bags that you wish, and it will display the total weight placed on it. However, you are permitted to use the scale only once. You will get only one chance to figure out which bag has the 1.1-ounce coins. How would you solve the problem?

Appendix A
Cognitive Bias

The term "cognitive" refers to various mental activities such as perception, attention, thinking, memory, learning, and reasoning. Although we are capable of *conscious logical reasoning*, we are also subject to some *unconscious psychological factors* that can impede our rational abilities. Researchers who study the factors that *diminish* our ability to interpret information, form judgments, make predictions, arrive at decisions, and evaluate arguments, refer to the factors as **cognitive biases**. As we shall see, biases occur in a variety of settings.

> **Cognitive biases** The factors that diminish our ability to interpret information, form judgments, make predictions, arrive at decisions, and evaluate arguments.

It is important to distinguish *cognitive biases* from *fallacies*. Arguments are constructed to offer evidence for a conclusion, but they can fail, and some special cases of failure are classified as fallacies. A *formal fallacy* is a logical error that occurs in the *form* or structure of an argument; they are restricted to deductive arguments. An *informal fallacy* is a mistake in reasoning that occurs in ordinary language and concerns the content of the argument rather than its form. Since *cognitive biases* are psychological factors that hinder our ability to *reason*, they are often involved in *fallacious reasoning*.

Over time, human abilities have evolved to help us survive. Some of these abilities involve making quick judgements based on our observation of the world. If we perceive something that *appears* to be dangerous, then we need to act quickly. The word *"appears"* is in italics to illustrate that our quick assessment of the situation might have been in error; the situation might *not* have been dangerous after all. Nevertheless, the ability to act quickly is important when we don't have the time to deliberate.

HEURISTICS

The term **heuristic** originates from the Greek language meaning "to discover, or to find out." Although modern uses of the term have broadened the original meaning to include various problem-solving methods such as trial and error experimentation, the general idea is that it is a natural way to make decisions, one that draws on personal experience. We can see this approach to decision making by noting that it is implicit in the phrase "common sense," where a decision is justified by appeal to extensive experience. An appeal to common sense often relies on assuming that the future will resemble past, even though we also know that things change, quite often drastically. The general idea of a heuristic can also be understood by the term "educated guess," which happens when we rely on experience and knowledge about a

> **Heuristic** From the Greek language meaning "to discover, or to find out." The general idea is that it is a natural way to make decisions, one that draws on personal experience.

subject or situation to make a decision without doing exhaustive research. But when we make decisions we are also making judgments; therefore, if a judgment is driven by a cognitive bias, then it will affect the decision.

Many factors contribute to the judgments we make. For example, a *change in context* can affect our judgments and behavior. Suppose two students meet at a party on campus. It is common for students to quickly identify their majors, so one might say, "I'm a physics major," while the other might say, "I'm a dance major." An initial judgment based on this information may lead the two people to think they have little in common, so they might have a short conversation and then move on to meet other people at the party. But if those same two people met in a foreign country while they were traveling on their own, then they might be happy to meet someone from their home country and might wind up spending a lot of time together. In the first context (the party) their judgments are based on their *differences* (academic majors), while in the second context their judgments are based on their *similarities* (being from the same country) to decide that they should spend more time together.

Heuristics are shortcuts that we call on when we are confronted with quick decisions about *what to do* or *what to believe*. Relying on these "mental shortcuts" or "rules of thumb" allows us to estimate—without a long deliberation—the likelihood of something happening. For example, suppose you are told there is an accident on the normal route you take driving to school. Based on your belief that accidents often cause long delays, you might decide to take a normally longer route. This quick decision illustrates the role of heuristics. However, the decision may not prove to be the best one. It is possible the accident is already being cleared up. If so, then by the time you would have arrived at where the accident occurred, the driving time to school would not have been affected. Although these "rule of thumb strategies" are helpful in many situations, the simple mental estimates regarding the *probability* of outcomes can lead to judgment errors, as the example illustrates. Hence they cannot guarantee that our decisions, actions, or beliefs are correct, and, as such, they can lead to either trivial or important mistakes, depending on the circumstances.

Heuristics are commonly used by physicians. For example, when examining a patient who reports experiencing general fatigue and bodily pain, a physician might begin by asking the patient to describe any other specific symptoms. The physician might also ask how long the symptoms have persisted, or whether the patient experienced these symptoms before, or whether the patient traveled recently. The answers to these questions allows the physician to draw on her general knowledge in order to diagnose *possible causes* of the patient's current physical problems.

The physician's initial questions try to connect the patient's symptoms with other patients who experienced similar symptoms. By doing this, the physician is relying on a *heuristic*: Similar symptoms (effects) are a good indicator of similar causes. The second step might be to treat the symptoms using methods that were successful with previous patients, such as medication, physical therapy, or even surgery. However, since the physician also knows that similar symptoms may actually be the result of different diseases, the diagnosis is not guaranteed to be correct.

Here is an example from everyday life: When you try to find a lost item in your house, you generally start looking for it in the last place you recall seeing it. This simple strategy is a heuristic, and its success depends on a number of factors, such as how sure you are that your memory is correct, or whether someone else moved the item since you last saw it.

Two psychologists, Daniel Kahneman and Amos Tversky, did pioneering research into the relationship between heuristics and cognitive biases. They recognized that a *positive* aspect of using heuristics is the ability to simplify decision making, and in doing so, some heuristics are quite reliable. However, they also recognized that a *negative* aspect of using heuristics is that they can lead to bias and erroneous judgment.

> In making predictions and judgments under uncertainty, people do not appear to follow the calculus of chance or statistical theory of prediction. Instead, they rely on a limited number of heuristics which sometimes yield reasonable judgments and sometimes lead to severe and systematic errors.
>
> Daniel Kahneman and Amos Tversky, "On the Psychology of Prediction,"
> *Psychological Review*, 80, no. 4, 1973

Although heuristics can offer a rational approach to problem-solving, they cannot ensure that our decisions are correct. This means that not only must we be *cautious* when we use them, we must also be aware that we *are* in fact constantly using them. This realization led Kahneman and Tversky to claim that if we can uncover the *systematic mistakes* that we make, then we can identify the *heuristics* (rules of thumb) involved in those errors; this will enable us to recognize the existence of specific *cognitive biases*. Although they were psychologists, their work was recognized as being important to many fields. In fact, their research proved to be highly useful to economists, so much so that Daniel Kahneman was awarded the Nobel Prize in Economic Sciences in 2002. Amos Tversky would most likely have shared the award with Kahneman, but Tversky died in 1996, and, unfortunately, Nobel Prizes are not awarded posthumously.

As we shall see when we look at specific examples of cognitive biases, a rigid reliance on certain kinds of heuristics can be detrimental to our decision making, and this unconscious psychological factor is involved with both cognitive biases and fallacious reasoning. Even when we have adequate time to deliberate, cognitive biases may still interfere with our reasoning process. Although we often have difficulty in recognizing *our* mistakes, we are sometimes able to recognize other people's mistakes. One explanation for this is that if we have no personal or psychological attachment to someone else's arguments, we can assess their reasoning *objectively*. This is where logic and critical thinking can help, by providing us with skills needed to interpret information accurately and evaluate arguments correctly.

HEURISTICS AND ALGORITHMS

We are more likely to use heuristics than algorithms in everyday life situations. For example, if a lamp in your room doesn't work, you might go out and buy a new one.

But before you do that, you might want to apply some simple trial and error methods. For instance, you might check whether any other electrical objects are working in the room. If they are not, then the problem is probably not with the lamp. But if other objects are working properly, then you might change the light bulb. If the lamp works, you are finished; but if it still doesn't work, then you might plug the lamp into another socket. If the lamp works, you are finished; but if it still doesn't work, and you are handy with fixing things, you might try changing the lamp's wiring. Of course, a lot of this depends on whether you have the time and inclination to solve the problem by trial and error. Some people will simply go out and buy a new lamp.

Algorithm A set of instructions that includes a step-by-step procedure designed to go consistently from a starting point to an end point.

An **algorithm** is a set of instructions that includes a step-by-step procedure designed to go consistently from a starting point to an end point. An algorithm can be as simple as a recipe that leads you from a list of ingredients to a finished meal, or it can be as complex as a chess program that searches through millions of possible moves in a game.

Here is an example of a mathematical algorithm that most people have used. To calculate the mean (average) of a set of numbers, follow these two steps:

> Step 1: Add the numbers.
> Step 2: Divide the total by the number of objects in the set.

For example, to calculate the mean score on an exam, you first add the score of each student who took the exam, and then divide by the number of students.

Here is a more advanced mathematical example of an algorithm. To calculate the standard deviation in a set of numerical values, follow these six steps:

> Step 1: Calculate the mean value.
> Step 2: Calculate the difference between each value in the set and the mean value.
> Step 3: Multiply each difference by itself (square each difference).
> Step 4: Add the results of the squaring process in step 3.
> Step 5: Divide the result of step 4 by one fewer than the number of members in the set.
> Step 6: The square root of the total variance is the standard deviation.

Algorithms can also be used to solve non-mathematical problems. For example, in order to diagnose an engine problem, auto mechanics often initiate a specific sequence of tests to identify the cause of the problem. The mechanic follows a step-by-step checklist to rule out anything that is not the cause. This procedure is usually more effective than just randomly trying different ideas because of the methodical elimination of potential causes. Procedures like this are generally developed over time from an analysis of large databases of past engine problems.

Some computer programs that have been developed to play games have proven to be very successful. For example, two world chess champions have been defeated by sophisticated chess programs (Garry Kasparov was defeated by a program called Deep Blue in 1997; Vladimir Kramnik was defeated by a program called Deep Fritz in 2006). Some chess grandmasters (the top-rated chess players in the world) claim to be able to think fifteen to twenty moves ahead in a game. But since there are potentially millions of possible future moves during a game, chess grandmasters ultimately rely on heuristics to identify general patterns based on their knowledge of past games. Some chess programs (also called "engines") rely on algorithms that effectively use "brute force" to compute possible outcomes for a fixed number of future moves. Although modern chess engines can make millions of calculations per second, they are also programmed with *heuristic* decision-making points to eliminate certain moves based on large databases of previous games and outcomes.

Computer programs have also proved to be successful in other venues. For example, in 2017 a program called AlphaGo defeated Ke Jie, the world's highest ranked *Go* player (a game of *Go* has considerably more potential moves than a game of chess). In a different type of game that relies on quick access to facts, a program called Watson defeated *Jeopardy!* champions Brad Rutter and Ken Jennings in 2011.

You have probably heard about how some companies use algorithms to gather data about people who use the Internet. The algorithms gather data about you by keeping track of your web searches or the ads that you click on. They can even track your movements and locations through your GPS devices. Algorithms not only analyze your data to predict your future behavior, they also drive your online experiences, thereby potentially affecting your beliefs and worldview.

THE LINK BETWEEN HEURISTICS AND COGNITIVE BIASES

Tversky and Kahneman conducted some of the earliest investigations of the connection between heuristics and cognitive biases in the 1970s. They designed experiments in which subjects were given verbal descriptions of problems that involved probability assessments or rules of logic. Tversky and Kahneman interpreted the results of their experiments as showing that many of the subjects' decisions either deviated from a correct probability calculation or violated a rule of logic. The two researchers then explained the results as stemming from the unconscious reliance on cognitive biases. The publication of their 1974 paper "Judgment Under Uncertainty: Heuristics and Biases" influenced many others to discover the range of possible cognitive biases, and how this impacts the generally accepted idea that humans are "rational actors." However, over the years, other scientists have challenged their claims, pointing out that at least some of the original findings can be explained by the confusing nature of many of the verbal descriptions posed to the subjects. That is, critics contend that when the probability or logical aspects of the problems are clearly exposed, subjects are better able to give the correct answers. Although the initial criticism focused on the specific experiments, many researchers accepted the existence of cognitive biases. Therefore, subsequent experiments concentrated on accurate ways to reveal the nature and extent of human cognitive biases. Research continues to fine-tune the linkage between our obvious need to rely on heuristics and how cognitive biases can negatively affect our judgment.

THEORIES OF JUDGMENT

Many of our responses to the physical world are automatically handled by our brains and nervous systems to coordinate our actions, reflexes, and sensations. For example, if someone throws you a ball, you don't have to consciously compute the ball's trajectory and speed. In a different situation, if we are asked to choose between two colors of a shirt, we might make a quick decision. Such a decision is probably the result of the automatic *intuitive* judgment system. These kinds of fast decisions are contrasted with decisions that require more deliberation, decisions that rely on the self-aware *reflective* system. For example, we might spend days or weeks trying to decide whether to continue working for a company or to quit.

There are competing theories of human judgment that center around the basic question of the rationality of our reliance on heuristics. One theory argues that the heuristic mental shortcuts we employ are the inevitable result of evolution and the inherent limitations of the human brain. However, many people argue that since humans have successfully adapted and thrived, the heuristics we employ are quite rational, even though they can lead to errors. Predicting the future often forces us to deal with a great deal of uncertainty. Nevertheless, evolutionary theory argues that the brute fact that we have managed to survive as a species is evidence that our reliance on mental shortcuts has been a successful adaptive feature—even if that reliance can sometimes lead to drastic and tragic mistakes. The cognitive researcher Gerd Gigerenzer argues that an evolutionary perspective regarding heuristics suggests that our mental capacity to create divisions of labor for different kinds of judgment situations is an efficient way to deal with the world. He claims that this ability is "directed at solving important adaptive problems, such as attachment development, mate search, parenting, social exchange, coalition formation, and maintaining and upsetting dominance hierarchies" (Gerd Gigerenzer, *Adaptive Thinking*, Oxford University Press, 2000).

A second theory argues that since our brains are capable of some very complex automatic calculations (the thrown ball, for example), it is rational for us to rely on these automatic processes to help us make many everyday decisions and judgments; this is called "the attribute substitution theory." The basic idea behind this theory is that we can often successfully solve complicated problems or decision-making situations by using heuristics to simplify the process. In other words, we unconsciously substitute a simple problem for a complex one. The thrust of this is that if a process has proven to be successful, then it is rational to rely on it. Of course, the theory *does not* claim that we will always be successful. However, the *unconscious* automatic nature of the substitution process helps explain why we can remain unaware of our biases and why they can persist even when we *are* made aware of their existence. In other words, the substitution occurs in the automatic *intuitive* judgment system, and *not* in the self-aware *reflective* system.

Here is an example of how people may unconsciously apply a heuristic to a simple math problem. Suppose you are told that a stick of gum and a candy bar together cost $1.10. You are also told that the candy bar costs $1 more than the stick of gum. You are then asked to determine how much the stick of gum costs. Did you answer 10 cents? If so, your answer is incorrect. If the stick of gum costs 10 cents, then according to the problem, the candy bar would cost $1 more, but that would mean the candy bar costs $1.10; given this, together the two items would cost $1.20. The correct answer is the stick of gum costs 5 cents, and the candy bar costs $1 more, so it costs $1.05; together they cost $1.10. The attribute substitution theory argues that instead of taking your time to consciously calculate various possible costs of the two items and their sums, you unconsciously (and incorrectly, in this case) "simplified" the problem by seeing it as just a large amount ($1) and a small amount (10 cents). This unconscious quick process resulted in the incorrect answer.

COGNITIVE BIASES

1. Belief Bias

A *valid deductive argument* is defined as an argument in which, assuming the premises are true, it is *impossible* for the conclusion to be false. In other words, the conclusion follows necessarily from the premises. An *invalid deductive argument* is defined as an argument in which, assuming the premises are true, it is *possible* for the conclusion to be false. In other words, the conclusion does not follow necessarily from the premises. Determining the *strength* of an *argument* requires an analysis of the *logical relationship* between the premises and the conclusion. However, if we judge the *strength* of an argument by focusing simply on whether we think the conclusion is true, or whether it fits with our values or beliefs, then we can fall prey to **belief bias.** For example, consider this argument:

> No cats are reptiles.
> <u>No reptiles are humans.</u>
> No cats are humans.

Belief bias When we judge the *strength* of an argument by focusing simply on whether we think the conclusion is true, or whether it fits with our values or beliefs.

The premises are both true, and so is the conclusion, but if you judged this to be a *valid* argument, then your assessment is incorrect; it is *invalid*. The invalidity is revealed by a logical analysis, the first step of which is to display the argument form:

> No X are Y.
> <u>No Y are Z.</u>
> No X are Z.

The next step is to create a counterexample. This is done by consistently substituting terms for the X, Y, and Z in the argument form. For example, we can make X = humans, Y = reptiles, and Z = mammals. This gives us the following:

> No humans are reptiles.
> <u>No reptiles are mammals.</u>
> No humans are mammals.

Although both premises are true, the conclusion is false; the counterexample reveals the invalidity of the argument. If you were fooled by the first argument, it is probably because your *belief bias* focused on the truth of the conclusion, "No cats are humans." Therefore, you determined, incorrectly, that the argument was valid. This illustrates the importance of learning how to critically and logically analyze information and arguments.

Substantial research has revealed the extent of belief bias. For example, in one experiment subjects were shown several arguments similar to the one above regarding cats and humans. Their task was to determine whether the arguments were valid or invalid. Most of the subjects displayed a tendency to misjudge not only invalid arguments with believable conclusions as being valid, but also valid arguments with unbelievable conclusions as invalid (J. St. B. T. Evans, Julie L. Barston, and Paul Pollard, "On the Conflict Between Logic and Belief in Syllogistic Reasoning," *Memory and Cognition*, 11, 1983).

2. Confirmation Bias

Confirmation bias
The habit of seeking out information that supports our existing beliefs and avoiding or rejecting information that might undermine those beliefs.

The habit of seeking out information that supports our existing beliefs and avoiding or rejecting information that might undermine those beliefs is called **confirmation bias**. The bias acts like a reflex in its immediate dismissal of information that threatens to challenge a strong belief. This tendency effectively shuts out opposing viewpoints, thus closing us off from a wider worldview. It shrinks our perspective and considers only evidence that reinforces our settled beliefs. For example, the Internet provides the opportunity to explore opposing views, but many people search only for information they know supports their beliefs, so they return to the same sources over and over again. This tendency provides an effective shield, but it also contributes to inflexible thinking. It manifests itself in political, ethical, and religious rigidity, making us unable or unwilling to even try to understand an opposing view. It reveals itself in what we read, what we watch on TV, what movies we go to, and even those with whom we associate.

An example of how confirmation bias can affect our assessment of information can be seen in *psychic readings*, one kind of which is called "cold reading," where the self-advertised psychic gives what appears to be specific information about an individual. What typically happens is the psychic starts by making a few vague or ambiguous statements, such as "You are often misunderstood by people" or "Some people have taken advantage of you." The psychic looks for visual cues that can reveal whether the individual agrees or disagrees with the statements, allowing the psychic to pursue a certain line of analysis. Since in the course of the reading the psychic makes numerous claims, this provides the opportunity for some of the statements to "hit home." Research shows that when subjects are asked their assessment of the reading, those who had a prior belief in this kind of psychic phenomena tend to show a strong selective recall of the statements that "hit home." Their prior belief was reinforced by their heightened recollection of the *confirming* instances.

3. Status Quo Bias

Heuristics save time. In many situations, they make our lives easier to manage. For example, if you walk down the cereal aisle in a supermarket, you will encounter dozens of different cereals. But many people ignore the dizzying display and zero in on one item. They rely on past experience to make quick decisions. Previous enjoyment of a certain cereal drives their focus to that product again, allowing them to ignore the other cereals.

As the cereal example shows, when we are confronted with a decision, some ideas will naturally come to mind before others. The allure of these first ideas is based on the psychological heuristic involved in the **status quo bias,** which tells us that when something comes to mind quickly, we should probably rely on it. In other words, we rely on the *unconscious* notion that the swift retrieval from our memory is the result of it having been successful many times in the past, so we should trust it.

But this ignores the *possibility* that the reason it came to mind quickly was actually a red flag. For example, although we normally choose the favorite cereal based on past experience (familiarity), it might be that we have been recently contemplating changing cereals because we want to reduce our sugar or sodium intake, and we recently learned that our favorite is not the best choice to help us reduce those items. In this case, the familiarity aspect makes it likely that our favorite will come to mind as we enter the cereal aisle, but without deliberation we might misinterpret the speed of the idea coming to mind with its being the right thing to do. This means that the status quo bias can sometimes hinder us from making a change that would ultimately benefit us.

It often takes a great effort to change our lives. For example, we might stay in a relationship that is unsatisfying, or even dangerous, simply because doing so seems easier than ending it, which can involve substantial changes to our everyday routines. In other situations, worrying about losing a job, or changing a career, or alienating friends and relatives, might deter us from acting in a way that might actually be beneficial in the long run. In politics, it is quite common for voters to stick to a candidate even though they have reservations about that person's performance, simply because the alternative might prove to be worse. Familiarity is often a powerful psychological driver of decisions. It contributes to a strong tendency to keep things the same; it is the fear of the unknown simply because it is unknown.

> **Status quo bias**
> This bias is based on the psychological heuristic that tells us that when something comes to mind quickly, we should probably rely on it.

4. Availability Bias

The nature of the information we receive can lead us to *overestimate* the likelihood of its happening again. For example, if we hear about a recent airplane crash, we might believe that airplane travel is less safe than travel by car. However, assessments based on objective statistical data show that air travel is much safer. Although we probably hear about car fatalities on a regular basis (through television news, for example), an airplane crash usually results in a high number of deaths. The scale of the airplane tragedy may lead us to overestimate the probability of a similar occurrence happening in the future. The vividness of an airplane crash that results in a large number of deaths can bias our thinking so much that we ignore objective evidence regarding the safety of air travel when compared to car travel. Therefore, the degree to which the memory is affected by its emotional impact on us might cause us to *unconsciously overestimate* the probability of it occurring again is referred to as the **availability bias**.

This bias has been tested in a variety of experiments. For example, researchers Mark deTurck, Lynne Texter, and Janet Harszlak wanted to see how jurors might respond to witnesses who lie, so they set up a fictional trial in which "mock jurors" listened to testimony ("Effects of Information Processing Objectives on Judgments of Deception Following Perjury" *Communication Research*, 16, no. 3, 1989). The jurors were presented with two kinds of witnesses: (a) those who *testified truthfully before lying*, and (b) those who were *caught lying before telling the truth*. The researchers wanted to know whether the jurors "would rate a witness to be more deceptive if the witness testified truthfully before lying than when the witness was caught lying first before telling the truth." The results of the experiment showed that when jurors relied on their memory to recall a witness's testimony, they rated a witness as *more deceptive* when the witness testified truthfully before lying. Since the lie was the most recent act the jurors recalled, their judgment was influenced by the availability bias.

Availability bias The degree to which the memory is affected by its emotional impact on us might cause us to *unconsciously overestimate* the probability of it occurring again.

5. Halo Bias

Edward Thorndike was the first researcher to identify the halo bias. When Thorndike looked at how people rate specific characteristics in another person, he found that the *specific ratings* were often influenced by the *overall* impression they had of the person they were rating; this has come to be known as the **halo bias** (or halo effect). For example, if a person was judged to be physically attractive, then they seemed to also get high rankings when they were rated for things such as discipline and initiative. It appeared that the specific high rankings were a result of the general impression. Thorndike remarked that "a halo of general merit is extended to influence the rating for the special ability." He also said that even highly experienced supervisors and managers are "unable to view an individual as a compound of separate qualities and assign a magnitude to each of these in independence of the others" (Thorndike, "A Constant Error in Psychological Ratings," *Journal of Applied Psychology*, 4, 1920).

Halo bias This bias occurs when our *specific* judgments or ratings of a person's abilities, skills, or characteristics are the result of the *overall impression* we have of that person.

Other studies have shown that "rapid judgments about the personality traits of political candidates, based solely on their appearance, can predict their electoral success. This suggests that voters rely heavily on appearances when choosing which candidate to elect" (Christopher Olivola and Alexander Todorov, "Elected in 100 Milliseconds: Appearance-Based Trait Inferences and Voting," *Journal of Nonverbal Behavior*, 34, 2010).

Studies by other researchers also found that attractiveness influenced voter preference. An experiment revealed that voters' judgments were strongly affected by a 1-second viewing of side-by-side photos of two U.S. congressional candidates (Brad Verhulst, Milton Lodge, and Howard Lavine, "The Attractiveness Halo: Why Some Candidates Are Perceived More Favorably than Others," *Journal of Nonverbal Behavior*, 34, 2010).

6. Functional Fixedness Bias

Francis Bacon said that "human understanding is like a false mirror, which, receiving rays irregularly, distorts and discolors the nature of things by mingling its own nature with it." (Francis Bacon is featured in a *Profiles in Logic* box in Chapter 4.) One way to begin understanding functional fixedness is to look at example of how our judgments are influenced by what we see. Here is a classic example:

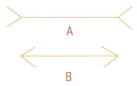

If you haven't seen a similar display before, you will most likely judge the horizontal line in A to be longer than the horizontal line in B. In fact, the two horizontal lines are identical in length. This optical illusion shows that our minds can be tricked into misjudging what we see. Although we cannot correct the way the optical illusion appears to us, once we confirm by simple measurement that the two horizontal lines are of equal length, we can recall it at a later time. We will still *see* the lengths as being different, but we will *know* that the lengths are the same.

Functional fixedness bias refers to the tendency to judge certain familiar objects as having only one particular use or function. This results from our seeing the world through a narrow lens. The alternative is being flexible about objects. For example, we all rely on cups or glasses to drink water, but if none are available, we can simply *cup our hands* to hold water. This is sometimes called "thinking outside the box," and it results from seeing objects as being capable of having multiple functions. The narrow focus tendency was studied by the psychologist Abraham Maslow, who wrote the following: "I suppose it is tempting, if the only tool you have is a hammer, to treat everything as if it were a nail" (*The Psychology of Science*, HarperCollins, 1966). In the television program *MacGyver*, the main character solves problems by recognizing that some objects at hand can be used outside their normal function; thus he is able to avoid the functional fixedness bias.

A functional fixedness bias can also manifest itself when it comes to pigeonholing people. For example, a manager may fail to recognize that a worker has supervisory potential, or parents may fail to see that their child has talents or interests that are not valued by the parents.

Functional fixedness bias The tendency to judge certain familiar objects as having only one particular use or function. This results from our seeing the world through a narrow lens.

7. Anchoring Bias

The **anchoring bias** occurs when our reliance on one piece of information about a subject (often the first thing we hear or learn) affects our subsequent thinking. For example, suppose you see on the Internet that the "average" price of a certain type of

Anchoring bias This occurs when our reliance on one piece of information about a subject (often the first thing we hear or learn) affects our subsequent thinking.

used motorcycle that you are interested in buying is $5000. This information might bias your judgment of two used motorcycles—one that costs less than the average, and another that costs more than the average—leading you to believe that the lower-priced one is a "better buy." If your judgment is anchored on price alone, then you might overlook the quality of the two motorcycles. Maybe the cheaper one has high mileage, or was in an accident, or wasn't well maintained; and maybe the more expensive one has low mileage and was serviced regularly.

Tversky and Kahneman ran several experiments that revealed the anchoring effect. In one experiment, they asked a group of students to estimate the product of $8 \times 7 \times 6 \times 5 \times 4 \times 3 \times 2 \times 1$ (the students were given only a few seconds to make their decision, not enough time for them to do a thorough calculation). They asked a second group of students to estimate the same product, but they gave the numbers in reverse order— $1 \times 2 \times 3 \times 4 \times 5 \times 6 \times 7 \times 8$. Although both groups considerably underestimated the correct answer by a large margin, the second group's average estimate was significantly smaller than the first. The psychologists interpreted these results as follows: "Because the result of the first few steps of multiplication (performed from left to right) is higher in the descending sequence than in the ascending sequence, the former expression should be judged larger than the latter. Both predictions were confirmed. The median estimate for the ascending sequence was 512, while the median estimate for the descending sequence was 2,250. The correct answer is 40,320" ("Judgment Under Uncertainty: Heuristics and Biases," *Science*, 185, 1974). The explanation in terms of anchoring is that people multiply the first few terms of each product and anchor the estimate on that figure.

8. Gambling Biases

When judging future outcomes, we naturally rely on past results. However, in certain circumstances involving judgment about probabilities, we repeatedly make very basic mistakes, some of which are grouped under the heading called **gambling biases**. For example, suppose you flipped a coin 10 times with these results: 7 heads, 3 tails (70% heads, 30% tails). Although most people accept that, *in the long run*, the ratio of heads to tails will approach 50-50, some people believe that in the example above tails are "overdue" to come up. They seem to believe two things:

Gambling biases
When judging future outcomes, we naturally rely on past results. However, in certain circumstances involving judgment about probabilities, we repeatedly make very basic mistakes.

Belief 1: In order to approach the 50:50 ratio, more tails than heads will have to come up on *future tosses*.

Belief 2: There is a greater chance (higher probability) that tails will come up on *the next coin toss*.

Let's see why *both* of these beliefs are unwarranted. Our analysis will illustrate the gambling effect.

The key to understanding the effect of the bias is to analyze the phrase "in the long run." All we need to do is extend the initial 10 coin tosses above (7 heads, 3 tails; 70% heads, 30% tails) to a much longer run. Suppose we toss the coin an additional

90 times, and in that run heads and tails come up the *same number* of times (each comes up 45 times). We add these results to the initial 10 tosses. We originally got 7 heads and 3 tails; next we got 45 heads and 45 tails; thus, out of 100 tosses, we got 52 heads and 48 tails. This means that of the 100 tosses, heads came up 52% and tails 48%. We went from 70% heads and 30% tails (the initial 10 tosses) to 52% heads and 48% tails, and this result happened when the next 90 tosses *did not have more tails than heads* (they both came up 45 times). Therefore, the ratio of heads to tails is already approaching 50-50 without tails having to come up more than heads. Thus, the belief that more tails than heads need to come up in the future to approach a 50–50 split is incorrect. This result also shows that even if a short run of tosses results in more heads than tails, both belief 1 and belief 2 above are incorrect.

A related mistake occurs in what is called the *positive expectation bias*. It concerns the psychological belief that since bad luck cannot go on forever, good luck is "overdue." This kind of thinking contributes to many kinds of addictions. For example, it can lead to a gambling addiction when the person believes that good luck is soon to happen (perhaps on the next roll of dice). And the longer the losing streak continues, the more the belief is reinforced ("My next bet will surely start a winning streak"). Interestingly, the bias can also feed the opposite belief, that a winning streak will likely continue, leading the gambler to make larger bets riding the "winning wave."

9. Frequency Bias

If you or someone close to you buys a car, you might suddenly begin to notice lots of similar cars. If you learn a new word, or hear about a person, place, or thing that you didn't know before, you might begin to see or hear other instances of it. A **frequency bias** occurs when we make a mistaken judgment regarding the extent to which something exists based on recent experience. In other words, before the effect takes hold of us, we might give a low estimate of the number of objects referred to, but once the effect takes hold and we begin to notice more and more instances of the object, our estimate of the number of objects might rise considerably. What happens is that in our daily life we are probably experiencing the *same* frequency of the object, but now we *notice* instances more frequently; our minds have become more selective and active in observing the object.

Frequency bias This occurs when we make a mistaken judgment regarding the extent to which something exists based on recent experience.

10. Ingroup Bias

The **ingroup bias** concerns the human tendency to look at the world through a tribalistic lens, to assign *positive* stereotypes to the members of our *ingroup*, and *negative* stereotypes to members of *outgroups*. This cognitive bias contributes to psychological factors such as suspicion of the outgroup, and fear that the outgroup will overrun us and destroy our culture. It also affects how we judge ourselves and our groups, such as believing that our group is superior (more intelligent, honest, hard-working, among other things) than members of the outgroup.

Ingroup bias This concerns the human tendency to look at the world through a tribalistic lens, to assign *positive* stereotypes to the members of our *ingroup*, and *negative* stereotypes to members of *outgroups*.

The ingroup bias has the capacity to insulate our thinking so much that even when confronted with evidence that goes against a stereotype, instead of admitting that our generalizations are flawed, we often resort to saying, "The exception proves the rule." Although the ingroup bias draws on some related psychological factors as the confirmation bias, the ingroup bias has a narrower focus.

The researcher Henri Tajfel devised some simple experiments to test the effect of ingroup bias. Tajfel took forty-eight students *who knew each other* and placed them randomly into two equal groups. The groups were given simple tasks that required them to make decisions that would affect hypothetical rewards for each group. Tajfel found that when the members of each group were given the choice between maximizing the profit for *both* groups, or maximizing the profit of *their own* group, they acted on behalf of their own group. Tajfel remarked that since the subjects already knew each other, "neither an objective conflict of interests nor hostility had any relevance whatever to what our subjects were asked to do. It was enough for them to see themselves as clearly categorized into an ingroup and an outgroup" (Tajfel, "Experiments in Intergroup Discrimination," *Scientific American*, 223, no. 5, 1970).

11. Fundamental Attribution Bias

Fundamental attribution bias
This bias manifests itself in situations in which we take *full credit* for something good that happened to us, while in other situations we look for *excuses* to explain why something bad happened to us.

The **fundamental attribution bias** manifests itself in situations in which we take *full credit* for something good that happened to us, while in other situations we look for *excuses* to explain why something bad happened to us. In other words, we have a tendency to believe that the good outcomes are a direct result of our *internal* abilities, intelligence, and skills, but the bad outcomes are the result of *external forces*. We praise ourselves for success, and blame the world for failures. For example, someone playing a board game such as Monopoly might attribute a win to knowledge of optimal game-playing strategies, but attribute a loss to unlucky dice tosses.

A study was conducted to see how teachers and students might interpret success or failure on an exam. Researchers had college students simulate what might happen in a typical classroom. Participants were randomly assigned to either the teacher group or the student group. The teacher group had to create a written lesson for the student group to study. The student group then had to take an exam based on the lesson material. The results showed that members of both groups "made self-serving attributions taking credit for success, but not for failure." These results reveal the possibility of conflict between teachers and students, especially if neither group is willing to take personal responsibility for the outcomes. On the one hand, teachers may blame students for not spending enough time preparing for the assignment; on the other hand, students may blame teachers for creating confusing or difficult assignments (Hunter McAllister, "Self-Serving Bias in the Classroom: Who Shows It? Who Knows It?" *Journal of Educational Psychology*, 88, 1996).

Fundamental attribution bias can manifest itself in several ways. As we saw earlier, it occurs when we explain away *our mistakes or failures* as being the result of *external factors*. But in other situations, it occurs when we attribute *other people's mistakes or failures* as resulting from *their personality flaws*. For example, if I drop a plate of food,

I might claim that the plate was slippery because it wasn't dried properly, or claim that someone had bumped me. But if someone else drops a plate, I might attribute that to the person's carelessness.

The bias also occurs when we misjudge the role of the *environment* in shaping our behavior and that of others. For example, we might believe that a person's criminal behavior resulted from innate character flaws, not because of an impoverished upbringing. In contrast, we might believe that if we had grown up in that same poor area, then our innate character would have ensured that we would not have become criminals.

In a series of experiments by Edward Jones and Victor Harris, participants listened to people expressing opinions about a politician. Afterward, they were asked to estimate each speaker's attitude; that is, whether or not the speaker was supportive of the politician. When participants *assumed* that the speakers were truly expressing a favorable opinion of the politician, they judged those speakers to be *genuinely* supportive of the politician. Similarly, when participants *assumed* that the speakers were truly expressing a negative opinion of the politician, they judged those speakers to be *genuinely* against the politician. Afterward, when participants were told that the speakers were merely acting out their roles—that a coin toss determined whether they would speak for or against the politician—they continued to believe that the speakers showed at least *some* genuine attitude toward the politician. The results indicate that the *initial assumptions* of a fundamental attribution of speaker sincerity remained, even in the face of contrary evidence (Jones and Harris, "The Attribution of Attitudes," *Journal of Experimental Social Psychology*, 3, 1967).

CAN WE OVERCOME COGNITIVE BIASES?

As has been shown by many types of research into the role of cognitive biases, we often disregard objective statistical evidence in favor of a small number of vivid individual experiences. But current research is trying to answer some important questions: Can we train ourselves, or be taught, not to let cognitive biases influence our judgment, decisions, and predictions? Can we slow down the cognitive processing of information to overcome our unconscious biases?

Although certain cognitive biases seem to be hardwired into us, there is encouraging work that indicates that we can overcome that hardwiring. For example, when given problems or information involving probabilities, students who have learned how to do basic probability calculations are able to rely on the reflexive system to slow down their judgments. This enables them to work carefully through problems and to analyze information, thus avoiding simple mistakes. Similarly, students who take courses in statistics are less likely to make simple statistical judgment errors than students who have not taken statistics courses. In addition, studies have shown that students who take logic or critical thinking courses typically score higher on the Law School Admission Test (LSAT) than students who have not been exposed to such experiences.

Appendix B

The LSAT and Logical Reasoning

INTRODUCTION

The Law School Admission Council describes the Law School Admission Test (LSAT) as follows:

> The test consists of five 35-minute sections of multiple-choice questions. Four of the five sections contribute to the test taker's score. These sections include one Reading Comprehension section, one Analytical Reasoning section, and two Logical Reasoning sections. The unscored section, commonly referred to as the variable section, typically is used to pretest new test questions or to preequate new test forms. The placement of this section will vary. Identification of the unscored section is not available until you receive your score report. A 35-minute, unscored writing sample is administered at the end of the test. Copies of your writing sample are sent to all law schools to which you apply. (https://www.lsac.org/jd/lsat/about-the-lsat)

Since law schools require you to take the LSAT, you should practice taking past exams, which are available for purchase or through your school and local libraries. Doing so will familiarize you with several key points:

a. the number of minutes allowed for each section;
b. the directions for each section;
c. typical terminology used;
d. how well you respond to the pressure of taking an actual LSAT exam, especially if you adhere to real-time scenarios for each section; and
e. the answers and explanations for the questions.

An old joke captures this nicely: A world-famous violinist was walking in New York City when a young person asked her, "How do I get to Carnegie Hall?" The violinist replied, "Practice, practice, practice!"

Because getting a law degree requires the ability to comprehend and analyze complex material, it is not surprising that the LSAT asks you to do two things: *read* and *analyze*. And because the LSAT is a timed test, you need to *read efficiently* and *analyze with precision*. Your ability to work *efficiently* is crucial because you have 35 minutes to answer approximately twenty-five questions, meaning you have roughly a minute and a half for each question. This fact reinforces the need for you to practice as much as you can. Your ability to *analyze with precision* can be strengthened by using this book because many of the techniques presented apply directly to the skills required to do well on the LSAT. The chapters in *Logic* provide precise definitions, explanations, examples, and exercises for the logical terms and types of reasoning tasks you will encounter in the LSAT. A thorough knowledge of this content will give you a firm foothold by allowing you to zero in on the logical issues at play in each question.

We will point out how various chapters in *Logic* teach skills that are applicable specifically to the two *logical reasoning* sections, which, as the Law School Admission Council point out, contain questions that "assess the ability to analyze, critically evaluate, and complete arguments as they occur in ordinary language." If you have already worked through the relevant chapters in *Logic*, you can use this guide as a refresher and revisit the exercise sets with an eye toward the specific needs of LSAT questions. If you have not yet worked through these chapters, you can use this guide as a bridge to each chapter's exercise sets and the types of questions asked in the LSAT.

The LSAT has evolved over the years. Today, *most of the LSAT logical reasoning questions involve inductive arguments*. There are many kinds of inductive arguments, such as analogical arguments, statistical arguments, causal arguments, legal arguments, moral arguments, and scientific arguments. *Analogical arguments* (see Chapter 10) are based on the idea that when two things share some relevant characteristics, they probably share other characteristics as well. *Statistical arguments* (see Chapter 13) are based on our ability to generalize. When we observe a pattern, we often create an argument that relies on a statistical regularity. *Causal arguments* (see Chapter 14) are arguments based on knowledge of either causes or effects. For example, a team of medical scientists may conduct experiments to determine if a new drug (the potential cause) will have a desired effect on a particular disease.

As we proceed, we will look at several specific examples of inductive and deductive arguments. We will analyze the arguments in many ways to identify the conclusion and premises, what additional information would strengthen (or weaken) the argument, what assumptions are being made by the person making the argument, specific reasoning flaws, and argument patterns. *You should try analyzing the examples before you look at the answers.* This will give you valuable experience and practice to see how you are doing. You can then compare your answers with the ones we provide.

1. LOGICAL REASONING

A typical logical reasoning section contains around 25 multiple-choice questions. A short *argument* is often given consisting of three or four *statements*. Recall the following definitions from Chapter 1:

- An **argument** is a group of *statements* in which the *conclusion* is claimed to follow from the *premise(s)*.
- A **statement** is a sentence that is either true or false.
- A **premise** is the information intended to provide support for the *conclusion*.
- A **conclusion** is a statement that is claimed to follow from the *premises* of an argument; the *main point* of an argument.

Argument A group of statements in which the conclusion is claimed to follow from the premise(s).

Statement A sentence that is either true or false.

Premise The information intended to provide support for a conclusion.

Conclusion The statement that is claimed to follow from the premises of an argument; the main point of an argument.

The most important thing to remember is that *statements are true or false but arguments are neither true nor false.*

Each LSAT *logical reasoning question* is followed by five possible answers. Your job is *not* to determine whether the *statements* that make up the *argument* are true or false. Instead, your job is to *identify* the *conclusion* and to *assume* that the *premises* are true. Why? Because the LSAT is not a test about facts, it is a test of *logical reasoning*. In other words, what follows from a set of *premises* that are *assumed to be true*?

As most study guides will tell you, *read the question before you read the argument*. The reason is that the LSAT uses several common question types, so if you know what type of question you are required to answer, you can then read the argument with that in mind. Here are some of the most common question types:

- Which one of the following *most accurately expresses* the *main conclusion* of the argument?
- If the *statements* in the argument are *true*, then which one of the following *must also* be true?
- Which one of the following is an *assumption* that is required by the argument?
- Which one of the following, *if true, most weakens* the argument?
- Which one of the following, *if true, most strengthens* the argument?
- Which one of the following is a *reasoning flaw* in the argument?
- Which one of the following exhibits a *reasoning pattern* that is *most like* the one exhibited in the argument?

Notice that many of the question types previously listed use the term "most" (*most accurately expresses; most weakens; most strengthens; most like*). This means that although several of the answer choices might, for example, strengthen the argument, your job is to choose the answer that *strengthens it the most*. In multiple-choice questions, the wrong answers are appropriately called *distractors* because their purpose is to distract you from the correct answer. They will often sound reasonable, but that shouldn't be surprising. The LSAT questions ask you to choose the best answer over the several possibly good answers.

2. DEDUCTIVE AND INDUCTIVE ARGUMENTS

Earlier we said that arguments are *neither true nor false*. Some of the ways logicians classify arguments are *strong, weak, valid,* or *invalid*. We can now further define arguments as being deductive or inductive. A **valid deductive argument** is one in which it is *impossible* for the conclusion to be false, *assuming* the premises are true. In other words, the conclusion *follows necessarily* from the premises. On the other hand, an **invalid deductive argument** is one in which it is *possible* for the conclusion to be false, *assuming* the premises are true. In other words, the conclusion *does not follow necessarily* from the premises (see Chapter 1, section 1F).

In contrast, a **strong inductive argument** is such that if the premises are *assumed* to be true, then the conclusion is *probably* true. In other words, the *probable truth*

Valid deductive argument An argument in which, *assuming* the premises are true, it is *impossible* for the conclusion to be false. In other words, the conclusion follows *necessarily* from the premises.

Invalid deductive argument An argument in which, *assuming* the premises are true, it is *possible* for the conclusion to be false. In other words, the conclusion does not follow necessarily from the premises.

Strong inductive argument An argument such that if the premises are *assumed* to be true, then the conclusion is *probably* true. In other words, the *probable truth* of the conclusion *follows from* the truth of the premises.

of the conclusion *follows from* the truth of the premises. On the other hand, a **weak inductive argument** is such that either (a) if the premises are *assumed* to be true, then the conclusion is *probably not true*, or (b) a *probably true* conclusion *does not follow from the premises* (see Chapter 1, section 1G).

Let's look at some arguments:

A. All Y are Z.
All X are Y.
All X are Z.

B. All Z are Y.
All X are Y.
All X are Z.

Upon analysis, no matter what terms we substitute for X, Y, and Z in example A, it will always turn out to be a valid argument. In other words, if we *assume* the two premises are true, then *necessarily* the conclusion is true. However, the same doesn't hold for argument B. Even if we *assume* that all Z's and all X's are Y's, it *does not necessarily follow* that all X's are Z's; thus argument B is invalid. For example, although it is true that all whales are mammals, and it is also true that all humans are mammals, it is false that all humans are whales. This is a counterexample to argument B. A **counterexample** to an argument shows that the conclusion *does not follow necessarily* from the premises. A single counterexample to a deductive argument is enough to show that the argument is invalid. Since argument A is valid, it has no counterexamples. If we look once again at argument A, then we can see that the conclusion *does not* amplify or expand the scope of the information in the premises. The first premise states that *every* Y is a Z; the second premise states that every X is a Y. Therefore, under the *assumption* that the premises are true, the conclusion *does not go beyond* what is already contained in the premises. (Exercises 1F.I can be used for practice.)

Let's now look at two different kinds of arguments:

C. Most X are Y.
I have an X.
Probably I have a Y.

D. Some X are Y.
I have an X.
Probably I have a Y.

Upon analysis, if we *assume* the two *premises* in argument C are *true*, then the conclusion is *probably true*; thus, it is a *strong* argument. This is very different from a *valid* argument. A *valid* argument *guarantees* that *if the premises are true*, then the conclusion is true. A *strong inductive argument* cannot offer that guarantee. In other words, the conclusion of a strong inductive argument might be false even if the premises are true.

Analysis also shows that argument D is weak. The key difference is that the term "some" does not carry the same weight as the term "most" did in argument C. Even if we *assume* that both *premises* are *true*, then the conclusion is *not probably true*.

Inductive arguments *amplify* the scope of the information in the premises. For example, the first premise in argument C provides information about *most* X's, but it *does not* make a claim about *every* X. The second premise picks out my X. It is in this sense that we say that the conclusion regarding my X *goes beyond* the information in the premises; thus, it is *possible* that the *conclusion is false* even under the *assumption* that the *premises are true*. (Exercises 1G can be used for practice.)

Weak inductive argument An argument such that either (a) if the premises are *assumed* to be true, then the conclusion is *probably not true*, or (b) a *probably true* conclusion *does not follow from the premises.*

Counterexample A counterexample to a statement is evidence that shows the statement is false. A counterexample to an argument shows that the conclusion does not follow necessarily from the premises. A single counterexample to a deductive argument is enough to show that the argument is invalid.

In all four previous examples, the *logical analysis* focused on the *relationship* between the premises and the conclusion. We simply had to *assume* the premises were true, then analyze either (a) whether the conclusion was *guaranteed* to be true (valid or invalid argument), or (b) whether the conclusion was *probably* true (strong or weak argument).

3. IDENTIFYING CONCLUSIONS AND PREMISES

Conclusion indicators Words and phrases that indicate the presence of a conclusion (the statement claimed to follow from premises).

Premise indicators Words and phrases that help us recognize arguments by indicating the presence of premises (statements being offered in support of a conclusion).

Every argument has a conclusion, so it helps to identify that first. Here are some **conclusion indicator** words and phrases that may appear in the argument: *therefore, thus, so, consequently, suggests that, it follows that, implies that, hence*. If you are not sure which sentence is the conclusion, you can simply place the word "therefore" in front of each of them to see which works best. On the other hand, the argument might have some **premise indicator** words and phrases: *because, since, as shown by, given that, it follows from*. If you are not sure which sentences are the premises, you can simply place the word "because" in front of each of them to see which works best (see Chapter 1, section 1B). Here is an example of an argument without any indicator words:

> We should boycott that company. They have been found guilty of producing widgets that they knew were faulty, and that caused numerous injuries.

In this case, the first sentence seems to be the point of the argument, and the second sentence seems to offer reasons in support of the conclusion. In other words, *because* the company has been found guilty of producing widgets that they knew were faulty, and that caused numerous injuries, *therefore* we should boycott the company. (Exercises 1B can be used for practice.)

A. Identifying the Conclusion

LSAT questions might ask you to identify the conclusion in a passage. Alternatively, you might have to identify *missing* premises or conclusions (this is covered in Chapter 1, section 1H). Here is a simple example where all you have to do is identify the conclusion:

> There is no reason for you not to start exercising regularly. Exercise helps strengthen your cardiovascular system. It also lowers your cholesterol, increases the blood flow to the brain, and enables you to think longer.

The conclusion is the first sentence. The other two sentences are the premises (support, evidence) offered as *reasons* to accept the conclusion. If you place the word "therefore" in front of each of the three sentences, then the first sentence stands out as the most logical choice. Another way to get the same result is to see that the second and third sentences *work together*. The second sentence states a benefit of exercise, and the third sentence adds three more benefits. (Another tipoff: The third sentence starts out by stating that "It [exercise] also ...," which indicates that it is another *reason* that is being put forward.) Let's analyze another argument, but this time we will provide five answer choices. As we pointed out earlier, you should approach each example as if it were an actual LSAT test question. If you try analyzing each example before you look at the answer, then you gain valuable experience and practice.

> I don't like movies that rely on computer-generated graphics to take the place of intelligent dialogue, interesting characters, and an intricate plot. After watching the ads on TV, I have the feeling that the new movie *Bad Blood and Good Vibes* is not very good. I predict that it will not win any Academy Awards.

Which of the following is the main point of the argument?

> **A.** The author claims that only movies that have intelligent dialogue, interesting characters, and an intricate plot win Academy Awards.
> **B.** The author does not like movies that rely on computer-generated graphics.
> **C.** The author feels that the new movie is not very good.
> **D.** The author predicts that the movie will not win any Academy Awards.
> **E.** The author obviously watches a lot of movies.

Did you read the question before you read the argument? Doing so would have alerted you that your task is to identify the *main point* (the conclusion) of the argument. It is common to forget this advice; however, with enough practice it will become second nature, so when you start taking practice LSAT exams you will have trained yourself *to read the question first.*

Let's go through the five choices one by one. Although the author does predict that the movie will not win any Academy Awards, nowhere in the argument does the author claim that *only* movies that have intelligent dialogue, interesting characters, and an intricate plot win Academy Awards. Thus, we can eliminate choice A. Although choice B is a statement made by the author, it is a premise, not the conclusion of the argument; thus, we can eliminate it. This is a very important point to remember. An answer choice might be true, but that alone doesn't make it correct. What counts is that it is the *best choice for a particular task*, which in this case is the identification of the main point of the argument. Notice that choice C is also a statement made by the author, but it, too, is a premise, not the conclusion of the argument; thus, we can eliminate it. Choice D seems to be the conclusion, especially if we add the word "therefore" in front of it. Nevertheless, we should still look at choice E. Although the statement may be true, there is no evidence that supports this claim as being the main point of the argument. Therefore, choice D is the correct answer. Let's analyze another example.

> Wild hogs often damage newly planted seedlings and food crops by rooting, and that also causes soil erosion. In addition, hogs compete with other animals that also forage, usually crowding them out. Lastly, hogs are vectors for diseases communicable to humans and livestock. Farmers should always take vigorous action to reduce wild hog populations near their land.

Which of the following is the main point of the argument?

> **A.** Wild hogs offer farmers a great return on investment.
> **B.** Wild hogs compete with other foraging animals.

    C. Wild hogs spread disease to humans and livestock.
    D. Farmers need to take action to reduce wild hog populations.
    E. Farmers should take the advice of government funded scientific studies.

The key to solving this question is to recognize that the first three sentences offer support for the conclusion, which can be seen if we add the word "because" in front of them and the word "therefore" in front of the last sentence. All we need to do is locate the answer that most closely mirrors the conclusion: *Farmers should always take vigorous action to reduce wild hog populations near their land.* Choice A does not reflect the conclusion, so it is eliminated. Choices B and C are premises, so they are eliminated. Choice D restates the conclusion, making it the best choice so far. Choice E refers to government studies, but that was not part of the argument, so it is eliminated. Therefore, choice D is the correct answer.

B. Choosing the Best Missing Conclusion

Another type of question has a passage containing premises but no conclusion, requiring you to choose the answer that offers the best conclusion given the stated premises. *Don't waste time* trying to decide whether the premises are *actually true or false*—for the purposes of the LSAT just *assume* that the premises are true. Here is an example of a simple argument with a *missing conclusion*:

> Banks lend money. We're a bank.

If we *assume* it is true that "Banks lend money," and we *assume* it is also true that "We're a bank," then the *conclusion* is "We lend money."

    Another type of question might ask you to choose the conclusion that is *most strongly supported* by the given premises. These kinds of question rely on your ability to analyze subtle uses of everyday words, as illustrated in the next example:

> I have a headache. I just took two aspirins. Aspirins can relieve headaches.

The key to solving this is to understand the force of the third sentence. The word "can" implies that aspirin has the ability to relieve a headache, but it *does not* imply that aspirin will always relieve a headache. Therefore, the conclusion that is most strongly supported by the given premises is "My headache will probably be relieved." Here is another example for analysis:

> He set three new world record times in the 100-meter sprint this year alone. In almost all cases, when someone has done something remarkable like that in the history of track and field they have later been found guilty of doping.

Which one of the following is the most logical conclusion for this passage?

    A. If someone is doping, then they set world records.
    B. He is definitely guilty of doping.
    C. He is probably guilty of doping.
    D. Doping is becoming the major problem in all athletics.
    E. Anyone caught doping should be stripped of his or her world record performances.

The key to solving this question is to recognize that the conclusion needs to connect the *person who set the three records* to *people who have later been found guilty of doping*. With this in mind, choice A reverses the connection between setting records and doping, so it is eliminated. Choice B goes too far; the term "definitely" does not conform with the premise that states "In almost all cases," so it is eliminated. Choice C uses the term "probably," which conforms with the premise that states "In almost all cases," making it the best answer so far. Choice D does not make the connection that we want, so it is eliminated. Choice E makes an assertion about anyone who has already been caught doping, going beyond what the premises tell us, so it is eliminated. Therefore, choice C is the correct answer. Let's analyze another example.

> My phone isn't an iPhone, nor is it an Android, and those are the only phones that have state-of-the-art voice recognition personal assistant programs. I can't just ask my phone to find stuff for me, but I need that capability for my research.

Which one of the following is the most logical conclusion for this passage?

- **A.** iPhones and Androids are the most user-friendly phones available.
- **B.** I should get either an iPhone or Android.
- **C.** No other phones offer state-of-the-art voice recognition personal assistant programs.
- **D.** I cannot ask my phone to find stuff.
- **E.** I'm sure other companies will start competing in the personal assistant program market.

The key to solving this question is seeing how the premises work together. The first sentence states that there are only two kinds of phones that offer state-of-the-art voice recognition personal assistant programs (it *doesn't matter* whether this or any other premise is true or false). The next sentence states two important things: (1) The person can't just ask her/his phone to find stuff, and (2) she/he needs that capability for research. The conclusion should be a statement that follows from all the information in the premises; in this case, it should be something that states an action that the speaker will most likely do. With this in mind, choice A doesn't offer any course of action, so it is eliminated. Choice B seems to offer what we need, so we can keep it for now. Choices C and D simply restate a premise, so they are eliminated. Choice E might be something that will happen in the future; however, it doesn't state an action that the *speaker* will most likely do, so it is eliminated. Therefore, choice B is the correct answer.

C. Assumptions: Choosing the Best Missing Premise

Some questions provide stated premises and a conclusion but leave out important information that is needed to support the conclusion. Your job is to determine the *missing assumption*. Here is a simple example:

> Judy must be an honest person because she has an advanced degree.

The premise indicator word "because" lets us know that the statement "she (Judy) has an advanced degree" is used to support the conclusion "Judy must be an honest person." However, in order to connect the given premise to the conclusion we need to supply some missing information. Since the conclusion makes a strong claim, the missing premise is "Every person who has an advanced degree is honest." (Alternatively, "All people who have an advanced degree are honest.") We are *not* concerned with whether the missing premise is actually true; we simply need to determine what needs to be *assumed* in order to derive the conclusion. What would happen if the argument had been slightly different?

> Judy is probably an honest person because she has an advanced degree.

The word "probably" indicates the conclusion might be false, so we don't need the strong words "every" or "all" in the missing premise. This will work: "Most people with an advanced degree are honest." The term "most" means more than 50%. Once again, we are *not* concerned with whether the missing premise is actually true; thus, if we *assume* both *premises* are true, then they make the conclusion *likely to be true*.

Why can't the missing premise be "Some people with an advanced degree are honest"? The term "some" is defined as *at least one*, but the upper limit is unspecified. Since the term allows for the possibility of less than 50%, it does *not* make the *conclusion* likely to be true. The following is an example that requires you to fill in a *missing assumption*:

> **A.** Every dog is a mammal. Therefore, every dog is an animal.

In order for the conclusion to logically follow, we need to connect *mammals* to *animals* such that there can be no doubt that the conclusion follows. This will work: Every mammal is an animal. In other words, the conclusion needs information that connects *every* mammal to the class of animals, and that is what the missing assumption does.

On the other hand, an argument may not need such a strong connection. Here is an example:

> **B.** I have a new car. Therefore, my car probably uses gasoline.

The conclusion needs additional information that, if assumed to be true, makes the conclusion *likely to be true* because the conclusion contains the key word "probably." We need to connect *new cars* to *uses gasoline* such that the conclusion is likely to be true. This will work: Most new cars use gasoline. The missing assumption uses the word "most" to make the connection. As stated earlier, the word "some" would not work because it is too weak (it can mean less than 50%, whereas "most" means more than 50%).

Compare argument B with the following:

> **C.** I have a new car. Therefore, my car definitely uses gasoline.

The term "definitely" implies a much stronger claim than the term "probably" in argument B. Given this, we need to find a missing assumption that supports the stronger conclusion: Every new car uses gasoline. If we assume the original premise and the missing assumption are both true, then the conclusion follows.

You might be thinking, "But that missing assumption is factually false—not every new car uses gasoline." Although your intuition is correct, it is misplaced here. Remember, the LSAT is *not* asking you questions about what is factually true or false. All the questions are artificial; they are *not* designed to assess what you *know*, they are designed to assess how well you can *reason*. Here is an argument and five choices for you to analyze:

> Earmarks are provisions in congressional legislation that direct federal funds to specific projects. Earmarks are meant to benefit all the residents of a particular state. My investigation thus shows that earmarks really benefit only those who make the largest campaign contributions.

Which one of the following, if assumed, enables the argument's conclusion to be properly inferred?

- **A.** Recent congressional legislation takes entirely too long to enact.
- **B.** I have evidence that shows that earmarks are actually written by congressional aides.
- **C.** I have evidence that shows a direct correlation between campaign contributions and earmark benefits to rich donors.
- **D.** I have evidence that shows the largest states get the most earmarks.
- **E.** Congressional legislation can be vetoed by the president.

Did you read the question before you read the argument? Let's go through the five choices. Even though the information in choice A may be true, it does not support the conclusion that "earmarks really benefit only those who make the largest campaign contributions," so we can eliminate it. We can apply the same analysis to choice B, thus eliminating it. Choice C does offer evidence, *if it is assumed to be true*, that supports the conclusion, so we can keep it for now. Even if choice D were true, that the largest states get the most earmarks, it can simply indicate that the states with the largest populations need more money to help with infrastructure, among other things, than states with smaller populations; this does not add the missing support for the conclusion, so we can eliminate it. Finally, choice E states a fact about legislation but it does not support the conclusion. Therefore, choice C is the correct answer.

Here is another argument for analysis:

> Eating meat is natural, so it's unobjectionable to eat meat.

On which one of the following assumptions does the argument rely?

- **A.** Some people are vegetarians.
- **B.** Human beings have teeth that help chew meat so it can be easily digested.
- **C.** Eating uncooked meat is dangerous.
- **D.** Natural activities are unobjectionable.
- **E.** Meat is a good source of usable protein.

To solve this question, we must recognize that a missing premise (assumption) is needed to connect the natural part of eating meat with its being unobjectionable.

Keeping that in mind, choice A does not make the needed connection (it does *not* help support the conclusion), so it is eliminated. The information provided in choice B does not make the needed connection either, so it is eliminated. Choice C does not help make the needed connection, so it is eliminated. Choice D connects *natural* to *unobjectionable*, making it the best choice so far. Choice E offers a reason to eat meat, but does not make the needed connection, so it is eliminated. Therefore, choice D is the correct answer. (Exercises 1H can be used for practice for missing conclusions and missing premises.)

4. ADDITIONAL INFORMATION THAT STRENGTHENS OR WEAKENS AN ARGUMENT

Some questions will ask you to determine whether additional evidence, *if assumed to be true*, either *strengthens* or *weakens* a given argument (see Chapter 1, "The Role of New Information"). Sometimes adding an additional premise to a weak argument can create a strong argument. For example, consider the following:

> There are green and black marbles in a box. Thus, a marble picked at random will probably be green.

Since we do not know how many marbles of each color are in the box, the premise *does not* make the conclusion likely to be true; thus, it is a weak argument. However, suppose we are given some additional information:

> There are green and black marbles in the box. *Eight of the marbles are green and two are black*. Thus, a marble picked at random will probably be green.

If the additional information is *assumed to be true*, then there is an 80% (8/10) chance of picking a green marble. Since the conclusion is now highly likely to be true, the assumed evidence *strengthens* the original argument. Here is another example for analysis:

> The gas pump stopped pumping gas into Jane's car; therefore, her car's gas tank is full.

Which one of the following, if true, would most strengthen the argument?

- **A.** Jane prepaid $10 for gas.
- **B.** Jane usually buys gas every 3 days.
- **C.** The electricity that runs the gas pump housing stopped working.
- **D.** Jane unknowingly bumped the dispenser, which shut off the gas being pumped.
- **E.** Jane's gas tank holds twenty gallons, and nineteen gallons was pumped into the gas tank.

Choice A can explain why the gas pump automatically stopped pumping gas (once it reached $10), but it does *not* help strengthen the conclusion because it is unlikely that Jane would have known that exactly $10 would fill the gas tank, so it is eliminated. Choice B tells us when Jane buys gas but it doesn't add support to the conclusion, so it is eliminated. Choices C and D actually weaken the argument as to why the pump stopped, so they are eliminated. Choice E tells us that nineteen gallons was administered into a twenty-gallon tank, which is enough to fill Jane's gas tank in most normal cases; since this offers the *most strength* of all the answers, it is the correct answer.

On the other hand, it is also possible that additional information will *weaken* an argument. For example, consider the following:

> I just drank a bottle of Sunrise Spring Mineral Water. Since it has been shown that most bottled water is safe, I can conclude, with some confidence, that the water was safe.

Assuming the premises are true, this is a strong argument. However, suppose we are given this additional evidence:

> Happy Sunshine Manufacturing Corporation has announced that it is recalling all of its Sunrise Spring Mineral Water due to a suspected contamination at one of its bottling facilities.

If we assume that this additional information is true, then the original conclusion is unlikely to be true; thus its addition weakens the original argument. Here is another example for analysis:

> The large box of cereal I bought says that it contains twenty-four ounces. But when I opened it, there was at least three inches of empty space instead of it being full to the top of the inner bag. The manufacturers are obviously guilty of false labeling.

Which one of the following, if true, would most weaken the argument?

- **A.** The cereal is number one in sales in the United States.
- **B.** Some cereals are lighter in weight than others.
- **C.** The box says that the contents might settle as a result of shipping.
- **D.** Cereals are boxed by an automatic dispenser.
- **E.** Empty space in packaging usually means contents do not meet specifications.

Choice A does nothing to weaken the argument, so we can eliminate it. Choice B sounds promising until we realize that it does not affect the argument's conclusion, so it is eliminated. Choice C provides evidence to explain the empty space, which weakens the conclusion, so we can keep it while we analyze the rest of the choices. Choice D does not help us understand why the empty space is there and it doesn't weaken the argument, so it can be eliminated. Choice E actually strengthens the argument, so it can't be correct. Therefore, choice C is the correct answer.

Of course, not all additional information will affect an argument. Thus, you must also be able to rule out additional evidence that is *irrelevant to the strength of the conclusion*. Eliminating wrong choices makes your final decision much easier. For example, consider the earlier argument:

> I just drank a bottle of Sunrise Spring Mineral Water. Since it has been shown that most bottled water is safe, I can conclude, with some confidence, that the water was safe.

We already know that this is a strong argument. Now suppose we are given this additional evidence:

> The bottle of water I just drank contained sixteen ounces.

If we assume that this additional information is true, then the original conclusion is unaffected because the additional evidence is *irrelevant* to the strength of the conclusion. Of course, in another context this additional information might be relevant. For example, if further information states that only the sixteen-ounce bottles of the water are contaminated, then this would be relevant to the strength of the argument. (Exercises 1G can be used for practice.)

5. ARGUMENTS THAT USE EITHER ANALOGICAL, STATISTICAL, OR CAUSAL REASONING

A. Analogical Reasoning

Analogy To draw an analogy is simply to indicate that there are similarities between two or more things.

Analogical reasoning One of the most fundamental tools used in creating an argument. It can be analyzed as a type of inductive argument— it is a matter of probability, based on experience, and it can be quite persuasive.

Some questions that ask which piece of evidence, if true, would most weaken (or strengthen) a given argument rely on *analogical reasoning*, the subject of Chapter 10. To draw an **analogy** is simply to indicate that there are similarities between two or more things. **Analogical reasoning** can be analyzed as a type of inductive argument; it is a matter of *probability*, based on experience.

If a question asks you to choose the answer that most *strengthens* a given analogical argument, then the correct answer will provide additional evidence of *similarities* between the items mentioned. In contrast, if a question asks you to choose the answer that most *weakens* a given analogical argument, then the correct answer will provide additional evidence of *differences* between the items mentioned. Let's look at a few examples.

> **A.** We both bought new vehicles. My vehicle averages 40 miles per gallon of gasoline. Therefore, your vehicle will probably average 40 miles per gallon of gasoline.

Suppose you are given this new information:

> We both bought the same make and model car with identical engine size.

This information, if true, *strengthens* the original analogical argument because the two cars share some additional *similar* characteristics that are relevant to gas mileage.

However, suppose you are given this new information:

> I bought a hybrid car, and you bought a heavy-duty pickup truck.

This information, if true, *weakens* the original analogical argument because the two vehicles have some additional *different* characteristics that are relevant to gas mileage.

Questions that rely on analogical reasoning can be asked in different ways. Here is an example:

> The new *Batman* movie set a box-office record. The last movie that set a box-office record won the Oscar for Best Picture. So, the new *Batman* movie is probably going to win the Oscar for Best Picture.

Which one of the following, if true, would most support the argument?

- **A.** The *Batman* movie is rated PG-13.
- **B.** The last movie to set a box-office record was based on a comic book hero.
- **C.** The previous Best Picture movie was made in England; the *Batman* movie was made in the United States.
- **D.** No movie based on a comic book character has ever won Best Picture.
- **E.** No movie that runs for more than 2 hours has ever won the Best Picture award.

The argument relies on an analogy between the *Batman* movie and a past Best Picture winner. It offers one common characteristic between the two movies—namely, the fact that they both set a box-office record. Since you are asked to locate the answer that would most support the argument, you need to find an additional relevant characteristic that the two movies have in common.

Choice A does not connect the *Batman* movie to the previous Best Picture movie, so it can be eliminated. Choice B provides an additional characteristic that both movies have in common, so it is the best choice so far. Choice C weakens the argument because it shows how the two movies differ; it can be eliminated. Choice D weakens the argument because it makes it unlikely that such a movie will win the Best Picture award; it can be eliminated. Choice E is irrelevant in this context because we don't know the running time of the *Batman* movie, so it can be eliminated. Therefore, choice B is the correct answer.

Let's analyze another example:

> If you like the taste of Russ's Steaks, then you'll like the taste of Mutt's Burgers. Mutt gets his burger meat from the same supplier that Russ gets his steaks. Russ gets his meat fresh daily. So does Mutt. Russ grills his steaks. Mutt grills his burgers.

Which one of the following, if true, would most weaken the argument?

- **A.** Both restaurants are well within your price range for eating out.
- **B.** Russ's Steaks is closer to your apartment than Mutt's Burgers.
- **C.** At Russ's Steaks you can buy beer, but not at Mutt's Burgers.
- **D.** Neither of the two restaurants has won any awards.
- **E.** Russ uses a special sauce on the steaks that is not available to Mutt.

The argument relies on an analogy between Russ's Steaks and Mutt's Burgers and offers three common characteristics (same supplier; fresh meat daily; grilled). Since you are asked to locate the answer that most weakens the argument, you need to find a relevant characteristic that the restaurants *do not share*. Choice A strengthens the argument, so it can be eliminated. Choice B provides a difference between the two restaurants, but the difference is *irrelevant* to whether you will like the taste of the food, which is what the conclusion claims, so it can be eliminated. Choice C offers a difference between the two restaurants, but it doesn't speak to the taste of the steaks and burgers; let's see if we can locate a better answer. Choice D tells us something that the two restaurants have in common, so it doesn't weaken the argument; it can be eliminated. Choice E shows a relevant difference between the two restaurants— the sauce—which can directly affect the taste of the steaks but which is lacking in the burgers. Since the two restaurants *do not share this relevant characteristic*, this information, if true, most weakens the argument. Therefore, choice E is the correct answer. (Exercises 10A, 10B, and 10C can be used for practice.)

B. Statistical Reasoning

Some questions that ask which piece of evidence, if assumed to be true, would most weaken (or strengthen) a given argument rely on *statistical reasoning*, the subject of Chapter 13. Evaluating arguments that rely on statistical evidence requires the correct interpretation of the statistical evidence as it relates to the conclusion of the argument.

The most important items to consider in an analysis of a statistical argument concern the population and sample. *Population* refers to any group of objects, not just human populations. A *sample* is a subset, or part, of a population. For example, if the *population* in question were the student body of a large university, say, 10,000 students, then a *sample* would be any portion of that population. A *representative sample* accurately reflects the characteristics of the population as a whole. Let's look at an example.

> Nearly 90% of a sample of registered voters said that they will vote for the Democratic nominee for mayor. Therefore, we can confidently predict that the Democratic nominee will be elected mayor.

Suppose you are given this new information:

> The sample was large, random, and had an equal number of registered Democrats, Republicans, and Independents.

This information, if true, *strengthens* the original statistical argument because the sample gave equal representation to Democrats, Republicans, and Independents. However, suppose you are given this new information:

> The sample included only registered Democrats.

This information, if true, *weakens* the original statistical argument because it is a biased sample; it only surveyed registered Democratic voters.

Questions that rely on statistical reasoning can be asked in different ways. For example:

> Nine out of ten students surveyed claimed the graduation requirements for a baccalaureate degree were too stringent. Therefore, graduation requirements at colleges nationwide are too stringent.

Which one of the following, if true, would most weaken the argument?

    A. The students surveyed were from one small community college in Iowa.
    B. The students surveyed had at least twenty-four credits.
    C. The survey consisted of 10,000 students from all across the United States.
    D. College students can choose from a wider variety of courses than ever before.
    E. Today's graduates have an average college debt of $24,000.

The argument relies on the results of a single survey (the *sample*) to support a claim about colleges nationwide (the *population*). Since you are asked to locate the answer that most weakens the argument, the answer must demonstrate that the sample is *not* representative of the population. Choice A, if true, clearly shows that the sample (one community college in Iowa) is unlikely to be representative of the population (all colleges in the United States), so it may be the answer we are looking for. Let's examine the other choices to be sure. Choice B tells us that the sample did not include students with fewer than twenty-four credits, so it does weaken the argument somewhat; however, it does not tell us the size of the sample or where it was conducted, so it is not as good an answer as choice A. Choice C strengthens the argument, so it can be eliminated. Choices D and E do *not* discuss the issue of whether graduation requirements for a baccalaureate degree are too stringent, so these choice can be eliminated. Therefore, choice A is the correct answer. Let's analyze another example:

> Last year, more than 5000 people in the northeastern United States contracted a rare and sometimes fatal tick disease called babesiosis. The microscopic organism infects red blood cells, and symptoms take anywhere from 1 to 8 weeks to manifest. Thus, we can conclude that people with autoimmune problems are especially vulnerable to this tick-borne disease.

Which one of the following, if true, would most strengthen the argument?

    A. Babesiosis is fatal only if medical treatment is not started within 48 hours after the tick bite.
    B. Researchers found that 80% of the 5000 people infected with babesiosis were over 12 years old.
    C. Researchers found that 72% of the 5000 people infected with babesiosis had preexisting autoimmune disorders.
    D. Babesiosis occurs in people of all ages.
    E. Very few cases of babesiosis occur in other parts of the United States.

The argument relies on statistics regarding 5000 people in the northeastern United States to conclude that people with autoimmune problems are especially vulnerable to a disease. Since you are asked to locate the answer that most strengthens the argument, the answer must connect autoimmune problems to the disease. Choices A and B, although interesting, do not directly connect autoimmune problems to the disease; therefore, they can be eliminated. Choice C tells us that 72% of the 5000 people infected with babesiosis had preexisting autoimmune disorders, making it the best answer so far. Choices D and E do not connect autoimmune problems to the disease, so they are eliminated. Therefore, choice C is the correct answer. (Exercises 13A and 13E can be used for practice.)

C. Causal Reasoning

Some questions that ask which piece of evidence, if assumed to be true, would most weaken (or strengthen) a given argument rely on *causal reasoning*, the subject of Chapter 14. Simply put, a *cause* is a set of conditions that bring about an effect. A common error is to confuse a *correlation* with *causation*. For example, it is a fact that most people who go swimming wear swimsuits. Also, people tend to put on their swimsuits *before* they go swimming, so there is a strong correlation between the two things. Nevertheless, *correlation does not guarantee causation*. In our example, merely putting on a swimsuit does not cause you to go swimming (you might simply be trying on a new swimsuit in a store). In other words, just because one thing happens before another thing does not guarantee that the first thing caused the second thing. At best, a correlation reveals a *possible* case of causality. Let's look at a few simple examples:

> The lamp in your room does not work. Therefore, the light bulb is defective.

Determine whether the following new information strengthens or weakens the argument.

> **A.** The ceiling light works.

If we assume this information is true, then there is electricity available in the room; thus, the new information *strengthens* the argument. However, suppose we were given this new information instead:

> **B.** The ceiling light does not work.

If we assume this information is true, then perhaps there is no electricity available anywhere in the room; thus, the new information *weakens* the argument.

An LSAT question regarding causality will contain an argument based on some cause-and-effect scenario. If you are asked to pick an answer that will *weaken* the argument, then you are expected to locate an *alternative explanation*—some other cause that could have brought about the effect. Any causal claim can be challenged by suggestions of alternative potential causes. On the other hand, you might be asked to pick an answer that will *strengthen* the argument. If so, then you are expected to locate the answer that either (a) most supports the causal claim offered in the given argument, or (b) best eliminates other alternative explanations.

Questions that rely on causal reasoning can be asked in different ways. Here is an example:

> Shortly after purchasing a new synthetic scarf, Carolyn developed a rash around her neck. She decided to stop wearing the scarf. In a few days, the rash went away. She concluded that she is allergic to the synthetic material used to make the scarf.

Which one of the following, if true, would most weaken the argument?

A. Carolyn had a similar allergic reaction to a sweater that contained synthetic material.
B. On the same day she purchased the scarf, Carolyn ate a new brand of bread that contained an allergen.
C. The scarf manufacturer recommends that you wash the scarf before wearing.
D. Carolyn often wears scarves, especially when it is cold outside.
E. Research has shown that some synthetic materials can cause allergic reactions.

The argument relies on a *conjectured* causal connection between the synthetic material in a new scarf and a rash (an allergic reaction). It offers a correlation—the rash occurred *after* she wore the scarf. Since you are asked to locate the answer that most weakens the argument, the answer must provide an *alternative explanation*—some other cause that could have brought about the effect. Choice A *supports* the conclusion, so it cannot be the correct answer. Choice B provides an alternative explanation (cause) for the rash—the bread contains an allergen that could have brought about the effect. This is the best answer so far. Choice C would be relevant if we knew whether Carolyn washed the scarf before she wore it. Without this additional information, the answer, by itself, doesn't weaken the argument. Choice D does not provide an alternative explanation for the rash, so it can be eliminated. Choice E *supports* the conclusion, so it cannot be the correct answer. Therefore, choice B is the correct answer. Let's analyze another example:

> Jill claims that her longevity (she is 85 years old) is the result of a rigorous exercise program and a healthy diet. Jill had two siblings who died before they reached 50 years of age.

Which one of the following, if true, would most strengthen the argument?

A. Jill and her siblings all lived in different cities throughout their adult lives.
B. All of Jill's siblings liked the same kinds of food as Jill.
C. Jill and her siblings got married before they were 24 years old.
D. Jill's two siblings died from different causes.
E. None of Jill's siblings exercised.

The argument relies on a *conjectured* causal connection between a rigorous exercise program and a healthy diet and Jill's longevity. Since you are asked to locate the answer that most strengthens the argument, the answer must either (a) most support the causal claim offered in the given argument, or (b) best eliminate other alternative explanations. Choice A offers an alternative explanation for Jill's longevity (life expectancy is often different for many cities), which weakens the argument. You can eliminate it. Choice B also weakens the argument since it offers evidence that all the siblings ate similar food; it can be eliminated. Choice C offers a similarity between the siblings, so it doesn't offer an alternative explanation for Jill's longevity; it can be eliminated. Choice D does not provide additional support for Jill's causal claim, and it doesn't tell us how the siblings died (perhaps as the result of accidents), so it can be eliminated. Choice E shows how Jill differed from her siblings in one important way—the rigorous exercise program. Although it doesn't mention anything about a healthy diet, it is the best choice available. Therefore, choice E is the correct answer. (Exercises 14H can be used for practice.)

6. EXPLAINING OR RESOLVING GIVEN INFORMATION

Some questions will *not* contain an argument. Instead, you will be given a few pieces of information that appear to conflict with each other, but which you must assume to be true. Your job is to pick an answer that *explains* or *resolves* the apparent discrepancy between the pieces of information. Let's analyze an example:

> Upon responding to a burglary, Jacob's fingerprints were found at the scene of a crime. However, Jacob's sister testified that Jacob was at her house fifty miles away at the time of the burglary.

Which one of the following, if true, most helps to resolve the apparent discrepancy in the passage?

- **A.** Jacob has never been arrested before for a crime.
- **B.** Jacob's sister is lying to protect Jacob.
- **C.** The burglary took place at a gated community.
- **D.** The police responded to the burglary within 15 minutes of the report.
- **E.** Jacob owns several pairs of gloves.

Remember that you must *assume* that two pieces of information are true: (1) Jacob's fingerprints were found at the scene of a crime, and (2) Jacob's sister testified that Jacob was at her house fifty miles away at the time of the burglary. Your job is to locate the answer that, *if true*, best explains or reconciles (1) and (2). Choice A doesn't explain why Jacob's fingerprints were found at the crime scene, so we can eliminate it. Choice B explains why Jacob's sister's *testified* as she did—*she lied*—and it explains why Jacob's fingerprints were found at the crime scene (he was not fifty miles away), so this is possibly the best answer. Choice C does not explain why Jacob's fingerprints were found at the crime scene, so it is eliminated. Although choice D seems to support the sister's claim that Jacob was fifty miles away (it would be quite difficult for Jacob to travel fifty miles in 15 minutes), nevertheless, it doesn't explain why Jacob's fingerprints were found at the crime scene, nor does choice E. Thus, choice B is the correct answer. Let's analyze another example:

> People whose income places them within the government's guidelines for "living in poverty," are, by definition, those who have the lowest income. However, studies show that this group spends more proportionally on state-run lottery tickets than any other socioeconomic group.

Which one of the following, if true, most helps to resolve the apparent discrepancy in the passage?

- **A.** The federal government should make state-run lotteries unconstitutional.
- **B.** Playing the lottery is a good way to have fun.
- **C.** Many of those living in poverty view winning the lottery as their only hope of getting out of poverty.
- **D.** You have a greater chance of being struck by lightning than winning the lottery.
- **E.** A lot of money is spent on television advertisements for state lotteries.

To solve this problem, we need something that can *reconcile* the (assumed) facts that those in poverty have the lowest incomes, *but* they spend the most (proportionally) on lottery tickets. The answer must explain *why* they spend the little money that they have on lottery tickets. Choice A offers a recommendation but it doesn't explain the actions of people living in poverty, so it is eliminated. Choice B seems to apply to all socioeconomic groups, not just those living in poverty; however, let's leave it for now. Choice C offers an explanation that directly focuses on the actions of those living in poverty, so it is the best choice so far. Choice D also doesn't explain the actions of people living in poverty, so it is eliminated. Choice E can be eliminated because television advertisements are accessible to all socioeconomic groups. Thus, choice C is the correct answer.

7. ARGUMENT FLAWS

Some questions require you to expose the *reasoning flaw* in an argument. These kinds of questions *do not* ask you to determine any factual issues. You simply need to figure out *why the argument is weak*, which is a logical issue, not a factual one. This is different from questions that ask you to choose an answer that would *weaken* an argument. A *flawed-argument* question asks you to choose the answer that correctly describes why the argument is weak.

Some of these questions involve informal fallacies, the subject of Chapter 4, which presents twenty-four fallacies. An *informal fallacy* is a mistake in reasoning that occurs in ordinary language and concerns the content of the argument rather than its form. Informal fallacies include mistakes of relevance, assumption, ambiguity, and diversion. We will mention only a few fallacies here, so you should work through the chapter and answer all the exercise sets; this will give you a good foundation for these types of LSAT questions.

A. Fallacies Based on Personal Attacks or Emotional Appeals

The strength of an argument should be judged on objective grounds. If an argument is based solely on an attack against the person making the argument, not on the merits of the argument itself, then a reasoning flaw occurs and the argument is weak.

The *ad hominem abusive fallacy* is distinguished by an attack on alleged character flaws of a person instead of the person's argument. Generally speaking, a person's character is irrelevant to the determination of the truth or falsity of her claims or the strength of her argument. Here is an example:

> You should not believe what she says about our economy because she is a left-leaning, card-carrying liberal.

An economic argument should be judged on the merits of the advice and strength of the argument presented, not by vague labels denigrating a person's character. The fallacy occurs because it avoids a logical analysis of whether the opponent's arguments are strong or weak. Let's analyze another example:

> You can be sure the senator's tax plan is not going to benefit the country as a whole because he's a multimillionaire and stands to benefit from extending the current tax cuts.

Which of the following most accurately describes a *reasoning flaw* in the argument?

- **A.** Tax increases generally result in a recession.
- **B.** The senator has recently been divorced.
- **C.** The senator is the highest ranking member of his party.
- **D.** Whether someone stands to benefit from his own tax plan does not give a reason why that tax plan will or will not benefit the country as a whole.
- **E.** Most proposed legislation never makes it out of committee.

Since you need to figure out *why the argument is weak*, the key to solving this problem is to see why the *conclusion* ("the senator's tax plan is not going to benefit the country as a whole") is *not* supported by the *single premise* ("he's a multimillionaire and stands to benefit from extending the current tax cuts"). The argument talks about tax cuts, not tax increases, so choice A is irrelevant to the discussion of an argument flaw. Choice B does not pertain to an argument flaw either, so it can be eliminated. Choice C does not directly connect to the conclusion, so it can be eliminated. Choice D shows that the reasoning is flawed; the *premise*, even if true, does not support the *conclusion* because the tax plan may still benefit the country as a whole. Choice E also does not talk about the connection of the premise to the conclusion, so it can be eliminated. Thus, choice D is the correct answer. (Exercises 4B can be used for practice.)

B. Weak Inductive Argument Fallacies

A *generalization* fallacy occurs when an argument relies on a mistaken use of the principles behind making a generalization. For example, it is not unusual for someone to have a negative experience with members of a group and then quickly stereotype the other members by assigning derogatory characteristics to all or most of the group. An argument that relies on a small sample that is unlikely to represent the population commits the *fallacy of hasty generalization*. Here is an example:

> I saw a fraternity guy act rudely to a fast-food employee in the food court. Probably most fraternity and sorority members are rude and arrogant.

The premise reports the observation of a single instance, but the conclusion generalizes the observed behavior to most fraternity *and* sorority members, even though no sorority members were observed. Thus, the conclusion was based on the mistaken belief that a single observation is representative of the entire group. The evidence in this case is not adequate to make such a generalization, so the premise cannot provide a good reason to support the conclusion.

Scientific advances owe much to experiments that verify cause-effect relationships. Science also has methods that confirm the existence of patterns that help us to understand the world and to predict future events. *Fallacies of false cause* occur when a causal connection is assumed to exist between two events when none actually exists, or when the assumed causal connection is unlikely to exist. Since causal claims require strong evidence, a cause-effect claim based on insufficient evidence commits the fallacy of false cause. Here is an example:

> Last week I bought a new car, and today I found out that I am being laid off at work. I shouldn't have bought that car; it brought me bad luck.

The person *incorrectly infers* that buying the new car caused him to be laid off. The fallacious reasoning relies on the *mistaken causal assumption* that simply because X occurred *before* Y, therefore X *caused* Y. Let's analyze an example:

> The Dow Jones Industrial Average surged by 200 points this afternoon. This proves my theory that the stock market is sensitive to solar activity, because there was a substantial solar flare this morning.

Which of the following most accurately describes a *reasoning flaw* in the argument?

- **A.** The argument uses the sun as an analogy to explain the Dow surge.
- **B.** The argument is based on the authority of the stock market.
- **C.** No mechanism is offered for a causal link between the sun and the stock market, so this is best classified as a coincidence.
- **D.** The argument begs the question because the evidence for the conclusion is already smuggled into the premises.
- **E.** Since the argument uses terms that change in the premises and the conclusion, the argument suffers from the fallacy of equivocation.

Since you need to figure out *why the argument is weak*, the key to solving this problem is to see why the *conclusion* ("This proves my theory that the stock market is sensitive to solar activity") is *not* supported by the *premises* ("The Dow Jones Industrial Average surged by 200 points this afternoon"; "there was a substantial solar flare this morning"). Since the argument makes a *causal claim* (the solar flare caused the Dow to surge), the answer must hit on this point. Choice A claims the flaw is based on an *analogy*, but the argument involves a cause-effect claim, so this choice is incorrect. Choice B claims the argument is based on *authority*, but again, the argument involves a cause-effect claim, thus eliminating this choice. Choice C identifies that the argument does not offer a plausible mechanism for the conjectured causal link, making it the best choice so far. Choice D claims the argument *begs the question*, while choice E claims the argument is flawed because of *equivocation*, but since we know the argument involves a cause-effect claim, both choices can be eliminated. Thus, choice C is the correct answer. (Exercises 4C can be used for practice.)

C. Fallacies of Unwarranted Assumption or Diversion

Fallacies of unwarranted assumption exhibit a special kind of reasoning error: They assume the truth of some unproved or questionable claim. The fallacies become apparent when the assumptions and lack of support are exposed, thus revealing the weak points of the argument.

Arguments often rely on the opinions of experts, specialists whose education, experience, and knowledge provide relevant support for a claim. When an argument uses expert testimony that is backed by strong evidence with no hint of impropriety, then the argument is most likely strong (as long as the testimony falls within the realm of the expert's field). On the other hand, arguments that rely on the opinions of people who either have *no* expertise, training, or knowledge relevant to the issue at hand, or whose testimony is not trustworthy, are arguments that **appeal to an unqualified authority**. Here is an example:

> I'm Nick Panning, quarterback of the Los Angeles Seals. I've been eating *Oaties* for breakfast since I was a kid. *Oaties* taste great, and they have all the nutrition kids need. You should get some for your kids today.

Appeal to an unqualified authority An argument that relies on the opinions of people who either have *no* expertise, training, or knowledge relevant to the issue at hand, or whose testimony is not trustworthy.

Merely being famous does not qualify someone to pronounce the merits of a product. An athlete generally has no expertise in the nutritional value of a breakfast cereal. On the other hand, a person with a Ph.D. in nutrition would presumably be in a good position to offer a fair assessment of the breakfast cereal (provided the opinion is not based on monetary compensation). Let's analyze the following example:

> Given its voracious appetite, a great white shark eats more than any person does. Additionally, great white sharks are more massive than adult humans. Therefore, it follows that great white sharks as a whole consume more food than human beings do.

Which of the following most accurately describes a *reasoning flaw* in the argument?

- **A.** The argument assumes a causal link between shark size and how much food it consumes.
- **B.** Just because individual sharks eat more than people do, it does not mean sharks as a whole eat more than humans do. There are many more people than there are sharks.
- **C.** The argument relies on a false analogy between sharks and humans.
- **D.** The argument generalizes from one shark to all sharks; it overlooks the possibility that some sharks eat less than some humans.
- **E.** A red herring is smuggled into the premises; this results in attention being diverted from the apparent false conclusion.

Since you need to figure out *why the argument is weak*, the key to solving this problem is to see why the *conclusion* ("great white sharks *as a whole* consume more food than human beings do") is *not* supported by the *premises* ("a great white shark eats more than any person";

"great white sharks are more massive than adult humans"). From evidence about the *individual members of two groups*, the argument concludes with a statement about the *groups as a whole*. In other words, it assumes that the two groups in question have the same number of members. Choice A claims the flaw is based on a faulty causal link, but it is not a causal argument so it can be eliminated. Choice B correctly points out that although an individual shark eats more than an individual person, there are many more people than there are sharks, making it the best answer so far. Choice C claims the flaw is based on a false analogy, but it is not an analogical argument so it can be eliminated. Choice D misses the point of the conclusion, which talks about two groups, sharks and humans, so it can be eliminated. Choice E claims the argument is flawed because of a red herring fallacy, but because this not what occurs in the argument, it is eliminated. Thus, choice B is the correct answer. (Exercises 4D can be used for practice.)

8. RECOGNIZING REASONING PATTERNS

Some questions will ask you to choose the answer that *mirrors* the reasoning pattern of a given argument. To do so, you must know how to *identify* reasoning patterns. Learning to symbolize the *logical form* (structure) of the argument by substituting capital letters for either *class terms* or *statements* in the argument can help you answer these types of questions. The techniques required for these skills are presented in Chapters 1, 5, and 7.

A. Class Terms

Here are two examples that use class terms:

A. All *dogs* are *mammals*.   **B.** All *mammals* are *dogs*.
All *beagles* are *dogs*.   All *beagles* are *dogs*.
All *beagles* are *mammals*.   All *beagles* are *mammals*.

For the purposes of our analysis, we italicized the *class terms* in the argument. Remember that when taking the LSAT, you will *not* be asked to determine whether the statements are true or false. Any time spent thinking about this shortens the time you have to identify the correct answer. Additionally, *it does not matter whether either argument A or B is valid or invalid*. All you need to do is identify the reasoning pattern. To do this, use capital letters to represent *class terms*; for example, D = *dogs*, M = *mammals*, and B = *beagles*.

A. All D are M.   **B.** All M are D.
All B are D.   All B are D.
All B are M.   All B are M.

Once you reveal the given argument's pattern, you simply have to identify which of the five choices mirrors that reasoning pattern. Let's analyze an example.

> Some ingredients in soap are things known to cause cancer. Some ingredients in hair shampoo are things known to cause cancer. It follows that some ingredients in soap are the same as some ingredients in hair shampoo.

Which of the following exhibits a reasoning pattern that is most similar to the argument?

   A. Some vegetables are low-calorie foods. Most low-calorie foods are organic plants. It follows that most vegetables are organic plants.

   B. Some vegetables are low-calorie foods. All low-calorie foods are organic plants. Thus, most vegetables are organic plants.

   C. Nearly all vegetables are organic plants. That's because some vegetables are low-calorie foods, and some organic plants are low-calorie foods.

   D. Some vegetables are low-calorie foods, and some organic plants are low-calorie foods. So, no vegetables are organic plants.

   E. Some vegetables are organic plants. That's because some vegetables are low-calorie foods, and some organic plants are low-calorie foods.

To solve this problem, we must identify the reasoning pattern in the given argument. Let's start by substituting letters for the terms: S = *ingredients in soap*, C = *things known to cause cancer*, and H = *ingredients in hair shampoo*:

   Some S are C. Some H are C. *It follows that* some S are H.

We italicized "It follows that" to emphasize that it is a *conclusion indicator phrase*. It is important to note that the answer *may have* a different conclusion indicator word or phrase, such as "thus" or "therefore," which will *not* affect the overall reasoning pattern. Also, the answer *may have* the conclusion appear first instead of last. Again, this will *not* affect the overall reasoning pattern because it doesn't matter where the conclusion appears. However, to make it easier to find the correct answer you could reconstruct the arguments in the five answers so the conclusion occurs last as it does in the given argument.

   Choice A uses the word "most," which means more than 50%, instead of the word "some," which means "at least one," making this a crucial difference; thus, this choice is eliminated. Choice B uses the word "all" instead of the word "some" which is also a crucial difference; thus, this choice is eliminated. Choice C uses the phrase "nearly all" instead of the word "some" and Choice D uses the word "no," both of which make a crucial difference, so these choices are eliminated. In choice E, the conclusion comes first, but if we reconstruct the argument, then we can see that it has the same reasoning pattern as the given argument. Therefore, choice E is the correct answer. (Exercises 1F.I can be used for practice.)

B. Conditional Statements

So far, we have been using letters to represent class terms (for example, D = *dogs*). We can now expand this technique to different types of statements. Let's compare the following two examples:

   H. All *pizza toppings* are *delicious morsels*.

   I. If *Sherry lives in Los Angeles*, then *Sherry lives in California*.

In example H, the two italicized words are *class terms*, which *by themselves* are neither true nor false. However, the two italicized parts of example I are *statements* that are either true or false (we call them *simple statements*). In addition, example I contains the logical vocabulary words "if" and "then." Taken as a whole, example I is a *compound statement* and it, too, is either true or false. We can use letters to represent the simple statements in example I while keeping the logical vocabulary in place. For example, if we let *L = Sherry lives in Los Angeles* and *C = Sherry lives in California*, then we get the following for example I: If *L*, then *C*.

C. Translating Conditional Statements

A thorough grasp of conditional statements can help you navigate many LSAT questions. As we discussed, it is important to avoid thinking about whether LSAT question statements are true or false, and having a technique for translating conditional statements using simple symbols can help. We use the horseshoe symbol ($\supset$) to translate conditional statements. For example, the ordinary language statement "If you smoke two packs of cigarettes a day, then you have a high risk of getting lung cancer" can be translated as $S \supset L$, with *S = you smoke two packs of cigarettes a day*, and *L = you have a high risk of getting lung cancer*. When you read the ordinary language statement, the *meaning* of the statement might tempt you to think about whether it is true or false. However, when you read the symbolic translation consisting of only two letters and a symbol, the meaning of the statement or whether it is true or false does not distract you.

The statement that follows "if" is the *antecedent*, and the statement that follows "then" is the *consequent*. Therefore, whatever phrase follows "if" must be placed *first* in the translation. Here are two examples to illustrate this point:

- If you wash the car, then you can go to the movies. $W \supset M$
- You can go to the movies, if you wash the car. $W \supset M$

The word "if" immediately reveals the existence of a conditional statement, making it a clear indicator word. There are additional English words and phrases that can indicate a conditional statement. For example, consider this statement: "Whenever it snows, my water pipes freeze," which can be translated as $S \supset F$. (Chapter 7 presents more words and phrases that indicate conditionals.) Learning to recognize conditional statements makes the task of translation easier.

Another important technique that can help you analyze some LSAT questions is to understand that two kinds of statements that use *class terms* can be translated as *conditional statements*. The first type of *categorical* statement uses the word "all" (see Chapter 5 for more details regarding categorical statements). For example, the statement "*All* scientists *are* people trained in mathematics" can be translated as "*If* a person is a scientist, *then* that person is trained in mathematics." Likewise, the statement "*All* unicorns *are* mammals" can be translated as "*If* something is a unicorn, *then* that thing is a mammal." The second type of *categorical* statement uses the word "no." For example, the statement "*No* slackers *are* reliable workers" is translated as "*If* a person is a slacker, *then* that person is not a reliable worker." (We will see these types of translations in action later in section F.)

D. Distinguishing "If" from "Only If"

As discussed in Chapter 7, section 7A, the word "if" precedes the *antecedent* of a conditional, while "only if" precedes the *consequent* of a conditional. Here are some examples:

- You will get the bonus only if you finish by noon. $B \supset F$
  (B = *You will get the bonus,* and F = *you finish by noon.*)
- Only if she has a 10% down payment will she get a mortgage. $M \supset P$
  (M = *she will get a mortgage,* and P = *she has a 10% down payment.*)

E. Conditionals and Arguments

We can apply the translating techniques to understand and analyze arguments that use conditional statements. For example:

Argument J:	Argument Form:
If Sherry lives in Los Angeles, then Sherry lives in California.	$L \supset C$
<u>Sherry lives in California.</u>	<u>C</u>
Sherry lives in Los Angeles.	L

At this stage, the most important thing to recognize is that a conditional statement *does not assert* that either the antecedent or the consequent is true. What is asserted is that *if* the antecedent is true, *then* the consequent is true. Given this understanding of a conditional statement, we can start by assuming that the first premise is true. Why? Because it *does not assert* that Sherry actually lives in Los Angeles, it just asserts that *if* she lives in Los Angeles, then she lives in California. Next, let's assume that the second premise is also true (Sherry lives in California). We can now ask: Does the conclusion follow necessarily from the two premises? No, because it is *possible* that Sherry lives in San Francisco. Thus, argument J is invalid. The *argument form* for argument J is referred to as the *fallacy of affirming the consequent.* It is a *formal fallacy,* a logical error that occurs in the form of an argument. Formal fallacies are restricted to *deductive* arguments. (Formal fallacies are discussed in Chapters 1, and 6–8.) Let's look at another argument.

Argument K:	Argument Form:
If Sherry lives in Los Angeles, then Sherry lives in California.	$L \supset C$
<u>Sherry lives in Los Angeles.</u>	<u>L</u>
Sherry lives in California.	C

Relying on our understanding of a conditional statement, we can analyze argument K. As with argument J, we can start by assuming that the first premise is true. Now, *if* the second premise is true, then the conclusion follows necessarily from the premises. Thus, argument K is valid. The *argument form* for argument K is referred to as *modus ponens.* In order to fully appreciate this result, we need to understand that since argument K is valid, no counterexample exists. This is an important claim, and we will explain it with the apparatus we currently have.

We were able to create a counterexample to Argument J by recognizing that even if both premises were true, it is possible that the conclusion is false (that Sherry lives in

San Francisco). Let's try that with argument K. As before, we can assume that the first premise is true. Now if we assume that the second premise is true, then the conclusion follows necessarily. (You can learn about different methods for demonstrating validity, as well as other methods for showing invalidity, in Part III, "Formal Logic.")

Let's look at a few more examples. To do this, we need to introduce a new symbol, "~" which stands for "not" or "it is not the case that." We use this when we want to negate a given statement. For example, we can symbolize the statement "Today is Monday" as M, and its negation, "Today is not Monday" as $\sim M$.

Argument M:	Argument Form:
If Sherry lives in Los Angeles, then Sherry lives in California.	$L \supset C$
<u>Sherry does not live in Los Angeles.</u>	$\sim L$
Sherry does not live in California.	$\sim C$

We have been using "L" to represent the simple statement "Sherry lives in Los Angeles." In order to represent the statement "Sherry does *not* live in Los Angeles," we place the phrase "It is not the case that" in front of "L." Similarly, we have been using "C" to represent the simple statement "Sherry lives in California." In order to represent the statement "Sherry does *not* live in California," we place the phrase "It is not the case that" in front of "C."

Let's analyze argument M. We can start by assuming that the two premises are true. Does the conclusion follow necessarily from the two premises? No, because it is possible that Sherry lives in San Francisco. Thus, argument M is invalid. The *argument form* for argument M is referred to as the *fallacy of denying the antecedent*, and it is a *formal fallacy*. Here is another example:

Argument N:	Argument Form:
If Sherry lives in Los Angeles, then Sherry lives in California.	$L \supset C$
<u>Sherry does not live in California.</u>	$\sim C$
Sherry does not live in Los Angeles.	$\sim L$

Let's analyze argument N. We can start by assuming that the premises are true. Given this, the conclusion follows necessarily from the premises. Thus, argument N is valid. The *argument form* for argument N is referred to as *modus tollens*. Since argument N is valid, no counterexample exists. Let's look at one more example.

Argument P:	Argument Form:
If Sherry lives in Los Angeles, then Sherry lives in California.	$L \supset C$
<u>If Sherry lives in California, then Sherry lives in the United States.</u>	$C \supset U$
If Sherry lives in Los Angeles, then Sherry lives in the United States.	$L \supset U$

Let's analyze argument P. We start by assuming that the premises are true. Given this, the conclusion follows necessarily from the premises. Thus, argument P is valid. The *argument form* for argument P is referred to as *hypothetical syllogism*. Since argument P is valid, no counterexample exists.

Let's see if you can determine whether the following argument (a) has a flaw (invalid) or (b) has no flaw (valid). Try translating the argument using symbols, then refer back to the different argument forms that we discussed. Work out your answer before reading the analysis that follows. Here is the argument:

Argument Q:

I will buy you dinner if you clean my room. You did not clean my room, so I will not buy you dinner.

The first step is the translation. If we let C = *you clean my room* and D = *I'll buy you dinner*, then here is the argument form:

$$C \supset D$$

$$\underline{\sim C}$$

$$\sim D$$

You might have recognized this as an instance of the *fallacy of denying the antecedent.* If so, then you know that it is an invalid argument. (Exercises 1F.II can be used for practice.) However, we can add to our understanding of the argument flaw by introducing some new logical concepts, the subject of the next section.

F. Sufficient and Necessary Conditions

The first premise of the previous argument Q, "I will buy you dinner if you clean my room," claims that cleaning the room will lead to dinner. But what the premise *does not* claim is that cleaning the room is the *only way* to get dinner. This is a crucial difference. If the premise had been "I will buy you dinner *only if* you clean my room," then it would be translated as "$D \supset C$" instead of "$C \supset D$." If so, then the argument would have been valid (it would be an instance of *modus tollens*). This illustrates how apparently simple differences can dramatically change the strength of an argument.

We can now use our basic understanding of conditional statements to explore two important concepts: *sufficient and necessary conditions* (see Chapters 7, 11, and 14.) To begin our discussion, consider this statement:

A. If you live in New Jersey, then you live in the United States. $N \supset U$

Let's look at the relationship between the antecedent and the consequent in the foregoing statement. If it is true that you live in New Jersey, then it is true that you live in the United States. In other words, living in New Jersey is *sufficient* for living in the United States. Of course, if you live in any of the other forty-nine states, then you also live in the United States. A *sufficient condition* occurs whenever one event ensures that another event is realized. In other words, the truth of the antecedent guarantees the truth of the consequent. The principle behind a sufficient condition can be captured by the phrases "is enough for" or "guarantees." Here is another example of a sufficient condition:

B. If my car engine starts, then I have gasoline. $S \supset G$

Of course, we must stipulate that it is not an electric car (the car needs gasoline to start and run). Given this stipulation, if the antecedent is true, then the consequent is true. Consider the next example:

C. If my dog is a poodle, then today is Monday. $P \supset M$

If the antecedent is true, it would *not* guarantee that the consequent is true. Therefore, this is not an example of a sufficient condition.

Suppose that the law of the state in which you are driving states that anyone caught driving with a blood alcohol level above 0.08% will be subject to a citation for driving while intoxicated (DWI) or, in some states, driving under the influence (DUI). If you are stopped by the police and agree to take a breath-analyzer test, then the following indicates a sufficient condition:

If your blood alcohol level exceeds 0.08%, then you are cited for DWI.

In other words, anyone caught driving with a blood alcohol level above 0.08% has met a *sufficient condition* for being issued a citation for DWI. Compare these results with a new case:

If you are cited for DWI, then your blood alcohol level exceeds 0.08%.

Even though it might be true that you were cited for a DWI, this is *not sufficient* information to determine that your blood alcohol level exceeds 0.08%. You might have refused to take a breath-analyzer test, so your blood alcohol level was not determined. Or you might have been given a variety of field sobriety tests, such as walking a straight line and turning, standing on one foot, or closing your eyes and touching the tip of your nose. If in the officer's opinion you failed the field sobriety test, then you may have been cited for DWI.

In contrast, a *necessary condition* means that one thing is *essential*, *mandatory*, or *required* in order for another thing to be realized. Consider this statement from earlier:

D. If you live in New Jersey, then you live in the United States. $N \supset U$

You cannot live in New Jersey unless you live in the United States. Given this, we can say that living in the United States is a *necessary condition* for living in New Jersey. If you *do not* live in the United States, then you *do not* live in New Jersey. This can also be written using the phrase "only if":

E. You live in New Jersey *only if* you live in the United States. $N \supset U$

It is important to remember that a necessary condition exists when the falsity of the consequent ensures the falsity of the antecedent. Here is another example of a necessary condition:

F. My car engine starts only if I have gasoline. $S \supset G$

Once again, we stipulate that my car needs gasoline to start and run. Given this, we can see that having gasoline is a necessary condition for my car engine to start. Of course, there are many other things that are necessary for my car engine to start, such as a battery, spark plugs, and ignition wires, to name only a few. So, although gasoline is not the only necessary condition for my car engine to start, it is definitely required.

This example also illustrates the fact that in many real-life circumstances multiple necessary conditions are required to bring something about. The principle behind a necessary condition can be captured by the words "mandatory," "essential," and the phrase "is required for." Let's look at one more example:

> **G.** If my dog is a poodle, then today is Monday. $P \supset M$

If the consequent is false, then the antecedent might be true or false. Therefore, this is *not* an example of a necessary condition.

The word "cause" has several meanings, and in everyday situations the possibility of ambiguity arises. For example, parents often tell their children that they must take vitamins because vitamins will help them grow. The claim is not that vitamins alone will cause children to grow; it is that vitamins are a *necessary condition* for children's growth. In another situation, a child might complain of a stomachache. The parent could suggest that the child stop drinking so much soda. Of course, the parent could also give the child some medicine to ease the pain. The parent relies on an understanding that several methods of reducing or eliminating the stomachache are possible. In other words, the parent is offering a *sufficient condition* to bring about a desired effect. A basic knowledge of sufficient and necessary conditions can help in the overall understanding and analysis of causal arguments. Here is an example for analysis:

> All acids are carbon-based compounds. Stignoric is a carbon-based compound, so it is an acid.

It doesn't matter whether you know if any of the statements that make up the argument are true or false. All you need to do is determine the *reasoning process*, which you can do if you translate the statements using symbols. The first premise, "All acids are carbon-based compounds" can be translated as a conditional: If *A* then *C*. The second premise, "Stignoric is a carbon-based compound" can be translated as: *S* is a *C*. The conclusion, "it (Stignoric) is an acid," can be translated as: *S* is an *A*.

The flaw is in mistaking a necessary condition for a sufficient condition. The first premise, if true, tells us that being a carbon-based compound is a necessary condition for being an acid; in other words, something cannot be an acid unless it is carbon-based. What the first premise *does not assert* is that all carbon-based compounds are acids. But that is exactly what the conclusion asserts, so that is where the flaw occurs.

Let's put all this together and analyze another example. Suppose you were given this argument question on the LSAT:

> John deposited a check for $1 million into his bank account. Thus, he won the lottery.

The conclusion follows logically if which one of the following is assumed?

> **A.** If anyone wins the lottery, then he deposits a check for $1 million into his bank account.
> **B.** All millionaires make bank deposits.
> **C.** You must have a bank account in order to make a deposit of $1 million.

D. John has always been a lucky person.
E. If anyone deposits a check for $1 million into his bank account, then he won the lottery.

The key to solving this problem is to recognize that the missing information has to connect two things: (1) depositing a check for $1 million and (2) winning the lottery. It is also important to suspend your judgment as to whether any of the information is actually true. Choice A sounds appealing. However, if we symbolize the argument using this choice we get the following: *L = anyone wins the lottery* and *D = he deposits a check for $1 million into his bank account*. Given this, the argument form is $L \supset D, D$, thus L. Since this is an invalid argument form (*affirming the consequent*), the conclusion *does not follow logically*, so it can't be the correct answer. Choices B, C, and D cannot be correct because they fail to connect the bank deposit to winning the lottery. Choice E is a conditional statement that has what we need. The *antecedent* connects depositing a check for $1 million to the *consequent* winning the lottery. It creates the valid argument form *modus ponens*, so the conclusion follows logically. (Exercises 7A.II and 7A.III can be used for practice.)

9. CONTINUING THE PROCESS

In order to continue the process begun with this short guide, you should go through the relevant chapters of *Logic* mentioned along the way. The text of each chapter will provide clear definitions, explanations, and examples of the kinds of skills needed for the LSAT *logical reasoning* sections. You should also do as many of the exercise sets as possible. Although the chapter exercise sets were not created to mirror the way LSAT questions are written, they do apply the basic *reasoning principles* on which the logical reasoning sections of the LSAT rely. The exercises also provide direct application of the important logical skills, which will sharpen and focus your ability to analyze LSAT questions.

Glossary

A

A priori theory of probability Ascribes to a simple event a fraction between 0 and 1.

A-proposition A categorical proposition having the form "All S are P."

Abduction The process that occurs when we infer explanations for certain facts.

Abnormal state A drastic change in the normal state regarding an object.

Ad hominem abusive The fallacy is distinguished by an attack on alleged character flaws of a person instead of the person's argument.

Ad hominem circumstantial When someone's argument is rejected based on the circumstances of the person's life.

Addition (Add) A rule of inference (implication rule).

Affidavit A written statement signed before an authorized official.

Affirmative conclusion/negative premise A formal fallacy that occurs when a categorical syllogism has a negative premise and an affirmative conclusion.

Algorithm A set of instructions that includes a step-by-step procedure designed to go consistently from a starting point to an end point.

Analogical argument The argument lists the characteristics that two (or more) things have in common and concludes that the things being compared probably have some other characteristic in common.

Analogical reasoning One of the most fundamental tools used in creating an argument. It can be analyzed as a type of inductive argument—it is a matter of probability, based on experience, and it can be quite persuasive.

Analogy To draw an analogy is simply to indicate that there are similarities between two or more things.

Anchoring bias This occurs when our reliance on one piece of information about a subject (often the first thing we hear or learn) affects our subsequent thinking.

Appeal to an unqualified authority An argument that relies on the opinions of people who either have *no* expertise, training, or knowledge relevant to the issue at hand, or whose testimony is not trustworthy.

Appeal to fear or force A threat of harmful consequences (physical or otherwise) used to force acceptance of a course of action that would otherwise be unacceptable.

Appeal to ignorance An argument built on a position of ignorance claims either that (1) a statement must be true because it has not been proven to be false or (2) a statement must be false because it has not been proven to be true.

Appeal to pity The fallacy results from an exclusive reliance on a sense of pity or mercy for support of a conclusion.

Appeal to the people The fallacy occurs when an argument manipulates a psychological need or desire, such as the desire to belong to a popular group, or the need for group solidarity, so that the reader or listener will accept the conclusion.

Appellate courts of appeal that review the decisions of lower courts.

Argument A group of statements in which the conclusion is claimed to follow from the premise(s).

Argument form (1) In categorical logic, an argument form is an arrangement of logical vocabulary and letters that stand for class terms such that a uniform substitution of class terms for the letters results in an argument. (2) In propositional logic, an argument form is an arrangement of logical operators and statement variables.

Association (Assoc) A rule of inference (replacement rule).

Asymmetrical relationship Illustrated by the following: If A is the father of B, then B is not the father of A.

Availability bias The degree to which the memory is affected by its emotional impact on us might cause us to *unconsciously overestimate* the probability of it occurring again.

B

Begging the question In one type, the fallacy occurs when a premise is simply reworded in the conclusion. In a second type, called *circular reasoning*, a set of statements seem to support each other with no clear beginning or end point. In a third type, the argument assumes certain key information that may be controversial or is not supported by facts.

Belief bias When we judge the *strength* of an argument by focusing simply on whether we think the conclusion is true, or whether it fits with our values or beliefs.

Biased sample An argument that uses a nonrepresentative sample as support for a statistical claim about an entire population.

Biconditional A compound statement consisting of two conditionals—one indicated by the word "if" and the other indicated by the phrase "only if." The triple bar symbol is used to translate a biconditional statement.

Bound variables Variables governed by a quantifier.

C

Categorical imperative The basic idea is that your actions or behavior toward others should always be such that you would want everyone to act in the same manner.

Categorical proposition A proposition that relates two classes of objects. It either affirms or denies total class inclusion, or else it affirms or denies partial class inclusion.

Categorical syllogism A syllogism constructed entirely of categorical propositions.

Causal network A set of conditions that bring about an effect.

Change of quantifier (CQ) The rule allows the removal or introduction of negation signs. (The rule is a set of four logical equivalences.)

Class A group of objects.

Cogent argument An inductive argument is cogent when the argument is strong and the premises are true.

Cognitive biases The factors that diminish our ability to interpret information, form judgments, make predictions, arrive at decisions, and evaluate arguments.

Cognitive meaning Language that is used to convey information has cognitive meaning.

Commutation (Com) A rule of inference (replacement rule).

Complement The set of objects that do not belong to a given class.

Complex question The fallacy occurs when a single question actually contains multiple parts and an unestablished hidden assumption.

Composition There are two forms of the fallacy: (1) the mistaken transfer of an attribute of the individual *parts of an object* to the *object as a whole* and (2) the mistaken transfer of an attribute of the individual *members of a class* to the *class itself.*

Compound statement A statement that has at least one simple statement and at least one logical operator as components.

Conclusion The statement that is claimed to follow from the premises of an argument; the main point of an argument.

Conclusion indicators Words and phrases that indicate the presence of a conclusion (the statement claimed to follow from premises).

Conditional probability The calculation of the probability that one event will occur given the knowledge that another event has already occurred.

Conditional proof (CP) A method that starts by assuming the antecedent of a conditional statement on a separate line and then proceeds to validly derive the consequent on a separate line.

Conditional statement In ordinary language, the word "if" typically precedes the *antecedent* of a conditional, and the statement that follows the word "then" is referred to as the *consequent.*

Confirmation bias The habit of seeking out information that supports our existing beliefs and avoiding or rejecting information that might undermine those beliefs.

Conjunction A compound statement that has two distinct statements (called *conjuncts*) connected by the dot symbol.

Conjunction (Conj) A rule of inference (implication rule).

Consequentialism A class of moral theories in which the moral value of any human action or behavior is determined exclusively by its outcomes.

Consistent statements Two (or more) statements that have at least one line on their respective truth tables where the main operators are true.

Constructive dilemma (CD) A rule of inference (implication rule).

Contingent statements Statements that are neither necessarily true nor necessarily false (they are sometimes true, sometimes false).

Contradictories In categorical logic, pairs of propositions in which one is the negation of the other.

Contradictory statements Two statements that have opposite truth values under the main operator on every line of their respective truth tables.

Contraposition An immediate argument formed by replacing the subject term of a given proposition with the complement of its predicate term, and then replacing the predicate term of the given proposition with the complement of its subject term.

Contraposition by limitation Subalternation is used to change a universal E-proposition into its corresponding particular O-proposition. We then apply the regular process of forming a contrapositive to this O-proposition.

Contraries Pairs of propositions that cannot both be true at the same time, but can both be false at the same time.

Control group The group in which the variable being tested is withheld.

Controlled experiment One in which multiple experimental setups differ by only one variable.

Convergent diagram A diagram that reveals the occurrence of independent premises.

Conversion An immediate argument formed by interchanging the subject and predicate terms of a given categorical proposition.

Conversion by limitation We first change a universal **A**-proposition into its corresponding particular **I**-proposition, and then we use the process of conversion on the **I**-proposition.

Copula The words "are" and "are not" are referred to as copula; they are simply forms of "to be" and serve to link (to "couple") the subject class with the predicate class.

Correlation A correspondence between two sets of objects, events, or data.

Counteranalogy A new, competing argument—one that compares the thing in question to something else.

Counterexample A counterexample to a statement is evidence that shows the statement is false. A counterexample to an argument shows that the conclusion does not follow necessarily from the premises. A single counterexample to a deductive argument is enough to show that the argument is invalid.

D

De Morgan (DM) A rule of inference (replacement rule).

Decreasing extension A sequence of terms in which each term after the first denotes a set of objects with fewer members than the previous term.

Decreasing intension A sequence of terms in which each term after the first connotes fewer attributes than the previous term.

Deductive argument An argument in which the inferential claim is that the conclusion follows *necessarily* from the premises. In other words, under the *assumption* that the premises are true it is *impossible* for the conclusion to be false.

Definiendum Refers to that which is being defined.

Definiens Refers to that which does the defining.

Definite description Describes an individual person, place, or thing.

Definition A definition assigns a meaning to a word, phrase, or symbol.

Definition by genus and difference Assigns a meaning to a term (the species) by establishing a genus and combining it with the attribute that distinguishes the members of that species.

Definition by subclass Assigns meaning to a term by naming subclasses (species) of the class denoted by the term.

Deontology The theory that duty to others is the first and foremost moral consideration.

Dependent premises Premises are dependent when they work together to support a conclusion. In other words, the falsity of one dependent premise weakens the support that the other dependent premises give to the conclusion.

Disanalogies To point out differences between two things.

Disjunction A compound statement that has two distinct statements (called *disjuncts*) connected by the wedge symbol.

Disjunctive syllogism (DS) A rule of inference (implication rule).

Distributed If a categorical proposition asserts something about every member of a class, then the term designating that class is said to be distributed.

Distribution (Dist) A rule of inference (replacement rule).

Divergent diagram A diagram that shows a single premise supporting independent conclusions.

Division There are two forms of the fallacy: (1) the mistaken transfer of an attribute of an *object as a whole* to the individual *parts of the object* and (2) the mistaken transfer of an attribute of a *class* to the individual *members of the class*.

Domain of discourse The set of individuals over which a quantifier ranges.

Double negation (DN) A rule of inference (replacement rule).

E

E-proposition A categorical proposition having the form "No S are P."

Egoism The basic principle that everyone should act in order to maximize his or her own individual pleasure or happiness.

Emotive meaning Language that is used to express emotion or feelings has emotive meaning.

Emotivism A theory that asserts that moral value judgments are merely expressions of our attitudes or emotions.

Empty class A class that has zero members.

Enthymemes Arguments with missing premises, missing conclusions, or both.

Enumerative definition Assigns meaning to a term by naming the individual members of the class denoted by the term.

Equiprobable When each of the possible outcomes has an equal probability of occurring.

Equivocation The fallacy occurs when the conclusion of an argument relies on an intentional or unintentional shift in the meaning of a term or phrase in the premises.

Exceptive propositions Statements that need to be translated into compound statements containing the word "and" (for example, propositions that take the form "All except S are P" and "All but S are P").

Exclusive disjunction When we assert that *at least one* disjunct is true, but *not* both. In other words, we assert that the truth of one *excludes* the truth of the other. Given this, an exclusive disjunction is true when only one of the disjuncts is true; otherwise it is false.

Exclusive premises A formal fallacy that occurs when both premises in a categorical syllogism are negative.

Existential fallacy A formal fallacy that occurs when a categorical syllogism has a particular conclusion and two universal premises.

Existential generalization (EG) A rule that permits the valid introduction of an existential quantifier from either a constant or a variable.

Existential import A proposition has existential import if it presupposes the existence of certain kinds of objects.

Existential instantiation (EI) A rule that permits giving a name to a thing that exists. The name can then be represented by a constant.

Existential quantifier Formed by putting a backward E in front of a variable, and then placing them both in parentheses.

Experimental group The group that gets the variable being tested.

Experimental science Tests the explanations proposed by theoretical science.

Explanation An explanation provides reasons for why or how an event occurred. By themselves, explanations are not arguments; however, they can form part of an argument.

Exportation (Exp) A rule of inference (replacement rule).

Extension The class or collection of objects to which the term applies. In other words, what the term denotes (its reference).

Extensional definition Assigns meaning to a term by indicating the class members denoted by the term.

F

Factual dispute Occurs when people disagree on a matter that involves facts.

Fallacy of affirming the consequent An invalid argument form; it is a formal fallacy.

Fallacy of denying the antecedent An invalid argument form; it is a formal fallacy.

False dichotomy A fallacy that occurs when it is assumed that only two choices are possible, when in fact others exist.

Figure The middle term can be arranged in the two premises in four different ways. These placements determine the figure of the categorical syllogism.

Finite universe method The method of demonstrating invalidity that assumes a universe, containing at least one individual, to show the possibility of true premises and a false conclusion.

Formal fallacy A logical error that occurs in the form or structure of an argument; it is restricted to deductive arguments.

Free variables Variables that are not governed by any quantifier.

Frequency bias This occurs when we make a mistaken judgment regarding the extent to which something exists based on recent experience.

Functional definition Specifies the purpose or use of the objects denoted by the term.

Functional fixedness bias The tendency to judge certain familiar objects as having only one particular use or function. This results from our seeing the world through a narrow lens.

Fundamental attribution bias This bias manifests itself in situations in which we take *full credit* for something good that happened to us, while in other situations we look for *excuses* to explain why something bad happened to us.

G

Gambling biases When judging future outcomes, we naturally rely on past results. However, in certain circumstances involving judgment about probabilities, we repeatedly make very basic mistakes.

General conjunction method The method that is used for calculating the probability of two or more events occurring together, regardless of whether the events are independent.

General disjunction method The method that is used for calculating the probability when two or more events are not mutually exclusive.

H

Halo bias This bias occurs when our *specific* judgments or ratings of a person's abilities, skills, or characteristics are the result of the *overall impression* we have of that person.

Hasty generalization An argument that relies on a small sample that is unlikely to represent the population.

Heuristic From the Greek language meaning "to discover, or to find out." The general idea is that it is a natural way to make decisions, one that draws on personal experience.

Hypothesis Provides an explanation for known facts and a way to test an explanation.

Hypothetical syllogism (HS) A rule of inference (implication rule).

I

I-proposition A categorical proposition having the form "Some S are P."

Identity relation A binary relation that holds between a thing and itself.

Illicit major A formal fallacy that occurs when the major term in a categorical syllogism is distributed in the conclusion but not in the major premise.

Illicit minor A formal fallacy that occurs when the minor term in a categorical syllogism is distributed in the conclusion but not in the minor premise.

Immediate argument An argument that has only one premise.

Implication rules Valid argument forms that are validly applied only to an entire line.

Inclusive disjunction When we assert that *at least one* disjunct is true, and *possibly both* disjuncts are true. Given this, an inclusive disjunction is false when both disjuncts are false, otherwise it is true.

Inconsistent statements Two (or more) statements that do not have even one line on their respective truth tables where the main operators are true (but they can be false) at the same time.

Increasing extension A sequence of terms in which each term after the first denotes a set of objects with more members than the previous term.

Increasing intension A sequence of terms in which each term after the first connotes more attributes than the previous term.

Independent premises Premises are independent when the falsity of one does not nullify any support the others would give to the conclusion.

Indictment A formal accusation presented by a grand jury.

Indirect proof (IP) A method that starts by assuming the negation of the required statement and then validly deriving a contradiction on a subsequent line.

Individual constants The subject of a singular statement is translated using lowercase letters. The lowercase letters act as names of individuals.

Individual variables The three lowercase letters x, y, and z.

Inductive argument An argument in which the inferential claim is that the conclusion is *probably true* if the premises are true. In other words, under the *assumption* that the premises are true it is *improbable* for the conclusion to be false.

Inference A term used by logicians to refer to the reasoning process that is expressed by an argument.

Inference to the best explanation Reasoning from the premise that a hypothesis would explain certain facts to the conclusion that the hypothesis is the best explanation for those facts.

Inferential claim If a passage expresses a reasoning process—that the conclusion follows from the premises—then we say that it makes an inferential claim.

Informal fallacy A mistake in reasoning that occurs in ordinary language and concerns the content of the argument rather than its form.

Ingroup bias This concerns the human tendency to look at the world through a tribalistic lens, to assign *positive* stereotypes to the members of our *ingroup*, and *negative* stereotypes to members of *outgroups*.

Instantial letter The letter (either a variable or a constant) that is introduced by universal instantiaton or existential instantiation.

Instantiation When instantiation is applied to a quantified statement, the quantifier is removed, and every variable that was bound by the quantifier is replaced by the same instantial letter.

Intension The intension of a term is specified by listing the properties or attributes that the term connotes—in other words, its sense.

Intensional definition Assigns a meaning to a term by listing the properties or attributes shared by all the objects that are denoted by the term.

Intransitive relationship Illustrated by the following: If A is the mother of B, and B is the mother of C, then A is not the mother of C.

Invalid deductive argument An argument in which, *assuming* the premises are true, it is *possible* for the conclusion to be false. In other words, the conclusion *does not follow necessarily* from the premises.

Irreflexive relationship An example of an irreflexive relationship is expressed by the statement "Nothing can be taller than itself."

J

Joint method of agreement and difference If two or more instances of an event have only one thing in common, while the instances in which it does *not* occur all share the absence of that thing, then the item is a likely cause.

Justification Refers to the rule of inference that is applied to every validly derived step in a proof.

L

Lexical definition A definition based on the common use of a word, term, or symbol.

Linked diagram A diagram that reveals the occurrence of dependent premises.

Logic The systematic use of methods and principles to analyze, evaluate, and construct arguments.

Logical analysis Determines the strength with which the premises support the conclusion.

Logical operators Special symbols that can be used as part of ordinary language statement translations.

Logical truth A statement that is necessarily true; a tautology.

Logically equivalent statements Two truth-functional statements that have identical truth tables under the main operator.

M

Main operator The operator that has the *entire* well-formed formula in its scope.

Major premise The first premise of a categorical syllogism (it contains the major term).

Major term The predicate of the conclusion of a categorical syllogism.

Material equivalence (Equiv) A rule of inference (replacement rule).

Material implication (Impl) A rule of inference (replacement rule).

Mean A statistical average that is determined by adding the numerical values in the data concerning the examined objects, then dividing by the number of objects that were measured.

Median A statistical average that is determined by locating the value that separates the entire set of data in half.

Mediate argument An argument that has more than one premise.

Method of agreement The method that looks at two or more instances of an event to see what they have in common.

Method of concomitant variations The method that looks for two factors that vary together.

Method of difference The method that looks for what all the instances of an event do not have in common.

Method of residues The method that subtracts from a complex set of events those parts that already have known causes.

Middle term The term that occurs only in the premises of a categorical syllogism.

Minor premise The second premise of a categorical syllogism (it contains the minor term).

Minor term The subject of the conclusion of a categorical syllogism.

Misleading precision A claim that appears to be statistically significant but is not.

Missing the point When premises that seem to lead logically to one conclusion are used instead to support an unexpected conclusion.

Mode A statistical average that is determined by locating the value that occurs most.

Modus ponens (MP) A rule of inference (implication rule). A valid argument form (also referred to as *affirming the antecedent*).

Modus tollens (MT) A rule of inference (implication rule). A valid argument form (also referred to as *denying the consequent*).

Monadic predicate A one-place predicate that assigns a characteristic to an individual.

Mood The mood of a categorical syllogism consists of the type of categorical propositions involved (**A**, **E**, **I**, or **O**) and the order in which they occur.

Mutually exclusive Two events, such that if one event occurs, then the other cannot.

N

Natural deduction A proof procedure by which the conclusion of an argument is validly derived from the premises through the use of rules of inference.

Naturalistic fallacy Value judgments cannot be logically derived from statements of fact.

Naturalistic moral principle Since it is natural for humans to desire pleasure (or happiness) and to avoid pain, human behavior ought to be directed to these two ends.

Necessary condition Whenever one thing is *essential*, *mandatory*, or *required* in order for another thing to be realized. In other words, the falsity of the consequent ensures the falsity of the antecedent.

Negation The word "not" and the phrase "it is not the case that" are used to deny the statement that follows them, and we refer to their use as negation.

Negation method The method that is used once the probability of an event occurring is known; it is then easy to calculate the probability of the event not occurring.

Negative conclusion/affirmative premises A formal fallacy that occurs when a categorical syllogism has a negative conclusion and two affirmative premises.

Noncontingent statements Statements such that the truth values in the main operator column do not depend on the truth values of the component parts.

Nonreflexive relationship A relationship that is neither reflexive nor irreflexive.

Nonsymmetrical relationship When a relationship is neither symmetrical nor asymmetrical, then it is nonsymmetrical. Illustrated by the following: If Kris loves Morgan, then Morgan may or may not love Kris.

Nontransitive relationship Illustrated by the following: If Kris loves Morgan and Morgan loves Terry, then Kris may or may not love Terry.

Nontrivial prediction A prediction that requires reference to background knowledge, which is everything we know to be true.

Normal state The historical information regarding an object.

Normative statement A statement that establishes standards for correct moral behavior, determining norms or rules of conduct.

O

O-proposition A categorical proposition having the form "Some S are not P."

Obversion An immediate argument formed by changing the quality of the given proposition, and then replacing the predicate term with its complement.

Operational definition Defines a term by specifying a measurement procedure.

Opposition When two standard-form categorical propositions refer to the same subject and predicate classes but differ in quality, quantity, or both.

Order of operations The order of handling the logical operators within a proposition; it is a step-by-step method of generating a complete truth table.

Ostensive definition Involves demonstrating the term—for example, by pointing to a member of the class that the term denotes.

P

Particular affirmative An I-proposition. It asserts that at least one member of the subject class is a member of the predicate class.

Particular negative An O-proposition. It asserts that at least one member of the subject class is not a member of the predicate class.

Persuasive definition Assigns a meaning to a term with the direct purpose of influencing attitudes or opinions.

Plaintiff The person who initiates a lawsuit.

Poisoning the well The fallacy occurs when a person is attacked *before* she has a chance to present her case.

Population Any group of objects, not just human populations.

Post hoc The fallacy occurs from the mistaken assumption that just because one event occurred before another event, the first event *must have caused* the second event.

Precedent A judicial decision that can be applied to later cases.

Precipitating cause The object or event directly involved in bringing about an effect.

Precising definition Reduces the vagueness and ambiguity of a term by providing a sharp focus, often a technical meaning, for a term.

Predicate logic Integrates many of the features of categorical and propositional logic. It combines the symbols associated with propositional logic with special symbols that are used to translate predicates.

Predicate symbols Predicates are the fundamental units in predicate logic. Uppercase letters are used to symbolize the units.

Predicate term The term that comes second in a standard-form categorical proposition.

Prejudicial effect Evidence that might cause some jurors to be negatively biased toward a defendant.

Premise The information intended to provide support for a conclusion.

Premise indicators Words and phrases that help us recognize arguments by indicating the presence of premises (statements being offered in support of a conclusion).

Prescriptive statement A statement that offers advice either by specifying a particular action that ought to be performed or by providing general moral rules, principles, or guidelines that should be followed.

Principle of charity We should choose the reconstructed argument that gives the benefit of the doubt to the person presenting the argument.

Principle of replacement Logically equivalent expressions may replace each other within the context of a proof.

Probability calculus The rules for calculating the probability of compound events from the probability of simple events. The results can be displayed as fractions, percentages, ratios, or a decimal between 0 and 1.

Probative value Evidence that can be used during a trial to advance the facts of the case.

Proof A sequence of steps (also called a deduction or a derivation) in which each step either is a premise or follows from earlier steps in the sequence according to the rules of inference.

Proposition The information content imparted by a statement, or, simply put, its meaning.

Propositional logic The basic components in propositional logic are statements.

Q

Quality When we classify a categorical proposition as either affirmative or negative, we are referring to its quality.

Quantifier The words "all," "no," and "some" are quantifiers. They tell us the extent of the class inclusion or exclusion.

Quantity When we classify a categorical proposition as either universal or particular, we are referring to its quantity.

R

Random sample A sample in which every member of the population has an equal chance of getting in.

Red herring A fallacy that occurs when someone completely ignores an opponent's position and changes the subject, diverting the discussion in a new direction.

Reflexive property The idea that *anything is identical to itself* is expressed by the reflexive property.

Relational predicate Establishes a connection between individuals.

Relative frequency theory of probability The theory that some probabilities can be computed by dividing the number of favorable cases by the total number of observed cases.

Relativism First, all moral value judgments are determined by a society's beliefs toward actions or behavior. Second, there are no objective or universal moral value judgments.

Remote cause Something that is connected to the precipitating cause by a chain of events.

Replacement rules Pairs of logically equivalent statement forms.

Representative sample A sample that accurately reflects the characteristics of the population as a whole.

Restricted conjunction method The method that is used in situations dealing with two or more independent events, where the occurrence of one event has no bearing whatsoever on the occurrence or nonoccurrence of the other event.

Restricted disjunction method The method that is used to calculate probability when two (or more) events are independent of each other, and the events are mutually exclusive.

Rigid application of a generalization When a generalization or rule is inappropriately applied to the case at hand. The fallacy results from the belief that the generalization or rule is universal (meaning it has no exceptions).

Rule-based reasoning Legal reasoning is also referred to as "rule-based reasoning."

Rules of inference The function of rules of inference is to justify the steps of a proof.

Rules of law The legal principles that have been applied to historical cases.

S

Sample A subset of a population.

Scope The statement or statements that a logical operator connects.

Self-contradiction A statement that is necessarily false.

Serial diagram A diagram that shows that a conclusion from one argument is a premise in a second argument.

Simple diagram A diagram consisting of a single premise and a single conclusion.

Simple statement One that does not have any other statement or logical operator as a component.

Simplification (Simp) A rule of inference (implication rule).

Singular proposition A proposition that asserts something about a specific person, place, or thing.

Slippery slope An argument that attempts to connect a series of occurrences such that the first link in a chain leads directly to a second link, and so on, until a final unwanted situation is said to be the inevitable result.

Sorites A special type of enthymeme that is a chain of arguments. The missing parts are intermediate conclusions, each of which, in turn, becomes a premise in the next link in the chain.

Sound argument A deductive argument is sound when the argument is valid, and the premises are true.

Standard-form categorical proposition A proposition that has one of the following forms: "All S are P," "Some S are P," "No S are P," "Some S are not P."

Standard-form categorical syllogism A categorical syllogism that meets three requirements: (1) All three statements must be standard-form categorical propositions. (2) The two occurrences of each term must be identical and have the same sense. (3) The major premise must occur first, the minor premise second, and the conclusion last.

Standard deviation A measure of the amount of diversity in a set of numerical values.

Statement A sentence that is either true or false.

Statement form (1) In categorical logic, a statement form is an arrangement of logical vocabulary and letters that stand for class terms such that a uniform substitution of class terms for the letters results in a statement. (2) In propositional logic, an arrangement of logical operators and statement variables such that a uniform substitution of statements for the variables results in a statement.

Statement function A pattern for a statement. It does not make any universal or particular assertion about anything, and it has no truth value.

Statement variable A statement variable can stand for any statement, simple or compound.

Status quo bias This bias is based on the psychological heuristic that tells us when something comes to the mind quickly we should probably rely on it.

Stipulative definition Introduces a new meaning to a term or symbol.

Strategy Referring to a greater, overall goal.

Straw man The fallacy occurs when someone's argument is misrepresented in order to create a new argument that can be easily refuted. The new argument is so weak that it is "made of straw." The arguer then falsely claims that his opponent's real argument has been defeated.

Strong inductive argument An argument such that if the premises are *assumed* to be true, then the conclusion is *probably* true. In other words, the *probable truth* of the conclusion *follows from* the truth of the premises.

Subalternation The relationship between a universal proposition (referred to as the *superaltern*) and its corresponding particular proposition (referred to as the *subaltern*).

Subcontraries Pairs of propositions that cannot both be false at the same time, but can both be true; also, if one is false, then the other must be true.

Subject term The term that comes first in a standard-form categorical proposition.

Subjectivist theory of probability The theory that some probability determinations are based on the lack of total knowledge regarding an event.

Substitution instance (1) In categorical logic, a substitution instance of a *statement* occurs when a uniform substitution of class terms for the letters results in a statement. A *substitution instance* of an *argument* occurs when a uniform substitution of class terms for the letters results in an argument. (2) In propositional logic, a substitution instance of a *statement* occurs when a uniform substitution of statements for the variables results in a statement. A substitution instance of an *argument* occurs when a uniform substitution of statements for the variables results in an argument.

Sufficient condition Whenever one event ensures that another event is realized. In other words, the truth of the antecedent guarantees the truth of the consequent.

Syllogism A deductive argument that has exactly two premises and a conclusion.

Symmetrical relationship Illustrated by the following: If A is married to B, then B is married to A.

Synonymous definition Assigns a meaning to a term by providing another term with the same meaning; in other words, by providing a synonym.

T

Tactics The use of small-scale maneuvers or devices.

Tautology A statement that is necessarily true.

Tautology (Taut) A rule of inference (replacement rule).

Teleology The philosophical belief that the value of an action or object can be determined by looking at the purpose or the end of the action or object.

Term A single word or a group of words that can be the subject of a statement; it can be a common name, a proper name, or even a descriptive phrase.

Theoretical definition Assigns a meaning to a term by providing an understanding of how the term fits into a general theory.

Theoretical science Proposes explanations for natural phenomena.

Transitive relationship Illustrated by the following: If A is taller than B, and B is taller than C, then A is taller than C.

Transposition (Trans) A rule of inference (replacement rule).

Truth-functional proposition The truth value of any compound proposition using one or more of the five logical operators is a function of (that is, uniquely determined by) the truth values of its component propositions.

Truth table An arrangement of truth values for a truth-functional compound proposition that displays for every possible case how the truth value of the proposition is determined by the truth values of its simple components.

Truth value Every statement is either true or false; these two possibilities are called *truth values*.

Truth value analysis Determines if the information in the premises is accurate, correct, or true.

Tu quoque The fallacy is distinguished by the specific attempt of one person to avoid the issue at hand by claiming the other person is a hypocrite.

U

Uncogent argument An inductive argument is uncogent if either or both of the following conditions hold: The argument is weak, or the argument has at least one false premise.

Undistributed If a proposition does not assert something about every member of a class, then the term designating that class is said to be undistributed.

Undistributed middle A formal fallacy that occurs when the middle term in a categorical syllogism is undistributed in both premises of a categorical syllogism.

Unintended consequences If you can show that something unacceptable to a person presenting an analogy follows from that analogy, then you put that person in a difficult position.

Universal affirmative An **A**-proposition. It affirms that every member of the subject class is a member of the predicate class.

Universal generalization (UG) A rule by which we can validly deduce the universal quantification of a statement function from a substitution instance with respect to the name of any arbitrarily selected individual (subject to restrictions).

Universal instantiation (UI) The rule by which we can validly deduce the substitution instance of a statement function from a universally quantified statement.

Universal negative An **E**-proposition. It asserts that no members of the subject class are members of the predicate class.

Universal quantifier The symbol used to capture the idea that universal statements assert something about every member of the subject class.

Universalizability The notion that the same principles hold for all people at all times.

Unsound argument A deductive argument is unsound when the argument is invalid, or when at least one of the premises is false.

Utilitarianism It can be summed up in the famous dictum "the greatest good for the greatest number."

V

Valid deductive argument An argument in which, *assuming* the premises are true, it is *impossible* for the conclusion to be false. In other words, the conclusion *follows necessarily* from the premises.

Value judgment A claim that a particular human action or object has some degree of importance, worth, or desirability.

Venn diagram A diagram that uses circles to represent categorical proposition forms.

Verbal dispute Occurs when a vague or ambiguous term results in a linguistic misunderstanding.

Verifiable prediction A prediction that, if true, must include an observable event.

W

Weak inductive argument An argument such that either (a) if the premises are *assumed* to be true, then the conclusion is *probably not true*, or (b) a *probably true* conclusion *does not follow from the premises*.

Well-formed formula Any statement letter standing alone, or a compound statement such that an arrangement of operator symbols and statement letters results in a grammatically correct symbolic expression.

Word origin definition Assigns a meaning to a term by investigating its origin. The study of the history, development, and sources of words is called *etymology*.

Answers to Selected Exercises

CHAPTER 1

Exercises 1B

I.

5. **Premises:**
    (a) True friends are there when we need them.
    (b) They suffer with us when we fail.
    (c) They are happy when we succeed.

Conclusion: We should never take our friends for granted. Although there are no indicator words, the first statement is the conclusion, the point of the passage, for which the other statements offer support.

9. **Premises:**
    (a) At one time Gary Kasparov had the highest ranking of any chess grand master in history.
    (b) He was beaten in a chess tournament by a computer program called Deep Blue.

Conclusion: The computer program should be given a ranking higher than Kasparov.
The indicator word "So" identifies the conclusion. The other statements are offered as support.

13. **Premises:**
    (a) My guru said the world will end on August 6, 2045.
    (b) So far everything she predicted has happened exactly as she said it would.

Conclusion: The world will end on August 6, 2045.
The indicator word "because" identifies the premises, so the first statement is the conclusion.

II.

5. Argument. The phrase "It follows that" identifies the premise, which is offered as support for the conclusion "she must be a vegetarian."

9. Not an argument. The statements do not act as either premises or conclusions; they simply convey information.

13. Argument. The conclusion is "The handprint on the wall had not been made by the librarian himself." The premises are "there hadn't been blood on his hands" and "the print did not match his [the librarian's]."

17. Not an argument.

21. Argument. The conclusion (as indicated by the word "Thus") is "we do not necessarily keep eBooks in compliance with any particular paper edition."

25. Not an argument. The passage provides a definition of "authoritarian governments" and a definition of "democratic governments." Although there is no direct conclusion, the author's choice of definitions indicates his point of view.

29. Not an argument

33. Not an argument; the information is offered as advice

37. Not an argument

41. Not an argument

45. Not an argument

49. Not an argument

Exercises 1C

5. Argument. The term "clearly" is used as a conclusion indicator.

9. Argument. A reason is given to support the claim "texting discourages thoughtful discussion or any level of detail."

13. Explanation. The information is offered to explain why "the iPhone and Android are popular."

17. Explanation. The information is offered to explain why Twain "gave up the idea" of making a lecturing trip through the antipodes and the borders of the Orient.

Exercises 1E

5. Deductive. The first premise tells us something about *all* fires. If both premises are assumed to be true, then the conclusion follows necessarily.

9. Deductive. The first premise tells us something about *all* elements with atomic weights greater than 64. If both premises are assumed to be true, then the conclusion follows necessarily.

13. Deductive. The first premise specifies the minimum age when someone can legally play the slot machines in Las Vegas. The second premise tells us Sam is 33 years old. If both premises are true, then the conclusion follows necessarily.

17. Inductive. We are told something about *most* Doberman dogs. Also, the use of the word "probably" in the conclusion indicates that it is best classified as an inductive argument.

21. Inductive. The conclusion is *not* meant to follow necessarily from the premise.

25. Inductive. The use of the phrase "you're more likely" in the conclusion indicates that it is best classified as an inductive argument.

29. Deductive. The decision is intended to follow necessarily from the Supreme Court's arguments for the unconstitutionality of the law in question.

Exercises 1F

I.

5. If we let C = *computers*, E = *electronic devices*, and A = *things that require an AC adapter*, then the argument form is the following:

   All C are E.
   All A are E.
   All C are A.

The following substitutions create a counterexample: let C = *cats*, E = *mammals*, and A = *dogs*.

   All cats are mammals.
   All dogs are mammals.
   All cats are dogs.

Both premises are true, and the conclusion is false. Therefore, the counterexample shows that the argument is invalid.

9. If we let U = *unicorns*, I = *immortal creatures*, and C = *centaurs*, then the argument form is the following:

   No U are I.
   No C are I.
   No U are C.

The following substitutions create a counterexample: let U = *cats*, I = *snakes*, and C = *mammals*.

   No cats are snakes.
   No mammals are snakes.
   No cats are mammals.

Both premises are true, and the conclusion is false. Therefore, the counterexample shows that the argument is invalid.

13. We must make sure that whatever birth dates we assign to Fidelix and Gil the premises must turn out to be *true*. Suppose Fidelix was born in 1989 and Gil was born in 1988. Both premises are then true. However, the conclusion is then *false*.

17. If we let S = *strawberries*, F = *fruit*, and P = *plants*, then the argument form is the following:

   All S are F.
   All S are P.
   All F are P.

The following substitutions create a counterexample: let S = *puppies*, F = *mammals*, and P = *dogs*.

   All puppies are mammals.
   All puppies are dogs.
   All mammals are dogs.

Both premises are true, and the conclusion is false. Therefore, the counterexample shows that the argument is invalid.

II.

5. If we let S = *birds can swim*, and A = *birds are aquatic animals*, then the argument form is the following:

   If S, then A.
   It is not the case that A.
   It is not the case that S.   *Modus tollens.* The argument is valid.

9. If we let L = *you are lost*, and C = *you are confused*, then the argument form is the following:

   L or C.
   It is not the case that L.
   C.   Disjunctive syllogism. The argument is valid.

13. If we let S = *I can save $1000*, and C = *I can buy a car*, then the argument form is the following:

   If S, then C.
   S.
   C.   *Modus ponens.* The argument is valid.

Exercises 1G

I.

5. Weak. The fact that it came up heads ten times in a row has no bearing on the next toss; each coin toss is an independent event, each having a 50-50 chance of heads or tails.

9. Strong. If we assume the premises are true, then the conclusion is probably true.

II.

5. *Weakens the argument.* If the lamp is not plugged in correctly, then electricity is probably not getting to the lamp.

9. *Strengthens the argument.* If every other electrical fixture in the room works, then electricity is probably getting to the lamp.

13. *Strengthens the argument.* Since the battery is so old, it is likely to be defective or worn out; therefore, we can determine that this new evidence strengthens the argument.

17. *Weakens the argument.* The loose terminal clamps are probably not relaying the battery power; therefore, we can determine that this new evidence weakens the argument.

Exercises 1H

I.

5. *Missing conclusion:* My headache will be relieved.

This makes the argument valid, provided the third premise means that in *all instances* taking aspirin relieves a headache. However, since this interpretation is false, this reconstruction is an unsound argument.

Missing conclusion: My headache will probably be relieved.

This makes the argument strong, provided we interpret the third premise as asserting that *in most cases* taking aspirin relieves a headache. However, we would have to gather data to see if this assertion is true or false. If it is true, then the argument is cogent; if it is false, then the argument is uncogent.

9. *Missing conclusion:* The penicillin pills Jill took will have no effect on her viral infection.

This makes the argument valid. The argument is unsound if any premise is false.

Missing conclusion: The penicillin pills Jill took will probably have no effect on her viral infection.

This makes the argument strong. The argument is uncogent if any premise is false.

13. *Missing premise:* All safe drivers have low insurance rates.

This makes the argument valid.

Missing premise: Most safe drivers have low insurance rates.

This makes the argument strong.

17. In the passage "urban dwellers with little access to green spaces have a higher incidence of psychological problems than people living near parks," the term "higher incidence" indicates a statistical result. Given this, a charitable reconstruction of the missing conclusion would make the argument inductive rather than deductive. Something like the following is appropriate:

Missing conclusion: The results strongly suggest that getting out into natural environments could be an easy and almost immediate way to improve moods for city dwellers.

This makes the argument strong. If the premises are true, then the argument is cogent.

II.

5. [He suddenly gained forty pounds of muscle.]
[He doubled his average home run total.]
[He has taken steroids.]

The rhetorical forces are the two assertions "he suddenly gained forty pounds of muscle" and "he doubled his average home run total." Given this, it seems to be indicating that the conclusion should be that he has taken steroids.

9. [There is no trace of gunpowder on her hands.]
[She did not commit suicide by shooting herself.]

The rhetorical force behind the assertion "there is no trace of gunpowder on her hands" seems to be indicating that the conclusion should be negative in tone.

13. *Rhetorical conditional*
[You want to get rich quick.]
[You should buy more lottery tickets.]

CHAPTER 2

Exercises 2A

I.

5. head of state, executive officer, elected official, commander-in-chief

9. produces food from photosynthesis, multicellular, rigid cell walls, manufacturing business

II.

5. Socrates, Plato, Aristotle

9. Lake Superior, Lake Tanganyika, Lake Erie

III.

5. Great Pyramid of Giza, Colossus of Rhodes, Lighthouse of Alexandria, Hanging Gardens of Babylon, Statue of Zeus at Olympia, Mausoleum at Halicarnassus, Temple of Artemis at Ephesus

9. January, March, May, July, August, October, December

IV.

5. robin, thrush, bird, flying animal, animal

9. Cherry Jell-O, Jell-O, chilled dessert, dessert, food

Exercises 2C

5. Synonymous
9. Enumerative
13. Subclass
17. Subclass
21. Operational
25. Enumerative
29. Ostensive
33. Synonymous

Exercises 2D

5. Theoretical
9. Lexical
13. Precising
17. Stipulative
21. Precising
25. Precising
29. Stipulative
33. Functional
37. Lexical
41. Precising
45. Functional
49. Theoretical

Exercises 2E

5. The definition uses figurative language (Guideline 7). In addition, it fails to provide the essential meaning of the term (Guideline 2).

9. We can use Guideline 1 to add quotation marks: "Grade point average."

13. We can add quotation marks (Guideline 1): "Romanticism."
17. The definitions use ambiguous and vague language (Guideline 6).

Exercises 2F

5. Cognitive meaning
9. Both cognitive meaning and emotive meaning. The claims about the wealth of some players provide cognitive meaning. However, an emotional twinge is provided by the claim "I don't feel we owe anybody anything monetarily. Some of these players are wealthier than their bosses."
13. Emotive meaning

Exercises 2G

5. Verbal dispute
9. Verbal dispute
13. Verbal dispute
17. Verbal dispute

CHAPTER 3

Exercises 3B

I.
5. [1] We should never take our friends for granted. [2] True friends are there when we need them. [3] They suffer with us when we fail, and [4] they are happy when we succeed.

9. [1] At one time Gary Kasparov had the highest ranking of any chess grandmaster in history. However, [2] he was beaten in a chess tournament by a computer program called Deep Blue, so [3] the computer program should be given a ranking higher than Kasparov.

13. [1] The world will end on August 6, 2045. I know this because [2] my guru said it would, and [3] so far everything she predicted has happened exactly as she said it would.

II.
5. [1] Sue hesitated; and then impulsively told the woman that [1] her husband and herself had been unhappy in their first marriages, [2] after which, terrified at the thought of a second irrevocable union, and lest the conditions of the contract should kill their love, yet wishing to be together, they had literally not found the courage to repeat it, [3] though they had attempted it two or three times. Therefore, [4] though in her own sense of the words she was a married woman, in the landlady's sense she was not.

9. [1] We are intelligent beings: [2] intelligent beings cannot have been formed by a crude, blind, insensible being: [3] there is certainly some difference between the ideas of Newton and the dung of a mule. [4] Newton's intelligence, therefore, came from another intelligence.

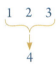

13. [1] After supper she got out her book and learned me about Moses and the Bulrushers, and [2] I was in a sweat to find out all about him; but by and by [3] she let it out that Moses had been dead a considerable long time; so then [4] I didn't care no more about him, because [5] I don't take no stock in dead people.

17. [1] It may be no accident that sexual life forms dominate our planet. True, [2] bacteria account for the largest number of individuals, and the greatest biomass. But [3] by any reasonable measures of species diversity, or individual complexity, size, or intelligence, sexual species are paramount. And [4] of the life forms that reproduce sexually, the ones whose reproduction is mediated by mate choice show the greatest biodiversity and the greatest complexity. [5] Without sexual selection, evolution seems limited to the very small, the transient, the parasitic, the bacterial, and the brainless. For this

reason, [6] I think that sexual selection may be evolution's most creative force.

III.

5. [1] Death is not an event in life: we do not live to experience death. [2] If we take eternity to mean not infinite temporal duration but timelessness, then eternal life belongs to those who live in the present. [3] Our life has no end in just the way in which our visual field has no limits.

9. Because [1] there is a law such as gravity, [2] the universe can and will create itself from nothing. [3] Spontaneous creation is the reason [4] there is something rather than nothing, [5] why the universe exists, [6] why we exist. [7] It is not necessary to invoke God to light the blue touch paper and set the universe going.

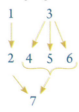

13. [1] The line that I am urging as today's conventional wisdom is not a denial of consciousness. [2] It is often called, with more reason, a repudiation of mind. [3] It is indeed a repudiation of mind as a second substance, over and above body. [4] It can be described less harshly as an identification of mind with some of the faculties, states, and activities of the body. [5] Mental states and events are a special subclass of the states and events of the human or animal body.

17. [1] It has only just begun to dawn on us that in our own language alone, not to speak of its many companions, the past history of humanity is spread out in an imperishable map, just as the history of the mineral earth lies embedded in the layers of its outer crust. But [2] there is this difference between the record of the rocks and the secrets which are hidden in language: [3] whereas the former can only give us knowledge of outward dead things—such as forgotten seas and the bodily shapes of prehistoric animals— [4] language has preserved for us the inner living history of man's soul. [5] It reveals the evolution of consciousness.

21. [1] It is a commonplace that all religion expresses itself in mythological or metaphorical terms; [2] it says one thing and means another; [3] it uses imagery to convey truth. But [4] the crucial fact about religion is not that it is metaphor, but [5] that it is unconscious metaphor. [6] No one can express any thought without using metaphors, but [7] this does not reduce all philosophy and science to religion, because [8] the scientist knows that his metaphors are merely metaphors and [9] that the truth is something other than the imagery by which it is expressed, whereas [10] in religion the truth and the imagery are identified. [11] To repeat the Creed as a religious act it is necessary not to add "All this I believe in a symbolical or figurative sense": [12] to make that addition is to convert religion into philosophy.

CHAPTER 4

Exercises 4B

I.
5. False
9. True

II.
5. *Ad hominem* abusive
9. *Ad hominem* circumstantial
13. Appeal to the people

17. *Ad hominem* circumstantial
21. *Ad hominem* abusive
25. Poisoning the well
29. No fallacy
33. Poisoning the well
37. *Ad hominem* abusive
41. *Ad hominem* circumstantial
45. *Ad hominem* circumstantial
49. No fallacy

Exercises 4C

I.
5. True
9. False

II.
5. No fallacy
9. Slippery slope
13. Biased sample
17. No fallacy
21. Biased sample
25. No fallacy
29. Biased sample
33. Division
37. *Post hoc* fallacy
41. Division
45. Composition
49. Division

Exercises 4D

I.
5. False
9. False
13. False

II.
5. Begging the question
9. No fallacy
13. Straw man fallacy
17. Complex question
21. No fallacy
25. Straw man
29. Red herring
33. Appeal to ignorance
37. False dichotomy
41. Appeal to an unqualified authority
45. Straw man
49. Equivocation

Exercises 4E

5. Red herring fallacy. Notice that Brewster does not deny the allegations. Also, he says, "Until I see the materials,

it's hard to comment." But he does offer comments: "It's obviously a piece completely out of context slanted for the purposes of the organization that caused somebody to deceptively be hired by the Asmussen stable."

9. False dichotomy. The disjunction offers two choices, but it neglects to acknowledge that other possibilities exist.
13. *Post hoc* (coincidence). The fallacy occurs from the mistaken assumption that just because one event occurred before another event, the first event *must have caused* the second event.
17. *Ad hominem* abusive. The argument uses purported character flaws of people's lives to reject their claims.
21. Hasty generalization. The generalization is created on the basis of one instance.
25. No fallacy
29. *Post hoc*. A fallacy involving either a short-term or long-term pattern that is noticed *after the fact*.
33. Two possibilities. (1) *Post hoc* (coincidence). The fallacy occurs from the mistaken assumption that just because one event occurred before another event, the first event *must have caused* the second event. (2) *Post hoc* (common cause). The mistake occurs when the writer thinks that one event causes another when both events are the result of a common cause (perhaps the rise of economies).
37. Appeal to an unqualified authority. The argument relies on the opinions of people who have no expertise, training, or knowledge relevant to the issue at hand.
41. Appeal to the people. The avoidance of objective evidence in favor of an emotional response.
45. No fallacy
49. No fallacy

CHAPTER 5

Exercises 5A

5. Subject term: *malicious murderers*
   Predicate term: *evil people*
   This is an example of an **A**-proposition.
9. Subject term: *lottery winners*
   Predicate term: *lucky people*
   This is an example of an **E**-proposition.
13. Subject term: *amendments to the U.S. Constitution*
   Predicate term: *unconstitutional acts*
   This is an example of an **E**-proposition.

Exercises 5B

I.
5. Universal negative; subject term distributed; predicate term distributed.
9. Universal affirmative; subject term distributed; predicate term undistributed.

13. Universal negative; subject term distributed; predicate term distributed.

II.

5. All high-definition TV shows are shows for children.
9. No karaoke bars are noisy rooms.

III.

5. Some wood-burning stoves are warmth givers.
9. Some tuna fish sandwiches are high-protein meals.

IV.

5. Some dancers are not physically gifted athletes.
9. Some movie special effects are not scenes generated by a computer.

Exercises 5D

5. Let S = *psychics*, and P = *frauds*. All S are P.

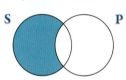

9. Let S = *teachers*, and P = *miserable wretches*. All S are P.

13. Let S = *sea creatures*, and P = *bivalves*. All S are P.

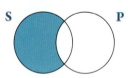

17. Let S = *scientific researchers*, and P = *people with impeccable credentials*. Some S are P.

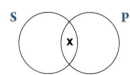

21. Let S = *French pastries*, and P = *baked items*. All S are P.

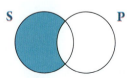

25. Let S = *dogs*, and P = *faithful pets*. All S are P.

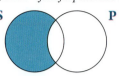

29. Let S = *teachers*, and P = *inspired orators*. All S are P.

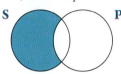

33. Let S = *designer jeans*, and P = *genetically engineered objects*. All S are P.

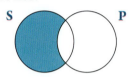

37. Let S = *traffic accidents*, and P = *speeding incidents*. Some S are P.

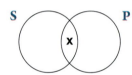

41. Let S = *ice cream toppings*, and P = *diet-friendly products*. No S are P.

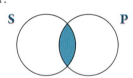

45. Let S = *French fries*, and P = *grease-laden spuds*. All S are P.

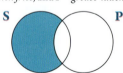

Exercises 5E

I.

5. A. *Converse:* No people likely to go to prison are greedy politicians. *Valid*
   B. *Obverse:* All greedy politicians are non-people likely to go to prison. *Valid*
   C. *Contrapositive:* No non-people likely to go to prison are non-greedy politicians. *Invalid*

9. A. *Converse:* All days when banks close are public holidays. *Invalid*
    B. *Obverse:* No public holidays are non-days when banks close. *Valid*
    C. *Contrapositive:* All non-days when banks close are non-public holidays. *Valid*
13. A. *Converse:* No diet-busters are ice cream toppings. *Valid*
    B. *Obverse:* All ice cream toppings are non-diet-busters. *Valid*
    C. *Contrapositive:* No non-diet-busters are non-ice cream toppings. *Invalid*
17. A. *Converse:* All grease-laden products are French fries. *Invalid*
    B. *Obverse:* No French fries are non-grease-laden products. *Valid*
    C. *Contrapositive:* All non-grease-laden products are non-French fries. *Valid*
21. A. *Converse:* Some great works of art are tattoos. *Valid*
    B. *Obverse:* Some tattoos are not non-great works of art. *Valid*
    C. *Contrapositive:* Some non-great works of art are non-tattoos. *Invalid*
25. A. *Converse:* No acts left unrewarded are good deeds. *Valid*
    B. *Obverse:* All good deeds are non-acts left unrewarded. *Valid*
    C. *Contrapositive:* No non-acts left unrewarded are non-good deeds. *Invalid*

II.
5. Here is the diagram of the premise, an **E**-proposition:

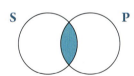

In order for the conclusion, an **I**-proposition, to be true, there would have to be an X in the area where S and P overlap. Since there is none, the immediate inference is invalid.

9. Here is the diagram of the premise, an **I**-proposition:

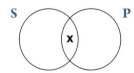

In order for the conclusion, an **O**-proposition, to be true, there would have to be an X in the area of S that is outside P. Since there is none, the immediate inference is invalid.

Exercises 5F.1

I.
5. True.

II.
5. a. True. Since these fall under *subalternation*, if the universal (in this case an **E**-proposition) is true, then the corresponding particular (in this case an **O**-proposition) is true too.

III.
5. c. Undetermined. No immediate inference can be made about the subaltern of a false **A**-proposition.

IV.
5. c. Undetermined. Since these fall under *subalternation*, if the universal is false, then the corresponding particular could be either true or false.
9. a. True. Since these fall under *subalternation*, if the universal is true, then the corresponding particular is true.
13. c. Undetermined. Since these fall under *subalternation*, if the particular is true, then the corresponding universal could be either true or false.
17. a. True. Since they are *contradictories*, if one is false, then the other is true.
21. c. Undetermined. Since they are *subcontraries*, they can both be true at the same time.

Exercises 5F.2

I.
5.

No S are P.

Under the *traditional interpretation*, in order for the conclusion to be true (an **I**-proposition) an X needs to be in the area where *S* and *P* overlap. Since this is not the case, this is an invalid argument.

9.

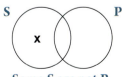

Some S are not P.

In order for the conclusion to be true (an **I**-proposition) there needs to be an X in the area where *S* and *P* overlap. Since this is not the case, this is an invalid argument.

13.

All S are P.

Under the *traditional interpretation*, in order for the conclusion to be true (an **E**-proposition) the area where S and P overlap needs to be shaded. Since this is not the case, this is an invalid argument.

17.

All S are P.

Under the *traditional interpretation*, in order for the conclusion to be true (an **I**-proposition) there would have to be an X in the area where S and P overlap. As we can see, the assumption of existence symbol (the circled X) is in the area. Now we need to see if the circled X represents something that actually exists. Since the S stands for *abominable snowmen*, and they do not exist, the assumption of existence symbol does not represent something that actually exists. Therefore, the argument is invalid under the traditional interpretation.

II.

5.   No S are P.
     Some S are P.

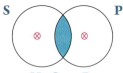

No S are P.

In order for the conclusion, an **I**-proposition, to be true, there would have to be an X in the area where S and P overlap. Since there is none, the argument is invalid.

9.   Some S are P.
     Some S are not P.

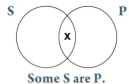

Some S are P.

In order for the conclusion, an **O**-proposition, to be true, there would have to be an X in the area of S that is outside of P. Since there is none, the argument is invalid.

Exercises 5G

5.   A.   *Converse:* No people likely to go to prison are greedy politicians. *Valid*

     B.   *Obverse:* All greedy politicians are non-people likely to go to prison. *Valid*

     C.   *Contrapositive:* Some non-people likely to go to prison are not non-greedy politicians. *Valid by limitation*

9.   A.   *Converse:* Some days when banks close are public holidays. *Valid by limitation*

     B.   *Obverse:* No public holidays are non-days when banks close. *Valid*

     C.   *Contrapositive:* All non-days when banks close are non-public holidays. *Valid*

13. A.   *Converse:* No diet-busters are ice cream toppings. *Valid*

     B.   *Obverse:* All ice cream toppings are non-diet-busters. *Valid*

     C.   *Contrapositive:* Some non-diet-busters are not non–ice cream toppings. *Valid by limitation*

17. A.   *Converse:* Some grease-laden products are French fries. *Valid by limitation*

     B.   *Obverse:* No French fries are non-grease-laden products. *Valid*

     C.   *Contrapositive:* All non-grease-laden products are non-French fries. *Valid*

21. A.   *Converse:* Some great works of art are tattoos. *Valid*

     B.   *Obverse:* Some tattoos are not non-great works of art. *Valid*

     C.   *Contrapositive:* Some non-great works of art are non-tattoos. *Invalid*

25. A.   *Converse:* No acts left unrewarded are good deeds. *Valid*

     B.   *Obverse:* All good deeds are non-acts left unrewarded. *Valid*

     C.   *Contrapositive:* Some non-acts left unrewarded are not non-good deeds. *Valid by limitation*

Exercises 5H

5.   All happy people are dancers.

9.   Some novels are not satires.

13. Some final exams in calculus are not challenging tests.

17. No young children are people protected from the dangers of war.

21. All video game companies are companies that hire game-testers.

25. All people who laugh last are people who laugh best.

29. All persons identical to Marie Curie are persons identical to the winner of Nobel Prizes in two different sciences, and all persons identical to the winner of Nobel Prizes in two different sciences are persons identical to Marie Curie.

33. Some diamond mines are places in California.
37. No best intentions are defeated things.
41. All legitimate religions are religions certified by the government.
45. All times you can get electricity in your apartment are times you pay your electric bill.
49. All orangutans are animals native to Borneo.
53. All improvements made to the gas engine are things that decrease our need for oil.
57. Some people are not people who bowl.
61. All beliefs worth having are beliefs that must withstand doubt.
65. All endings are new beginnings.
69. All people over 30 years are people to be trusted.
73. All people winning at the moment are people who will seem to be invincible.

CHAPTER 6

Exercises 6B

I.

5. *major term:* independent creatures; *minor term:* lovable pets; *middle term:* cats; *mood:* **OOO**; *figure:* **3**
9. *major term:* surgical tools; *minor term:* blunt instruments; *middle term:* hammers; *mood:* **EIO**; *figure:* **1**
13. *major term:* brain food; *minor term:* sporting events; *middle term:* math problems; *mood:* **AEE**; *figure:* **1**

II.

5. **OOO-3**
9. **AEO-1**

Exercises 6C

I.

5. Some M are not P.
   Some M are not S.
   Some S are not P.

Answer: Invalid

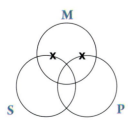

9. All M are P.
   No S are M.
   Some S are not P.

Answer: Invalid

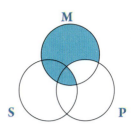

13. All M are P.
    All S are M.
    All S are P.

Answer: Valid

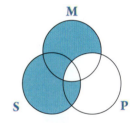

17. All P are M.
    No S are M.
    All S are P.

Answer: Invalid

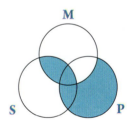

21. All P are M.
    Some S are not M.
    No S are P.

Answer: Invalid

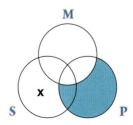

25. All M are P.
     No S are M.
     Some S are P.

Answer: Invalid

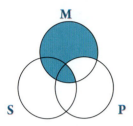

29. No M are P.
     All S are M.
     All S are P.

Answer: Invalid

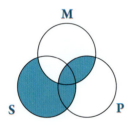

II.

5. No septic tanks are swimming pools. No sewers are swimming pools. Therefore, no septic tanks are sewers.

Answer: Invalid. Let S = *septic tanks*, P = *swimming pools*, and W = *sewers*.

     No W are P.
     No S are P.
     No S are W.

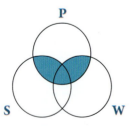

9. Some buildings are poorly constructed domiciles. Some buildings are architectural nightmares. So, some architectural nightmares are poorly constructed domiciles.

Answer: Invalid. Let B = *buildings*, P = *poorly constructed domiciles*, and A= *architectural nightmares*.

Some B are P.
Some B are A.
Some A are P.

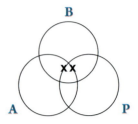

III.

5. **AEE-2**

Answer: Valid

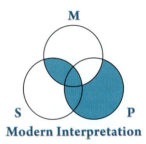

Modern Interpretation

9. **AII-3**

Answer: Valid

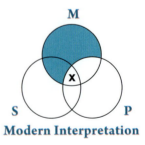

Modern Interpretation

13. **AEE-4**

Answer: Valid

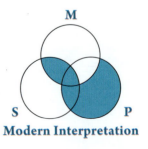

Modern Interpretation

IV.

5. **AAI-3**

Answer: Invalid under the modern interpretation.

Modern Interpretation

9. **EAO-4**

Answer: Invalid under the modern interpretation.

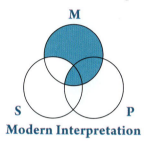

Modern Interpretation

Exercises 6D

I.

5. **AEE-2**

Answer: All six rules are met.

Rule 1: The middle term is distributed in the second premise.

Rule 2: The major term is distributed in the conclusion and in the major premise.

Rule 3: It does not have two negative premises.

Rule 4: It has a negative premise and a negative conclusion.

Rule 5: It has a negative conclusion and a negative premise.

Rule 6: It does not have universal premises and a particular conclusion.

9. **AII-3**

Answer: All six rules are met.

Rule 1: The middle term is distributed in the first premise.

Rule 2: The major term is not distributed in the conclusion.

Rule 3: It does not have two negative premises.

Rule 4: It does not have a negative premise.

Rule 5: It does not have a negative conclusion.

Rule 6: It does not have universal premises and a particular conclusion.

13. **AEE-4**

Answer: All six rules are met.

Rule 1: The middle term is distributed in the second premise.

Rule 2: The major term is distributed in the conclusion and in the major premise.

Rule 3: It does not have two negative premises.

Rule 4: It has a negative premise and a negative conclusion.

Rule 5: It has a negative conclusion and a negative premise.

Rule 6: It does not have universal premises and a particular conclusion.

II.

5. Some furry creatures are lovable pets. Some eccentric people are lovable pets. So, some eccentric people are furry creatures.

Answer: Let F = *furry creatures*, L = *lovable pets*, and E = *eccentric people*.

Some F are L.
Some E are L.
Some E are F.

III-2. Invalid. Rule 1 is broken: The middle term is not distributed in at least one premise.

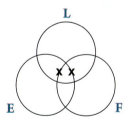

Exercises 6E

I.

5. Some M are not P.
No M are S.
Some S are not P.

Answer: Invalid

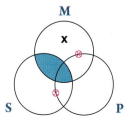

9. All M are P.
    No S are M.
    Some S are not P.

Answer: Invalid

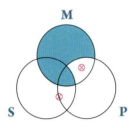

13. All M are P.
    All S are M.
    Some S are not P.

Answer: Invalid

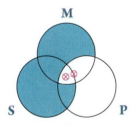

II.
5. No septic tanks are swimming pools. No sewers are swimming pools. Therefore, some septic tanks are not sewers.

Answer: Invalid. Let S = *septic tanks*, P = *swimming pools*, and W = *sewers*.

    No W are P.
    No S are P.
    Some S are not W.

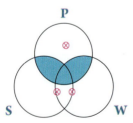

9. Some buildings are poorly constructed domiciles. No buildings are architectural nightmares. So, some architectural nightmares are poorly constructed domiciles.

Answer: Invalid. Let B = *buildings*, P = *poorly constructed domiciles*, and A = *architectural nightmares*.

Some B are P.
No B are A.
Some A are P.

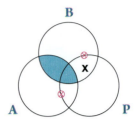

III.
5. **AEE-2**
Answer: Valid

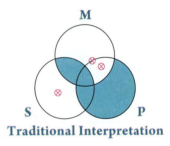
Traditional Interpretation

9. **AII-3**
Answer: Valid

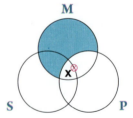
Traditional Interpretation

13. **AEE-4**
Answer: Valid

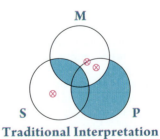
Traditional Interpretation

IV.

5. **AAI-3**

Answer: Provisionally valid under the traditional interpretation.

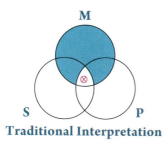

Traditional Interpretation

9. **EAO-4**

Answer: Provisionally valid under the traditional interpretation.

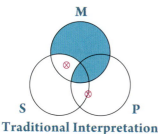

Traditional Interpretation

Exercises 6F

5. Some furry creatures are lovable pets. Some eccentric people are lovable pets. So, some eccentric people are furry creatures.

Answer: Let F = *furry creatures*, L = *lovable pets*, and E = *eccentric people*.

Some F are L.
Some E are L.
Some E are F.

III-2. Invalid. Rule 1 is broken: The middle term is not distributed in at least one premise.

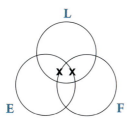

Exercises 6G.1

I.

5. Some A are non-B.
    All C are non-B.
    Some C are not A.

The syllogism violates Rule 1: The middle term must be distributed in at least one premise.

The syllogism violates Rule 2: If a term is distributed in the conclusion, then it must be distributed in a premise.

The syllogism violates Rule 5: A negative conclusion must have a negative premise.

The following Venn diagram shows that the syllogism is invalid:

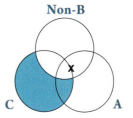

9. No A are B.
    All C are A.
    All C are B.

The syllogism violates Rule 4: A negative premise must have a negative conclusion.

The following Venn diagram shows that the syllogism is invalid:

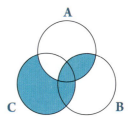

13. All C are A.
     All A are B.
     All B are C.

The syllogism violates Rule 2: If a term is distributed in the conclusion, then it must be distributed in a premise.

The following Venn diagram shows that the syllogism is invalid:

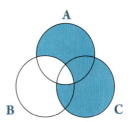

II.

5. Let S = *self-motivated students*, I = *students using their intellectual capabilities*, D = *disinterested students*, non-D = *interested students*.

All S are I.   All S are I.
No D are I.   Rewritten as: No D are I.
All S are non-D.   No S are D.

The syllogism does not violate any of the six rules.

The following Venn diagram shows that the syllogism is valid:

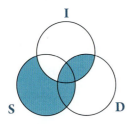

9. Let P = *preschool children*, S = *severely overweight students*, O = *obese students*, and D = *people susceptible to diabetes*.

Since the term "severely overweight students" and the term "obese students" are synonyms, we can use the same letter for both when we rewrite the syllogism.

Some O are D.   Rewritten as: Some S are D.
Some P are S.   Some P are S.
Some P are not D.   Some P are not D.

The syllogism violates Rule 1: The middle term must be distributed in at least one premise.

The syllogism violates Rule 2: If a term is distributed in the conclusion, then it must be distributed in a premise.

The following Venn diagram shows that the syllogism is invalid:

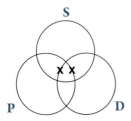

Exercises 6G.2

5. Let R = *refurbished computers*, E = *expensive things*, and U = *computers bought by my uncle*.

All U are non-E.   All U are non-E.
All U are R.   Rewritten as: All U are R.
No R are E.   All R are non-E.

The syllogism violates Rule 2: If a term is distributed in the conclusion, then it must be distributed in a premise.

The following Venn diagram shows that the syllogism is invalid:

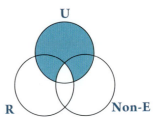

9. Let S = *starvation diets*, E = *effective ways to lose weight*, and B = *things that are bad for your heart*.

All S are B.
Some S are E.
Some E are B.

The syllogism does not violate any of the six rules.

The following Venn diagram shows that the syllogism is valid:

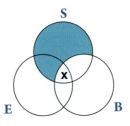

13. Let T = *traditional Western philosophy*, F = *footnotes to Plato*, and A = *Asian philosophy*.

All T are F.
No A are T.
No A are F.

The syllogism violates Rule 2: If a term is distributed in the conclusion, then it must be distributed in a premise.

The following Venn diagram shows that the syllogism is invalid:

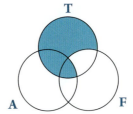

Exercises 6H

I.

5. Let R = *replaced broken cell phones*, A = *broken cell phones accompanied by a sales slip*, and I = *cell phones identical to my broken cell phone*.

Missing conclusion: My broken cell phone will not be replaced.

All R are A.
No I are A.
No I are R.

The syllogism does not violate any of the six rules.

The following Venn diagram shows that the syllogism is valid:

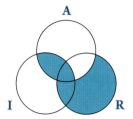

9. Let S = *people who can successfully find their way home,* L = *people who can learn logic,* and C = *students in this class.*

Missing conclusion: All the students in this class can learn logic.

All S are L.
All C are S.
All C are L.

The syllogism does not violate any of the six rules.

The following Venn diagram shows that the syllogism is valid:

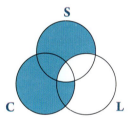

13. Let S = *state laws,* U = *unconstitutional laws,* and O = *laws overturned by the Supreme Court.*

Missing premise: All unconstitutional laws are laws overturned by the Supreme Court.

All U are O.
Some S are U.
Some S are O.

The syllogism does not violate any of the six rules.

The following Venn diagram shows that the syllogism is valid:

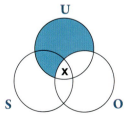

17. Let A = *airline companies,* G = *companies that take their customers for granted,* and R = *companies that refuse to give a refund on a purchase.*

Missing premise: Some airline companies are companies that refuse to give a refund on a purchase.

All R are G.
Some A are R.
Some A are G.

The syllogism does not violate any of the six rules.

The following Venn diagram shows that the syllogism is valid:

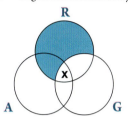

II.

5. Let K = *countries identical with the two Koreas,* W = *countries still technically at war,* and T = *war that ended only with a truce.*

Missing premise: All wars that ended only with a truce are countries still technically at war.

All T are W.
All K are T.
All K are W.

The syllogism does not violate any of the six rules.

The following Venn diagram shows that the syllogism is valid:

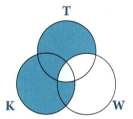

9. Let P = *people who failed,* D = *people with dreams of perfection,* and I = *splendid failures to do the impossible.*

Missing premise: All people with dreams of perfection are splendid failures to do the impossible.

All D are I.
All P are D.
All P are I.

The syllogism does not violate any of the six rules.

The following Venn diagram shows that the syllogism is valid:

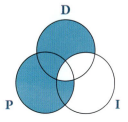

Exercises 6I

I.

5.   All B are D.   All B are D.
     No E are C.   No E are C.
     No A are non-C.   Rewritten as: All A are C.
     All non-A are non-B.   All B are A.
     All D are non-E.   No D are E.

     No E are C.
     All A are C.
     No A are E. (*Intermediate conclusion*)

The syllogism does not violate any of the six rules.

The following Venn diagram shows that the syllogism is valid:

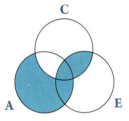

     No A are E.
     All B are A.
     No B are E. (*Intermediate conclusion*)

The syllogism does not violate any of the six rules.

The following Venn diagram shows that the syllogism is valid:

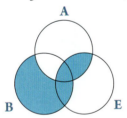

     No B are E.
     All B are D.
     No D are E.

The syllogism violates Rule 2: If a term is distributed in the conclusion, then it must be distributed in a premise.

The following Venn diagram shows that the syllogism is invalid:

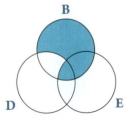

9.   All D are C.
     All C are A.

All four possible categorical statements (**A, E, I, O**) as the conclusion will result in an invalid syllogism.

For example, if either **E** or **O** is used, then the subsequent syllogisms will violate Rule 5: A negative conclusion must have a negative premise. On the other hand, if **A** is used, then the syllogism will violate Rule 2: If a term is distributed in the conclusion, then it must be distributed in a premise. Finally, if **I** is used, then the syllogism will violate Rule 6: Two universal premises cannot have a particular conclusion.

II.

5.   Let F = *famous sitcoms*, C = *controversial shows*, M = *shows written for mass audiences*, and X = *X-rated movies*.

     No F are C.   No F are C.
     All F are M.   Rewritten as: All F are M.
     All X are non-M.   No X are M.
     All X are C.   All X are C.

     No F are C.
     All F are M.

All four possible categorical statements (**A, E, I, O**) as the conclusion will result in an invalid syllogism.

For example, if either **A** or **I** is used, then the subsequent syllogisms will violate Rule 4: A negative premise must have a negative conclusion. On the other hand, if **E** is used, then the syllogism will violate Rule 2: If a term is distributed in the conclusion, then it must be distributed in a premise. Finally, if **O** is used, then the syllogism will violate Rule 6: Two universal premises cannot have a particular conclusion.

9.   Let N = *all neighbors identical to my neighbor*, L = *people who play loud music*, D = *drum sounds*, H = *hearts of songs*, M = *people who play music that has a melody*, and Y = *music that you can hear*.

     All N are L.
     All D are H.
     All N are M.
     All Y are L.
     All M are D.
     All Y are H.

     All D are H.
     All M are D.
     All M are H. (*Intermediate conclusion*)

The syllogism does not violate any of the six rules.
The following Venn diagram shows that the syllogism is valid:

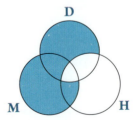

All M are H.
All N are M.
All N are H. (*Intermediate conclusion*)

The syllogism does not violate any of the six rules.

The following Venn diagram shows that the syllogism is valid:

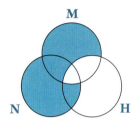

All N are H.
All N are L.

All four possible categorical statements (**A, E, I, O**) as the conclusion will result in invalid syllogisms.

For example, if either **E** or **O** is used, then the subsequent syllogisms will violate Rule 5: A negative conclusion must have a negative premise. On the other hand, if **A** is used, then the syllogism will violate Rule 2: If a term is distributed in the conclusion, then it must be distributed in a premise. Finally, if **I** is used, then the syllogism will violate Rule 6: Two universal premises cannot have a particular conclusion.

CHAPTER 7

Exercises 7A

I.

5. Let C = *My car does look great*, and M = *it gets great gas mileage*: ~ C · M

Although you could translate the first statement simply as C (where C = *My car does not look great*), nevertheless, ~ C captures the English more accurately.

9. Let C = *candy is bad for your teeth*, and Q = *tobacco is bad for your teeth*: C ∨ Q
13. Let T = *Toothpaste is good for your teeth*, and B = *tobacco is good for your teeth*: T · ~ B
17. Let R = *My room could use a good cleaning*, and L = *I am too lazy to do anything about it*: R · L
21. Let T = *I will leave a big tip*, and E = *the dinner is excellent*: T ⊃ E
25. Let G = *Grover Cleveland was the greatest U.S. president*: ~ G

Although you could translate the statement simply as G (where G = *It is false that Grover Cleveland was the greatest U.S. president*); nevertheless, ~ G captures the English more accurately.

29. Let B = *Barbara is going to lose her football bet*, and J = *Johnny will get a night at the ballet*: B · J
33. Let D = *driving too fast is hazardous to your health*, and B = *driving without buckling up (is hazardous to your health)*: D ⊃ B
37. Let R = *my room could use a good cleaning*, and L = *I am too lazy to do anything about it*: L ⊃ R
41. Let R = *it rains tomorrow*, and W = *I will have to water my plants*: R ⊃ ~ W
45. Let O = *My car is old*, and R = *it is still reliable*: O · R

II.

5. Sufficient condition. Since June has exactly 30 days, if the antecedent is true, then the consequent will be true as well.
9. Sufficient condition. Since 100 pennies is the equivalent of $1, if the antecedent is true, then the consequent will be true as well.
13. Sufficient condition. Since a banana is a fruit, if the antecedent is true, then the consequent will be true as well.

III.

5. Necessary condition. June has exactly 30 days. Given this, if this month does *not* have exactly 30 days, then this month is *not* June.
9. Necessary condition. If I do *not* have *at least* the equivalent of $1, then I have *at most* 99 cents. Given this, I do *not* have exactly 100 pennies.
13. Necessary condition. If I am *not* eating a fruit, then I am *not* eating a banana.

Exercises 7B.1

5. L ⊃ ~ P   This is a *WFF*.

9. [(P Q] ∨ ~ R   This is not a *WFF*. **Rule 1:** The dot, wedge, horseshoe, and triple bar must always go *between* two statements (simple or compound). **Rule 4:** *Parentheses* must be used to indicate the main operator.

13. P Q   This is not a *WFF*. **Rule 1:** The dot, wedge, horseshoe, and triple bar must always go *between* two statements (simple or compound).

Exercises 7B.2

The *main operator* is circled in each example.

5. L ⊃ ~ P
9. (P · Q) ∨ ~ R
13. ~ K ⊃ ~ P
17. [(M ∨ P) ⊃ (Q ∨ R)] ∨ (S · ~ P)
21. ~ Q · P
25. L ⊃ (~ P ⊃ Q)

Exercises 7B.3

I.

5. Let S = *you can save $100 a month,* A = *you can afford the insurance,* and B = *you can buy a motorcycle.*

$$S \supset (A \supset B)$$

The second use of a conditional, $A \supset B$, must be placed within parentheses so it becomes the consequent of the conditional that has S as the antecedent.

9. Let W = *Walter can drive to Pittsburgh next weekend,* S = *Sandy can drive to Pittsburgh next weekend,* J = *Jessica will come home,* and F = *Jennifer is able to arrive on time.*

$$\sim (W \vee S) \supset (\sim J \vee F)$$

The antecedent is the negation of a disjunction, and it must be placed within parentheses; the consequent is a disjunction, so it too must be placed within parentheses.

13. Let D = *your disc player breaks,* B = *I will get you a new one for your birthday,* and F = *you can see about getting it fixed.*

$$(D \supset B) \vee F$$

The first disjunct is a conditional, so it has to be placed in parentheses.

17. Let S = *you will eat a lot of salads,* and V = *you will absorb a lot of vitamins.*

$$\sim (S \supset V) \cdot \sim (V \supset S)$$

The main operator is a dot, so parentheses must be placed around each conjunct with the negation sign outside of each set of parentheses.

21. Let S = *Sally got a promotion,* L = *Louis asks for a raise,* and J = *he [Louis] looks for another job.*

$$S \cdot (L \vee J)$$

25. Let M = *Mary owns a motorcycle,* P = *she [Mary] passes the motorcycle driver's test,* B = *she [Mary] will buy her own motorcycle,* and T = *she [Mary] will use Tom's [motorcycle].*

$$\sim M \cdot [P \supset (B \vee T)]$$

29. Let C = *Prison populations will continue to grow,* S = *longer prison sentences will be imposed,* N = *new laws are created,* P = *profiling is stopped,* R = *punishment is seen as retribution,* and D = *punishment can work as a deterrent.*

$$[(C \cdot S) \supset (N \cdot \sim P)] \cdot (R \supset \sim D)$$

II.

5. Let S = *a spirit of harmony will survive in America,* and D = *each of us remembers that we share a common destiny:*
$$S \supset D$$

9. Let F = *I have failed,* and W = *I've just found 10,000 ways that won't work:* $\sim F \cdot W$

13. Let H = *the only tool you have is a hammer,* and N = *you tend to see every problem as a nail:* $H \supset N$

17. Let B = *The bankrupt New York City Off-Track Betting Corporation will close all of its branches in the city's five boroughs,* S = *shutter its account-wagering operation at the close of business on Friday,* and R = *the company gets some relief:* $(B \cdot S) \vee R$

Exercises 7C.1

5. (a) R is true. The negation denies the truth value of whatever follows it.

9. (a) Yes. A disjunction is true if at least one disjunct is true.

13. (c) S could be true or false. A conditional can be true if the antecedent is true and the consequent true, or if the antecedent is false.

17. (c) S could be true or false. A biconditional is true when both components have the same truth value (either both true or both false).

Exercises 7C.2

I.

5.

Q	S	Q ≡ S
F	F	**T**

9.

Q	R	S	(Q ⊃ R) · S
F	T	F	T **F** F

13.

R	S	P	(R · ~S) · P
T	F	T	TT **T** T

17.

P	Q	R	S	[P ∨ (Q · R)] ∨ ~S
T	F	T	F	T F **T** T

II.

5. Cannot be determined. Since Q is true, one component of the biconditional is true. However, because S is unassigned, it could be either true or false. Therefore, if S is true, then the compound proposition is true; but if S is false, then the compound proposition is false.

9.

Q	R	S	(Q ⊃ R) · S
T	F		F **F**

13.

R	S	P	(R · ~S) · P
F		T	F **F**

17.

P	Q	R	S	[P ∨ (Q · R)] ∨ ~S
T	T	F		T F **T**

Exercises 7D

5.

R	S	Q	(R · S) ∨ Q
T	T	T	T T
T	T	F	T T
T	F	T	F T
T	F	F	F F
F	T	T	F T
F	T	F	F F
F	F	T	F T
F	F	F	F F

9.

Q	R	P	~(Q · R) ⊃ P
T	T	T	F T T
T	T	F	F T T
T	F	T	T F T
T	F	F	T F F
F	T	T	T F T
F	T	F	T F F
F	F	T	T F T
F	F	F	T F F

13.

P	S	R	P ≡ (~S ∨ ~R)
T	T	T	F F F F
T	T	F	T F T T
T	F	T	T T T F
T	F	F	T T T T
F	T	T	T F F F
F	T	F	F F T T
F	F	T	F T T F
F	F	F	F T T T

17.

P	Q	R	~[P ⊃ (Q ∨ R)]
T	T	T	F T T
T	T	F	F T T
T	F	T	F T T
T	F	F	T F F
F	T	T	F T T
F	T	F	F T T
F	F	T	F T T
F	F	F	F T F

21.

P	Q	P ⊃ ~Q
T	T	F F
T	F	T T
F	T	T F
F	F	T T

25.

Q	S	Q ≡ S
T	T	T
T	F	F
F	T	F
F	F	T

29.

Q	R	S	(Q ⊃ R) · ~S
T	T	T	T F T
T	T	F	T T T
T	F	T	F F F
T	F	F	F F T
F	T	T	T F F
F	T	F	T T T
F	F	T	T F F
F	F	F	T T T

33.

R	S	P	(R · ~S) ∨ P
T	T	T	F F T
T	T	F	F F F
T	F	T	T T T
T	F	F	T T T
F	T	T	F F T
F	T	F	F F F
F	F	T	F T T
F	F	F	F T F

37.

P	Q	R	S	[P ∨ (Q · R)] ∨ ~S
T	T	T	T	T T T F
T	T	T	F	T T T T
T	T	F	T	T F T F
T	T	F	F	T F T T
T	F	T	T	T F T F
T	F	T	F	T F T T
T	F	F	T	T F T F
T	F	F	F	T F T T
F	T	T	T	T T T F
F	T	T	F	T T T T
F	T	F	T	F F F F
F	T	F	F	F F T T
F	F	T	T	F F F F
F	F	T	F	F F T T
F	F	F	T	F F F F
F	F	F	F	F F T T

Exercises 7E

5. Tautology

P	Q	(P v ~ P) v Q
T	T	T F T
T	F	T F T
F	T	F T T
F	F	T T T

9. Tautology

R	S	~ (R · ~ R) v ~ (S v ~ S)
T	T	T FF T F T F
T	F	T FF T F T T
F	T	T FT T F T F
F	F	T FT T F T T

13. Tautology

P	P ⊃ P
T	T
F	T

17. Tautology

R	S	(R · ~ R) ⊃ (S v ~ S)
T	T	FF T T F
T	F	FF T T T
F	T	FT T T F
F	F	FT T T T

Exercises 7F.1

5. Logically equivalent

P	Q	R	P v (Q v R)	(P v Q) v R
T	T	T	T T	T T
T	T	F	T T	T T
T	F	T	T T	T T
T	F	F	T F	T T
F	T	T	T T	T T
F	T	F	T T	T T
F	F	T	T T	F T
F	F	F	F F	F F

9. Logically equivalent

P	P	~ ~ P
T	T	T F
F	F	F T

13. Logically equivalent

P	Q	P ≡ Q	(P · Q) v (~ P · ~ Q)
T	T	T	T T F FF
T	F	F	F F F FT
F	T	F	F F T FF
F	F	T	F T T TT

17. Not logically equivalent

P	Q	~ (P · Q)	~ P · ~ Q
T	T	F T	F F F
T	F	T F	F F T
F	T	T F	T F F
F	F	T F	T T T

21. Not logically equivalent

P	Q	P ≡ Q	(P ⊃ Q) v (Q ⊃ P)
T	T	T	T T T
T	F	F	F T T
F	T	F	T T F
F	F	T	T T T

25. Not logically equivalent

P	Q	P ⊃ Q	~ Q v P
T	T	T	F T
T	F	F	T T
F	T	T	F F
F	F	T	T T

Exercises 7F.2

I.

5. Consistent

T	U	T ≡ U	T · U
T	T	T	T
T	F	F	F
F	T	F	F
F	F	T	F

9. Contradictory

C	D	C·D	~Cv~D
T	T	T	F F F
T	F	F	F T T
F	T	F	T T F
F	F	F	T T T

13. Consistent

M	Mv~M	M
T	T F	T
F	T T	F

17. Consistent

Q	R	S	(Q⊃~R)⊃S	S≡(Q·R)
T	T	T	F F T	T T
T	T	F	F F T	F T
T	F	T	T T T	F F
T	F	F	T T F	T F
F	T	T	T F T	F F
F	T	F	T F F	T F
F	F	T	T T T	F F
F	F	F	T T F	T F

II.

5. The truth table analysis reveals that in line 4 the main operators are all true (there are other lines where this is the case, too). Statements are consistent if there is *at least one* line on their respective truth tables where the main operators are all true; therefore, this is a set of consistent statements.

P	Q	S	P⊃Q	Q⊃~P	Qv~S
T	T	T	F F	F F	T F
T	T	F	F F	F F	T T
T	F	T	T T	T F	F F
T	F	F	T T	T F	T T
F	T	T	T F	T T	T F
F	T	F	T F	T T	T T
F	F	T	T T	T T	F F
F	F	F	T T	T T	T T

9. The truth table analysis reveals that in line 5 the main operators are all true (there are other lines where this is the case, too). Statements are consistent if there is *at least one* line on their respective truth tables where the main operators are all true; therefore, this is a set of consistent statements.

R	P	S	Q	Rv(~P·S)	Qv~P	Q⊃~P
T	T	T	T	T F F	T F	F F
T	T	T	F	T F F	F F	T F
T	T	F	T	T F F	T F	F F
T	T	F	F	T F F	F F	T F
T	F	T	T	T T T	T T	T T
T	F	T	F	T T T	T T	T T
T	F	F	T	T T F	T T	T T
T	F	F	F	T T F	T T	T T
F	T	T	T	F F F	T F	F F
F	T	T	F	F F F	F F	T F
F	T	F	T	F F F	T F	F F
F	T	F	F	F F F	F F	T F
F	F	T	T	T T T	T T	T T
F	F	T	F	T T T	T T	T T
F	F	F	T	F T F	T T	T T
F	F	F	F	F T F	T T	T T

Exercises 7G.1

I.

5. Invalid. Line 2 has the premise true and the conclusion false.

R	S	~Rv~S	/~R
T	T	F F F	F
T	F	F T T	F √
F	T	T T F	T
F	F	T T T	T

9. Valid

R	S	~(RvS)	~R	/~S
T	T	F T	F	F
T	F	F T	F	T
F	T	F T	T	F
F	F	T F	T	T

13. Valid

S	Q	R	S v (Q v R)		~Q	~R	/ S
T	T	T	T	T	F	F	T
T	T	F	T	T	F	T	T
T	F	T	T	T	T	F	T
T	F	F	T	F	T	T	T
F	T	T	T	T	F	F	F
F	T	F	T	T	F	T	F
F	F	T	T	T	T	F	F
F	F	F	F	F	T	T	F

13. Invalid

P	R	S	~(R·S)		~R⊃P		/~S	
T	T	T	F	T	F	T	F	
T	T	F	T	F	F	T	T	
T	F	T	T	F	T	T	F	✓
T	F	F	T	F	T	T	T	
F	T	T	F	T	F	T	F	
F	T	F	T	F	F	T	T	
F	F	T	T	F	T	F	F	
F	F	F	T	F	T	F	T	

II.

5. Valid

P	Q	R	S	(P⊃Q)·(R⊃S)			P v R	/Q v S
T	T	T	T	T	T	T	T	T
T	T	T	F	T	F	F	T	T
T	T	F	T	T	T	T	T	T
T	T	F	F	T	T	T	T	T
T	F	T	T	F	F	T	T	T
T	F	T	F	F	F	F	T	F
T	F	F	T	F	F	T	T	T
T	F	F	F	F	F	T	T	F
F	T	T	T	T	T	T	T	T
F	T	T	F	T	F	F	T	T
F	T	F	T	T	T	T	F	T
F	T	F	F	T	T	T	F	T
F	F	T	T	T	T	T	T	T
F	F	T	F	T	F	F	T	F
F	F	F	T	T	T	T	F	T
F	F	F	F	T	T	T	F	F

17. Invalid

S	Q	R	[(S·Q)·R]⊃Q			Q	R	/~S	
T	T	T	T	T	T	T	T	F	✓
T	T	F	T	F	T	T	F	F	
T	F	T	F	F	T	F	T	F	
T	F	F	F	F	T	F	F	F	
F	T	T	F	F	T	T	T	T	
F	T	F	F	F	T	T	F	T	
F	F	T	F	F	T	F	T	T	
F	F	F	F	F	T	F	F	T	

9. Invalid

R	S	R≡S	/R	
T	T	T	T	
T	F	F	T	
F	T	F	F	
F	F	T	F	✓

21. Valid

P	Q	R	P⊃(Q v ~R)			Q⊃~R		/P⊃~R	
T	T	T	T	T	F	F	F	F	F
T	T	F	T	T	T	T	T	T	T
T	F	T	F	F	F	T	F	F	F
T	F	F	T	T	T	T	T	T	T
F	T	T	T	T	F	F	F	T	F
F	T	F	T	T	T	T	T	T	T
F	F	T	T	F	F	T	F	T	F
F	F	F	T	T	T	T	T	T	T

25.   Invalid

P	Q	S	(P v Q)	≡ S	/ P
T	T	T	T	T	T
T	T	F	T	F	T
T	F	T	T	T	T
T	F	F	T	F	T
F	T	T	T	T	F √
F	T	F	T	F	F
F	F	T	F	F	F
F	F	F	F	T	F √

III.

5.   Invalid. Let S = we stop interfering in other countries' internal affairs, and E = we will find ourselves with more enemies than we can handle.

S	E	S v E	S	/~E
T	T	T	T	F √
T	F	T	T	T
F	T	T	F	F
F	F	F	F	T

9.   Invalid. Let P = the prosecuting attorney's claims are correct, and G = the defendant is guilty.

P	G	P ⊃ G	~G	/ P
T	T	T	F	T
T	F	F	T	T
F	T	T	F	F
F	F	T	T	F √

13.   Invalid. Let U = UFOs exist, and L = there is life on other planets.

U	L	U ⊃ L	~U	/ L
T	T	T	F	T
T	F	F	F	F
F	T	T	T	T
F	F	T	T	F √

17.   Invalid. Let V = you take 1000 mg of vitamin C every day, and C = you will get a cold.

V	C	V ⊃ ~C	~C	/ V
T	T	F F	F	T
T	F	T T	T	T
F	T	T F	F	F
F	F	T T	T	F √

Exercises 7G.2

5.   Valid. Let R = you are right, and W = you are wrong.

R	W	R v W	~R	/ W
T	T	T	F	T
T	F	T	F	F
F	T	T	T	T
F	F	F	T	F

9.   Invalid. Let J = Joyce went south on I-15 from Las Vegas, and L = Joyce got to Los Angeles.

J	L	J ⊃ L	~J	/~L
T	T	T	F	F
T	F	F	F	T
F	T	T	T	F √
F	F	T	T	T

13.   Valid. Let E = Eddie can vote, and R = he (Eddie) is registered.

E	R	E ≡ R	~R	/~E
T	T	T	F	F
T	F	F	T	F
F	T	F	F	T
F	F	T	T	T

Exercises 7H.1

I.

5.   Invalid

P	Q	R	S	[P v (Q v S)] ⊃ R	~P	~Q	~S	/~R
F	F	T	F	F F T	T	T	T	F √

9. Valid

P	Q	R	S	~(P∨Q)∨~(R·S)	P·Q	R	/~S
T	T	T	T	F T [F]F T	[T]	[T]	[F]

The only assignments available to get the conclusion false and the second and third premises true make it impossible to then get the first premise true. Since it is impossible to get all the premises true and the conclusion false at the same time, we have shown that the argument is valid.

13. Although there is only one way to get the conclusion false, there are three ways to get each premise true. Therefore, we might need to explore all the possibilities:

(Option 1)

R	Q	S	(R∨Q)⊃~S	Q∨S	/R
F	T	T	T [F]F	[T]	[F]

This assignment of truth values makes the conclusion false, and the second premise true. However, since the first premise is false with this assignment, this cannot give us all true premises and a false conclusion. Therefore, we must try the next option.

(Option 2)

R	Q	S	(R∨Q)⊃~S	Q∨S	/R
F	T	F	T [T]T	[T]	[F] √

This assignment of truth values makes the conclusion false, and all the premises true; therefore, the argument is invalid. (Thus, it is not necessary to try the other option.)

17. Invalid

R	Q	S	~(~R∨~Q)⊃~S	Q⊃S	/~R⊃S
F	F	F	F T TT [T]T	[T]	T [F] √

II.
5. Invalid. Let *C* = *animals are conscious*, *P* = *animals do feel pain*, and *R* = *animals do have rights.*

C	P	R	(~C∨~P)⊃~R	~R	~P	/~C
T	F	F	F TT [T]T	[T]	[T]	[F] √

9. Invalid. Let *E* = *Elvis sold the most records of all time*, *B* = *the Beatles sold the most records of all time*, and *C* = *I won the contest.*

E	B	C	(E∨B)⊃~C	~B	/C
F	F	F	F [T]T	[T]	[F] √

13. Invalid. Let *J* = *Joyce went south on I-15 from Las Vegas*, and *L* = *Joyce got to Los Angeles.*

J	L	J⊃L	~J	/~L
F	T	[T]	[T]	[F] √

17. Valid. Let *E* = *Eddie can vote*, and *R* = *he (Eddie) is registered.*

E	R	E≡R	E	/R
T	F	[F]	[T]	[F]

Since the only way to get the conclusion false is for *R* to be false, and the only way to get the second premise true is for *E* to be true, it will be impossible to then get the first premise true. Thus, the argument is valid.

Exercises 7H.2
5. Consistent

R	P	S	Q	R∨(~P·S)	Q∨~P	Q⊃~P
T	F	T	T	[T]T T	[T]T	[T]T

9. Consistent

M	P	Q	R	~M∨~P	~M∨Q	P∨R
F	T			T [T]	T [T]	[T]

13. Consistent

Q	R	S	~(Q⊃R)⊃S	S∨(Q·R)
	T		[T]	[T]

CHAPTER 8

Exercises 8B
I.
[5] 3. ~Q	1, 2, MT
[9] 3. P⊃Q	1, 2, DS
[13] 3. R⊃P	1, 2, HS

II.
[5] 3. Q·S	1, 2, DS
[9] 3. ~(T⊃R)	1, 2, MT
[13] 3. ~(P·~R)	1, 2, MT

III.

[5] 5. $P \supset S$ 1, 4, HS
     6. $P \supset Q$ 3, 5, HS
     7. Q 2, 6, MP
[9] 5. $P \supset Q$ 3, 4, HS
     6. $\sim R$ 2, 5, MP
     7. $\sim S$ 1, 6, DS

IV.

[5] 5. $\sim S$ 1, 3, DS
     6. $P \supset Q$ 2, 5, MP
     7. R 4, 6, MP
[9] 5. $\sim P$ 2, 3, MT
     6. $\sim S$ 4, 5, MT
     7. $P \vee Q$ 1, 6, DS
     8. Q 5, 7, DS

Exercises 8C

I.

[5] 1. $\sim P \supset (Q \vee R)$
     2. $(\sim P \supset \sim S) \supset \sim L$
     3. $(Q \vee R) \supset \sim S$ / $\sim L$
     4. $\sim P \supset \sim S$ 1, 3, HS
     5. $\sim L$ 2, 4, MP
[9] 1. $R \vee S$
     2. $\sim (P \vee Q)$
     3. $R \supset (P \vee Q)$
     4. $S \supset (Q \vee R)$ / $Q \vee R$
     5. $\sim R$ 2, 3, MT
     6. S 1, 5, DS
     7. $Q \vee R$ 4, 6, MP
[13] 1. $P \vee (S \supset Q)$
     2. $\sim Q$
     3. $P \supset Q$
     4. $\sim S \supset R$ / R
     5. $\sim P$ 2, 3, MT
     6. $S \supset Q$ 1, 5, DS
     7. $\sim S$ 2, 6, MT
     8. R 4, 7, MP
[17] 1. $Q \supset P$
     2. S
     3. $(Q \vee \sim R) \supset \sim P$
     4. $S \supset (Q \vee \sim R)$ / $\sim R$
     5. $Q \vee \sim R$ 2, 4, MP
     6. $\sim P$ 3, 5, MP
     7. $\sim Q$ 1, 6, MT
     8. $\sim R$ 5, 7, DS

II.

[5] 1. $S \supset (C \supset H)$
     2. $E \supset S$
     3. $E \vee (S \vee C)$
     4. $\sim (C \supset H)$ / C

     5. $\sim S$ 1, 4, MT
     6. $\sim E$ 2, 5, MT
     7. $S \vee C$ 3, 6, DS
     8. C 5, 7, DS
[9] 1. $(C \vee M) \supset L$
     2. $S \supset (\sim E \supset \sim L)$
     3. $E \vee S$
     4. $\sim E$ / $\sim (C \vee M)$
     5. S 3, 4, DS
     6. $\sim E \supset \sim L$ 2, 5, MP
     7. $\sim L$ 4, 6, MP
     8. $\sim (C \vee M)$ 1, 7, MT

Exercises 8D

I.

[5] 3. $\sim P \cdot (T \supset U)$ 1, 2, Conj
[9] 3. $P \cdot Q$ 1, 2, Conj
[13] 3. $P \cdot [(R \supset S) \vee Q]$ 1, 2, Conj

II.

[5] 2. P 1, Simp
[9] 3. $(P \supset Q) \cdot (R \vee S)$ 1, 2, Conj
[13] 2. $\sim P \vee \sim S$ 1, Simp

III.

[5] 1. P
     2. $(P \vee Q) \supset R$
     3. $R \supset S$ / S
     4. $P \vee Q$ 1, Add
     5. R 2, 4, MP
     6. S 3, 5, MP
[9] 1. $P \cdot (S \vee Q)$
     2. $(P \vee R) \supset M$ / M
     3. P 1, Simp
     4. $P \vee R$ 3, Add
     5. M 2, 4, MP
[13] 1. $(P \supset Q) \cdot (R \supset S)$
     2. $P \vee L$
     3. $(L \supset M) \cdot (N \supset K)$ / $Q \vee M$
     4. $P \supset Q$ 1, Simp
     5. $L \supset M$ 3, Simp
     6. $(P \supset Q) \cdot (L \supset M)$ 4, 5, Conj
     7. $Q \vee M$ 2, 6, CD
[17] 1. $S \vee P$
     2. $(R \vee S) \supset L$
     3. $(P \vee Q) \supset R$
     4. $\sim S$ / L
     5. P 1, 4, DS
     6. $P \vee Q$ 5, Add
     7. R 3, 6, MP
     8. $R \vee S$ 7, Add
     9. L 2, 8, MP

[21]
1. $R \supset P$
2. $(Q \cdot \sim R) \supset (S \cdot \sim R)$
3. $\sim P$
4. $P \vee Q$ — / S
5. Q — 3, 4, DS
6. $\sim R$ — 1, 3, MT
7. $Q \cdot \sim R$ — 5, 6, Conj
8. $S \cdot \sim R$ — 2, 7, MP
9. S — 8, Simp

[25]
1. $(M \vee N) \supset (P \cdot K)$
2. $(P \vee \sim Q) \supset [(R \supset L) \cdot S]$
3. M — / $P \cdot (R \supset L)$
4. $M \vee N$ — 3, Add
5. $P \cdot K$ — 1, 4, MP
6. P — 5, Simp
7. $P \vee \sim Q$ — 6, Add
8. $(R \supset L) \cdot S$ — 2, 7, MP
9. $R \supset L$ — 8, Simp
10. $P \cdot (R \supset L)$ — 6, 9, Conj

[29]
1. $P \cdot \sim Q$
2. $(P \vee \sim R) \supset (\sim S \cdot M)$
3. $(\sim S \cdot P) \supset (P \supset N)$ — / N
4. P — 1, Simp
5. $P \vee \sim R$ — 4, Add
6. $\sim S \cdot M$ — 2, 5, MP
7. $\sim S$ — 6, Simp
8. $\sim S \cdot P$ — 4, 7, Conj
9. $P \supset N$ — 3, 8, MP
10. N — 4, 9, MP

IV.

[5]
1. $\sim B \vee \sim H$
2. $P \supset S$
3. $(\sim B \supset F) \cdot (\sim H \supset \sim A)$
4. $(F \vee \sim A) \supset \sim S$ — / $\sim P$
5. $F \vee \sim A$ — 1, 3, CD
6. $\sim S$ — 4, 5, MP
7. $\sim P$ — 2, 6, MT

[9]
1. $G \supset C$
2. $U \supset \sim S$
3. G
4. $C \supset U$ — / $\sim S$
5. C — 1, 3, MP
6. U — 4, 5, MP
7. $\sim S$ — 2, 6, MP

Exercises 8E

I.

[5] 2. $\sim \sim S$ — 1, DN
[9] 2. $P \cdot (Q \vee R)$ — 1, Dist
[13] 2. $S \cdot (Q \cdot R)$ — 1, Assoc

II.

[5] 2. $\sim (P \vee Q)$ — 1, DM
[9] 2. $R \vee [S \vee (P \supset Q)]$ — 1, Assoc
[13] 2. $\{[R \supset (P \cdot Q)] \vee L\} \vee M$ — 1, Assoc

III.

[5]
1. $P \supset (Q \cdot R)$
2. $\sim Q \cdot S$ — / $\sim P$
3. $\sim Q$ — 2, Simp
4. $\sim Q \vee \sim R$ — 3, Add
5. $\sim (Q \cdot R)$ — 4, DM
6. $\sim P$ — 1, 5, MT

[9]
1. $\sim (P \cdot Q)$
2. $(\sim P \vee \sim Q) \supset (R \cdot S)$
3. $(R \vee \sim Q) \supset \sim T$ — / $\sim T$
4. $\sim P \vee \sim Q$ — 1, DM
5. $R \cdot S$ — 2, 4, MP
6. R — 5, Simp
7. $R \vee \sim Q$ — 6, Add
8. $\sim T$ — 3, 7, MP

[13]
1. $\sim P$
2. $Q \vee (R \cdot P)$ — / Q
3. $(Q \vee R) \cdot (Q \vee P)$ — 2, Dist
4. $Q \vee P$ — 3, Simp
5. Q — 1, 4, DS

[17]
1. $P \vee Q$
2. $(R \cdot S) \cdot L$ — / $[(L \cdot R) \cdot P] \vee [(L \cdot R) \cdot Q]$
3. $L \cdot (R \cdot S)$ — 2, Com
4. $(L \cdot R) \cdot S$ — 3, Assoc
5. $L \cdot R$ — 4, Simp
6. $(L \cdot R) \cdot (P \vee Q)$ — 1, 5, Conj
7. $[(L \cdot R) \cdot P] \vee [(L \cdot R) \cdot Q]$ — 6, Dist

[21]
1. $P \supset \sim \sim R$
2. $P \cdot \sim (S \cdot R)$ — / $\sim S$
3. P — 2, Simp
4. $\sim \sim R$ — 1, 3, MP
5. $\sim (S \cdot R)$ — 2, Simp
6. $\sim S \vee \sim R$ — 5, DM
7. $\sim S$ — 4, 6, DS

[25]
1. $\sim (P \cdot Q)$
2. R
3. $[S \supset (P \cdot Q)] \cdot (R \supset L)$
4. $S \vee R$ — / $\sim P \vee (\sim Q \cdot L)$
5. $(P \cdot Q) \vee L$ — 3, 4, CD
6. L — 1, 5, DS
7. $\sim P \vee \sim Q$ — 1, DM
8. $L \vee \sim P$ — 6, Add
9. $(\sim P \vee \sim Q) \cdot (L \vee \sim P)$ — 7, 8, Conj
10. $(\sim P \vee \sim Q) \cdot (\sim P \vee L)$ — 9, Com
11. $\sim P \vee (\sim Q \cdot L)$ — 10, Dist

[29]
1. $P \supset \sim Q$
2. $P \cdot (R \vee Q)$
3. $R \supset S$ — / S
4. P — 2, Simp
5. $\sim Q$ — 1, 4, MP
6. $R \vee Q$ — 2, Simp
7. R — 5, 6, DS
8. S — 3, 7, MP

[33]
1. $\sim (J \equiv M) \cdot R$
2. $[S \supset (L \cdot M)] \vee (N \cdot J)$
3. $[S \supset (L \cdot M)] \supset (J \equiv M)$ — / $(J \vee K) \cdot (R \vee \sim H)$
4. $\sim (J \equiv M)$ — 1, Simp

5. $\sim[S \supset (L \cdot M)]$ 3, 4, MT
6. $N \cdot J$ 2, 5, DS
7. J 6, Simp
8. $J \vee K$ 7, Add
9. R 1, Simp
10. $R \vee \sim H$ 9, Add
11. $(J \vee K) \cdot (R \vee \sim H)$ 8, 10, Conj

IV.

[5] 1. $(\sim A \cdot L) \vee (\sim A \cdot F)$
2. $\sim F$ / L
3. $\sim A \cdot (L \vee F)$ 1, Dist
4. $L \vee F$ 3, Simp
5. L 2, 4, DS

[9] 1. $N \supset (R \cdot M)$
2. $(N \cdot P) \vee (N \cdot F)$ / $N \cdot M$
3. $N \cdot (P \vee F)$ 2, Dist
4. N 3, Simp
5. $R \cdot M$ 1, 4, MP
6. M 5, Simp
7. $N \cdot M$ 4, 6, Conj

Exercises 8F

I.

[5] 2. $(R \supset S) \cdot (S \supset R)$ 1, Equiv
[9] 2. $P \supset Q$ 1, Impl
[13] 2. $[(S \vee L) \cdot (Q \vee K)] \vee [\sim (S \vee L) \cdot \sim (Q \vee K)]$ 1, Equiv

II.

[5] 2. $S \supset P$ 1, Impl
[9] 2. $[(R \vee K) \supset (Q \vee S)] \cdot [(Q \vee S) \supset (R \vee K)]$ 1, Equiv

III.

[5] 1. $S \supset (P \supset Q)$
2. $\sim Q$ / $\sim (S \cdot P)$
3. $(S \cdot P) \supset Q$ 1, Exp
4. $\sim (S \cdot P)$ 2, 3, MT

[9] 1. $P \equiv S$ / $P \supset S$
2. $(P \supset S) \cdot (S \supset P)$ 1, Equiv
3. $P \supset S$ 2, Simp

[13] 1. $(S \cdot T) \cdot R$ / S
2. $S \cdot (T \cdot R)$ 1, Assoc
3. S 2, Simp

IV.

[5] 1. $\sim Q \supset \sim P$
2. $(P \cdot R) \supset S$
3. P / $Q \vee S$
4. $P \supset Q$ 1, Trans
5. Q 3, 4, MP
6. $Q \vee S$ 5, Add

[9] 1. $\sim P \cdot Q$
2. $Q \supset (R \supset P)$ / $\sim R$
3. Q 1, Simp
4. $R \supset P$ 2, 3, MP
5. $\sim P$ 1, Simp
6. $\sim R$ 4, 5, MT

[13] 1. $[P \supset (Q \cdot R)] \cdot [S \supset (L \cdot Q)]$
2. $P \cdot R$ / $Q \cdot (R \vee L)$
3. P 2, Simp
4. $P \vee S$ 3, Add
5. $(Q \cdot R) \vee (L \cdot Q)$ 1, 4, CD
6. $(Q \cdot R) \vee (Q \cdot L)$ 5, Com
7. $Q \cdot (R \vee L)$ 6, Dist

[17] 1. $\sim (P \cdot Q) \supset (R \vee S)$
2. $\sim P \vee \sim Q$
3. T / $(T \cdot R) \vee (T \cdot S)$
4. $\sim (P \cdot Q)$ 2, DM
5. $R \vee S$ 1, 4, MP
6. $T \cdot (R \vee S)$ 3, 5, Conj
7. $(T \cdot R) \vee (T \cdot S)$ 6, Dist

[21] 1. $(P \vee Q) \vee \sim R$
2. $[(P \vee Q) \supset Q] \cdot (\sim R \supset S)$
3. $\sim P$ / $Q \vee (S \cdot \sim R)$
4. $Q \vee S$ 1, 2, CD
5. $P \vee (Q \vee \sim R)$ 1, Assoc
6. $Q \vee \sim R$ 3, 5, DS
7. $(Q \vee S) \cdot (Q \vee \sim R)$ 4, 6, Conj
8. $Q \vee (S \cdot \sim R)$ 7, Dist

[25] 1. $\sim P \supset Q$
2. $\sim R \supset (\sim S \vee P)$
3. $Q \supset \sim S$ / R
4. $\sim P \supset \sim S$ 1, 3, HS
5. $S \supset P$ 4, Trans
6. $\sim S \vee P$ 5, Impl
7. $\sim \sim (\sim S \vee P)$ 6, DN
8. $\sim \sim R$ 2, 7, MT
9. R 8, DN

[29] 1. $\sim R \vee \sim S$
2. $P \vee [Q \vee (R \cdot S)]$
3. $L \supset \sim P$ / $L \supset Q$
4. $(P \vee Q) \vee (R \cdot S)$ 2, Assoc
5. $\sim (R \cdot S)$ 1, DM
6. $P \vee Q$ 4, 5, DS
7. $\sim \sim P \vee Q$ 6, DN
8. $\sim P \supset Q$ 7, Impl
9. $L \supset Q$ 3, 8, HS

[33] 1. $S \supset Q$
2. $R \cdot S$
3. $Q \supset (L \vee \sim R)$ / L
4. S 2, Simp
5. Q 1, 4, MP
6. $L \vee \sim R$ 3, 5, MP
7. R 2, Simp
8. $\sim \sim R$ 7, DN
9. L 6, 8, DS

[37] 1. $Q \vee (P \supset S)$
2. $S \equiv (R \cdot T)$
3. $P \cdot \sim Q$ / $P \cdot R$
4. P 3, Simp
5. $\sim Q$ 3, Simp
6. $P \supset S$ 1, 5, DS

7. S — 4, 6, MP
8. $[S \supset (R \cdot T)] \cdot [(R \cdot T) \supset S]$ — 2, Equiv
9. $S \supset (R \cdot T)$ — 8, Simp
10. $R \cdot T$ — 7, 9, MP
11. R — 10, Simp
12. $P \cdot R$ — 4, 11, Conj

[41] 1. $P \vee R$
2. $\sim P \vee (Q \cdot R)$
3. $R \supset (Q \cdot S)$ — $/ Q \cdot S$
4. $R \vee P$ — 1, Com
5. $\sim R \supset P$ — 4, Impl
6. $P \supset (Q \cdot R)$ — 2, Impl
7. $\sim R \supset (Q \cdot R)$ — 5, 6, HS
8. $\sim\sim R \vee (Q \cdot R)$ — 7, Impl
9. $R \vee (Q \cdot R)$ — 8, DN
10. $(R \vee Q) \cdot (R \vee R)$ — 9, Dist
11. $R \vee R$ — 10, Simp
12. R — 11, Taut
13. $Q \cdot S$ — 3, 12, MP

[45] 1. $P \supset Q$
2. $Q \supset \sim(R \vee P)$
3. $\sim S \supset Q$
4. $S \supset (M \supset L)$
5. R
6. $M \vee P$ — $/ L$
7. $R \vee P$ — 5, Add
8. $\sim\sim(R \vee P)$ — 7, DN
9. $\sim Q$ — 2, 8, MT
10. $\sim P$ — 1, 9, MT
11. M — 6, 10, DS
12. $\sim\sim S$ — 3, 9, MT
13. S — 12, DN
14. $S \cdot M$ — 11, 13, Conj
15. $(S \cdot M) \supset L$ — 4, Exp
16. L — 14, 15, MP

[49] 1. $\sim(S \supset Q)$
2. $(M \cdot N) \supset (O \vee P)$
3. $\sim[O \vee (N \cdot P)]$
4. $N \equiv \sim(Q \cdot R)$ — $/ \sim(M \vee Q)$
5. $\sim(\sim S \vee Q)$ — 1, Impl
6. $\sim\sim S \cdot \sim Q$ — 5, DM
7. $\sim O \cdot \sim(N \cdot P)$ — 3, DM
8. $\sim Q$ — 6, Simp
9. $\sim Q \vee \sim R$ — 8, Add
10. $\sim(Q \cdot R)$ — 9, DM
11. $[N \supset \sim(Q \cdot R)] \cdot [\sim(Q \cdot R) \supset N]$ — 4, Equiv
12. $\sim(Q \cdot R) \supset N$ — 11, Simp
13. N — 10, 12, MP
14. $\sim(N \cdot P)$ — 7, Simp
15. $\sim N \vee \sim P$ — 14, DM
16. $\sim\sim N$ — 13, DN
17. $\sim P$ — 15, 16, DS
18. $\sim O$ — 7, Simp
19. $\sim O \cdot \sim P$ — 17, 18, Conj
20. $\sim(O \vee P)$ — 19, DM
21. $\sim(M \cdot N)$ — 2, 20, MT
22. $\sim M \vee \sim N$ — 21, DM

23. $\sim M$ — 16, 22, DS
24. $\sim M \cdot \sim Q$ — 8, 23, Conj
25. $\sim(M \vee Q)$ — 24, DM

V.
[5] 1. $\sim M$ — $/ \sim G \supset \sim M$
2. $\sim M \vee G$ — 1, Add
3. $M \supset G$ — 2, Impl
4. $\sim G \supset \sim M$ — 3, Trans

[9] 1. $F \supset O$
2. $F \supset W$ — $/ F \supset (W \cdot O)$
3. $\sim F \vee W$ — 2, Impl
4. $\sim F \vee O$ — 1, Impl
5. $(\sim F \vee W) \cdot (\sim F \vee O)$ — 3, 4, Conj
6. $\sim F \vee (W \cdot O)$ — 5, Dist
7. $F \supset (W \cdot O)$ — 6, Impl

[13] 1. $\sim(H \vee Y)$
2. $I \supset \sim(\sim Y \vee H)$ — $/ \sim I$
3. $\sim(Y \vee H)$ — 1, Com
4. $\sim Y \cdot \sim H$ — 3, DM
5. $\sim Y$ — 4, Simp
6. $\sim Y \vee H$ — 5, Add
7. $\sim\sim(\sim Y \vee H)$ — 6, DN
8. $\sim I$ — 2, 7, MT

Exercises 8G

I.
[5] 1. $(P \cdot Q) \supset S$
2. $P \supset Q$ — $/ P \supset S$
3. $\quad P$ — *Assumption (CP)*
4. $\quad Q$ — 2, 3, MP
5. $\quad P \cdot Q$ — 3, 4, Conj
6. $\quad S$ — 1, 5, MP
7. $P \supset S$ — 3–6, CP

[9] 1. $P \supset (Q \cdot R)$
2. $S \supset (Q \cdot T)$ — $/ (S \vee P) \supset Q$
3. $\quad S \vee P$ — *Assumption (CP)*
4. $\quad [S \supset (Q \cdot T)] \cdot [P \supset (Q \cdot R)]$ — 1, 2, Conj
5. $\quad (Q \cdot T) \vee (Q \cdot R)$ — 3, 4, CD
6. $\quad Q \cdot (T \vee R)$ — 5, Dist
7. $\quad Q$ — 6, Simp
8. $(S \vee P) \supset Q$ — 3–7, CP

[13] 1. $[(P \vee Q) \vee R] \supset (S \vee L)$
2. $(S \vee L) \supset (M \vee K)$ — $/ Q \supset (M \vee K)$
3. $\quad Q$ — *Assumption (CP)*
4. $\quad Q \vee P$ — 3, Add
5. $\quad P \vee Q$ — 4, Com
6. $\quad (P \vee Q) \vee R$ — 5, Add
7. $\quad S \vee L$ — 1, 6, MP
8. $\quad M \vee K$ — 2, 7, MP
9. $Q \supset (M \vee K)$ — 3–8, CP

[17] 1. $Q \supset \sim P$
2. $\sim P \vee (Q \vee R)$ — $/ P \supset (R \vee \sim S)$

	3. P	Assumption (CP)
	4. $\sim\sim P$	3, DN
	5. $Q \vee R$	2, 4, DS
	6. $\sim Q$	1, 4, MT
	7. R	5, 6, DS
	8. $R \vee \sim S$	7, Add
	9. $P \supset (R \vee \sim S)$	3–8, CP

[21] 1. $[(A \cdot B) \cdot C] \supset D$ $/ A \supset [B \supset (C \supset D)]$

		2. A	Assumption (CP)
		3. B	Assumption (CP)
		4. C	Assumption (CP)
		5. $A \cdot B$	2, 3, Conj
		6. $(A \cdot B) \cdot C$	4, 5, Conj
		7. D	1, 6, MP
		8. $C \supset D$	4–7, CP
		9. $B \supset (C \supset D)$	3–8, CP

10. $A \supset [B \supset (C \supset D)]$ 2–9, CP

[25] 1. $(P \vee Q) \supset (R \cdot S)$
     2. $(R \vee \sim L) \supset [M \cdot (K \vee N)]$ $/ P \supset [R \cdot (K \vee N)]$

	3. P	Assumption (CP)
	4. $P \vee Q$	3, Add
	5. $R \cdot S$	1, 4, MP
	6. R	5, Simp
	7. $R \vee \sim L$	6, Add
	8. $M \cdot (K \vee N)$	2, 7, MP
	9. $K \vee N$	8, Simp
	10. $R \cdot (K \vee N)$	6, 9, Conj

11. $P \supset [R \cdot (K \vee N)]$ 3–10, CP

[29] 1. $R \supset \sim U$
     2. $P \supset (Q \vee R)$
     3. $(Q \supset S) \cdot (S \supset T)$ $/ P \supset (\sim U \vee T)$

	4. P	Assumption (CP)
	5. $Q \vee R$	2, 4, MP
	6. $Q \supset S$	3, Simp
	7. $S \supset T$	3, Simp
	8. $Q \supset T$	6, 7, HS
	9. $(Q \supset T) \cdot (R \supset \sim U)$	1, 8, Conj
	10. $T \vee \sim U$	5, 9, CD
	11. $\sim U \vee T$	10, Com

12. $P \supset (\sim U \vee T)$ 4–11, CP

[33] 1. $P \supset Q$
     2. $(P \cdot Q) \equiv S$ $/ P \equiv S$
     3. $[(P \cdot Q) \supset S] \cdot [S \supset (P \cdot Q)]$ 2, Equiv

	4. P	Assumption (CP)
	5. Q	1, 4, MP
	6. $P \cdot Q$	4, 5, Conj
	7. $(P \cdot Q) \supset S$	3, Simp
	8. S	6, 7, MP

9. $P \supset S$ 4–8, CP

	10. S	Assumption (CP)
	11. $S \supset (P \cdot Q)$	3, Simp
	12. $P \cdot Q$	10, 11, MP
	13. P	12, Simp

14. $S \supset P$ 10–13, CP
15. $(P \supset S) \cdot (S \supset P)$ 9, 14, Conj
16. $P \equiv S$ 15, Equiv

[37] 1. $\sim P \supset (R \supset \sim T)$
     2. $U \supset (\sim Q \supset \sim R)$
     3. $\sim Q \cdot T$ $/ \sim R \vee (\sim U \cdot P)$

	4. $\sim P$	Assumption (CP)
	5. $R \supset \sim T$	1, 4, MP
	6. T	3, Simp
	7. $\sim\sim T$	6, DN
	8. $\sim R$	5, 7, MT

9. $\sim P \supset \sim R$ 4–8, CP
10. $\sim\sim P \vee \sim R$ 9, Impl
11. $P \vee \sim R$ 10, DN
12. $\sim R \vee P$ 11, Com

	13. U	Assumption (CP)
	14. $\sim Q \supset \sim R$	2, 13, MP
	15. $\sim Q$	3, Simp
	16. $\sim R$	14, 15, MP

17. $U \supset \sim R$ 13–16, CP
18. $\sim U \vee \sim R$ 17, Impl
19. $\sim R \vee \sim U$ 18, Com
20. $(\sim R \vee \sim U) \cdot (\sim R \vee P)$ 12, 19, Conj
21. $\sim R \vee (\sim U \cdot P)$ 20, Dist

II.

[5] 1. $L \supset A$
     2. $U \supset (P \supset L)$ $/ U \supset (P \supset A)$

	3. U	Assumption (CP)
	4. $P \supset L$	2, 3, MP
	5. $P \supset A$	1, 4, HS

6. $U \supset (P \supset A)$ 3–5, CP

Exercises 8H

I.

[5] 1. $\sim Q \vee P$
     2. $\sim (P \vee S)$ $/ \sim Q$

	3. Q	Assumption (IP)
	4. $\sim\sim Q$	3, DN
	5. P	1, 4, DS
	6. $P \vee S$	5, Add
	7. $(P \vee S) \cdot \sim (P \vee S)$	2, 6, Conj

8. $\sim Q$ 3–7, IP

[9] 1. $[P \supset (Q \cdot R)] \cdot (S \supset L)$
     2. S $/ L$

	3. $\sim L$	Assumption (IP)
	4. $S \supset L$	1, Simp
	5. $\sim S$	3, 4, MT
	6. $S \cdot \sim S$	2, 5, Conj

7. $\sim\sim L$ 3–6, IP
8. L 7, DN

[13] 1. $\sim P \supset \sim (Q \vee \sim P)$ $/ P$

	2. $\sim P$	Assumption (IP)
	3. $\sim (Q \vee \sim P)$	1, 2, MP
	4. $\sim Q \cdot \sim\sim P$	3, DM
	5. $\sim\sim P$	4, Simp
	6. P	5, DN
	7. $P \cdot \sim P$	2, 6, Conj

8. $\sim\sim P$ 2–7, IP
9. P 8, DN

[17]
1. ~P · ~T
2. ~(P · ~Q) ⊃ R   / R v T
3. ~R   Assumption (IP)
4. ~~(P · ~Q)   2, 3, MT
5. P · ~Q   4, DN
6. P   5, Simp
7. ~P   1, Simp
8. P · ~P   6, 7, Conj
9. ~~R   3–8, IP
10. R   9, DN
11. R v T   10, Add

[21]
1. P ⊃ (~P ≡ ~Q)
2. ~P v Q   / ~P
3. P   Assumption (IP)
4. ~~P   3, DN
5. ~Q   2, 4, DS
6. ~P ≡ ~Q   1, 3, MP
7. (~P ⊃ ~Q) · (~Q ⊃ ~P)   6, Equiv
8. ~Q ⊃ ~P   7, Simp
9. ~P   5, 8, MP
10. P · ~P   3, 9, Conj
11. ~P   3–10, IP

[25]
1. P ⊃ Q
2. (R · S) v L
3. L ⊃ ~Q   / (~S v ~R) ⊃ ~P
4. ~S v ~R   Assumption (CP)
5. P   Assumption (IP)
6. ~(S · R)   4, DM
7. ~(R · S)   6, Com
8. L   2, 7, DS
9. ~Q   3, 8, MP
10. Q   1, 5, MP
11. Q · ~Q   9, 10, Conj
12. ~P   5–11, IP
13. (~S v ~R) ⊃ ~P   4–12, CP

[29]
1. P ⊃ Q
2. ~R ⊃ (P · S)
3. S ⊃ ~Q   / R
4. ~R   Assumption (IP)
5. P · S   2, 4, MP
6. P   5, Simp
7. Q   1, 6, MP
8. ~~Q   7, DN
9. ~S   3, 8, MT
10. S   5, Simp
11. S · ~S   9, 10, Conj
12. ~~R   4–11, IP
13. R   12, DN

[33]
1. (P ⊃ Q) ⊃ ~(S ⊃ R)
2. ~(P v T)   / S
3. ~S   Assumption (IP)
4. ~S v R   3, Add
5. S ⊃ R   4, Impl
6. ~~(S ⊃ R)   5, DN
7. ~(P ⊃ Q)   1, 6, MT
8. ~(~P v Q)   7, Impl
9. ~~P · ~Q   8, DM

10. P · ~Q   9, DN
11. P   10, Simp
12. ~P · ~T   2, DM
13. ~P   12, Simp
14. P · ~P   11, 13, Conj
15. ~~S   3–14, IP
16. S   15, DN

[37]
1. P ⊃ (Q · S)
2. Q ⊃ (R v S)
3. P v (Q ⊃ R)   / Q ⊃ R
4. Q   Assumption (CP)
5. R v ~S   2, 4, MP
6. ~R   Assumption (IP)
7. ~S   5, 6, DS
8. ~S v ~Q   7, Add
9. ~Q v ~S   8, Com
10. ~(Q · S)   9, DM
11. ~P   1, 10, MT
12. Q ⊃ R   3, 11, DS
13. R   4, 12, MP
14. R · ~R   6, 13, Conj
15. ~~R   6–14, IP
16. R   15, DN
17. Q ⊃ R   4–16, CP

[41]
1. (S · N) ⊃ ~E
2. S v L
3. N
4. K
5. L ⊃ M
6. (M · K) ⊃ R
7. R ⊃ ~E   / ~E
8. E   Assumption (IP)
9. ~~E   8, DN
10. ~R   7, 9, MT
11. ~(M · K)   6, 10, MT
12. ~M v ~K   11, DM
13. ~~K   4, DN
14. ~M   12, 13, DS
15. ~L   5, 14, MT
16. S   2, 15, DS
17. ~(S · N)   1, 9, MT
18. ~S v ~N   17, DM
19. ~~S   16, DN
20. ~N   18, 19, DS
21. N · ~N   3, 20, Conj
22. ~E   8-21, IP

[45]
1. K ⊃ (L v M)
2. H ⊃ (G v K)
3. (M v F) ⊃ ~(H · K)
4. (G · H) ⊃ (K · L)   / H ⊃ [K · (L · ~M)]
5. H   Assumption (CP)
6. G v K   2, 5, MP
7. ~K   Assumption (IP)
8. G   6, 7, DS
9. G · H   5, 8, Conj
10. K · L   4, 9, MP
11. K   10, Simp
12. K · ~K   7, 11, Conj

13.	$\sim\sim K$	7-12, IP
14.	K	13, DN
15.	$L \vee M$	1, 14, MP
16.	$H \cdot K$	5, 14, Conj
17.	$\sim\sim(H \cdot K)$	16, DN
18.	$\sim(M \vee F)$	3, 17, MT
19.	$\sim M \cdot \sim F$	18, DM
19.	$\sim M$	19, Simp
20.	L	15, 19, DS
21.	$L \cdot \sim M$	19, 20, Conj
22.	$K \cdot (L \cdot \sim M)$	14, 21, Conj
23.	$H \supset [K \cdot (L \cdot \sim M)]$	5-22, CP

II.

[5]
1.	$\sim(\sim J \cdot F)$	
2.	$\sim J \supset F$	$/ J$
3.	$\sim J$	Assumption (IP)
4.	F	2, 3, MP
5.	$\sim\sim J \vee \sim F$	1, DM
6.	$J \vee \sim F$	5, DN
7.	$\sim F$	3, 6, DS
8.	$F \cdot \sim F$	4, 7, Conj
9.	J	3–8, IP

Exercises 8I

[5]
1.	$(S \supset \sim S) \cdot (\sim S \supset S)$	Assumption (IP)
2.	$(\sim S \vee \sim S) \cdot (\sim S \supset S)$	1, Impl
3.	$(\sim S \vee \sim S) \cdot (\sim\sim S \vee S)$	2, Impl
4.	$(\sim S \vee \sim S) \cdot (S \vee S)$	3, DN
5.	$\sim S \cdot (S \vee S)$	4, Taut
6.	$\sim S \cdot S$	5, Taut
7.	$\sim[(S \supset \sim S) \cdot (\sim S \supset S)]$	1–6, IP

[9]
1.	$\sim(L \cdot \sim M) \cdot \sim M$	Assumption (CP)
2.	$\sim(L \cdot \sim M)$	1, Simp
3.	$\sim L \vee \sim\sim M$	2, DM
4.	$\sim L \vee M$	3, DN
5.	$\sim M$	1, Simp
6.	$\sim L$	4, 5, DS
7.	$[\sim(L \cdot \sim M) \cdot \sim M] \supset \sim L$	1–6, CP

[13]
1.	$\sim[(R \vee \sim R) \supset (S \vee \sim S)]$	Assumption (IP)
2.	$\sim[\sim(R \vee \sim R) \vee (S \vee \sim S)]$	1, Impl
3.	$\sim\sim(R \vee \sim R) \cdot \sim(S \vee \sim S)$	2, DM
4.	$\sim(S \vee \sim S)$	3, Simp
5.	$\sim S \cdot \sim\sim S$	4, DM
6.	$\sim S \cdot S$	5, DN
7.	$\sim\sim[(R \vee \sim R) \supset (S \vee \sim S)]$	1–6, IP
8.	$(R \vee \sim R) \supset (S \vee \sim S)$	7, DN

[17]
1.	$K \supset (L \supset M)$	Assumption (CP)
2.	$K \supset L$	Assumption (CP)
3.	K	Assumption (CP)
4.	$L \supset M$	1, 3, MP
5.	L	2, 3, MP
6.	M	4, 5, MP
7.	$K \supset M$	3–6, CP
8.	$(K \supset L) \supset (K \supset M)$	2–7, CP
9.	$[K \supset (L \supset M)] \supset [(K \supset L) \supset (K \supset M)]$	1–8, CP

[21]
1.	$\sim\{[(B \cdot \sim C) \vee (D \cdot \sim G)] \vee [(C \cdot G) \vee (\sim B \vee \sim D)]\}$	
		Assumption (IP)
2.	$\sim[(B \cdot \sim C) \vee (D \cdot \sim G)] \cdot \sim[(C \cdot G) \vee (\sim B \vee \sim D)]$	
		1, DM
3.	$\sim[(B \cdot \sim C) \vee (D \cdot \sim G)]$	2, Simp
4.	$\sim[(C \cdot G) \vee (\sim B \vee \sim D)]$	2, Simp
5.	$\sim(B \cdot \sim C) \cdot \sim(D \cdot \sim G)$	3, DM
6.	$\sim(C \cdot G) \cdot \sim(\sim B \vee \sim D)$	4, DM
7.	$\sim(B \cdot \sim C)$	5, Simp
8.	$\sim(D \cdot \sim G)$	5, Simp
9.	$\sim(C \cdot G)$	6, Simp
10.	$\sim(\sim B \vee \sim D)$	6, Simp
11.	$\sim B \vee \sim\sim C$	7, DM
12.	$\sim\sim B \cdot \sim\sim D$	10, DM
13.	$\sim\sim B$	12, Simp
14.	$\sim\sim D$	12, Simp
15.	$\sim\sim C$	11, 13, DS
16.	$\sim C \vee \sim G$	9, DM
17.	$\sim G$	15, 16, DS
18.	$\sim D \vee \sim\sim G$	11, DM
19.	$\sim\sim D$	12, Simp
20.	$\sim\sim G$	18, 19, DS
21.	$\sim G \cdot \sim\sim G$	17, 20, Conj
22.	$\sim\sim\{[(B \cdot \sim C) \vee (D \cdot \sim G)] \vee [(C \cdot G) \vee (\sim B \vee \sim D)]\}$	
		1-21, IP
23.	$[(B \cdot \sim C) \vee (D \cdot \sim G)] \vee [(C \cdot G) \vee (\sim B \vee \sim D)]$	
		22, DN

CHAPTER 9

Exercises 9A

5. As

9. $(x)\{Ux \supset [Gx \equiv (Mx \cdot Lx)]\}$

13. $(x)(Cx \supset \sim Ux)$

17. $(x)(Cx \supset \sim Px)$

21. $(x)(Lx \supset Ax)$

25. $(x)(Bx \supset \sim Cx)$

29. $(\exists x)(Sx \cdot \sim Ex)$

33. $(x)(Fx \supset \sim Cx)$

37. $(x)[Wx \supset (Ex \vee Ox)]$

41. $(\exists x)(Tx \cdot Wx) \supset (x)(Tx \supset Ix)$

45. $(x)(Ax \supset Mx)$

49. $(Mt \cdot Ms) \supset \sim(Mf \vee Mr)$

53. $\sim Pp \supset \sim Gp$

57. $(Ds \cdot Da) \cdot (\sim Ps \cdot \sim Pa)$

Exercises 9B

III.

[5]
1.	$(\exists x) Hx$	
2.	$(x)(Hx \supset Px)$	$/ (\exists x)(Hx \cdot Px)$
3.	Hc	1, EI
4.	$Hc \supset Pc$	2, UI

5. Pc 3, 4, MP
6. $Hc \cdot Pc$ 3, 5, Conj
7. $(\exists x)(Hx \cdot Px)$ 6, EG

[9]
1. $(x)(Ux \supset Sx)$
2. $(\exists x)(Ux \cdot Tx)$ / $(\exists x)(Tx \cdot Sx)$
3. $Ua \cdot Ta$ 2, EI
4. $Ua \supset Sa$ 1, UI
5. Ua 3, Simp
6. Sa 4, 5, MP
7. Ta 3, Simp
8. $Ta \cdot Sa$ 6, 7, Conj
9. $(\exists x)(Tx \cdot Sx)$ 8, EG

[13]
1. $(\exists x)(Px \cdot Qx)$
2. $(x)(Px \supset Rx)$ / $(\exists x)(Qx \cdot Rx)$
3. $Pa \cdot Qa$ 1, EI
4. Pa 3, Simp
5. $Pa \supset Ra$ 2, UI
6. Ra 4, 5, MP
7. Qa 3, Simp
8. $Qa \cdot Ra$ 6, 7, Conj
9. $(\exists x)(Qx \cdot Rx)$ 8, EG

[17]
1. $(x)[\sim (Fx \lor Gx) \supset Hx]$
2. $(x)(Hx \supset Lx)$
3. $(x) \sim Fx$ / $(x)(Gx \lor Lx)$
4. $\sim (Fx \lor Gx) \supset Hx$ 1, UI
5. $Hx \supset Lx$ 2, UI
6. $\sim (Fx \lor Gx) \supset Lx$ 4, 5, HS
7. $\sim \sim (Fx \lor Gx) \lor Lx$ 6, Impl
8. $(Fx \lor Gx) \lor Lx$ 7, DN
9. $Fx \lor (Gx \lor Lx)$ 8, Assoc
10. $\sim Fx$ 3, UI
11. $Gx \lor Lx$ 9, 10, DS
12. $(x)(Gx \lor Lx)$ 11, UG

IV.
[5]
1. $(x) \sim Rx$
2. $(x)[(Bx \lor Ex) \equiv Rx]$ / $(\exists x)(Ex \equiv Bx)$
3. $(Ba \lor Ea) \equiv Ra$ 2, UI
4. $[(Ba \lor Ea) \supset Ra] \cdot [Ra \supset (Ba \lor Ea)]$ 3, Equiv
5. $(Ba \lor Ea) \supset Ra$ 4, Simp
6. $\sim Ra$ 1, UI
7. $\sim (Ba \lor Ea)$ 5, 6, MT
8. $\sim (Ea \lor Ba)$ 7, Com
9. $\sim Ea \cdot \sim Ba$ 8, DM
10. $(\sim Ea \cdot \sim Ba) \lor (Ea \cdot Ba)$ 9, Add
11. $(Ea \cdot Ba) \lor (\sim Ea \cdot \sim Ba)$ 10, Com
12. $Ea \equiv Ba$ 11, Equiv
13. $(\exists x)(Ex \equiv Bx)$ 12, EG

Exercises 9C

I.
5. $\sim (\exists x)(Px \supset Qx)$
9. $(\exists x) \sim (Px \supset Qx)$

II.
[5]
1. $\sim (\exists x) Gx$
2. $(\exists x) Fx \lor (\exists x)(Gx \cdot Hx)$ / $(\exists x) Fx$

---

3. $(x) \sim Gx$ 1, CQ
4. $\sim Gx$ 3, UI
5. $\sim Gx \lor \sim Hx$ 4, Add
6. $\sim (Gx \cdot Hx)$ 5, DM
7. $(x) \sim (Gx \cdot Hx)$ 6, UG
8. $\sim (\exists x)(Gx \cdot Hx)$ 7, CQ
9. $(\exists x) Fx$ 2, 8, DS

[9]
1. $\sim (x) Gx$
2. $(x)(Fx \supset Gx)$
3. $\sim (x) Hx \lor (x) Fx$ / $(\exists x) \sim Hx$
4. $(\exists x) \sim Gx$ 1, CQ
5. $\sim Ga$ 4, EI
6. $Fa \supset Ga$ 2, UI
7. $\sim Fa$ 5, 6, MT
8. $(\exists x) \sim Fx$ 7, EG
9. $\sim (x) Fx$ 8, CQ
10. $\sim (x) Hx$ 3, 9, DS
11. $(\exists x) \sim Hx$ 10, CQ

[13]
1. $\sim (\exists x) Lx$
2. $(\exists y) My$
3. $(x)[(Kx \supset \sim Mx) \lor La]$ / $\sim (y) Ky$
4. $(x) \sim Lx$ 1, CQ
5. Ma 2, EI
6. $\sim La$ 4, UI
7. $(Ka \supset \sim Ma) \lor La$ 3, UI
8. $Ka \supset \sim Ma$ 6, 7, DS
9. $\sim \sim Ma$ 5, DN
10. $\sim Ka$ 8, 9, MT
11. $(\exists y) \sim Ky$ 10, EG
12. $\sim (y) Ky$ 11, CQ

[17]
1. $\sim (\exists x) Cx$
2. $(\exists x)(Dx \cdot \sim Gx) \supset (x)(Hx \lor Cx)$
3. $\sim (x)(\sim Gx \supset Hx)$ / $\sim (x) Dy$
4. $(\exists x) \sim (\sim Gx \supset Hx)$ 3, CQ
5. $\sim (\sim Ga \supset Ha)$ 4, EI
6. $\sim (\sim \sim Ga \lor Ha)$ 5, Impl
7. $\sim (Ga \lor Ha)$ 6, DN
8. $\sim Ga \cdot \sim Ha$ 7, DM
9. $\sim Ga$ 8, Simp
10. $\sim Ha$ 8, Simp
11. $(x) \sim Cx$ 1, CQ
12. $\sim Ca$ 11, UI
13. $\sim Ha \cdot \sim Ca$ 10, 12, Conj
14. $\sim (Ha \lor Ca)$ 13, DM
15. $(\exists x) \sim (Hx \lor Cx)$ 14, EG
16. $\sim (x)(Hx \lor Cx)$ 15, CQ
17. $\sim (\exists x)(Dx \cdot \sim Gx)$ 2, 16, MT
18. $(x) \sim (Dx \cdot \sim Gx)$ 17, CQ
19. $\sim (Da \cdot \sim Ga)$ 18, UI
20. $\sim Da \lor \sim \sim Ga$ 19, DM
21. $\sim Da \lor Ga$ 20, DN
22. $\sim Da$ 9, 21, DS
23. $(\exists y) \sim Dy$ 22, EG
24. $\sim (x) Dy$ 23, CQ

III.
[5]
1. $\sim (\exists x)(Hx \lor Gx)$
2. $(x)(Fx \cdot \sim Gx) \supset (\exists x) Hx$ / $(\exists x) \sim Fx$

3.	$(x) \sim (Hx \vee Gx)$	1, CQ
4.	$\sim (Hx \vee Gx)$	3, UI
5.	$\sim Hx \cdot \sim Gx$	4, DM
6.	$\sim Hx$	5, Simp
7.	$(x) \sim Hx$	6, UG
8.	$\sim (\exists x) Hx$	7, CQ
9.	$\sim (x) (Fx \cdot \sim Gx)$	2, 8, MT
10.	$(\exists x) \sim (Fx \cdot \sim Gx)$	9, CQ
11.	$\sim (Fa \cdot \sim Ga)$	10, EI
12.	$\sim Fa \vee \sim \sim Ga$	11, DM
13.	$\sim Fa \vee Ga$	12, DN
14.	$\sim Gx$	5, Simp
15.	$(x) \sim Gx$	14, UG
16.	$\sim Ga$	15, UI
17.	$\sim Fa$	13, 16, DS
18.	$(\exists x) \sim Fx$	17, EG

Exercises 9D

I.

[5]

1.	$(x) (Fx \supset Hx)$	
2.	$(x) (Fx \supset Gx)$	$/ (x) [Fx \supset (Gx \cdot Hx)]$
3.	Fx	Assumption (CP)
4.	$Fx \supset Gx$	2, UI
5.	$Fx \supset Hx$	1, UI
6.	Gx	3, 4, MP
7.	Hx	3, 5, MP
8.	$Gx \cdot Hx$	6, 7, Conj
9.	$Fx \supset (Gx \cdot Hx)$	3–8, CP
10.	$(x) [Fx \supset (Gx \cdot Hx)]$	9, UG

[9]

1.	$\sim (\exists y) Ky \supset \sim (\exists z) Mz$	
2.	$(\exists x) [Hx \supset (y) \sim Ky]$	$/ (x) Hx \supset (z) \sim Mz$
3.	$(x) Hx$	Assumption (CP)
4.	$Ha \supset (y) \sim Ky$	2, EI
5.	Ha	3, UI
6.	$(y) \sim Ky$	4, 5, MP
7.	$\sim (\exists y) Ky$	6, CQ
8.	$\sim (\exists z) Mz$	1, 7, MP
9.	$(z) \sim Mz$	8, CQ
10.	$(x) Hx \supset (z) \sim Mz$	3–9, CP

[13]

1.	$(x) [Gx \supset (Hx \cdot Lx)]$	$/ (x) (Fx \supset Gx) \supset (x) (Fx \supset Lx)$
2.	$(x) (Fx \supset Gx)$	Assumption (CP)
3.	Fx	Assumption (CP)
4.	$Fx \supset Gx$	2, UI
5.	Gx	3, 4, MP
6.	$Gx \supset (Hx \cdot Lx)$	1, UI
7.	$Hx \cdot Lx$	5, 6, MP
8.	Lx	7, Simp
9.	$Fx \supset Lx$	3–8, CP
10.	$(x) (Fx \supset Lx)$	9, UG
11.	$(x) (Fx \supset Gx) \supset (x) (Fx \supset Lx)$	2–10, CP

[17]

1.	$(\exists x) (Dx \vee Mx) \supset (x) Fx$	
2.	$(\exists x) Bx \supset (\exists x) (Cx \cdot Dx)$	$/ (x) (Bx \supset Fx)$
3.	Bx	Assumption (CP)
4.	$(\exists x) Bx$	3, EG
5.	$(\exists x) (Cx \cdot Dx)$	2, 4, MP

6.	$Ca \cdot Da$	5, EI
7.	Da	6, Simp
8.	$Da \vee Ma$	7, Add
9.	$(\exists x) (Dx \vee Mx)$	8, EG
10.	$(x) Fx$	1, 9, MP
11.	Fx	10, UI
12.	$Bx \supset Fx$	3–11, CP
13.	$(x) (Bx \supset Fx)$	12, UG

[21]

1.	$\sim (\exists x)(Kx \cdot \sim Px)$	
2.	$(\exists x) Gx \supset (x)(Hx \supset Kx)$	
3.	$(\exists x) Lx \supset (x)(Px \supset \sim Hx)$	$/ (\exists x)(Gx \cdot Lx) \supset \sim (\exists x) Hx$
4.	$(\exists x)(Gx \cdot Lx)$	Assumption (CP)
5.	$Ga \cdot La$	4, EI
6.	Ga	5, Simp
7.	La	5, Simp
8.	$(\exists x) Gx$	6, EG
9.	$(x)(Hx \supset Kx)$	2, 8, MP
10.	$(\exists x) Lx$	7, EG
11.	$(x)(Px \supset \sim Hx)$	3, 10, MP
12.	$(x) \sim (Kx \cdot \sim Px)$	1, CQ
13.	$\sim (Kx \cdot \sim Px)$	12, UI
14.	$\sim Kx \vee \sim \sim Px$	13, DM
15.	$\sim Kx \vee Px$	14, DN
16.	$Kx \supset Px$	15, Impl
17.	$Hx \supset Kx$	9, UI
18.	$Hx \supset Px$	16, 17, HS
19.	$Px \supset \sim Hx$	11, UI
20.	$Hx \supset \sim Hx$	18, 19, HS
21.	$\sim Hx \vee \sim Hx$	20, Impl
22.	$\sim Hx$	21, Taut
23.	$(x) \sim Hx$	22, UG
24.	$\sim (\exists x) Hx$	23, CQ
25.	$(\exists x)(Gx \cdot Lx) \supset \sim \exists x) Hx$	4–24, CP

II.

[5]

1.	$(x) (Ux \supset Sx)$	
2.	$(\exists x) Sx \supset (\exists x) Ax$	$/ (\exists x) Ux \supset (\exists x) Ax$
3.	$\sim (\exists x) Ax$	Assumption (CP)
4.	$\sim (\exists x) Sx$	2, 3, MT
5.	$(x) \sim Sx$	4, CQ
6.	$\sim Sx$	5, UI
7.	$Ux \supset Sx$	1, UI
8.	$\sim Ux$	6, 7, MT
9.	$(x) \sim Ux$	8, UG
10.	$\sim (\exists x) Ux$	9, CQ
11.	$\sim (\exists x) Ax \supset \sim (\exists x) Ux$	3–10, CP
12.	$(\exists x) Ux \supset (\exists x) Ax$	11, Trans

Exercises 9E

I.

[5] Some dinosaurs were meat-eaters.
Therefore, all dinosaurs were meat-eaters.

[9] Every fruit is a plant.
Therefore, everything is either a fruit or a plant.

II.

[5] A universe containing one individual:

La	Ma	La ⊃ Ma	Ma	/ La
F	T	$\boxed{T}$	$\boxed{T}$	$\boxed{F}$ √

[9] A universe containing one individual:

Ha	Fa	Ga	Ha ⊃ Fa	Fa ⊃ Ga	/ Ga ⊃ Ha
F	T	T	$\boxed{T}$	$\boxed{T}$	$\boxed{F}$ √

[13] A universe containing one individual:

Ga	La	Ha	Ga · La	Ga · Ha	/ La ⊃ Ha
T	T	F	$\boxed{T}$	$\boxed{F}$	$\boxed{F}$

A universe containing two individuals:

Ga	La	Ha	Gb	Lb	Hb	(Ga · La) ∨ (Gb · Lb)	(Ga · Ha) ∨ (Gb · Hb)	/ (La ⊃ Ha) · (Lb ⊃ Hb)
T	T	F	T		T	T $\boxed{T}$	F $\boxed{T}$ T	F $\boxed{F}$ √

III.

[5] 1. (∃x)(Cx · ~ Bx)
    2. (∃x)(Wx · Cx)   / (∃x)(Bx · ~ Wx)
A universe containing one individual:

Ba	Ca	Wa	Ca · ~ Ba	Wa · Ca	/ Ba · ~ Wa
F	T	T	$\boxed{T}$T	$\boxed{T}$	$\boxed{F}$F √

Exercises 9F.1

5. (∃x) (y) Dxy
9. (x) (Rxt ⊃ Rxd)
13. (x) (∃y) Cxy
17. (x) [Gx ⊃ (∃y) (∃z) (Pyz · Pxy)]

Exercises 9F.2

[5] 1. (x) (y) (Fxy ⊃ ~ Fyx)
    2. Fba   / ~ Fab
    3. (y) (Fby ⊃ ~ Fyb)   1, UI
    4. Fba ⊃ ~ Fab   3, UI
    5. ~ Fab   2, 4, MP
[9] 1. ~ (∃x) [Fx · (∃y) (Fy · Bxy)] / (x) [Fx ⊃ (y) (Fy ⊃ ~ Bxy)]
    2. (x) ~ [Fx · (∃y) (Fy · Bxy)]   1, CQ
    3. ~ [Fa · (∃y) (Fy · Bay)]   2, UI
    4. ~ Fa ∨ ~ (∃y) (Fy · Bay)   3, DM
    5. ~ Fa ∨ (y) ~ (Fy · Bay)   4, CQ
    6. ~ Fa ∨ (y) (~ Fy ∨ ~ Bay)   5, DM
    7. Fa ⊃ (y) (~ Fy ∨ ~ Bay)   6, Impl
    8. Fa ⊃ (y) (Fy ⊃ ~ Bay)   7, Impl
    9. (x) [Fx ⊃ (y) (Fy ⊃ ~ Bxy)]   8, UG

[13]
   1. (x) (∃y) (Mx · Py)   / (x) Mx
   ⎡ 2. ~ (x) Mx   Assumption (IP)
   ⎜ 3. (∃x) ~ Mx   2, CQ
   ⎜ 4. ~ Ma   3, EI
   ⎜ 5. (∃y) (Ma · Py)   1, UI
   ⎜ 6. Ma · Pb   5, EI
   ⎜ 7. Ma   6, Simp
   ⎣ 8. Ma · ~ Ma   4, 7, Conj
   9. ~ ~ (x) Mx   2–8, IP
   10. (x) Mx   9, DN

[17] 1. Fa   / (x) [(Gx · Hxa) ⊃ (∃y) (Fy · Hxy)]
   ⎡ 2. Gx · Hxa   Assumption (CP)
   ⎜ ⎡ 3. ~ (∃y) (Fy · Hxy)   Assumption (IP)
   ⎜ ⎜ 4. (y) ~ (Fy · Hxy)   3, CQ
   ⎜ ⎜ 5. ~ (Fa · Hxa)   4, UI
   ⎜ ⎜ 6. ~ Fa ∨ ~ Hxa   5, DM
   ⎜ ⎜ 7. ~ ~ Fa   1, DN
   ⎜ ⎜ 8. ~ Hxa   6, 7, DS
   ⎜ ⎜ 9. Hxa   2, Simp
   ⎜ ⎣ 10. Hxa · ~ Hxa   8, 9, Conj
   ⎜ 11. ~ ~ (∃y) (Fy · Hxy)   3–10, IP
   ⎣ 12. (∃y) (Fy · Hxy)   11, DN

13. $(Gx \cdot Hxa) \supset (\exists y)(Fy \cdot Hxy)$ 2–12, CP
14. $(x)[(Gx \cdot Hxa) \supset (\exists y)(Fy \cdot Hxy)]$ 13, UG

Exercises 9G.1

5. $c = k$
9. $(\exists x)(Fx \cdot Sx)$
13. $(\exists x)(\exists y)[(Px \cdot Py) \cdot x \neq y]$
17. $Vk \cdot Mk \cdot (x)[(Vx \cdot Mx) \supset x = k]$

Exercises 9G.2

[5] 1. Fb

    2. $(x)(Fa \supset x \neq a)$ / $a \neq b$
    3. $a = b$ Assumption (IP)
    4. $b = a$ 3, Id
    5. Fa 1, 4, Id
    6. $Fa \supset b \neq a$ 2, UI
    7. $b \neq a$ 5, 6, MP
    8. $b = a \cdot b \neq a$ 4, 7, Conj
  9. $a \neq b$ 3–8, IP

[9] 1. $\sim Lb$
  2. $(x)[Hx \supset (Lx \cdot x = b)]$ / $\sim Ha$
    3. Ha Assumption (IP)
    4. $Ha \supset (La \cdot a = b)$ 2, UI
    5. $La \cdot a = b$ 3, 4, MP
    6. La 5, Simp
    7. $a = b$ 5, Simp
    8. Lb 6, 7, Id
    9. $Lb \cdot \sim Lb$ 1, 8, Conj
  10. $\sim Ha$ 3–9, IP

[13] 1. $(Fb \cdot Gab) \cdot (x)[(Fx \cdot Gax) \supset x = b]$
  2. $(\exists x)[(Fx \cdot Gax) \cdot Hx]$ / Hb
  3. $(Fc \cdot Gac) \cdot Hc$ 2, EI
  4. $(x)[(Fx \cdot Gax) \supset x = b]$ 1, Simp
  5. $(Fc \cdot Gac) \supset c = b$ 4, UI
  6. $Fc \cdot Gac$ 3, Simp
  7. $c = b$ 5, 6, MP
  8. Hc 3, Simp
  9. Hb 7, 8, Id

[17]

1. $(Fb \cdot Hab) \cdot (x)[(Fx \cdot Hax) \supset x = b]$
2. $(\exists x)\{(Fx \cdot Gx) \cdot (y)[(Fy \cdot Gy) \supset y = x] \cdot Hax\}$
    / $(\exists x)\{(Fx \cdot Gx) \cdot (y)[(Fy \cdot Gy) \supset y = x] \cdot x = b\}$
3. $(Fc \cdot Gc) \cdot (y)[(Fy \cdot Gy) \supset y = c] \cdot Hac$ 2, EI
4. $(x)[(Fx \cdot Hax) \supset x = b]$ 1, Simp
5. $(Fc \cdot Hac) \supset c = b$ 4, UI
6. $Fc \cdot Gc$ 3, Simp
7. Fc 6, Simp
8. Hac 3, Simp
9. $Fc \cdot Hac$ 7, 8, Conj
10. $c = b$ 5, 9, MP
11. $(Fc \cdot Gc) \cdot (y)[(Fy \cdot Gy) \supset y = c]$ 3, Simp
12. $(Fc \cdot Gc) \cdot (y)[(Fy \cdot Gy) \supset y = c] \cdot c = b$ 10, 11, Conj
13. $(\exists x)\{(Fx \cdot Gx) \cdot (y)[(Fy \cdot Gy) \supset y = x] \cdot x = b\}$ 12, EG

[21] 1. $Cj \cdot Uj \cdot (x)[(Cx \cdot Ux) \supset x = j]$
  2. Aj / $(x)[(Cx \cdot Ux) \supset Ax]$

3. $(x)[(Cx \cdot Ux) \supset x = j]$ 1, Simp
4. $(Cj \cdot Uj) \supset x = j$ 3, UI
5. $Cj \cdot Uj$ 1, Simp
6. $x = j$ 4, 5, MP
    7. $Cx \cdot Ux$ Assumption (CP)
    8. Ax 2, 6, Id
9. $(Cx \cdot Ux) \supset Ax$ 7–8, CP
10. $(x)[(Cx \cdot Ux) \supset Ax]$ 9, UG

[25] 1. $(\exists x)(Hx \cdot \sim Gx)$
2. $(\exists x)(\exists y)(Gx \cdot Kx \cdot Gy \cdot Ky \cdot x \neq y)$
3. $(x)(y)(z)[(Kx \cdot Ky \cdot Kz) \supset (x = y \lor x = z \lor y = z)]$
    / $\sim (x)(Hx \supset Kx)$
4. $(\exists y)(Ga \cdot Ka \cdot Gy \cdot Ky \cdot a \neq y)$ 2, EI
5. $Ga \cdot Ka \cdot Gb \cdot Kb \cdot a \neq b)$ 4, EI
6. $Hc \cdot \sim Gc$ 1, EI
    7. $(x)(Hx \supset Kx)$ Assumption (IP)
    8. $Hc \supset Kc$ 7, UI
    9. Hc 6, Simp
    10. Kc 8, 9, MP
    11. Ka 5, Simp
    12. Kb 5, Simp
    13. $Ka \cdot Kb$ 11, 12, Conj
    14. $Ka \cdot Kb \cdot Kc$ 12, 13, Conj
    15. $(y)(z)[(Ka \cdot Ky \cdot Kz) \supset (a = y \lor a = z \lor y = z)]$ 3, UI
    16. $(z)[(Ka \cdot Kb \cdot Kz) \supset (a = b \lor a = z \lor b = z)]$ 15, UI
    17. $(Ka \cdot Kb \cdot Kc) \supset (a = b \lor a = c \lor b = c)]$ 16, UI
    18. $a = b \lor a = c \lor b = c$ 14, 17, MP
    19. $a \neq b$ 5, Simp
    20. $a = c \lor b = c$ 18, 19, DS
      21. $a = c$ Assumption (IP)
      22. Ga 5, Simp
      23. Gc 21, 22, Id
      24. $\sim Gc$ 6, Simp
      25. $Gc \cdot \sim Gc$ 23, 25, Conj
    26. $a \neq c$ 21-25, IP
    27. $b = c$ 20, 26, DS
    28. Gb 5, Simp
    29. Gc 27, 28, Id
    30. $\sim Gc$ 6, Simp
    31. $Gc \cdot \sim Gc$ 29, 30, Conj
32. $\sim (x)(Hx \supset Kx)$ 7–31, IP

CHAPTER 10

Exercises 10A

5. **Premise 1:** X, the junior, and Y, the fifth grader, have the following attributes in common: *a*, eat the same food; *b*, have their own bedrooms; *c*, get the same amount of allowance.

Premise 2: X has *d*: has to do housework.

Conclusion: Therefore, *probably* Y should have *d*: has to do housework.

The structure of the argument:

> X and Y have *a*, *b*, *c*, in common.
> X has *d*.
> Therefore, *probably* Y should have *d*.

9. **Premise 1:** X, fruit, and Y, Chocolate Peanut Gooies, have the following attributes in common: *a*, provides energy; *b*, roughage; *c*, sugar; *d*, citric acid; *e*, vitamins; *f*, minerals.

   Premise 2: X has *g*: is good for your health.

   Conclusion: Therefore, *probably* Y has *g*: is good for your health.

The structure of the argument:

> X and Y have *a*, *b*, *c*, *d*, *e*, *f*, in common.
> X has *g*.
> Therefore, *probably* Y has *g*.

13. **Premise 1:** X, fruit trees and vegetables, and Y, seaweed, have the following attribute in common: *a*, they are plants.

    Premise 2: X has *b*: adding fertilizer helps them to grow better.

    Conclusion: Adding fertilizer should help seaweed grow better.

The structure of the argument:

> X and Y have *a* in common.
> X has *b*.
> Therefore, *probably* Y has *b*.

17. **Premise 1:** X, my assertion and belief that between the Earth and Mars there is a china teapot revolving about the sun in an elliptical orbit, and Y, received dogmas, have the following attributes in common: *a*, they are purposely devised to be incapable of disproof by physical and scientific methods; *b*, based on pure belief without any physical evidence to support them; *c*, since the assertions cannot be disproved it is an intolerable presumption on the part of human reason to doubt them.

    Premise 2: We know that for X, *d*, I should rightly be thought to be talking nonsense.

    Conclusion: Therefore, it is probable that for Y, a received dogma, *d*, it should rightly be thought to be talking nonsense.

The structure of the argument:

> X and Y have *a*, *b*, *c*, in common.
> X has *d*.
> Therefore, *probably* Y has *d*.

Exercises 10B

I.

5. (a) *Number of entities:* The high school student and the fifth grader.

   (b) *Variety of instances:* Just two people are being compared.

   (c) *Number of characteristics:* Food; bedroom; allowance.

   (d) *Relevancy:* They seem relevant to the question of chores.

9. (a) *Number of entities:* Fruit and Chocolate Peanut Gooies.

   (b) *Variety of instances:* It is assumed that many kinds of fruit are referred to in the example.

   (c) *Number of characteristics:* Providing energy; roughage; sugars; citric acid; vitamins; minerals.

   (d) *Relevancy:* The characteristics listed are relevant to the issue of health.

13. (a) *Number of entities:* Fruit trees, vegetables, plants, and seaweed.

    (b) *Variety of instances:* Some are grown on land and some in water.

    (c) *Number of characteristics:* All are plants.

    (d) *Relevancy:* This characteristic is probably related to plant growth.

17. (a) *Number of entities:* Many received dogmas and one contrived assertion.

    (b) *Variety of instances:* Received dogmas differ in their age and popularity.

    (c) *Number of characteristics:* Three are mentioned.

    (d) *Relevancy:* All the characteristics are relevant to the point being made.

II.

5. Since we are not offered any information regarding the average time it took for the brakes to fail, this does not weaken the argument. The evidence is strong enough to warrant having your brakes replaced.

Exercises 10C

5. (a) *Disanalogies:* The age difference is considerable when one factors in the probable difference in size, strength, capabilities, stamina, and level of responsibility.

   (b) *Counteranalogy:* The high school student is more like the parents. The high school student is nearly an adult, and adults are expected to accept responsibility. They are expected to take care of a house and everything in it. They are expected to relieve children of the burdens of adulthood and let the children be children.

   (c) *Unintended consequences:* Since the high school student wants equal treatment, then perhaps the parents should make both children go to bed or be in the house at the same time at night. Since the fifth grader is not permitted to drive the car, then the high school student should not have that privilege either.

9. (a) *Disanalogies*: The candy bar probably contains numerous artificial ingredients whose health benefits may be questioned. Fruit contains no artificial ingredients. The sugar that grows in fruit is not the same as that put in most candy bars.

(b) *Counteranalogy*: The candy bar is like cotton candy. They both taste good to most people, usually because they contain so much sugar (or artificial sugar substitute). They both provide a quick burst of energy. This kind of energy causes a backlash when its effects wear off. The person usually feels lethargic, and his or her attention and focus is disrupted. Both foods are artificial and not organic, natural products. If cotton candy is not healthy, then neither are Chocolate Peanut Gooies.

(c) *Unintended consequences*: Since the candy bar is just as good as fruit, we can eliminate the need for fruit in our diets and substitute the candy bar to meet our minimum daily requirements.

13. (a) *Disanalogies*: All the plants that the fertilizer worked on were grown on land. Fertilizer has not yet been tried on plants grown in water.

(b) *Counteranalogy*: Seaweed grows in saltwater. It has been shown that the fertilizer does not work in saltwater. So, adding the fertilizer will probably not help the seaweed to grow better.

(c) *Unintended consequences*: The fertilizer alters the genetic structure of the plants. If you alter the genetic structure of seaweed, it might disrupt the ecosystem in the sea and prove harmful.

17. (a) *Disanalogies*: The assertion and belief that between the Earth and Mars there is a china teapot revolving about the sun in an elliptical orbit and received dogmas are different in the main sense that the received dogmas have long histories of being believed; also, received dogmas are usually classified as "religions" and are established beliefs that are protected by many democratic societies. Many received dogmas are a source of comfort and hope for the followers.

(b) *Counteranalogy*: The teapot belief offers no hope of an afterlife and provides no moral guides to acting as a human. Therefore, it will not offer hope or comfort to people.

(c) *Unintended consequences*: At most times in history there were scientific hypotheses that could not be tested because the technology was not available. Given this, if we are to discard any belief that cannot be disproved, then some of theoretical science will have to be discarded; for example, if string theory is not testable, then physicists should abandon it.

CHAPTER 11

Exercises 11E

5. (A) The credibility of a witness may be attacked **or** (B) supported by evidence in the form of opinion **or** (C) reputation, **but** subject to these limitations: (D) the evidence may refer **only** to (E) character for truthfulness **or** (F) untruthfulness, **and** (G) evidence of truthful character is admissible **only** after (H) the character of the witness for truthfulness has been attacked by opinion **or** (I) reputation evidence **or** (J) otherwise.

[A or (B or C)] and [If D, then (E or F)] and
[If G, then (H or I or J)].

9. (A) Evidence of juvenile adjudications is generally **not** admissible under this rule. (B) The court may **however**, in a criminal case allow evidence of a juvenile adjudication of a witness other than the accused **if** (C) conviction of the offense would be admissible to attack the credibility of an adult **and** (D) the court is satisfied that admission in evidence is necessary for a fair determination of the issue of guilt **or** (E) innocence.

A or [If C and (D or E), then B].

13. (A) Cross-examination should be limited to the subject matter of the direct examination **and** (B) matters affecting the credibility of the witness. (C) The court may, in the exercise of discretion, permit inquiry into additional matters as if on direct examination.

The information in C gives the court the option to allow "inquiry into additional matters" by referring to those matters "as if" they were being conducted on direct examination. In other words, the "additional matters" are to be understood as being *similar to* those under direct examination.

(A and B) and C.

17. (A) Extrinsic evidence of a prior inconsistent statement by a witness is **not** admissible **unless** (B) the witness is afforded an opportunity to explain **or** (C) deny the same **and** (E) the opposite party is afforded an opportunity to interrogate the witness thereon, **or** (F) the interests of justice otherwise require. (G) This provision does **not** apply to admissions of a party-opponent as defined in rule 801(d)(2).

{If not [(B or C) and (E or F)], then A} and G.

21. (A) At the request of a party (B) the court shall order witnesses excluded so that they cannot hear the testimony of other witnesses, **and** (C) it may make the order of its own motion. This rule does **not** authorize exclusion of (1) (E) a party who is a natural person, **or** (2) (F) an officer **or** (G) employee of a party which is **not** a natural person designated as its representative by its attorney, **or** (3) (H) a person whose presence is shown by a party to

be essential to the presentation of the party's cause, **or** (4) (I) a person authorized by statute to be present.

The use of the word "and" in the phrase "**and** it may make the order of its own motion" is being used to indicate another way that "the court shall order witnesses excluded." In other words, the rule is *not* stating that "the court shall order witnesses excluded" if both A and C occur at the same time; only one of them needs to occur.

[If (A or C), then B] and
[If (E or F or G or H or I), then not B].

Exercises 11G

I.

5. (1) U.S. Common law courts also provided judicial review of the size of damage awards. They deferred to jury verdicts, **but** *they recognized that juries sometimes awarded damages so high as to require correction.*
(2) If the plaintiff did *not* agree to a reduction in his damages, then Justice Story ordered a new trial.
(3) The court may grant a new trial for excessive damages; however, it *is indeed an exercise of discretion full of delicacy and difficulty.*
(4) [**if**] (A) it should clearly appear that the jury have committed a gross error, **or** (B) have acted from improper motives, **or** (C) have given damages excessive in relation to the person **or** (D) the injury, [**then**] (E) it is as much the duty of the court to interfere, to prevent the wrong, as in any other case:

If (A or B or C or D), then E.

9. (A) An Oregon trial judge, **or** (B) an Oregon Appellate Court, may order a new trial **if** (C) the jury was **not** properly instructed, [**or**] **if** (D) error occurred during the trial, **or if** (E) there is no evidence to support any punitive damages at all:

If (C or D or E), then (A or B).

But **if** (F) the defendant's only basis for relief is the *amount* of punitive damages the jury awarded, [**then**] (G) Oregon provides no procedure for reducing **or** (H) setting aside that award:

If F, then (G or H).

The precedent evidence is then added to: "This has been the law in Oregon at least 1949 when the State Supreme Court announced its opinion in *Van Lom v. Schneiderman,* definitively construing the 1910 amendment to the Oregon Constitution. In that case the court held that it had *no power to reduce or set aside an award* of both compensatory and punitive damages that was admittedly excessive."

13. (A) Oregon's abrogation of a well-established common law protection against arbitrary deprivations of property raises a presumption that its procedures violate the Due Process Clause. (B) As this Court has stated from its first Due Process cases, traditional practice provides a touchstone for constitutional analysis. **Because** (C) the basic procedural protections of the common law have been regarded as so fundamental, [**therefore**] (D) very few cases have arisen in which a party has complained of their denial:

(B and C), therefore D.

In fact, (E) most of our Due Process decisions involve arguments that traditional procedures provide too little protection **and** (F) that additional safeguards are necessary to ensure compliance with the Constitution. **Nevertheless,** (G) there are a handful of cases in which a party has been deprived of liberty or property without the safeguards of common law procedure:

(E and F) and G.

(H) When the absent procedures would have provided protection against arbitrary **and** inaccurate adjudication, (I) this Court has **not** hesitated to find the proceedings violative of Due Process:

If H, then I.

17. The Court then begins its response to the argument in 16: (A) The first, limitation of punitive damages to the amount specified, is hardly a constraint at all, **because** (B) there is no limit to the amount the plaintiff can request, **and** (C) it is unclear whether an award exceeding the amount requested could be set aside. (D) See *Tenold v. Weyerhaeuser Co:* Oregon Constitution bars court from examining jury award to ensure compliance with $500,000 statutory limit on noneconomic damages:

(B, C, D), therefore A.

II.

5. Precedent case example: (A) "The guaranty of the right to jury trial in suits at common law, incorporated in the Bill of Rights as one of the first ten amendments of the Constitution of the United States, was interpreted by the Supreme Court of the United States to refer to jury trial as it had been theretofore known in England; **and so** (B) it is that the federal judges, like the English judges, have always exercised the prerogative of granting a new trial when the verdict was clearly against the weight of the evidence, whether it be **because** (C) excessive damages were awarded **or** (D) for any other reason."

[A and (C or D)], therefore B.

III.

5. Second, (A) Oberg was **not** allowed to introduce evidence regarding Honda's wealth until he "presented evidence sufficient to justify to the court a prima facie claim of punitive damages. (B) During the course of

trial, evidence of the defendant's ability to pay shall **not** be admitted **unless and until** (C) the party entitled to recover establishes a prima facie right to recover [punitive damages]." (D) This evidentiary rule is designed to lessen the risk "that juries will use their verdicts to express biases against big businesses," to take into account "[t]he total deterrent effect of other punishment imposed upon the defendant as a result of the misconduct":

> A and (B only if C).

9. The passage lays out the facts and issues, but the direct conclusion needs to be added:

(A) The Court's opinion in *Haslip* went on to describe the checks Alabama places on the jury's discretion *postverdict*—through excessiveness review by the trial court, **and** appellate review, which tests the award against specific substantive criteria. (B) While postverdict review of that character is **not** available in Oregon, (C) the seven factors against which Alabama's Supreme Court tests punitive awards strongly resemble the statutory criteria Oregon's juries are instructed to apply. **And** (D) this Court has often acknowledged, **and** generally respected, the presumption that juries follow the instructions they are given. (E) As the Supreme Court of Oregon observed, *Haslip* "determined only that the Alabama procedure, as a whole and in its net effect, did **not** violate the Due Process Clause."

> A, B, C, D, E.

Therefore, [The Honda decision did **not** violate the Due Process Clause].

13. In short, (A) Oregon has enacted legal standards confining punitive damage awards in product liability cases. (B) These state standards are judicially enforced by means of comparatively comprehensive preverdict procedures but markedly limited postverdict review, (C) for Oregon has elected to make fact-finding, once supporting evidence is produced, the province of the jury.... (D) The Court today invalidates this choice, largely **because** (E) it concludes that English and early American courts generally provided judicial review of the size of punitive damage awards. (F) The Court's account of the relevant history is **not** compelling.

> A and B and C.
> E and F.
> Therefore D.

17. **Furthermore,** (A) common law courts reviewed punitive damage verdicts extremely deferentially, if at all. (B) See *Day* v. *Woodworth*: assessment of "exemplary, punitive, **or** vindictive damages ... has been always left to the discretion of the jury, as the degree of punishment to be thus inflicted must depend on the peculiar circumstances of each case"; (C) *Missouri Pacific R. Co.* v. *Humes*: "[t]he discretion of the jury in such cases is **not** controlled by any very definite rules"; (D) *Barry* v. *Edmunds*: in "actions

for torts where no precise rule of law fixes the recoverable damages, it is the peculiar function of the jury to determine the amount by their verdict." (E) True, 19th century judges occasionally asserted that they had authority to overturn damage awards upon concluding, from the size of an award, that the jury's decision must have been based on "partiality" **or** "passion and prejudice." **But** (F) courts rarely *exercised* this authority.

> B, C, D, E, F.
> Therefore A.

21. (A) Oregon's procedures adequately guide the jury charged with the responsibility to determine a plaintiff's qualification for, **and** (B) the amount of, punitive damages, **and on that account** (C) do **not** deny defendants procedural due process; (D) Oregon's Supreme Court correctly refused to rule that "an award of punitive damages, to comport with the requirements of the Due Process Clause, *always* must be subject to a form of postverdict or appellate review" for excessiveness; (E) the verdict in this particular case, considered in light of this Court's decisions in *Haslip* and *TXO*, hardly appears "so 'grossly excessive' as to violate the substantive component of the Due Process Clause," *TXO*. **Accordingly,** (F) the Court's procedural directive to the state court is neither necessary nor proper. (G) The Supreme Court of Oregon has **not** refused to enforce federal law, **and** (H) I would affirm its judgment.

> (A and B), therefore C.
> Therefore D.
> E, therefore (G and H).
> Therefore F.

CHAPTER 12

Exercises 12A

5. Factual claim
9. Personal value claim
13. Moral value claim

Exercises 12B

5. False
9. False
13. True

Exercises 12E

I.
5. stealing
   Argument: *Emotivism:* Stealing is sometimes justified. For example, if a society is corrupt and the economy is such that survival is difficult, then stealing from those

who have amassed their wealth through corrupt means is morally justified.

Discussion of the argument: Stealing is never justified. If a society is corrupt, then all citizens must do their best to change it by moral means. That includes protest and civil disobedience. Stealing simply copies a behavior that is unjustified, no matter who does it and for whatever purpose.

9. animal rights

Argument: *Relativism:* Since there are no universal objective rights even for humans, it stands to reason that animals do not have any rights either. Besides, any "right" is provided by a collective agreement among people with free will, those capable of making rational decisions. There is no evidence that animals act on anything other than instinct; therefore, any talk of "animal rights" is misguided.

Discussion of the argument: Even if there are no universal objective rights, we can still agree to establish certain basic rights for others. For example, most people agree that humans have basic rights regardless of their physical or mental capabilities. Likewise, we can choose to designate certain basic rights to animals.

13. freedom of speech

Argument: *Emotivism:* Even though most people believe that freedom of speech is a fundamental right of all humans, that "social fact" does not make it objective. In other words, people have a strong *emotional* attachment to the idea of freedom of speech, but that in no way makes it an objective fact of the world.

Discussion of the argument: The "social fact" aspect of freedom of speech is important for people to be able to recognize repressive and dictatorial regimes, and to take steps to remedy the situations. The ability to criticize a government through freedom of speech is a sign of a healthy and mature society.

17. birth control

Argument: *Emotivism:* Birth control is an effective way to control overpopulation, especially in undeveloped countries where children have no real hope of long-term survival. It takes pressure off individual families who may not be able to feed another mouth. It allows people to decide when and if they want to have children, and thereby take better control over their lives.

Discussion of the argument: Birth control can also mean stopping pregnancies for any reason whatsoever. There are many countries where female children are not wanted, so couples take it upon themselves to abort female fetuses. In the future, people might decide to eliminate any fetus if it doesn't conform to their expectations.

II.

5. **Argument:** The nation's underlying divides are still ideological, but we rarely fight them honestly as philosophical differences. We just accuse the other side of corruption. Politics is no longer a debate; it's an attempt to destroy lives through accusation.

Discussion: *Deontology* holds that we have a duty not to harm others. Although there are political divides in our country, if we want democracy to succeed, we must stop accusing each other of corruption and stop trying to destroy lives through accusation. Instead, we have a duty to engage in honest and rational debate.

9. **Argument:** Different cultures have different views on concussions and different views on identifying concussions, or even what the symptoms are that may suggest concussion. We know from research, for example, that the reporting of symptoms varies by language of origin. We have determined that players from different nationalities and cultural backgrounds report concussions in different manners. Different cultures also put more or less importance around different symptoms. One culture may not consider a headache to be important and won't report it, but they will report dizziness. Meanwhile, headaches can be one of the indicators for post-concussion syndrome. [Therefore, we should be more cautious and explore different ways of identifying possible concussion cases.]

Discussion: According to *relativism*, we should not expect people from different cultures, people with different languages and different nationalities, to agree on when a concussion occurred. But since a concussion can be medically defined with some degree of precision, we should apply those medical standards and the appropriate tests to determine the objective aspect of a concussion, instead of relying on people's subjective opinions on whether they think they have suffered a concussion.

CHAPTER 13

Exercises 13A

5. *Sample:* 6000 urban public high school seniors throughout the United States
    Population: All U.S. high school seniors
    Sample size: The sample is large and taken from throughout the United States. This raises the likelihood that the sample is representative of the population.
    Potential bias: The sample excludes private high schools. This reduces the likelihood that the sample is representative of the population, because there may be a significant difference between the two groups' test scores. Their exclusion from the study may bias the results in one direction or another.
    Randomness: This is a random sample. This raises the likelihood that the sample is representative of the

population. However, it would be better for the researchers to generalize to public school seniors because that is what they studied.

9. *Sample:* The results of the World Series from 1903 to 2008 and the correlation to sales
Population: Future World Series winners
Sample size: The sample includes the results from 105 years. The sample is certainly large enough to be representative of the past winners, since it includes nearly the entire past population. However, since the researchers are projecting into the future, there may be reasons to think that future society may not be the same as that represented in the sample.
Potential bias: The sample clearly shows a past trend. However, since we know that cigarette and liquor sales are affected by many social factors, the extended trend may be a simple correlation and not an indication of any real connection (the issue of *correlation* will be explored further in the next chapter). This allows us to question the likelihood that the sample is representative of the population.
Randomness: In a sense, randomness is not an issue here. If all the World Series results are included, then no data are missing regarding other World Series.

Exercises 13B

I.
5. Mean: 186.7; Median: 200; Mode: 200

II.
5. Mean: $1200.30; Median: $1000; Mode: $1000

III.
5. Mean: 3.13; Median: 3.16; Mode: 3.16

IV.
5. Mean: 55.29″; Median: 74″; Modes: 74″, 80″

Exercises 13C

I.
5. The standard deviation is 73.67.
Step 1: 186.7
Step 2: −86.7; −76.7; 13.3; 13.3; 23.3; 113.3
Step 3: 7516.9; 5882.9; 176.9; 176.9; 542.9; 12,836.9
Step 4: 27,133.4
Step 5: 5426.68
Step 6: 73.67

II.
5. The standard deviation is 1642.90.
Step 1: 1200.30
Step 2: −1199.80; −1199.30; −200.30; −200.30; 2799.70
Step 3: 1,439,520.04; 1,438,320.49; 40,120.09; 40,120.09; 7,838,320.09

Step 4: 10,796,400.80
Step 5: 2,699,100.20
Step 6: 1642.90

III.
5. The standard deviation is 0.17.
Step 1: 3.13
Step 2: −0.27; −0.17; 0.03; 0.03; 0.13; 0.23
Step 3: 0.07; 0.03; 0.00; 0.00; 0.02; 0.05
Step 4: 0.17
Step 5: 0.03
Step 6: 0.17

IV.
5. The standard deviation is 27.22.
Step 1: 55.29
Step 2: −31.29; −28.29; −27.29; 18.71; 18.71; 24.71; 24.71
Step 3: 979.06; 800.32; 744.74; 350.06; 350.06; 610.58; 610.58
Step 4: 4445.40
Step 5: 740.90
Step 6: 27.22

Exercises 13E

5. First, we are told that the "hundreds of millions of dollars" are wasted, presumably because of late penalties incurred with the IRS. Second, "workers have forgone huge amounts of money in matching 401(k) contributions because they never got around to signing up for a retirement plan." However, no accurate figures are given to support this claim. Third, we are told that "Seventy percent of patients suffering from glaucoma risk blindness because they don't use their eyedrops regularly." However, no information is given to show how this figure was arrived at; we are not told the kind of study, the sample size, or whether it was random. Fourth, the claim that "Procrastination also inflicts major costs on businesses and governments" has no supporting evidence. Also, the term "major costs" is vague. Finally, the claim that "the bankruptcy of General Motors was due in part to executives' penchant for delaying tough decisions" has no supporting evidence.

9. The sample is eight power plants closed between 2001 and 2011 in California; the population is all coal- and oil-fired power plants in the world (since the study cites the World Health Organization). We don't know whether the eight plants in California are substantially different from those in other parts of the United States (or the rest of the world); for example: Were they substantially older than average? Had they been upgraded to meet the latest pollution standards? Although eight plants is not a large number, it may be sufficient if we can determine whether those eight plants are representative of other power plants still in use.

Exercises 13G

5. Using the restricted conjunction method we get the following:

$$1/7 \times 1/7 = 1/49$$

9. Using the restricted conjunction method we get the following:

$$1/2 \times 1/2 = 1/4$$

13. Using the restricted conjunction method we get the following:

$$4/15 \times 4/15 = 16/225$$

17. Question 1: 2/52, or 1/26
    Question 2: 4/52, or 1/13

21. $1/4 \times 1/4 \times 1/4 \times 1/4 = 1/256$.

25. Let A be the event of drawing a brown sock on the first attempt. The probability, $P(A)$, of this occurring is 4/15. Now if A occurs, then there will be only fourteen socks left in the drawer, three of which will be brown (because one brown sock has been removed). The probability of getting a brown sock on the second attempt, called B, is 3/14. We calculate the probability of getting two brown socks in succession as the joint occurrence of A and (B if A), which is the product of the probabilities of their separate occurrence: $4/15 \times 3/14 = 12/210$. Dividing both by 6, we get 2/35.

Exercises 13I

5. $A = $ graduating with a GPA greater than 3.5, and $B = $ scoring above 1200 on the MADT:

$$Pr\ A,\ if\ B = \frac{.70 \times .20}{Pr\ (B)}$$

$$= \frac{.14}{Pr\ (B)}$$

$$Pr\ (B) = (.70 \times .20) + (.15 \times .80)$$
$$Pr\ (B) = .14 + .12$$
$$Pr\ (B) = .26$$
$$Pr\ A,\ if\ B = \frac{.14}{.26}$$

$Pr\ A,\ if\ B = .54$ Therefore, it is a strong measure.

CHAPTER 14

Exercises 14A

I.

5. Sufficient condition. Since June has exactly 30 days, if the antecedent is true, then the consequent will be true as well.

9. Sufficient condition. Since 100 pennies is the equivalent of $1, if the antecedent is true, then the consequent will be true as well.

13. Sufficient condition. If it is true that I am eating a banana, then it must be true that I am eating a fruit.

II.

5. Necessary condition. June has exactly 30 days. Given this, if this month does *not* have exactly 30 days, then this month is *not* June.

9. Necessary condition. If I do *not* have *at least* the equivalent of $1, then I have *at most* 99 cents. Given this, I do *not* have exactly 100 pennies.

13. Necessary condition. If I am *not* eating a fruit, then I am *not* eating a banana.

Exercises 14C

I.

5. False
9. True

II.

5. The joint method of agreement and difference

III.

5. **Possible Causes**

The **Effect**	Dinner	Groceries	Gas	Lent to Friend	Lost the Money
Missing $20					√

The chart displays the *method of agreement*. We can conclude that losing the money is probably causally connected to the missing $20.

9. **Possible Causes**

Instances of the **Effect**	Batch of Seeds	Soil	Watering Schedule	Amount of Water	Sun	Fertilizer
Plant 1: Twice the pounds as plant 2.	√	√	√	√	√	√
Plant 2: Half the pounds as plant 1.	√	√	√	√	√	

The **chart** displays the *method of difference*. We can conclude that spraying the plant with a fertilizer once a week is probably causally connected to producing twice as many pounds of tomatoes.

13.

Minutes Boiling an Egg

	3	4	5	6	7	8	9	10
Hardness of Egg	Runny	Thicker	Perfect	Harder	Harder	Harder	Harder	Perfect

The chart displays the *method of concomitant variations*. We can conclude that the number of minutes boiling an egg is probably causally connected to the hardness of the egg.

Exercises 14H

I.

5. True
9. False

II.

5. *Hypothesis 1:* Your friend forgot to water the plants.
Experiment 1: Check for moisture in the dirt.
Hypothesis 2: Your plants have contracted a disease.
Experiment 2: Check with a plant nursery.

9. *Hypothesis 1:* The service was interrupted and you are both calling at the same time.
Hypothesis 2: Your mother took another call and accidentally disconnected your call.
Experiment: Wait for a few minutes and try dialing again.

III.

5. *Hypothesis:* The battery in Joe's car is dead.
Experiment: Replace the battery.
Prediction: If the hypothesis is correct, then the car will start.
Confirm/Disconfirm: The prediction was true, and the evidence confirms the hypothesis.
Alternative Explanations: The clamps on either the positive or negative terminal heads might have been loose. If so, the battery might not have been dead or defective. The battery could have (and should have) been tested. It may have simply needed recharging. Without having evidence to rule out these possibilities, we must be careful not to assign too much weight to the existing evidence.

9. *Hypothesis:* Becky is allergic to her cat.
Experiment: Two experiments: (A) Becky will give the cat to a neighbor for a day, during which time Becky will see if she stops sneezing. (B) Becky will take allergy medicine to control the sneezing.
Prediction: For the first experiment, if the hypothesis is correct, then Becky should stop sneezing. For the second experiment, provided the medicine is effective, Becky should stop sneezing.
Confirm/Disconfirm: Both predictions turned out true, and Becky was convinced that the evidence confirmed her hypothesis.
Alternative Explanations: We are told that the sneezing started about the same time as Becky's husband started using a new flea powder, and the sneezing stopped when he started using the old brand of flea powder. This evidence certainly weakens Becky's hypothesis, but it does not mean that her hypothesis cannot be true. We would have to do additional experiments with combinations of old and new flea powder and the allergy medicine to be able to gather the strongest possible evidence to confirm or disconfirm either Becky's hypothesis or the alternative flea powder hypothesis.

13. *Hypothesis:* There is a causal connection between elevated levels of activity in the amygdala and heart health.
Experiment: Researchers tracked the health of nearly 300 people for an average of about 4 years. Brain scans monitored elevated levels of activity in the amygdala and the incidence of chest pain and heart attacks.
Prediction: The people with heightened activity in the amygdala will have a higher incidence of heart problems.
Confirm/Disconfirm: The prediction turned out to be true; therefore, the hypothesis was confirmed.
Alternative Explanations: Other factors need to be accounted for and ruled out, such as age, diet, and type of work performed.

17. *Hypothesis:* Perhaps dolphins have a type of sonar that can do what human sonar cannot.
Experiment: Researchers modeled the types of echolocation pulses that dolphins emit and processed them using nonlinear mathematics instead of the standard way of processing sonar returns. The math involved is complex. Essentially it relies upon sending out pulses that vary in amplitude. The first may have a value of 1, while the second is one-third that amplitude. If the dolphin remembers what the ratios of the two pulses were, and can multiply the second echo by that and add the echoes together, it can make the fish "visible" to its sonar.
Prediction: The modeling technique worked, and could explain how dolphins achieve hunting success with bubbles.
Confirm/Disconfirm: Since the prediction was true, the hypothesis was confirmed.
Alternative Explanations: Although the computer modeling worked, the dolphins' ability might be a function of a different and non-mathematical method of hunting.

Index

Index entries preceded by an asterisk (*) may also be found in the glossary. Page numbers followed by "**b**" refer to text boxes.

TRUTH TABLES FOR PROPOSITIONAL OPERATORS

Negation

p	$\sim p$
T	F
F	T

Conjunction

p	q	$p \cdot q$
T	T	T
T	F	F
F	T	F
F	F	F

Disjunction

p	q	$p \vee q$
T	T	T
T	F	T
F	T	T
F	F	F

Conditional

p	q	$p \supset q$
T	T	T
T	F	F
F	T	T
F	F	T

Biconditional

p	q	$p \equiv q$
T	T	T
T	F	F
F	T	F
F	F	T

THE EIGHT IMPLICATION RULES

Modus Ponens (MP)

$$p \supset q$$
$$\underline{p \quad\quad}$$
$$q$$

Modus Tollens (MT)

$$p \supset q$$
$$\underline{\sim q \quad\quad}$$
$$\sim p$$

Hypothetical Syllogism (HS)

$$p \supset q$$
$$\underline{q \supset r}$$
$$p \supset r$$

Disjunctive Syllogism (DS)

$$p \vee q \qquad p \vee q$$
$$\underline{\sim p \quad\quad} \qquad \underline{\sim q \quad\quad}$$
$$q \qquad\quad p$$

Simplification (Simp)

$$\underline{p \cdot q} \qquad \underline{p \cdot q}$$
$$p \qquad\quad q$$

Conjunction (Conj)

$$p$$
$$\underline{q \quad\quad}$$
$$p \cdot q$$

Addition (Add)

$$\underline{p \quad\quad}$$
$$p \vee q$$

Constructive Dilemma (CD)

$$(p \supset q) \cdot (r \supset s)$$
$$\underline{p \vee r \quad\quad}$$
$$q \vee s$$

THE TEN REPLACEMENT RULES

De Morgan (DM)

$\sim(p \cdot q) :: \sim p \vee \sim q$

$\sim(p \vee q) :: \sim p \cdot \sim q$

Double negation (DN)

$p :: \sim\sim p$

Commutation (Com)

$p \vee q :: q \vee p$

$p \cdot q :: q \cdot p$

Association (Assoc)

$p \vee (q \vee r) :: (p \vee q) \vee r$

$p \cdot (q \cdot r) :: (p \cdot q) \cdot r$

Distribution (Dist)

$p \cdot (q \vee r) :: (p \cdot q) \vee (p \cdot r)$

$p \vee (q \cdot r) :: (p \vee q) \cdot (p \vee r)$

Transposition (Trans)

$p \supset q :: \sim q \supset \sim p$

Material implication (Impl)

$p \supset q :: \sim p \vee q$

Material equivalence (Equiv)

$p \equiv q :: (p \supset q) \cdot (q \supset p)$

$p \equiv q :: (p \cdot q) \vee (\sim p \cdot \sim q)$

Exportation (Exp)

$(p \cdot q) \supset r :: p \supset (q \supset r)$

Tautology (Taut)

$p :: p \vee p$

$p :: p \cdot p$

QUANTITY, QUALITY, AND DISTRIBUTION

A: All S are P.
Universal
Affirmative
Subject term distributed
Predicate term undistributed

E: No S are P.
Universal
Negative
Subject term distributed
Predicate term distributed

I: Some S are P.
Particular
Affirmative
Subject term undistributed
Predicate term undistributed

O: Some S are not P.
Particular
Negative
Subject term undistributed
Predicate term distributed

LOGICALLY EQUIVALENT STATEMENT FORMS

CONVERSION

E: No S are P.	**E**: No P are S.
I: Some S are P.	**I**: Some P are S.

OBVERSION

A: All S are P.	**E**: No S are non-P.
E: No S are P.	**A**: All S are non-P.
I: Some S are P.	**O**: Some S are not non-P.
O: Some S are not P.	**I**: Some S are non-P.

CONTRAPOSITION

A: All S are P.	**A**: All non-P are non-S.
O: Some S are not P.	**O**: Some non-P are not non-S.

FOUR FIGURES OF CATEGORICAL SYLLOGISMS

M P	P M	M P	P M
S M	S M	M S	M S
S P	S P	S P	S P
Figure 1	Figure 2	Figure 3	Figure 4

RULES FOR CATEGORICAL SYLLOGISMS

Rule 1: The middle term must be distributed in at least one premise.
Rule 2: If a term is distributed in the conclusion, then it must be distributed in a premise.
Rule 3: A categorical syllogism cannot have two negative premises.
Rule 4: A negative premise must have a negative conclusion.
Rule 5: A negative conclusion must have a negative premise.
Rule 6: Two universal premises cannot have a particular conclusion.

INFORMAL FALLACIES

1. **Ad hominem abusive:** The fallacy is distinguished by an attack on alleged character flaws of a person instead of the person's argument.

2. **Ad hominem circumstantial:** The fallacy occurs when someone's argument is rejected based on the circumstances of the person's life.

3. **Poisoning the well:** The fallacy occurs when a person is attacked *before* she has a chance to present her case.

4. **Tu quoque:** The fallacy is distinguished by the specific attempt of one person to avoid the issue at hand by claiming the other person is a hypocrite.

5. **Appeal to the people:** The fallacy occurs when an argument manipulates a psychological need or desire, such as the desire to belong to a popular group, or the need for group solidarity, so that the reader or listener will accept the conclusion.

6. **Appeal to pity:** The fallacy results from an exclusive reliance on a sense of pity or mercy for support of a conclusion.

7. **Appeal to fear or force:** The fallacy occurs when a threat of harmful consequences (physical or otherwise) is used to force acceptance of a course of action that would otherwise be unacceptable.

8. **Rigid application of a generalization:** When a generalization or rule is inappropriately applied to the case at hand. The fallacy results from the mistaken belief that a generalization or a rule is universal (meaning it has no exceptions).

9. **Hasty generalization:** An argument that relies on a small sample that is unlikely to represent the population.

10. **Composition:** There are two forms of the fallacy: (1) The mistaken transfer of an attribute of the individual *parts of an object* to the *object as a whole*. (2) The mistaken transfer of an attribute of the individual *members of a class* to the *class itself.*

11. **Division:** There are two forms of the fallacy: (1) The mistaken transfer of an attribute of an *object as a whole* to the individual *parts of the object.* (2) The mistaken transfer of an attribute of a *class* to the individual *members of the class.*

12. **Biased sample:** An argument that uses a nonrepresentative sample as support for a statistical claim about an entire population.

13. **Post hoc:** The fallacy occurs from the mistaken assumption that just because one event occurred before another event, the first event *must have caused* the second event.

14. **Slippery slope:** An argument that attempts to connect a series of occurrences such that the first link in a chain leads directly to a second link, and so on, until a final unwanted situation is said to be the inevitable result.

15. **Begging the question:** In one type, the fallacy occurs when a premise is simply reworded in the conclusion. In a second type, called circular reasoning, a set of statements seem to support each other with no clear beginning or end point. In a third type, the argument assumes certain key information that may be controversial or is not supported by facts.

16. **Complex question:** The fallacy occurs when a single question actually contains multiple parts and an unestablished hidden assumption.

17. **Appeal to ignorance:** An argument built on a position of ignorance claims either that (1) a statement must be true because it has not been proven to be false or (2) a statement must be false because it has not been proven to be true.

18. **Appeal to an unqualified authority:** An argument that relies on the opinions of people who either have *no* expertise, training, or knowledge relevant to the issue at hand, or whose testimony is not trustworthy.

19. **False dichotomy:** The fallacy occurs when it is assumed that only two choices are possible, when in fact others exist.

20. **Equivocation:** The fallacy occurs when the conclusion of an argument relies on an intentional or unintentional shift in the meaning of a term or phrase in the premises.

21. **Straw man:** The fallacy occurs when an argument is misrepresented in order to create a new argument that can be easily refuted. The new argument is so weak that it is "made of straw." The arguer then falsely claims that his opponent's real argument has been defeated.

22. **Red herring:** The fallacy occurs when someone completely ignores an opponent's position and changes the subject, diverting the discussion in a new direction.

23. **Misleading precision:** A claim that appears to be statistically significant but is not.

24. **Missing the point:** When premises that seem to lead logically to one conclusion are used instead to support an unexpected conclusion.

INFERENCE RULES FOR PREDICATE LOGIC

Universal instantiation (UI)

$$\frac{(x)\mathcal{S}x}{\mathcal{S}y} \qquad\qquad \frac{(x)\mathcal{S}x}{\mathcal{S}a}$$

Universal generalization (UG)

Not Permitted

$$\frac{\mathcal{S}y}{(x)\mathcal{S}x} \qquad\qquad \frac{\mathcal{S}a}{(x)\mathcal{S}x}$$

Restrictions on UG:

1. *Universal generalization cannot be used within an indented proof sequence, if the instantial variable is free in the first line of the sequence.*
2. *Universal generalization cannot be used if the instantial variable y is free in any line that was obtained by existential instantiation (EI).*

Existential instantiation (EI)

Not Permitted

$$\frac{(\exists x)\mathcal{S}x}{\mathcal{S}a} \qquad\qquad \frac{(\exists x)\mathcal{S}x}{\mathcal{S}y}$$

Restriction on EI: The existential name (a) cannot be a name that appears in any previous line of the proof, and it cannot appear in the line that indicates the conclusion to be derived.

Existential generalization (EG)

$$\frac{\mathcal{S}a}{(\exists x)\mathcal{S}x} \qquad\qquad \frac{\mathcal{S}y}{(\exists x)\mathcal{S}x}$$

Change of quantifier (CQ)

$$(x)\mathcal{S}x \;::\; \sim(\exists x)\sim\mathcal{S}x$$
$$\sim(x)\mathcal{S}x \;::\; (\exists x)\sim\mathcal{S}x$$
$$(\exists x)\mathcal{S}x \;::\; \sim(x)\sim\mathcal{S}x$$
$$\sim(\exists x)\mathcal{S}x \;::\; (x)\sim\mathcal{S}x$$

Identity rules (Id)

1. Premise
$$\Phi = \Phi$$

2. $\Phi = \Psi \;::\; \Psi = \Phi$

3. $\dfrac{\mathcal{S}\Phi}{\Phi = \Psi}$
$$\mathcal{S}\Psi$$

*Φ, Ψ are any individual *variables* or individual *constants**

TYPES OF DEFINITIONS

Intensional definition: Assigns a meaning to a term by listing the properties or attributes shared by all the objects that are denoted by the term.

Synonymous definition: Assigns a meaning to a term by providing another term with the same meaning; in other words, by providing a synonym.

Word origin definition: A meaning can be assigned to a term by investigating its origin. The study of the history, development, and sources of words is called *etymology*.

Operational definition: Defines a term by specifying a measurement procedure.

Definition by genus and difference: Assigns a meaning to a term (the species) by establishing a genus and combining it with the attribute that distinguishes the members of that species.

Extensional definition: Assigns meaning to a term by indicating the class members denoted by the term.

Ostensive definition: Involves demonstrating the term—for example, by pointing to a member of the class that the term denotes.

Enumerative definition: Assigns meaning to a term by naming the individual members of the class denoted by the term.

Definition by subclass: Assigns meaning to a term by naming subclasses (species) of the class denoted by the term.

Stipulative definition: Introduces a new meaning to a term or symbol.

Lexical definition: A definition based on the common use of a word, term, or symbol.

Functional definition: Specifies the purpose or use of the objects denoted by the term.

Precising definition: Reduces the vagueness and ambiguity of a term by providing a sharp focus, often a technical meaning, for a term.

Theoretical definition: Assigns a meaning to a term by providing an understanding of how the term fits into a general theory.

Persuasive definition: Assigns a meaning to a term with the direct purpose of influencing attitudes or opinions.

SIX STEPS FOR
CALCULATING STANDARD DEVIATION

Step 1: Calculate the mean value.

Step 2: Calculate the difference between each value in the set and the mean value.

Step 3: Multiply each difference by itself (square each difference).

Step 4: Add the results of the squaring process in step 3.

Step 5: Divide the result of step 4 by one fewer than the number of members in the set.

Step 6: The square root of the total variance is the standard deviation.

PROBABILITY METHODS

Restricted conjunction method: $Pr\ (A\ and\ B) = Pr\ (A) \times Pr\ (B)$

General conjunction method: $Pr\ (A\ and\ B) = Pr\ (A) \times Pr\ (B, if A)$

Restricted disjunction method: $Pr\ (A\ or\ B) = Pr\ (A) + Pr\ (B)$

General disjunction method: $Pr\ (A\ or\ B) = [Pr\ (A) + Pr\ (B)] - [Pr\ (A) \times Pr\ (B)]$

Negation method: $Pr\ (\sim A) = 1 - Pr\ (A)$

Bayes's Theorem: $Pr\ (A, if\ B) = \dfrac{Pr\ (B, if\ A)\ \times\ Pr\ (A)}{Pr\ (B)}$

MILL'S METHODS

Method of agreement: The method that looks at two or more instances of an event to see what they have in common.

Method of difference: The method that looks for what all the instances of an event do not have in common.

Joint method of agreement and difference: If two or more instances of an event have only one thing in common, while the instances in which it does *not* occur all share the absence of that thing, then the item is a likely cause.

Method of residues: The method that subtracts from a complex set of events those parts that already have known causes.

Method of concomitant variations: The method that looks for two factors that vary together.